Exploring AutoCAD Civil 3D 2018

(8th Revised and Updated Edition)

Sham Tickoo
Professor
Purdue University Northwest
Hammond, Indiana, USA

Contributing Authors
Manash Chatterjee
BIM Specialist

Tickoo Institute of Emerging Technologies (TIET)
Gurgaon, India

ISBN: 978-93-87284-13-5
8th Revised and Updated Edition
(For distribution in SAARC countries only)

Limits of Liability and Disclaimer of Warranty

The information contained in this book is the best of Author's & Publisher's knowledge. We are committed to serve students with best of our knowledge and resources. We have taken utmost care and attention while editing and printing of this book but Author and Publisher should not be held responsible for errors, omissions and any other unintentional mistake that might have crept in. However, errors brought to our notice shall be gratefully acknowledged and attended to.

All trademarks referred to in the book are acknowledged as properties of their respective owners. This book is written solely for the benefit and guidance of the students.

Distributors

BPB PUBLICATIONS
20, Ansari Road, Darya Ganj
New Delhi-110002
Ph: 23254990/23254991

DECCAN AGENCIES
4-3-329, Bank Street
HYDERABAD-500195
Ph: 24756967/24756400

MICRO MEDIA
Shop No. 5, Mahendra Chambers
150 DN Rd. Next to Capital Cinema
V.T (C.S.T.) Station
MUMBAI-400001
Ph: 22078296/22078297

BPB BOOK CENTRE
376 Old Lajpat Rai Market
DELHI-110006
Ph: 23861747

COMPUTER BOOK CENTRE
12, Shrungar Shopping Centre
M.G. Road
BENGALURU–560001
Ph: 25587923/25584641

Published by Manish Jain for BPB Publications, 20 Ansari Road, Darya Ganj
New Delhi-110002 and Printed by Repro India Pvt. Ltd, Mumbai

DEDICATION

To teachers, who make it possible to disseminate knowledge
to enlighten the young and curious minds
of our future generations

To students, who are dedicated to learning new technologies
and making the world a better place to live in

SPECIAL RECOGNITION

A special thanks to Mr. Denis Cadu and the ADN team of Autodesk Inc.
for their valuable support and professional guidance to
procure the software for writing this textbook

THANKS

To employees at CADCIM Technologies and
Tickoo Institute of Emerging Technologies (TIET)
for their valuable help

To Bhawna Kathpalia for technical editing this manuscript

To Rajendra Badola, Anju Jethwani, and Kusha Gupta
for copy editing this manuscript

Note

If you are a faculty member, you can register by clicking on the following link to access the teaching resources: ***http://www.cadcim.com/Registration.aspx***. The student resources are available at ***http://www.cadcim.com***. We also provide ***Live Virtual Online Training*** on various software packages. For more information, write us at ***sales@cadcim.com***.

Table of Contents

Chapter 2: Working with Points

Chapter 3: Working with Surfaces

Chapter 5: Alignments

Chapter 6: Working with Profiles

Chapter 7: Working with Assemblies and Subassemblies

Chapter 8: Working with Corridors and Parcels

Chapter 9: Sample Lines, Sections, and Quantity Takeoffs

Chapter 10: Feature Lines and Grading

Chapter 11: Pipe Networks

Chapter 12: Pressure Networks

Chapter 13: Working with Plan Production Tools and Data Shortcuts

Preface

AutoCAD Civil 3D 2018

AutoCAD Civil 3D is one of the leading civil engineering software developed by Autodesk Inc., USA. This software provides a comprehensive solution for various infrastructure works such as earthwork, subdivision, highways, land development, survey, drainage, and different areas related to project management. AutoCAD Civil 3D has the ability to dynamically link various objects created in it. As a result any changes or revisions made in the design are instantly updated by a click of mouse. This powerful feature saves a lot of time, thereby enabling the engineers and designers involved in the project to assess various conditions that can affect their design process.

Exploring AutoCAD Civil 3D 2018 textbook has been written with the intention of helping the readers effectively usc AutoCAD Civil 3D. Structured in a pedagogical sequence, the chapters in this textbook cover the basic as well as advanced concepts of AutoCAD Civil 3D such as alignments, surfaces, gradings, corridor modeling, and earthwork calculations to name only a few. The civil engineering industry examples that are used as tutorials and the related additional exercises at the end of each chapter will help the users to understand the techniques used in the industry to design a project.

The salient features of this textbook are as follows:

- **Tutorial Approach**
  The author has adopted the tutorial point-of-view and the learn-by-doing approach throughout the textbook. This approach guides the users through the process of creating models in the tutorials.

- **Real-World Models as Projects**
  The author has used about 36 real-world projects as tutorials in this textbook. This enables the readers to relate the models in the tutorials to the real-world. In addition, there are about 20 exercises that can be used by the readers to assess their knowledge.

- **Tips and Notes**
  Additional information related to various topics is provided to the users in the form of tips and notes.

- **Heavily Illustrated Text**
  The text in this textbook is heavily illustrated with about 750 diagrams and screen capture images.

- **Learning Objectives**
  The first page of every chapter summarizes the topics that are covered in the chapter.

- **Self-Evaluation Test, Review Questions, and Exercises**
  Each chapter ends with Self-Evaluation Test so that the users can assess their knowledge of the chapter. The answers to Self-Evaluation Test are given at the end of the chapter. Also, the Review Questions and Exercises are given at the end of each chapter and they can be used by the Instructor as test questions and assignments.

Symbols Used in the Textbook

Note

The author has provided additional information to the users about the topic being discussed in the form of notes.

Tip

Special information and techniques are provided in the form of tips that help in increasing the efficiency of the users.

Enhanced

This symbol indicates that the command or tool being discussed has been enhanced in AutoCAD Civil 3D 2018.

New

This symbol indicates that the command or tool being discussed has been new in AutoCAD Civil 3D 2018.

Formatting Conventions Used in the Textbook

Please refer to the following list for the formatting conventions used in this textbook.

• Names of tools, buttons, options, browser, palette, panels, and tabs are written in boldface.	Example: The **Create Surface** tool, the **Modify** button, the **Create Design** panel, the **Home** tab, **Properties Palette**, **Content Browser**, and so on.
• Names of dialog boxes, drop-downs, drop-down lists, list boxes, areas, edit boxes, check boxes, and radio buttons are written in boldface.	Example: The **Table Style** dialog box, the **Points** drop-down of **Create Ground Data** panel in the **Home** tab, the **Name** edit box of the **Surface Properties** dialog box, and so on.
• Values entered in edit boxes are written in boldface.	Example: Enter **EG Surface** in the **Name** edit box.
• Names of the files saved are italicized.	Example: *c03_tut1a.dwg*

- The methods of invoking a tool/option from the ribbon, Application Menu, or the shortcut keys are given in a shaded box.

Ribbon: Home > Create Ground Data > Surface drop-down > Create Surface
Command: CREATESURFACE

Naming Conventions Used in the Textbook

Tool

If you click on an item in a panel of the ribbon and a command is invoked to create/edit an object or perform some action then that item is termed as **tool**.

For example:
Create Corridor tool, **Create Surface** tool, **Create Surface Profile** tool

If you click on an item in a panel of the ribbon and a dialog box is invoked wherein you can set the properties to create/edit an object then that item is also termed as **tool**, refer to Figure 1.

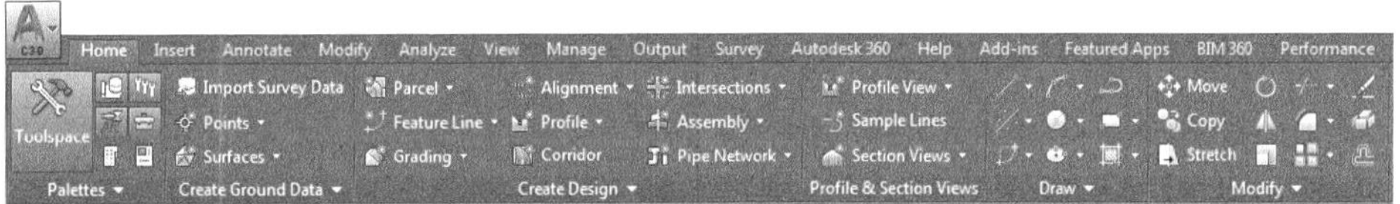

Figure 1 *Tools in the Ribbon*

For example:
Create Surface tool, **Create Feature Line** tool
Water Drop tool, **Bounded Volumes** tool

Dialog Box

In this textbook, different terms are used for referring to the components of a dialog box. Refer to Figure 2 for the terminology used.

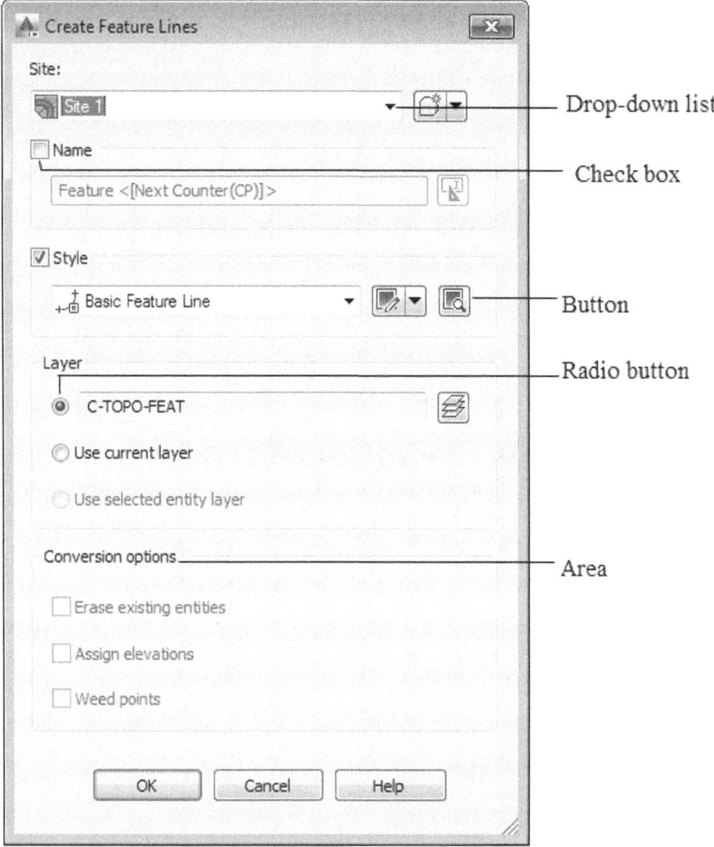

Figure 2 Different terminologies used in a dialog box

Button

The item in a dialog box that has a 3D shape like a button is termed as **button**. For example, **OK** button, **Cancel** button, **Apply** button, and so on. If the item in a ribbon is used to exit a tool or a mode, it is also termed as button. For example, **Modify** button, **Finish Editing System** button, **Cancel Editing System** button, and so on, refer to Figure 2.

Drop-down

A drop-down is one in which a set of common tools are grouped together. You can identify a drop-down with a down arrow on it. These drop-downs are given a name based on the tools grouped in them. For example, **Surfaces** drop-down, **Points** drop-down, **Grading** drop-down, and so on, refer to Figure 3.

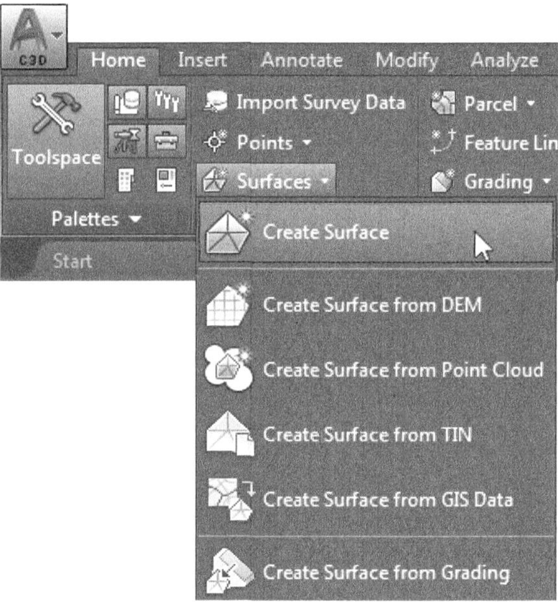

Figure 3 Choosing a tool from drop-down

Drop-down List

A drop-down list is one in which a set of options are grouped together. You can set various parameters using these options. You can identify a drop-down list with a down arrow on it. For example, **Type Selector** drop-down list, **Units** drop-down list, and so on, refer to Figure 4.

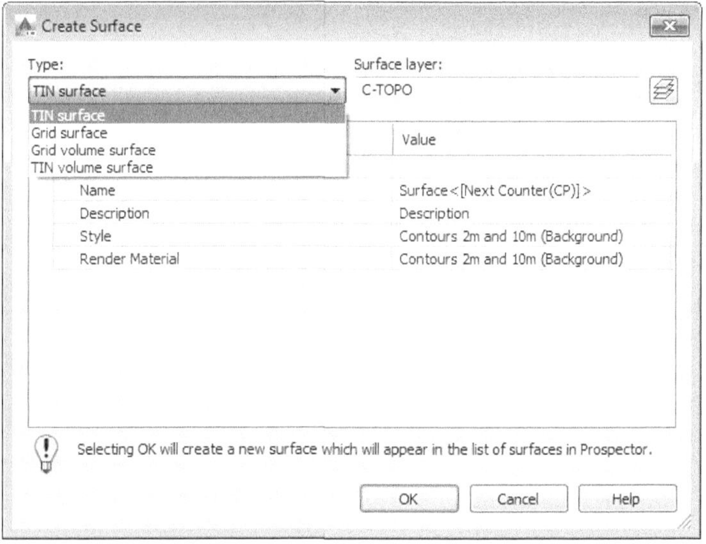

Figure 4 Selecting an option from the ***Type*** *drop-down list*

Options

Options are the items that are available in shortcut menu, drop-down list, dialog boxes, and so on. For example, choose the **Alignment Properties** option from the shortcut menu displayed on right-clicking in the drawing area, refer to Figure 5.

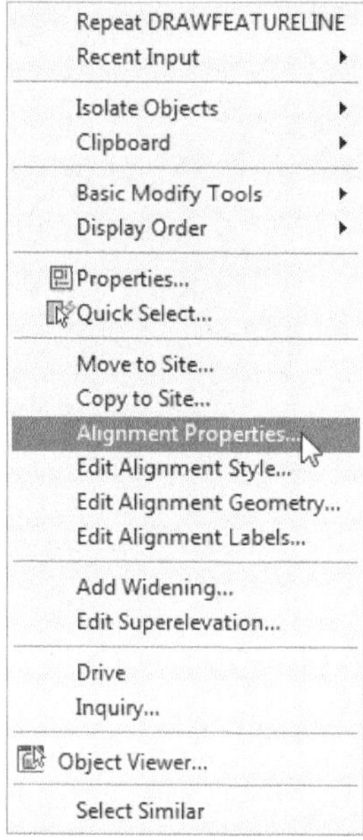

***Figure 5** Choosing an option from the shortcut menu*

Free Companion Website

It has been our constant endeavor to provide you the best textbooks and services at affordable price. In this endeavor, we have come out with a Free Companion website that will facilitate the process of teaching and learning of AutoCAD Civil 3D 2018. If you purchase this textbook, you will get access to the files on the Companion website.

The following resources are available for the faculty and students in this website:

Faculty Resources

- **Technical Support**
  You can get online technical support by contacting ***techsupport@cadcim.com***.

- **Instructor Guide**
  Solutions to all review questions and exercises in the textbook are provided in the Instructor Guide to help the faculty members test the skills of the students.

- **PowerPoint Presentations**
  The contents of the book are arranged in PowerPoint slides that can be used by the faculty for their lectures.

- **Civil 3D Files**
  The Civil 3D files used in illustration, tutorials, and exercises are available for free download.

Student Resources

- **Technical Support**
  You can get online technical support by contacting ***techsupport@cadcim.com***.

- **Civil 3D Files**
  The Civil 3D files used in illustrations and tutorials are available for free download.

If you face any problem in accessing these files, please contact the publisher at *sales@cadcim.com* or the author at *stickoo@pnw.edu* or *tickoo525@gmail.com*

Stay Connected

You can now stay connected with us through Facebook and Twitter to get the latest information about our textbooks, videos, and teaching/learning resources. To get such updates, follow us on Facebook (***www.facebook.com/cadcim***) and Twitter (***@cadcimtech***). You can also subscribe to our YouTube channel (***www.youtube.com/cadcimtech***) to get the information about our latest video tutorials.

This page is intentionally left blank

Chapter 1

Introduction to AutoCAD Civil 3D 2018

Learning Objectives

After completing this chapter, you will be able to:

- *Understand the basic features of AutoCAD Civil 3D 2018*
- *Understand AutoCAD Civil 3D 2018 screen components*
- *Get familiar with different workspaces in AutoCAD Civil 3D 2018*

INTRODUCTION TO AutoCAD Civil 3D 2018

AutoCAD Civil 3D is a powerful Building Information Modeling (BIM) tool that is used for designing, analyzing, and documenting engineering projects such as land development, transportation, and environmental projects.

This software includes various sets of tools for designing a civil engineering project along with the tools from other Autodesk products such as AutoCAD and Map 3D. It also has interfacing application such as Trimble Link™, Carlson Connect™, Infraworks, and Leica Exchange for transferring and converting data set into Civil 3D environment. These tools can be accessed through toolbars and Ribbon provided in the software interface. Civil 3D also supports the traditional commands that exist in AutoCAD software to invoke various tools. These commands are executed using the command prompt in the software.

AutoCAD Civil 3D 2018 provides a model-centric technology at the core that enables the entire team in a project to coordinate and work on a single updated model. Data sharing is conducted through various approaches ranging from Xrefs and data shortcuts to integrated data management controls. These approaches help team members to work in parallel, connected locally or remotely, on the latest updated model. As a result, a project can be managed well and the budget can also be controlled.

BASIC FEATURES OF AutoCAD Civil 3D

AutoCAD Civil 3D features a range of design and analysis objects within its three-dimensional dynamic engineering model. These Civil 3D objects include points, surfaces, parcels, alignments, profiles, and gradings. All objects in this model have a hierarchical interaction mechanism with each other. This mechanism ensures that modifications carried out in one object are truly reflected in other objects that are connected to it.

A Civil 3D object is a drawing element that maintains a relationship with another Civil 3D objects. For example, an alignment object is a combination of lines and curves in a horizontal plane that collectively defines the location of a project component such as the centerline of a road. This alignment can be an independent object or it can be a parent object of other Civil 3D objects such as profiles and cross-sections. If you edit this alignment object it will result in the change of other related Civil 3D objects.

Civil 3D has other objects such as points, surfaces, alignments, profiles, sites, parcels, gradings, corridors, assemblies, and subassemblies. All these objects have a designated hierarchy that can be viewed in an interface component called the **TOOLSPACE** palette.

AutoCAD Civil 3D also features various other object components such as tables, object labels, and the analysis results that are derived from the model. These object components are associated with the core model and they can be dynamically updated so as to reflect any change made in the core model.

Some of the various objects required to create a Civil 3D model are discussed next.

Points

Points are the basic building blocks in AutoCAD Civil 3D. In Civil 3D, points are coordinate geometry points and are also known as the COGO points. In a civil engineering project, points are used to represent the existing ground locations and design elements. A Civil 3D point object is different from the AutoCAD point object. An AutoCAD point merely displays the location of an object. A Civil 3D point has a unique identification number and properties such as northing, easting, elevation, and description. These points can also have additional properties to control their appearance such as point style, point label style, and layer.

Point Groups

The point groups allow you to group the COGO points together. The groups are created by using the point objects that have similar characteristics. This helps you to control the overall appearance of the points. Point group objects make it easy to change the point number, point style, and other properties of a large number of points.

Surfaces

Surfaces are key objects in AutoCAD Civil 3D. They are the three-dimensional geometric representation of a land terrain. In Civil 3D, you can calculate a composite volume surface that represents the difference between two surface areas.

The surfaces are created using points, point files, DEM data, existing AutoCAD objects, contours, breaklines, and boundaries. You can also import the information regarding the surfaces from LandXML, TIN (Triangulated Irregular Network), and DEM (Digital Elevation Model) files.

In AutoCAD Civil 3D, you can perform various surface analyses to show different height ranges, slopes, and watershed areas. This is done to ensure that there are no unwanted point in the design.

Alignments

The alignment objects in civil engineering projects represent the geometry of features like the pipeline, road, canal, railway, or construction baselines in a horizontal plane. Creating and defining the alignment is the first step in the design process of highway, railway, or other engineering projects.

In AutoCAD Civil 3D, an alignment object can be created from a polyline or by using the **Alignment Layout Tools** toolbar. The alignment objects can also be edited using the grips or commands in the **Alignment Layout Tools** toolbar.

Profiles

The profiles (or long sections) are used to show surface levels along a selected horizontal alignment using the specified surfaces. After creating a profile in Civil 3D, you can design the vertical alignment directly on it by using standard alignment tools, grips, or editors.

Profile Views

The profile views are used to represent the graph lines which form the grid along which the profile is plotted. One profile view object can be used to represent multiple profiles. Profile view object also includes data bands. Data bands can be used to display additional information about the profile view.

Assemblies and Subassemblies

Assemblies constitute the primary structure of an AutoCAD Civil 3D corridor model. The subassemblies are the building blocks for creating an assembly. The assembly objects are composed of subassemblies. The assembly forms the primary structure of a corridor model. The subassemblies can be carriage ways, curbs, and slopes that can be added to the assembly baseline to create an assembly.

Corridors

A corridor represents a path such as a road, railway, or canal. The horizontal and vertical geometry of a corridor is defined by the alignment and the profile.

The corridor objects are created along one or more baselines (alignments). These are then created by placing a 2D section (assembly) at incremental locations along the baselines and by creating matching slopes that reach a surface model at each incremental location. The corridor models can be edited on the basis of sections.

Parcels

The parcels represent any closed boundary that is spatially referenced to a geographical location. However, the major use of parcel is to represent a tract of land which could be a lot in a subdivision. Parcel can also be a water body or even a lot in a given site which is termed as site parcel.

Grading

In AutoCAD Civil 3D, the grading tools enable the engineers to grade a surface by applying different grading criteria. On applying grading to a surface, you can analyze the grading and balance the cut and fill volumes of a surface.

Sections

In AutoCAD Civil 3D, sections or cross-sections provide a view of the terrain that is cut at an angle across a linear feature such as a proposed road. The sections are cut across the horizontal alignments at specified station intervals. These sections can be plotted individually for a specified station or as a group for a specified range of stations, depending on the purpose of a plot. You can generate the section volumes from a design for earthworks and materials using the **Quantity Take Off** tools.

Pipe Networks

You can use pipe networks to design the utility system such as the storm and wastewater system which carry fluids under the effect of gravity. The pipe networks are created from design catalogs and can be edited in plan views. You can also display the pipe network parts in profile and section views. Therefore, if a change is made to the pipe networks in plan view, the profile and section views are dynamically updated.

Pressure Pipe Networks

In Civil 3D, the pressure pipe network consists of objects that are used to design a pipe network that carries fluids under pressure, such as water supply network. In this category, various tools are provided to design the network in plan and profile layout. Similar to pipe network, the pressure pipe network is created from the parts that are available in a parts list. This parts list is derived from the AutoCAD catalog which is a master collection of various available parts.

Superelevation View

Superelevation or banking is defined as the transverse inclination to the road pavement surface created to counter the centrifugal forces that are exerted on the vehicle while travelling along a curved path. The superelevation view in Civil 3D is used to represent the superelevation. It is also used to perform the superelevation calculations and edit the superelevation data.

STARTING AutoCAD Civil 3D 2018

Enhanced

You can start AutoCAD Civil 3D 2018 by double-clicking on its shortcut icon on the desktop or from the taskbar. To start it from the taskbar, click on Windows icon and then choose **Civil 3D 2018 Imperial/Metric** from the menu displayed (for Windows 10), refer to Figure 1-1; AutoCAD Civil 3D 2018 will start and a window will be displayed with the **Start Tab** chosen by default.

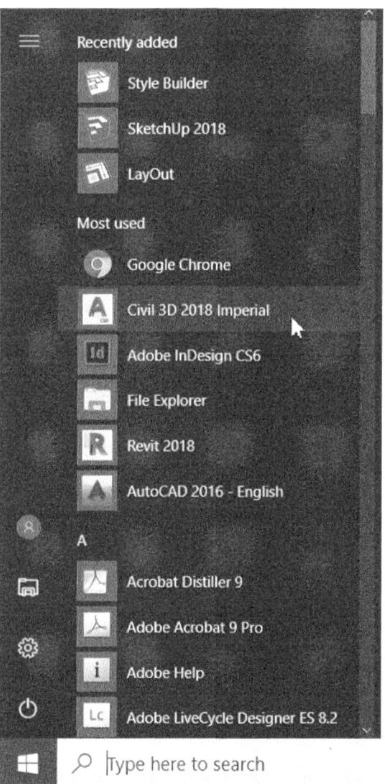

Figure 1-1 *Starting AutoCAD Civil 3D 2018 from the taskbar*

This tab contains two other tabs: **Learn** and **Create**. The **Learn** tab consists of two panes. The left pane of this tab contains a list of video links in **Getting Started Videos**. These links and videos can be used as additional learning resources. The right pane of the **Learn** tab contains the links for learning tips and check online resources in the **Learning Tips** and **Online Resources** areas, respectively.

The **Create** tab consists of three panes: **Get Started**, **Recent Documents**, and **Connect**. This tab provides information such as how to start Civil 3D, list of recently opened documents and notifications, and feedback. The third pane enables you to sign in to Autodesk.

AutoCAD Civil 3D 2018 USER INTERFACE

The Civil 3D interface consists of various components such as the drawing area, command window, toolbars, Ribbon, model and layout tabs, Status Bar, **TOOLSPACE** palette, and **PANORAMA** window, as shown in Figure 1-2. The title bar is displayed on the top of the screen and displays the current drawing name.

The AutoCAD Civil 3D interface components are discussed next.

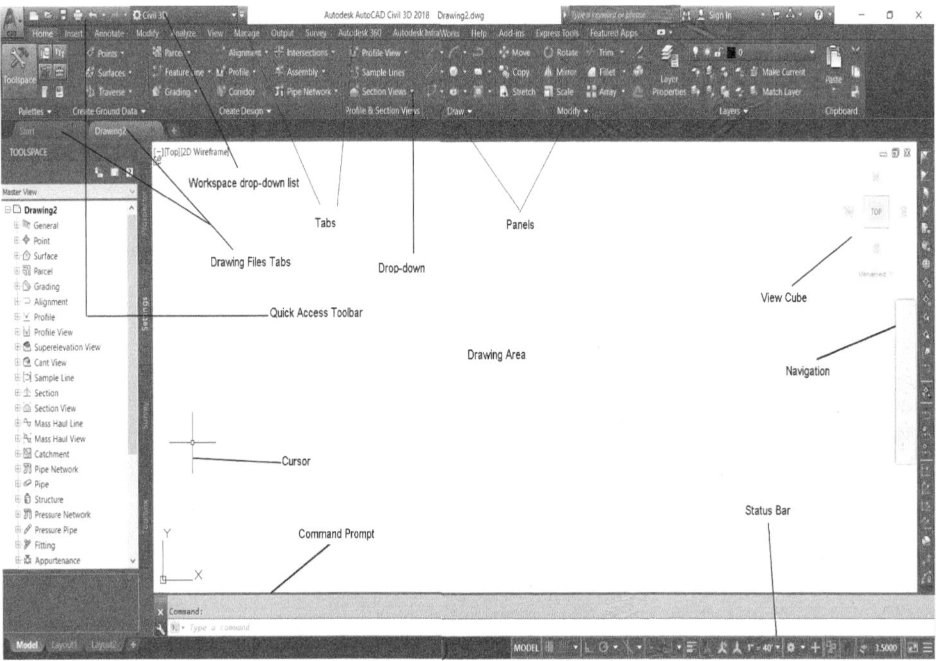

Figure 1-2 AutoCAD Civil 3D 2018 interface components

Drawing Area

The drawing area covers the major portion of the screen. Here, you can draw various objects and use commands. To draw the objects, you need to define the coordinate points that can be selected by using a pointing device. The position of the pointing device is represented on the screen by the cursor. There is a coordinate system icon at the lower left corner of the drawing area. The window also has standard Windows buttons such as close, minimize, scroll bar, and so on at the top right corner. These buttons have the same functions as in any other standard window.

Ribbon

The Ribbon interface in AutoCAD Civil 3D has a collection of tools that are grouped into various tabs based on their functionality. This interface provides an alternative to the layered menus, toolbars, and task panes which were used previously for displaying tools. The tools in the tabs are further sub grouped and placed into various panels depending on their usage and functionality.

To invoke a command, choose the required tool from the Ribbon. Figure 1-3 shows the typical **Home** tab of the AutoCAD Civil 3D Ribbon.

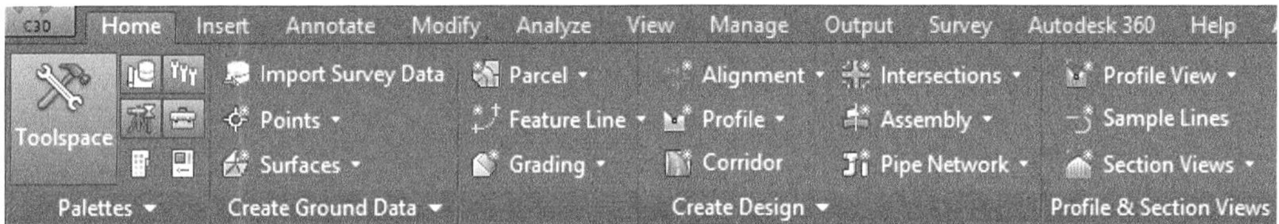

***Figure 1-3** Partial view of the Ribbon showing the **Home** tab*

When you start a Civil 3D session for the first time, by default the Ribbon is displayed horizontally below the **Quick Access Toolbar**. The panels in the Ribbon have various tools arranged in rows. Some of the tools have a small white down arrow displayed on their right. This arrow indicates that there are other tools as well that have similar functions and are grouped together in this drop-down. Click on the down arrow; a list of tools will be displayed. Note that if you choose a tool from the drop-down, the corresponding command will be invoked and the tool that you have chosen will be displayed in the panel. For example, to create a surface using the **Create Surface** tool, click on the down arrow next to the **Surfaces** drop-down in the **Create Ground Data** panel of the **Home** tab. Choose the **Create Surface** tool from the drop-down; the **Create Surface** dialog box will be displayed. Next, specify the various options in this dialog box to create the required surface.

In this book, the tool selection sequence is written as: choose the **Create Surface** tool from **Home > Create Ground Data > Surfaces** drop-down.

Some panels have a down arrow displayed on the right of their name. This indicates that more tools are available. To access these tools, click on the down arrow to expand the panel. You will notice that a push pin is available at the left of the panel. Click on the push pin to keep the panel in the expanded state. Also, some of the panels have an inclined arrow at the lower right corner. When you click on an inclined arrow, a dialog box will be displayed. You can define the setting of the corresponding panel in the dialog box.

You can reorder the panels in the tab. To do so, press and hold the left mouse button on the panel to be moved and then drag it to the required position in the tab. To undock the Ribbon, right-click on the blank space in the Ribbon; a shortcut menu is displayed. Choose the **Undock** option from the shortcut menu. Civil 3D allows you to customize the display and the contents of the tabs and panels in the Ribbon. To customize the Ribbon, right-click in the Ribbon; a shortcut menu will be displayed. Hover the cursor over an option in the menu; a flyout will be displayed. For example, if you hover the cursor over the **Show Tabs** option, a flyout will be displayed with the list of names of tabs that are available in the Ribbon. In the flyout, by default, a check mark is displayed beside those tab names that are available in ribbon. The check indicates that the corresponding panel will be displayed in the Ribbon. If you clear the check, the corresponding tab will get hidden in the Ribbon.

The options in the **Autodesk InfraWorks** tab are shown in Figure 1-4. The AutoCAD Civil 3D 2018 gives you access to InfraWorks-related commands and enables you to launch InfraWorks directly from the Ribbon.

*Figure 1-4 The options in the **Autodesk Infraworks** tab*

Application Menu

The **Application Menu**, shown in Figure 1-5, will be displayed when you choose the **Application** button located on the top left corner of the Civil 3D window.

It contains some of the tools that are available in the **Standard** toolbar. You can search a command using the search field in the **Application Menu**. To search a tool, enter the complete or partial name of the command in the search field; the possible tool list will be displayed. If you click on a tool from the list, the corresponding command will get activated.

By default, the **Recent Documents** button is chosen in the **Application Menu**. As a result, the list of recently opened drawings will be displayed in the menu. If you have opened multiple drawing files, choose the **Open Documents** button; the documents that are opened will be listed in the **Application Menu**. To set the preferences of the file, choose the **Options** button available at the bottom right of the **Application Menu**. To exit Civil3D, choose the **Exit Autodesk AutoCAD Civil 3D 2018** button next to the **Options** button.

*Figure 1-5 The **Application Menu***

Command Window

The command window located at the bottom of the drawing area has the command prompt where you can enter the commands. It also displays the subsequent prompt sequences and messages, refer to Figure 1-2. You can change the size of the window by placing the cursor on the top edge (double line bar known as the Grab bar) and then dragging it. This way you can increase its size to see the previous commands that you have used. By default, the command window displays only three lines. You can also press the F2 function key to display the **AutoCAD Text** window.

Drawing File Tabs

The drawing file tabs are displayed above the drawing area, refer to Figure 1-2, shows drawing that are currently opened. Using these drawing tabs, you can quickly switch between the drawings. The order in which these tabs are displayed is based on the sequence in which the files are opened.

Status Bar

The Status bar is displayed at the bottom of the screen, as shown in Figure 1-6. It contains some useful information and buttons that will make it easier for you to change the status of some AutoCAD functions. You can toggle between on and off states of most of these functions by choosing buttons from this bar.

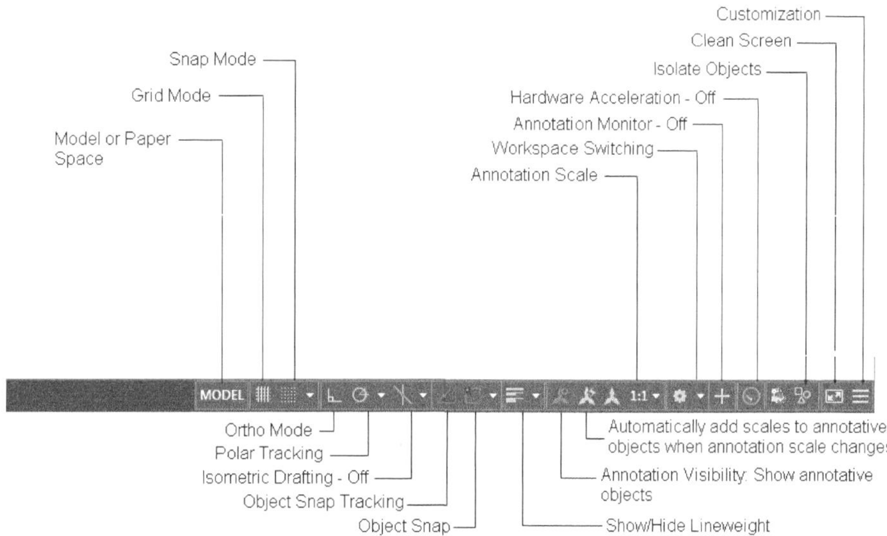

Figure 1-6 *The Status bar displayed in the Civil 3D workspace*

Model

The **Model** button is chosen by default because you work in the model space to create drawings. You will learn more about the model space in later chapters.

Display drawing grids

The grid lines are used as reference lines to draw objects in AutoCAD. If the **GRIDMODE** button is chosen, the display drawing grid will be on and the grid lines will be displayed on the screen. The F7 function key can be used to turn the grid display on or off.

Snap Mode

You can choose this button to turn on the snap mode. In this mode, the cursor moves in fixed increments. The F9 function key acts as a toggle key to turn the snap off or on.

Ortho Mode

You can choose this button to draw lines at right angles only. You can use the F8 function key to turn ortho mode on or off.

Polar Tracking

If you turn the polar tracking on, the movement of the cursor is restricted along a path based on the angle set as the polar angle. Choose the **Polar Tracking** button to turn the polar tracking on. You can also use the F10 function key to turn on this option. Note that turning the polar tracking on, automatically turns off the ortho mode.

Isometric Drafting

In AutoCAD, you can activate the required working plane. To activate the required working plane, choose the **Isometric Drafting** button from the Status bar. On choosing this button, a flyout is displayed with the **isoplane Left**, **isoplane Top**, and **isoplane Right** options. You can choose the required option from this flyout to activate the respective work plane.

Object Snap Tracking

When you choose this button, the inferencing lines will be displayed. Inferencing lines are dashed lines that are displayed automatically when you select a sketching tool and track a particular keypoint on the screen. Choosing this button turns the object snap tracking on or off. You can also use the F11 function key to turn the object snap tracking on or off.

Object Snap

When the **Object Snap** button is chosen, you can use the running object snaps to snap on to a point. You can also use the F3 function key to turn the object snap on or off. The status of **OSNAP** (off or on) does not prevent you from using the immediate mode object snaps.

Show/Hide Lineweight

This button in the Status Bar allows you to toggle on or off the display of lineweights in the drawing. If this button is not chosen, the display of lineweight will be turned off.

Show annotation objects

This button is used to control the visibility of the annotative objects that do not support the current annotation scale in the drawing area.

Add Scales to annotative objects when the annotative scale changes

On choosing this button, the annotation scales that are set current will be added to all the annotative objects present in the drawing.

Annotation Monitor

The **Annotation Monitor** button helps you to identify and address the disassociated annotations in the drawing. When this button is activated, you are automatically notified about the non associative dimensions, leaders, and associated model geometry.

Isolate Objects
This button is used to hide or isolate objects from the drawing area. On choosing this button, a flyout will be displayed. Choose the required option from this flyout and then select the objects to hide or isolate. To end isolation or display a hidden object, choose this button again and choose the **End Object Isolation** option.

Hardware Acceleration On
This button is used to set the performance of the software to an acceptable level.

Clean Screen
The **Clean Screen** button is available at the lower right corner of the screen. When you choose this button, it displays an expanded view of the drawing area by hiding all the toolbars except the command window, Status Bar, and menu bar. Choose the **Clean Screen** button again to restore the previous display rate.

Customization
The **Customization** button is available on the right corner of the Status Bar. Using this button, you can add or remove tools in the **Status Bar**.

TOOLSPACE Palette
In AutoCAD Civil 3D, you can view the project data and its status at any time in the **TOOLSPACE** palette. The data in the palette updates itself dynamically to show the status of the data within the drawing. To display the **TOOLSPACE** palette in a drawing, choose the **TOOLSPACE** button from the **Palettes** panel of the **Home** tab or type **SHOWTS** in the command line. There are four tabs in the palette: **Prospector**, **Settings**, **Survey**, and **Toolbox**. These tabs are discussed next.

Prospector Tab
The **Prospector** tab is used to manage project files. You can choose the **Prospector** tab in the **TOOLSPACE** palette. The options in the **Prospector** tab, as shown in Figure 1-7, are used to view, edit, and manage drawings. You can also edit the object data for the Civil 3D objects that are present in the drawing. In this tab, all the objects in a drawing or project are arranged in a hierarchy.

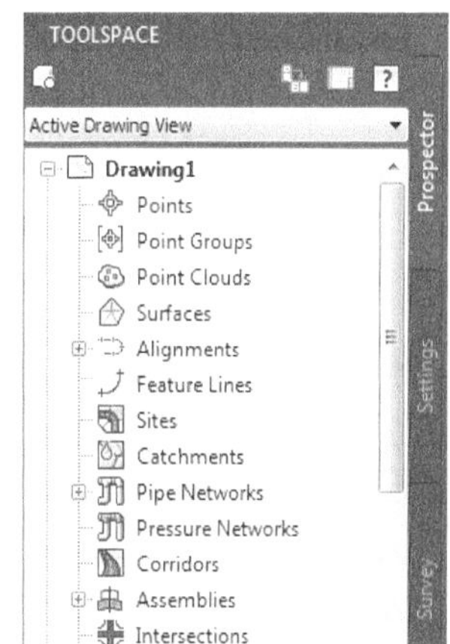

*Figure 1-7 The options displayed in the **Prospector** tab*

The drop-down list displayed at the top of the **Prospector** tab displays various options. The content displayed in the **Prospector** tab depends on the option selected from this drop-down list. Select the **Master View** option from the drop-down list; all project and drawing items, including drawing templates are displayed in a hierarchical order in the **Prospector** tab. If more than one Civil 3D drawing file are opened then the name of the active drawing is highlighted. Select the **Active Drawing View** option in the drop-down list; hierarchy of all the items in the active drawing is displayed in the **Prospector** tab, refer to Figure 1-7. You can toggle the display of the **Prospector** tab in the **TOOLSPACE** palette by choosing the **Prospector** button from the **Palettes** panel of the **Home** tab.

Settings Tab

Choose the **Settings** tab from the **TOOLSPACE** palette; various options in this tab will be displayed, as shown in Figure 1-8. You can also invoke this tab by choosing the **Settings** button from the **Palettes** panel of the **Home** tab. You can use this tab to view, create, and modify different styles for different object types in Civil 3D. This tab is also used to control the settings for drawings and commands.

Survey Tab

Choose the **Survey** tab from the **TOOLSPACE** palette; various options in this tab will be displayed. You can also invoke this tab by choosing the **Survey** button from the **Palettes** panel of the **Home** tab. The **Survey** tab shows the survey data present in the AutoCAD Civil 3D projects folder. This survey data can be accessed from multiple drawings. This tab displays a collection of databases such as **Survey Databases**, **Equipment Databases**, **Figure Prefix Databases**, and **Linework Code Sets**, as shown in Figure 1-9.

*Figure 1-8 The **Settings** tab chosen in the **TOOLSPACE** palette*

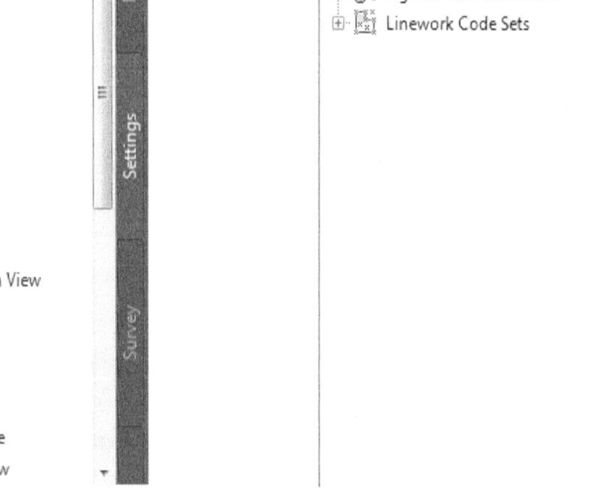

*Figure 1-9 The **Survey** tab chosen in the **TOOLSPACE** palette*

The survey databases consist of the records of survey points whereas the equipment database records the standard deviations and other operational parameters of the equipment used for the survey. The figure prefix databases record the conversion routines that are used while creating site features from the survey points.

Toolbox Tab

Choose the **Toolbox** button from the **Palettes** panel of the **Home** tab; the options in this tab will be displayed in the **TOOLSPACE** palette, as shown in Figure 1-10. This tab manages reports for each type of object in Civil 3D. These reports provide you useful engineering information regarding the objects in the drawing. The data available in these reports can be in Land XML format with custom/predefined XSL style sheets or in a .NET format.

Figure 1-10 The ***Toolbox*** *tab chosen in the* ***TOOLSPACE*** *palette*

The TOOLSPACE Item View

The TOOLSPACE Item View is used to view the contents of a given node or subnode in a list. This pane is displayed below the tree in the **TOOLSPACE** palette. For example, the **Points** node has a set of points which are displayed in the Toolspace Item View at the bottom of the toolspace.

Shortcut Menu

AutoCAD Civil 3D provides you with shortcut menus that are an easy and convenient way of invoking tools and the recently used commands. These shortcut menus are context-sensitive which means that the commands present in them are dependent on the place or object for which they are displayed. A shortcut menu is invoked by right-clicking and is displayed at the cursor location. You can right-click anywhere in the drawing area to display the general shortcut menu. The shortcut menus are also displayed when you right-click on one or more drawing objects or on an individual item from the **TOOLSPACE** palette. Figure 1-11 shows a shortcut menu displayed on right-clicking on the **Points** node in the **Prospector** tab.

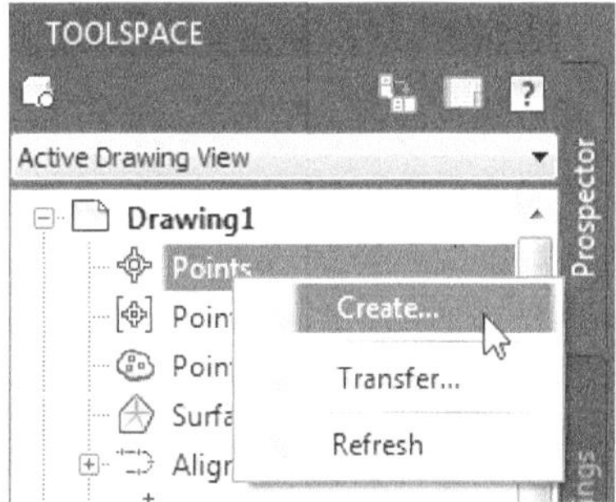

Figure 1-11 *Shortcut menu displayed on right-clicking on the* ***Points*** *node in the* ***Prospector*** *tab*

Layout Tools

In AutoCAD Civil 3D, you can use various layout toolbars to create and edit the Civil 3D objects such as alignments, grading, points, profiles, pipes, pressure pipes, and parcels. These toolbars provide access to object-specific designs and edit commands. To invoke a toolbar, choose the drop-down corresponding to the object. Next, choose the layout or creation method from the options that will be displayed in the flyout. Figure 1-12 shows the **Alignment Layout Tools - <alignment name>** toolbar invoked by choosing **Alignment Creation Tools** from **Home > Create Design > Alignment** drop-down.

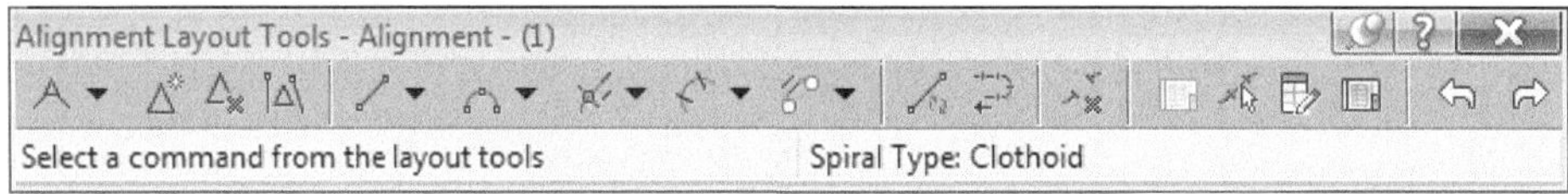

Figure 1-12 *The **Alignment Layout Tools - <alignment name>** toolbar*

Autodesk 360

Autodesk 360 is a cloud computing platform introduced by Autodesk. This platform provides a set of cloud services and products that can help you share, simulate, visualize, and design your work. You can access the Autodesk 360 services using your Autodesk ID. To login to your Autodesk 360 account, choose the **Sign In** button in the **InfoCenter** toolbar; a drop-down list will be displayed. Next, choose the **Sign In to Autodesk 360** option from this list; the **Autodesk-Sign In** dialog box will be displayed, as shown in Figure 1-13. Enter your credentials in this dialog box and choose the **Sign In** button; Autodesk will validate your credentials and then provide access to your account.

Tip

*You can sign up for a free Autodesk ID by choosing the **Need an Autodesk ID?** link in the **Autodesk - Sign In** dialog box.*

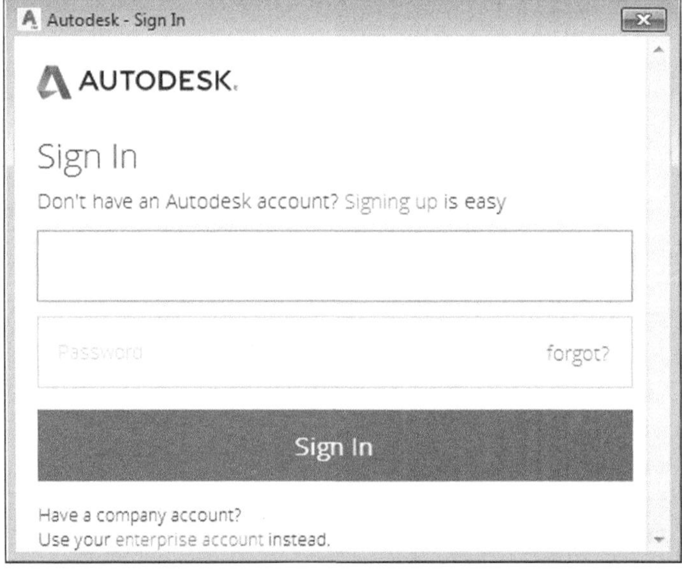

Figure 1-13 *The **Autodesk - Sign In** dialog box*

PANORAMA Window

This window can be used to display the entities of the objects such as alignments and profiles in a tabulated form. The **PANORAMA** window is a floating, dockable window that can be kept open while working. This window includes several tables called vistas on different tabs. In the **PANORAMA** window, the data displayed in black is editable and the data displayed in grey is non-editable.

Civil 3D WORKSPACES

Workspaces are the set of toolbars, menus, and Ribbon that are grouped and organized together to work in a custom and task-oriented environment. A workspace controls the layout of the Civil 3D user interface. When you use a specific workspace, you can view the Ribbon, toolbars, and other applications that have been specified for the selected workspace. To invoke the applications and tools that are specified in other workspaces, enter the commands in the command line.

You can select workspaces at the beginning when you start the Civil 3D application or anytime during the drawing session. When you start AutoCAD Civil 3D, you are prompted to select a specific workspace and then continue. Once you are done, you can switch to other workspace settings at any time by choosing the **Workspace Switching** button that is located in the Status Bar. On doing so, a flyout will be displayed, as shown in Figure 1-14.

Choose an option from this flyout for specifying different workspace settings in the current drawing environments. After you choose the required option, the drawing interface will change according to the setting of the workspace you have chosen.

In AutoCAD Civil 3D, there are four default workspaces such as **Civil 3D**, **Planning and Analysis**, **2D Drafting & Annotation**, and **3D Modeling**. These default workspaces are designed considering the tools that a user might use for that kind of project. You can also create your own customized workspace and save it using the **Save Current As** tool from the flyout, refer to Figure 1-14.

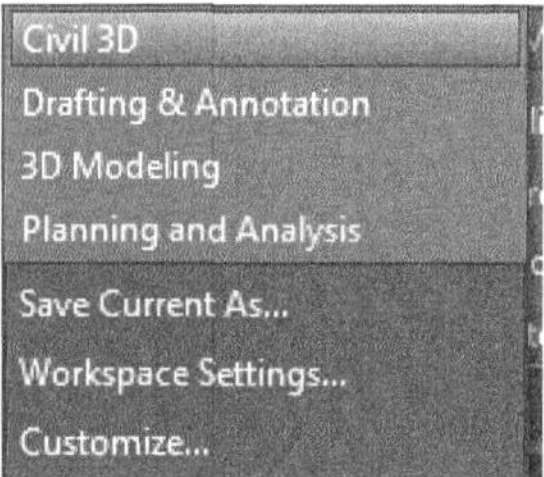

Figure 1-14 *The flyout displaying various options for choosing a workspace*

The default workspaces that are available in AutoCAD Civil 3D are discussed next.

Civil 3D

The Civil 3D workspace includes all the necessary tools and applications that required for designing a civil engineering project such as the road, railway, or a pipe network designing project.

2D Drafting & Annotation

This workspace is used for the purpose of documentation of a project. The **Annotation** tab is included in the Ribbon in this workspace. All the tools related to annotation are available in this tab so that you can annotate easily as per your requirement.

3D Modeling

This workspace contains all the tools and applications that are available in the AutoCAD and can be useful in AutoCAD Civil 3D.

Planning and Analysis

This workspace contains all the tools and features that are available in AutoCAD Map 3D and can be used directly in AutoCAD Civil 3D.

GETTING STARTED WITH AutoCAD Civil 3D

Before you create a new project or start working on the existing project, you should be familiar with various tools and concepts that can be applied to create the initial setup of the project. The basic setup tools like drawing templates and setting units are discussed next.

Drawing Templates

Drawing templates are very useful tools for AutoCAD Civil 3D users. These tools help in maintaining consistency throughout the drawings in the project.

To use a template in a drawing, choose the **Prospector** tab of the **TOOLSPACE** palette and then select the **Master View** option from the drop-down list at the top. Now, expand the **Drawing Templates** node and right-click on a template; a shortcut menu will be displayed, as shown in Figure 1-15.

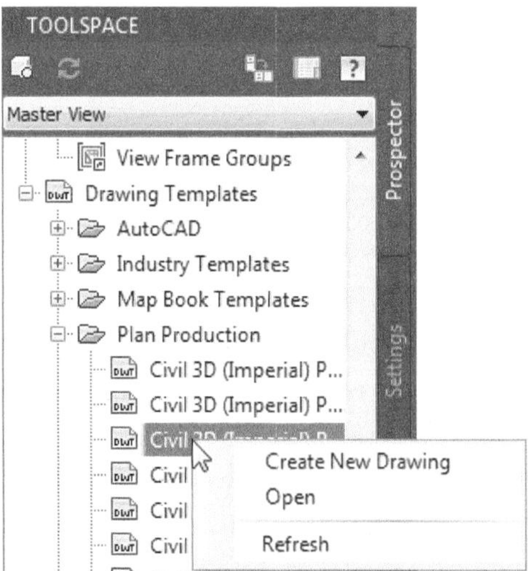

Figure 1-15 *Choosing a drawing template from the* ***Drawing Templates*** *node of the* ***Prospector*** *tab*

To create a new drawing file, choose the **Create New Drawing** option from the shortcut menu displayed; a new drawing file will be created using the settings of the drawing template file that you had selected.

You can also open the existing drawing template in AutoCAD Civil 3D. To do so, choose the **Open** option from the shortcut menu; the template will open in the drawing area.

An AutoCAD Civil 3D drawing template file contains information of the standard AutoCAD settings such as layers, text styles, dimension styles, and so on. It also contains AutoCAD objects such as lines and texts. The drawing template files also carry AutoCAD Civil 3D drawing information that is listed in the **Settings** and **Prospector** tabs of the **TOOLSPACE** palette.

Drawing Settings

Drawing settings allow the user to review or modify settings specified for a drawing. To edit the current drawing settings, right-click on the drawing name that is displayed in the **Settings** tab of the **TOOLSPACE** palette; a shortcut menu will be displayed. Choose the **Edit Drawing Settings** option from this shortcut menu, as shown in Figure 1-16; the **Drawing Settings - <drawing name>** dialog box will be displayed, refer to Figure 1-17. This dialog box contains five tabs that are discussed next.

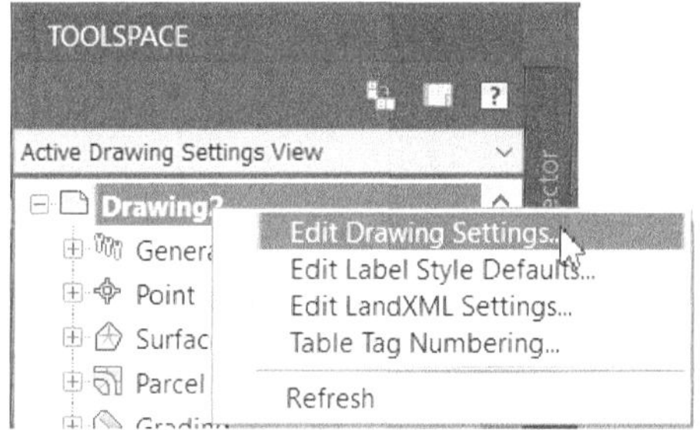

Figure 1-16 *Choosing the* ***Edit Drawing Settings*** *option*

Units and Zone Tab

This tab is used to set linear and angular units, intended plot scale, and coordinate zone for the current drawing.

Transformation Tab

This tab is primarily used to specify the parameters for the projection and coordinate system of the drawing.

Object Layers Tab

This tab provides a table in which the objects can be directly assigned a layer. To change the layer of an object, click in the field of the **Layer** column corresponding to that object; the **Layer Selection** dialog box will be displayed. In this dialog box, select the layer name that you want to assign to the selected object and choose the **OK** button; the dialog box will be closed and the selected layer name will be assigned to the object.

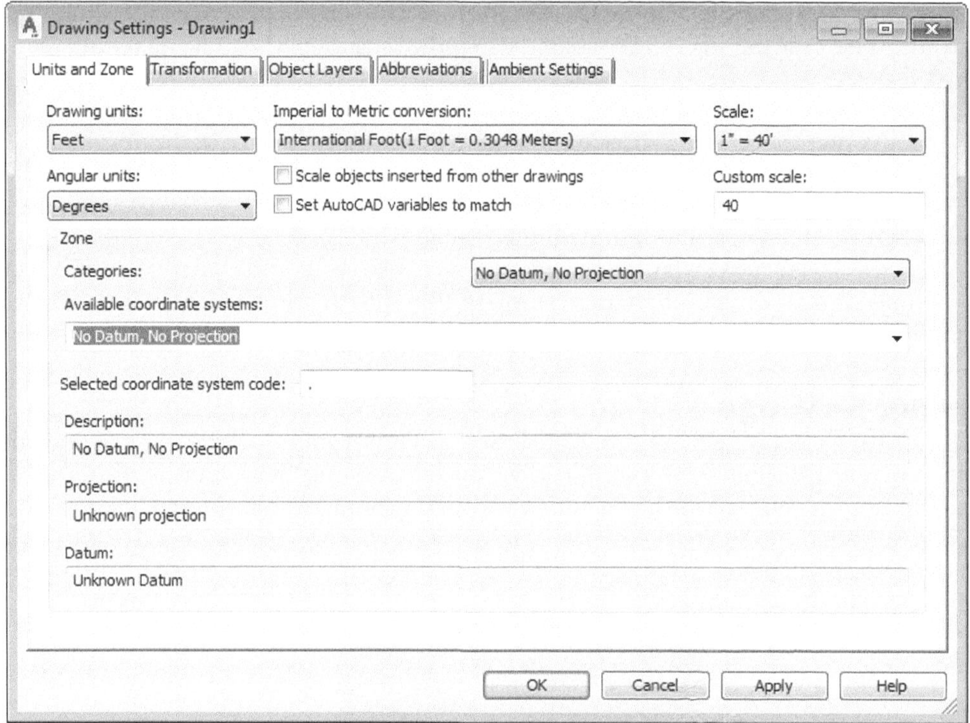

*Figure 1-17 The **Drawing Settings** dialog box*

The layer of an object controls various properties such as color, linetype, and lineweight of an object to which it is assigned. As a result, the object to which a layer is assigned can have maximum flexibility in its display.

Abbreviations Tab

In this tab, you can set the abbreviations used in object labels, especially for alignment and profile geometry points.

Ambient Settings Tab

This tab provides global default settings such as precision, unit, rounding of the numeric values, visibility of tooltips, and so on. You can expand various properties and make the required settings in the **Value** column of this tab. The ambient settings made in the **Ambient** tab are used throughout the drawing unless they are overridden at the feature or command level.

After configuring the settings in the **Drawing Settings** dialog box, you need to examine the default styles for each feature and its labels, the feature name format, and other settings that you may want to modify. To do so, go through point, surface, and other features in the **Settings** tab and right-click on each feature. Next, choose the **Edit Feature Settings** option from the shortcut menu to invoke the **Edit Feature Settings** dialog box. You can examine various settings of the selected feature by using the options in this dialog box.

Self-Evaluation Test

Answer the following questions and then compare them to those given at the end of this chapter:

1. The horizontal and vertical geometry of a corridor is defined by its _________ and profile.

2. The ___________ palette is used to view the project data and its status at any time.

3. You can use the _________ tab in the **TOOLSPACE** palette to view, create, and modify different styles for different object types in Civil 3D.

4. When you select the **Active Drawing View** option from the drop-down list in the **Prospector** tab only the items in the _________ drawing will be displayed.

5. You can switch between the workspaces by choosing the _________ button in the Status Bar.

6. In Civil 3D, each defined point has a unique number. (T/F)

7. The **Planning and Analysis** workspace displays all the tools and toolbars that are available in AutoCAD Civil 3D. (T/F)

8. You can invoke the **Survey** tab by choosing the **Survey** button from the **Palettes** panel of the **Home** tab. (T/F)

9. The annotation scale controls the size and display of the annotative objects in the model space. (T/F)

10. The **SHOWTS** command is used to display the **TOOLSPACE** palette. (T/F)

Review Questions

Answer the following questions:

1. In AutoCAD Civil 3D, the _________ tool enables the engineers to grade a surface by applying criteria such as slope to a surface or grade to a distance.

2. The _________ tab in the **TOOLSPACE** palette manages reports for each type of object in Civil 3D.

3. In AutoCAD Civil 3D, the _________ workspace is used for the purpose of drafting and annotating features.

4. In AutoCAD Civil 3D, __________ provides you with a view of the terrain that is cut at an angle across a linear feature.

5. The **Transformation** tab in the **Drawing Settings** dialog box is used to transform the coordinate system to local specifications. (T/F)

Answers to Self-Evaluation Test

1. alignment, **2. TOOLSPACE**, **3. Settings**, **4.** active, **5. Workspace Switching**, **6.** T, **7.** F, **8.** T, **9.** T, **10.** T

Chapter 2

Working with Points

Learning Objectives

After completing this chapter, you will be able to:

- *Understand the concept of points in Civil 3D*
- *Create points using different methods*
- *Create point styles*
- *Create point label styles*
- *Understand file formats*
- *Edit points*
- *Understand description keys*

POINT OBJECT

A point object represents a location in 3D space, and is defined by its X, Y, and Z coordinates. Each civil engineering project starts with data collection. This data is imported into Civil 3D workspace as points by using a suitable coordinate system. Generally, points specify the location of different features on the site such as trees, road geometry points, property corners, edge of pavements, and so on. However, Civil 3D points offer you more than just specifying the location of different objects on the site. In Civil 3D, each point represents an individual object with different information and has a unique point number. The information displayed by a Civil 3D point object depends upon the point settings, which will be discussed later in the chapter.

Components of Point Object

In AutoCAD Civil 3D, a point object has two major components, marker and label. Marker represents the location of point object whereas label displays information about that point object. The display of point marker is controlled by point style and the display of the point label is controlled by the point label style. Figure 2-1 shows a point with number, elevation, and description.

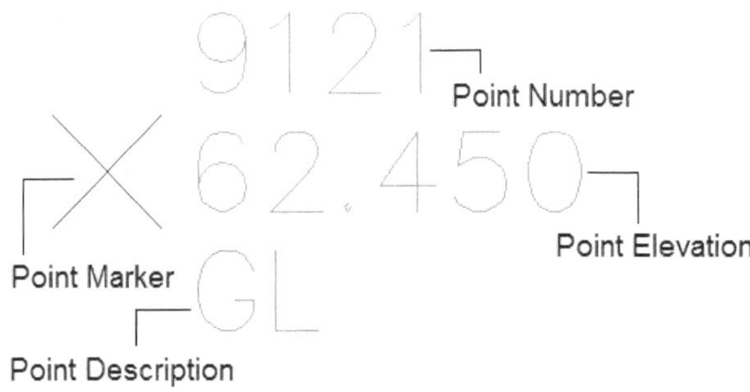

Figure 2-1 *A point with number, elevation, and description*

The properties of an individual Civil 3D point can be viewed in the **PROPERTIES** palette, refer to Figure 2-2. You can modify the properties of the selected point(s) such as color, layer, linetype, and point elevation.

Creating Points

In AutoCAD Civil 3D, you can create points using various methods. These methods of point creation involve conversion of AutoCAD points into Civil 3D points, importing points from external point files, and creation of points using input parameters specified by the user.

These methods for point creation have been broadly classified into six categories which are discussed next.

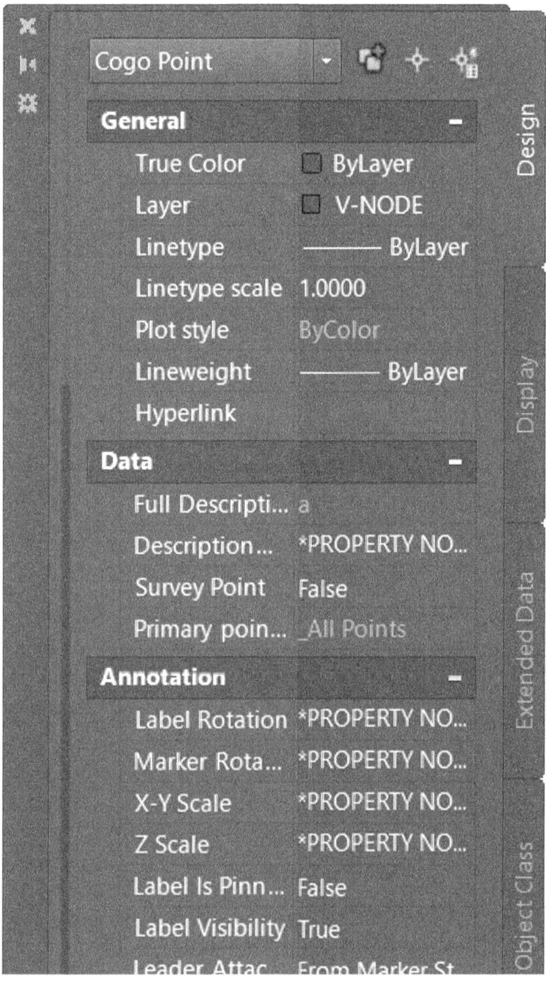

Figure 2-2 Partial view of the ***PROPERTIES*** *palette showing different point properties*

The Miscellaneous Category

Ribbon:	Home > Create Ground Data > Points drop-down > Create Points-Miscellaneous

The tools in the **Miscellaneous** category are used to create points by manually specifying the point location in the drawing. The tools in the **Miscellaneous** category are the most commonly used tools to create points. To access these tools, choose the **Create Points-Miscellaneous** option from the **Create Ground Data** panel; a flyout will be displayed with different tools, as shown in Figure 2-3. Some of the tools in this category are discussed next.

Manual

Ribbon: Home > Create Ground Data > Points drop-down > Create Points- Miscellaneous > Manual
Command: CREATEPOINTMANUAL

The **Manual** tool is used to manually create points. To create points using this tool, invoke this tool from the **Create Ground Data** panel; the **Create Points** toolbar will be displayed and you will be prompted to specify the location of the point. Click in the drawing to specify the location.

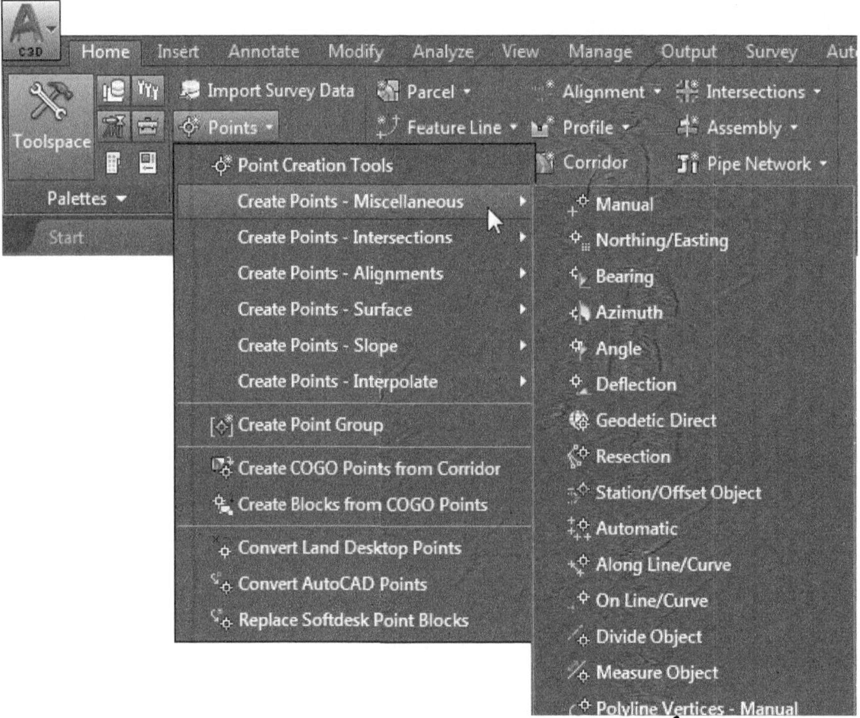

***Figure 2-3** The tools in the **Miscellaneous** category*

Next, enter description of the point in the command line or in the dynamic input edit box and right-click; you will be prompted to specify the elevation of the point. Now, specify the elevation of the point and right-click again to continue or press ENTER to terminate the command.

Geodetic Direct

Ribbon: Home > Create Ground Data > Points drop-down > Create Points- Miscellaneous > Geodetic Direct
Command: CREATEPTGEODETICDIR

The **Geodetic Direct** tool is used to create points by using geodetic direction and azimuth. Before using this tool, you need to assign a coordinate system and a zone to the current drawing. To do so, choose the **Settings** tab in the **TOOLSPACE** palette. In the **Settings** tab, right-click on the current drawing name; a shortcut menu will be displayed.

Choose the **Edit Drawing Settings** option from the shortcut menu; the **Drawing Settings - <drawing name>** dialog box will be displayed. In the dialog box, choose the **Units and Zone** tab. Next, in the **Zone** area of this tab, select the required geographic zone from the **Categories** drop-down list. Also, select the coordinate system within the selected zone category from the **Available coordinate systems** drop-down list. Choose the **Apply** button and then the **OK** button to close the dialog box.

Once the coordinate system has been assigned, choose the **Geodetic Direct** tool from the **Create Ground Data** panel; you will be prompted to specify the start point. Click in the drawing to specify the start point; you will be prompted to specify the azimuth. Azimuth is the angle measured with respect to the true north. Specify azimuth; you will be prompted to specify the geodetic distance. The geodetic distance is the shortest path between two points along the ellipsoid of the earth at sea level. Specify distance; you will be prompted to enter description. Enter the point description. Next, specify elevation for the point. Press ENTER to terminate the command.

Note

*1. The **Geodetic Direct** tool is also known as the **Geodetic Direction and Distance tool** when accessed through the **Create Points** toolbar.*

*2. If the coordinate system is not assigned to the drawing and you invoke the **Geodetic Direct** tool to create points then an **AutoCAD Civil 3D 2018** warning message will be displayed.*

Automatic

Ribbon:	Home > Create Ground Data > Points drop-down > Create Points- Miscellaneous > Automatic
Command:	CREATEPOINTAUTOMATIC

The **Automatic** tool is used to create points automatically at the endpoints of single or multiple lines, feature lines, or lot lines. In case of an arc, a point is also created at the center. To create points using this tool, choose the **Automatic** tool from the **Create Ground Data** panel. Next, select the required entity and press ENTER; you will be prompted to specify the description and elevation for the points to be generated. Enter the point description and elevation at the Command prompt. You will notice that points are displayed at endpoints, center of arc, and vertices of the selected entity. Next, press ENTER to exit the command.

Polyline Vertices - Manual

Ribbon:	Home > Create Ground Data > Points drop-down > Create Points- Miscellaneous > Polyline Vertices - Manual
Command:	CREATEPTPLYLINECTRVERTMAN

The **Polyline Vertices - Manual** tool is used to create points at each vertex of a polyline at the specified elevation. To do so, choose the **Polyline Vertices - Manual** tool from the **Create Ground Data** panel; you will be prompted to specify the default elevation of all points to be created. Enter the elevation at the command prompt; you will be prompted to select polyline. Next, select the required polyline; you will be prompted to enter a description. Enter a description for the point either at the Command prompt or in the dynamic input edit box and press ENTER; a point will be created at the first vertex of the polyline. Similarly, enter description for other points on the polyline and then press ENTER to exit the command.

Polyline Vertices - Automatic

Ribbon:	Home > Create Ground Data > Points drop-down > Create Points- Miscellaneous > Polyline Vertices - Automatic
Command:	CREATEPTPLYLNCTRVERTAUTO

The **Polyline Vertices - Automatic** tool is used to create points automatically at each vertex of a polyline. To do so, choose the **Polyline Vertices - Automatic** tool and select the required polyline. Next, enter a point description in the command line. Press ENTER to end the command or continue it by specifying the description of all points on the polyline. On doing so, points will be created at vertices of the selected polyline and the elevation of the generated points will be the same as that of the selected polyline.

The Intersections Category

Ribbon:	Home > Create Ground Data > Points drop-down > Create Points-Intersections

The tools in the **Intersections** category are used to create points at the intersection of direction lines of two points, intersection of distances of two points, intersection of two alignments, and so on. To access tools in the **Intersections** category, choose the **Create Points - Intersections** option from the **Create Ground Data** panel; a flyout will be displayed with different tools, as shown in Figure 2-4. Some of the tools in this category are discussed next.

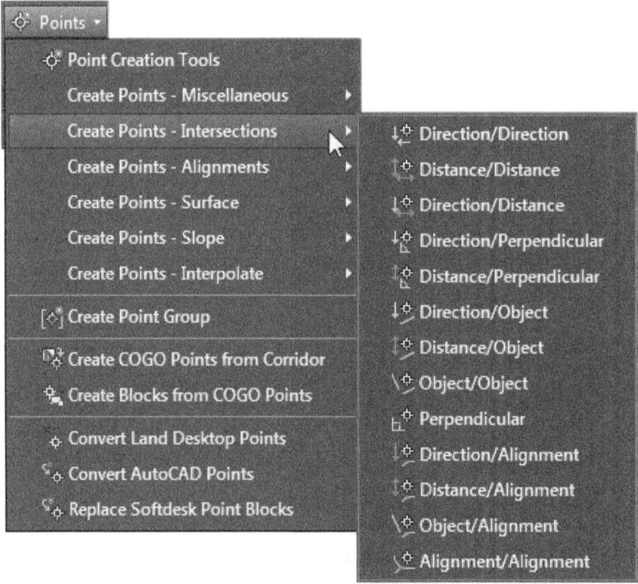

*Figure 2-4 The tools in the **Intersections** category*

Direction/Direction

Ribbon: Home > Create Ground Data > Points drop-down > Create Points - Intersections > Direction/Direction
Command: CREATEPOINTDIRECTIONDIR

The **Direction/Direction** tool is used to create points at specified offset distance from the point where the direction lines meet, refer to Figure 2-5.

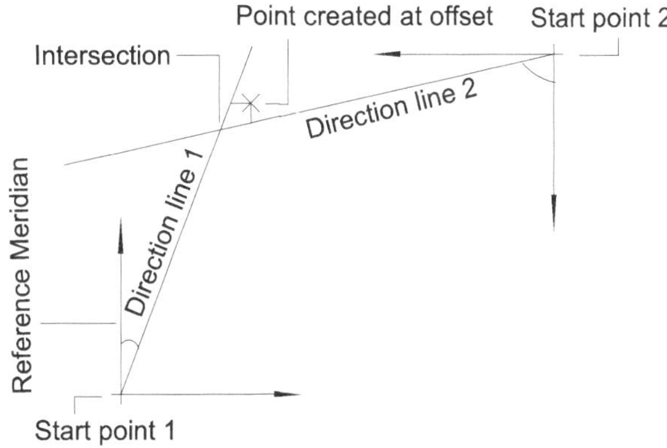

Figure 2-5 The point created at the specified offset distance from the intersection of direction lines of two points

To create points using this tool, choose the **Direction/Direction** tool from the **Create Ground Data** panel; you will be prompted to specify the start point in the drawing. Specify the point by clicking in the drawing. On doing so, you will be prompted to specify the direction at the start point. You can specify direction using the **Bearing** or **Azimuth** option. You can use the **Bearing** option to specify the direction with reference to a particular quadrant, or the **Azimuth** option to specify the direction with reference to the North meridian. Enter **B** to select **Bearing** or **Z** to select **Azimuth**. If you select the **Bearing** option, a quadrant will be displayed at the specified point. Move the cursor in the required quadrant and click to select the quadrant.

Next, click again to specify the bearing by clicking in the drawing or by entering the bearing in the command line; you will be prompted to specify the offset from the point of intersection. Enter the offset distance in the command line or specify the distance by picking points from the drawing.

Specify the second point by following same procedure. Once you specified the offset for the second point, you will be prompted to specify the point description and elevation. Enter the description and elevation of the point. On doing so, you will notice that a point is displayed at the specified offset distance from the intersection of direction lines of points, refer to Figure 2-5.

Distance/Distance

Ribbon:	Home > Create Ground Data > Points drop-down > Create Points-Intersections > Distance/Distance
Command:	CREATEPOINTDISTANCEDIST

The **Distance/Distance** tool is used to create a point at the intersection of arcs of given radial distances from specified points. On choosing this tool, you will be prompted to specify the location of the radial point. Click in the drawing to specify the location; you will be prompted to specify the radius. Enter the radius in the command line using the dynamic input or pick points in the drawing to specify the radius. Similarly, specify the location of the second point and enter a radius; two cross marks indicating two points at the apparent intersection of arcs will be displayed. Click near the intersection, where you want to create point or press ENTER to accept the default **ALL** option to enable you to create points at both intersections. Next, follow the prompts and specify the point description and elevation. On doing so, the point(s) will be created at the intersection of the arcs, refer to Figure 2-6. Press ESC to exit the command.

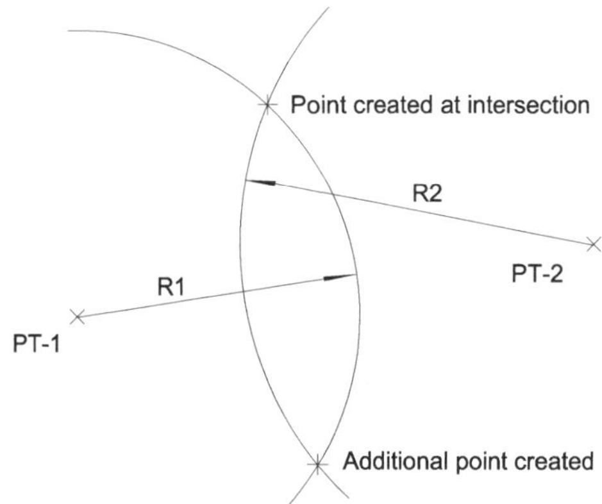

Figure 2-6 *Points created at the intersection of arcs of specified radial distances defined from two points*

Note

Cross-marks, indicating the intersections of two points, will not be displayed if the radii are non-intersecting.

Direction/Perpendicular

Ribbon:	Home > Create Ground Data > Points drop-down > Create Points-Intersections > Direction/Perpendicular
Command:	CREATEPOINTDIRECTIONPERP

The **Distance/Perpendicular** tool is used to create a point at the intersection of the direction line and the perpendicular line that passes through the specified location. Choose this tool from the **Create Ground Data** panel; you will be prompted to specify the start point. Click in the drawing to specify the start point; you will be prompted to specify the direction at the start point. Specify the direction by specifying bearing or azimuth. On doing so, you will be prompted to specify the offset distance. Specify the offset distance from the direction line or press ENTER to accept the default value **0**. Next, specify the location of the perpendicular point; a cross mark will be displayed perpendicular to the specified point. Follow the prompts and specify the point description and elevation; a point coinciding with the cross mark will be created, as shown in Figure 2-7.

Distance/Object

Ribbon:	Home > Create Ground Data > Points drop-down > Create Points-Intersections > Distance/Object
Command:	CREATEPOINTDISTANCEOBJECT

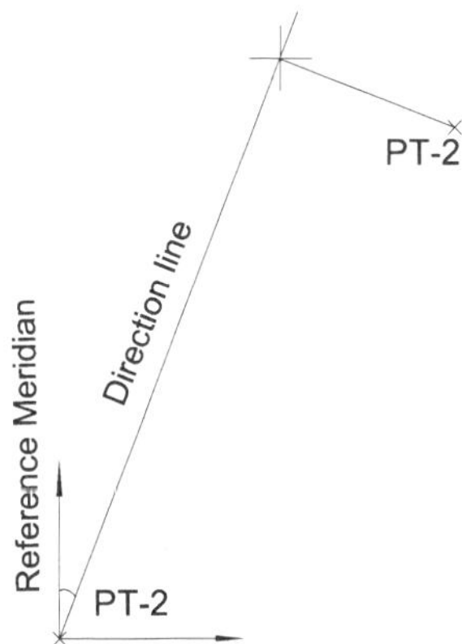

Figure 2-7 *The point created in the specified direction at a perpendicular distance from the specified point*

The **Distance/Object** tool is used to create a point at the intersection of an object such as line, arc, feature line, polyline, or plot line and an arc of specified radial distance of given point. To create a point using this tool, choose the **Distance/Object** tool from the **Create Ground Data** panel; you will be prompted to select the specified line, arcs, or any other objects from the drawing. Select the object from the drawing.

Next, specify an offset distance of the point from the selected object by entering a suitable value in the command line. Alternatively, you can specify the distance by picking points from the drawing. If no offset is required, enter **0** as the offset value. On doing so, you will be prompted to specify the radial point. Click at the required location in the drawing to specify the radial point. Next, specify the radial distance by entering the required value in the command line or by picking points from the drawing; you will notice that two cross marks are displayed at the apparent intersection of the object and the arc of specified radial distance. Click near the cross-mark where you want to add a point or press ENTER to accept the default **All** option to add points at all intersections. Enter a description and elevations for the points and then press ENTER to end the command. Figure 2-8 shows the points created at 0 offset distance from the arc object.

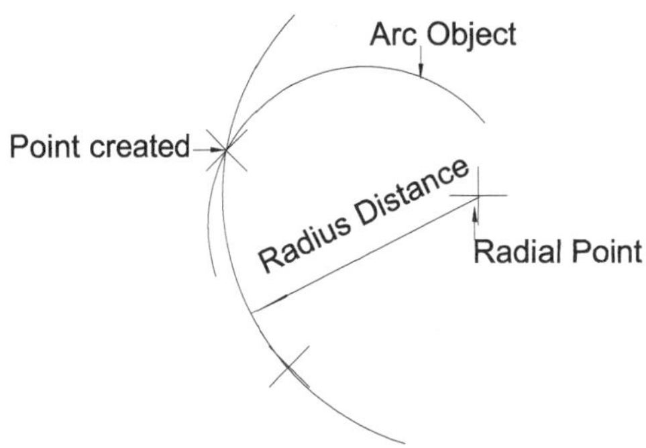

Figure 2-8 Point created at the intersection of the arc object and the radial distance from a point

The Alignments Category

Ribbon: Home > Create Ground Data > Points drop-down > Create Points - Alignments

The tools in the **Alignments** category are used to create points on or along the horizontal alignment at a given offset distance. To access tools in the **Alignments** category, choose the **Create Points - Alignments** option from the **Create Ground Data** panel; a flyout will be displayed with different tools, as shown in Figure 2-9. Some of the tools in this category are discussed next.

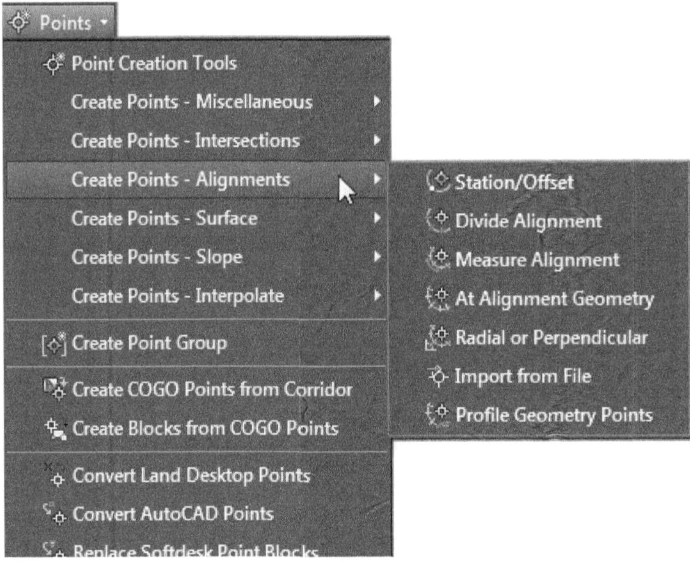

Figure 2-9 Partial view of flyout displaying tools in the ***Alignments*** *category*

Station/Offset

Ribbon: Home > Create Ground Data > Points drop-down > Create Points - Alignments > Station/Offset
Command: CREATEPOINTSTATIONOFFSET

The **Station/Offset** tool is used to create a point at a given offset from the point station selected on the alignment. To create a point, invoke this tool from the **Create Ground Data** panel; you will be prompted to select an alignment. Next, click on a station on the alignment and then specify an offset distance. Also, specify the description and elevation of the point when prompted; a point will be created and displayed at the specified offset distance from the station that was selected on the alignment. This tool is useful for creating points for right of way, lanes, and shoulders.

Divide Alignment

Ribbon: Home > Create Ground Data > Points drop-down > Create Points - Alignments > Divide Alignment
Command: CREATEPOINTDIVIDEALIGN

The **Divide Alignment** tool is used to create points at equal divisions of an alignment. Using this tool, you can create points at vertex or endpoints of each segment. Choose the **Divide Alignment** tool from the **Create Ground Data** panel; you will be prompted to select the required alignment from the drawing. Select the alignment from the drawing; you will be prompted to specify the number of segments. Specify the number of segments; you will be prompted to specify the offset distance. Specify the offset distance or enter **0** if the points are not required to be created at an offset; you will be prompted to specify the description and elevation for all the points that will be created at the vertex of each segment. Enter the description and elevation; the points will be created, as shown in Figure 2-10.

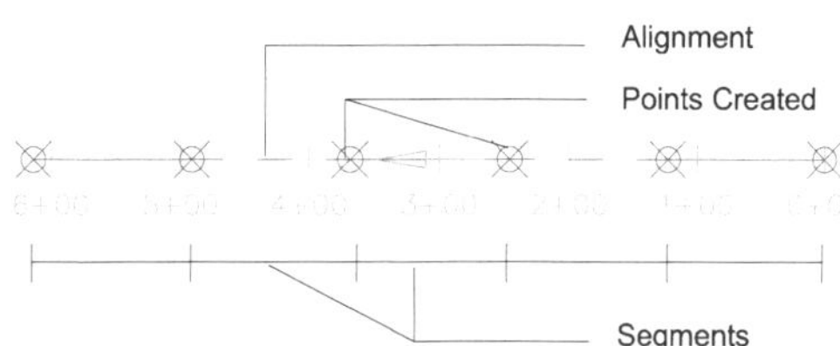

Figure 2-10 *Points created at 0 offset distance at each vertex of all five segments*

Measure Alignment

Ribbon: Home > Create Ground Data > Points drop-down > Create Points - Alignments > Measure Alignment
Command: CREATEPOINTMEASUREALIG

The **Measure Alignment** tool is used to create points at fixed intervals along an alignment. To create points using this tool, you need to specify an interval and an offset distance from the alignment at which the points will be created. Choose the **Measure Alignment** tool from the **Create Ground Data** panel and select the required alignment. Next, specify the starting station from where you want to start creating points or press ENTER to accept the default option. Similarly, specify the end station.

Note

To enter a user-specified station through command bar, type station value in the xx+xx.xx format. For example, to enter a station value of 1024.75, use 10+24.75 as input value.

Note

You can specify the start and end station values manually to replace the default values.

On doing so, you will be prompted to specify the offset from the alignment. Next, enter the offset distance in the command line or press ENTER to create points on the alignment. Similarly, specify the interval at which you want to create these points. Now, enter the point description and elevation; points will be created at specified interval along the entire alignment. Note that once you specify the description and elevation for points, they will be created and displayed automatically.

At Alignment Geometry

Ribbon:	Home > Create Ground Data > Points drop-down > Create Points - Alignments > At Alignment Geometry
Command:	CREATEPOINTATPTPCSCETC

The **At Alignment Geometry** tool is used to create points at each geometry point such as start and end points of alignment (EP, BO), spiral tangents (TS, ST), spiral curves (SC, CS) as well as point of intersections (PI), point of Curvature (PC), and so on. This tool is named as **At Geometry Points** in the **Create Points** toolbar. To create points, choose the **At Alignment Geometry** tool from the **Create Ground Data** panel. Next, select the required alignment from the drawing. Next, specify the starting station from where you want to start creating points. Similarly, specify the second station and end station and press ENTER. On doing so, you will be prompted to enter a point description. Specify the point description and elevation till all the points are created. Next, press ENTER to terminate the command.

Tip

You can automatically extract the point description such as alignment and surfaces from any of the Civil 3D objects. To do so, select the ***Automatic - Object*** *option in the* ***Prompt for Description*** *drop-down list displayed under the* ***Points Creation*** *head in the* ***Create Points*** *toolbar.*

Import from File

Ribbon:	Home > Create Ground Data > Points drop-down > Create Points - Alignments > Import from File
Command:	CREATEPOINTIMPORTFROMFILE

The **Import From File** tool is used to create points from the text file (*.txt*) containing information about the station, offset, and elevation of an alignment. To create points using this tool, choose the **Import from File** tool from the **Create Ground Data** panel; the **Import Alignment Station and Offset File** dialog box will be displayed. Browse to the required location and open the required file. On doing so, the **Enter file format** dynamic input prompt will be displayed, as shown in Figure 2-11.

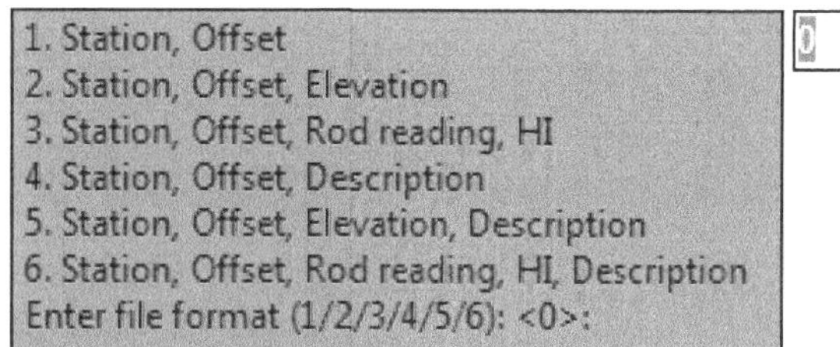

***Figure 2-11** The **Enter file format** dynamic input prompt*

Note

The station value in the text file should have a xxxx.xx format. For example, station 4+57.28 in a text file should be written as 457.28.

Also, six different file formats in the prompt will be displayed. Specify the required format by entering the corresponding number of the format starting from 1 to 6 in the text box, as shown in Figure 2-11. For example, if the text file consists of the Station and Offset information, enter **1** in the text box. Next, specify delimiter type of the text file using **1** for space delimiter and **2** for comma delimiter. After specifying the delimiter, specify the invalid indicator for elevation, station, or offset. Next, select the required alignment along which points will be created using the text file; Civil 3D will import points from the selected file and create points along the alignment.

Note

*To get the dynamic input, ensure that the **Dynamic Input** in the status bar is selected and turned on.*

The Surface Category

Ribbon: Home > Create Ground Data > Points drop-down > Create Points - Surface

The tools in the **Surface** category are used to create points on the horizontal alignment or at a certain offset distance from it. To access tools in the **Surface** category, choose the **Create Points - Surface** option from the **Create Ground Data** panel; a flyout will be displayed with different tools, as shown in Figure 2-12. Some of the tools in this category are discussed next.

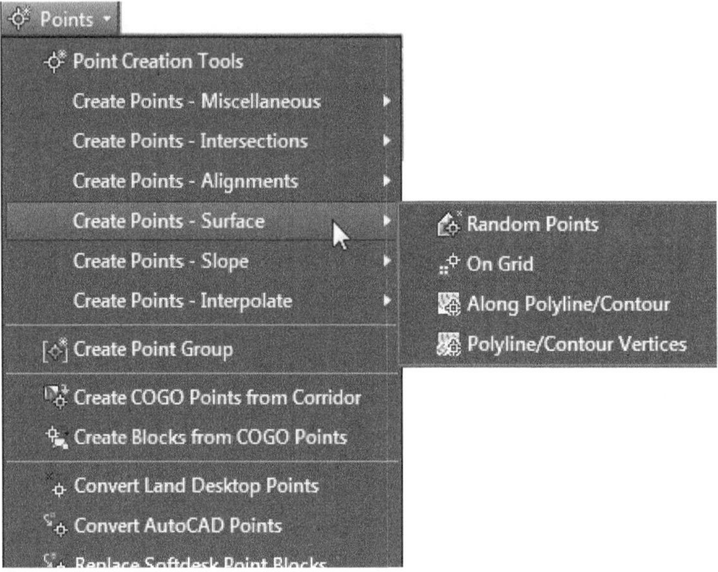

***Figure 2-12** Partial view of flyout displaying tools in the **Surface** category*

Random Points

Ribbon: Home > Create Ground Data > Points drop-down > Create Points - Surface > Random Points
Command: CREATEPOINTRANDOMPOINTS

The **Random Points** tool is used to add points anywhere on the surface. The points that are added acquire their elevation from the surface itself. You can invoke the **Random Points** tool from the **Points** drop-down. On doing so, you will be prompted to specify a location for the new point. Next, click at the required location inside the surface and specify the description of the point. Continue adding these points or press ENTER to end the command.

Note

AutoCAD Civil 3D calculates the elevation for a point using the surface and assigns it to the point.

On Grid

Ribbon: Home > Create Ground Data > Points drop-down> Create Points - Surface > On Grid
Command: CREATEPOINTONGRID

The **On Grid** tool is used to create points on a surface by specifying the spacing along the X and Y axes of the grid. To do so, choose the **On Grid** tool from the **Points** drop-down; you will be prompted to specify a grid base point. Now, click on the surface to specify the base point of the grid; you will be prompted to specify the rotation of the grid in the command line. Press ENTER to accept the default value. Now, specify the spacing between each point in the X direction in the command line or pick the points on the screen.

Similarly, specify the spacing along the Y direction. Now, specify the upper right corner of the grid; a single boundary of the grid will be displayed. Also, you will be prompted to change the spacing or the rotation of the grid. Press ENTER to accept the default option **No**. Follow the prompts and enter description for points. As you continue to enter description in the command line, you will notice that points will be displayed in a grid. These points will be added at the surface elevation, as shown in Figure 2-13.

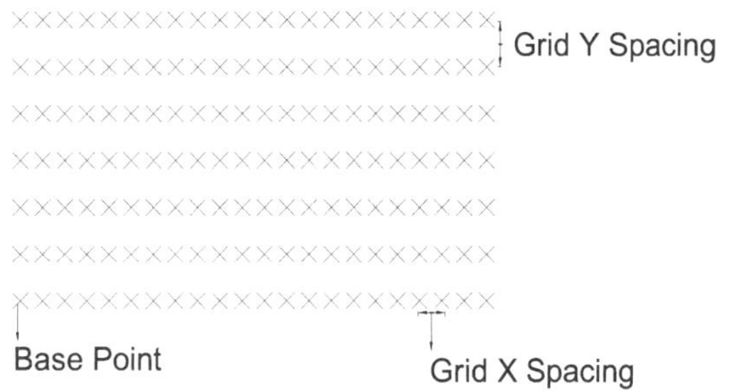

Figure 2-13 The points added at the surface elevation

Along Polyline/Contour

Ribbon:	Home > Create Ground Data > Points drop-down > Create Points - Surface > Along Polyline/Contour
Command:	CREATEPTALONGPOLYCONTOUR

The **Along Polyline/Contour** tool is used to create points along a polyline or a contour on a surface. To create points using this tool, choose the **Along Polyline/Contour** tool from the **Create Ground Data** panel and select the required surface. Next, specify the distance between the points in the command line. Now, select the required polyline or contours in the surface; you will be prompted to specify the point description. Specify the description for the points and then press ENTER. The point will be created and you will be again prompted to enter description for the next point. Continue doing this until you are prompted to select a new polyline or contour. Press ESC to exit the command.

The Slope Category

Ribbon:	Home > Create Ground Data > Points drop-down > Create Points - Slope

The tools in the **Slope** category are used to create points based on the slope, grade intersections, elevations, or distances. To access tools in the **Slope** category, choose the **Create Points - Slope** option from the **Create Ground Data** panel; a flyout will be displayed with different tools, as shown in Figure 2-14. Some of the tools in this category are discussed next.

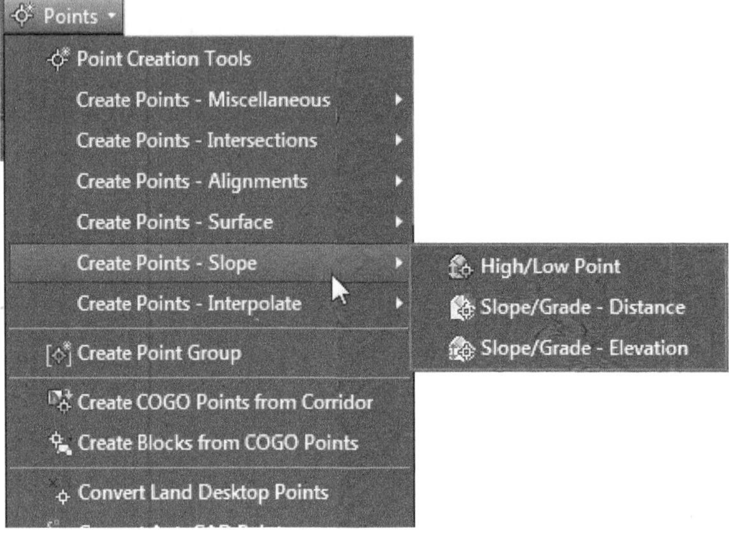

***Figure 2-14** Partial view of flyout displaying tools in the **Slope** category*

High/Low Point

Ribbon:	Home > Create Ground Data > Points drop-down > Create Points - Slope > High/Low Point
Command:	CREATEPOINTHIGHLOWPOINT

The **High/Low Point** tool is used to create a high or low elevation point by specifying the slope or grade of two points. These points are created at a location where the slopes or grades of two points intersect. Choose this tool from the **Create Ground Data** panel and click in the drawing to specify the first point. Click again to specify the second point. Next, you need to specify the required slope or grade for the first point in the drawing area by entering a value in the command line or by using the dynamic input. To do so, enter **S** in the command line to specify the slope (in ratio) or enter **G** to specify the grade (percent) and press ENTER. Similarly, specify the required slope or grade for the second point; a cross mark will be displayed. Now, press ENTER to accept the default option **Yes** after being prompted to add a point at the intersection. Next, enter the point description; a new point will be added at the intersection of the forward slope/grade of the first point and the back slope from the second point, as shown in Figure 2-15.

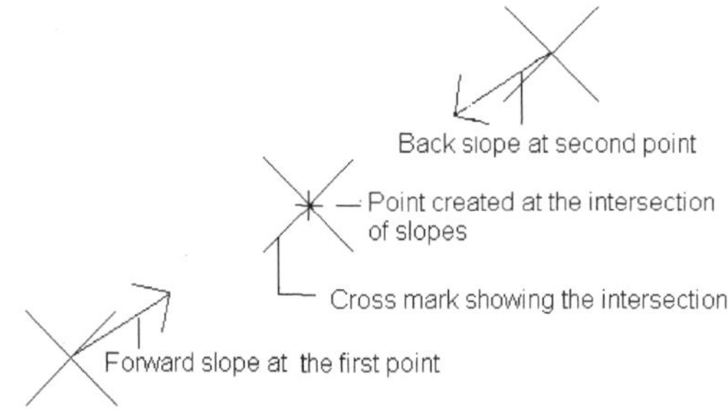

***Figure 2-15** Point created at the intersection of slopes*

Slope/Grade-Distance

Ribbon: Home > Create Ground Data > Points drop-down > Create Points - Slope > Slope/Grade - Distance
Command: CREATEPOINTSLOPEGRADEDIST

The **Slope/Grade-Distance** tool is used to create specified number of points at a desired slope or grade from a given point at the specified direction and distance. To do so, choose the **Slope/Grade-Distance** tool from the **Create Ground Data** panel and click in the drawing to specify the start point. Next, click in the required direction again to specify the direction of intermediate points. Now, specify the required slope or grade at that point. Next, enter the distance at which you want to create multiple points in the command line. Enter the number of points in the command line and press ENTER. Specify the offset distance or press ENTER to accept the default value. Optionally, press ENTER to add the endpoint. Follow the prompts and enter the point description or continue pressing ENTER to skip description. As you continue pressing ENTER, points will be displayed in the drawing in the specified direction.

Slope/Grade Elevation

Ribbon: Home > Create Ground Data > Points drop-down > Create Points - Slope > Slope/Grade - Elevation
Command: CREATEPOINTSLOPEGRADEELEV

The **Slope/Grade Elevation** tool is used to create multiple points in a specific direction by specifying grade/slope at a specified distance and elevation. Choose the **Slope/Grade - Elevation** tool from the **Create Ground Data** panel and click in the drawing to specify the start point. Click again to specify the direction in which points will be created. Next, specify the required grade or slope in the command line and press ENTER. Specify the end elevation in the command line and press ENTER. Now, enter the number of points to be created. Optionally, specify the offset distance in the command line and press ENTER. Again, press ENTER to add the endpoint, if required. Follow the prompts and enter the description for all the points. As you enter the description, points will be created and displayed.

The Interpolate Category

Ribbon: Home > Create Ground Data > Points drop-down > Create Points - Interpolate

The tools in the **Interpolate** category are used to add points to the drawing by interpolation. To access tools in this category, choose the **Create Points - Interpolate** option from the **Create Ground Data** panel; a flyout will be displayed with different tools, as shown in Figure 2-16. Some of the tools in this category are discussed next.

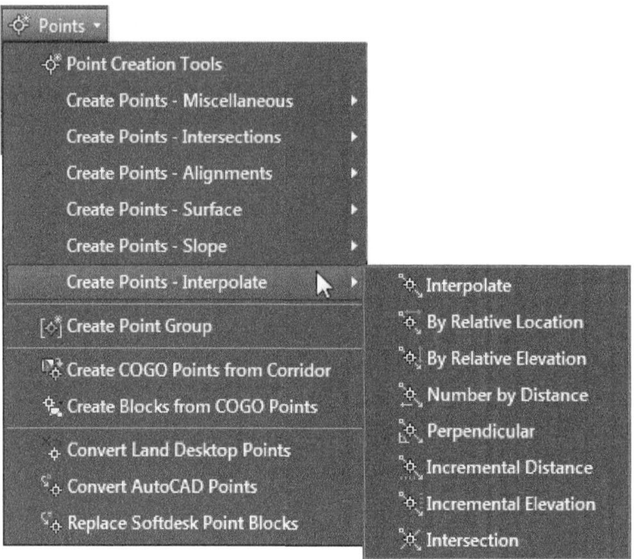

***Figure 2-16** The flyout displaying tools in the **Interpolate** category*

Interpolate

Ribbon:	Home > Create Ground Data > Points drop-down > Create Points - Interpolate > Interpolate
Command:	CREATEPOINTINTERPOLATE

The **Interpolate** tool is used to create specified number of points between two existing points by interpolation. To create points using the **Interpolate** tool, choose the **Interpolate** tool from the **Create Ground Data** panel; you will be prompted to select the object. Select the first point; you will be prompted to specify the second point. Specify the second point. Next, specify the number of points that you want to create in the command line and press ENTER. Then, specify the offset and press ENTER. Now, enter the description for each point and press ENTER; the points will be created between the two points through interpolation and will be added to the drawing between these two points.

By Relative Location

Ribbon:	Home > Create Ground Data > Points drop-down > Create Points - Interpolate > By Relative Location
Command:	CREATEPOINTBYRELLOCATION

The **By Relative Location** tool is used to create a point by interpolating a point between two given points based on the distance specified. To create points, choose the **By Relative Location** tool from the **Create Ground Data** panel and click in the drawing to specify the first control point. Next, specify the elevation of the point in the command line and press ENTER. Similarly, specify the second control point; you will be prompted to specify the distance at which you want to create the point. You can specify the distance either by entering the required value in the command line or by using the dynamic input. Next, specify the offset distance of the point from the arbitrary line or the arc joining two control points. Now, specify the point description in the command line and press ENTER; the point will be created and displayed at the specified distance from the first control point and at the specified offset distance from the arbitrary line joining two control points. Press ENTER to end the command.

Intersection

Ribbon: Home > Create Ground Data > Points drop-down > Create Points - Interpolate > Intersection
Command: CREATEPTINTERPOLINTERSEC

The **Intersection** tool is used to create points by interpolation at the intersection of two existing entities such as arc or line. If there are no existing entities in the drawing, you can create arbitrary regions for two entities by picking points from the drawing. To create points, choose the **Intersection** tool from the **Create Ground Data** panel. Next, click in the drawing at the required location to specify the first point for the first region. The first control point of the first entity will be created. Next, specify the elevation for the first control point in the command line or press ENTER to skip the elevation; you will be prompted to specify the second point. Click to specify the second point; you will be prompted to specify elevation. To specify the elevation of the second point using the elevation difference between the first and second point, enter **D** in the command line, enter **S** to specify the slope between the two points, or enter **G** to specify the grade between two points. This is called the second control point of the first entity. Thus, you have created an arbitrary region for the first entity. Next, specify the offset distance of the point to be created from the entity. To do so, follow the prompts and specify two more control points for the second entity. On doing so, green colored cross marks indicating the intersection of two points will be displayed and you will be prompted to specify the description for the point. If the entities intersect only at one point, one cross-mark will be displayed and if the entities intersect at two points, two cross marks will be displayed. Specify the description or press ENTER to skip the description; a point will be interpolated and displayed on the cross mark. Press ENTER to end the command. Figure 2-17 shows the interpolated points created at the intersection.

To create a point from the existing entities, choose the **Intersection** tool from the **Create Points** toolbar. Next, enter **E** in the command line and press ENTER; you will be prompted to select the existing line, arc, lot line, feature line, or polyline entity. Select the required existing entities and follow the prompts to create points by the intersection of two entities.

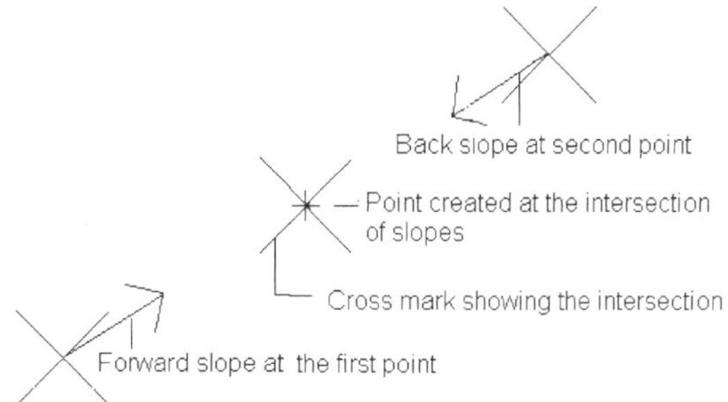

Figure 2-17 *The interpolated points created at the intersection*

Import Points

Ribbon:	Insert > Import > Points from File
Command:	IMPORTPOINTS

The **Points from File** tool is used to create points by using the point data contained in the imported files. The point data is generally imported from the ASCII (.txt) or Microsoft Access (.mdb) files. Creating points using the point data collected by the data collector or surveyor is the most convenient way to create points. Before importing points, you need to specify the file format according to the point data in the file.

To import the point data file, choose the **Points from File** tool from the **Import** panel; the **Import Points** dialog box will be displayed, as shown in Figure 2-18. In this dialog box, you can select a file format and specify other necessary options prior to importing points. The options in this dialog box are discussed next.

Selected Files

The **Selected Files** list box displays the name and path of the selected file to be imported as points. To add a source file, choose the button on the right of the **Selected Files** list box; the **Select Source File** dialog box will be displayed. Browse to the required folder and then select the file to be imported. Also, select the file type from the **Files of type** drop-down list and choose the **Open** button to open the file; the name and path of the file will be displayed in the **Selected Files** list box.

Specify point file format

The **Point File Format** dialog box displays various file formats supported by Civil 3D. A file format describes the sequence or arrangement of point data in the file to be imported. It is important to select file format similar to point file before importing, exporting, or transferring points. For example, if the point file consists of the northing, easting, and elevation information of points, you need to select the NEZ file format.

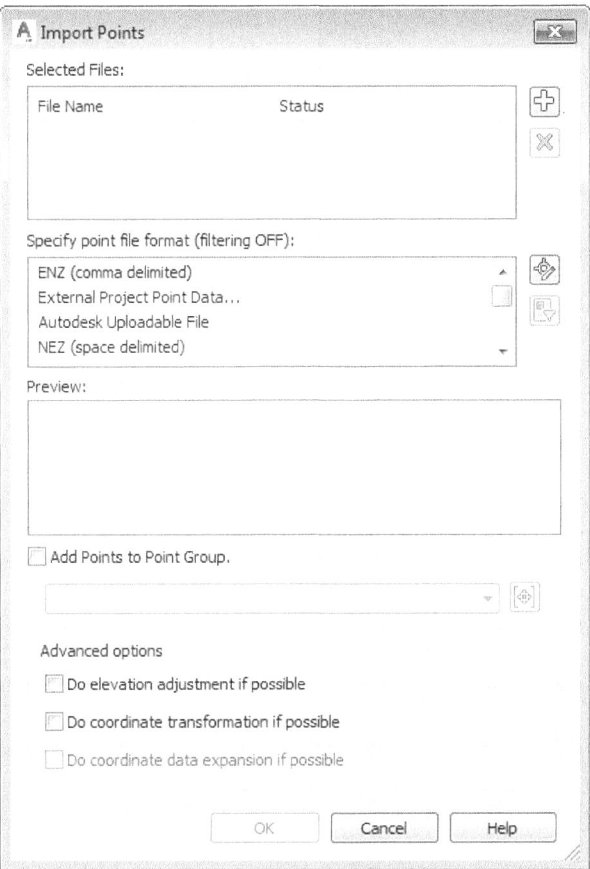

*Figure 2-18 The **Import Points** dialog box*

There are two main types of file formats, **User point Database** and **User Point File**. The **User Point Database** format is used to specify the arrangement of point data in the Microsoft Access database file and the **User Point File** is used to specify the arrangement in the .txt file. You can use the in-built file formats depending upon the type of file used or create your own formats. The methods of creating new formats are discussed later in this chapter.

Add Points to Point Group

Select the **Add Points to Point Group** check box to add the points of the selected file to an existing point group. You can select a point group from the drop-down list located below the **Add Points to Point Group** check box, if the drawing consists of any predefined point groups. If the drawing does not consist of a point group, you can create a point group. To create a point group, choose the button on the right of the drop-down list; the **Point File Formats - Create Group** dialog box will be displayed. Enter the name of the point group that you want to create in the edit box and choose the **OK** button; the point group will be created and the points will be added to the point group.

Advanced options

Selecting the **Do elevation adjustment if possible** check box from the **Advanced options** area enables the elevation adjustment of the points being imported. For adjusting elevation data using this option, the point file format must contain Z+, Z-, or thickness columns.

Here, the value in the Z+ column will be added to the value in the **Elevation** column. The value in the Z- column for a point will be subtracted from the value in the **Elevation** column. This results in new elevation values for the points when they are imported or transferred. The Thickness column is used to store data for layer thickness and thickness value will be subtracted from the value in the **Elevation** column for the points.

Selecting the **Do coordinate transformation if possible** check box enables the coordinate transformation for the imported point file. This option is applicable only if the imported point file and the drawing in which the point file is imported has a defined coordinate system. The imported points are transformed to match the coordinate system of the current drawing.

After specifying the file format and other options in the **Import Points** dialog box, choose the **OK** button; the dialog box will be closed and points will be imported. The appearance of the imported points will depend on the point settings.

Tip

You can also create points using the ***Create Points*** *toolbar. To invoke the toolbar, choose the* ***Points Creation Tools*** *tool from* ***Home > Create Ground Data > Points*** *drop-down, refer to Figure 2-19. Alternatively, invoke the* ***Create Points*** *toolbar by right-clicking on the* ***Points*** *node in the* ***Prospector*** *tab in the* ***TOOLSPACE*** *palette and then choose* ***Create*** *from the shortcut menu displayed.*

*Figure 2-19 The **Create Points** toolbar*

Note

If you do not specify a point group, the points created or imported in the drawing will be added to the default ***_All Point*** *point group. The* ***_All Point*** *group is displayed in the* ***Prospector*** *tab of the* ***TOOLSPACE*** *palette.*

POINT SETTINGS AND STYLES

AutoCAD Civil 3D has some in-built point styles that control the visibility and appearance of Civil 3D points. Besides controlling the visibility and display of points, these styles help you manage the workability of points. Point styles can be assigned after the points are imported or created. Alternatively, you can use a drawing template with the required point settings and then import or create points according to industry standards. Civil 3D has some default settings for points. These settings control display, elevation, layer, visibility, size, dimension, and so on. You can view and edit these default settings as per your requirement. To edit these settings, choose the **Settings** tab in the **TOOLSPACE** palette and right-click on the **Point** node; a shortcut menu will be displayed. Choose the **Edit Feature Settings** option from the shortcut menu, as shown in Figure 2-20; the **Edit Feature Settings - Point** dialog box will be displayed, as shown in Figure 2-21.

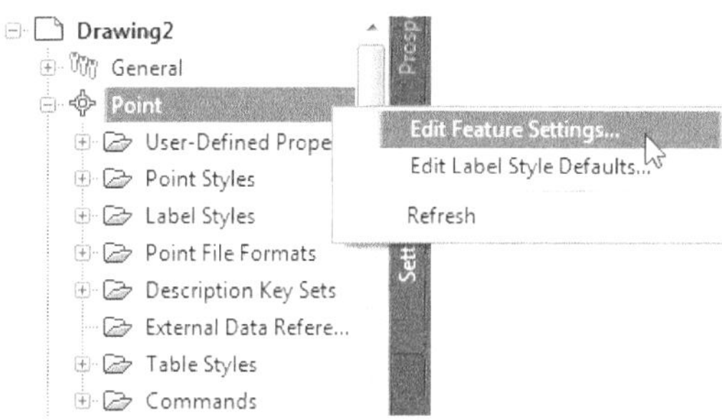

*Figure 2-20 Choosing the **Edit Feature Settings** option from the shortcut menu*

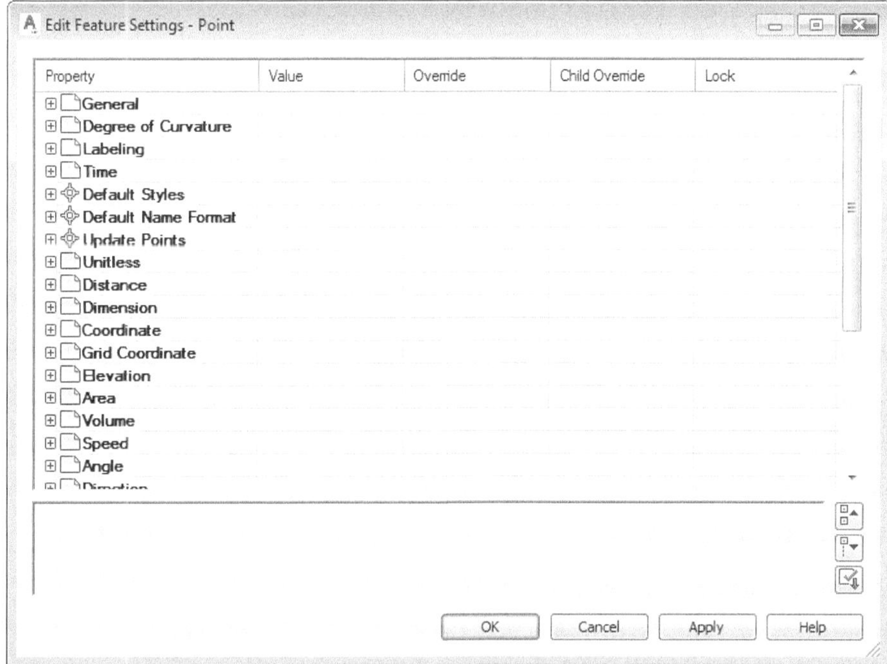

*Figure 2-21 The **Edit Feature Settings - Point** dialog box*

This dialog box is used to edit the settings of points. Every Civil 3D object has some default settings that can be viewed and modified using the **Edit Feature Settings - Point** dialog box. You can expand various categories in the dialog box and click in the **Value** field of properties to modify values.

For example, expand the **Default Styles** node and then click in the **Value** field of the **Point Style** property; The **Browse** button will be displayed. Choose the **Browse** button to display the **Point Style** dialog box. Select the required option from the drop-down list, as shown in Figure 2-22. Next, choose the **OK** button; the dialog box will be closed and the default point style will be modified. Now, when you create or import points in the drawing or template, the selected point style will be assigned automatically to points.

Similarly, you can modify the other default values related to the point object in this dialog box and choose the **OK** button to close the dialog box.

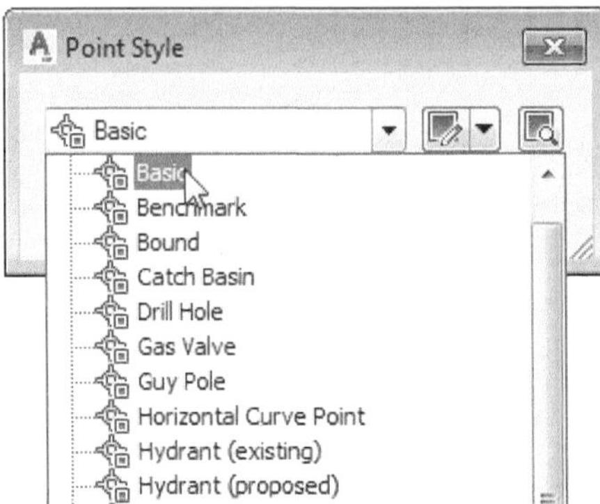

Figure 2-22 *Selecting a point style from the drop-down list*

Note

*The drop-down list displayed in the **Point Style** dialog box will be based on the type of drawing template selected while creating the drawing file.*

Point Styles

Point styles control the shape, size, color, and location of the point marker. It also controls the visibility of the point label. Point styles are created and assigned before or after points are created in the drawing. As discussed earlier, AutoCAD Civil 3D provides you with some in-built point styles. However, you can create your own point styles as per the project requirements and use them in the drawing. Point styles are created and managed in the **Settings** tab of the **TOOLSPACE** palette.

Creating a Point Style

You can create a point style by using the options in the **Point Style - New Point Style** dialog box. To invoke the **Point Style - New Point Style** dialog box, choose the **Settings** tab in the **TOOLSPACE** palette and expand the **Point** node. Next, right-click on **Point Styles** and then choose the **New** option from the shortcut menu displayed, as shown in Figure 2-23. On doing so, the **Point Style - New Point Style** dialog box will be displayed with the **Information** tab chosen, as shown in Figure 2-24. The options in different tabs of this dialog box are discussed next.

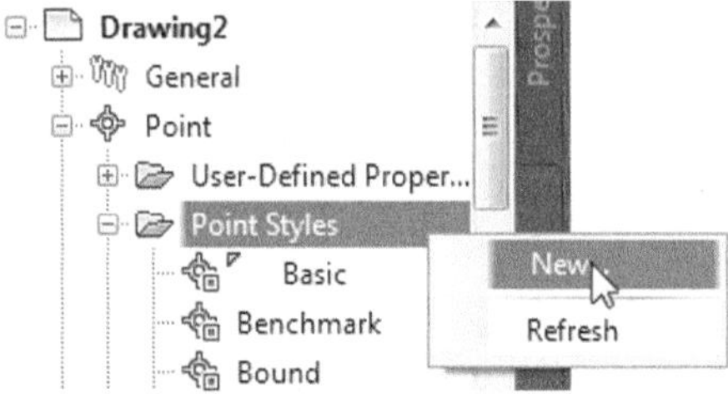

Figure 2-23 *Choosing the **New** option from the shortcut menu*

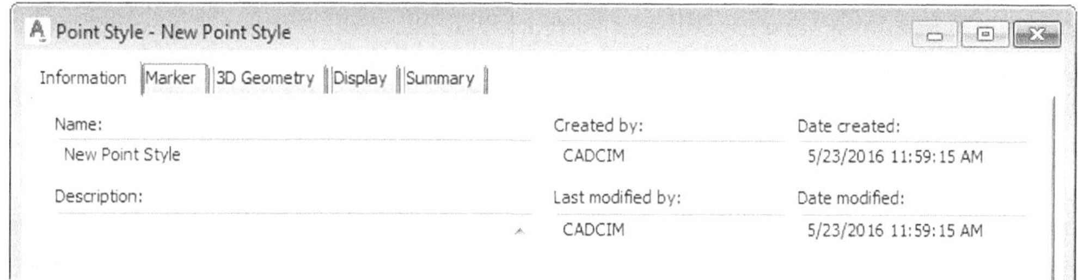

*Figure 2-24 Partial view of the **Information** tab of the **Point Style - New Point Style** dialog box*

Information Tab

This tab is chosen by default and is used to specify name for a point style. Enter a name for the new point style in the **Name** edit box. If no name is specified, the point style will be created with the default name **New Point Style**. You can also enter a description about the point style in the **Description** text box.

Marker Tab

The **Marker** tab, as shown in Figure 2-25, is used to specify the appearance of the marker point in the drawing. Using this tab, you can specify the point marker as that of the AutoCAD point style or you can use the AutoCAD blocks to represent them in the drawing. In this tab, you can also use the custom defined point markers to represent as a point marker in the drawing. Various options in the **Marker** tab are discussed next.

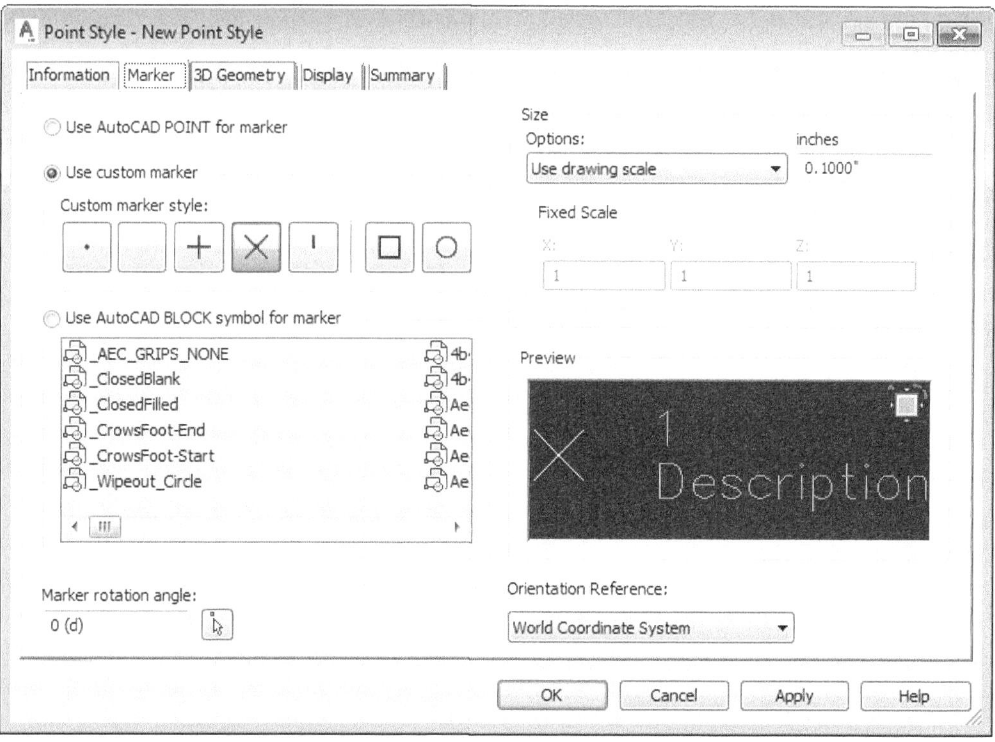

*Figure 2-25 The **Marker** tab in the **Point Style - New Point Style** dialog box*

In the **Marker** tab, you can specify the marker point using the current AutoCAD point symbol, which can be specified by the AutoCAD PDMODE and PDSIZE system variables. To do so, select the **Use AutoCAD POINT for marker** radio button and see its preview in the **Preview** area. In this tab, you can also use a specified symbol to represent a point marker in the drawing. To do so, select the **Use custom marker** radio button. On selecting this radio button, different symbols to represent the point marker will be displayed as buttons in the **Custom marker style** area. You can choose any one of the five buttons on the left to be used as a base symbol and then choose either sixth or seventh button or both. The last two buttons that are chosen individually or in combination superimposes over the base symbol to form a combined symbol. As you choose these buttons, you can preview them in the **Preview** area of the **Marker** tab.

You can also display the point marker in the drawing using a block reference of an AutoCAD block. To do so, select the **Use AutoCAD BLOCK symbol for marker** radio button; the list of blocks defined in the drawing are listed in the text box below the radio button. Choose any of the blocks from the list and preview it in the **Preview** area.

After selecting the marker style, specify the size of the marker in the **Size** area. You can set the size of the markers using four different options available in the **Options** drop-down list. Select the **Use drawing scale** option to specify the size of the marker by multiplying a specified value with the current drawing scale. Enter the required value in the **inches** edit box. You can select the **Use Fixed Scale** option from the drop-down list to set the size of the point marker by specifying the fixed scale values in the **X**, **Y**, and **Z** edit boxes. Enter a suitable value in these edit boxes to assign a fixed display scale to the marker.

You can also select the **Use size in absolute units** option from the **Options** drop-down list to set the marker size in an absolute value, based on the units displayed. Enter the required value for the size in the edit box next to the drop-down list. The **Use size relative to screen** option in the **Options** drop-down list is used to set the size of the marker as percentage of the drawing screen size. Enter the percentage in the **percent** edit box.

Optionally, specify the marker rotation in the **Marker rotation angle** edit box or choose the button on the right to specify the rotation by picking points from the drawing. Also, specify the orientation of the marker by selecting the option from the **Orientation Reference** drop-down list. If you select the **World Coordinate System** option, it ensures that the marker rotation angle will be relative to the world coordinate system. If the **Object** option is selected from the drop-down list then the marker rotation angle will be relative to the object it is attached to. If you select the **View** option from the **Orientation Reference** drop-down list, the marker rotation angle will be relative to the current AutoCAD view direction.

3D Geometry Tab

This tab is used to specify the display of points in the Model view or 3D views. The **Point Display Mode** property specifies the display of point in 3D view. Click in the **Value** field of this property and select any of the three display modes from the drop-down list. Select the **Use Point Elevation** mode to display points at their actual elevation. The **Flatten Points To Elevation** mode is used to flatten or project points to the specified elevation. On selecting this option, the **Point Elevation** property will be enabled. You can specify the required elevation in the **Value** field of this property. The **Exaggerate Points By Scale Factor** mode is used to raise or exaggerate the elevation of point by a specified scale factor. On selecting this option, the **Scale Factor** property will be available and you can enter the required scale factor in the **Value** field of this property.

Display Tab

This tab is used to set the visibility and display of the point marker and label. Using this tab, you can set different display settings for points in different views such as plan view (2D), model (3D), section, or profile view. You can select the required view from the **View Direction** drop-down list. To do so, select the required view from the **View Direction** drop-down list and then set the display settings in the **Component Display** area.

The **Component display** area is used to display the point component and different display settings in different columns. The **Component Type** column in this area lists the components of point object. The number of components in the **Component Type** column varies according to the types of object present in the drawing. The **Visibility** column specifies the visibility of component. Click on the light bulb icon in this column to control the visibility. The bulb in yellow color indicates that the component is visible. Click on the bulb to turn it off; the select component will now become invisible in the drawing.

The **Layer** column specifies the layer assigned to the component. Click on the default layer value to display the **Layer Selection** dialog box. You can use this dialog box to specify the required layer for the component and choose **OK** to exit the dialog box. The **Color** column specifies the color of the component. Click on the default value in the **Color** column to display the **Select Color** dialog box. You can use this dialog box to select a color for the component.

The **Linetype** column specifies the linetype for the component. Click on the default value in this column to display the **Select Linetype** dialog box. Select the required linetype from the dialog box. Note that the **Show Linetypes in Drawing** radio button is selected by default in this dialog box. As a result, the linetypes loaded in the current drawing are displayed. To view more linetypes, select the **Show Linetypes in File** radio button.

The **LT Scale** column specifies the linetype scale for the component. Click on the default value and enter the scale in the **LT Scale** column.

The **Lineweight** column specifies the lineweight for the component. Click on the default **Value** in this column to display the **Lineweight** dialog box. Select the required lineweight from this dialog box and choose the **OK** button; the specified lineweight will be applied on the component. The **Plot Style** column specifies the plot style of the component. You can edit the value for the plot style.

The Summary Tab

This tab is used to review or edit the values of properties, if required. After you have specified settings in the point style, choose the **OK** button; the **Point Style** dialog box will be closed and the point style will be added in the **Point Styles** node in the **Settings** tab.

POINT LABEL STYLES

Point label styles control the behavior and appearance of point labels. Point labels provide information about points. Like point styles, point label styles are created and managed in the **Settings** tab of the **TOOLSPACE** palette.

Creating a Point Label Style

Civil 3D provides you with some in-built label styles such as the point styles. But you can create your own point label styles and use them in the drawing. To create a new point label, choose the **Settings** tab and expand **Point** and select **Label Styles** to view the in-built label styles. Right-click on the **Label Styles** option; a shortcut menu will be displayed. Choose **New** from the shortcut menu; the **Label Style Composer dialog box - New Point Label Style** dialog box will be displayed. The options in this dialog box are discussed next.

Information Tab

This tab displays information about point label style such as name, date of creation, and so on. Enter a name for the required point label style in the **Name** edit box in this tab.

General Tab

The **General** tab is used to specify if label is displayed as label or tag. In addition, it specifies the visibility, orientation reference, and so on for the label. The properties in this tab are listed in the **Properties** column under three different categories: **Label**, **Behavior**, and **Plan Readability**. The default values of properties are listed in the **Value** column. The **Preview** pane in this tab displays the preview of the point and point label style. You can use the **ViewCube** tool in this pane to view the point style and point label style in different directions. Various properties displayed under these three categories are discussed next.

Text Style

The **Text Style** property is used to specify the default text style for the label text. Click in the **Value** field of this property; The **Browse** button will be displayed. Choose the **Browse** button to display the **Select Text Style** dialog box. Select the required style from this dialog box and then choose the **OK** button to apply the specified style.

Label Visibility

This property is used to control the visibility of the entire label. By default, the value of this property is set to **true**. As a result, the label will be visible in the drawing. To hide the point label in the drawing, set the value of this property to **false**.

Layer

The **Layer** property is used to specify the default layer for all label components. To modify the layer, click in the **Value** field and choose the browse button available on the right of this field; the **Layer Selection** dialog box will be displayed. You can use this dialog box to select or create the required layer.

Orientation Reference

This property is used to specify the orientation for the point label. By default, orientation is set to **Object**, which indicates that the label will be oriented according to object such as line or arc. To change the orientation of the point label, click in the **Value** field and select the required options from the drop-down list. The options have been explained earlier in this chapter.

Forced Insertion

This property is used to specify the position for a point label relative to an object such as line or arc segment. This property will be active only when the **Orientation Reference** property is set to **Object**. To specify the value for the **Forced Insertion** property, click in its **Value** field; a drop-down list will be displayed. You can select any of the following three options from the drop-down list: **None**, **Bottom**, and **Top**. The **None** option is selected by default. As a result, the point label is placed at its original location. You can select the **Bottom** or **Top** option to add the label at the bottom or top of the object.

Plan Readable

This property is used to specify whether to rotate the label text to make it easily readable in the plan view. By default, the value of this property is set to **true**, which indicates that the label will be rotated in the plan view to make it easily readable. If you set the value of this property to **false** then the **Readability Bias** and **Flip Anchors with Text** properties will not be highlighted

Layout Tab

The options in the **Layout** tab, as shown in Figure 2-26, are used to specify the layout of the point label by creating and editing label components. The options in this tab are discussed next.

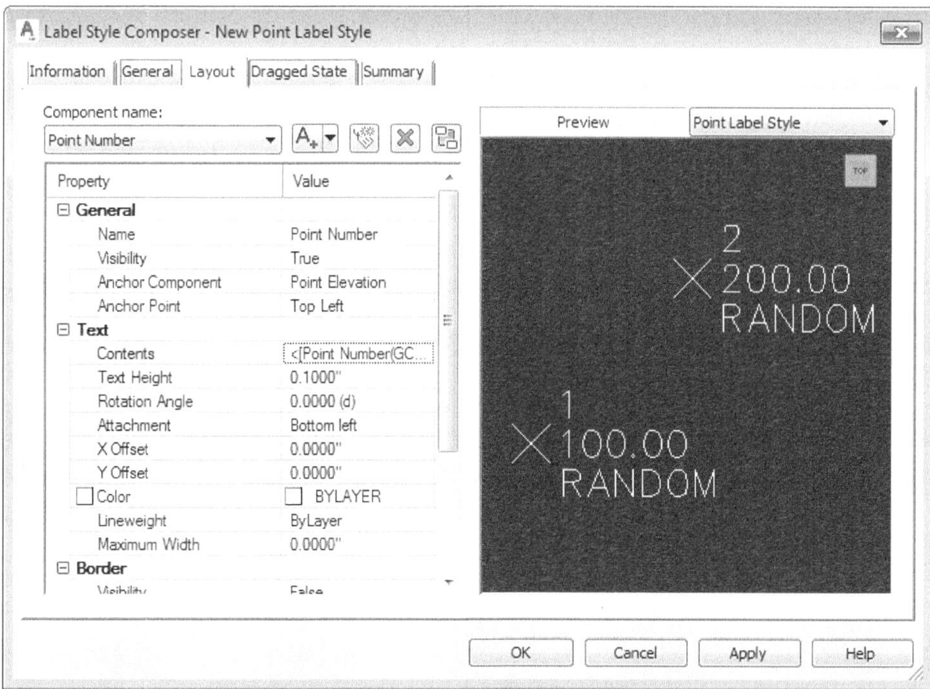

*Figure 2-26 The options in the **Layout** tab*

Component name

The **Component name** drop-down list is used to display the components of point label. By default, the point label has three components **Point Number**, **Point Elevation**, and **Point Description**. Select the required label component from the **Component name** drop-down list to view its properties in the **Property** column. Different label properties in this tab are discussed next.

Name

This property of the **General** category is used to specify the name of the selected label component. Click in the **Value** field of this property and specify the name of the newly created component or the existing label components. Note that you cannot change the name of **Point Elevation**.

Visibility

This property is used to specify whether the component is visible or not. By default, the value of this property is set to **true**. As a result, the component will be visible in the drawing. Click in the **Value** field of this property and select **false** from the drop-down list to hide the selected component.

Anchor Component

This property is used to specify a reference for positioning the component. There are three options available for **Anchor Component**: **Feature**, **Point Description**, and **Point elevation**. Click in the **Value** field of this property and select the required component from the drop-down list to use it as an anchor for the label. The default option **<Feature>** helps you anchor the label to a feature. A point is called a feature, if a label style is created for it.

Anchor Point

This property is used to specify the location where the text of the label style will be attached on the component. To assign a value to this property, click in its **Value** field and select any of the options from the drop-down list displayed. The options available in the drop-down list are: **Top Left**, **Top Center**, and so on. For example, if you select **Feature** as the anchor component for the **Point Description** component and **Top Left** as the anchor point, the **Point Description** will be placed at top left corner of the existing feature (point).

Contents

This property of the **Text** category is used to specify the content of label component. Click in the **Value** field of this property and choose the **Browse** button; the **Text Component Editor - Content** dialog box will be displayed. You can use this dialog box to create label text. The procedure to add text to the label is discussed later in this chapter.

Text Height

This property is used to specify height of the text in the label. Click in the **Value** field of the **Text Height** property and specify the required text height.

Rotation Angle

This property is used to specify the angle of rotation or inclination of the text component. Click in the **Value** field of this property and enter value of rotation. Alternatively, choose the button displayed on the right to specify the rotation by picking points from the drawing. The positive angle direction is always counterclockwise.

Attachment

This property is used to specify the attachment point for the label component attached to the anchor point. Click in the **Value** field and select the required attachment point from the drop-down list that is displayed.

X Offset

This property is used to specify the offset distance of the component from anchor point in the X direction. Click in the **Value** field of this property and enter the offset value to adjust label, if required.

Y Offset

This property is used to specify the offset distance of the component from anchor point in the Y direction. Click in the **Value** field of this property and enter the offset value to adjust the label, if required.

Color

This property is used to specify the default color of the label component. To change the default color, click on the value, and choose the **Browse** button; the **Select Color** dialog box will be displayed. Select the required color from this dialog box and choose the **OK** button.

Lineweight

This property is used to specify the lineweight of the text. Click in the **Value** field of **Lineweight** and choose the button displayed on the right; the **Lineweight** dialog box will be displayed. Select the required lineweight from the dialog box and choose **OK**; the **Lineweight** dialog box will be closed.

Visibility

This property of the **Border** category is used to specify whether the label component text will be displayed with a border or not. By default, the value of this property is set to **false**. As a result, the border will be invisible. To display label in a border, click in the **Value** field of this property and select **true** from the drop-down list to make the border visible. You can view the border in the **Preview** window.

Type

This property is used to specify the shape of the border. The **Rectangular** is the default border type. To select a border shape, click in the **Value** field of the **Type** property and select the required shape for the border from the drop-down list. You can view the shape of the border in the **Preview** panel after setting the visibility of the border to **true**.

Background Mask

This property is used to specify whether or not a background mask will be applied to the label. Click in the **Value** field of this property and select **true** from the drop-down list to apply the background mask. If you apply the background mask to the component, the background of the label, such as surface contours, will be hidden by mask.

Gap

This property is used to specify the distance between label component and border. Click in the **Value** field of this property and specify the distance between label and border.

Color

This property is used to specify the color of the border. The default value of this property is **By Layer**, which indicates that the current color assigned to the label is controlled by the layer property of the border.

Linetype

This property is used to specify the linetype of the border. The default value of the **Linetype** property is **By Block**.

Lineweight

This property specifies the lineweight of the border.

Create component

To create a new label component, choose the required option from the **Component name** drop-down; a flyout will be displayed. You can choose the required component to be added from the flyout. You can add a new text component, a line component, or a block component and then set its properties as required.

Copy component

Choose the **Copy component** button to create a copy of the selected component. Specify a name in the **Value** column for the copied component; the component will be added in the **Component** name drop-down list.

Delete component

Choose the **Delete component** button to delete the selected label component from the **Component name** drop-down list.

Component draw order

Choose the **Component draw order** button; the **Component Draw Order** dialog box will be displayed, as shown in Figure 2-27.

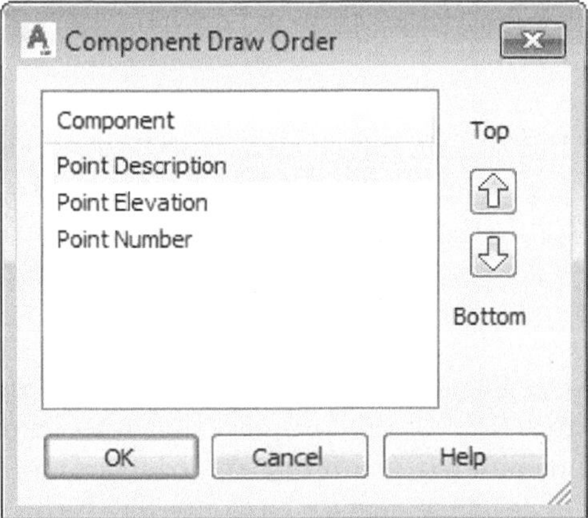

Figure 2-27 The ***Component Draw Order*** *dialog box*

You can use this dialog box to specify the order in which label components will be displayed in the multicomponent label. Select the required component from the **Component** area and choose the **Top** or **Bottom** button to move the selected component to the top or bottom in the label. Note that the component at the top of the dialog box is the last component displayed in the label.

Dragged State Tab

This tab is used to specify the properties and display of label when it is dragged from its insertion point. You may drag the label from its original insertion point due to the lack of space in the drawing. When you drag label to a different position, it is followed by a leader with an arrow head. The properties of this tab are listed under two categories, **Leader** and **Dragged State Components**. The **Leader** category contains leader properties where as the **Dragged State Components** category contains label properties. Some of the properties of this tab are discussed next.

Arrow Head Style

This property of the **Leader** category is used to specify the default arrow head style for the leader attached to the dragged label. Click in the **Value** field of this property and select the required style from the drop-down list. The **None** option is used to create a leader without arrow head.

Arrow Head Size

This property is used to specify the default arrow head size of the leader. Click in the **Value** field and change the size, if required.

Visibility

The **Visibility** property controls the visibility of the leader. By default, the value is set to **true**. If you do not want the leader to be displayed when the label is dragged, set the visibility of the leader to **false**.

Type

This property is used to specify the type of leader that will be drawn after dragging the label. Click in the **Value** field of this property and then select the **Straight Leader** or **Spline Leade**r type from the **Value** field of this property.

Display

This property of the **Dragged State Components** category is used to control the display of label after it is dragged. There are two options to display the dragged label: **As Composed** and **Stacked Text**. Select the **As Composed** option to display the label the way it is originally composed and oriented. On selecting this option, all other properties in the **Dragged State Components** category will disappear. Select the **Stacked Text** option to display the label based on the settings of the properties specified in the **Dragged State Components** category. On selecting this option, label components will be stacked or arranged vertically in the order they are defined in the label style.

Leader Attachment

This property is used to specify the attachment location of the leader with reference to the label content. Click in the **Value** field of this property and select the required option to attach the leader from the drop-down list.

Leader Justification

This property specifies whether the label text is justified according to the leader or not. Set the value of this property to **true** to enable the left justification of the text if the leader is on the left and vice versa. If the leader justification is set to **false**, the text will always be left-justified, irrespective of the leader position.

Summary Tab

This tab is used to review and edit the properties of all the components of a label. Expand the categories in this tab to view properties and values.

After you have specified the settings of the label style, choose the **OK** button to close the **Label Style Composer - New Point Label Style** dialog box. The label style will be added in the **Label Styles** node of the **Settings** tab.

Adding the Text Component to the Label

To add a new text component to a label, choose the **Layout** tab from the **Label Style Composer - New** dialog box and then choose the default **Create Text component** button available on the right of the **Component name** drop-down; the component with the default name **Text.1** will be added to the **Component name** drop-down list and its properties will be displayed in the **Property** column. Next, click in the **Value** field of the **Contents** property. In the **Text** category, choose the browse button displayed in the **Value** field, as shown in Figure 2-28. On doing so, the **Text Component Editor - Contents** dialog box will be displayed, as shown in Figure 2-29.

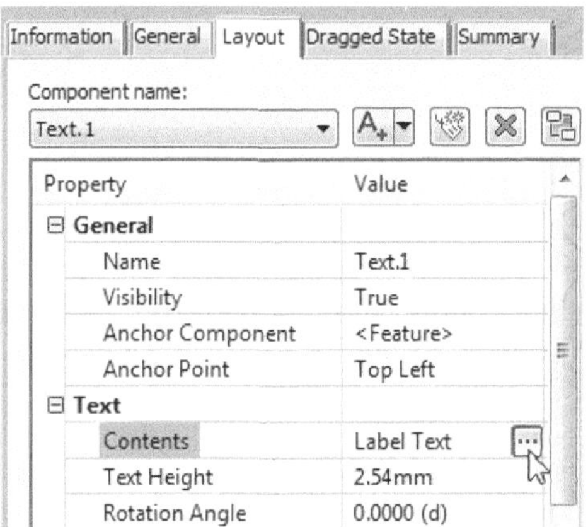

*Figure 2-28 Choosing the browse button displayed in the **Value** field of the **Contents** property*

In this dialog box, the **Properties** tab is chosen by default. In this tab, click in the **Properties** drop-down list and then select the property to be added to the label text; the property modifiers and their respective values will be displayed in the **Modifier** and **Value** columns, respectively. Change the property modifier value if required and then choose the right-arrow button next to the **Properties** drop-down list to add the selected property in the **Text Component Editor** window.

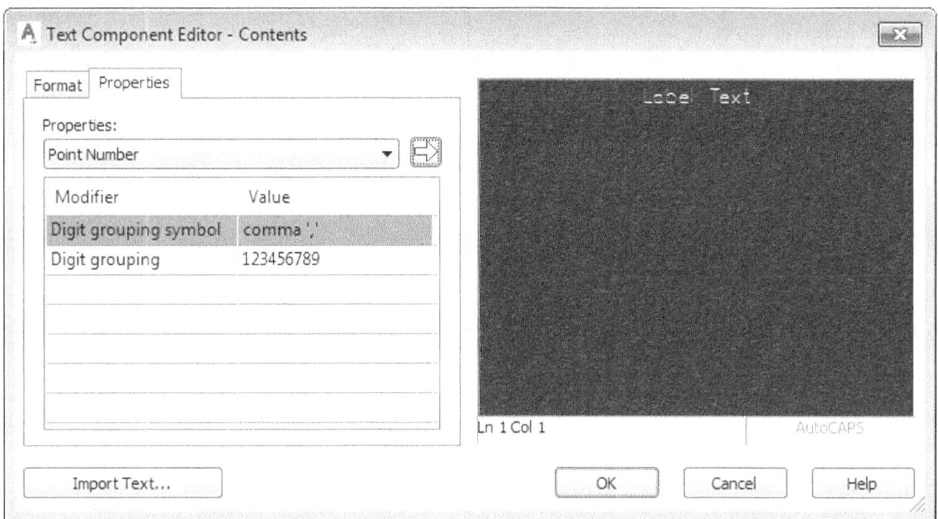

Figure 2-29 The ***Text Component Editor - Contents*** *dialog box*

Note

You can edit the modifier values of a property after it has been added to the right pane of the ***Text Component Editor - Contents*** *dialog box. To do so, select the text for the property to be edited in the right pane; the property corresponding to the selected text is displayed in the left pane. Now, edit the required modifier value in the left pane.*

To format the text, choose the **Format** tab. Select the text in the **Editor** window in the right pane of the **Text Component Editor - Contents** dialog box and choose the options in the **Format** tab to format the text as required. After you have formatted the text, choose the **OK** button from the **Text Editor Component - Contents** dialog box; the dialog box will be closed and you can preview the label content in the **Preview** window.

To view and edit the default settings of point label styles, expand the **Point** node and right-click on the **Label Styles** sub-node in the **Settings** tab; a shortcut menu will be displayed. Choose the **Edit Label Style Defaults** option from the shortcut menu; the **Edit Label Style Defaults - Point Label Style** dialog box will be displayed, as shown in Figure 2-30. Expand the categories in this dialog box to view and edit the default values of label properties. You can assign point style or point label style to a group of points. The point groups are discussed later in this chapter.

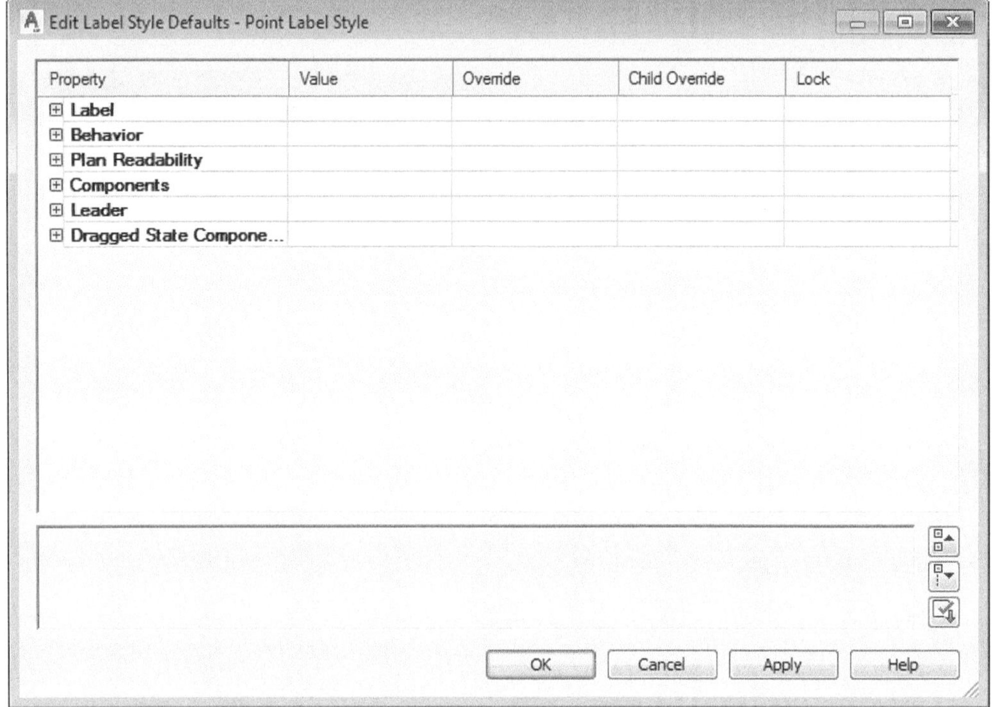

Figure 2-30 The ***Edit Label Style Defaults - Point Label Style*** *dialog box*

EDITING POINTS

Ribbon: Modify > Ground Data > Points
Command: EDITPOINTS

You can edit the properties of a point. There are various tools that can be used to edit the properties of a point. To edit a property, choose the **Points** tool from the **Ground Data** panel of the **Modify** tab; the **COGO Point** contextual tab will be displayed in the Ribbon, as shown in Figure 2-31.

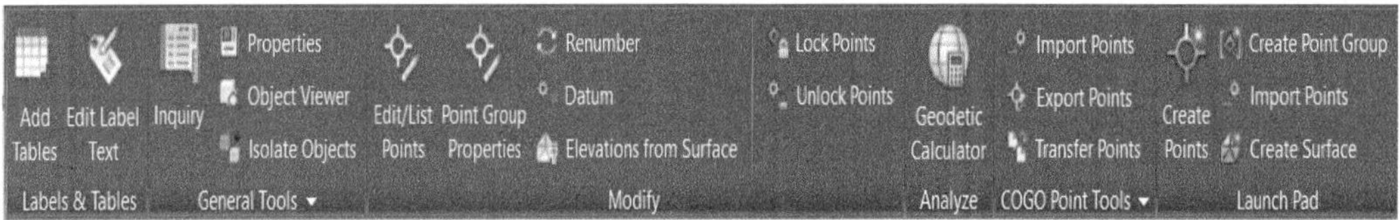

Figure 2-31 The ***COGO Point*** *contextual tab*

This tab contains various editing tools. These tools are discussed next.

Renumbering a Point

Ribbon: COGO Point > Modify > Renumber
Command: SELECTANDEDITPOINTNUMBERS

To renumber a point, choose the **Renumber** tool from the **Modify** panel; you will be prompted to specify a method for selecting points. Press ENTER to accept the default **<All>** option to renumber all the points. Enter **N** in the command line to specify the required point number to renumber, **G** to select the point group to renumber points in the point group, or **S** to renumber the selected points from the drawing. Alternatively, you can renumber a point in the **PANORAMA** window. To do so, right-click on the required point number in the **Point Number** column of this window and then choose the **Renumber** option from the shortcut menu; you will be prompted to enter an additive factor. Enter an integer value in the command line and press ENTER; the point will be renumbered according to the integer value specified. The value (additive factor) specified will be added to the existing point number to renumber it.

Changing the Elevation of the Point

Ribbon: COGO Point > Modify > Datum
Command: EDITPOINTDATUM

You can change the elevation of a point(s) with respect to a specified datum. To do so, choose the **Datum** tool from the **Modify** panel; you will be prompted to enter a new elevation or select a reference. Enter the required elevation in the command line or **R** in the command line to select the **Reference** option and then press ENTER. The elevation of the selected point will be modified in the **Point Elevation** column. If you select the **Reference** option, you need to specify the reference elevation and then the new elevation. The elevation of the selected point will be modified on the basis of difference between the two elevations.

Tip

You can also change the elevation of a point by changing the datum. To change elevation using datum, select the point and right-click on it; a shortcut menu will be displayed. Choose ***Datum*** *from the shortcut menu. Then, choose* ***change in Elevation*** *or* ***Reference*** *option and press ENTER.*

Changing the Point Elevation with Respect to a Surface

Ribbon: COGO Point > Modify > Elevation from Surface
Command: EDITPOINTSURFACEELEVS

You can change the point elevation based on the surface elevation. To do so, select the required point number(s) and choose the **Elevations from Surface** tool from the **Modify** panel; the **Select surface** dialog box will be displayed. Select the required surface from the dialog box and choose the **OK** button to close the dialog box. The **Point Elevation** column will display the elevation from the surface. After selecting the required surface, you will be prompted to specify the points to be edited. Choose the required points and press ENTER. Note that Civil 3D will display a message if there is no surface in the drawing. Alternatively, right-click on the point number(s) and then choose the **Elevation from Surface** option from the shortcut menu displayed; the **Select surface** dialog box will be displayed. Select the desired surface from the drop-down list and then choose the **OK** button to close the dialog box. The **Point Elevation** column will display the elevation from the surface.

Deleting a Point

To delete a point from the drawing, right-click on the point number to be deleted in the item view of **TOOLSPACE**; a shortcut menu will be displayed. Choose the **Delete** option from the shortcut menu; the **Autodesk AutoCAD Civil 3D 2018** message box will be displayed. Choose the **Yes** button to delete the required point(s). Alternatively, select the point object and press DELETE to delete.

Zooming to a Point

To zoom to a point(s), select it in the item view of the **TOOLSPACE** and then right-click; a shortcut menu will be displayed. Choose the **Zoom to** option from the shortcut menu to zoom to the selected point(s).

Locking/Unlocking Points

Ribbon:	COGO Point > Modify > Lock Points/Unlock Points
Command:	LOCK POINTS / UNLOCK POINTS

Locking the points prevents you from changing the properties of points. You cannot delete, move, edit, or even change the point style and the point label style of the locked points. To lock points, right-click on the required point numbers from the **Point Number** column of the **Point Editor**; a shortcut menu will be displayed. Choose **Lock** from the shortcut menu; the selected point will be locked and a red colored symbol will be displayed next to the selected point in the **Point Editor** tab, as shown in Figure 2-32.

Similarly, you can choose **Unlock** from the shortcut menu to unlock points to edit. The locked points will be displayed in the **Point Editor** as well as in the **Prospector** List view. Alternatively, the points can be locked or unlocked using the **Lock Points** or **Unlock Points** tools that are available in the **Modify** panel of the **COGO Point** tab.

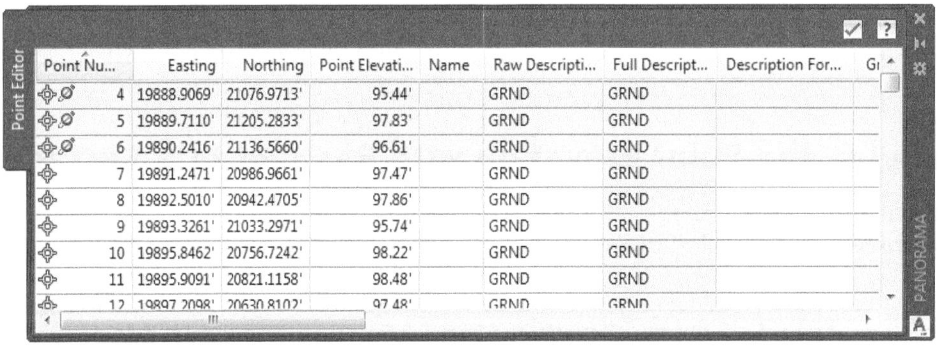

Point Nu...	Easting	Northing	Point Elevati...	Name	Raw Descripti...	Full Descript...	Description For...	Gi
4	19888.9069'	21076.9713'	95.44'		GRND	GRND		
5	19889.7110'	21205.2833'	97.83'		GRND	GRND		
6	19890.2416'	21136.5660'	96.61'		GRND	GRND		
7	19891.2471'	20986.9661'	97.47'		GRND	GRND		
8	19892.5010'	20942.4705'	97.86'		GRND	GRND		
9	19893.3261'	21033.2971'	95.74'		GRND	GRND		
10	19895.8462'	20756.7242'	98.22'		GRND	GRND		
11	19895.9091'	20821.1158'	98.48'		GRND	GRND		
12	19897.2098'	20630.8102'	97.48'		GRND	GRND		

Figure 2-32 *A red colored symbol displayed next to the selected point in the* ***Point Editor*** *tab*

Using the Geodetic Calculator

Ribbon: COGO Point > Analyze > Geodetic Calculator
Command: SHOWGEODETICCALCULATOR

You can use the **Geodetic Calculator** tool to calculate geodetic information about points. To do so, the drawing must have a defined coordinate system. Civil 3D will display a warning message if no coordinate zone is assigned to the drawing. To calculate geodetic information, choose the **Geodetic Calculator** tool from the **Analyze** panel; the **Geodetic Calculator** dialog box will be displayed, as shown in Figure 2-33. Choose the **Specify point** button at top left corner of the dialog box and click in the drawing to specify the point; the geodetic information of the point will be displayed in the dialog box. Alternatively, enter the point number in the **Value** column.

You can also specify the required geodetic information such as **Latitude**, **Longitudes** or **Grid Easting** or **Grid Northing** and create the point with specified geodetic information. To do so, specify the geodetic information and choose the **Create Points** button from top right corner of the dialog box; you will be prompted to specify the point description. Enter the point description in the command line and press ENTER; the point with the specified geodetic information will be created.

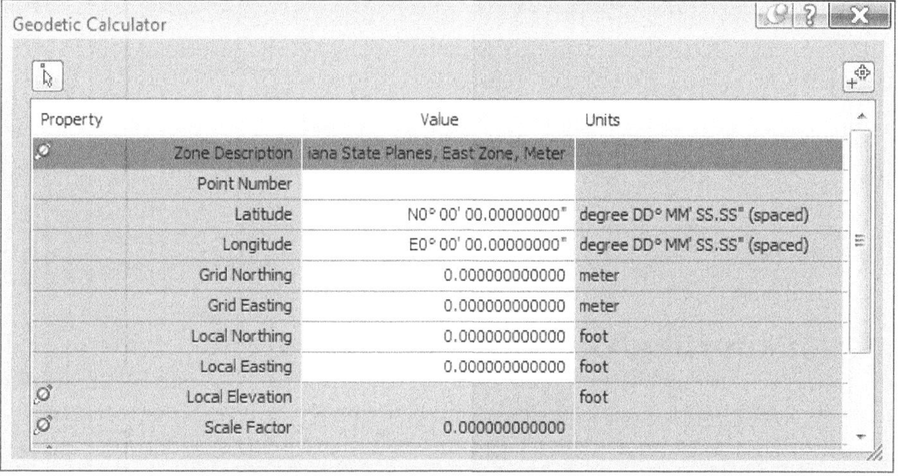

*Figure 2-33 The **Geodetic Calculator** dialog box*

Editing Points Using the PANORAMA Window

You can edit individual points either graphically in the drawing or by using the **Point Editor** tab in the **PANORAMA** window. To edit points using the **Point Editor** tab, choose the **Edit/List Points** tool from the **Modify** panel of the **COGO Point** tab; the **PANORAMA** window with the **Point Editor** tab will be displayed, as shown in Figure 2-34.

Point Nu...	Easting	Northing	Point Elevati...	Name	Raw Descripti...	Full Descript...	Description For...	Gı
4	19888.9069'	21076.9713'	95.44'		GRND	GRND		
5	19889.7110'	21205.2833'	97.83'		GRND	GRND		
6	19890.2416'	21136.5660'	96.61'		GRND	GRND		
7	19891.2471'	20986.9661'	97.47'		GRND	GRND		
8	19892.5010'	20942.4705'	97.86'		GRND	GRND		
9	19893.3261'	21033.2971'	95.74'		GRND	GRND		
10	19895.8462'	20756.7242'	98.22'		GRND	GRND		
11	19895.9091'	20821.1158'	98.48'		GRND	GRND		
12	19897.2098'	20630.8102'	97.48'		GRND	GRND		

*Figure 2-34 The **PANORAMA** window with the **Point Editor** tab*

The **Point Editor** tab in the **PANORAMA** window is used to display information about points such as its Elevation, Northing, Easting, Number, and others that are relevant to it. Click in the required cell and edit a new value of the point property. For example, to change the elevation of point number 1, click in the corresponding cell of the **Point Elevation** column and enter a new value for this number. Similarly, you can change the **Easting**, **Northing**, **Elevation** and other properties of individual points. You can also use different point editing commands in the **Point Editor** tab. To do so, right-click on any point number in the **Point Number** column of the **Point Editor** tab; a shortcut menu will be displayed. You can also use the **AutoCAD** commands such as rotate, copy, move, and erase to edit points graphically.

Tip

*You can also invoke the **PANAROMA** window from the **TOOLSPACE**. To do so, right-click on the **Points** node in the **Prospector** tab and then choose the **Edit Points** option from the shortcut menu.*

Importing/Exporting/Transferring Points

Civil 3D allows you to import, export, and even transfer points from one file to another. Points can be imported and exported in the ASCII (*.txt*) format or in the Microsoft Access database (*.mdb*) format. Importing points is the easiest method to create and add points in the drawing. The surveyor collects the point data and then imports it to Civil 3D as an ASCII file.

Importing Points

Ribbon: COGO Point > COGO Point Tools> Import Points
Command: IMPORTPOINTS

To import points in the **AutoCAD Civil 3D** workspace, choose the **Import Points** tool from the **COGO Point Tools** panel; the **Import Points** dialog box will be displayed. While importing, exporting, and transferring points, you need to select the right type of file format. **AutoCAD Civil 3D** will display a check mark next to the path of the file if the file format selected is correct. Select the required file format from the **Specify point file format** list box in the **Import Points** dialog box and then import the required point file. You can also create your own file format. The method of creating file format is discussed later in this chapter.

Exporting Points

Ribbon: COGO Point > COGO Point Tools > Export Points
Command: EXPORTPOINTS

You can export specific points from AutoCAD Civil 3D to ASCII file or a Microsoft Access database. Before exporting points, you need to select the appropriate file format depending upon the point data and then export points. To export Civil 3D points, choose the **Export Points** tool from the **COGO Point Tools** panel; the **Export Points** dialog box will be displayed, as shown in Figure 2-35. Note that the default file format selected is **Autodesk Uploadable File**.

Next, select the required file format from the **Format** drop-down list in the dialog box. You can also create your own file format, which will be discussed later in this chapter. Next, enter the name and path of the file to which points will be exported or choose the button on the right of the **Destination File** text box; the **Select Destination File** dialog box will be displayed. Browse to the required location where the file is saved. Select the file and then choose the **Open** button; the file name and path will be displayed in the **Destination File** text box. You can export files by using any of the two file format options: **Columnated** or **Delimited**. These option are discussed later in this chapter.

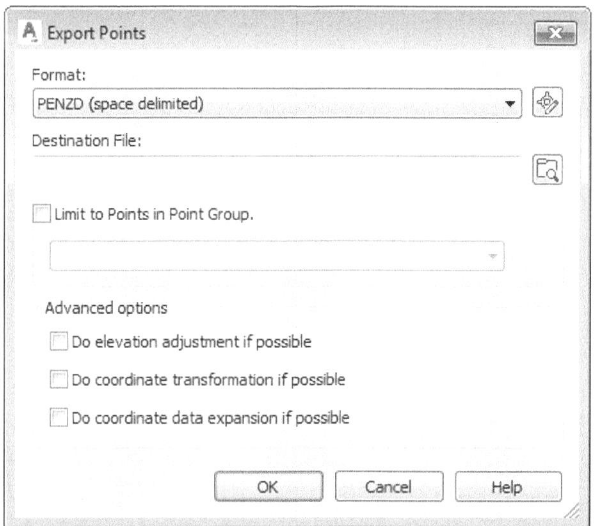

*Figure 2-35 The **Export Points** dialog box*

Next, in the **Export Points** dialog box, you can also select the **Limit to Points in Point Group** check box; the drop-down list will be activated. Select the required point group from the drop-down list below it. On doing so, points will be added to the required point group. Now, choose the **OK** button; the dialog box will be closed and points will be exported.

Tip

*You can also invoke the **Export Points** dialog box from the **TOOLSPACE** palette. To do so, right-click on the **Points** node in the **Prospector** tab; a shortcut menu will be displayed. Choose the **Export** option from the menu; the **Export Points** dialog box will be displayed.*

Transferring Points

Ribbon: COGO Point > COGO Point Tools > Transfer Points
Command: TRANSFERPOINTS

AutoCAD Civil 3D allows you to transfer points from the source file to the destination file. A source file is a file from which points are transferred and destination file is a file to which points will be transferred. The source and destination files can be *.txt* files or *.mdb* files. Before transferring points, ensure that the file format of both the files are same. Before transferring points, you need to create two types of file formats for both the source and destination files to specify the layout or arrangement of the point data in files.

After you have created the file formats for both the files, choose the **Transfer Points** tool in the **COGO Points Tools** panel; the **Transfer Points** dialog box will be displayed, as shown in Figure 2-36.

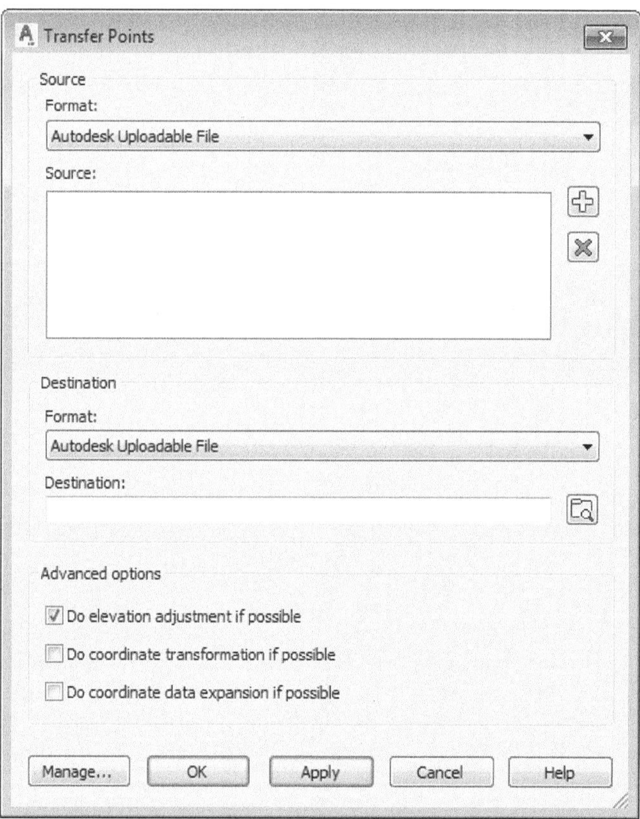

Figure 2-36 *The* ***Transfer Points*** *dialog box*

In the **Source** area of the dialog box, select the required file format of the source file from the **Format** drop-down list. Choose the (+) sign button on the right of the text box of this area to display the **Select Source File** dialog box. Select the required file from this dialog box and choose the **OK** button to close it. Similarly, select the required file format and select the destination file from the **Destination** area.

Tip

*You can also invoke the **Transfer Points** dialog box from the **TOOLSPACE** palette. To do so, right-click on **Points** in the **Prospector** tab and then choose the **Transfer** option from the shortcut menu.*

Now, select the required check boxes from the **Advanced options** area to enable the elevation, coordinate adjustment, or data expansion of the point data while transferring point from the source file to the destination file. Note that you can create a new file format by choosing the **Manage** button in the **Transfer Points** dialog box. After selecting the file formats and the files, choose the **OK** button; the **Transfer Points** dialog box will be closed and the point will be transferred to the destination file. The method of creating a new file format is discussed next.

Creating a New File Format

A file format defines the structure of file in which it holds (encodes) data. For example, the point properties in the source point file are arranged in the order, point number, easting, elevation, and description. To import or export the point to or from this file, the file format to which points are imported or exported should have the same format. If the order of properties in the destination file is easting, elevation, and description, the point numbers of the source file will not be transferred to the destination file.

Civil 3D has some in-built file formats that can be used before importing, exporting, or transferring the points. However, you can also create your own file formats as per the requirement. The new file formats are created by using the **Point File Formats** dialog box that can be accessed by choosing the button on the right of the **Format** edit box either in the **Import Points** or **Export Points** dialog box.

To create a new point file format, choose the **Settings** tab in the **TOOLSPACE** palette and expand the **Point** collection. Next, right-click on the **Point File Formats** node and the choose **New** from the shortcut menu displayed; the **Point File Formats - Select Format Type** dialog box will be displayed, as shown in Figure 2-37.

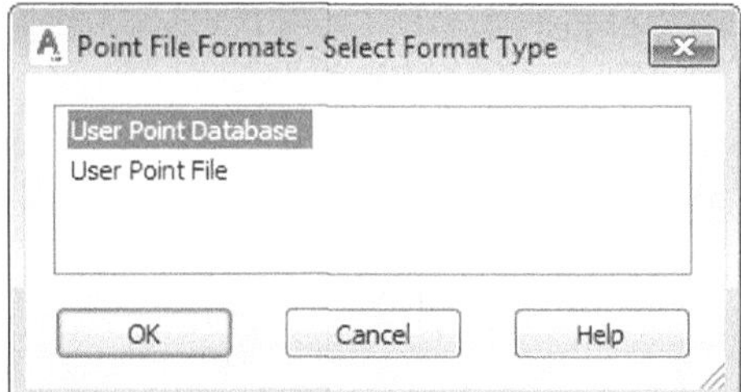

***Figure 2-37** The **Point File Formats - Select Format Type** dialog box*

You can select any of the two file format types from the dialog box. The **User Point Database** format type is used to describe the arrangement of points in the Microsoft Access database file (*.mdb*) and the **User Point File** option is used to describe the arrangement of points in the ASCII or Text(.txt) file. The methods of creating file formats using these two format types are discussed next.

Creating the User Point Database File Format

To create the user point database point file format, right-click on the **Point File Format** node in the **Settings** tab; a shortcut menu will be displayed. Choose the **New** option from it; the **Point File Formats - Select File Format Type** dialog box will be displayed. Choose the **User Point Database** option from this dialog box and then choose the **OK** button; the **User Point Database Format** dialog box will be displayed, as shown in Figure 2-38. This dialog box is used to view or edit the properties space of the user point database format used to import points from *.mdb* files or export points from *.mdb* files. In the **Format name** edit box, enter a name of the file format; the name of the file format will be displayed in the **Point File Format** node in the **Settings** tab. Select the required table from the **Table name** drop-down list. Note that if the table name is not available in the drop-down list, choose the **Load** button and load the required *.mdb* file from the **Select Source Database** dialog box displayed. You can browse to the location where you have saved the *.mdb* file and choose the **Open** button from this dialog box to load the file. On doing so, the table name will be displayed in the **Table name** drop-down list and the data will be displayed in columns. You can refer it for creating format.

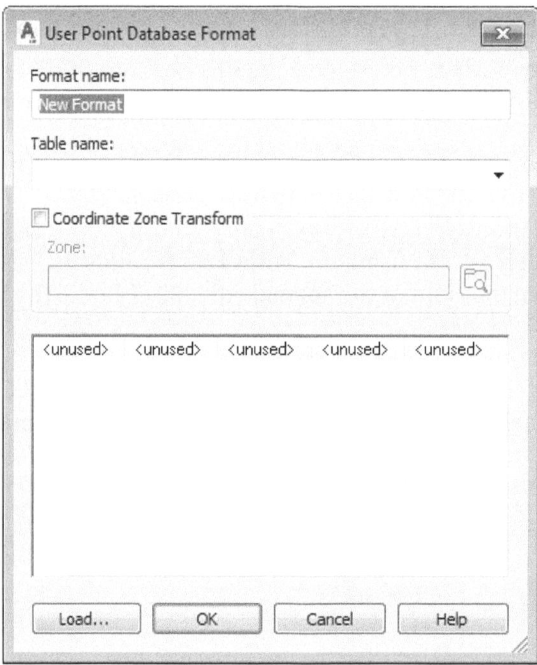

Figure 2-38 The ***User Point Database Format*** *dialog box*

Optionally, select the check box in the **Coordinate Zone Transform** area to assign a coordinate zone to the file format. Choose the button on the right of the **Zone** edit box and then select the required zone from the **Select Coordinate Zone** dialog box. Next, you need to format the column names. To do so, click on the default unused column in the dialog box; the **Point File Formats - Select Column Name** dialog box will be displayed. Select the required option according to the point data from the **Column name** drop-down list, as shown in Figure 2-39.

If you do not want any data to be imported and exported, accept the default **<unused>** option from the drop-down list and choose the **OK** button. Similarly, select the name for all columns in the dialog box. To change the order of columns, simply click and drag the column to the required position. Next, choose the **OK** button; the **User Point Database Format** dialog box will be closed and the name of format will be added in the **Point File Format** node of the **Points** collection in the **Settings** tab.

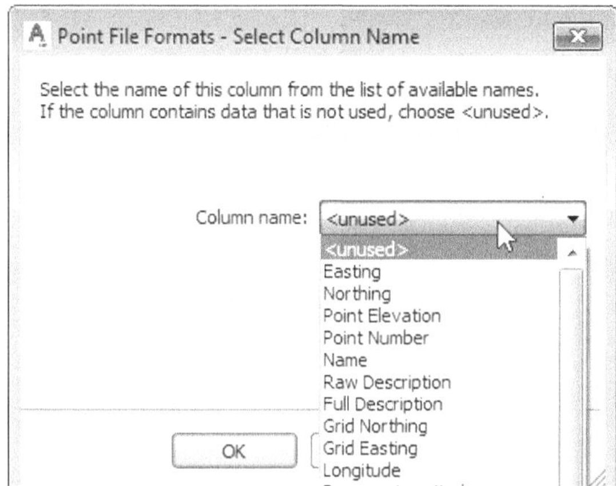

***Figure 2-39** Selecting the column name from the **Column name** drop-down list*

Creating the User Point File Format

To create the user point file format, right-click on the **Point File Formats** sub-node in the **Point** node of the **Settings** tab; a shortcut menu will be displayed. In the dialog box, choose the **New** option from it; the **Point File Formats - Select Format Type** dialog box will be displayed. Choose the **User Point File** option from the text box and then choose the **OK** button; the **Point File Format** dialog box will be displayed, as shown in Figure 2-40.

Enter the format name in the **Format name** edit box. In the **Default file extension** drop-down list of this dialog box, select the required file extension of the point data file. You can select any of the following extensions from the drop-down list:

.auf: Autodesk Uploadable File, comma delimited. Required values in the file are point number, northing, easting, elevation, and description (in the order).

.csv: Comma Separated Value file; ASCII (text) file comma-delimited

.nez: Northing, Easting, and Elevation data

.pnt: Point file

.prn: Formatted text, space delimited

.txt: Delimited ASCII (text) file

.xyz: Coordinates X, Y, and Z

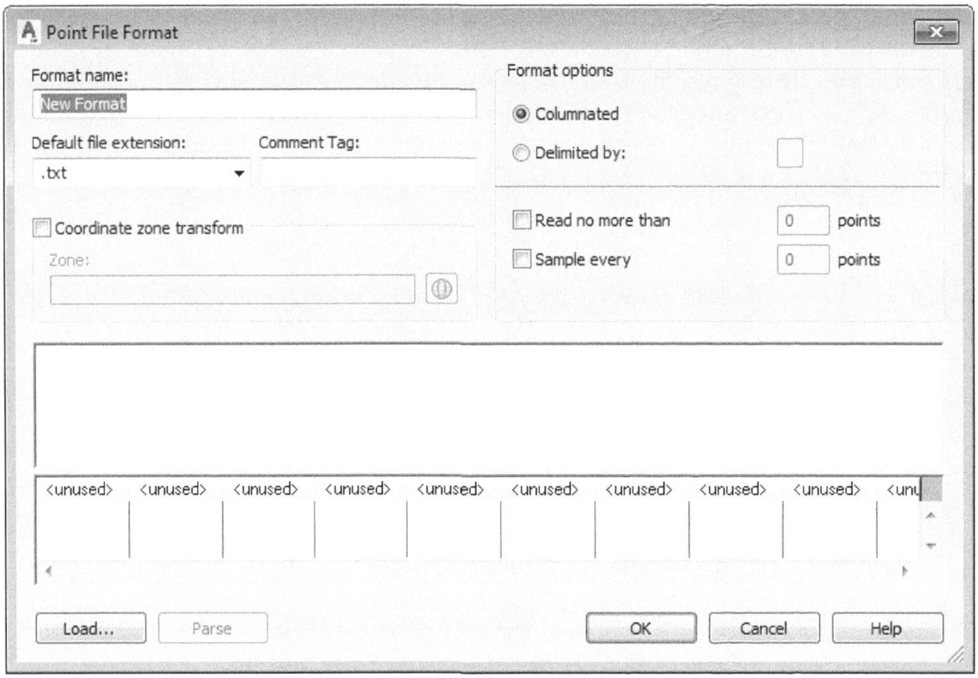

***Figure 2-40** The **Point File Format** dialog box*

After selecting the default extension, choose the **Load** button; the **Select Source File** dialog box will be displayed. Select the point file from this dialog box and load the point data. You can refer the point data in the file while creating the format. Optionally, assign a coordinate zone to the file format, as explained earlier. Now, in the **Format options** area, select the required format option. There are two types of format options: **Columnated** and **Delimited by**. By default, the **Columnated** radio button is selected. As a result, the imported point data will be arranged in columns and rows, separated by tabs. If you select the **Delimited by** radio button, the point data will be separated by a delimiter such as comma(,) or a space. Figures 2-41 and 2-42 show a typical comma separated value file and a space delimited point file, respectively.

```
1,715.1150,184.6870,-99999,
2,728.2360,222.1870,-99999,
3,737.6090,265.3130,-99999,
4,743.2320,312.1870,-99999,
5,752.6050,359.0620,-99999,
6,750.7300,411.5620,-99999,
7,728.2360,449.0620,-99999,
8,685.1230,460.3130,-99999,
9,651.3830,454.6880,-99999,
10,628.8890,445.3120,-99999,
11,600.7720,439.6880,-99999,
12,563.2820,420.9380,-99999,
13,546.4120,392.8120,-99999,
14,520.1690,349.6880,-99999,
15,497.6750,321.5620,-99999,
16,480.8050,282.1880,-99999,
```

***Figure 2-41** Typical comma separated file format*

```
1       184.687 715.115 102.000
2       222.187 728.236 102.000
3       265.313 737.609 102.000
4       312.187 743.232 102.000
5       359.062 752.605 102.000
6       411.562 750.730 102.000
7       449.062 728.236 102.000
8       460.313 685.123 102.000
9       454.688 651.383 102.000
10      445.312 628.889 102.000
11      439.688 600.772 102.000
12      420.938 563.282 102.000
13      392.812 546.412 102.000
14      349.688 520.169 102.000
15      321.562 497.675 102.000
16      282.188 480.805 102.000
17      252.187 448.938 102.000
18      209.063 430.194 102.000
19      164.062 447.064 102.000
20      141.563 486.428 102.000
21      115.312 523.918 102.000
```

***Figure 2-42** Typical space delimited file format*

To specify the maximum number of points to be imported or exported, select the **Read no more than** check box and enter a value in the **points** edit box next to it. Civil 3D imports or exports only the specified number of points. For example, if you enter **1000** in the **points** edit box, only 1000 points will be imported or exported from the file. Similarly, to sample the point data with the specified number and import or export the points accordingly; select the **Sample every** check box and enter a number in the **points** edit box next to it. For example, if you enter a value of **50**, every 50th point will be imported or exported from the file.

Adding Point Tables

Ribbon: COGO Point > Labels & Tables > Add Tables
Command: ADDPOINTTABLE

Point tables help you view point information in tabular form. You can create different point table styles and use them to create tables. To add point tables, choose the **Add Tables** tool from the **Labels & Tables** panel; the **Point Table Creation** dialog box will be displayed, as shown in Figure 2-43.

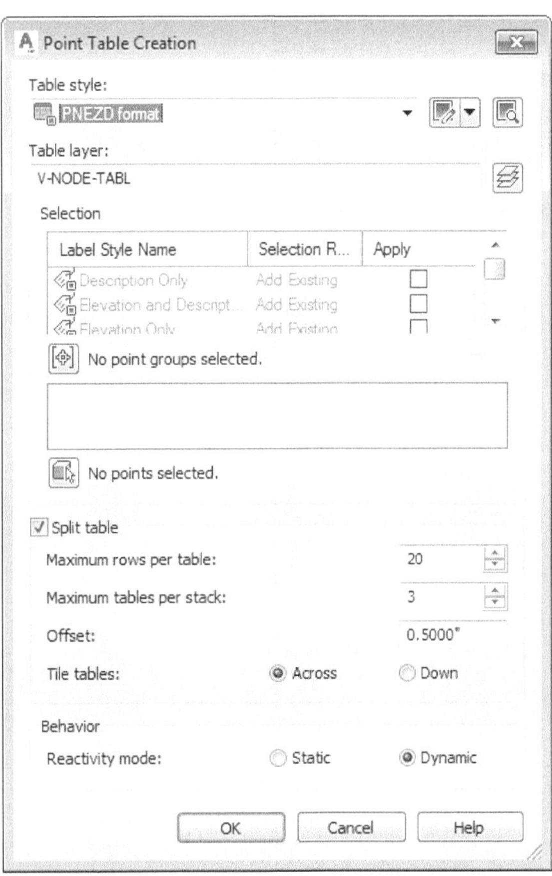

*Figure 2-43 The **Point Table Creation** dialog box*

From the **Table style** drop-down list, select the required table style. The **Table layer** option is used to display the default layer on which the table will be created. To modify the default layer, choose the button on the right of this option; the **Object Layer** dialog box will be displayed. You can use this dialog box to select or create a new layer for the table.

The options in the **Selection** area are used to select the points to be labeled. The **Selection** area displays the list of existing point label styles in the **Label Style Name** column. To select the required point label style, select the corresponding check box in the **Apply** column. The label content of the selected point label style will be used to create point table.

Now, choose the **Select Point Groups** button to display the **Point Groups** dialog box. Select the required point group from the dialog box and choose the **OK** button; the points of the selected point group will be added in the table and the total number of point group(s) will be displayed next to the **Select Point Groups** button. You can choose the **Pick On-Screen** button and select the required points from the drawing by using any window selection method and then press ENTER; the selected points will be added in the table and displayed next to the **Pick On-Screen** button.

Optionally, choose the options in the **Split table** to format the table and choose the **OK** button; the **Point Table Creation** dialog box will be closed and you will be prompted to specify the upper left corner of the table. Click at the required location in the drawing area; the point table will added in the drawing.

POINT GROUPS

As mentioned earlier, a point group is a collection of similar points. Point groups help you control, organize, and manage a point easily. Like points, point groups also have their own styles and label styles. You can assign different point styles and point label styles to each point group and control the appearance of points of a point group. It helps you quickly identify and modify point styles or point label styles of the required points of any point group. For example, you can group surface points that are used for creating surface in a group and assign a point style to them. Also, you can create another point group containing points of the centerline of an alignment and assign them a different point style and label style. Now, you can easily identify and distinguish the surface creation points from the centerline points in the drawing. These points can then be easily edited or managed in the drawing as required.

Creating Point Groups

Ribbon: Home > Create Ground Data > Points drop-down > Create Point Group
Command: CREATEPOINTGROUP

Point groups are created based on point properties. You can group points based on their point numbers, elevation, description, and so on. To create a point group, choose the **Create Point Group** tool from the **Create Ground Data** panel; the **Point Group Properties - Point Group - (1)** dialog box will be displayed, as shown in Figure 2-44. The options in the dialog box are discussed next.

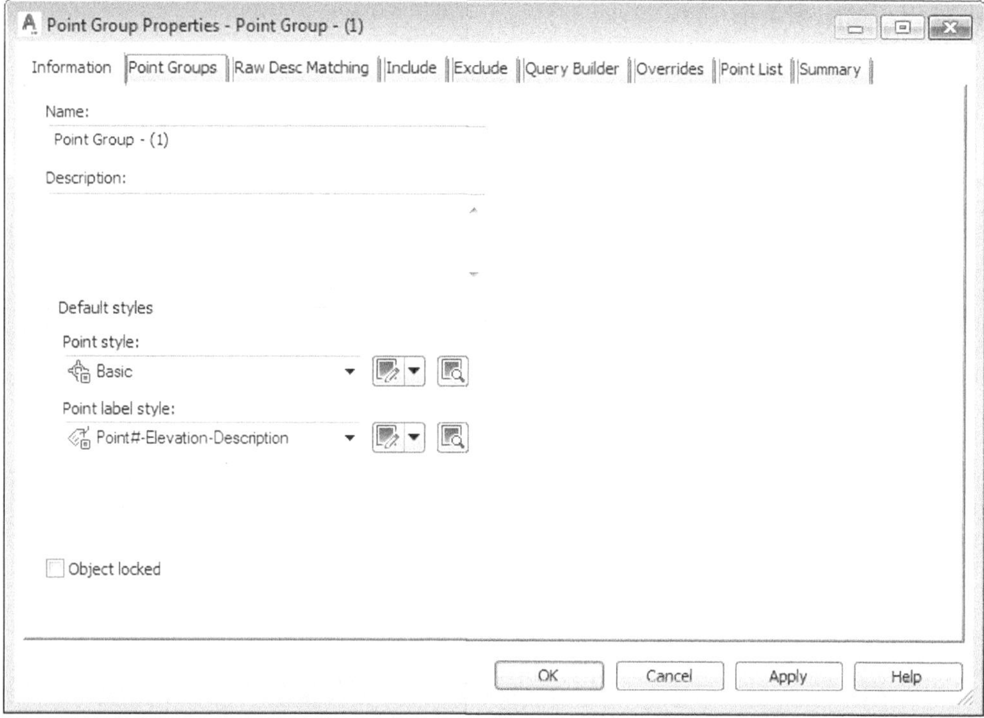

*Figure 2-44 The **Point Group Properties - Point Group - (1)** dialog box*

Information Tab

The **Information** tab in this dialog is chosen by default. Enter a name of the point group in the **Name** edit box. Optionally, enter a short description about the point group in the **Description** text box. Next, in the **Default styles** area, select the point style from the **Point style** drop-down list for the points included in the point group. Similarly, select a point label style from the **Point label style** drop-down list to label the points included in the point group. On selecting the **Object locked** check box, the **Name** and **Description** areas will become inactive.

Tip

*You can also create your own **Point Style** and **Point Label Style** by selecting **Create New** from the drop-down lists available on the right of the **Point Style** and **Point Label Style** drop-down lists.*

Point Groups Tab

This tab is used to list the existing point groups in the drawing. To select a particular point group from the list, select the check box on the left of the point group name in the **Point Group** column. The **_All Points** point group is the default point group.

Raw Desc Matching Tab

This tab is used to list the codes that are used for description keys in the drawing. You can use this tab to include the points whose raw description match with the description key codes displayed in this tab. You can select the required description key code by selecting the check box next to it. The points whose raw description matches with the selected codes will be included in the point group. Note that codes will be displayed in this only if the drawing contains description keys. The description keys and their functions are discussed later in this chapter.

Include Tab

This tab is used to specify the criteria to include points based on their point numbers, elevations, names, raw description, full description either in the respective edit boxes or by selecting them from the drawing. The options are discussed next.

With numbers matching

Select the **With numbers matching** check box to include points based on specified point numbers. You can enter point numbers in the edit box next to the check box. The point numbers should be separated by comma. You can also enter a point number range separated by hyphen. For example, you can enter point numbers like, 100, 150, 200. On doing so, the points with the point numbers matching to 100, 150, 200 will be included in the point group. Enter the point range as 50-500; all the points with point numbers starting from 50 to 500 will be included in the drawing. Alternatively, choose the **Selection Set in Drawing** button and select the required points from the drawing using the window selection method and press ENTER; the point numbers or the ranges will be displayed in the edit box after the selection.

With elevations matching

Select this check box to include points in the point group based on their elevations. You can enter elevations of points in different ways in your drawing. First, you can enter the elevation by using a comma separated values. For example, if you enter **100**, **500**, **1000** these points will be included in the point group. Second, you can also use the greater than symbol (**>**) followed by the elevation value to include points whose elevation value is greater than the specified value. For example, if you enter **>-500**, the points having elevation greater than **-500** will be included in the point group. Third, you can use the (**<**) less than symbol to include points having elevation less than the specified elevation. For example, if you enter **<1000>**, all points having elevation less than **1000** will be included in the point group. Fourth, you can also use range for specifying the points to be included in the point group. For example, 100-1000 will include points having elevation varying from **10** to **1000**.

With names matching

Select this check box to include points based on name. Enter point names in the edit box next to this check box. The point names should be separated by a comma.

With raw descriptions matching

Select this check box to include points in the point group based on their raw description. Enter the comma separated description in the edit box next to the **With raw descriptions matching** check box; for example, GRND, STN, BLDG. The raw descriptions are not case-sensitive. You can also use wild cards after the raw description, for example, STN*.

With full description matching

Select this check box to include those points that match with the specified full description of points. Enter the required full description in the edit box next to the **With full description matching** check box.

Include all points

Select the **Include all points** check box to include all the points of the drawing in the point group. On selecting this check box, all other options are disabled.

Exclude Tab

This tab is used to specify the criteria for excluding points from point groups. The options in this tab are the same as discussed in the **Include** tab.

Query Builder Tab

This tab is used to create point groups using a set of query. Query is a set of combined logical expressions that use logical operators such as OR, NOT, AND and so on, using the query builder.

Overrides Tab

The **Overrides** tab is used to display the existing properties of points in a point group and allows you to override the properties of points in a point group that is required. Select the check box on the left of the property that you want to override. To modify **Raw Description**, select the check box in the **Property** column. Next, click in the **Overrides** column and enter a new value in the column. Similarly, enter a new value in the **Overrides** column for the **Point Elevation** property. To override the **Point Style** or **Point Label Style** properties, select the corresponding check boxes in the **Property** column and double-click in the **Overrides** column; the **Point Style** or **Point Label Style** dialog box will be displayed. Select the required style from the dialog box and choose the **OK** button.

Point List Tab

This tab is used to display the list of all points and their properties in the point group. You cannot edit any information in this tab. You can change the sequence of columns by dragging column heads to the desired position.

Summary Tab

This tab is used to review information about point group properties and also lists point group query. After you have specified the point style, point label style, included the points, and specified other properties in the dialog box, choose the **OK** button; the **Point Group Properties - Point Group (1)** dialog box will be closed and the point group name will be added to the **Point Group** collection in the **Prospector** tab of the **TOOLSPACE** palette.

Editing Point Groups

To edit point group properties, right-click on the point group in the **Point Group** node in the **Prospector** tab and choose the **Properties** option from the shortcut menu; the **Point Group Properties - <point group name>** dialog box will be displayed. In the **Information** tab of the dialog box, you can modify the point group name, point style, point label style of points included in the point group. Choose the **Include** or **Exclude** tab from the dialog box to include and exclude points. Choose the **Apply** button to apply the changes and choose **OK** to close the dialog box.

Tip

You can also open the ***Point Group Properties - <point group name>*** *dialog box from the drawing. To do so, select any point of the point group in the drawing and then right-click to display a shortcut menu. Choose the* ***Point Group Properties*** *option from the shortcut menu.*

The options discussed earlier for editing points are used to edit points of any point group. To access the editing options, expand the **Point Groups** collection in the **Prospector** tab and right-click on the required point group to display a shortcut menu, as shown in Figure 2-46. You can choose the required options from the shortcut menu and edit the points of the point group as discussed earlier.

Out of Date Points Groups

A point group is called out of date if you add or delete points, or modify properties such as elevation or description of points included in the point group. The out of date point groups are indicated by a yellow symbol displayed in the **Prospector** tab on the left of the point group name, as shown in Figure 2-45. The **Point Group - (1)** is out of date as indicated by the symbol on the left. This shows that some changes have been made in the point group.

To view changes made in the point group, choose the **Show Point Group Differences** button in the **Point Groups** dialog box; the **Point Group Changes** dialog box will be displayed. This dialog box is used to list the changes made in the points of a point group. To update the point group, choose the **Update Point Group** button in the **Point Group Changes** or the **Point Groups** dialog box; the point group will be updated and the out of date symbol will disappear. Alternatively, right-click in the **Prospector** tab and choose the **Show Changes** option to view the changes made in a point group or choose the **Update** option to update the point group from the shortcut menu. The various editing options in **Point Groups** are shown in Figure 2-46.

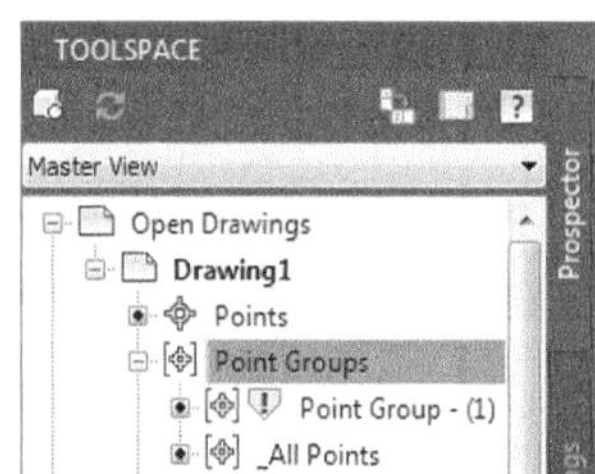

Figure 2-45 *The symbol corresponding to the* ***Point Groups*** *indicating the out of date point group*

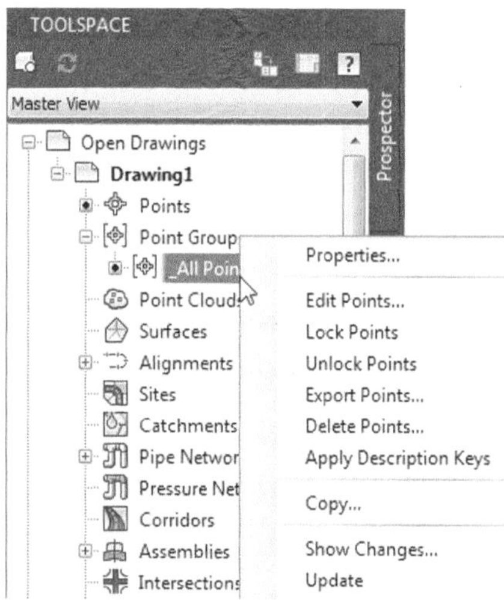

Figure 2-46 *The* ***Point Groups*** *editing options*

Description Keys

This key is used to control the visibility and appearance of points. Unlike point groups, the description keys cannot be used for controlling and appearance of the existing points. You can use these keys for creating and importing new points in the drawing or converting points in the drawing. The point groups are used to control the style and label of all points in a point group but the description keys are applied to individual points as an override. On importing or creating new points, the points are assigned the styles based on the raw description of points matching with the code and format of description keys.

Creating Description Keys

To create a description key, choose the **Settings** tab of the **TOOLSPACE** palette and expand the **Point** node. Next, right-click on **Description Key Sets** sub-node; a shortcut menu will be displayed. Next, choose the **New** option from the shortcut menu; the **Description Key Set - New DescKey Set** dialog box will be displayed. Enter a description key set name in the **Name** edit box. Optionally, enter a short description about the key set in the **Description** text box and then choose the **OK** button; the dialog box will be closed and a name for the description key set will be added in the **Description Key Sets** node of the **Settings** tab. After creating and naming a description key set, you will create a description key to the description key set. To do so, expand the **Description Key Sets** node, right-click on **New desckey set** that you have created and then choose **Edit Keys** from the shortcut menu, as shown in Figure 2-47.

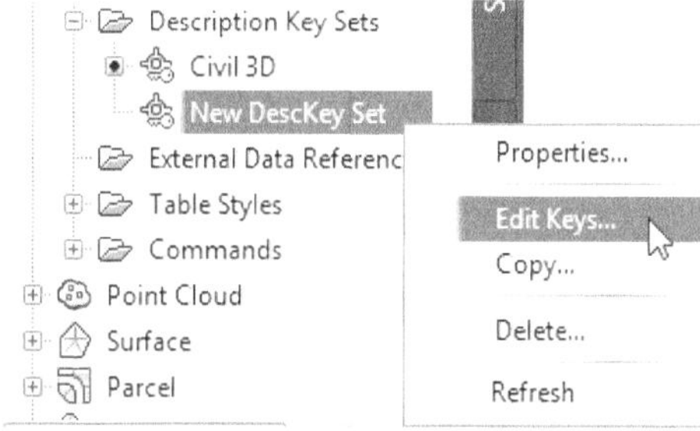

***Figure 2-47** Choosing the **Edit Keys** option*

On doing so, the **PANORAMA** window with the **DescKey Editor** tab will be displayed, as shown in Figure 2-48. In the **DescKey Editor PANORAMA** window, you will add the raw descriptions that will match the description keys. The columns used for creating description keys in the **DescKey Editor PANORAMA** window are discussed next.

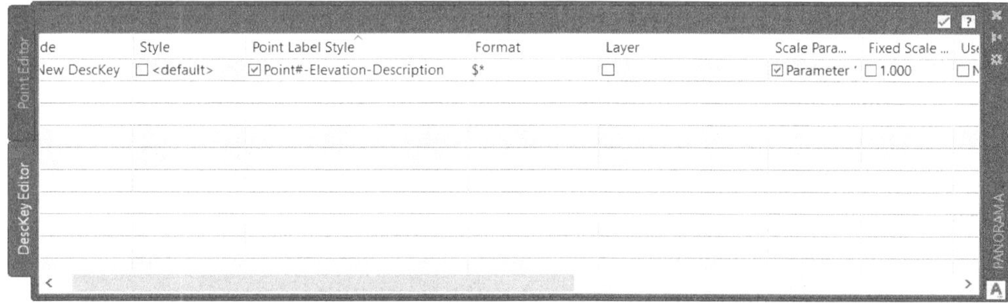

***Figure 2-48** The **PANORAMA** window with **DescKey Editor** tab*

Code

This column specifies the raw description of points. A raw description is a code that is used for points by a person who has created points from the site or field. To enter a code, double-click in the **Code** field to activate it and enter the required code in the **Code** column. You can also use the wild cards characters within the codes. These characters are used to expand the matching capabilities of description keys. Some of the common wild card characters used are *(asterisk), # (pound), and so on. For example, the MH raw description for the Manhole points can have raw descriptions as MHole, MH-1, MH-2, and so on. Thus, if you want to assign the same points style, label style and description to all the manhole points, you can use wild card characters with code such as MH*. Adding this wild character (*) means that code MH * will match with all raw description that match with MH such as MH-1, MH-2, MHole, and so on. Thus, all manhole points when imported into drawing will be identified automatically and assigned the same style and label styles.

You can specify the description in the **Code** column. Unlike the raw description of points in a point group, the description keys to be matched are case sensitive. This means the raw description MHole will not match with the description key code, MHOLE. Some of the wild cards used are; **?** for specifying number, **#** for single digit, @ for single alphabetical character only, **.** for non- alphanumeric character, [ ] for a list, and so on. Note that wild cards characters are always added after the description key code.

Point Style

This column specifies the default point style to be assigned to points matching with description key codes. To modify the point style, select the check box in the **Point Style** column field and click on the **Point Style** field; the **Point Style** dialog box will be displayed. You can use this dialog box to select the required point style or create a new point style using the options in the dialog box.

Point label Style

To specify the required point label style, select the check box in the **Point label Style** field and click in the **Point Label Style** field; the **Point Label Style** dialog box will be displayed. The **Point Label Style** dialog box displays the default point label style to be assigned to the points matching with the description key code. Select the required point label style or create a new point label style using this dialog box.

Format

This column specifies the format used for translating the raw description of points matching the description key into full description. As a result, you can make the raw description more meaningful and comprehensive. As discussed earlier, raw descriptions refer to the point description that is specified by the surveyor on the field and may not give the proper description of points. So, to create a full description of points, you can use the **Format** code of description keys.

The raw description of a point can be translated into full description in three ways. The first way is to keep the full description same as that of the raw description. For example, **GRND** is both the full description and raw description of ground points. To do so, enter $* in the **Format** field to accept the raw description as full description.

The second way is to change the raw description into full description. For example, the **IP** raw description will be replaced by **Iron Pin**. The third way is to change the order and adding information or parameters to the full description. For example, a point has a raw description **TREE OAK 5** in which **OAK** is a parameter of the raw description. This raw description matches with a description key code **Tree** in the key set. Assume that the format for the key is $2"$1tree. Now, this format will help you create a full description in a specified order. The full description of the point will be **5"OAK tree**.

During the description key match, the raw description **TREE OAK 5** will match the description key having the code **TREE** and format code, **$2"$1tree**. This format code will translate the raw description into full description, **5"OAK tree**. $2 refers to the second parameter in the raw description, **5,** whereas **$1** refers to the first parameter, **OAK**. The added information in the format code is " and tree. Thus, the full description is created by replacing the values of **$2** to **5"** and **$1** to **OAK** to create the **5"OAK tree** as the full description.

To create new description keys in the description key set, right-click in any of the fields and choose **New** from the shortcut menu; a new key will be added to the **Code** column of the **DescKey Editor PANORAMA** window, as shown in Figure 2-49. After you have specified the code, point style, point label styles, and format, choose the green colored button at top right corner of the **PANORAMA** window to close it. Figure 2-50 shows an example of a description key set having different keys.

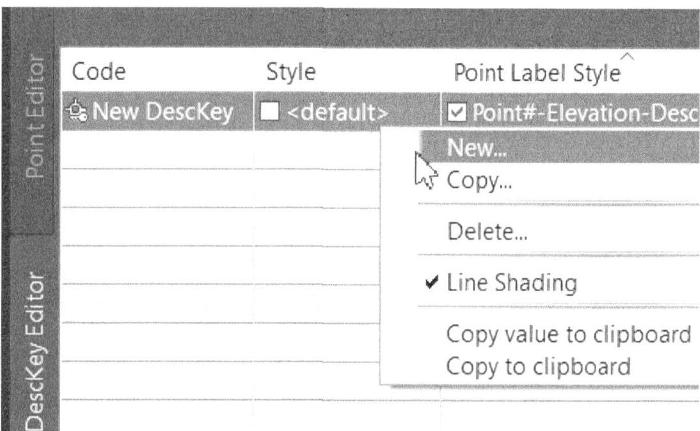

***Figure 2-49** Choosing the **New** option from the shortcut menu*

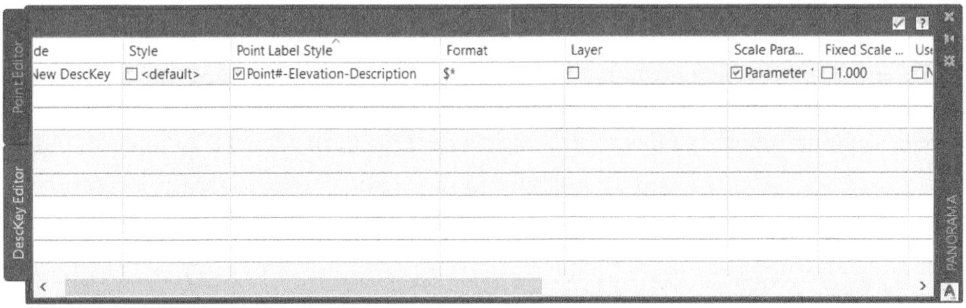

*Figure 2-50 The **Deskey Editor** tab in the **PANORAMA** window showing different keys of a description key set*

Activating the Description Key Matching

To activate the process of description key matching, choose the **Settings** tab from the **TOOLSPACE** palette and expand the **Commands** sub-node of the **Points** node in the **Settings** tab. Next, right-click on **Create Points** and choose the **Edit Command Settings** option from the shortcut menu; the **Edit Command Settings - Create Points** dialog box will be displayed. Expand the **Point Creation** category and ensure that the **Disable Description Keys** property is set to **false**. Choose the **OK** button to exit the dialog box, as shown in Figure 2-51.

Alternatively, choose the **Point Creation Tools** option from the **Points** drop-down in **Create Ground Data** panel from the **Home** tab; the **Create Points** toolbar will be displayed. Expand the toolbar and then expand the **Points Creation** category in it. Next, ensure that the **Disable Description Keys** property is set to **False**.

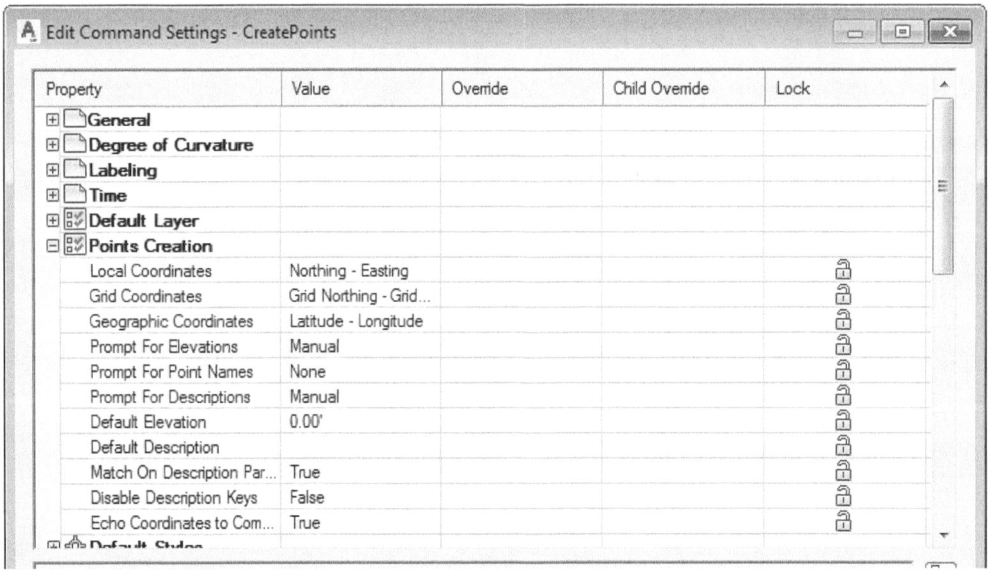

*Figure 2-51 The **Disable Description Keys** property set to **False***

TUTORIALS

Before starting the tutorial, you need to download and save the tutorial files on your computer. To do so, follow the steps given below:

1. Log on to *www.cadcim.com* and browse to *Textbooks > Civil/GIS > Civil 3D > Exploring AutoCAD Civil 3D 2018*. Next, select *c02_c3d_2018_tut.zip* file from the **Tutorial Files** drop-down list. Choose the corresponding **Download** button to download the data file.

2. Now, save and extract the downloaded folder to the following location:

   C:\c3d_2018

Note

*While opening the tutorial file, the **PANORAMA** window may appear with an error message. Close this window to proceed further.*

Tutorial 1 — Creating Points I

In this tutorial, you will create points using various tools that are available in the **Create Points** toolbar, as shown in Figure 2-52. **(Expected time: 20 min)**

The following steps are required to complete this tutorial:

a. Open the file.
b. Create points using different options in the **Points** drop-down.
c. Save the file.

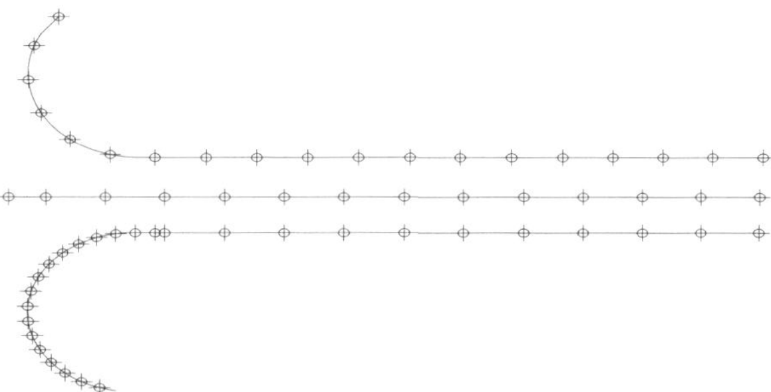

Figure 2-52 *Points created by using various tools in the **Create Points** toolbar*

Opening the File

1. Choose **Open > Drawing** from the **Application Menu**; the **Select File** dialog box is displayed.

2. In this dialog box, browse to the location *C:\c3d_2018\c02_c3d_2018_tut*.

3. Select the file *c02_c3d_2018_tut01.dwg* and then choose the **Open** button to open the file.

The opened drawing file consists of an alignment and two lines on both sides.

Creating Points Using the Options in the Alignment Category

1. Choose the **Create Points - Alignments** option from **Home > Create Ground Data > Points** drop-down; a flyout is displayed.

2. Choose the **Station/Offset** tool from the flyout to create points at some offset distance from the stations on an alignment; the **Create Points** toolbar is displayed and you are prompted to select the alignment.

3. Select the **Centreline** alignment in the drawing; you are prompted to specify the station along the baseline.

4. As you move the cursor over the alignment, a tooltip showing the first stations is displayed, as shown in Figure 2-53. Zoom in to view the alignment and click on **0+00** at the start of the alignment. Now you are prompted to specify the offset distance.

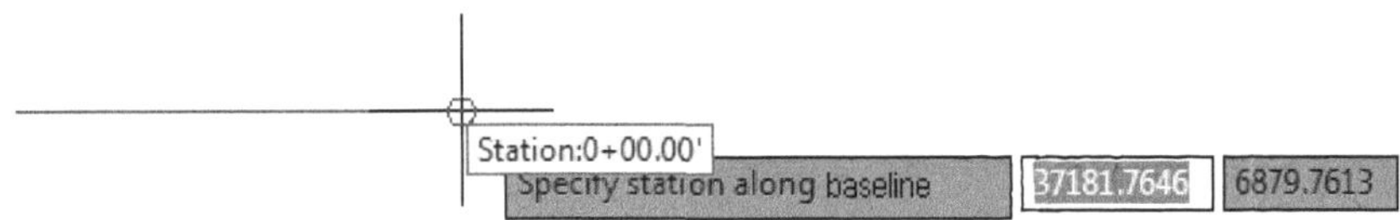

Figure 2-53 *A tooltip showing the first station*

Tip

You can also create a point at the start of an alignment by specifying ***0.00*** *in the command line and then press* ENTER.

5. Press ENTER to accept the default offset value; you are prompted to enter the point description.

6. Next, enter **CL** as the point description in the command line and press ENTER; you are prompted to specify elevation.

7. Specify the point elevation value as **100** in the command line, and press ENTER; a blue colored point is displayed at the first station of the alignment. Also, you are prompted to specify another station in the command line.

8. Pan to the next station **30+00** on the alignment and click on it.

9. Press ENTER to accept the default offset value; you are prompted to specify the description.

10. Repeat the procedure followed in steps 6 and 7 and add a new point at station **30+00**. On creating the point, you are again prompted to specify the next station.

Continue creating points till you reach the other end of the alignment, as shown in Figure 2-54.

11. Press ESC to terminate the command.

In this way, you have created points from the alignment.

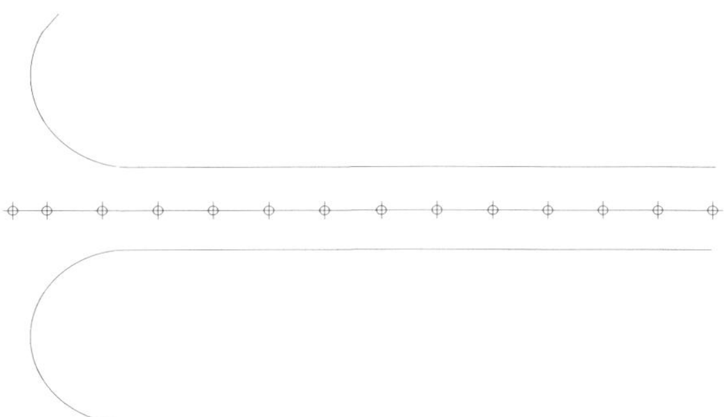

Figure 2-54 Points created at each selected station

Creating Points Using the Options in the Miscellaneous Category

1. Choose the **Create Points - Miscellaneous** option from **Home > Create Ground Data > Points** drop-down; a flyout is displayed.

2. Choose the **Divide Object** tool from the flyout; the **Create Points** toolbar is displayed and you are prompted to select an arc, line, polyline, lot line, or feature line.

3. Select the line above the alignment; you are prompted to enter the number of segments.

4. Enter **12** in the command line and press ENTER; you are prompted to specify the offset.

5. Press ENTER to accept the default offset value; you are prompted to specify the point description.

6. Enter **OSP** and press ENTER; you are prompted to specify the point elevation.

7. Enter **100** and press ENTER; a blue colored point is displayed at the endpoint of the selected line; you are prompted to specify the description and elevation.

8. Repeat the procedure given in steps 6 and 7 and keep on specifying the point description and elevation till you are prompted to select an arc, line, polyline, or feature line.

9. Next, select the arc object above the alignment; you are prompted to specify the number of segments. Enter **6** in the command line and press ENTER; you are prompted to specify the offset.

10. Enter **5** as the offset distance in the command line and press ENTER; you are prompted to specify the point description.

11. Enter **OSP** in the command line and press ENTER; you are prompted to specify the point elevation.

12. Enter **100** in the command line and press ENTER; you are prompted to specify the point description.

13. Repeat the procedure given in steps 11 and 12 to create points at an offset along the selected arc.

14. Press ESC to terminate the command.

Figure 2-55 shows points created from the line and arc objects by dividing these objects into specified segments.

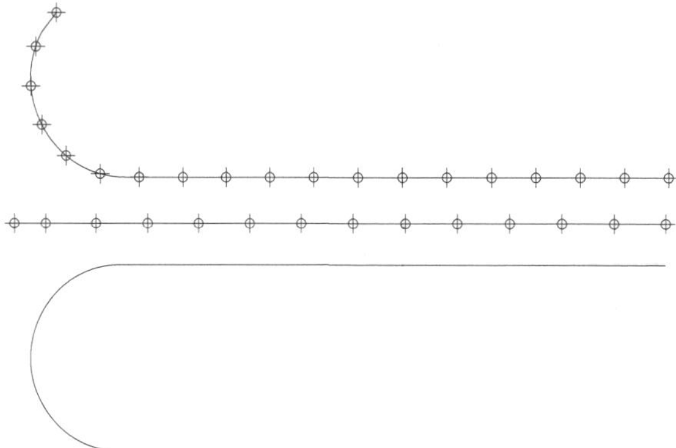

Figure 2-55 *Points created from the line and arc objects*

Creating Points Using the Options in the Intersection Category

1. Choose the **Create Points-Intersections** option from **Home > Create Ground Data > Points** drop-down; a flyout is displayed

2. Choose the **Direction/Perpendicular** tool from the flyout; you are prompted to specify the start point.

3. Click at the first point of the alignment to specify the first point; you are prompted to specify the direction.

4. Drag the cursor vertically downward and click on the line just below the point on alignment; an arrow showing the direction is displayed and you are prompted to specify the offset.

5. Press ENTER to accept the default offset value; you are prompted to specify the location for the perpendicular point.

6. Click on the line object just below the first point on the alignment; a green cross-mark indicating the position of the point is displayed on the screen. Also, you are prompted to specify the point description.

Note

*Ensure that the **OSNAP** or **ORTHO** command is activated to specify the perpendicular point. You can also use the transparent commands to specify the perpendicular points.*

7. Enter **PP** (perpendicular point) and press ENTER; you are prompted to specify the elevation.

8. Enter **100** in the command line and press ENTER; a point is displayed on the line and you are prompted again to specify the start point.

9. Now, click at the second point on the alignment; you are prompted to specify the direction.

10. Again, drag the cursor downward and click on the line just below the selected point; an arrow is displayed and you are prompted to specify the offset.

11. Press ENTER to accept the default offset distance; you are prompted to specify the location of the perpendicular point.

12. Click on the line just below the second point; you are prompted to specify the point description.

13. Specify the description and the elevation as specified in steps 7 and 8; a point is displayed on the line, refer to Figure 2-56.

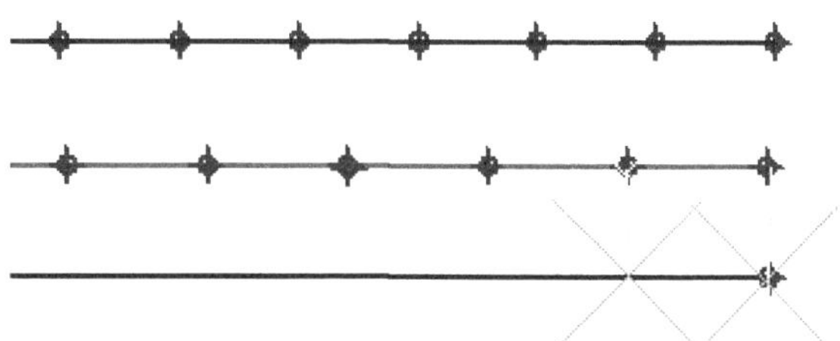

Figure 2-56 *Cross-marks indicating the location of the point*

14. Using the procedure followed in steps 3 to 8, create points in the perpendicular direction of the alignment points.

    Figure 2-57 shows the points created at the intersection of the direction specified from alignment points and the perpendicular points specified on the line.

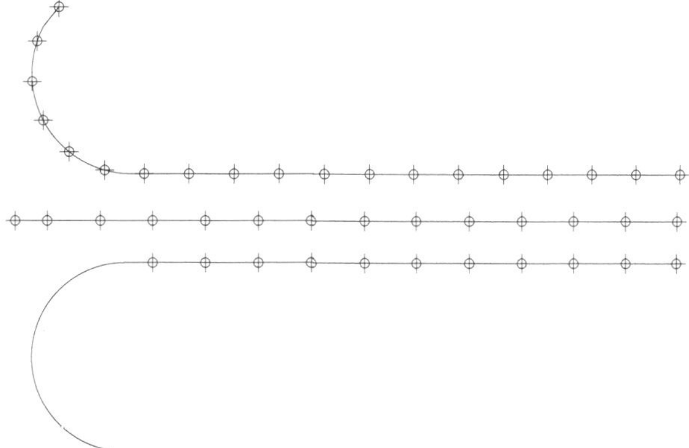

Figure 2-57 *Points created by intersection*

15. Choose the **Create Points - Miscellaneous** option from **Home > Create Ground Data > Points** drop-down; a flyout is displayed.

16. Choose the **Measure Object** tool from the flyout; you are prompted to select an arc, line, polyline, lot line, or feature line. Select the arc below the alignment; you are prompted to specify the starting station.

17. Press ENTER to accept the default value **<0.000>**. On doing so, the ending station is displayed in the command line.

18. Next, press ENTER; you are prompted to specify the offset distance.

19. Again, press ENTER; the default value is accepted as offset and you are prompted to specify the interval.

20. Enter **1000** in the command line and press ENTER; you are prompted to specify the point description.

21. Enter **OSP** in the command line and press ENTER; you are prompted to specify the elevation.

22. Enter **100** in the command line and press ENTER; you are again prompted to specify the description and elevation.

23. Repeat steps 21 and 22 till you are prompted to select an arc again. Thus, Civil 3D creates the point first by measuring the arc object by identifying the start and end stations of the arc and then divides the arc at specified intervals. Points are created at the end of each interval including the start and end stations of the arc, refer to Figure 2-58.

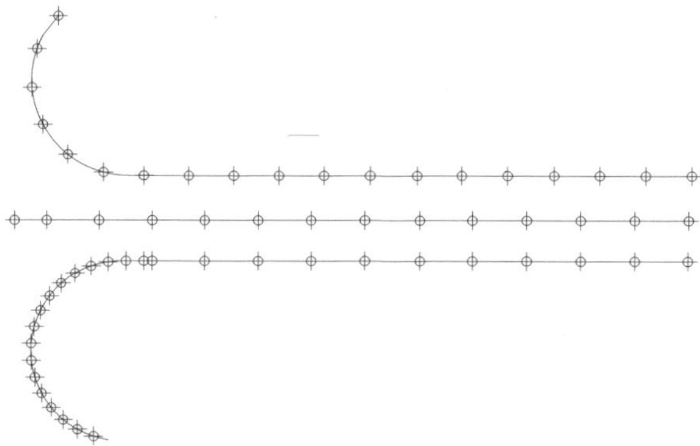

Figure 2-58 *Points created along the arc object below the alignment*

Saving the File

1. Choose **Save As** from the **Application Menu**; the **Save Drawing As** dialog box is displayed.

2. In this dialog box, browse to the following location:

   C:\c3d_2018\c02_c3d_2018_tut

3. In the **File name** edit box, enter **c02_tut01**.

4. Choose the **Save** button; the file is saved with the name *c02_tut01.dwg* at the specified location.

Tutorial 2 — Importing Points

In this tutorial, you will import points into a drawing, create a point group, create a new point style, and a point label style for points, as shown in Figure 2-59. **(Expected time: 30 min)**

The following steps are required to complete this tutorial:

a. Open a new template.
b. Import points from the point file.
c. Create a point group.
d. Create a new point style and assign it.
e. Create a new label style and assign it.
f. Save the drawing.

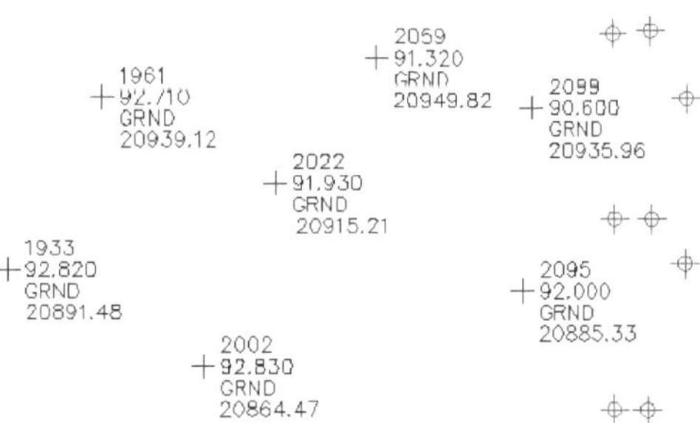

Figure 2-59 *Points created with a new point style and point label style*

Opening the New Template

1. Choose **New** from the **Application Menu**; the **Select template** dialog box is displayed.

2. Select the *_AutoCAD Civil 3D (Imperial) NCS.dwt* template file and choose the **Open** button to open the template file.

Importing Points

1. Choose the **Point Creation Tools** tool from **Home > Create Ground Data > Points** drop-down; the **Create Points** toolbar is displayed.

2. Choose the **Import Points** button from the **Create Points** toolbar; the **Import Points** dialog box is displayed.

3. Select the **PENZD (space delimited)** option from the **Specify point file format (filtering OFF)** list box.

Note

*By selecting the **PENZD (space delimited)** option, the points will be arranged in the order of the point number, easting, northing, elevation, and description. The points will be separated by a space delimiter.*

4. Choose the **Add files** button on the right of the **Selected Files** list box; the **Select Source File** dialog box is displayed. Browse to *C:\c3d_2018\c02_c3d_2018_tut* location.

5. Select the *c02_c3d_2018_tut02.txt* file and choose the **Open** button; the dialog box is closed and the path of the selected file is displayed in the **Import Points** dialog box.

6. Next, choose the **OK** button in the **Import Points** dialog box; the dialog box is closed and the points are imported.

7. Choose the **Prospector** tab in the **TOOLSPACE** palette and notice a black colored symbol on the left of the **Points** node, refer to Figure 2-60. This indicates that the points have been added in the drawing.

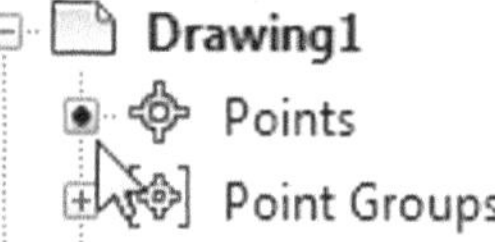

***Figure 2-60** The symbol indicating points addition*

8. Enter **ZE** in the command line and press ENTER; the points are displayed in the drawing. Next, close the **Create Points** toolbar.

9. Expand the **Point Groups** node. You will notice that all the points are added to the default **_All Points** group.

Creating a Point Group

1. Choose the **Points** tool from the **Ground Data** panel of the **Modify** tab; the **COGO Point** tab is displayed in the Ribbon.

2. Choose the **Edit/List Points** tool from the **Modify** panel of the **COGO Point** tab; the **PANORAMA** window with the **Point Editor** tab is displayed.

3. Scroll the bar in the **PANORAMA** window to view the description of points. On scrolling the bar, you will notice that some of the points have **GRND** as the point description. Now, you need to create a new point group that will include all the points with **GRND** as the description.

4. Close the **PANORAMA** window after viewing the point description of all the points that you have imported.

5. Now, right-click on **Point Groups** in the **Prospector** tab of the **TOOLSPACE** palette; a shortcut menu is displayed. Choose the **New** option from the shortcut menu; the **Point Group Properties - Point Group - (1)** dialog box is displayed.

6. In the **Information** tab, enter **Ground Points** in the **Name** edit box.

7. Choose the **Include** tab and then select the **With raw descriptions matching** check box. Enter **GRND** in the corresponding edit box.

8. Next, choose the **OK** button; the dialog box is closed. All the points with **GRND** as the raw description are added to the **Ground Points** point group in the **Point Groups** node.

9. Expand the **Point Groups** node and select the **Ground Points** point group; all the ground points are displayed in the **TOOLSPACE** list view.

Creating a Point Style

1. Choose the **Settings** tab of the **TOOLSPACE** palette and expand **Point > Point Styles**; a triangular symbol on the left of the style name is displayed, as shown in Figure 2-61. This symbol indicates that the style being used is an existing style named **Basic**.

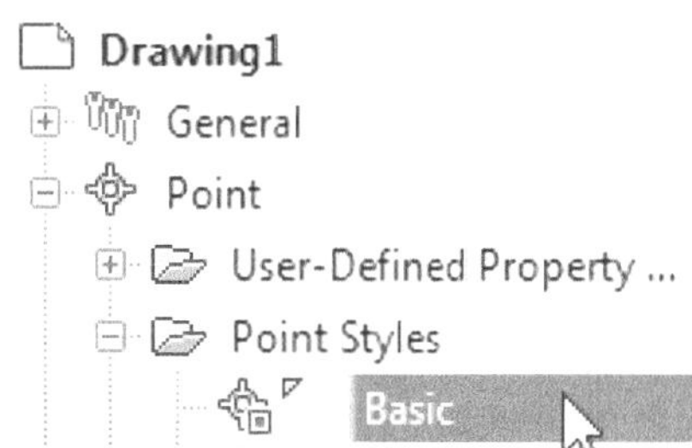

*Figure 2-61 The triangular symbol displayed on the left of the **Basic** point style*

2. Right-click on the **Point Styles** node and then choose the **New** option from the shortcut menu; the **Point Style - New Point Style** dialog box is displayed.

3. Accept the default point group name in the **Name** edit box and choose the **Marker** tab from the dialog box.

4. Ensure that the **Use custom marker** radio button is selected and then choose the third button from the **Custom marker style** options.

5. Select the **Use size relative to screen** option from the **Options** drop-down list in the **Size** area.

6. Enter **4** in the **percent** edit box.

7. Now, choose the **Display** tab and make sure that the **Plan** option is selected in the **View Direction** drop-down list.

8. In the **Component display** region, click on the color of the **Marker** component; the **Select Color** dialog box is displayed.

9. Select the **blue** color from the dialog box and choose the **OK** button to exit the dialog box.

10. Now, choose **Apply** and then **OK** from the **Point Style - New Point Style** dialog box; the dialog box is closed and the point style name is added to the **Point Styles** node in the **Settings** tab.

Creating a Point Label Style

1. Choose the **Settings** tab of the **TOOLSPACE** palette and expand **Point > Label Styles** in the tab. You will notice that **Point#-Elevation-Description** is the current point label style.

2. Right-click on **Label Styles** and then choose the **New** option from the shortcut menu displayed; the **Label Style Composer - New Point Label Style** dialog box is displayed.

3. In the **Label Style Composer - New Point Label Style** dialog box, accept the default label style name displayed in the **Name** edit box and choose the **Layout** tab from this dialog box.

4. Now, choose the **Create Text component** button on the right of the **Component name** drop-down list; a new component **Text.1** is created and added to the **Component name** drop-down list.

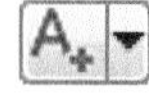

5. Click in the **Value** field of the **Name** property and enter **Northing** as the name of the component.

6. Click in the **Value** field of the **Anchor Component** property and select the **Point Description** option from the drop-down list. Note the position of the component in the **Preview** window.

7. Similarly, set the value of the **Anchor Point** property to **Bottom Center**. Note the position of the component.

8. Set the values of the **X Offset** and **Y Offset** properties in the **Text** category to **0.1500"** and **-0.0700"**, respectively. Again, note the position of the component in the **Preview** window.

9. Now, click in the **Value** field of the **Contents** property; a browse button is displayed.

10. Choose the browse button; the **Text Component Editor - Contents** dialog box is displayed.

11. In the **Text Component Editor - Contents** dialog box, select **Northing** from the **Properties** drop-down list and set the value of the **Precision** modifier to **0.01**.

12. Select **Label Text** in the **Text Editor**.

13. Choose the button next to the **Properties** drop-down list; the selected property is added to the **Text Editor** window available on the right pane of the **Text Component Editor - Contents** dialog box, refer to Figure 2-62.

Figure 2-62 *Partial view of the* ***Text Component Editor - Contents*** *dialog box showing the northing label text*

14. Next, choose the **OK** button to close the **Text Component Editor - Contents** dialog box.

15. Again, choose the **OK** button to close the **Label Style Composer - New Point Label Style** dialog box.

Assigning Point Style and Point Label Style to the Point Group

1. Choose the **Prospector** tab of the **TOOLSPACE** palette and expand the **Point Groups** node.

2. Right-click on the **Ground Points** group; a shortcut menu is displayed. Choose the **Properties** option from the shortcut menu; the **Point Group Properties - Ground Points** dialog box is displayed.

3. In the **Information** tab, select the **New Point Style** option from the **Point style** drop-down list in the **Default styles** area, as shown in Figure 2-63.

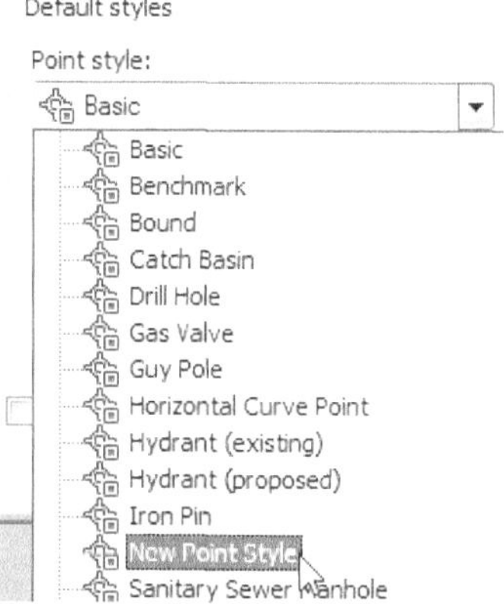

***Figure 2-63** Selecting the **New Point Style** option from the **Point style** drop-down list*

4. Choose the **Apply** button from the **Point Group Properties - Ground Points** dialog box; you will notice that all the ground points are displayed in blue color with the selected marker style.

5. Similarly, select the **New Point Label Style** option from the **Point label style** drop-down list.

6. Next, choose the **OK** button; the **Point Group Properties - Ground Points** dialog box is closed. The ground points are displayed with a new point style and label style. Note that the point label displays the point number, elevation, description, and northing of each point, as shown in Figure 2-64.

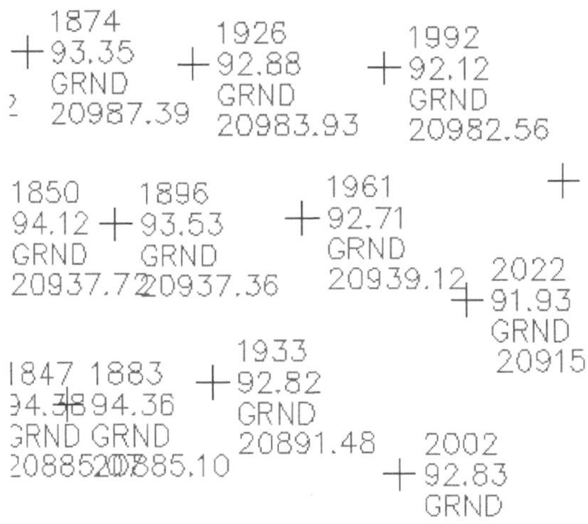

Figure 2-64 *Ground points displaying the point number, elevation, description, and northing of each point*

Saving the File

1. Choose **Save As** from the **Application Menu**; the **Save Drawing As** dialog box is displayed.

2. In this dialog box, browse to the following location:

   C:\c3d_2018\c02_c3d_2018_tut

3. In the **File name** edit box, enter **c02_tut02**.

4. Choose the **Save** button; the file is saved with the name *c02_tut02.dwg* at the specified location.

Tutorial 3 — Creating Points II

In this tutorial, you will verify the drawing settings, create points manually using the coordinate data in latitude and longitude format, and create points using the **Slope/Grade - Elevation** tool, refer to Figure 2-65. **(Expected time: 40 min)**

The following steps are required to complete this tutorial:

a. Open the drawing.
b. Specify the drawing settings.
c. Create points manually using the coordinate data specified in latitude and longitude.
d. Apply point style and label style.
e. Create points using the Slope/Grade - Elevation method.
f. Save the drawing file.

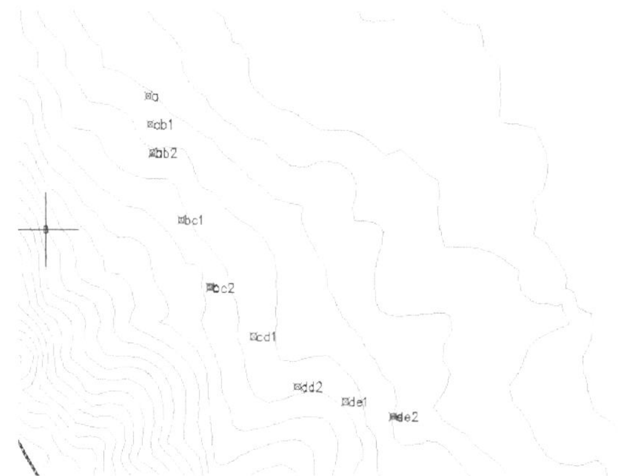

Figure 2-65 *Points created using the* ***Slope/Grade - Elevation*** *tool*

Opening the Drawing File and Specifying its Drawing Settings

In this tutorial, you first need to specify the drawing settings for the project.

1. Choose **Open > Drawing** from the **Application Menu**; the **Select File** dialog box is displayed.

2. In this dialog box, browse to the location *C:\c3d_2018\c02_c3d_2018_tut*.

3. Select the file *c02_c3d_2018_tut03.dwg* and choose the **Open** button to open the file.

4. Choose the **Settings** tab in the **TOOLSPACE** palette. Right-click on the drawing name *c02_c3d_2018_tut03* in the **TOOLSPACE** palette; a shortcut menu is displayed. Choose the **Edit** Drawing Settings option from the shortcut menu; the Drawing Settings - <drawing name> dialog box is displayed.

5. In the **Units and Zone** tab of the **Drawing Settings** dialog box, refer to Figure 2-66, ensure the settings as follows:

   Drawing units: **Meters**
   Imperial to Metric Conversion: **International Foot (1 Foot = 0.3048 Meters)**
   Angular units: **Degrees**
   Categories: **UTM, NAD83 Datum**
   Available coordinate systems: **UTM with NAD83 datum, Zone 11, Meter; Central Meridian 117d W**

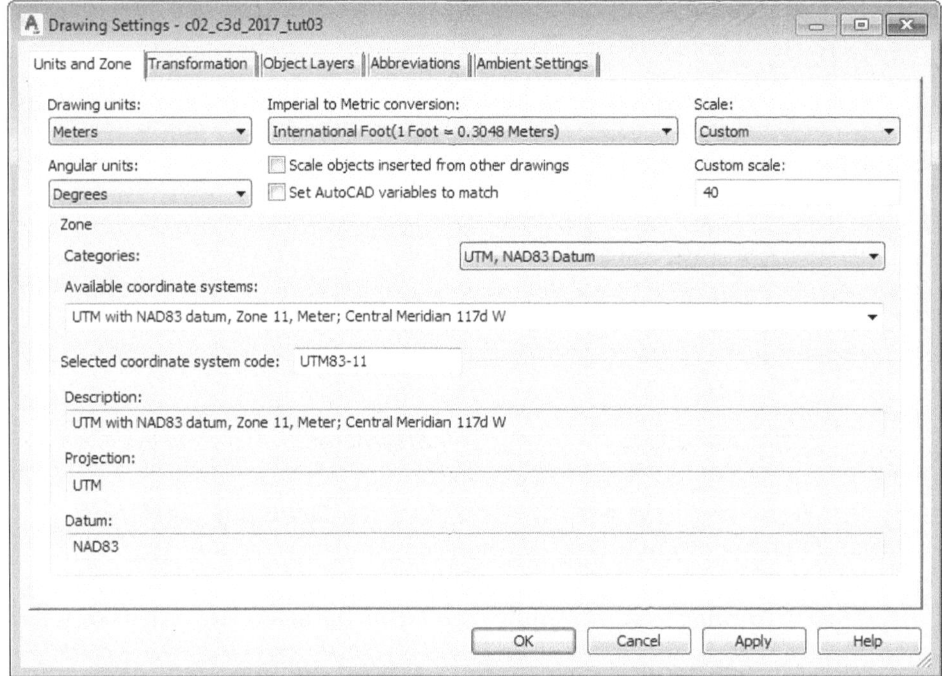

***Figure 2-66** The **Units and Zone** tab of the **Drawing Settings** dialog box*

6. In the **Ambient Settings** tab of the **Drawing Settings** dialog box, expand the **Coordinate** node. By default, the value for **Unit** is set to **meter**. If it is not so, click on the corresponding **Value** cell of the **Unit** property and choose the **meter** option from the drop-down list displayed.

7. Ensure that the value of the **Unit** property in the **Elevation** node is set to **meter**.

8. In the **Lat Long** node, set the value of **Unit** and **Format** as **degree** and **decimal**, respectively, if they are not so.

9. Choose the **OK** button to save and exit the **Drawing Settings** dialog box.

Note

*If the options in the **Drawing Settings** dialog box are not configured as mentioned in step 5 to 8, you need to set the values as specified in these steps.*

Creating Points Manually Using Point Coordinates

1. Invoke the **Create Points** toolbar by choosing the **Point Creation Tools** tool from **Home > Create Ground Data > Points** drop-down.

2. Choose the **Manual** button from the **Create Points** toolbar; you are prompted to specify a location for the new point.

3. Enter command **'LL** in the command line; the current lat/long unit and input format information are displayed and you are prompted to enter the value for latitude.

Note

The points can also be created with the ***Northing*** *and* ***Easting*** *coordinate values. To create points using these values, choose the* ***Manual*** *tool from the* ***Create Points*** *toolbar and then enter* ***'NE*** *at the Command prompt.*

4. Specify **N33.229010** in the command line and press ENTER; you are prompted to enter the value for longitude.

5. Specify **E-116.758552** in the command line and press ENTER; you are prompted to specify the point description.

6. Enter **a** as the point description; you are prompted to specify the point elevation.

7. Enter **849.13** in the command line and press ENTER.

8. Create points b, c, d, and e by using the procedure followed in steps 4 to 6 and the data given in the following table:

Point	Latitude	Longitude	Elevation
b	N 33.228168	E -116.758706	860.70
c	N 33.226149	E -116.757575	875.79
d	N 33.224642	E -116.755833	869.28
e	N 33.224198	E -116.753949	849.99

Tip

E- *or* ***W*** *as prefix in the value of longitude indicates the location of the point to the west of prime meridian.*

9. Press ESC twice to exit the **Create Points** command.

Applying the Point Style and Point Label Style

1. Select the **Points** node in the **Prospector** tab of the **TOOLSPACE**; a list of points in the drawing is displayed in the **TOOLSPACE** item view.

2. Right-click the first point in the **TOOLSPACE** item view; a shortcut menu is displayed. Choose the **Select** option from the shortcut menu; the selected point is displayed with the grip editor markers in the drawing area.

3. Keeping the point selected, right-click in the drawing area; a shortcut menu is displayed. Choose the **Point Group Properties** option from the shortcut menu; the **Point Group Properties- _All Points** dialog box is displayed.

4. In the **Information** tab of the dialog box, select the **Tutorial3-Point Style** option from the **Point style** drop-down list and the **Description Only** option from the **Point label style** drop-down list.

5. Choose **OK** to apply the selected settings and exit the dialog box. The surface with the **COGO** points is displayed, as shown in Figure 2-67.

Figure 2-67 *Surface with* ***COGO*** *points*

6. Hover the mouse over the first **COGO** point; the information of the point is displayed in the tooltip, as shown in Figure 2-68.

Cogo Point	
Number	1
Layer	0
Description	a
Easting	522496.6435m
Northing	3676701.4565m
Elevation	849.13m
Grid Easting	522496.6435m
Grid Northing	3676701.4565m
Latitude	N33.229010 (d)
Longitude	W116.758552 (d)
Scale Factor	1.000
Convergence	0.132311 (d)
Layer	0

Figure 2-68 *Information of the* ***COGO*** *point displayed in tooltip*

Creating Points Using the Slope/Grade - Elevation Tool

1. Turn on the **Object Snap** with the **Node** option selected.

Note

You can toggle the options for snapping in the ***Object Snap*** *tab of the* ***Drafting Settings*** *dialog box. To invoke the dialog box, enter* ***OSNAP*** *in the command bar.*

Tip

Final image can vary according to the scale of drawing.

2. Choose the **Slope/Grade - Elevation** tool from the **Slope: High/Low Point** drop-down in the **Create Points** toolbar; you are prompted to specify the start point. 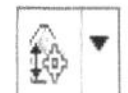

3. Select point **a**; you are prompted to specify a point to define the direction of the intermediate points. Select point **b**; you are prompted to specify slope/grade between points **a** and **b**. The points created will be along the line joining points **a** and **b**.

4. Specify **-8.13334** as slope in the command line and press ENTER; you are prompted to specify the ending elevation.

   The slope is negative as the point **b** (860.70m) is on a higher level than point **a** (849.13m).

5. Enter **860.70** as the ending station elevation; you are prompted to specify the number of intermediate points.

6. Enter **2** as the number of intermediate points and press ENTER; you are prompted to specify offset.

7. Accept the default value of **0.00**; you are prompted to add the end point.

8. Enter **NO** in the command line; you are prompted to add description for the first point.

9. Specify **ab1** as the point description and press ENTER; you are prompted to specify description for the point.

10. Enter **ab2** as the description of the second point; you are prompted to specify the point for defining the direction.

11. Use ESC to terminate the create points command.

12. Using the procedure followed in steps 2 to 10, create points between points **b** and **c**, points **c** and **d**, and points **d** and **e** based on the data given in the following table:

Points between	Start point	Slope	End elevation
bc	b	-16.48	875.79
cd	c	27.39	867.28
de	d	10.57	849.99

Figure 2-69 shows the final result for the points created using the provided data.

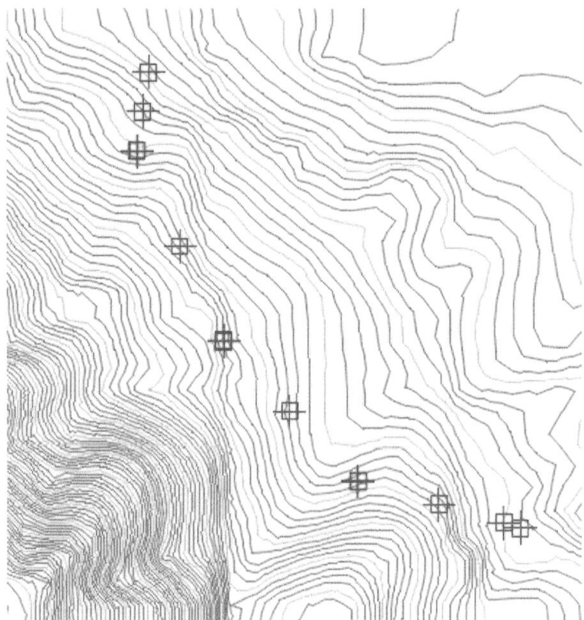

Figure 2-69 *COGO points created using the* ***Slope/Grade - Elevation*** *tool*

Saving the File

1. Choose **Save As** from the **Application Menu**; the **Save Drawing As** dialog box is displayed.

2. In this dialog box, browse to the following location:

   C:\c3d_2018\c02_c3d_2018_tut

3. In the **File name** edit box, enter **c02_tut03**.

4. Choose the **Save** button; the file is saved with the name *c02_tut03.dwg* at the specified location.

Self-Evaluation Test

Answer the following questions and then compare them to those given at the end of this chapter:

1. Which of the following tools is used to create points by specifying the distances along the X and Y axes of the grid?

   a) **Along Polyline/Contour** b) **Direction/Direction**
   c) **On Grid** d) None of these

2. Which of the following properties is used to specify the orientation of the point label?

   a) **Plan Readable** b) **Orientation Reference**
   c) **Forced Insertion** d) None of these

3. Which of the following properties is used to specify a reference to position the component of the point label?

   a) **Anchor Component** b) **Anchor Point**
   c) **Attachment** d) None of these

4. Which of the following categories is used to create points by selecting the point location manually in the drawing?

   a) **Create Point - Miscellaneous** b) **Create Point - Intersections**
   c) **Create Point - Alignments** d) None of these

5. Which of the following tools is used to create a point at the intersection of two grades or slopes?

   a) **High/Low Point** b) **By Relative Location**
   c) **Slope/Grade Distance** d) **Direction/Direction** 1.

6. Points specify the _________of different features.

7. The two main components of a Civil 3D point are _________ and _________.

8. The _________ category has the most commonly used options for creating points.

9. Besides controlling the visibility and display of points, ________ help you manage the workability of points.

10. Point styles control the shape, size, color, location of the point marker as well as the _________ of the point label.

11. To calculate geodetic information, choose the _________ tool from the **Analyze** panel in the **COGO Points** contextual tab.

12. To import points to AutoCAD Civil 3D, choose the ________ tool from the **COGO Point Tools** panel in the **COGO Points** contextual tab.

13. Points are the building blocks of all civil engineering projects and designs. (T/F)

14. For creating points, you need to invoke the **Create Points** toolbar from **Home > Create Ground Data > Points** drop-down. (T/F)

15. For editing a point in a drawing, you need to invoke the **Edit/List Points** tool from the **COGO Points** panel in the **Modify** tab. (T/F)

Review Questions

Answer the following questions:

1. The __________ option is used to create points by using the point data contained in point files.

2. The __________ dialog box displays various file formats supported by Civil 3D.

3. There are two main types of file formats, __________ and **User Point File**.

4. The __________ window displays all points in the drawing and is also used to edit them.

5. The __________ dialog box is used to export points from AutoCAD Civil 3D.

6. The __________ tab is used to specify criteria to include points in a point group based on their properties.

7. You cannot import points from file. (T/F)

8. In Civil 3D, each point is an individual object with different information. (T/F)

9. You cannot convert AutoCAD points into Civil 3D points. (T/F)

10. Locking the points prevents you from changing the point style of the points. (T/F)

EXERCISES

Before starting the exercises, you need to download and save the exercise files on your computer. To do so, follow the steps given below:

1. Log on to *www.cadcim.com* and browse to *Textbooks > Civil/GIS > Civil 3D > Exploring AutoCAD Civil 3D 2018*. Next, select *c02_c3d_2018_exer.zip* file from the **Exercise Files** drop-down list. Choose the corresponding **Download** button to download the data file.

2. Now, save and extract the downloaded folder to the following location:

   C:\c3d_2018

Note

While opening the exercise files, the **PANORAMA** *window may appear with an error message. Close this window to proceed further.*

Exercise 1

Open the *c02_c3d_2018_ex01.dwg* file and create a point style and label style for points. Next, assign these styles to points using the following parameters: **(Expected time: 30 min)**

Point Style name: **New Style**
Marker Style: **default**
Marker Color: **blue**
Point Label Style Name: **New Label Style**
Color of all the label components: **blue**
Save the file as *c02_ex01a.dwg*.

Exercise 2

Using the *c02_ex01a.dwg* file, create a point group and edit the points in the point group using the **Point Editor**. Use the following parameters: **(Expected time: 30 min)**

Point Group Name: **Tower points**
Raw Description to include Points: **Tower**
Edit the elevation of the first five points, as shown in Figure 2-70
Save the file as *c02_ex02a.dwg*.

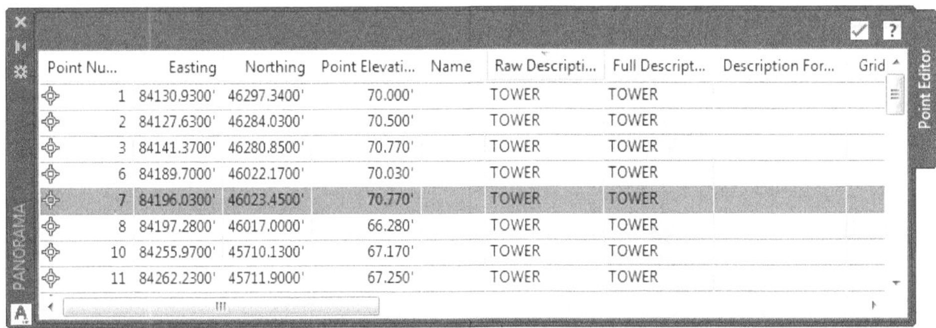

Point Nu...	Easting	Northing	Point Elevati...	Name	Raw Descripti...	Full Descript...	Description For...	Grid
1	84130.9300'	46297.3400'	70.000'		TOWER	TOWER		
2	84127.6300'	46284.0300'	70.500'		TOWER	TOWER		
3	84141.3700'	46280.8500'	70.770'		TOWER	TOWER		
6	84189.7000'	46022.1700'	70.030'		TOWER	TOWER		
7	84196.0300'	46023.4500'	70.770'		TOWER	TOWER		
8	84197.2800'	46017.0000'	66.280'		TOWER	TOWER		
10	84255.9700'	45710.1300'	67.170'		TOWER	TOWER		
11	84262.2300'	45711.9000'	67.250'		TOWER	TOWER		

Figure 2-70 *The **Point Editor** window showing the edited elevations*

Answers to Self-Evaluation Test

1. c, **2.** b, **3.** a, **4.** a, **5.** a, **6.** location, **7.** marker, label, **8. Miscellaneous**, **9.** point styles, **10.** visibility, **11. Geodetic Calculator**, **12. Import Points**, **13.** T, **14.** T, **15.** T

Chapter 3

Working with Surfaces

Learning Objectives

After completing this chapter, you will be able to:

- *Create various types of surfaces*
- *Create surfaces by adding data*
- *Add data from different sources*
- *Create and edit surface styles*
- *Apply surface properties*

SURFACES

In Civil 3D, a surface is considered as a building block and is created from triangular networks or grid data. Each triangle on the surface is created by connecting three nearest points of elevation. Also, each triangle has a defined slope.

A surface is a basic requirement of any Civil 3D project. All volume calculations, profiles, corridors, sections, and grading objects that are generated in a project are based on the surface created. You can create a surface by importing data from Triangular Irregular Network (TIN) files, Digital Elevated Model (DEM) files, points, point files, existing AutoCAD objects, contours, breaklines, point groups, and also from Google Earth.

Types of Surfaces

There are four types of surfaces in Civil 3D: TIN Surface, TIN Volume Surface, Grid Surface, and Grid Volume Surface. The TIN Volume Surface and Grid Volume Surface are used for calculating volumes. Types of surfaces are discussed next.

TIN Surface

A TIN surface is generated by the triangulation of points. The TIN surface is a set of contiguous non-overlapping triangles. The edges that form the triangles of the surface connect points to form an irregular triangular network. Each edge of the triangle is bound by two vertices. Each vertex in the surface has a definite coordinate and elevation. The elevation of any point on the surface is calculated by interpolating the elevation of the vertices of the triangle in which the point lies. The TIN surfaces are mostly used in case of irregular and variable surfaces such as streams, roads, and so on.

TIN Volume Surface

A TIN volume surface is created by computing the difference between two surfaces: the base surface and the comparison surface. The TIN volume surface is used for calculating the cut, fill, and net volumes between the two surfaces (base and comparison). The elevation of any point in the TIN volume surface is defined by the difference in the elevation of the base surface and the comparison surface at that point.

Grid Surface

A grid surface is created from the points that lie on the grid. A grid comprises points with elevation information spaced at regular intervals. You can either create or import a grid surface. You can also use a grid surface for mapping the surfaces that have uniform topography.

Grid Volume Surface

A grid volume surface is created by computing the difference between the comparison surface and the overlaying base surface. The elevation value of a grid volume surface is the difference between the elevation values of the comparison and base surfaces. The grid volume surface helps you to quickly generate a volume that can be used for iterative site design. Figure 3-1 shows a grid volume surface.

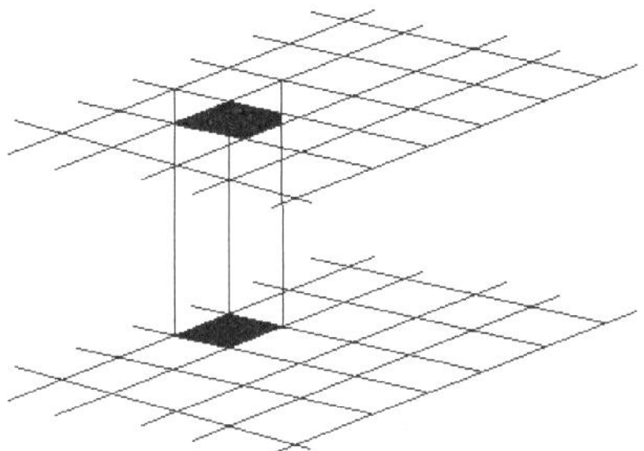

Figure 3-1 The grid volume surface

CREATING AND EDITING SURFACES

A surface can be created by using points, point groups, AutoCAD objects, and boundaries. A surface can also be created directly by importing the DEM and TIN files that are generated from the survey. The methods of creating a surface and its different aspects are discussed next.

Creating a Surface

Ribbon:	Home > Create Ground Data > Surfaces drop-down > Create Surface
Command:	CREATESURFACE

You can create a surface by using the **Create Surface** tool. Invoke the **Create Surface** tool from the **Create Ground Data** panel in the **Surfaces** drop-down; the **Create Surface** dialog box will be displayed, as shown in Figure 3-2.

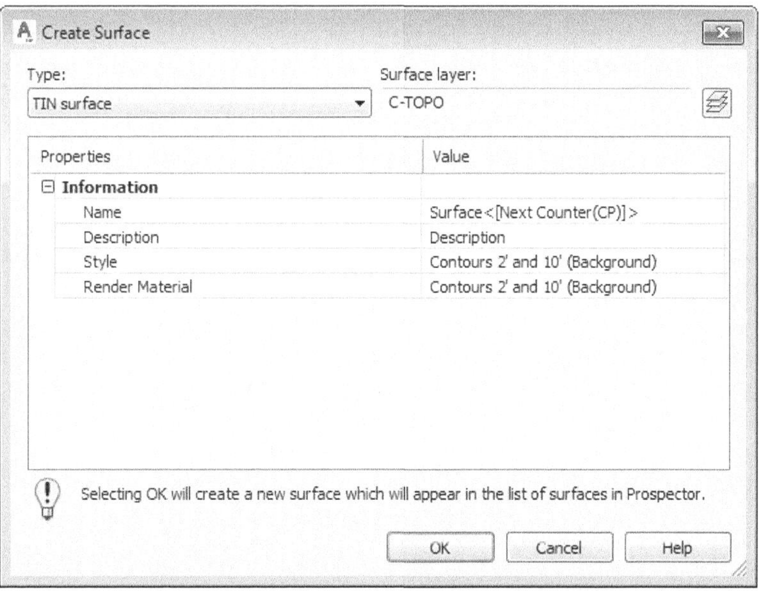

*Figure 3-2 The **Create Surface** dialog box*

Alternatively, you can invoke the **Create Surface** dialog box by using the **TOOLSPACE** palette. To do so, select the **Surfaces** node from the **Prospector** tab of the **TOOLSPACE** palette and right-click; a shortcut menu will be displayed. Choose the **Create Surface** tool from the shortcut menu to display the **Create Surface** dialog box. In this dialog box, you can specify the surface type, name, and description of the surface. The options in this dialog box are discussed next.

Type

The **Type** drop-down list shows four different types of surfaces that you can create in Civil 3D. Select the required surface type from this drop-down list.

Surface layer

The **Surface layer** text box displays the default layer on which the surface will be created. By default, the **C-TOPO** layer is used as the surface layer. To assign a different layer, choose the button on the right of the text box to display the **Object Layer** dialog box. You can use this dialog box to assign a new layer to the surface.

The surface properties displayed under the **Information** node of the **Create Surface** dialog box are discussed next.

Name

This property specifies the default name of the surface. Click on the **Value** field of the **Name** property; a button will be displayed on the right of the default name. Choose the button; the **Name Template** dialog box will be displayed. Specify a name in the **Name** edit box and choose the **OK** button. You can also specify a name directly in the **Value** field after clicking on the default surface name.

Description

This property is used to briefly describe the surface. Click on the **Value** field of the **Description** property and enter a short description of the surface, if required.

Style

This property specifies the default surface style assigned to the surface. To modify the surface style, click in the **Value** field of this property; the browse button will be displayed. Choose the browse button; the **Select Surface Style** dialog box will be displayed. You can use one of the options from the **Select a style** drop-down list in this dialog box to define the surface style based on the project requirement.

You can create a new surface style in Civil 3D. To do so, click in the **Value** field of the **Style** property; a drop-down list will be displayed. Select the **Create New** option from the drop-down list. You will learn how to create a new surface in detail later in this chapter.

Note

*The styles available in the **Select Surface Style** dialog box vary depending on the template used.*

Render Material

This property specifies the default material value applied to the surface. Click on the default render material in the **Value** column and choose the button that will be displayed on the right; the **Select Render Material** dialog box will be displayed. You can select the required option from the **Select from list** drop-down list in this dialog box. Select the **By Block** option to use the render material of an associated block. You can also select the **By Layer** option from the drop-down list to use the render material assigned to the layer on which the object is created or select the **Global** option to use the global render material for the surface. In the **Select Render Material** dialog box, you can choose the **Select from Drawing** button to select the file from the drawing area.

On specifying the values of the surface properties, choose the **OK** button; the **Create Surface** dialog box will be closed and a new TIN surface will be created and added to the **Surfaces** node in the **Prospector** tab of the **TOOLSPACE** palette. To view the newly created surface, expand the **Surfaces** node by clicking on the + button next to it. The new surface with the name **Surface1** is added to the **Surface** node.

Note

As the added surface does not contain any data, so it will not be visible in the drawing area.

Adding Data from Different Sources to a Surface

You can add data to a surface from different sources such as points, point files, DEM and contours. The data obtained from these objects will be used to create a surface. The **Definition** subnode in the **Prospector** tab of the **TOOLSPACE** palette lists the different sources that can be used to add data in a surface. Expand the **Definition** subnode to view the sources, as shown in Figure 3-3. The methods of adding different types of data are discussed next.

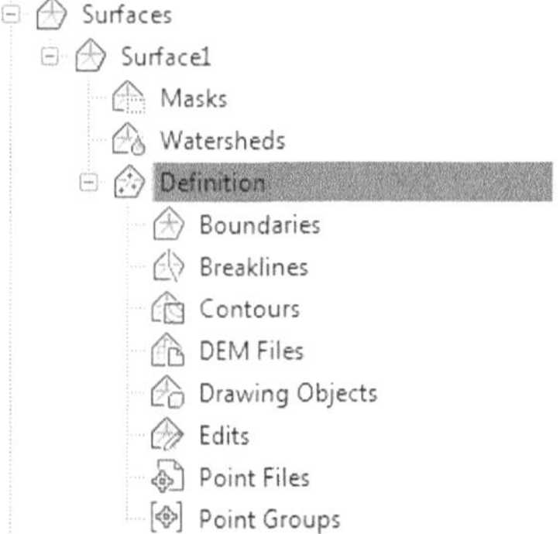

Figure 3-3 *Expanded* ***Definition*** *subnode*

Adding DEM Files (Creating a Surface from DEM)

Ribbon: Surface > Modify > Add Data drop-down > DEM Files
Command: ADDSURFACEDEMFILE

Digital Elevation Model or DEM is defined as the digital representation of a continuously varying surface. DEM represents the elevation or height of any point in the data from a datum. The DEM file stores and transfers large amount of data related to the topographic relief information of the land. This information can be used in surveying, planning, and other engineering projects. The DEM files basically consists of XYZ coordinates of points at regular grid spacing intervals.

To add the DEM files, choose the **DEM Files** tool from the **Modify** panel; the **Add DEM File** dialog box will be displayed. Alternatively, expand the **Definition** subnode of the surface in the **Prospector** tab of the **TOOLSPACE** palette, select the **DEM Files** option, and right-click; a shortcut menu will be displayed. Choose the **Add** button from the shortcut menu; the **Add DEM File** dialog box will be displayed, as shown in Figure 3-4. Next, click on the button next to the **DEM file name** edit box; the **Grid Surface from DEM** dialog box will be displayed. Next, browse to the required location and select the required DEM file and then choose the **Open** button in the dialog box; the DEM file will be added to the current drawing file.

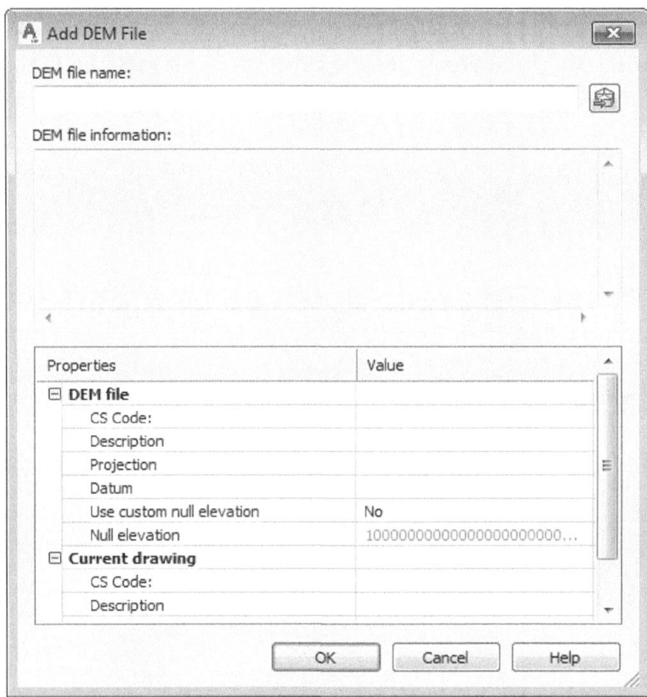

*Figure 3-4 The **Add DEM File** dialog box*

The **Properties** column of the **Add DEM File** dialog box displays various properties such as the coordinate system of the DEM file, description of the coordinate system, projection used, and so on. The properties and their respective values for both the DEM file and the current drawing are displayed in the **Add DEM File** dialog box under two categories. **DEM file** and **Current drawing**. By default, no coordinate system is assigned to the DEM file. You can assign a coordinate system to it to match with the coordinate system of the current drawing, especially if you are creating a grid surface from the DEM file.

To change the coordinate system of the DEM file, click in the **Value** field of the **CS Code** property and choose the button that is displayed on the right; the **Select Coordinate Zone** dialog box will be displayed. Select the required category from the **Categories** drop-down list. Next, select the coordinate zone from the **Available coordinate systems** drop-down list and choose the **OK** button; the **Select Coordinate Zone** dialog box will be closed. Again, choose the **OK** button from the **Add DEM file** dialog box; the DEM data will be added to the drawing and the surface will be created. To view the surface, enter **ZE** in the command line and press ENTER. The surface will be displayed based on the surface style set.

Note

*You can directly create a surface from the DEM file by using the options available in the **TOOLSPACE** palette. To do so, choose the **Surface** option in the **Prospector** tab of the **TOOLSPACE** palette and right-click; a shortcut menu will be displayed. Next, choose the **Create Surface from DEM** option from the shortcut menu; the **Grid Surface from DEM** dialog box will be displayed. In this dialog box, select the required DEM file and choose the **Open** button; the surface will be created from the selected DEM file.*

Adding Data to Surface by using Drawing Objects

Ribbon: Surface > Modify > Add Data drop-down > Drawing Objects
Command: ADDSURFACEDRAWINGOBJECTS

You can add surface data from different types of AutoCAD drawing objects. To do so, choose the **Surface** tool from the **Ground Data** panel, as shown in Figure 3-5. On doing so, the **Surface** tab will be displayed in the ribbon.

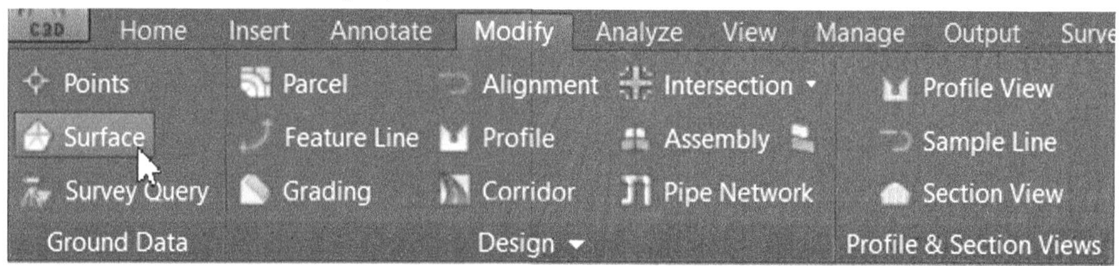

***Figure 3-5** The **Surface** tool chosen from the **Ground Data** panel*

Next, choose the **Drawing Objects** tool from the **Modify** panel; the **Add Points From Drawing Objects** dialog box will be displayed, as shown in Figure 3-6. To add the drawing object, select the object type from the **Object type** drop-down list. The drop-down list contains six different types of drawing objects such as lines, points, blocks and so on. The points from these objects are then added to the surface. For example, on selecting the **Points** option from the **Object type** drop-down list, the XYZ coordinates of the AutoCAD points will be used for creating the surface points.

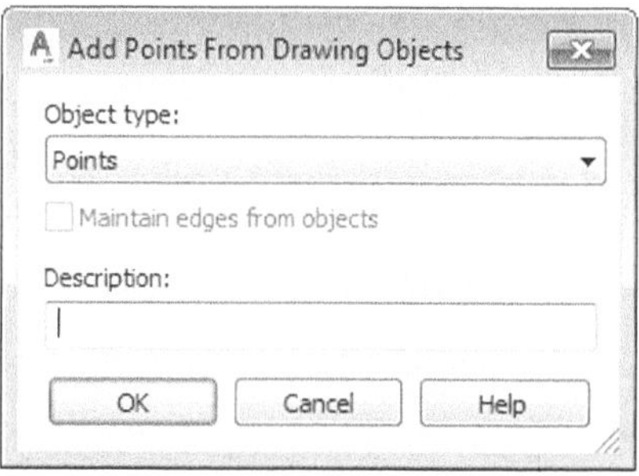

***Figure 3-6** The **Add Points From Drawing Objects** dialog box*

Similarly, on selecting the **Lines** option, the XYZ coordinates of the endpoints of the line project will be used to create the surface points. By default, the **Maintain edges from objects** check box in the **Add Points From Drawing Objects** dialog box is inactive. If you select the **Lines**, **Polyface**, or **3D faces** options from the **Object type** drop-down list, the **Maintain edges from objects** check box will be activated. This check box is used to maintain a distance between the surface edges and the edges of the drawing objects. On selecting this check box, the edges of the surface will be created at a distance from the edges of the drawing object selected. If this check box is not selected, the edges of the surface will coincide with the edges of the drawing object. Optionally, you can enter the description of the point data in the **Description** text box and choose the **OK** button; the dialog box will be closed and the surface will be created with the surface border visible (according to the surface style settings) in the drawing.

You can also add objects to the surface by using the **TOOLSPACE** palette. To do so, right-click on the **Drawing Objects** option in the **Definition** subnode of the surface in the **Prospector** tab; a shortcut menu will be displayed. Choose the **Add** option from the shortcut menu; the **Add Points From Drawing Objects** dialog box will be displayed. To add the drawing object, select the object type from the **Object type** drop-down list. The points from these objects are then added to the surface.

Note that whenever you add data to a surface, a symbol will be displayed on the left of the data option in the **Definition** subnode. This symbol indicates that the data has been added and it also symbolizes the type of data added to the surface. For example, on adding data to the surface by using the **Drawing Objects** option, a symbol will be displayed on the left of the **Drawing Objects** option in the **Definition** subnode of the surface, as shown in Figure 3-7.

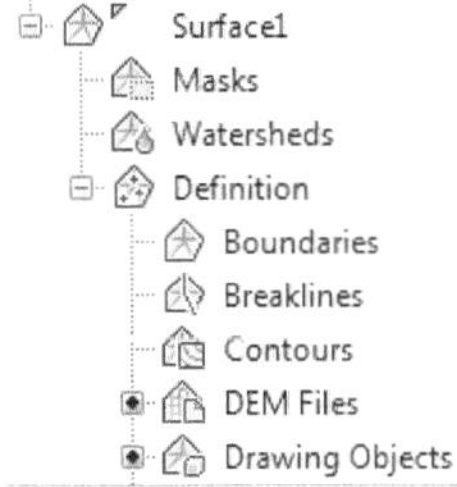

***Figure 3-7** The symbol displayed on the left of the **Drawing Objects** option*

Note

*AutoCAD objects can be added only in case of the **TIN surface** type.*

Adding Point Files

Ribbon: Surface > Modify > Add Data drop-down > Point Files
Command: ADDPOINTFILE

You can create surface data by adding point files consisting of point data. Point files can be added to the surface only after selecting the right file format. AutoCAD Civil 3D supports many types of file formats. You can select a point file format for the surface depending upon the point data format in the file. The point files can be added only to the TIN surfaces.

To add a point file data to a surface, choose the **Point Files** tool from the **Modify** panel; the **Add Point File** dialog box will be displayed, as shown in Figure 3-8. From the **Specify point file format** list box in the dialog box, select the format to import the point file. For example, the **PENZ (space delimited)** format will include point numbers, easting, northing, and elevation values separated by space. Next, choose the button available on the right of the **Selected Files** list box in the **Add Point File** dialog box; the **Select Source File** dialog box will be displayed. Select the required point file from the dialog box and choose the **Open** button; the file name and its path will be displayed in the **Selected Files** area. Choose **OK** in the **Add Point File** dialog box; the data in the point file will be added to the surface.

Alternatively, you can add point file data by using the options in the **TOOLSPACE** palette. To do so, expand the **Definition** subnode and right-click on **Point Files**; a shortcut menu will be displayed. Choose the **Add Files** option from the shortcut menu; the **Add Point File** dialog box will be displayed. Select the relevant format to import the point file data.

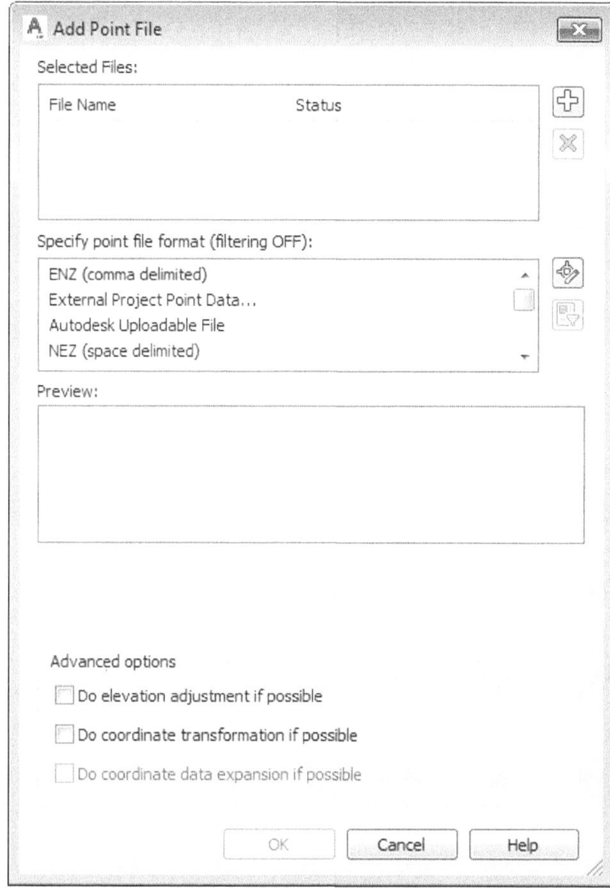

Figure 3-8 The **Add Point File** dialog box

Adding Point Groups

Ribbon: Surface > Modify > Add Data drop-down > Point Groups
Command: ADDSURFACEPOINTGROUP

AutoCAD Civil 3D allows you to create a surface from a group of points or use the existing point groups to add the required point data to a surface.

To add a point group to a surface, choose the **Point Groups** tool from the **Modify** panel; the **Point Groups** dialog box will be displayed, as shown in Figure 3-9. Next, select the point group that you want to add to the surface. Note that by default, the point group **_All Points** is created when you import points. Choose the **OK** button; the points of the selected point group will be added to the surface. Point file and point groups are the most common types of data sources that are added to the surfaces.

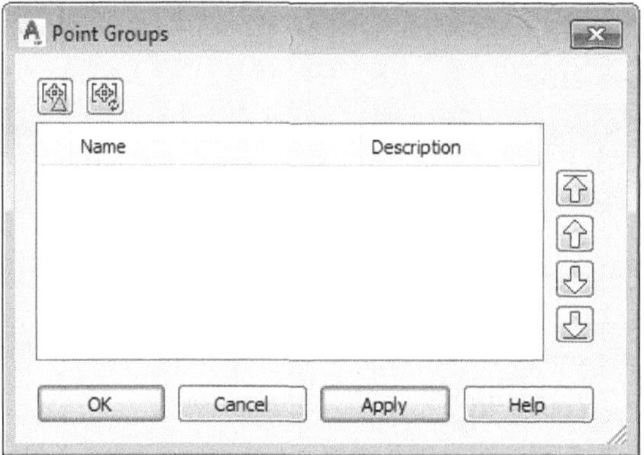

*Figure 3-9 The **Point Groups** dialog box*

Adding Contours

Ribbon: Surface > Modify > Add Data drop-down > Contours
Command: ADDSURFACECONTOURS

Apart from the point files and point groups, contours also provide the data that can be used to create a surface. To add contours to a surface, choose the **Contours** tool from the **Modify** panel; the **Add Contour Data** dialog box will be displayed, as shown in Figure 3-10.

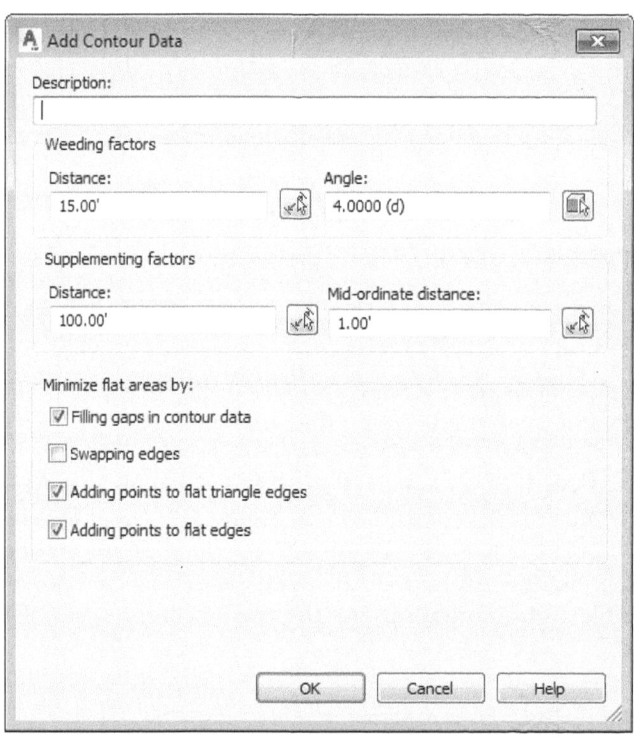

*Figure 3-10 The **Add Contour Data** dialog box*

Alternatively, you can add contours using the **TOOLSPACE** palette. To do so, right-click on **Contours** in the **Definition** subnode; a shortcut menu will be displayed. Choose the **Add** option from the shortcut menu; the **Add Contour Data** dialog box will be displayed.

You can use the options in this dialog box to add contour data to a surface. Enter a description about the contour data in the **Description** text box. The options in the **Weeding factors** and **Supplementing factors** areas are used to remove or add vertices along the contours. Specify the weeding distance in the **Distance** edit box or choose the button on the right of this edit box to specify the weeding distance in the drawing. Similarly, you can specify the weeding angle in the **Angle** edit box. In the **Supplementing factors** area, specify the supplementing distance and the mid-ordinate distance in the **Distance** and **Mid-ordinate distance** edit boxes, respectively. In the **Minimize flat areas by** area, the **Filling gaps in contour data**, **Adding points to flat triangle edges**, and **Adding points to flat edges** check boxes are selected by default to enable the filling of small gaps in contours and adding new vertices at the required locations.

After you have specified the required data, choose the **OK** button; the dialog box will be closed and you will be prompted to select the contours. Select the required contours and press ENTER; the contour data will be added to the surface and the surface will be displayed according to the surface style used.

Adding Surface Boundaries

Ribbon: Surface > Modify > Add Data drop-down > Boundaries
Command: ADDSURFACEBOUNDARIES

A boundary can be defined as a closed polygon entity used to represent the edge or limit of a surface. You can control the visibility of the surface triangulation within or outside the boundary. Any closed polygon or polyline object can be added to the surface as a surface boundary. To add a boundary to a surface, choose the **Boundaries** tool from the **Modify** panel; the **Add Boundaries** dialog box will be displayed, as shown in Figure 3-11.

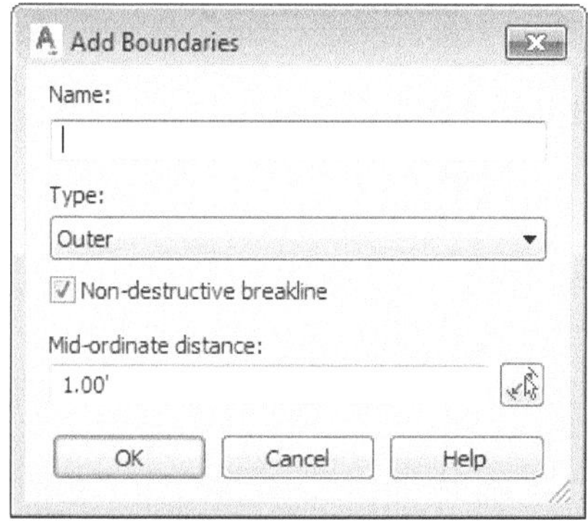

***Figure 3-11** The **Add Boundaries** dialog box*

Alternatively, you can add a boundary to a surface by using the options in the **TOOLSPACE** palette. To do so, expand the **Definition** subnode of the surface from the **Prospectors** tab and right-click on **Boundaries**; a shortcut menu will be displayed. Choose the **Add** option from the shortcut menu; the **Add Boundaries** dialog box will be displayed. In the dialog box, you can specify a name for the boundary in the **Name** edit box. Next, select the type of boundary from the **Type** drop-down list. A surface can have four different types of boundaries that are discussed next.

Outer

By default, the **Outer** option is selected in the **Type** drop-down list. As a result, the boundary is created such that all the TIN lines outside the boundary are deleted and the TIN lines inside the boundary are retained. Figures 3-12 and 3-13 show the surface before and after adding the outer boundary, respectively.

Figure 3-12 *Surface before adding the outer boundary*

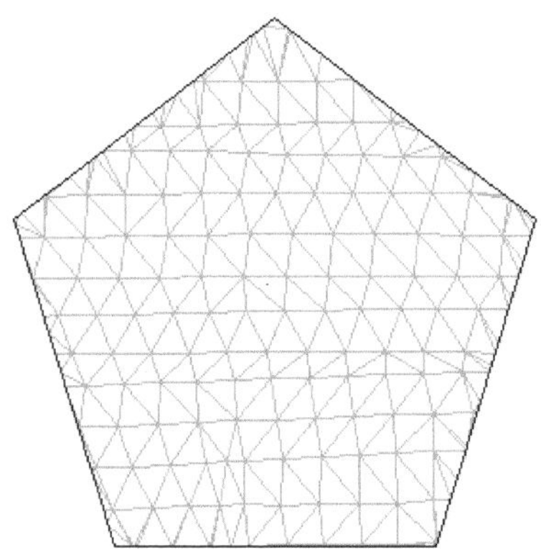

Figure 3-13 *Surface after adding the outer boundary*

Note that the **Non-destructive breakline** check box in the **Add Boundaries** dialog box is selected by default. As a result, a new surface is created by cutting the triangles lying across the boundary. If this check box is cleared, an internal border will be created and the triangles that are lying completely inside the boundary will be retained. In other words, the internal border will include only those triangles whose all three edges are inside the boundary. Figure 3-14 shows the internal border of the surface created after adding the outer boundary by clearing the **Non-destructive breakline** check box.

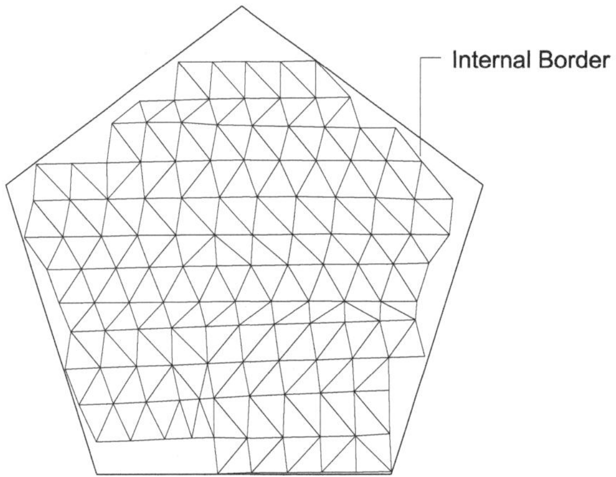

Figure 3-14 *Adding the outer boundary after clearing the* ***Non-destructive breakline*** *check box*

Note

You can create multiple outer boundaries. However, in such a case, Civil 3D surface will display only the last boundary created. To switch between multiple outer boundaries, select the check box corresponding to the add boundary in the ***Definition*** *tab of the* ***Surface Property - <Surface Name>*** *dialog box.*

Hide

The **Hide** option from the **Type** drop-down list enables you to hide the surface triangulation in a particular area. The triangles lying inside the related boundary will not be displayed. You can use this boundary to create voids or holes for some areas such as wetlands and buildings. The surface inside the boundary will not be included in the area and volume calculations. Figure 3-15 shows the surface after adding the boundary with the **Hide** option and the **Non-destructive breakline** check box selected. Figure 3-16 shows the surface after selecting the **Hide** option from the **Type** drop-down list and clearing the **Non-destructive breakline** check box in the **Add Boundaries** dialog box. In Figure 3-15, the triangles are deleted exactly at the boundary as the **Non-destructive breaklines** check box was selected by default. In Figure 3-16, an internal border is created and all the triangles that were lying completely inside the boundary are affected, thus making them hidden.

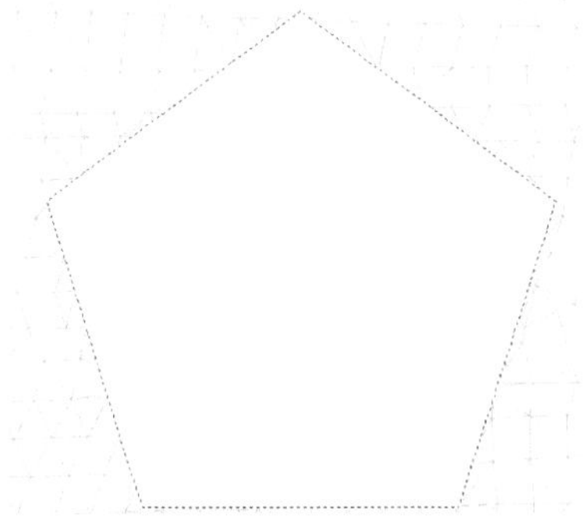

Figure 3-15 *Surface created after selecting the* ***Non-destructive breakline*** *check box*

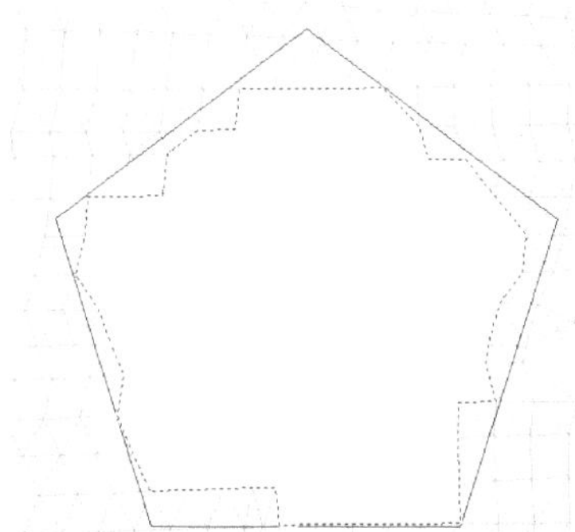

Figure 3-16 *Surface created after clearing the* ***Non-destructive breakline*** *check box*

Show

Selecting the **Show** option from the **Type** drop-down list enables you to display the triangles inside the hide boundary. You can use this option to display the hidden triangles when the **Hide** option is selected.

Data Clip

Selecting the **Data Clip** boundary option from the **Type** drop-down list helps you to create a surface boundary using the polygon object from the drawing itself such as feature lines, parcels, circles, and so on. This type of boundary is used to define a region on a surface where you want to import a set of surface data exclusively. For example, if you want to import a high resolution Light Detection and Ranging (LIDAR) data to a corridor only but not to the surrounding surface then you can use the **Data Clip** boundary option. The data imported will be clipped at the **Data Clip** boundary.

First, select the boundary type from the **Type** drop-down list in the **Add Boundaries** dialog box and then choose the OK button; will be closed and you will be prompted to select the objects. Select the required polygon or polyline object and then press ENTER; the selected boundary will be added to the surface. Note that the boundaries that you add to the surface will be listed along with their names and types in the **TOOLSPACE** Item View, as shown in Figure 3-17.

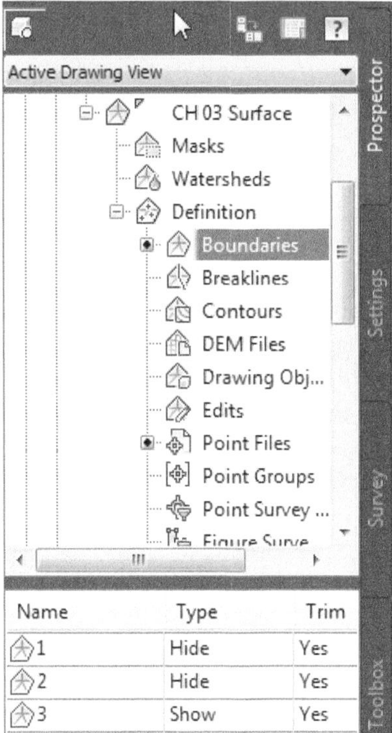

*Figure 3-17 The **TOOLSPACE** Item View of the **TOOLSPACE** palette displaying the added boundaries*

To view the properties of the boundary, select the required boundary in the **TOOLSPACE** Item View and right-click on it; a shortcut menu will be displayed. Choose the **Properties** option from the shortcut menu; the **Boundary Properties** dialog box will be displayed. You can also use this dialog box to edit the name of the boundary view. To do so, enter the desired name in the **Name** edit box in this dialog box.

Deleting a Boundary

To delete a boundary, select it from the **TOOLSPACE** Item View and right-click to display a shortcut menu. Choose the **Delete** option from the shortcut menu; a warning message will be displayed, as shown in Figure 3-18. Choose the **OK** button; the boundary will be deleted from the drawing as well as from the **TOOLSPACE** Item View. Remember that the **Delete** option will not be displayed in the shortcut menu if you are trying to delete the current boundary. A small triangular symbol on the left of the boundary name in the **TOOLSPACE** item view indicates that a boundary is currently in use.

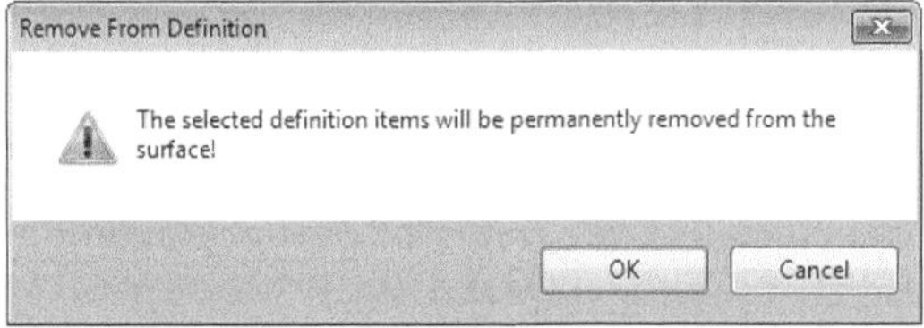

*Figure 3-18 The **Remove From Definition** warning message window*

If you remove a boundary from the surface or make any changes in the surface, a yellow symbol will be displayed on the left of the surface name, as shown in Figure 3-19. This symbol indicates that a change has been made in the surface and the surface is out of date. To update the surface, select the surface in the **Prospector** tab and right-click to display a shortcut menu. Choose the **Rebuild** option from the shortcut menu; the surface will be updated automatically and the symbol will disappear.

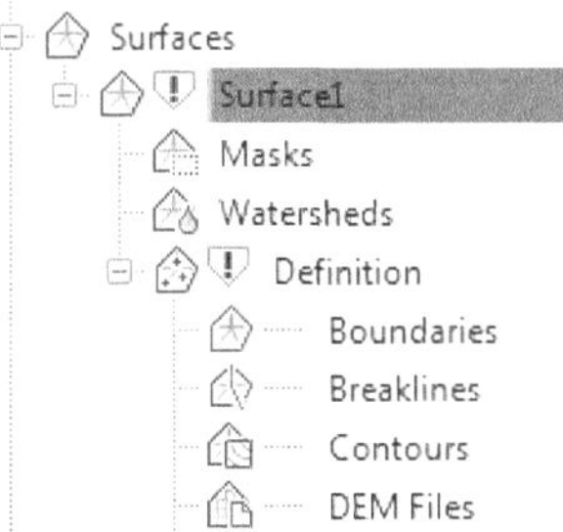

Figure 3-19 The symbol displayed on the left of ***Surface1***

Adding Breaklines to the Surface

Ribbon: Surface > Modify > Add Data drop-down > Breaklines
Command: ADDSURFACEBREAKLINES

Breaklines are polylines, feature lines, or 3D lines used to restrict the triangulation of the surface along the breakline. Breaklines basically represent the features such as streams, retaining walls, ditches, and so on. They can be added only to TIN surfaces. To add breaklines, choose the **Breaklines** tool from the **Modify** panel; the **Add Breaklines** dialog box will be displayed, as shown in Figure 3-20.

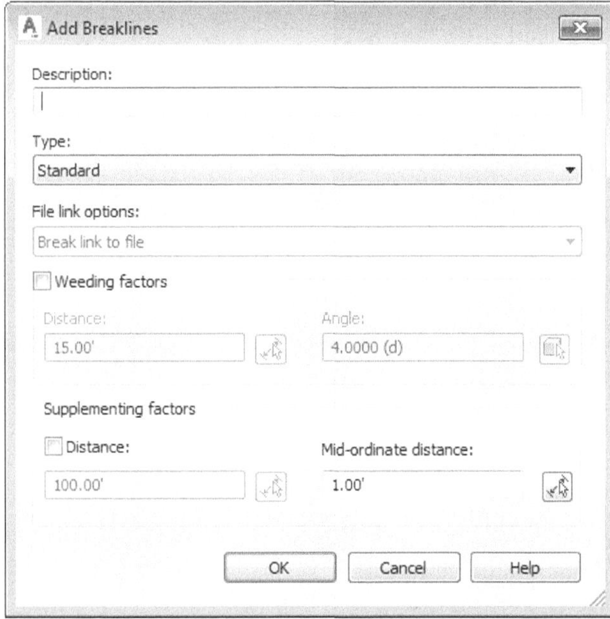

Figure 3-20 The ***Add Breaklines*** *dialog box*

Alternatively, right-click on the **Breaklines** option in the **Definition** node of the surface in the **Prospector** tab of the **TOOLSPACE** palette; a shortcut menu will be displayed. Choose the **Add** option from the shortcut menu; the **Add Breaklines** dialog box will be displayed. Enter a short description or name for the breakline in the **Description** text box. This description will be displayed in the **Description** column of the **TOOLSPACE** Item View. The description will help you identify the breaklines. If you do not enter any description, Civil 3D will automatically name it as **Breakline set1:1**. Next, select the type of breakline that you want to add to the surface from the **Type** drop-down list. There are five types of breaklines, which are discussed next.

Standard

This type of breakline is a three-dimensional object created from 3D lines, polylines, and feature lines. The **standard** breaklines are created by connecting the existing elevation points of polylines or feature lines. Therefore, you do not need to associate point objects with their vertices. The breaklines used for defining a marshy area or swales are good examples of **Standard** breaklines. The **Standard** breaklines can also have arc segments. For a breakline of the **Standard** type, you can specify the weeding and supplementing factors by selecting the **Weeding factors** check box and **Supplementing factors** area respectively. You specify the weeding distance and angle in the **Distance** and **Angle** edit boxes, respectively. Alternatively, choose the buttons on the right of the **Distance** and **Angle** edit boxes to specify the distance and angle. Similarly, specify the distance and mid-ordinate distance for the curved segments in the respective edit boxes in the **Supplementing factors** area. The mid-ordinate distance is used to tessellate the polyline arcs from which the breakline will be created. The supplementing factors are used to add more triangles along the straight segments of the breakline to make the surface smoother. Figures 3-21 and 3-22 illustrate the effect of adding breaklines after clearing and selecting the **Distance** check box.

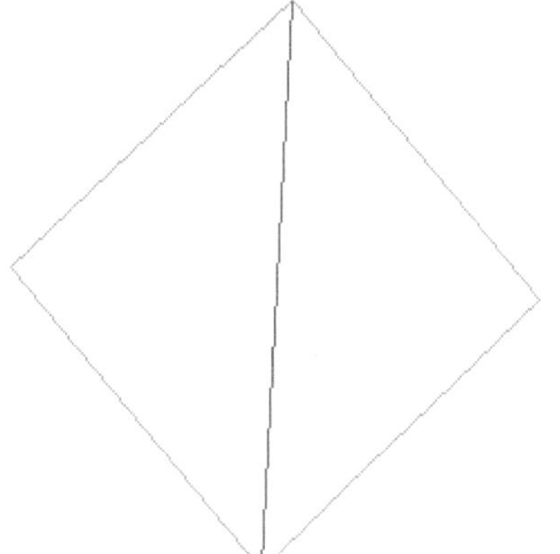

*Figure 3-21 Breaklines created after clearing the **Distance** check box*

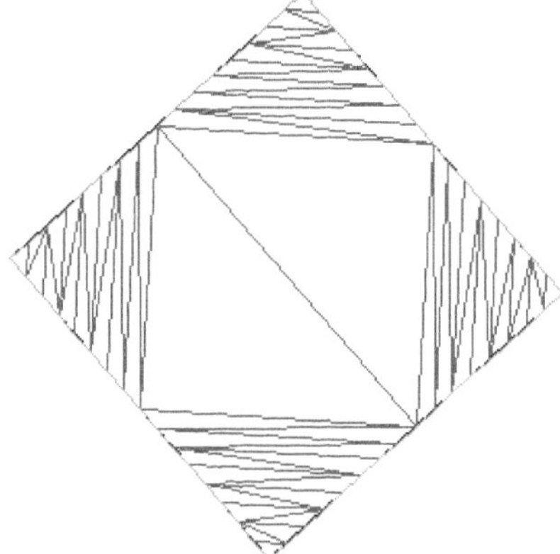

*Figure 3-22 Breaklines created after selecting the **Distance** check box*

Proximity

The **Proximity** breakline is a two-dimensional object created from polylines or feature lines. The XYZ coordinates or northing, easting, and elevations of the proximity breakline are calculated for each vertex of the parent polyline in reference to the TIN surface point that is nearest to the vertex. These types of breaklines cannot have curved segments.

Wall

Like the **Standard** breakline, the **Wall** breakline is also a three-dimensional object created from an existing polyline and representing the top or bottom of the wall. The **Wall** breaklines can be used in areas where there is vertical face in the surface such as retaining walls, curbs, and so on. These breaklines help you to represent the surface in a more accurate way. For example, for a retaining wall, you can define the differences in the elevations between the materials on both sides of the wall.

After selecting the **Wall** breakline from the **Type** drop-down list, choose the **OK** button; the **Add Breaklines** dialog box will be closed and you will be prompted to select the objects. Select the required polyline objects and press ENTER; you will be prompted to pick the offset side. Click on any side of the first polyline vertex; you will be prompted to select an option for specifying the wall height. You can enter **ALL** or **Individual**. Enter **A** for ALL and **I** for Individual. If you press ENTER, the **ALL** option will be selected by default. and you will be prompted to enter elevation difference for offset points or elevation. Next, enter the required elevation value and press ENTER; all vertices of the polyline object will have the same elevation and the **Wall** breaklines will be created.

The **Individual** option is used to specify the offset elevations of each vertex of the polyline. To specify the elevations using this option, enter **I** in the command line and press ENTER; you will be prompted to specify the elevation at the offset points individually. Specify the elevation in the command line and press ENTER until the elevation for all points is specified. Note that adding the **Wall** breaklines can change the surface slope values.

From file

The **From file** breakline is created directly from the FLT(*.flt) file format without drawing the breaklines. The FLT file consists of the name, type, coordinates, and elevations of the breakline. On selecting the **From file** option from the **Type** drop-down list, the **File link options** drop-down list in the **Add Breaklines** dialog box will be enabled. There are two types of file linking options in this drop-down list. The **Break link to file** option in this drop-down list is used to add the breakline to the **Definition** subnode of the surface. If you select this option, then after importing the breaklines from the file, the link to the file will be broken. However, on selecting the **Maintain link to file** option, the link to the file will be maintained.

After selecting the required file link option, choose the **OK** button; the **Import Breakline File** dialog box will be displayed. You can use this dialog box to select the required FLT file and import it to the drawing.

Non-destructive

The **Non-destructive** breaklines are used to restrict the surface triangulations along its length, without affecting the surface elevation at the intersections and surface triangulation.

After selecting the type of breakline and other required options in the **Add Breaklines** dialog box, choose the **OK** button; you will be prompted to select the object in the drawing. Select the polyline or 3D lines in the drawing and press ENTER; the breaklines will be added to the surface and **Breakline set1:1** will be displayed in the **TOOLSPACE** Item View.

Editing a Surface

You can perform various surface edits manually. To view various edit operations, choose the **Edit Surface** drop-down from the **Modify** panel; all the edit tools will be displayed. Choose any of the tools and perform the desired edit operation on the surface. Alternatively, you can edit surface by selecting the **Edits** option from the **Definition** subnode of the surface in the **Prospector** tab and right-click; a shortcut menu will display all surface edit options. The entire history of the edit operations performed on the surface will be added and can be viewed in the **TOOLSPACE** Item View. The **Edit Surface** tools are discussed next.

Note

*The options in the shortcut menu displayed on choosing the Edits option of the **Prospector** tab are displayed based on the type of the surface selected.*

Add Line

Ribbon:	Surface > Modify > Edit Surface drop-down > Add Line
Command:	ADDSURFACELINE

The **Add Line** tool is used to add a line to the TIN surface by connecting two endpoints of the existing surface lines. It helps you to modify the surface triangulation. Before using the **Add Line** edit option, make sure that the surface triangles are visible in the drawing. To add a new line to the surface, choose the **Add Line** tool from the **Modify** panel; you will be prompted to select the endpoints. Select the endpoints of the TIN lines of the triangles that cross the other TIN lines; the TIN lines will be added. Note that adding the TIN line affects the surface triangulation. Figure 3-23 shows the surface before adding the TIN lines and Figure 3-24 shows the surface after adding the TIN lines.

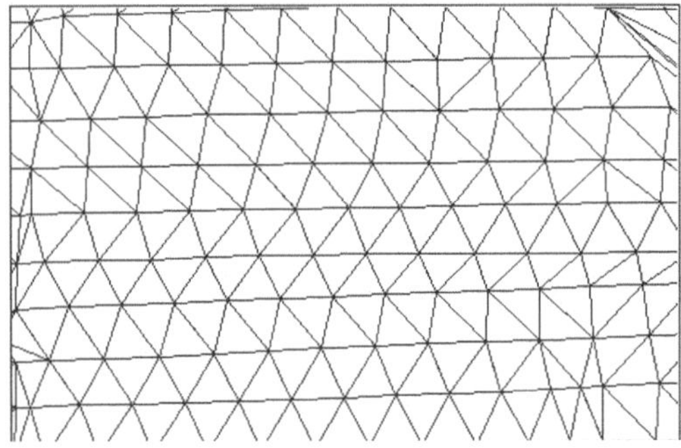

Figure 3-23 *Surface before adding TIN lines*

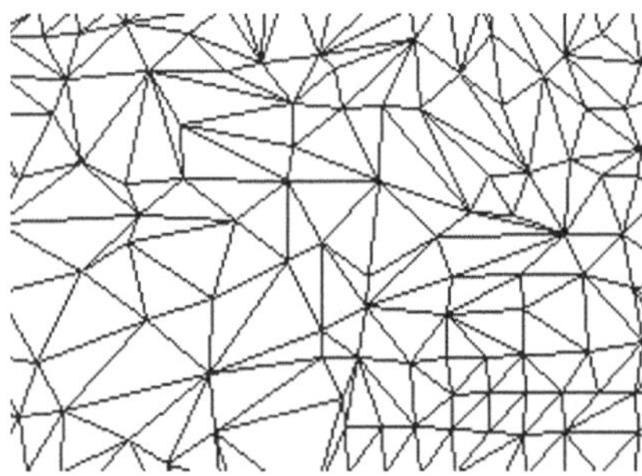

Figure 3-24 *Retriangulation of the surface after adding TIN lines*

Continue selecting the endpoints of TIN lines to add more lines or press ENTER to end the command. The **Add Line** operation will be listed in the Edits column of the **TOOLSPACE** Item View. The coordinates of the selected points will also be displayed in the **Description** column of the **TOOLSPACE** Item View, as shown in Figure 3-25.

Note

*The **Add Line** edit option can be used in all four types of surfaces.*

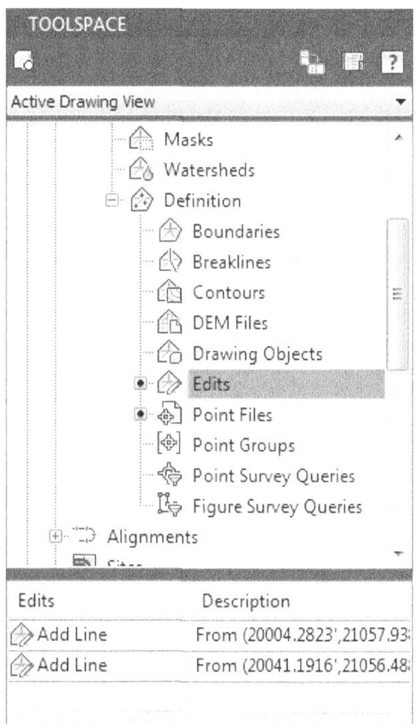

***Figure 3-25** The **TOOLSPACE** Item View displaying the **Add Line** operations in the **Edits** column and the coordinates in the **Description** column*

Tip

*Alternatively, to use the **Add Line** edit option, expand the **Definition** subnode of the surface and right-click on **Edits**; a shortcut menu will be displayed. Choose **Add Line** from the shortcut menu to add a line. Similarly, you can use other edit options.*

Delete Line

Ribbon: Surface > Modify > Edit Surface drop-down > Delete Line
Command: DELETESURFACELINE

The **Delete Line** tool is used to delete TIN or Grid lines from an existing surface. To delete the required entity, choose the **Delete Line** tool from the **Modify** panel; you will be prompted to select the edges. Select the edges or TIN lines that you want to remove and press ENTER; the edges will be removed from the surface and a boundary will be created in the area from where the lines or edges of the triangles are deleted. This tool is useful to reduce the unwanted TIN or Grid lines so that an accurate surface is created. Moreover, it can be used to delete the lines where the surface is not required at all such as a pond or any other water resource. For example, using the **Delete Line** tool, you can create a surface only with the center line points of the road survey. On deleting lines from a surface, an interior border will be created around the area from where the lines are deleted. Figures 3-26 and 3-27 shows the TIN surface before and after deleting the TIN lines, respectively.

Note

*The **Delete Line** tool can be used for all types of surfaces. However, you need to ensure that the surface triangles visibility is turned on before using this tool.*

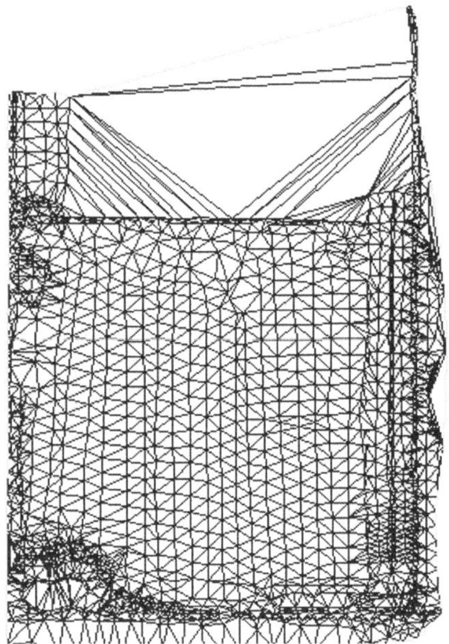

Figure 3-26 *The TIN surface before deleting TIN lines*

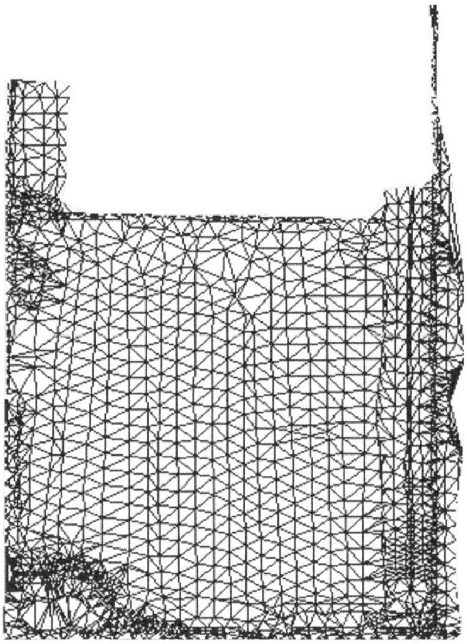

Figure 3-27 *The TIN surface with an interior border after deleting TIN lines*

Swap Edge

Ribbon: Surface > Modify > Edit Surface drop-down > Swap Edge
Command: EDITSURFACESWAPEDGE

The **Swap Edge** tool is used to swap or change the direction of the two triangular faces by changing the direction of the common edge. To swap the edge of the triangles, choose the **Swap Edge** tool from the **Modify** panel; you will be prompted to select an edge. Select the required edge(s); the orientation of the edge and the facing of the triangles will be changed. Press ENTER to end the command. Note that this tool cannot be used in the grid and grid volume surfaces. Figures 3-28 and 3-29 show a surface before and after swapping the edges.

Figure 3-28 *Surface before swapping the edges*

Figure 3-29 *Surface after swapping the edges*

Note

*If there are multiple surfaces, you need to select the relevant surface. To do so, press ENTER; the **Select a Surface** dialog box will be displayed. Now, select the surface and then choose **OK**.*

Add Point

Ribbon: Surface > Modify > Edit Surface drop-down > Add Point
Command: ADDSURFACEPOINT

The **Add Point** tool is used to add a point data manually to the surface by specifying the location and elevation of a point. To add a point, choose the **Add Point** tool from the **Modify** panel; you will be prompted to select a point. Click inside or outside the existing surface to add a point; you will be prompted to specify the elevation of the point. Enter the required elevation in the command line and press ENTER; the point will be added to the surface and the surface will re-triangulate accordingly. Figure 3-30 shows a surface after adding a point on its exterior border. In this figure, the surface has retriangulated according to the elevation of the added point.

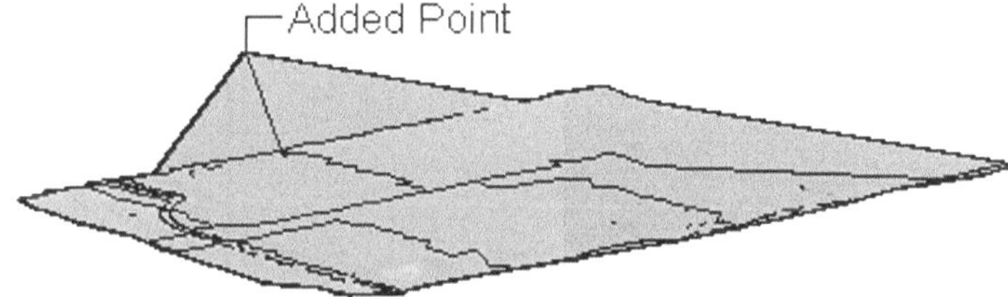

Figure 3-30 *Surface after adding a point on its exterior border*

The added point and its coordinates will be displayed in the **TOOLSPACE** Item View on clicking the edit option in **Definition** Sub-node. The **Add Point** tool can be used in all types of surfaces. You can also use this tool to add elevation to the surfaces with flat slopes.

Note

In case of grid surfaces, you can perform this operation only if you add points outside the existing surface, holes, or areas that have no existing points.

Delete Point

Ribbon: Surface > Modify > Edit Surface drop-down > Delete Point
Command: DELETESURFACEPOINT

This tool is used to remove unnecessary or unwanted surface points. To delete surface points, the visibility of the **Points** component should be turned on in the **Display** tab of the **Surface Style** dialog box. You will learn more about the surface styles later in this chapter. If you try to delete the points in the surface without turning the **Points** visibility on, Civil 3D will display a message box, as shown in Figure 3-31.

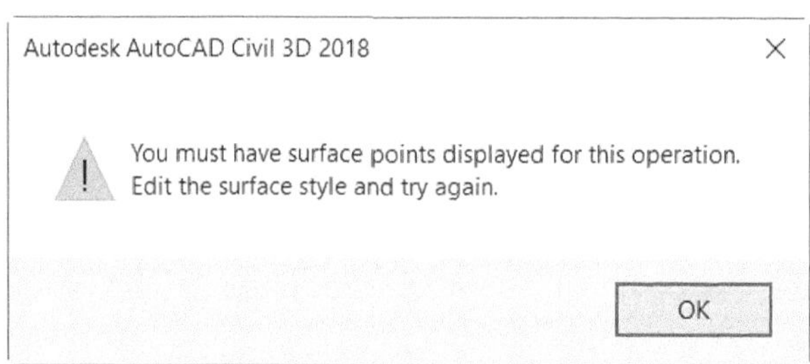

*Figure 3-31 The **Autodesk AutoCAD Civil 3D 2018** message box*

To delete points from a surface, choose the **Delete Point** tool from the **Modify** panel; you will be prompted to select the points. Select the points that you want to delete from the surface and press ENTER; the selected points will be deleted from the surface and the surface will be updated automatically.

Modify Point

Ribbon: Surface > Modify > Edit Surface drop-down > Modify Point
Command: EDITSURFACEPOINT

The **Modify Point** tool is used to modify the elevation of surface points. To change the elevation of surface points, choose the **Modify Point** tool from the **Modify** panel; you will be prompted to select the points to modify. Select the points that you want to modify and press ENTER; you will be prompted to specify the new elevation for the selected points. Specify the new elevation in the command line and press ENTER. You can continue selecting more points on the surface or press ENTER to end the command.

Alternatively, you can modify the elevation of surface points by selecting **Edits** in the surface **Definition** subnode in the **Prospector** tab of the **TOOLSPACE** palette and right-click; a shortcut menu will be displayed. Choose the **Modify Point** option from the shortcut menu; you will be prompted to select the point and specify the new elevation.

Note

*Before using the **Modify Point** tool, make sure that the points are visible in the drawing.*

Move Point

Ribbon: Surface > Modify > Edit Surface drop-down > Move Point
Command: MOVESURFACEPOINT

The **Move Point** tool is used to change the location of the existing surface points. To move a point to a new location, choose the **Move Point** tool from the **Modify** panel; you will be prompted to select the point that you want to move. Select the required point from the surface by clicking on the point. Click again to specify the new location for the point. You can also specify the location in the command line by entering its coordinates. The surface retriangulates and updates automatically according to the new location of the point. Press ENTER to end the command. Note that this tool can be used only in case of TIN surfaces and TIN volume surfaces.

Minimize Flat Areas

Ribbon: Surface > Modify > Edit Surface drop-down > Minimize Flat Areas
Command: MINIMIZESURFACEFLATAREAS

This tool is used to minimize the flat areas in a surface as these areas can make the surface inaccurate. These flat areas are the surface triangles whose points are obtained from a contour at same elevation. These points of the triangles will have the same elevation and therefore, the triangles will have no slope. This type of problem occurs when a contour data is added to a TIN surface.

The **Minimize Flat Areas** tool helps you to remove the triangles whose all three points are at the same elevation, thus creating a flat area. Also, you can find and remove the triangle edges connecting the points on the contours that have the same elevation. To do so, choose the **Minimize Flat Areas** tool from the **Modify** panel; the **Minimize Flat Areas** dialog box will be displayed, as shown in Figure 3-32. This dialog box displays different options under the **Minimize flat areas by** area. Some of these options are discussed next.

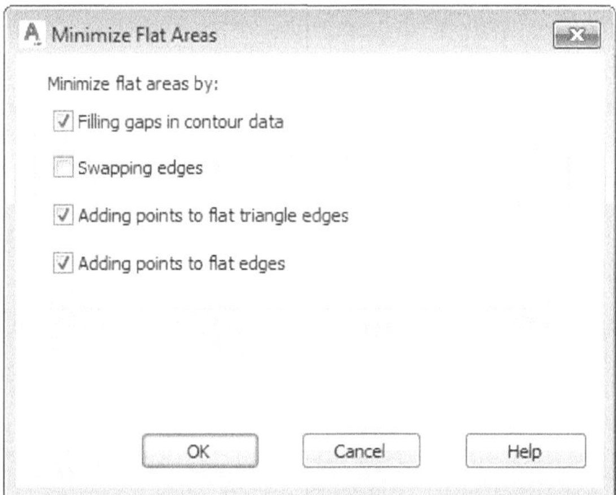

*Figure 3-32 The **Minimize Flat Areas** dialog box*

Filling gaps in contour data

This option is used to fill small gaps that can occur between two consecutive contours. If the contours lie close to each other, Civil 3D will join their ends by adding a triangular edge in the gap. This will make the contour a single continuous contour.

Note

This option is applicable only on the contours that are displayed in the drawing. It does not affect the original contour data added to the surface.

Swapping edges

On selecting this option, Civil 3D will find all flat triangles that share a non-contour edge with the non-flat triangles in the surface. If the two triangles of the surface that share a common edge form a convex quadrilateral, the common edge will be swapped creating two non-flat triangles. This option removes most of the flat triangles from the surface without affecting the number of surface triangles and points. In this way, the original size of the surface will be retained.

Adding points to flat triangle edges

On selecting this option, a new point will be created. The point will be created on the flat edge that is between the two triangles. In this case, instead of swapping the common edge of the two triangles, a point will be added at the midpoint of the common edge. The elevation of the point will be automatically calculated by Civil 3D. The surface will retriangulate automatically. This option helps you remove the flat areas more effectively than the **Swapping edges** option. This results in the increase of the number of triangles and points, thus affecting the size of the surface.

Raise/Lower Surface

Ribbon: Surface > Modify > Edit Surface drop-down > Raise/Lower Surface
Command: RAISELOWERSURFACE

This tool is used to raise or lower the elevation of a surface by increasing or decreasing the value of the elevation of surface points. You can raise the surface by adding a positive value and lower the surface by adding a negative value for the elevation in the command line. This tool can be used for testing the gradings and adjusting the surfaces at the required elevation to calculate the cut and fill volumes.

To change the elevation of a surface, choose the **Raise/Lower Surface** tool from the **Modify** panel; you will be prompted to add the amount to all elevations. Enter a value (positive or negative) in the command line and press ENTER; the surface will be raised or lowered as per the specified elevation value. This tool is mainly used in TIN and Grid surfaces.

Smooth Surface

Ribbon: Surface > Modify > Edit Surface drop-down > Smooth Surface
Command: SMOOTHSURFACE

This tool is used to smoothen the surface contours by adding additional points to the surface. You can calculate the elevation of the added points using two methods: NNI (Natural Neighbor Interpolation) and Krigging.

The NNI method is used to calculate the elevation of the arbitrary points by interpolating the elevations of the neighboring points. This method can also interpolate the elevation lying within the surface. The Krigging method is a complex method as compared to the NNI method. This method would require information about the spatial continuity and a sample of surface data to interpolate the elevations making it more complex than the NNI method.

To smoothen a surface using NNI method, choose the **Smooth Surface** tool from the **Modify** panel; the **Smooth Surface - <surface name>** dialog box will be displayed, as shown in Figure 3-33. Click and select the **Natural neighbor interpolation** option from the drop-down list in the **Value** column of the **Select method** property. On doing so, the options in the **Krigging Method** category will be disabled.

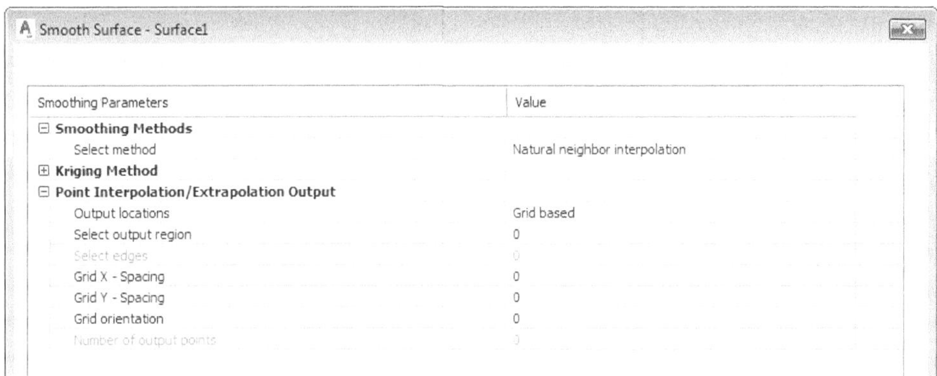

Figure 3-33 *Partial view of the **Smooth Surface** dialog box*

Click in the **Value** field of the **Output locations** property and select the required option from this drop-down list. If you select the **Grid based** option, the generated points will lie on a grid defined within the specified polygon areas selected in the drawing. The **Centroids** option can be selected from the drop-down list to interpolate the points at the centroids of the triangles of the surface. The **Random points** option can be selected to interpolate number of points within the boundary of the polygon. The **Edge midpoints** option can be used to interpolate the points at the midpoints of the triangle edges. To use this option, the visibility of the surface triangles should be turned on.

Next, click in the **Value** field of the **Select output region** property and choose the **Browse** button displayed on the right; the dialog box will disappear and you will be prompted to select an output region. Select the required surface or region bounded by a rectangle or polygon and then specify the value of **Grid X-Spacing** and **Grid Y-Spacing properties** by clicking in the **Value** field.Choose the **OK** button from the **Smooth Surface - <surface name>** dialog box; Civil 3D will start smoothening the surface. Similarly, you can use the **Krigging** method to smoothen the surface. Figures 3-34 and 3-35 show the surface before and after smoothening using the **NNI** method.

Figure 3-34 *Surface contours before smoothening using the **NNI** method*

Figure 3-35 *Surface contours after smoothening using the **NNI** method*

Paste Surface

Ribbon: Surface > Modify > Edit Surface drop-down > Paste Surface
Command: EDITSURFACEPASTE

The **Paste Surface** tool can be used to paste one surface over another surface. This tool is useful for creating composite surfaces such as creating corridor surfaces and then pasting the corridor surface on the existing surface.

This tool is also useful in surface gradings and comparing the design surface with the existing surface. To paste a surface on another surface, choose the **Paste Surface** tool from the **Modify** panel; the **Select Surface to Paste** dialog box will be displayed. In the dialog box, select the surface to be pasted on the existing surface from the list box and then choose **OK** to exit the dialog box.

Simplify Surface

Ribbon: Surface > Modify > Edit Surface drop-down > Simplify Surface
Command: SIMPLIFYSURFACE

This tool is used to simplify a surface by reducing the number of points on the surface or by contracting the triangle edges on a TIN surface. To simplify a surface, choose the **Simplify Surface** tool from the **Modify** panel; the **Simplify Surface - <surface name>** wizard will be displayed. By default, the **Simplify Methods** page will be displayed in the wizard, as shown in Figure 3-36.

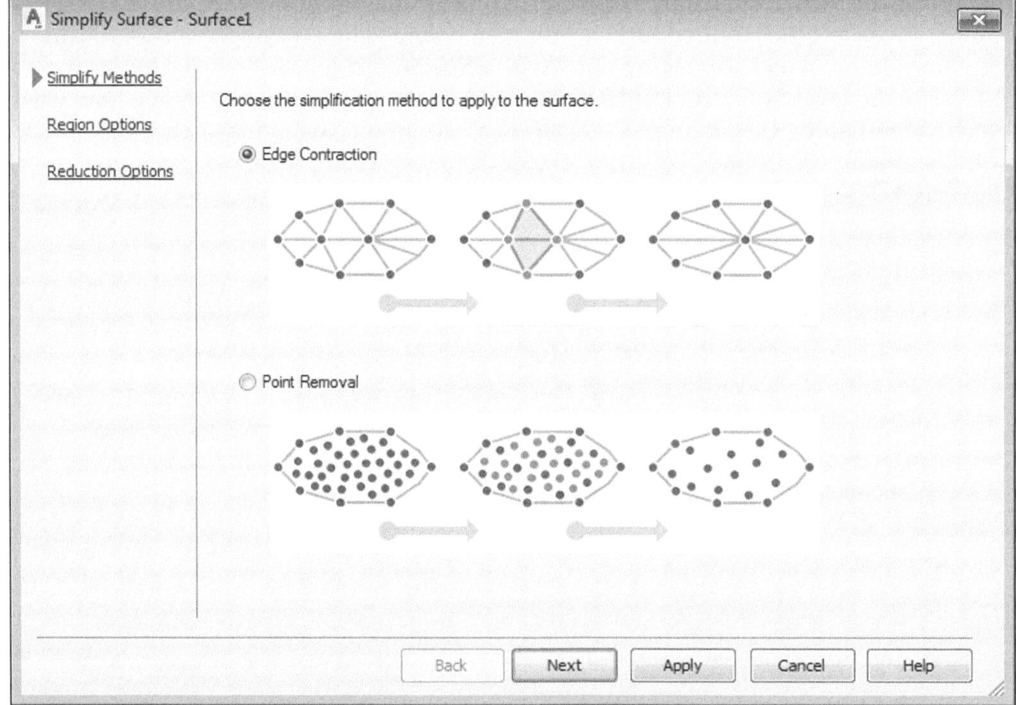

***Figure 3-36** The **Simplify Surface-Surface1** wizard with the **Simplify Methods** page displayed*

Select the required method for simplifying the surface and choose the **Next** button; the **Region Options** page will be displayed. Specify the region that you want to simplify in this page. You can select the surface border to simplify the entire surface or select polygons or objects from a specific region to simplify it. Choose the **Next** button to display the **Reduction Options** page. Specify the percentage of the points to be removed from the surface or the selected region using the slider bar in the **Reduction Options** area of this page.

Next, choose the **Finish** button; the wizard will be closed and the surface will be simplified. You will notice a change in the surface triangulation due to the removal of surface points. Note that this option does not affect the accuracy of the surface. Figures 3-37 and 3-38 show a surface before and after using the **Simplify Surface** option.

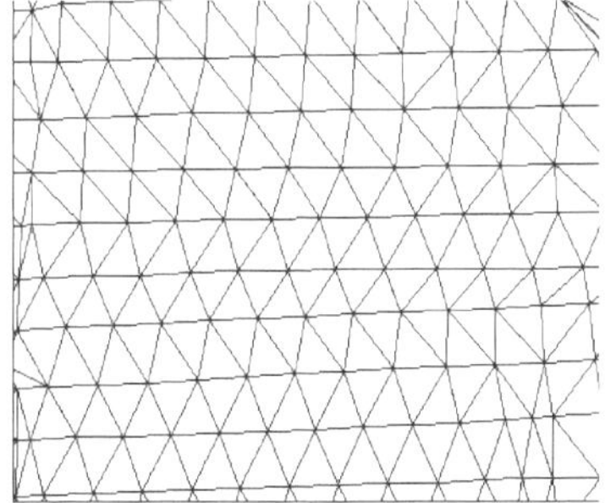

Figure 3-37 *Surface before using the* ***Simplify Surface*** *option*

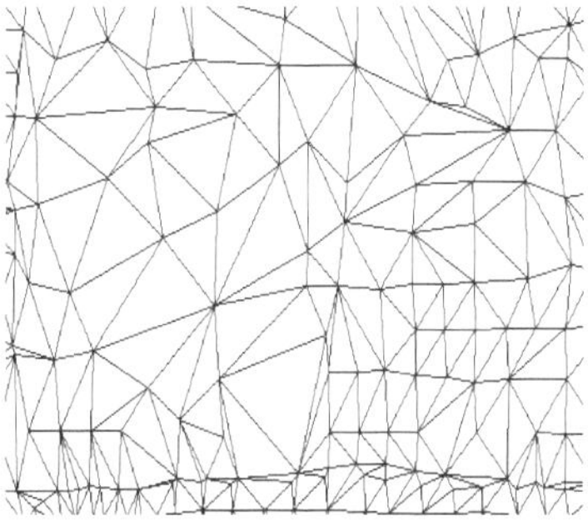

Figure 3-38 *Surface after using the* ***Simplify Surface*** *option*

Creating Surface Masks

Surface masks are used to block the display of a surface or specific area on the surface and to assign it a different render material. The masking region can be defined by using closed polygons, polylines, 3D polylines, rectangles, feature lines, surfaces, and so on. To create a mask, expand the **Surfaces** node in the **Prospecto**r tab of the **TOOLSPACE** palette and then expand the required surface node. Next, right-click on **Masks** to display a shortcut menu and choose the **Create Mask** option from it; you will be prompted to select objects. Select the required polyline or other objects to define the boundary of the masking region and press ENTER; the **Create Mask** dialog box will be displayed. Specify a name, masking type, render material, and other values in the dialog box and choose the **OK** button; the masked region will be created.

The surface outside or inside the masking region will be hidden depending upon the type of mask used. You can create two types of masks: inside and outside. On creating the inside mask type;the area inside the polygon boundary will be hidden. On creating the outside mask, the area outside the polygon will be hidden. The surface masks are listed under the **Masks** head in the respective surface node.

Creating Volume Surfaces

To create a volume surface, you need minimum two surfaces; base surface and comparison surfaces. Volume surfaces are classified into two types: TIN volume surfaces and Grid volume surfaces.

To create a volume surface, expand the **Surfaces** node in the **Prospector** tab of the **TOOLSPACE** palette and right-click; a shortcut menu will be displayed. Choose the **Create Surface** option from the shortcut menu; the **Create Surface** dialog box will be displayed. In this dialog box, select the **TIN volume surface** option from the **Type** drop-down list; the properties of the TIN volume surface will be displayed in the dialog box. Click in the **Value** field of the **Base Surface** property; a browse button will be displayed. Choose the browse button; the **Select Base Surface** dialog box will be displayed. Select the surface that is to be assigned as the base surface from the list of surfaces in the dialog box and choose the **OK** button. Similarly, click in the **Value** field of the **Comparison Surface** property and then select a surface to be assigned as the comparison surface from the **Create Surface** dialog box. Specify values of the other properties in this dialog box and choose the **OK** button; the dialog box will be closed and the volume surface will be created and listed in the **Surfaces** node. Similarly, you can also create grid volume surface using the **Create Surface** dialog box.

Note

Civil 3d will show error message box if surfaces overlap each other.

SURFACE STYLES

The surface styles control the display of the surfaces. You can create different types of surface styles as per your project requirements. The surface styles are created and managed by using the options in the **Surface Style** subnode in the **Settings** tab of the **TOOLSPACE** palette. Civil 3D also has some in-built surface styles that are listed in the **Surface Styles** node of the **Settings** tab. The surface styles that are listed in the **Surface Styles** node depend upon the type of template selected.

Creating a Surface Style

You can create a new surface style based on the project requirement. To create a new surface style**,** expand the **Surface** node in the **Settings** tab of the **TOOLSPACE** palette; the **Surface Styles** subnode will be displayed. Now, right-click on the subnode; a shortcut menu will be displayed. Choose the **New** option from the shortcut menu; the **Surface Style-New Surface Style** dialog box will be displayed, as shown in Figure 3-39. The options in different tabs in this dialog box are discussed next.

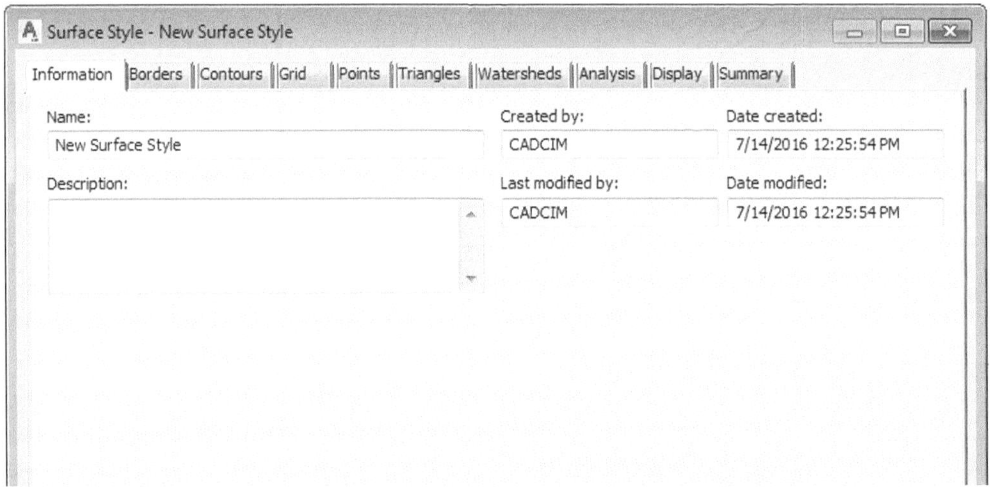

Figure 3-39 *Partial view of the* ***Surface Style - New Surface Style*** *dialog box*

Information Tab

The options in this tab are used to specify the name of the surface style, date of creation, description, and other basic information about the surface style. Specify the name for the surface style in the **Name** edit box. Optionally, you can specify the description in the **Description** text box.

Borders Tab

This tab is used to set the display settings of the surface border by specifying the values of the border properties. These properties are listed under three categories: **3D Geometry**, **Border Types**, and **Datum**. These properties are discussed next.

3D Geometry

The properties in this category control the display of surface of the border. To control the display of the border, click in the **Value** field of the **Border Display Mode** property, and select the required mode from the drop-down list that will be displayed. The **Use Surface Elevation** option in this drop-down list is used to display the surface border at its original elevation. The **Flatten Elevations** option is used to display the border at the specified elevation. If you select this option from the drop-down list, the **Flatten Border to Elevation** property will be enabled in the dialog box. Specify the required elevation in the **Value** field of this property. If you select the **Exaggerate Elevation** option from the drop-down list, you will be able to exaggerate and scale the border according to the scale factor. You can specify the scale factor in the **Value** field of the **Exaggerate Borders by Scale Factor** property that will be enabled on selecting the **Exaggerate Elevation** option.

Border Types

The properties in this category help you control the visibility of the borders. The visibility of the outer border of the surface can be controlled by using the **Display Exterior Borders** property. The outer border is the border that represents the extents of the surface. By default, the value of this property is set to **True**. To hide the surface border, click in the **Value** field of this property and select **False** from the drop-down list.

The **Display Interior Borders** property in this category controls the visibility of the interior borders such as borders of ponds, wells, holes, or areas, where no data is available. By default, the value of this property is set to **True**. To make the interior border invisible, click on the **Value** field and select **False** from the drop-down list; the interior border of the surface will be hidden. Figure 3-40 shows the exterior and interior borders of a surface.

Figure 3-40 *Surface displaying the exterior and interior borders*

Datum

The **Datum** category is used to specify whether to use a datum or not. By default, the value of this property is set to **False**. To show the datum, set the value to **True** and specify the datum elevation in the **Value** field of the **Datum Elevation** property. To project this boundary to the datum, set the value of the **Project Grid to Datum** property to **True**. The datum projection is visible only in the 3D view, as shown in Figure 3-41.

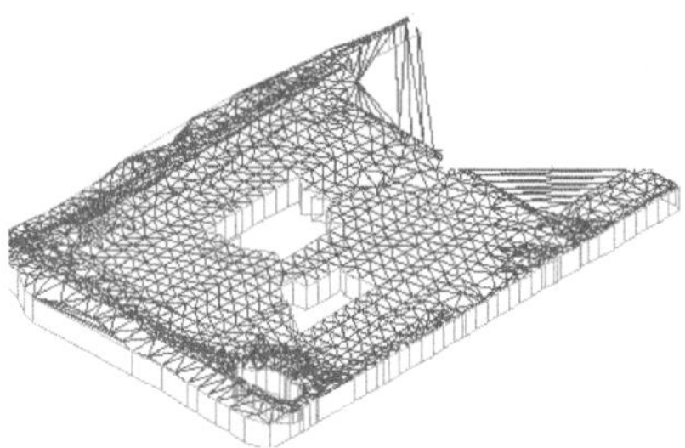

Figure 3-41 *A surface border projected to the datum in 3D view*

Contours Tab

This tab is used to define the settings for the display of the surface contours. The properties in the **Contours** tab are listed under six different categories that are discussed next.

Contour Ranges

Expand the **Contour Ranges** category to display various properties that control the display of the contours in the contour analysis. Contour analysis will be explained in detail in the next chapter. In the **Contour Ranges** category, the **Group Values by** property specify the grouping of contours. In the **Value** field of the **Group Values by** property, the **Quantile** option is selected by default. This option is used to divide the data equally in the number of contour ranges specified. The **Number of Ranges** property specifies the number of ranges in which the contours will be divided. To set the number of ranges, click in the **Value** field of this property and set the value using the spinner displayed on the right of this property. The **Range Precision** property specifies the rounding value for the contour ranges. To specify the range precision, click in the **Value** field of this property and select the required option from the drop-down list. The **Use Color Scheme** property specifies whether or not to use a color scheme for the contour range. To use the color schemes, click in the **Value** field and select **True** from the drop-down list. On doing so, the **Major Color Scheme** and **Minor Color Scheme** properties will be enabled. Click on the **Value** field of these properties and select the required color scheme from the drop-down lists displayed.

3D Geometry

Expand the **3D Geometry** category. The properties in this node are similar to those explained in the **3D Geometry** category of the **Borders** tab.

Legend

Expand the **Legend** category. The property in this category specifies the default contour legend style. The contour legend provides information of the surface contours in a consolidated form. To modify the contour style, click on the **Value** field of this property and choose the browse button displayed on the right. On doing so, the **Contour Legend Style** dialog box will be displayed. Select the required style from the dialog box and choose the **OK** button; the specified style will be applied to the contour legends.We can also create our own **New Legend Style.**

Contour Intervals

Expand the **Contour Intervals** category to view properties in this category. There are three properties under this category. The **Base Elevation** property specifies the relative base elevation for the major or minor contour intervals which are defined with base elevation as the reference. Click on the **Value** field of the **Base Elevation** property and specify the required elevation or choose the button displayed on the right to specify the base elevation from the drawing area. Similarly, you can specify the minor contour interval in the **Value** field of the **Minor Interval** property. Note that when you change the value of the **Minor Interval** property, the value of the **Major Interval** property will change automatically. The value of the major contour interval depends upon the minor contour interval and is always a multiple of the minor contour interval value. For example, if the **Minor Interval** value is **5**, the value for the **Major Interval** should be **25**.

Contour Depressions

Expand the **Contour Depressions** category. The properties in this category are used to control the display of the depression contours. The **Display Depression Contours** property in this category controls the display of depression in the contours. By default, the value of this property is set to **False**. Click on the **Value** field of this property and select **True** from the drop-down list to make the depression contours visible on the surface. The depression contours are indicated by tick marks around the contour boundary. You can set the interval between the tick marks in the **Tick Mark Interval** property. This property controls the distance between the tick marks displayed along the contour periphery. The number of tick marks generated along the contour boundary will vary according to the distance. To specify the interval between tick marks, click on the **Value** field and choose the button displayed on the right; you will be prompted to specify the distance. Specify the distance in the command line and press ENTER or pick points on the drawing to specify the distance. Similarly, specify the length of the tick marks in the **Value** field of the **Tick Mark Length** property to view them clearly. Figure 3-42 shows the depression contours displayed after setting the value of the **Display Depression Contours** property to **true** and with the tick marks facing inward.

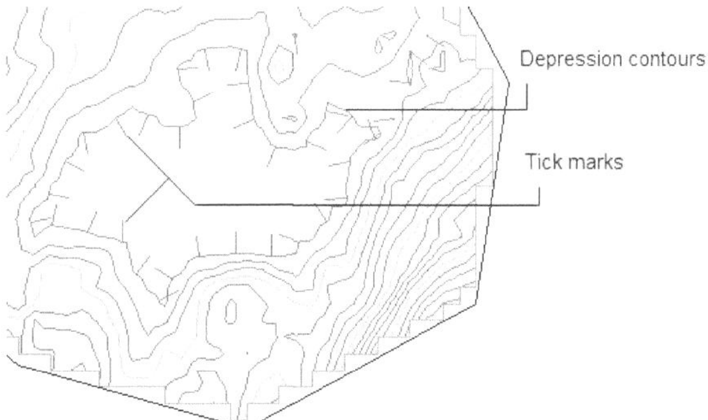

Figure 3-42 *Depression contours on the surface with the tick marks facing inward*

Note

Contours will be displayed on the surface only if the visibility of the ***Major Contour*** *and* ***Minor Contour*** *layers is turned on in the* ***Display*** *tab of the* ***Surface Style - New Surface Style*** *or* ***Surface Style - <surface>*** *dialog box.*

Contour Smoothing

Expand the **Contour Smoothing** category to view the properties available in this category. The **Smooth Contours** property enables smoothing of contour lines by adding new vertices or drawing contours as spline curve. By default, the contour smoothening value is set to **False**. To enable contour smoothening, click in the **Value** field of this property and select **True** from the drop-down list that is displayed. This action will activate the **Smoothing Type** property in the **Contour Smoothing** category. Next, click in the **Value** field of the **Smoothing Type** property to select the type of contour smoothening. The **Add vertices** type of smoothening adds vertices on the contours to give them a smooth appearance. The **Spline curve** type of smoothening creates a spline curve through the contour points.

You can also control smoothening by using the slider bar in the **Contour smoothing** area at the bottom of the **Surface Style** dialog box. Note that this slider is available only for the **Add vertices** type of smoothening.

The **Display table** at the bottom of the tab shows the properties of the contour range in different columns. The **Number** column in this table displays the contour ranges specified. The number displayed in the **Number** column corresponds to the value specified in the **Number of Ranges** property. The **Major Display** and the **Minor Display** columns specify the display of the major and minor contours in that particular range.

You can specify the linetype, lineweight, and color for the contours by using the three buttons in the **Minor Display** and **Major Display** columns. To specify the linetype for the major contour, choose the first button out of the three buttons in the **Major Display**column; the **Select Linetype** dialog box will be displayed. In this dialog box select the required **Linetype** and then choose the **OK** button; the dialog box will be closed and the selected linetype will be assigned to the major contour. Similarly, you can specify the line weight and color for the contour by using the options available in the **Lineweight** and **Select Color** dialog boxes, respectively. These dialog boxes can be invoked by choosing the second and third button, respectively.

Grid Tab

This tab controls the grid display of the grid surface. The grid properties are divided under three categories: **3D Geometry**, **Primary Grid**, and **Secondary Grid**. These categories are discussed next.

3D Geometry

Expand the **3D Geometry** category. The properties in this node are similar to those explained in the **3D Geometry** category of the **Borders** tab.

Primary Grid

The properties in this category control the display of the primary grid on the surface. The primary grid represents the grid lines along the Y direction. The **Use Primary Grid** property in this category specifies whether to display the primary grid in the drawing or not. By default, the display of the primary grid is set to **true**, which means the primary grid lines will be displayed automatically.

The **Interval** property of the primary grid specifies the distance between the primary grid lines. Click in the **Value** field of this property and choose the button displayed on the right; you will be prompted to specify the distance. Specify the distance in the command line and press ENTER or pick points in the drawing.

The **Orientation** property specifies the direction or orientation of the primary grid lines. Specify the orientation for the grid lines in the **Value** column of this property. You can also use the button displayed on the right of this field to specify the orientation.

Secondary Grid

The secondary grid represents the grid lines along the X direction. The properties in this category are same as those of the primary grid.

Points Tab

This tab is used to control the display of the surface points. The categories and their properties in this tab are discussed next.

3D Geometry

The properties in this category are same as those discussed in the **Borders** tab except that here they are used for the surface points.

Point Size

The properties in this category specify the units and size of the surface points. The **Point Scaling Method** property in this category specifies the scaling method to determine the point size. To select the scaling method, click on the **Value** field of this property and select the required method from the drop-down list. The **Point Units** property specifies the value used for the point size. To specify the point size, click on the **Value** field of this property and specify the value or choose the button displayed on the right to specify the point units by picking points in the drawing.

Point Display

The properties in this category are used to control the display of surface points. The **Data Point Symbol** property in this category specifies the symbols used to display the surface point. Click in the **Value** field of this property; a button will be displayed on the right. On choosing this button, different symbols for the point display will be displayed, as shown in Figure 3-43. You can select the required symbol to display the surface points.

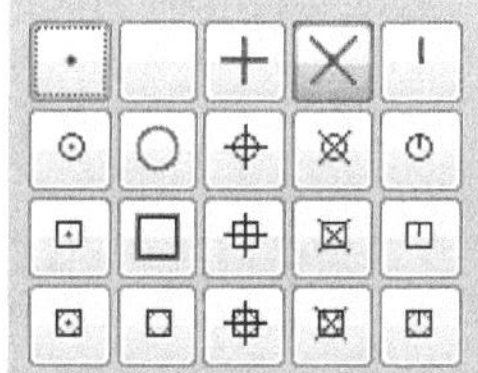

Figure 3-43 *Different symbols available for the point display*

The **Data Point Color** property specifies the color of the surface points. Click in the Value field of this property; a button will be displayed on the right. Choose the button; the **Select Color** dialog box will be displayed. Select the desired color for the data points from this dialog box and choose the **OK** button. The **Derived Point Symbol** property is used to specify the symbol for the display of the derived points. The derived points are the points that are added during surface smoothening and other calculations. You can select the required symbol and color for the derived points in the same way as discussed for the surface data points. Similarly, select a symbol and color for the non-destructive points. The non-destructive points are the points that are created when the non-destructive breaklines are added to the surface.

Note

*The surface points will be visible in the drawing only if the visibility of points is turned on in the **Display** tab of the **Surface Style** dialog box.*

Triangles Tab

This tab is used to specify the properties of the triangle components of the TIN surface. The properties in this tab are discussed next.

3D Geometry

The **Triangle Display Mode** property specifies the mode by which the triangles will be displayed. You can select the options to assign a specific display mode for the triangles on the surface from the drop-down list available in the **Value** column of this property. There are three options available in this drop-down list: **Use Surface Elevation**, **Flatten Elevations**, and **Exaggerate Elevation**.

On selecting the **Use Surface Elevation** mode from the drop-down list, the triangles will be displayed at the surface elevation which is the actual surface elevation, as shown in Figure 3-44. On selecting the **Flatten Elevations** mode, the triangles will be flattened upto a specified elevation on the surface, as shown in Figure 3-45. Note that the elevated areas in the surface have been flattened and the surface has shifted from its original elevation.

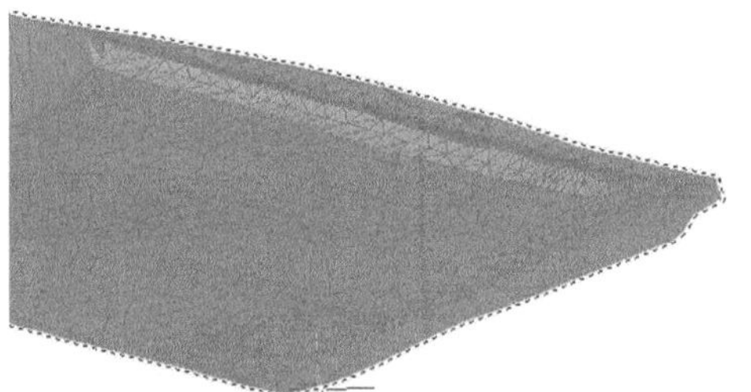

Figure 3-44 *Surface border and triangles created after using the **Use Surface Elevation** option*

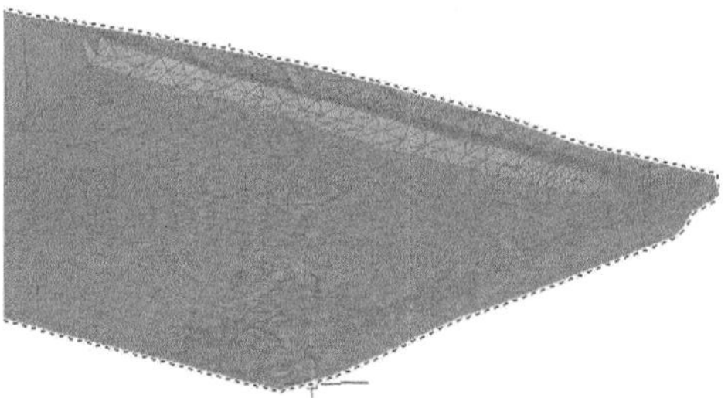

Figure 3-45 *Surface border and triangles created after using the **Use Surface Elevation** and **Flatten Elevations** option*

On selecting the **Exaggerate Elevation** mode, the triangles on the surface will be exaggerated by a specified scale factor, as shown in Figure 3-46. In this surface, the elevated areas have been exaggerated and elevated by a specified scale factor. Also, the surface has been elevated from its original elevation that is displayed by the surface border.

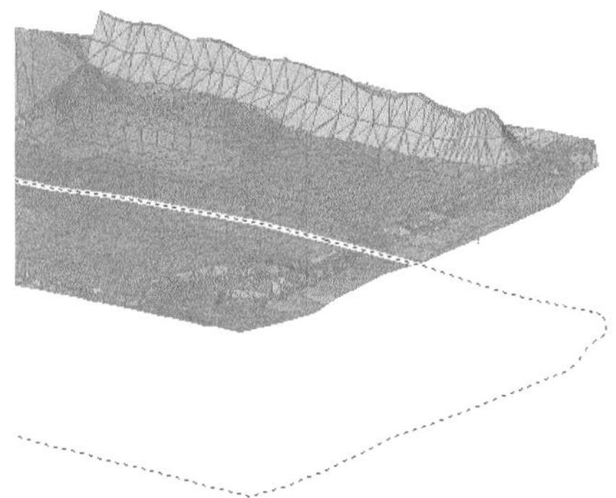

***Figure 3-46** Surface triangles created using the **Exaggerate Elevation** option and the border below the exaggerated surface*

Watersheds Tab

Watershed is an area drained by a river or any other watercourse. The watershed areas help you to determine the drain points. The **Watersheds** tab is used to control the display of watersheds in a surface. The watershed properties are listed in different categories, as shown in Figure 3-47. The properties in this tab are discussed in detail in the next chapter.

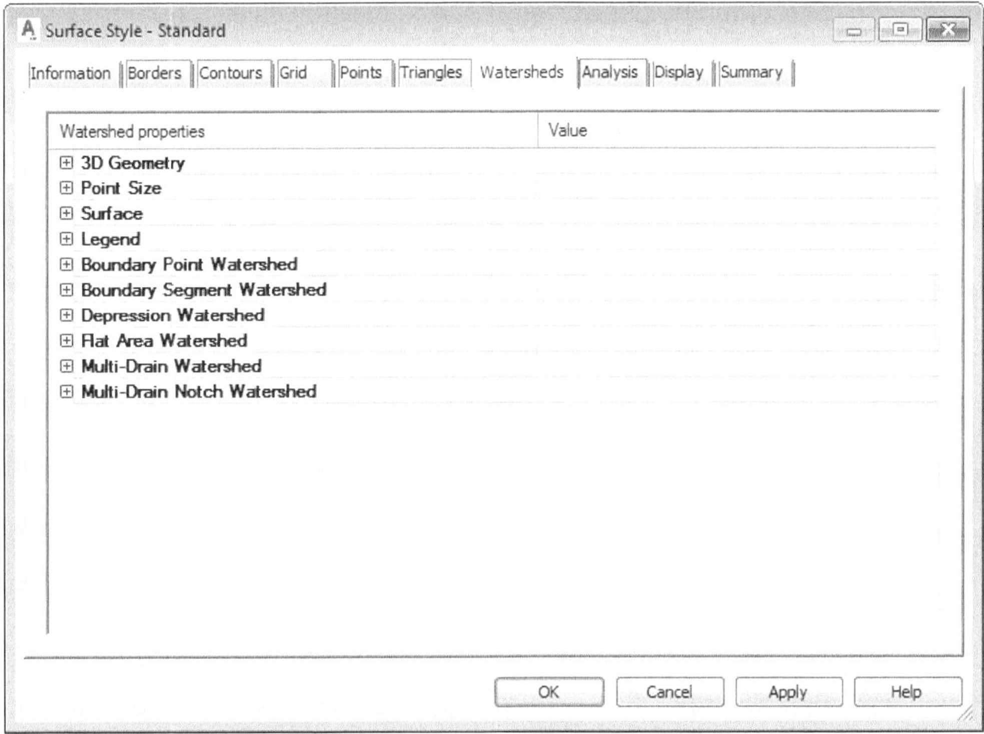

***Figure 3-47** The properties in **Watersheds** tab of the **Surface Style - Standard** dialog box*

Analysis Tab

This tab is used to specify the parameters that control the display of the surface analysis. There are four main types of analyses that can be used to study a surface. These are directions, elevations, slopes, and slope arrows. The properties in this tab are discussed next.

Directions/Elevations/Slopes/Slope Arrows Categories

Expand these categories. The properties in these categories specify the display settings of the directional type of surface analysis (discussed in the next chapter). The **Scheme** property specifies the color scheme of the ranges. Click in the **Value** field of the respective category and select the required color scheme from the drop-down list. The **Group by** property specifies the method to create and group the direction ranges. Click in the **Value** field of this property and select the grouping method from the drop-down list. To specify the number of ranges in which the directions will be grouped, click on the **Value** field of the **Number of Ranges** property and use the spinner on the right of this field to set the number. Note that the default value for this property is **8**.

To set the range precision, click in the **Value** field of the **Range Precision** property and select the value for the precision from the drop-down list. The **Display Type** property specifies the entity created during surface analysis. Click in the **Value** field and select the required entity from the drop-down list. You can create Hatch solid, 3D faces, 2D solids, or meshes using the options in this drop-down list. However, only the meshes and 3D faces can be viewed in the 3D mode.

To set the legend style for these categories, click in the **Value** field of the **Legend Style** property of the respective category and choose the button that is displayed on the right; the **Legend Style** dialog box will be displayed. Select the required legend style using the options in this dialog box and choose the **OK** button to close this dialog box. The different types of surface analyses and the process to execute them are discussed in detail in next chapter.

Display Tab

This tab controls the visibility and display settings of the surface components. You can use the properties under this tab to change the visibility, color, or layer for the surface components at various phases of the project and also in a specific view direction. The options in this tab are discussed next.

View Direction

This option specifies the direction in which you can specify the display settings and view the surface. The **Plan** view is the default view direction that helps you to view the drawing in the 2D mode. The **Model** view helps you specify the settings in 3D view. The **Section** option helps you to view the surface in a section. You can specify the settings of the surface components in all the three view directions.

Component Display Area

The **Component display** area displays various components and view properties of the surface components in different columns. The **Component Type** column lists the names of all components of the surface or any Civil 3D object. The **Visible** column specifies the visibility of the components. To turn the visibility of a component on or off, click on the bulb icon in the **Visible** column. The yellow color of the bulb icon indicates that the component's visibility is turned on. As a result, the component will be displayed on the surface.

The **Layer** column displays the layers of the component. By default, the **0** layer is assigned to all components. Click on the default layer value for a specific component in the **Layer** column; the **Layer Selection** dialog box will be displayed. Select or create a new layer for the component by using this dialog box. You can also set the color, linetype, and lineweight for all the components displayed in the **Layer** column.

Summary Tab

This tab displays the summary of surface style properties and the assigned parameters in the **Value** columns under different categories. You can expand the categories to view and edit the properties.

On specifying the values of the surface style properties, choose the **OK** button from the **Surface Style - New Surface Style** dialog box; the dialog box will be closed and the selected surface style will be added to the **Surface > Surface Styles** subnode of the **Settings** tab.

Editing Surface Styles

Ribbon: Surface > Modify > Surface Properties drop-down > Edit Surface Style
Command: EDITSURFACESTYLE

To edit a surface style, choose the **Edit Surface Style** tool from the **Modify** panel; you will be prompted to select the surface. Select the required surface and press ENTER; the **Surface Style - <style name>** dialog box will be displayed. You can edit the properties of the surface style in this dialog box as per your requirement and choose the **OK** button to close it.

Tip
*Alternatively, choose the **Settings** tab in the **TOOLSPACE** palette and expand **Surface > Surface Styles** subnode. Select the required surface style and right-click on it; a shortcut menu will be displayed. Choose the **Edit** option from the shortcut menu; the **Surface Style - <style name>** dialog box will be displayed.*

Editing Surface Properties

Ribbon: Surface > Modify > Surface Properties drop-down > Surface Properties
Command: EDITSURFACEPROPERTIES

Every Civil 3D surface has some properties that can be viewed and edited at any stage of the project. The surface properties can be viewed in the **Surface Properties** dialog box. To view and edit the surface properties, choose the **Surface Properties** tool from the **Modify** panel; the **Surface Properties - <surface name>** dialog box will be displayed.

Alternatively, to display this dialog box, choose the **Prospector** tab of the **TOOLSPACE** palette and expand the **Surfaces** node. Next, select the required surface and right-click; a shortcut menu will be displayed. Choose the **Surface Properties** option from the shortcut menu; the **Surface Properties - <surface name>** dialog box will be displayed. The dialog box has four tabs that are discussed next.

Information Tab

This tab displays the general information about the surface such as surface name, description, surface style, and render material. The options in this tab are as follows:

Name

This option specifies the default name of the surface. Specify the name of the surface in the **Name** edit box.

Description

You can optionally enter the description of the surface in the **Description** text box.

Default styles

The **Default styles** area is used to specify the default surface style and render material style. Select the desired option from the **Surface style** and **Render Material** drop-down lists in this area to specify the surface style and render material. Instead of selecting an in-built surface style in Civil 3D, you can also create a new style, or copy and edit the current surface style in the **Default styles** area. To do so, choose the down arrow on the right from the respective drop-down list; a flyout will be displayed. Choose the required option from the flyout to perform the corresponding operations.

Object locked

If you select this check box, you will not be able to edit a surface. Clear the check box to edit the surface.

Show tooltips

This check box is selected by default. It displays the tooltips for the objects in the drawing. The tooltips display the information about the objects such as elevation, coordinates, and description.

Definition Tab

This tab is used to edit the surface definition items. The options in this tab are discussed next.

Build: Expand the **Build** options. The properties in this category are discussed next.

Copy deleted dependent objects: This property specifies whether the object information is to be copied to the surface definition in case the object is deleted. For example, if the polyline used for creating a boundary is deleted, the boundary is also deleted from the surface and its definition. If you set the value of this property to **Yes**, the objects such as boundary, breaklines or a point group will be retained even if you remove the parent polyline or any other object. The information of the deleted component will be copied and saved in the surface's definition.

Exclude elevations less than: This property is used to set the minimum limit of the surface elevation such that the value less than the specified value will be excluded while creating the surface. Click in the **Value** field of this property and select **Yes** from the drop-down list to exclude the points that have elevations less than the specified value.

Elevation: This property will be activated only if you have set the value for the **Exclude elevation less than** property to **Yes**. In the **Value** column of this property, you can set the value for the minimum limit of the surface elevation such that the value less than the specified value will be excluded while creating the surface.

Exclude elevations greater than: This property sets the maximum limit of the surface elevation such that the values greater than the specified value will be excluded from the surface. Click in the **Value** field of this property and select **Yes** from the drop-down list to exclude the elevations greater than the specified value. Specify the maximum value in the **Value** field of the **Elevation** property. The elevation greater than this value will be excluded from the surface.

Use maximum angle: This property sets the maximum limit of the angle between the adjacent TIN lines such that values greater than the specified values will be excluded from the surface. Click in the **Value** field of this property and select **Yes** to exclude the angles greater than the specified value. Specify the maximum value in the **Value** field of **Maximum angle between adjacent TIN lines** property. The angle greater than this value will be excluded from the surface.

Maximum angle between adjacent TIN lines: This property will be activated only if you have set the value for the **Use maximum angle** property to **Yes**. In this property, you can specify the limit value in the **value** column for the maximum angle between the adjacent TIN lines when the surface is built.

Use maximum triangle length: This property specifies whether the triangles that have length more than the specified length should be removed from the surface or not. Click in the **Value** field of this property and select **Yes** from the drop-down list to remove the triangles with a length greater than the specified length of the triangle.

Maximum triangle length: This option is activated after you select **Yes** for the **Use maximum triangle length** option in the **Value** field. Click in the **Value** field and specify the value for the length. The triangles with length greater than the length specified in the column will be removed while creating the surface.

Convert proximity breaklines to standard: This option specifies whether to convert the proximity breaklines into standard breaklines or not. Click in the **Value** field of this property; a down arrow will be displayed. Choose the down arrow and select **Yes** from the drop-down list to convert the proximity breaklines into standard breaklines.

Allow crossing breaklines. This property is used to specify whether to allow the crossing of breaklines or not. If you set the value of this property to **Yes** then you need to specify the elevation at the point of intersection.

Elevation to use: This property is available only when the value for **Allow crossing breaklines** property is set to **Yes**. Click in the **Value** field of this property and select any one of the following options from the drop-down list. Select the **Use first breakline elevation at intersection** option to use the elevation of the first breakline to determine the elevation at the intersection. Select the **Use last breakline elevation at intersection** option to use the elevation of the last breakline to determine the elevation at the intersection. Select the **Use average elevation at intersection** option to use the average of the first and last breakline elevation values to determine the elevation at the intersection.

Data operations

Expand the **Data operations** options to view the data operations performed on a surface. You can specify whether or not to include the data operations in the surface build. To include the required data operation, select the check box next to it from the **Operation Type** list box at the bottom of the dialog box. You can change the visibility, color, or layer for the surface components at various phases of a project. By default, the value for all the data operations is set to **Yes**. Click in the **Value** field of a data operation; a down arrow will be displayed. Choose the down arrow and select **No** to exclude the data operation from the surface build.

Edit operations

Expand the **Edit operations** options to view different surface edit operations. By default, the value for all the edit operations is set to **Yes**. Click in the **Value** field of a data operation; a down arrow will be displayed. Next, choose the down arrow and select **No** to exclude the edit operation from the surface build. You can also specify whether or not to include the edit operations in the surface build by using the **Operation Type** list box. To do so, select or clear the edit operations check boxes in this list box.

Operation Type

The **Operation Type** area of the **Surface Properties** dialog box displays all surface operations and their parameters in the order in which these operations were performed. These parameters are listed in the **Parameters** column. You can clear the check box for any surface operation listed in the **Operation Type** column to exclude it from the surface build.

Analysis Tab

This tab is used to specify the properties of the surface analysis. You can also modify the properties of existing surface analysis using the options in this dialog box. Various options in the **Analysis** tab are discussed next.

Analysis type

This option specifies the type of analysis selected. You can select the type of surface analysis from the **Analysis type** drop-down list. By default, **Elevations** is selected from the drop-down list. The properties of the selected analysis type will be displayed in the **Range Detail Area**

Legend

This option specifies the legend style for the selected analysis type. Select the required legend style from the **Select a Style** drop-down list in the **Legend** area.

Preview

Select the **Preview** check box to display the legend style in the **Preview** area, as shown in Figure 3-48. You can use the **ViewCube** in the **Preview** area to rotate and adjust the legend table.

Ranges

The **Ranges** area displays the number of ranges required for the surface analysis. These ranges will be displayed in the **Range Details** area below the **Create ranges by** drop-down list. Use the **Number** spinner in this area to set the number of ranges. The default value displayed in the spinner is **8**. You can use the **Run analysis** button to run the surface analysis after specifying the required properties. The **Range Details** area of this tab displays the result of analysis in tabular form.

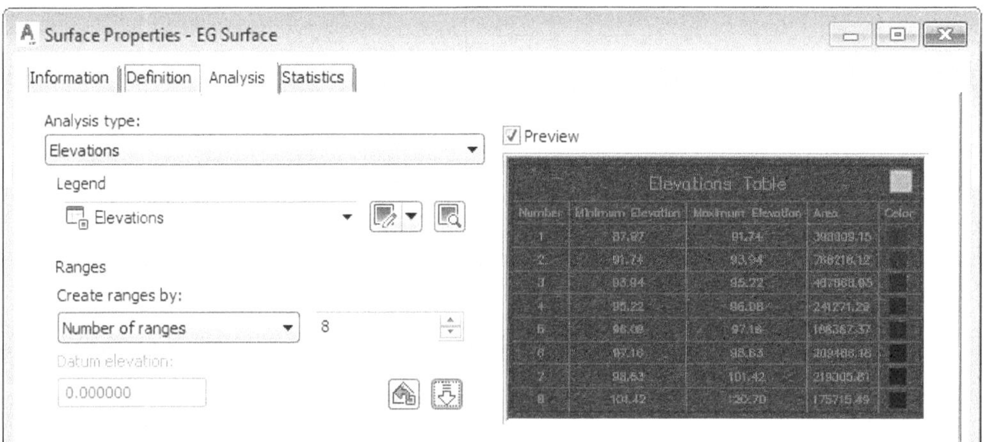

*Figure 3-48 Partial view of the **Surface Properties - EG Surface** dialog box with the **Preview** check box selected and legend style displayed*

Statistics Tab

The **Statistics** tab displays the statistical information about the surface grouped in categories. This information includes maximum and minimum values for elevation, slope/grade, coordinate in X and Y direction, number of triangles, and number of points.

Note

*The information displayed in the third category in the **Statistics** tab varies according to the type of surface created. For example, in case of TIN surface, the number of triangles, maximum triangle area, and so on will be displayed in the TIN category. If the surface is a grid surface or volume surface then properties displayed will vary accordingly.*

SURFACE TOOLS

AutoCAD Civil 3D provides various tools which make the surface object more interactive. These tools can be accessed from the **Surface Tools** panel in the **Surface** contextual tab. To display the **Surface** tab, choose the **Surface** tool from the **Ground Data** panel of the **Modify** tab. The surface tools are discussed next.

Drape Image

Ribbon:	Surface > Surface Tools > Drape Image
Command:	DRAPEIMAGE

This tool is used to drape an image imported from Google Earth over an existing surface. Before using this tool, you need to import and insert an image from the Google Earth into Civil 3D and then overlay the image on the surface using the **Drape Image** tool.

To drape an image, choose the **Drape Image** tool from the **Surface Tools** panel; the **Drape Image** dialog box will be displayed, as shown in Figure 3-49.

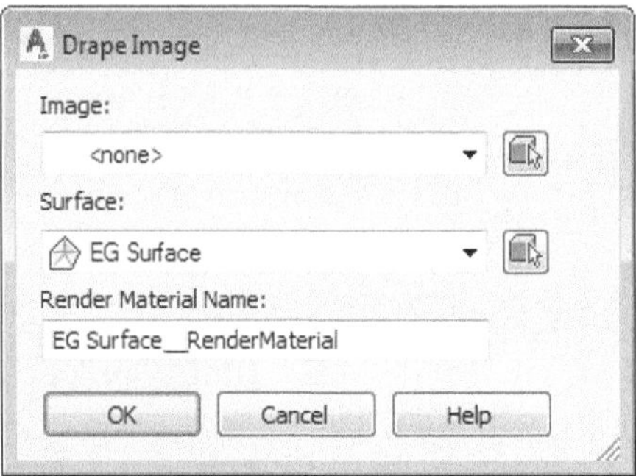

*Figure 3-49 The **Drape Image** dialog box*

This dialog box is used to select the required image and overlay it over the surface. Select the required image from the drop-down list in the **Image** area. You can also choose the **Select from the drawing** button on the right of this drop-down list and select the image from the drawing. Note that the images imported from Google Earth are named automatically when imported to Civil 3D. Next, select a surface from the **Surface** drop-down list or select it from the drawing by choosing the **Select from the drawing** button on the right of the drop-down list. The render material is created automatically as Civil 3D renders the image draped over the surface. Now, choose the **OK** button; the dialog box will be closed. The image will be draped but you will not be able to view it. Before you view the image, select the imported image and right-click to display a shortcut menu. Choose **Isolate Objects > Hide Selected Objects** from the shortcut menu; the image will disappear and you will see the surface only. At this stage, you can view the surface in 3D mode only. To view the rendered image, choose the **View** tab and then select the **Realistic** visual style from the **Visual Style** drop-down list in the **Views** panel, as shown in Figure 3-50. The gray scale Google Image will be draped over the surface and the image will be clipped according to the surface.

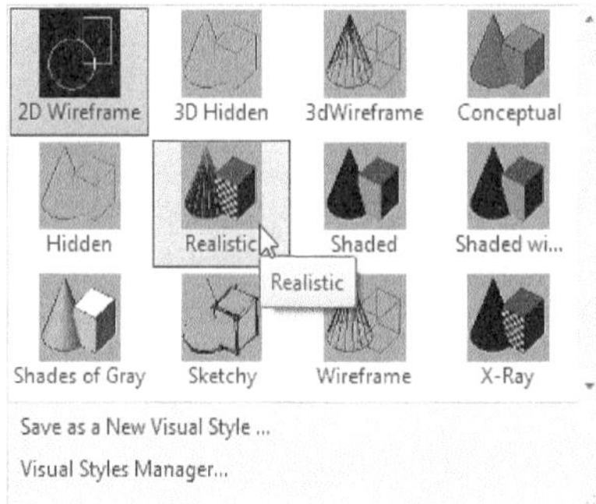

*Figure 3-50 The **Realistic** visual style selected from the **Visual Style** drop-down list*

Extract Solids from Surface

Ribbon: Surface > Surface Tools > Extract from Surface drop down>Extract Solids from Surface
Command: EXPORTSURFACETOSOLID

This tool is used to extract solids from the surface based on the surface triangles and surface borders. To extract a solid from a surface, choose the **Extract Solids from Surface** tool from **Surface Tools** panel; the **Extract Solid from Surface** dialog box will be displayed, as shown in Figure 3-51.

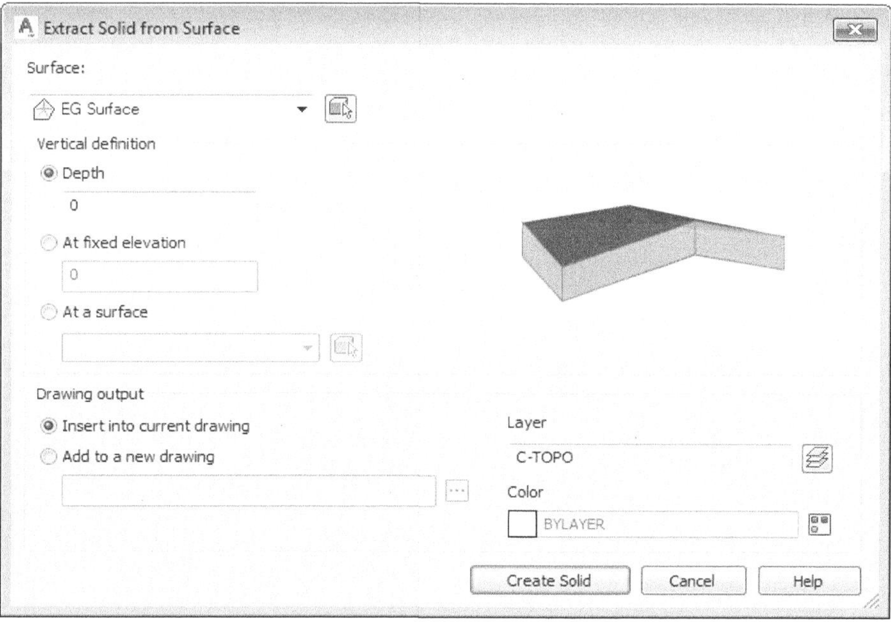

*Figure 3-51 The **Extract Solid from Surface** dialog box*

Select the surface from the **Surface** drop-down list or choose the **Select from the drawing** button to select the surface from drawing.

In the **Vertical definition** area, the **Depth** radio button is selected by default. Enter the negative or positive integer value for the depth.. If you enter a positive value, the solid is extruded upward from the surface. If you enter a negative value, the solid is extruded downward from the surface. Select the **At fixed elevation** radio button to specify that the bottom of solid is at a fixed elevation. On doing so, the edit box below will be activated. Enter the required elevation value in the edit box. Select the **At a surface** radio button to create a solid from a surface. On selecting this radio button, the edit box below will be activated. Enter the required value int he edit box. Alternatively choose, the **Select from the drawing** button; next to the edit box. The solid defined is at a relative distance from another surface.

In the **Drawing output** area, the **Insert Into Current Drawing** radio button is selected by default and is used to create the solid in the current drawing. To create solid in another drawing, select the **Add to a new drawing** radio button and browse to open the **Specify new drawing** dialog box, where you can specify the drawing name and location.

In the **Layer** area, specify the layer on which the solid is created and in the **Color** area, specify the color for the solid. Now, choose the **Create Solid** button. The solid surface will be saved with *.dwg* file extension.

Export to DEM

Ribbon: Surface > Surface Tools >Extract from Surface drop down>Export to DEM
Command: SURFACEEXPORTTODEM

AutoCAD Civil 3D allows you to export the surface data to DEM files that can be used in different programs such as AutoCAD Map 3D, ArcGIS, and Raster Design. To export the surface data to a DEM file, choose the **Export to DEM** tool in the **Surface Tools** panel; the **Export Surface to DEM** dialog box will be displayed, as shown in Figure 3-52. This dialog box is used to specify the parameters to export a file. The **Selected Surface** category of this dialog box displays information of the surface to be exported and the **Export** category displays the properties of the DEM file to be created.

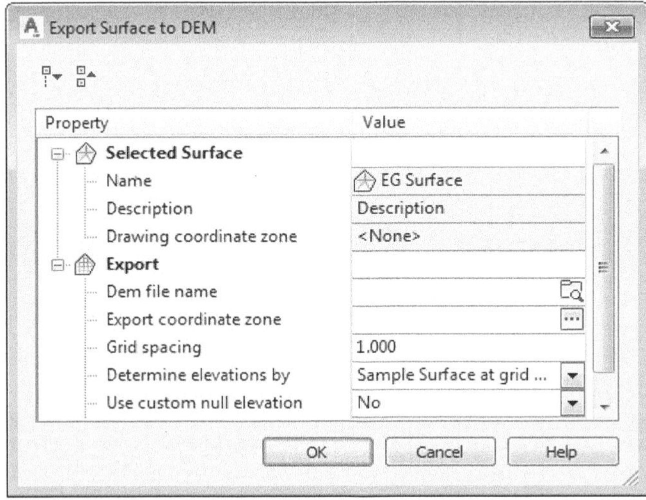

*Figure 3-52 The **Export Surface to DEM** dialog box*

To specify the DEM file name, click on the folder symbol in the **Value** field of the **Dem file name** property; the **Export Surface to DEM** dialog box will be displayed. In this dialog box, browse to the required location and specify a file name in the **File name** edit box. Next, select the file type from **Files of type** drop-down list. You can either select the **.dem* or **.tif* file format. Choose the **Save** button to close the dialog box. Similarly, click on the browse button in the **Value** field of the **Export coordinate zone** property; the **Select Coordinate System** dialog box will be displayed. Specify a coordinate zone for the DEM file in the dialog box and choose the **OK** button to return to the **Export Surface to DEM** dialog box. Choose the **OK** button; the **Export Surface to DEM** dialog box will be displayed until the surface is exported to DEM file. The file will be saved with **.tif* or **.dem* file extension. You can now import and use this DEM file in other programs supporting the USGS (.dem) or GEOTIFF (.tif) file types.

Extract Objects

Ribbon: Surface > Surface Tools >Extract from Surface drop down> Extract Objects
Command: SURFACEEXTRACTOBJECTS

The **Extract Objects** tool is used to extract the surface components and modify them without exploding them. In such cases, the extracted components retain their original properties. These components can be modified and used for developing further designs. For example, catchment areas, water drop paths, watersheds, and so on can be extracted and the data obtained from these objects can be used to design ponds, sewers, and so on. These components can be used by the Hydrological department for further investigations.

To extract objects from a surface, choose the **Extract Objects** tool from the **Surface Tools** panel; the **Extract Objects from Surface - <surface name>** dialog box will be displayed, as shown in Figure 3-53.

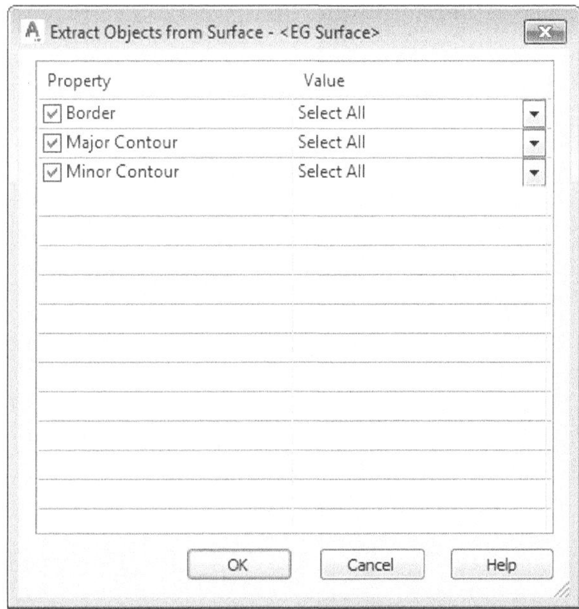

*Figure 3-53 The **Extract Objects from Surface - <EG Surface >** dialog box*

The dialog box displays the existing components of the surface in the **Property** column. By default, Civil 3D will extract all components. To extract the desired components, choose the down-arrow in the **Value** field of the corresponding property and then select the **Select from Drawing** option from the drop-down list; the **Select from Drawing** button will be displayed on the right. Choose the button; you will be prompted to select the required components. Select the required components and then press ENTER; the **Extract Objects from Surface - <Surface 1>** dialog box will be displayed with the required objects selected. Next, choose the **OK** button; the selected objects will be extracted. Now, enter **List** in the command line and press ENTER; you will be prompted to select the objects. Select the required extracted object and press ENTER; the **AutoCAD Text Window** will be displayed showing the information of the component that has been extracted.

TUTORIALS

1. Download the *c03_c3d_2018_tut.zip* file from *http://www.cadcim.com*. The path of the file is as follows: *Textbooks > Civil/GIS > AutoCAD Civil 3D > Exploring AutoCAD Civil 3D 2018.*

2. Now, save and extract the downloaded file at the following location:

   C:\c3d_2018

Note

*While opening the tutorial file, the **PANORAMA** window with an error message may appear. Close this window to proceed further.*

Tutorial 1 — Creating Surface

In this tutorial, you will create a surface, as shown in Figure 3-54, and add point data to it. Then, you will apply a surface style and perform edit operations on it. **(Expected time: 30 min)**

The following steps are required to complete this tutorial:

a. Open a template file.
b. Create a TIN surface.
c. Create and assign a new surface style to the surface.
d. Save the file.

Opening the New Template File

1. Choose **New** from the **Application Menu**; the **Select template** dialog box is displayed.

2. In the **Select template** dialog box, select *_AutoCAD Civil3D (Imperial) NCS.dwt* template and choose the **Open** button.

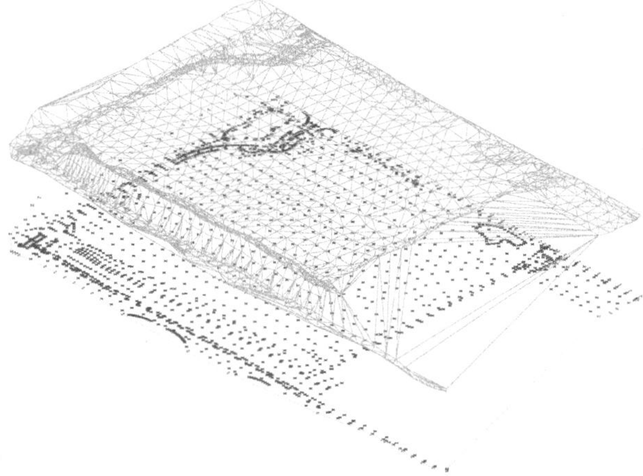

Figure 3-54 *The surface displayed in 3D view*

Creating the Surface

1. Choose the **Create Surface** tool from **Home > Create Ground Data > Surfaces** drop-down; the **Create Surface** dialog box is displayed.

2. Click in the **Value** field of the **Name** property and choose the **Browse** button displayed on the right; the **Name Template** dialog box is displayed, as shown in Figure 3-55.

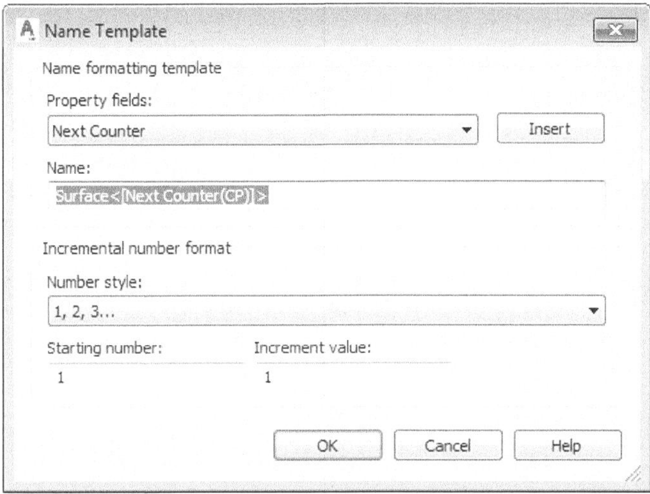

*Figure 3-55 The **Name Template** dialog box*

3. Enter the name **EG Surface** in the **Name** edit box of the dialog box and choose the **OK** button to close the dialog box.

4. Now, ensure that the **TIN surface** option is selected in the **Type** drop-down list of the **Create Surface** dialog box and choose the **OK** button; the dialog box is closed. Also, the surface is created and added to the **Surfaces** node of the **Prospector** tab of the **TOOLSPACE** palette, as shown in Figure 3-56.

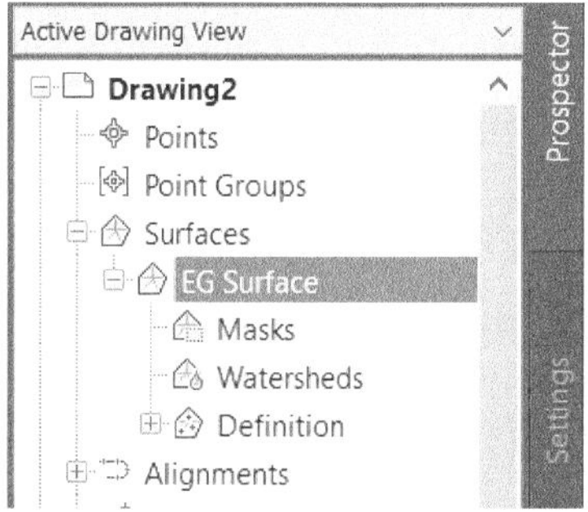

*Figure 3-56 The **EG Surface** added to the **Surfaces** node of the **Prospector** tab*

Note

You cannot see the surface at this stage because it is empty and you need to add data to make it visible.

Adding Point File to the Surface

1. Expand **Surfaces > EG Surface > Definition** in the **Prospector** tab of the **TOOLSPACE** palette.

2. Select **Point Files** from the **Definition** node and right-click; a shortcut menu is displayed.

3. Choose **Add** from the shortcut menu; the **Add Point File** dialog box is displayed.

4. From the **Specify point file format** list box, select the **PENZD (space delimited)** option. This file format is used for the point files that are saved with the extension *.txt*, as shown in Figure 3-57.

Note

If you select the wrong format for the point file from the ***Specify point file format*** *list box, Civil 3D will display an error message indicating that the wrong file format has been selected.*

5. Next, choose the button on the right of the **Selected Files** list box; the **Select Source File** dialog box is displayed. 

6. Browse to the folder *c03_c3d_2018_tut* and select the *c03 _c3d_2018_tut01- PENZD* .txt file. Choose the **Open** button; the file name and path is displayed in the **Selected Files** list box, refer to Figure 3-57.

7. Choose the **OK** button from the **Add Point File** dialog box; the data is added to the surface.

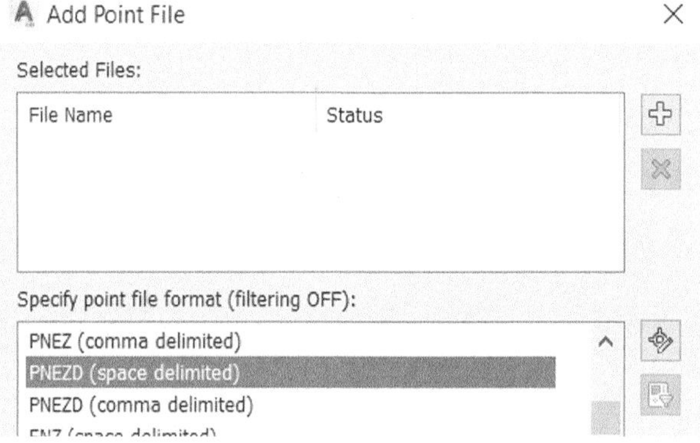

Figure 3-57 Partial view of the ***Add Point File*** *dialog box*

Viewing the Surface

1. Enter **ZE** in the command line and then press ENTER; the surface is displayed with a surface border and the major and minor contours, as shown in Figure 3-58. This is due to the default surface style settings of the template file.

Figure 3-58 The ***EG Surface*** *displayed in the drawing area*

Creating a New Surface Style

1. Choose the **Settings** tab of the **TOOLSPACE** palette; the items in the tab are displayed.

2. In the **Settings** tab, expand **Surface > Surface Styles**; you will notice that an orange triangular symbol is displayed on the left of the three surface styles namely: **Contours 1' and 5' (Design)**, **Contours 2' and 10' (Background)**, and **Contours 2' and 10' (Design)** indicating that these surface styles are currently in use.

3. Select **Surface Styles** and right-click; a shortcut menu is displayed.

4. Choose **New** from the shortcut menu; the **Surface Styles - New Surface Style** dialog box is displayed. The **Information** tab is chosen by default in this dialog box.

5. Enter **EG Style** in the **Name** edit box of the **Information** tab.

6. Choose the **Apply** button; the name of the dialog box is changed to **Surface Style - EG Style**.

7. Next, choose the **Points** tab from the **Surface Style - EG Style** dialog box.

8. Click on the **Value** field of the **Point Units** property and enter **7.00'**.

9. Next, expand the **Point Display** category and click in the **Value** field of the **Data Point Symbol** property; a **Browse** button is displayed on the right of this field.

10. Choose the **Browse** button; a small window with different point symbols is displayed. Retain the default settings.

11. Next, choose the **Display** tab. Make sure that the **Plan** option is selected in the **View Direction** drop-down list of the **Display** tab. The settings of the surface style can only be viewed in the plan.

12. Click on the bulb icon in the **Visible** column and turn on the visibility of **Points** and **Triangles**. Also, ensure that the **Major Contour** and **Minor Contour** layers are turned on so that the objects in these layers are visible when viewed in the plan view. 

13. Choose the **Apply** button to configure the settings for the plan view of the surface.

14. Next, select the **Model** option from the **View Direction** drop-down list.

15. In the **Display** tab, turn on the visibility of **Points** and **Border**. Also, ensure that the visibility of **Triangles** is turned on.

16. Choose the **Triangles** tab and click in the **Value** field of the **Triangle Display Mode** property and select the **Exaggerate Elevation** option from the drop-down list. Next, enter **5.000** in the **Value** field of the **Exaggerate Triangles by Scale Factor** property.

17. Choose the **Apply** button; the settings are configured for the 3D view/model of the surface.

18. Next, choose the **OK** button in the **Surface Styles - EG Style** dialog box; the **EG Style** is created and added to the **Surface Styles** node of the **Settings** tab.

Assigning the EG Style to the Surface

1. Choose the **Prospector** tab of the **TOOLSPACE** palette and expand the **Surfaces** node.

2. Select **EG Surface** and right-click; a shortcut menu is displayed.

3. Choose **Surface Properties** from the shortcut menu; the **Surface Properties - EG Surface** dialog box is displayed. The **Information** tab is chosen by default in this dialog box.

4. In the **Default styles** area of the tab, select **EG Style** from the **Surface style** drop-down list, as shown in Figure 3-59.

5. Choose the **Apply** button; a TIN surface is displayed with the surface points.

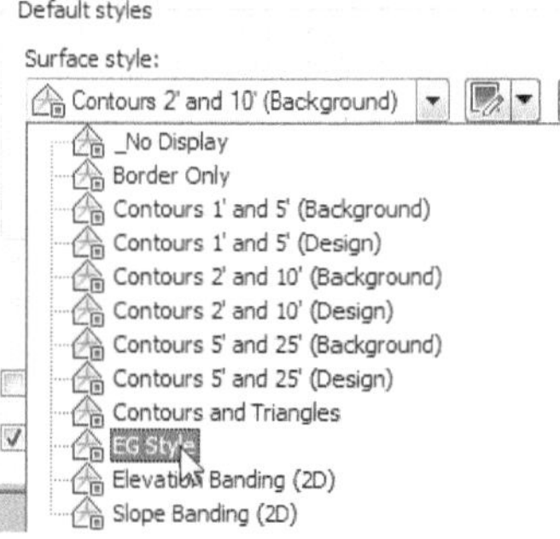

Figure 3-59 *Selecting the* ***EG Style*** *option from the* ***Surface style*** *drop-down list*

6. Choose the **OK** button to close the **Surface Properties - EG Surface** dialog box. Figures 3-60 and 3-61 show the TIN surface with the surface points and the point style selected, respectively. Note that the surface points are represented by the symbol that was selected for the point display in the surface style.

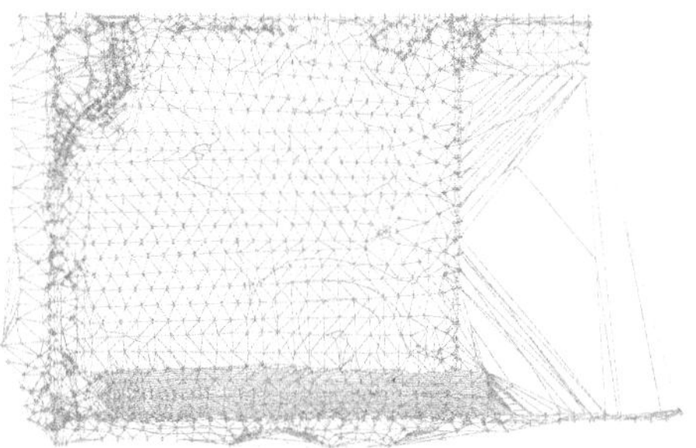

Figure 3-60 *The TIN surface with the surface points*

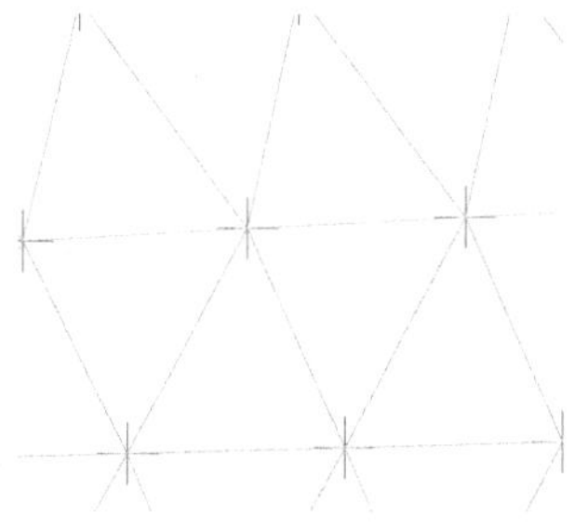

Figure 3-61 *Points represented by the selected point symbol*

7. Choose the **SE Isometric** button from the **Views** panel of the **View** tab, as shown in Figure 3-62 to view the surface in 3D view; the surface is displayed with triangles at an exaggerated elevation, and the surface border and points are displayed at the original elevation, as shown in Figure 3-63.

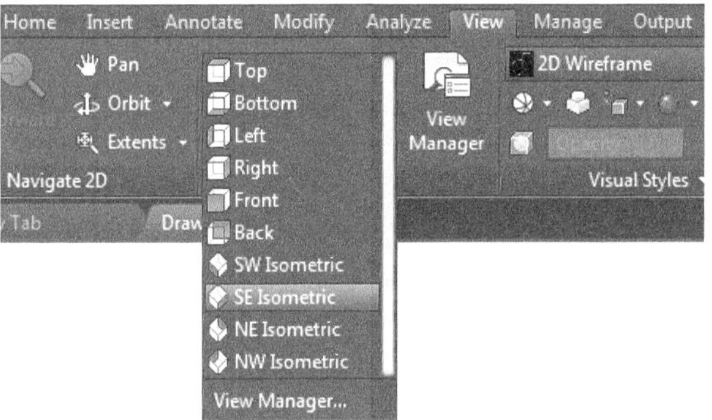

Figure 3-62 The ***SE Isometric*** *button chosen from the* ***View*** *tab*

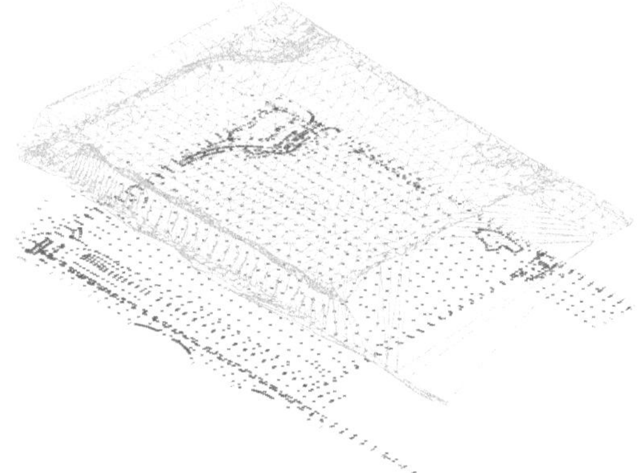

Figure 3-63 The ***SE Isometric*** *view of the* ***EG Surface***

Note

Figure 3-63 displays the model view of the surface using the model view settings previously defined for surface style.

Saving the Drawing

1. Choose the **Save As** from the **Application Menu**; the **Save Drawing As** dialog box is displayed.

2. In this dialog box, browse to the following location:

   C:\c3d_2018\c03_c3d_2018_tut

3. In the **File name** edit box, enter **c03_c3d_2018_tut01a**.

4. Next, choose the **Save** button; the file is saved with the name *c03_c3d_2018_tut01a* at the specified location.

Tutorial 2 Surface Pasting

In this tutorial, you will create two surfaces by using the point group and breaklines. Also, you will use some of the surface editing commands and paste the surface, as shown in Figure 3-64.

(Expected time: 30 min)

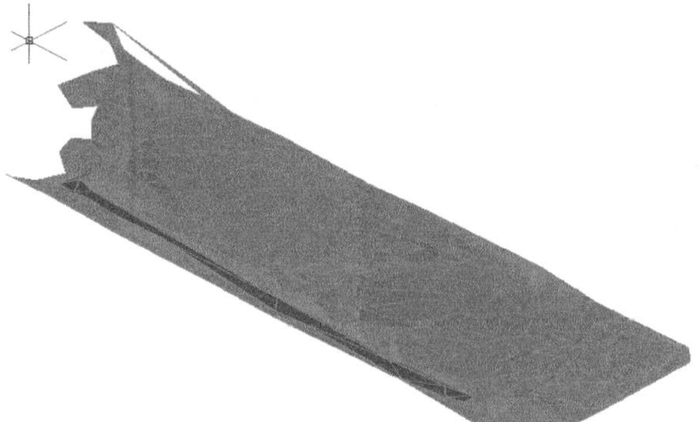

Figure 3-64 The pasted surface

The following steps are required to complete this tutorial:

a. Open the file.
b. Create a surface by using breaklines.
c. Create a surface by using point groups.
d. Use the **Delete Line** tool to edit the surface.
e. Paste the surface.
f. Save the file.

Opening the File

1. Choose **Open > Drawing** from the **Application Menu**; the **Select File** dialog box is displayed.

2. In the dialog box, browse to the location *C:\c3d_2018\c03_c3d_2018* where you have saved the file.

3. Select the file *c03_c3d_2018_tut02.dwg* and then choose the **Open** button to open the file.

Creating E Street Surface using Breaklines

1. Choose the **Create Surface** tool from **Home > Create Ground Data > Surfaces** drop-down; the **Create Surface** dialog box is displayed.

2. Select the **TIN surface** option in the **Type** drop-down list of the displayed dialog box, if it is not selected by default.

3 Enter **E Street** in the **Value** field of the **Name** property.

4. Click on the browse button in the **Value** field of the **Style** property; the **Select Surface Style** dialog box is displayed. In this dialog box, select the **E Style** option from the drop-down list and then choose the **OK** button; the selected style is displayed in the **Value** field of the **Style** property.

5. Next, choose the **OK** button from the **Create Surface** dialog box; the dialog box is closed and a surface is created. Now, you will add data to this surface.

6. Choose the **Prospector** tab and expand **Surfaces > E Street > Definition**.

7. In the **Definition** node, right-click on **Breaklines** and choose **Add** from the shortcut menu displayed; the **Add Breaklines** dialog box is displayed.

8. Enter **E Lines** in the **Description** text box and ensure that the **Standard** option is selected in the **Type** drop-down list.

9. Next, choose the **OK** button; the dialog box is closed and you are prompted to select the objects.

10. Select the two polylines from the drawing and then press ENTER; the breaklines are added to the **E Street** surface, as shown in Figure 3-65.

Note

*The breaklines are added to the **Breaklines** subnode of the **E Street** surface's **Definition** node and they are also displayed in the List View.*

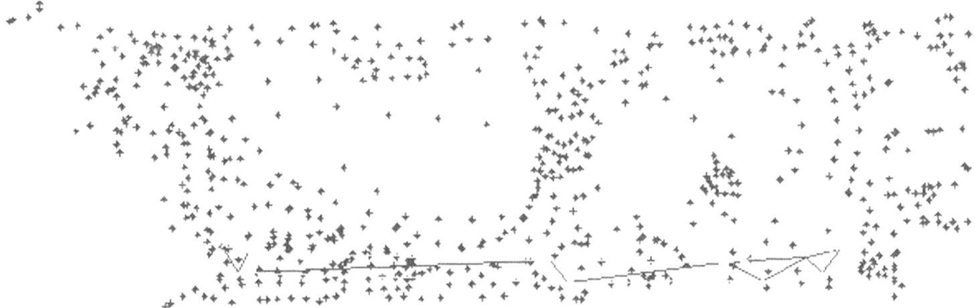

Figure 3-65 *Points and the **E Street** surface after adding breaklines*

Creating the Existing Ground Surface Using Point Groups

1. Repeat steps 1 to 4 given in the previous section and then set the following values in the **Create Surface** dialog box:

   Surface type: **TIN surface** Name: **EG** Style: **Basic**

2. Now, choose the **OK** button; the **EG** surface is created.

3. Expand **Surfaces > EG > Definition** in the **Prospector** tab of the **TOOLSPACE** palette.

4. Right-click on **Point Groups** and choose **Add** from the shortcut menu displayed; the **Point Groups** dialog box is displayed.

5. Select the **_All Points** group and choose the **OK** button; the point group is added as the definition to the surface, as shown in Figure 3-66.

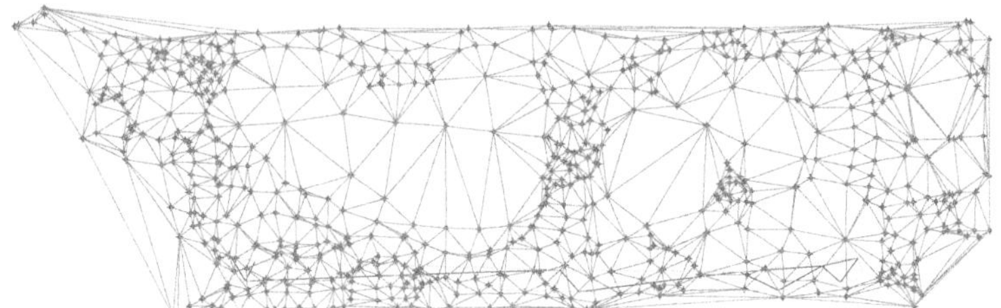

Figure 3-66 *The* ***EG*** *surface created after adding the point group*

Editing the EG surface

1. Choose the **Surface** tool from the **Ground Data** panel of the **Modify** tab; the **Surface** contextual tab is displayed.

2. Next, choose the **Delete Line** tool from **Surface > Modify > Edit Surface** drop-down; you are prompted to select the surface from which you want to delete the lines.

3. Press ENTER; the **Select a Surface** dialog box is displayed.

4. Select the **EG** surface from the dialog box and choose the **OK** button; the dialog box is closed and you are prompted to select the required edges.

5. Select all the longer edges on the left side of the surface and shorter edges on the top left corner, as shown in Figure 3-67.

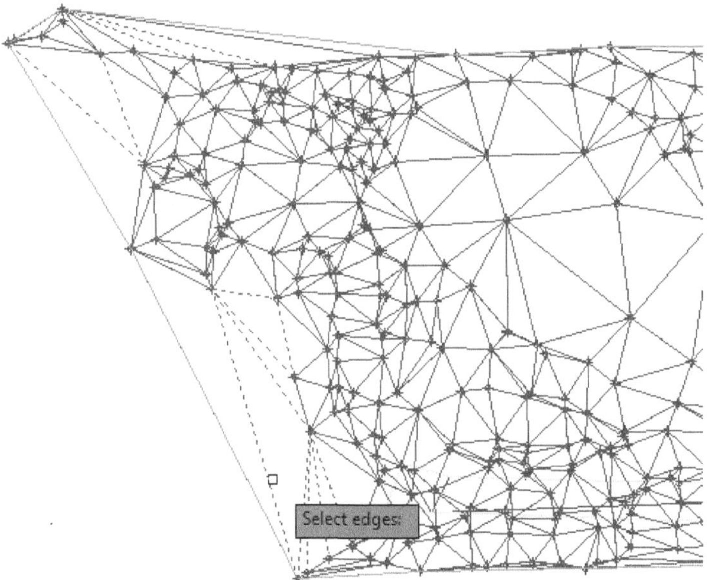

Figure 3-67 *Selecting the longer edges of the triangles*

6. Press ENTER; the selected lines are deleted and the surface is displayed, as shown in Figure 3-68. Press ENTER to exit the command.

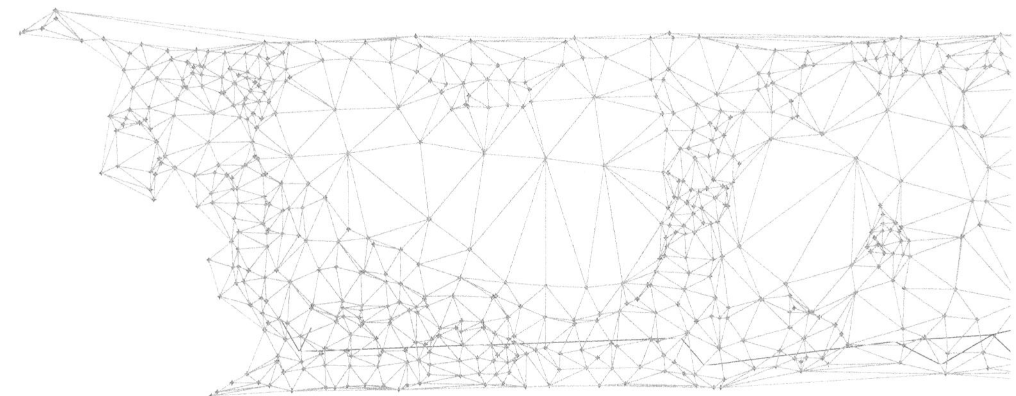

Figure 3-68 *The* ***EG*** *surface after deleting the TIN lines*

7. Before you paste the **E Street** surface on the **EG** surface, it is better to view the surfaces in a 3D view. To do so, select the **SE Isometric** option from the **Views** panel of the **View** tab; the **EG** surface is displayed in an isometric view, as shown in Figure 3-69.

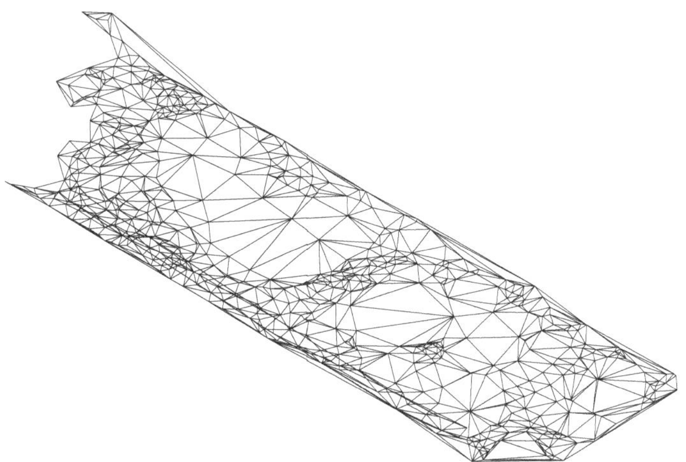

Figure 3-69 *The* ***EG*** *surface before pasting the* ***E Street*** *surface*

Pasting the Surface

1. Choose the **Paste Surface** tool from **Surface > Modify > Edit Surface** drop-down; you are prompted to select a surface.

2. Press ENTER; the **Select a Surface** dialog box is displayed.

3. In the dialog box, select the **EG** surface and choose the **OK** button; the **Select Surface to Paste** dialog box is displayed.

4. Select **E Street** from the dialog box and choose the **OK** button; the dialog box is closed and the **E Street** surface is pasted on the **EG** surface. Civil 3D has now recalculated triangulation and has built the **EG** surface taking breaklines into account. Notice the change of the **EG** surface in the region of added breaklines, refer to Figure 3-70.

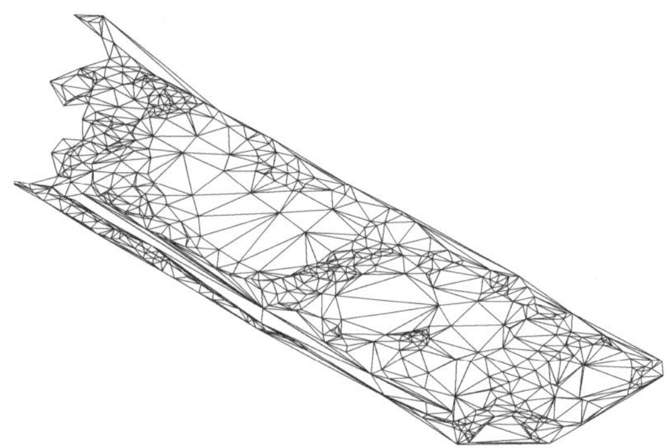

Figure 3-70 The ***EG*** *surface after pasting the* ***E Street*** *surface*

5. Choose the **View** tab and then select the **Realistic** visual style from the **Visual Style** drop-down list in the **Views** panel; the **E Street** surface is displayed, as shown in Figure 3-71.

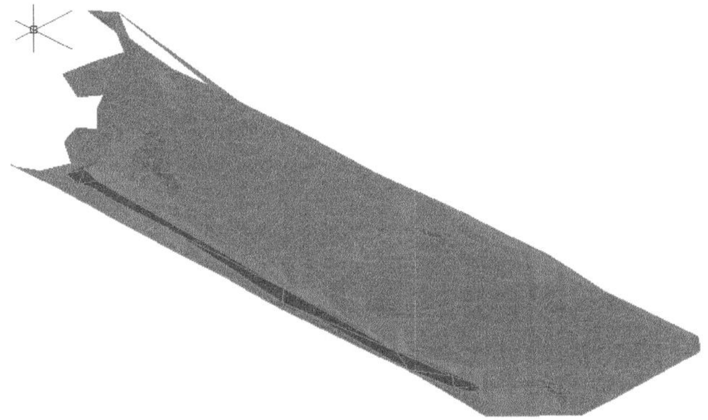

Figure 3-71 The realistic view of the surface after pasting the ***E Street*** *surface over the* ***EG*** *surface*

Note

1. The ***E Street*** *surface will disappear as soon as you choose another command or zoom in or out the surface.*

2. Sometimes you may not be able to paste one surface over another. This happens due to the difference in the elevation of the two surfaces.

Saving the File

1. Choose **Save As** from the **Application Menu**; the **Save Drawing As** dialog box is displayed.

2. In this dialog box, browse to the following location:

   C:\c3d_2018\c03_c3d_2018_tut

3. In the **File name** edit box, enter **c03_c3d_2018_tut02a** .

4. Next, choose the **Save** button; the file is saved with the name *c03_c3d_2018_tut02a* at the specified location.

Tutorial 3 Creating Surface from GIS Data

In this tutorial, you will create a surface using a shape file, import a raster image, and drape it over the surface, refer to Figure 3-72. **(Expected time: 45 min)**

The following steps are required to complete this tutorial:

a. Open a new drawing file.
b. Set the parameters of the drawing.
c. Create a surface from GIS data.
d. Insert the geo-referenced image.
e. Drape the raster image.
f. View the result of draping.
g. Save the file.

Figure 3-72 *The isometric view of the surface with the draped raster image*

Opening a New Drawing File

1. Choose **New** from the **Application Menu**; the **Select template** dialog box is displayed.

2. In this dialog box, select the **_AutoCAD Civil 3D (Imperial) NCS.dwt** template; a new file is opened.

Setting the Drawing Parameters

In this section, you will specify the drawing settings such as the coordinate system, drawing units, and the ambient settings for the drawing.

1. Right-click on the drawing name in the **Settings** tab of the **TOOLSPACE** palette; a flyout is displayed. Choose the **Edit Drawing Settings** option from the displayed flyout; the **Drawing Settings - <Drawing Name>** dialog box is displayed.

2. Choose the **Units and Zone** tab in the dialog box. Next, select the **Meters** option from the **Drawing Units** drop-down list and the **UTM, NAD 83 Datum** option from the **Categories** drop-down list.

3. In the **Available coordinate systems** drop-down list, select the **UTM with NAD83 Datum, Zone 11, Meter; Central Meridian 117d W** option and then choose the **Apply** button from the **Drawing Settings** dialog box. The drawing is set to UTM Zone 11 projection and the datum is set to NAD 83, refer to Figure 3-73.

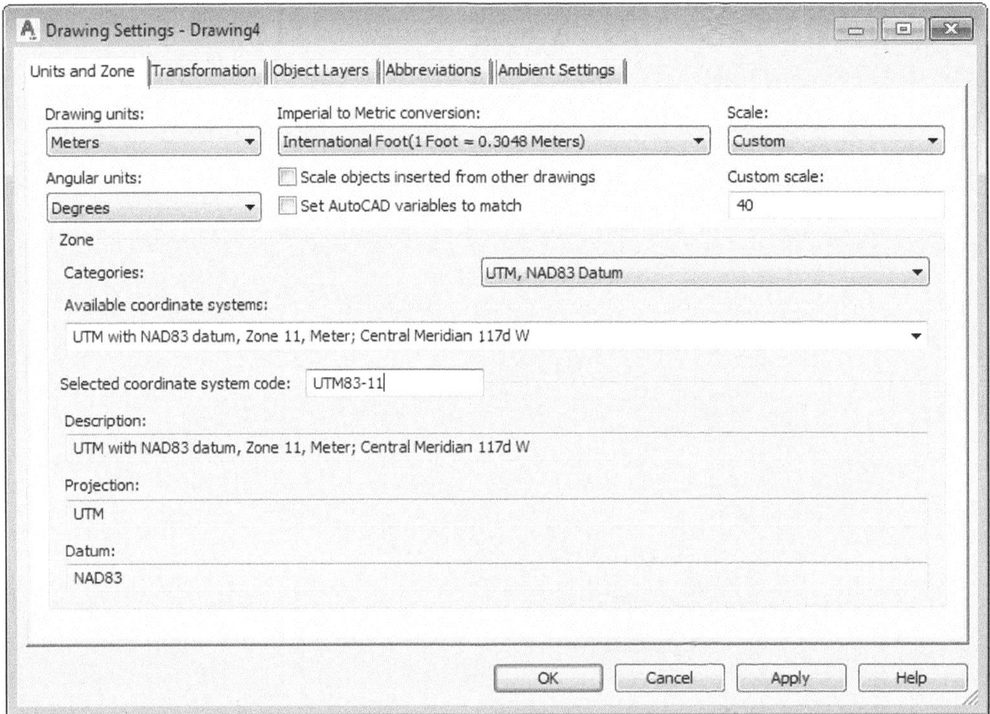

Figure 3-73 The settings in the ***Units and Zone*** *tab of the* ***Drawing Settings - Drawing 4*** *dialog box*

4. Next, choose the **Ambient Settings** tab. Expand the **Coordinate** node and click on the cell in the **Value** column corresponding to the **Unit** property; a drop-down list is displayed. Select the **meter** option from the drop-down list, as shown in Figure 3-74.

5. Expand the **Elevation** node and click on the cell in the **Value** column corresponding to the **Unit** property; a drop-down list is displayed. Select the **meter** option from the drop-down list.

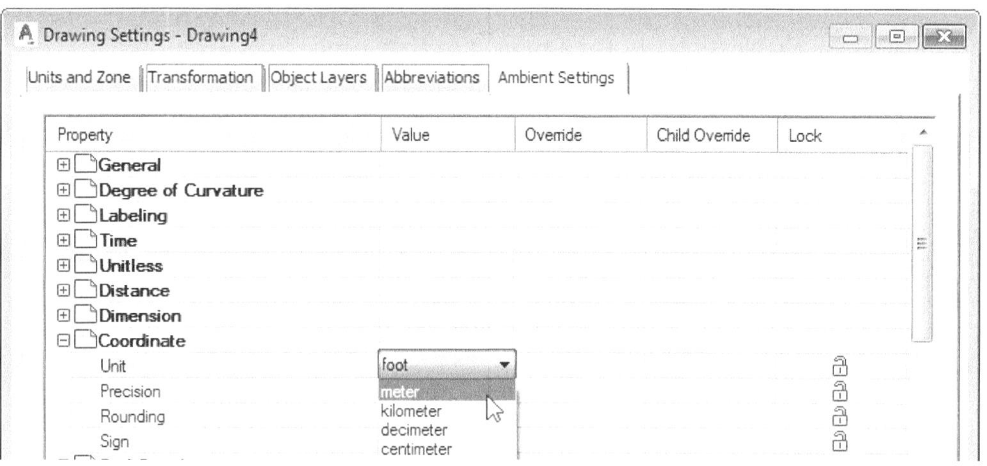

Figure 3-74 *Selecting the* ***meter*** *option for the* ***Unit*** *cell from the drop-down list*

6. Expand the **Lat Long** node and click on the cell in the **Value** column corresponding to the **Format** property; a drop-down list is displayed. Select the **decimal** option from the drop-down list.

7. Choose the **Apply** button to set the parameters and then choose the **OK** button; the **Drawing Settings** dialog box is closed.

Creating a Surface from GIS Data

1. Choose the **Create Surface from GIS Data** tool from **Home > Create Ground Data > Surfaces** drop-down; the **Object Options** page of the **Create Surface from GIS Data** wizard is displayed, as shown in Figure 3-75.

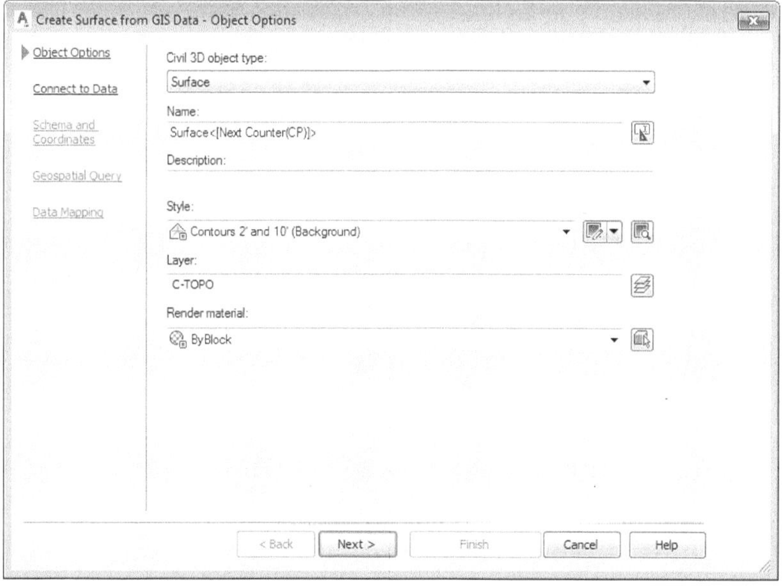

Figure 3-75 *The* ***Object Options*** *page of the* ***Create Surface from GIS Data*** *wizard*

2. In the **Name** text box, delete the existing text and type **LakeHenshawRegion** as the surface name. Choose the **Next** button; the **Connect to Data** page of the wizard is displayed.

3. In the **Data source type** area of this dialog box, select the **SHP** radio button.

4. In the **Connection parameter** area, choose the browse button corresponding to the **SHP path** edit box; the **Select a SHP file** dialog box is displayed.

5. Browse to the location *C:\c3d_2018\c03_c3d_2018_tut* and select the *LakeHenshaw-ElevationPoints* file. Choose the **Open** button; the **Select a SHP File** dialog box is closed and the path of the selected file is displayed in the **SHP path** text box.

6. Choose the **Login** button in the **Connect to Data** page; the **Schema and Coordinates** page of the wizard is displayed. In the **Schema and Coordinates** page, notice that the **LakeHenshaw-ElevationPoints** file is displayed under the **Feature class** column and its CRS is displayed under the **Coordinate system** column.

7. Now, select the check box for the **LakeHenshaw-ElevationPoints** file and choose the **Next** button; the **Geospatial Query** page of the wizard is displayed.

8. Accept the default settings in the **Geospatial Query** page and choose the **Next** button; the **Data Mapping** page is displayed.

9. In the **Map GIS data to Civil3D properties** list box of the **Data Mapping** page, click in the **Civil3D Property** cell corresponding to the **Contour** property; a drop-down list is displayed. Select **Elevation** from this drop-down list and choose **Finish** to exit the wizard.

10. Enter **ZE** at the Command prompt and press ENTER to zoom to the extent of the drawing. The surface created from GIS data is displayed, as shown in Figure 3-76.

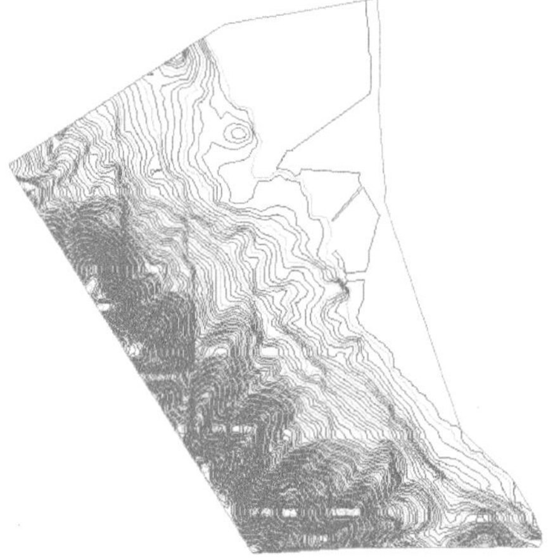

Figure 3-76 *Surface created from GIS data*

Inserting the Georeferenced Image

For the purpose of overlaying the raster on the surface, you shall use the **MAPIINSERT** command.

1. Enter **MAPIINSERT** command in the command line and press ENTER; the **Insert Image** dialog box is displayed.
2. In this dialog box, browse to the location *C:\c3d_2018\c03_c3d_2018_tut* and select the *LakeHenshaw.tif* file.
3. Next, choose the **Open** button; the **Insert Image** dialog box is closed and the **Image Correlation** dialog box is displayed.
4. In the **Source** tab of the **Image Correlation** dialog box, select the **World File** option from the **Correlation Source** drop-down list, if it is not selected. Make sure the values of the parameters in the **Source** tab of the dialog box are set, as shown in Figure 3-77.
5. Choose **OK** to close the **Image Correlation** dialog box.
6. Select the image and right-click; a shortcut menu is displayed. From the shortcut menu, choose the **Display Order** option; a flyout is displayed, as shown in Figure 3-78.

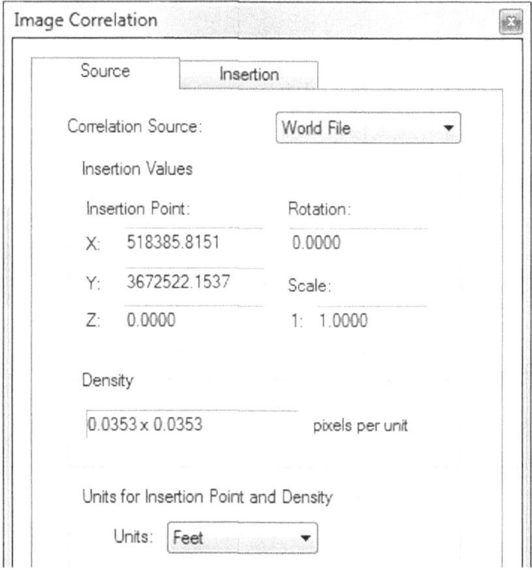

Figure 3-77 *The partial view of the* ***Image Correlation*** *dialog box*

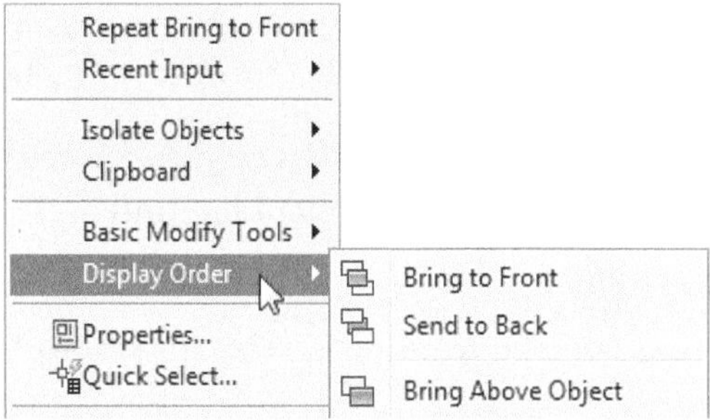

*Figure 3-78 The flyout showing the **Display Order** options*

7. Choose the **Send to Back** option from this flyout; the surface is now displayed over the image, as shown in Figure 3-79.

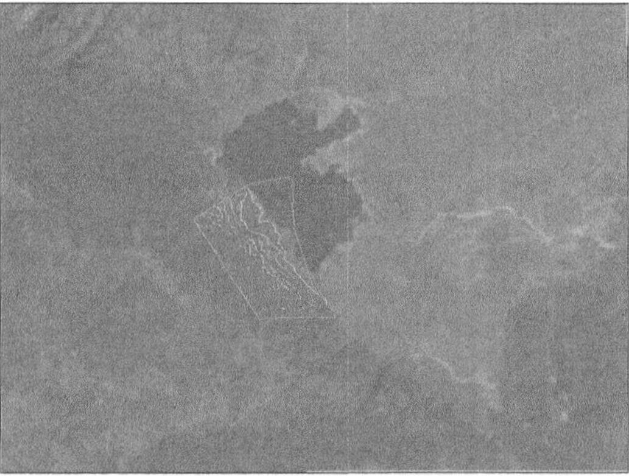

Figure 3-79 Surface displayed over the inserted raster image

Draping the Image

1. Choose the **Surface** tool from the **Ground Data** panel of the **Modify** tab; the **Surface** tab is displayed in the ribbon.

2. In this tab, choose the **Drape Image** tool from the **Surface Tools** panel; the **Drape Image** dialog box is displayed, as shown in Figure 3-80. Accept the default values in the dialog box and choose the **OK** button; the dialog box is closed and the image is draped over the surface.

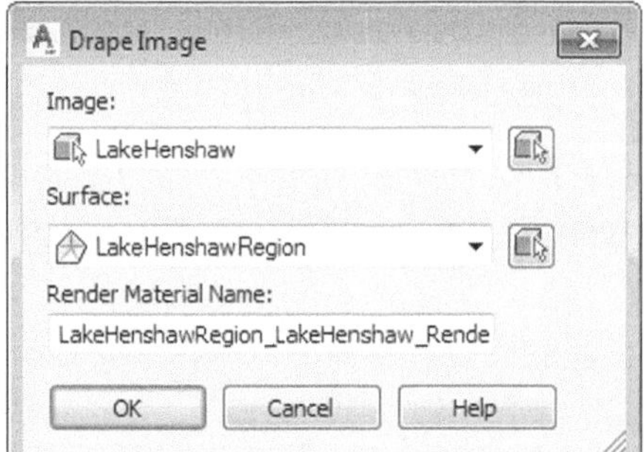

*Figure 3-80 The **Drape Image** dialog box*

Viewing the Image

1. Select the raster image and right-click; a shortcut menu is displayed.

2. Choose **Isolate Objects > Hide Selected Objects** from the shortcut menu.

3. Select the **Realistic** visual style from the **Visual Style** drop-down list in the **View** tab in the Ribbon.

4. Choose the **Orbit** tool from the **Navigation 2D** panel of the **View** tab and orient the drawing to a suitable viewing angle. Exit the **Orbit** tool by pressing the ESC key. The drawing area now shows the surface with draped raster image, as shown in Figure 3-81.

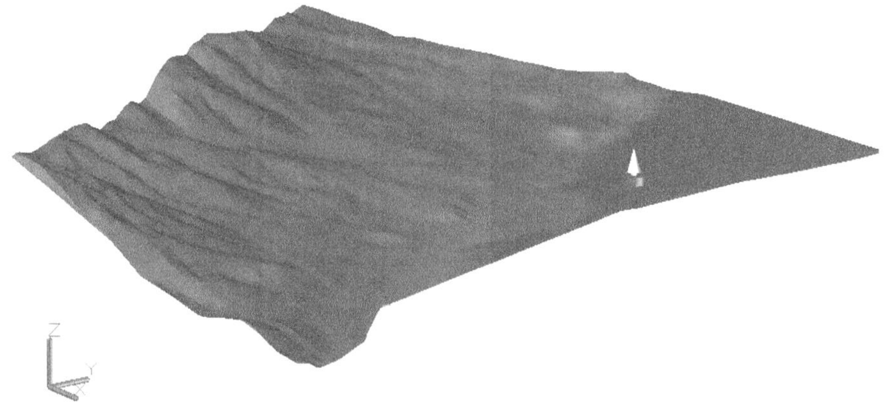

Figure 3-81 *The surface with the draped raster image*

Saving the File

1. Choose **Save As** from the **Application Menu**; the **Save Drawing As** dialog box is displayed.

2. In this dialog box, browse to the following folder:

   C:\c3d_2018\c03_c3d_2018_tut

3. In the **File name** edit box, enter **c03_tut03a**.

4. Next, choose the **Save** button; the file is saved with the given name at the specified location.

Self-Evaluation Test

Answer the following questions and then compare them to those given at the end of this chapter:

1. Which of the following tools is used to create a surface from a digital elevation model?

   a) **Create Surface**
   b) **Create Surface from DEM**
   c) **Create Surface from TIN**
   d) **Create Surface from GIS Data**

2. Which of the following properties in the **Add DEM Files** dialog box is used to change the coordinate system of the DEM file?

   a) **CS Code**
   b) **Datum**
   c) **Projection**
   d) None of these

3. Which of the following features can be represented by breaklines?

   a) Streams
   b) Retaining walls
   c) Ditches
   d) All of the above

4. Which of the following types of analysis places a slope directional arrow at the centroid of each triangle?

   a) **Slopes**
   b) **Slope Arrows**
   c) **Directions**
   d) **Elevations**

5. Which of the following options is used to control the visibility of the surface triangulation within or outside a defined region?

   a) **Boundaries**
   b) **Drawing Objects**
   c) **Breaklines**
   d) **Surface Styles**

6. The DEM is used to represent the ____________ of a continuously varying surface.

7. A surface boundary is a _________ entity and is also used to control the visibility of the surface triangulation.

8. In a Civil 3D drawing file, the _________ tab of the **TOOLSPACE** palette lists the available surface styles.

9. The _________ node in the **Prospector** tab of the **TOOLSPACE** palette lists the surfaces in the current drawing file.

10. A surface can be defined as a network of grids or TIN lines. (T/F)

11. You can use only point data to create a Civil 3D surface. (T/F)

12. The surface is not visible unless the data is added to it. (T/F)

13. You can create a volume surface by comparing two surfaces. (T/F)

14. You can add breaklines only to a TIN surface. (T/F)

15. The **Extract Objects** tool is used only to extract the triangles from the TIN surface. (T/F)

Review Questions

Answer the following questions:

1. The __________ tool is used to identify the flat areas and gaps in the surface after adding the contour data.

2. The __________ tab of the **Surface Properties** dialog box displays the overall view of the surface.

3. You need to use the __________ tool to create a surface from an SHP file.

4. You can create the __________ and __________ volume surfaces using the **Create Surface** tool.
5. The surface name is displayed in both the **Prospector** and **Settings** tabs of the **TOOLSPACE** palette. (T/F)

6. The volume surface is also known as differential surface. (T/F)

7. You can change the location of a surface point. (T/F)

8. You can change the display of the surface at any stage of the project by modifying the surface styles and surface properties. (T/F)

9. The objects which are extracted from the surface do not retain their original properties. (T/F)

10. The **Definition** subnode provides you with the surface edit options. (T/F)

EXERCISES

1. Log on to *www.cadcim.com* and browse to *Textbooks > Civil/GIS > Civil 3D > Exploring AutoCAD Civil 3D 2018*. Next, select *c03_c3d_2018_exer.zip* file from the **Exercise Files** drop-down list. Choose the corresponding **Download** button to download the data file.

2. Now, save and extract the downloaded folder to the following location:

   C:\c3d_2018

Note

While opening the exercise files, the ***PANORAMA*** *window may appear with an error message. Close this window to proceed further.*

Exercise 1 DEM Surface

Create a surface from *c03_c3d_2018_ex01.dem* file. Also, create a new surface style in the **Contours** tab of the **Surface Style - New Surface Style** dialog box using the following parameters:

(Expected time: 30 min)

1. Contour Display Mode: **Exaggerate Elevations**
2. Scale Factor: **3**
3. Minor Interval: **10**
4. Contour Smoothening: **True**
5. Smoothening type: **Spline curve**

Hint:

Settings in the **Display** tab

1. In **Plan** view direction, turn on the visibility of **Borders**, **Minor Contours**, and **Major Contours**.

2. Set the color of **Border** to **blue**, **Minor Contour** to **red**, and **Major Contour** to **green**.

3. In the **Model View** direction, turn off the visibility of **Border** and turn on the visibility of **Major Contour** and **Minor Contour** and set the color of **Minor Contour** to **magenta** and **Major Contour** to **cyan**.

Assign the newly created surface style to the surface and then choose the **SE Isometric** option from the list box in the **Views** panel of the **View** tab to view the surface. The SE Isometric view of the DEM Surface after assigning the new surface style is displayed, as shown in Figure 3-82.

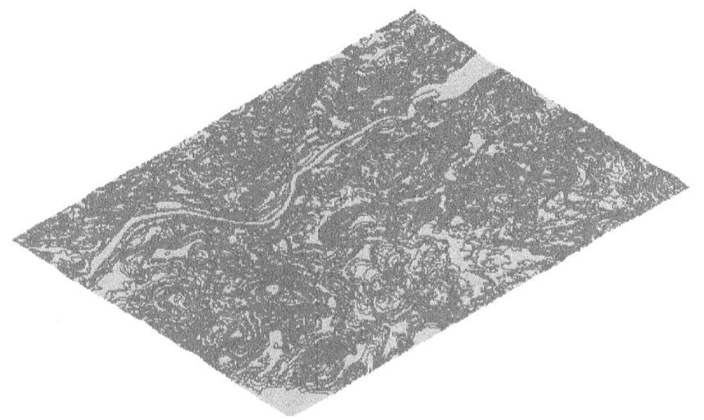

Figure 3-82 The SE Isometric view of the DEM Surface after assigning the new surface style

Exercise 2 Drape Image

Create a surface from *c03_c3d_2018_ex02.dem* file, and insert and drape *c03_c3d_2018_ex02_image.tif* file over the surface using the following parameters: **(Expected time: 45 min)**

1. Coordinate System: **UTM with NAD27 datum, Zone 10, Meter**

2. Drawing Units: **Meter**

Hint:

Set the units for insertion point and density in feet during image insertion.

Answers to Self-Evaluation Test

1. b, **2.** a, **3.** d, **4.** b, **5.** a, **6.** Surface elevation, **7.** Polygon, **8.** **Settings**, **9.** **Surfaces**, **10.** T, **11** F, **12.** T, **13.** T, **14.** T, **15.** F

Chapter 4

Surface Volumes and Analysis

Learning Objectives

After completing this chapter, you will be able to:

- *Understand the concept of surface volumes*
- *Compute surface volumes*
- *Understand the concept of surface analysis*
- *Perform surface analysis*
- *Create and add legend tables*

SURFACE VOLUMES

Earthwork estimation is an important part of any Civil Engineering project. Civil 3D provides you with a streamlined method to calculate total cut, fill, and net volumes of earthwork between two surfaces. The earthwork volumes between two surfaces can be calculated either by creating a volume surface (third surface) or by directly calculating the total cut and fill volumes between them.

Civil 3D makes earthwork calculations simple and fast. For earthwork calculations, you need two surfaces. Civil 3D analyzes both surfaces and calculates the total volume of cut and fill by comparing the vertical distance between points in these surfaces. The distance between the elevations of two surfaces can then be used to create a third surface, known as volume surface. The various methods to calculate the surface volumes are discussed next.

Volumes Dashboard

Ribbon: Analyze > Volumes and Materials > Volumes Dashboard
Command: VOLUMESDASHBOARD

Using the Volumes dashboard, you can break the surfaces in phases or parcels for volume analysis. The tools in the dashboard can be used to calculate and analyze the volume in multiple volume surfaces and bounded areas, which fall within the boundary of the volume surfaces. In the dashboard, you can save and use the information of the analysis across multiple drawing sessions. The result of volume analysis can be exported as a summary report or can be inserted into the drawing using the dashboard.

To calculate surface volumes, choose the **Volumes Dashboard** tool from the **Volumes and Materials** panel of the **Analyze** tab; the **PANORAMA** window with the **Volumes Dashboard** tab will be displayed, as shown in Figure 4-1.

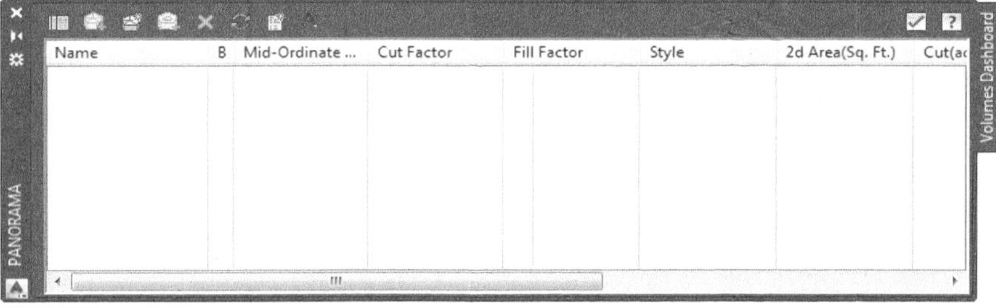

***Figure 4-1** The **PANORAMA** window with the **Volumes Dashboard** tab*

Components of Volumes Dashboard

The various tools displayed in the **Volumes Dashboard** tab of the **PANORAMA** window that are used to calculate volume surfaces and generate report are discussed next.

Toggle Net Graph Panel

The **Toggle Net Graph Panel** button is used to toggle the display of the auxiliary panel. This panel displays the total volume (cut and fill), net volume, and cut and fill graph for the selected volume surfaces or bounded areas. To display the surface statistics in the panel, select one or more surfaces using the corresponding check box.

Add Volume Surface

You can choose the **Add Volume Surface** button to add an existing volume surface to the Volumes dashboard.

Note

*The **Add Volume Surface** button remains inactive if no volume surface exists in the current drawing.*

Create new volume surface

You can choose the **Create new volume surface** button to create and add a new volume surface to the Volumes dashboard. On choosing this button, the **Create Surface** dialog box will be displayed. Select the appropriate volume surface type from the options in the **Type** drop-down list. Specify base surface and comparison surface in the **Volume Surface** node. To specify the base surface, click in the corresponding **Value** cell; a browse button appears in the cell. Choose the browse button; the **Select Base Surface** dialog box is displayed. In the dialog box, select the required surface and choose the **OK** button. The dialog box closes and the name of the selected surface now appears in the **Value** cell of the base surface in the **Create Surface** dialog box.

Note

*You are required to specify the values for the **Grid Parameters** when you choose the **Grid volume surface** option from the **Type** drop-down list.*

Add Bounded Volume

You can choose the **Add Bounded Volume** button to limit the area for volume calculation of a surface to a specified region. You can use AutoCAD entities such as Polyline, Polyline (3D), Polyline (2D), Parcel Segment, Feature Line, Circle, Ellipse, Survey Figure, and Parcel to define the boundary of the area.

Note

*You must create and select a volume surface in the **Volumes Dashboard** tab to activate the **Add Bounded Volume** button.*

To add a bounded volume to the surface, choose the **Add Bounded Volume** button; you will be prompted to select the bounding object.Select the bounding object in the drawing area; the bounded volume is added to the surface and the volume calculations are displayed in the surface node.

Remove Selected Entry

You can choose the **Remove Selected Entry** button to delete the selected row from the **Volumes Dashboard** tab of the **PANORAMA** window.

Re-compute volumes

You can choose the **Re-compute volumes** button to recalculate the volume. This tool is useful where an updated surface requires recalculations of volume.

Generate Cut/Fill Report

You can choose this button to generate the cut or fill reports from the selected volume surfaces and bounded areas.

Note

*The **Cut/Fill Report** is generated and displayed in a new browser. You can save the report as a file to include in your project report.*

Insert Cut/Fill Summary

You can choose this button to insert the result of surface volume calculations into the drawing in tabular form. To insert the table, choose the **Insert Cut/Fill Summary** button; you will be prompted to specify the point of insertion. Click in the drawing area to specify insertion point; the **Cut/Fill Summary** will be added at the specified location.

Composite Volumes

In the composite volume method, the cut, fill, and net volumes are calculated by using a pair of surfaces consisting of a top (Comparison) and a bottom (Base) surface. The Base surface is the existing ground surface and the Comparison surfacc will bc thc proposed surface. Civil 3D analyzes and compares the two surfaces to calculate the difference of elevation between each vertex point of the TIN or a cell in the Grid surfaces or at the intersection of the triangle edges of two surfaces. This elevation difference is then used to create a TIN volume or a TIN grid surface.

To use the composite volume method, type **reportsurfacevolume** in the command line; the **PANORAMA** window with the **Composite Volumes** tab will be displayed, as shown in Figure 4-2. The components of the tab and the method used for computing composite volume are discussed next.

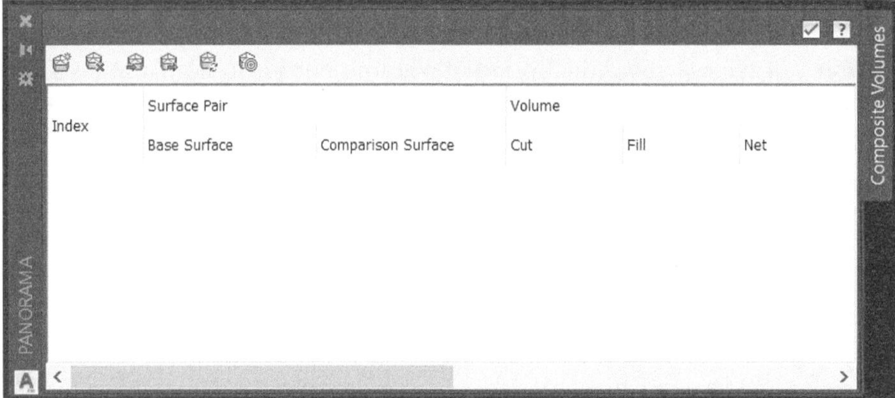

*Figure 4-2 The **PANORAMA** window with the **Composite Volumes** tab*

Components of Composite Volumes Tab

The components in this tab help you to calculate the volume based on the existing and proposed surface. The components are used to calculate the net volume by comparing the two surfaces. Volumes are also calculated for the purpose of cut and fill. The options available in this tab are discussed next.

Create new volume entry

You can choose the **Create new volume entry** button to create a new composite volume entry.

Delete volume entry

You can choose the **Delete volume entry** button to delete the existing composite volume entry from the **PANORAMA** window.

Import volume entries from file

You can choose the **Import volume entries from file** button to import the existing composite volume entries from a file. The file should be in XML format. On choosing this button, the **Import Volume Entries** dialog box will be displayed. Select the required XML file of the volume entry from this dialog box and choose the **Open** button; the volume entries will be imported and added to the **PANORAMA** window.

Export volume entries to file

You can choose the **Export volume entries to file** button to export volume entries. On choosing this button, the **Export Volume Entries** dialog box will be displayed. Specify a name for the file in the **File name** edit box and choose the **Save** button; the file will be saved in the XML format at the specified location.

Recompute volumes

You can choose the **Recompute volumes** button to recalculate volumes. This button is used when you have updated or edited any surface of the surface pair. Civil 3D recomputes the volumes based on the changes made in the surface.

Create new volume entry from surfaces

You can choose the **Create new volume entries from surfaces** button to create a volume entry by selecting surfaces from the drawing. Civil 3D prompts to select a base and a comparison surface when the **Create new volume entries from surfaces** button is chosen. Select the surfaces from the drawing; the cut and fill volumes will be displayed in the **PANORAMA** window.

Computing Composite Volumes

To calculate composite volumes, first you need to make a composite volume entry in the **PANORAMA** window. To add a new volume entry, choose the **Create new volume entry** button; the new volume entry will be displayed in the list box. Next, in the **Surface Pair** column, click on **<select surface>** in the **Base Surface** sub-column and select the required base surface from the drop-down list. Similarly, select a comparison surface from the **Comparison Surface** column and press ENTER or click on the free space in the window. The total cut and fill volumes will be calculated and then displayed in the **Volume** column of the following sub-columns:

Cut

The **Cut** sub-column displays the quantity of material to be removed from the Base surface to make it equal to the Comparison surface.

Fill

The **Fill** sub-column displays the quantity of earth material to be added to the Base surface, thus making it equal to the Comparison surface.

Net

The **Net** sub-column displays the net difference between the cut and fill volume of the two surfaces.

Net Graph

The **Net Graph** column shows the percentage representation of the net volume, net cut volume, and net fill volume. The red bar in this graph indicates the net cut volume, which signifies the extra material that needs to be removed from the existing site. The green bar indicates that the material needs to be added to the existing site.

The **Cut Factor** and **Fill Factor** columns display the cut and fill factor values for the specified surface. These values are used to calculate the net volume of material required to cut or fill the base surface so as to make it conform to the planned (Comparison) surface. The net material required to cut or fill the base surface on applying the cut or fill factor is displayed in the **Cut (adjusted)** and **Fill (adjusted)** columns, respectively.

Bounded Volumes

This method helps you to calculate the volume of a surface or specified part of a surface. The area, whose volume has to be calculated, can be defined by a bounding polygon or a parcel. The bounded volume can be calculated using a volume surface or any other surface. In case of volume surfaces, the volume is calculated using the difference in elevation between two surfaces. For terrain surfaces, the volume is calculated from zero elevation to the elevation in the area bounded by a polygon or parcel.

To calculate the bounded volume between two specified areas, enter **reportsurfboundedvolume** in the command line; you will be prompted to select the bounding polygon. Select the polygon that bounds the required area; the cut, fill, and net volumes will be displayed in the command line. Alternatively, press the F2 key to display the bounded volume results in the **AutoCAD Text Window**.

CREATING VOLUME SURFACES

The volume surfaces help you review earthwork calculations of a site. The volume surface is a surface that is created by using the elevation difference between two surfaces. You can then analyze the surface and review the total amount of the cut or fill volume so that a balance between the total cut and fill volumes can be produced on the site. Civil 3D allows you to create two types of volume surfaces. The methods to create these volume surfaces are discussed next.

Creating the TIN Volume Surface

Ribbon:	Home > Create Ground Data > Surfaces drop-down > Create Surface
Command:	CREATESURFACE

To create a TIN volume surface, you need a pair of TIN surfaces. In Civil 3D, you can create a TIN volume surface by choosing the **Create Surface** tool from the **Create Ground Data** panel, as discussed in the previous chapter. On doing so, the **Create Surface** dialog box will be displayed. Next, select the **TIN volume surface** option from the **Type** drop-down list in this dialog box. Specify the name, style, and description of the surface in the respective **Value** fields. Next, click in the **Value** field of the **Base Surface** property; a browse button will be displayed. Choose this button to display the **Select Base Surface** dialog box. In this dialog box, select the required option from the list box and then choose the **OK** button; the **Select Base Surface** dialog box will be closed. Similarly, select the Comparison surface from the **Select Comparison Surface** dialog box. Specify the cut and fill factors for the material. Now, choose the **OK** button from the **Create Surface** dialog box; the dialog box will be closed and a TIN volume surface will be created and added to the **Surfaces** node. You can edit and analyze this surface the same way as you analyze to any other surface.

Note

*Due to increase in volume, the **Cut Factor** for the excavated material will be greater than 1 while the **Fill Factor** will be less than 1 as the volume of the filling material decreases due to compaction.*

Creating the Grid Volume Surface

Ribbon: Home > Create Ground Data > Surfaces drop-down > Create Surface
Command: CREATESURFACE

You can create a grid volume surface by using a pair of grid surfaces. To create a Grid volume surface, first you need to create a grid surface, as discussed in previous chapter. Next, choose the **Create Surface** tool from the **Create Ground Data** panel; the **Create Surface** dialog box will be displayed. Select **Grid volume surface** from the **Type** drop-down list; the properties of the grid volume surface will be displayed in the **Properties** column of the dialog box. Specify the information such as name, description, and style for the grid volume surface in the respective **Value** fields. Similarly, you can specify the grid parameters such as grid spacing in both X and Y directions and also in the grid's orientation. Next, select the Base surface as well as the Comparison surface as explained in the previous section. Enter the cut and fill factors and then choose the **OK** button. The **Create Surface** dialog box will be closed and the grid volume surface will be added in the **Surfaces** node.

SURFACE ANALYSIS

Ribbon: Surface > Modify > Surface Properties drop-down > Surface Properties
Command: EDITSURFACEPROPERTIES

After creating a surface, you need to analyze it for collecting information from it. This information can be used in the development of the project design. Surface analyses helps you understand and visualize the surface topography in a better way. For example, if you are generating the slope analyses of a surface, it would help you to find slopes of various points in the surface. Civil 3D supports seven ways to analyze a surface. These are Contours, Directions, Elevations, Slopes, Slope Arrows, Watersheds, and User-defined contours.

To carry out a surface analysis, choose the **Surface Properties** tool from the **Modify** panel; the **Surface Properties - <surface name>** dialog box will be displayed. In this dialog box, choose the **Analysis** tab; the options in this tab will be displayed, as shown in Figure 4-3.

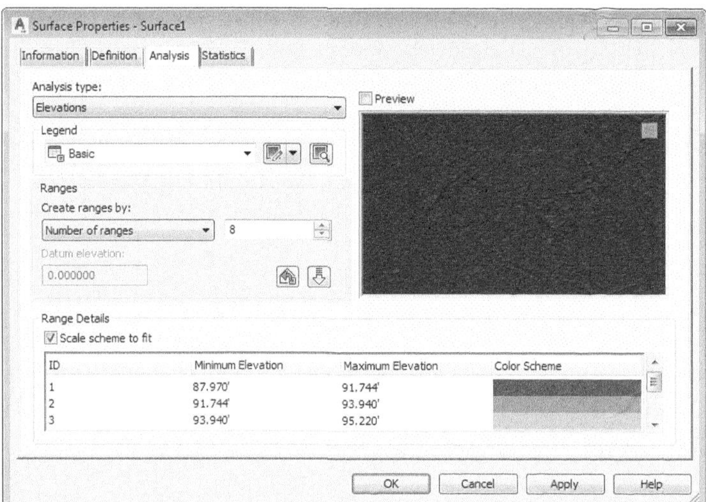

Figure 4-3 *The options displayed in the* ***Analysis*** *tab of the* ***Surface Properties*** *dialog box*

Note

If there are multiple surfaces in the drawing, you will be prompted to select a surface. To select a surface from the list, press ENTER; the ***Select a Surface*** *dialog box will be displayed. Select the required surface using this dialog box.*

Alternatively, choose the **Prospector** tab in the **TOOLSPACE** palette and expand the **Surfaces** node. Right-click on the required surface in the **Surfaces** node; a shortcut menu will be displayed. Choose the **Surface Properties** option from the shortcut menu; the **Surface Properties - <surface name>** dialog box will be displayed.

In the **Analysis** tab, select the required option from the **Analysis type** drop-down list. The options in this drop-down list are used to analyze the elevation, contour, slope, directions, Slope Arrows, and Watershed. After selecting the analysis type, select the legend style from the drop-down list in the **Legend** area. Legend is a tabular representation of the Surface analysis data. You can create legend style depending upon the information that you want to display in the legend table. You can select the **Preview** check box to preview the created legend style. Note that the preview of the legend is displayed only after running the analysis. Next, in the **Ranges** area, specify the number of ranges in the **Number** spinner; the surface data will be divided into the specified number of ranges and analyzed accordingly. After specifying the number of ranges, choose the **Run analysis** button; the result of the analysis will be displayed in tabular form in the **Range Details** area. This result table may have different columns depending on the analysis type selected. In the **Range Details** area, the **Scale scheme to fit** check box is selected by default. This check box scales the number of entries in the **Scheme** column of the **Range Details** area to cover the ranges uniformly. This implies that a uniform sampling is taken from the scheme between the first and last entries in the **Scheme** column. After performing the analysis, you can preview the information of the legend in the **Preview** area. Choose the **OK** button to close the dialog box.

To visualize the analysis results in the drawing, select the surface that you have analyzed and right-click to display a shortcut menu and then choose the **Edit Surface Style** option from it; the **Surface Style - <style name>** dialog box will be displayed. By default, the **Display** tab is chosen in the dialog box. In this tab, turn on the layers of those components whose results you want to view from the analysis. For example, if you run the Elevation analysis of the surface, you need to turn on the visibility of the **Elevations** component in the **Surface Style** dialog box. The methods for performing various types of analyses by using the options in the **Analysis type** drop-down list are discussed next.

Contour Analysis

The **Contours** option in the **Analysis type** drop-down is used to analyze and display surface contours by using different colors and linetypes. To analyze contours, select the **Contours** option from the **Analysis type** drop-down list of the **Surface Properties - <surface name>** dialog box. The **Legend** area displays the default legend style for the selected analysis type. Civil 3D has an in-built legend style for each of its analysis types. However, you can create your own legend style and display the required information in the legend. This is discussed later in this chapter. In the **Analysis** tab, you can also preview the legend style. To preview the legend tables with analysis information, select the **Preview** check box. You can also add legend tables to the drawing, which is also discussed later in this chapter.

In the Contour analysis, you can divide and group surface contours in different number of ranges based on their elevations. To do so, specify the desired value in the **Number** spinner in the **Ranges** area of the **Analysis** tab. The contours will be grouped depending on the value specified in the **Number** spinner.

In the **Range Details** area of the **Analysis** tab, each contour range is assigned a maximum and a minimum elevation. The major and minor ranges of this contour range are assigned a specific color, linetype, and lineweight. The value of the results can be modified in this area.

On specifying the legend properties and the number of ranges, perform the Contour analysis by choosing the **Run analysis** button. Next, choose the **Apply** button and then the **OK** button to close the **Surface Properties - <surface name>** dialog box. To view contours in the surface, you need to turn on the visibility of the major and minor contours in the **Display** tab of the **Surface Styles** dialog box.

Note

*The **Range** area of the **Analysis** tab is used to display the default value of the number of ranges for each analysis type. This default value is derived from the range settings in the **Surface Style** dialog box.*

Direction Analysis

The **Directions** option in the **Analysis type** drop-down list of the **Analysis** tab is used to classify surface triangles on the basis of the direction they face. Direction analysis generates aspect map that graphically displays the surface slopes with reference to the cardinal direction. For analyzing the surface, select the **Directions** option from the **Analysis type** drop-down list of the **Surface Properties - <surface name>** dialog box. Specify the options in the **Legend** area, as discussed earlier. In the **Ranges** area, specify the value in the **Number** spinner and choose the **Run analysis** button; the result of this analysis will be displayed in terms of maximum and minimum directions of each range with the assigned color scheme in the **Range Details** area of the **Analysis** tab.

You can modify the maximum and minimum direction values and the color scheme for a particular range by double-clicking on default values in the respective columns of the **Range Details** area. After modifying these values, choose **Apply** and then the **OK** button to close the dialog box. To view the results of the Direction analysis, turn on the visibility of the **Directions** component in the **Surface Style** dialog box.

Elevations Analysis

The Elevations analysis is the most important type of Surface analysis. It is used to group the surface triangles based on their elevation. It helps the site planners review and judge the total amount of earthwork required to create a leveled finished surface. To run this type of analysis, select the **Elevations** option from the **Analysis type** drop-down list in the **Analysis** tab of the **Surface Properties - <surface name>** dialog box. Specify the options in the **Legend** area as discussed earlier. In the **Ranges** area, select the required option from the **Create ranges by** drop-down list. You will need to set the value in the spinner, if you select the **Number of ranges** option from the drop-down list. Next, run the analysis; the details such as maximum elevation, minimum elevation, and color scheme for each range of elevation will be displayed in the **Range Details** area of the **Analysis** tab. Also, elevation bands will be displayed in different shades of color specified in the **Color Scheme** property of the **Analysis** tab in the **Surface Style** dialog box. You can also modify the color scheme in the **Surface Style** dialog box. Note that the default color scheme selected is **Blue**.

Alternatively, in the **Analysis** tab of the **Surface Properties - <surface name>** dialog box, you can change the color of each range by double-clicking on the default color in the column and selecting the color from the **Select Color** dialog box. After modifying the color or elevation values of a range, choose the **Apply** button in the **Select Color** dialog box. To view the Elevation analysis results, turn on the visibility of **Elevations** in the **Display** tab of the **Surface Style <name>** dialog box. To invoke this dialog box, select the required surface from the **Surfaces** node in the **Prospector** tab and right-click; a shortcut menu will be displayed. Choose the **Edit Surface Style** option from the shortcut menu; the **Surface Style <name>** dialog box will be displayed. In this dialog box, choose the **Display** tab and turn on the visibility of the **Elevations** layer. Choose **Apply** and then the **OK** button. On doing so, you will see different elevation bands represented by different colors, as shown in Figure 4-4.

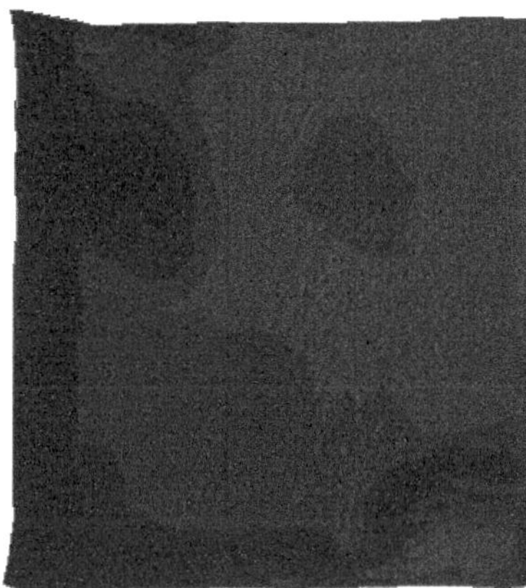

Figure 4-4 *Elevation bands represented by different colors*

Slopes Analysis

The Slopes analysis is another important analysis carried out to analyze varying slopes in the surface. The slope of a surface is defined as a change in its elevation over a certain distance. It can be expressed as a ratio or a percentage (grade). For example, slope of 4:1 means an elevation raise of one unit for a distance of four units. In percentage, it can be expressed as 25% of grade. Similarly, a slope of 3: -1 means an elevation fall of one unit for a distance of three units. In percentage, it can be expressed as a grade of -33%. The **Slopes** option in the **Analysis type** drop-down is used to display the slope of the ground. In Slope analysis, the surface triangles are grouped according to their slope. Each range is assigned a color and the triangles in a particular slope based on range will be displayed using the same color scheme.

To analyze slopes, select the **Slopes** option from the **Analysis type** drop-down list of the **Surface Properties - <surface name>** dialog box. Specify the options in the **Legend** area as discussed earlier. In the **Ranges** area, specify the value in the **Number** spinner as discussed earlier and choose the **Run analysis** button; the result of this analysis will be displayed in terms of the minimum and maximum slope values in the **Range Details** area.

Turn on the visibility of **Slopes** in the **Display** tab of the **Surface Style** dialog box; triangles will be displayed according to the color scheme of the slope range they belong to. Civil 3D calculates the slopes of triangles of the TIN surface at their centroids. The result of the Slope analysis helps the designers and engineers in designing the drainage and sewer systems.

Slope Arrows Analysis

The **Slope Arrows** option in the **Analysis type** drop-down list is used to perform Surface analysis on the basis of the directions of slopes of the triangles. The result of this analysis is displayed using the direction arrows. These arrows show the slope direction and are placed at the centroid of each triangle in a TIN surface. The slope arrows pointing each other represent a valley whereas the arrows pointing away from each other signify a hill. In the Watershed analysis, the slope arrows represent the direction of the water flow across the surface.

To analyze slope directions, select the **Slope Arrows** option from the **Analysis type** drop-down list of the **Surface Properties-<surface name>** dialog box. Specify the options in the **Legend** area as discussed earlier. In the **Ranges** area, specify the value in the **Number** spinner, as discussed earlier and choose the **Run analysis** button; the result of this analysis will be displayed in terms of the minimum and maximum slope values in the **Range Details** area.

After performing the analysis, turn on the visibility of **slopes arrows** in the **Display** tab of the **Surface Style** dialog box. You will notice that the slope arrows are displayed according to their color range. Figure 4-5 shows the slope arrows after running the Slope Arrows analysis.

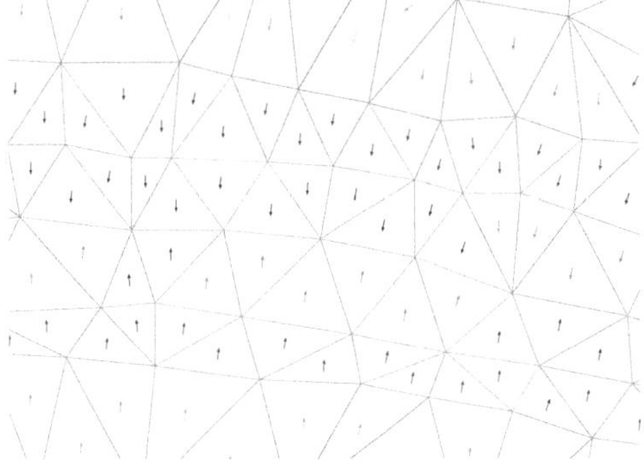

Figure 4-5 *Slope arrows displayed on performing the Slopes Arrows analysis*

Note

*The **Slopes** analysis and the **Slope Arrows** analysis display the same information. But the Slope analysis displays results through colored triangles, whereas the Slope Arrows analysis displays results using the coloured slope arrows.*

User-defined Contours Analysis

The **User-defined contours** option in the **Analysis type** drop-down is used to carry out the analysis for the User-defined contour lines of the surface. These contour lines are defined according to their elevation ranges. For example, consider that the site on which you are working has contour lines upto 100 feet of elevation and your project requires analyzing contours upto 70 feet. In such a case, you can use the User-defined contours analysis. This analysis divides the surface and displays contour lines at specified contour intervals upto the elevation range defined by the user. As a result, in the example discussed above, after performing this analysis, the surface will display contour lines upto a range of 70 feet at specific contour intervals. Moreover, the contour lines are displayed in different colors, linetype, and lineweight.

To analyze User- defined contours, select the **User-defined contours** option from the **Analysis type** drop-down list of the **Surface Properties - <surface name>** dialog box. Specify the options in the **Legend** area as discussed earlier. In the **Ranges** area, specify the value in the **Number** spinner as discussed earlier and choose the **Run analysis** button; the result of this analysis is displayed in terms of elevation in the **Range Details** area. In this analysis, the contour lines are segregated according to a specific elevation assigned with a unique combination of colors, linetype, and lineweight upto a range that can be modified. To view the contours, turn on the visibility of **Use Contours** in the **Display** tab of the **Surface Style** dialog box.

Figures 4-6 and 4-7 show the **Range Details** area of the Contour analysis and the User-defined Contours analysis, respectively. A comparison between these two analysis types shows that the Contour analysis displays the maximum and minimum elevations for a range whereas the User-defined analysis shows contour lines at a specified interval and elevation and within a defined range.

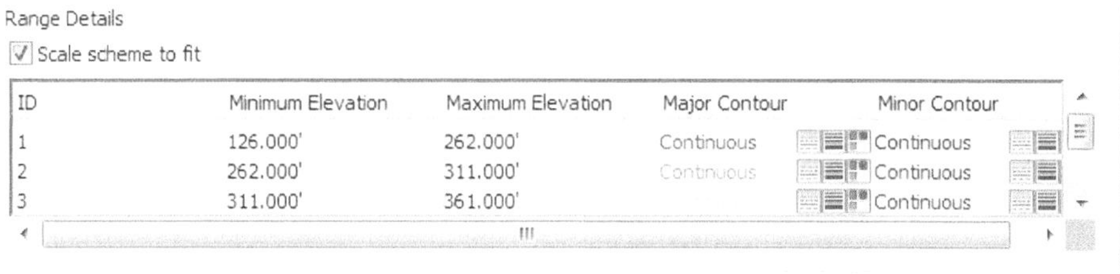
Range Details

☑ Scale scheme to fit

ID	Minimum Elevation	Maximum Elevation	Major Contour	Minor Contour
1	126.000'	262.000'	Continuous	Continuous
2	262.000'	311.000'	Continuous	Continuous
3	311.000'	361.000'		Continuous

Figure 4-6 *The* ***Range Details*** *area of the Contour analysis*

Range Details

ID	Description	Elevation	Display
1	Contour 1	20.000'	Continuous
2	Contour 2	30.000'	Continuous
3	Contour 3	40.000'	

Figure 4-7 *The* ***Range Details*** *area of the user-defined Contour analysis*

Watersheds Analysis

Watershed is an area that is drained by watercourse. It is the area of land that catches rain, snow, and other forms of precipitation, and then drains it to another watercourse such as river, lake, and so on. The TIN lines of the surface are used to calculate the areas through which the water would flow along the surface. These areas help you determine the drain targets. Drain target is an area from where the water flow stops or passes over the surface. The region of the surface from where water drains to these targets is called a watershed.

In Civil 3D, the Watersheds analysis helps you analyze the flow of water along and off the surface by determining the regions or watersheds. Various types of watersheds and Watershed Analyses are discussed next.

Type of Watersheds

Depending on the type of drain targets, watershed is classified into six types. These types are discussed next.

Boundary Point Watershed

In this type of watershed, the drain target point is the boundary point. The boundary point is the lowest point at the end of the channel.

Boundary Segment Watershed

If an edge on the surface boundary belongs to a triangle that slopes down toward it, the water flow will find its path along this edge and flows off the surface. A boundary segment watershed is a sequence of connection of such edges, which are the drain target of the water flow.

Depression Watershed

A depression is a set of connected points that are at the same elevation and whose neighbors are at higher elevation. This connected set of points is a single drain target where the water flow has no downhill place to go.

In a Depression watershed, the drain target is determined by a set of points at lower elevation than the surrounding points. This type of watershed is classified into two types, namely Ambiguous Depression and Shallow Depression.

The Ambiguous Depression watershed does not include any drain targets but water flowing on it can reach more than one drain target. This type of watershed is created when the depth of the Depression watershed is less than the threshold depth of the watershed and there are multiple neighboring watersheds at the points of minimum elevation of the boundary.

The Shallow Depression watershed is determined by the average depth of Depression watershed when it is filled to overflow. The average depth of depression is determined by dividing the volume of water in the depression by the area of the top surface of water. When this depth is less than the user-specified threshold depth, the Depression watershed is known as Shallow Depression watershed.

Flat Area Watershed

The Flat Area watershed is defined as the flat region from where the water can drain to other drain targets besides the flat area. A flat area is defined as a connected set of triangles in which vertices of all the triangles have the same elevation.

Multi-drain Watershed

The Multi-drain watershed is a split channel and water flowing through it can drain into multiple channels. Civil 3D keeps a record of the watersheds into which the water from the Multi-drain watersheds can drain.

Multi-drain Notch Watershed

In this type of watershed, a notch is formed by the two points of a flat edge and the water can flow to multi drains from the notch.

Running the Watershed Analysis

To run the Watershed analysis, select the **Watersheds** option from the **Analysis type** drop-down list of the **Surface Properties** dialog box. The options displayed in the **Analysis** tab of the **Surface Properties** dialog box are discussed next.

In the **Watershed Parameters** area of this tab, the **Merge depressions into single drain targets when Minimum Average Depth is less than** edit box is used to specify the minimum average depth of a depression in the surface on which a watershed can be created. This will avoid the minor depression depths from being defined as watersheds. Enter a value in this edit box to specify the minimum average depth of the depression in the surface at which a watershed is to be created. All the depressions with a depth less than the specified value will be ignored automatically, and therefore will not be considered as watersheds.

Alternatively, select the **Merge adjacent boundary watersheds** check box to enable all the boundary segments or boundary point watersheds along the outer boundary surface to be merged. Now, choose the **Run analysis** button to run the **Watershed** analysis; the details of the analysis will be displayed in various columns of the **Range Details** area, as shown in Figure 4-8.

In the **Range Details** area, the **ID** column displays the index number of every range. The **Type** column displays the type of watershed in that range. The bulb icon in this column indicates the visibility of the watershed. You can turn the visibility of the watershed on or off at any range. The **Drains Into** column specifies the sub areas into which the watershed drains.

For example, 101,103 indicate that the watershed drains into the sub-areas 101,103. The **Segment Display** column shows the segments of the watershed sub-areas. You can change the display of these segments by changing the lineweight, linetype, and color of the sub-area segments. To do so, choose the required button from the **Segment Display** column. The **Area Display** column specifies the hatch pattern that is used to represent the watershed sub-area. Choose the required button from this column to display the **Hatch Properties** dialog box. You can use this dialog box to specify a hatch pattern. To change the color of the hatch pattern, choose the button on the right of the hatch pattern and select the color from the **Select Color** dialog box that will be displayed after choosing the button.

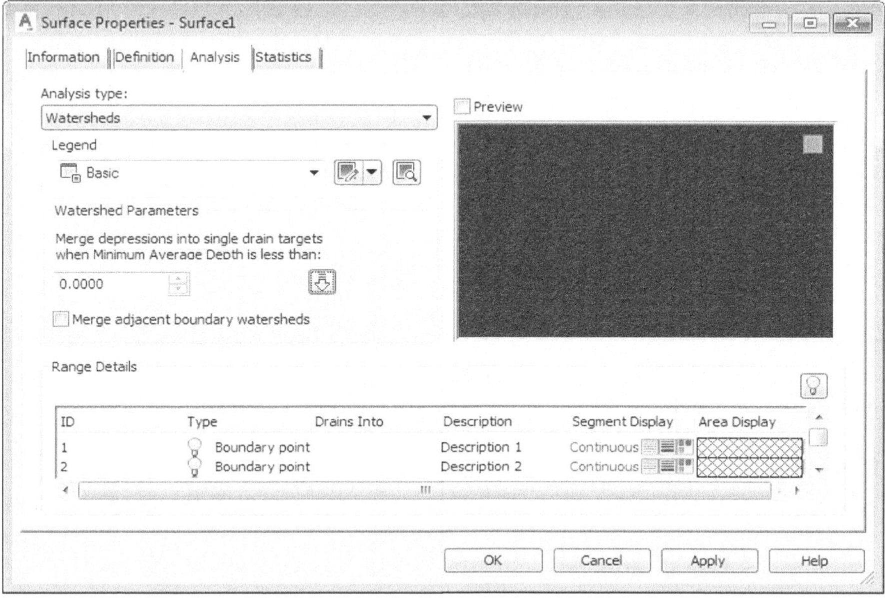

***Figure 4-8** The analysis details shown in the **Range Details** area for the **Watersheds** analysis*

Once the analysis is done, choose the **Apply** button. Next, choose the **OK** button to close the dialog box. The **Watersheds** analysis is completed. To view the results of the **Watersheds** analysis, turn on the visibility of **Watersheds** in the **Display** tab of the **Surface Style** dialog box. On doing so, watersheds are displayed in different hatch patterns and colors. Each watershed displays a tag inside it, which shows the range ID, type of watershed, and watershed area. Figure 4-9 shows the watershed with different hatch patterns and Figure 4-10 shows the watershed tags with watershed information.

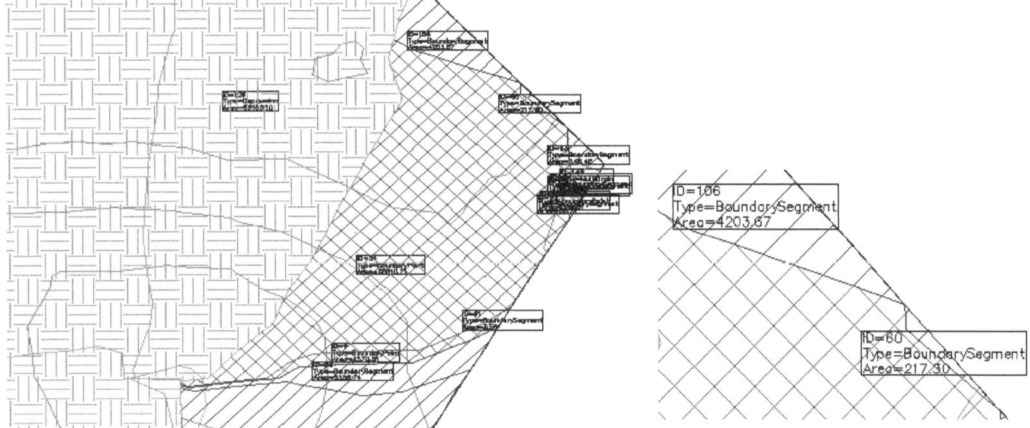

***Figure 4-9** Hatch patterns representing the watersheds*

***Figure 4-10** Watershed tag displaying the watershed information*

SURFACE ANALYSIS TABLES

In Civil 3D, data collected after performing a Surface analysis is divided into ranges that have different colors assigned to them. The surface legend table is used to organize and consolidate the data in a tabular form. You can create surface legend tables for all types of surface analyses, such as **Directions**, **Elevations**, **Slopes**, **Slope Arrows**, **Contours**, **and Watersheds**. You can add a surface legend table to your drawing only after you have performed the Surface analysis, modified the surface style to display the analysis type, and set up a surface legend table style to display the surface data. The method of creating a legend table style and adding a legend table to the drawing is discussed next.

Creating Legend Table Styles

Civil 3D offers a default legend table style for each type of Surface analysis. However, you can create your own legend table style and view the required information in the table.

The **Table Styles** are created, edited, and managed in the **Settings** tab of the **TOOLSPACE** like any other Civil 3D object. To create a new legend table style, expand the **Surface > Table Style** node in the **Settings** tab and then expand the subnode for which you want to create a style. For example, expand the **Elevation** node to create the legend style for the Elevation analysis of the surface. Next, you will notice that a default **Elevations** legend style name appears in the **Elevation** node. Now, right-click on **Elevation** and then choose **New** from the shortcut menu; the **Table Style - New Elevation Table Style** dialog box will be displayed, as shown in Figure 4-11. The tabs in this dialog box are discussed next.

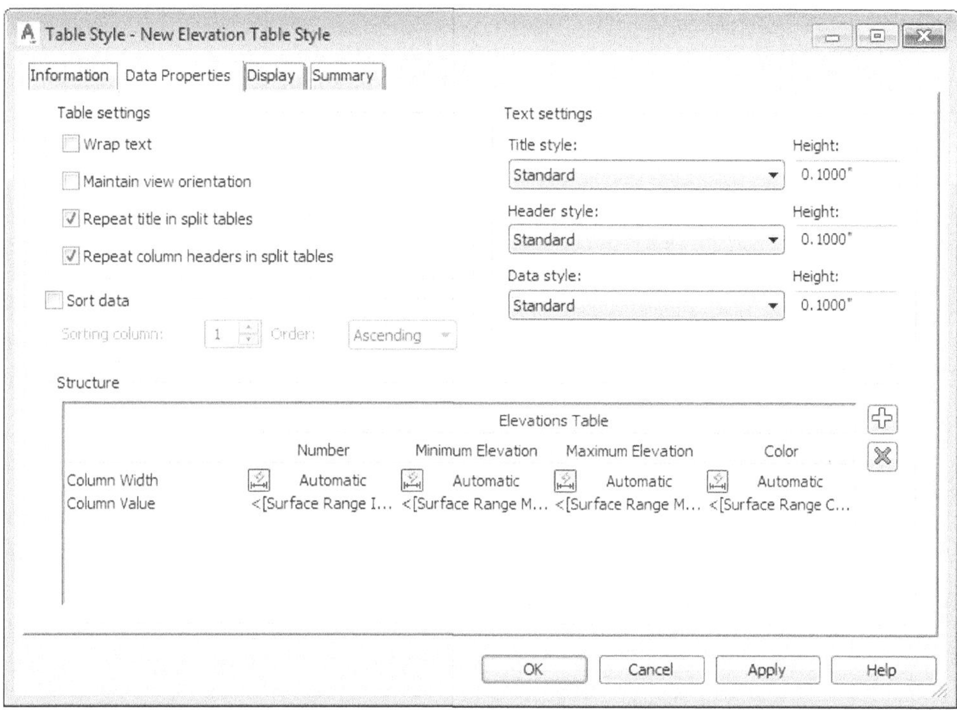

*Figure 4-11 The **Table Style - New Elevation Table Style** dialog box*

Information Tab

This tab is used to edit the name of the table style and to give description about the style, if required. Enter a name of the legend style in the **Name** edit box.

Data Properties Tab

This tab is used to define the table settings and the text style of the text in the table. The areas in this tab are discussed next.

Table settings Area

The options in this area are used to set the table format. Select the **Wrap text** check box to wrap text in the **Elevation Table** when the column width is set to **Manual** in the **Structure** area. Select the **Maintain view orientation** check box to align the legend table according to the orientation of the drawing view. The legend will be aligned according to the drawing, if rotated. Select the **Repeat titles in split tables** check box to enable the title of the legend to be repeated, if the legend is split into different sections. Select the **Repeat column headers in split tables** check box to ensure that the column headers of the legend repeat when they are split into different sections.

Text settings Area

The options in the **Text Settings** area are used to set the display option of the text in the table. Select the text style from the **Title style** drop-down list for the title and then specify the height of the text title in the **Height** edit box. Similarly specify the text style and height for the column header and data using the respective drop-down list and edit boxes.

Sort data Area

The options in this area are used to sort data based on the specified column of the table. To do so, select the **Sort data** check box in this area; the **Sorting column** spinner and the **Order** drop-down list will be available. Use the spinner to specify the number of columns to sort out the data. Next, select the order from the **Order** drop-down list to sort the data.

Structure Area

The **Structure** area is used to specify the composition of the legend data in columns of the table. It allows you to add or delete columns from the table. The table title and the column headers vary according to the type of analysis being used. To modify the header or title text, double-click on the column header or title to open the respective text component editor window. For example, double-click on the **Number** header for the **Number** column indicating the range IDs, refer to Figure 4-11. On clicking a header column, the **Text Component Editor - Column Contents** window will be displayed. You can use this window to edit the header text, color, and style. Choose the **OK** button after editing the header text. Similarly, you can change the header text for other columns also.

To add a new column in the table structure, choose the **Add column** button on the right of the **Structure** area. Note that the added column does not have any header text. Next, double-click in the header area and specify the header for the column. For example, if you want to display the area of the elevation band, you can add **2D Area** as the column header.

Next, to specify the width for the column, click on the default **Automatic** symbol displayed in the **Column Width** row and then choose **Manual** from the flyout. Specify the column width in the edit box. By default, the column width is set to **Automatic**, which means the column width will be adjusted automatically. After specifying the column width, you need to specify the column value as the composition of that column. To do so, double-click on the **Column Value** cell in the required column; the **Text Component Editor - Column Contents** window will be displayed. Next, select the required option from the **Properties** drop-down list; the properties and values of the selected option will be displayed in the **Modifier** and **Value** columns, respectively. Modify the required values and then choose the arrow button to add the selected property in the **Text Editor**. Finally, choose the **OK** button; the selected value column will be displayed in the column.

Display Tab

This tab is used to specify the visibility, layer, color, linetype, and lineweight for the table components.

Summary Tab

The **Summary** tab is used to get the review of the legend style settings. After you have specified the settings for the table style, choose the **OK** button from the **Table Style - New Elevation Table Style** dialog box; the dialog box will be closed and the table style will be added in the respective subnode in the **Table Styles**.

Adding Surface Legend Tables

Ribbon: Annotate > Labels & Tables > Add Tables drop-down > Add Surface Legend Table
Command: ADDSURFACELEGENDTABLE

To add the result table of Surface analysis in the current drawing, choose the **Add Surface Legend Table** tool from the **Labels & Tables** panel; you will be prompted to enter the table type. Specify the type of table by entering a value in the command line or by selecting it dynamically from the dynamic input prompt; you will be prompted to specify the behavior of the table. Select the **Dynamic** option so that the legend table is updated automatically when you modify the surface. If you select the **Static** option, the legend table will not be updated automatically when you modify the surface. On selecting the behavioral option for the legend table, you will be prompted to specify the upper left corner of the table. Click in the drawing to specify the upper left corner; the legend table will be added in the drawing.

Note

While adding the legend table if there are multiple surfaces, you will be prompted to select the surface or press ENTER; the ***Select a Surface*** *dialog box will be displayed with the name of the surfaces available. Select the required surface from the list and choose the* ***OK*** *button to close the dialog box.*

To assign a new table style to the added legend table, select the table from the drawing and right-click; a shortcut menu will be displayed. Choose **Table Properties** from the shortcut menu; the **Table Properties** dialog box will be displayed, as shown in Figure 4-12.

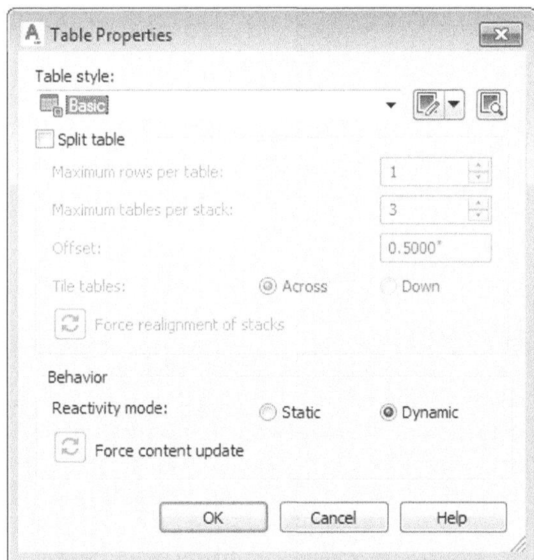

Figure 4-12 *The* ***Table Properties*** *dialog box*

Select the required table style from the **Table style** drop-down list. Next, you can select the **Split table** checkbox to split the table, if required. On doing so, the options in this dialog box will be activated. Specify the number of rows in each section of the split by using the **Maximum rows per table** spinner. Also, specify the number of splits using the **Maximum tables per stack** spinner.

Next, specify the distance between the split sections of the table in the **Offset** edit box. In the **Tile tables** area, select the **Across** radio button to tile the split sections horizontally or select the **Down** radio button to tile the split sections vertically. Choose the **OK** button after selecting the table style and specifying the settings. The legend table will be displayed according to the assigned legend style.

Editing Legend Table Styles

You can edit the style settings for any legend table. To edit the legend table, expand the **Table Styles** subnode from the **Surface** node in the **Settings** tab of the **TOOLSPACE** palette. Next, expand the required legend table node for which you want to edit the legend table. Right-click on the current legend table style name and choose **Edit** from the shortcut menu; the **Table Style <style name>** dialog box will be displayed. Edit the table style settings such as data properties and the table component display in the **Data Properties** and **Display** tabs. Also, edit the table style name if required. Choose the **Apply** button. Next, choose the **OK** button to close the dialog box.

Tip

Select the required legend table in the drawing and right-click to display a shortcut menu. Choose ***Edit Table Style*** *from the shortcut menu to edit the legend table style.*

SURFACE LABELS

Ribbon:	Annotate > Labels & Tables > Add Labels drop-down > Surface > Add Surface Labels
Command:	ADDSURFACELABELS

After you have created and analyzed the surface, you can display the surface information by using surface labels. Surface labels have two components: labels and tag. The label component contains text and the tag component is used to mark surfaces with numbers. Surface labels are created and managed in the **Settings** tab of the **TOOLSPACE** palette. You can add labels for surface contours, slopes, and spot elevations by using the **Add Surface Labels** tool. The various label types are discussed next.

Adding Contour Labels

To add contour labels to a surface, choose the **Add Surface Labels** tool from the **Labels & Tables** panel; the **Add Labels** dialog box will be displayed. Select **Surfaces** from the **Feature** drop-down list and then select **Contour - Multiple at Interval** from the **Label type** drop-down list. Next, select the major contour label, minor contour label, and user contour label styles from the respective drop-down lists. Now, choose the **Add** button from the dialog box; you will be prompted to pick the first point. Click in the drawing to specify the first point of the line along which you want to label contours. Click again to specify the second point of the line. Next in the command line, specify the contour interval at which you want to label contours. Press ENTER; Civil 3D will label contours along the line at specified contour. Similarly, you can label multiple contours or a single contour by selecting the **Contour - Multiple** or **Contour - Single** option from the **Label type** drop-down list. Alternatively, you can label contours by choosing the **Contour - Multiple**, **Contour - Single**, or **Contour - Multiple at Interval** tool from the **Add Labels** drop-down, refer to Figure 4-13.

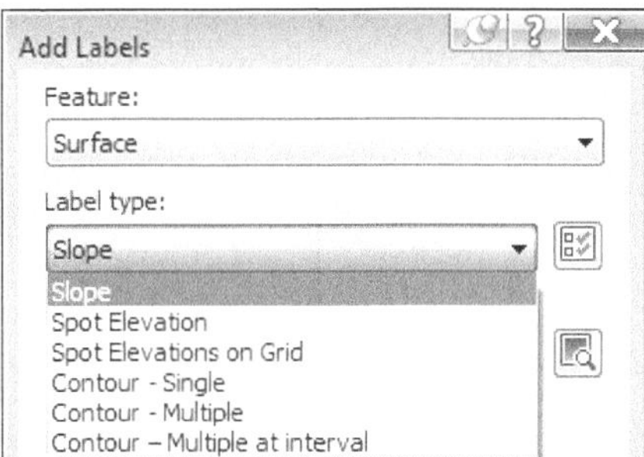

Figure 4-13 *Various options for labeling a surface*

Adding Slope Labels

You can add slope labels to a surface. To do so, choose the **Add Surface Labels** tool from the **Labels & Tables** panel; the **Add Labels** dialog box will be displayed. Select the **Surface** option from the **Feature** drop-down list in the dialog box. Next, select **Slope** from the **Label type** drop-down list.

Select the required slope label style from the **Slope label style** drop-down list. Now, choose the **Add** button; you will be prompted to choose between one point or two point method for specifying point.

The **One-point** slope label allows you to add a slope label by selecting a single point. The slope and direction are determined normal to the selected point. Press ENTER to accept the default **One-point** slope label and then pick a point in the drawing to add a slope label. The **Two-point** slope label allows you to add a slope label by selecting two points, the first point is the origin and the second point indicates the slope and the direction. To add a **Two-point** slope label, press the T key and then press ENTER. Pick the first point to add slope label and then pick the second point in the required direction; the slope label will be added to the specified direction.

Adding Spot Labels

Civil 3D allows you to add spot elevation labels and view the elevation of the surface at the spot. To add spot elevation labels, select the **Spot Elevation** option from the **Label type** drop-down list in the **Add Labels** dialog box. Select the required spot elevation label style option from the **Spot elevation label style** drop-down list. Also, select a marker style from the **Marker style** drop-down list to add a marker at the spot elevation label. Now, choose the **Add** button; you will be prompted to select the surface. Select the surface; you will be prompted to select a point in the drawing. Select the point in the drawing; the spot elevation along with the marker will be placed in the drawing for the selected point. Now, choose the **Close** button, the **Add Labels** dialog box will be closed. You can also use the **Spot Elevation on Grid** option from the **Label type** drop-down list in the **Add Labels** dialog box to add the spot elevation in a grid surface.

SURFACE LABEL STYLES

Surface styles control the display of surface, while label styles control the display of surface label styles. Civil 3D has various in-built label styles but you can also create your own label styles to label surface contours, slopes, watersheds, and spot elevations. These label styles control the visibility and display of surface labels. To create a surface label style, choose the **Settings** tab of the **TOOLSPACE** palette. Expand the **Label Styles** subnode from the **Surface** node in the **Settings** tab. Next, expand the required surface component node for which you want to create a label style. For example, in the **Contour** subnode, you will notice some in-built contour label styles. Now, if you want to create a new label style for contours, right-click on the **Contour** subnode to display a shortcut menu. Choose **New** from the shortcut menu; the **Label Style Composer - New Surface Contour Label Style** dialog box will be displayed, as shown in Figure 4-14. Various tabs in this dialog box are discussed next.

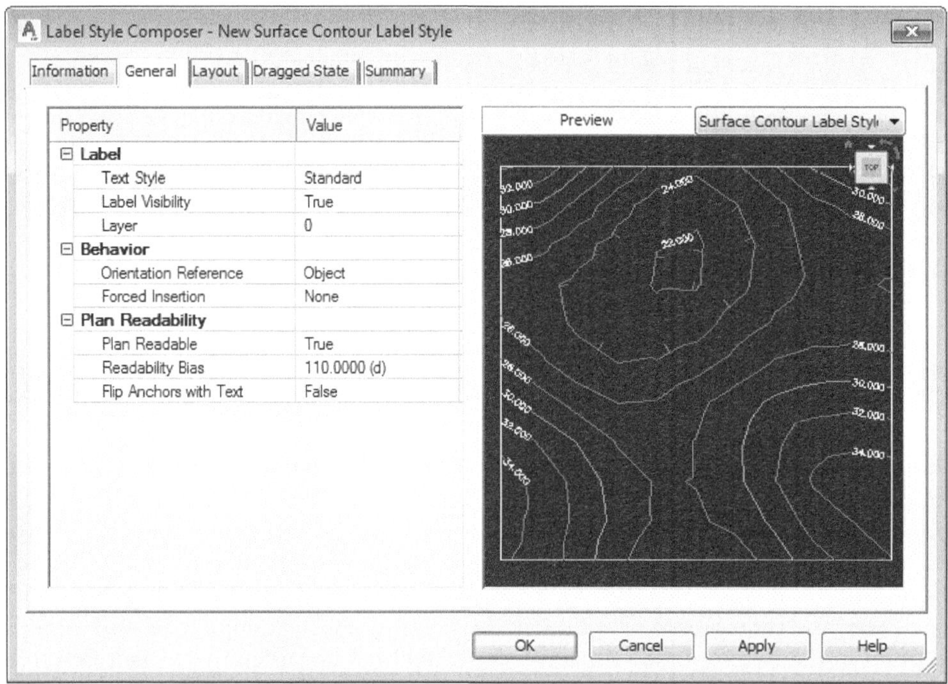

Figure 4-14 The ***Label Style Composer - New Surface Contour Label Style*** *dialog box*

Information Tab

Using this tab, you can specify the contour label style name in the **Name** edit box. Optionally, enter a description for the label style in the **Description** box. This tab also provides details about the label style.

General Tab

This tab is used to specify the general properties of label style such as label text style, label visibility, and label orientation. Properties of the label style are displayed in the **Property** column and values are displayed in the **Value** column in three different categories. These categories are discussed next.

Label

Expand the **Label** category. The **Text Style** property in this category specifies the text style of all the text components of a label. **Standard** is the default value of the text style. Click in the **Value** field of this property and choose the browse button; the **Select Text Style** dialog box will be displayed. Select the required type of text style from this dialog box. The **Label Visibility** property controls the visibility of the labels in the drawing. By default, its value is set to **True**. You can click in the **Value** field of this property and select **False** from the drop-down list to hide the label in the drawing. The **Layer** property specifies the layer of all components of the label. You can modify the layer on which the label will be placed.

Behavior

The **Orientation Reference** property specifies the orientation of the label. Click in the **Value** field of this property and select the required option from the drop-down list displayed. The **Object** option is selected by default in this drop-down list. The **View** option is used to realign a label to the current view orientation in both the model and plan views. The **World Coordinate System** option is used to adjust labels with respect to the angle between the current view and world view. The **Forced Insertion** property is used to specify the position of a label relative to an object. This property is applicable only when the **Orientation Reference** property is set to **Object** and the objects are lines, arc segments, or spline segments. The **None** value maintains the label position as composed, relative to the object. The **Top** option is used to add label above the object and the **Bottom** option is used to add label below the object.

Plan Readability

The **Plan Readable** property of this category specifies the text rotation to ensure that all the text components in labels are read easily in a specified view. Click in the **Value** field of the property and select **True** or **False** from the drop-down list. If you select **True**, the text in the label will be rotated so that it can be read easily in a specified view. Select the **False** option to keep the label in its original position, irrespective of the view.

Preview

The preview window displays the view of the label style. To change the view, select any option from the **Preview** drop-down list. Next, right-click on the preview window to access the view-related options in the shortcut menu.

Layout Tab

This tab is used to create, delete, or edit label components. You can also use this tab to add new components to a label, if required, and specify the text for the component. In this tab, you can specify text contents, height, color, and other related properties as well.

Dragged State Tab

This tab is used to specify label properties in the dragged state. You can control the display and appearance of labels when they are dragged from their insertion points.

Summary Tab

The **Summary** tab is used to displays all the components of labels and the specified values of various label properties. After you have specified the label style properties, choose the **OK** button; the **Label Style Composer** dialog box will be closed and the new contour style will be added to the **Contour** node in the **Settings** tab of the **TOOLSPACE** palette. To view the label style, choose the **New Surface Contour Label Style** subnode from the **Label Styles** node in the **Settings** tab of the **TOOLSPACE** palette, as shown in the Figure 4-15.

***Figure 4-15** Choosing the **New Surface Contour Label Style** subnode from the **Label Style** node*

Select the label style that you have created from the **Add Labels** dialog box before adding contour labels to the surface. Similarly, you can create your own styles for spot elevations, slopes, and watersheds and use them to label the surface.

TUTORIALS

1. Download the *c04_c3d_2018_tut.zip* file from *http://www.cadcim.com*. The path of the file is as follows: *Textbooks > Civil/GIS > AutoCAD Civil 3D > Exploring AutoCAD Civil 3D 2018.*

2. Save and extract the downloaded file at the following location:

   C:\c3d_2018

Note

*While opening the tutorial file, the **PANORAMA** window with an error message may appear. Close this window to proceed further.*

Tutorial 1 — Surface Volume

In this tutorial, you will calculate the composite volume and create a TIN volume surface. Also, you will calculate the volume of an area bounded by a polygon. Figure 4-16 shows the surface whose volume has been determined. **(Expected time: 45 min)**

The following steps are required to complete this tutorial:

a. Open the file.
b. Compute Composite Volume.
c. Create a TIN volume surface.
d. Create the new legend style.
e. Add the legend table to the drawing.
f. Calculate the volume of the area bounded by the polygon.
g. Save the file.

Figure 4-16 Surface with the determined net volume

Opening the File

1. Choose **Open** from the **Application Menu**; the **Select File** dialog box is displayed.

2. In this dialog box, browse to the location *C:\c3d_2018\c04_c3d_2018_tut,* where you have saved the file.

3. Select the file *c04_c3d_2018_tut01.dwg* and choose the **Open** button to open it.

   The drawing file consists of two TIN surfaces: the **Existing Ground** surface with borders and contours, and the **Proposed Ground** surface with triangles. You will notice a magenta colored polygon in the **Proposed Ground** surface.

Computing Composite Volumes

1. Enter **REPORTSURFACEVOLUME** at the command prompt and press ENTER; the **Composite Volumes** tab in the **PANORAMA** window is displayed.

2. Choose the **Create new volume entry** button from the **Composite Volumes** tab of the **PANORAMA** window; a new volume entry is added to the list box.

3. Double-click on the **<select surface>** cell in the **Base Surface** column; a drop-down list is displayed. Select the **Existing Ground** option from this drop-down list, as shown in Figure 4-17.

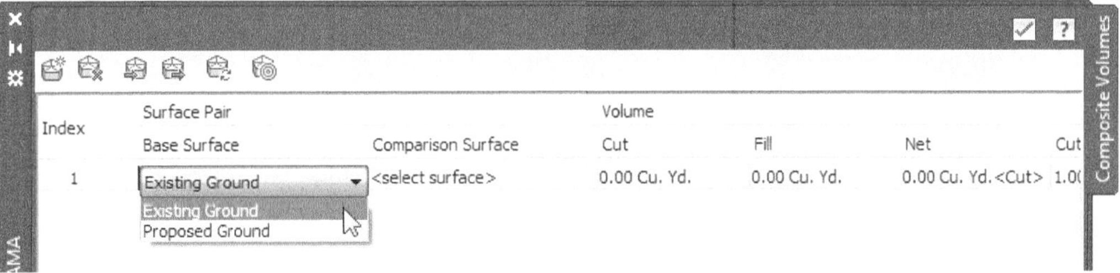

Figure 4-17 Selecting the ***Existing Ground*** *option from the drop-down list*

4. Similarly, select the **Proposed Ground** option from the drop-down list in the **Comparison Surface** column. On specifying the base and comparison surfaces, the net cut and fill volumes are displayed in the **Cut** and **Fill** columns, respectively, as shown in Figure 4-18.

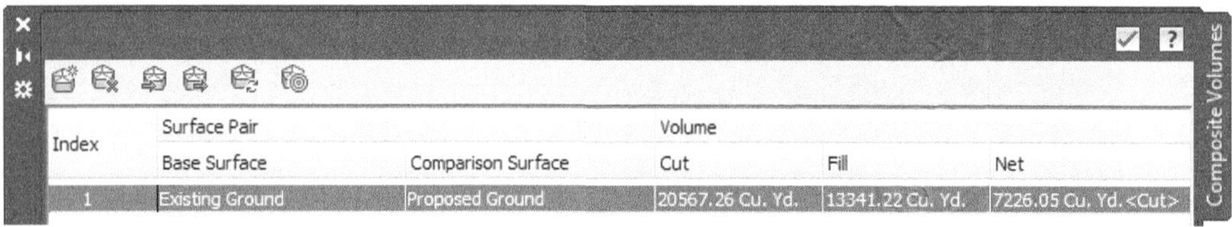

Figure 4-18 *The net cut and fill volumes displayed in the* ***Cut*** *and* ***Fill*** *columns.*

The total volume of material to be removed from the existing ground is **20567.26 Cu. Yd.** and the total material required to be filled is **13341.22 Cu. Yd**.

5. Accept the default cut and fill factor values. Move the slider of the **PANORAMA** window to pan across the window to view the adjusted values for the cut, fill and net material required. The net volume of material is **7226.05 Cu Yd<Cut>**.

   This means that to create a balanced proposed ground, the **7226.05 Cu Yd** of material needs to be removed from the existing ground. Note that the red graph in the **Net Graph** column indicates that the material needs to be removed from the base surface.

6. Close the **PANORAMA** window.

Creating the TIN Volume Surface

1. Choose the **Create Surface** tool from **Home > Create Ground Data > Surfaces** drop-down; the **Create Surface** dialog box is displayed.

2. In this dialog box, select the **TIN volume surface** option from the **Type** drop-down list.

3. Set the values of the TIN volume surface properties as follows:

   Name: **Volume Surface** Base Surface: **Existing Ground**
   Comparison Surface: **Proposed Ground**

4. Choose the **OK** button; the **Create Surface** dialog box is closed. The surface is created and displayed in different colored bands.

5. Now, expand the **Surfaces** node in the **Prospector** tab of the **TOOLSPACE** palette.

6. Right-click on the **Volume Surface** node; a shortcut menu is displayed. From the shortcut menu, choose the **Surface Properties** option; the **Surface Properties - Volume Surface** dialog box is displayed.

7. Choose the **Statistics** tab from this dialog box, if it is not selected by default.

8. Expand the **Volume** category in this tab; the cut, fill, and net volumes are displayed, as shown in Figure 4-19.

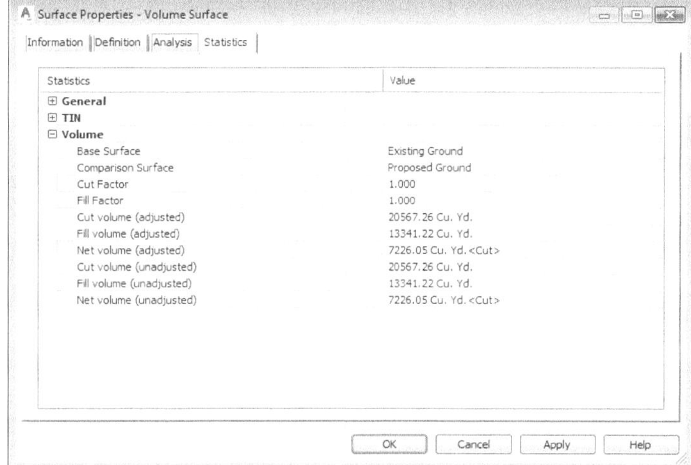

Figure 4-19 *The cut, fill and net volumes displayed in the **Volume** category*

Next, you will perform the Elevations analysis to visually differentiate various ranges of altitude in the surface.

9. Next, choose the **Analysis** tab in the **Surface Properties - Volume Surface** dialog box.

10. Ensure that the **Elevations** option is selected from the **Analysis type** drop-down list.

11. In the **Ranges** area, retain the default settings and choose the **Run analysis** button; the results are displayed in the **Range Details** area. Choose the **Apply** button; the volume surface shows elevation bands in different colors, as shown in Figure 4-20. Different color bands represent various elevation ranges in the surface.

Figure 4-20 *The volume surface with elevation band*

Now perform analysis using two bands of elevation ranges.

12. Set the value in the spinner located next to the **Create ranges by** drop-down list to **2** and choose the **Run analysis** button; the analysis is performed. The range details are displayed in the **Range Details** area, as shown in Figure 4-21. Choose the **Apply** button to apply the changes to the drawing.

Range Details

☑ Scale scheme to fit

ID	Minimum Elevation	Maximum Elevation	Color Scheme
1	-13.012'	0.000'	
2	0.000'	7.299'	

Figure 4-21 *Partial view of the* ***Range Details*** *area for Elevation analysis with two bands*

Creating the New Legend Style

In this section, you will create a new legend style.

1. In the **Analysis** tab, choose the down arrow button from the **Legend** area and then choose the **Create New** option from the flyout displayed, as shown in Figure 4-22. On doing so, the **Table Style - New Elevation Table Style** dialog box is displayed.

Figure 4-22 *Choosing the* ***Create New*** *option from the flyout*

2. In the **Information** tab, enter **Cut and Fill Levels** in the **Name** edit box.

3. Choose the **Data Properties** tab from the dialog box. In the **Structure** area of this tab, double-click on the table name **Elevations Table**; the **Text Component Editor - Column Contents** dialog box is displayed.

4. Delete the existing text in the **Text Editor** text box and then enter **Cut and Fill Levels** in it, as shown in Figure 4-23.

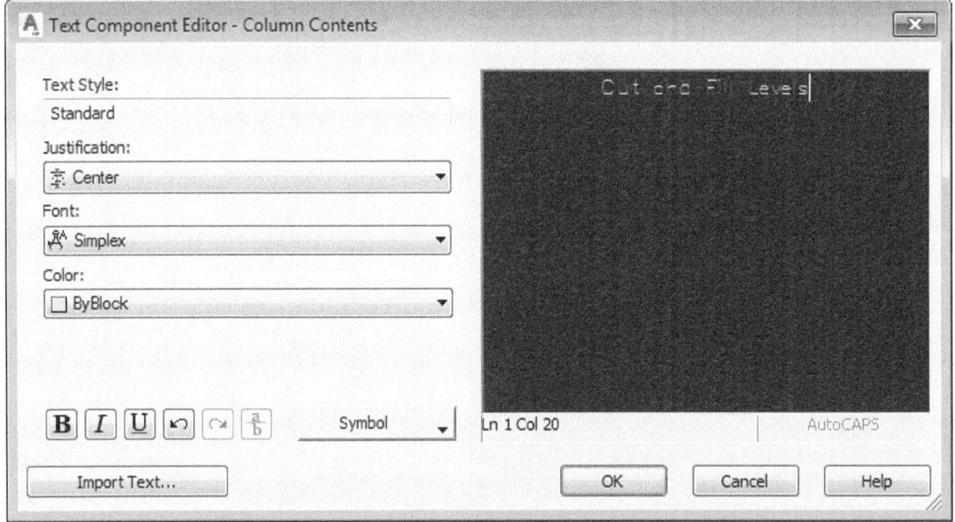

Figure 4-23 *The text entered in the* ***Text Editor*** *text box*

5. Choose the **OK** button to close the dialog box; the **Table Style - Cut and Fill Levels** dialog box is displayed. Notice that the name of the table in the **Structure** area is changed to **Cut and Fill Levels**.

6. In this dialog box, double-click on the **Minimum Elevation** header in the **Structure** area; the **Text Component Editor - Column Contents** dialog box is displayed.

7. Delete the existing text in the **Text Editor** text box and then enter **Cut Level** in it. Next, choose the **OK** button; the dialog box is closed. Notice that the **Minimum Elevation** column in the **Structure** area of the **Table Style - Cut and Fill Levels** dialog box is renamed as **Cut Level**.

8. Double-click on the **Maximum Elevation** header; the **Text Component Editor - Column Contents** dialog box is displayed.

9. Select and then delete the existing text in the **Text Editor** text box and enter **Fill Level**.

10. Next, choose the **OK** button; the **Text Component Editor - Column Contents** dialog box is closed.

11. Choose the **Add Column** button; a new column is added to the **Structure** area. 

12. Double-click on the header of the newly added column; the **Text Component Editor - Column Contents** dialog box is displayed.

13. In the **Text Editor** text box of the dialog box, enter **Net Volume** and then choose the **OK** button; the **Text Component Editor - Column Contents** dialog box is closed.

14. Now, double-click in the **Column Value** cell of the **Net Volume** column; the **Text Component Editor - Column Contents** dialog box is displayed.

15. Now, select the **Surface Range Volume** option from the **Properties** drop-down list, as shown in Figure 4-24.

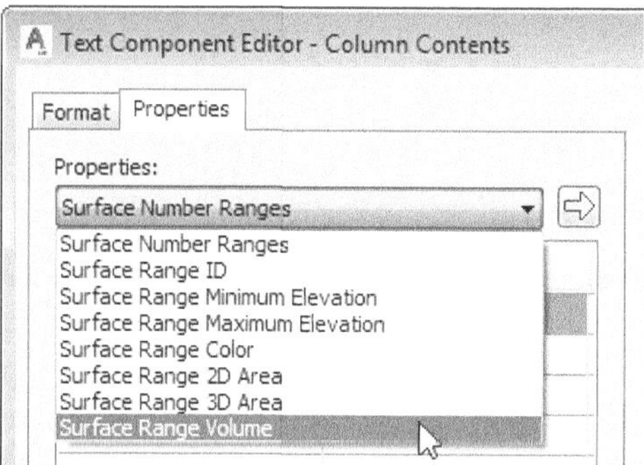

Figure 4-24 *Selecting the* ***Surface Range Volume*** *option from the* ***Properties*** *drop-down list*

16. Choose the arrow button to add this property to the **Text Editor** window.

17. Next, choose the **OK** button; the **Text Component Editor - Column Contents** dialog box is closed.

18. Now, choose the **Display** tab from the **Table Style - Cut and Fill Levels** dialog box.

19. Set the **Overall Border** color display to **By Layer**. Also set color for the **Title Separator**, **Header Separator**, and **Data Separator** components to **blue**. Next, set the color of the **Title Text**, **Header Text**, and **Data Text** components to **red**.

20. Next, click on the bulb icon in the **Visible** column of the **Title Area Fill**, **Header Area Fill**, and **Data Area Fill** to turn off the display. Next, choose the **OK** button to close the **Table Style - Cut and Fill Levels** dialog box.

21. Select the **Preview** check box in the **Analysis** tab of the **Surface Properties - Volume Surface** dialog box to view the new **Cut and Fill Levels** legend table in the preview, as shown in Figure 4-25.

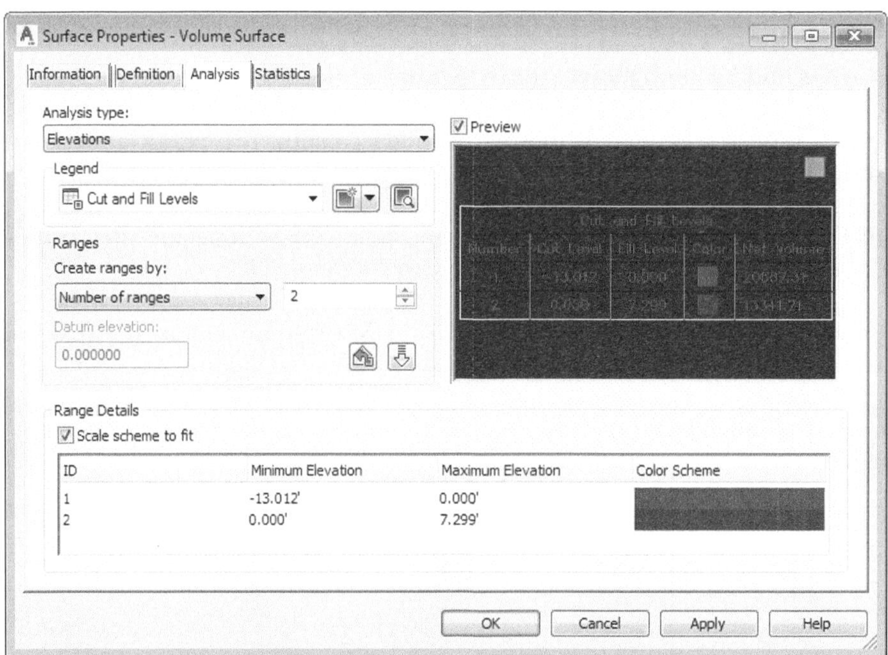

*Figure 4-25 The **Analysis** tab displaying the **Cut and Fill Levels** legend table in the **Preview** window*

22. Choose the **OK** button to close the **Surface Properties - Volume Surface** dialog box.

Adding the Legend Table to the Drawing

1. Choose the **Add Surface Legend Table** tool from **Annotate > Labels & Tables > Add Tables** drop-down; you are prompted to select the surface.

2. Press ENTER; the **Select a Surface** dialog box is displayed.

3. Select **Volume Surface** and choose **OK**; the dialog box is closed. Also, you are prompted to specify the type of the table.

4. Press ENTER to accept the default **Elevations** option; you are prompted to specify the behavior of the table.

5. Press ENTER to accept the default **Dynamic** option; you are prompted to select the upper left corner.

6. Click at the required location in the drawing; the legend table is added to the drawing and displays the cut and fill levels along with net volume, as shown in Figure 4-26.

Cut and Fill Levels				
Number	Cut Level	Fill Level	Color	Net Volume
1	−13.012	0.000		20567.31
2	0.000	7.299		13341.21

Figure 4-26 *The legend table displaying the cut and fill levels along with net volume*

Computing the Bounded Volume

1. In the **Prospector** tab of the **TOOLSPACE** palette, choose the **Volume Surface** subnode from the **Surfaces** node and right-click on it; a shortcut menu is displayed.

2. Choose the **Edit Surface Style** option from the shortcut menu; the **Surface Style - Elevation Banding (2D)** dialog box is displayed.

3. In this dialog box, choose the **Display** tab. Turn off the visibility of **Elevations** component in this tab. Choose the **OK** button to close the dialog box.

4. Enter **ReportSurfBoundedVolume** in the command line and press ENTER; The **Select a Surface** dialog box is displayed.

5. Choose the **Volume Surface** option from this dialog box.

6. Choose the **OK** button; the dialog box is closed and you are prompted to select the bounding polygon.

7. Select the **Finished Ground** displayed in magenta color from the drawing, as shown in Figure 4-27.

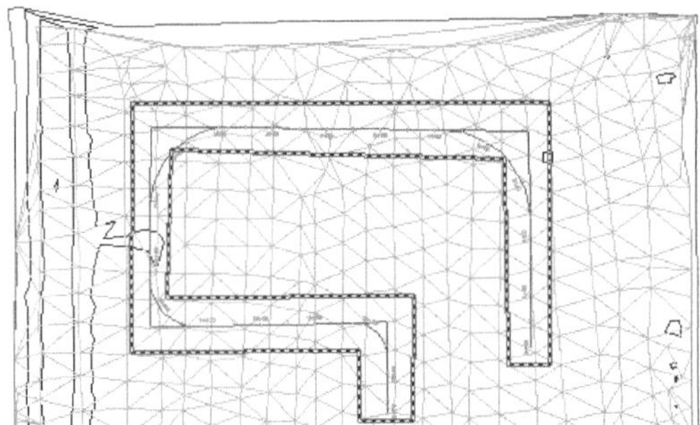

Figure 4-27 *Selecting the* ***Finished Ground*** *from the drawing*

8. Press the F2 key; the **AutoCAD Text Window** is displayed showing the cut, fill, and net volumes of the area bounded by the polygon, as shown in Figure 4-28.

```
Select a surface <or press enter key to select from list>:

Surface:  Existing Ground
Current datum elevation: 0.000'
Select bounding polygon or [Datum]: *Cancel*

Command: *Cancel*

Command: REPORTSURFBOUNDEDVOLUME


Select a surface <or press enter key to select from list>:

Surface:  Volume Surface
Current datum elevation: 0.000'
Select bounding polygon or [Datum]:
          Net volume = 35.00 Cu. Yd.<Cut>
                 Cut = 35.00 Cu. Yd.
                Fill = 0.00 Cu. Yd.
Net volume (adjusted) = 35.00 Cu. Yd.<Cut>
      Cut (adjusted) = 35.00 Cu. Yd.
     Fill (adjusted) = 0.00 Cu. Yd.
Current datum elevation: 0.000'
Select bounding polygon or [Datum]:
```

Figure 4-28 *The* ***AutoCAD Text Window*** *displaying the cut, fill, and net volumes of the bounded area*

Saving the File

1. Choose **Save As** from the **Application Menu**; the **Save Drawing As** dialog box is displayed.

2. In this dialog box, browse to the following location:

   C:\c3d_2018\c04_c3d_2018_tut

3. In the **File name** edit box, enter **c04_tut01a**.

4. Choose the **Save** button; the file is saved with the name *c04_tut01a.dwg* at the specified location.

5. Choose **Close** from the **Application Menu** to close the file.

Tutorial 2 Elevation Analysis

In this tutorial, you will carry out the Elevation analysis using two different methods of ranging elevations and viewing elevation bands in the surface, refer to Figure 4-29.

(Expected time: 30 min)

The following steps are required to complete this tutorial:

a. Open the file.
b. Create Surface Elevation analysis styles.
c. Add elevation legend.
d. Apply surface style and perform Surface analysis
e. Save the file.

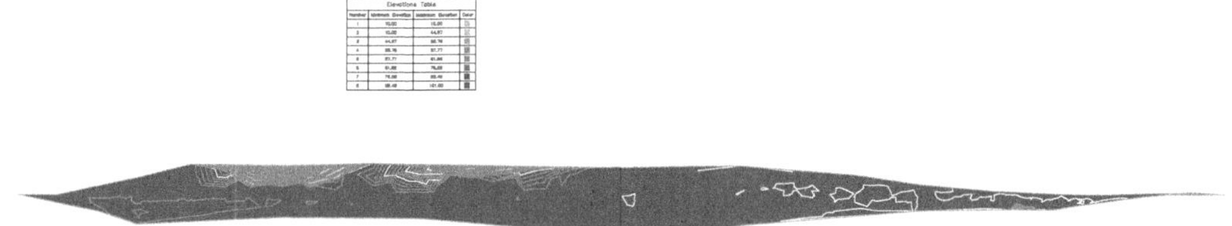

Figure 4-29 *Surface1 elevation bands*

Opening the File

1. Choose **Open** from the **Application Menu**; the **Select File** dialog box is displayed.

2. In this dialog box, browse to the location *C:\c3d_2018\c04_c3d_2018_tut,* where you have saved the file.

3. Select the file *c04_c3d_2018_tut02.dwg* and choose the **Open** button from the dialog box.

The file contains a surface displaying its contours and border.

Creating a Surface Analysis Style

1. Choose the **Settings** tab from the **TOOLSPACE** palette.

2. Expand **Surface > Surface Styles** in the **Settings** tab to view the existing surface style (**Basic**).

3. Right-click on **Basic** and choose the **Edit** option from the shortcut menu displayed; the **Surface Style - Basic** dialog box is displayed.

4. Choose the **Information** tab and then enter **Elevation-Quantile** in the **Name** edit box.

5. Choose the **Analysis** tab and expand the **Elevations** category node in it.

6. Click in the **Value** cell corresponding to the **Range color scheme** option; a drop-down list is displayed. Select the **Greens** option from this drop down list.

7. Ensure that the values of the properties in the **Elevations** category match the values shown in Figure 4-30.

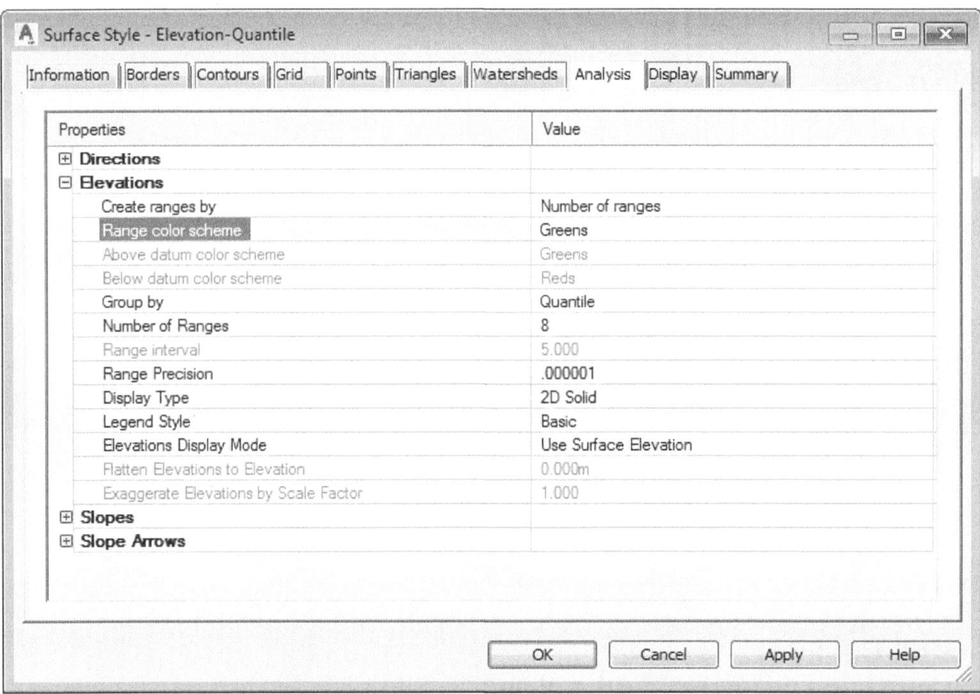

*Figure 4-30 Properties in the **Elevations** category of the **Analysis** tab*

8. Now, choose the **Display** tab from the **Surface Style - Elevation - Quantile** dialog box and turn on the visibility of the **Elevations** component.

9. Choose **Apply** and then the **OK** button; the dialog box is closed. The **Elevation-Quantile** style is added to the **Surface Styles** node, as shown in Figure 4-31. Also, elevation band are displayed in the surface, as shown in the Figure 4-32. Elevations in the surface are grouped by the Quantile method and displayed in different shades of green, representing elevations of different ranges.

*Figure 4-31 The **Elevation-Quantile** style added to the **Surface Styles** node*

Figure 4-32 ***Surface1*** *surface displaying elevation bands*

Adding the Elevation Legend

1. Choose **Add Surface Legend Table** from **Annotate > Labels & Tables > Add Tables** drop-down.

2. Select **Elevations** from the dynamic input prompt is not selected by default; the table type is specified and you are prompted to specify the behavior type of the legend.

3. Press ENTER to select **Dynamic** from the dynamic input prompt; you are prompted to specify the upper left corner of the table.

4. Click at the required location in the drawing area to add the legend table; the Elevations table showing eight ranges of elevations with a color assigned to each range is added to the drawing, refer to Figure 4-33.

Elevations Table			
Number	Minimum Elevation	Maximum Elevation	Color
1	10.00	98.37	■
2	98.37	98.94	■
3	98.94	99.32	■
4	99.32	99.53	■
5	99.53	99.74	■
6	99.74	99.93	■
7	99.93	100.21	■
8	100.21	101.00	■

Figure 4-33 *The Elevations table*

In this case, the dark shade represents the highest elevation range (101.00) whereas the light shade represents the ranges with lower elevations.

5. In the **Settings** tab, expand **Surface Styles** in the **Surface** node. Right-click on the **Elevation-Quantile** subnode; a shortcut menu is displayed.

6. Choose the **Copy** option from the shortcut menu; the **Surface Style - Elevation-Quantile [Copy]** dialog box is displayed.

7. Choose the **Information** tab. Enter **Elevations-Equal Interval** in the **Name** edit box.

8. Next, choose the **Analysis** tab. Expand the **Elevations** category.

9. Set the value of the **Range color scheme** property to **Greens** and the **Group by** property to **Equal interval**.

10. Choose the **Display** tab and turn on the visibility of **Elevations** if not turned on by default.

11. Choose the **OK** button; the dialog box is closed and **Elevations - Equal Interval** is added to the **Surface Styles** node.

Applying Surface Style and Performing Surface Analysis

1. Select the surface in the drawing area and right-click; a shortcut menu is displayed.

2. Choose the **Surface Properties** option from the shortcut menu; the **Surface Properties - Surface1** dialog box is displayed.

Tip

You can also invoke the ***Surface Properties - Surface1*** *dialog box using the* ***Prospector*** *tab. To do so, expand the* ***Surfaces*** *node and then right-click; a shortcut menu is displayed. In this menu, choose the* ***Surface Properties*** *option.*

3. In the **Information** tab, select the **Elevations - Equal Interval** option from the **Surface style** drop-down list in the **Default styles** area.

4. Choose the **Apply** button.

5. Choose the **Analysis** tab and make sure the **Elevations** option is selected in the **Analysis type** drop-down list.

6. In the **Ranges** area of the tab, retain the default settings and then choose the **Run Analysis** button to run the analysis; the details are displayed in the **Range Details** area.

7. Choose the **OK** button to close the dialog box. Notice the difference in representation of the surface. Also, notice the updated values in the **Elevations** table.

   As the Dynamic option is selected, the values are updated while specifying the behavior of the legend.

Saving the File

1. Choose **Save As** from the **Application Menu**; the **Save Drawing As** dialog box is displayed.

2. In this dialog box, browse to the following location:

   C:\c3d_2018\c04_c3d_2018_tut

3. In the **File name** edit box, enter **c04_tut02a**.

4. Next, choose the **Save** button; the file is saved with the name *c04_tut02a.dwg* at the specified location.

Tutorial 3 Slope Analysis

In this tutorial, you will create a style for the Slope analysis. Next, you will run the Slope analysis and the Slope Arrows analysis on the surface, as shown in Figure 4-34.

(Expected time: 30 min)

The following steps are required to complete this tutorial:

a. Open the file.
b. Perform the Slope analysis.
c. Add the slope legend table.
d. Perform the Slope Arrow analysis.
e. Save the file.

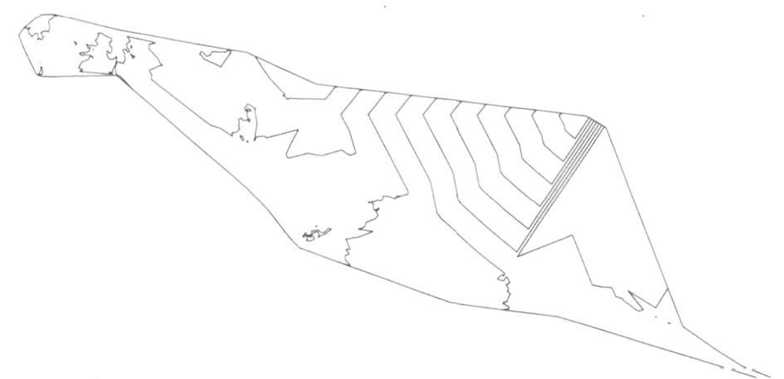

Figure 4-34 *The surface used for slope analysis and slope arrows analysis*

Opening the File

1. Choose **Open** from the **Application Menu**; the **Select File** dialog box is displayed.

2. In this dialog box, browse to the location *C:\c3d_2018\c04_c3d_2018,* where you have saved the file.

3. Select the file *c04_c3d_2018_tut03.dwg* and choose the **Open** button to open it. The file consists of a surface that displays contours and border, refer to Figure 4-34.

Performing the Slope Analysis

1. Select **Existing Surface** from the drawing and right-click; a shortcut menu is displayed.

2. Choose the **Surface Properties** option from the shortcut menu; the **Surface Properties - Existing Surface** dialog box is displayed.

3. Choose the **Analysis** tab from the dialog box if not selected by default and then select the **Slopes** option from the **Analysis type** drop-down list.

4. Set the value to **5** in the **Number** spinner in the **Ranges** area of the dialog box if not set by default.

5. Choose the **Run analysis** button; the information about minimum and maximum values of different ranges of slopes is displayed in the Range Details area. Five different ranges in the area are represented by different color shades.

6. Double-click on the color for the range ID **1** in the **Range Details** area; the **Select Color** dialog box is displayed.

7. Select the **red** color from the dialog box and then choose the **OK** button; the **Select Color** dialog box is closed and the color representing the range is changed to red.

8. Follow the procedure used in steps 6 and 7 to modify the color of ranges 2, 3, 4, and 5 to **yellow**, **green**, **cyan**, and **blue** respectively.

9. Choose **Apply** and then the **OK** button; the **Surface Properties - Existing Surface** dialog box is closed.

10. Now, expand the **Surface** node in the **Prospector** tab and right-click on **Existing Surface**; a shortcut menu is displayed.

11. Choose the **Edit Surface Style** option from the shortcut menu; the **Surface Style - Standard** dialog box is displayed.

12. Turn on the visibility of **Slopes** in the **Display** tab and choose **OK** to close the dialog box. Figure 4-35 shows different colors representing different slope bands created on the surface.

Figure 4-35 *Different colors representing different slope bands*

Adding the Slope Legend

1. Choose the **Add Surface Legend Table** tool from **Annotate > Labels & Tables > Add Tables** drop-down; you are prompted to select the table type.

2. Select **Slopes** from the dynamic input prompt to select the table type; you will be prompted to specify the table behavior. Now, press ENTER; the **Dynamic** option is accepted as the default behavior and you are prompted to specify the top left corner of the table.

3. Click in the drawing area to add slope legend table; the slope legend table is added to the drawing showing information about the minimum/maximum slope of a range and the color representing the range.

4. Select the legend table and right-click; a shortcut menu is displayed.

Tip

*The table displayed in the drawing area is very small due to the view scale. Use the **Zoom Selected objects** option to zoom in the table for easy viewing. To do so, enter **Z** at the command line; you are prompted to select the mode of zooming. Enter **O** at the command line for specifying **Object**; you are prompted to select the object. Select the slope legend table from the drawing and press ENTER, the slope legend table in the drawing area is zoomed in.*

5. Choose the **Edit Table Style** option from the shortcut menu; the **Table Style - Standard** dialog box is displayed.

6. Choose the **Summary** tab from the dialog box and expand the **General** category.

7. Set the following values in the **General** category:

   Text Height: Title: **20.0000"** Text Height: Header: **18.0000"**

   Text Height: Data: **15.0000"**

8. Choose the **Apply** button and then the **OK** button to close the dialog box; the **Slopes Table** is displayed, as shown in Figure 4-36.

Slopes Table			
Number	Minimum Slope	Maximum Slope	Color
1	0.00%	1.32%	
2	1.32%	2.65%	
3	2.65%	4.46%	
4	4.46%	8.27%	
5	8.27%	75058.83%	

Figure 4-36 The Slopes Table

Performing the Slope Arrows Analysis

1. Select **Existing Surface** from the drawing and right-click; a shortcut menu is displayed.

2. Choose the **Surface Properties** option from the shortcut menu; the **Surface Properties - Existing Surface** dialog box is displayed.

3. Choose the **Analysis** tab from the dialog box and select the **Slope Arrows** option from the **Analysis type** drop-down list.

4. Next, set the value to **5** in the **Number** spinner of the **Ranges** area of the dialog box if not set by default.

5. Choose the **Run analysis** button; the information about the slope area is displayed in the **Range Details** area. It displays the minimum and maximum slopes for each range. Slope arrows are divided into five different ranges represented by different color shades.

6. Double-click on the currently selected color for the range ID **1**; the **Select Color** dialog box is displayed.

7. Select red from the dialog box if not selected by default and then choose the **OK** button; the **Select Color** dialog box is closed and the color representing the range is changed to red.

8. Using the procedure followed in steps 6 and 7 to modify the color of ranges **2**, **3**, **4**, and **5** to **yellow**, **green**, **cyan**, and **blue**, respectively.

9. Choose **Apply** and then the **OK** button; the **Surface Properties - Existing Surface** dialog box is closed.

10. Select the surface in the drawing area and right-click; a shortcut menu is displayed. Select the **Edit Surface Style** option from the shortcut menu; the **Surface Style - Standard** dialog box is displayed. In the dialog box, choose the **Display** tab and ensure that the visibility of **Slopes** is turned off and the visibility of **Slope Arrows** component is turned on. You can toggle the visibility state of the selected component by choosing the bulb icon in the **Visible** column.

11. Choose the **OK** button; the dialog box is closed and the drawing now displays the result of the Slope Arrows analysis**.** The result is displayed using different colored arrows that correspond to different slope ranges, as shown in Figure 4-37.

Figure 4-37 *The arrows displaying the Slope Arrows analysis*

12. Zoom in to view the **Slope Arrows** legend table. On doing so, arrows of different colors pointing in different directions are displayed.

Saving the File

1. Choose **Save As** from the **Application Menu**; the **Save Drawing As** dialog box is displayed.

2. In this dialog box, browse to the following location:

   C:\c3d_2018\c04_c3d_2018_tut

3. In the **File name** edit box, enter **c04_tut03a**.

4. Next, choose the **Save** button; the file is saved with the name *c04_tut03a.dwg* at the specified location.

Tutorial 4 Watershed and Water Drop Analyses

In this tutorial, you will perform the Watershed and Water Drop analyses for the given surface. You will also extract objects from the given surface, refer to Figure 4-38
(Expected time: 30 min)

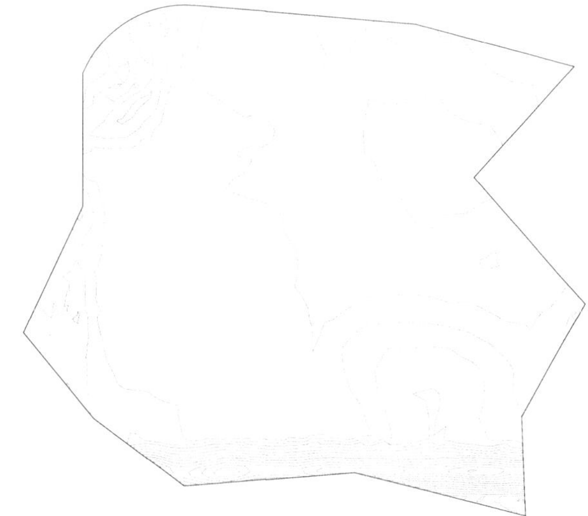

Figure 4-38 *Surface for Watershed and Water Drop analyses*

The following steps are required to complete this tutorial:

a. Open the file.
b. Create surface style.
c. Perform the Watersheds analysis.
d. Add the Watershed legend.
e. Extract objects from the surface.
f. Perform the Water Drop analysis.
g. Save the file.

Opening the File

1. Choose **Open** from the **Application Menu**; the **Select File** dialog box is displayed.

2. In this dialog box, browse to the location *C:\c3d_2018\c04_c3d_2018_tut,* where you have saved the file.

3. Select the file *c04_c3d_2018_tut04.dwg* and choose the **Open** button to open the file. The file consists of a surface that displays its contours and surface border, refer to Figure 4-38.

Creating the Surface Style

1. Select the surface from the drawing area and right-click; a shortcut menu is displayed.

2. Choose the **Edit Surface Style** option from the shortcut menu; the **Surface Style - New Surface Style** dialog box is displayed.

3. In the dialog box, choose the **Watersheds** tab and expand the **Boundary Point Watershed** category.

4. Next, set the following values of properties as given below:

   Color: **red** (default color) Use Hatching: **True**
   Hatch Pattern: **ANS137**

5. Now, expand the **Boundary Segment Watershed** category and ensure that the following values of properties are set:

   Color: **blue** Use Hatching: **True**
   Hatch Pattern: **ANS131**

6. Next, expand the **Depression Watershed** category and set the following values:

   Color: **green** (default color) Use Hatching: **True**
   Hatch Pattern: **EARTH**

7. Expand the **Multi-Drain Watershed** category and set the following values:

   Color: **magenta** Use Hatching: **True** Hatch Pattern: **ANS132**

8. Choose the **Apply** button.

9. Now, choose the **Display** tab and turn on the visibility for the **Watersheds** option.

10. Choose the **OK** button to close the **Surface Style - New Surface Style** dialog box.

Performing the Watersheds Analysis

1. Select **Surface 1** from the drawing and right-click; a shortcut menu is displayed.

2. Choose the **Surface Properties** option from the shortcut menu; the **Surface Properties - Surface1** dialog box is displayed.

3. Ensure that the **Analysis** tab is selected and then select the **Watersheds** option from the **Analysis type** drop-down list.

4. Choose the **Run analysis** button; the details of the **Watershed** analysis are displayed in the **Range Details** area.

5. Choose the button with a bulb icon at the top right corner of the **Range Details** area; the **Watershed Display** dialog box is displayed.

6. Click on the bulb icons next to the **Flat area** and **Multi-drain notch** watershed types to turn off the display of these watersheds in the drawing, refer to Figure 4-39.

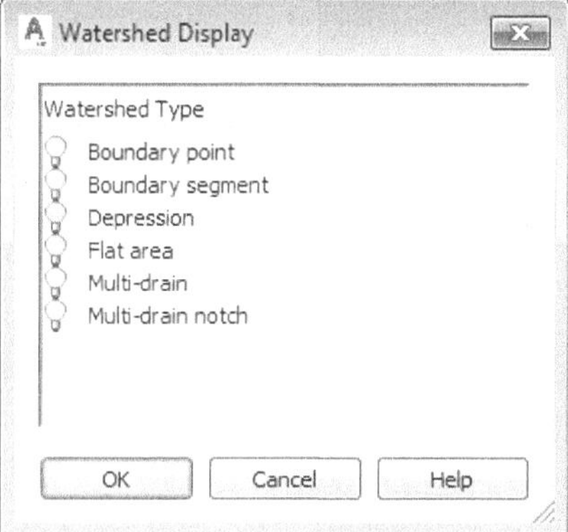

Figure 4-39 *Display turned off for the* ***Flat area*** *and* ***Multi -Drain notch*** *watershed*

7. Choose the **OK** button to close the dialog box.

8. Again, choose OK to close the Surface Properties - Surface1 dialog box; different hatch patterns representing different watershed regions in the surface are displayed, as shown in Figure 4-40. Each watershed area has a tag that displays information about that watershed.

9. Zoom in to view the watershed tag in each area, refer to Figure 4-41. The watershed tag displays the ID, type, and area of the watershed.

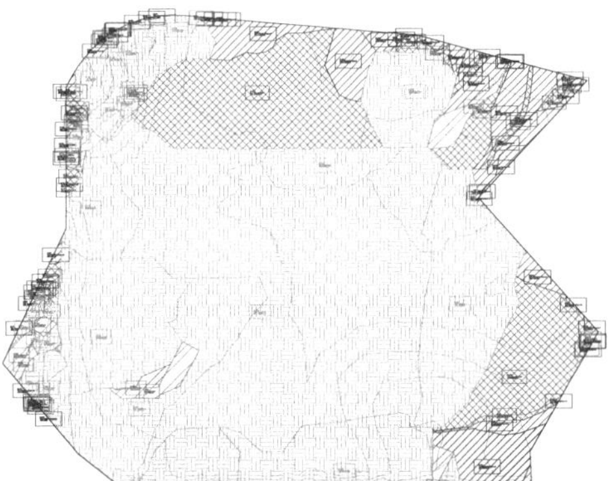

Figure 4-40 *Watersheds displayed after performing the* ***Watersheds*** *analysis*

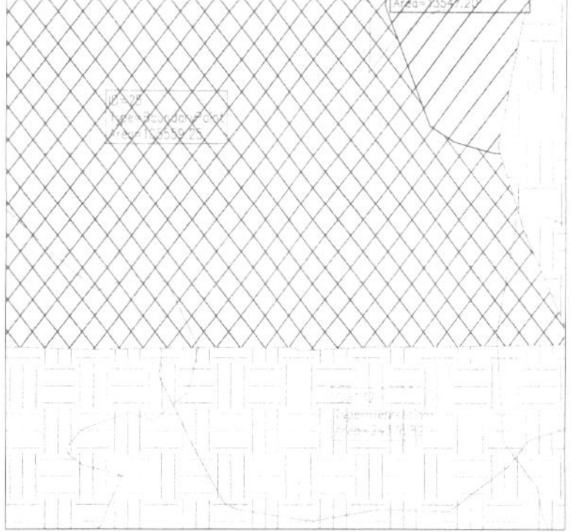

Figure 4-41 *The watershed tag for the given watershed*

Adding the Watershed Legend

1. Choose the **Add Surface Legend Table** tool from **Annotate > Labels & Tables > Add Tables** drop-down; you are prompted to select the table type.

2. Select **Watersheds** from the **Enter table type** dynamic input prompt displayed in the screen, as shown in Figure 4-42; you are prompted to specify the top left corner of the table.

Note

Dynamic input is displayed only if the ***Dynamic Input*** *option is turned on.*

Figure 4-42 *Selecting the* ***Watersheds*** *option from the* ***Enter table type*** *dynamic input prompt*

3. Select **Dynamic** as the behavior of the table from the input prompt.

4. Click at the required location in the drawing; the watershed legend table is added to the drawing and also the information about the watersheds is displayed in 155 ranges, refer to Figure 4-43.

Watersheds Table						
ID	Type	Drains Into	Description	Segment Display	Area Display	Area
1	Boundary point		Description 1	———	179.80 Sq. Ft.	179.80
2	Boundary point		Description 2	———	11.02 Sq. Ft.	11.02
3	Boundary point		Description 3	———	78.29 Sq. Ft.	78.29
4	Boundary point		Description 4	———	5.91 Sq. Ft.	5.91
5	Boundary point		Description 5	———	146.03 Sq. Ft.	146.03
6	Boundary point		Description 6	———	413.02 Sq. Ft.	413.02
7	Boundary point		Description 7	———	722.31 Sq. Ft.	722.31
8	Boundary point		Description 8	———	3304.61 Sq. Ft.	3304.61
9	Boundary point		Description 9	———	2570.51 Sq. Ft.	2570.51
10	Boundary point		Description 10	———	338.51 Sq. Ft.	338.51

Figure 4-43 *Partial view of the Watersheds Table*

5. Now, select the **Watersheds Table** and right-click on it; a shortcut menu is displayed.

6. Choose the **Edit Table Style** option from the shortcut menu; the **Table Style - Basic** dialog box is displayed.

7. In the **Data Properties** tab, select the **Description** column from the **Structure** area and choose the **Delete column** button to delete the selected column. 

8. Choose **Apply** and then the **OK** button to close the dialog box. The **Description** column is removed from the watershed legend table.

9. Again, select the **Watersheds Table** and right-click; a shortcut menu is displayed. Choose the **Table Properties** option from the shortcut menu; the **Table Properties** dialog box is displayed, as shown in Figure 4-44.

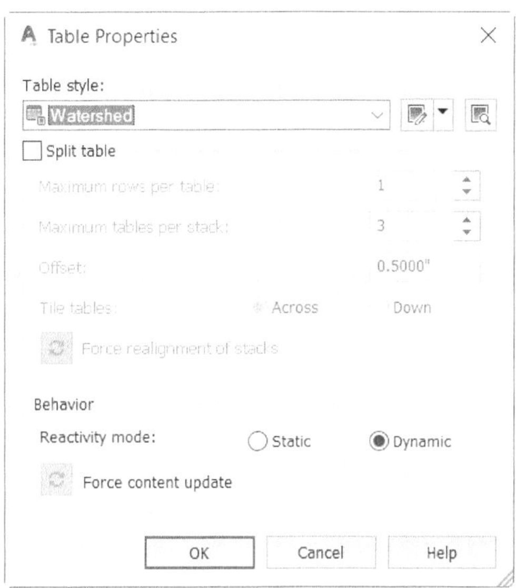

*Figure 4-44 The **Table Properties** dialog box*

10. Select the **Split table** check box if not selected by default. Set the value to **10** in the **Maximum rows per table** spinner and **3** in the **Maximum tables per stack** spinner.

11. Choose the **OK** button; the dialog box is closed and the **Watersheds Table** is divided into three columns.

Extracting Objects from Surface

1. Choose the **Surface** tool from the **Ground Data** panel of the **Modify** tab; the **Surface** tab is displayed.

2. Choose the **Extract Objects** tool from the **Extract From Surface** drop down in the **Surface Tools** panel of the **Surface** tab; the **Extract Objects from Surface - <Surface1>** dialog box is displayed.

3. Clear all the check boxes except the **Watersheds** check box in the dialog box and then choose the **OK** button; the dialog box is closed and watersheds are extracted from the objects.

4. Move the cursor over the surface and click on any watershed area; you will notice that you can select the watershed areas individually. Also, on selecting an individual watershed area, a blue grip is displayed around the watershed area. This indicates that you have selected an individual object.

5. Keeping the watershed area selected, enter **LIST** in the command line and then press ENTER; the AutoCAD Text Window showing the parameters of the selected watershed area is displayed, as shown in Figure 4-45.

6. Press ENTER; you are prompted to select an object. Select another watershed and press ENTER to view the parameter of the selected watershed in the **AutoCAD Text Window**. Now, close the **AutoCAD Text Window**.

```
Command: LIST
1 found
                  HATCH      Layer: "0"
                             Space: Model space
                   Color: 3 (green)    Linetype: "BYLAYER"
                   Handle = 2890
                 Hatch pattern EARTH
                 Annotative: No
                 Hatch scale  100.0000
                 Hatch angle      0
                 Not associative
                 Area       96160.1000
                 Origin     X=   0.0000  Y=   0.0000  Z=   0.0000
```

*Figure 4-45 The **AutoCAD Text Window** showing parameters of the selected watershed area*

Performing the Water-Drop Analysis

1. Choose the **Water Drop** tool from **Analyze > Ground Data > Flow Paths** drop-down; the **Water Drop** dialog box is displayed.

2. Click in the **Value** field of the **Path Layer** property; a **Browse** button is displayed. Choose the **Browse** button; the **Layer Selection** dialog box is displayed.

3. In this dialog box, choose the **New** button; the **Create Layer** dialog box is displayed.

4. In the **Create Layer** dialog box, click in the **Value** field of the **Layer Name** property and enter **C-TOPO-WDRP** in the text box displayed. Next, choose the **OK** button; a new layer is added to the **Layer Selection** dialog box.

5. Select the **C-TOPO-WDRP** layer in the **Layer Selection** dialog box and choose the **OK** button; the selected layer name is displayed in the **Value** field of the **Path Layer** property of the **Water Drop** dialog box.

6. In the **Water Drop** dialog box, click in the **Value** field corresponding to the **Place Marker at Start Point** property; a drop-down list is displayed. Select the **Yes** option from the drop-down list, refer to Figure 4-46.

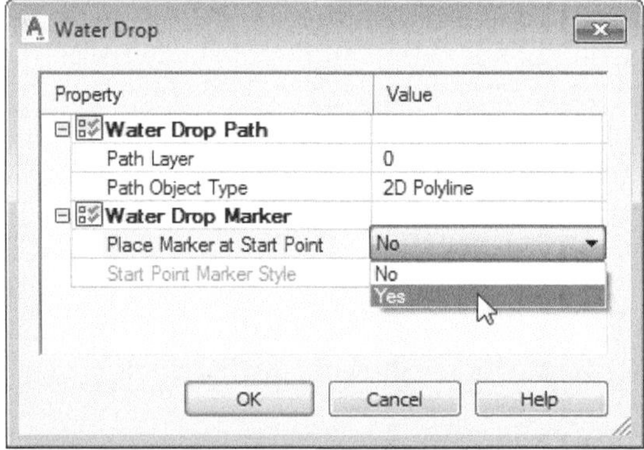

*Figure 4-46 The **Yes** option selected in the **Place Marker at Start Point** drop-down list*

7. Choose the **OK** button; the dialog box is closed and you are prompted to select the point.

8. Zoom in the bottom of the surface and click at different locations; the polylines and markers are displayed, as shown in Figure 4-47.

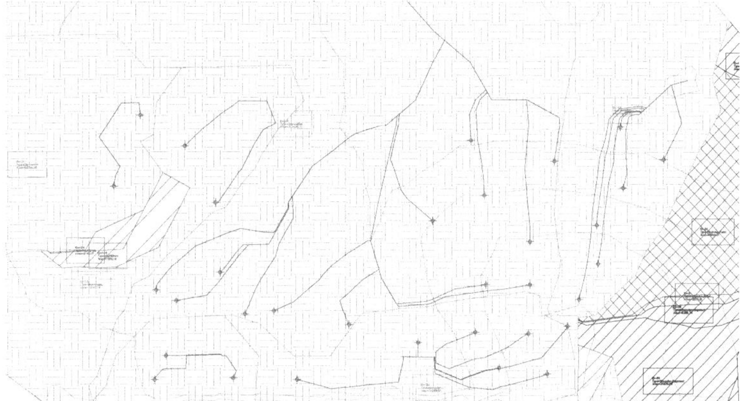

Figure 4-47 *Polyline and markers displaying the path of water flow*

9. The marker specifies the start point of the path and the polyline shows the path followed by water.

Saving the File

1. Choose **Save As** from the **Application Menu**; the **Save Drawing As** dialog box is displayed.

2. In this dialog box, browse to the following location:

   C:\c3d_2018\c04_c3d_2018_tut

3. In the **File name** edit box, enter **c04_tut04a**.

4. Next, choose the **Save** button; the file is saved with the name *c04_tut04a.dwg* at the specified location.

Self-Evaluation Test

Answer the following questions and then compare them to those given at the end of this chapter:

1. Which of the following analysis is used to determine the direction of slope?

   a) Slope b) Slope Arrow
   c) Contours d) Elevation

2. The __________ is used to investigate different properties of a surface.

3. The __________ tab in the **Surface Properties - <Surface Name>** dialog box is used to run the Surface analysis.

4. In the **Surface Properties** dialog box, you can view the legend table in the __________ area by selecting the **Preview** check box.

5. The __________ provide you an organized way to view information about the Surface analysis.

6. The __________ area in the **Surface Properties** dialog box is used to specify the contents and the properties of the result table for the Surface analysis.

7. The __________ tab in the **Label Style Composer** dialog box is used to define the layout of a label by creating, deleting, or editing label components and their properties.

8. The __________ tab is used to define the properties for labels when they are dragged from their original position or insertion point.

9. The __________ tool is used to calculate the cut and fill quantities for a pair of surfaces.

10. The __________ and __________ factors are used for calculating the **Cut (adjusted)** and **Fill (adjusted)** volumes.

11. The Slope Arrows analysis is based on the slope directions. (T/F)

12. After carrying out the Slope Arrows analysis, an arrow will be displayed at the centroid of every triangle. (T/F)

13. In the Watersheds analysis, the depth less than the value specified in the **minimum average depth value** edit box is automatically ignored from being considered as watershed. (T/F)

14. The boundary point is the lowest drain target point at the end of the channel through which water continues to flow off the surface. (T/F)

15. The Multi-Drain Notch watershed is found on a surface where a flat edge exists between two points forming a notch and water flows into multiple drains from the notch. (T/F)

Review Questions

Answer the following questions:

1. Which of the following types of Surface analysis is carried out to analyze the flow of water across a surface?

   a) **Slope** b) **Slope Arrows**
   c) **Elevations** d) **Watersheds**

2. Which of the following are modes of a label?

a) Label mode and tag mode
b) Dragged mode and invisible mode
c) Text mode and insertion mode
d) None of these

3. Which of the following options allows you to create contour labels at specified interval?

a) **Contour- Single**
b) **Add Labels**
c) **Contour -Multiple**
d) **Contour -Multiple at Interval**

4. The _________ method is used to compute the volumes of a specific area in the surface.

5. The _________ tab in the **Surface Properties** dialog box is used to display the computed volumes of a TIN volume surface.

6. The _________ key is used to display the result of the bounded volume in the **AutoCAD Text Window**.

7. The___________ analysis is used to divide elevation into bands of different colors representing various elevations.

8. The legend table styles are created, edited, and managed in the **Prospector** tab of the **TOOLSPACE** palette. (T/F)

9. The labels in the drawing can update automatically with a change in the surface. (T/F)

10. Watershed labels are added automatically when watersheds are displayed. (T/F)

EXERCISES

1. Log on to *www.cadcim.com* and browse to *Textbooks > Civil/GIS > Civil 3D > Exploring AutoCAD Civil 3D 2018*. Next, select *c04_c3d_2018_exer.zip* file from the **Exercise Files** drop-down list. Choose the corresponding **Download** button to download the data file.

2. Now, save and extract the downloaded folder to the following location:

C:\c3d_2018

Note

*While opening the exercise files, the **PANORAMA** window may appear with an error message. Close this window to proceed further.*

Exercise 1

Open the *c04_c3d_2018_ex01.dwg* file and run the Contour analysis. Also, add contour labels. Figures 4-48 and 4-49 are given for your reference.

(Expected time: 30 min)

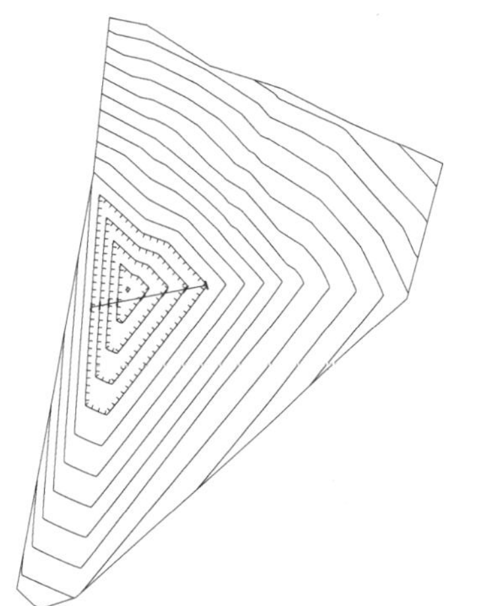

Figure 4-48 *Surface after contour analysis*

Figure 4-49 *Depression contours and contour labels*

Right-click on **Surface 1** in the **Prospector** tab and choose **Edit Surface Style** from the shortcut menu. Specify the following settings in the **Contours** tab of the **Surface Style** dialog box:

Number of Ranges: **5**
Minor Interval: **15.000'**
Display Depression Contours: **True**
Tick Mark Length: **3.000'**
Smooth Contours: **True**

Exercise 2

Open the *c04_c3d_2018_ex02.dwg* file and compute the volume between the surface1 and pool surface. Also, create a TIN volume surface. Assign the volume style to the TIN volume surface, refer to Figure 4-50. **(Expected time: 30 min)**

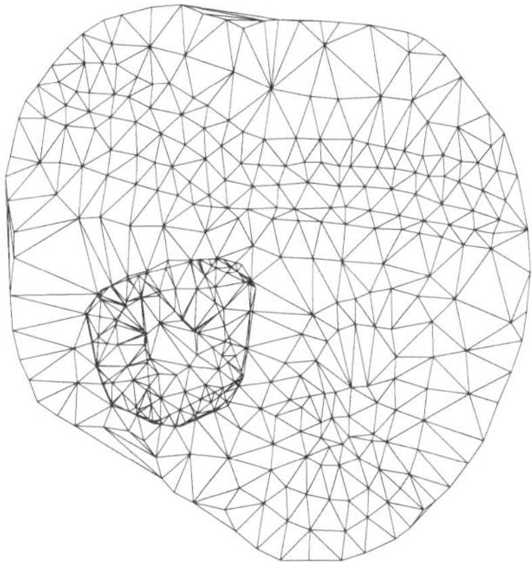

Figure 4-50 *The TIN volume surface*

Answers to Self-Evaluation Test

1. b, **2. Surface analysis**, **3. Analysis**, **4. Preview**, **5.** Range Details, **6.** Legends, **7. Layout**, **8. Dragged State**, **9. Volumes Dashboard**, **10.** Cut, Fill, **11.** T, **12.** T, **13.** T, **14.** T, **15.** T

Chapter 5

Alignments

Learning Objectives

After completing this chapter, you will be able to:

- *Create alignment and its components*
- *Understand factors affecting an alignment*
- *Understand methods of creating alignments*
- *Use alignment layout tools*
- *Use different methods of editing alignment*
- *Create best fit alignment entities*
- *Understand and create superelevation view*

ALIGNMENTS

An alignment is a linear Civil 3D object with coordinates and consists of lines, curves, and spirals. The alignment represents features such as the center line of a road, highway, tunnel, pavement edges, sidewalks, pipe lines, and so on. Alignment can represent existing or proposed features. It helps surveyors and engineers in creating the layouts of the projects easily and effectively. Defining the alignment is the first and basic step in designing a road or a pipeline. While starting up a new transportation project, the alignments should be designed carefully as they also serve as the geometries that control the layout and construction of the highway. A well designed road alignment reduces the cost of maintenance and vehicle operations. It also provides comfortable driving and road safety.

In AutoCAD Civil 3D, an alignment can exist as an independent object or as an object dependent on other Civil 3D objects such as profiles, cross-sections, and parcels. Alignments are dynamic in nature implying that the changes made by the user are dynamically reflected in all inter-related Civil 3D objects. In AutoCAD Civil 3D, the process of drafting and modifying an alignment layout is easy.

Types of Alignments

Alignments can be categorized into two types: vertical and horizontal. Horizontal alignment represents the geometry of an object in a plan view. It includes geometry of the object along straight paths and curves in a horizontal plane. Vertical alignment represents the elevation of points along the length of the object. The vertical alignment is represented by the longitudinal profile of the object and it includes the vertical curves and gradients.

The vertical and horizontal alignments should meet the required design standards so as to yield maximum efficiency. The criterion for designing alignments is discussed next.

Key Points for Designing an Alignment

Creating an alignment requires careful and thorough study of the area. The key points which should be considered while designing a road alignment are discussed next.

1. Designed alignment should be short and straight. The construction along the designed alignment should require minimum cutting and embankment. It should also avoid region with poor soil structure for a stable foundation of the structure.

2. An alignment should be safe for construction, operation, and maintenance from the stability point of view of the constructed structure. It should also be safe for the traffic operation and must have smooth curves and gradients.

3. An alignment should be designed on a higher ground so as to allow good drainage. Also, it should have a minimum number of cross drainages along its length.

4. The structure when constructed along the proposed alignment should add to the aesthetic beauty of the region.

5. Finally, the alignment should be such that the cost of construction, maintenance, and operation of the project is economized leading to a good project cost benefit ratio.

Components of Alignment

The two main components of an alignment are stations and offsets. Stations represent segments or distances into which an alignment is divided. Each alignment starts and terminates at a station. Each station is represented by a value that specifies the distance of that station from the start or the first station of the alignment. For example, the value 5+40 denotes that the station is located at 540' from the start of the alignment. The specification of the first station in an alignment depends on its length or the project requirement. The values of the stations automatically increase toward the last station of the alignment.

Offsets, the other important components of an alignment, represent the location of the existing or proposed objects in the site. These offsets help the surveyors to locate the nearby objects by taking the alignment as the reference or the base line. If we take the direction of the increasing stations as the reference then the offsets on the right of the alignment have a positive value and the offsets on the left have a negative value. For example, a tree with a station 2+50 and an offset -16.3 indicates that it is located at a distance of 250' from the first station and at a distance of 16.3' to the left of the alignment.

Factors Affecting an Alignment

The factors that control the alignment are discussed next.

Traffic

The alignment should comport with the traffic requirements and should be designed keeping the traffic flow, future expansions, and the shortest paths in mind.

Control Points

The control points or the obligatory points are the points through which the alignment should or should not pass. The obligatory points such as an intermediate towns or settlements through which the alignment should connect or pass can cause the alignment to deviate from the shortest path. The obligatory points through which the alignment should not pass such as monuments, graveyards, and so on can also cause the alignment to deviate from the straight and the shortest paths. Figure 5-1 shows the alignment deviating from the straight path AB to a longer path ACB to include the obligatory point C, which represents an intermediate town.

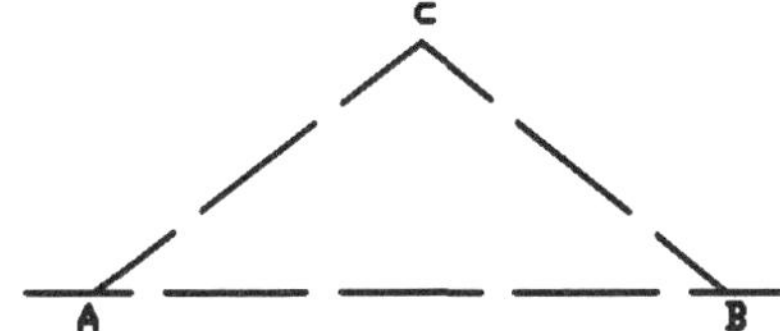

Figure 5-1 *Alignment deviating from the straight path AB*

Geometric Design

The geometric design factors that affect the design of an alignment are gradient, radius of curve, and sight distance. While aligning a road or highway, the gradient should be flat as far as possible and should be less than the design gradient. The sight distance is the actual distance at which an obstruction, stationary or moving, is clearly visible to the driver for the safe and smooth running of vehicles on the roads. In other words, the sight distance represents the distance at which the fast moving vehicles can stop or overtake safely. The alignment of a road or a highway should be designed in such a way that the sight distance requirements are fulfilled.

Economy

The alignment, apart from fulfilling the above requirements should also be economical. In other words, while designing an alignment, the initial cost of construction, cost of maintenance, and the cost of vehicle operation should be kept in mind.

The cost of construction can be controlled if the alignment is designed to balance the total cut and fill ratio of the surface in which it is created.

Apart from these, the other factors that affect the design of an alignment are the drainage, hydrological, and topographical features. The drainage considerations can control the vertical alignment of a road or highway in particular.

CREATING ALIGNMENTS

You can create alignments from polylines or by using the **Alignment Layout** tools. You can also create an alignment from the pipe network or by importing the data from landXML files. The basic information required to create an alignment are the name, type, and the style of the alignment. Civil 3D also allows you to use the criteria-based designs for creating alignments.

Once an alignment is created, it is added to the **Alignment** node in the **Prospector** tab of the **TOOLSPACE** palette.

Creating Alignments Using Polylines

Ribbon: Home > Create Design > Alignment drop-down > Create Alignment from Objects
Command: CREATEALIGNMENTENTITIES

The simplest and the most common method of creating an alignment is by using polylines. Using this method, you can automatically add curves between the tangents in the alignments. You can create an alignment from a polyline in two steps. The first step is to sketch the polyline and the second step is to convert the polyline into an alignment. To sketch the polyline, invoke the **Polyline** tool from the **Draw** panel of the **Home** tab; you will be prompted to specify the start point of the polyline. Click in the drawing area to specify the start point of the polyline. Click again when prompted to specify the next point. You can continue clicking to specify the points or press ENTER to terminate the command. On exiting the command, a polyline will be created. Now to convert this polyline into an alignment, choose the **Create Alignment from Objects** tool from the **Create Design** panel; you will be prompted to select a line, an arc, or a polyline object. In the drawing, select the polyline that you have drawn. Also, you can enter **X** in the command line to select the polyline from within the Xref drawing. On selecting the polyline from the drawing or from the Xref drawing, you will be prompted to press ENTER to accept the alignment direction or to enter **R** to reverse the direction. Press ENTER to accept the default alignment direction; the **Create Alignment from Objects** dialog box will be displayed, as shown in Figure 5-2. This dialog box is used to specify the information about the alignment. The options in this dialog box are discussed next.

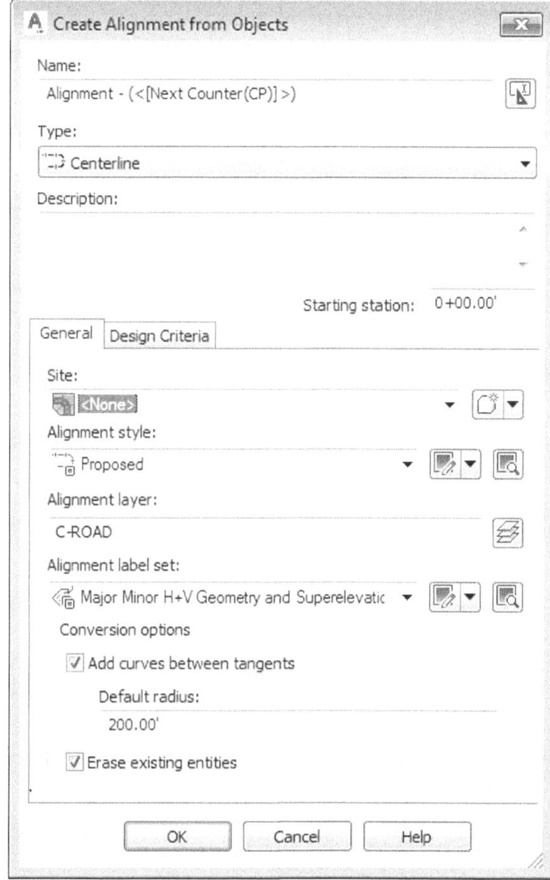

Figure 5-2 *The* ***Create Alignment from Objects*** *dialog box*

Name

The **Name** edit box displays the default name of the alignment. To specify a name for the alignment, choose the button on the right of this edit box; the **Name Template** dialog box will be displayed. Enter a name in the **Name** edit box of this dialog box and choose the **OK** button. Note that if you do not specify a name, Civil 3D will automatically name the alignment and number it. By default, **Alignment (1)** will be the default name assigned to the first alignment you create.

Description

The **Description** text box is used to specify optional description about the alignment. Specify a short description in this text box, if required. The name and description of the alignment help you easily identify different alignments in a drawing with multi-alignment.

Starting station

The **Starting station** edit box displays the station value of the starting station. The **0+00.00'** value is the default starting station value and can be changed to any user specific value. For example, to assign a value of 50' to the start station, enter **0+50.00** in the edit box.

General Tab

The options in this tab are used to specify the information about the alignment such as its site name, alignment style, and layer.

The **Site** drop-down list in this tab is used to select the required site associated with the alignment. Alternatively, you can select the site directly from the drawing or create a new site by choosing the down arrow on the right of the **Site** drop-down list to display a flyout. Choose the **Pick from Drawing** option to select the site from the drawing or choose the **Create New** option from the flyout to create a new site. On selecting the **Pick from Drawing** option, you will be prompted to select an object from the site. Select the object created in the site; the **Create Alignment - From polyline** dialog box will be displayed again and the site name will be selected in the **Site** drop-down list.

The **Alignment style** drop-down list displays the default alignment style. The alignment styles control the display of various alignment components such as lines, curves, tangents, and curve extension. Select the required alignment style from this drop-down list. You can also create a new style or edit the existing alignment style by choosing the required option from the flyout that is displayed when you choose the down arrow on the right of the **Alignment style** drop-down list.

Tip

*<None> is the default option displayed in the **Site** edit box. This means that the alignment will not interact with other Civil 3D objects. Accept this option if you do not want the alignment to interact with other objects such as parcels or profiles. The alignment will be added to the **Alignment** collection of the **Prospector** tab.*

Note

The alignment styles are available in the drop-down list only if there are some predefined alignment styles. The availability of the style depends on the type of template that you have selected.

The **Alignment layer** text box displays the default layer (**C-ROAD**) on which the alignment will be created. To select a new layer, choose the button on the right of the **Alignment layer** text box; the **Object Layer** dialog box is displayed. You can use this dialog box to select a new layer for the alignment.

The **Alignment label set** drop-down list in the **Create Alignment from Objects** dialog box displays the default label set. Select the required **Alignment label set** from this drop-down list. Alternatively, you can choose the down arrow on the right of this drop-down list to display a flyout. Choose the required option from the flyout to create a new label set or edit the existing label set. The alignment label set helps you to label different components of an alignment such as the major and minor stations and the station equations, both simultaneously.

Note

*The options in the **Alignment styles and Alignment label set** drop-down lists vary depending upon the template selected at the start of the project and the alignment style and alignment label sets defined by the user in the drawing.*

The **Conversion options** area in the **Create Alignment from Objects** dialog box consists of two check boxes. If the **Add curves between tangents** check box is selected, you can automatically add curves between the tangents. The radius of these curves will be equal to a fixed percentage of the tangent length and the deflection angle. Select the **Erase existing entities** check box to delete the entities such as polylines that are used to create the alignment. Clear the check box to retain the entity.

Design Criteria Tab

You can use the options in this tab to specify the design criteria settings for the alignment. You can select and apply the required design criteria, superelevation attainment method, design speed, and other design parameters in this tab to create a design-based alignment. The options in this tab and the method of creating a design-based alignment are discussed later in this chapter.

After specifying the required information in the **Create Alignment from Objects** dialog box, choose the **OK** button; the dialog box will be closed and the selected polyline entity will be converted into an alignment without any design criteria.

Creating Alignments Using the Alignment Layout Tools

Ribbon: Home > Create Design > Alignment drop-down > Alignment Creation Tools
Command: CREATEALIGNMENTLAYOUT

AutoCAD Civil 3D allows you to create an alignment based on some intricate designs by using the alignment layout tools. These tools can be accessed from the **Alignment Layout Tools** toolbar. These tools enable you to incorporate your engineering designs in the alignment and create an alignment according to the design criteria. For example, if you want the alignment curve to pass through a particular point, you can create the layout of the alignment accordingly by using the required curve tool from the toolbar. These sophisticated layout tools help you create an alignment layout using the curves, spirals, points of intersection (PIs), and so on.

Creating an alignment using the alignment layout tools is a two-step process. The first step includes naming the alignment, specifying the site on which the alignment will be created, selecting the alignment style, and the alignment label style. The second step involves the use of the alignment layout tools to draft the alignment.

To create an alignment using the layout tools, choose **Alignment Creation Tools** from the **Create Design** panel; the **Create Alignment - Layout** dialog box will be displayed, as shown in Figure 5-3. The options in this dialog box are the same as those discussed earlier for the **Create Alignment from Objects** dialog box.

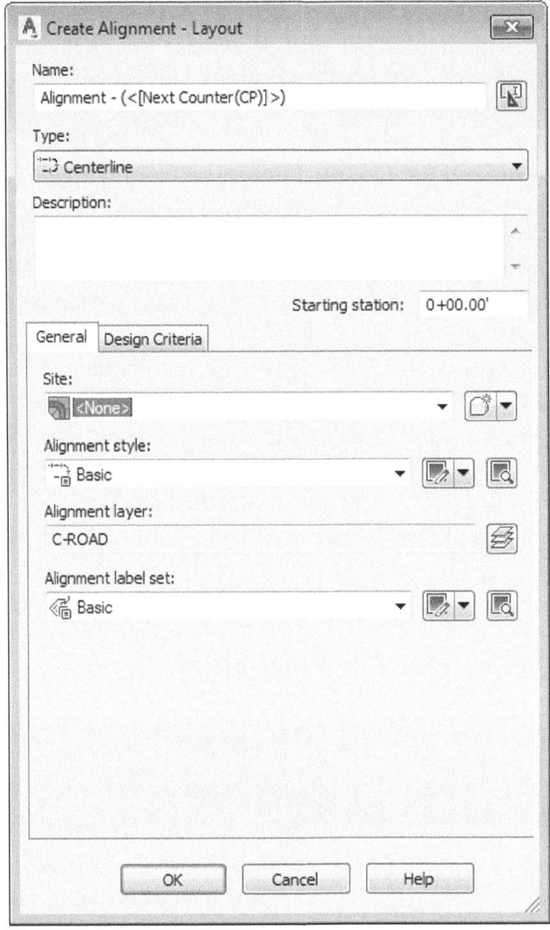

*Figure 5-3 The **Create Alignment - Layout** dialog box*

After specifying the required information about the alignment and the design criteria in the **Create Alignment - Layout** dialog box, choose the **OK** button; the **Alignment Layout Tools - <alignment name>** toolbar will be displayed. This will conclude the initial step of setting an alignment. The second step is to create the alignment using the alignment layout tools from the **Alignment Layout Tools** toolbar. The tools in this toolbar will be discussed in detail in the next section.

The **Alignment Layout Tools** toolbar provides you with a wide range of tools to design and edit the alignment. The constraint-based alignment entities such as curves, spirals, tangents, and lines can be used to solve various design problems by adding design constraints. These tools help you to be more creative by enabling you to use fixed, floating, or free entities, while designing the alignments. These layout tools also help you convert the AutoCAD lines and arcs to alignment entities. The wide range of curves, tangents, lines, and spiral tools in this toolbar help you design not only the road alignments but also the railway alignments. The components that constitute an alignment (curves, lines, spirals, and tangents) can be divided into three different entities, which are discussed next.

Fixed Entity

The fixed entity is the one whose properties remain static even if the properties of the other alignment entities are changed. A fixed entity is defined by specifying its points or radius. It is not dependent on another entity for its geometry or tangency. Therefore, you can add a fixed entity as and when required. Figure 5-4 shows a fixed curve entity that is created independent of any other entity by specifying the start, second, and the end points of the fixed curve.

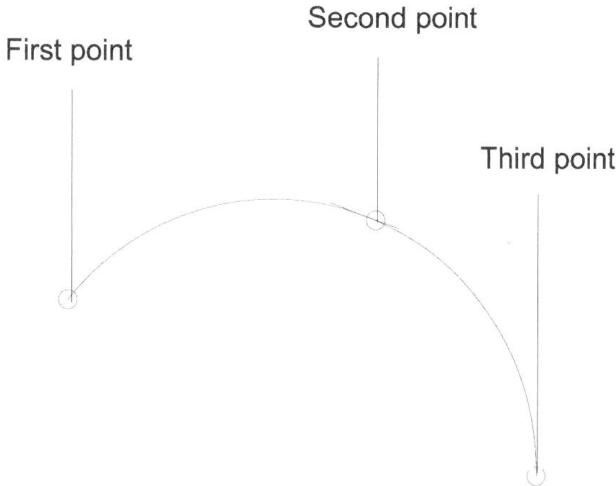

Figure 5-4 A fixed curve entity created by using three points

Floating Entity

A floating entity is defined as the entity that is always tangent to one of the entities to which it is connected. The geometry of such entity is defined by the set of parameters provided or is dependent on the other entity. A floating entity can be attached only to a fixed entity or another floating entity. Figure 5-5 shows a fixed curve entity with a floating curve attached to it and passing through a point in a specified direction.

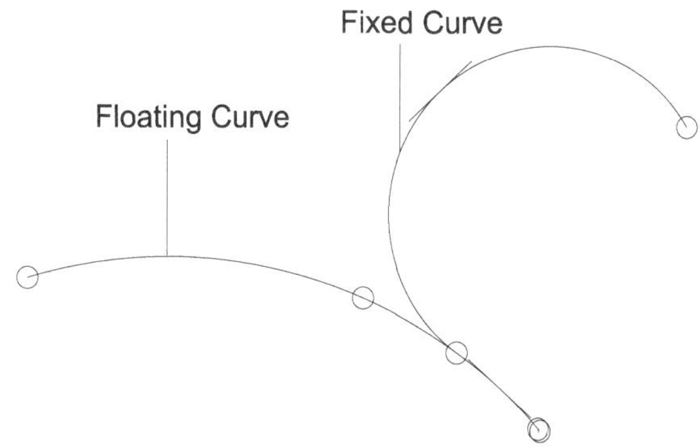

Figure 5-5 A floating curve attached to a fixed curve entity

Free Entity

A free entity is an entity which is always tangent to the attached entities at its start point and end point. It is defined by a set of user specified parameters. A free entity can be added to two fixed, two floating, or one fixed and floating entity. Figure 5-6 shows a free line added between two fixed curves.

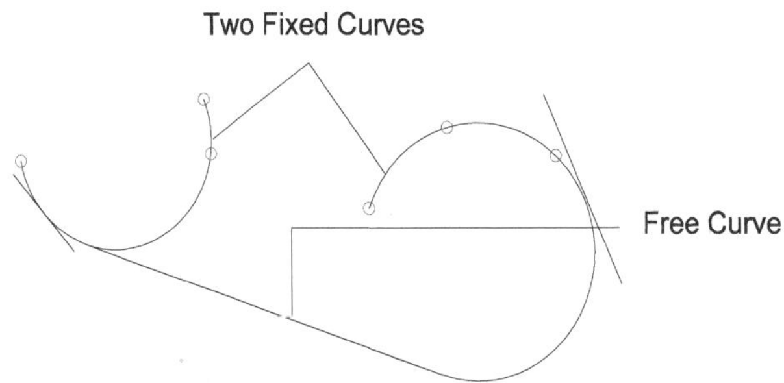

Figure 5-6 A free line entity added between two fixed curve entities

Note

*Every time you move the cursor near the **Alignment Layout Tools** toolbar, a tooltip with the name of the tool is displayed.*

ALIGNMENT LAYOUT TOOLS TOOLBAR

The tools in the **Alignment Layout Tools** toolbar are used to design an alignment using various constraints explained earlier. The tools available in this toolbar are discussed next. Figure 5-7 shows the **Alignment Layout Tools - <alignment name>** toolbar.

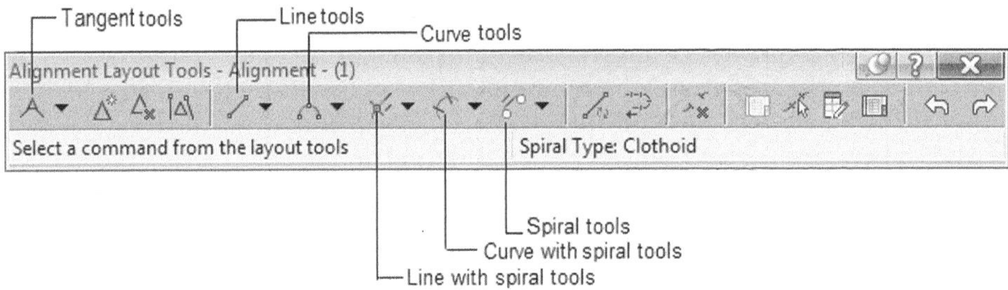

*Figure 5-7 The **Alignment Layout Tools - Alignment - (1)** toolbar*

Tangent Tools

The **Tangent** tools can be accessed by choosing the down arrow on the right of the first tool in the toolbar. The **Tangent** tools are discussed next.

Tangent-Tangent (No curves) Tool

This tool is used to create an alignment that consists of tangents without curves. The alignment is created by selecting and joining the consecutive points end-to-end. To invoke this tool, choose the **Draw Tangent-Tangent without Curve** button from the **Alignment Layout Toolbar**; you will be prompted to specify the start, intermediate, and end point. Click in the drawing area to specify the points and press ENTER to end the command.

Tangent-Tangent (With curves) Tool

This tool is used to create a tangent-tangent alignment with curves by selecting points in the drawing. To create the tangent-tangent alignment, invoke the **Tangent-Tangent (With curves)** tool from the **Draw Tangent Tangent without curve** drop-down; you will be prompted to specify the start, intermediate, and the end point. Click in the drawing area to specify the points and press ENTER to end the command.

Curve and Spiral Settings Tool

This tool is used to specify the curve settings to create an alignment consisting of curves and spirals. To create an alignment, invoke **Curve and Spiral Settings** tool from the **Draw Tangent-Tangent without Curve** drop-down; the **Curve and Spiral Settings** dialog box will be displayed. You can select the type of spiral to be added to the alignment from the **Type** drop-down list. There are eight different types of spirals in this list that you can use in your design. The **Clothoid** is the most commonly used type of spiral for both highways and railways.

Tip

In AutoCAD Civil 3D 2018, a new type of modified cubic parabola is added. You can define the settings for the modified cubic parabola by selecting the ***NSW Cubic Parabola*** *option from the* ***Type*** *drop-down list. This option has been added to meet the requirements of New South Wales (Australia) standards.*

Point of Intersection Tools (PI)

The **Point of Intersection** tools can be used to add, delete, or break apart the PI of the tangents. The PI tools are discussed next.

Insert PI

This tool is used to create a point of intersection (PI) by breaking a fixed line into two adjacent fixed lines. To insert PI, choose the **Insert PI** button from the **Alignment Layout Tools** toolbar; you will be prompted to pick a point near to PI to insert the PI. Click at the location where you want to add the PI. Figure 5-8 shows a PI added to a fixed line.

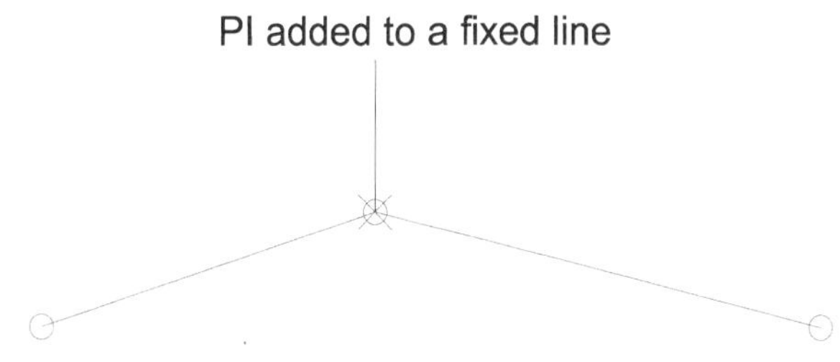

Figure 5-8 *PI added to a fixed line*

Delete PI

This tool is used to delete a point of intersection and create a single tangent from two adjacent tangents. If you remove a PI between two tangents, the result will be a combination of the two tangents. To delete a PI, choose the **Delete PI** button from the **Alignment Layout Tools** toolbar; you will be prompted to pick a point near the PI that you want to delete. Click in the drawing area near a PI; the PI will be removed. Press ENTER to end the command.

Break-apart PI

This tool is used to separate the point of intersection at which the endpoints of two tangents meet resulting in two separate tangents. To do so, choose the **Break-apart PI** button from the **Alignment Layout Tools** toolbar; you will be prompted to pick a point near a PI that you want to split. Click in the drawing near the PI, and then specify the distance by which you want to split it by specifying the points in the drawing or by entering the distance in the command line; the tangent or the fixed line will split into two different parts. Figure 5-9 shows the two split parts of the fixed line split up using the **Break-apart PI** tool.

Figure 5-9 *Fixed line after breaking apart from the PI*

Line Tools

The Line tools in the **Alignment Layout Tools** toolbar can be used to add a fixed, floating, or free line for creating an alignment geometry. Some of the line tools are discussed next.

Fixed Line (Two Points) Tool

This is the default line tool that is used to add a fixed line between two specified points. To invoke this tool, choose the **Fixed Line (Two Points)** drop-down list from the **Alignment Layout Tools** toolbar; you will be prompted to specify the start point. Click in the drawing to specify the start point and then specify the next point. Press ENTER to end the command.

Fixed Line (From curve end, length) Tool

This tool is used to add a fixed line by selecting the end point and direction of a fixed or a floating curve entity and then specifying the length of the line to be created. To invoke this tool, choose the down arrow on the right of the **Fixed Line (Two Points)** drop-down list in the **Alignment Layout Tools** toolbar and select the **Fixed Line (From curve end, length)** tool; you will be prompted to select the entity for specifying the start point and the direction. Select a fixed or floating curve and then specify the length for the line by picking two points in the drawing or entering the length in the command line. Figure 5-10 shows a fixed line added to a fixed curve entity.

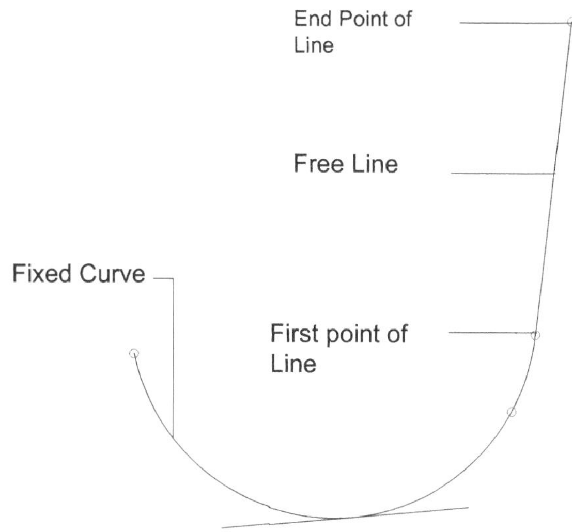

Figure 5-10 Fixed line added to a fixed curve entity

Floating Line (From curve, through point) Tool

This tool is used to add a floating line from a point which is on the existing curve to the specified point. To invoke this tool, choose the down arrow on the right of the **Draw Fixed Line (Two points)** tool and select the **Floating Line (From curve, through point)** tool from the drop-down menu; you will be prompted to select the entity to which the line needs to be attached. Select the entity in the drawing and then click to specify a point, through which the floating line passes when prompted to specify the end point in the command line, as shown in Figure 5-11.

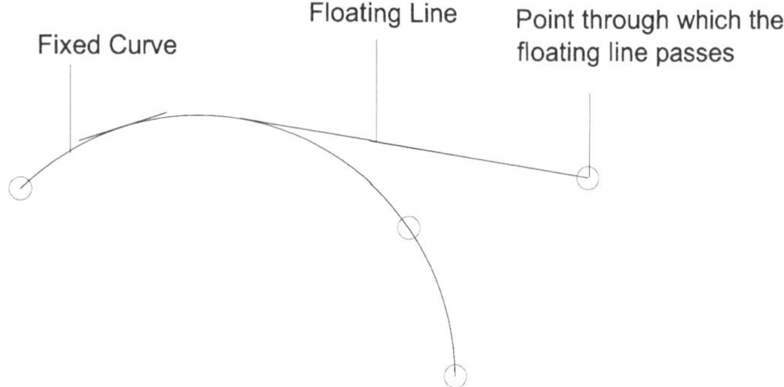

Figure 5-11 Floating line added to a fixed curve entity

Free Line (Between two curves) Tool

This tool is used to add a free line between two fixed or floating curves and is tangent to the curves at both the ends. To invoke this tool, choose the down arrow on the right of the **Draw Fixed Line-Two Points** tool and select **Free Line (Between two curves)** from the drop-down menu; you will be prompted to select the entity from which the free line is to be added. Select the first entity in the drawing and then select the second entity to which the free line is to be added. Figure 5-12 shows a free line added between two fixed curve entities.

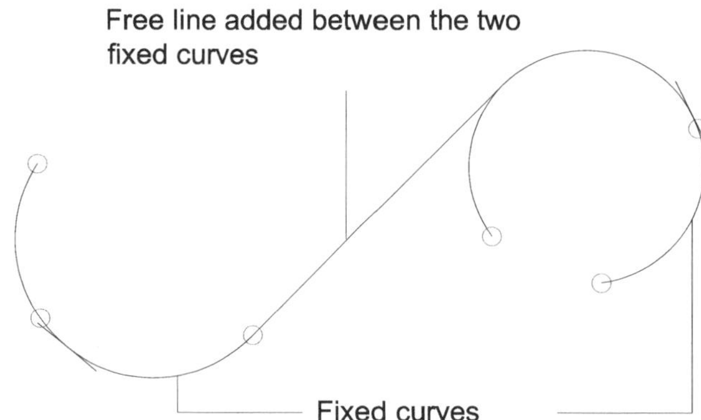

Figure 5-12 Free line added between the two fixed curve entities

Curve Tools

The curve tools are used to add fixed, floating, or free curves to the alignment geometry. Some of the curve tools are discussed next.

Fixed Curve (Three Points) Tool

This tool is used to add a fixed curve to the alignment geometry by specifying three points in the drawing. This tool is similar to the AutoCAD three point arc command. To draw a fixed curve, choose the default **Add Fixed Curve-Three Points** tool from the **Alignment Layout Tools - <alignment name>** toolbar; you will be prompted to specify the start point. Click in the drawing to specify the start point and then follow the prompts displayed in the command line to add a fixed arc.

There are other types of fixed curve tools to add the fixed curves to the alignment. To access them, choose the down arrow on the right of the **Fixed Curve (Three Points)** tool and select **More Fixed Curves** from the drop-down menu; a flyout with different curve tools will be displayed. Select the required tool from the cascading menu and follow the prompts displayed in the command line to add the curve to the alignment.

Floating Curve (From entity, radius, through point) Tool

This tool allows you to add a floating curve that will be tangent to the entity it is attached to. This curve is added by specifying the radius, a pass through point, and the angle range (less than or greater than 180 degrees). To add a floating curve, choose the down arrow on the right of the **Add Fixed Curve-Three point** tool and select it from the drop-down; you will be prompted to select the entity to which the floating curve will be attached. Next, specify the radius of the curve by picking two points in the drawing or by entering the radius in the command line. Next, specify the angle less than 180 degrees by accepting the default **<Less than180>** value or enter **G** in the command line and press ENTER to choose the **<Greater than180>** value to specify the angle more than 180 degrees. Next, specify the type of curve by accepting the default **<Compound>** value or entering **R** in the command line to choose the **Reverse** curve type.

There are other tools also that can be used to add the floating curves to the alignments. To view these tools, choose the down arrow on the right of the default tool, **Add Fixed Curve-Three point**, in the **Alignment Layout Tools** toolbar and select **More Floating Curves** from the drop-down; a flyout will be displayed. You can choose the required tool from the cascading menu to add the floating curve.

Free Curve Fillet (Between two entities, radius) Tool

This tool is used to add a free curve between two fixed or floating entities by specifying the radius for the curve. To add a free curve, choose the drop down arrow on the right of the **Floating Curve (From entity, radius, through point)** tool and select **Free Curve Fillet (Between two entities, radius)** from the drop-down; you will be prompted to select the entity to start the curve. First, select the entity in the drawing to start the curve and then the entity at which the curve will end. Next, specify the angle range, the curve type, and then radius of the curve. A free curve will be added between the two entities and it will always be tangent to these entities.

Line with Spiral Tools

These tools help you add a floating line with a spiral. There are two such types of tools available in the toolbar and these are discussed next.

Floating Line with Spiral (From curve, through point) Tool

This tool is used to attach a floating line with a spiral to a curve or a line passing through a point. On choosing this tool, you will be prompted to select the entity to attach the spiral. Once you select the entity, you will be prompted to specify the spiral length and a pass through point.

Floating Line with Spiral (From curve end, length) Tool

Use this tool to attach a floating line to a spiral that starts from the end of a curve. While using this tool, you need to specify the length of the floating line and spiral.

Curve with Spiral Tools

These tools help you add a spiral and a floating curve to the alignment. One such type of tool is discussed next.

Free Spiral - Curve - Spiral (Between two entities) Tool

This tool is chosen by default and is used to add a spiral between two entities by specifying the in and out lengths, curve type, and the radius of the spiral. Choose the down arrow on the right of this tool in the **Alignment Layout Tools** toolbar; a flyout with different tools will be displayed. You can choose the required tool from the flyout and add a curve with a spiral to the alignment.

Spiral Tools

Spiral tools are used to add fixed, free, or floating spirals to the alignment geometry. These tools can be accessed from the flyout that will be displayed on choosing the down arrow on the right of the **Free Compound Spiral - Spiral (Between two curves)** tool. Some of the spiral tools are discussed next.

Free Compound Spiral - Spiral (Between two curves) Tool

This tool is chosen by default and is used to add a compound spiral between two curves. Invoke this tool and select the entities in the drawing between which you want to add a spiral. If the curves are not in the same direction, a warning will be displayed on the screen. Choose **Yes** to continue or **No** to start the command again. While using this tool, you cannot specify the spiral length.

Fixed Spiral Tool

This tool is used to add a fixed spiral to the alignment. To add a fixed spiral, choose the down arrow on the left of the **Free Compound Spiral-Spiral (Between two curves)** tool; a drop-down will be displayed. Choose the **Fixed Spiral** tool from the drop-down; you will be prompted to select an entity to specify the start point and direction of the spiral. Select the entity in the drawing. Next, press ENTER to accept the default spiral type **Incurve**. Alternatively, enter **O** for the **Outcurve**, **P** for the **Point**, and **C** for the **Compound** spiral types in the command line. Next, press ENTER to accept the default curve direction **<Clockwise>** or enter **O** in the command line to choose the counterclockwise direction. Next, specify the spiral length by picking two points in the drawing or entering the value in the command line. Similarly, specify the radius for the spiral; the spiral will be added to the entity and will always be tangent to the alignment.

Free Reverse Spiral-Spiral (Between two curves) Tool

This tool is used to add a free reverse spiral between two curves. Choose this tool and select the entities between which you want to add a reverse spiral. Note that you cannot specify the spiral lengths in this case.

Convert AutoCAD line and arc Tool

Convert Autocad line and arc tool is used to convert the AutoCAD lines and arcs into an alignment entity.

Reverse Sub-entity Direction Tool

This tool is used to reverse the direction of a fixed line, curve, or an unconnected segment of the alignment. Invoke this tool, press and hold the CTRL key, and select the required single sub-entity; the directions of the entity will be reversed. Figures 5-13 and 5-14 show the direction of a fixed curve before and after using the **Reverse Sub-entity Direction** tool.

Delete Sub-entity Tool

This tool is used to delete an alignment sub entity. To delete an alignment sub entity, choose the **Delete Sub-entity** tool; you will be prompted to select the sub entity to be removed. Select the sub entity and the entity will be removed from the drawing.

Edit Best fit data for all entities Button

This tool is available only when the alignment consists of sub-entities that are created using the best fit tools. On invoking this tool, a table with the original regression data of the best fit sub-entities in the alignment will be displayed. You can edit the values in the data based on the design. The best fit entities are explained later in this chapter.

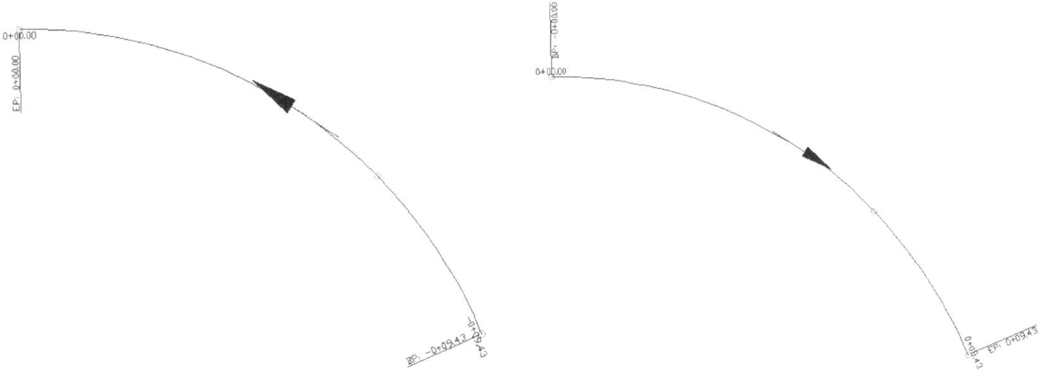

Figure 5-13 The direction of the fixed curve entity before reversing the direction

Figure 5-14 The direction of the fixed curve entity after reversing the direction

Pick Sub-entity Tool

The **Pick Sub-entity** tool is used to pick an alignment entity as well as to view and modify its parameters in the **Alignment Layout Parameters** window. Choose the **Pick Sub-entity** tool from the **Alignment Layout** toolbar; the **Alignment Layout Parameters** window will be displayed and you will be prompted to select the sub-entity. Select the required entity from the drawing; the parameters and their values will be displayed in the respective **Parameter** and the **Value** columns of the **Alignment Layout Parameters** window. You can view the parameters of the selected entity and also modify the values that are active.

Sub-entity Editor Tool

This tool is used to view and edit the parameters of the selected sub-entity of an alignment. Choose the **Sub-entity Editor** tool from the **Alignment Layout Tools** toolbar; the **Alignment Layout Parameters** window will be displayed. Next, invoke the **Pick Sub-entity** tool and select the required alignment sub-entity whose parameters you want to view and edit. On doing so, the **Alignment Layout Parameters** window will be populated with the parameters of the selected sub-entity. You can edit all the parameters that are displayed in black.

Alignment Grid View Tool

This tool is used to view an alignment entity in a table view. You can modify the values of the features that appear in boldface letters in the **PANORAMA** window. Choose the **Alignment Grid View** tool from the **Alignment Layout Tools** toolbar; the **PANORAMA** window with the **Alignment entities** tab will be displayed, as shown in Figure 5-15. The alignment entities will be displayed in rows and their features will be listed in columns. You can numerically edit all features that appear in bold.

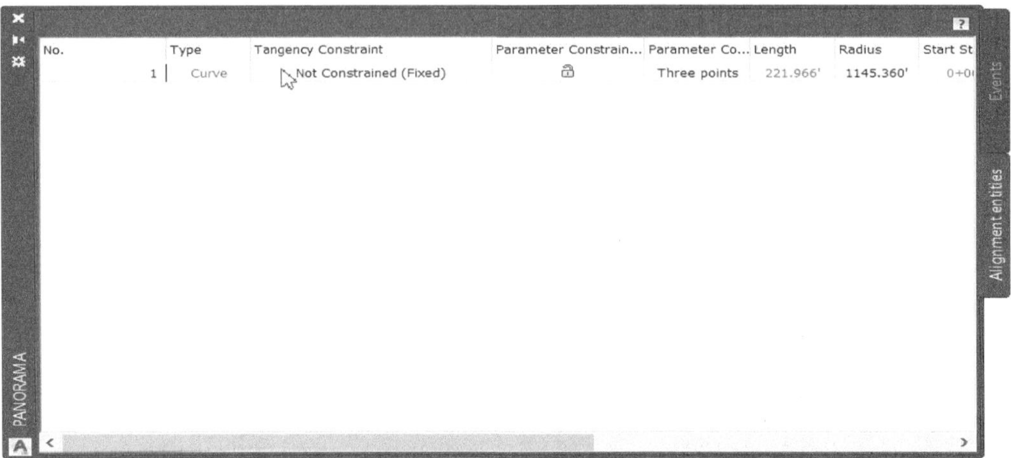

*Figure 5-15 The **PANORAMA** window with the **Alignment entities** tab*

Note that if the alignment consists of the sub-entities created from the best fit, the **PANORAMA** window with an extra **Regression Data** tab will be displayed, as shown in Figure 5-16.

Property	Value
Entity1	Line
Length	53.507'
Direc...	S1° 43' 38"E
Start ...	(20414.0768...
End P...	(20415.6895...

Pt No.	Exclude	Pass Throu...	Point Northing	Point Easting	Weight	Offset to
1	☐	☐	20837.1638'	20393.2472'	1.000	-20.839'
2	☐	☐	20828.9357'	20439.7661'	1.000	25.411'
3	☐	☐	20784.1713'	20411.1200'	1.000	-4.572'

Regression Graph:

*Figure 5-16 The **PANORAMA** window with the **Regression Data** tab showing the regression data from the **Best Fit** alignment entities*

This tab displays the regression data from the best fit entities. It also displays the regression graph at the bottom of the window and the attributes of the best fit entity in a tree structure in the left panel of this window. The **Regression Graph** displays the relationship between the regression data and the best fit entity created. The red line indicates the regression points and the green line represents the best fit entity. Some of the options in the **PANORAMA** window are discussed next.

Add more points

Choose the **Add more points** button to add more points by using various import options in the **Best Fit** dialog box.

Delete Selected Points

Choose the **Delete Selected Points** button to delete the selected points from the regression table. This tool will be activated only when you select a row in the regression table.

Click here to empty current regression sample data

Choose the **Click here to empty current regression sample data** button to clear the data in the regression table.

Click here to create entity and continue to edit the data

Choose the **Click here to create entity and continue to edit the data** button to create the line, arc, or parabola based on the data after editing the data in the regression table. The **PANORAMA** window will be displayed for further editing of the data if required.

Press to dismiss this vista

On choosing the **Press to dismiss this vista** button from the **PANORAMA** window, the entity is created using the data in the table and the **Regression Data** vista will be closed.

The **Undo** and **Redo** tools of the **Alignment Layout Tools** toolbar help you revert to the last edit operation made in the alignment entity. Thus, you can use the required tools from the toolbar to create the alignment based on the design requirement.

CREATING ALIGNMENTS USING THE BEST FIT METHOD

The best fit method is used to get the best fitting alignment using the various Civil 3D objects such as the COGO points, AutoCAD points, lines, and arcs. You can access the tools for creating the best fit entities from the **Best Fit** drop-down in the **Draw** panel of the **Home** tab. You can use these tools to easily complete the complex alignment designs. Besides polylines, Civil 3D also allows you to convert lines and curves into an alignment.

The tools in the **Best Fit** drop-down help you create lines, arcs, and parabolas from various AutoCAD entities. You can also create a best fit alignment by picking points from the screen. These tools are especially used for the rehabilitation projects where you need to resurvey the existing road. In these type of projects, the existing survey data may not match with the original survey data. This situation demands that you create an alignment from the available data. You can use the tools from the **Best Fit** drop-down to edit the lines and curves to match the actual survey data in the best possible way. These tools can also be used for both alignments and profiles. To access these tools, click on the down arrow next to the **Best Fit** drop-down in the **Draw** panel. On doing so, a list of tools will be displayed, as shown in Figure 5-17. Invoke the required tool from the drop-down. These tools are discussed next.

***Figure 5-17** The tools in the **Best Fit** drop-down*

Creating Lines, Arcs, and Points as Entities by Using the Best Fit Entities Tool

Ribbon: Home > Draw > Best Fit drop-down > Create Best Fit Line / Create Best Fit Arc / Create Best Fit Parabola
Command: CREATELINEBYBESTFIT / CREATEARCBYBESTFIT / CREATEPARABOLABYBESTFIT

To create a line of best fit, choose the **Create Best Fit Line** tool from the **Draw** panel; the **Line by Best Fit** dialog box will be displayed, as shown in Figure 5-18. You can create the best fit entity by selecting one of the four different options available in this dialog box.

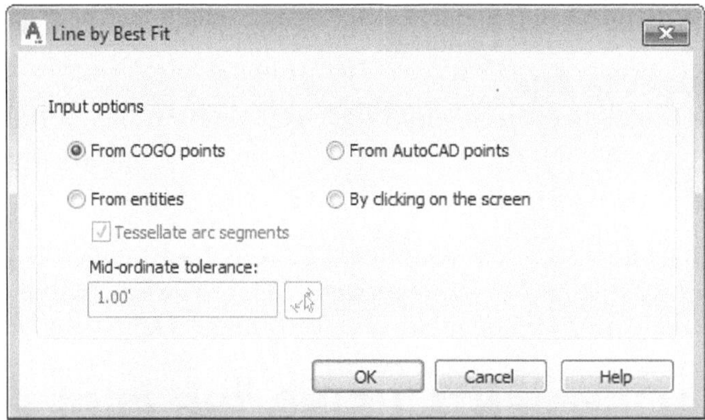

*Figure 5-18 The **Line by Best Fit** dialog box*

To create a line using the Civil 3D points, select the **From COGO points** radio button from the **Line by Best Fit** dialog box and then choose the **OK** button; the **Line by Best Fit** dialog box will close and you will be prompted to select the point objects. Select the point objects in the drawing and press ENTER; the **PANORAMA** window with the **Regression Data** will be displayed. You can edit the regression data in the **PANORAMA** window as required and choose the **Create Entity** button to create a line of best fit.

To create a line from the middle of an entity, select the **From entities** radio button; the **Mid-ordinate tolerance** edit box will be enabled in which you can specify the mid-ordinate distance.

Similarly, you can create the best fit arc and parabola entities by choosing the **Create Arc/Create Parabola** tool from the **Draw** panel. The steps involved in creating these entities are the same as those explained for creating the line entity.

To convert the **Best Fit** entities into an alignment, choose the **Convert AutoCAD line and arc** tool from the **Alignment Layout Tools** toolbar and select the required line and arc to convert them into an alignment.

CRITERIA-BASED ALIGNMENT DESIGN

In AutoCAD Civil 3D, you can use its criteria-based design feature to ensure that your design meets the required project standards. Before you understand the workflow of creating the criteria-based alignment design, it is important to understand various design criteria.

Design Criteria

The design criteria file is an XML file within AutoCAD Civil 3D that consists of the common and minimum design criteria for creating alignments and profiles. The design criteria values are specified for design speeds, minimum speed, superelevation, curve radius, and length of the individual alignment entities. There are two design criteria files available in Civil 3D, one in **Metric Units** and other in **Imperial Units**. These design criteria are based on AASHTO (American Association of State and Highway Transport Officials) standards. The design criteria files can be customized to match the required standards for the project and then saved on a local server. A design file on a server can be accessible to all members of the team. The design criteria for creating profiles and alignment are discussed next.

Minimum Radius at the Specified Design Speed

This criterion specifies a set of values for the minimum curve radius at different vehicle speed for a given superelevation. Figure 5-19 shows a Civil 3D design criteria file based on AASHTO standards for the minimum radii at the specified design speed for a fixed superelevation of 6%.

Superelevation Attainment Method

This criterion specifies the superelevation applied and the method used to calculate it. Civil 3D supports two methods to calculate superelevation, **Standard** and **Planar**. The **Standard** method is used to calculate superelevation for undivided crowned roads and divided roads. It also involves removal of the adverse crown. On the other hand, the **Planar** method does not involve the removal of the crown and is used only for the panel-section roads without crown. Each of these methods specifies the formulas to calculate the distance between the transition points. You will learn about superelevation in detail later in this chapter. Figure 5-20 shows the superelevation attainment method table created from the design criteria file to calculate the transition.


```
<MinimumRadiusTable name="AASHTO 2004 US Customary eMax 6%">
  <MinimumRadius speed="15" radius="39" />
  <MinimumRadius speed="20" radius="81" />
  <MinimumRadius speed="25" radius="144" />
  <MinimumRadius speed="30" radius="231" />
  <MinimumRadius speed="35" radius="340" />
  <MinimumRadius speed="40" radius="485" />
  <MinimumRadius speed="45" radius="643" />
  <MinimumRadius speed="50" radius="833" />
  <MinimumRadius speed="55" radius="1060" />
  <MinimumRadius speed="60" radius="1330" />
  <MinimumRadius speed="65" radius="1660" />
  <MinimumRadius speed="70" radius="2040" />
  <MinimumRadius speed="75" radius="2500" />
  <MinimumRadius speed="80" radius="3050" />
```


Figure 5-19 The minimum radius table from the design criteria file


```
- <TransitionStyleStandard>
    <TransitionFormula type="LCtoFS" formula="{t}" />
    <TransitionFormula type="LCtoBC" formula="{p}*{t}" />
    <TransitionFormula type="NCtoLC" formula="{t}*{c}/{e}" />
    <TransitionFormula type="LCtoRC" formula="{t}*{c}/{e}" />
    <TransitionFormula type="NStoNC" formula="{t}*({s}-{c})/{e}" />
  </TransitionStyleStandard>
</SuperelevationAttainmentMethod>
<SuperelevationAttainmentMethod name="Planar Roadway">
- <TransitionStylePlanar>
  - <Continuing>
      <TransitionFormula type="NCtoFS" formula="{t}-{t}*{c}/{e}" />
      <TransitionFormula type="NCtoBC" formula="{t}*({p}-{c}/{e})" />
    </Continuing>
  - <Opposing>
      <TransitionFormula type="LCtoFS" formula="{t}" />
      <TransitionFormula type="LCtoBC" formula="{p}*{t}" />
      <TransitionFormula type="NCtoLC" formula="{t}*{c}/{e}" />
    </Opposing>
```


***Figure 5-20** The superelevation attainment method table from the design criteria file*

Superelevation Rate at a Given Radius

This criterion specifies a set of values for superelevation and radii for a given speed. Figure 5-21 shows a reference from the design criteria file showing the superelevation rate at a fixed speed of 30 and varying curve radii.

Minimum Radius Length at a Given Radius

This criterion specifies the minimum transition length required at a given radius. The transition length varies according to the curve radius at a given speed. For example, at a road design speed of 15 and a curve radius of 605, the required transition length will be 34. On the other hand, if the curve radius is 496 and the road design speed is the same then the transition length will be 40. Figure 5-22 shows a reference from the design criteria file showing different transition lengths required at a fixed speed of 15 and varying curve radii.

```
- <SuperelevationDesignSpeed speed="30">
    <SuperelevationRate radius="3240" eRate="1.5" />
    <SuperelevationRate radius="2370" eRate="2.0" />
    <SuperelevationRate radius="2130" eRate="2.2" />
    <SuperelevationRate radius="1930" eRate="2.4" />
    <SuperelevationRate radius="1760" eRate="2.6" />
    <SuperelevationRate radius="1610" eRate="2.8" />
    <SuperelevationRate radius="1480" eRate="3.0" />
    <SuperelevationRate radius="1370" eRate="3.2" />
    <SuperelevationRate radius="1270" eRate="3.4" />
    <SuperelevationRate radius="1160" eRate="3.6" />
    <SuperelevationRate radius="1100" eRate="3.8" />
    <SuperelevationRate radius="1030" eRate="4.0" />
    <SuperelevationRate radius="955" eRate="4.2" />
    <SuperelevationRate radius="893" eRate="4.4" />
    <SuperelevationRate radius="834" eRate="4.6" />
    <SuperelevationRate radius="779" eRate="4.8" />
    <SuperelevationRate radius="727" eRate="5.0" />
    <SuperelevationRate radius="676" eRate="5.2" />
    <SuperelevationRate radius="627" eRate="5.4" />
    <SuperelevationRate radius="582" eRate="5.6" />
    <SuperelevationRate radius="542" eRate="5.0" />
```

Figure 5-21 The superelevation rate table from the design criteria file for the design speed

```
- <TransitionLengthTable name="2 Lane">
  - <TransitionLengthDesignSpeed speed="15">
      <TransitionLength radius="932" tLength="0" />
      <TransitionLength radius="676" tLength="31" />
      <TransitionLength radius="605" tLength="34" />
      <TransitionLength radius="546" tLength="37" />
      <TransitionLength radius="496" tLength="40" />
      <TransitionLength radius="453" tLength="43" />
      <TransitionLength radius="415" tLength="46" />
      <TransitionLength radius="382" tLength="49" />
      <TransitionLength radius="352" tLength="52" />
      <TransitionLength radius="324" tLength="55" />
      <TransitionLength radius="300" tLength="50" />
      <TransitionLength radius="277" tLength="62" />
      <TransitionLength radius="255" tLength="65" />
      <TransitionLength radius="235" tLength="68" />
      <TransitionLength radius="215" tLength="71" />
      <TransitionLength radius="193" tLength="74" />
      <TransitionLength radius="172" tLength="77" />
      <TransitionLength radius="154" tLength="80" />
      <TransitionLength radius="139" tLength="83" />
      <TransitionLength radius="126" tLength="86" />
      <TransitionLength radius="115" tLength="89" />
      <TransitionLength radius="105" tLength="92" />
```

***Figure 5-22** The transition length table from the design criteria file*

The design criteria files contain many tables specifying different design values based on the AASHTO standards. AutoCAD Civil 3D will display a warning symbol in the drawing if these standards are violated while creating the alignment. When you create an alignment from the **Alignment Layout Tools** toolbar, the minimum criteria values will be displayed automatically in the command line. You can accept the default values or enter new ones.

Note

*AutoCAD Civil 3D provides predefined and country-specific **Country Kits** or design templates. To download these templates, visit **www.autodesk.com**, enter **Country Kits** in the **Search** field and then press ENTER. Next, click on the **AutoCAD Civil 3D Services & Support - Templates & Libraries** link; the **Templates and Libraries** page will be displayed. Scroll down the page to view the country kits and download the required country kit. These lists are basically .exe files consisting of country specific drafting and design standards that you can use to create your designs.*

Creating Connected Alignments

New

Ribbon:	Home > Create Design > Alignment drop-down > Create Connected Alignment
Command:	CREATEALIGNMENTCONNECTED

The new connected alignment capabilities in AutoCAD Civil 3D 2018 allow you to create a new dynamically linked alignment and profile that enables transitions between two intersecting alignments and their profiles. You can use this feature to create a curb return, an exit ramp, a merging/diverging road, or to connect an existing road with a proposed road.

Choose the **Create Connected Alignment** tool from the **Alignment** drop-down in the **Create Design** panel of the **Home** tab; first you will be prompted to select the first alignment and then the second alignment from the drawing. Now, you will be prompted to pick a location for connected alignment and then press ENTER to accept the location; the **Create Connected Alignment** dialog box will be displayed, as shown in figure 5-23. In this dialog box, you need to make the required settings or accept the default settings and then choose the OK button; the connected alignment will be created, as shown in Figure 5-24.

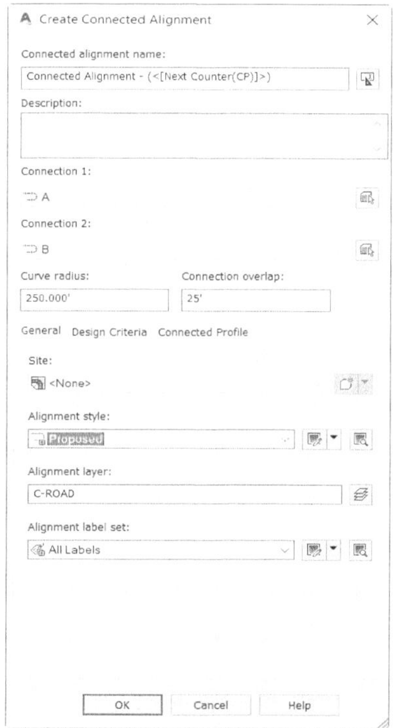

Figure 5-23 *The* ***Create Connected Alignment*** *dialog box*

Connnected alignment is defined as a connection between two alignments. Figure 5-24 shows connected aligmnent betweeen two different alignments.

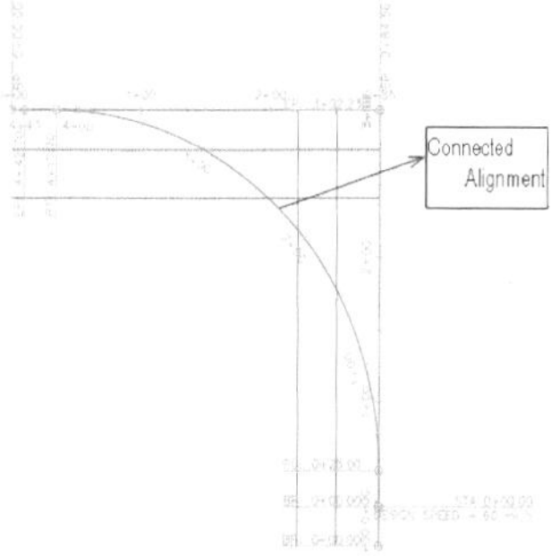

Figure 5-24 *The connected alignment between two different alignment.*

Design Checks

Design checks are created to check the criteria which are not included in the in-built design criteria files. These checks are basically mathematical expressions defined to verify that the alignment entities such as lines, curves, and spirals comply with the criteria set for the alignment. You can create individual design checks for lines, spirals, curves, and tangents and save them in a design check set that can be applied to an alignment. As explained earlier, a design check set is a collection of different design checks. You can create a new design check set or edit an existing one by choosing **Alignment > Design Checks > Design Check Sets** in the **Settings** tab in the **TOOLSPACE** palette. The detailed method of creating the design checks is discussed next.

Creating a Design Check

To create a new design check, choose the **Settings** tab and expand **Design Checks** sub node in **Alignment** node; you will notice different entities listed in the **Design Checks** node. You can create the design checks for any of those listed entities. To create a design check for the line sub-entity of an alignment, right-click on the **Line** subnode; a shortcut menu will be displayed. Choose **New** from the shortcut menu; the **New Design Check - New Alignment Design Check** dialog box will be displayed, as shown in Figure 5-25. The options in this dialog box are discussed next.

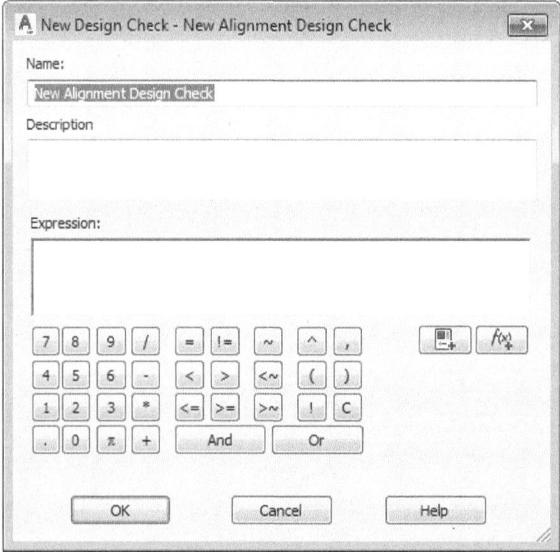

*Figure 5-25 The **New Design Check - New Alignment Design Check** dialog box*

Name

Use the **Name** edit box to specify the name for the current design check.

Description

Enter a short description about the design check in this text box.

Expression

The **Expression** edit box is used to enter the mathematical expressions for the design check using functions, properties, buttons, and logical operators. The different operators that can be used to create design checks are listed next.

Operator	Operation
=	logical equals
!=	logical not equals
!	logical not
<	logical less-than
>	logical greater-than
<=	logical less-than or equals
>=	logical greater-than or equals
~	logical approximately equal
<~	logical less-than or approximately equal
>~	logical greater-than or approximately equal

Operator	Operation
+	binary addition
-	binary subtraction
*	binary multiplication
/	binary division
AND	boolean **AND**
–	unary minus
+	unary plus
^	power

Insert property

The **Insert property** button is used to insert a property in the design check. Choose this button; a flyout with different options will be displayed. Choose the required property from the flyout to add it to the **Expression** edit box. For example, if you want that the length of any sub-entity of an alignment should be equal to or greater than 100, choose the **Insert property** button and then choose **Length** from the flyout and add the **>=** logical operator by choosing the respective button from the dialog box. You can also use the parenthesis at the start and end of the design check expression.

Insert function

The **Insert function** button is used to add a function in the design check expression. Choose the **Insert function** button; a flyout will be displayed. Choose the required function from the flyout to add it to the design check expression. Some of the functions are as follows:

Function	Description
ACOS(x)	Returns arccosine of x
ABS(x)	Returns absolute value of x
ASIN(x)	Returns arcsin of x
ATAN(x)	Returns arctangent of x
ATAN2(y,x)	Returns arctangent of y/x in the correct quadrant based on signs of x and y
COS(theta)	Returns the cosine of theta
SEC(theta)	Returns the secant of theta
COSH(theta)	Returns the hyperbolic cosine of theta
SECH(theta)	Returns the hyperbolic secant of theta

DEG2GRD(theta)	Converts theta in degrees to gradients
DEG2RAD(theta)	Converts theta in degrees to radians
EXP(x)	Returns exponential of x
TAN(theta)	Returns the tangent of theta
COT(theta)	Returns the cotangent of theta
TANH(theta)	Returns the hyperbolic tangent of theta
COTH(theta)	Returns the hyperbolic cotangent of theta
TRUNC(x)	Truncates x to an integer value
IF(test,true_val,false_val)	Evaluates test, if test is non-zero evaluates and returns true_val. Else, evaluates and returns false_val. True_val and false_val can be any expression

After you have created the design check expression, choose the **OK** button to close the **New Design Check - New Alignment Design Check** dialog box. The created design check will now be added to the **Line** node in the **Settings** tab. Similarly, you can create a design check for the curve, spiral, and tangent intersection entities listed in the **Design Checks** collection of the **Settings** tab. You can then add these design checks in a design check set and use them for creating alignments.

Working with Design Checks in a Design Check Set

To add a design check in a design check set, choose the **Settings** tab and expand the **Alignment** node. Now, choose the **Design Check Sets** subnode to view the default name of the design check set. Next, right-click on the **Design Check Sets** and choose **New** from the shortcut menu displayed; the **Alignment Design Check Set - New Alignment Check Set** dialog box will be displayed. The **Information** tab will be chosen by default in this dialog box. In this tab, enter a name of the check set in the **Name** edit box. Next, choose the **Design Checks** tab. In this tab, select the required option from the **Type** and **<Geometry Type> Checks** drop-down lists. Next, choose the **Add** button to add the selected design check and type in the respective columns, refer to Figure 5-26. Then, choose the **OK** button to close the dialog box.

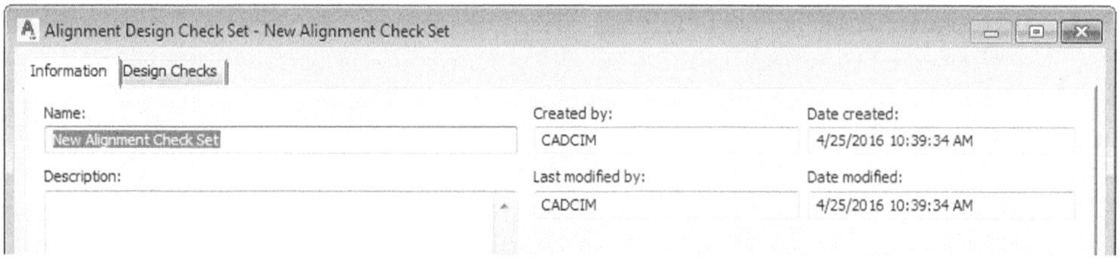

***Figure 5-26** The partial view of the **Alignment Design Check Set - New Alignment Check Set** dialog box showing some design checks*

To edit an existing **Design Check Sets**, right-click on the required design check in the **Alignment Design Check Set** dialog box; the choose **Edit** option from the shortcut menu displayed. The **Alignment Design Check Set - <Name>** dialog box will be displayed. On completion of edits, choose the **OK** button to save changes and exit the dialog box.

To assign a design check while creating the alignment, select the required design check set from the **Use design check set** drop-down in the **Design Criteria** tab of the **Create Alignment - Layout** or the **Create Alignment - From Object** dialog box.

Creating a Design-based Alignment

Ribbon: Home > Create Design > Alignment drop-down > Alignment Creation Tools
Command: CREATEALIGNMENTLAYOUT

To create a design-based alignment, choose the **Alignment Creation Tools** tool in the **Create Design** panel from the **Home** tab; the **Create Alignment - Layout** dialog box will be displayed. Choose the **Design Criteria** tab in this dialog box. The **Design Criteria** tab is used to specify the options for creating the criteria-based alignment. The options in this tab are discussed next.

Starting design speed

The **Starting design speed** edit box displays the default value of the design speed at the starting station of the alignment. Enter the starting design speed in the edit box. If you do not specify the design speed for other stations in the alignment, the design speed specified at the first station will be applied throughout the alignment.

Use criteria-based design

Select the **Use criteria-based design** check box to apply the design criteria to the alignment; the options in the **Use design criteria file** area will be activated.

Use design criteria file

The **Use design criteria file** check box is selected by default if the **Use criteria-based design** check box is selected. Also, a design criteria file is selected by default and displayed in the textbox of the **Use design criteria file** area. This design criteria file is located in the Autodesk installation folder C:*Program data\Autodesk\C3D 2018\enu\Data\Corridor Design Standards\Imperial_Autodesk Civil 3D Imperial (2011) Roadway Design Standards.xml*

To choose a different design criteria file, click the browse button; the **Select Design Speed Table** dialog box will be displayed. Browse and open the required design criteria file. From this file, you can specify the superelevation attainment method, minimum radius, and transition (spiral) length in their respective tables.

Default criteria

The **Default criteria** table displays the properties and default values included in the criteria file. You can change the default values of these properties by clicking in the corresponding **Value** field of the properties and selecting an option from the drop-down list displayed, as shown in Figure 5-27.

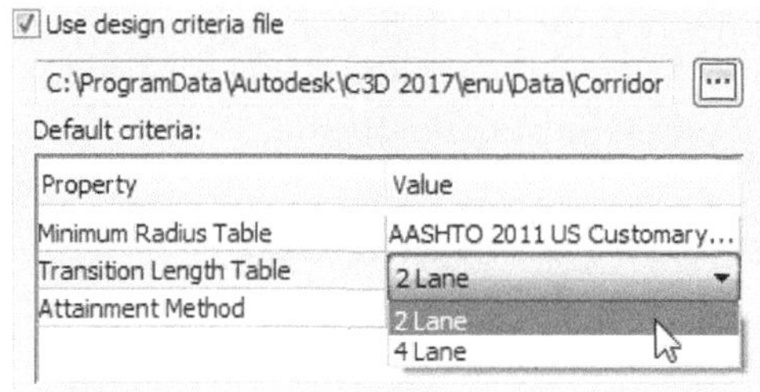

Figure 5-27 Selecting an option from the drop-down list displayed

Use design check set

The **Use design check set** check box is selected by default. As a result, you can use and select an alignment design check set. Select the required design check set from the drop-down list below this check box. While drafting an alignment, if the design parameters of any sub-entity do not comply with the minimum values specified in the design criteria file, Civil 3D will display a warning symbol on that sub-entity, as shown in Figure 5-28.

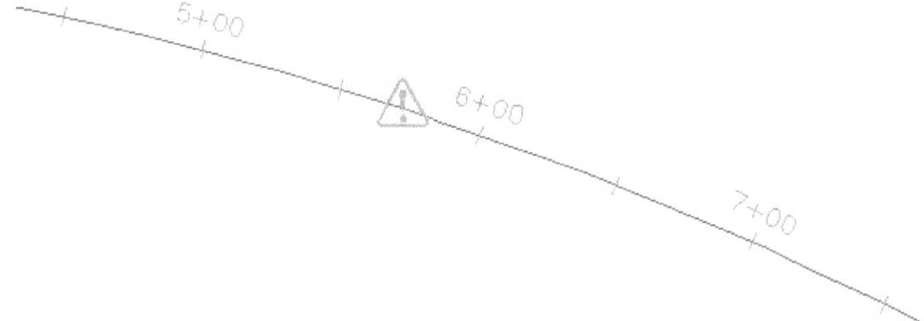

Figure 5-28 The warning symbol displayed on the curve

If you hover the cursor over the warning symbol, a tooltip will be displayed showing the standard that has been violated and also the values that are required to rectify the violation. The warning message is also displayed in the **Alignment Entities** tab of the **PANORAMA** window displayed on choosing the **Alignment Grid View** tool from the **Alignment Layout Tools** toolbar.

Editing the Design Criteria

You can edit and customize the design criteria according to your required standards. To edit design criteria, select the required alignment in the current drawing; the **Alignment:<Alignment name>** tab will be displayed. In this tab, choose the **Design Criteria Editor** tool from the **Modify** panel; the **Design Criteria Editor - <design criteria file name.xml>** dialog box will be displayed, as shown in Figure 5-29.

On the left pane of this dialog box, three collections are displayed: **Units**, **Alignments**, and **Profiles**. Expand the **Alignments** collection; four sub-collection will be displayed namely the minimum radius tables, superelevation attainment methods, superelevation tables, and widening methods. You can expand the required sub-collection for which you want to edit the design criteria. For example, to change the minimum radius in the design, expand the **Minimum Radius Table** sub-collection and select any of the tables listed in it. On doing so, the values of different design speeds and the minimum radii will be displayed in columns on the right pane of the dialog box. Click on the required radius value and change it at the specified design speed according to the design criteria.

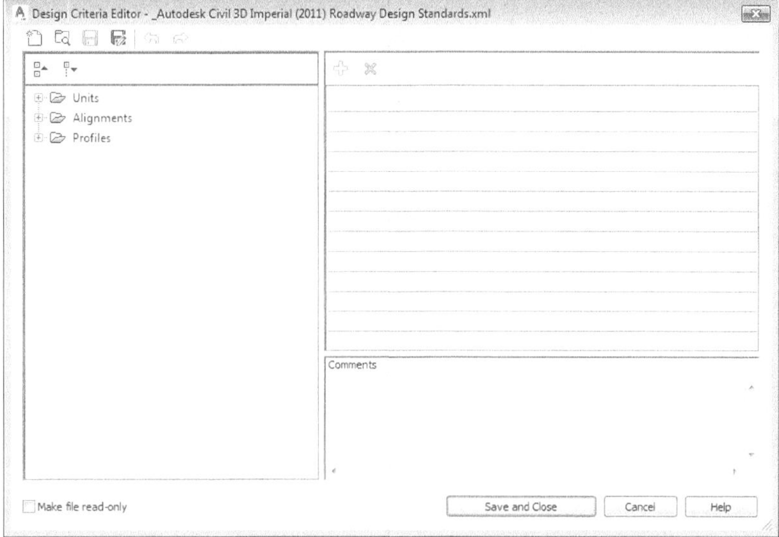

Figure 5-29 The ***Design Criteria Editor - _Autodesk Civil 3D Imperial (2011) Roadway Design Standards.xml*** *dialog box*

Similarly, expand other sub-collections. Select them to display the design parameters in columns on the right pane of the dialog box. You can edit the values as required. You can also modify the units for the design criteria file by using the **Units** collection. The **Profiles** collection allows you to edit the profile criteria if the alignment consists of any profiles. This will be discussed later in the chapter. The different buttons in the **Design Criteria Editor** dialog box are discussed next.

New

Choose the **New** button to create a new design criteria file; an empty file without any design parameter will be displayed.

Open

The **Design Criteria Editor** dialog box is displayed with the default design criteria in a file. If you want to edit the design criteria of any other design criteria file that you have customized, choose the **Open** button; the **Select a Design Criteria File** dialog box will be displayed. Select and open the required design criteria file using this dialog box.

Save

This button is activated only after you edit a design parameter. Choose the **Save** button to save the changes made in the design criteria file.

Save As

Choose the **Save As** button to save the current design criteria file using a different file name; the **Enter a file name to save** dialog box will be displayed. Enter a name in the **File name** edit box and choose the **Save** button to save the file.

Add

Choose the **Add** button to add a new row above the selected row or at the end of the parameters table if you have not selected one.

Delete

Choose the **Delete** button to delete the required rows from the table.

Note

*The **Undo** and **Redo** buttons can be used to revert to the change made recently in the design parameter value and the recent undo operation performed.*

Comments

The **Comments** text box is used to add a comment about the selected design parameters from the left pane of the dialog box. These comments will be saved with the file and are displayed every time you select the design criteria.

Make file read-only

Select the **Make file read-only** check box to prevent the design criteria file from being modified. On selecting this check box, the values displayed on the right pane will be deactivated.

Save and Close

Choose the **Save** and **Close** button to save the changes made in the design criteria and close the **Design Criteria Editor- <design criteria file name>** dialog box, respectively.

ALIGNMENT PROPERTIES

Ribbon:	Alignment > Modify > Alignment Properties drop-down > Alignment Properties
Command:	EDITALIGNMENTPROPERTIES

To view and edit the alignment properties, select the required alignment from the drawing; the **Alignment:<Alignment Name>** tab will be displayed. Next, choose the **Alignment Properties** tool from the **Modify** panel; the **Alignment Properties - <alignment name>** dialog box will be displayed. This dialog box is used to assign new name and object style, and set station equations, design criteria, and superelevation properties to an alignment. You can also view the profile information if the alignment consists of profiles. You will learn about the profiles in the next chapter. The tabs in this dialog box are discussed next.

Tip

*You can also select the required alignment name from the **Alignments** collection in the **Prospector** tab of the **Toolspace** palette and right-click to display the shortcut menu. Choose **Properties** from the shortcut menu to display the **Alignment Properties** dialog box.*

Information Tab

The **Information** tab displays the name and object style of the selected alignment. You can modify the name by using the **Name** edit box. The style can be changed by selecting an option from the **Object style** drop-down list.

Station Control Tab

This tab help you to change the station reference point and add station equations along an alignment. The options in this tab are discussed next.

Reference point Area

The **Reference point** area displays the XY coordinates of the default station reference point and displays the starting station of the alignment. By default, the starting station of the alignment is considered as the station reference point and its coordinates are displayed in the **X** and **Y** edit boxes, as shown in Figure 5-30.

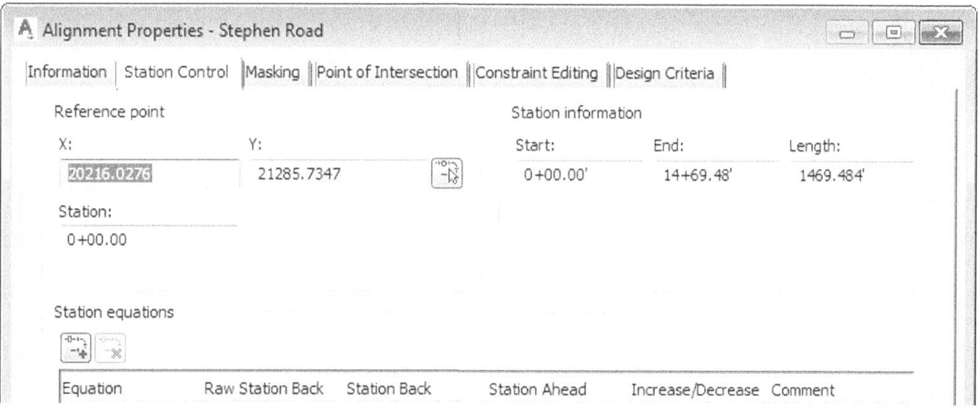

Figure 5-30 *The coordinates displayed in the* ***X*** *and* ***Y*** *edit boxes in the* ***Reference point*** *area*

You can modify the reference point for the alignment. To do so, choose the **Pick reference point** button on the right and specify the reference point by picking a station along the alignment from the drawing. To change the default station value of the alignment, enter the required station value in the **Station** edit box of this area. Note that the information displayed in the **Station information** area changes according to the values entered in the **Station** edit box.

Note

The start station of the alignment can be specified before creating the alignment by entering the value in the ***Starting station*** *edit box of the* ***Create Alignment - Layout/from Objects*** *dialog boxes. However, if you did not specify the start station in the beginning, you can do it in the* ***Alignment Properties*** *dialog box.*

Station equations Area

This area allows you to display and create the station equations. To create a new station equation, choose the **Add station equation** button; the **Alignment Properties** dialog box will disappear and you will be prompted to specify a station along the alignment. Pick the required station from the alignment; the **Alignment Properties** dialog box will be displayed again and the information will displayed in the **Station equations** area. You can change the values in the **Raw Station Back**, **Station Ahead** and **Increase/Decrease** columns by clicking in the respective column cells. To add more station equations, choose the **Add station equation** button again; the new station equation will be added before the previously added station. Note that the station equation added first becomes your last station equation.

Note

*The **Autodesk Autocad Civil 3D 2018** warning message box will be displayed, if any changes are done in the **stations control** tab. Choose **OK** to continue or choose **Cancel** to terminate the command.*

Design Criteria Tab

This tab is used to assign or edit the design criteria and speeds. This tab can also be used to assign variable speed limits for stations along an alignment. However, only one design speed can be assigned to any given station.

Design Speeds Area

The **Design Speeds** area allows you to specify the design speeds at a station. Note that a default design speed is already added in the **Design Speed** column of this area. To change the default value, double-click on it in the **Design Speed** column and enter the value you require. Next, specify the station at which you want to assign the speed by clicking in the **Start Station** column and choosing the pick button displayed there; you will be prompted to specify the station. Select the required station from the drawing; the selected station will be displayed in the **Start Station** column.

To add a new design speed at a station, choose the **Add design speed** button; a new record is added to the table. Edit the values for **Start Station** and **Design Speed**. To delete a record for design speed, select the record and then choose the **Delete design speed** button.

You can also add a comment or instructions about the design speeds in the **Comment** column. To apply a design criterion, select the **Use criteria-based design** check box. If the criterion is already assigned, you can change the design criteria file and the design check set.

Note

*If you select the **Use criteria-based design** check box without assigning a single design speed, Civil 3D will display a warning message box informing you to assign a design speed. This message is displayed because you need to specify at least one design speed to create a design-based alignment. Choose the **Yes** button from the dialog box to proceed further.*

ALIGNMENT STYLES

Alignment styles help you control the appearance of the objects, labels, and tables of an alignment. AutoCAD Civil 3D consists of various in-built styles that are applied automatically to alignment objects. You can also create new alignment styles and control the display of alignment objects, alignment labels, and tables as required. The alignment styles are created and managed in the **Settings** tab of the **TOOLSPACE** palette.

Creating an Alignment Style

The alignment styles control the visual display of the alignment entities such as lines, arcs, curves, and tangents. To create alignment styles, choose the **Settings** tab of the **TOOLSPACE** palette and expand the **Alignment** node. Right-click on the **Alignment Styles** option and choose **New** from the shortcut menu displayed; the **Alignment Style - New Alignment Style** dialog box will be displayed, as shown in Figure 5-31. The tabs in this dialog box are discussed next.

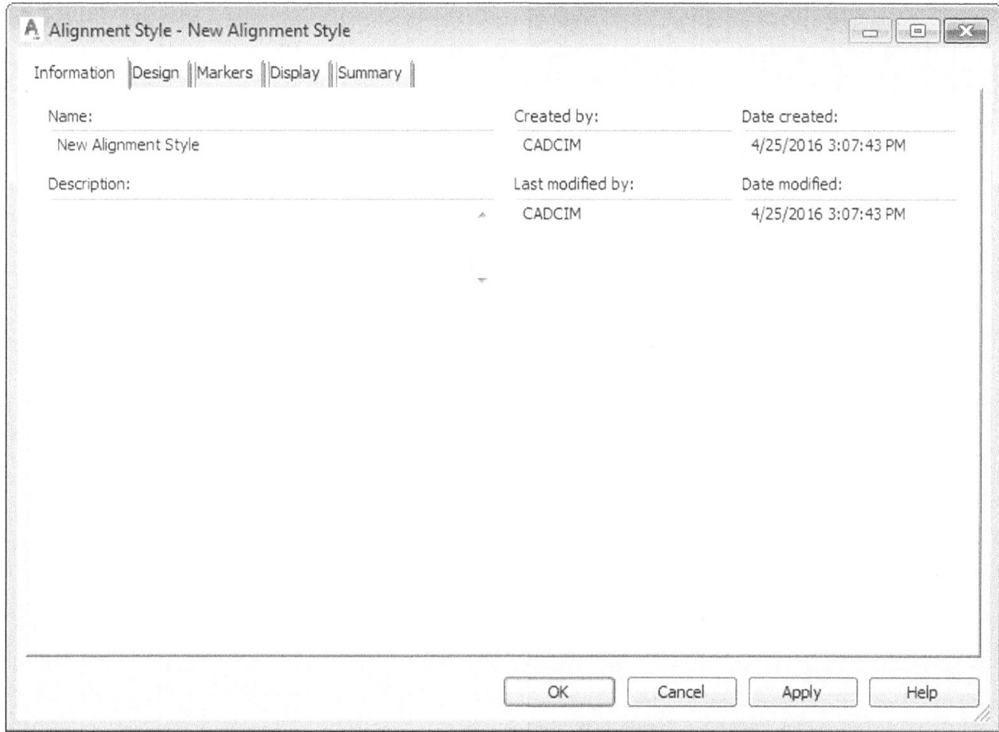

*Figure 5-31 The **Alignment Style - New Alignment Style** dialog box*

Information Tab

This tab is used to specify the name and description of the alignment style. Use the **Name** and **Description** edit boxes to specify the name and description of the alignment style.

Design Tab

This tab is used to specify the grip behavior for alignment curves while editing the alignment. Select the **Enable radius snap** check box in the **Grip edit behavior** area to enable the cursor to snap to a specified increment value of the free curve while editing; the **Radius snap value** edit box will be displayed. Enter the radius snap value in the **Radius snap value** edit box. The cursor will snap to the specified radius value when you grip edit the curves in the alignment. For example, if you enter the value 5 when the radius is 100, the cursor will snap to the position where the radius value is equal to 105. The snap value is always a whole number such as 10, 20, 100 and so on. The cursor will not snap to the values given in the decimal form such as 105.5.

Markers Tab

This tab is used to specify the appearance for alignment points such as PI, start point and end point, spiral curve and mid points. The **Name** column in the **Alignment points** list box displays various alignment points. The **Marker Style** column specifies the marker style for the points. Double-click in the **Marker Style** column; the **Pick Marker Style** dialog box will be displayed. You can select a marker style for the point or create a new style using the options in this dialog box. The **Arrowhead** area displays various options to specify the appearance of the arrowhead used for the alignment direction arrows. You can select any type of arrowhead from the **Type** drop-down list. On selecting the style for the arrowhead, you can also specify the size of the arrowhead using the **Size** Option and enter the value in the **Inches** edit box in the **Arrowhead** area.

Display Tab

This tab is used to specify the display characteristics and visibility for the alignment components such as lines, arcs, curves, and so on. The options in this tab are discussed next.

View Direction

You can view the drawing in two dimensions and three dimensions with different display settings of the components. You can also specify the display settings for both two and three dimensions. To select a specific view for the display setting, select the **Plan**, **Section**, or **Model** options from the **View Direction** drop-down list in the **Display** tab.

Component display area

The **Component display** area lists the names and the display properties of the alignment components in different columns. The alignment components such as lines, arrows, curves, and spirals are listed in the **Component Type** column. You can set the visibility, color, lineweight, and linetype of the alignment components in the view direction selected. Note that the properties for the component displayed are configured for the selected view direction only. For example, if you have selected **Plan** from the **View Direction** drop-down list and set the color of the **Line** component to red, the line component of the alignment will be displayed in red only in the plan view of the alignment.

Summary Tab

The options in this tab display the summary of the settings made in the other tabs of the **Alignment Style** dialog box. For example, the **Information** node displays the name, description, and other information about the style and the **Direction Arrow** node specifies the arrow head style. The **Design** collection displays the information about the specifications made in the **Design** tab. Similarly, the **Marker** node shows the settings defined in the **Marker** tab. Set the required options in the **Alignment Style** dialog box and choose the **OK** button; the alignment style will be created and added in the **Alignment Styles** subnode of the **Alignment** node of the **Settings** tab.

Editing the Current Alignment Style

Ribbon:	Alignment > Modify > Alignment Properties drop-down > Edit Alignment Style
Command:	EDITALIGNMENTSTYLE

To edit an existing style, select the alignment from the drawing; the **Alignment:<Alignment Name>** tab will be displayed. Next, choose the **Edit Alignment Style** tool from the **Modify** panel; the **Alignment Style** dialog box with the alignment style name will be displayed. Edit the alignment style as required and choose the **OK** button to close the dialog box.

Tip
*You can also edit the alignment style using the **Settings** tab. To do so, choose the **Settings** tab and expand the **Alignments** node. In this node, expand the **Alignment Styles** sub node. Next, right-click on the existing alignment style name and choose **Edit** from the shortcut menu displayed.*

ALIGNMENT LABEL STYLES

The alignment style is created to control the display of the alignment objects whereas the alignment label styles are created to control the display of text and labels of these alignment objects. The alignment labels are automatically generated in Civil 3D along the alignment at some specified points such as start and end points of the alignment, major and minor stations, at the point of intersections, and so on. The display of the alignments is controlled by the alignment styles. Civil 3D has a number of in-built label styles to label different components of an alignment such as stations, station offsets, lines, curves, spirals, points of intersections, and so on. You can manage alignment label style by specifying the required alignment label set. A label set is a group of label styles that are defined for various alignment components. The label set is created by using the options in the **Settings** tab of the **TOOLSPACE** palette.

Creating an Alignment Label Style

To create a label style, expand the **Alignment** collection and then expand the **Label Styles** node. You will see that the **Label Styles** node consists of different subnodes of various alignment objects such as stations, station offsets, lines and curves. Each of these alignment objects has varied label styles.

The first step to create an alignment label style is to define a label style for each of these elements and then add these label styles to the label set. The label set is a combination of different label styles that you want to apply to the alignment. It helps you easily assign the labels to the alignment.

To create a label style, expand the **Alignment** node from the **Settings** tab and then expand the **Label Styles** node; the different subnodes will be displayed. Expand the required subnode for which you want to define the label style. For example, to define a label style for the stations and the station offsets of the alignment, expand the **Station** and **Station Offsets** subnodes; the **Station** subnode consists of different elements such as the major and minor stations, geometry points and the design speeds for which you need to define the label styles. You can define labels for all the elements or the required elements. For example, to define a label style for the major station, select and right-click on **Major Station** and then choose **New** from the shortcut menu displayed; the **Label Style Composer - New Major Station Label Style** dialog box will be displayed, as shown in Figure 5-32.

The dialog box consists of five tabs, which are discussed next.

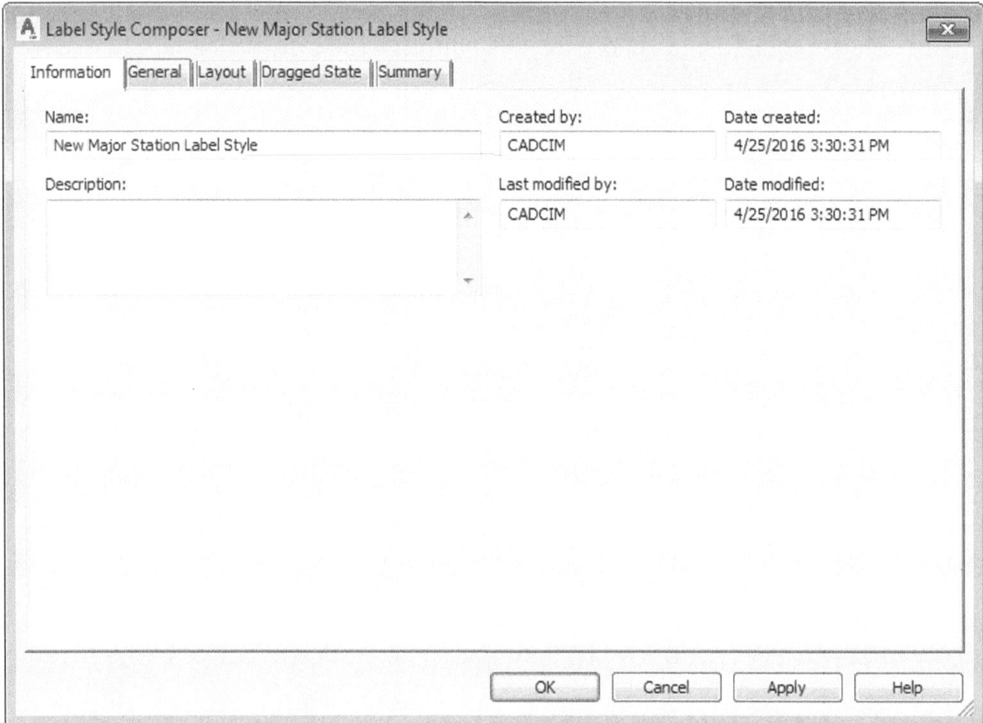

*Figure 5-32 The **Label Style Composer - New Major Station Label Style** dialog box*

Information Tab

This tab is used to specify the name of the label style. Specify the name of the label style in the **Name** edit box.

General Tab

The **General** tab is used to define the label text visibility, orientation, location, and label text settings. This tab consists of a **Preview** window that displays the current label style.

The label style properties and their values are listed in the **Property** and **Value** columns under three categories, **Label**, **Behavior**, and **Plan Readability**. You can expand or collapse the respective categories by clicking on the **+/-** sign on the left of each category. The properties in the **Label** category control the label text style, visibility, and layer. The properties in the **Behavior** category control the location and orientation of the label whereas the properties in the **Plan Readability** category help you define the settings for the label to be visible in the plan view.

Layout Tab

The **Layout** tab is used to create a label style for the components. The **Layout** tab consists of a **Preview** display box that shows the preview of the existing style and the **Component name** drop-down list to select the component for which you want to create the label style. The **Create Text component**, **Copy component**, **Delete component**, and **Component draw order** buttons are available on the right of the **Component name** drop-down list, refer to Figure 5-33.

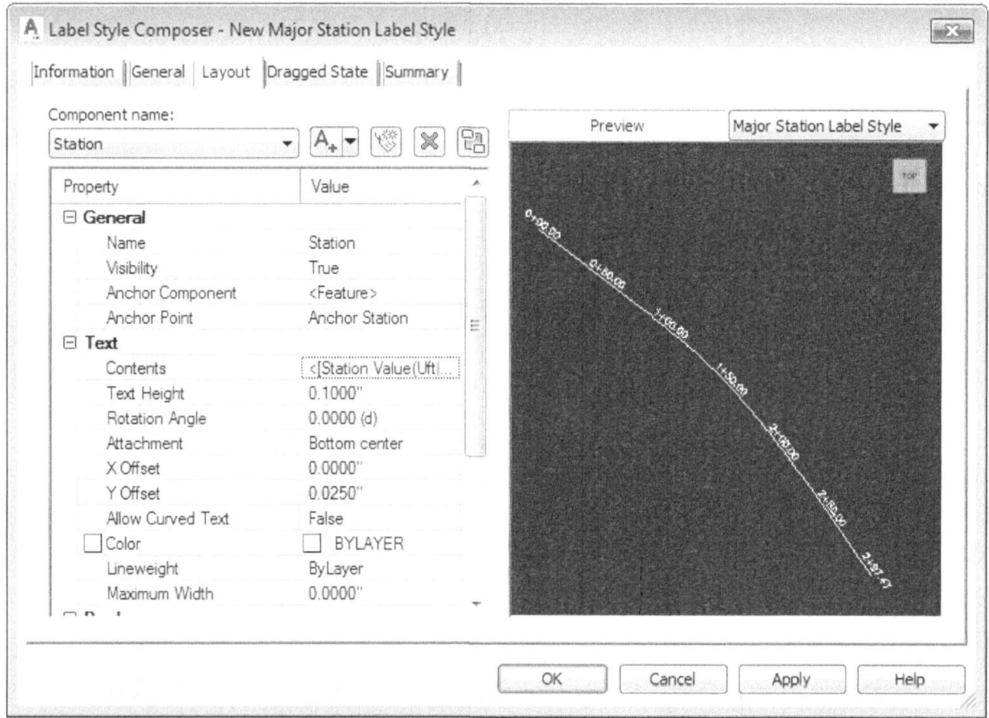

*Figure 5-33 The **Layout** tab of the **Label Style Composer - New Major Station Label Style** dialog box*

In the first step, you will create a component and then modify its properties that are displayed in the **Property** and **Value** columns of the dialog box. You can choose the main alignment label components such as **Text**, **Line**, **Block**, **Tick**, and **Reference Text** from the flyout that is displayed on choosing the **Create Text component** button. Once you add a component, it will be added to the **Component name** drop-down list and the properties and values of the component will be displayed accordingly in the **Property** and **Value** columns. The properties displayed in the **Property** column vary according to the component added. They are displayed in the three categories: **General**, **Text**, and **Border**.

The properties in the **General** category help you define the name and visibility of the component. The **Anchor Component** property in this category specifies the anchor component to which the component will be attached. The **Anchor Point** property specifies the point on the anchor component to which the selected component will be attached.

The properties in the **Text** category help you specify the content of the label text, text height, color weight, and so on. You can click in the property field of the **Value** column and modify the values of the label style properties. You can define the color, lineweight, layer, text height, rotation, and also the point where the label text would be attached to the anchor point by using the **Attachment** property.

You can add or change the content of the label style using the **Text Component Editor-Contents** dialog box. To invoke this dialog box, click in the value field of the **Contents** property in the **Text** category and choose the button displayed on the right; the **Text Component Editor - Contents** dialog box will be displayed, as shown in Figure 5-34. There are two tabs in this dialog box: **Format** and **Properties**. It also has a text editor window on the right where you can type the text. The **Properties** tab is chosen by default and is used to add property fields to the label style. Select the property of the feature from the **Properties** drop-down list. Every property has some modifier associated with it, listed in the **Modifier** column. The values of these modifiers can be changed to create a customized label text. For example, to change the value of the **Unit** modifier, click in the **Value** field corresponding to this modifier; a drop-down list will be displayed on the field. Select the required unit from the drop-down list to modify the existing value.

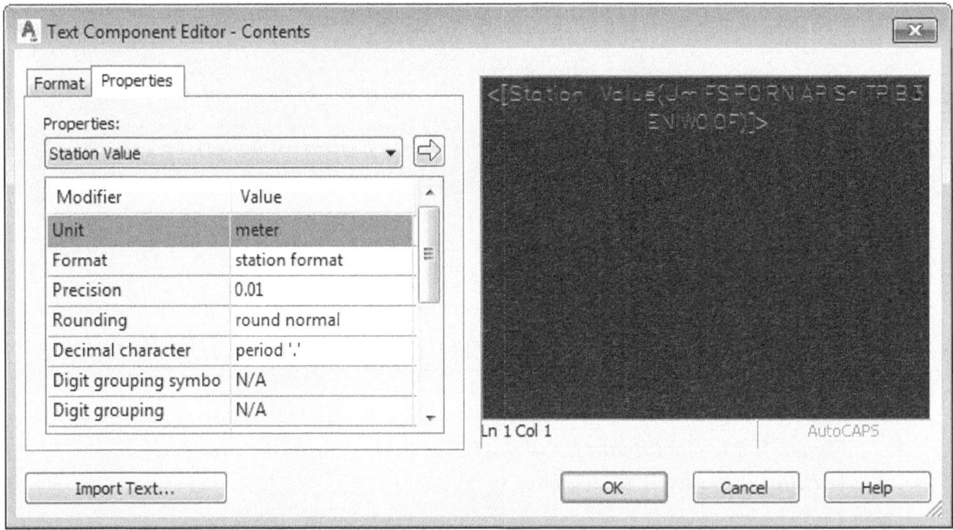

*Figure 5-34 The **Text Component Editor - Contents** dialog box*

Once you have set the values of the modifiers, choose the right arrow button on the right of the **Properties** drop-down list; the property field with the coding will be added to the Text Editor window, as shown in Figure 5-35.

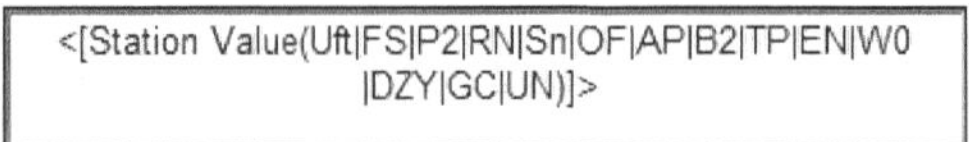

*Figure 5-35 The **Station Value** property added to the Text Editor window*

The codes of the property field added in the Text Editor window are actually the abbreviations of the modifiers and their values. For example, the **Station Value** property code added in the text editor window is *<[Station Value(Uft|FS|P2|RN|Sn|OF|AP|B2|TP|EN|W0|DZY|GC|UN)]>*. Some of the abbreviations and values in this code are:

Abbreviation	Modifier	Value
Uft	Unit	Foot
FS	Format	Station
P2	Precision	2
RN	Rounding	Normal

AP	Decimal Character	Period
Sn	Sign	Negative
OF	Output	Full

The characters such as **</**, **(**,**)**, **|**, and **/>** are used to specify the beginning and end of the property field, modifier, and the modifier separator. You can add the text manually in the beginning. To edit the text added manually, right-click in the text editor window and choose the required editing options from the shortcut menu.

Note

While adding the text manually, do not use the characters such as <>.

To set the formatting of the label text, choose the **Format** tab. The **Justification**, **Font**, and **Color** options in this tab are used to align the label text, select a font, and select the color for the text, respectively. The **Text Style** is the same as set in the **General** tab and cannot be modified in this tab.

Once you have added the label text component and set other parameters in the **Text Component Editor - Contents** dialog box, choose the **OK** button to return to the **Label Style Composer - New Major Station Label Style** dialog box.

The properties in the **Border** category help you set the display of a border around the label or the component to be edited. In this category, set the value for the **Visibility** property to **True** to make the border visible. You can select the type of border in the **Type** property of this category. You can add a rectangular, rounded rectangular, or a circular type of border to the labels or the components using this property. The properties in the **Border** category also help you display a background mask by setting the value of the **Background Mask** to **True**. The background mask is used to hide the objects in the background of the label. You can set the distance between the text and the border of the label by entering the required value in the **Value** column of the **Gap** property. You can also modify the color, linetype, and lineweight of the border in the respective **Value** columns. Similarly, you can add the **Line**, **Block**, **Tick**, and **Reference Text** components from the flyout that is displayed by choosing the **Create Text component** button. You can also modify the properties displayed on the **Property** column based on the component added.

To delete a component from the label, select the component from the **Component name** drop-down list and choose the **Delete Component** button represented by the red cross mark on the right of the **Component name** drop-down list. To set the order of various components in the label, choose the **Component draw order** button. On doing so, the **Component Draw Order** dialog box with various components of the label will be displayed. Set the draw order of these components using the **Top** and **Bottom** arrows displayed on the right of this dialog box and choose the **OK** button to return to the **Label Style Composer** dialog box.

Dragged State Tab

This tab is used to specify the appearance for the label in the dragged state when it is dragged or moved from its original position. The dragged state properties of the label are listed under two categories: **Leader** and **Dragged State Components**.

The properties in the **Leader** category help you make the leader visible or invisible when the label is dragged. Set the value of the **Visibility** property to **True** or **False** to make the leader visible or invisible in the dragged state. You can also set the properties of the **Arrow Head Style**, **Color**, **Linetype**, **Lineweight**, and so on in their respective **Value** fields.

The **Display** property in the **Dragged State Components** category helps you specify the display of the label after it is dragged. Click in the **Value** field of this property and select **As Composed** from the drop-down list to view the original settings of the label. On selecting this option, other properties will become unavailable and you will not be able to modify them. Select the **Stacked Text** option for the **Display** property to display the text components of the label in a vertically stacked way. On selecting this option, all blocks, ticks, and direction arrows will be removed and the label components will be stacked according to the draw order specified in the label style. Similarly, specify the values for the other properties as required. Once you have defined the settings for the label in the dragged state, select the label in the drawing and drag it to a new location using the grips and view the label in the dragged state.

Summary Tab

This tab is used to review and modify the settings of the label style. You can modify only those values that appear in bold. Expand the required categories in the **Summary** tab to view or modify the settings.

After creating the label style of the required alignment components, the next step is to group these styles using the **Label Sets** to make it easy to apply various styles to the alignment.

Creating a Label Set

To create a label set, expand the **Alignment** node from the **Settings** tab. Next, expand the **Label Styles** node and right-click on the **Label Sets**; a shortcut menu will be displayed. Choose **New** from the shortcut menu; the **Alignment Label Set - New Alignment Label Set** dialog box will be displayed. This dialog box consists of two tabs, **Information** and **Labels**, which are discussed next.

Information Tab

This tab is used to specify the name for the label set as well as to review the information associated with it such as the date when it was created or modified, and so on. You can specify the name in the **Name** edit box.

Labels Tab

This tab is used to specify the labels to the label types to be included in the set. The options in this tab are discussed next.

Type

The **Type** drop-down list provides you with the label types options that can be selected or added to the label set. You can configure and select the label type to add to the label set.

Label Style

The **Label Style** drop-down list contains the set of available styles for the selected type. The options in this drop-down list are type dependent. Once you select a label type from the **Type** drop-down list, the corresponding label styles will be displayed in the **Label Style** list.

Style selection

This button is used to create a new label style, copy or edit the existing style of the label type, or pick the style from the drawing. Choose the down-arrow on the right of this button to display a flyout. You can choose an option from the flyout to select the style. To view the style of the label type, choose the button on the right of this button. On doing so, the **Style Detail** dialog box will be displayed with the preview of the label style in the **Preview** window.

Add

Once you have selected the label type and the label style, choose the **Add** button to add them in the label set. These selected types and styles will be listed in the **Type** column and the **Style** column in the **Labels** tab. To remove the label type from the label set, select it from the **Type** column and choose the button on the right of the **Add** button. On doing so, the selected label type and label style will be deleted from the **Type** and **Style** columns.

The **Increment** column specifies the increment values at which the major and minor station labels can be added. This column is available only for the station labels. Click in the **Increment** column and specify the increment value for stations.

Once you have specified the name for the label set in the **Information** tab, select the label types, the label styles, and specify the increment values if required, and then choose the **OK** button. On doing so, the **Alignment Label Set - New Alignment Label Set** dialog box will be closed and the label set will be added to the **Label Sets** subnode under the **Label Styles** node in the **Settings** tab of the **TOOLSPACE** palette.

To apply a label set to an alignment you have created, select the required alignment from the drawing and right-click. Choose the **Edit Alignment Labels** option from the shortcut menu displayed; the **Alignment Labels - <alignment name>** dialog box will be displayed. Choose the **Import label set** button located at the lower right of the dialog box; the **Select Label Set** dialog box will be displayed. Select the required label set you have created from the drop-down list and choose the **OK** button; the label types and the corresponding styles will be displayed in the dialog box. Choose the **Apply** button from the **Alignment Labels - <alignment name>** dialog box to view the changes or the **OK** button to assign the label set to the alignment.

Adding Alignment Labels

Ribbon:	Annotate > Labels & Tables > Add Labels drop-down > Alignment > Add Alignment Labels
Command:	ADDALIGNLABELS

Once you have created and configured your own styles for the alignment objects, you can add them in the drawing. To do so, choose the **Add Alignment Labels** from the **Labels & Tables** panel; the **Add Labels** dialog box will be displayed, as shown in Figure 5-36.

Select the object to be labeled from the **Feature** drop-down list. Next, select the required label type and choose the **Add** button; you will be prompted to select the object to be labeled. You can label a single alignment segment or all segments together by selecting the **Single Segment** or **Multiple Segment** option from the **Label type** drop-down list. Similarly, you can select the **Station Offset**, **Station Offset-Fixed Point**, and other options to add labels to offset stations and tangent intersection points in the alignment. After selecting the label type, choose the **Add** button and follow the prompts to label the alignment segments. Next, choose the **Close** button to close the **Add Labels** dialog box.

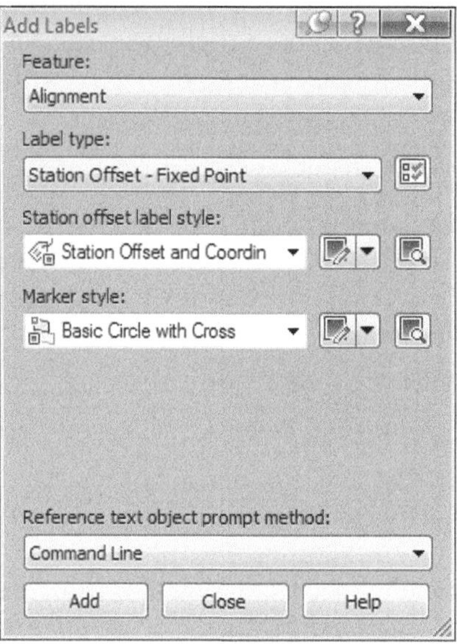

*Figure 5-36 The **Add Labels** dialog box*

EDITING ALIGNMENTS

You can edit an alignment using grip editing, the **PANORAMA** window, and the **Alignment Layout Tools** toolbar. Different methods of editing an alignment are discussed next.

Editing an Alignment Layout Using the Geometry Editor

Ribbon: Alignment > Modify > Geometry Editor
Command: EDITALIGNMENT

You can edit the alignment geometry by using different tools from the **Alignment Layout Tools** toolbar. You can do so by adding curves, spirals, tangents, and other sub-entities to the alignment. To edit the alignment geometry, select the required alignment from the drawing; the **Alignment:<alignment name>** tab will be displayed. Choose the **Geometry Editor** tool from the **Modify** panel; the **Alignment Layout Tools - <alignment name>** toolbar will be displayed. Figure 5-37 shows the alignment and the two points of intersection of tangents and Figure 5-38 shows the alignment after using the **Break- apart PI** tool to break the point of intersection.

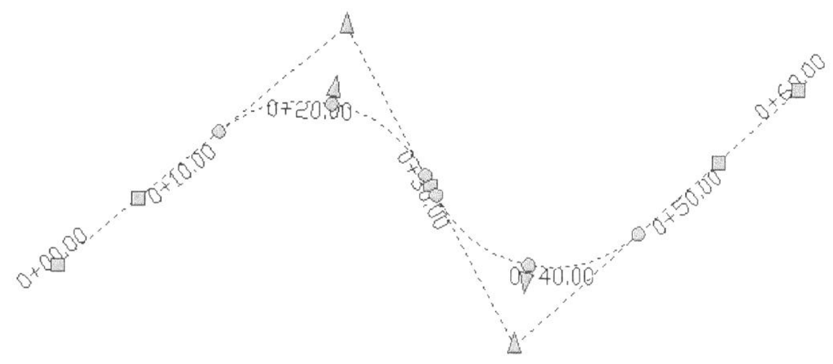

Figure 5-37 *The alignment and the two points of intersection of the tangents*

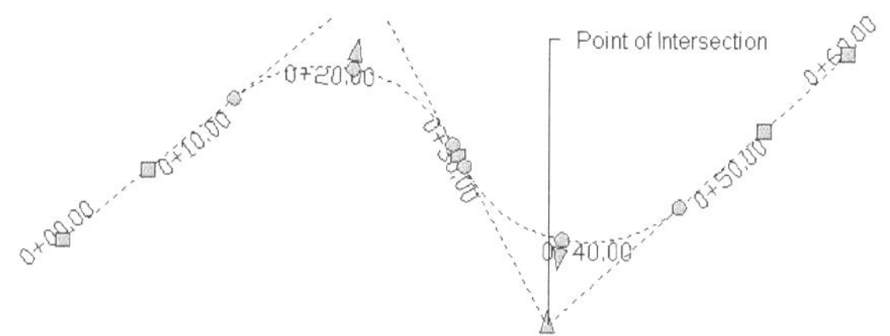

Figure 5-38 *The alignment after using the* ***Break- apart PI*** *tool*

Tip

You can also display the ***Alignment Layout Tools*** *toolbar using shortcut menu. To do so, select the alignment from the drawing and right-click; a shortcut menu will be displayed. Next, choose* ***Edit Alignment Geometry*** *from the shortcut menu; the* ***Alignment Layout Tools*** *toolbar will be displayed.*

Similarly, you can use other tools from the toolbar. For instance, if you want to delete any entity from the alignment, choose the **Delete Sub-entity** tool from the **Alignment Layout Tools** toolbar; you will be prompted to select the sub-entity to be removed. Press the CTRL key and click on the sub-entity to remove it. If you want to delete the point of intersection, choose the **Delete PI** tool from the **Alignment Layout Tools** toolbar. Figure 5-39 shows the alignment after removing the bottom PI.

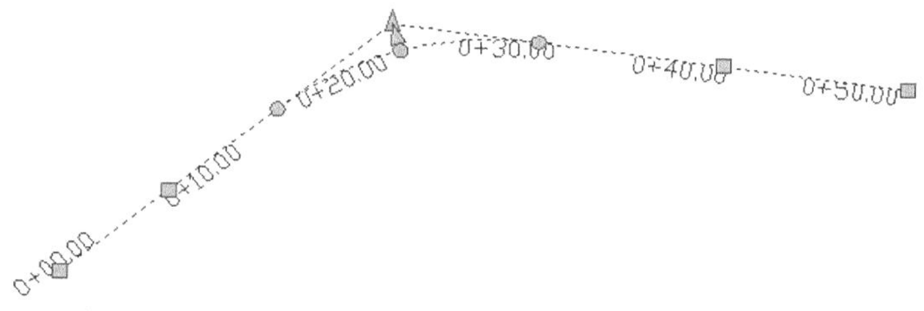

Figure 5-39 *The alignment after deleting the PI using the* ***Delete PI*** *tool*

Editing the Alignment Using the Layout Parameters Dialog Box

You can edit the alignment geometry by changing the values of the design parameters of the alignment entity in the **Alignment Layout Parameters** dialog box. To do so, select the alignment from the drawing and right-click; a shortcut menu will be displayed. Choose the **Edit Alignment Geometry** option from the shortcut menu; the **Alignment Layout Tools** toolbar will be displayed. Choose the **Sub-entity Editor** tool from this toolbar; the **Alignment Layout Parameters** dialog box will be displayed. Note that this dialog box will be activated only if a sub-entity is selected. To select the sub-entity, choose the **Pick Sub-entity** tool; you will be prompted to select the sub-entity. Click to select the entity. On doing so, the design parameters will be displayed in the **Alignment Layout Parameters** dialog box. Note that you cannot modify those parameters in the dialog box that are displayed faded. Figure 5-40 shows the **Alignment Layout Parameters** dialog box for the selected entity of the alignment. You can modify the values related to the tangency constraint and pass through point parameters of the selected entity in this dialog box.

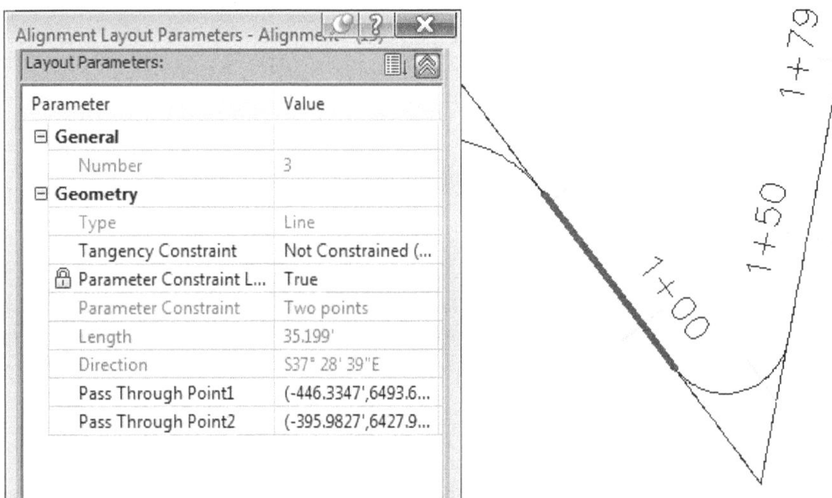

Figure 5-40 Partial view of the ***Alignment Layout Parameters*** *dialog box for the selected entity of the alignment*

Editing the Alignment Using the PANORAMA Window

Another method used for editing the alignment is the **Alignment Entities** tab of the **PANORAMA** window. To do so, choose the **Alignment Grid View** tool from the **Alignment Layout Tools** toolbar; the **PANORAMA** window will be displayed. This window displays the entities and the properties in separate rows. You can numerically edit the values that are highlighted in black, as shown in Figure 5-41. To edit a value, first unlock the **Parameter Constraint** subnode of a particular entity then double-click on it and enter a new value. For example, if you want to edit the length of the curve entity, double click on the curve length displayed in the **Length** column and enter a new value for the curve length.

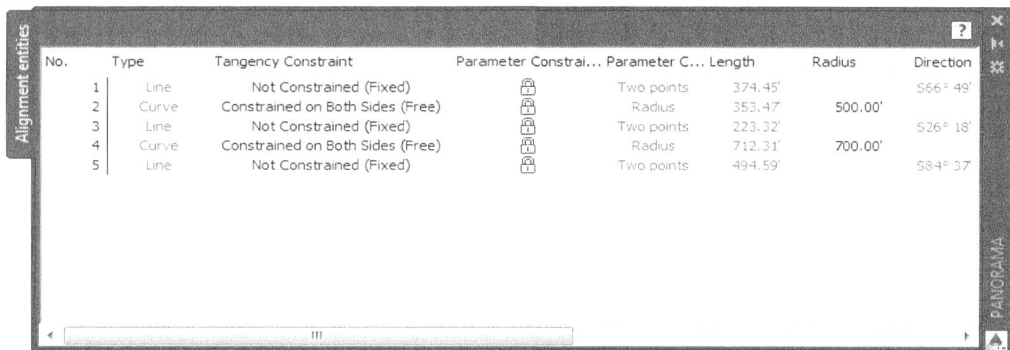

*Figure 5-41 The **Alignment entities** tab of the **PANORAMA** window for editing the values displayed in black*

Note

*An inactive **PANORAMA** window can be activated by selecting an entity from it.*

Changing the Direction of the Alignment and Sub-entities

Ribbon: Alignment > Modify drop-down > Reverse Direction
Command: REVERSEALIGNMENTDIRECTION

AutoCAD Civil 3D allows you to change and reverse the original direction of an alignment or an individual sub-entity irrespective of the method used for creating the alignment. Changing the direction of an alignment will change direction of all the objects that are dependent and associated with it.

To reverse the direction of an alignment, choose the **Reverse Alignment Direction** tool from the **Modify** panel; you will be prompted to select the alignment. Select the alignment from the drawing. Alternatively, press ENTER; the **Select Alignment** dialog box is displayed. Select the alignment from this dialog box and choose the **OK** button; the **Autodesk AutoCAD Civil 3D 2018** message box will be displayed, as shown in Figure 5-42. Choose **OK** to change the direction or choose **Cancel** to terminate the command.

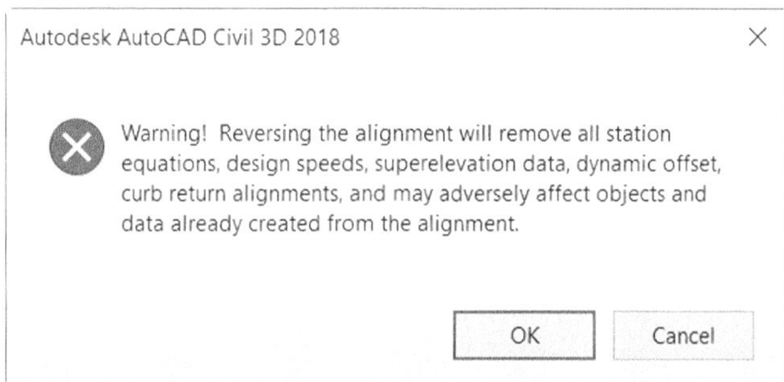

*Figure 5-42 The **Autodesk AutoCAD Civil 3D 2018** message box*

Figure 5-43 shows the original direction of the alignment and the sub-entity. Figure 5-44 shows the alignment and the sub-entity after reversing the direction. You can also reverse the direction of non-fixed entities of an alignment by choosing **Alignment > Reverse Alignment Direction** from the menu bar. Select the required curve or a line entity from the alignment; a warning dialog box will be displayed. Choose **OK** to proceed and change the direction of the selected sub-entity.

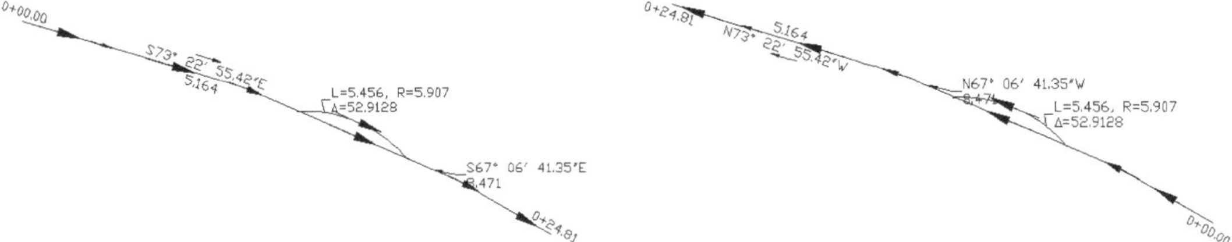

Figure 5-43 *Partial view of the alignment and its direction*

Figure 5-44 *The alignment after reversing its direction*

Editing the Alignment Using the Grip Edits

The simplest way of editing the alignment is by using the AutoCAD tools such as **Rotate**, **Move**, **Stretch**, and **Grip edits**. Every alignment has some grips that are displayed when you select it. The grips are displayed at the point of intersections, start points, end points, and center points of the curves and lines. To graphically edit the alignment, click on the grips and drag them to the required position; the alignment will be updated and redrawn. Figure 5-45 shows the alignment being redrawn after grip editing the point of intersection.

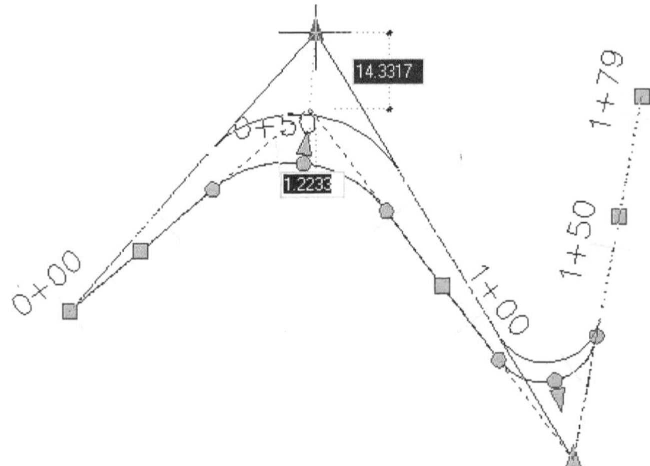

Figure 5-45 *The alignment after grip editing the point of intersection*

The alignment grips are useful in graphically editing the alignment curves and tangents. The following table displays the types of grips and their functions:

Grip Shape	Function
Square Grip	Moving the square grip located at the end of the line helps you to modify the length and angle of the line. If the grip is located at end of the curve then on moving the grip, the radius of the attached entity is affected. If the square grip is located at the center of the line, you can use this grip to change the location of the entire line.
Circular Grip	This grip, if located at the center of the curve, helps you move or change the center point of the curve to the required location. If the circular grip is displayed at a pass-through point then you can modify the pass-through point, thereby changing the radius of the curve.
Triangular Grip	This grip is displayed at the point of intersection of tangents and helps you modify the location of the PI. If the triangular grip is displayed at the end of the curve or line, you can use it to change the length of the directly editable lines and curves.
Triangular Grip and Circular Grip	This grip is used to edit the radius or the pass-through circular grip point of the curve. The triangular grip is displayed for the curves whose radius can be edited directly but the direction cannot be changed. The circular grip changes the location of the pass-through point and the radius of the curve.

Editing Alignment Styles and Label Styles

To edit an existing alignment style and alignment label styles, expand the **Alignment** node and then the **Alignment Styles** or **Label Styles** subnode in the **Settings** tab. Select the existing alignment style or the existing label style and right-click; a shortcut menu will be displayed. Choose the **Edit** option from the shortcut menu; the **Alignment Style** or **Alignment Label Sets** dialog box will be displayed. Modify the properties of the alignment style or labels style as required and choose the **Apply** button to view the changes in the drawing. Choose **OK** to accept the changes and close the dialog box.

ADDING ALIGNMENT TABLES

Ribbon: Annotate > Labels & Tables > Add Tables drop-down > Alignment

The alignment tables help you display the information about the alignment components such as the lines, curve, spiral, and segment of the alignment. The table for each component helps you to display the information in an organized way. You can create your own table styles and add the tables in the drawing.

Note

Before you add tables in the drawing, ensure that all alignment entities are labeled as you cannot create tables without labeling the alignment entities.

To add alignment tables for a line, choose the **Alignment** option from the **Add Tables** drop-down, as shown in Figure 5-46; a flyout will be displayed. Choose the **Add Line** tool from the flyout; the **Table Creation** dialog box will be displayed, as shown in Figure 5-47.

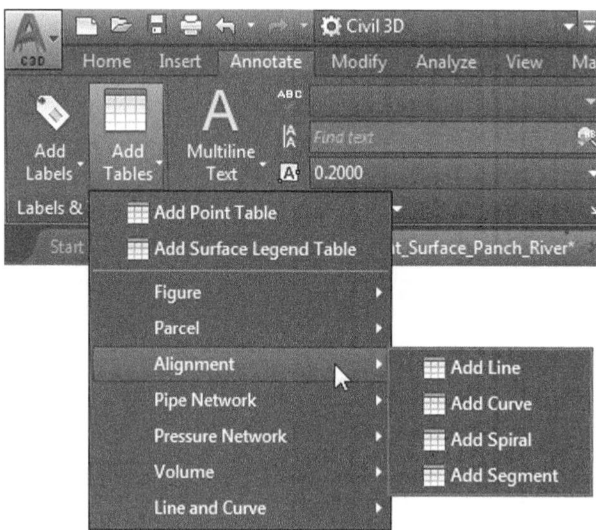

*Figure 5-46 Choosing the **Alignment** option from the **Add Tables** drop-down*

In the **Table Creation** dialog box, the **Table style** drop-down list displays the default table style for the line component. You can also create a new table style by choosing the down arrow on the right of the **Table Style** drop-down list to display a flyout. Choose **Create New** from the flyout; the **Table Style - New Alignment Line Table Style** dialog box will be displayed. You can use this dialog box to create your own table style and specify the data to be displayed. The table style name will be added in the **Table Style** drop-down list. The **Table layer** text box displays the layer on which the table will be created. To change the layer of the table to be created, choose the button on the right of this text box; the **Object Layer** dialog box will be displayed. Now, select a new layer from this dialog box.

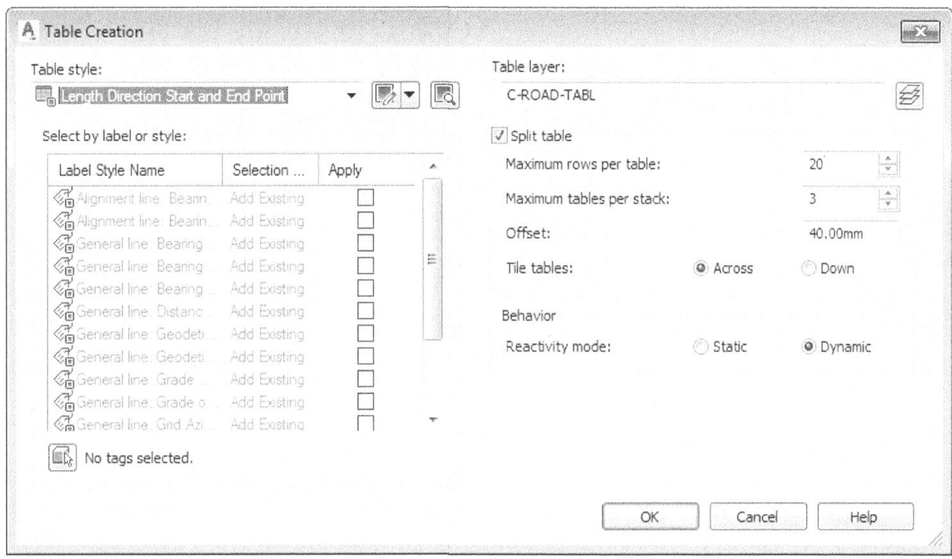

*Figure 5-47 The **Table Creation** dialog box*

The **Select by label or style** area of the **Table Creation** dialog box helps you to add data to the table from the objects labeled in the drawing. To do so, you need to select the label or the label style from which the data will be obtained and added to the table. Remember that the alignment entities should be labeled prior to creating the tables. The label style for the line will be displayed in the **Select by label or style** area. You can select the check box in the **Apply** column to select an existing label style. The **Pick On- Screen** button in this area helps you select the labels of only those entities that you want to add to the table. Choose this button and select the labels for the required alignment entities from the drawing. Next, press ENTER; the number of tags or labels selected will be displayed next to the **Pick On-Screen** button in the **Table Creation** dialog box.

You can use the options in the **Split table** area of the **Table Creation** dialog box to specify the table format. In the **Behavior** area, the **Dynamic** radio button is selected by default. It means that the table will be updated automatically if the alignment entities are modified. To retain the table data irrespective of the modifications made to the alignment entity, select the **Static** radio button. Now, choose the **OK** button from the **Table Creation** dialog box; the dialog box will be closed and you will be prompted to select the upper left corner of the table. Click in the drawing area at the required location to add the table. The information about the alignment entities will be displayed in the table. For example, if you have added a line table, all the line entities with their start points, end points, direction, and so on will be listed in the table. The data added in the table will vary according to the type of table added. Figure 5-48 shows the Line Table displaying information about the line component of an alignment.

Line Table: Alignments				
Line #	Length	Direction	Start Point	End Point
L4	5.127	N74° 18' 57.25"W	(17.8109,10.1993)	(12.8748,11.5853)
L3	4.183	N68° 46' 02.13"W	(21.7533,8.6699)	(17.8540,10.1849)
C1	1.066	N06° 39' 18.63"E	(21.9294,6.6942)	(22.0527,7.7506)

Figure 5-48 *The Line Table*

Similarly, to add data for other components of the alignment, choose the tool corresponding to the alignment component from the **Add Tables** drop-down.

SUPERELEVATION

Superelevation is the tilting of the road surface, achieved by raising the outer edge of the pavement over the inner edge. Superelevation helps in countering the centrifugal force that can cause the vehicle to overturn or skid when moving along a curve. As mentioned earlier in this chapter, the AASHTO standards have been included in Civil 3D as the XML design criteria files. These design files contain the minimum superelevation, curve radii, design speeds, and other required values under different tables. The amount of superelevation is inversely proportional to the radius of the curve. This means that the shorter the radius of the curve, the greater will be the amount of superelevation required to maintain the design speeds. Superelevation rate is expressed in percent.

The following table shows the minimum curve radii recommended for 6% superelevation for various design speeds. Note that with the increase in design speed, the length of the curve radii also increases.

-<MinimumRadiusTable name=**"AASHTO 2011 US Customary eMax 6%"**>
<MinimumRadius radius=**"15"** speed=**"10"**/>
<MinimumRadius radius=**"39"** speed=**"15"**/>
<MinimumRadius radius=**"81"** speed=**"20"**/>
<MinimumRadius radius=**"144"** speed=**"25"**/>
<MinimumRadius radius=**"231"** speed=**"30"**/>
<MinimumRadius radius=**"340"** speed=**"35"**/>

The methods used for analyzing and creating a view of superelevation are discussed next.

Analyzing Superelevation

In Civil 3D, you can analyze superelevation for a given alignment. You can calculate the superelevation of the alignment using the **Calculate/Edit Superelevation** tool. To modify the superelevation of the alignment, you can use the **View Tabular Editor** tool. The **Superelevation Curve Manager** can be used to specify the design criteria and edit the same for the recalculation of the superelevation. The tools for analyzing superelevation are discussed next.

Calculating Superelevation

Ribbon: Alignment (Contextual Tab) > Modify > Superelevation drop-down > Calculate/Edit Superelevation
Command: CALCEDITSUPERELEVATION

The **Calculate/Edit Superelevation** tool is used to calculate the superelevation for an alignment. This tool can also calculate the superelevation for a particular curve of the alignment. To calculate the superelevation, select the alignment from the drawing; the **Alignment:<alignment name>** tab will be displayed. Choose the **Calculate/Edit Superelevation** tool from the **Modify** panel of the **Alignment:<alignment name>** tab; the **Edit Superelevation - No Data Exists** message box will be displayed. In this message box, select the **Calculate superelevation now** option; the **Calculate Superelevation** wizard with the **Roadway Type** page will be displayed, as shown in Figure 5-49. The different pages of this wizard are discussed next.

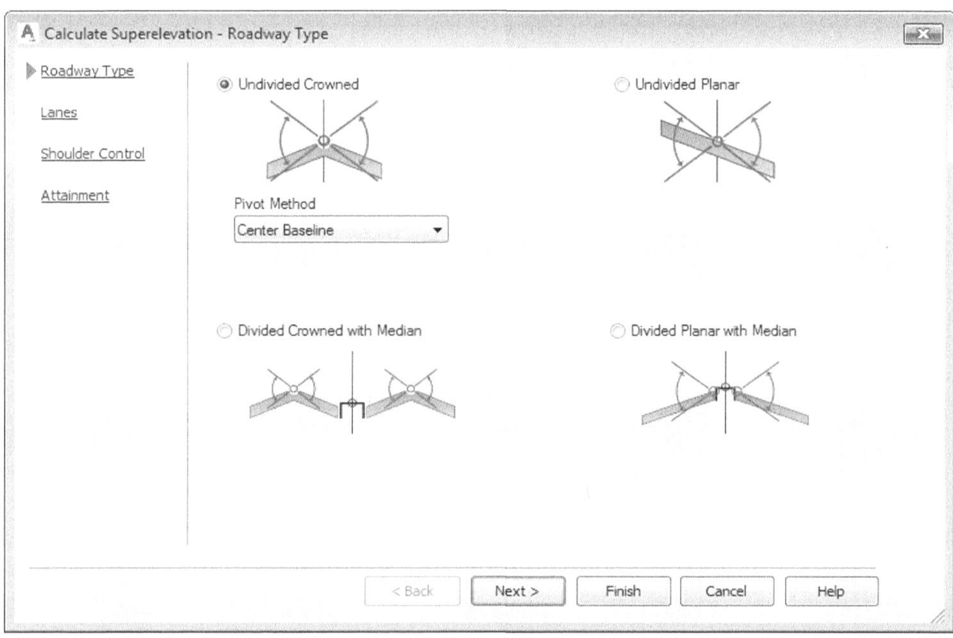

***Figure 5-49** The **Calculate Superelevation** wizard with the **Roadway Type** page*

Roadway Type Page

This page is used to specify the road type. Select the required road type radio button to specify the road type to be used for the calculation of superelevation. For example, if you select the **Undivided Crowned** radio button then you need to specify the pivot method. To specify the pivot method, select an option from the **Pivot Method** drop-down list. Similarly, if you select the **Undivided Planer** road type then the **High Side Location** drop-down list will be displayed. In this case, you need to define both the pivot method and the high side location. To define the high side location, select an option from the **High Side Location** drop-down list. Choose the **Next** button to go to the **Lanes** page.

Lanes Page

The **Lanes** page is used to specify the number of lanes for the road type selected in the **Road Type** page. The properties to be defined in this page will depend upon the type of road selected in the **Road Type** page. For example, if you select the undivided planar road type then you need to define the number of lanes, normal lane width, and normal lane slope. To define the number of lanes, select the required option from the **Number of lanes right** drop-down list. To define the normal lane width, enter the value in the **Normal lane width** edit box. Similarly, to define the normal lane slope, enter the value in the **Normal lane slope** edit box. Choose the **Next** button to go to the **Shoulder Control** page.

Shoulder Control Page

This page of the **Calculate Superelevation** wizard is used to define the properties of the shoulder. The portion which is beyond the edge of the road and is occasionally used for vehicular traffic is known as shoulder. The properties to be defined for the shoulder would depend upon the type of road selected. For example, if the undivided planar road type is selected, then the **Inside median shoulders** area will not be active. But if you select the divided planar with median road type then the **Inside median shoulders** area will be active. If you want to calculate the superelevation for the median shoulder, you need to select the **Calculate** check box and enter the values for various properties in the **Inside median shoulders** area. Similarly, to calculate the superelevation for the outside edge shoulders, you need to select the **Calculate** check box and enter the values for various properties in the **Outside edge shoulders** area. Choose the **Next** button to go to the **Attainment** page.

Attainment Page

This page is used to specify the design criteria file for the superelevation calculation. You can also specify the superelevation rate table, transition length table, and attainment method in this page.

To define the design criteria file, select the browse button next to the **Design criteria file** text box; the **Open** dialog box will be displayed. In this dialog box, select the relevant design file and choose the **Open** button; the design file will be displayed in this text box. To define the superelevation rate table, select an option from the **Superelevation rate table** drop-down list. To define the transition length table, select the required option from the **Transition length table** drop-down list. The options available in this drop-down list will depend upon the type of superelevation rate table selected. To define the attainment method, select the required option from the **Attainment Method** drop-down list. The options available in this drop-down list depend upon the type of road selected in the **Road Type** page.

In the **Transition formula for superelevation runoff** area of this page, you need to specify the percentage of transition length for the tangent. The transition length is the length for the tangent where the tangent is followed by a curve or vice-versa. Enter the value in the **% on tangent for tangent-curve** edit box. If a spiral is followed by a curve or vice-versa then you need to specify the transition length by entering a relevant value in the **% on spiral for spiral-curve** edit box.

You can also apply smoothing to a curve. To do so, select the **Apply curve smoothing** check box in the **Transition formula for superelevation runoff** area. This will make the **Curve**

length edit box active. Enter a value in this edit box to specify the curve length. To avoid the overlapping in the alignment, you need to select the **Automatically resolve overlap** check box. Choose the **Finish** button to exit the wizard.

Editing Superelevation

Ribbon: Alignment > Modify > Superelevation drop-down > View Tabular Editor
Command: CALLSETTABULARVIEWONALIGN

Once you have calculated the superelevation, you can use the **View Tabular Editor** tool to display or edit the calculated superelevation curve data in tabular format. To do so, choose the **View Tabular Editor** tool from the **Modify** panel; the **Superelevation Tabular Editor** tab will be displayed in the **PANORAMA** window, as shown in Figure 5-50.

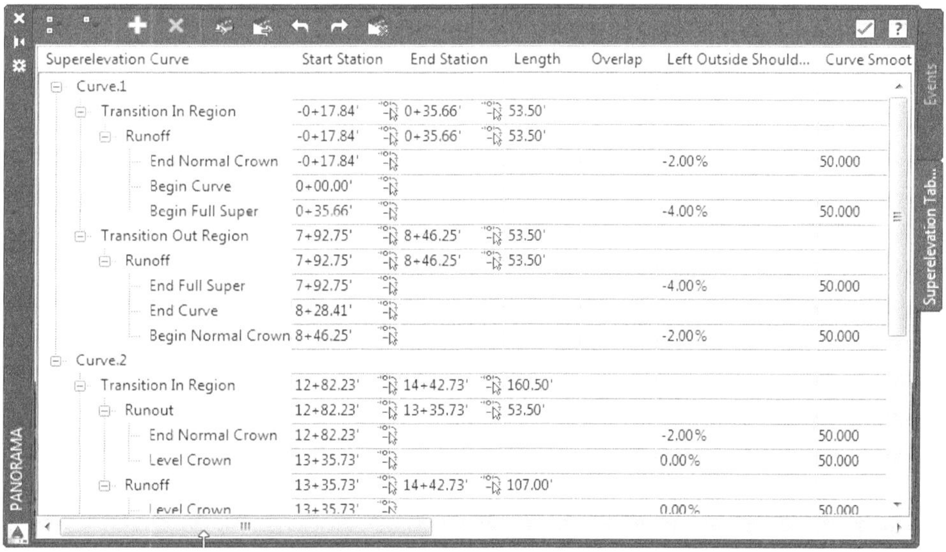

Superelevation Curve	Start Station	End Station	Length	Overlap	Left Outside Should...	Curve Smoot
Curve.1						
Transition In Region	-0+17.84'	0+35.66'	53.50'			
Runoff	-0+17.84'	0+35.66'	53.50'			
End Normal Crown	-0+17.84'				-2.00%	50.000
Begin Curve	0+00.00'					
Begin Full Super	0+35.66'				-4.00%	50.000
Transition Out Region	7+92.75'	8+46.25'	53.50'			
Runoff	7+92.75'	8+46.25'	53.50'			
End Full Super	7+92.75'				-4.00%	50.000
End Curve	8+28.41'					
Begin Normal Crown	8+46.25'				-2.00%	50.000
Curve.2						
Transition In Region	12+82.23'	14+42.73'	160.50'			
Runout	12+82.23'	13+35.73'	53.50'			
End Normal Crown	12+82.23'				-2.00%	50.000
Level Crown	13+35.73'				0.00%	50.000
Runoff	13+35.73'	14+42.73'	107.00'			
Level Crown	13+35.73'				0.00%	50.000

*Figure 5-50 The **Superelevation Tabular Editor** tab of the **PANORAMA** window*

The **Superelevation Tabular Editor** tab shows the details of the transition in region and the transition out region. You can edit the properties in these regions. For example, you can change the start station for the runout. To do so, click in the **Value** field of the **Runout** property in the **Start Station** column and enter the value. Alternatively, to change the start station for the runout, click on the button next to the **Value** field of the **Runout** property; you will be prompted to select the station along the alignment. Select the station; the **Superelevation Tabular Editor** tab will be displayed. Similarly, you can change or view other properties. To close this window, clear the check box on the upper right corner of the **PANORAMA** window.

Creating Superelevation View

Ribbon:	Alignment > Modify > Superelevation drop-down > Create Superelevation View
Command:	CREATESUPERELEVATIONVIEW

The **Create Superelevation View** tool is used to display the superelevation graphically. Choose this tool from the **Modify** panel and select the required alignment; the **Create Superelevation View** dialog box will be displayed, as shown in Figure 5-51. In this dialog box, click on the button next to the **Superelevation view name** edit box; the **Name Template** dialog box will be displayed. Enter a name in the **Name** edit box and choose the **OK** button to close the dialog box. Next, select an alignment from the **Alignment** drop-down list. Alternatively, you can select the alignment by using the **Select from the drawing** button. To do so, choose the **Select from the drawing** button on the right of the drop-down list; you will be prompted to select an alignment from the drawing. Select the alignment from the drawing; the **Create Superelevation View** dialog box will be displayed. To specify the superelevation layer, choose the button next to the **Superelevation view layer** text box. Next, to specify the style for the superelevation, select an option from the **Superelevation view style** drop-down list.

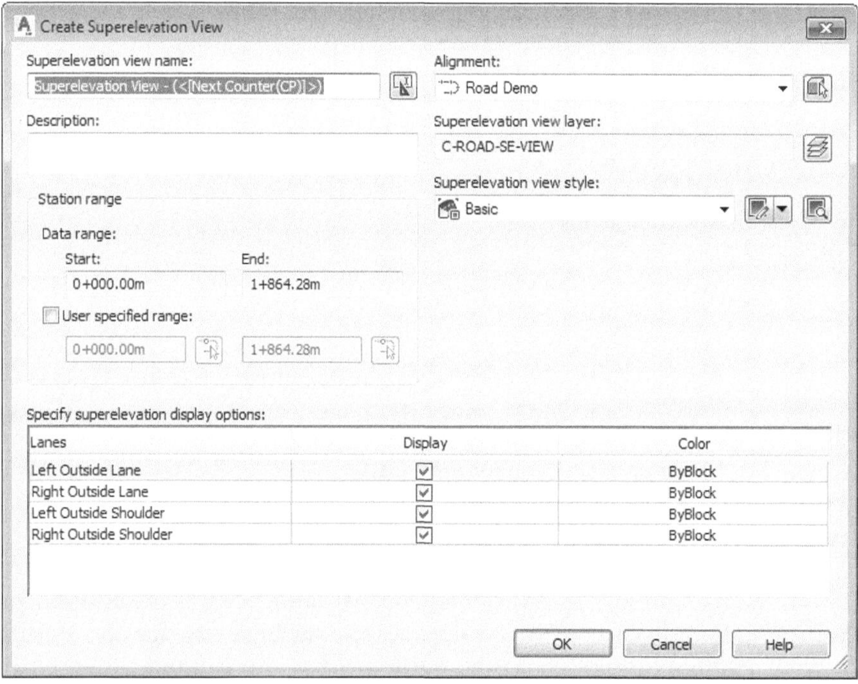

*Figure 5-51 The **Create Superelevation View** dialog box*

In the **Station range** area, select the **User specified range** check box to specify the start and end stations of the selected alignment. You can clear this check box to retain the default start and end stations. In the **Specify superelevation display options** list box, the **Lanes** column will list all the lanes in the alignment. You can clear the check box in the **Display** column corresponding to a particular lane if you do not want that lane to be displayed in the **Superelevation Tabular Editor** tab in the **PANORAMA** window. You can also specify the color for the lanes to be displayed in the superelevation view. To do so, select the **Color** column and specify the color for the selected lane. Then choose the **OK** button; the **Create Superelevation View** dialog box will be closed and you will be prompted to select the superelevation view origin in the drawing area. Specify the origin; the superelevation will be created, as shown in Figure 5-52.

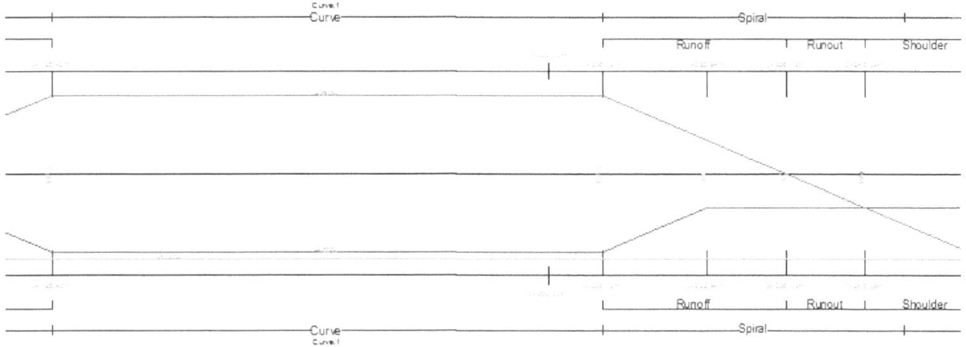

Figure 5-52 *Partial view of the superelevation created*

TUTORIALS

1. Download the *c05_c3d_2018_tut.zip* file from *http://www.cadcim.com,* as explained in Chapter 2.

2. Now, save and extract the downloaded file at the following location:

   c:\c3d_2018

Note
While opening the tutorial file, the ***PANORAMA*** *window with an error message may appear. Close this window to proceed further.*

Tutorial 1 Alignment from Polyline

In this tutorial, you will create an alignment from a polyline, as shown in Figure 5-53. You will also create and apply a new alignment style. **(Expected time: 30 min)**

The following steps are required to complete this tutorial:

a. Open the file.
b. Create alignment from a polyline.
c. Create a new alignment style.
d. Apply the new style to the alignment.
e. Save the file.

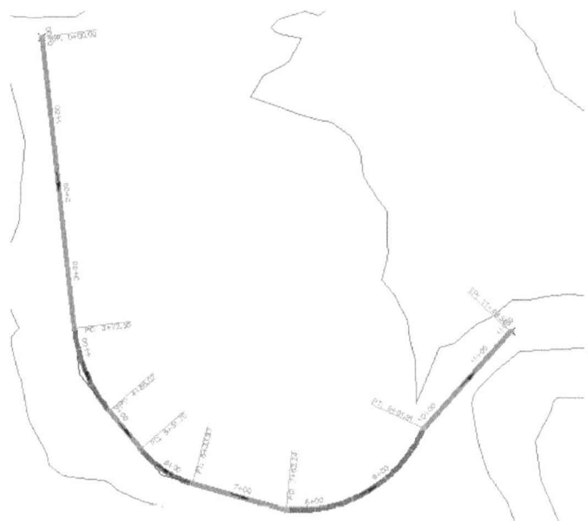

*Figure 5-53 The **Street A** alignment*

Opening the File

1. Choose **Open** from the **Application Menu**; the **Select File** dialog box is displayed.

2. In the dialog box, browse to the location *C:\c3d_2018\c05_c3d_2018_tut* where you have saved the tutorial file.

3. Select the file *c05_c3d_2018_tut01.dwg* and then choose the **Open** button to open the file. Ignore any error message, if displayed.

Creating an Alignment Polyline

1. To create an alignment from a polyline, choose the **Create Alignment from Objects** tool from **Home > Create Design > Alignment** drop-down; you are prompted to select the first line/arc/polyline or [Xref].

2. Select the red color polyline in the drawing and then press ENTER; you are prompted to specify the alignment direction.

3. Press ENTER again to select the default alignment direction; the **Create Alignment from Objects** dialog box is displayed.

4. Enter **Street A** as the alignment name in the **Name** edit box.

5. Select **Layout** from the **Alignment style** drop-down list.

6. Choose the **OK** button; the polyline is converted into an alignment with all geometry points and stations, as shown in Figure 5-54.

Figure 5-54 Alignment of ***Street A*** *created from polyline*

Creating a New Alignment Style

1. Choose **Alignment > Alignment Styles** from the **Settings** tab of the **TOOLSPACE** palette. You will notice a triangular symbol on the left of the **Layout** option indicating the current alignment style.

2. Select **Alignment Styles** and right-click on it; a shortcut menu is displayed.

3. Choose **New** from the shortcut menu; the **Alignment Style - New Alignment Style** dialog box is displayed.

4. Choose the **Markers** tab; various options in this tab are displayed.

5. Double-click on the button in the **Marker Style** column corresponding to the **Begin of Alignment** option; the **Pick Marker Style** dialog box is displayed. 

6. Select the **Basic X** option from the drop-down list in this dialog box, as shown in Figure 5-55. Choose the **OK** button.

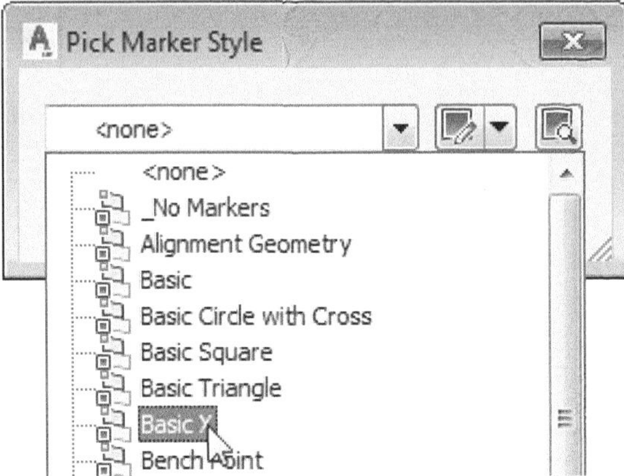

***Figure 5-55** Selecting the **Basic X** option from the drop-down list*

7. Repeat the procedure followed in steps 5 and 6 and make **Basic X** as the marker style for the **End of Alignment** option.

8. Next, choose the **Display** tab. Change the color for the **Line** component to **green**, **Curve** to **magenta,** and **Line Extensions** to **blue** in the **Color** column.

9. Change the lineweight of **Line**, **Curve**, and **Line Extensions** to **0.5** mm in the **Lineweight** column.

10. Choose the **OK** button to close the **Alignment Style - New Alignment Style** dialog box; the **New Alignment Style** is added to the **Alignment Styles** node in the **Settings** tab.

Applying the Alignment Style

1. Select the **Street A** alignment from the drawing and right-click; a shortcut menu is displayed.

2. Choose **Alignment Properties** from the shortcut menu; the **Alignment Properties - Street A** dialog box is displayed.

Tip

*You can also display the **Alignment Properties - Street A** dialog box from the **Prospector** tab of the **Toolspace** palette. To do so, expand the **Alignments** node and the **Centerline Alignments** sub node. Then, right-click on **Street A** node to display a shortcut menu. Choose **Properties** from the shortcut menu to display the **Alignment Properties - Street A** dialog box.*

3. In the **Information** tab, select the **New Alignment Style** option from the **Object style** drop-down list.

4. Choose the **Apply** button to apply the style to the alignment.

5. Then, choose the **OK** button; the **Alignment Properties - Street A** dialog box is closed and the alignment style is assigned to the **Street A** alignment.

6. Now, choose the **Show/Hide Lineweight** button from the status bar at the bottom right of the screen; the alignment entities are displayed with the assigned lineweight (0.5mm), as shown in Figure 5-56. 

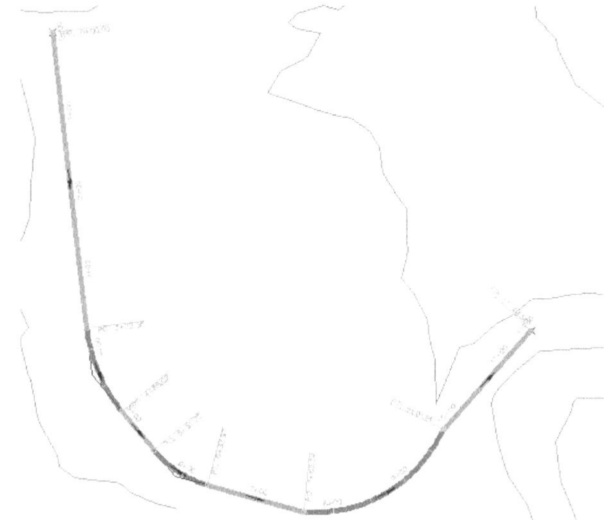

Figure 5-56 *The* ***Street A*** *alignment after assigning the New Alignment Style to it*

Saving the File

1. Choose **Save As** from **Application Menu**; the **Save Drawing As** dialog box is displayed.

2. In this dialog box, browse to the following location:

   C:\c3d _2018\c05_c3d_2018_tut

3. In the **File name** edit box, enter **c05_tut01a**.

4. Choose the **Save** button; the file is saved with the name *c05_tut01a.dwg* at the specified location.

Tutorial 2 Criteria-Based Alignment Layout

In this tutorial, you will create a criteria-based alignment, as shown in Figure 5-57 using the **Alignment Layout** tools from the **Alignment Layout Tools** toolbar. Also, you will rectify the violation errors. **(Expected time: 30 min)**

Figure 5-57 *The criteria-based* ***Road A*** *alignment layout*

The following steps are required to complete this tutorial:

a. Open the file.
b. Name the alignment and assign the alignment style.
c. Assign a design speed and design criteria.
d. Create the alignment.
e. Add the best fit curve.
f. Add free spiral to the alignment.
g. Add the fixed spiral curve.
h. View and correct the alignment design criteria violations.
i. Save the file.

Opening the File

1. Choose **Open** from the **Application Menu**; the **Select File** dialog box is displayed.

2. In the dialog box, browse to the location *C:\c3d_2018\c05_c3d_2018_tut* where you have saved the file.

3. Select the file *c05_c3d_2018_tut02.dwg* and then choose the **Open** button to open the file. Ignore the error message if displayed. The file consists of a surface border and a series of circles.

Naming the Alignment

1. Choose the **Alignment Creation Tools** tool from **Home > Create Design > Alignment** drop-down; the **Create Alignment - Layout** dialog box is displayed.

2. Enter **Road A** in the **Name** edit box.

3. Select the **New Alignment Style** option from the **Alignment style** drop-down list.

Assigning the Design Speed and Design Criteria

1. Choose the **Design Criteria** tab from the **Create Alignment - Layout** dialog box. This tab is used to specify the design speed and design criteria.

2. In the **Starting design speed** edit box, change the design speed to **55 mi/h**. This is the design speed at the first station of the alignment.

3. Select the **Use criteria-based design** check box.

4. Choose the browse button from the **Use design criteria file** area; the **Select Design Speed Table** dialog box is displayed.

5. Select the **_Autodesk Civil 3D Imperial (2011) Roadway Design Standards.xml** file and choose the **Open** button to open this file and exit the dialog box. On doing so, you have selected the in-built design criteria file to create an alignment using the design standards specified in this file.

6. In the **Default Criteria** area, click in the **Value** field of the **Minimum Radius Table** property and select the **AASHTO 2011 US Customary eMax 10%** table from the drop-down list.

7. Ensure that the **Use design check set** check box is selected and then choose the **OK** button; the **Create Alignment - Layout** dialog box is closed and the **Alignment Layout Tools - Road A** toolbar is displayed, as shown in Figure 5-58.

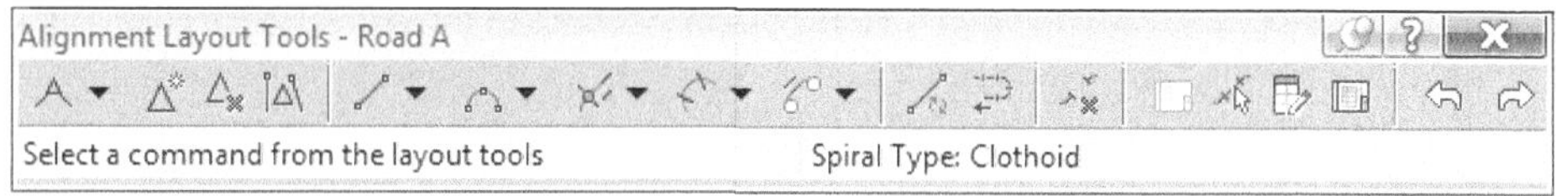

Figure 5-58 *The* ***Alignment Layout Tools - Road A*** *toolbar*

8. Enter **OSNAP** at the command bar and press ENTER; the **Object Snap** tab in the **Drafting Settings** dialog box is displayed. Ensure that the check box for the **Center** option for object snapping is selected.

9. Choose the **OK** button to close the **Drafting Settings** dialog box.

10. Zoom in the surface to view the circle A on the left of the surface.

Creating the Alignment

1. Choose the **Tangent-Tangent (No curves)** tool from the **Alignment Layout Tools - Road A** toolbar; you are prompted to specify the start point.

2. Snap to the center of the circle A and click to specify the start point, as shown in Figure 5-59.

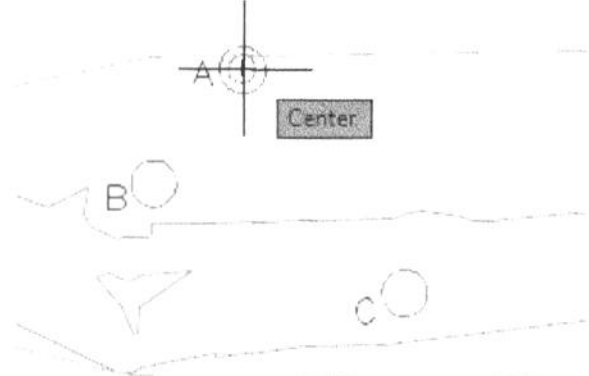

Figure 5-59 *Specifying the start point at the center of the first circle*

3. Next, click on the center of the circle B; the section of the alignment is created between the center of the circles A and B.

4. Continue creating the alignment between the circles C, D, E, and F (leave the last one which is circle G). Press ENTER to terminate the command at the circle F. The alignment is created, as shown in Figure 5-60.

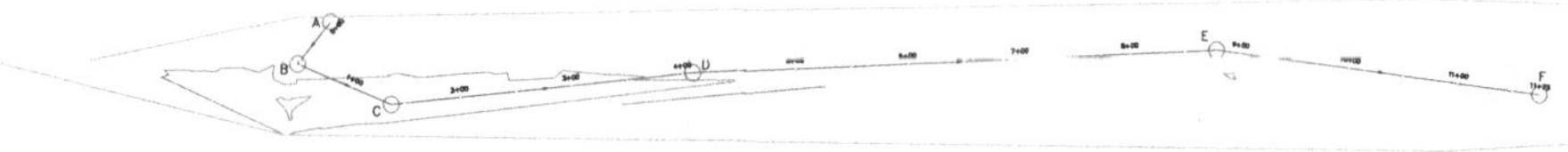

Figure 5-60 *The* ***Road A*** *alignment created*

Adding the Best Fit Curve

1. Zoom in the start of the alignment and choose the down arrow on the right side of the **Fixed Curve (Three point)** tool from the **Alignment Layout Tools - Road A** toolbar; a flyout is displayed. 

2. Choose the **Free Curve - Best Fit** option from the flyout, as shown in Figure 5-61; you are prompted to select the first entity.

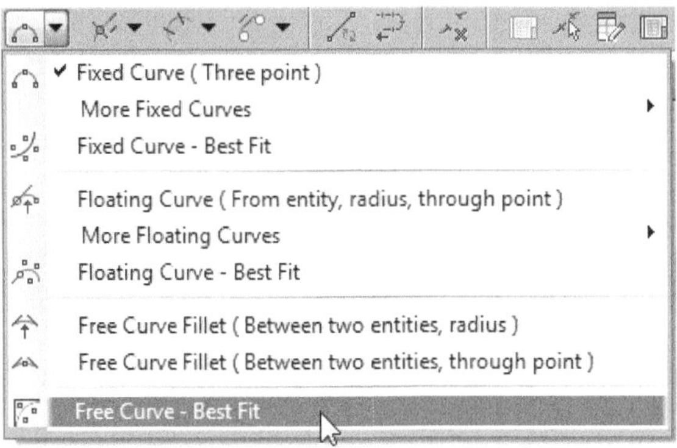

Figure 5-61 *Choosing the* ***Free Curve - Best Fit*** *option from the flyout*

3. Select the alignment section between circles A and B; you are prompted to specify the next entity.

4. Select the alignment section between circles B and C; the **Curve by Best Fit** dialog box is displayed.

5. Select the **By clicking on the screen** radio button from the dialog box and choose the **OK** button; the dialog box is closed and you are prompted to specify a point.

6. Click at the tick mark of the first station, **0+00**; an arc segment is displayed, as shown in Figure 5-62. Also, you are prompted to specify the next point of the arc.

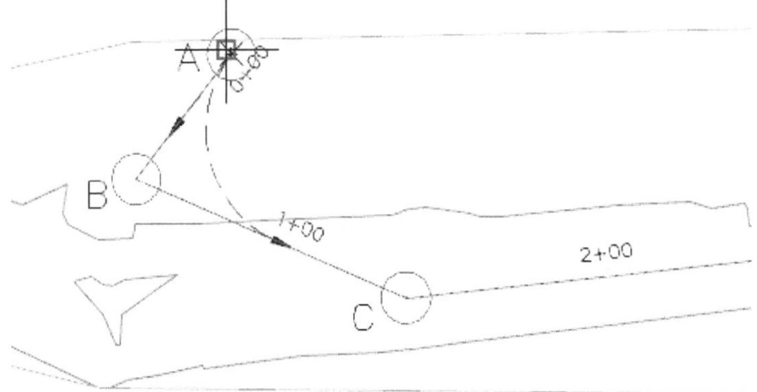

Figure 5-62 *The arc segment displayed on specifying the first point*

7. Now, click at the tick mark of station **2+00** and press ENTER; the **PANORAMA** window with the **Regression Data** tab is displayed, as shown in Figure 5-63.

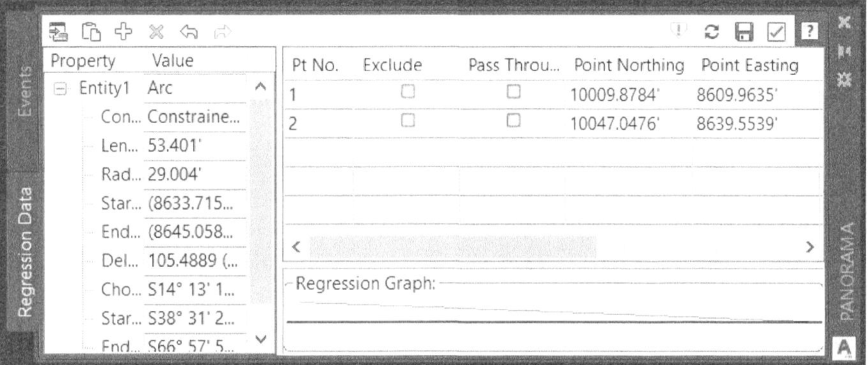

*Figure 5-63 The **PANORAMA** window with the **Regression Data** tab chosen*

8. Choose the **Save** button in the **PANORAMA** window to create the entity.

9. In the **Pass Through** column, select the first row; a cross mark and a line are displayed to graphically represent the location of the regression point in the **Regression Graph** area.

10. Choose the button with green tick mark to exit the **PANORAMA** window; the best fit curve is created and displayed on the alignment, as shown in Figure 5-64.

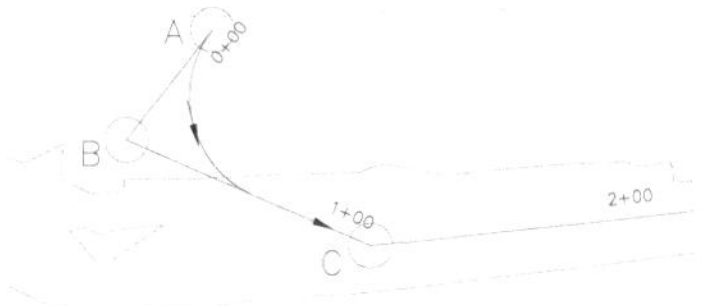

*Figure 5-64 The best fit curve added to the **Road A** alignment*

Adding Free Spiral to the Alignment

1. Zoom in the end of the alignment.

2. In the **Alignment Layout Tools - Road A** toolbar, choose the down-arrow on the right of the **Free Compound Spiral-Spiral (Between two curves)** tool and choose the **Free Spiral (Between two entities)** tool from the flyout displayed; you are prompted to select an entity.

3. Select the alignment section on the left of the circle E; you are prompted to specify the next entity. Select the alignment section on the right of the circle E; you are prompted to select the spiral type in the command line.

4. Press ENTER to accept the default **<Incurve>** option; you are prompted to specify the spiral length.

5. Press ENTER to accept the default **<200.000'>** spiral length; a spiral is added between two tangents. A violation symbol is displayed on the spiral indicating that the design criterion has been violated. Press ESC to exit the command.

6. To check the criterion that has been violated, hover the cursor over the violation symbol in the drawing; a tooltip stating the type of violation is displayed, as shown in Figure 5-63.

Note

The tooltip shows that the criterion for the ***Transition Length*** *in the spiral is violated. In this case, the tool tip shows the current spiral length and the minimum transition length for the selected design speed, which is 200.000' and 255.000', respectively, refer to Figure 5-65.*

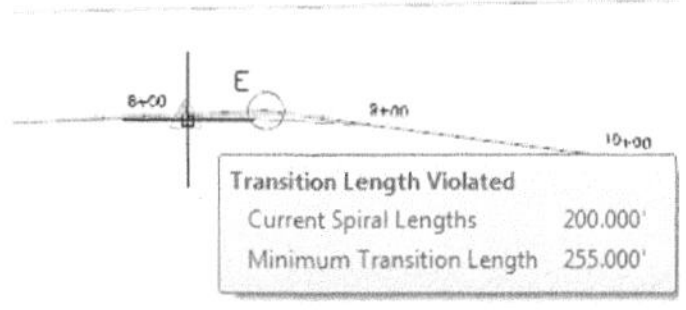

Figure 5-65 *The tooltip displaying the violation type*

Adding a Fixed Spiral

1. Choose the down arrow on the right of the **Free Spiral (Between two entities)** tool; a flyout is displayed. Choose the **Fixed Spiral** option from the flyout; you are prompted to select an entity to specify the start point and direction.

2. Select a segment of the alignment lying between station 10+00 and 11+00; you are prompted to specify the spiral type, as shown in Figure 5-66.

3. Select the **Point** option from the dynamic input; you are prompted to select the spiral.

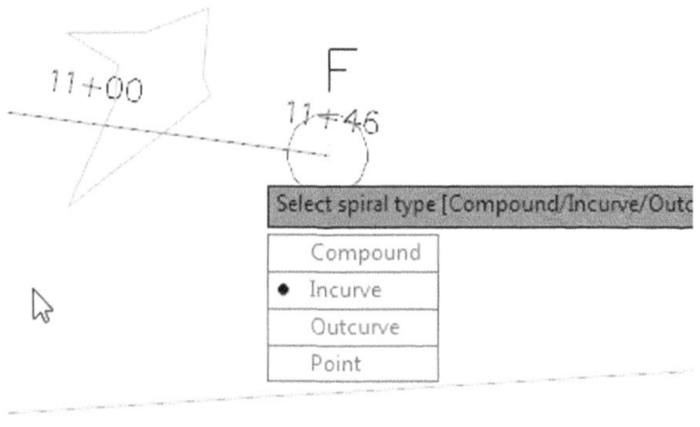

Figure 5-66 *Dynamic input prompted for selecting spiral type*

4. Press ENTER to select the **Incurve** type; you are prompted to specify the end point of the spiral. Click at the center of the circle G to specify the end point of the spiral, as shown in Figure 5-67.

Figure 5-67 *Specifying the end point to add a fixed spiral*

5. Press ENTER to terminate the command. You have now created a design-based alignment between circles A and G using different tools from the **Alignment Layout Tools** toolbar.

Correcting the Criteria Violation

1. Invoke the **Sub-entity Editor** tool from the **Alignment Layout Tools - Road A** toolbar; the **Alignment Layout Parameters - Road A** dialog box is displayed.

2. Invoke the **Pick Sub-entity** tool from the toolbar and select the green line curve between circles E and F containing the warning sign; the **Alignment Layout Parameters - Road A** dialog box is populated with different spiral parameters, as shown in Figure 5-68.

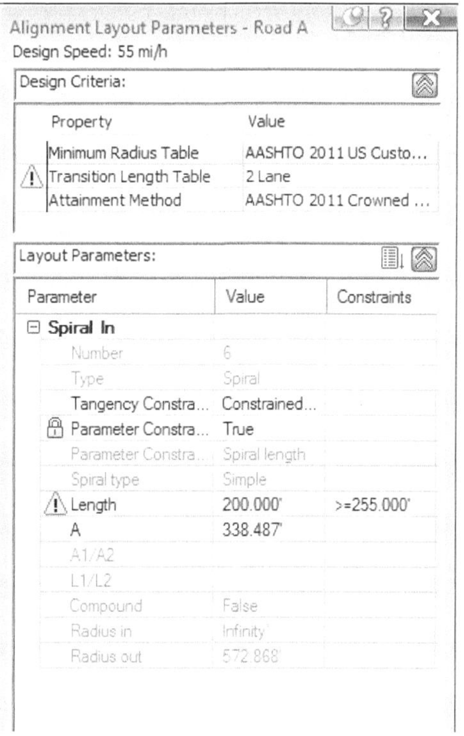

Figure 5-68 *Partial view of the* ***Alignment Layout Parameters - Road A*** *dialog box*

Note

*If the **Alignment Layout Tools - Road A** toolbar is not displayed, select the alignment from the drawing and then right-click; a shortcut menu is displayed. Choose the **Edit Alignment Geometry** option from the shortcut menu; the **Alignment Layout Tools - Road A** toolbar is displayed.*

Tip

*To hide/show the violation symbol, enter **OP** in the command prompt to display the **Option** dialog box and clear the **Drafting** check box from the **Solution Tips** area in the **AEC Editor** panel.*

3. Click in the value field of the **Length** parameter displayed in the **Value** column and change the length parameter to **500.000'** and then press ENTER; the violation symbol disappears and the violation error is rectified.

4. Close the **Alignment Layout Parameters - Road A** dialog box to view the alignment.

5. Zoom and pan to the free spiral and note that the violation symbol is removed, Figure 5-69 shows the **Road A** alignment after it is created.

Figure 5-69 *The **Road A** alignment*

Saving the File

1. Choose **Save As** from the **Application Menu**; the **Save Drawing As** dialog box is displayed.
2. In this dialog box, browse to the following location:

   C:\c3d _2018\c05_c3d_2018_tut

3. In the **File name** edit box, enter **c05_tut02a**.

4. Next, choose the **Save** button; the file is saved with the name *c05_tut02a.dwg* at the specified location.

Tutorial 3 Customizing Design Criteria

In this tutorial, you will apply a design criteria to an existing alignment and calculate the superelevation values. Also, you will create design criteria, label styles, and label set for different alignment entities. Figure 5-70 shows the alignment created. **(Expected time: 1 hr)**

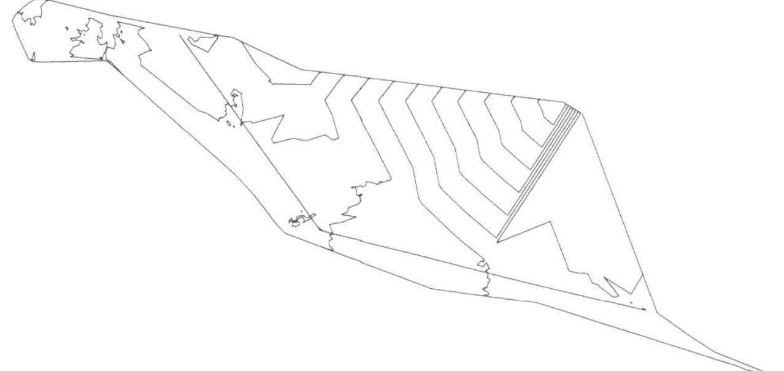

***Figure 5-70** The **Palkins Street** alignment*

a. Open the file.
b. Apply the design criteria file and calculate superelevation values.
c. Grip edit the alignment.
d. Create the design criteria.
e. Create label styles for major stations and minor stations.
f. Create a label set.
g. Save the file.

Opening the File

1. Choose **Open** from the **Application Menu**; the **Select File** dialog box is displayed.

2. In the dialog box, browse to the location *C:\c3d_2018\c05_c3d_2018_tut* folder.

3. Select the file *c05_c3d_2018_tut03.dwg* and then choose the **Open** button to open the file. Ignore the error message if displayed.

   This file consists of a surface and an alignment named Palkins Street. You will now assign a design criteria and calculate superelevation values.

Applying the Design Criteria and Calculating Superelevation Values

1. Select the **Palkins Street** alignment from the drawing if it is not selected and right-click; a shortcut menu is displayed.

2. Choose the **Alignment Properties** option from the shortcut menu displayed; the **Alignment Properties – Palkins Street** dialog box is displayed.

3. Choose the **Design Criteria** tab from the dialog box, if it is not selected by default.

4. Select the **Use criteria - based design** check box located on the right of the dialog box; the default design criteria file is applied to the alignment. Note that the default design speed is **60 mi/h**. Choose the **OK** button to close the dialog box.

Note

*The **_Autodesk Civil 3D Imperial (2011) Roadway Design Standards.xml** file is the default design criteria file applied to the alignment. You can access this file from the **Imperial** folder at C:\Documents and Settings\All Users\Application Data\Autodesk\C3D 2018\enu\Data\Corridor Design Standards\Imperial.*

5. Choose the **Calculate/Edit Superelevation** tool from **Alignment: Palkins Street > Modify > Superelevation** drop-down; the **Edit Superelevation - No Data Exists** window is displayed.

6. Choose the **Calculate superelevation now** option; the **Calculate Superelevation** wizard with the **Roadway Type** page is displayed.

7. Retain the default settings in this page and choose the **Next** button; the **Lanes** page is displayed. In the **Lanes** page, select the **2** option from the **Number of lanes right** drop-down list and retain the other default settings. Then, choose the **Next** button; the **Shoulder Control** page is displayed.

8. In the **Shoulder Control** page, enter **3** in the **Normal shoulder width** edit box and retain other default settings. Choose the **Next** button; the **Attainment** page is displayed.

9. In the **Attainment** page, choose the browse button next to the **Design criteria file** text box; the **Open** dialog box is displayed. Select the ***_Autodesk Civil 3D Imperial (2011) Roadway Design Standards.xml*** file and choose the **Open** button. The file path is displayed in the **Design criteria file** text box.

10. Now, select the **AASHTO 2011 US Customary eMax 4%** option from the **Superelevation rate table** drop-down list, if it is not selected by default.

11. Select the **2 Lane** option from the **Transition length table** drop-down list and the **AASHTO 2011 Crowned Roadway** option from the **Attainment method** drop-down list, if it is not selected by default.

12. Next, enter **65%** in the **% on tangent for tangent-curve** edit box and retain the default value in the **% on spiral for spiral-curve** edit box. Choose the **Finish** button; the **Calculate Superelevation** dialog box is closed and the **PANORAMA** window with the **Superelevation Tabular Editor** tab is displayed, as shown in Figure 5-71. Close the **PANORAMA** window.

13. The violation symbols are displayed at the curves. Move the cursor over the violation symbols and read the tooltip displaying the minimum radius violation message.

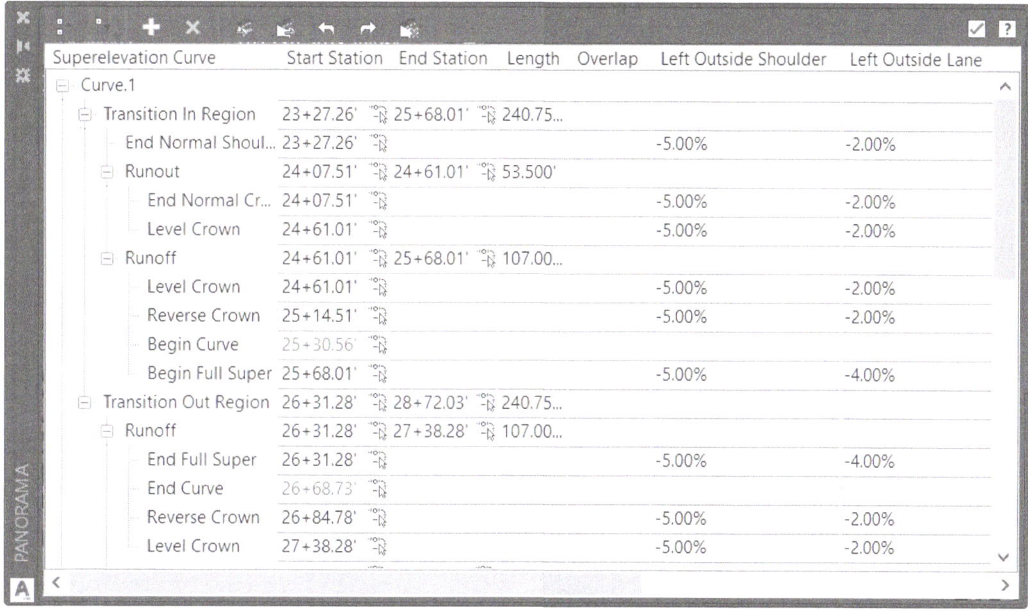

Superelevation Curve	Start Station	End Station	Length	Overlap	Left Outside Shoulder	Left Outside Lane
Curve.1						
Transition In Region	23+27.26'	25+68.01'	240.75...			
End Normal Shoul...	23+27.26'				-5.00%	-2.00%
Runout	24+07.51'	24+61.01'	53.500'			
End Normal Cr...	24+07.51'				-5.00%	-2.00%
Level Crown	24+61.01'				-5.00%	-2.00%
Runoff	24+61.01'	25+68.01'	107.00...			
Level Crown	24+61.01'				-5.00%	-2.00%
Reverse Crown	25+14.51'				-5.00%	-2.00%
Begin Curve	25+30.56'					
Begin Full Super	25+68.01'				-5.00%	-4.00%
Transition Out Region	26+31.28'	28+72.03'	240.75...			
Runoff	26+31.28'	27+38.28'	107.00...			
End Full Super	26+31.28'				-5.00%	-4.00%
End Curve	26+68.73'					
Reverse Crown	26+84.78'				-5.00%	-2.00%
Level Crown	27+38.28'				-5.00%	-2.00%

*Figure 5-71 The **Superelevation Tabular Editor** tab in the **PANORAMA** window*

Grip Editing the Alignment

1. Select the **Palkins Street** alignment and right-click; a shortcut menu is displayed.

2. Choose the **Edit Alignment Geometry** option from the shortcut menu; the **Alignment Layout Tools - Palkins Street** toolbar is displayed.

3. Zoom and pan to the first violation symbol.

4. Invoke the **Pick Sub-entity** tool; you are prompted to select the sub entity. Select the curve on which the violation symbol is displayed; the **Alignment Layout Parameters- Palkins Street** dialog box is displayed with relevant values, as shown in Figure 5-72.

5. Right-click in the drawing and select the alignment to display the alignment grips. Move the triangular grip on the curve toward the upper right direction. As you continue moving the grip, the radius value in the **Alignment Layout Parameters- Palkins Street** dialog box changes accordingly.

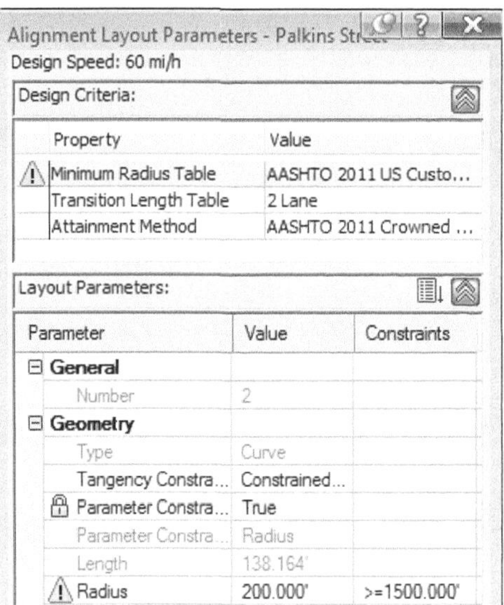

***Figure 5-72** The **Alignment Layout Parameters - Palkins Street** dialog box*

6. Click when the violation symbol disappears from the dialog box and the radius value displayed in the **Value** column is greater than **1500.000'** as per the design criteria.

7. Zoom and pan to the next violation symbol and select the triangular grip on the curve.

8. Move the grip upward till the violation symbol in the **Alignment Layout Parameters - Palkins Street** dialog box disappears and the value for the **Radius** parameter is greater than or equal to the minimum curve radius required.

Note

While using grip edit, make sure that you select the triangular grip ( ) on the curve.

Tip

*In the **Palkins Street** alignment, you will notice two violation symbols that appear due to out-of-date superelevation. To remove the symbols, select the alignment and then choose the **Calculate/Edit Superelevation** tool from **Alignment: Palkins Street > Modify > Superelevation** drop-down; the **SUPERELEVATION CURVE MANAGER - PALKINS STREET** window will be displayed. In this window, choose the **Recalculate** button; the **SUPERELEVATION CURVE MANAGER - PALKINS STREET** window will be closed and the violation symbols will be removed.*

Creating the Design Criteria

1. Choose the **Design Criteria Editor** tool from the **Modify** panel of the **Alignment:Palkins Street** tab; the **Design Criteria Editor - _Autodesk Civil 3D Imperial (2011) Roadway Design Standards.xml** dialog box is displayed.

2. Choose the **Save As** button to display the **Enter a file name to save** dialog box. 

3. Enter **Palkins Street Standards** in the **File name** edit box and then browse to *C:\c3d_2018\c05_c3d_2018_tut.*

4. Choose the **Save** button to save the default design criteria file with a different name before making any change in the file. The default design criteria file is saved with a different name at the specified location.

   Next, you will edit the design criteria file.

5. In the left pane of the **Design Criteria Editor - Palkins Street Standards.xml** dialog box, expand **Alignments > Minimum Radius Tables** to view the existing minimum radius tables.

6. Right-click on **Minimum Radius Tables**; a shortcut menu is displayed. Choose the **New Minimum Radius Table** option from the shortcut menu; a new table is added in the **Minimum Radius Tables** subnode with the name **New Minimum Radius Table**.

7. Double-click on the table **New Minimum Radius Table** and change the name to **Palkins Street at eMax 5%**. Then press ENTER; a new minimum radius table is created, as shown in Figure 5-73.

Figure 5-73 *The* ***Palkins Street at eMax 5%*** *table added in the* ***Minimum Radius Tables*** *subnode*

8. In the right pane of the dialog box, select the first row in the **Speed** column and click; a drop-down list is displayed.

9. Select **10** from the drop-down list.

10. Double click again in the **Speed** column in the second row and select **20** from the drop-down list.

11. Similarly, add **30**, **40**, **50**, **60**, and **70** values in the **Speed** column.

12. Click in the first row in the **Radius** column and enter **50** as the radius value.

13. Click in the second row in the **Radius** column and enter **100** as the radius for the speed value of **20** miles per hour.

14. Similarly, enter values **200**, **250**, **300**, **350**, and **400** as **Radius** for the **Speed** values of **30**, **40**, **50**, **60**, and **70**, respectively, as shown in Figure 5-74.

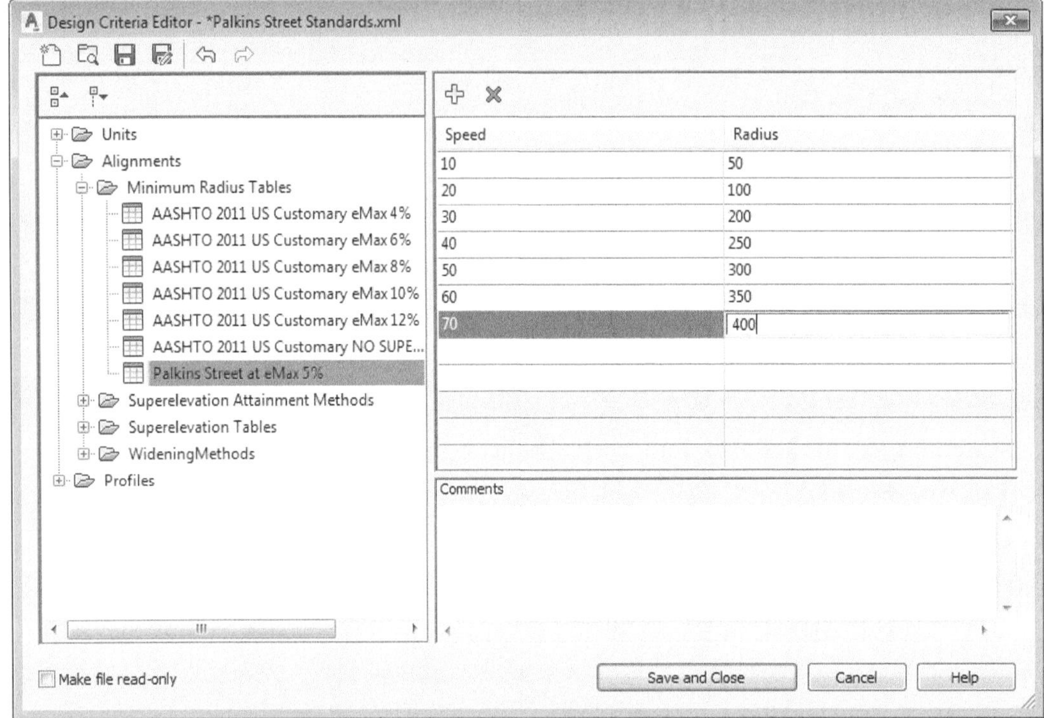

Figure 5-74 The radius defined for various design speeds

15. Choose the **Save and Close** button, a **Design Criteria Editor - Unsaved Changes** dialog box will appear. Choose the **Save changes and Exit** button to exit the **Design Criteria Editor – Palkins Street Standards.xml** dialog box. You have created a new design criteria by customizing the default design criteria file. Next, you will create label styles and label set.

Creating the Label Style for Major Stations

1. Expand **Alignment > Label Styles > Station** subnode in the **Settings** tab of the **TOOLSPACE** palette.

2. Select the **Major Station** subnode in the **Station** node and right-click; a shortcut menu is displayed.

3. Choose **New** from the shortcut menu; the **Label Style Composer - New Major Station Label Style** dialog box is displayed.

4. Enter **Palkins-major** as the style name in the **Name** edit box of the **Information** tab.

5. Next, choose the **Layout** tab.

6. In the **Layout** tab, set the values of the properties in the **Text** collection as given below:

   Text height: **10.000"** Color: **blue** Lineweight: **0.18mm**

7. Next, choose the **Dragged State** tab.

8. In the **Leader** category, set the color of the leader to **Red**.

9. In the **Dragged State Components** category, set the color of the dragged state component to **red**.

10. Choose the **OK** button; the **Label Style Composer – Palkins-major** dialog box is closed.

Tip
*The **Palkins-major** label style for the major station will be listed under the **Major Station** subnode of the **Station** node in the **Settings** tab.*

Creating the Label Style for Minor Stations

1. Expand **Alignments > Label Styles > Station** subnode in the **Settings** tab of the **TOOLSPACE** palette, if it is not expanded already.

2. Select the **Minor Station** subnode in the **Station** node and right-click to display a shortcut menu.

3. Choose the **New** option from the shortcut menu; the **Label Style Composer - New Minor Station Label Style** dialog box is displayed.

4. Enter **Palkins-minor** as the style name in the **Name** edit box of the **Information** tab.

5. Choose the **Layout** tab and set the values of the properties in the **Text** collection as given below:

   Text Height: **5.000"** Color: **magenta** Lineweight: **0.15mm**

6. Choose the **OK** button to close the **Label Style Composer – Palkins - minor** dialog box.

Creating the Label Set

1. Expand the **Alignments > Label Styles** subnode in the **Settings** tab of the **TOOLSPACE** palette.

2. Select the **Label Sets** subnode in the **Label Styles** node and right-click; a shortcut menu is displayed.

3. Choose **New** from the shortcut menu; the **Alignment Label Set - New Alignment Label Set** dialog box is displayed.

4. Enter **Palkins-Set** in the **Name** edit box of the **Information** tab.

5. Choose the **Labels** tab. Next, select the **Major Stations** option, if it is not selected from the **Type** drop-down list. Select the **Palkins-major** option from the **Major Station Label Style** drop-down list.

6. Choose the **Add** button to add **Major Stations** in the **Type** column and the style name in the **Style** column.

7. Select the **Minor Stations** option from the **Type** drop-down list and the **Palkins-minor** option from the **Minor Station Label Style** drop-down list.

8. Choose the **Add** button to add the **Minor Stations** in the **Type** column and the **Palkins-minor** label style in the **Style** column.

9. Choose the **OK** button in the **Alignment Label Set - Palkins-Set** dialog box; the **Palkins-Set** label set is added to the **Label Sets** subnode in the **Settings** tab.

10. Select the alignment in the drawing and right-click; a shortcut menu is displayed.

11. Choose **Edit Alignment Labels** from the shortcut menu; the **Alignment Labels - Palkins Street** dialog box is displayed.

12. Choose the **Import label set** button in the dialog box; the **Select Label Set** dialog box is displayed.

13. Select **Palkins-Set** option from the dialog box, if it is not selected by default and choose the **OK** button to close the dialog box.

14. Again, choose the **OK** button to close the **Alignment Labels - Palkins Street** dialog box. The major and minor stations of the **Palkins Street** alignment are labeled according to the **Palkins-major** and **Palkins-minor** label styles added in the **Palkins-Set**, as shown in Figure 5-75.

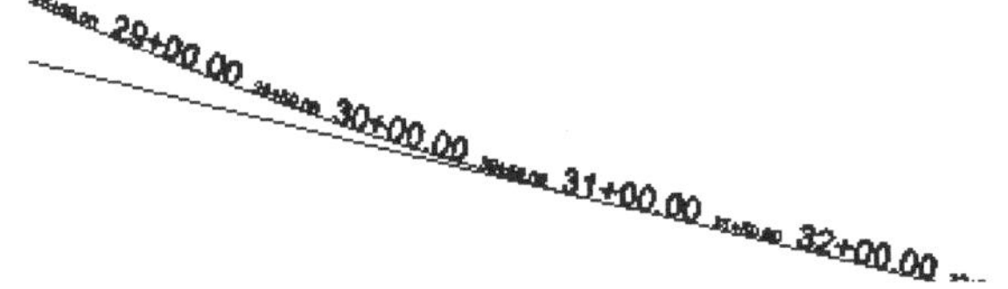

***Figure 5-75** The **Palkins Street** alignment with the label style added*

Saving the File

1. Choose **Save As** from the **Application Menu**; the **Save Drawing As** dialog box is displayed.

2. In this dialog box, browse to the location *C:\c3d_2018\c05_c3d_2018_tut*

3. In the **File name** edit box, enter **c05_tut03a**.

4. Next, choose the **Save** button; the file is saved with the name *c05_tut03a.dwg* at the specified location.

Self-Evaluation Test

Answer the following questions and then compare them to those given at the end of this chapter:

1. The simplest method of creating an alignment is by using the __________ tool.

2. When you create an alignment using the __________ toolbar, you can set the parameters for design criteria.

3. The __________ tools from **Alignment Layout Toolbar** are used to add a fixed line between two points for creating an alignment geometry.

4. __________ is one of the commonly used methods of editing an alignment manually.

5. The __________ tool is used to calculate superelevation for a given alignment.

6. Creating an alignment using the **Alignment Layout Tools** toolbar is a two-step process. (T/F)

7. The fixed entity is not a dynamic entity and its properties remain static even if the properties of other alignment entities are changed. (T/F)

8. A free entity is defined by using the parameters that you specify and is not dependent on the other two entities for its geometry. (T/F)

9. The **Pick Sub - entity** tool is used to select a sub-entity and edit its parameters. (T/F)

10. The **PANORAMA** window displays information only about the selected sub-entity of the selected sub-entity of the alignment. (T/F)

Review Questions

Answer the following questions:

1. Which of the following input options can be used to create an alignment entity using the **Best Fit** method?

   a) From COGO points b) AutoCAD Points
   c) From feature lines d) All of the these

2. Which of the following road types is listed in the **Calculate Superelevation - Roadway Type** page?

   a) Undivided Crowned b) Undivided Planner
   c) Divided Crowned with Median d) All of the these

3. The __________ tool from the **Alignment Layout Tools** toolbar is used to create an alignment that consists of tangents without curves.

4. Choose the _________ tool from the **Alignment Layout Tools** toolbar to display the **PANORAMA** window with the **Alignment Entities** tab chosen.

5. Choose the _________ tool from the **Alignment Layout Tools** toolbar to display the **Alignment Layout Parameters** dialog box.

6. Changing the _________ alignment style results in the change of display appearance of a given alignment.

7. Design criteria cannot be applied unless you select the _________ check box in the **Create Alignment- Layout** dialog box.

8. The _________ tool is used to change the direction of an alignment.

9. The _______ symbol displayed on the alignment, indicates violation of design criteria.

10. The position or layout of the center line of a highway and road on the ground is called an alignment. (T/F)

11. Stations represent the segments or the distances into which an alignment is divided. (T/F)

12. A floating entity can be attached only to a fixed entity or another floating entity. (T/F)

13. A design criteria file also contains superelevation attainment method. (T/F)

14. The **Best Fit** commands help you create lines, arcs, and parabolas using only the AutoCAD points. (T/F)

15. Before creating a table, the respective alignment entities should be labeled. (T/F)

EXERCISES

1. Log on to *www.cadcim.com* and browse to *Textbooks > Civil/GIS > Civil 3D > Exploring AutoCAD Civil 3D 2018*. Next, select *c05_c3d_2018_exer.zip* file from the **Exercise Files** drop-down list. Choose the corresponding **Download** button to download the data file.

2. Now, save and extract the downloaded folder to the following location:

   C:\c3d_2018

Note

*While opening the exercise files, the **PANORAMA** window may appear with an error message. Close this window to proceed further.*

Exercise 1

Open the *c05_c3d_2018_ex01.dwg* file and create an alignment using the **Create Alignment from Objects** tool. Also, calculate the superelevation values at the superelevation rate of 10%. Use the following parameters: **(Expected time: 30 min)**

1. Alignment name: **Lane 1**
2. Alignment style: **Basic**
3. Alignment label set: **Major and Minor only**
4. Design speed: **55mi/hr**
5. Minimum radius table: **AASHTO 2001 eMax 10%**
6. Save the file as *c05_ex01a.dwg*.

Exercise 2

Open the *c05_c3d_2018_ex02.dwg* file and complete the alignment by using the **Alignment Creation Tools**. Use the tools from the **Alignment Layout Tools** toolbar to add the sub-entities. Also, create a label style for major and minor stations of the alignment and add them to a label set. Use the following parameters: **(Expected time: 30 min)**

1. Choose the **Fixed Curve** tool to add a curve using the top vertices of the first three polygons.

2. Using the **Floating Curve (from entity end, through point)** tool, add a floating curve at the end of the alignment by using the last segment as the entity and top vertex of the last polygon as the pass-through point.

3. Design Speed: 60mi/h (**Design Speed** tab)

4. Major Station label Name: **Major ST**
   Text height: **0.2000"**
   Color: **green**

5. Minor Station Label Name: **Minor ST**
   Text height: **0.1000"**
   Color: **blue**

   Save the file as *c05_ex02a.dwg*.

Answers to Self-Evaluation Test

1. Create Alignment from Objects, **2. Alignment Layout Tools**, **3. Fixed Line (Two Points)**, **4.** Grip editing, **5. Calculate/Edit Superelevation**, **6.** T, **7.** T, **8.** F, **9.** T, **10.** F

Chapter 6

Working with Profiles

Learning Objectives

After completing this chapter, you will be able to:

- *Understand the concept of profiles*
- *Create a surface profile*
- *Create a layout profile*
- *Create multiple, stacked, and quick profiles*
- *Create profile label styles and view styles*
- *Create band sets and band styles*
- *Use profile properties*

PROFILES

Alignments and profiles are the main components of a road design project. Profiles are graphical representations of the surface elevations along the horizontal alignment, as shown in Figure 6-1. They help you view the terrain along a specified alignment. A profile view object is used to store and display the information about the profile. It displays and maintains the profiles along with its associated information such as the length, start and end points, and station and elevation data of the alignment that it represents. Moreover, a profile view object creates and controls the actual grid in which the profile data will be displayed along with the bands of data that you want to display.

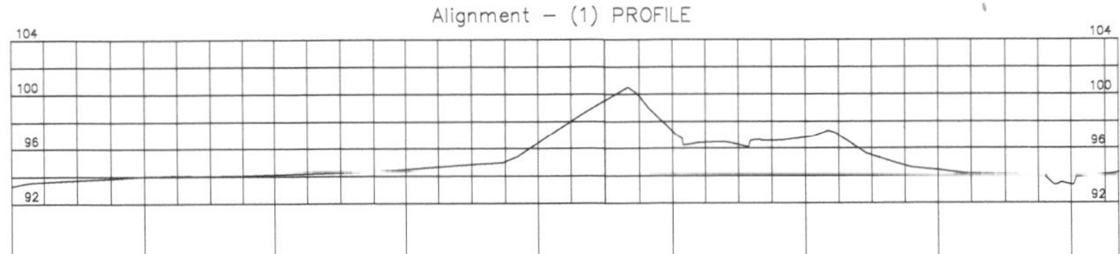

***Figure 6-1** A profile created from the alignment*

Types of Profiles

There are different types of profiles and these are discussed next.

Existing Ground/Surface Profile

The **Existing Ground** (EG) profile is created from an existing surface and shows the variations in the surface elevation along the required alignment.

Finished Ground/Layout/Design/Proposed Profile

The **Finished Ground** (FG) profile is created from an existing surface. This type of profile is created based on certain design requirements. You can draft the FG profile using the **Profile Layout Tools** toolbar in the same way as you create an alignment using the **Alignment Layout Tools** toolbar. You will learn how to use the **Profile Layout Tools** toolbar later in this chapter.

Superimposed Profile

A superimposed profile is created by superimposing one profile view on the other profile view.

Corridor Profile

A corridor profile is created from the feature line of a corridor. A profile can be displayed in a single profile view or multiple profile views. The single profile view displays the elevation variation (profile) of the selected station along the alignment in a single profile view. While, the multiple profile views displays shorter segments of a profile in individual profile view grids. All profile views grids displayed in the multiple profile view will be of consistent length and scale.

Creating a Surface Profile

Ribbon: Home > Create Design > Profile drop-down > Create Surface Profile
Command: CREATEPROFILEFROMSURFACE

You can create a surface profile and analyze the elevations along a horizontal path. To create a surface profile or an Existing Ground (EG) profile, choose the **Create Surface Profile** tool from the **Create Design** panel; the **Create Profile from Surface** dialog box will be displayed, as shown in Figure 6-2.

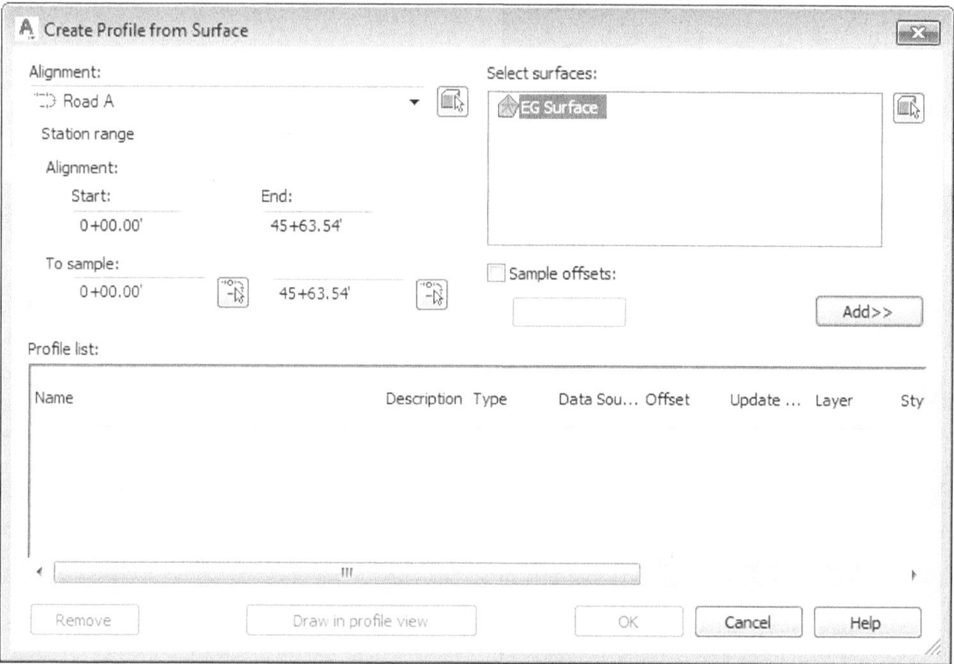

***Figure 6-2** The **Create Profile from Surface** dialog box*

Note

*The **Create Profile from Surface** dialog box will be invoked only if a surface object and an alignment object exists in the drawing.*

From the **Alignment** drop-down list, select the alignment along which you want to create the profile. Next, select the required surface from the **Select surfaces** list box. To select more than one surface, press and hold the CTRL key and select the required surfaces. The values displayed in the **Start** and **End** edit boxes in the **Station range** area show the start and end stations of the alignment respectively and you cannot edit these values. These values are selected by default for profile creation. In case you require to create a profile between stations other than the default stations, choose the buttons on the right of the **To sample** edit box and pick the stations directly from the alignment. Alternatively, you can type the required station value in the edit boxes. Next, choose the **Add** button; the profile will be added in the **Profile list** list box. You can also create surface profile for the offsets along the alignment. To do so, select the check box next to the **To sample** edit box and then enter the offset distance in the **Sample offsets** edit box. The

Sample offsets edit box becomes available only after you select the check box next to it. Next, choose the **Add** button to add the offset profile to the **Profile list** list box. Note that you can view and edit the profile data of the current profiles only. To remove a profile from the **Profile list** list box, select the profile from it and choose the **Remove** button. Note that the profiles removed in this manner are not available for drawing in the profile view.

Note

*You can also remove the **Profile** from the **Prospector** tab. To do so, expand the **Profiles** subnode from the **Alignments** node. Now, select the required profile and right-click; a shortcut menu will be displayed. Choose the **Delete** option from the shortcut menu; the profile will be deleted.*

Now, choose the **OK** button; the **Create Profile from Surface** dialog box will be closed and the **PANORAMA** window will be displayed with a message. At this stage, the profile is just sampled but not displayed and it will be added under **Alignments > Centerline Alignments > <Alignment Name> > Profiles** subnode in the **Prospector** tab. If offset alignment is created, then the profile will be sampled and added under the **Alignments > Offset Alignments > <Alignment Name> > Profiles** subnode.

Note

On entering a negative offset value, the offset profile will be displayed below the original profile.

Creating a Profile View

To view a profile, it has to be drawn in the profile view. To create the profile view, choose the **Create Profile View** tool from **Home > Profile & Section Views > Profile View** drop-down; the **General** page of the **Create Profile View** wizard will be displayed, as shown in Figure 6-3. You will use this wizard to create the profile view. The different pages of this wizard are discussed next.

Note

*You can also invoke the **Create Profile View** wizard by choosing the **Draw in profile view** button in the **Create Profile from Surface** dialog box.*

General Page

The options in this page are used to specify the basic profile view information such as the profile view name, style, and alignment. Select the name of the parent alignment from the **Select alignment** drop-down list. Alternatively, choose the corresponding **Select from the drawing** button to select an alignment directly from the drawing. The profile view will be created by sampling this alignment.

Next, enter a name for the profile view in the **Profile view name** edit box. Optionally, you can enter a brief profile description in the **Description** text box. The **Profile view style** drop-down list displays the default profile view style. You can select the required profile view style from this drop-down list. You can also create a new profile view style or edit the default view style. To edit or create a style, choose the down arrow button on the right of this drop-down list to display a flyout. Next, choose the required option from the flyout to edit or create a new profile view style. The **Profile view layer** text box displays the default layer on which the profile view will be created. Choose the button on the right of this option to display the **Object Layer** dialog box. You can use this dialog box to modify the layer.

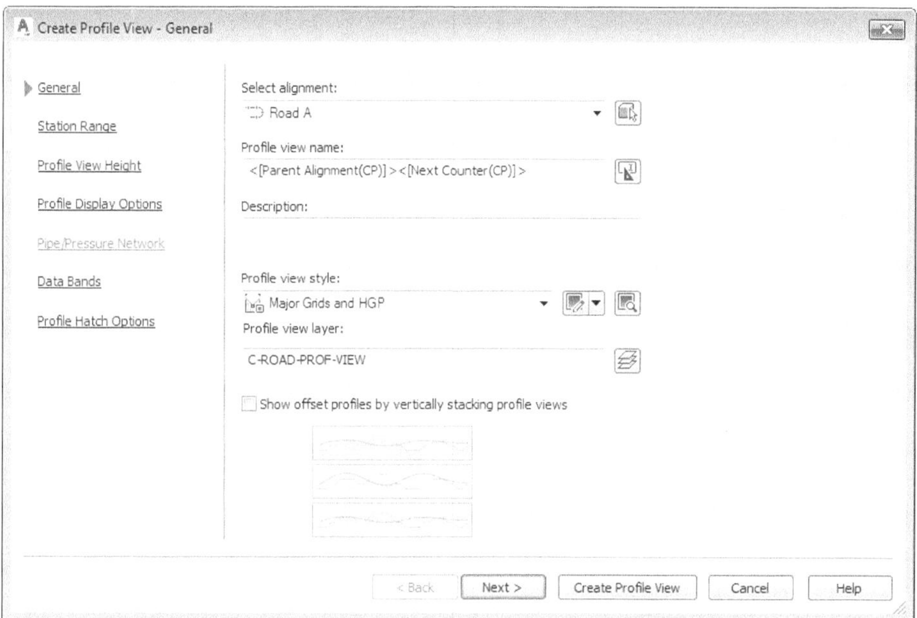

Figure 6-3 The ***General*** *page of the* ***Create Profile View*** *wizard*

Select the **Show offset profiles by vertically stacking profile views** check box to create stacked profile views. The stacked profile views are a collection of related profile views in which the offset profile views are drawn separately and placed vertically above or below the centerline profile view. Note that on selecting this check box, a link to the **Stacked Profile** page will be displayed on the left pane of the wizard.

Once you have specified the basic profile information in the **General** page, choose the **Next** button; the **Station Range** page of the **Create Profile View** wizard will be displayed, as shown in Figure 6-4.

Station Range Page

The **Station Range** page of the wizard is used to specify the station range along which the profile view will be drawn. If your alignment is very long and you want to create a profile view for only a few stations, you can do it by specifying the station range using the options in the **Station Range** page, refer to Figure 6-4.

In the **Station range** area of this page, the **Automatic** radio button is selected by default. This indicates that the profile view will be drawn from the first station to the end station of the parent alignment. Select the **User specified range** radio button in the **Station range** area to specify the station range as required. On selecting the radio button, the corresponding edit boxes will become active. Enter the start and end station values of the required station range in the edit boxes. Alternatively, you can choose the button on the right of the edit boxes to specify the station range by selecting the alignment stations directly from the drawing.

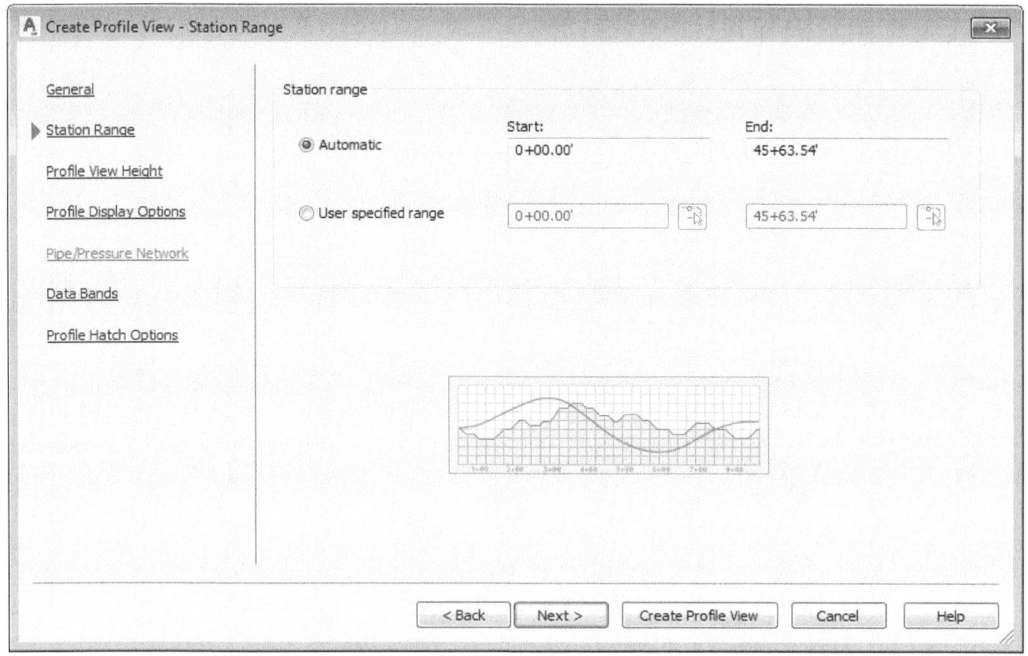

Figure 6-4 The ***Station Range*** *page of the* ***Create Profile View*** *wizard*

On specifying the station range in the **Station Range** page, choose the **Next** button; the **Profile View Height** page will be displayed, as shown in Figure 6-5.

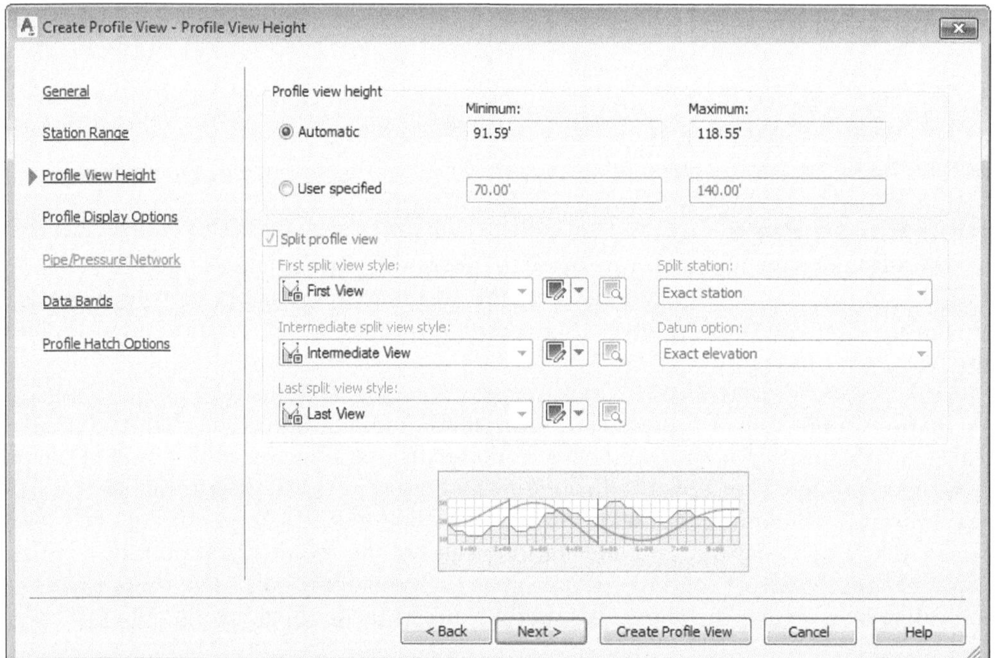

Figure 6-5 The ***Profile View Height*** *page of the* ***Create Profile View*** *wizard*

Profile View Height Page

This page is used to specify the height of the profile view and the settings for the split profile view, if required. In the **Profile view height** area, the **Automatic** radio button is selected by default and the full height of the highest profile view is displayed, refer to Figure 6-5. You can select the **User specified** radio button in this area to specify the minimum and maximum heights of the profile view in the **Minimum** and **Maximum** edit boxes, respectively.

Note

If the height of the profile view extends beyond the specified values, then the view will be split or clipped.

In the **Split profile view** area, you can specify the settings used for splitting a profile view. If you select the **User specified** radio button in the **Profile view height** area, the **Split profile view** check box in this page will be activated.

In this area, select the profile view style from the **First split view style** drop-down list to specify the display style of the first split profile view segment. The profile view styles control the display of the profile view by specifying the grid spacing, view direction and the title of profile views. You can create a new style for the first split profile view or edit the default profile view. To do so, choose the down arrow on the right of the drop-down list and select the required option from the flyout displayed. Similarly, select the profile view styles for the intermediate and last split profile views from the **Intermediate split view style** and **Last split view style** drop-down lists, respectively. To specify the start and end station for which the profile view segment will be created, select an option from the **Split station** drop-down list. To specify the vertical location for splitting the profile view, select an option from the **Datum option** drop-down list.

After specifying the profile height and split profile view settings in the **Profile View Height** page, choose the **Next** button; the **Stacked Profile** page of the **Create Profile View** wizard will be displayed. The **Stacked Profil**e page is discussed next.

Note

*The **Stacked Profile** page will appear as the next page after the **Profile View Height** page only if the **Show offset profiles by vertically stacking profile views** check box is selected in the **General** page of the wizard. If this check box is cleared, the **Profile Display Options** page of the **Create Profile View** wizard will be displayed as the next page, as shown in Figure 6-6.*

Stacked Profile Page

This page is used to specify the settings for the stacked profile views. In the **Number of stacked views** spinner, specify the number of views to be created. You can specify any number from 1 to 9. Enter a positive value for the spacing between various profile views in the **Gap between views** edit box. The **Top view style** drop-down list displays the default style used for the topmost profile view. Select the required style from this drop-down list. You can create a new style for the top profile view or edit the default style. To create a new style, click the down arrow button on the right of this drop-down list; a flyout will be displayed. Choose the **Create New** or **Edit Current Selection** option as per the requirement. Similarly, select a profile view style for the middle and bottom views from the **Middle view style** and **Bottom view style** drop-down lists, respectively.

Note that the preview on the right of this page displays the total number of profile views specified. Now, choose the **Next** button; the **Profile Display Options** page of the **Create Profile View** wizard will be displayed. This page is discussed next.

Profile Display Options Page

This page of the wizard is used to view and change the settings of the profiles associated with the parent alignment. The **Select stacked view to specify options for** list box of this page lists all stacked views and allows you to select the required profile view for which you want to specify the display options, refer to Figure 6-6. The number of profile views listed in this list box depends upon the number specified in the **Stacked Profile** page.

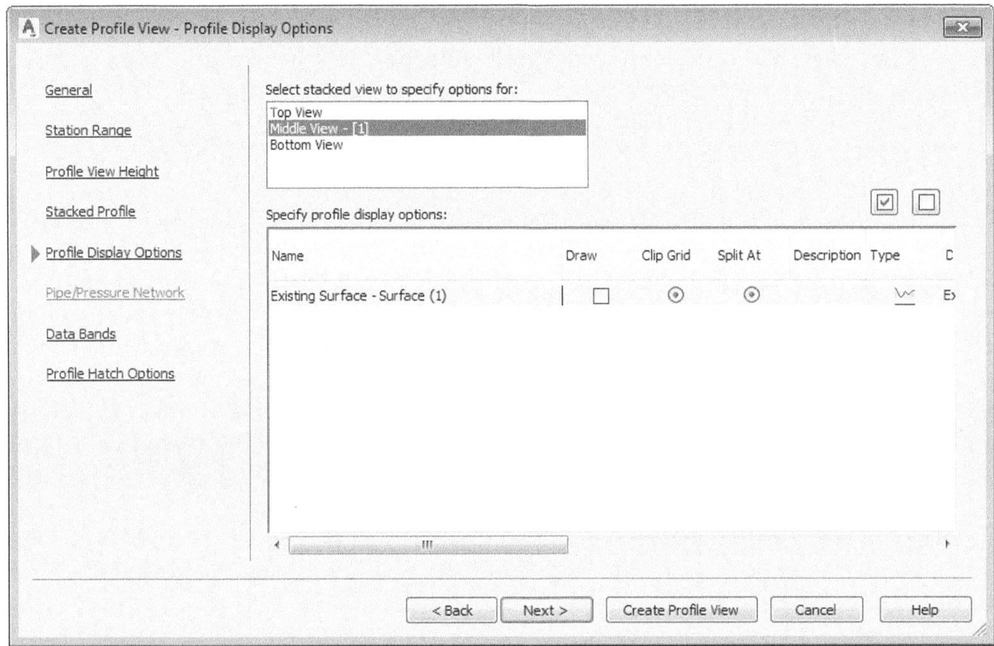

*Figure 6-6 The **Profile Display Options** page of the **Create Profile View** wizard*

Note

*The **Select stacked view to specify options for** list box will be available only if the **Show offset profiles by vertically stacking profile views** check box is selected in the **General** page of the wizard.*

The **Specify profile display options** area in this page allows you to specify the display options for the profile views associated with the alignment. The **Name** column in this area specifies the name of the profile views. The check boxes in the **Draw** column are used to select the profile that you want to draw in the profile view. You can select all check boxes in the **Draw** column by choosing the **Select All Profiles** button available at the top right corner of the **Specify profile display options** area. The **Clip Grid** column allows you to select the profile that will control the horizontal and vertical extents of the profile view grid by selecting the required radio button in this column. This option will be functional only if the **Grid Options** in the **Grid** tab of the **Profile View Style** dialog box are set to clip the grid in the profile view. The **Split At** column specifies where to split from a profile view that contains multiple profiles.

Tip

*A profile view consists of both the existing ground profile and the finished ground profile. If you select the radio button in the **Split At** column for the existing ground profile, the split will occur in the existing ground elevation.*

The **Description** column is used to provide the description of a profile. Click in this column and enter the required description about the profile. The **Type** column specifies the type of profile by displaying the respective icons.

Tip

The profile icon with a blue line indicates a surface profile, the profile with a red line indicates a layout profile, the icon with an orange line indicates a superimposed profile, and the green colored icon indicates a corridor profile.

The **Data Source** column specifies the name of the surface for which the profile is drawn in the profile view. In case of corridor profiles, it displays the name of the parent corridor. The **Offset** column specifies the offset distance from the centerline of the parent horizontal alignment. The **Update Mode** column specifies whether the surface profile will be updated dynamically or it will remain static. To specify a surface as dynamic or static, click in this column and specify the required update mode from the drop-down list for the surface profile only. The **Layer** column specifies the layer of the profile. To specify the layer, click in this column and select the required row from the **Layer Selection** dialog box displayed. Similarly, click in the **Style**, **Override**, and **Labels** columns and select the required profile style and profile label set from the dialog boxes displayed. To override the profile style for the current profile, select the **<Not Overridden>** check box in the **Override Style** column and then specify a suitable profile from the **Pick profile style** dialog box, as discussed in earlier chapters. The **Alignment** column specifies the parent alignment from which the profile is created. The **Station** columns specify the start and end station values of the profile while the **Elevation** columns specify the minimum and maximum elevation values along a profile.

After setting the required parameters in the **Profile Display Options** page of the wizard, choose the **Next** button; the **Data Bands** page of the **Create Profile View** wizard will be displayed.

Note

*If there are pipe networks in the drawing then the **Pipe Network Display** page will be enabled and displayed before the **Data Bands** page.*

Data Bands Page

The **Data Bands** page is used to specify the properties of the data band associated with the profile. You will learn about the data bands and data band sets later in this chapter. In this page, the **Select band set** drop-down list displays the default band set style for the profile view. You can select the required band set from this drop-down list. The options in the **Location** drop-down list of the **List of bands** area are used to specify where to add the data band in the profile view. You can place the data band either on the top or at the bottom of the profile view. The **Set band properties** list box displays the band properties. The **Band Type** column specifies the types of data band such as profile, vertical geometry, superelevation, and pipe data bands. The **Style** column displays the name of the data band style assigned to the band set. To select the required style, click at the right corner in the **Style** column; the **Pick Band Style** dialog box will be displayed. Select the required style from the drop-down list of this dialog box. The **Profile 1** and **Profile 2** columns display the names of the two profiles from which the band data is obtained. For example, if you select the existing ground and finished ground as profile 1 and profile 2, respectively, then each station in the data band will display the elevation values from both profiles. When you click in these columns the corresponding drop-down lists will be displayed. You can select the required profile from these drop-down lists. Choose the browse button in the **Geometry Points** column to display the **Geometry Points to Label in Band** dialog box. You can use this dialog box to select the alignment and profile of geometry points that you want to label in the data band.

After setting the required parameters in the **Data Bands** page of the wizard, choose the **Next** button; the **Profile Hatch Options** page of the **Create Profile View** wizard will be displayed.

Profile Hatch Options Page

The **Profile Hatch Options** page of the wizard is used to set the options for adding hatch patterns to show the cut and fill regions in the profile view. You can add hatch patterns for areas that are cut, filled, and have multiple boundaries defining the hatch region or in areas where quantity takeoff criteria is used to define a hatch region. To add a hatch in the profile, click on the button displayed under the hatch option name; a record is added in the hatch table and all buttons displayed above the table are also activated. In the **Profile** column of the hatch table, select the options in the drop-down list corresponding to the options in the **Hatch Area** column. Next, choose the **Create Profile View** button located at the bottom of the wizard; you will be prompted to specify the origin of the profile view. Click in the drawing area to specify the origin of the profile view; the profile view will be added to the drawing. To display the profile created, choose the **Prospector** tab in the **TOOLSPACE** palette, and expand the **Profiles** subnode in the **Alignments** node to view the profile and profile view name. Next, expand the **Profile Views** subnode in the **Alignments** node; the profile view will be listed in the **Profile Views** subnode. Thus, a surface profile is created by utilizing the elevation data of the surface at the points where the alignment crosses the lines of the TIN surface.

Creating a Layout or Criteria-Based Profile

Ribbon:	Home > Create Design > Profile drop-down > Profile Creation Tools
Command:	CREATEPROFILELAYOUT

The layout profiles are used to represent the design elevations along an alignment and are created on the existing profile grid view. A layout profile represents the proposed elevation changes to be made for a finished ground. The workflow to create a layout (Design profile) is similar to creating a criteria-based alignment using the **Profile Layout Tools** toolbar. You need to select and assign a design criteria file for the profile from which you can obtain the minimum **K** values. Remember that if you assign a design criteria file to the parent alignment, the same design criteria file will be assigned to the profile view. However, you can change the design criteria file to create the profile as per your design requirements.

To create a layout profile, choose the **Profile Creation Tools** tool from the **Create Design** panel; you will be prompted to select a profile view. Select the profile view on which you want to create the design profile; the **Create Profile - Draw New** dialog box will be displayed, as shown in Figure 6-7.

Tip

The K value is the ratio of the curve length and the algebraic distance between the incoming and the outgoing tangents. The K value represents the horizontal distance at which the grade on the vertical curve changes by 1%. The American Association of State Highway Transport Officials (AASHTO) has established some minimum K values according to which the curves can be designed. The length of the curves should not be less than the minimum K value for a particular distance.

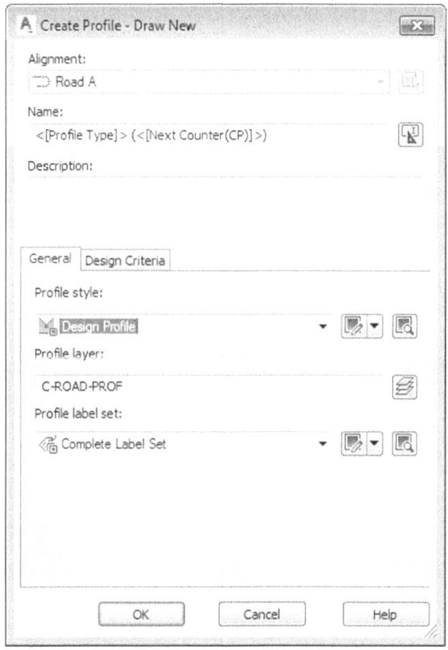

***Figure 6-7** The **Create Profile - Draw New** dialog box*

In this dialog box, the **Alignment** text box displays the name of the parent alignment. The **Name** edit box displays the default name of the profile. You can enter a new profile name in this edit box. Select the required profile style and the profile label set from the drop-down lists in the **Profile style** and **Profile label set** drop-down lists, respectively. You can also set the required layer for the profile in the **Profile layer** text box. The text box displays the default layer assigned to the profile. You can assign a new layer to the profile by choosing the button available on the right of the text box in the **Profile layer** text box.

The **General** tab in this dialog box is used to specify the display properties of the profile. The **Design Criteria** tab is used to specify the design criteria file for the layout profile. You can select the **Use criteria-based design** check box to apply a new design criteria file or change the existing file. This design criteria file will provide the minimum K values required to create the design profile.

After you have specified the profile information and design criteria file in the **Create Profile - Draw New** dialog box, choose the **OK** button; the **Profile Layout Tools** toolbar will be displayed with the profile name, as shown in Figure 6-8. Note that this profile name will be listed in the **Profiles** subnode of the **Alignments** node in the **Prospector** tab of the **TOOLSPACE** palette.

*Figure 6-8 The **Profile Layout Tools - Layout (1)** toolbar*

You can use the tools in the **Profile Layout Tools** toolbar to create a criteria-based profile design. The toolbar can also be used to create the layout profile and edit the surface profiles. You will notice that whenever you invoke a tool in this toolbar, the name of that tool will be displayed at the bottom of the toolbar. Some of the tools in this toolbar are discussed next.

Draw Tangents

Invoke the **Draw Tangents** tool from the toolbar to pick the Points of Vertical Intersection (PVI) on the profile view to draw tangents between the points without any curves. Choose the down arrow of the **Draw Tangents with Curves** tool to display the flyout that contains the other tools.

Draw Tangents With Curves

Invoke this tool to add a series of fixed tangents between the specified points. This tool also helps you add free curves automatically at the point of vertical intersection.

Curve Settings

Choose this tool to specify the curve parameters that will be used while using the **Draw Tangents With Curves** tool. On choosing this tool, the **Vertical Curve Settings** dialog box will be displayed, as shown in Figure 6-9. This dialog box is used to select the curve type to be added between the tangents and to configure the curve settings accordingly.

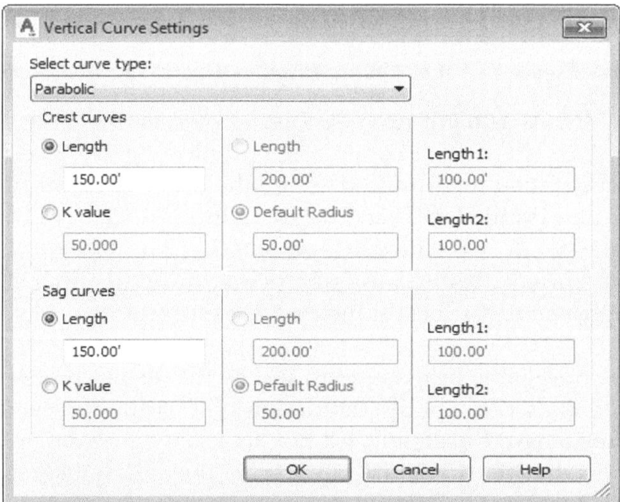

*Figure 6-9 The **Vertical Curve Settings** dialog box*

Convert Free Curve (Through Point)

Choose this option to convert the free vertical curves constrained by pass through points into PVI based curves that are compatible with previous versions of software.

Insert PVI

The **Insert PVI** tool breaks a tangent into two by adding a point of vertical intersection (PVI) at the specified location.

Delete PVI

The **Delete PVI** tool removes a point of vertical intersection between two adjacent tangents thereby creating one tangent.

Move PVI

The **Move PVI** tool enables the user to move an existing PVI to a new location in a profile view.

Fixed Tangents (Two points)

This tool is used to add tangents to the vertical profile by selecting the start and end points. Choose the down arrow on the right of this tool; a flyout will be displayed with other tangent creation tools. You can use the required tools to add tangents to the profile layout. For example, invoke the **Free Tangent** tool from this flyout to add a free tangent.

Fixed Vertical Curve (Three points)

This tool is used to add a curve to the profile by specifying three points.

Free Vertical Curve (Parabola)

This tool is used to add a free parabolic curve constrained to a specified pass-through point, curve length, radius, or K value between two entities.

Free Vertical Curve (Circular)

This tool is used to add a free circular curve constrained to a specified pass-through point, curve length, or radius between two tangents.

Note

*The **Free Vertical Curve (Circular)** tool cannot be used to create curve between two curves or between a tangent and a curve.*

Free Circular Curve (PVI based)

This tool is used to add a circular curve in the profile by specifying the length, radius, or a pass-through point. This tool is PVI-based, so the drawing must consist of points of vertical intersection (PVI). Invoke this tool from the toolbar and click near any PVI in a curve except the first and the last PVI. Next, specify the radius, length, or a pass-through point to add a circular curve.

You can use various other options to add the free vertical curves to the profile by invoking the other free vertical curve tools that are available in the **Profile Layout Tools** toolbar. You can also use the **Floating Vertical Curve** tools to add floating curves to the profile.

Insert PVIs - Tabular

This tool is used to add the PVI data numerically in a tabular form. Invoke this tool; the **Insert PVIs** dialog box will be displayed. Select the required radio button from the **Vertical curve type** area of this dialog box to specify the curve type and then specify the corresponding data in the columns. This tool helps you create points of vertical intersection (PVIs) at multiple locations at the same time.

Raise/Lower PVIs

This tool is used to increase or decrease the height of the PVI. Invoke this tool to display the **Raise/Lower PVI Elevation** dialog box. This dialog box is used to change the elevation of profiles. You can change the elevation of PVI either for the entire length of profile or for a specified station range. In the **Elevation change** edit box of the **Raise/Lower PVI Elevation** dialog box, specify a positive value to increase the elevation or a negative value to decrease the elevation of the profile or the PVIs. In the **PVI range** area, select the **All** radio button to modify the elevation of all PVIs, thereby changing the elevation of the entire profile or select the **Station range** radio button to specify the start and end station values. On doing so, the elevation of the PVIs within the specified station range will be modified.

Tip

*If the **Profile Layout Tools** toolbar is closed, select the profile from the drawing and right-click to display a shortcut menu. Now, choose the **Edit Profile Geometry** option from the shortcut menu to display the **Profile Layout Tools** toolbar again.*

Copy Profile

This tool is used to create a copy of the profile. Invoke this tool to display the **Copy Profile Data** dialog box. This dialog box is used to copy the entire profile or a part of the profile. The copy of the profile will be added in the **Profiles** subnode of the **Alignments** node in the **Prospector** tab of the **TOOLSPACE** palette. This copy can then be used to create a new profile or to overwrite an existing profile.

Displays PVI based data in grid and layout parameter editors

This tool is used in conjunction with the **Profile Grid View** tool in the **Profile Layout Tools** toolbar to edit the PVI based parameter of a profile. When you open the **PANORAMA** window by invoking the **Profile Grid View** tool, the PVI-based information will be displayed in it. This is because the **PVI based** option is selected by default from the flyout. To view the information about the profile entities such as tangents, curves, and so on, choose the down arrow on the right of this tool; a flyout will be displayed. Choose the **Entity based** option from the flyout; the profile entities and their information will be displayed in the **PANORAMA** window. You can use these options to toggle between the PVIs or the entity based parameters of a profile for editing or viewing the information about it.

You can use the required tools in the **Profile Layout Tools** toolbar and create a layout profile or edit the existing layout profile. You can rectify violation errors using the **Alignment Layout Parameters** and **PANORAMA** window. This is explained in detail later in this chapter.

Note

While drafting a layout profile, the violation icon will be displayed on the entity that violates the minimum design criteria, as discussed in Chapter 5.

Extend Entity

This tool is used to extend an entity (floating, fixed tangent, or parabola) to the extents of a profile.

Creating a Superimposed Profile

Ribbon: Home > Create Design > Profile drop-down > Create Superimposed Profile
Command: SUPERIMPOSEPROFILE

In AutoCAD Civil 3D, you can compare two profiles by superimposing one profile over the other. A superimposed profile is the one that is created by superimposing the profile of an alignment over the profile views of other alignments. Superimposing a profile helps you study the variations in elevation of profiles. For example, you can superimpose a highway alignment profile over the pipe network alignment to view and compare the elevations.

To create a superimposed profile, choose the **Create Superimposed Profile** tool from the **Create Design** panel; you will be prompted to select the source profile from the drawing area. Select the profile which you want to superimpose as the source profile; you will be prompted to select the destination profile view where the superimposed profile is displayed. Select the profile view; the **Superimpose Profile Options** dialog box will be displayed, as shown in Figure 6-10. The tabs in this dialog box are discussed next.

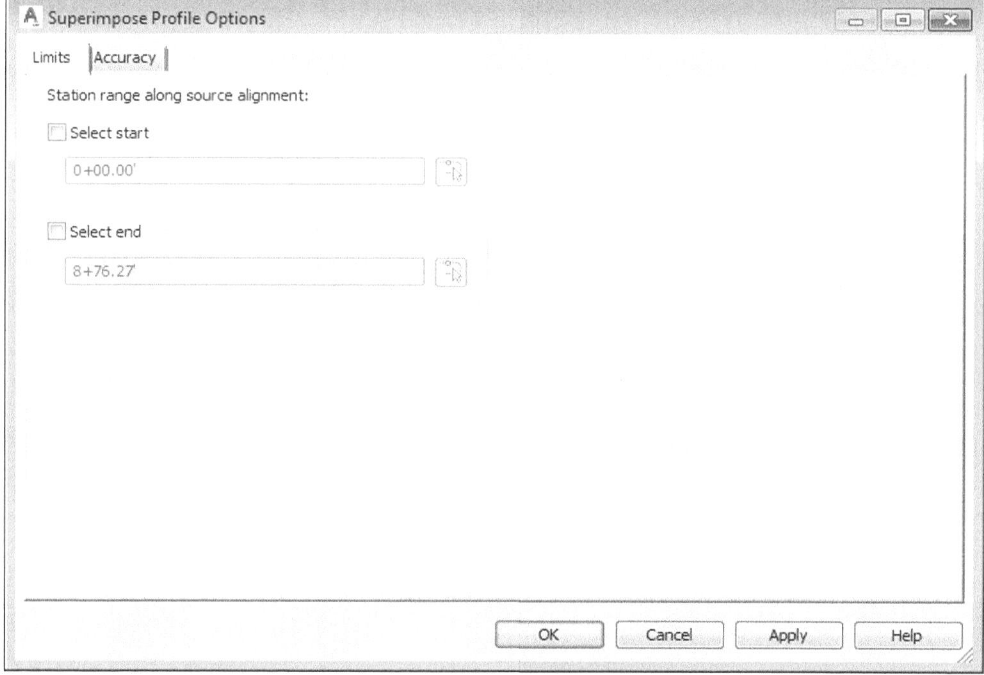

***Figure 6-10** The **Superimpose Profile Options** dialog box*

Limits Tab

The options in the **Limits** tab are used to specify the station range of the profile to be superimposed. By default, Civil 3D superimposes the entire length of the given source profile. If you want to superimpose the profile partially between any two stations, you are required to specify the start and end station values. To specify a start station, select the **Select start** check box in the **Limits** tab of this dialog box; the edit box below this check box will be activated. You can now enter the start station value in this edit box. Alternatively, choose the button on the right of this dialog box to specify the station value directly from the drawing. Similarly, select the **Select end** check box and specify the end station value. Defining the station range also prevents the superimposed profile to react whenever a change is made to the station range of the source profile. This is because the station range of the superimposed profile will remain fixed.

Accuracy Tab

The options in the **Accuracy** tab are used to specify the accuracy of curves in the superimposed profile. Enter the required mid-ordinate distance for both the horizontal and vertical curves in the respective **Horizontal** and **Vertical** edit boxes of the **Accuracy** tab. Smaller the value of this distance, more will be the number of line segments used to represent the curves.

After specifying the required parameters, choose the **OK** button; the **Superimpose Profile Options** dialog box will be closed and the required profile will be superimposed. Figures 6-11 and 6-12 show the source and destination profiles, respectively. Figure 6-13 shows the superimposed profile created by superimposing the profile shown in Figure 6-12 over the profile shown in Figure 6-11.

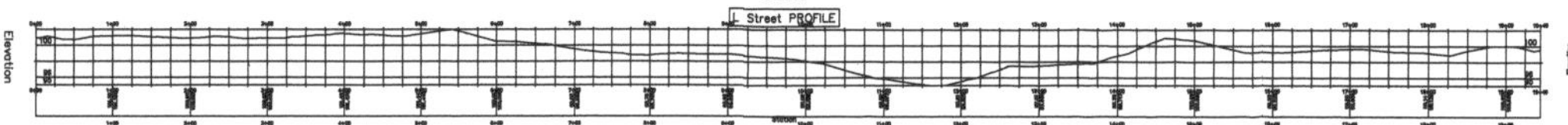

Figure 6-11 *The profile view of L Street*

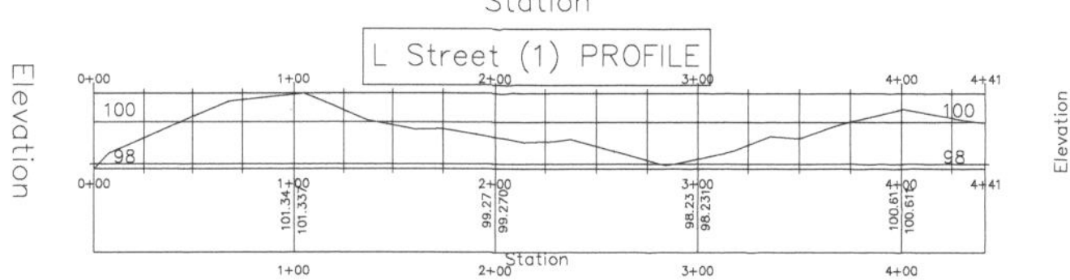

Figure 6-12 *The profile view of L Street (1)*

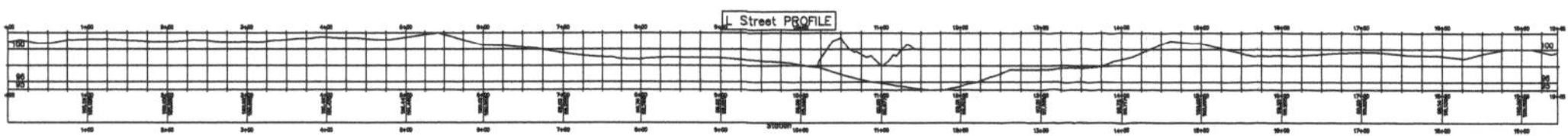

Figure 6-13 *The superimposed profile view of L Street (1) over L Street*

Creating Multiple Profile Views

Ribbon: Home > Profile & Section Views > Profile View drop-down > Create Multiple Profile Views
Command: CREATEMULTIPLEPROFILEVIEW

AutoCAD Civil 3D allows you to create multiple profile views by splitting the large profile view into smaller segments. To create multiple views, choose the **Create Multiple Profile Views** from the **Profile & Section Views** panel. On doing so, the **Create Multiple Profile Views** wizard along with the **General** page will be displayed, as shown in Figure 6-14. The different pages in this wizard are discussed next.

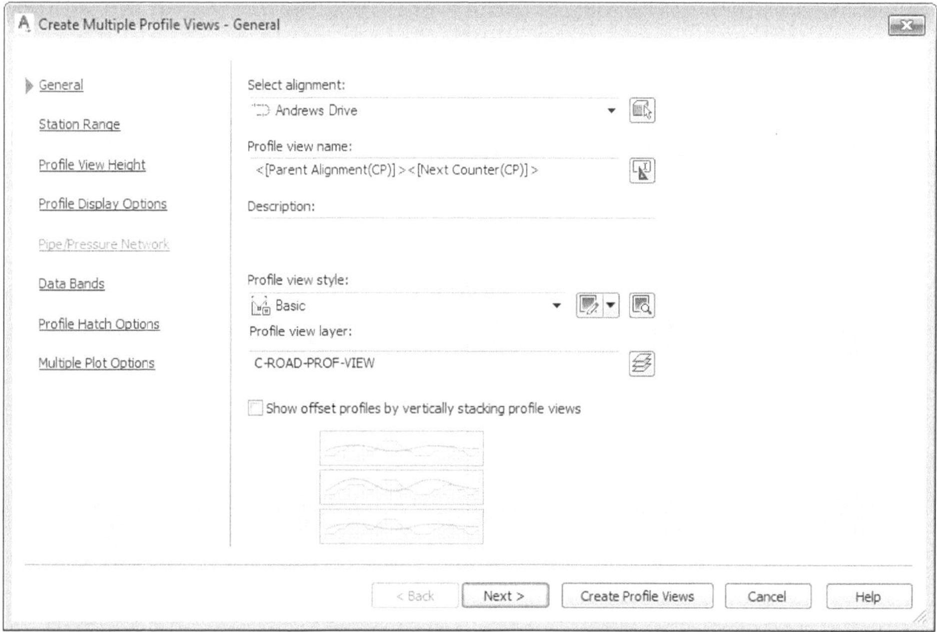

*Figure 6-14 The **General** page of the **Create Multiple Profile Views** wizard*

General Page

The **General** page is displayed by default and is used to specify the basic information about a profile such as name, parent alignment, layer, and profile style. The options in this page are same as those discussed in the **General** page of the **Create Profile View** wizard. Select the alignment for which you want to create the profile views from the **Select alignment** drop-down list of the **General** page. Next, specify the profile name in the **Profile view name** edit box. Optionally, you can enter a brief description about the profile in the **Description** text box. Next, select the style for the profile views from the **Profile view style** drop-down list. After entering the required parameters, choose the **Next** button to display the **Station Range** page of the **Create Multiple Profile Views** wizard.

Station Range Page

The **Station Range** page is used to specify the station range by which the profile view is drawn. By default, the **Automatic** radio button is selected in this area implying that the profile view will be drawn according to the station range specified in the **Start** and **End** text boxes beside it. If you select the **User specified range** radio button in this area, the **Start** and **End** edit boxes displayed on the right will be activated. You can accept the default values or enter numeric values in these edit boxes to limit the station range of the profile view. The **Length of each view** edit box in the **Station range** area specifies the length of each profile view segment in a multiple profile view. Now, choose the **Next** button to display the **Profile View Height** page of the **Create Multiple Profile Views** wizard.

Profile View Height Page

In this page, you can specify the height upto which the profile view will be drawn. In the **Profile view heigh**t area, the **Automatic** radio button is selected by default. As a result, the height of the profile view is drawn to the full height of the highest profile. The **Maximum** and **Minimum** edit boxes next to this radio button specify the limit of the height of the profile view.

You can select the **User specified** radio button to specify the height up to which the profile view is drawn. If a profile extends beyond the user-specified value, it is either split according to the **Split profile view** settings or clipped.

Next, you will specify how to place the datum for all profiles within the profile view. To do so select an option from the **Profile view datum by** drop-down list. Note that this drop-down list is activated only on selecting the **User specified** radio button. On selecting the **Minimum elevation** option from the drop-down list, the profile datum values will be based on the lowest datum values of elevation of all profiles in the profile view. This option is useful for profiles that have high elevation variation. If you select the **Mean elevation** option from the **Profile view datum by** drop-down list, the profile datum values will be based on the mean value of elevation of all profiles. Also, the profiles will be drawn at the center of the profile views with an equal space at the top and bottom of the profile.

Next, select the **Split profile view** check box to split the profile, if the profile height extends beyond the value specified in the edit box in the **Profile View Height** area. In the **Split profile view** area, select the profile view styles, required for the first, intermediate, and end profile view segments. You can specify the station and vertical locations where the profile view will split. To do so, use the **Split station** and the **Datum option** drop-down lists, respectively. After specifying the required parameters in the **Profile View Height** page of the **Create Multiple Profile View** wizard, choose the **Next** button; the **Profile Display Options** page will be displayed.

Profile Display Options Page

The options in this page are similar to those in the **Profile Display Options** page of the **Create Profile View** wizard and have been discussed earlier in the **Creating a Profile View** section. Specify the required options and choose the **Next** button; the **Data Bands** page will be displayed.

Data Bands Page

The options in this page are similar to those in the **Data Bands** page of the **Create Profile View** wizard and have already been discussed earlier in the **Creating a Profile View** section. Specify the required options and choose the **Next** button; the **Profile Hatch Options** page will be displayed.

Profile Hatch Options Page

The options in this page are similar to those in the **Profile Hatch Options** page of the **Create Profile View** wizard and have been discussed earlier in the **Creating a Profile View** section. Specify the required options and choose the **Next** button; the **Multiple Plot Options** page will be displayed.

Note

*In the **Create Profile View** wizard, if the **Show offset profiles by vertically stacking profile views** check box is selected in the **General** page, the link of the **Stacked Profiles** page will be displayed below the link of the **Profile View Height** page.*

Multiple Plot Options Page

This page is used to specify the layout of the plotted profile views. Note that this page is available only for the multiple profile views. The **Draw order** area of this page is used to specify whether you want to draw the profile view segments in different rows or columns. By default, the **By rows** radio button is selected in this area. As a result, the profile view segment is drawn in different rows. If the **By rows** radio button is selected, you can specify the maximum number of profile view segments in a row by using the **Maximum in a row** spinner. You can select the **By columns** radio button to draw the profile view segments in different columns. You can specify the maximum number of profile view segments in a column by using the **Maximum in a column** spinner. The **Start corner** drop-down list is used to specify the direction to draw the profile views. For example, on selecting the **Upper right** option, the profile views will be drawn in a row starting from the upper right corner, as indicated in the **Preview** area.

The **Gap between adjacent profile views** area is used to specify the space between adjacent profile views in a row or column in plotted units. To specify the space between the adjacent profile views, enter the required spacing values in the **Row** and **Column** edit boxes. After you have specified the required information in the **Create Multiple Profile Views** wizard, choose the **Create Profile Views** button; the wizard will close and you will be prompted to specify the origin of the profile view. Click in the drawing area at the required location; multiple views will be created in the drawing, as shown in Figure 6-15.

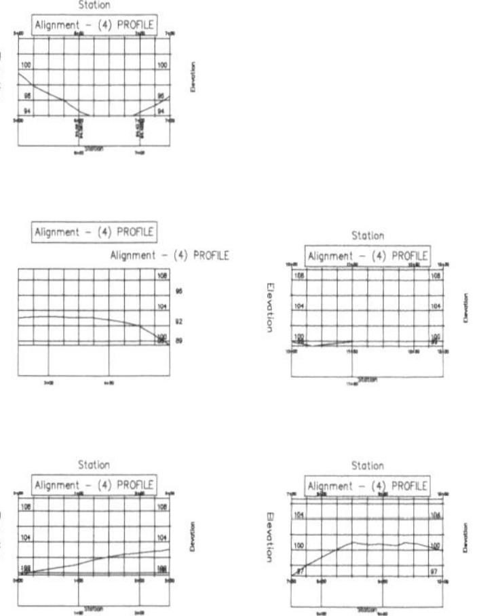

Figure 6-15 *Multiple profile views created using the **Create Multiple Profile View** tool*

Creating a Quick Profile

Ribbon: Home > Create Design > Profile drop-down > Quick Profile
Command: CREATEQUICKPROFILE

You can create a profile without creating an alignment by using the **Quick Profile** tool. A quick profile can be created along an existing AutoCAD object such as line, polyline, feature line, lot line or using points that are specified by clicking on the screen.

To create a quick profile, choose the **Quick Profile** tool from the **Create Design** panel; you will be prompted to select the object along which you want to create the profile. Select the required object; the **Create Quick Profiles** dialog box will be displayed, as shown in Figure 6-16.

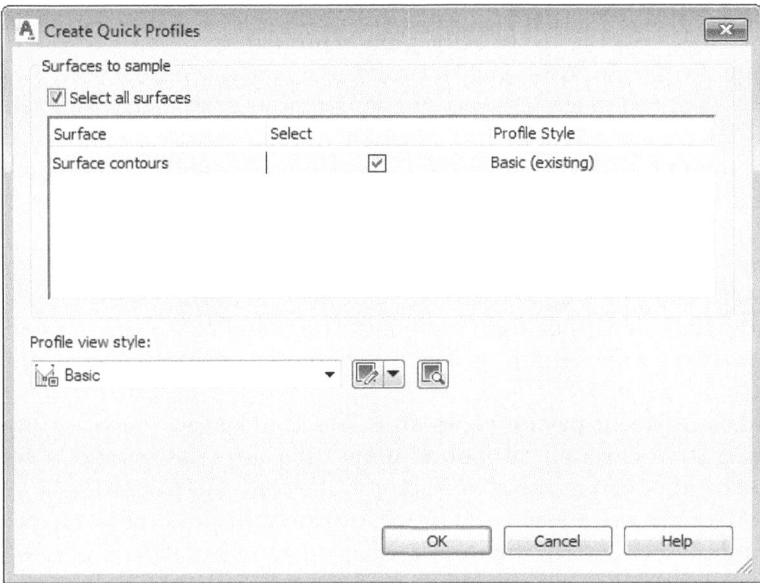

Figure 6-16 The ***Create Quick Profiles*** *dialog box*

In the **Create Quick Profiles** dialog box, the **Surfaces to sample** area lists all the existing surfaces in the drawing and allows you to select the required surface from which you want to create the profile. By default, the **Select all surfaces** check box is selected in this area. You can clear the respective check box in the **Select** column if you do not want to create the quick profile from a particular surface. The **Profile Style** column in the **Surfaces to sample** area specifies the current style for the profile. Click in this column; the **Pick profile style** dialog box will be displayed. Select the required profile style from this dialog box and choose the **OK** button; the **Pick profile style** dialog box will be closed.

Next, select the required style for the profile view from the **Profile view style** drop-down list and choose the **OK** button; you will be prompted to specify the origin of the profile view. Click in the drawing to place the profile view at the required location; the quick profile will be created. Once you click in the drawing to specify the location of the profile, the profile view will be placed at that location. Also, the **PANORAMA** window is displayed with the information that this profile is a temporary object and will be deleted on applying the **SAVE** command or on exiting from the current drawing.

Note

*If you have selected a 3D object, the **Draw 3D entity profile** area will be displayed in the **Create Quick Profiles** dialog box.*

You can also create a quick profile by selecting points on the required surface. To do so, choose the **Quick Profile** tool from the **Create Design** panel; you will be prompted to select object or points. Enter **P** in the command line; you will be prompted to select the first point. Select the desired first point; you will be prompted to specify the second point. Specify all the required points in the drawing. On specifying the points, press ENTER; the **Create Quick Profiles** dialog box will be displayed. Now, select the required surface from this dialog box and choose the **OK** button; the quick profile will be created. Click at the required location in the drawing area to place the required quick profile view.

Creating Dynamic Offset Profiles

You can create the dynamic offset profiles using the same command that you can use to create offset alignments. The geometry of the offset profile is created using a default cross slope which you can modify by editing the profile properties. You can create multiple offset alignments in a single operation including a different number on each side of the parent alignment. The offset distance can be different on each side of the parent alignment. It is used to show a borrow ditch, TBC profiles, or pretty much anything that is relative to your main profile.

To create an offset profile, choose the **Create Offset Alignments** tool from the **Alignments** drop-down in the **Create Design** panel; you will be prompted to select the alignment along which you want to create the offset profile. Select the required alignment; the **Create Offset Alignments** dialog box will be displayed. In this dialog box, select the **Create Profile for Offset Alignment** check box in the **Create Offset Profile** tab; the offset profile will be created, as shown in Figure 6-17.

To display the offset profile, choose the **Prospector** tab in the **TOOLSPACE** palette and expand the **Offset Alignments** and **Profiles** subnodes in the **Alignments** node to view the offset profile created.

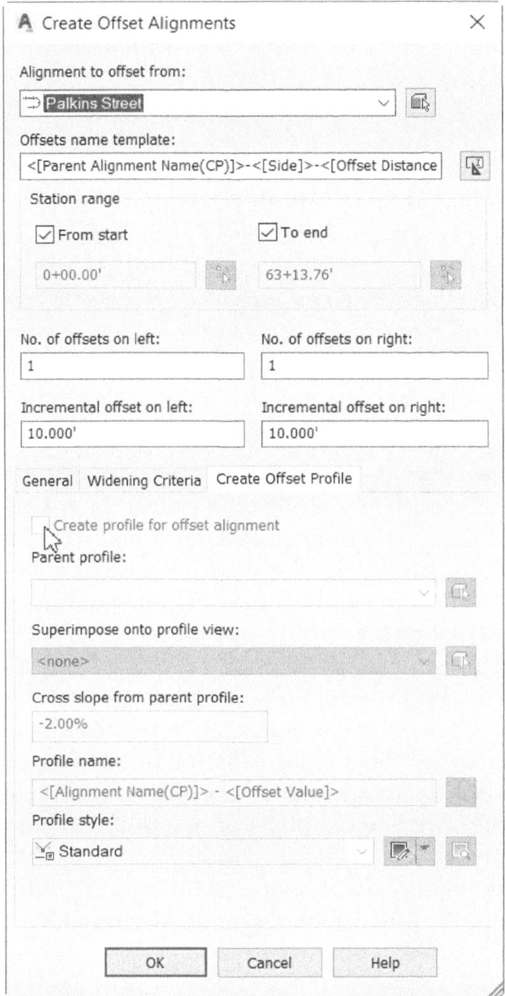

***Figure 6-17** The **Create Offset Profile** tab in the **Create Offset Alignment** dialog box*

DEFINING A PROFILE DESIGN CRITERIA

Ribbon: Profile (Contextual tab) > Modify Profile > Design Criteria Editor
Command: DESIGNCRITERIAEDITOR

The **Design Criteria Editor** tool is used to define or edit the design criteria for a design based profile. The **Design Criteria Editor** tool is available in the **Profile** (Contextual) tab. To create a new design criteria, choose the **Profile** tool from the **Design** panel of the **Modify** tab; the **Profile** tab will be displayed. Next, choose the **Design Criteria Editor** tool from the **Modify Profile** panel of the **Profile** tab; the **Design Criteria Editor - _Autodesk Civil 3D Imperial (2011) Roadway Design Standards.xml** dialog box will be displayed. Remember that the *_Autodesk Civil 3D Imperial (2011) Roadway Design Standards.xml* is the name of the default design criteria file that will be assigned to profiles. Before you create a new design criterion, choose the **Save As** button and save the default design criteria file with a different name at a different location.

Now, expand the **Profiles > Minimum K Tables > AASHTO 2011 Standard** node to display three options for the **Stopping Sight**, **Passing Sight**, and **Headlight Sight Distances** under it. Select any of the options; the **Speeds** and **K** values will be displayed in the columns on the right side of the dialog box, as shown in Figure 6-18.

To create a new table, right-click on **Minimum K Tables** and choose **New Minimum K Table** from the shortcut menu displayed; a new table will be added to the **Minimum K Tables** node. Now, right-click on the new table name added in the **Minimum K Tables** node; a shortcut menu will be displayed. Choose the **New Stopping Sight Distance**, **New Passing Sight Distance**, or **New Headlight Sight Distance** option from the displayed shortcut menu to create a new empty sight distance table. To add values in the sight distance table, select the sight distance table name in the **Minimum K Tables node**; the empty table is displayed in the right pane. Next, double-click on the first row of the **Speed** column and enter the required speed in the edit box displayed. Similarly add various speed values in the table. Next, specify the **K** value for the corresponding speed in the **K** column. After creating the table, choose the **Save and Close** button to save the design criteria file.

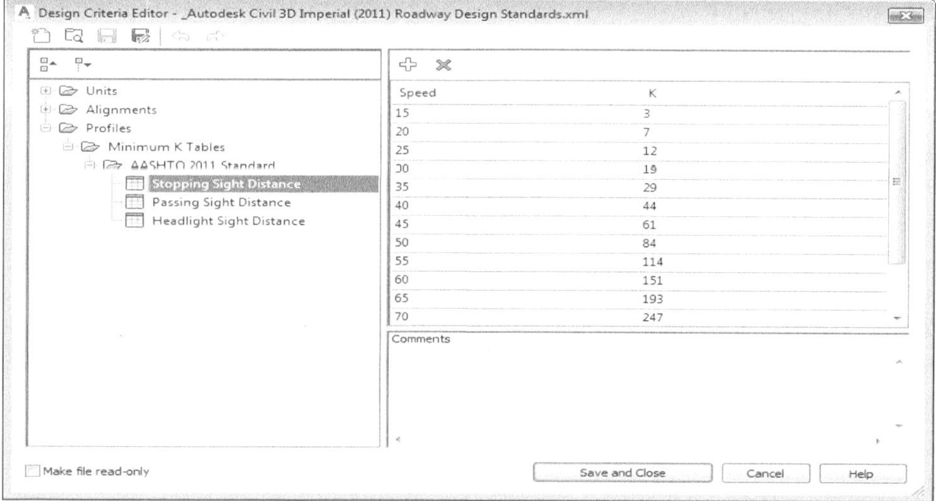

***Figure 6-18** The **Design Criteria Editor** dialog box showing the minimum K values at different speeds*

EDITING LAYOUT/DESIGN PROFILES

You can edit the design profile geometry and profile design criteria of a project at any stage. Civil 3D is compatible enough to quickly adjust to the changes made in the profile. You can edit the geometry of a profile either by grip editing or by using the **Profile Layout Parameters** dialog box, the **PANORAMA** window, and various other tools of the **Profile Layout Tools** toolbar. The profiles layout tools are described next.

Editing Profile Using the Profile Layout Tools Toolbar

The profile layout tools are used to modify the profile by editing the PVIs and profile entities individually. To do so, choose the **Profile** tool from the **Design** panel of the **Modify** tab; the **Profile** tab will be displayed in the Ribbon. In this tab, choose the **Geometry Editor** tool from the **Modify Profile** panel; you will be prompted to select the profile. Select the required profile from the drawing; the **Profile Layout Tools <layout name>** toolbar will be displayed.

To edit the PVIs in the layout profile, ensure that the **PVI based** tool is chosen in the **Profile Layout Tools** toolbar so that the PVI data of the selected profile is displayed in the **PANORAMA** window. To invoke the **PANORAMA** window, choose the **Profile Grid View** tool from the toolbar. The **PANORAMA** window contains the **Profile Entities** tab which lists all PVIs of the selected profile, refer to Figure 6-19.

Tip

You can also display the ***Profile Layout Tools <layout name>*** *toolbar from the drawing area. To do so, select the required layout profile from the profile view and right-click; a shortcut menu will be displayed. Choose* ***Edit Profile Geometry*** *from the shortcut menu; a toolbar will be displayed.*

No.	PVI Station	PVI Elevation	Grade In	Grade Out	A (Grade Change)	Profile Curve Type	Profile Curve Length	K Value
1	0+00.00'	98.569'		-0.02%				
2	0+04.25'	98.568'	-0.02%	2.06%	2.09%			
3	0+05.61'	98.596'	2.06%	3.61%	1.54%			
4	0+13.20'	98.870'	3.61%	2.46%	1.15%			
5	0+15.87'	98.935'	2.46%	3.62%	1.16%			
6	0+22.43'	99.173'	3.62%	-1.46%	5.08%			
7	0+28.58'	99.083'	-1.46%	-7.83%	6.38%			
8	0+31.55'	98.850'	-7.83%	-1.83%	6.00%			
9	0+33.45'	98.815'	-1.83%	-1.52%	0.31%			
10	0+34.30'	98.802'	-1.52%	11.89%	13.41%			
11	0+34.63'	98.841'	11.89%	12.21%	0.32%			

Figure 6-19 *The* ***Profile Entities*** *tab of the* ***PANORAMA*** *window*

You can edit the station, elevation, and grade values for the PVIs by double-clicking on the existing values and replacing them with the required values. To view and edit only the selected PVIs, invoke the **Select PVI** tool from the toolbar and click near the required PVI in the drawing; the PVI data will be displayed in the **Profile Layout Parameters <layout name>** dialog box. To edit PVI parameters, click on the cell corresponding to the parameter you want to change; an edit box is displayed. Enter the new value in the edit box.

Note that you can also edit the PVI using the **Profile Entities** tab of the **PANORAMA** window. To edit a PVI, select it in the **Number** column of the **PANORAMA** window; the data of the selected PVI will be displayed in the **Profile Layout Parameters** dialog box. You can edit the PVI station, grade, and the PVI elevation values in this dialog box.

To edit the profile entities, choose the down arrow on the right of the **PVI based** tool and then choose **Entity based** from the flyout displayed. This will help you view only the entity data in the **PANORAMA** window and the **Profile Layout Tools** toolbar.

Editing Profiles Using Grips

One of the easiest methods of editing the geometry of a profile is by using the grips that are displayed on selecting a layout profile. You can edit both the profile PVIs and profile entities using the grips displayed on selecting the design profile. Before you do so, ensure that you have invoked the required **PVI Based** or **Entity Based** tool from the **Profile Layout Tools** toolbar. Now, select the required profile from the profile view to activate profile grips; the square, circular, and triangular shaped grips will be displayed.

The square grip, if displayed at the end of the tangent, helps you to simultaneously modify the tangent length and the grade. Identify such a grip from the profile and select it; the grip will turn red. Move the grip to change the length of the tangent as required. If the square grip is displayed at the midpoint of the tangent then you can change the location of the tangent without affecting the tangent length and grade, however, the location of the adjacent PVIs and grade of the adjacent tangents will also be modified. To move the tangent to a new location, select the square grip at the midpoint of the tangent; the grip will turn red in color and you will be prompted to specify the stretch point in the command line. Now, you can specify a new location by entering a value in the command line or using the dynamic input. You can also enter the value using the **PANORAMA** window or the **Profile Layout Parameters** dialog box.

The circular grip enables you to modify the radius whereas the triangular grip is used to modify the PVIs at the point of intersection (marked red). Select the respective grips and stretch them to edit the geometry of the profile.

PROFILE AND PROFILE VIEW STYLES

You can control the appearance of a profile and its components by creating a profile style. You must remember that the profile styles and profile view styles are two separate entities. The profile styles and profile view styles are created and managed in the **Settings** tab of the **TOOLSPACE** palette. The methods of creating styles for profile and profile views are discussed next.

Creating a Profile Style

To create a new profile style, choose the **Settings** tab of the **TOOLSPACE** palette. Expand **Profile > Profile Styles** subnode to view the default profile styles. Now, select and right-click on **Profile Styles** to display a shortcut menu. Choose **New** from the shortcut menu; the **Profile Style - New Profile Style** dialog box will be displayed, as shown in Figure 6-20. This dialog box is used to create a new profile style. The tabs in this dialog box are discussed next.

***Figure 6-20** Partial view of the **Profile Style - New Profile Style** dialog box*

Information Tab
The **Information** tab is used to view and specify general information about a style such as its name and description. Enter the name of the style in the **Name** edit box. Optionally, you can enter the style description in the **Description** edit box.

Design Tab
This tab is used to specify the distance between the curve segments for a clear 3D display of the alignment data. Enter the required distance in the **Curve tessellation distance** edit box. Remember that smaller the value entered, smoother will be the display of the 3D curve.

Markers Tab
This tab is used to control the display of the markers representing different points in the profile. The **Name** column of the **Profile points** area displays the names of various points in the profile and the **Marker Style** column displays the marker styles that represent these points. You can select a marker style for points from the **Pick Marker Style** dialog box that is displayed when you double-click in the **Marker Style** column. If you do not want to display the points in the profile, set the marker style to **None**, if it is not selected by default.

The options in the **Arrowhead** area are used to set the size, type, and display of the arrowhead. Select the required arrowhead style from the **Type** drop-down list. Select an option from the **Size options** drop-down list to set the size of the arrowhead.

Display Tab
This tab is used to set the visibility and format of the profile components such as lines and curves. Select the required view from the **View Direction** drop-down list. The **Component display** area displays the names of different profile components in the **Component Type** column. By default, the visibility of all components is turned on which is indicated by the yellow colored bulb icon in the **Visible** column. To turn off the visibility of a component, click on the bulb icon in the **Visible** column. Similarly, you can click on the default values in the **Layer**, **Color**, **Lineweight**, **LT Scale**, and **Linetype** columns and change them as required.

Summary Tab
This tab displays different properties of a profile and is used to review and adjust the values of the profile style. Expand the required collection in this tab to review the values associated with the profile style. You can edit the values, if required. Note that only the values displayed in black can be edited. After setting the required parameters, choose the **OK** button; the **Profile Style - <style name>** dialog box will be closed and the style will be added in the **Profile styles** subnode of the **Settings** tab. Now, you can assign this newly created style to a profile by using the **Profile Properties** dialog box. The steps to assign a profile style are similar to that of assigning an alignment style, as explained in Chapter 5.

Creating a Profile View Style
The profile view style controls the display of the grid in which the profile is drawn. The profile view styles also control the grid and profile annotations. Like the profile style, the profile view styles are also created and managed in the **Settings** tab.

To create a profile view style, expand **Profile View > Profile View Styles** in the **Settings** tab; the existing profile view styles will be displayed. Next, right-click on the **Profile View Styles**; a shortcut menu will be displayed. Choose **New** from the shortcut menu; the **Profile View Style- New Profile View Style** dialog box will be displayed,

You can use this dialog box to create a customized profile view style by changing the default settings in different tabs of this dialog box. The tabs in the **Profile View Style - New Profile View Style** dialog box are discussed next.

Information Tab

This tab is used to view and enter general information about the profile view style. Enter a name for the style in the **Name** edit box. Optionally, you can enter a short description in the **Description** text box.

Graph Tab

This tab is used to specify the vertical scale and the direction of the profile view, as shown in Figure 6-21. The options in the **Vertical scale** area help you set the scale for the profile view so that the elevations are clearly visible in it. You can set the vertical scale by selecting the required scale option from the **Vertical scale** drop-down list. The vertical scale is a ratio of horizontal scale and vertical exaggeration. Note that you can also specify a scale other than those available in the drop-down list. To do so, select the **Custom** option from the **Vertical scale** drop-down list and enter the required scale in the **Custom scale** edit box.

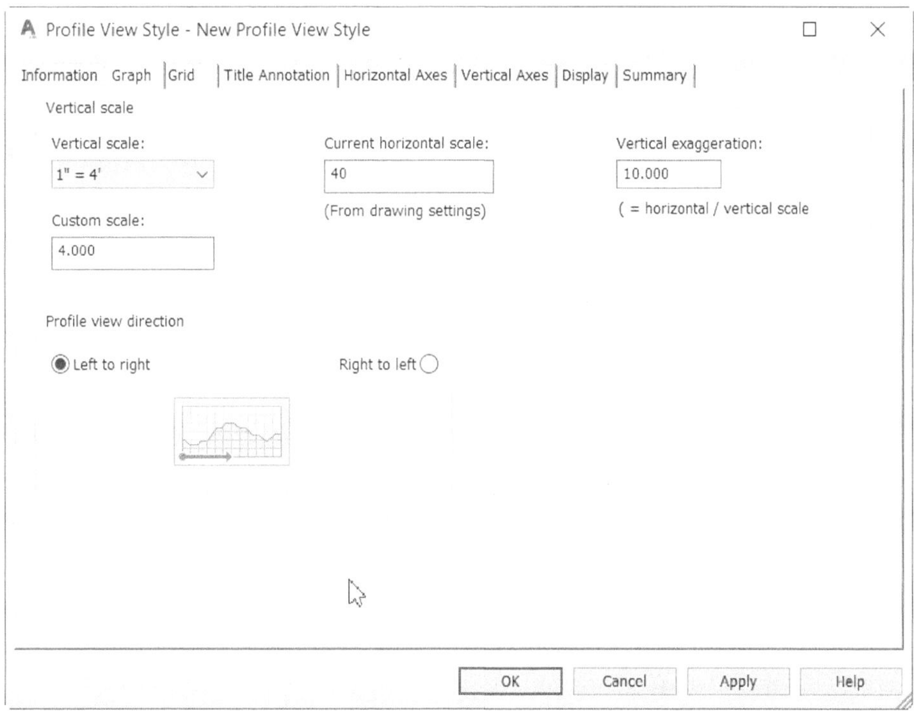

*Figure 6-21 The **Graph** tab in the **Profile View Style - New Profile View Style** dialog box*

The **Current horizontal scale** text box specifies the overall drawing scale. This value cannot be edited directly in this dialog box. The horizontal scale can be edited only in the **Drawing Settings** dialog box. You can specify the vertical exaggeration value in the **Vertical exaggeration** edit box. Enter the required value in the **Vertical exaggeration** edit box. This value is used to specify the amount by which the elevation values need to be increased in the profile view to gain greater visibility. You can either enter 1 for no change in scale or a value greater than 1 to increase the scale. The elevation values in the profile view are multiplied by this value. A greater value results in the increase of the amount of exaggeration in the profile view.

The **Profile view direction** area in this tab specifies the direction of the profile in the profile view. By default, the direction is set from left to right such that the lowest station number starts from the left and the highest station number is on the right. To reverse the direction, select the **Right to left** radio button in this area. On doing so, the highest station number will be aligned to the right and the smallest station number to the left.

Grid Tab

This tab is used to specify the options to clip, pad, and offset the axis in the profile grid view. The **Grid options** area in this tab allows you to select the grid type that you want to clip. By default, the **Clip vertical grid** check box is selected. This specifies that all the vertical grid lines will always be clipped or trimmed and will be drawn below the profile line. The graphic below this check box shows the preview of the profile view with vertical clipping of the grid. The **Omit grid in padding areas** check box is also the default selection in the **Grid options** area. As a result, the vertical grid lines will not be drawn in the padding areas on the left and right side of the profile view. If you select the **Clip to highest profile(s)** check box in this area, the vertical grid lines in the profile view will be drawn to the highest profile in the profile view.

Similarly, select the **Clip horizontal grid** check box to clip the horizontal grid. Figure 6-22 shows the clipping of vertical grid lines and Figure 6-23 shows the profile view with both the horizontal and vertical grid lines clipped after selecting the **Clip horizontal grid**, **Clip vertical grid**, and **Omit grid in padding areas** (for horizontal grids) check boxes.

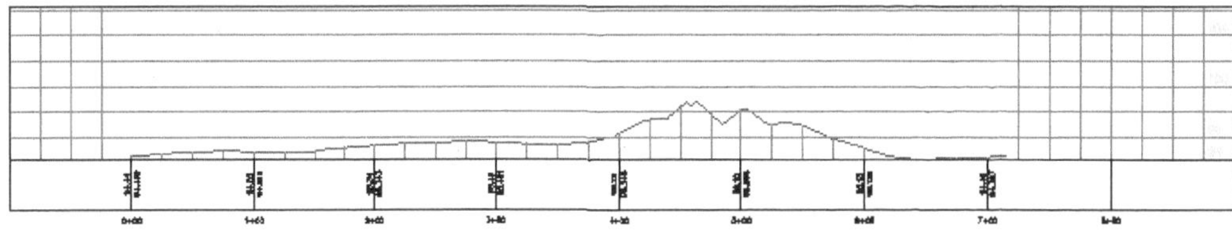

Figure 6-22 *The profile view with vertical grid lines clipped*

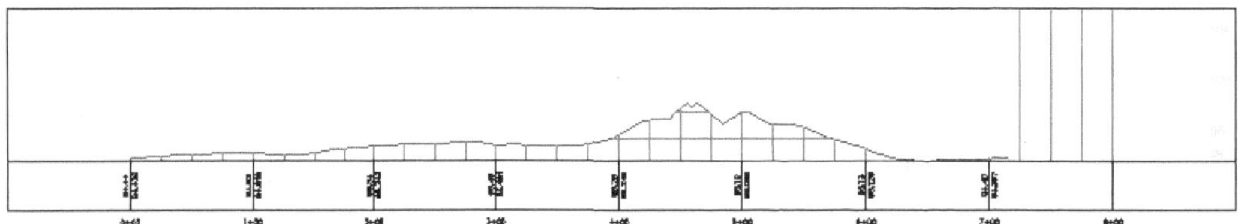

Figure 6-23 *The profile view showing the clipped vertical and horizontal grid lines*

In the **Grid padding (major grids)** area, you can specify the distance or the major grid blocks that can be added to the profile view to increase its extents. Enter the number of major grid blocks to be added above the profile in the **Above maximum elevation** edit box; the profile grid view will be extended accordingly. Similarly, you can enter a value in the **To left**, **To right**, and **Below datum** edit boxes to add the major grid blocks on the left, right, and bottom of the profile view, respectively. Similarly, specify the offset values for the axis in the **Axis offset (plotted units)** area.

Title Annotation Tab

This tab is used to control the appearance of the graph view and the titles along the axis of the view. In the **Graph view title** area of this tab, select the text style for the title from the **Text style** drop-down list. Specify the text height in the **Text height** edit box. The **Title content** text box displays the content of the title. To modify the content, choose the button on the right of this text box; the **Text Component Editor - Title Text** dialog box will be displayed. You can use this dialog box to modify the content of the title. The options in the **Title position** area are used to specify the position of the title of the profile view. Select the location and then specify the justification of the title using the **Location** and the **Justification** drop-down lists, respectively. Optionally, you can specify the horizontal and the vertical offset values from the specified location and justification in the **X offset** and **Y offset** edit boxes, respectively. Select the **Border around the title** check box to draw a border around the title. On doing so, the **Gap** edit box will be enabled and you can specify the distance between the border and the title in this edit box. Similarly, you can modify the default settings for the titles along the axis of the graph view. The titles of the axes will be displayed only if the visibility of the **Left Axis Title** and the **Right Axis Title** layers are turned on in the **Display** tab.

Horizontal Axes Tab

This tab is used to specify the settings for the tick marks placed along the top or bottom of the horizontal axis. Select the **Top** or **Bottom** radio button to select the axis along which you want to modify the settings for the tick marks. By default, the **Bottom** radio button is selected.

Note

*Before you specify the settings for the tick marks, make sure that you have turned on the display component of the required top, bottom, left, or right axis as well as the major and minor tick marks in the **Display** tab.*

In the **Major tick details** area, you can specify the interval or spacing between the Major ticks in the **Interval** edit box. You can specify the length of the tick marks in the **Tick size** edit box. From the **Tick Justification** drop-down list, select the position of the major ticks to place them on the top, bottom, or center of the axis. Next, enter a value in the **Text height** edit box to specify the height of the text used to label the ticks. The **Tick label text** edit box specifies the label content of the ticks. To modify the property on the basis of which the tick marks are labeled, choose the button on the right of this edit box; the **Text Component Editor - Major Tick Text** dialog box will be displayed. Select the style for the tick label text from the **Text style** edit box. If you want the label text to incline at a certain angle to the axis, specify the angle for the rotation in the **Rotation** edit box. Similarly, you can specify the distance between the label and the tick marks horizontally and vertically in the **X offset** and **Y offset** edit boxes, respectively. A negative value will move the label toward the left by the specified distance and a positive value will move the label to the right of the axis.

Note

You can display the annotations for both the major and minor axes in the left and right directions of the profile view by turning on the visibility of the ***Left Axis Annotation Major*** *and* ***Left Axis Annotation Minor*** *layers in the* ***Display*** *tab.*

In the same way, you can modify the default settings of the minor tick marks and the label text in the **Minor tick details** area of this tab.

Vertical Axes Tab

This tab is used to specify the settings for the tick marks placed along the left and right of the vertical axis. The options available in this tab are the same as those explained in the **Horizontal Axes** tab. You can select the **Tick and label start elevation** check box to place the tick mark and the tick label at the first station along the vertical axis.

Display Tab

This tab is used to control the visibility and display of the components that form a profile view. Before specifying the settings for the appearance of any component, make sure that you turn on the component in the **Display** tab so that you can easily view the changes made in the settings after choosing the **Apply** button.

Summary Tab

This tab helps you quickly review and change the settings specified in various tabs. In this tab, you can modify only those values that are highlighted in black. Once you have specified the settings for the profile view style, choose the **Apply** button to view the changes or choose the **OK** button to close the **Profile View Style - New Profile View Style** dialog box. On doing so, the profile view style name will be added in the **Settings** tab. If you want to view the style in the **Settings** tab, expand the **Profile View Styles** subnode of the **Profile View** node in the **Settings** tab.

Assigning the Profile View Style

You can assign a profile view style to the profile view by selecting the desired style from the **Profile view style** drop-down list available in the **General** page of the **Create Profile View** wizard, as shown in Figure 6-24.

Note

You can access the ***Create Profile View*** *wizard only if you create the profile by using the* ***Create Surface Profile*** *tool from the* ***Create Design*** *panel.*

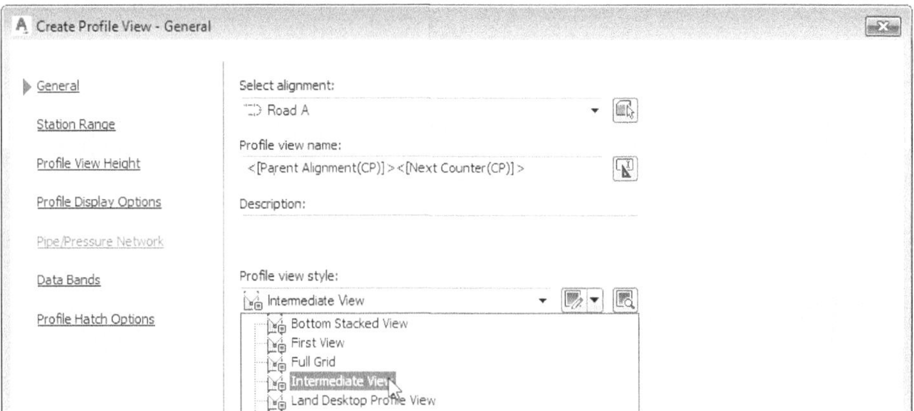

***Figure 6-24** Selecting the intermediate view from the **Profile view style** drop-down list in the **General** page of the **Create Profile View** wizard*

Alternatively, to assign the required profile view style, select the profile view from the drawing area and right-click; a shortcut menu will be displayed. Choose **Profile View Properties** from the shortcut menu; the **Profile View Properties - <Profile name>** dialog box will be displayed. In this dialog box, select the required profile view style from the **Object style** drop-down list in the **Information** tab, as shown in Figure 6-25. Next, choose the **Apply** button to view the changes. Choose the **OK** button to close the dialog box.

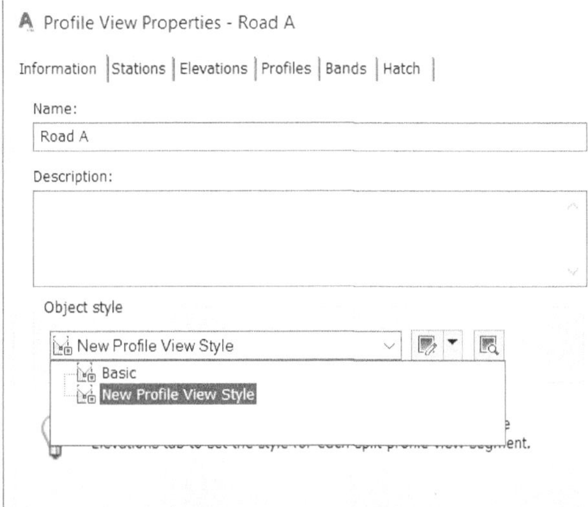

***Figure 6-25** Selecting the **New Profile View Style** from the **Object style** drop-down list in the **Profile View Properties - Road A** dialog box*

Tip

*You can also invoke the **Profile View Properties** dialog box by choosing the **Prospector** tab and expanding the **Alignments** collection. Now, expand the parent alignment node and then expand the **Profile Views** node under it to display the desired profile view. Select the desired profile view and right-click to display the shortcut menu. Choose the **Properties** option from the shortcut menu to display the **Profile View Properties - <profile name>** dialog box of the selected profile view.*

PROFILE LABELS

You can label a profile by using the in-built profile label styles. The layout profiles can be labeled automatically using the **Create Profile - Draw New** dialog box as explained earlier in this chapter. However, you need to use the **Edit Labels** command to label the other profiles. To label the layout profiles, select the **Complete Label Set** option from the **Profile label set** drop-down list of the **Create Profile - Draw New** dialog box, as shown in Figure 6-26.

This label set consists of labels for the lines, grade breaks, sag curves, and crest curves. Next, choose the **OK** button to close the **Create Profile - Draw New** dialog box. Once you draw the layout profile, all the lines, grade breaks, sag, and crest curves in the profile will be labeled automatically.

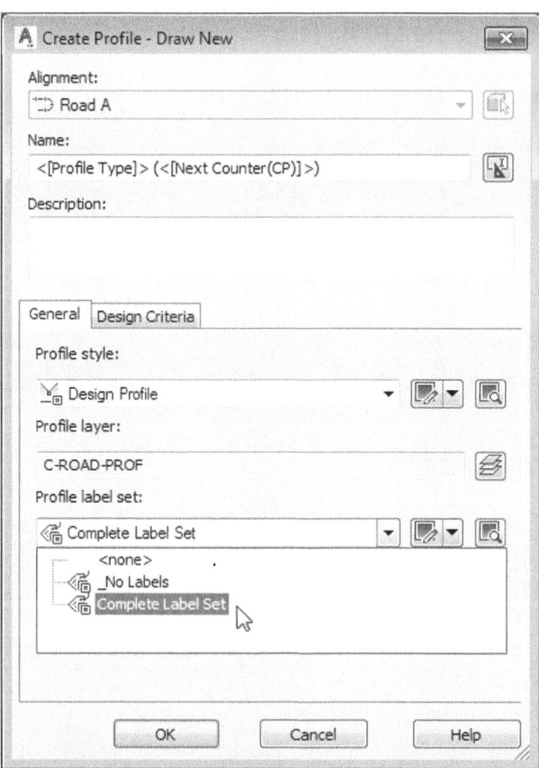

Figure 6-26 *Selecting the **Complete Label Set** from the **Profile label set** drop-down list*

To label other profiles such as surface profiles, superimposed profiles, and so on, select the profile (represented by a red line) in the profile view and right-click to display the shortcut menu. Choose **Edit Labels** from the shortcut menu; the **Profile Labels - <profile name>** dialog box will be displayed, as shown in Figure 6-27.

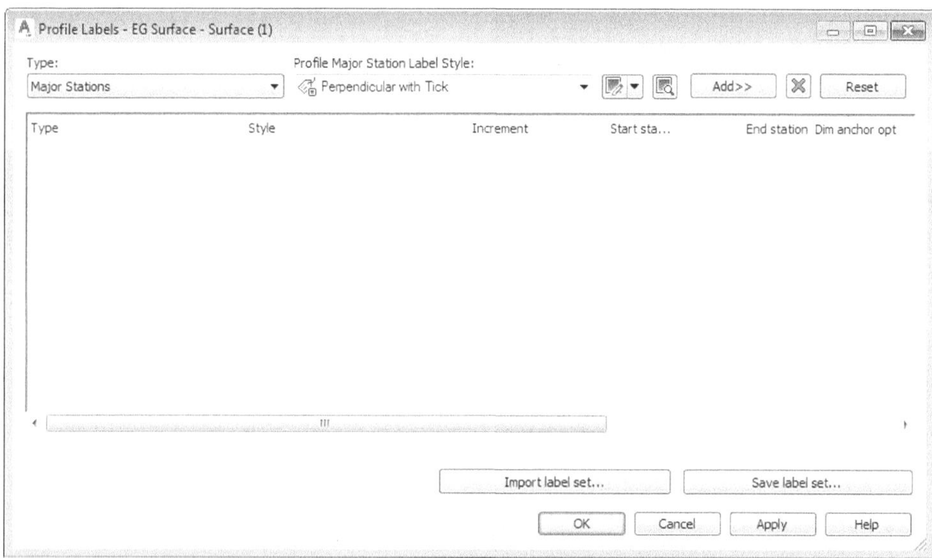

Figure 6-27 The ***Profile Labels - <profile name>*** *dialog box*

Select the type of label to be added in the profile view from the **Type** drop-down list. Next, select the corresponding label style from the **Profile <type> Label Style** drop-down list on the right of the **Type** drop-down list. Choose the **Add** button to add the selected label type and label style in the table to create a label set. Similarly, select the other types and their styles and add them in the table to create various label sets. Choose the **OK** button; the labels will be added to the profile in the profile view.

Select the type of label to be added in the profile view from the **Type** drop-down list. Next, select the corresponding label style from the **Profile <type> Label Style** drop-down list on the right of the **Type** drop-down list. Choose the **Add** button to add the selected label type and label style in the table to create a label set. Similarly, select the other types and their styles and add them in the table to create various label sets. Choose the **OK** button; the labels will be added to the profile in the profile view.

Note

If the ***Complete Label Set*** *option is not available in the* ***Profile Label Set*** *drop-down list then you have to create your own profile label set.*

Creating a New Profile Label Style

You can label the major and minor stations, sag and crest curves, horizontal geometry points, grade breaks, and lines in a profile view. You can also create your own label style to label all these components and then add them to label set. To create a new label for a curve, expand **Profile > Label Styles** node from the **Settings** tab. Next, select and right-click on **Curve** in the

Label Style subnode to display the shortcut menu. Choose **New** from the shortcut menu; the **Label Style Composer - New Profile Curve Label Style** dialog box will be displayed, as shown in Figure 6-28.

You can create a label style for the curves by assigning required values to various options in the **General** and **Layout** tabs. You can modify the values of the required properties and view the changes in the **Preview** area displayed in the **General**, **Layout** and the **Dragged State** tabs. Once you have defined the settings and specified the name of the new curve label style, choose the **OK** button; the new curve label style will be added in the **Curve** subnode of the **Profile** node. To view the label style name, expand **Profile > Label Styles > Curve** subnode in the **Settings** tab.

Similarly, you can create your own label styles for other profile components such as **Line**, **Station**, and **Grade Breaks** listed in the **Profile** node of the **Settings** tab. Once you have created new label styles, you can add them to a label set and save the label so that you can retrieve and use it again when required.

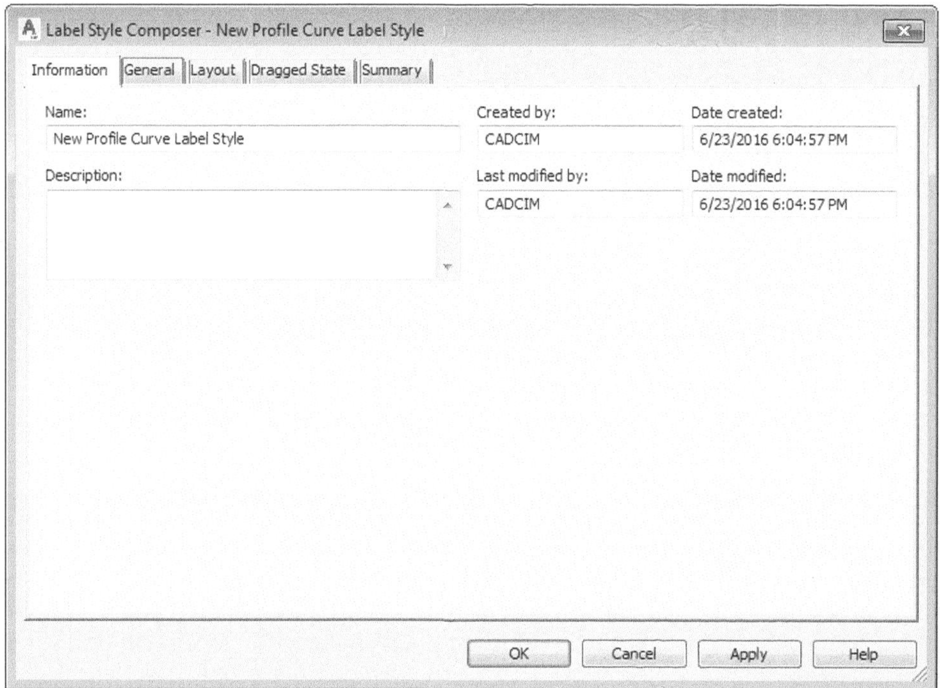

*Figure 6-28 The **Label Style Composer - New Profile Curve Label Style** dialog box*

Creating a Label Set

To create a label set, expand the **Profile > Label Styles** subnode in the **Settings** tab. Right-click on **Label Sets** in the **Label Styles** subnode of the **Profile** node; a shortcut menu will be displayed. Choose **New** from the shortcut menu; the **Profile Label Set - New Profile Label Set** dialog box will be displayed.

In this dialog box, the **Information** tab is chosen by default. You can enter a name for the label set in the **Name** edit box of this tab. Optionally, you can specify the description about the label set in the **Description** edit box. Next, choose the **Labels** tab and select the **Crest Curves** option from the **Type** drop-down list, as shown in Figure 6-29.

Select the label style from the **Profile Crest Curve Label Style** drop-down list. Now, choose the **Add** button to add **Crest Curves** and the selected label style in the label set. On doing so, the selected label type and label style will be added and displayed in the list box.

Similarly, you can select the label type and the label styles for other types of labels such as major stations, minor stations, and so on. Then, choose the **Add** button to add them in the label set. You can then use this label set to label the components with the selected label styles. Once you have created the label set, choose the **OK** button. The label style will be added in **Profiles > Label Styles > Label Sets** subnode in the **Settings** tab.

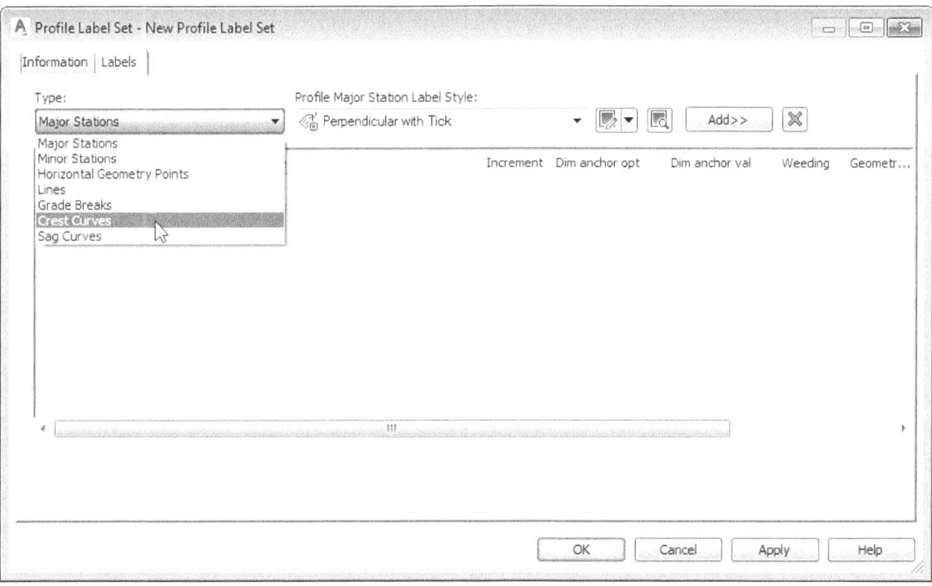

Figure 6-29 Selecting the ***Crest Curves*** *option from the* ***Type*** *drop-down list*

Assigning Labels to a Profile

Ribbon: Annotate > Labels & Tables > Add Labels drop-down > Add/Edit Profile Labels
Command: EDITPROFILELABELS

You can assign labels to a profile view as a label set. To do so, choose **Add/Edit Profile Labels** from the **Labels & Tables** panel; you will be prompted to select a profile from the drawing. Select the required profile line in the profile view grid; the **Profile Labels - <profile name>** dialog box will be displayed.

To assign a label set consisting of the required label types and label styles, choose the **Import label set** button at the bottom of the **Profile Labels - <profile name>** dialog box. On doing so, the **Select Label Set** dialog box will be displayed, as shown in Figure 6-30.

Figure 6-30 The Select Label Set dialog box

You can use this dialog box to select the required label set and assign it to a profile. After selecting the required label set from the **Select Label Set** dialog box, choose the **OK** button to close this dialog box; the label types and their corresponding styles will be displayed in the **Profile Labels - <profile name>** dialog box. Choose the **Apply** button to assign the labels and view them in the drawing. Choose the **OK** button to close the **Profile Labels - <profile name>** dialog box.

To assign a label set to a layout profile, choose the **Profiles Creation Tools** tool from the **Profile** drop-down in the **Create Design** panel; you will be prompted to select a profile view from the drawing. Select the desired profile view from the drawing; the **Create Profile - Draw New** dialog box will be displayed. Now, select the required label set from the drop-down list displayed in the **Profile label set** area of this dialog box and choose the **OK** button; the profile displayed in the drawing will be automatically labeled.

Tip

*You can also assign labels to a profile view as a label set using another method. To do so, select the profile from the profile view grid in the drawing and right-click to display a shortcut menu. Choose the **Edit Labels** option from the shortcut menu; the **Profile Labels - <profile name>** dialog box will be displayed. This dialog box will help you to create the label set.*

Creating a New Profile View Label Style

It is important to understand that the profile and profile views are two different things. Profiles are represented by a red line in the profile view. The profile view is the grid on which the profile is drawn. These styles can be accessed from the **Profile** and **Profile View** nodes in the **Settings** tab.

To create a new profile view label style, expand the **Profile View > Label Styles** subnode in the **Settings** tab of the **TOOLSPACE** palette. The profile labels are used to label the station elevation and depth properties of the station from the profile. Thus, you can create three types of profile view label styles; **Station Elevation**, **Depths**, and **Projection**. The **Station Elevation** labels are used to label the elevation of a particular station from the datum. The **Depth** labels help you label the depth and can be used in earthwork projects involving cut and fill. The **Station Elevation** label displays the station and its elevation at a selected point in a profile view. The **Depth** label displays the difference of elevation between the two points selected in a profile view. The **Projection** labels are used to label the station and elevation of the projected objects like points, feature lines, and survey figures. To create a new label style to label the station elevation of the profile view, select and right-click on the **Station Elevation** option under the **Label Styles** subnode of the **Profile View** node in the **Settings** tab. On doing so, a shortcut menu will be displayed. Choose **New** from the shortcut menu; the **Label Style Composer - New Profile Station and Elevation Label Style** dialog box will be displayed.

Choose the **General** tab in this dialog box to specify the general properties of the label style such as text style, visibility, and so on. Choose the **Layout** tab to specify the format of the label components and also create and edit them. In the **General** category of the **Layout** tab, specify the required name, anchor point, and anchor component for the label of the station and elevation component. In the **Text** category of the **Layout** tab, click in the **Value** field of the **Contents** property and choose the browse button displayed. On doing so, the **Text Component Editor - Contents** dialog box will be displayed. You can use this dialog box to edit the label content, if required. Next, in the **Label Style Composer** dialog box, you can set the color, text height, attachment, and other properties of the label style. After doing so, choose the **OK** button to close the **Label Style Composer - < Label Style name>** dialog box. The new label style will be added in the **Station elevation** subnode.

Similarly, you can create new **Depth** and **Projection** label styles.

Adding Profile View Labels

Ribbon: Annotate > Labels & Tables > Add Labels drop-down > Profile View > Add Profile View Labels
Command: ADDPROFILEVIEWLABELS

To add the profile view labels, choose the **Profile View** option from the **Labels & Tables** panel; a flyout will be displayed. Choose the **Add Profile View Labels** tool from the flyout; the **Add Labels** dialog box will be displayed, as shown in Figure 6-31.

To add the station elevation labels to the profile view, first ensure that **Profile View** is selected in the **Feature** drop-down list of this dialog box. Then, select **Station Elevation** from the **Label type** drop-down list. Select the required label style from the **Station elevation label style** drop-down list for the selected label type. From the **Marker style** drop-down list, select the marker to mark the station in the profile view grid that you want to label. Next, choose the **Add** button; you will be prompted to select a profile view. Select the required profile view; you will be prompted to specify the station. Note that a red line attached to the cursor will be displayed. Click in the profile view at the required location where you want to specify the station. Click again to specify the elevation; the station value and its elevation will be displayed in the profile view.

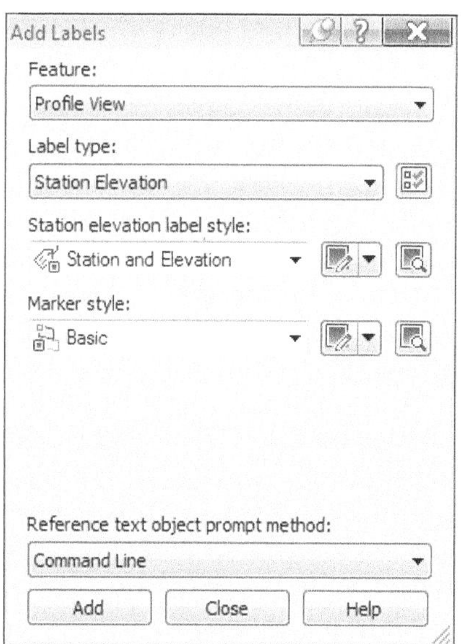

*Figure 6-31 The **Add Labels** dialog box*

To add the depth labels to the profile view, select **Depth** from the **Label type** drop-down list in the **Add Labels** dialog box and select the required label from the **Depth label style** drop-down list. Choose the **Add** button and follow the prompts; the **Depth** labels will be added at the specified positions. Once you have added the labels, choose the **Close** button to close the **Add Labels** dialog box.

Alternatively, you can directly add the **Station Elevation** and **Depth** labels in the profile view by first choosing the profile view from the drawing. On doing so, the **Profile Views: <profile name>** (Contextual) tab will be displayed. Next, choose the **Station Elevation and Depth** tool from the **Add view Labels** drop-down from the **Labels** panel and then follow the prompts.

BAND SETS AND BAND STYLES

Civil 3D allows you to add profile data such as profile, superelevation, cut and fill depths, vertical geometry, and so on in a consolidated form of band in the profile view. Band set is a collection of such profile data bands and band styles. Figure 6-32 shows a profile view with a band set at the bottom of the profile view.

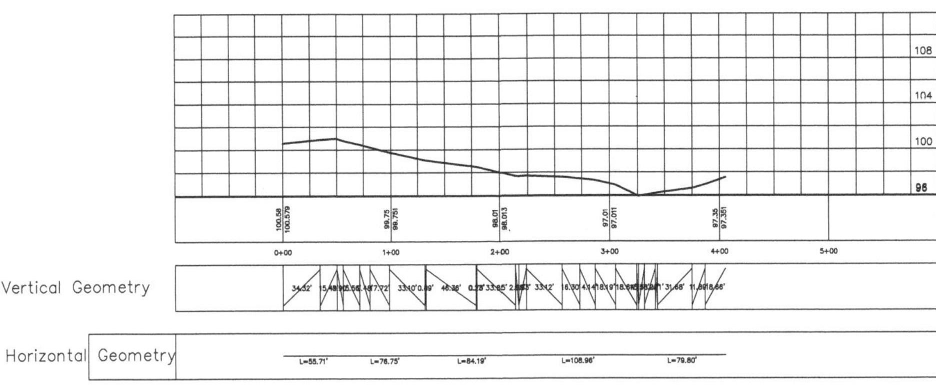

Figure 6-32 *Profile view with the band set at the bottom*

The profile bands can display the profile data for both the **Existing Ground** and **Finished Ground** profiles. To create a profile view band style, expand **Profile View > Band Styles** node in the **Settings** tab of the **TOOLSPACE** palette. Next, select the **Band Sets** subnode and right-click; a shortcut menu will be displayed. Choose **New** from the shortcut menu; the **Band Set - New Profile View Band Set** dialog box will be displayed. Specify a name for the new band set in the **Name** edit box. Next, choose the **Bands** tab. Select the required band type from the **Band type** drop-down list and select the respective band style from the **Select band style** drop-down list. Now, choose the **Add** button; the **Geometry Points to Label in Band** dialog box will be displayed. This dialog box is used to select the profile and alignment geometry points that you want to label in the data band. The alignment geometry points that can be labeled are displayed in the **Alignment Points** tab and the profile geometry points are displayed in the **Profile points** tab of the dialog box. By default, all alignment and profile geometry points available in their respective tabs are selected. If required, you can clear the check boxes for the geometry points that you do not want to label. After specifying the required settings, choose the **OK** button to close the **Geometry Points to Label in Band** dialog box and return to the **Band Set - New Profile View Band Set** dialog box. Again, choose **OK**; the **Band Set - New Profile View Band Set** dialog box will be closed and the new band set will be added in the **Band Set** subnode. Expand **Profile View > Band Styles > Band Sets** subnode in the **Settings** tab to view the new band set style that has been added.

Creating a Band Style (Framing a Band)

You can create a new band style for each individual band type component and add it to the band set. For example, to create a new style for the display of the vertical geometry data, expand **Profile View > Band Styles > Vertical Geometry** in the **Settings** tab to view the in-built style for the **Vertical Geometry**. To create a customized style, right-click on the **Vertical Geometry** node; a shortcut menu will be displayed. Choose **New** from the shortcut menu; the **Vertical Geometry Band Style - New Vertical Geometry Band Style** dialog box will be displayed. The tabs in this dialog box are discussed next.

Information Tab

In this tab, you can specify a name for the new band style in the **Name** edit box. Optionally, you can enter a short description about the style in the **Description** edit box.

Band Details Tab

You can use this tab to design the format and contents of the band style. This tab has various areas and options, as shown in Figure 6-33, and they are discussed next.

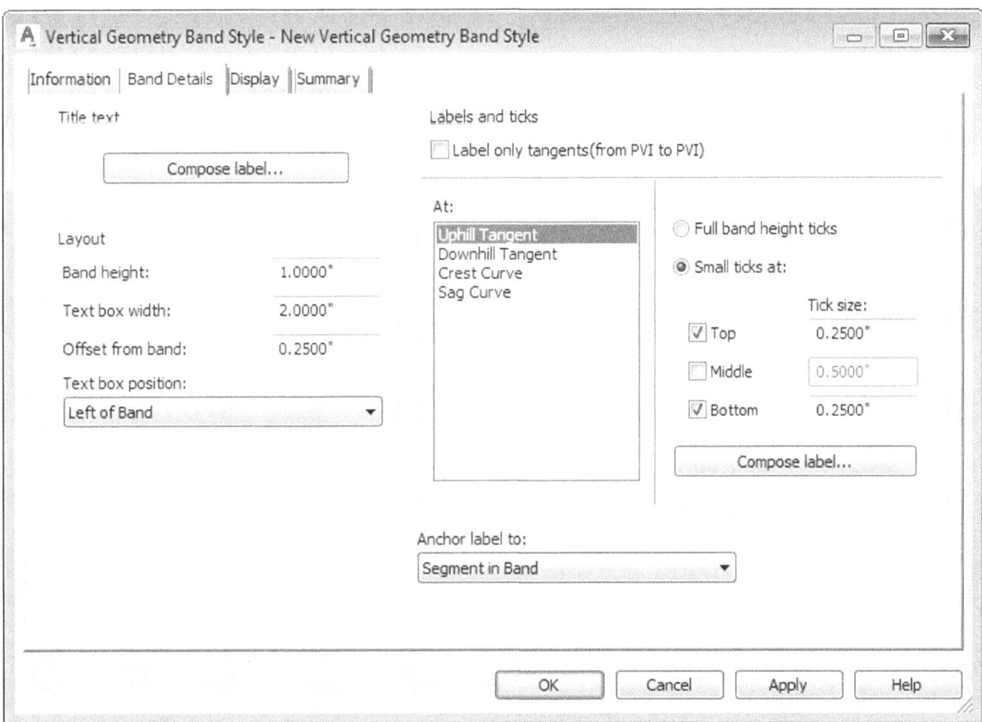

*Figure 6-33 The **Band Details** tab with various areas and options*

Title text Area

Choose the **Compose label** button from this area; the **Label Style Composer - Band Title** dialog box will be displayed, as shown in Figure 6-34.

In the **Text** category of this dialog box, you can modify the title, color, size, and other properties of the band title. To modify the title, click on the **Value** field of the **Contents** property; a browse button will be displayed on the right. Choose this button; the **Text Component Editor - Contents** dialog box will be displayed, as shown in Figure 6-35.

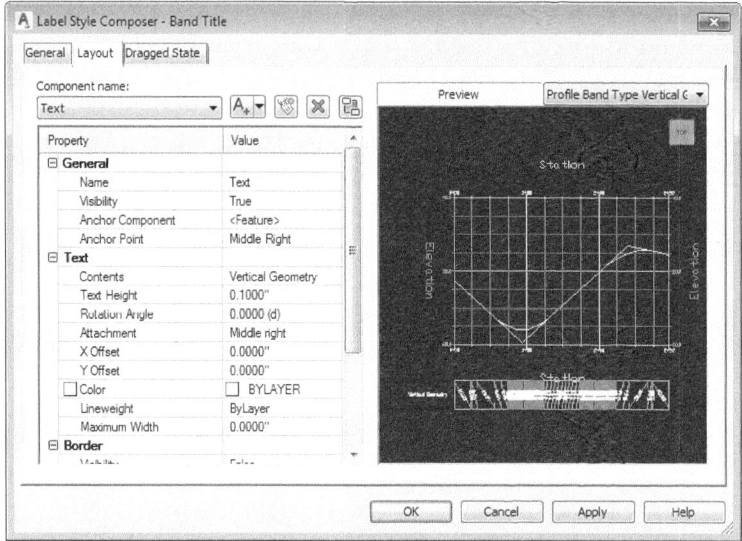

Figure 6-34 *The* ***Label Style Composer - Band Title*** *dialog box*

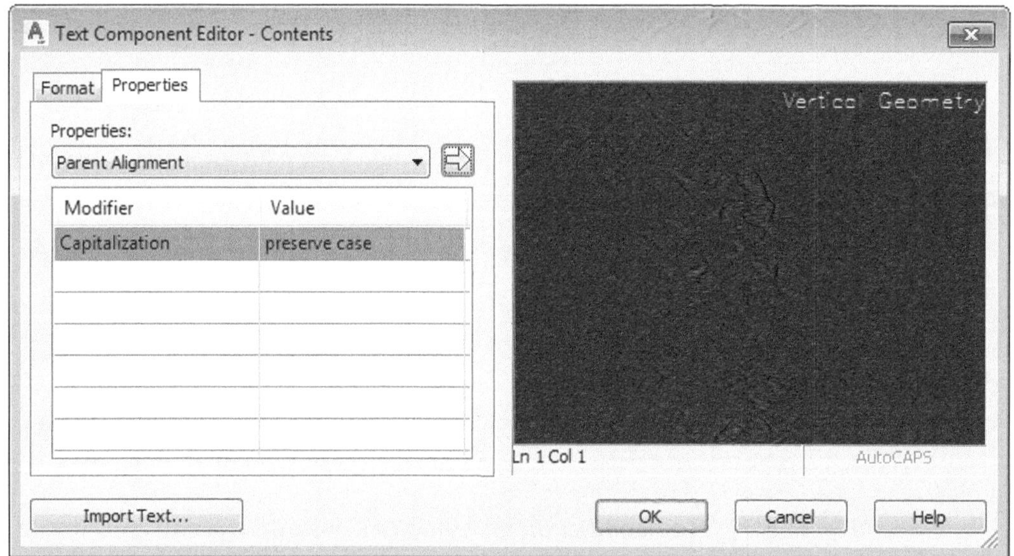

Figure 6-35 *The* ***Text Component Editor - Contents*** *dialog box*

Delete the existing title in the **Preview** display box and specify the required band title. You can choose the **Format** tab in the **Text Component Editor - Contents** dialog box and specify the settings for the format of the band title. Once you have modified and formatted the band title, choose the **OK** button; the new title will be displayed in the **Value** field of the **Contents** property and in the **Preview** display box. After modifying the default settings for the band title, choose the **OK** button to close the **Label Style Composer - Band Title** dialog box.

Labels and ticks Area

The options in the **Labels and ticks** area are used to specify the location and size of the ticks and labels in a profile view. The location where you add the labels and ticks differs according to the band label style selected. For creating vertical geometry band style, the ticks and labels can be added at different locations such as at uphill and downhill tangents, crest, and sag curves. Similarly, for creating a band style for the horizontal geometry, you can add the ticks and labels at tangents, curves, or spirals. After selecting the location, select the required options on the right of this area to specify the tick size. You can enter the tick size in the **Tick Size** edit box.

Layout Area

The options in the **Layout** area are used to specify the dimensions of the band and also the size and position of the text box relative to the band. You can specify the band height in the **Band height** edit box. Specify the width of the text box for the band title in the **Text box width** edit box. Specify the distance of the text box from the band in the **Offset from band** edit box. Select the position of the text box with respect to the band from the **Text box position** drop-down list. Once you have specified the settings for the new style for the **Vertical Geometry** band style, choose the **OK** button. The band style will be added in the **Vertical Geometry** subnodc of thc **Band Styles** nodc.

Choose the **Compose label** button to preview or edit the label text for the selected location. On choosing this button, the **Label Style Composer band title** dialog box will be displayed. You can use this dialog box to review or edit the label text properties and the content of the label text.

Anchor Label to Drop-down List

This drop-down list is used to specify profile labels at a specific location in the profile view bands. There are two options in this drop-down list, namely **Segment in Band** and **True Geometry Location**. Select any of these options to specify the location of the labels depending on where the profile labels need to be placed.

Display Tab

This tab is used to set the display properties of the band style components in the selected view direction. You can select the required view direction from the **View Direction** drop-down list. Similarly, you can set the visibility and other display properties of the profile view band style components listed in the **Component display** list box of this tab. You can also set different properties of the band style components such as the band border, band title box, ticks, and so on in this tab.

Summary Tab

This tab is used to review and edit the values of the band style, if required. You can expand the required node and edit the values in black.

After specifying and customizing the band style properties, choose the **OK** button to exit the **Vertical Geometry Band Style - New Vertical Geometry Band Style** dialog box. The new vertical geometry band style will be added in the **Vertical Geometry** node in the **Settings** tab. Similarly, you can create other band styles. Now to assign the created band style, select the required profile view from the drawing and right-click; a shortcut menu will be displayed. Choose **Profile View Properties** from the shortcut menu; the **Profile View Properties** dialog box for the selected profile will be displayed. Choose the **Bands** tab and then select **Vertical Geometry** from the **Band type** drop-down list. Choose the **Add** button to add it into the list box. Next, select the band style from the **Select band style** drop-down list. Choose the **Apply** button to update the profile and view the changes. Next, choose the **OK** button to close the **Profile View Properties** dialog box.

Similarly, you can create a band style for all band types, add them to a band set, and apply the band set consisting of the required band types and band styles to the profile view.

PROFILE PROPERTIES

Ribbon: Profile > Modify Profile > Profile Properties Drop Down> Profile Properties
Command: EDITPROFILEPROPERTIES

You can view the profile properties and the design criteria of the profile using the **Profile Properties** dialog box. To display the **Profile Properties** dialog box, choose the **Profile Properties** tool from the **Modify Profile** panel and select a profile from the drawing and press ENTER; the **Profile Properties - <profile name>** dialog box will be displayed, as shown in Figure 6-36.

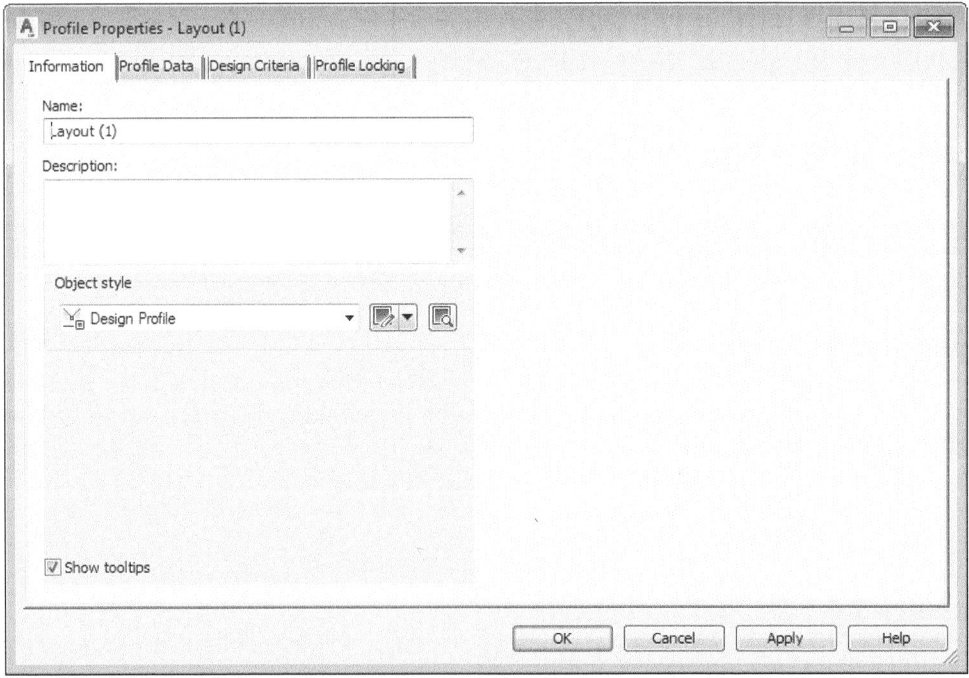

***Figure 6-36** The **Profile Properties - Layout (1)** dialog box*

In this dialog box, the **Information** tab displays the profile name. You can edit the profile name by specifying a new name in the **Name** edit box. Optionally, you can enter a short description in the **Description** text box. Select the required profile style from the **Object style** drop-down list.

The **Profile Data** tab displays the structural profile data such as the profile name, profile type, data source, and offset distance in a table. To change the display contents of the table right-click in the table region; a shortcut menu containing column names will be displayed. In this menu, tick or clear the required column names that you wish to display or hide in the table; the menu will be closed and the table will be updated to reflect the changes. You can also modify the settings for profile style, update mode, and layer of the profile in the **Profile Data** tab.

The **Design Criteria** tab helps you to view the design criteria used to create the design profile. If a design criterion is not already applied to the profile, select the **Use criteria-based design** check box and select the design criteria file. To apply a design check, select the **Use design check set** check box and then select the required design check set from the **Use design check set** drop-down list.

Tip

*You can also invoke the **Profile Properties** dialog box by selecting the profile from the drawing. On doing so, the **Profile Properties <profile name>** tab will be displayed. Next, choose the **Profile Properties** tool from the **Modify Profile** panel; the **Properties <profile name>** dialog box will be displayed.*

Note

If the parent horizontal alignment is not assigned any design criteria, you cannot assign design criteria to its profile as well.

The **Profile Locking** tab displays the options for anchoring the profile to the alignment. The **Anchor profile geometry points to alignment geometry points** radio button in this tab locks geometry point of each profile to geometry point of previous alignment. If changes are made to the horizontal alignment, the elevation of the profile geometry point is maintained and entities are modified or deleted as specified. If you choose the **Modify affected entities** radio button, the **Notify which entities are affected** check box will be enabled. By default, this check box is selected. As a result, you will be notified whenever the entities are affected. The **Anchor profile to alignment start** radio button locks the profile to the start of the alignment. If changes are made to the horizontal alignment, those changes are not reflected in the profile and they stay locked to the alignment start station.

Note

*While working in PVI mode, notifications are not displayed in the **PANORAMA** window.*

PROFILE VIEW PROPERTIES

Ribbon: Profile > Modify View > Profile View Properties Drop down > Profile View Properties
Command: EDITGRAPHPROPERTIES

A profile view also has its own properties. To view or edit the profile properties, select the required profile view grid in the drawing and right-click to display the shortcut menu. Choose **Profile View Properties** from the shortcut menu; the **Profile View Properties - <profile view name>** dialog box will be displayed, as shown in Figure 6-37.

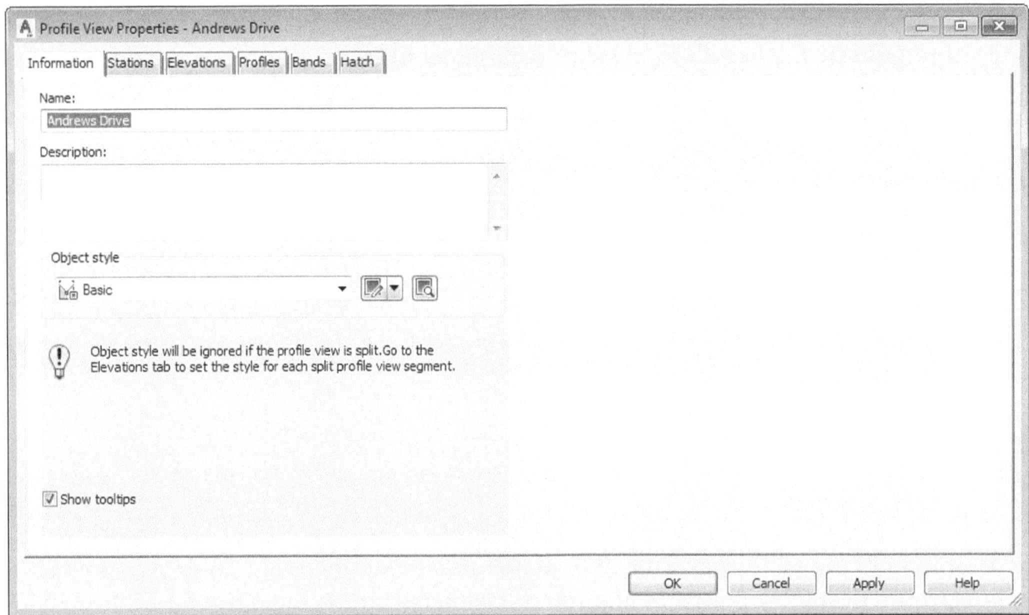

*Figure 6-37 The **Profile View Properties - Andrews Drive** dialog box*

The **Information** tab in this dialog box is used to view or edit the profile view name and the profile view style. Enter the required name in the **Name** edit box and select the required profile view style from the **Object style** drop-down list.

The **Stations** tab is used to view or edit the station range of the profile view. To modify the profile view range, select the **User specified range** radio button and choose the button on the right of the first edit box to pick the first station of the range from the drawing. Similarly, choose the button on the right of the second edit box and select the end station from the drawing directly. Now, choose the **Apply** button; the profile view will be modified based on the new station range.

The **Elevations** tab is used to view or edit the vertical range of the profile view and also specify the settings to split the profile view.

TUTORIALS

Tutorial 1 Existing Ground Profile

In this tutorial, you will create a ground profile by sampling a surface across the given alignment. You will also create an offset profile and a staggered/split profile view. The split profile view is shown in Figure 6-38. **(Expected time: 30 min)**

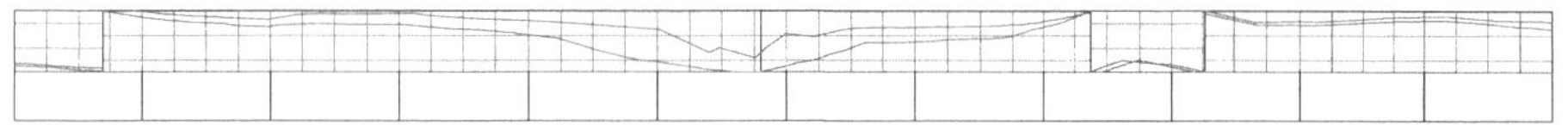

Figure 6-38 *The split profile view*

The following steps are required to complete this tutorial:

a. Download and open the file.
b. Create a profile using the **L Street** alignment.
c. Create the profile view.
d. Create the split/staggered profile view.
e. Save the file.

Downloading and Opening the File

1. Download *c06_c3d_2018_tut.zip* file from *http://www.cadcim.com*. Next, save and extract the file at *C:\c3d_2018*.

2. Choose **Open** from the **Application Menu**; the **Select File** dialog box is displayed.

3. In the dialog box, browse to the location *C:\c3d_2018\c06_c3d_2018_tut,* where you have saved the file.

4. Select the file *c06_c3d_2018_tut01.dwg* and then choose the **Open** button to open the file. The file consists of a surface (**Surface1**) and two alignments, **L Street** and **L Street (1)**, as shown in Figure 6-39.

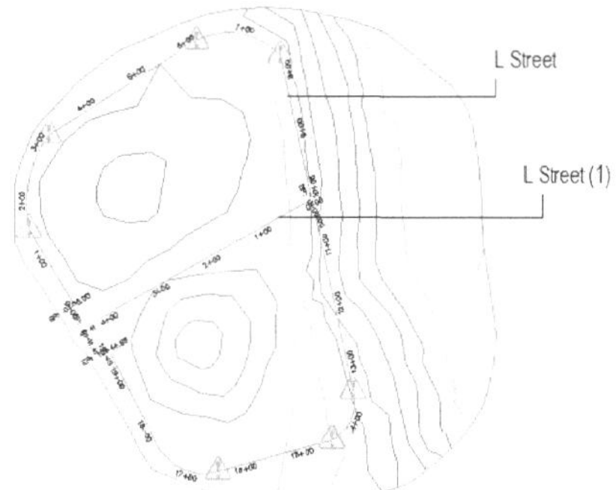

Figure 6-39 *The surface **(Surface1)** and the alignments displayed*

Creating a Profile

1. Choose the **Create Surface Profile** tool from **Home > Create Design > Profile** drop-down; the **Create Profile from Surface** dialog box is displayed.

2. In this dialog box, select the **L Street** option from the **Alignment** drop-down list if it is not selected by default.

3. Select **Surface1** from the **Select surfaces** list box and then choose the **Add** button; the selected profile is added to the **Profile list** list box.

4. Select the **Sample offsets** check box; the edit box below the **Sample offsets** check box is activated.

5. Enter **20** in the **Sample offsets** edit box and again select **Surface1** from the **Select surfaces** list box.

6. Choose the **Add** button; the offset profile is added to the **Profile list** list box.

Creating a Profile View

1. Choose the **Draw in profile view** button at the bottom of the **Create Profile from Surface** dialog box; the **General** page of the **Create Profile View** wizard is displayed.

2. Select **L Street** from the **Select alignment** drop-down list if it is not selected by default.

3. In the **Profile view name** edit box, enter **Street**.

4. Accept the default profile view style and choose the **Profile View Height** option from the left pane of the wizard; the **Profile View Height** page of the **Create Profile View** wizard is displayed.

5. In this page, select the **User specified** radio button from the **Profile view height** area of the **Profile View Height** page if not selected by default. Next, specify **97.00'** and **107.00'** in the **Minimum** and **Maximum** edit boxes, respectively, as shown in Figure 6-40.

Figure 6-40 *Specifying values for the Profile view height*

6. Next, choose the **Create Profile View** button from this page; you are prompted to select the origin of the profile view.

7. Click in the drawing area to place the profile view in the selected origin; the profile view and the offset are created. Figure 6-41 shows the **L Street** profile view created for the 20' offset profile and the original profile.

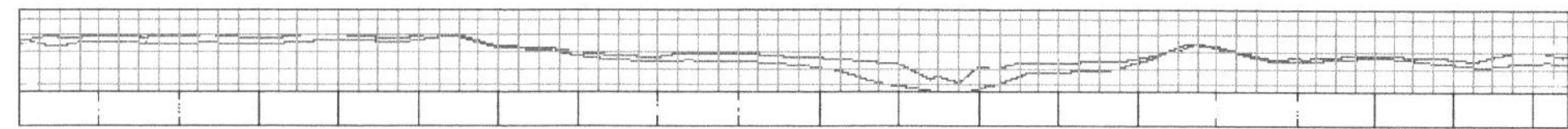

*Figure 6-41 The **L Street** profile view for the 20' offset and the original profile*

The two profiles, the offset profile and the original profile are added to the **Profiles** node of the parent **L Street** alignment collection as **Surface1 - 20.000** (at 20' offset) and **Surface1 - Surface (17)** in the **Prospector** tab, as shown in Figure 6-42. To view the profile, expand **Alignments > L Street > Profiles** in the **Prospector** tab of the **TOOLSPACE** palette. The profile view is added to the **Profile Views** node as **Street**, as shown in Figure 6-43.

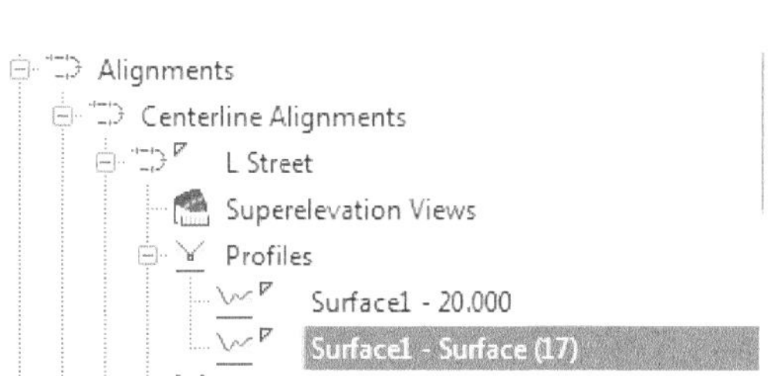

*Figure 6-42 Added profiles in the **Profiles** node of the **L Street** alignment*

Alignments
Centerline Alignments
L Street
Superelevation Views
Profiles
Surface1 - 20.000
Surface1 - Surface (17)
Profile Views
Street

*Figure 6-43 The **Street** profile view in the **Profile Views** node of the **L Street** alignment*

Creating a Split/Staggered Profile View

1. Choose the **Create Profile View** tool from **Home > Profile & Section Views > Profile View** drop-down; the **General** page of the **Create Profile View** wizard is displayed. Ensure that **L Street** is selected in the **Select alignment** drop-down list.

2. Enter **View L** in the **Profile view name** edit box.

3. Select the **Full Grid** option from the **Profile view style** drop-down list if it is not selected by default.

4. Choose the **Next** button; the **Station Range** page is displayed.

5. In the **Station range** area, select the **User specified range** radio button if it is not selected by default.

6. Next, choose the button on the right of the first edit box in the **Station range** area to pick the first station from the drawing. 

7. Zoom in on the drawing and click at **6+00.00'** station to pick the first station.

Tip

*You can also edit the station range using the **Station Range** edit box. Click in the edit box and type in the required station value.*

8. Choose the button on the right of the second edit box and click at **18+00.00'** station tick mark to pick the end station to sample.

9. Choose the **Next** button; the **Profile View Height** page is displayed.

10. In the **Profile View Height** area of this page; select the **User specified** radio button if not selected by default. Ensure that the **Split profile view** check box is selected.

11. Set the values in the **Minimum** and **Maximum** edit boxes on the right of the **User specified** radio button in the **Profile view height** area, as shown in Figure 6-44.

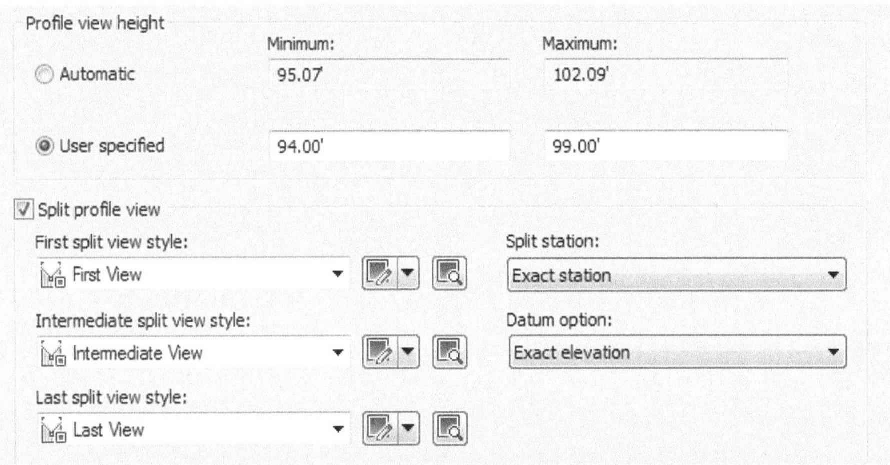

***Figure 6-44** Specifying the profile view height settings for split profiles*

12. Retain the default settings for the **Split profile view** area and choose the **Next** button in the **Create Profile View** wizard; the **Profile Display Options** page of the wizard is displayed. Make sure that the check box under the **Draw** column and the radio buttons in the **Clip Grid** and **Split At** columns corresponding to the **Surface1- Surface(17)** option in the **Name** column are selected.

13. Next, choose the **Create Profile View** button in the **Profile Display Options** page of the **Create Profile View** wizard; you are prompted to select the origin for the profile view.

14. Click in the drawing area to specify the origin of the profile view; the profile view is displayed and the profile is split in multiple views, as shown in Figure 6-45.

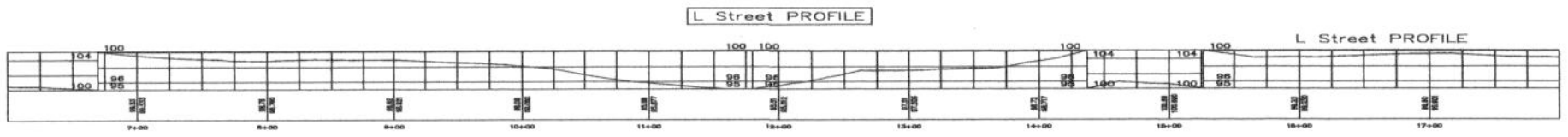

***Figure 6-45** The split profile view for the **L Street** alignment*

Saving the File

1. Choose **Save As** from the **Application Menu**; the **Save Drawing As** dialog box is displayed.

2. In this dialog box, browse to the following location:

   C:\c3d_2018\c_06_c3d_2018_tut

3. In the **File name** edit box, enter **c06_tut01a**.

4. Next, choose the **Save** button; the file is saved with the name *c06_tut01a.dwg* at the specified location.

Tutorial 2 — Layout Profile

In this tutorial, you will create a layout profile for **Road A** alignment using the **Profile Layout Tools** toolbar and the design criteria, as shown in Figure 6-46. Also, you will rectify the design error. **(Expected time: 30 min)**

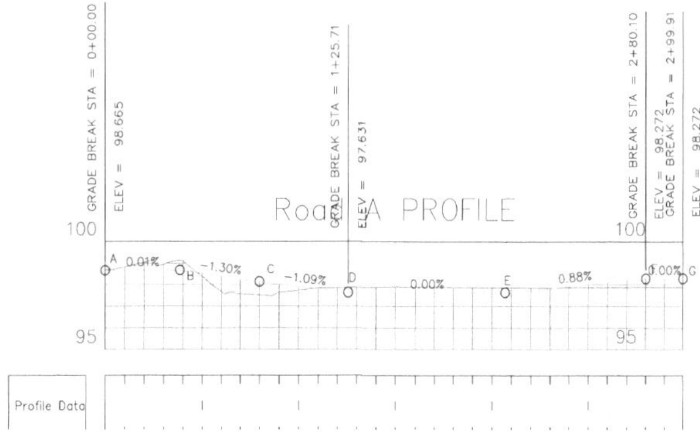

*Figure 6-46 The **Road A** profile*

The following steps are required to complete this tutorial:

a. Download and open the file.
b. Create a layout profile.
c. Create the profile using the **Draw Tangents** tool.
d. Add curves.
e. Correct the violation error.
f. Save the file.

Downloading and Opening the File

1. Download *c06_c3d_2018_tut.zip* file if not downloaded earlier from *http://www.cadcim.com*. Next, save and extract the file at *C:\3d_2018*.

2. Choose **Open** from the **Application Menu**; the **Select File** dialog box is displayed.

3. In this dialog box, browse to the location *C:\c3d_2018\c06_c3d_2018_tut.*

4. Select the file *c06_c3d_2018_tut02.dwg* and then choose the **Open** button to open the file. The *c06_c3d_2018_tut02.dwg* file consists of a surface and **Road A** profile view. Ignore the error message if displayed.

Creating a Layout Profile

1. Choose the **Profile Creation Tools** tool from **Home > Create Design > Profile** drop-down; you are prompted to select a profile view.

2. Select the **Road A** profile view from the drawing; the **Create Profile - Draw New** dialog box is displayed.

3. Enter **Profile A** in the **Name** edit box of this dialog box.

4. In the **General** tab of this dialog box, retain the default settings. Next, choose the **Design Criteria** tab.

5. In the **Design Criteria** tab, select the **Use criteria-based design** check box to apply the design criteria to the layout profile.

6. Choose the **OK** button; the **Create Profile - Draw New** dialog box is closed and the **Profile Layout Tools - Profile A(1)** toolbar is displayed.

Creating the Profile Using the Draw Tangents Tool

1. Invoke the **Draw Tangents** tool from the toolbar; you are prompted to specify the start point.

2. Turn on the **OSNAP** (F3) option and zoom on to the profile view.

3. Move the cursor to the center of the circle **A** in the profile view; the cursor snaps to the center of the circle. Specify the start point of the tangent; you are prompted to specify the end point of the tangent, refer to Figure 6-47.

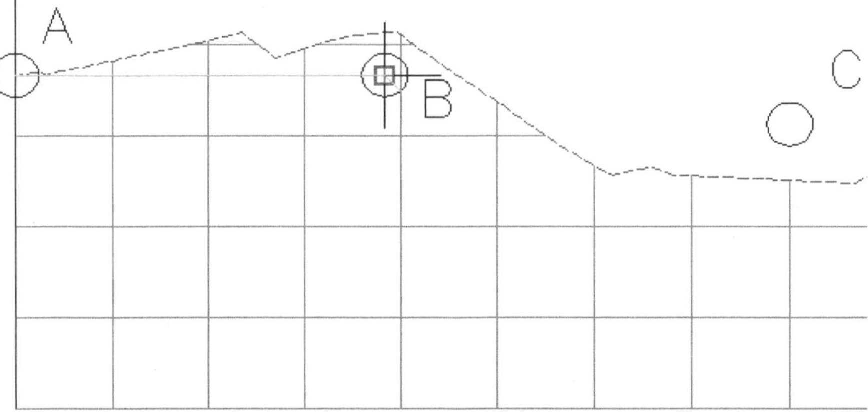

Figure 6-47 *The Specifying the end point of tangent at the center of circle* ***B***

4. Click at the center of circle **B**; a cyan colored tangent is displayed connecting the centers of two circles **A** and **B**.

5. Repeat the procedure followed in steps 3 and 4 to create a tangent between all the circles.

6. After creating the tangent between circles **F** and **G**, right-click to exit the command.

   Notice that, a profile has been created consisting of tangents connecting the point of vertical intersections (PVIs), as shown in Figure 6-48.

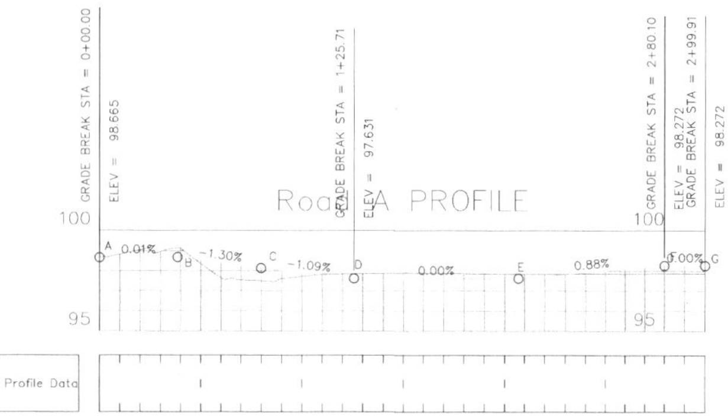

***Figure 6-48** The **Road A** profile created*

Adding Curves

1. Choose the **Free Vertical Curve (Parabola)** tool from the **Profile Layout Tools - Profile A(1)** toolbar, as shown in Figure 6-49; you are prompted to select the first entity.

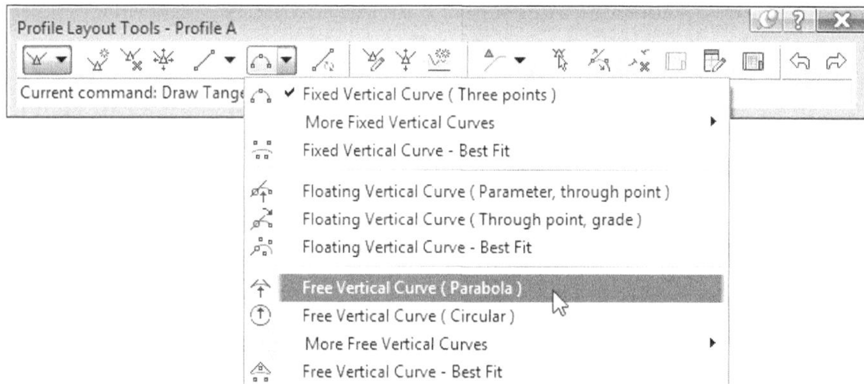

***Figure 6-49** Invoking the **Free Vertical Curve (Parabola)** tool*

2. Zoom in the circle **B**. To add a curve, select the tangent to the left of circle **B**; you are prompted to select the next entity.

3. Now, select the tangent to the right of circle **B**; you are prompted to specify the curve length or radius.

4. Enter **R** for radius in the command line and press ENTER; you are prompted to specify a radius.

Note

The default radius values displayed in the command line are obtained from the design criteria file and may vary depending on the design criteria file assigned to the project.

5. Enter **5000** in the command line and press ENTER; a free vertical curve is added between the selected tangents. Note that a violation symbol is displayed on the curve, as shown in Figure 6-50.

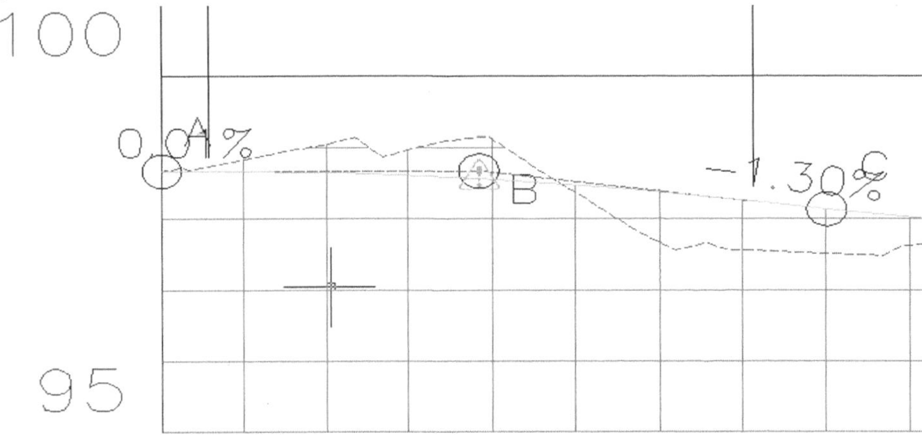

***Figure 6-50** The violation symbol displayed on the vertical curve*

6. Select the **More Free Vertical curves** option from the **Free Vertical curve** tool area in the **Profile Layout Tools - Profile A(1)** toolbar; a flyout is displayed. Choose the **Free Vertical Parabola (PVI based)** tool from the flyout; you are prompted to pick a point near a PVI.

7. Zoom in to circle **E** in the profile view and click near this circle, refer to Figure 6-51; you are prompted to specify the curve length.

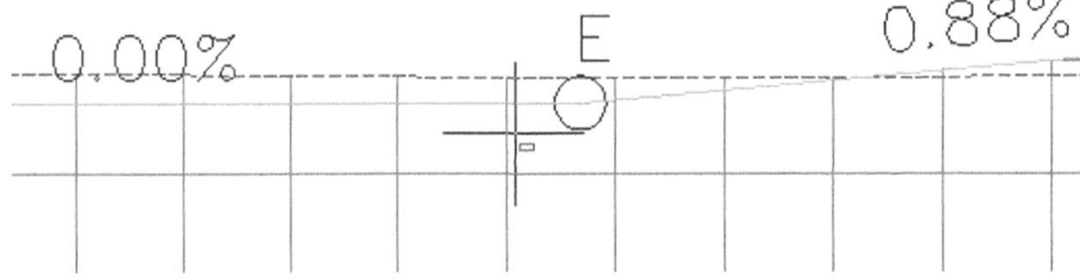

***Figure 6-51** Picking a point near a PVI*

8. Press ENTER to accept the default value of the curve length displayed in the command line; a free PVI-based curve is labeled and added between the tangents, as shown in Figure 6-51.

9. Now, press ENTER to terminate the command. Notice that the curve is also labeled, as shown in Figure 6-52.

Tip

*If the **Profile Layout Tools** toolbar is not displayed, select the layout profile (cyan colored) from the profile view in the drawing and right-click; a shortcut menu will be displayed. Choose the **Edit Profile Geometry** option from the shortcut menu; the **Profile Layout Tools** toolbar is displayed.*

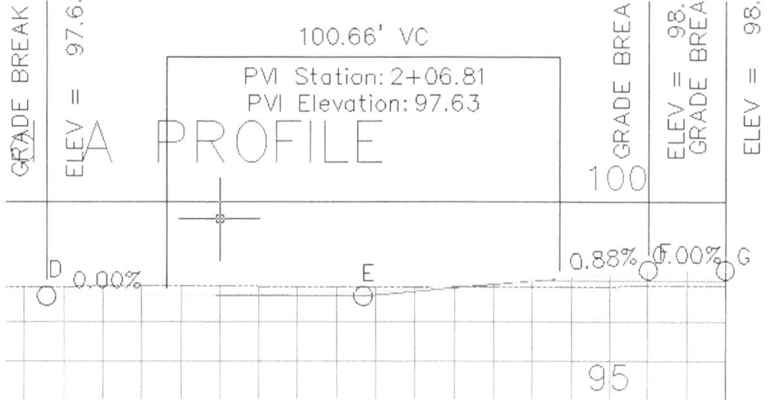

*Figure 6-52 The **Free Vertical Curve (PVI based)** added between the tangents*

Correcting the Violation Error

1. Invoke the **Entity based** tool from the **Profile Layout Tools - Profile A** toolbar.

2. Next, invoke the **Profile Layout Parameters** tool; the **Profile Layout Parameters - Profile A(1)** dialog box is displayed.

Note

Hover the cursor over the violation symbol, a tooltip with the type of error is displayed, as shown in Figure 6-53. The message in the tooltip informs that the minimum K value for Stopping Sight Distance criterion is violated.

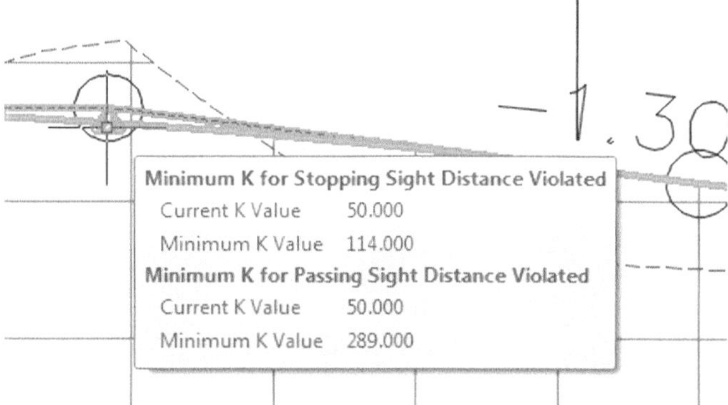

Figure 6-53 The tooltip showing the type of error

3. Now, invoke the **Select Entity** tool and select the curve on which the violation symbol is displayed; the curve parameters and their values are displayed in the **Profile Layout Parameters** dialog box, as shown in Figure 6-54.

In this dialog box, you can see that a violation symbol is displayed along with the **K** value parameter. This symbol is displayed at the top of the dialog box showing that the minimum **K** value is violated for both the **Stopping Sight Distance** and **Passing Sight Distance** parameters.

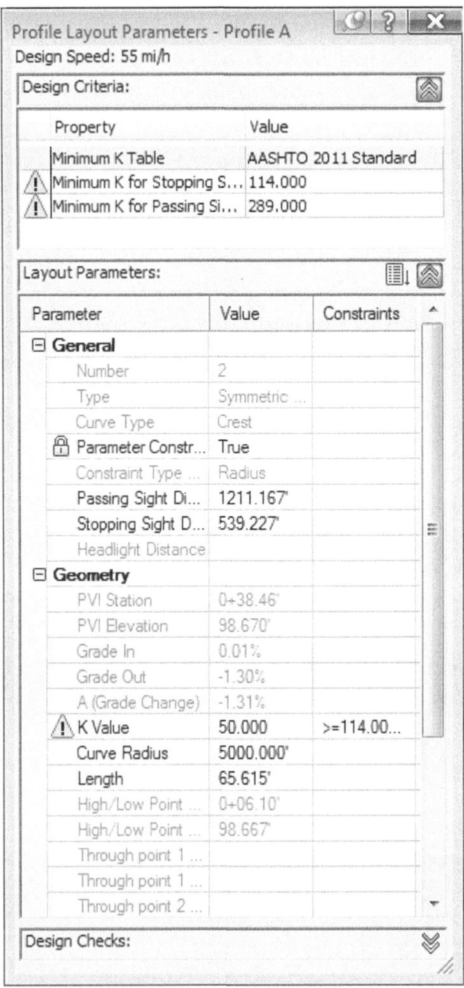

*Figure 6-54 The **Profile Layout Parameters** dialog box*

You will also observe that the minimum K value required to meet the criteria is displayed in the tooltip and in the **Constraints** column. Therefore, in this case, the violation symbol will be removed only if the K value for both the **Stopping Sight Distance** and **Passing Sight Distance** rules is satisfied. The minimum K value required for the **Stopping Sight Distance** should be greater than or equal to 114.00, and the minimum K value for the **Passing Sight Distance** should be 289.00.

When there are two types of design criteria violation at the same station then there are two ways to solve this problem. The first one is to assign a new design speed at the station where the curve starts violating the criterion. The second option is to annotate the station range of the curve as the **No Passing Zone**. You can try any of these two ways and proceed further. In the current tutorial, assigning a new design speed at the station where the alignment begins will not solve the problem. So you will have to follow the second option.

Saving the File

1. Choose **Save As** from the **Application Menu**; the **Save Drawing As** dialog box is displayed.

2. In this dialog box, browse to the following location:

   C:\c3d_2018\c06_c3d_2018_tut

3. In the **File name** edit box, enter **c06_tut02a**.

4. Next, choose the **Save** button; the file is saved with the name *c06_tut02a.dwg* at the specified location.

Tutorial 3 Superimposed Profile

In this tutorial, you will create superimpose a profile on another profile and examine the elevation difference between the two profiles. You will also create multiple views and stacked profile views, as shown in Figure 6-55. **(Expected time: 30 min)**

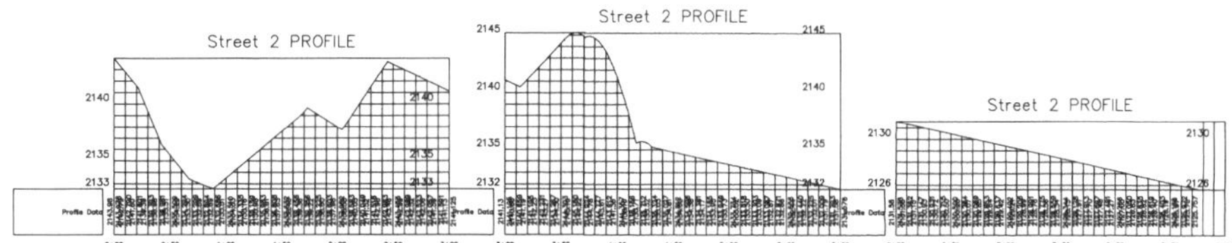

***Figure 6-55** The multiple profile views*

The following steps are required to complete this tutorial:

a. Download and open the file.
b. Superimpose the **Street 2** profile over the **Andrews Drive** profile view.
c. Create multiple views of the **Andrews Drive** profile view.
d. Save the file.

Downloading and Opening the File

1. Download *c06_c3d_2018_tut.zip* file, if not downloaded earlier, from *http://www.cadcim.com*. Next, save and extract the file at *C:\c3d_2018*.

2. Choose **Open** from the **Application Menu**; the **Select File** dialog box is displayed.

3. In the dialog box, browse to the location *C:\c3d_2018\c06_c3d_2018_tut* folder where you have saved the file.

4. Select the file *c06_c3d_2018_tut03.dwg* and then choose the **Open** button to open the file. The file consists of a surface and two profile views, **Andrews Drive** and **Street 2**, as shown in Figure 6-56. You will now superimpose the **Street 2** profile over the **Andrews Drive** profile view.

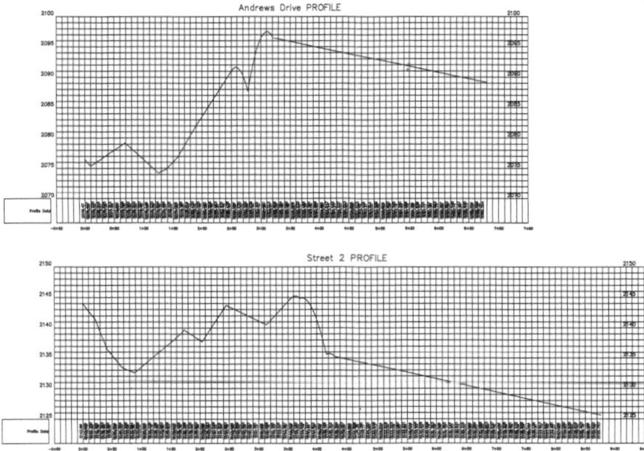

***Figure 6-56** The **Andrews Drive** and the **Street 2** profile views*

Superimposing the Profile

1. Choose the **Create Superimposed Profile** tool from **Home > Create Design > Profile** drop-down; you are prompted to select the source profile.

2. Select the profile from the **Street 2** profile view; you are prompted to select the destination profile view.

3. Next, select the **Andrews Drive** profile view to superimpose the **Street 2** profile; the **Superimpose Profile Options** dialog box is displayed.

4. Accept the default values in the **Limits** tab of the **Superimpose Profile Options** dialog box. Choose the **OK** button; the **Superimpose Profile Options** dialog box is closed and the profile information of the **Street 2** profile is superimposed over the **Andrews Drive** profile view, as shown in Figure 6-57.

Creating Multiple Views

1. Choose the **Create Multiple Profile Views** tool from **Home > Profile & Section Views > Profile View** drop-down; the **Create Multiple Profile Views** wizard with the **General** page is displayed.

2. Select **Street 2** from the **Select alignment** drop-down list in the **General** page of this wizard.

3. Enter **Street 2** profile in the **Profile view name** edit box of the same page.

4. Choose the **Next** button; the **Station Range** page of the wizard is displayed.

5. Enter **300** in the **Length of each view** edit box for each of these views. Note that the length of each view can be decided based on the station range along the horizontal axis and the number of views to be created.

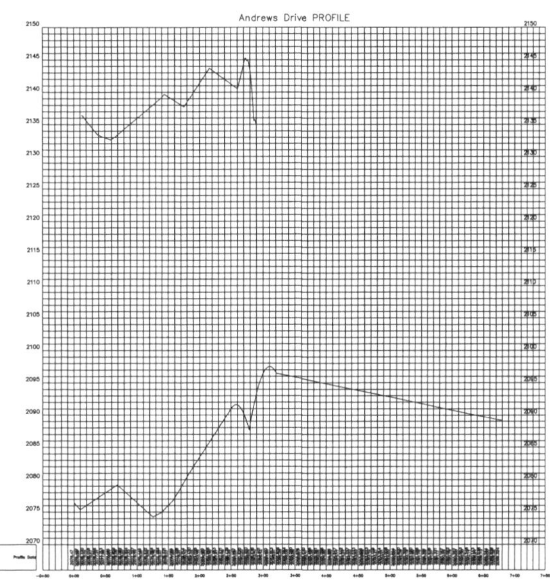

Figure 6-57 *The* ***Street 2*** *profile superimposed over the* ***Andrews Drive*** *profile view*

6. Next, choose the **Multiple Plot Options** option from the **Create Multiple Profile Views** wizard.

7. In the **Gap between the adjacent profile views** area of this page, enter **50** in both the **Row** and **Column** edit boxes.

8. Ensure that the **By rows** radio button is selected in the **Draw order** area and the value in the **Maximum in a row** edit box is set to **4**. Next, choose the **Create Profile Views** button; you are prompted to specify the origin of the profile view. Click in the drawing area to add multiple profile views.

9. Select the first profile view and right-click; a shortcut menu is displayed. Choose **Edit Profile View Style** from the shortcut menu; the **Profile View Style - Basic** dialog box is displayed.

10. Choose the **Grid** tab and then select the **Clip vertical grid** and **Clip horizontal grid** check boxes in the **Grid options** area.

11. Choose the **OK** button; the dialog box is closed and the profile views are displayed, as shown in Figure 6-58.

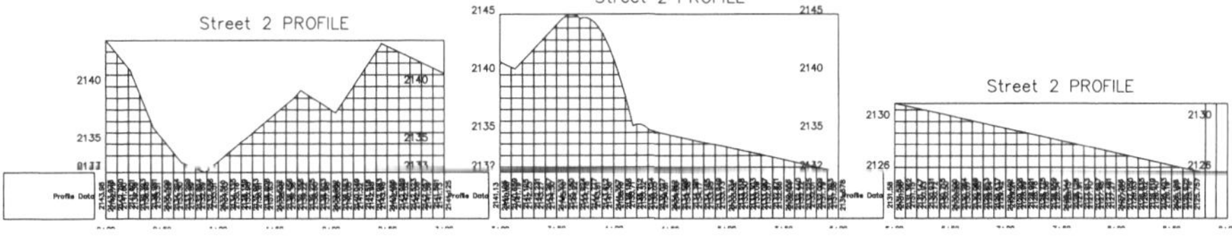

Figure 6-58 *The multiple views for the* ***Street 2*** *profile*

Creating Stacked Views

1. Choose the **Create Surface Profile** tool from **Home > Create Design > Profile** drop-down; the **Create Profile from Surface** dialog box is displayed.

2. Select **Andrews Drive** from the **Alignment** drop-down list if it is not selected by default. Select **Surface contours** from the **Select surfaces** area and then choose the **Add** button; the profile with the name **Surface contours - Surface (8)** is added to the **Profile list** list box.

3. Next, choose the **Draw in profile view** button; the **Create Profile from Surface** dialog box is closed and the **Create Profile View** wizard with the **General** page is displayed.

4. Enter **Andrews Stacked** in the **Profile view name** edit box of the **General** page.

5. Now, select the **Show offset profiles by vertically stacking profile views** check box; the link to the **Stacked Profile** page is added to the **Options** panel of the wizard.

6. Choose the **Stacked Profile** option from the wizard; the **Create Profile View - Stacked Profile** page of the wizard is displayed.

7. In this page, set the value to **3** in the **Number of stacked views** spinner if it is not set by default. Enter **10** as the gap distance in the **Gap between views** edit box.

8. Choose the **Next** button; the **Profile Display Options** page is displayed.

9. Ensure that the **Middle View - [1]** option is selected in the **Select stacked view to specify options for** list box.

10. Next, select the check box for the **Surface contours - Surface (6) - [Street 2] - (16)** (third row) in the **Draw** column of the **Specify profile display options** list box.

11. Now, select the **Top View** option from the **Select stacked view to specify options for** list box.

12. Select the check box for the **Surface contours - Surface (5)** (first row) in the **Draw** column of the **Specify profile display options** area.

13. Select the **Bottom View** option from the **Select stacked view to specify options for** list box and the check box for the **Surface contours - Surface (6) - [Street 2] - (16)** (third row) in the **Draw** column.

14. Choose the **Create Profile View** button; the wizard is closed and you are prompted to specify the origin of the profile view.

15. Click at the required location; the three stacked profile views are created, as shown in Figure 6-59.

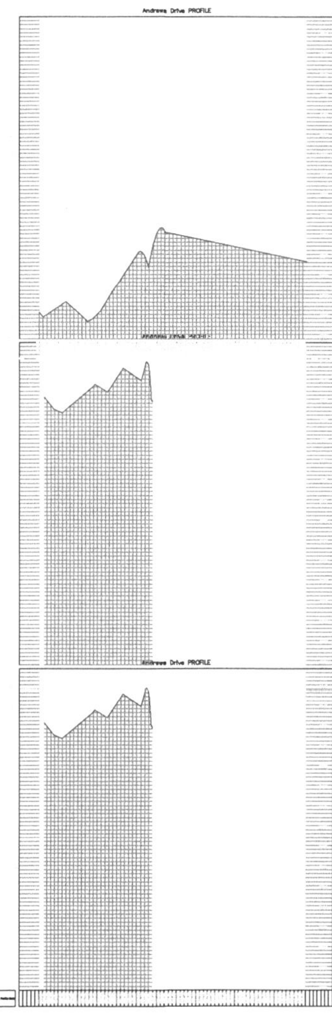

Figure 6-59 *The top, middle, and bottom stacked profile views*

Saving the File

1. Choose **Save As** from the **Application Menu**; the **Save Drawing As** dialog box is displayed.

2. In this dialog box, browse to the following location:

   C:\c3d_2018\c06_c3d_2018_tut

3. In the **File name** edit box, enter **c06_tut03a**.

4. Next, choose the **Save** button; the file is saved with the name *c06_tut03a.dwg* at the specified location.

Tutorial 4 Profile Style

In this tutorial, you will create a profile label style and a profile label set. You will then assign the profile label set to the **Road A** profile, as shown in Figure 6-60. **(Expected time: 30 min)**

The following steps are required to complete this tutorial:

a. Download and open the file.
b. Create profile label style.
c. Create profile label set.
d. Assign profile label style to the profile.
e. Save the file.

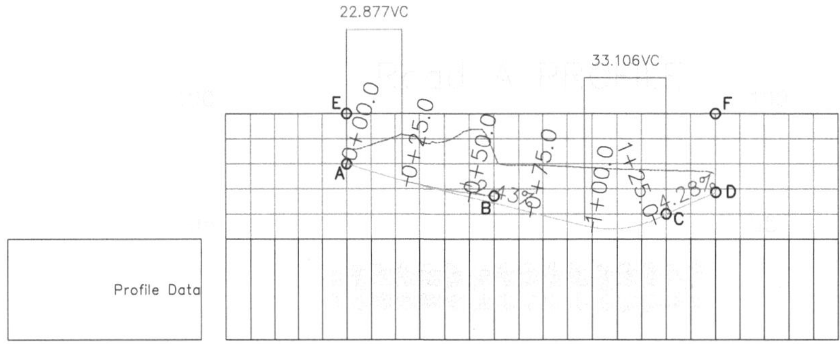

***Figure 6-60** The profile label set assigned to the **Road A** profile*

Downloading and Opening the File

1. Download *c06_c3d_2018_tut.zip* file, if not downloaded earlier, from *http://www.cadcim.com*. Next, save and extract the file at *C:\c3d_2018*.

2. Choose **Open** from the **Application Menu**; the **Select File** dialog box is displayed.

3. In the dialog box, browse to the location *C:\c3d_2018\c06_c3d_2018*.

4. Select the file *c06_c3d_2018_tut04.dwg* and then choose the **Open** button to open it. Ignore any error message if displayed. The file consists of the **Road A** layout profile and the **Road A** profile view of the specified station range.

Creating a New Profile Label Style

1. Choose the **Settings** tab from the **TOOLSPACE** palette and expand the **Profile** node.

2. Next, expand **Label Styles > Station** in the **Profile** node.

3. Right-click on the **Major Station** subnode and choose the **New** option from the shortcut menu displayed; the **Label Style Composer - New Profile Major Station Label Style** dialog box is displayed.

4. Enter **Road A Major** in the **Name** edit box of the **Label Style Composer - New Profile Major Station Label Style** dialog box.

5. Choose the **Layout** tab from the dialog box. Notice that the dialog name is modified as **Label Style Composer - Road A Major**.

6. Click in the **Value** column for the **Contents** property; a browse button is displayed.

7. Choose the browse button; the **Text Component Editor - Contents** dialog box is displayed.

8. Select the text displayed in the **Text Editor** window of this dialog box, as shown in Figure 6-61, and then press DELETE.

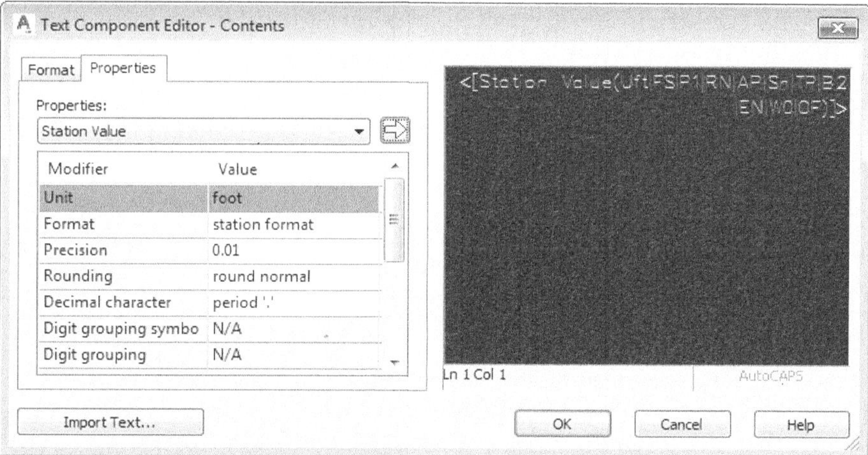

Figure 6-61 *The* ***Text Component Editor - Contents*** *dialog box*

9. Next, double-click in the **Value** column of the **Precision** modifier; a drop-down list is displayed.

10. Select **0.1** from the drop-down list, as shown in Figure 6-62.

11. Next, choose the button next to the **Properties** drop-down list to add the selected value in the **Text Editor** window.

12. Choose the **OK** button; the **Text Component Editor - Contents** dialog box is closed.

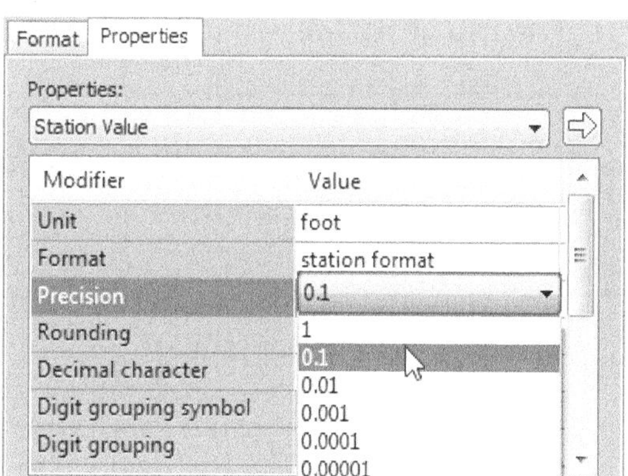

Figure 6-62 *Selecting the* ***0.1*** *value for the* ***Precision*** *modifier*

13. Set the following properties in the **Text** node of the **Label Style Composer - Road A Major** dialog box:

    Text Height: **0.1500"** Color: **blue**

14. Click on the down-arrow on the right of the **Create Text Component** button; a flyout is displayed. Choose the **Tick** option from the flyout, as shown in Figure 6-63; the tick component is added to the component type list and its properties are displayed in the **Property** column.

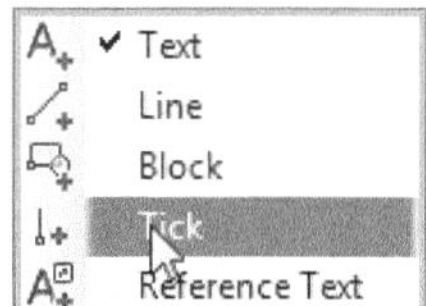

Figure6-63 Choosing the ***Tick*** *option*

15. In the **Tick** node, click in the **Value** column for the **Block name**; a browse button is displayed on the right.

16. Choose the browse button; the **Select a Block** dialog box is displayed.

17. Select the **AeccTickLine** option from the **Blocks** list box and choose the **OK** button; the **Select a Block** dialog box is closed.

18. Choose the **OK** button; the **Label Style Composer - Road A Major** dialog box is closed and the **Road A Major** label style is added to the **Major Station** node of the **Settings** tab, as shown in Figure 6-64.

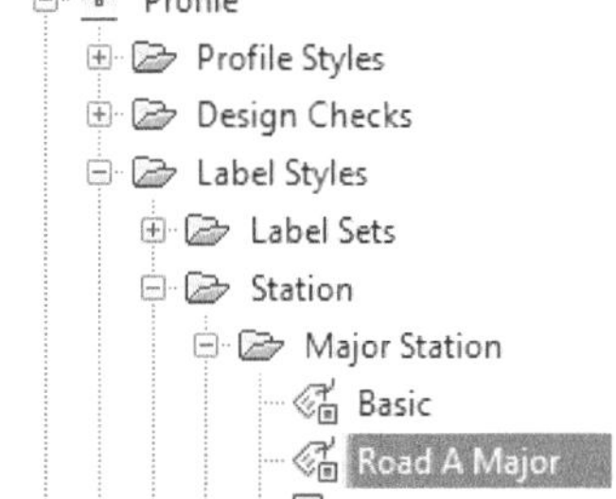

Figure 6-64 *The* ***Road A Major*** *label style added to the* ***Major Station*** *node*

19. Select the **Line** subnode in the **Label Styles** node and right-click; a shortcut menu is displayed.

20. Choose **New** from the shortcut menu; the **Label Style Composer - New Profile Tangent Label Style** dialog box is displayed.

21. Enter **Road A Line** in the **Name** edit box of the dialog box.

22. Choose the **Layout** tab. Notice that the dialog name is modified as **Label Style Composer - Road A Line**. In the **Layout** tab, set the values in the **Text** node as follows:

    Text Height: **0.1400"** Color: **red**

23. Choose the **Dragged State** tab. In the **Dragged State Components** category of this tab, set the value of the **Color** property to green.

24. Choose the **OK** button; the **Label Style Composer - Road A Line** dialog box is closed and the **Road A Line** label style is added to the **Line** subnode of the **Settings** tab.

25. Right-click on the **Curve** subnode of the **Label Styles** node; a shortcut menu is displayed. Choose the **New** option from the shortcut menu; the **Label Style Composer - New Profile Curve Label Style** dialog box is displayed.

26. Enter **Road A Curve** in the **Name** edit box of the dialog box.

27. Choose the **Layout** tab. In this tab, select the **Dimension Line** option from the **Component name** drop-down list if it is not selected by default.

28. Set the value of the **Color** property of the default **Dimension Line** component to **red**.

29. Next, select **Start Line**, **End Line**, and **Length** from the **Component name** drop-down list and set their colors to red.

30. Choose the **OK** button; the **Label Style Composer - Road A Curve** dialog box is closed and the **Road A Curve** label style for curve is added to the **Curve** subnode of the **Settings** tab.

Creating a Label Set

1. Right-click on the **Label Sets** subnode in the **Label Styles** node and choose the **New** option from the shortcut menu displayed; the **Profile Label Set - New Profile Label Set** dialog box is displayed.

2. In the **Information** tab, enter **Road A Label Set** in the **Name** edit box.

3. Next, choose the **Labels** tab. By default, the **Major Stations** option is selected in the **Type** drop-down list of this tab.

4. Select the **Road A Major** option from the **Profile Major Station Label Style** drop-down list.

5. Now, choose the **Add** button to add the selected label style to the label set.

6. Next, select **Lines** from the **Type** drop-down list and the **Road A Line** option from the **Profile Tangent Label Style** drop-down list.

7. Choose the **Add** button; a row is added to the list box of the **Labels** tab.

8. Select the **Sag Curves** option from the **Type** drop-down list and the **Road A Curve** option from the **Profile Sag Curve Label Style** drop-down list.

9. Choose the **Add** button; a row is added to the list box of the **Labels** tab.

10. Set the **Increment** value for the **Major stations** to **25.000'**, as shown in Figure 6-65.

11. Now, choose the **OK** button; the **Profile Label Set - Road A Label Set** dialog box is closed and the **Road A Label Set** is added to the **Label Sets** subnode.

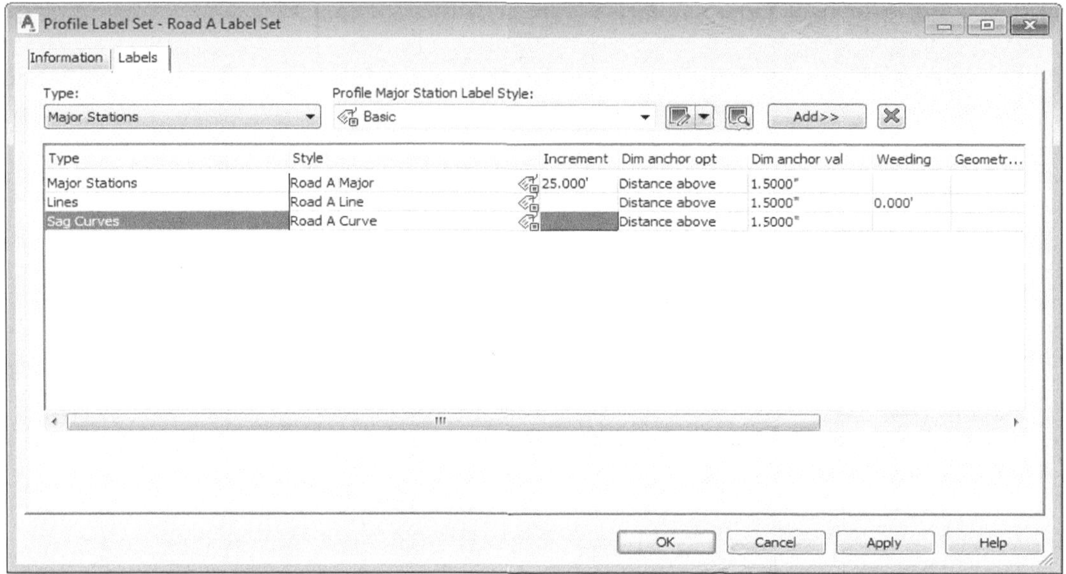

*Figure 6-65 The increment value for the **Major Stations** set to **25.000'***

Assigning the Profile Label Style

1. Select the **Road A** profile (cyan colored layout profile) and right-click; a shortcut menu is displayed.

2. Next, choose the **Edit Labels** option from the shortcut menu; the **Profile Labels - Road A** dialog box is displayed.

3. Choose the **Import label set** button located at the bottom of the **Profile Labels - Road A** dialog box; the **Select Label Set** dialog box is displayed.

4. Select the **Road A Label Set** option from the drop-down list displayed in the **Select Label Set** dialog box, as shown in Figure 6-66.

5. Next, choose the **OK** button in the **Select Label Set** dialog box; the dialog box is closed and the labels of the label set are displayed in a tabular format in the **Profile Labels - Road A** dialog box.

6. Next, choose the **Apply** button to assign the label set to the profile and view the change.

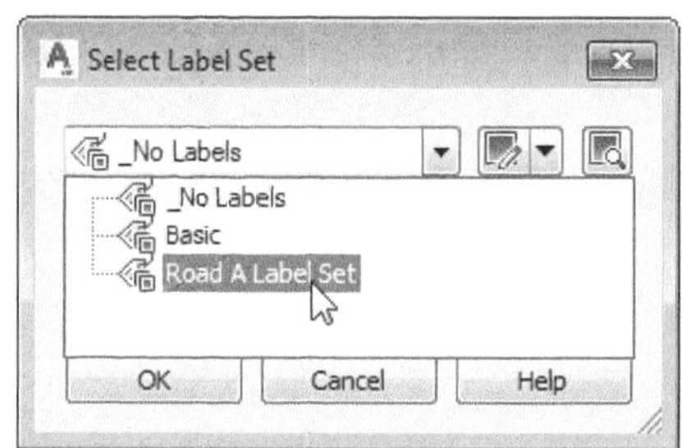

*Figure 6-66 Selecting the **Road A Label Set** option from the drop-down list*

7. Choose the **OK** button in the **Profile Labels - Road A** dialog box; the dialog box is closed. You will notice that the profile is labeled according to the settings defined, as shown in Figure 6-67.

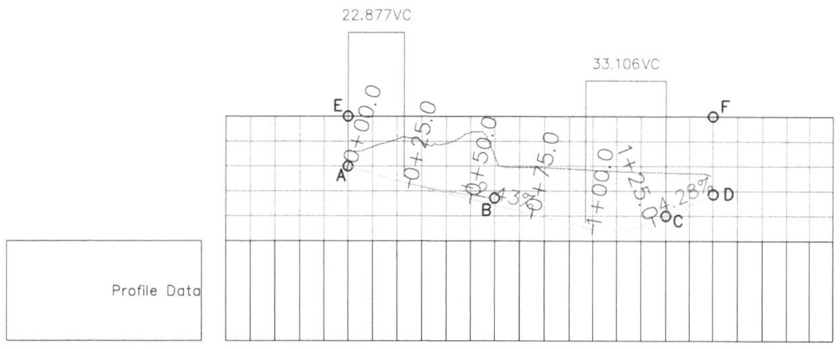

*Figure 6-67 The Profile label set assigned to the **Road A** Profile*

Saving the File

1. Choose **Save As** from the **Application Menu**; the **Save Drawing As** dialog box is displayed.

2. In this dialog box, browse to the following location:

   C:\c3d_2018\c06_c3d_2018_tut

3. In the **File name** edit box, enter **c06_tut04a**.

4. Next, choose the **Save** button; the file is saved with the name *c06_tut04a* at the specified location.

Tutorial 5 Profile View Style

In this tutorial, you will create profile view label style and band style. You will then create the profile band set and assign it to the profile view, as shown in Figure 6-68.

(Expected time: 60 min)

The following steps are required to complete this tutorial:

a. Download and open the file.
b. Create profile view label style.
c. Create band style.
d. Create band set.
e. Save the file.

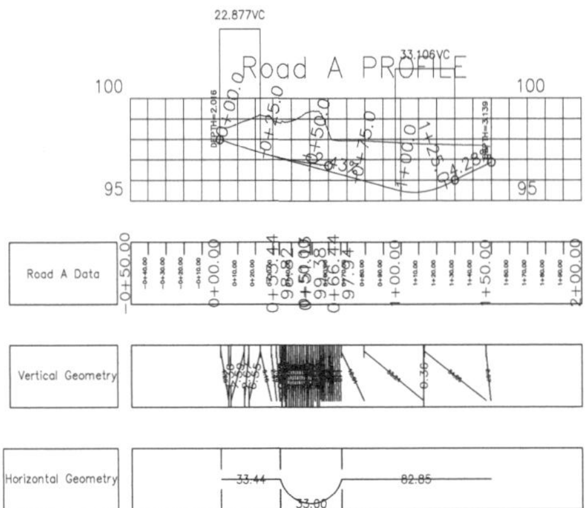

*Figure 6-68 The **Road A** profile view with the specified data bands added*

Downloading and Opening the File

1. Download *c06_c3d_2018_tut.zip* file, if not downloaded earlier, from *http://www.cadcim*.com. Next, save and extract the file at *C:\c3d_2018*.

2. Choose **Open** from the **Application Menu**; the **Select File** dialog box is displayed.

3. In the dialog box, browse to the location *C:\c3d_2018\c06_c3d_2018_tut.*

4. Select the file *c06_c3d_2018_tut05.dwg* and then choose the **Open** button to open it. Ignore the error message displayed, if any. The file consists of the **Road A** layout profile and the **Road A** profile view of the specified station range.

Creating a Profile View Label Style

1. Expand the **Profile View > Label Styles** subnode in the **Settings** tab.

2. Right-click on the **Depth** subnode; a shortcut menu is displayed.

3. Choose the **New** option from the shortcut menu; the **Label Style Composer - New Profile Depth Label Style** dialog box is displayed.

4. In the **Information** tab of this dialog box, enter **Road A Depth** in the **Name** edit box. Next, choose the **Layout** tab.

5. In this tab, set the **Color** property of the **Line** component to magenta.

6. Select the **Depth** option from the **Component name** drop-down list; the corresponding properties are displayed in the **Property** column.

7. Set the **Text Height** property to **0.0700′** and the **Color** property to magenta.

8. Choose the **OK** button; the **Label Style Composer - Road A Depth** dialog box is closed and the **Road A Depth** style is added to the **Depth** subnode of the **Settings** tab.

9. Now, choose the **Profile View** option from **Annotate >Labels & Tables > Add Labels** drop-down; a flyout is displayed. Choose the **Profile View** option from the flyout; another flyout is displayed. Choose the **Add Profile View Labels** tool from this flyout; the **Add Labels** dialog box is displayed.

10. In this dialog box, select the **Depth** option from the **Label type** drop-down list, as shown in Figure 6-69.

11. Select the **Road A Depth** from the **Depth label style** drop-down list.

12. Now, choose the **Add** button; you are prompted to select a profile view.

13. Select the **Road A** profile view from the drawing; you are prompted to pick the first point on the screen.

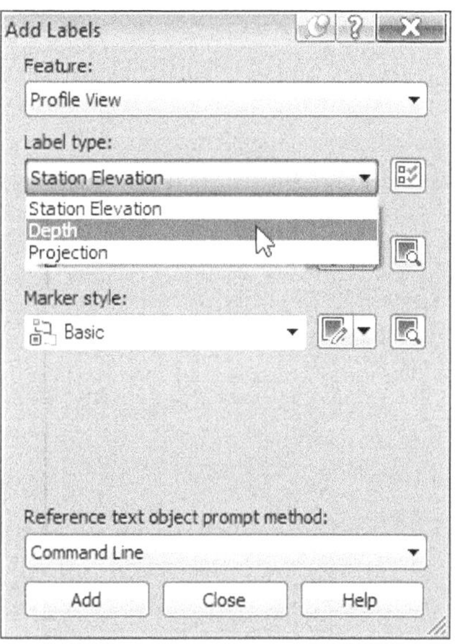

Figure 6-69 *Selecting the **Depth** option*

14. Click at the center of the circle **A** in the profile view; you are prompted to pick the second point on the screen.

Tip

*You can turn on the object snap mode with the **Center** snap option selected to easily select the center of circle.*

15. Next, click at the center of circle **E** to specify the second point; the depth between the selected points is displayed as the depth label, as shown in Figure 6-69.

16. Similarly, add a depth label by selecting the center point of the circle **D** and circle **F.**

17. Choose the **Close** button to close the **Add Labels** dialog box. Notice, the depth is displayed in the profile view, refer to Figure 6-70.

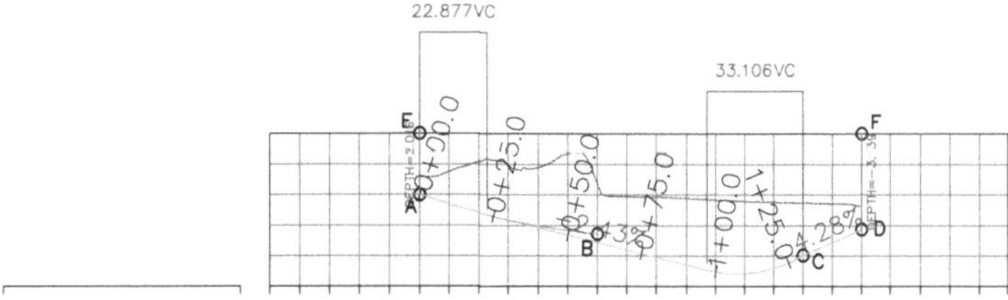

Figure 6-70 *The profile view for **Road A** displaying the depth label*

Creating a Band Style

1. Expand **Profile View > Band Styles > Profile Data** subnode in the **Settings** tab of the **TOOLSPACE** palette.

2. Right-click on the **Profile Data** subnode; a shortcut menu is displayed.

3. Next, choose the **New** option from the shortcut menu; the **Profile Data Band Style - New Profile Data Band Style** dialog box is displayed, as shown in Figure 6-71.

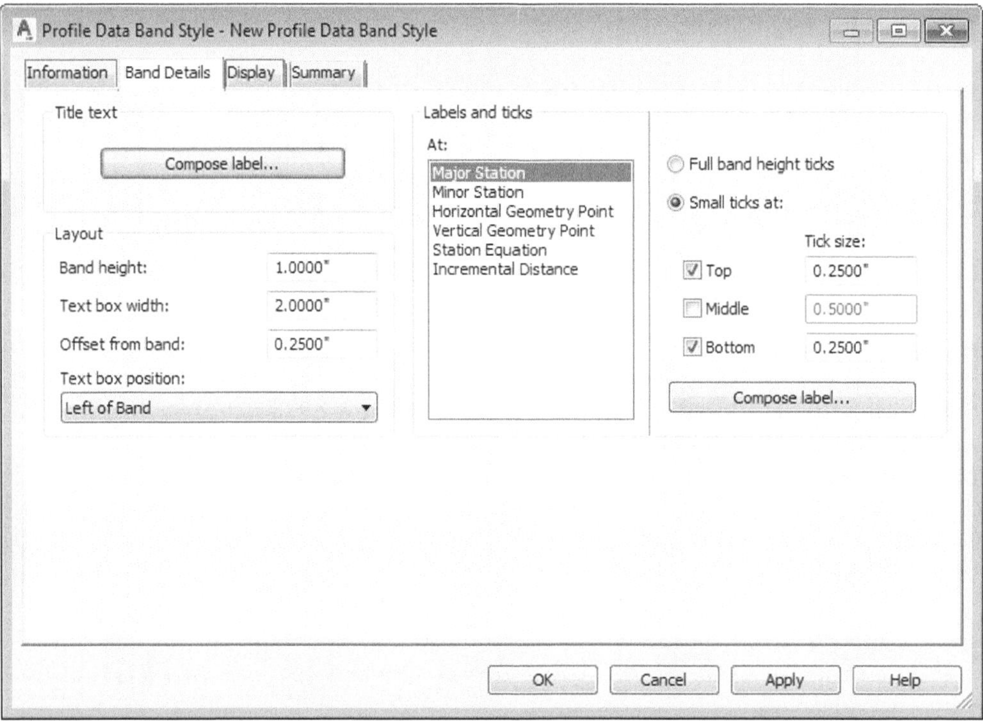

*Figure 6-71 The **Band Details** tab of the **Profile Data Band Style- New Profile Data Band Style** dialog box*

4. Enter **Road A Data** in the **Name** edit box of the dialog box.

5. Choose the **Band Details** tab.

6. From the **Title text** area, choose the **Compose label** button; the **Label Style Composer - Band Title** dialog box is displayed.

7. Click in the **Value** field for the **Contents** property in the **Layout** tab; a browse button is displayed on the right.

8. Choose the browse button; the **Text Component Editor - Contents** dialog box is displayed.

9. Delete the text from the **Text Component Editor - Contents** dialog box and enter **Road A Data** in the editor window, as shown in Figure 6-72.

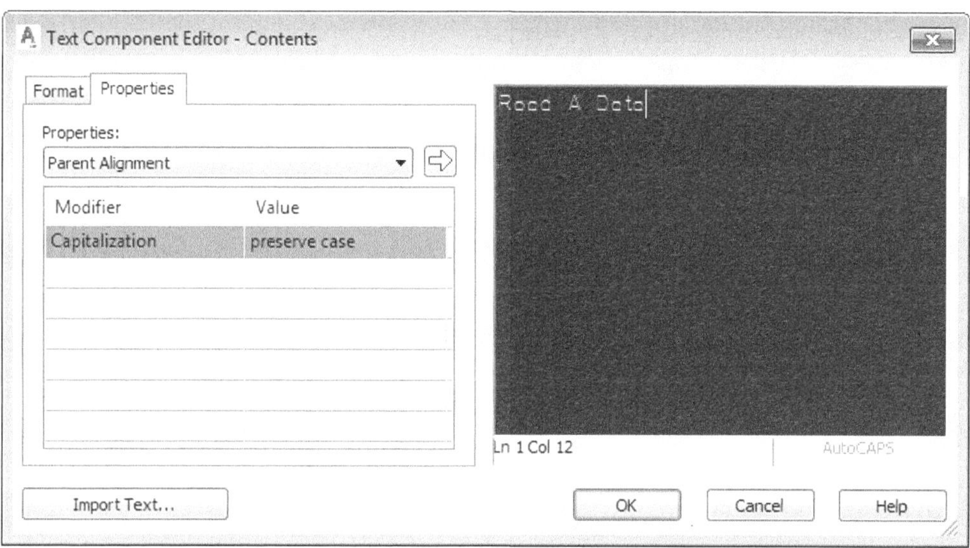

***Figure 6-72** The **Road A Data** text added in the editor window*

10. Next, choose the **OK** button; the **Label Style Composer - Band Title** dialog box is displayed.

11. In the **Value** column of the **Text** node of the **Label Style Composer - Band Title** dialog box, set the value of the **Color** property to red.

12. Next, choose the **OK** button; the **Label Style Composer - Band Title** dialog box is closed.

13. In the **Layout** area of the **Band Details** tab of the **Profile Data Band Style - Road A Data** dialog box, set the values as follows:

    Band height: **0.7500″** Text box width: **1.5000″** Offset from band: **0.2000″**

14. In the **Labels and ticks** area, select **Major Station** from the **At** list box and then select the **Small ticks at** radio button displayed on the right of the **At** list box.

15. In the area next to the **At** list box, select the **Top** check box, if not selected by default. Next, you need to clear all other check boxes. Then, set the tick size to **0.1500″** in the edit box of the **Tick size** column.

16. Next, choose the **Compose label** button; the **Label Style Composer - Major Station** dialog box is displayed.

17. Set the value of the **Text Height** property of the **Station Value** component to **0.1300″**.

18. Select the **Profile 1 Elevation** option from the **Component name** drop-down list and choose the **Delete component** button placed on the right of the **Component name** drop-down list.

19. Next, choose the **OK** button; the **Label Style Composer - Major Station** dialog box is closed.

20. Select the **Minor Station** option from the **Labels and ticks** area in the **Profile Data Band Style - Road A Data** dialog box.

21. Also, select the **Small ticks at** radio button and the **Bottom** check box to place the ticks. Clear all other check boxes in this area and enter **0.1500"** in the **Tick size** edit box on the right of the **Bottom** check box.

22. Choose the **Compose label** button; the **Label Style Composer - Minor Station** dialog box is displayed.

23. In this dialog box, set the **Text Height** to **0.05"** and the **Color** to red in the **Text** node.

24. Select **Profile 1 Elevation** from the **Component name** drop-down list and choose the **Delete component** button to delete it.

25. Next, choose the **OK** button; the **Label Style Composer - Minor Station** dialog box is closed.

26. Repeat the procedure followed in steps 21 to 25 to specify the settings for the **Horizontal Geometry Point** option displayed in the **At** list box in the **Labels and ticks** area.

27. Now, choose the **Display** tab.

28. In this tab, for the **Band Border** and **Band Title Box** components, modify the color to red in the **Color** column of the **Component display** area.

29. Next, choose the **OK** button; the **Profile Data Band style - Road A Data** dialog box is closed.

30. Next, right-click on the **Vertical Geometry** subnode in the **Band Styles** node in the **Settings** tab; a shortcut menu is displayed.

31. Choose **New** from the shortcut menu; the **Vertical Geometry Band Style - Road A Band Set** dialog box is displayed.

32. Enter **Road A Vertical** in the **Name** edit box of the **Information** tab.

33. Choose the **Band Details** tab and set the following values in the respective edit boxes of the **Layout** area:

    Band height: **0.7500"** Text box width: **1.5000"** Offset from band: **0.2000"**

34. Now, select **Downhill Tangent** from the **At** list box in the **Labels and ticks** area and set the parameters mentioned in step 33 if it is not set.

35. Next, choose the **Display** tab.

36. For the **Band Border** component, change the color to blue in the **Color** column.

37. Choose the **OK** button to close the **Vertical Geometry Band Style - Road A Vertical** dialog box. Thus, you have finished creating a band style for the **Vertical Geometry** band.

38. Right-click on the **Horizontal Geometry** subnode in the **Band Styles** node in the **Settings** tab and choose the **New** option from the displayed shortcut menu; the **Horizontal Geometry Band Style - New Horizontal Geometry Band Style** dialog box is displayed.

39. Set the following parameters in this dialog box:

    Information tab-

    Name: **Road A Horizontal**

    Band Details tab-

    Band height: **0.7500″**
    Text box width: **1.6000″** Offset from band: **0.2000″**

    Display tab-

    Band Border color: **magenta** Band Title Box: **magenta**

40. Next, choose the **OK** button in the **Horizontal Geometry Band Style - Road A Horizontal** dialog box; the dialog box is closed.

Creating a Band Set

1. Expand **Profile View > Band Styles** in the **Settings** tab, if it is not expanded.

2. Right-click on the **Band Sets** subnode; a shortcut menu is displayed.

3. Choose **New** from the shortcut menu; the **Band Set - New Profile View Band Set** dialog box is displayed.

4. Enter **Road A Band Set** in the **Name** edit box of the **Information** tab.

5. Next, choose the **Bands** tab.

6. In this tab, select **Profile Data** from the **Band type** drop-down list, if it is not selected and then select the **Road A Data** style from the **Select band style** drop-down list.

7. Next, choose the **Add** button; the **Geometry Points to Label in Band** dialog box is displayed.

8. Choose the **OK** button to accept all the points selected by default; the **Geometry Points to Label in Band** dialog box is closed and the **Profile Data** band type and the **Road A Data** style are added to the table in the **List of bands** area in the **Band Set - Road A Band Set** dialog box.

9. Using the procedure followed in steps 6 and 7, add **Vertical Geometry**, **Horizontal Geometry** and their respective band styles to the table, refer to Figure 6-73.

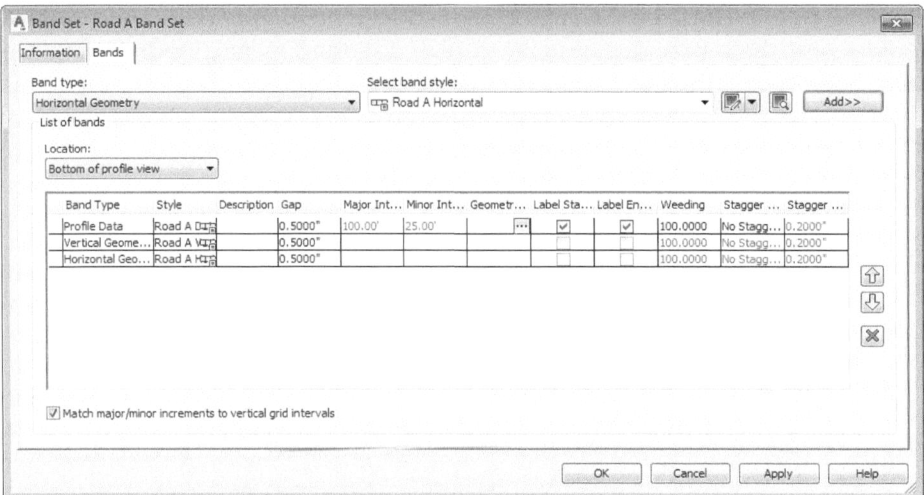

*Figure 6-73 The **Bands** tab of the **Band Set - Road A Band Set** dialog box*

10. Next, choose the **OK** button; the **Band Set - Road A Band Set** dialog box is closed and the **Road A Band Set** is added to the **Band Sets** node in the **Settings** tab.

Assigning the Band Set

1. Select the **Road A** profile view from the drawing and right-click; a shortcut menu is displayed.

2. Choose the **Profile View Properties** option from the shortcut menu, as shown in Figure 6-74; the **Profile View Properties - Road A** dialog box is displayed.

3. In this dialog box, choose the **Bands** tab, if it is not selected by default, and then choose the **Import band set** button; the **Band Set** dialog box is displayed.

4. In **Band Set** dialog box, select the **Road A Band Set** option from the drop-down list, as shown in Figure 6-75.

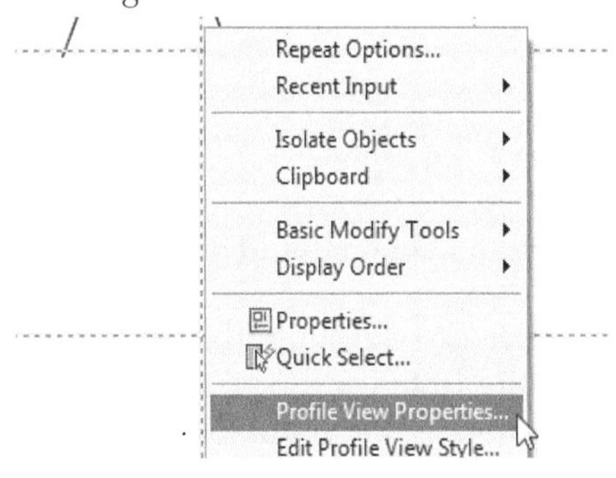

*Figure 6-74 Choosing the **Profile View Properties** option*

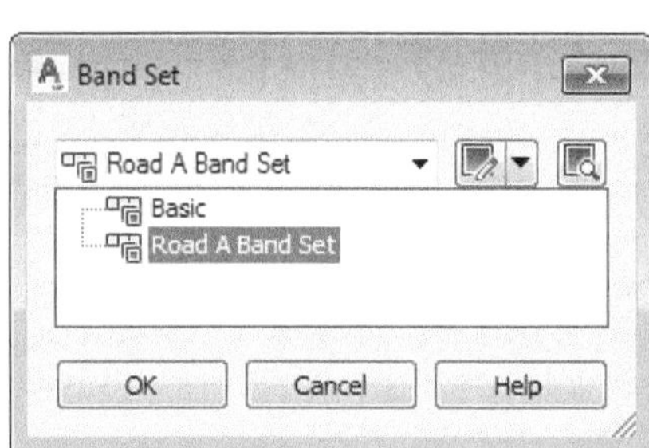

*Figure 6-75 Selecting the **Road A Band Set** option from the drop-down list*

5. Choose the **OK** button; the **Band Set** dialog box is closed and the band styles are added to the list box of the **Profile View Properties - Road A** dialog box.

6. Choose the **Apply** button to assign the band set styles to the profile view and then choose **OK** to close the dialog box. The bands are added to the drawing with the selected band styles, as shown in Figure 6-76.

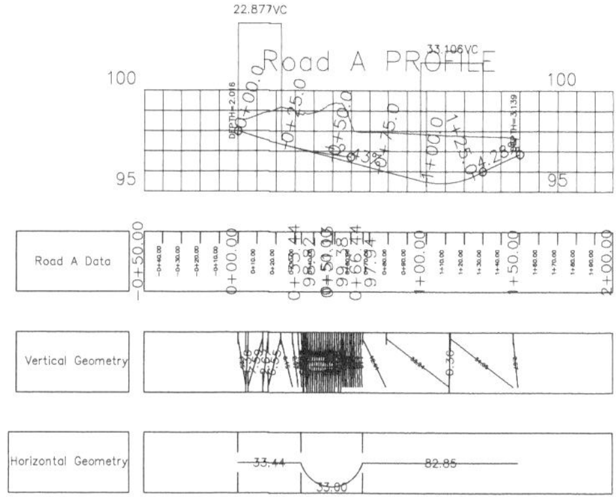

***Figure 6-76** The **Road A** profile view with the specified data bands added*

Note that the vertical geometry band added to the drawing contains data for surface profile and the band needs to display the data for design profile. In the next steps, you will modify the band style for vertical geometry band.

7. Select the **Road A** profile view from the drawing and right-click; a shortcut menu is displayed.

8. Choose **Profile View Properties** option from the shortcut menu displayed; the **Profile View Properties - Road A** dialog box is displayed.

9. Ensure that the **Bands** tab is selected. In the **List of bands** area, scroll to the right of the list box and click in the profile 1 field of the **Vertical Geometry** band type; a drop-down list is displayed.

10. Select **Road A** from the drop-down list and choose **OK**; the **Profile View Properties - Road A** dialog box is closed and the vertical geometry band is updated.

Saving the File

1. Choose **Save As** from the **Application Menu**; the **Save Drawing As** dialog box is displayed.

2. In this dialog box, browse to the following location:

   C:\c3d_2018\c06_c3d_2018_tut

3. In the **File name** edit box, enter **c06_tut05a**.

4. Next, choose the **Save** button; the file is saved with the name *c06_tut04a* at the specified location.

Tutorial 6 Editing Profiles

In this tutorial, you will edit the layout profile, as shown in Figure 6-77, using different editing methods. **(Expected time: 30 min)**

The following steps are required to complete this tutorial:

a. Download and open the file.
b. Use the **Profile Layout Parameters** dialog box and the **PANORAMA** window to edit the profile.
c. Edit the profile using the grip edits.
d. Save the file.

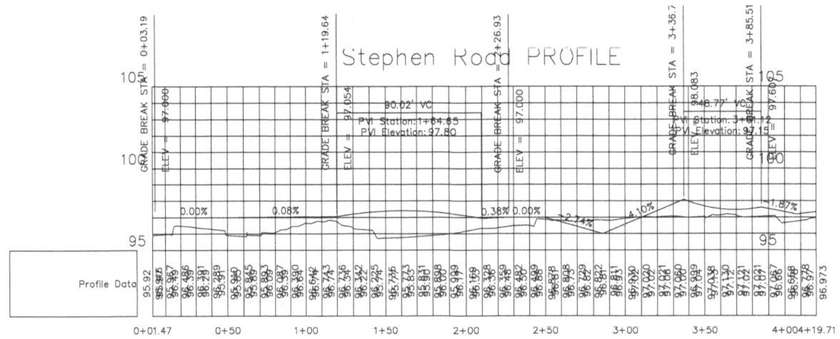

*Figure 6-77 The **Stephen Road Layout** profile*

Downloading and Opening the File

1. Download *c06_c3d_2018_tut.zip* file, if not downloaded earlier, from *http://www.cadcim.com*. Next, save and extract the file at *C:\c3d_2018*.

2. Choose **Open** from the **Application Menu**; the **Select File** dialog box is displayed.

3. In the dialog box, browse to the location *C:\c3d_2018\c06_c3d_2018_tut* folder.

4. Select the file *c06_c3d_2018_tut06.dwg* and then choose the **Open** button to open the file. Ignore any warnings if displayed. The drawing file consists of a TIN surface, **Surface 1**, the **Stephen Road** profile view, and a layout profile.

Editing the Profile Using the PANORAMA Window

1. In the **Stephen Road** profile view, select and right-click on the **Stephen layout** profile that is displayed in cyan color; a shortcut menu is displayed. Choose the **Edit Profile Geometry** option from the shortcut menu; the **Profile Layout Tools - Stephen layout** toolbar is displayed, as shown in Figure 6-78.

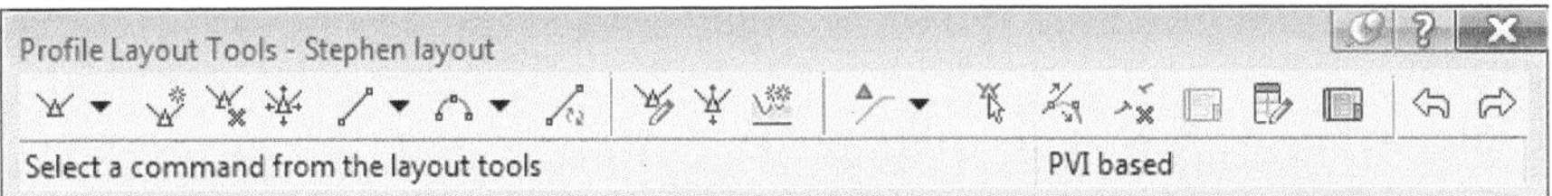

*Figure 6-78 The **Profile Layout Tools - Stephen layout** toolbar*

2. In this toolbar, choose the **Profile Layout Parameters** button; the **Profile Layout Parameters - Stephen layout** dialog box is displayed. 

3. Now, invoke the **Select PVI** tool from the toolbar and click near the PVI at station 0+55. On doing so, the **Profile Layout Parameters** dialog box is populated with the parameters of the selected PVI, as shown in Figure 6-79. 

Note

*The values shown for the **Geometry** property of the **Profile Layout Parameters - Stephen layout** may vary based on the PVI selected.*

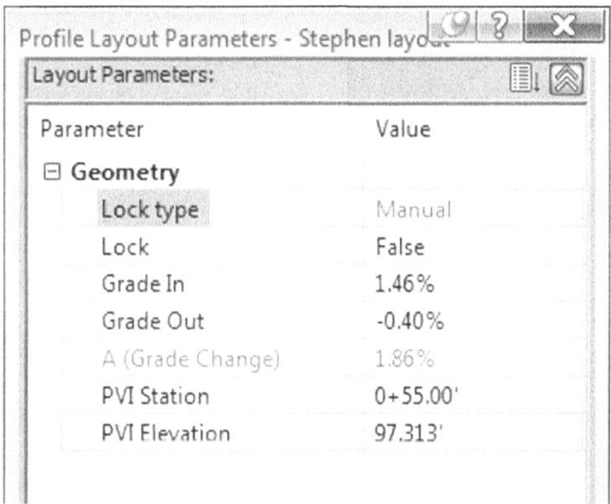

***Figure 6-79** The **Profile Layout Parameters - Stephen layout** dialog box displaying the parameters of the selected PVI*

4. Modify the value of the **PVI Elevation** parameter to **98.000'** and press ENTER.

Note

*You have modified the parameters of a single PVI using the **Profile Layout Parameters** dialog box. You can modify only those values that are highlighted in black color in this dialog box. The other values are derived from in-built mathematical calculations and therefore, cannot be modified.*

5. Next, close the **Profile Layout Parameters - Stephen layout** dialog box.

6. Next, choose the **Profile Grid View** button from the **Profile Layout Tools - Stephen layout** toolbar; the **PANORAMA** window with the **Profile Entities** tab is displayed. 

7. Enter **96.70** in the **Value** field of the **PVI Elevation** column for the first PVI station, as shown in Figure 6-80.

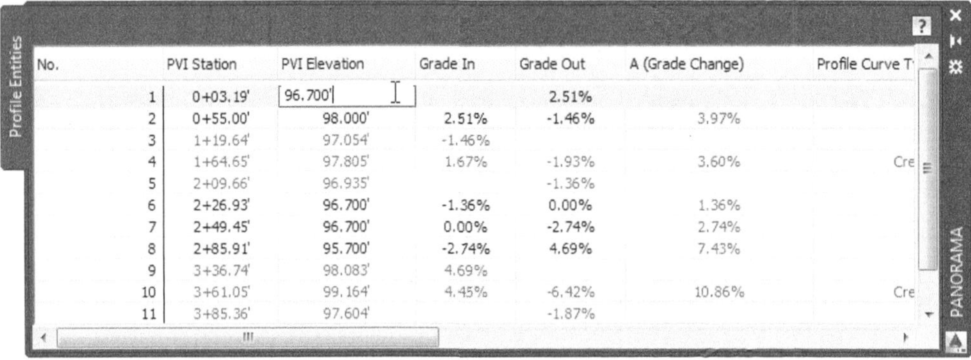

No.	PVI Station	PVI Elevation	Grade In	Grade Out	A (Grade Change)	Profile Curve T
1	0+03.19'	96.700'		2.51%		
2	0+55.00'	98.000'	2.51%	-1.46%	3.97%	
3	1+19.64'	97.054'	-1.46%			
4	1+64.65'	97.805'	1.67%	-1.93%	3.60%	Cre
5	2+09.66'	96.935'		-1.36%		
6	2+26.93'	96.700'	-1.36%	0.00%	1.36%	
7	2+49.45'	96.700'	0.00%	-2.74%	2.74%	
8	2+85.91'	95.700'	-2.74%	4.69%	7.43%	
9	3+36.74'	98.083'	4.69%			
10	3+61.05'	99.164'	4.45%	-6.42%	10.86%	Cre
11	3+85.36'	97.604'		-1.87%		

Figure 6-80 Modifying the PVI elevation value in the ***PANORAMA*** *window*

8. Modify the values of the 6th, 7th, and 8th **PVI Elevation** values to **97.000'** as done in the previous step and press ENTER.

9. Close the **PANORAMA** window.

10. Invoke the **Raise/Lower PVIs** tool from the **Profile Layout Tools - Stephen layout** toolbar; the **Raise/Lower PVI Elevation** dialog box is displayed, refer Figure 6-81.

11. Enter **-1.000'** in the **Elevation change** edit box and select the **Station range** radio button from the **PVI range** area.

12. Enter **2+50.00** and **3+00.00** in the **Start** and **End** edit boxes, respectively, to lower the elevation value of the PVIs that lie within the specified station range.

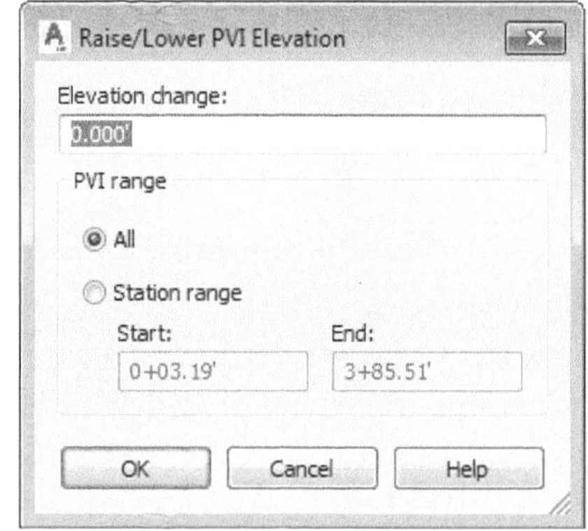

Figure 6-81 The ***Raise/Lower PVI Elevation*** *dialog box*

13. Choose the **OK** button; the dialog box is closed and the PVIs are lowered by the value specified in the **Elevation change** edit box.

Note

You can specify a positive value in the ***Elevation change*** *edit box to raise the elevation of PVIs.*

Editing the Profile Using the Profile Layout Parameters Dialog Box

1. Click on the down-arrow on the right of the **PVI based** button in the **Profile Layout - Stephen layout** toolbar and choose the **Entity based** option from the flyout displayed, as shown in Figure 6-82.

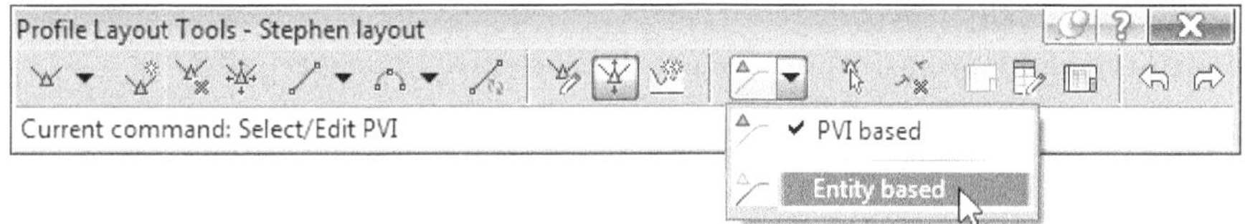

*Figure 6-82 Selecting the **Entity based** option from the flyout*

2. Now, choose the **Profile Layout Parameters** button from the **Profile Layout Tools - Stephen layout** toolbar; the **Profile Layout Parameters** dialog box is displayed.

3. Choose the **Select Entity** button from the **Profile Layout Tools** toolbar. 

4. Select the curve from the profile view. On selecting the curve, the **Profile Layout Parameters** dialog box is populated with the selected curve parameters, refer to Figure 6-83.

5. Enter **2500.000'** in the **Value** field of the **Curve Radius** parameter, as shown in Figure 6-83, and press ENTER.

6. Close the **Profile Layout Parameters** dialog box and press ESC to exit.

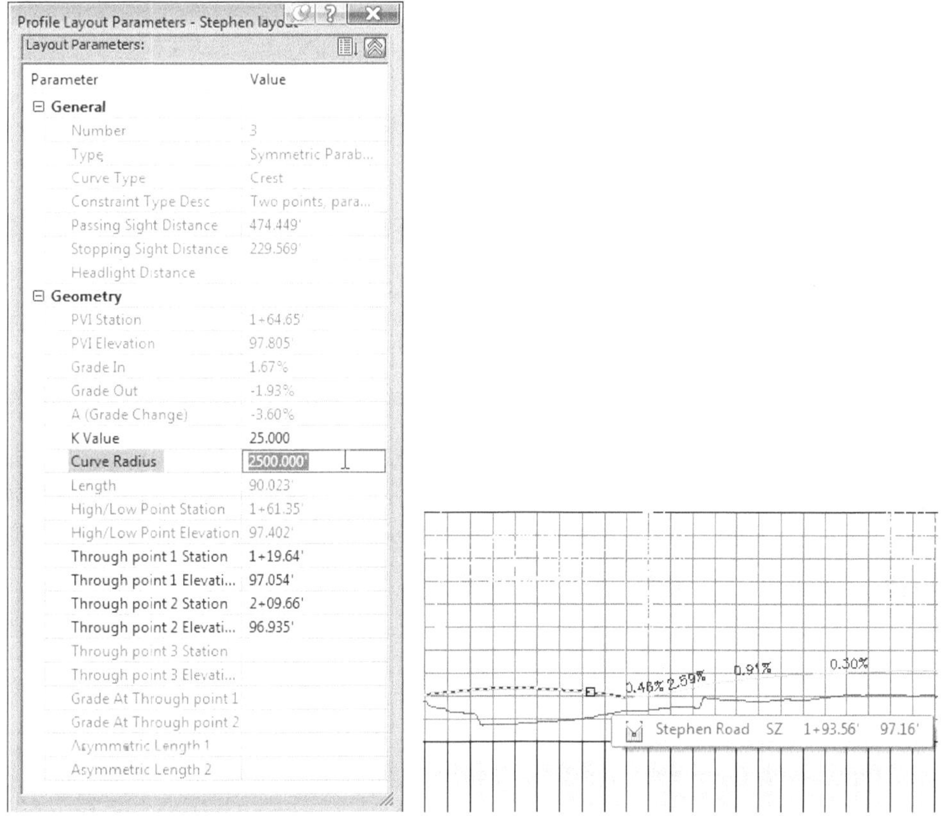

*Figure 6-83 The value **2500.00'** entered in the **Curve Radius** parameter*

Editing Profile Using Grips

1. Select the **Stephen layout** profile; the profile grips are displayed.

2. Select the circular grip of the curve at the end of the profile and drag the cursor upward.

3. Now, click in the profile view, refer to Figure 6-84; the elevation is modified for the selected PVI. Press ESC to exit.

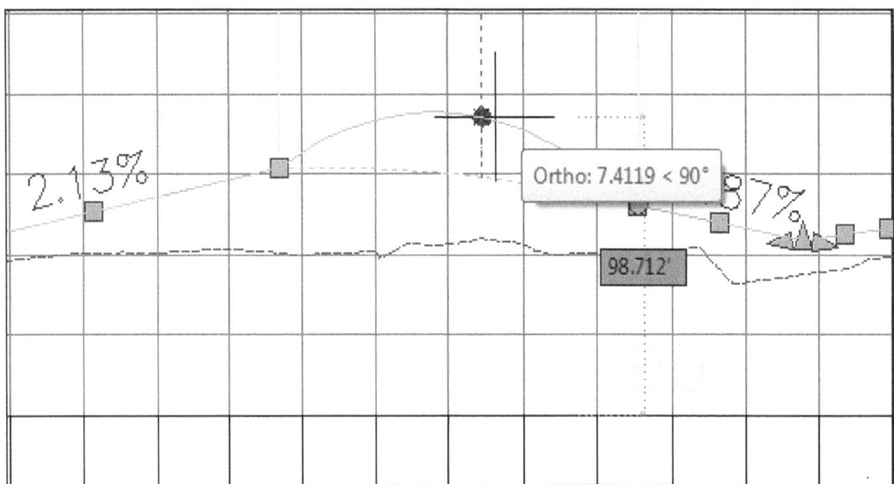

Figure 6-84 *Selecting the circular curve grip*

Saving the File

1. Choose **Save As** from the **Application Menu**; the **Save Drawing As** dialog box is displayed.

2. In this dialog box, browse to the following location:

   C:\c3d_2018\c06_c3d_2018_tut

3. In the **File name** edit box, enter **c06_tut06a**.

4. Next, choose the **Save** button; the file is saved with the name *c06_tut06a.dwg* at the specified location.

Self-Evaluation Test

Answer the following questions and then compare them to those given at the end of this chapter:

1. Which of the following tools in the **Profile Layout Tools** toolbar is used to specify the curve parameters to be used with the **Draw Tangents with Curves** tool?

   a) **Curve Settings** b) **Fixed Vertical Curve (Three Points)**
   c) **Free Circular Curve (PVI Based)** d) **Free Vertical Curve - Best Fit**

2. Which of the following is achieved by using the **Create Superimposed Profile** tool?

   a) Show one profile in relation to another
   b) Hide the overlaid profile
   c) Create profiles from two different surfaces
   d) None of these

3. Which of the following profile view parameters can be edited using the **Profile View Properties** dialog box?

   a) Information, summary, profile and station
   b) Name, Hatch
   c) Information, stations, elevation, profiles, bands and hatch
   d) Information

4. Which of the following objects can be used to create profiles using the **Quick Profile** tool?

   a) Corridor
   b) Alignment
   c) Line, arc, polyline, or points
   d) Sample lines

5. Which of the following is a graphical representation of the surface elevations along a horizontal alignment?

   a) Alignment
   b) Profile
   c) Cross Section
   d) Assembly

6. The criteria-based design feature allows a __________ profile to be created according to the design standards.

7. The __________ dialog box is used to create the surface profile.

8. The __________ dialog box helps you create a temporary profile to view elevation information along a line, polyline, feature or lot line, survey figure, or surface.

9. In the __________ edit box, you can specify a positive value to increase or a negative value to decrease the elevation of a profile or a PVIs.

10. The __________ tool is used to change the elevation of a profile.

11. You can add labels to a profile view by using the __________ dialog box.

12. You can create a layout profile by choosing the **Profile Creation Tools** tool from the **Create Design** panel. (T/F)

13. The **Profile Style - New Profile Style** dialog box is used to create a new profile style. (T/F)

14. Profiles represent surface levels or elevations at different intervals along a horizontal alignment. (T/F)

15. A profile view does not control the grid in which the profile is displayed. (T/F)

Review Questions

Answer the following questions:

1. The __________ dialog box is used to view the properties of a selected profile.

2. The ___________button is used to insert the PVI data numerically.

3. The display and appearance of a profile is controlled by the __________.

4. The __________ style controls the display of the grid representation of the profiles.

5. You can view the new band style in the **Settings** tab by expanding the **Profile View > Band Styles >** __________nodes.

6. You can specify the start station and end station values in the __________ area of the **Station Range** page in the **Create Profile View wizard**.

7. The __________ dialog box is used to add the profile view labels.

8. The ___________ dialog box is used to view and modify the layout parameters of the selected profile component.

9. One of the easiest methods of editing the geometry of a profile is by using the __________ window.

10. Civil 3D has separate in-built styles for both profile and profile view. (T/F)

EXERCISES

1. Log on to *www.cadcim.com* and browse to *Textbooks > Civil/GIS > Civil 3D > Exploring AutoCAD Civil 3D 2018*. Next, select *c06_c3d_2018_exer.zip* file from the **Exercise Files** drop-down list. Choose the corresponding **Download** button to download the data file.

2. Now, save and extract the downloaded folder to the following location:

   C:\c3d_2018

Note

*While opening the exercise files, the **PANORAMA** window may appear with an error message. Close this window to proceed further.*

Exercise 1

Open the *c06_c3d_2018_ex01.dwg* file and create a split profile using the parameters given next.
(Expected time: 30 min)

1. Profile view name: **ST. Road**
2. Profile view height: Minimum: **94.483'** Maximum: **101.483'**
3. Split profile view: **Default settings**
4. Save the drawing as *c06_ex01a*.

Exercise 2

Open the *c06_c3d_2018_ex02.dwg* file and create a layout profile using the following tools and parameters:
(Expected time: 30 min)

1. Profile name: **Road A**
2. Profile style: **Default**
3. Profile label set: **Default**

Profile Layout Tools:

Curve: **Fixed Vertical Curve (Two points, parameter)**
Curve type: **Crest**
Curve radius: **35**

Answers to Self-Evaluation Test

1. a, **2**. a, **3**. c, **4**. c, **5**. b, **6**. Layout, **7. Create Profile from Surface**, **8. Create Quick Profiles**, **9. Elevation change**, **10. Raise/Lower PVIs**, **11. Add Labels**, **12.** T, **13.** T, **14.** T, **15.** F

Chapter 7

Working with Assemblies and Subassemblies

Learning Objectives

After completing this chapter, you will be able to:

- *Understand and create assemblies*
- *Create different assembly styles*
- *Use codes*
- *Understand subassemblies*
- *Create customized subassemblies*
- *Create styles for the subassembly components*

INTRODUCTION TO ASSEMBLIES AND SUBASSEMBLIES

After creating alignments and profiles, you will learn to create assemblies that are required to create a road model. A road model or corridor is formed by the combination of alignments, surface, and assemblies (discussed in next chapter). After designing the horizontal and vertical alignments of a roadway, you will now learn to define the cross-section of the roadway using assemblies.

An assembly is a collection of smaller units called subassemblies. These subassemblies are parametric in nature and are the building blocks of any road cross-section. A typical road section assembly consists of subassemblies such as lanes, sidewalks, and curbs. Figure 7-1 shows a road assembly cross-section.

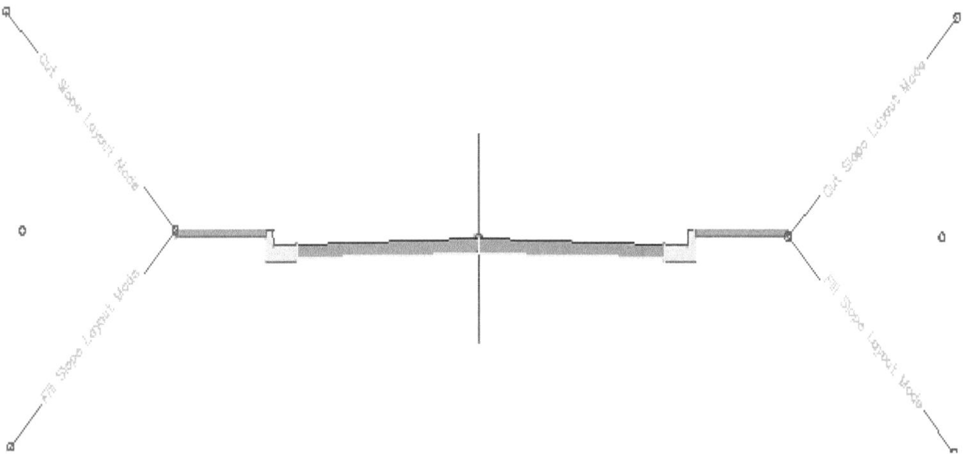

Figure 7-1 *A typical road assembly cross-section*

The subassemblies are attached to the left and right of the assembly and have some parameters associated with them. These parameters can be modified as per the requirements of the project. In short, assemblies together with subassemblies form the basic components of a road or other alignment based designs.

ASSEMBLIES

An assembly is a Civil 3D object that consists of subassemblies. The subassemblies are used to form the basic structure of a corridor. An assembly has a baseline with an attachment point indicated by a marker. A subassembly is attached to the baseline using this attachment point. Subassembly objects also have attachment points, that can be used to attach one subassembly to another.

Components of an Assembly

The primary components of an assembly are baseline and subassemblies. An assembly can also have a baseline point, insertion point, and offset line. The main components of assembly are discussed next.

Insertion Point

The insertion point is the first point specified for creating the assembly. This point helps you to define the center line of the final corridor.

Baseline

Baseline is a vertical line with a marker in an assembly.

Baseline Point

The baseline point (marker) is a point on the baseline where you can attach the first subassembly. The baseline point and the insertion point always coincide with each other.

Offset Line

The offset line is a vertical line with a marker which passes through the offset point.

Offset Point

The offset point represents the ground reference point of the assembly along with a specified offset alignment. The subassemblies attached to this point follow the offset alignment.

Creating Assemblies

Ribbon: Home > Create Design > Assembly drop-down > Create Assembly
Command: CREATEASSEMBLY

To create an assembly, choose the **Create Assembly** tool from the **Create Design** panel; the **Create Assembly** dialog box will be displayed, as shown in Figure 7-2.

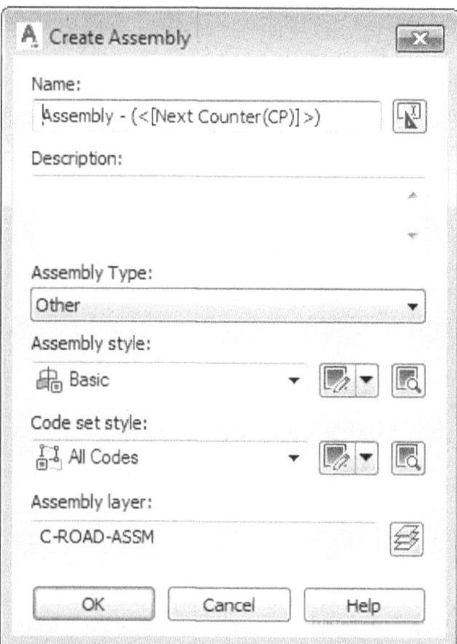

Figure 7-2 *The* ***Create Assembly*** *dialog box*

Specify a name for the assembly in the **Name** edit box. Optionally, you can enter a description for the assembly in the **Description** edit box. Select the assembly type from the **Assembly Type** drop-down list. Select the assembly style from the **Assembly style** drop-down list. In the **Assembly layer** option, specify the layer in which the assembly will be created. Next, choose the **OK** button; the dialog box will be closed and you will be prompted to specify the location for the assembly baseline. Click on the screen to specify the location of the assembly baseline. On doing so, the assembly baseline, as shown in Figure 7-3, will be displayed at the specified location in the drawing.

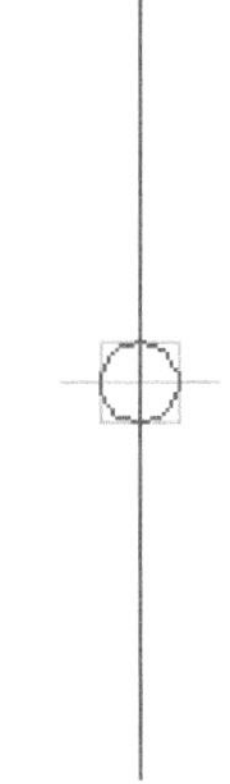

Figure 7-3 An assembly baseline

After creating an assembly, you need to add the subassemblies. AutoCAD Civil 3D has various in-built subassemblies which are parametric and can be modified as required. Apart from the in-built parametric assemblies, AutoCAD Civil 3D also allows you to create customized subassemblies from polylines. The in-built subassemblies can be selected from the **TOOL PALETTES**. To select subassemblies, choose the **Tool Palettes** button from the **Palettes** panel of the **Home** tab; the **TOOLPALETTES-CIVIL IMPERIAL SUBASSEMBLIES** palette will be displayed, as shown in Figure 7-4. Next, choose and place the required subassembly from the **TOOL PALETTES**; the **PROPERTIES** window will be displayed, as shown in Figure 7-5.

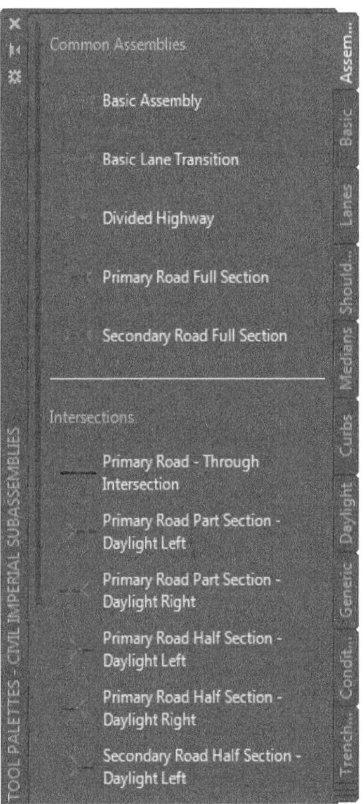

*Figure 7-4 The **TOOL PALETTES-CIVIL IMPERIAL SUBASSEMBLIES** palette*

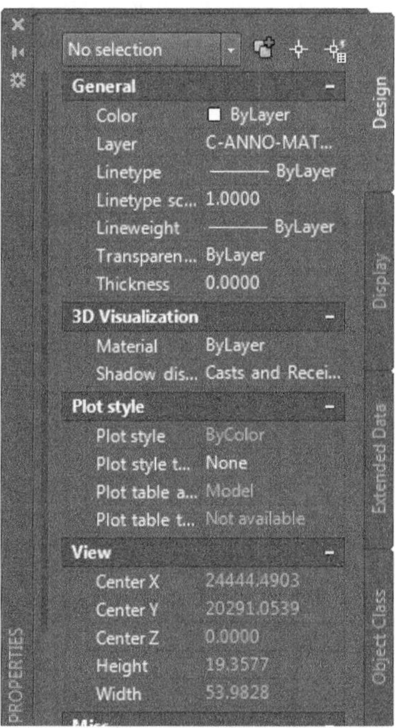

*Figure 7-5 The **PROPERTIES** window of a subassembly*

You can also change the parameters of a subassembly. To do so, select the subassembly and right-click; a shortcut menu is displayed. From this menu, select the **Properties** option. In this window, the **ADVANCED** rollout of the **Design** tab displays the basic parameters of the selected subassembly. The **Side** parameter specifies the side on which the subassembly will be attached. If you want to add the subassembly to the right of the baseline, set the **Side** parameter to **Right**. The **Width** and **Depth** parameters specify the width and depth of the subassembly, respectively. You can modify the values of these parameters as required. In the command line, you will be prompted to select the marker point to attach the subassembly. Click on the marker of the baseline; the subassembly will be attached to the assembly baseline on the side specified in the **Side** parameter. You can change the **Side** parameter to **Left** and attach the subassembly to the left of the baseline marker. Figure 7-6 shows the subassemblies attached to both sides of an assembly baseline.

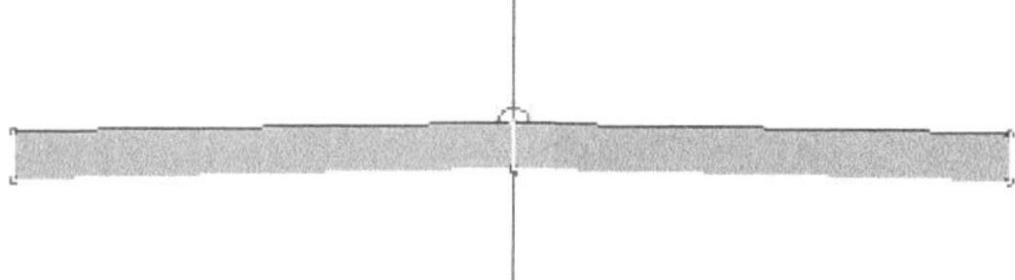

Figure 7-6 *An assembly baseline with the* ***BasicLane Transition*** *subassemblies attached on both sides*

Note

AutoCAD Civil 3D allows you to use the AutoCAD commands such as ***Copy****,* ***Paste****, and* ***Mirror*** *for editing the subassemblies. For example, you can use the* ***Mirror*** *command to replicate the existing subassemblies on the other side of an assembly baseline.*

To create an independent or a detached subassembly, select the required subassembly from the **TOOL PALETTES**; you will be prompted to select marker point within the assembly. Enter **D** to create the detached subassembly and press ENTER; you will be prompted to specify a location for the subassembly. Click on the screen to specify the location for the subassembly; the subassembly will be placed independent of the assembly baseline. Also, you will notice that every subassembly has circular markers at the corners. These markers help you attach the subassemblies with each other at the exact location.

Tip

You can also use the keyboard shortcut CTRL + 3 to open the ***TOOL PALETTES****.*

Similarly, specify the **Side** parameter and then select the circular markers to which the subassemblies will be attached. Figure 7-7 shows a road assembly consisting of different subassemblies.

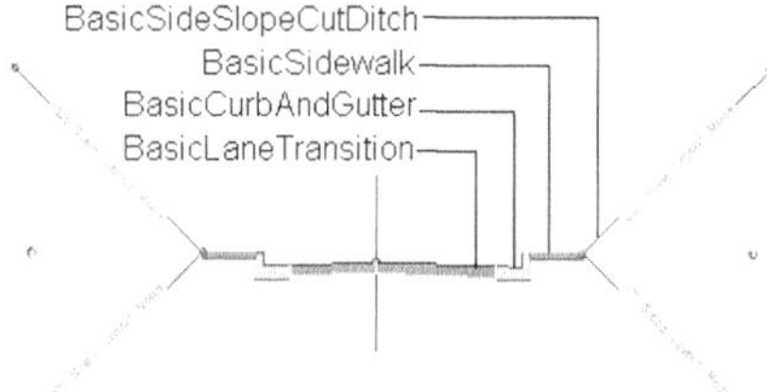

Figure 7-7 *A road assembly consisting of different subassemblies*

The assemblies that you create will be listed in the **Prospector** tab of the **TOOLSPACE** in the **Assemblies** node with the name you assign to them.

Assembly Properties

To access the assembly properties, choose the **Prospector** tab in the **TOOLSPACE**. Expand the **Assemblies** node. Right-click on the existing assembly in the node and choose the **Properties** option from the shortcut menu displayed; the **Assembly Properties - <Assembly Name>** dialog box will be displayed, refer to Figure 7-8.

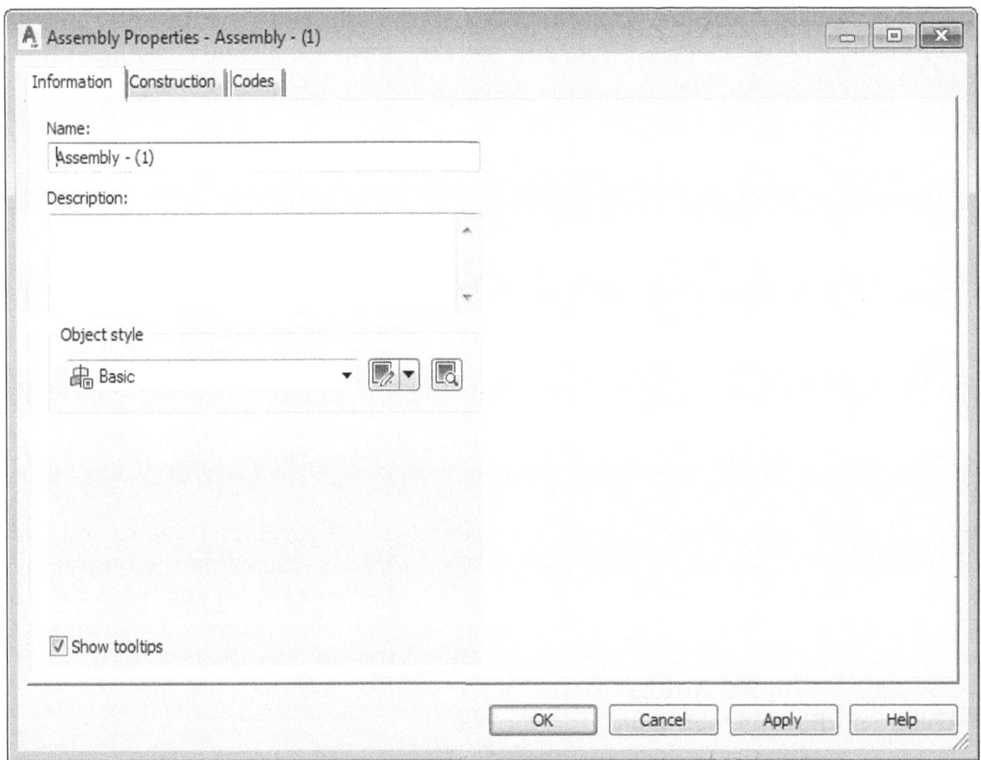

*Figure 7-8 The **Assembly Properties - Assembly - (1)** dialog box*

You can modify the name of the assembly in the **Name** edit box. Optionally, you can specify a description for the assembly in the **Description** edit box. Select the required option from the drop-down list in the **Object style** area to specify the style.

Choose the **Construction** tab to view and edit the subassemblies that constitute the assembly. You can select an option from the **Assembly Type** drop-down list to specify the type of assembly to be created. The **Item** area lists the subassemblies under two groups, on the left and right sides of the assembly. It displays the organizational hierarchy in the order in which the subassemblies are processed or added to the assembly. Select the subassembly from the **Item** area; the parameters of the selected subassembly will be displayed in the **Input values** area, as shown in Figure 7-9.

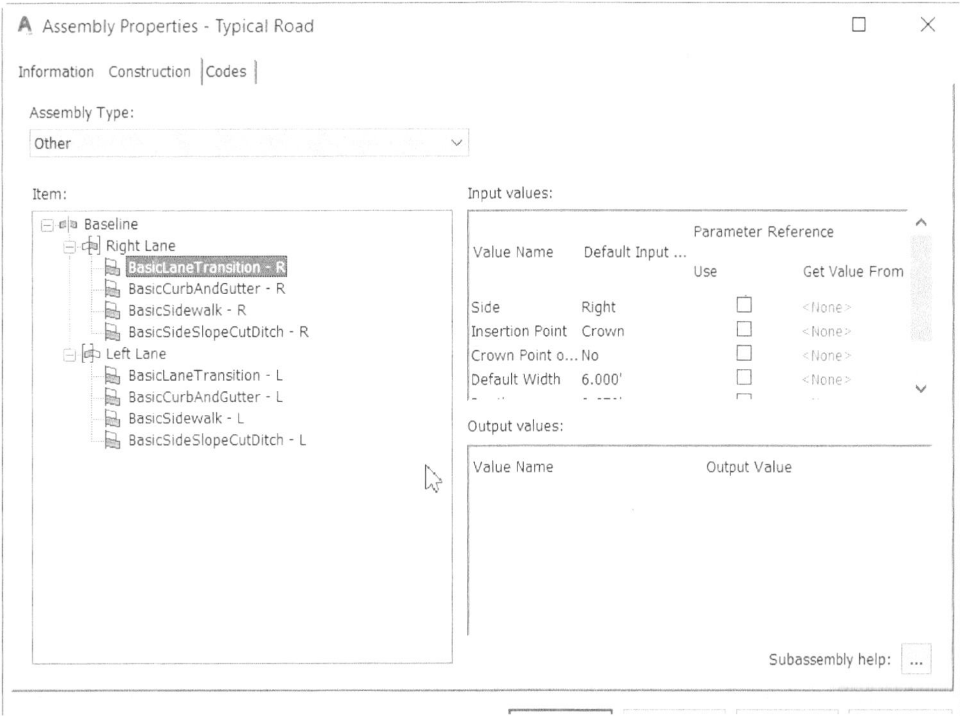

***Figure 7-9** The **Construction** tab displaying the input values of the selected subassembly*

The **Value Name** and **Default Input Value** columns of the **Input values** area display the names and default values of all the input parameters of the selected subassembly. To modify a non numeric value, such as **Side**, click on the corresponding value cell of the required parameter; the **Pick Default Value** dialog box will be displayed, refer to Figure 7-10.

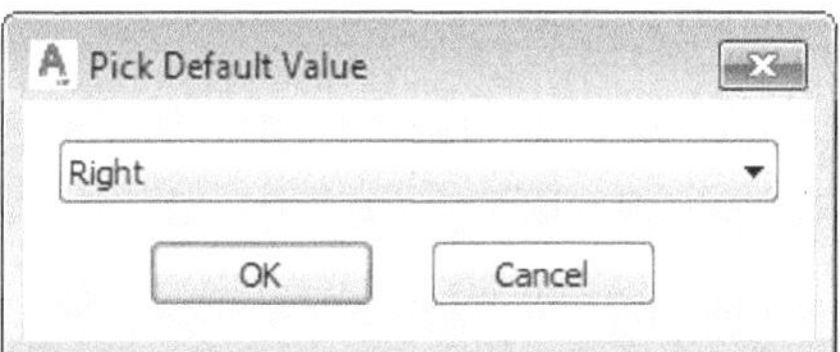

***Figure 7-10** The **Pick Default Value** dialog box*

Select the required option from the drop-down list in the **Pick Default Value** dialog box and then choose the **OK** button to exit. To modify a numeric value, click on the value cell of the respective parameter and enter the value. The **Parameter Reference** column in the **Assembly Properties** dialog box specifies the values referred to as the input parameters. Select the check box in the **Use** column for the required parameter. Civil 3D allows you to use the output value of other subassemblies as the input parameter value for the selected subassembly. Click in the **Get Value From** column and select the required output value from the drop-down list. To view details about the required subassembly, choose the **Subassembly help** button; the AutoCAD help window will be displayed. This window gives detailed information about the selected subassembly and its properties.

To delete a subassembly, select it from the **Item** list area and right-click on it. Choose the **Delete** option from the shortcut menu displayed. Next, choose the **Apply** button; the selected subassembly will be deleted. Similarly, you can rename the required subassembly by selecting the **Rename** option from the shortcut menu.

In the **Assembly Properties** dialog box, choose the **Codes** tab to view the styles of the codes associated with the assembly. The codes are explained in detail later in this chapter. After viewing and modifying the assembly properties, choose the **OK** button to save the changes and exit the dialog box.

Assembly Styles

Like other Civil 3D objects, assemblies also have styles that control the display of the assemblies. The assembly styles are listed in the **Assembly** node of the **Settings** tab of the **TOOLSPACE**. You can create a new assembly style or edit the existing assembly style using the **Settings** tab.

Creating a New Assembly Style

To create a new assembly style, choose the **Settings** tab and expand the **Assembly** node. Right-click on the **Assembly Styles** subnode and choose **New** from the shortcut menu displayed; the **Assembly Style - New Assembly Style** dialog box will be displayed. By default, the **Information** tab will be chosen in the dialog box. In this tab, specify a name for the assembly style in the **Name** edit box. Optionally, you can specify the description about the assembly in the **Description** edit box.

Next, choose the **Marker** tab. This tab is used to specify the display settings of the assembly components. From the **Component** drop-down list of this tab, select the required assembly component for which you want to change the display settings, refer to Figure 7-11.

After selecting the required component, select the marker style and specify the size of the marker. For the **Insertion Point**, **Baseline Point**, and **Offset Point** components, you can use different options for the display of the marker. Select the **Use AutoCAD POINT for marker** radio button to enable Civil 3D to use the AutoCAD point as the marker for the selected component. Select the **Use custom marker** radio button to select a custom marker style. You can also select the **Use AutoCAD BLOCK symbol for marker** radio button and select the AutoCAD block from the list box to be used as a marker. After specifying the marker style, set the marker size by choosing the required options from the **Size** area. Choose the **Display** tab to specify the view direction, visibility, and other display properties of the assembly components. You can turn off the visibility of any assembly component as well as modify its color and other properties. The **Summary** tab lists the information about the style used for assembly. Choose the **OK** button; the **Assembly Style** dialog box will be closed and the assembly style will be added in the **Assembly Styles** subnode of the **Assembly** node.

To edit the style of an existing assembly, expand **Assembly > Assembly Styles** subnode in the **Settings** tab of the **TOOLSPACE**. Right-click on the existing assembly style; a shortcut menu will be displayed. Choose **Edit** from the shortcut menu; the **Assembly Style - <name>** dialog box will be displayed for the selected style. Modify the settings for the existing assembly style and choose the **Apply** button to view the changes in the assembly. Next, choose the **OK** button to accept the changes and close the dialog box.

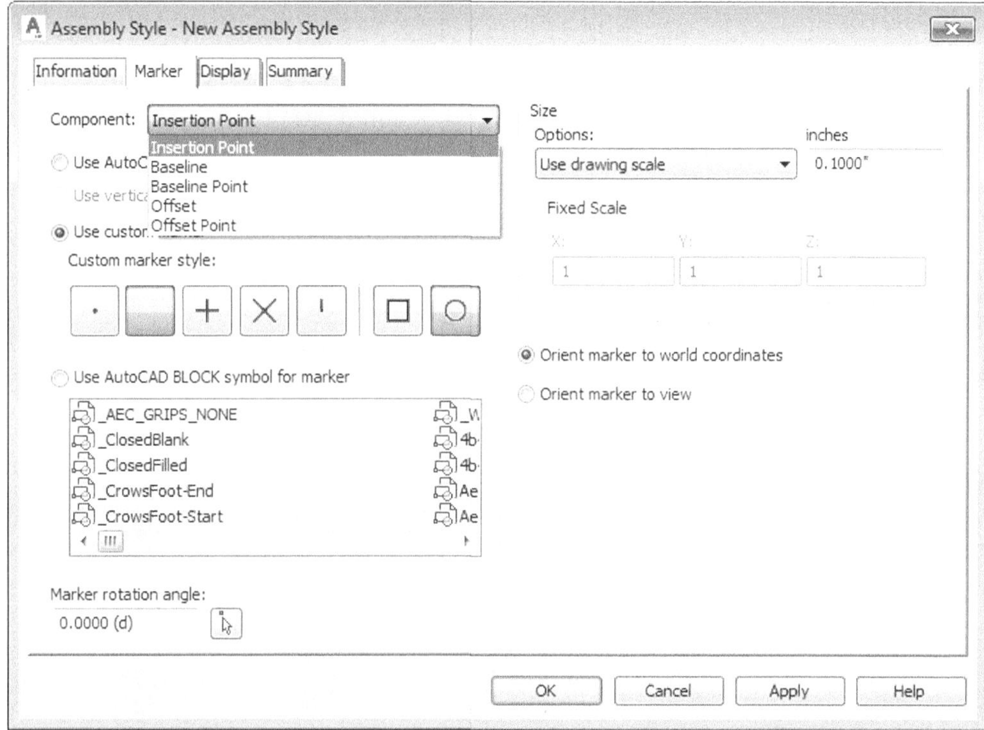

*Figure 7-11 Selecting the required assembly component from the **Component** drop-down list*

USING CODES

Codes are used to display parameters of three main components of a subassembly namely, points, links, and shapes. These components are assigned with some values (annotation, style, labels) that are called codes. Codes identify the point, link, and shape in a subassembly and form the basic component of the three-dimensional corridor model. These codes also help create and arrange assemblies. There are three types of subassembly codes and they are discussed next.

Point Codes

Point codes define the vertices or the end points of a subassembly. These end points or vertices are called assembly points. For example, each crown point on a corridor will have the same point code and likewise, points on the edge of a pavement will have the same point code. These codes also help you create an offset or elevation label in road cross-sections. Figure 7-12 shows the points, links, and shapes in a subassembly.

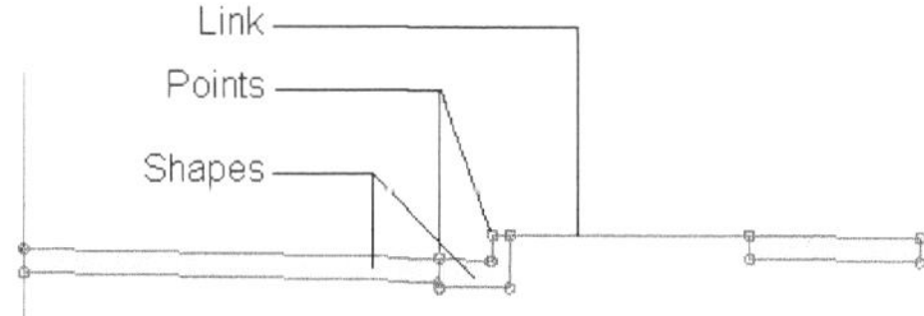

Figure 7-12 Points, links, and shapes in a subassembly

Link Codes

Links are basic lines that are used to join the points of a subassembly. These lines then connect with each other to form a planar structural surface of a corridor. Link codes are the codes assigned to the line segments joining the points. There are different types of link codes such as the Top link, Base link code, Datum link code, and Sub base link code. The Top link code connects all the points on the finished grade surface. Similarly, the Base link connects all the points located on the base layer. The link codes help you create grade or slope labels.

The link codes are used for tasks such as grading, visualization, and earthwork and volume calculations. You can use the links of a paved surface, finished grade surface, or sub-base surface and extract the required information from these links joining the point of a subassembly. In a subassembly, the points are represented by circles and the links are represented by straight lines joining the points.

Shape Codes

Shape of a subassembly is defined as a 2D closed area created by combining points and links. Shapes can represent a curb, sidewalk, pavement, and so on. The shape codes are used for quantity calculations based on the area of the shapes. Shape codes are used to identify the material and the hatch patterns.

Figure 7-13 shows the assembly with the point, link, and shape codes. The point codes are represented by P, the link codes by L, and the shape codes are represented by the name of the shape of the subassembly.

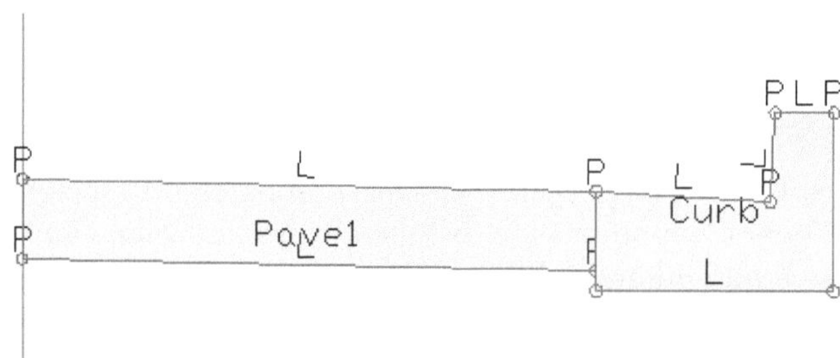

Figure 7-13 *Subassembly with the point (P), link (L), and shape codes*

The representation of these codes depends upon the code style assigned to them. You can use the in-built code styles or create your own customized code styles for an assembly, subassembly, or corridor. There are about 48 standard point codes, 18 standard link codes, and 10 standard shape codes that can be used in AutoCAD Civil 3D for representing subassemblies and corridor modeling.

Code Set Styles

Code set styles are similar to label set style or band set styles that have been explained in the earlier chapters. Code set style is a collection or a set of multiple code styles that are created and applied to objects once. You can create a customized style for links, points, or shape. You can add them in a code set and then add the styles together to a subassembly object. You can also create a label style for these components and add them to the code set. The code set styles are created and managed in the **Settings** tab of the **TOOLSPACE**. The code set styles are listed under the **Code Set Styles** subnode in the **Multipurpose Styles** node of the **General** node in the **Settings** tab, as shown in Figure 7-14. Before you create a code set style, create a style for different components of the subassembly such as point style, shape, and so on. You can then add these multiple styles in a code set to create a code set style.

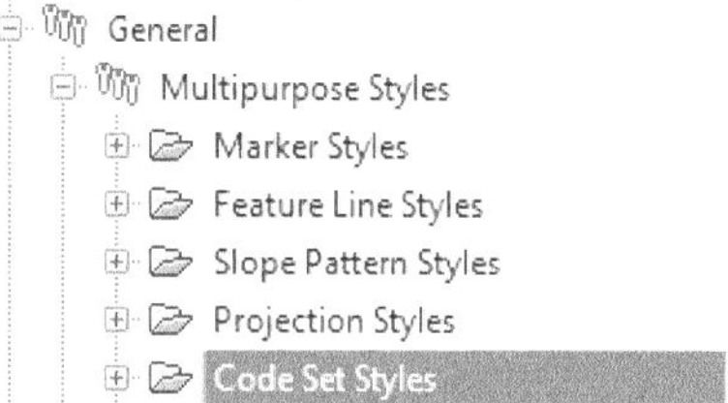

Figure 7-14 The ***Code Set Styles*** *subnode*

Creating a Point Style

To create a new style for the subassembly point, choose the **Settings** tab of the **TOOLSPACE**. Next, expand **General > Multipurpose Styles > Marker Styles** subnode in the **Settings** tab. Now, right-click on the **Marker Styles** node and choose **New** from the shortcut menu displayed; the **Marker Style - New Marker Style** dialog box will be displayed, as shown in Figure 7-15.

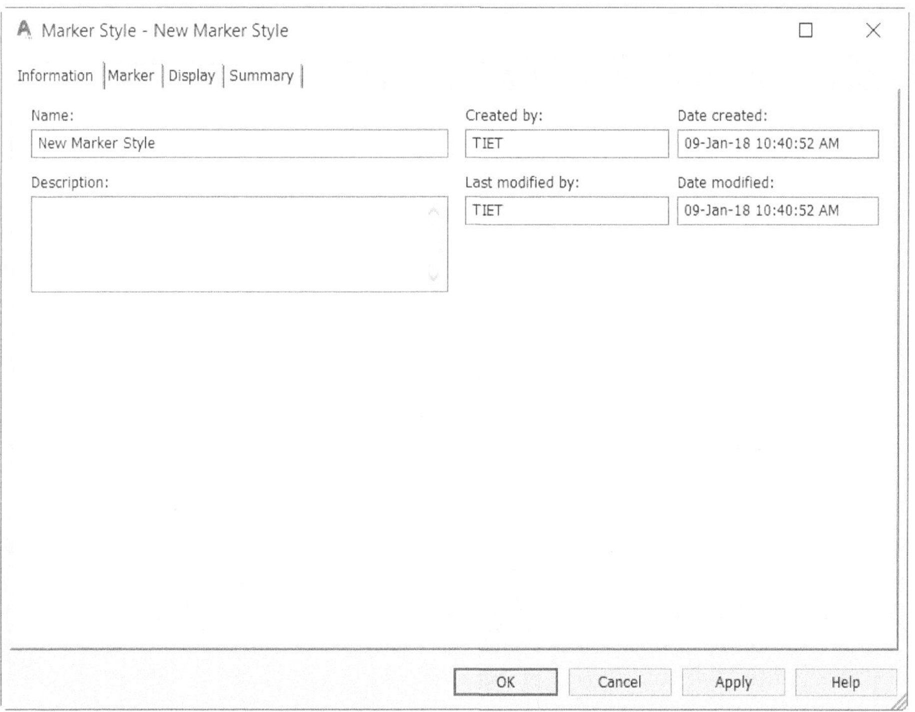

Figure 7-15 The ***Marker Style - New Marker Style*** *dialog box*

In this dialog box, the **Information** tab is chosen by default. The **Name** edit box in this tab is used to specify a name for the new style. By default, the **New Marker Style** text is displayed in this edit box. You can also enter description for the new style in the **Description** edit box. Next, choose the **Marker** tab. Choose the required marker style to display the subassembly points from the options given in this tab. Set the size of the marker using the options in the **Size** area.

After defining the marker style, choose the **Display** tab. In this tab, you can specify display options. Select a view direction from the **View Direction** drop-down list and set the visibility, color, lineweight, and layer for the marker in the selected view direction. Next, choose the **Summary** tab to review or modify some values, if required. Now, choose the **OK** button; the dialog box will be closed and the point style will be added to the **Markers Styles** subnode in the **Settings** tab.

Creating Links and Shape Styles

To create a new link style, expand **General > Multipurpose Style > Link Styles** subnode in the **Settings** tab of the **TOOLSPACE**. Right-click on the **Link Styles** subnode in the **Settings** tab and choose the **New** option from the shortcut menu; the **Link Style - New Link Style** dialog box will be displayed with three tabs, namely **Information**, **Display**, and **Summary**. You can use this dialog box to create a new style similar to the ones you created for the point style. The new styles will be listed in the respective **Link Styles** subnode of the **Settings** tab.

To create a new shape style, expand **General > Multipurpose Style > Shape Styles** subnode in the **Settings** tab of the **TOOLSPACE**. Right-click on the **Shape Styles** subnode in the **Settings** tab and choose the **New** option from the shortcut menu; the **Shape Style - New Shape Style** dialog box will be displayed. You can use this dialog box to create a new style. The new styles will be listed in the respective **Shape Styles** subnode of the **Settings** tab.

Creating Label Styles

You can also create label styles for point, link and shape components. The label styles control the display of labels and annotations used for these components. You can create label style for point, link, and shape. These labels represent the codes assigned to these components. They are created and managed in the **Settings** tab of the **TOOLSPACE**.

Creating a Point Code Label Style

To create a label style for the point code, expand **General > Label Styles > Marker** subnode in the **Settings** tab of the **TOOLSPACE**. Next, right-click on the **Marker** subnode to display a shortcut menu and choose the **New** option from the shortcut menu displayed; the **Label Style Composer - New Subassembly Marker Label Style** dialog box will be displayed.

In this dialog box, the **Information** tab is chosen by default. Enter a name and description of the point label style in the **Name** and **Description** edit boxes of this tab, respectively. Next, choose the **Layout** tab to display the properties of the label style. By default, the **Text** option is selected in the **Component name** drop-down list. You can select other options from this drop-down list. The properties of the **Text** component of the label style are listed in the **Property** column. You can modify the **General** and **Text** properties of the label style. To display a border around the label, set the value of the **Visibility** property to **True** in the **Border** category. You can also add new components for the label style by using the **Text Component Editor - Contents** dialog box, as shown in Figure 7-16. To do so, click in the **Value** field of the **Contents** property; a browse button will be displayed. Choose the browse button; the **Text Component Editor - Contents** dialog box will be displayed. In this dialog box, you can select the required option from the **Properties** drop-down list in the **Properties** tab and add it to the text editor. Choose the **OK** button to close the dialog box.

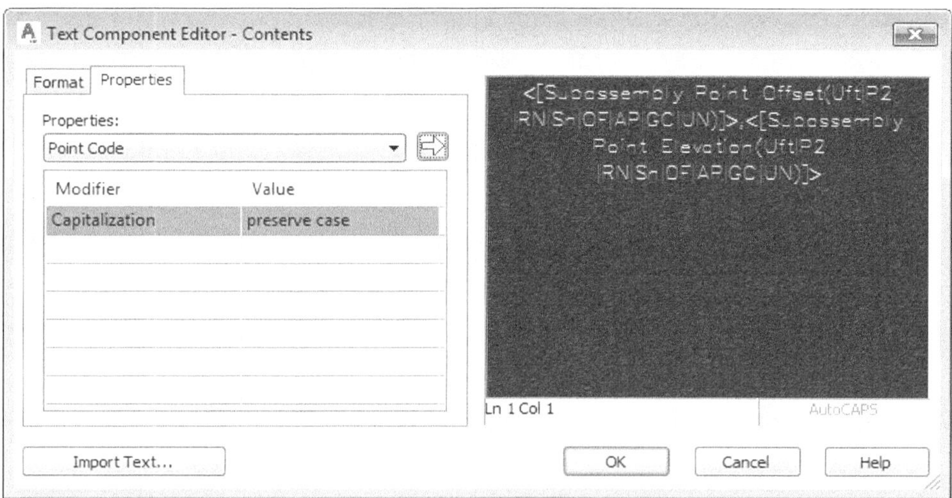

Figure 7-16 The ***Text Component Editor - Contents*** *dialog box*

Choose the **Dragged State** tab in the **Label Style Composer** dialog box. Modify the values of the label style properties as required. These properties determine how a label will be displayed when it is dragged. Choose the **Summary** tab to review the settings and modify the values if required. You can modify the values that are given in black color only. Choose the **OK** button; the dialog box will be closed and the label style will be added in the **Marker** subnode of the **Label Styles** node in the **Settings** tab.

Creating a Label Style for the Link or Shape Codes

To create a label style for the link or shape codes, right-click on the respective **Link** or **Shape** subnode in the **Label Styles** node in the **Settings** tab; a shortcut menu will be displayed. Choose **New** from the shortcut menu; the corresponding **Label Style Composer - New Subassembly Link Label Style** or the **Label Style Composer - New Subassembly Shape Label Style** dialog box will be displayed. Specify the settings for the styles in the dialog box and choose the **OK** button to close the dialog box. The styles created will be added in the **Link** or **Shape** subnodes.

Once you have created the styles and their respective label styles for different components, you can add them in the code set to create a code set style.

Creating Code Set Styles

To create a code set style, expand **General > Multipurpose Styles > Code Set Styles** subnode in the **Settings** tab of the **TOOLSPACE**. Next, right-click on the **Code Set Styles** node to display a shortcut menu and choose the **New** option from it; the **Code Set Style - New Code Set Style** dialog box will be displayed.

By default, the **Information** tab is chosen in this dialog box. In this tab, enter a name for the code set style in the **Name** edit box. Next, choose the **Codes** tab. This tab is used to view and change the default code styles as well as add new codes in the drawing. Code set styles can be associated with subassemblies, assemblies, corridors, and section views. Specify the code name, code style, and code label styles in the **Name**, **Style**, and **Label Style** columns, respectively, of the **Codes** tab, as shown in Figure 7-17.

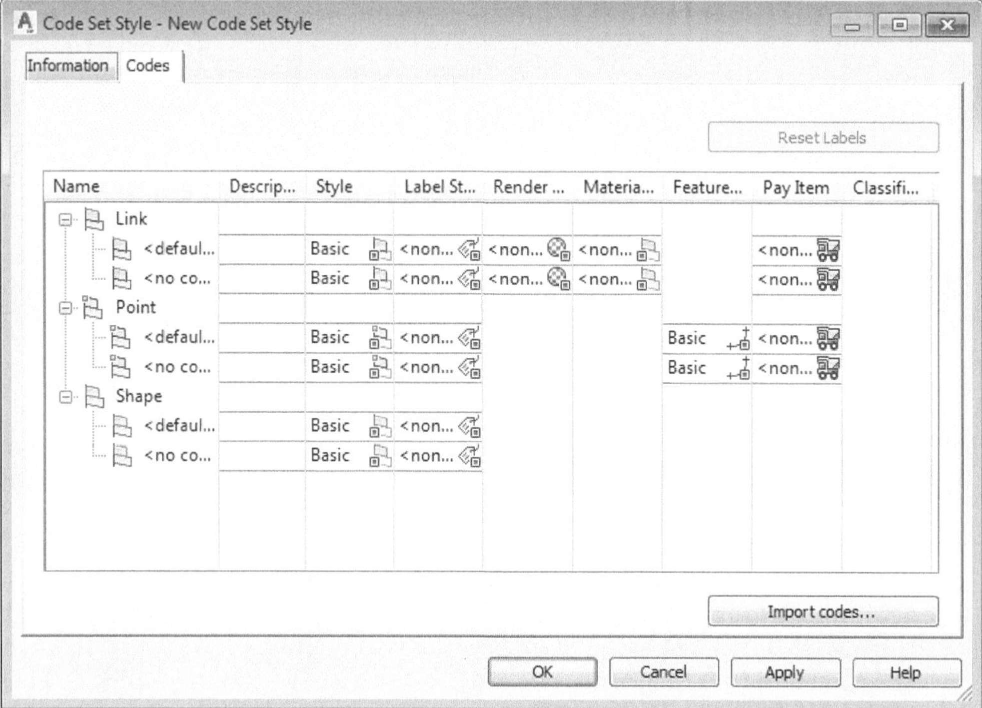

*Figure 7-17 The **Codes** tab of the **Code Set Style - New Code Set Style** dialog box*

To add the required codes, right-click on the node in the **Name** column; a shortcut menu is displayed. Choose **Add** from it, as shown in Figure 7-18. On doing so, the **Pick Link Style** or **Pick Marker Style** or **Pick Shape Style** dialog box for the required code will be displayed. Select a style from the relevant dialog box and choose the **OK** button; the **NEW CODE** name will be added to the relevant collection. Double-click on **NEW CODE** and specify a name for the code.

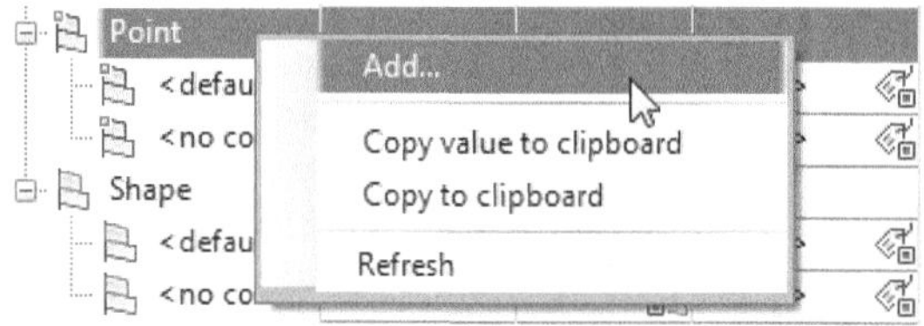

*Figure 7-18 Choosing the **Add** option from the shortcut menu displayed*

To change the style of an existing entry, click on the icon in the style cell of the required entry; the **Pick Marker Style**, **Pick Link Style**, or **Pick Shape Style** dialog box will be displayed depending on the code you have selected. Select a style and choose the **OK** button. Similarly, click in the **Label Styles** column to display the **Pick Style** dialog box. Select a label style from the respective dialog box and choose the **OK** button.

To import codes from a subassembly, assembly, or a corridor to the code set, choose the **Import codes** button in the **Code Set Style - New Code Set Style** dialog box; the dialog box will close and you will be prompted to select the required subassemblies, assemblies, or corridor to import the codes. Select the required object from the drawing and press ENTER to return to the **Code Set Style - New Code Set Style** dialog box. On doing so, the codes used in the selected subassembly, assembly, or a corridor object will be automatically added in the **Codes** tab. You can modify the code style and the label styles for the imported codes or accept the existing styles. Choose the **OK** button to close the **Code Set Style - New Code Set Style** dialog box. The code set style that you have created will be added in the **Code Set Style** subnode of the **Multipurpose Styles** node in the **Settings** tab.

Note

*The default value of the code style in the **Style** column is set to **Standard** and the default value of the code label style in the **Label Style** column is set to **None**. The default values depend upon the type of drawing template you use. If you are working on the **_AutoCAD Civil 3D (Imperial) NCS** template, the default value for the **Style** column in this template will be **Basic**.*

To assign the code set style that you have created, select the subassembly in the drawing and right-click to display the shortcut menu and choose **Subassembly Properties** from it; the **Subassembly Properties <name>** dialog box will be displayed. Choose the **Codes** tab. Next, select the required code set style option from the **Code set style (from assembly)** drop-down list and choose the **Apply** button to view the change. Choose the **OK** button to close the **Subassembly Properties <name>** dialog box.

To create an assembly at some distance from the existing assembly and add different subassemblies or even modify the parameters of the existing subassemblies, you can create an assembly offset. To do so, choose the **Add Assembly Offset** tool from the **Home > Create Design > Assembly** drop-down; you will be prompted to select an assembly from the drawing. Select an assembly graphically in the drawing by clicking on the required assembly. You can also choose the assembly from a list of existing assemblies. To do so, press ENTER; the **Select an Assembly** dialog box will be displayed. Select the required assembly from the drop-down list and choose the **OK** button; you will be prompted to specify the offset distance. Click in the drawing area to specify the location for the offset; an offset point is created at the specified location.

WORKING WITH SUBASSEMBLIES

As explained earlier in this chapter, a subassembly is the main building block for corridor modeling and it represents the geometry of the components used for designing a corridor. AutoCAD Civil 3D has different in-built subassemblies for different components of a corridor such as lanes, ditches, and slopes. These ready-to-use subassemblies can adapt automatically to different superelevations, cut, or fill changes.

Besides the built in subassemblies, AutoCAD Civil 3D also allows you to create your own customized subassemblies using the polylines or .NET language. As discussed earlier, the subassemblies can be accessed from the **TOOL PALETTES**, as shown in Figure 7-19. The **TOOL PALETTES** contains various tabs with different subassemblies. When you hover the cursor over a tab, a tooltip is displayed with the name of the tab and type of subassemblies.

The **TOOL PALETTES** consists of ready-to-use subassemblies for different components of corridor design such as lanes, channels and ditches, curbs and gutters, and so on. You can choose the required tab and select the subassembly from the palette.

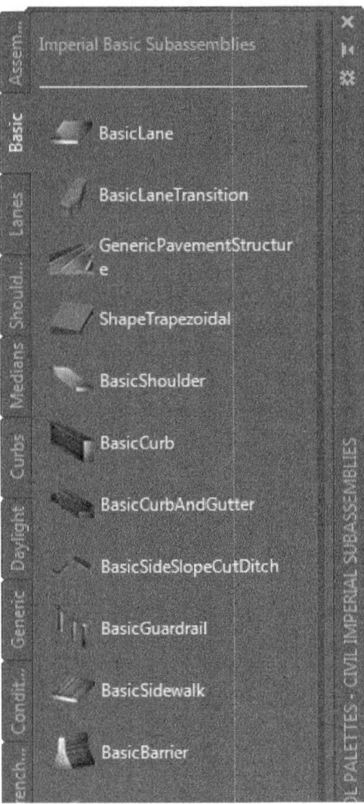

Figure 7-19 The ***TOOL PALETTES - CIVIL IMPERIAL SUBASSEMBLIES*** *palette*

The **Lanes** tab of the **TOOL PALETTES - CIVIL IMPERIAL SUBASSEMBLIES** displays the subassemblies for different shapes of travel lanes for the roadway. Figure 7-20 shows the **LaneBrokenBack** subassembly from this tab. This subassembly is used to create a cross-section of a two-lane roadway. The two lanes, inner and outer, have different slopes. Select the **LaneBrokenBack** subassembly from the **TOOL PALETTES**; the **Properties** window will be displayed. Move the scroll bar of the **Properties** window to view the parameters in the **ADVANCED** section. The slope values for the inner and outer lanes of the **LaneBrokenBack** subassembly are displayed in this section.

The **Basic** tab displays the subassemblies for the lane component of a roadway. Figure 7-21 shows the **BasicLane** subassembly. It is also used to create a simple lane. This subassembly is most widely used for creating top and datum surfaces. In the **ADVANCED** section of the **Properties** window of this assembly, you can modify the width, depth, and the slope parameters.

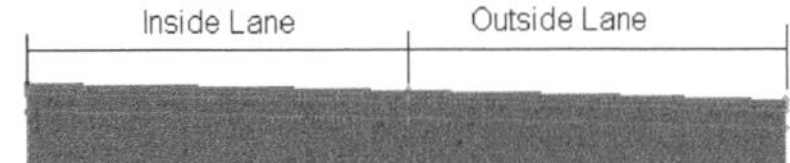

Figure 7-20 *The* ***LaneBrokenBack*** *subassembly from the* ***Lanes*** *tab*

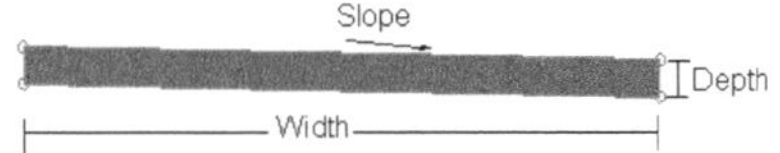

Figure 7-21 *The* ***BasicLane*** *subassembly*

The **Curbs** tab displays the subassemblies for the advanced roadway structures with advance parameters. Figure 7-22 shows the **UrbanCurbGutterGeneral** subassembly from the **Curbs** tab. This subassembly has the depth, slope, extension and other parameters that can be modified according to the design of the subassembly. These parameters are also used to calculate the quantity takeoffs of the subbase layer. Unlike the **BasicCurbandGutter** subassembly, it has more dimension parameters that can be adjusted in the **Properties** window based on the design requirements. The dimension parameters for the **BasicCurbandGutter** subassembly are listed below:

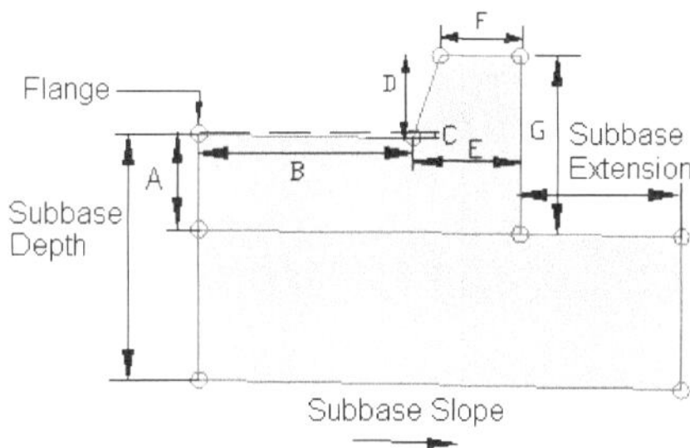

Figure 7-22 *The **UrbanCurbGutterGeneral** subassembly*

A= Depth of the gutter at the flange point
B= Width of flange point to gutter flowline
C= Depth from the flange point to the gutter flowline
D= Height of curb from the gutter flowline to the top-of-curb
E= Width from the gutter flowline to the back-of-curb
F= Width of the top-of-curb
G= Height of the back-of-curb

The **Daylight** tab displays the available daylight subassemblies which are used to add daylight to the road assemblies. A daylight typically represents where the existing ground and the proposed design ground meet and it is usually the limit of construction. It is a function performed by a specific type of subassembly, where a slope is extended from that subassembly until it intersects with a surface. Figure 7-23 shows a **DaylightStandard** subassembly.

Figure 7-23 *The **DaylightStandard** subassembly*

The **Generic** tab displays the subassembly that is used to add connected links for the roadway structures. These subassemblies provide you with the basic flexible components that can be used to create a perfect component to suit your design criteria. For example, you can use generic assemblies to create a 5' wide buffer with 2% slope and a 4' sidewalk with 1.5% slope.

You cannot use a **BasicSideWalk** subassembly to create this assembly because it does not have a slope parameter. Also, the **UrbanSideWalk** subassembly cannot be used, as it has the same buffer slope as that of the sidewalk. So in this case, the **LinkWidthandSlope** subassembly can be used to meet the criteria. Figure 7-24 shows the left side of the assembly consisting of a buffer strip of 5' width with 2% slope and **UrbanSidewalk** of 4' width and 1.5% slope.

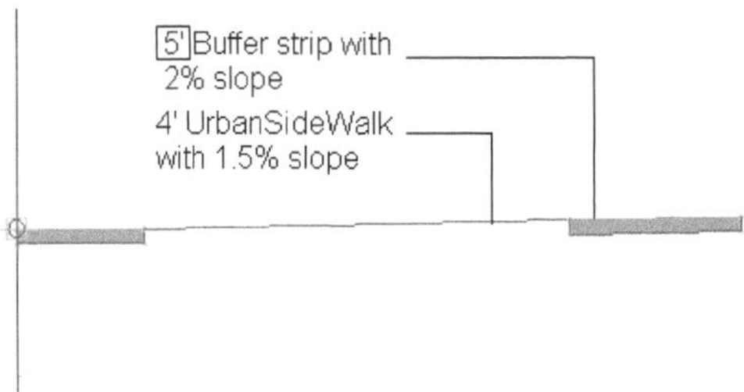

Figure 7-24 *The left side of an assembly*

The **Trench Pipe Subassemblies** tab displays different subassemblies for adding channels and trench pipes which are used to accommodate the storm runoff. If this tab is not added in the **TOOL PALETTES** by default then you can add it manually. The procedure to add a subassembly to the **TOOL PALETTES** is discussed in detail further in this chapter.

The **Channel** subassembly in the **Trench Pipe Subassemblies** tab is used to create an open channel. You can edit various properties of the **Channel** subassembly such as depth, lining depth, and side slope. To do so, select the subassembly from **TOOL PALETTES**; the **Properties** window will be displayed. In this window, you can specify various properties in the **ADVANCE** rollout. Figure 7-25 shows a **Channel** subassembly.

Figure 7-25 *The **Channel** subassembly*

Subassembly Properties

You can view the properties of the subassembly in the **Subassembly Properties** dialog box. To invoke this dialog box, select the subassembly in the drawing and right-click to display the shortcut menu. Choose **Subassembly Properties** from the shortcut menu; the **Subassembly Properties - <Subassembly Name>** dialog box will be displayed. The tabs in this dialog box are discussed next.

The Information Tab

The **Name** edit box in the **Information** tab displays the name of the subassembly. You can specify a new name in this edit box. Optionally, you can enter a description in the **Description** edit box.

The Parameters Tab

This tab is used to view and modify the input and output parameters of the **Properties** window. To modify an input or output parameter value, double-click on the required input value in the **Default Input Value** column and enter a new value, refer to Figure 7-26. You can also choose the **Subassembly help** button to display the **Autodesk AutoCAD Civil 3D 2018- Help** window. You can use this window to browse through various topics related to subassembly.

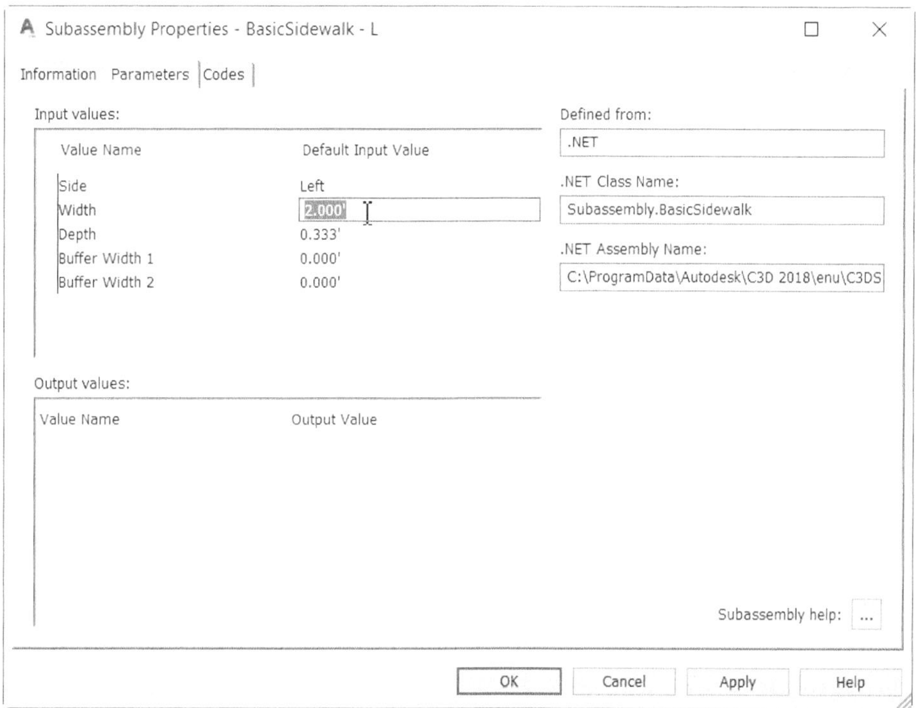

*Figure 7-26 Editing the input value for **Width** of a subassembly in the **Parameters** tab*

The Codes Tab

This tab is used to view the code styles and the code label styles in a code set assigned to a subassembly. The **Code set style (from assembly)** drop-down list in the **Codes** tab displays the code set style. When a subassembly is attached to an assembly, the code set style is determined by the code set style of the assembly object. In such a case, all controls on this tab such as the **Code set style (from assembly)** drop-down list and the **Reset Labels** button are disabled. The codes are displayed under three heads: **Link**, **Point**, and **Shape**, as shown in Figure 7-27. Choose the **OK** button after reviewing and editing the subassembly properties.

You have learned to add subassemblies using the **TOOL PALETTES**. Now, you will learn to create the subassemblies using the AutoCAD polyline objects.

Tip

*If a subassembly is detached independently or then you can change the code styles from the **Code set styles** drop-down list in the **Codes** tab.*

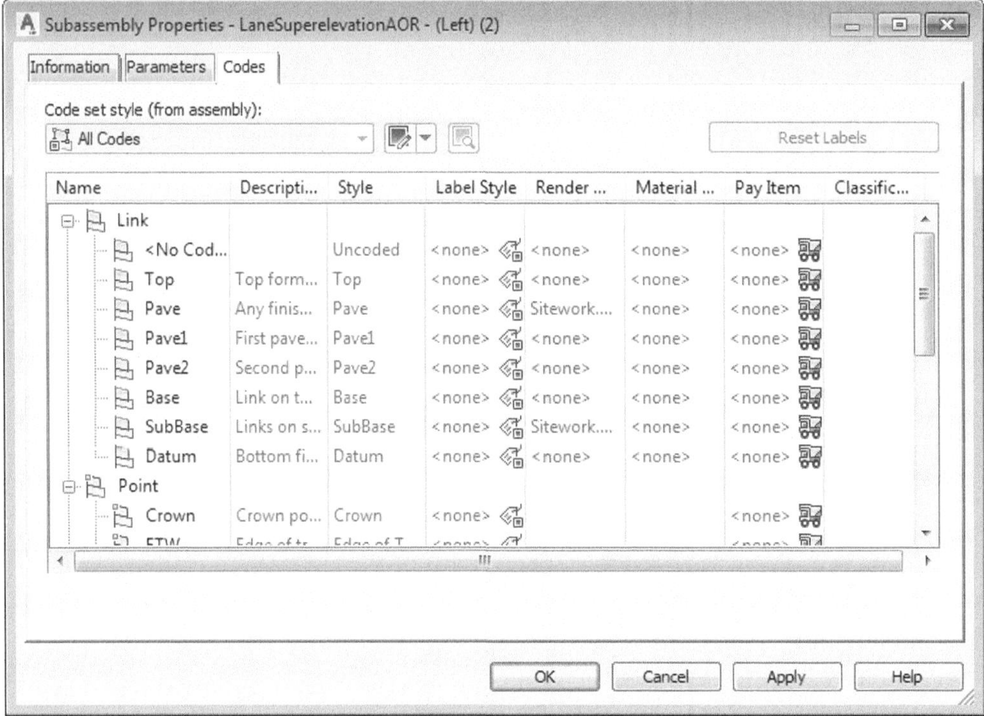

*Figure 7-27 The **Link**, **Point**, and **Shape** heads in the **Codes** tab*

Creating Subassemblies using Polylines

You can create a customized subassembly using polylines. To do so, create the required object using the **Polyline** tool. Next, choose the **Create Subassembly from Polyline** tool from the **Create Design** panel of the **Home** tab; you will be prompted to select the entity. Select the polyline entity from the drawing area; the **Create Subassembly - From Polyline** dialog box will be displayed, as shown in Figure 7-28. The options in this dialog box are discussed next.

Name

The **Name** edit box displays the default name of the subassembly. You can specify a name for the subassembly in this edit box.

Description

This text box is used to specify a description about the subassembly.

Code set style

The **Code set style** drop-down list displays the code set styles for the subassembly codes. You can select a code set style from this drop-down list.

Subassembly layer

Choose the button on the right of the **Subassembly layer** text box to select a layer that will be assigned to the subassembly. By default, the layer assigned to a subassembly is **C-ROAD-ASSM**.

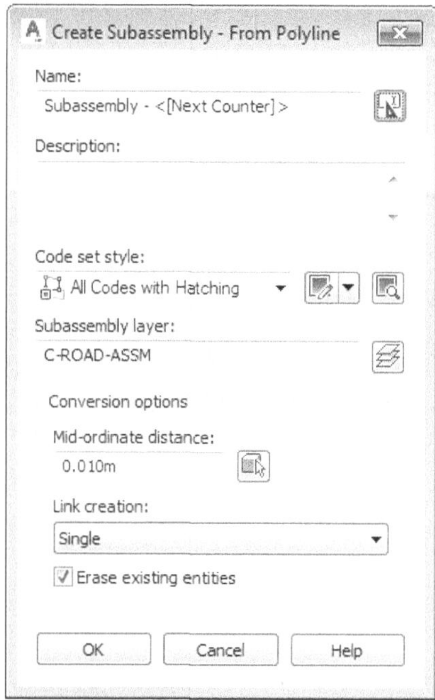

Figure 7-28 The ***Create Subassembly - From Polyline*** *dialog box*

Conversion options Area

In the **Conversion options** area, the **Mid-ordinate distance** edit box is used to specify the length of the tessellated segments in the curve. Specify this distance if the subassembly consists of curves and arcs. From the **Link creation** drop-down list, select the option for creating a single or multiple links. The default option displayed for creating links is **Multiple**.You can use the **Single** option to create one link from all the components of the subassembly or the **Multiple** option to create multiple links from all the components of the subassembly. If you select the **None** option, you will not be able to create any link. Clear the **Erase existing entities** check box to retain the original polyline object from which you want to create the subassembly.

Once you have specified the parameters for the subassembly in the **Create Subassembly - From Polyline** dialog box, choose the **OK** button; the dialog box will be closed and the name of the subassembly will be added to the **Assemblies** node of the **Prospector** tab, as shown in Figure 7-29. Also, the polyline object will be converted to a subassembly. You can now assign codes to the subassembly, add shape to it and then add it to the assembly baseline.

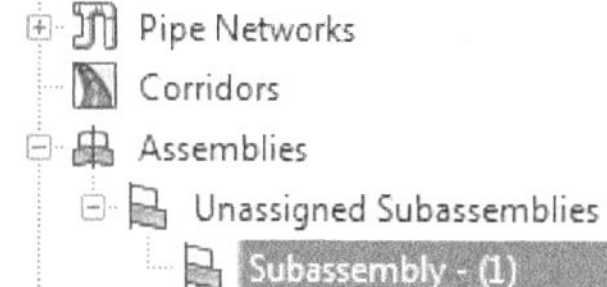

Figure 7-29 The ***Assemblies*** *subnode displaying the added subassembly*

Adding Codes to the Subassembly

After creating a subassembly from a polyline, you need to add codes to the subassembly. To add code, select the subassembly which is created from the polyline, and then right-click on it; a shortcut menu is displayed. Choose **Add Code** from the shortcut menu; you will be prompted to enter a code. Specify a code in the command line and press ENTER; you will be prompted to select a link, point, or shape. Select a point, link, or shape of the subassembly; the code will be assigned to the selected subassembly.

To view the assigned codes, select the assembly in the drawing and right-click to display the shortcut menu. Choose **Subassembly Properties** from the shortcut menu; the **Subassembly Properties - <assembly name>** dialog box will be displayed. Choose the **Codes** tab to view the assigned codes.

Adding Shape and Shape Codes

To add a shape to the subassembly created from a polyline, select it in the drawing. Right-click and choose the **Add Shape** option from the shortcut menu; you will be prompted to select the subassembly links. Select the required subassembly links in the drawing; a subassembly shape will be created. Figures 7-30 and 7-31 show the subassembly before and after adding a shape, respectively.

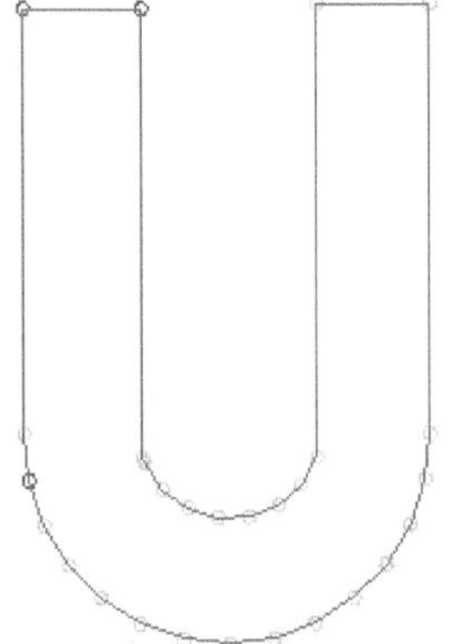

Figure 7-30 *The subassembly before adding a shape*

Figure 7-31 *The subassembly after adding a shape*

Adding Subassembly to an Assembly

You can add a customized subassembly to an assembly. To do so, select the assembly from the drawing; the **Assembly : <name>** (Contextual) tab will be displayed in the Ribbon. In this tab, choose the **Add to Assembly** tool from the **Modify Subassembly** panel; you will be prompted to select the subassembly. Select the subassembly; you will be prompted to select the required marker point in the assembly. Select the marker point in the assembly, the subassembly will be attached to it.

Subassembly Catalog Library

The subassembly catalog displays different subassembly tools that can be used for the corridor modeling. These subassemblies are created using the .NET programming language. To access the subassembly catalogs, select the assembly from the drawing; the **Sub-Assembly<name>** tab will be displayed. Choose the **Catalog** button from **Launch Pad** panel of this tab; the **<user name> Catalog Library - Autodesk Content Browser 2018** window will be displayed, as shown in Figure 7-32.

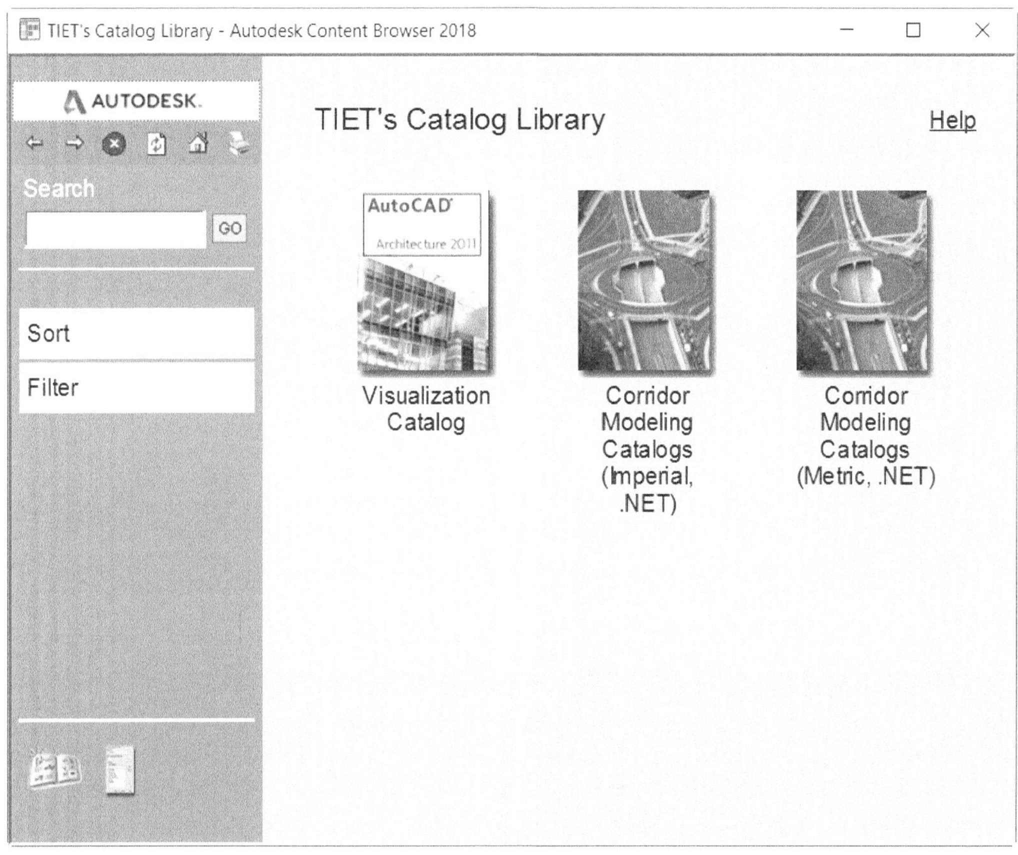

***Figure 7-32** The window displaying the **Catalog Library - Autodesk Content Browser 2018** window*

The catalog library shows three corridor catalogs: **Visualization Catalog**, **Corridor Modeling Catalogs (Metric.NET)**, and **Corridor Modeling Catalogs (Imperial .NET)**. Choose the **Corridor Modeling Catalogs (Metric .NET)** or the **Corridor Modeling Catalogs (Imperial .NET)** catalog to display the subassembly tools with Metric or Imperial units. On doing so, the subassemblies in the respective catalog will be displayed.

The **Corridor Modeling Catalogs** window displays different subassembly catalogs such as **Channel and Trench Pipe Subassemblies**, **Generic Subassemblies**, **Retaining Wall Subassemblies**, and so on.

You can choose the required catalog to view the subassembly. Each catalog consists of a number of subassemblies. You can choose the required subassembly and add it in the **TOOL PALETTES**.

To add the subassemblies to **TOOL PALETTES**, open the required catalog to view the subassemblies. Every subassembly has an i-drop symbol with the text '**i**' at the bottom right corner. You can use this i-drop symbol to add the required subassembly to the **TOOL PALETTES**. To do so, press and hold the left mouse button on the '**i**' text, and drag it to the **TOOL PALETTES**, refer to Figure 7-33. Similarly, you can add the entire catalog to **TOOL PALETTES**.

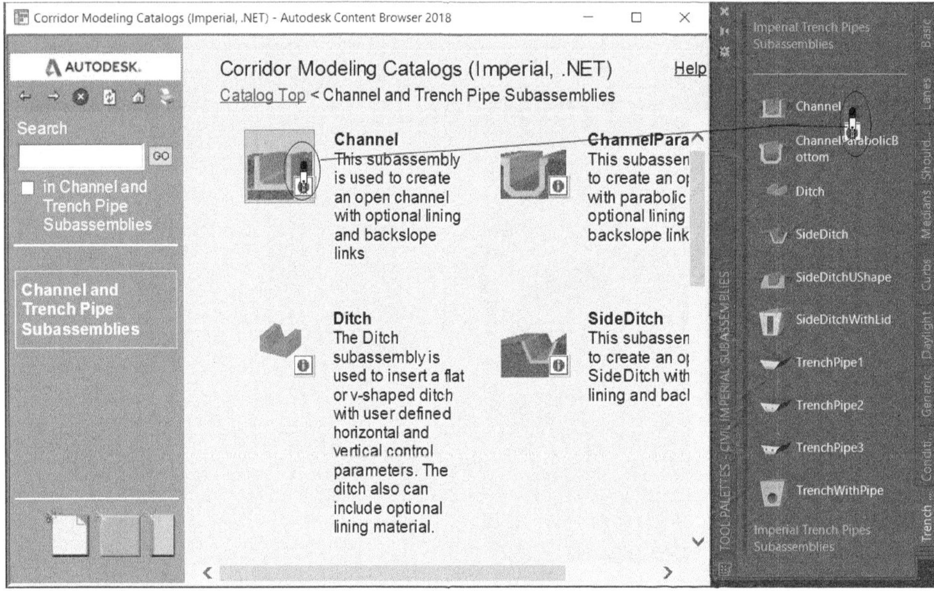

Figure 7-33 Adding a subassembly to TOOLPALETTES

ADDING ASSEMBLIES TO TOOL PALETTES

Once you have created the assembly for your corridor model, you can save it in the **TOOL PALETTES**. To do so, enter **B** at the command prompt and press ENTER; the **Block Definition** dialog box will be displayed. You need to convert the entire assembly into one block. Enter a name for the assembly in the **Name** edit box. Choose the **Pick Point** button from the **Base point** area; the **Block Definition** dialog box will be closed and you will be prompted to specify the insertion base point. Select the insertion base point from the assembly by clicking on the assembly at the required point; the **Block Definition** dialog box will be displayed again and the coordinates of the selected insertion point will be displayed in the **Base point** area. Next, clear the **Specify On-screen** check box from the **Objects** area. Ensure that the **Open in block editor** check box is cleared so as to make the resulting block non-editable. Choose the **Select objects** button; the **Block Definition** dialog box will be closed and you will be prompted to select the objects. Select the complete assembly and the baseline with a crossing window. Press ENTER to return to the dialog box. Next, choose the **OK** button to close the **Block Definition** dialog box and convert the assembly into a block. Save the file at the required location. Next, enter **Insert** in the command line and press ENTER; the **Insert** dialog box will be displayed. Select the block from the **Name** drop-down list. Choose the **Browse** button and open the saved file from the **Select Drawing File** dialog box displayed. Select the **Explode** check box and choose the **OK** button; the **Select Drawing File** dialog box will be closed and you will be prompted to specify the insertion point. Click in the drawing at the suitable location. Specify the scale factor and press ENTER. The assembly block will be added to the drawing. You can zoom in or zoom out to view the assembly clearly. Save the file again.

Next, choose the required palette in which you want to add the assembly block from the **TOOL PALETTES**. You can also create a new palette to save the assembly block. To do so, right-click in the space of any palette and choose **New Palette** from the shortcut menu displayed; a new blank palette with a box will be created. Enter a name for the palette in the box and press ENTER. Next, to add the assembly to the palette, select the assembly block and press and hold the left mouse button until an arrow is displayed. Drag the arrow attached with the assembly block and drop it on the palette. The assembly block will be added to the **TOOL PALETTES**. Figure 7-34 shows the assembly added to the **New** palette in the **TOOL PALETTES**. Select the assembly in the palette, right-click to display the shortcut menu, and choose **Properties** from it; the **Tools Properties** dialog box will be displayed. You can modify the name, enter a description, view, and edit the parameters of the assembly in this dialog box.

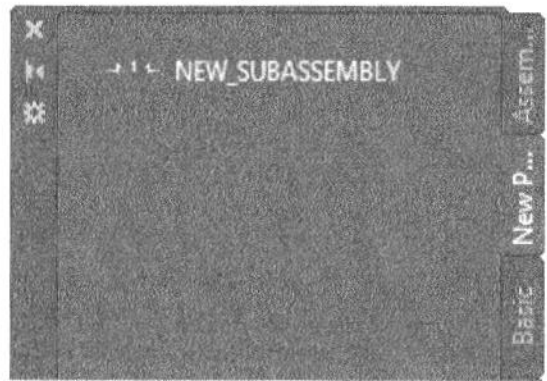

Figure 7-34** The assembly added in the **New** palette of the **TOOLPALETTES

TUTORIALS

Tutorial 1 Typical Road Assembly

In this tutorial, you will create a typical road assembly consisting of different subassemblies, as shown in Figure 7-35 and then rename the subassemblies in the created road assembly.

(Expected time: 30 min)

The following steps are required to complete this tutorial:

a. Download and open the file.
b. Create an assembly.
c. Add the required subassemblies after modifying their parameters.
d. Rename the subassemblies.
e. Save the file.

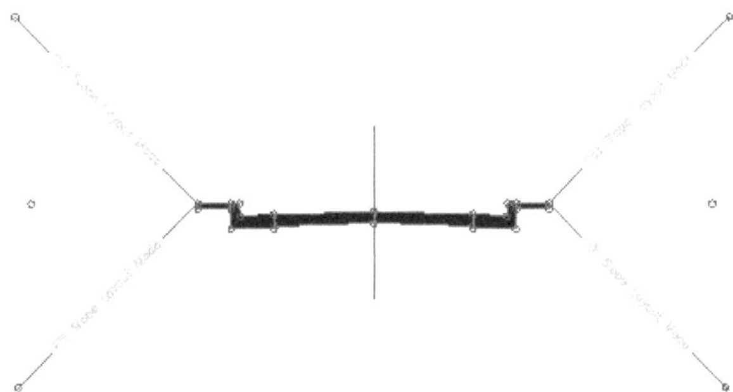

***Figure 7-35** A typical road assembly*

Downloading and Opening the File

1. Download *c07_c3d_2018_tut.zip* file from *www.cadcim.com*. Next, save and extract the file at *C:\c3d_2018*.

2. Choose **Open** from the **Application Menu**; the **Select File** dialog box is displayed.

3. In this dialog box, browse to *C:\c3d_2018\c07_c3d_2018_tut* where you have saved the file.

4. Select the file *c07_c3d_2018_tut01.dwg* and then choose the **Open** button to open it.

Ignore any error message if displayed.

Creating an Assembly

1. Choose the **Create Assembly** tool from **Home > Create Design >Assembly** drop-down; the **Create Assembly** dialog box is displayed.

2. Enter **Typical Road** in the **Name** edit box.

3. Next, choose the **OK** button; the **Create Assembly** dialog box is closed and you are prompted to specify the assembly baseline location.

4. Click in the drawing area to specify the location for the assembly baseline; the assembly baseline is added, as shown in Figure 7-36.

Adding Subassemblies

1. Choose the **Tool Palettes** button from the **Palettes** panel of the **Home** tab; the **TOOL PALETTES** is displayed.

2. Choose the **Basic** tab from the **TOOL PALETTES** and select the **BasicLaneTransition** subassembly from it; the **Properties** window is displayed.

3. Set the value of the **Default Width** parameter to **6.000′** in the **ADVANCED** rollout of the **Properties** window. Set the value of the **Side** property to **Right**.

Note

You can press CTRL + 1 to display the ***Properties*** *window if not displayed.*

Figure 7-36 *The assembly baseline*

4. Next, click on the marker of the assembly baseline; the **BasicLaneTransition** subassembly is added to the right of the baseline.

5. Set the **Side** parameter in the **Properties** window to **Left**, refer to Figure 7-37.

6. Ensure that the value of the **Default Width** property is **6.000′** and then press ENTER.

7. Click on the assembly marker; the **BasicLaneTransition** subassembly is added to the left of the assembly baseline. Figure 7-38 shows the **BasicLaneTransition** subassembly added to both sides of the assembly baseline.

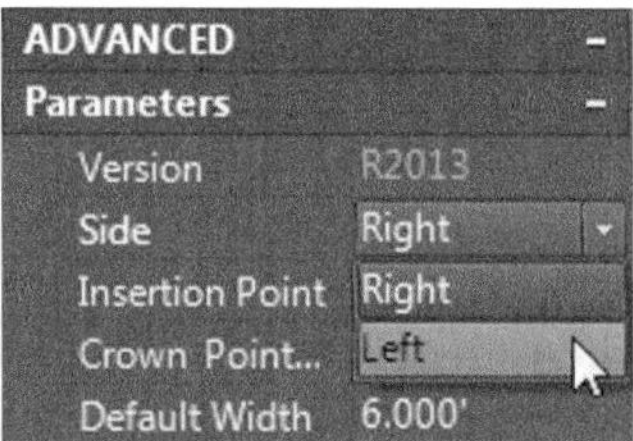

Figure 7-37 *Setting the* ***Side*** *parameter to* ***Left***

Note

*You must check the side in the **Properties** window and then click on the respective side of the assembly baseline to add the subassembly.*

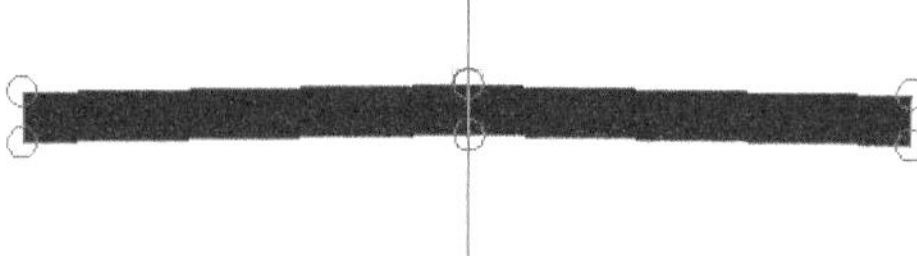

Figure 7-38 *The **BasicLaneTransition** subassemblies added to both sides of the assembly baseline*

8. In the **Basic** tab of the **TOOL PALETTES**, select the **BasicCurbAndGutter** subassembly; the **Properties** window for the subassembly is displayed. Ensure that the **Side** parameter is set to **Right** in the **ADVANCED** rollout of the **Properties** window.

9. Click on the circular marker on the top right edge of the **BasicLaneTransition** subassembly, as shown in Figure 7-39; the **BasicCurbAndGutter** subassembly is added to the right of the **BasicLaneTransition** subassembly.

Figure 7-39 *Selecting the top circular mark of the **BasicLaneTransition** subassembly*

10. Next, set the **Side** parameter for the **BasicCurbAndGutter** subassembly to **Left** in the **Properties** window.

11. Click on the circular mark on the top left edge of the **BasicLaneTransition** subassembly. The **BasicCurbAndGutter** subassembly is added to the left of the assembly baseline.

    Now, you have added a curb and gutter to the pavement. Zoom out to see the entire cross section of the pavement, refer to Figure 7-40.

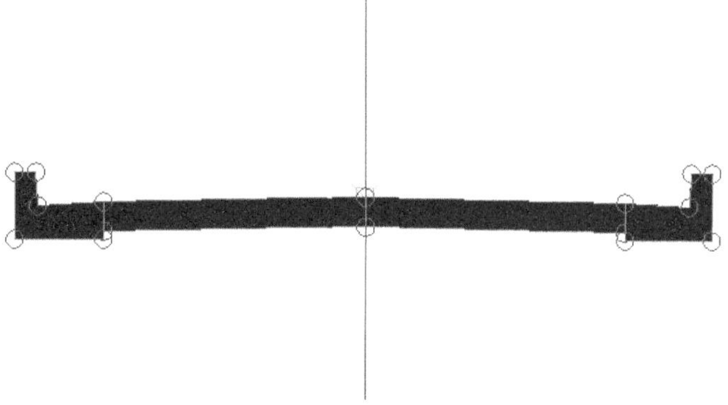

Figure 7-40 *The **BasicCurbAndGutter** subassembly added to the assembly*

12. Select the **BasicSidewalk** subassembly from the **Basic** tab in **TOOL PALETTES**. 

13. Set the **Width** parameter value to **2.000'** in the **Properties** window and press ENTER.

14. Set the **Side** parameter value to **Right** in the **Properties** window.

15. Next, click on the circular marker on the top right edge of the **BasicCurbAndGutter** subassembly, as shown in Figure 7-41; a 2' wide sidewalk is added to the right side of the assembly.

Figure 7-41 *Selecting the circular marker on the right side of the top edge of the* ***BasicCurbAndGutter*** *subassembly*

16. In the **TOOL PALETTES**, change the value of the **Side** parameter to **Left** and ensure that the **width** parameter is set to **2'**. Now, click on the circular marker on the top left edge of the **BasicCurbAndGutter** subassembly. A sidewalk of width 2' is added to left side of the assembly. Figure 7-42 displays **BasicSidewalk** subassembly added to both sides.

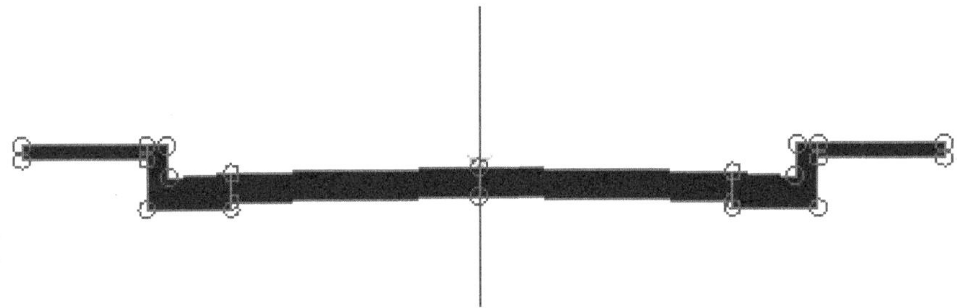

Figure 7-42 *The* ***BasicSidewalk*** *subassembly added to both sides of the assembly baseline*

17. Next, select the **BasicSideSlopeCutDitch** subassembly in the **Basic** tab of the **TOOL PALETTES**.

18. Set the **Cut Slope** parameter value to **4.00:1** in the **Properties** window and press ENTER.

19. Ensure that the **Side** parameter is set to **Right**.

20. Click on the marker on the top right edge of the **BasicSidewalk** subassembly; the **BasicSideSlopeCutDitch** subassembly is added to the right of the assembly.

21. Repeat steps 17 and 18, change the **Side** parameter to **Left** and add the **BasicSideSlopeCutDitch** subassembly to the left of the assembly. Now, you have finished creating a **Typical Road** assembly consisting of the **BasicLaneTransition**, **BasicCurbAndGutter**, **BasicSidewalk**, and **BasicSideSlopeCutDitch** subassemblies, as shown in Figure 7-43. Next, close the **Properties** window and the **TOOL PALETTES**, and press ESC to exit the command.

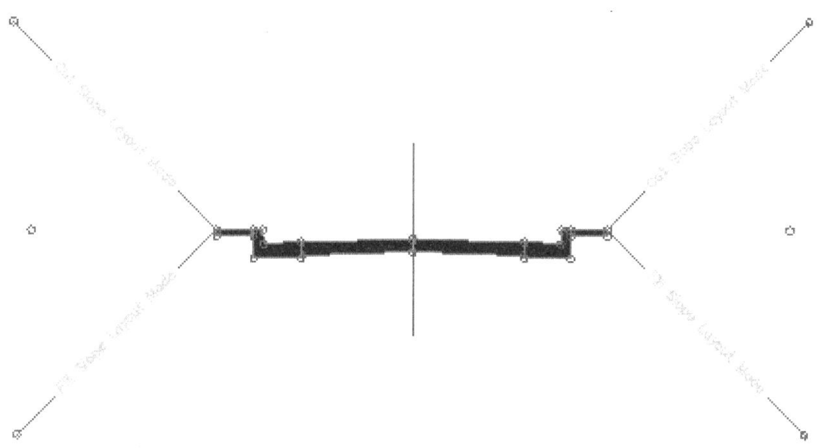

Figure 7-43 *A typical road assembly*

Tip

*To invoke the **Assembly Properties - <Assembly Name>** dialog box, select the required assembly baseline in the drawing and right-click; a shortcut menu is displayed. Choose **Assembly Properties** from the shortcut menu.*

Renaming the Subassemblies

1. Choose the **Prospector** tab of the **TOOLSPACE**.
2. Expand the **Assemblies** node.
3. Right-click on **Typical Road** in the **Assemblies** node; a shortcut menu is displayed.
4. Choose the **Properties** option from the shortcut menu; the **Assembly Properties - Typical Road** dialog box is displayed.
5. Choose the **Construction** tab; the subassemblies are listed under the **Item** area.
6. Right-click on the **Right** subnode in the **Item** area; a shortcut menu is displayed. Choose the **Rename** option from the shortcut menu; the selected text becomes editable.
7. Enter **Right Lane** in the displayed edit box and press ENTER.
8. Using the procedure followed in steps 6 and 7, rename the **Left** subnode as **Left Lane**.
9. Next, right-click on the **BasicLaneTransition** subassembly under the **Right Lane** and choose **Rename** from the shortcut menu displayed; the selected text becomes editable.
10. Enter **BasicLaneTransition - R** in the displayed edit box and press ENTER.

11. Next, right-click on the first **BasicLaneTransition** subassembly under the **Left Lane** subnode and choose **Rename** from the shortcut menu displayed; the subassembly name becomes editable.

12. Enter **BasicLaneTransition - L** and press ENTER. Similarly add suffixes **- R** and **- L** to the other subassembly names under the **Right Lane** and **Left Lane** subnodes, respectively, refer to Figure 7-44.

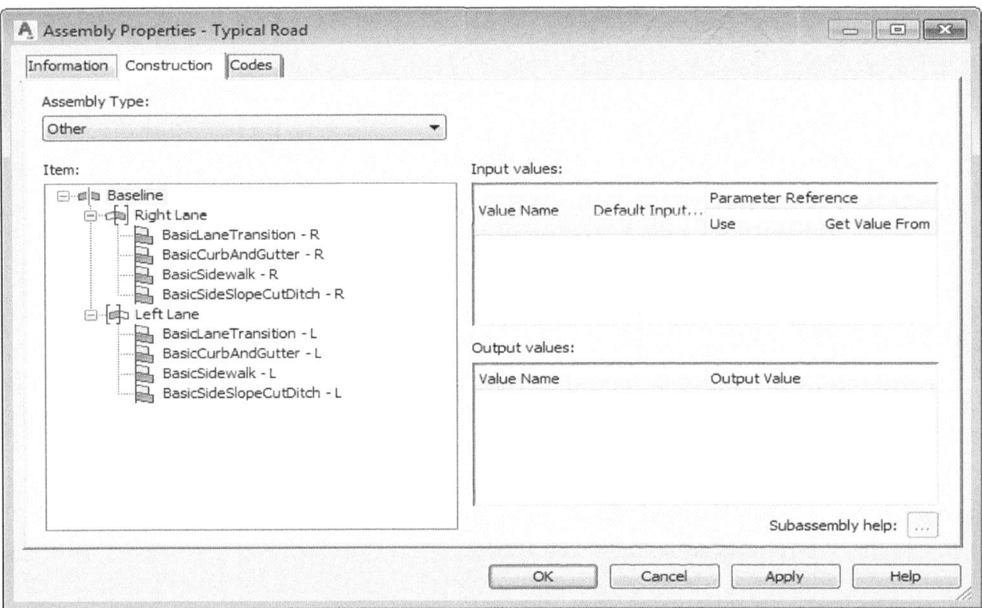

Figure 7-44 *The **Item** area of the **Construction** tab displaying the renamed subassemblies*

13. Next, choose the **OK** button in the **Assembly Properties - Typical Road**; the dialog box is closed.

14. Expand the **Assemblies** node and its subnodes in the **Prospector** tab; the subassemblies are renamed and displayed, as shown in Figure 7-45.

Note

*You can also rename the subassemblies by selecting each of them individually in the drawing and then renaming them in the **Subassembly Properties** dialog box. To display the **Subassembly Properties** dialog box, select the subassembly in the drawing, right-click on it and choose **Subassembly Properties** from the shortcut menu displayed.*

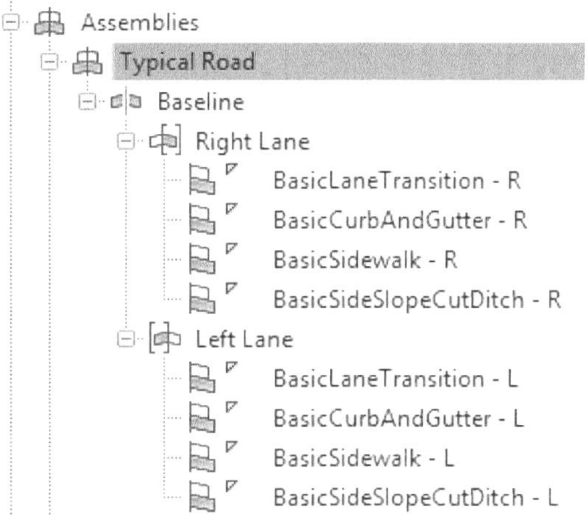

Figure 7-45 *The renamed subassemblies in the* ***Assemblies*** *node in the* ***Prospector*** *tab*

Saving the File

1. Choose **Save As** from the **Application Menu**; the **Save Drawing As** dialog box is displayed.
2. In this dialog box, browse to the following location:

   C:\c3d_2018\c07_c3d_2018_tut

3. In the **File name** edit box, enter **c07_tut01a**.
4. Choose the **Save** button; the file is saved with the name *c07_tut01a.dwg* at the specified location.

Tutorial 2 Canal Assembly

In this tutorial, you will create a canal assembly, as shown in Figure 7-46. Also, you will create a marker style, a shape style, and code set style. **(Expected time:1 h 15 min)**

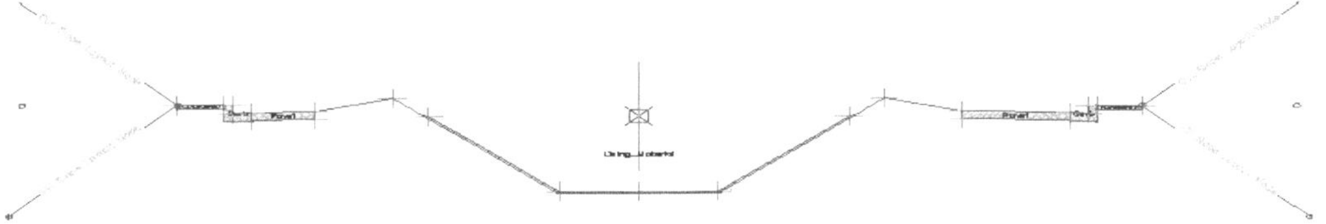

Figure 7-46 *The Canal assembly*

The following steps are required to complete this tutorial:

a. Download and open the file.
b. Create an assembly.
c. Add subassemblies to the canal assembly.

d. Create an assembly style.
e. Create a new marker, link, shape, and code set style for the assembly.
f. Assign the assembly and code set style.
g. Save the file.

Downloading and Opening the File

1. Download *c07_c3d_2018_tut.zip* file, if not downloaded earlier, from *http://www.cadcim.com*. Next, save and extract the file at *C:\c3d_2018*.

2. Choose **Open** from the **Application Menu**; the **Select File** dialog box is displayed.

3. In this dialog box, browse to the location *C:\c3d_2018\c07_c3d_2018* where you have saved the file.

4. Select the file *c07_c3d_2018_tut02.dwg* and then choose the **Open** button to open the file. The *c07_c3d_2018_tut02.dwg* file consists of a surface and **Road A** profile view.

Creating an Assembly

1. Choose the **Create Assembly** tool from **Home > Create Design > Assembly** drop-down; the **Create Assembly** dialog box is displayed.

2. Enter **Canal** in the **Name** edit box of the dialog box.

3. Next, choose the **OK** button; the dialog box is closed and you are prompted to specify the location for the assembly baseline.

4. Click in the drawing area to specify the location for the assembly baseline; the assembly baseline is created. The assembly name **Canal** is added to the **Assemblies** node in the **Prospector** tab of the **TOOLSPACE**.

Adding Subassemblies to the Canal Assembly

1. Choose the **Tool Palettes** button from the **Palettes** panel of the **Home** tab; the **TOOL PALETTES - CIVIL IMPERIAL SUBASSEMBLIES** palette is displayed.

2. Select the **Channel** subassembly from the **Trench Pipes** tab in the **TOOL PALETTES**; the **Properties** window is displayed and you are prompted to select a marker point. 

Tip

*In case, the **Channel** subassembly is not displayed in the **TOOL PALETTES**, you can use the Autodesk's catalog library to insert the subassembly in the **TOOL PALETTES**. To insert the required subassembly, select the assembly baseline from the drawing; the **Assembly: Canal** tab is displayed. Choose the **Catalog** button from the **Launch Pad** panel of this tab; the **<user name> Catalog Library - Autodesk Content Browser 2018** window is displayed.*

*In this window, select the **Corridor Modeling Catalogs (Imperial, .NET)** thumbnail view; the **Corridor Modeling Catalogs (Imperial, .NET) - Autodesk Content Browser 2018** page is displayed.*

*In this page, choose the **Channel and Trench Pipe** Subassemblies; the subassemblies in this catalog are displayed. Next, place the cursor on the i text in the **Channel** subassembly thumbnail; the cursor changes to an i-drop symbol, as shown in Figure 7-47. Press and hold the left mouse button on the i-text, drag this symbol, and add it to the subassembly in the required tab of the **TOOL PALETTES**, refer to Figure 7-48. The **Channel** subassembly is now added to the chosen tab in the **TOOL PALETTE**.*

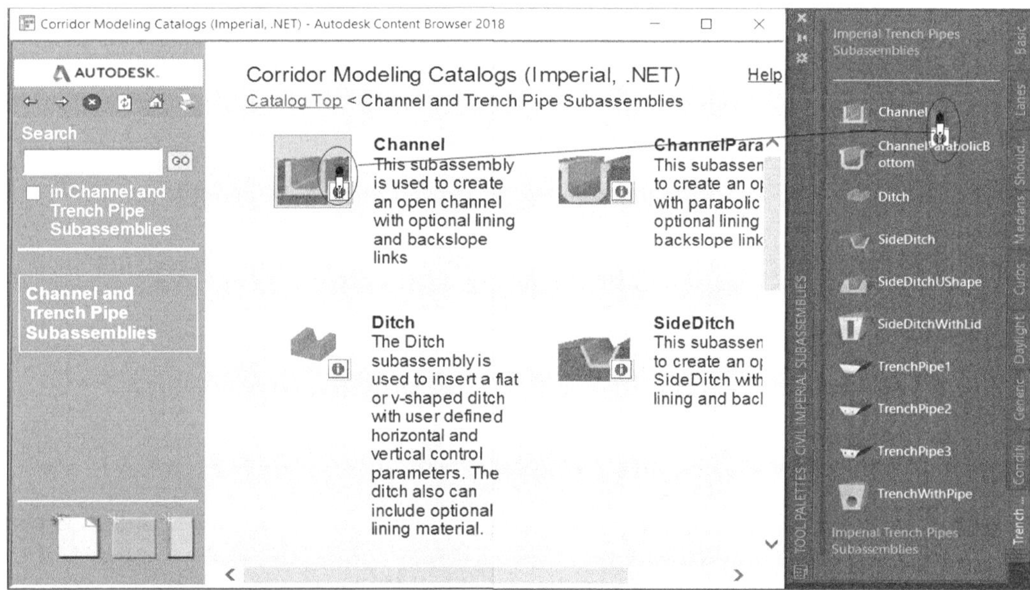

Figure 7-47 *Adding the **Channel** subassembly to the **TOOL PALETTE***

Note

*Adjust and dock the **Properties** window and the **TOOL PALETTES** to view the drawing area clearly. You can turn on the **Auto-hide** command to hide the **TOOL PALETTES**.*

3. In the **Properties** window, scroll down to view the **ADVANCED** rollout.

4. Modify the values of the **Channel** parameters as given below:

Depth: **9.000'** Bottom Width: **9.000'**

Note

Ensure that you press ENTER every time you modify a value. You can view the changes in the subassembly whenever you modify a parameter.

5. Close the **Properties** window.

6. Click on the marker on the assembly baseline; the **Channel** subassembly is added, as shown in Figure 7-48.

Figure 7-48 *The* ***Channel*** *subassembly added to assembly baseline*

7. Choose the **Basic** tab in the **TOOL PALETTES - CIVIL IMPERIAL SUBASSEMBLIES** if not chosen by default.

8. Choose the **BasicLaneTransition** subassembly from this tab; the **Properties** window is displayed. Ignore any error messages if displayed.

9. In the **PROPERTIES** window, set the **Default Width** parameter value to **9.000'** and press ENTER. Ensure that the **Side** parameter is set to **Right** if not set by default.

10. Click on the circular marker on the right backslope of the channel; the lane is added on the right side, as shown in Figure 7-49.

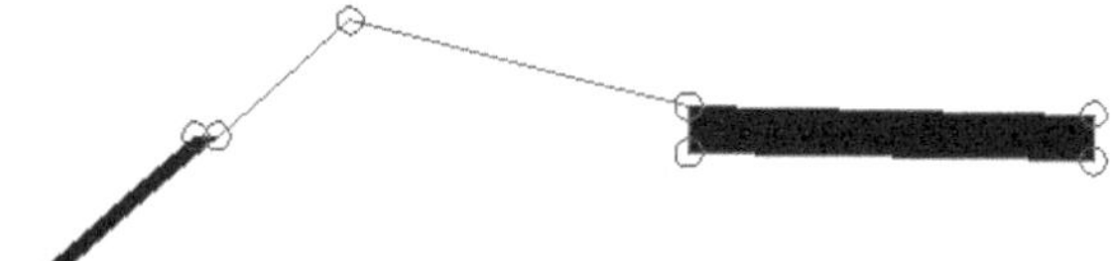

Figure 7-49 *The* ***BasicLaneTransition*** *subassembly added on the right side of the channel*

11. In the **Properties** window, set the **Side** parameter to **Left**.

12. Click on the marker on the left backslope of the **Channel** subassembly to add the **BasicLaneTransition** subassembly on the left side of the **Channel** subassembly.

13. Next, select the **BasicCurbAndGutter** subassembly from the **Basic** tab; the **Properties** window is updated and shows parameters for the **BasicCurbAndGutter** subassembly.

14. In the **Properties** window, set the **Gutter Width** value to **1.300'**. Set the **Side** parameter to **Right**.

15. Click on the circular marker on the top right edge of the **BasicLaneTransition** subassembly lane; the **BasicCurbAndGutter** subassembly is added to the right.

16. In the **Properties** window, set the **Side** parameter to **Left** and then click on the top left edge of the **BasicLaneTransition** subassembly on the left of assembly line; the **BasicCurbAndGutter** subassembly is added to the left side. Figure 7-50 shows the **Canal** assembly after adding the subassemblies.

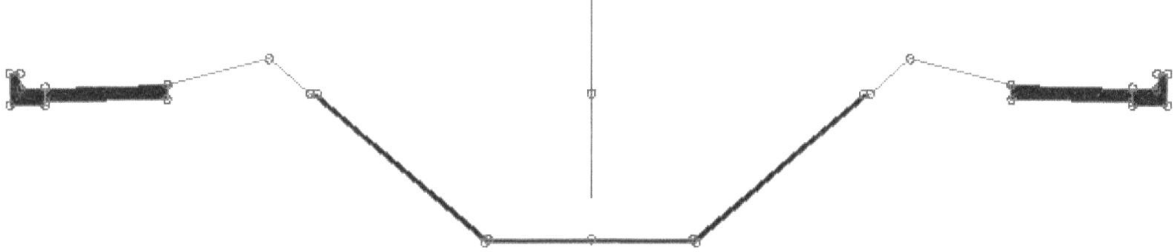

***Figure 7-50** The **Canal** assembly after adding three subassemblies*

17. Now, choose the **BasicSidewalk** subassembly from the **Basic** tab; the **Properties** window is updated accordingly. In this window, set the **Width** parameter value to **4.000'** and press ENTER. Set the **Side** parameter to **Right**.

18. Click on the circular mark on the top right edge of the **BasicCurbAndGutter** subassembly; the **BasicSidewalk** subassembly is added to the right of the baseline. Figure 7-51 shows the **BasicSidewalk** subassembly added to the right side.

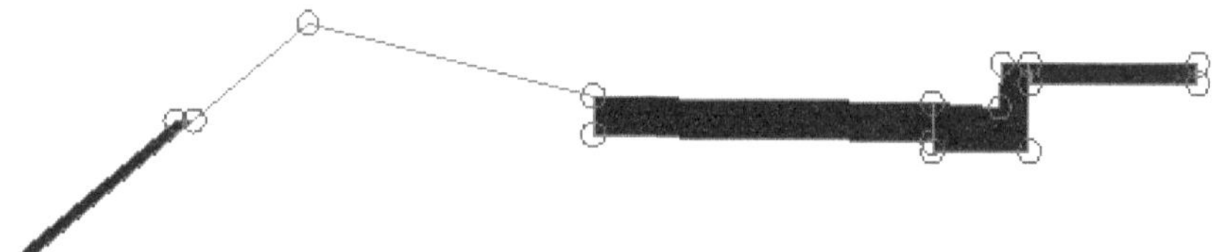

***Figure 7-51** The **BasicSideWalk** subassembly added on the right side*

19. In the **Properties** window, ensure that the **Width** parameter value is set to **4.000'** and press ENTER. Set the **Side** parameter to **Left**.

20. Click on the circular mark on the top left edge of the **BasicCurbAndGutter** subassembly on the left of the baseline; the **BasicSidewalk** subassembly is added to the left side of the baseline.

21. Next, select the **BasicSideSlopeCutDitch** subassembly from the **TOOL PALETTES**. Set the **Side** parameter to **Right** in this window.

22. Click on the marker on the top right edge of the **BasicSidewalk** subassembly; the **BasicSideSlopeCutDitch** subassembly is added, as shown in Figure 7-52.

23. Set the **Side** parameter to **Left** in the **PROPERTIES** window. Select the marker on the top left edge of the **BasicSidewalk** subassembly; the **BasicSideSlopeCutDitch** subassembly is added to the left. Figure 7-53 shows the **Canal** assembly with the added subassemblies.

24. Close the **Properties** windows and **TOOL PALETTES**, and press ESC to exit.

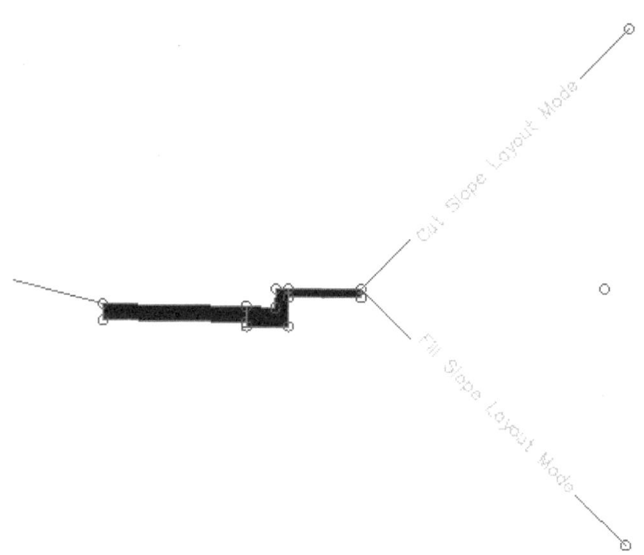

*Figure 7-52 The **BasicSideSlopeCutDitch** subassembly added to the right of the assembly baseline*

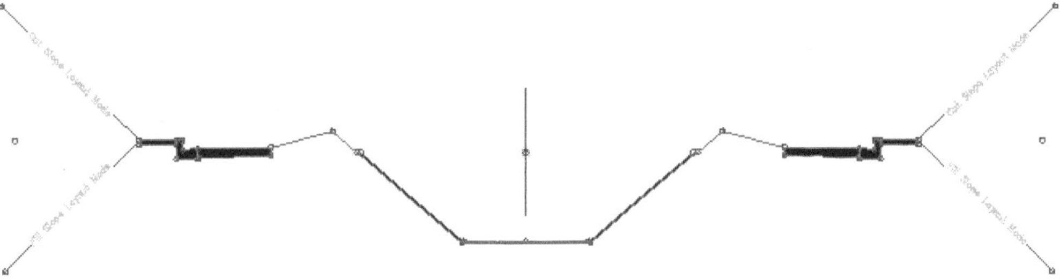

*Figure 7-53 The **Canal** assembly*

25. Choose the **Prospector** tab in the **TOOLSPACE** and expand the **Assemblies** node; the subassemblies that you have used are added to the **Canal** assembly, as shown in Figure 7-54.

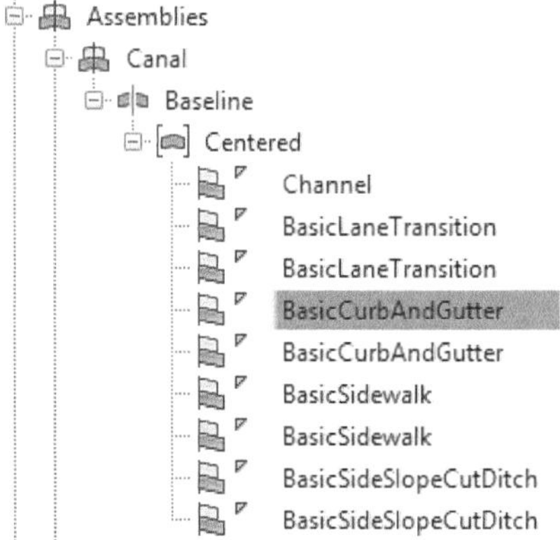

*Figure 7-54 The subassemblies in the **Canal** assembly node*

Creating a New Style for the Assembly

1. Choose the **Settings** tab in the **TOOLSPACE**.
2. Expand **Assembly > Assembly Styles** in the **Settings** tab. Note that **Basic** is the only assembly style available in this node.
3. Now, right-click on the **Assembly Styles** node; a shortcut menu is displayed.

4. Choose the **New** option from this shortcut menu; the **Assembly Style - New Assembly Style** dialog box is displayed.

5. Enter **Canal Style** in the **Name** edit box of the **Information** tab.

6. Next, choose the **Marker** tab. By default, the **Insertion Point** option is selected in the **Component** drop-down list.

7. From the **Use custom marker** area, choose the last button with a circle to override the default marker style, which is a circular marker style. 

8. Next, choose the fourth button, which is a button with a cross marker style, for the insertion point of the assembly. 

9. In the **Size** area of the **Marker** tab, select **Use size relative to screen** from the **Options** drop-down list, as shown in Figure 7-55.

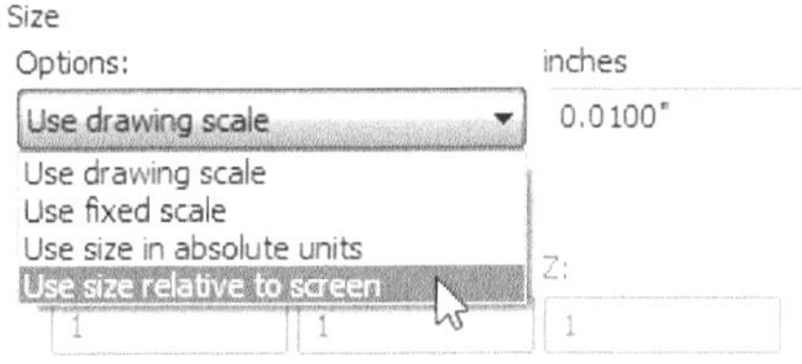

Figure 7-55 *Selecting the* ***Use size relative to screen*** *option from the* ***Options*** *drop-down list*

10. Now, assign a marker style to the baseline by selecting the **Baseline Point** option from the **Component** drop-down list, as shown in Figure 7-56.

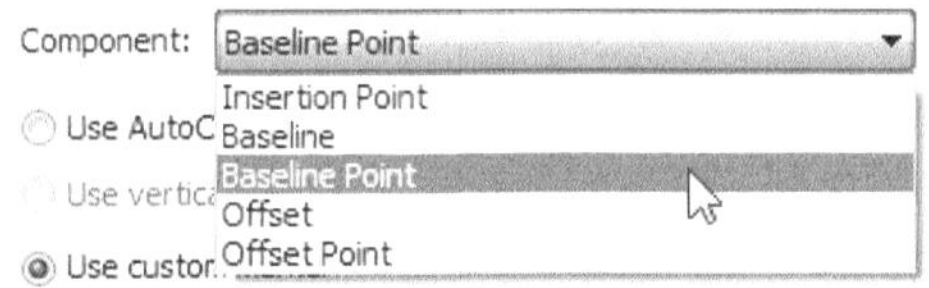

Figure 7-56 *Selecting the* ***Baseline Point*** *option from the* ***Component*** *drop-down list*

11. Next, select the **Use Custom marker** radio button if not selected by default; the **Custom marker style** buttons are activated.

12. Now, choose the default chosen button to deactivate it. Next, choose the button with a square symbol to activate it as the marker style for the **Baseline Point**. Next, choose the **Apply** button.

13. Now, choose the **Display** tab.

14. Click on the default color value of **Insertion Point** in the **Color** column; the **Select Color** dialog box is displayed.

15. Select **blue** and then choose the **OK** button from the **Select Color** dialog box.

16. Repeat the procedure followed in steps 14 and set the color of the **Baseline Point** to **magenta**.

17. Next, choose the **OK** button from the **Assembly Style - Canal Style** dialog box; the dialog box is closed and **Canal Style** is added to the **Assembly Styles** subnode in the **Settings** tab, as shown in Figure 7-57.

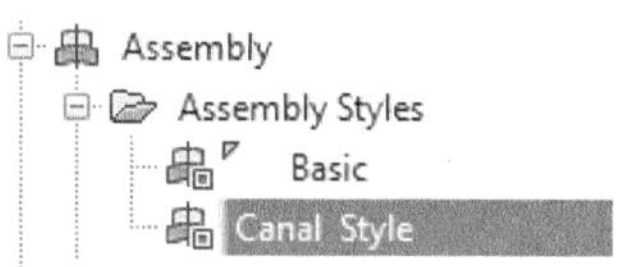

Figure 7-57 *The* ***Canal Style*** *added to the* ***Assembly Styles*** *subnode*

Creating a Style for Subassembly Components - Points

1. Expand **General > Multipurpose Styles > Marker Styles** in the **Settings** tab of the **TOOLSPACE**. Notice the existing styles for all the subassembly points used in this tutorial. The subassembly points are represented by the selected marker style.

2. Now, right-click on the **Marker Styles** subnode; a shortcut menu is displayed.

3. Choose the **New** option from this shortcut menu; the **Marker Style - New Marker Style** dialog box is displayed.

4. Enter **Canal Points** in the **Name** edit box in the **Information** tab.

5. Next, choose the **Marker** tab. In this tab, the **Use custom marker** radio button is selected by default.

6. Now, choose the button with a circle symbol to disable the circular marker style that is chosen by default.

7. Choose the third button from right with a plus sign. +

8. In the **Size** area, select the **Use size relative to screen** option from the **Options** drop-down list.

9. Enter **2.5** in the **Percent** edit box.

10. Next, choose the **Display** tab. In this tab, the **Plan** option is selected by default in the **View Direction** drop-down list.

11. In the **Component display** list box of this tab, set the color of the **Marker** component type to **green**.

12. Choose the **OK** button; the **Marker Style - Canal Points** dialog box is closed and the **Canal Points** style is added to the **Marker Styles** subnode of the **Settings** tab.

Creating a Style for the Subassembly Links

1. Right-click on the **Link Styles** subnode of the **Multipurpose Styles** node; a shortcut menu is displayed.

2. Choose the **New** option from the shortcut menu displayed; the **Link Style - New Link Style** dialog box is displayed.

3. Set the following parameters in the **Link Style - New Link Style** dialog box.

   Information tab
   Name: **Canal Link**

   Display tab
   Color: **red** Lineweight: **0.35mm**

4. Next, choose the **OK** button in the **Link Style - New Link Style** dialog box; the dialog box is closed and the new style is added to the **Link Styles** subnode in the **Settings** tab.

Creating a Style for Subassembly Shapes

1. Right-click on the **Shape Styles** subnode in the **Multipurpose Styles** node; a shortcut menu is displayed.

2. Choose the **New** option from the shortcut menu displayed; the **Shape Style - New Shape Style** dialog box is displayed.

3. Enter **Canal Shape** in the **Name** edit box in the **Information** tab. Next, choose the **Display** tab.

4. In the **Component display** list box of the **Display** tab, set the color of the **Shape Area Fill** component type to **cyan**.

5. In the **Component hatch display** list box of this tab, click on the default pattern in the **Pattern** column; the **Hatch Pattern** dialog box is displayed.

6. Now, select the **Predefined** option from the **Type** drop-down list in the **Pattern** area.

7. Next, select the **ANSI35** option from the **Pattern Name** drop-down list.

8. Choose the **OK** button to close the **Hatch Pattern** dialog box.

9. Next, choose the **OK** button; the **Shape Style - Canal shape** dialog box is closed and **Canal Shape** is added to the **Shape Styles** subnode of the **Settings** tab.

Creating a Label Style for the Subassemblies - Shape Labels

1. Expand **General > Label Styles > Shape** subnode in the **Settings** tab.

2. Right-click on the **Shape** subnode to display a shortcut menu and then choose the **New** option from it; the **Label Style Composer - New Subassembly Shape Label Style** dialog box is displayed.

3. In the **Information** tab, enter **Canal Label** in the **Name** edit box. Next, choose the **Layout** tab.

4. Click in the **Value** field of the **Contents** property; a browse button is displayed.

5. Choose the browse button; the **Text Component Editor - Contents** dialog box is displayed.

6. In the **Properties** tab, ensure that the **Shape Codes** option is selected from the **Properties** drop-down list and the shape code is added to the **Text Editor**.

7. Next, clear the text in the **Text Editor** (right pane). Select the **Shape Area** option from the **Properties** drop-down list and choose the right arrow button to add the shape area to the content of the shape label.

8. Now, choose the **OK** button; the **Text Component Editor - Contents** dialog box is closed.

9. In the **Label Style Composer - Canal Label** dialog box, set the **Text Height** to **0.0100"** and the **Color** property to **blue**.

10. Choose the **OK** button; the dialog box is closed and **Canal Label** is added to the **Shape** subnode of the **Settings** tab.

Creating a Code Set Style

1. Right-click on the **Code Set Styles** subnode in the **Multipurpose Styles** node in the **Settings** tab of the **TOOLSPACE**; a shortcut menu is displayed.

2. Choose the **New** option from the shortcut menu; the **Code Set Style - New Code Set Style** dialog box is displayed.

3. In the **Name** edit box of the **Information** tab of this dialog box, enter **Canal Code Set**.

4. Next, choose the **Codes** tab.

5. Click on the symbol in the **Style** column corresponding to the **<default>** option in the **Link** node; the **Pick Link Style** dialog box is displayed, as shown in Figure 7-58.

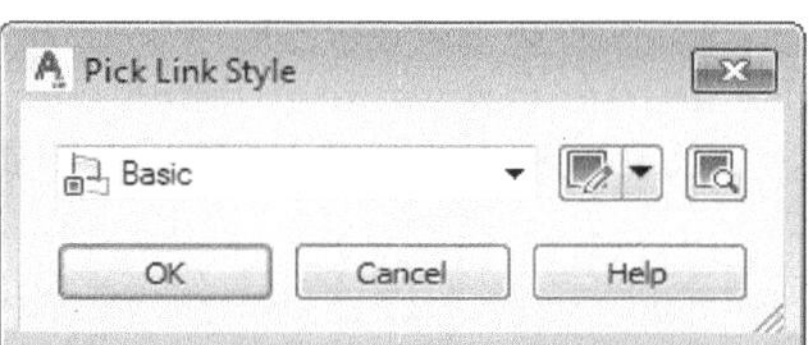

*Figure 7-58 The **Pick Link Style** dialog box*

6. Select the **Canal Link** option from the drop-down list in the **Pick Link Style** dialog box and choose the **OK** button; the **Pick Link Style** dialog box is closed.

7. Again, click on the symbol in the **Style** column corresponding to the **<default>** option in the **Point** node of the **Canal Code Set** dialog box; the **Pick Marker Style** dialog box is displayed.

8. Select **Canal Points** from the drop-down list in the **Pick Marker Style** dialog box and choose the **OK** button; the dialog box will be closed.

9. Click on the symbol in the **Style** column corresponding to the **<default>** option in the **Shape** node; the **Pick Shape Style** dialog box is displayed. Select the **Canal Shape** option from the drop-down list in the dialog box and then choose the **OK** button to close this dialog box.

10. Now, click on the symbol in the **Label Style** column corresponding to the **<default>** option in the **Shape** node; the **Pick Style** dialog box is displayed.

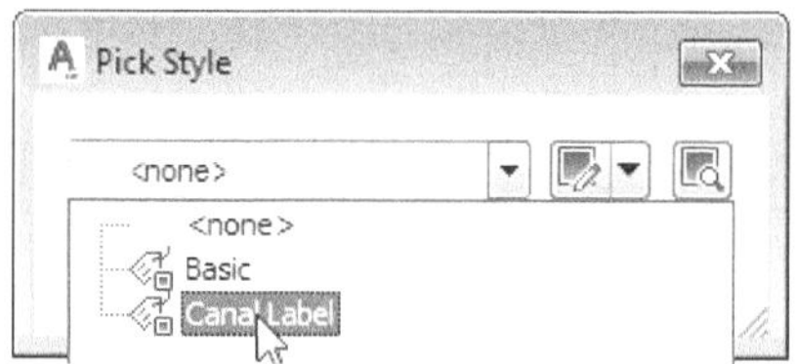

Figure 7-59 *Selecting the* ***Canal Label*** *option from the* ***Pick Style*** *dialog box*

11. Select the **Canal Label** option from the drop-down list in the **Pick Style** dialog box, as shown in Figure 7-59. Next, choose the **OK** button in the **Pick Style** dialog box; the dialog box is closed. Next, choose the **OK** button in the **Code Set Style** dialog box; the dialog box is closed and the code set style is created.

Assigning the Assembly and Code Set Styles

1. Select the assembly baseline in the drawing and right-click; a shortcut menu is displayed.

2. Choose the **Assembly Properties** option from the shortcut menu; the **Assembly Properties - Canal** dialog box is displayed.

3. In the **Information** tab of the dialog box, select the **Canal Style** option from the drop-down list in the **Object style** area.

4. Next, choose the **Codes** tab.

5. Select the **Canal Code Set** option from the **Code set style** drop-down list.

6. Next, choose the **Apply** button to apply the style to the assembly in the drawing. Next, choose the **OK** button; the **Assembly Properties - Canal** dialog box is closed. Figure 7-60 shows the assembly after assigning the **Canal Style** style. Figure 7-61 shows the **Canal** assembly with the **Canal Code Set** style assigned to the subassemblies.

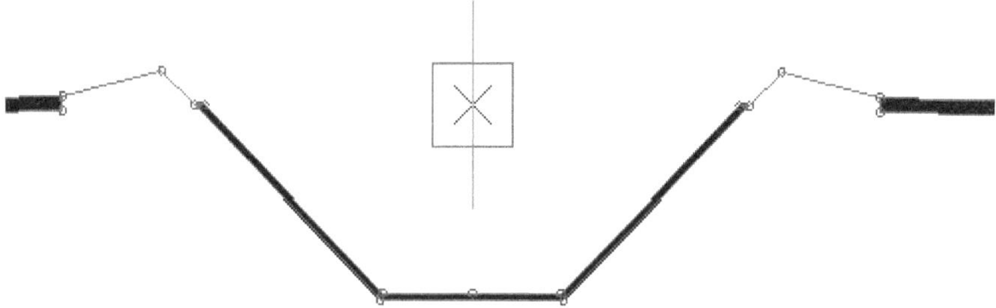

Figure 7-60 *Assemblies after assigning* ***Canal Style***

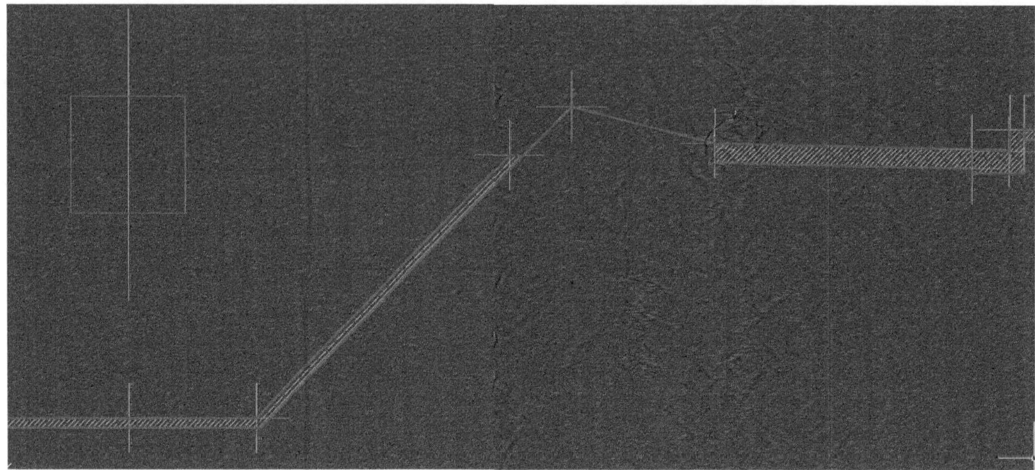

Figure 7-61 Subassemblies after assigning the ***Canal Code Set*** *style*

Note
Styles can be created before creating assembly and subassemblies.

Saving the File

1. Choose **Save As** from the **Application Menu**; the **Save Drawing As** dialog box is displayed.

2. In this dialog box, browse to the following location:

   C:\c3d_2018\c07_c3d_2018_tut

3. In the **File name** edit box, enter **c07_tut02a**.

4. Next, choose the **Save** button; the file is saved with the name *c07_tut02a.dwg* at the specified location.

Tutorial 3 Customized Subassembly

In this tutorial, you will create a customized **UShapeDitch** subassembly, as shown in Figure 7-62 using the **Create Subassembly from Polyline** tool. **(Expected time: 30 min)**

The following steps are required to complete this tutorial:

a. Download and open the file.
b. Convert the polyline object into the subassembly.
c. Create the label styles.
d. Add the subassembly to the assembly.
e. Save the file.

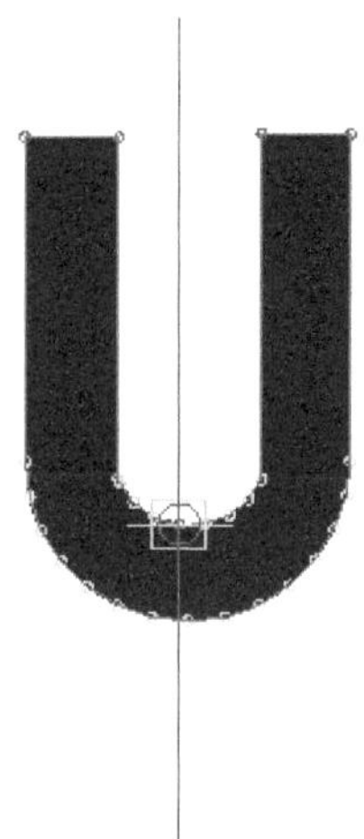

*Figure 7-62 The **UShapeDitch** subassembly to be created*

Downloading and Opening the File

1. Download *c07_c3d_2018_tut.zip* file if not downloaded earlier, from *www.cadcim.com*. Next, save and extract the file at *C:\c3d_2018*.

2. Choose **Open** from the **Application Menu**; the **Select File** dialog box is displayed.

3. In the dialog box, browse to the location *C:\c3d_2018c07_c3d_2018_tut* where you have saved the file.

4. Select the file *c07_c3d_2018_tut03.dwg* and then choose the **Open** button to open the file.

Creating the Subassembly

1. Choose the **Create Subassembly - From Polyline** tool from the **Create Design** panel of the **Home** tab; you are prompted to select an entity.

2. Next, select the polyline object from the drawing; the **Create Subassembly - From Polyline** dialog box is displayed.

3. Enter **UShapeDitch** in the **Name** edit box of this dialog box, as shown in Figure 7-63.

4. Select the **Single** option from the **Link creation** drop-down list if not selected by default. Ensure that the **Code set style** is set to **All Codes with Hatching**.

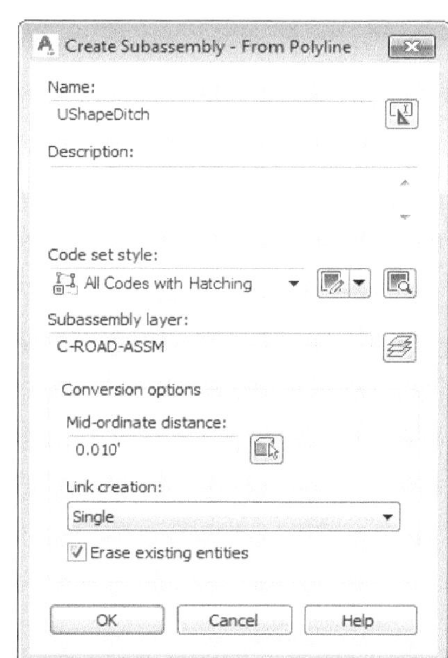

*Figure 7-63 Entering the text in the **Name** edit box*

5. Next, choose the **OK** button; the U-shaped object is changed to a subassembly, as shown in Figure 7-64.

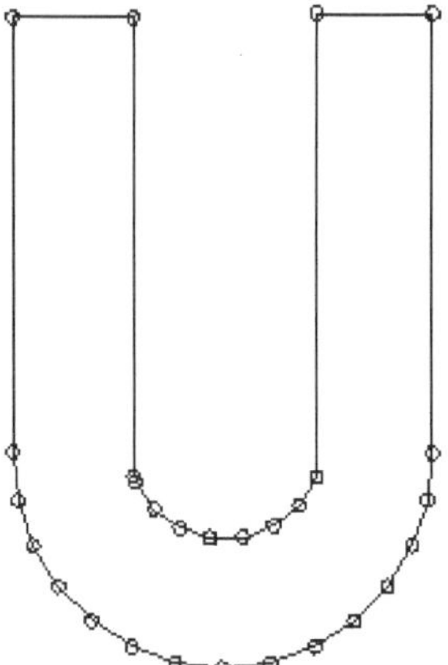

*Figure 7-64 The **UShapeDitch** subassembly*

Note

You will notice circles are attached along the subassembly boundary. These circles are the subassembly points, and the lines joining these points are the subassembly links.

Adding Point Codes

1. Select the subassembly and right-click; a shortcut menu is displayed.
2. Choose the **Add Code** option from the shortcut menu; you are prompted to enter the code.
3. Enter **p1** in the command line and press ENTER; you are prompted to select subassembly point, links, or shape.
4. Next, select the subassembly point at **A** by clicking on the circle at **A**, refer to Figure 7-65; the color of the circle is changed to purple and the code **p1** is assigned to the selected point.
5. Repeat the procedure followed in steps 1 through 4 to assign **p2** to **p5** codes to points B, C, D and E respectively.
6. Place the cursor over the assigned point; a tooltip with the subassembly name, layer, and other details is displayed, as shown in Figure 7-66. Before assigning the point codes, you can check the point numbers displayed in the tooltip.

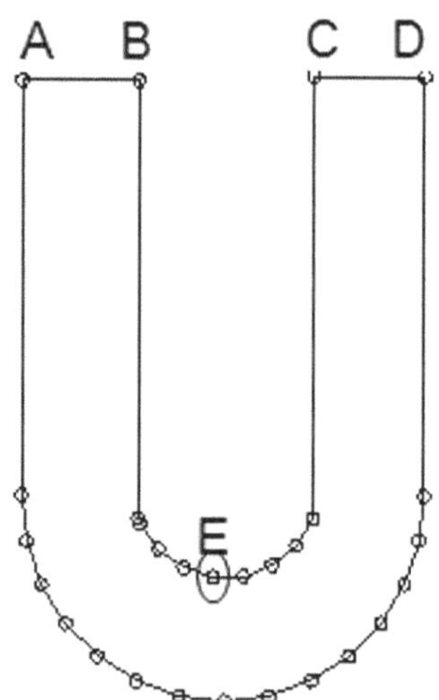

Figure 7-65 Points labeled for assigning the point codes

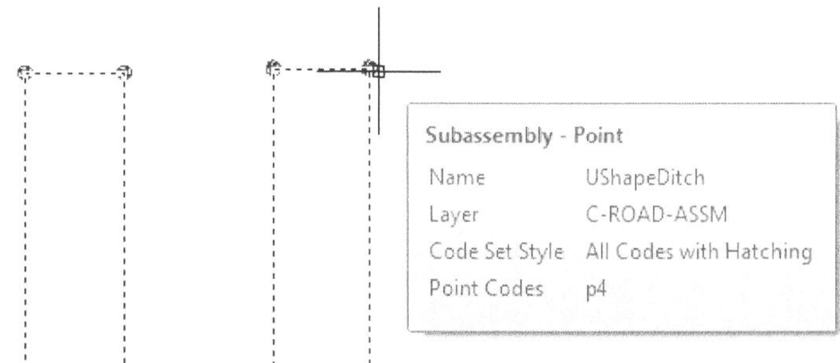

Figure 7-66 *The tooltip displayed on placing the cursor on the point*

Adding the Link Codes

1. Select the subassembly and right-click; a shortcut menu is displayed.

2. Choose the **Add Code** option from the shortcut menu displayed.

3. Enter **l1** in the command line and press ENTER; you are prompted to select either a subassembly point, links, or shape.

4. Select a line joining the points; the **l1** code is assigned to the subassembly links (lines joining the points) and the color of the lines changes to blue.

5. Place the cursor over the subassembly link; a tooltip is displayed with the subassembly information such as link code, subassembly name and other details, refer to Figure 7-67.

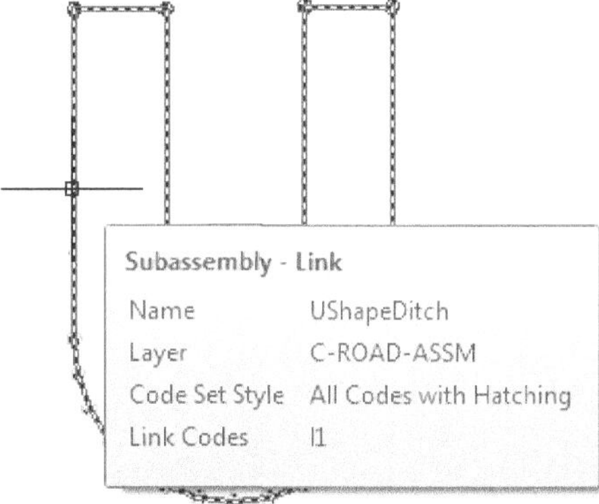

Figure 7-67 *The tooltip displaying the subassembly link information*

Note

*All the subassembly links have the same link number and the same link code assigned to them. This is because, while creating subassembly, the **Single** option is selected from the **Link creation** drop-down list in the **Conversion options** area of the **Create Subassembly - Polyline** dialog box.*

Adding the Shape and the Shape Code

1. Select the subassembly and right-click; a shortcut menu is displayed.

2. Choose the **Add Shape** option from the shortcut menu displayed; you are prompted to select the subassemblies links.

3. Select the subassembly link (line joining the subassembly points) and right-click; the subassembly is filled with a fill pattern and the shape is added, as shown in Figure 7-68.

4. Select the subassembly and right-click; a shortcut menu is displayed. Next, choose the **Add Code** option from the displayed menu.

5. Enter **U-Ditch** in the command line and press ENTER; you are prompted to select a subassembly point, link, or shape.

6. Next, click on the fill material of the subassembly to select the shape; the **U-Ditch** shape code is assigned to the subassembly. To verify, place the cursor over the fill pattern; a tooltip is displayed with the subassembly information.

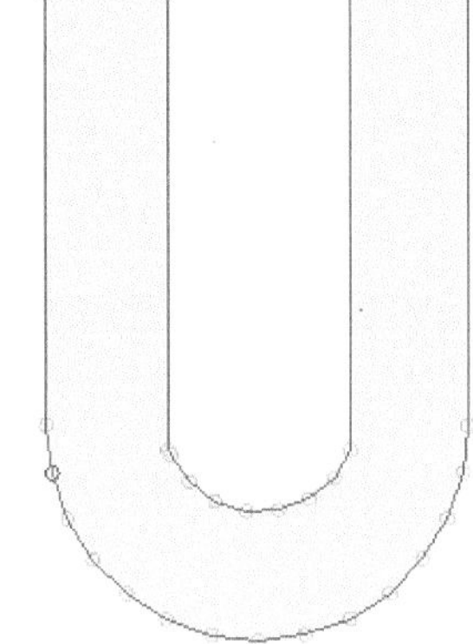

***Figure 7-68** The **UShapeDitch** subassembly after adding the shape*

Modifying the Origin

1. Select the subassembly; a blue colored square marker is displayed, as shown in Figure 7-69. This marker represents the origin or the insertion point of the subassembly.

***Figure 7-69** Partial view of the **UShapeDitch** subassembly displaying the square marker*

2. Select the subassembly and right-click; a shortcut menu is displayed.

3. Choose the **Modify Origin** option from this menu; you are prompted to specify a new hook point.

4. Select the point labeled **E (p5)**, refer to Figure 7-65. On doing so, the origin is modified and the **Subassembly hook point has been modified** message is displayed in the command line.

5. Select the subassembly again to view the modified origin. The origin is displayed at the point **E** of the subassembly.

Creating a New Point Label Style

1. Expand **General > Label Styles > Marker** in the **Settings** tab of the **TOOLSPACE**. The existing marker label style used is **Offset Elevation**.

2. Right-click on the **Marker** node; a shortcut menu is displayed.

3. Choose the **New** option from the shortcut menu; the **Label Style Composer - New Subassembly Marker Label Style** dialog box is displayed.

4. Enter **New Marker Label Style** in the **Name** edit box and then choose the **Layout** tab.

5. Click in the value field of the **Contents** property in the **Layout** tab; a browse button is displayed on the right of this field.

6. Choose the browse button displayed; the **Text Component Editor - Contents** dialog box is displayed.

7. Delete the text displayed in the **Text Editor** window of the **Properties** tab of the **Text Component Editor - Contents** dialog box.

8. Next, select the **Point Code** option from the **Properties** drop-down list and then choose the arrow button displayed on the right of this drop-down list. 

9. Next, choose the **OK** button; the **Text Component Editor - Contents** dialog box is closed.

10. Next, set the **Text Height** to **0.0030"** and **Color** to **blue** in the **Label Style Composer - New Marker Label Style** dialog box.

11. Choose the **OK** button; the **Label Style Composer- New Marker Label Style** dialog box is closed.

Creating a New Shape Label Style

1. Expand **General > Label Styles > Shape** subnode in the **Settings** tab.

2. Right-click on the **Shape** node; a shortcut menu is displayed.

3. Choose the **New** option from the shortcut menu; the **Label Style Composer - New Subassembly Shape Label Style** dialog box is displayed.

4. In this dialog box, specify the following parameters:

   Name: **New Shape Label Style** Color: **red (Layout tab)**

   Text Height: **0.0030" (Layout tab)**

5. Next, choose the **OK** button; the dialog box is closed and a new shape label style is created.

Editing the Code Set Style

1. Select the subassembly and right-click; a shortcut menu is displayed.

2. Choose the **Subassembly Properties** option from the shortcut menu; the **Subassembly Properties - UShapeDitch** dialog box is displayed.

3. Next, choose the **Codes** tab in this dialog box.

4. Select the **Basic** option from the **Code set style** drop-down list.

5. Choose the **OK** button; the **Subassembly Properties - UShapeDitch** dialog box is closed.

6. Next, expand **General > Multipurpose > Code Set Styles** subnode.

7. Right-click on the **Basic** subnode and choose the **Edit** option from the shortcut menu; the **Code Set Style - Basic** dialog box is displayed.

8. Choose the **Codes** tab in this dialog box.

9. Next, choose the **Import codes** button displayed on the lower right corner of this tab; the **Code Set Style - Basic** dialog box is closed and you are prompted to select the subassemblies, assemblies, or corridor from which you want to import the codes.

10. Select the subassembly from the drawing and press ENTER; the **Code Set Style - Basic** dialog box is displayed again and all the codes assigned to the **U-shaped Ditch** subassembly are added to the code set. Note that the label style for the point, link, and the shape codes is set to **None**.

11. Click on the symbol in the **Label Style** column for the **p1** code; the **Pick Style** dialog box is displayed.

12. Next, select the **New Marker Label Style** option from the drop-down list in the **Pick Style** dialog box and then choose **OK** button; the dialog box is closed.

13. Repeat steps 11 and 12. Set the label style for other point codes (**p2** to **p5**) to **New Marker Label Style**, and the shape code label style to **New Shape Label Style**.

14. Similarly, set the label style for **U-Ditch** to **New Shape Label Style**, as shown in Figure 7-70.

15. Choose the **OK** button; the **Code Set Style - Basic** dialog box is closed. The point code and the shape code labels are added to the subassembly, as shown in Figure 7-71.

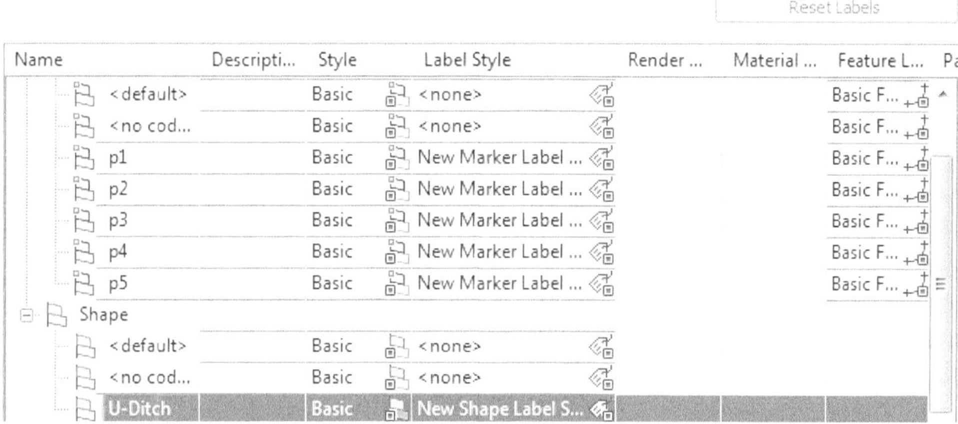

*Figure 7-70 The **New Marker Label Style** and the **New Shape Label Style** label style assigned to the point codes and the shape code*

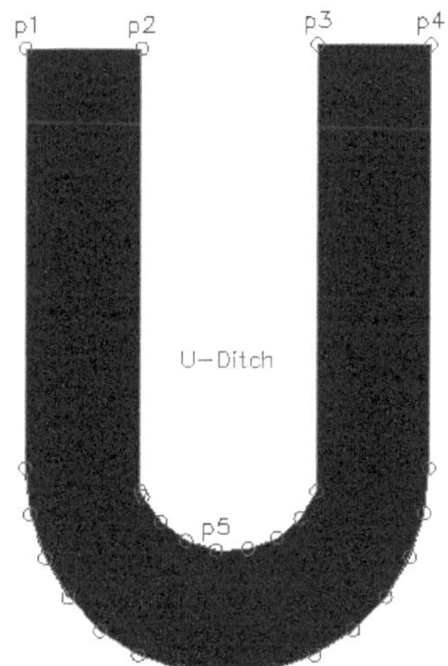

*Figure 7-71 The **UShapeDitch** subassembly with the point and shape code labels*

Adding the Customized U-shaped Ditch to the Assembly

1. Choose the **Create Assembly** tool from **Home > Create Design > Assembly** drop-down; the **Create Assembly** dialog box is displayed.

2. Enter **Baseline** in the **Name** edit box and choose the **OK** button to close the dialog box; you are prompted to specify the baseline location. Specify the baseline location in the drawing.

3. Next, select the **UShapeDitch** subassembly and right-click; a shortcut menu is displayed.

4. Choose the **Add to Assembly** option from the shortcut menu; you are prompted to select a marker point within the assembly.

5. Select the marker of the baseline; the **UShapeDitch** subassembly is added to the assembly at the origin, as shown in Figure 7-72.

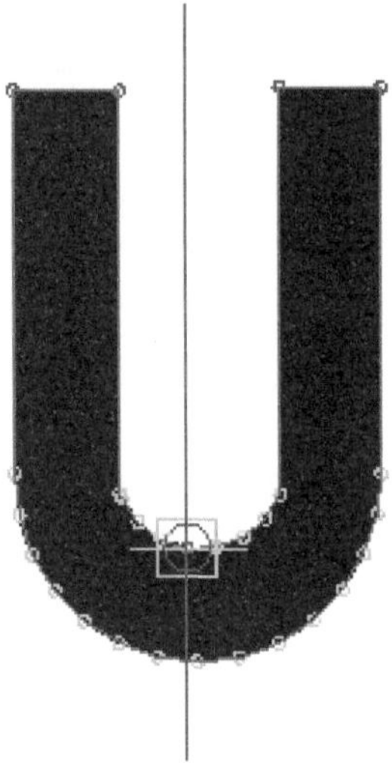

*Figure 7-72 The **UShapeDitch** subassembly attached to the assembly baseline*

Saving the File

1. Choose **Save As** from the **Application Menu**; the **Save Drawing As** dialog box is displayed.

2. In this dialog box, browse to the following location:

   C:\c3d_2018\c07_c3d_2018_tut

3. In the **File name** edit box, enter **c07_tut03a**.

4. Next, choose the **Save** button; the file is saved with the name *c07_tut03a.dwg* at the specified location.

Tutorial 4 Divided Lane

In this tutorial, you will create an assembly for the lane.

(Expected time: 30 min)

The following steps are required to complete this tutorial.

a. Download and open the file.
b. Create an assembly baseline.
c. Add subassemblies.
d. Save the file.

Downloading and Opening the File

1. Download *c07_c3d_2018_tut.zip* file, if not downloaded earlier, from *http://www.cadcim.com*. Next, save and extract the file at *C:\c3d_2018*.

2. Choose **Open** from the **Application Menu**; the **Select File** dialog box is displayed.

3. In the dialog box, browse to the location *C:\c3d_2018\c07_c3d_2018_tut* where you have saved the file.

4. Select the file *c07_c3d_2018_tut04.dwg* and then choose the **Open** button to open the file. Ignore any error message if displayed.

Creating an Assembly

1. Choose the **Create Assembly** tool from the **Home > Create Design > Assembly** drop-down; the **Create Assembly** dialog box is displayed.

2. Enter **Divided Lane** in the **Name** edit box.

3. Choose the **OK** button; the dialog box is closed and you are prompted to specify the location of the assembly baseline.

4. Click in the drawing area; an assembly baseline is created and the **Divided Lane** is added in the **Assemblies** node in the **Prospector** tab of the **TOOLSPACE**.

Adding Subassemblies

1. Choose the **Tool Palettes** button from the **Palettes** panel of the **Home** tab; the **TOOL PALETTES - CIVIL IMPERIAL SUBASSEMBLIES** is displayed.

2. Choose the **Medians** tab from the **TOOL PALETTES - CIVIL IMPERIAL SUBASSEMBLIES**.

3. Next, choose the **MedianDepressedShoulderExt** subassembly; the **PROPERTIES** window is displayed.

   In this tutorial, you will use the subassembly with its default property values.

4. Select the marker on the assembly baseline and then click; the subassembly is added, as shown in Figure 7-73.

Tip
*Right-click on the **MedianDepressedShoulderExt** subassembly in the **TOOL PALETTES**; a shortcut menu is displayed. Choose **Help** from the shortcut menu to get familiarized with the subassembly parameters.*

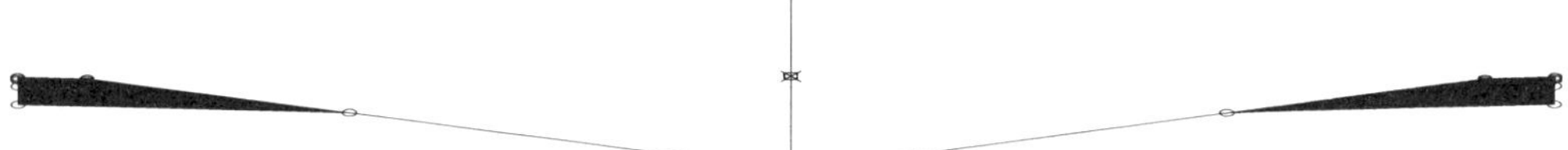

Figure 7-73 *The **MedianDepressedShoulderExt** subassembly added to the assembly*

5. Next, choose the **LaneOutsideSuperWithWidening** subassembly from the **Lanes** tab of the **TOOL PALETTES- CIVIL IMPERIAL SUBASSEMBLIES**.

6. Ensure that the **Side** property in the **PROPERTIES** window is set to **Right**. Select the top circle on the right edge of the **MedianDepressedShoulderExt** subassembly and then click; the **LaneOutsideSuperwithWidening** subassembly is added to the right side of the assembly baseline.

7. Set the **Side** parameter in the **PROPERTIES** window to **Left** and add the **LaneOutsideSuperWithWidening** subassembly on the left side, as explained previously, refer to Figure 7-74.

Figure 7-74 *The* ***LaneOutsideSuperWithWidening*** *subassembly added*

8. Choose the **ShoulderExtendAll** subassembly from the **Shoulders** tab of the **TOOL PALETTES-CIVIL IMPERIAL SUBASSEMBLIES**.

9. Set the **Side** parameter to **Right** in the **PROPERTIES** window.

10. Click on the circle on the top right edge of the **LaneOutsideSuperWithWidening** subassembly; the **ShoulderExtendAll** subassembly is added to the right side of the assembly baseline.

11. Set the **Side** parameter to **Left** in the **PROPERTIES** window and add the **ShoulderExtendAll** subassembly to the left side. The subassembly is added on both sides, as shown in Figure 7-75.

Figure 7-75 *The* ***ShoulderExtendAll*** *subassembly added on both sides*

12. Now, choose the **Daylight** tab from the **TOOL PALETTES**.

13. Choose the **DaylightStandard** subassembly; the **PROPERTIES** window is displayed. In this window, set the **Side** parameter in the **PROPERTIES** window to **Right**.

14. Click on the circle on the lower right edge of the **ShoulderExtendAll** subassembly; the **DaylightStandard** subassembly is added, as shown in Figure 7-76.

*Figure 7-76 The **DaylightStandard** subassembly added*

15. Set the **Side** parameter in the **PROPERTIES** window to **Left** to add the **DaylightStandard** subassembly on the left side of the assembly baseline.

16. Press ESC to exit the command and close the **TOOL PALETTES**; the **Divided Lane** assembly is created and displayed, as shown in Figure 7-77.

*Figure 7-77 The **Divided Lane** assembly*

Saving the File

1. Choose **Save As** from the **Application Menu**; the **Save Drawing As** dialog box is displayed.

2. In this dialog box, browse to the following location:

   C:\c3d_2018\c07_c3d_2018

3. In the **File name** edit box, enter **c07_tut04a**.

4. Next, choose the **Save** button; the file is saved with the name *c07_tut04a.dwg* at the specified location.

Self-Evaluation Test

Answer the following questions and then compare them to those given at the end of this chapter:

1. Which of the following defines a set of style for the point, link, and shape code for an assembly?

   a) **Design Check Sets** b) **Label Sets**
   c) **Band Sets** d) **Code Set Styles**

2. Which of the following tools is used to create an assembly for a service road on either side of a highway?

   a) **Create Assembly** b) **Add Assembly Offset**
   c) **Offset** d) **Create Subassembly from Polyline**

3. Which of the following styles cannot be defined using the **Assembly Style <Assembly Name>** dialog box?

   a) **Insertion Point**
   b) **Baseline** and **Baseline Point**
   c) **Offset** and **Offset Point**
   d) **Point Code, Link code and Shape Code**

4. In which panel of the **Assembly <Assembly Name>** (contextual) tab, you can find the **Catalog** tool which is used to invoke the AutoCAD Catalog Library?

   a) **Launch Pad**
   b) **Modify Assembly**
   c) **Modify Subassembly**
   d) **General Tools**

5. An assembly is a collection of smaller units called _________.

6. When you select a subassembly from the **TOOL PALETTES**, the _________ window is displayed.

7. To create an assembly, you need to first define the _________ and then add subassemblies to it.

8. The points on a subassembly represent the ______________ or the end points of a subassembly.

9. A line joining any two points of the subassembly is called _________.

10. An assembly consists of a baseline and the subassemblies attached to the baseline. (T/F)

11. A baseline is an inclined line with a marker. (T/F)

12. The subassemblies are added to the left and right of the assembly baseline. (T/F)

13. Each subassembly has two components: points and links. (T/F)

14. In-built subassemblies can be accessed using the **TOOL PALETTES**. (T/F)

Review Questions

Answer the following questions:

1. Civil 3D allows you to create customized subassemblies using the _________ tool.

2. The _________ language is used to create customized and parametric subassemblies.

3. Before adding the subassembly to a baseline, you need to specify the side in the _________ parameter of the **PROPERTIES** window.

4. You can view the properties of a subassembly in the _________ dialog box.

5. The __________ subassembly catalog consists of subassembly tools that help you in creating the corridor model for the first time.

6. The **Create Subassembly from Polyline** dialog box is used to create a subassembly using a polyline. (T/F)

7. The Code set style is a collection or a set of multiple code styles. (T/F)

8. The **PROPERTIES** window displays all the parameters of the selected subassembly. (T/F)

9. The **Corridor Modeling Catalog** window displays six different catalogs. (T/F)

10. You can use the **i-drop** symbol to add the required subassembly to the **TOOL PALETTES**. (T/F)

EXERCISES

Exercise 1

Create a Road assembly, refer to Figure 7-78 using the following subassemblies and parameters: **(Expected time: 30 min)**

Road Assembly Name: **Perkins Road**

Subassembly 1: **BasicLaneTransition**
Default Width: **10.000'**

Subassembly 2: **BasicCurbAndGutter**
Gutter Width: **1.500'**

Subassembly 3: **UrbanSidewalk**
Sidewalk Width: **3.000'**

Subassembly 4: **SideDitch**
Inside Extension Height: **0.000'**
Inside Backslope Width: **0.000'**

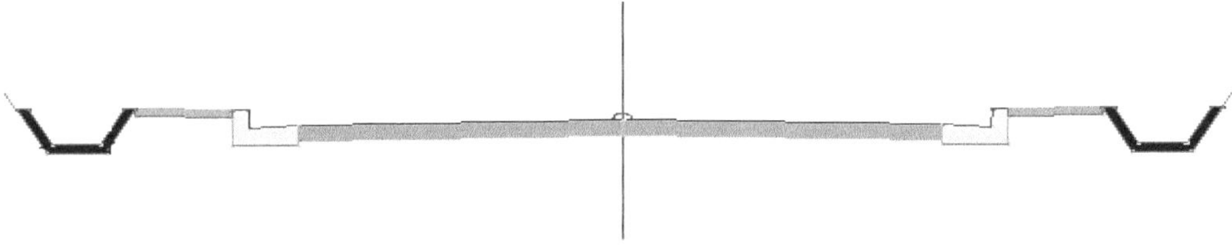

***Figure 7-78** The **Perkins Road** assembly*

Exercise 2

Create a pipe trench assembly, as shown in Figure 7-79 using the following subassembly and parameters: **(Expected time: 30 min)**

Assembly Name: **PipeTrench**
Subassembly: **TrenchPipe1**

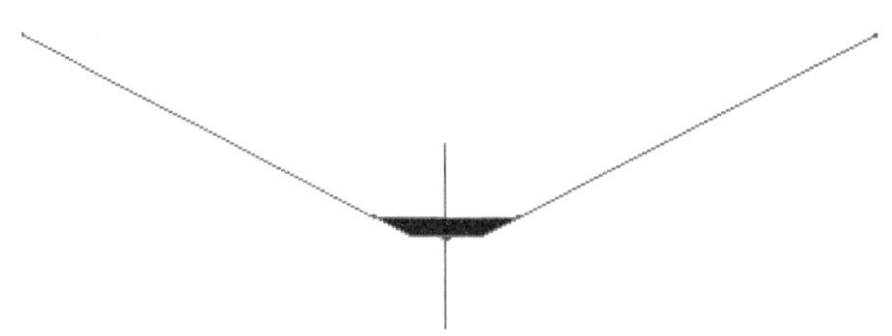

*Figure 7-79 The **PipeTrench** assembly*

Tip
*Select the subassembly after adding to the assembly and right-click to display the shortcut menu. Choose the **Subassembly Properties** from it. Next, choose the **Parameters** tab from the **Subassemblies Properties - Trench Pipe1** dialog box. Choose the **Subassembly help** button to display the **AutoCAD Civil 3D 2018 - English - Help** window. Study and understand the parameters and the subassembly diagram. Choose the **OK** button to close the dialog box. Next you can modify the input parameters in the **Properties** window.*

After understanding the input parameters of the **TrenchPipe1** subassembly, change the following input parameters in the **PROPERTIES** window:

Bedding Depth: **1.000'**
Sideslope: **2.00:1**
Width: **4.000'**

Answers to Self-Evaluation Test

1. d, **2.** b, **3.** d, **4.** a, **5.** subassemblies, **6. Properties**, **7.** assembly basepoint, **8.** vertices, **9.** link, **10.** T, **11.** F, **12.** T, **13.** F, **14.** T

Chapter 8

Working with Corridors and Parcels

Learning Objectives

After completing this chapter, you will be able to:
- *Create simple and complex corridors*
- *Edit corridors*
- *Calculate earthwork volumes for the corridor*
- *Create corridor surfaces*
- *Add corridor boundaries*
- *Extract corridor solids and bodies*
- *Create parcels using objects*
- *Create parcels using the layout tools and the Right of Way tool*
- *View and edit parcel properties*

OVERVIEW

A corridor is a three-dimensional model of a design encompassing the horizontal, vertical, and the cross-sectional geometries. In other words, a corridor is a combination of an alignment that provides horizontal geometry, a profile that provides vertical geometry, and an assembly that provides cross-sectional geometry. These Civil 3D objects are combined together to create a dynamic three-dimensional corridor model.

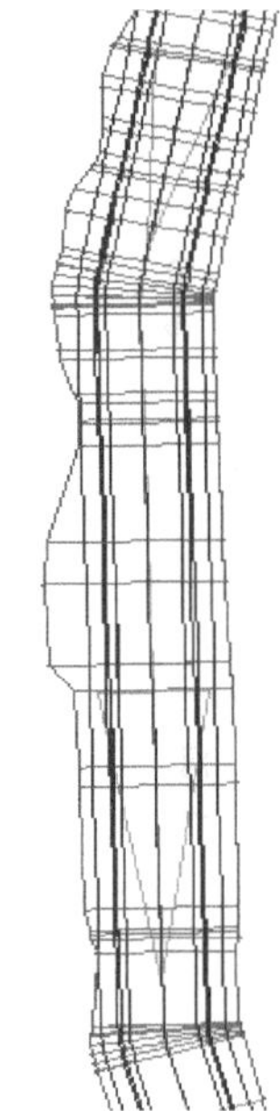

Figure 8-1 2D view of a corridor model

Corridors for intersections, cul-de-sacs, and branching streams are complex models as they use multiple alignments and assemblies for their creation. Figure 8-1 shows the 2D view of a corridor in a plan view.

A corridor model displays different components such as points, point codes, links, link codes, subassemblies, feature lines, and surfaces that are using link codes and feature lines. These points and links are derived from subassemblies. Feature lines are the longitudinal lines that connect the identical point codes. These lines are created automatically when a corridor model is built. Each feature line is assigned the code similar to the point codes that the line connects to. Thus, feature line codes add a fourth dimension to the corridor model. Figure 8-2 shows the feature lines connecting the point codes and the 2D cross-section of assemblies placed after fixed intervals.

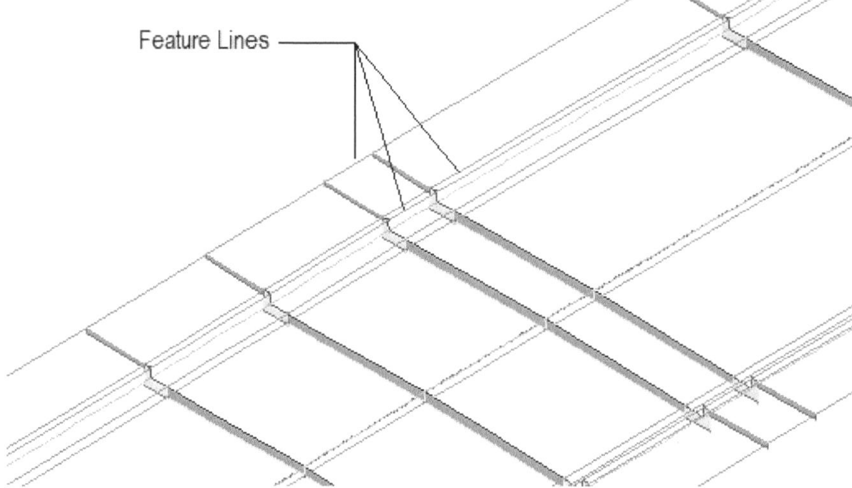

Figure 8-2 Feature lines of the corridor

CORRIDORS

A corridor can be a simple model created from a single alignment or a complex model created using multiple alignments. An alignment used for creating a corridor is called a baseline. Next, you will learn to create a corridor model using the **Create Corridor** interface in AutoCAD Civil 3D.

Creating Corridor

Ribbon: Home > Create Design > Corridor
Command: CREATECORRIDOR

The **Create Corridor** dialog box is used to specify the settings for creating a corridor. To create a corridor, choose the **Corridor** tool from the **Create Design** panel; the **Create Corridor** dialog box will be displayed, as shown in Figure 8-3.

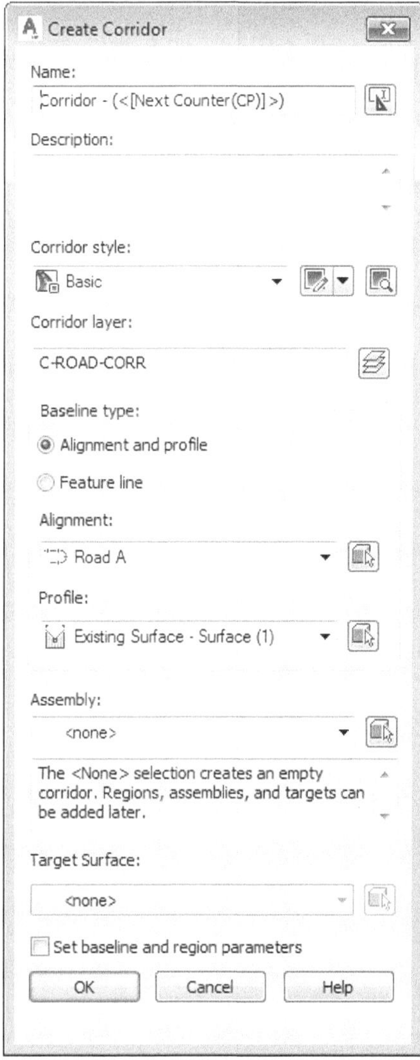

***Figure 8-3** The **Create Corridor** dialog box*

Note that to create a corridor in a drawing, you need to have a surface, an alignment, and a profile object in your drawing.

The options in the **Create Corridor** dialog box are discussed next.

Name

You can specify a name for the corridor in the **Name** edit box.

Description

You can enter the description about the corridor in the **Description** edit box.

Corridor style

You can select a corridor style from the **Corridor style** drop-down list. To create a new style or edit the existing style, click on the down arrow next to the **Corridor style** drop-down list; a flyout will be displayed. Choose the required option from the flyout to create or edit the corridor style.

Corridor layer

The **Corridor layer** text box displays the default layer on which the corridor will be created. To assign a different layer or to create a new layer for the corridor, choose the button displayed on the right of **Corridor layer** text box; the **Object Layer** dialog box will be displayed. Choose the appropriate options in this dialog box to select or create a layer for the corridor creation.

Baseline type

In AutoCAD Civil 3D, you can specify a feature line or an alignment and a profile as the baseline for the corridor.

Alignment and profile

You can select an alignment and a profile as the baseline for creating the corridor by selecting the **Alignment and profile** radio button in the **Baseline type** area. On doing so, the **Alignment** and **Profile** drop-downs will be displayed. Choose the required alignment from the **Alignment** drop-down and the required profile from the **Profile** drop-down. Alternatively, you can select the alignment from the drawing by choosing the **Select from the drawing** button that is displayed on the right of the **Alignment** drop-down. On doing so, you will be prompted to select an alignment from the drawing. On selecting the alignment, Civil 3D updates the available options in the **Profile** drop-down with the list of the profiles associated with the selected alignment, refer to Figure 8-4. Similarly, you can choose the profile from the drawing by choosing the **Select from the drawing** button that is displayed on the right of the **Profile** drop-down list.

Feature line

You can select a feature line as the baseline for creating the corridor by selecting the **Feature line** radio button in the **Baseline type** area. On doing so, the **Site** and **Feature line** drop-downs will be displayed. Choose the required site from the **Site** drop-down and the required feature line from the **Feature line** drop-down. Alternatively, you can select the site from the drawing by choosing the **Select from the drawing** button that is displayed on the right of the **Site** drop-down. On doing so, you will be prompted to select a site from the drawing. On selecting the site, Civil 3D updates the available options in the **Feature line** drop-down with the list of the feature lines associated with the selected site. Similarly, you can choose the feature line from the drawing by choosing the **Select from the drawing** button that is displayed on the right of the **Feature line** drop-down list.

Note

When you select a profile that is not associated with the selected alignment in the drawing, Civil 3D displays a message at the command prompt that the selected profile is not associated with the currently selected alignment.

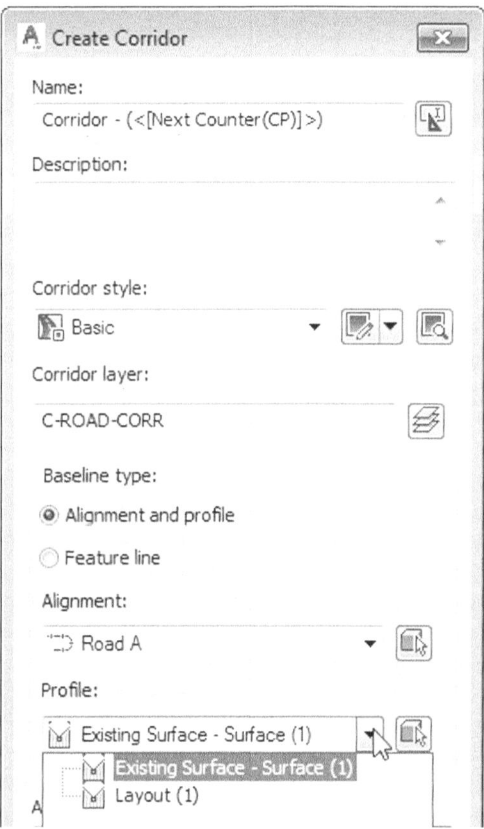

Figure 8-4 *Displaying the list of the profiles associated with the selected alignment*

Assembly

You can specify an assembly to be used for creating the corridor by selecting an option from the **Assembly** drop-down list.

You can also create a corridor without defining an assembly in the **Create Corridor** dialog box by selecting the **<none>** in the **Assembly** drop-down of the dialog box. If you select the **<none>** option, the **Autodesk AutoCAD Civil 3D 2018** warning message box will be displayed notifying that a corridor has been created without any defined region, refer to Figure 8-5.

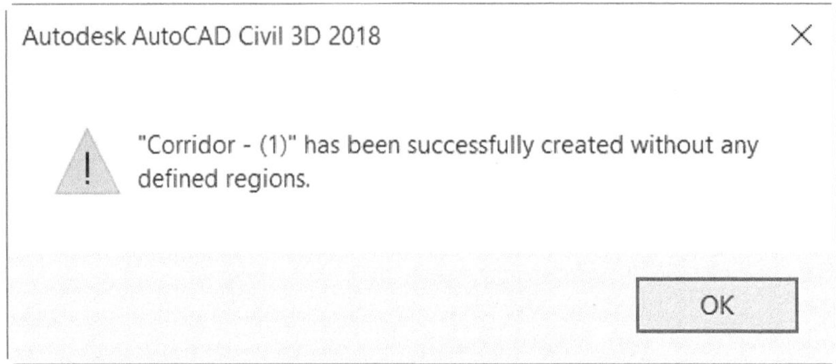

*Figure 8-5 The **Autodesk AutoCAD Civil 3D 2018** message box*

You can also select the assembly from the drawing. To do so, choose the **Select from the drawing** button that is displayed on the right of **Assembly** drop-down list; the **Create Corridor** dialog box will be closed and you will be prompted to select the assembly. Click on the required assembly in the drawing; the **Create Corridor** dialog box will be displayed again with the name of selected assembly in the **Assembly** drop-down list.

Note

1. The regions, assemblies, and targets can be added later to the created corridor.

*2. When no assembly is selected in the **Assembly** drop-down list, the **Target Surface** drop-down is disabled and the **Set Baseline and Region Parameters** check box is cleared.*

Target Surface

You can select the required target surface from the **Target Surface** drop-down list in the **Create Corridor** dialog box. Note that this drop-down displays a list of all surfaces available in the drawing. Alternatively, you can select the target surface from the drawing. To do so, choose the **Select from the drawing** button that is displayed on the right of **Target Surface** drop-down list. On choosing the button, you will be prompted to select the surface from the drawing.

Set baseline and region parameters

Select this check box in the **Create Corridor** dialog box and then choose the **OK** button; to display the **Baseline and Region Parameters** dialog box will be displayed, refer to Figure 8-6. You can specify targets and frequencies, and also add multiple baselines and regions in the corridor model using the options in this dialog box.

The various options and parameters in the dialog box are discussed next.

Add Baseline

Choose the **Add Baseline** button to add a new baseline in the corridor model. On choosing this button, the **Create Corridor Baseline** dialog box will be displayed, refer to Figure 8-7. Select the required radio button for the baseline type in the **Baseline type** area. For alignment as the baseline type, select the **Alignment and profile** radio button; the **Alignment** drop-down will be displayed. Select the required alignment from the **Alignment** drop-down list and choose the **OK** button; the selected alignment will be added in the **Name** column of the **Baseline and Region Parameters** dialog box. Similarly, to add a feature line as the baseline type, select the **Feature line** radio button; the **Site** and **Feature line** drop-downs will be displayed. Select the site containing the feature line from the **Site** drop-down. On selecting the site, Civil 3D updates the available options in the **Feature line** drop-down with the list of the feature lines associated with the selected site.

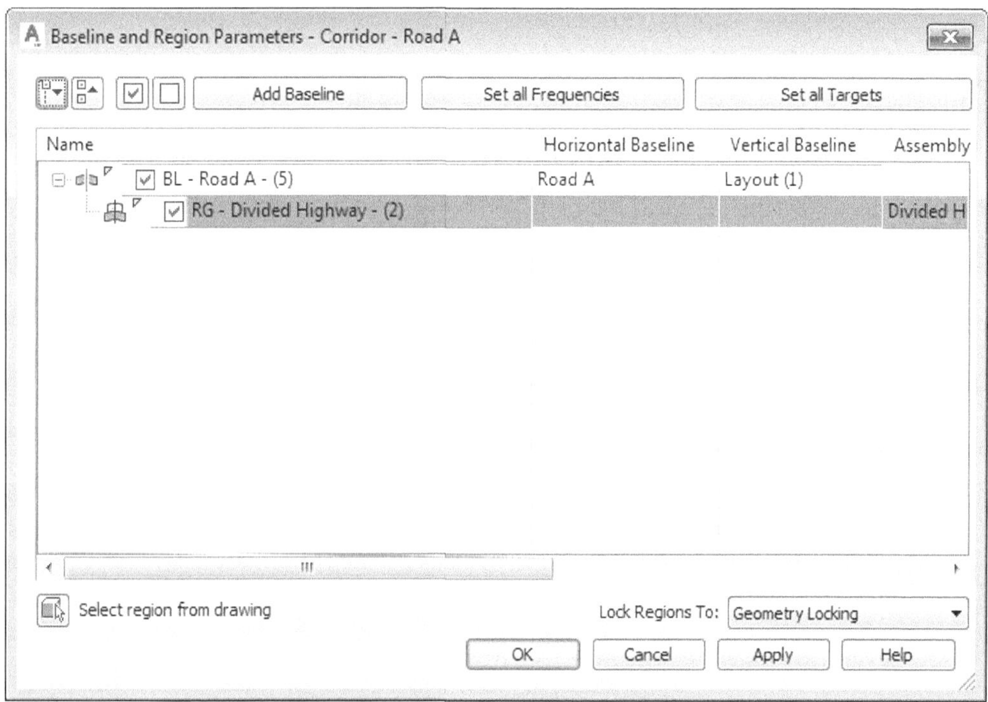

Figure 8-6 The ***Baseline and Region Parameters*** *dialog box*

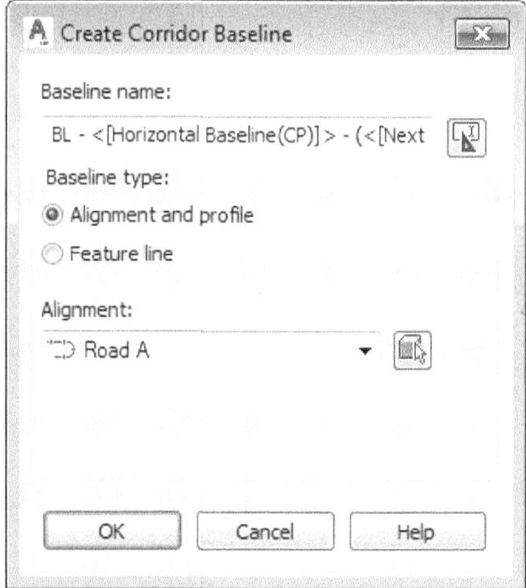

Figure 8-7 The ***Create Corridor Baseline*** *dialog box*

To delete an existing baseline from the **Baseline and Region Parameters** dialog box, right-click on the required baseline name; a shortcut menu will be displayed. Choose the **Remove Baseline** option, the selected baseline will be deleted, refer to Figure 8-8.

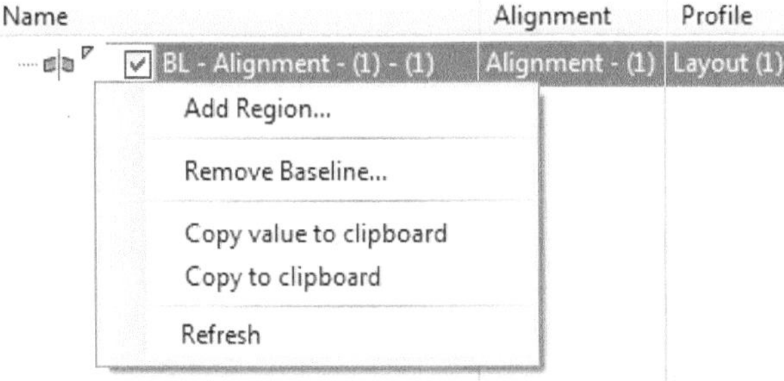

Figure 8-8 *The shortcut menu displayed by right clicking on the baseline*

Add Region

The region in a corridor model is used to associate assemblies to a given station range along the corridor.

To add a region to a corridor model, right-click on the required baseline name in the **Baseline and Region Parameters** dialog box; a shortcut menu will be displayed, refer to Figure 8-8. Select the **Add Region** option from the shortcut menu; the **Create Corridor Region** dialog box will be displayed, refer to Figure 8-9.

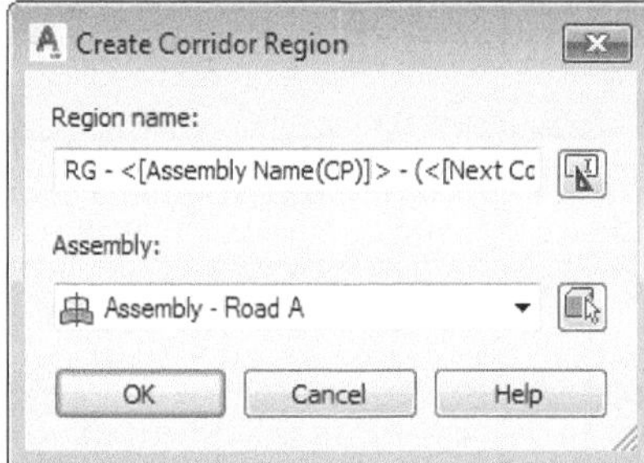

Figure 8-9 *The* ***Create Corridor Region*** *dialog box*

You can assign the region name in the **Region name** edit box. Select the assembly for the region in the **Assembly** drop-down list. Alternatively, you can select the assembly from the drawing. To do so, choose the **Select from the drawing** button displayed on the right of the drop-down list. On doing so, you will be prompted to select the required assembly in the drawing.

On specifying the required options in the **Create Corridor Region** dialog box, choose the **OK** button; the dialog box will be closed and new region will be added under the selected baseline node, refer to Figure 8-10.

Tip

1. To expand and collapse all the nodes of all the categories in the ***Baseline and Region Parameters*** *dialog box, choose the* ***Expand All Categories*** *and* ***Collapse All Categories*** *buttons, respectively.*

2. To view the created region in the ***Baseline and Region Parameters*** *dialog box, expand the baseline (alignment) node by clicking on the* **+** *icon.*

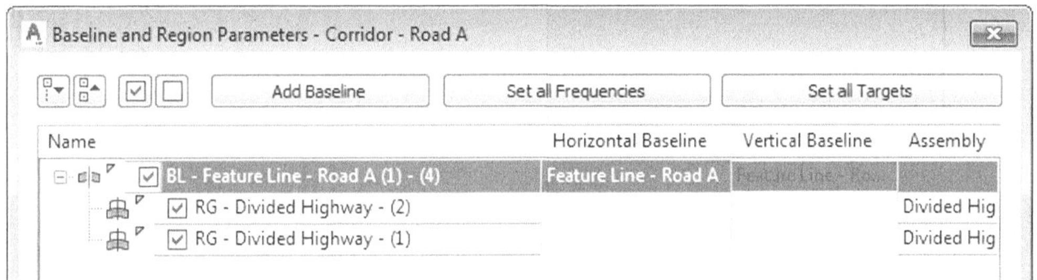

Figure 8-10 *The partial view of the* ***Baseline and Region Parameters*** *dialog box showing new region added to the baseline node*

Name

The **Name** column displays the hierarchy that lists all baselines, regions, and their corresponding offset alignments included in the corridor model. In this column, the check boxes are placed beside the listed baselines and regions in the hierarchy. The selected check box implies that the corresponding baseline or region is visible in the corridor model. If you clear the check box, the corresponding region or baseline will be invisible in the corridor. Note that the section of the corridor to which these invisible baselines and regions belong will not be updated with the change in the underlying elements such as alignment, surfaces and subassemblies.

In the **Name** column, the baseline can hold more than one region. By default, the baseline has only one region.

Horizontal Baseline

This column displays the name of the horizontal baseline used for the baseline creation. To edit the properties of the baseline, click on the horizontal baseline name in this column; the **Edit Corridor Baseline** dialog box will be displayed. Use the **Baseline name** edit box and the options in the **Baseline type** area to edit the name and horizontal baseline for the selected baseline. Choose the **OK** button to apply the changes and close the dialog box.

Note that, if horizontal baseline comprises a feature line, the column for vertical baseline will become unavailable.

Vertical Baseline

This column specifies the vertical baseline associated with the selected horizontal baseline. To change the vertical baseline, click on the name in the **Vertical Baseline** column; the **Select a Profile** dialog box will be displayed. The **Select a profile** drop-down list of this dialog box displays the list of all the vertical baselines associated with the selected horizontal baseline. Select the required vertical baseline from this list and then choose the **OK** button to apply settings and close the dialog box.

Assembly

This column displays the assembly used for the selected corridor region. To change the assembly, click on the assembly name in the **Assembly** column; the **Edit Corridor Region** dialog box will be displayed. In this dialog box, select the required assembly from **Assembly** drop-down list and then choose the **OK** button to close the dialog box. Alternatively, to select the assembly from the drawing, choose the **Select from the drawing** button in the **Edit Corridor Region** dialog box. On choosing the button, you will be prompted to select the assembly in the drawing. Now, you can select the assembly in the drawing.

Start Station

This column specifies the start station of a region or the controlling offset. By default, the start station of a region is the start station of the baseline. If there are more than one corridor regions along a baseline then the end station of the last region will be the start station of the following region. To modify the start station, click on the station value in the **Start Station** column; an edit box is displayed. Enter the required start station value in the displayed edit box. Alternatively, click on the button on the right of the value to select the station in the drawing.

End Station

This column specifies the end station of a region or controlling offset. To specify the end station, click in the **End Station** column and enter the required value. Alternatively, click on the button on the right of the station value to specify the station in the drawing.

Frequency

This column specifies the frequency at which assemblies will be placed for a given baseline and region in a corridor. The default value of the frequency in this column is **25.000'**. As a result, the assemblies will be placed along the baseline in the corridor after every 25.000'. To modify the value of the frequency, choose the browse button on the right of that value; the **Frequency to Apply Assemblies** dialog box will be displayed, as shown in Figure 8-11.

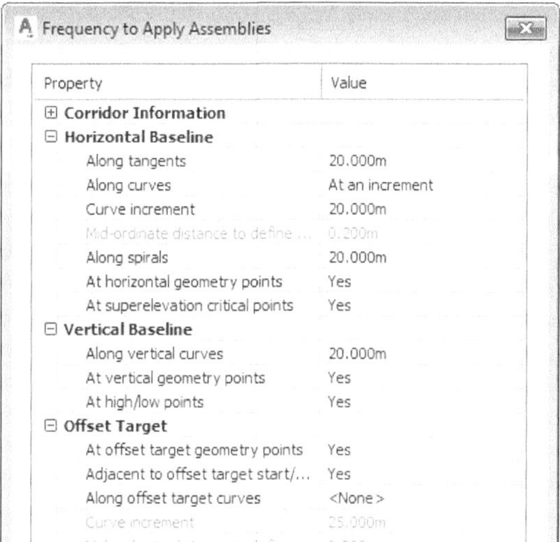

***Figure 8-11** Partial view of the **Frequency to Apply Assemblies** dialog box*

You can use this dialog box to specify the frequency of the assemblies along with different properties such as tangents, curves, and spirals in the corridor. To specify the frequency of a property, click on the frequency value in the **Value** field corresponding to the required property; an edit box will be displayed. Enter a new frequency value in the displayed edit box. Alternatively, click on the required field in the **Value** column; a browse button will be displayed on the right of this field. Choose this button; you will be prompted to specify distance in the drawing. Pick two points in the drawing to specify the frequency distance.

Civil 3D also allows you to place or remove assemblies at geometry points such as start and end of curves, superelevation critical points, profile geometry points, and high and low geometry points. By default, assemblies are placed at all these points. If you do not want to place assemblies at these points, click on the corresponding field of the **Value** column and select the **No** option from the drop-down list displayed.

Target

The **Target** column is used to specify the target objects such as surface, alignment, and profile. A target is required when the geometry of a subassembly requires a surface, offset or elevation targets for defining the geometry.

To set the target, choose the browse button displayed in this column; the **Target Mapping** dialog box will be displayed. You can use this dialog box to set the mapping of targets in subassemblies to the objects in the drawing. In the dialog box, set the targets such as the surface, offset, and elevation targets in the corresponding **Object Name** fields for the required subassembly. Choose the **OK** button to close the dialog box.

Overrides

You can view and delete existing assembly overrides to the station using this column. When you create a corridor, if there are no overrides, the **Value** field in this column will be disabled.

After specifying the settings for the corridor, choose the **OK** button to close the dialog box. Civil 3D will start the process of generating the corridor model. As the process ends, the corridor model is created and the name of the corridor is added to the **Corridors** node in the **Prospector** tab of the **TOOLSPACE** palette.

Tip

You can also edit the corridor baseline and region parameters after the creation of the corridor using the options in the ***Baseline and Region Parameters*** *dialog box. To invoke the dialog box, right-click on the baseline name in the* ***Corridors*** *node of the* ***Prospector*** *tab; a shortcut menu will be displayed. Choose the* ***Properties*** *option from the displayed shortcut menu; the* ***Baseline and Region Parameters*** *dialog box will be displayed.*

Corridor Properties

You can view and edit the corridor properties using the **Corridor Properties** dialog box. To invoke this dialog box, expand the **Corridors** node in the **Prospector** tab and then right-click on the existing corridor; a shortcut menu will be displayed. Choose the **Properties** option from the shortcut menu; the **Corridor Properties** dialog box will be displayed. The options in the dialog box are discussed next.

Information Tab

The **Information** tab is chosen by default. You can use this tab to view or modify the general information of the corridor using various settings such as name, description, and object style. In this tab, you can view and change the name of the current corridor by entering a suitable name in the **Name** edit box. Optionally, you can enter a description for the corridor in the **Description** edit box.

The **Object style** area in this tab specifies the corridor style that is used to control the display of corridor components such as region boundaries and assembly insertion stations. You can change the default style and assign a new style to the selected corridor by selecting the required option from the drop-down list in the **Object style** area.

Parameters Tab

This tab is used to view and edit the parameters of the current corridor including the baselines, regions, controlling offsets, and setting targets.

Codes Tab

This tab is used to view the points, links, and shape codes, label styles, and fill material used in creating the corridor model. These codes are derived from the subassemblies that are used to create the corridor model. In this tab, you can only modify the code set style by selecting the required option from the **Code set style** drop-down list.

Feature Lines Tab

This tab is used to control the display of feature lines and also to specify the settings for the connection of feature lines. The **Code** column in this tab displays the point codes that are used in the subassemblies for creating the corridor. The **Connect** column displays check boxes that specify whether or not the point codes at each station are connected. By default, all identical point codes are connected as longitudinal feature lines. If the check box in the **Connect** column is selected, then the corresponding point will be connected by the feature line to the corridor. If you want to delete the feature lines connecting to a point code, clear the check box corresponding to that point between point codes. For example, if you clear the check box for the **Ditch_Out** code, refer to Figure 8-12, the feature line will not connect to the **Ditch_Out** point codes while creating the corridor.

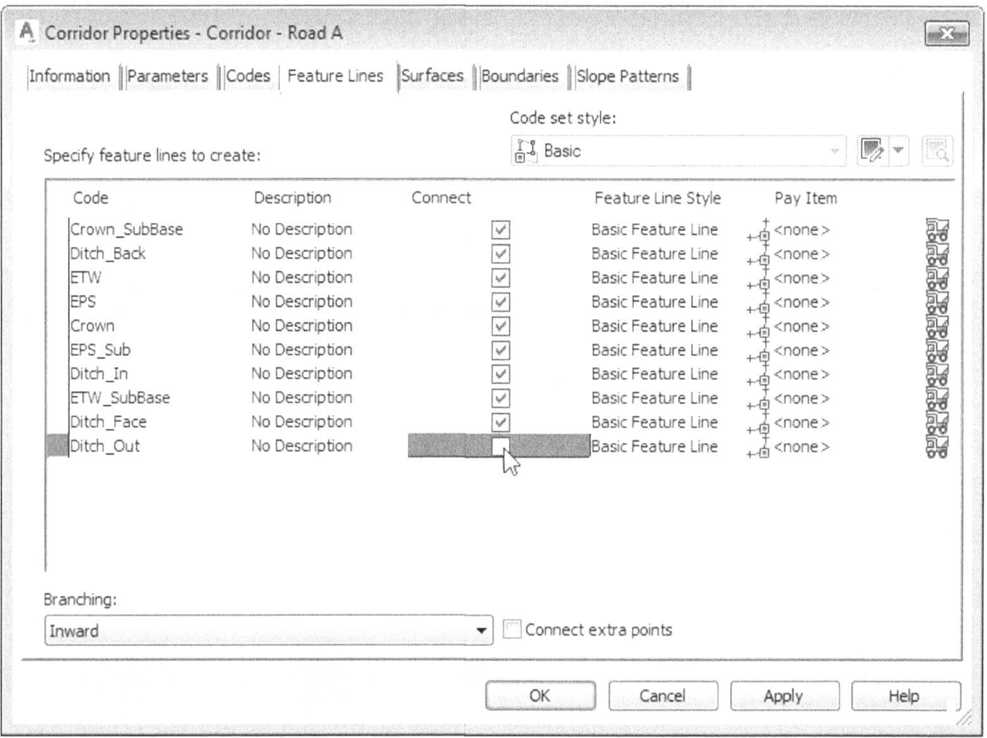

Figure 8-12 *The* ***Connect*** *column check box cleared for the* ***Ditch_Out*** *code in the* ***Feature Lines*** *tab*

Every feature line has a style that controls the display of the feature line. The **Feature Line Style** column displays the style assigned to a feature line. To edit the existing style, click on the button on the right of the existing style in the **Feature Line Style** column; the **Pick Feature Line Style** dialog box will be displayed. Select the required option from the drop-down list in this dialog box and then choose the **OK** button to close the dialog box. The **Pay Item** column specifies the unit of work for which the cost is paid to the contractor involved in the construction project. You can choose the button in the pay item cell to specify any pay item attached to the code.

The **Branching** drop-down list in the **Feature Lines** tab specifies the method of branching feature lines, where a point code has been used varyingly at different stations. You can set the branching by selecting the required option from the drop-down list. If you select the **Inward** option from the drop-down list, the feature lines branch inward joining the innermost point codes. On selecting the **Outward** option, the feature lines branch outward joining the outermost point codes. Selecting the **Connect extra points** check box allows the feature line to join the stations that have varying number of same point codes.

Surfaces Tab

This tab is used to create the corridor surfaces that are used to perform volume calculations. You can specify a set of parameters in the **Surfaces** tab, which is used to generate a corridor surface. You can also specify the surface style and the render material for the surface in this tab. The **Name** column in this tab displays the name of the corridor surface created. The **Surface Style** column displays the surface style associated with the corridor surface. To modify the surface style, click on the required surface style; the **Pick Corridor Surface Style** dialog box will be displayed. Select the required option from the drop-down list in the dialog box and then choose the **OK** button to exit the dialog box. The **Render Material** column displays the render material assigned to the surface. To specify a different render material, click on the default value in the **Render Material** column; the **Select Render Material** dialog box will be displayed. Select the render material from the drop-down list in the dialog box and then choose the **OK** button. The **Add as Breakline** column specifies whether breaklines are used in the corridor surface. The **Overhang Correction** column specifies if the overhang is to be corrected when rendered. It also specifies whether the top links or bottom links are to be followed in order to correct the overhang. If you do not want the overhang to be corrected, click in this column and select the **None** option from the drop-down list that is displayed. The **Description** column in this tab shows the description about the corridor surface. To enter the description, click in the column and enter the description in the edit box that is displayed.

The method to create a corridor surface is discussed in detail later in this chapter.

Boundaries Tab

You can use this tab to add boundaries to the corridor surface. By adding boundaries, you can prevent the triangulation outside the corridor. The method of adding boundaries to the corridor is explained in detail later in this chapter.

Slope Patterns Tab

This tab is used to add slope patterns between feature lines. Slope patterns are the lines that indicate the slopes. To add a slope pattern between a set of feature lines, choose the **Add slope pattern** button; the **Corridor Properties** dialog box will be closed and you will be prompted to select the first feature line. Select the first feature line from the corridor model. Next, you will be prompted to select the second feature line. Select the second feature line from the corridor model; the **Corridor Properties <corridor name>** dialog box will be displayed again with the information about the selected feature lines, slope pattern style, start and end stations, refer to Figure 8-13.

The **Feature Line1** and **Feature Line2** columns display the codes of the first and second feature lines. The **Slope Pattern Style** column displays the style name for the slope pattern. To modify the slope pattern style, click on the symbol given on the right of the style name in the column; the **Pick Style** dialog box will be displayed. Next, select the required option from the drop-down list in this dialog box and choose the **OK** button to exit the dialog box; the slope pattern style will be changed to the selected style and the style name will be displayed in the **Slope Pattern Style** column.

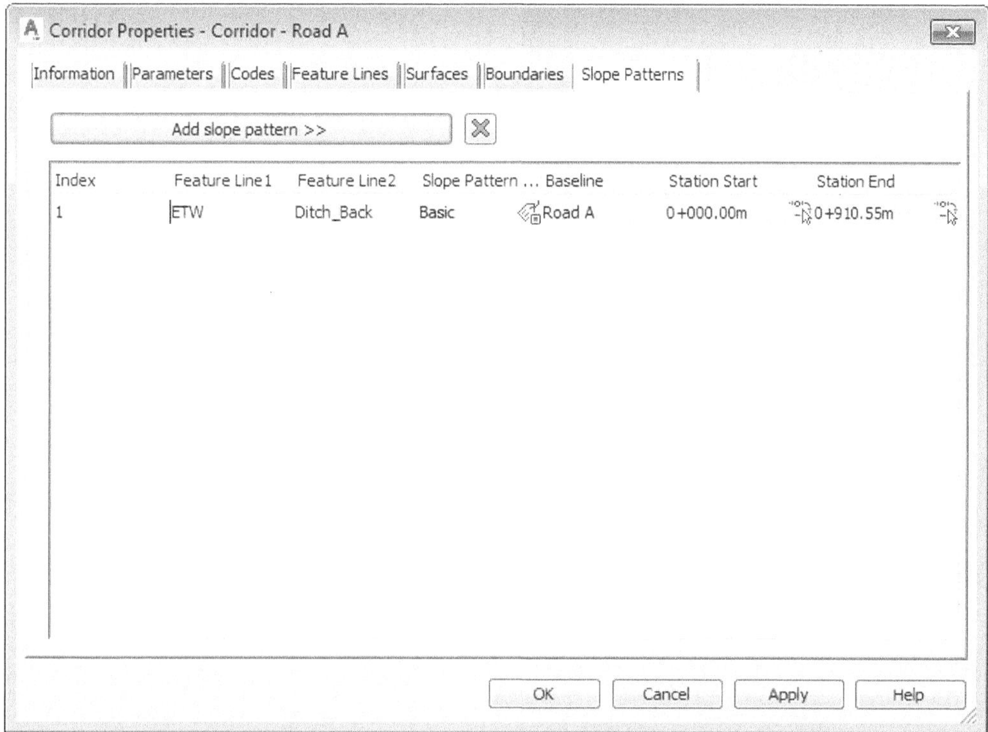

Figure 8-13 *The* ***Slope Patterns*** *tab displaying the information of added slope pattern between the selected feature lines*

The **Baseline** column displays the name of the baseline that is used to create the corridor. The **Station Start** and **Station End** columns specify the start and end stations of slope patterns. To modify the station values, click on the value displayed in the respective column and then enter the new value in the displayed edit box. Alternatively, click on the button displayed on the right side of the column; the **Corridor Properties** dialog box will be closed and you will be prompted to specify the station. Pick the station from the alignment; the dialog box will be displayed again and the selected station will be displayed in the station column.

After you have specified the slope pattern style and the stations, choose the **Apply** button to view the pattern. Next, choose the **OK** button; the **Corridor Properties** dialog box will be closed and the slope pattern will be displayed between the station range, as shown in Figure 8-14. Notice that the slope pattern is applied between the first and the second feature lines selected.

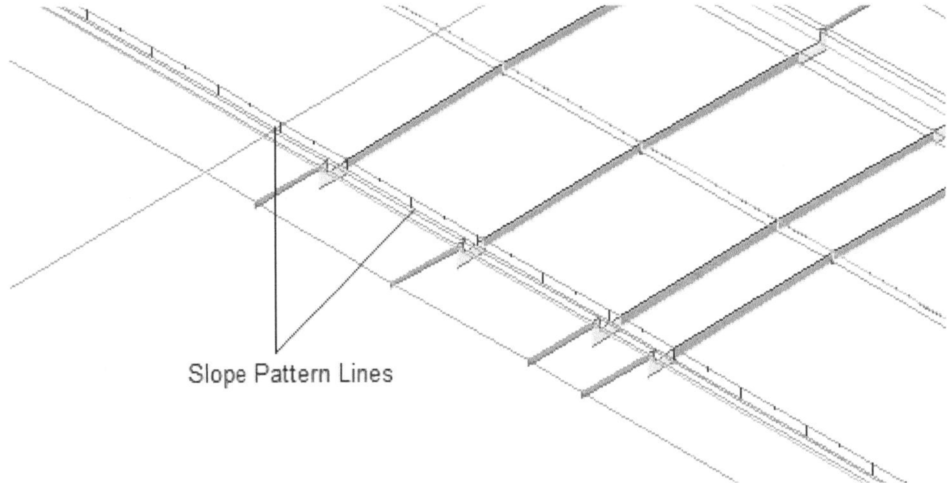

Figure 8-14 Slope pattern lines of the basic slope pattern style

CORRIDOR SURFACE

A corridor surface is a component of corridor object in which the surface is created using the corridor subassembly point and link codes. You can create a corridor surface by using the feature line data, link data, or both in the **Surfaces** tab of the **Corridor Properties <corridor name>** dialog box. To invoke this dialog box, select the corridor from the drawing and right-click; a shortcut menu will be displayed. Choose the **Corridor Properties** from the shortcut menu; the **Corridor Properties <corridor name>** dialog box will be displayed. Next, choose the **Surfaces** tab from the dialog box and then use various options from it to create a corridor surface.

Options in the Surfaces Tab

The **Surfaces** tab of the **Corridor Properties** dialog box consists of various options and tools for creating a corridor surface. These options are discussed next.

Create a corridor surface

Choose the **Create a corridor surface** button to create an empty corridor surface to which you can add data using the options in the **Add data** area. On doing so, a surface with a default name will be added in the **Name** column of the **Surfaces** tab. You can specify a new name for the corridor surface in this column surfaces.

If you select the check box corresponding to the surface name, then the corridor surface created will be visible in the drawing. This surface will dynamically update if changes are made to the corridor model. If the check box is cleared, the surface will not be displayed in the model.

Create a corridor surface for each link

Choose the **Create a corridor surface for each link** button to create individual corridor surfaces using all the link codes of the corridor. On doing so, the corridor surfaces will be created using each link code data and will be added in the **Name** column. You can expand the surface nodes to view the link code from which the surface will be created. Figure 8-15 shows the link codes of the first three corridor surfaces.

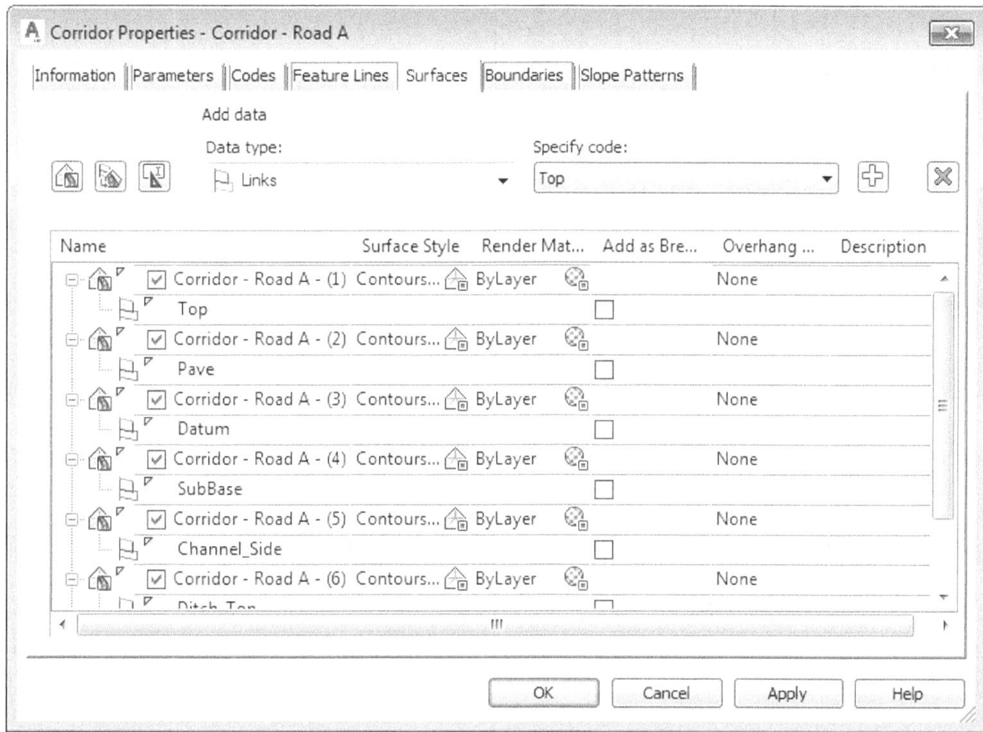

*Figure 8-15 The **Surfaces** tab displaying the list of surfaces and the link codes*

Surface name template

The **Surface name template** button is used to specify the name of the corridor surface. Choose this button to display the **Name Template** dialog box and specify the name of the corridor surface. Note that you need to choose this button before creating the corridor surface.

You can also change the name of the corridor surface after you add it to the **Name** column. To do so, double-click on the existing name of the corridor surface that is displayed in the **Name** column and enter a new name in the edit box that is displayed.

Add data Area

The options in the **Add data** area are used to add the data type and code to the corridor surface from which the corridor surface will be created.

To add a data type from which you want to create a corridor surface, select the **Links** or **Feature Lines** option from the **Data type** drop-down list. Next, you need to specify the code. To do so, select the required option from the **Specify code** drop-down list in the **Add data** area. For example, selecting **Feature Lines** from the **Data type** drop-down list and **Top_Curb** from the **Specify code** drop-down list will create a corridor surface data from the feature lines that connect the points with **Top_Curb** code.

Add surface item

Choose the **Add surface item** button to add data that is specified using the options selected from the **Data type** and **Specify code** drop-down lists to the selected corridor surface.

Delete surface item

If you want to delete a corridor surface, click on the surface name in the **Name** column and choose the **Delete surface item** button to delete the corridor surface.

Creating a Corridor Surface

You can create a corridor surface that is dynamic in nature by using the options in the **Surfaces** tab of the **Corridor Properties** dialog box. To do so, choose the **Surface name template** button in the **Surfaces** tab of the **Corridor Properties <corridor name>** dialog box; the **Name Template** dialog box will be displayed. In the **Name Template** dialog box, enter the name of the corridor surface in the **Name** edit box and choose the **OK** button; the dialog box will be closed. Next, choose the **Create a corridor surface** button from the **Surfaces** tab in the **Corridor Properties <corridor name>** dialog box; a surface name will be added in the **Name** column of the table in the **Corridor Properties** dialog box. This surface will be empty, therefore, you need to add data to it to create a surface.

To add data to this empty surface, first you need to select the type of data to be added. To do so, select the **Links** or **Feature Lines** option from the **Data type** drop-down list to create the surface using the links or corridor feature lines. Next, select the required links or the feature lines codes from the **Specify Code** drop-down list. These codes provide the data to create the corridor surface.

After selecting the code, choose the **Add surface item** button to add data to the surface. The selected code will be added to the **Surface** node of the **Name** column. Similarly, select other required codes and add them to the surface. Assign the surface style to the surface by selecting the surface style from the drop-down list in the **Surface Style** column as explained earlier. Next, add the breakline in the surface. To add a required code as breakline in the surface, select the check box corresponding to the code in the **Add as Breakline** column. Next, choose the **OK** button; the **Corridor Properties <corridor name>** dialog box will be closed and the **Corridor Properties- Rebuild** message box will be displayed. Choose the **Rebuild the Corridor** option in this window. Civil 3D will generate a triangulated corridor surface using the parameters defined earlier.

You can also create a corridor surface using both the link and feature data. To do so, create an empty surface and then select the **Links** option from the **Data type** drop-down list and add it with a specific code to the surface. Next, select the **Feature Lines** option from the **Data type** drop-down list and also add it with a specific code selected from the **Specify code** drop-down list to the same surface. Now, choose the **OK** button to exit the dialog box; a corridor surface will be created connecting both the link codes and feature line codes. Figure 8-16 shows the 3D view of the corridor surface created using the **Top** codes of the **Links** data. Figure 8-17 shows the 3D view of the corridor surface using the **ETW** and **Sidewalk_In** codes of the feature lines.

Note

*Once you create the corridor surface, it will be added to the **Surfaces** node of the **Prospector** tab. You can edit the style, add surface labels, and perform other surface editing operations in the same way as you do with other surfaces. If you make any changes in the corridor surface, make sure that the corridor surface is rebuilt. To rebuild the surface, expand the **Surfaces** node. Select and right-click the surface for corridor; a shortcut menu will be displayed. Choose the **Rebuild** option from the shortcut menu; the corridor surface will be updated accordingly.*

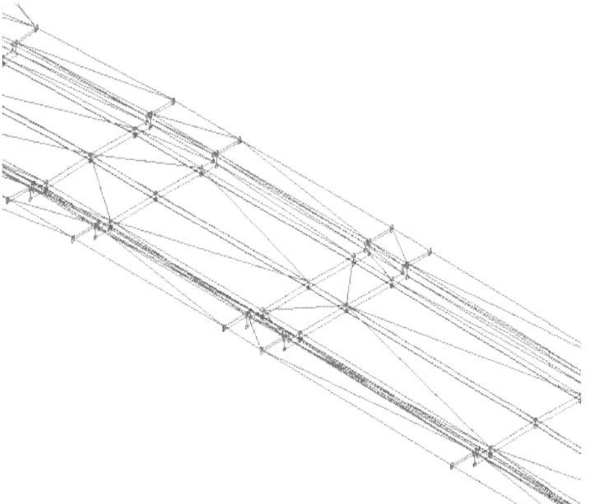

Figure 8-16 *The 3D view of the corridor surface created using the **Top** codes of the **Links** data*

Figure 8-17 *The 3D view of the corridor surface created using the **ETW** and **Sidewalk_In** codes of the feature lines*

Adding the Surface Boundary

You can add boundaries to the corridor surface to prevent the formation of excess triangulation outside the corridor design. Figure 8-18 shows the corridor surface created by joining two codes and the extra surface triangulation formed outside the corridor surface.

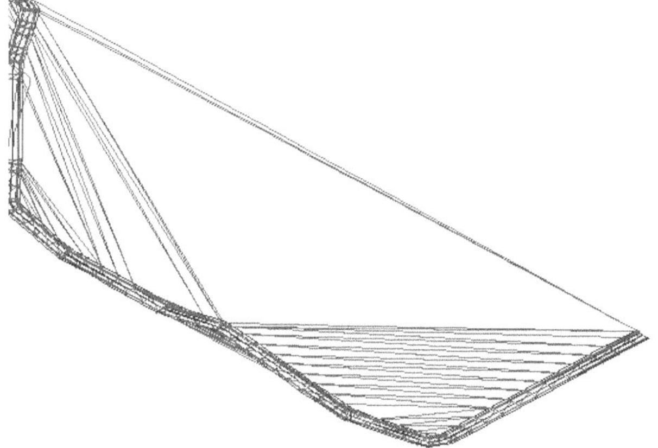

Figure 8-18 *The corridor surface created before adding the boundary*

To prevent this excess triangulation in the surface, add boundaries to the corridor surface. You can add surface boundaries using the **Boundaries** tab of the **Corridor Properties <corridor name>** dialog box. Invoke this dialog box by using the method explained in the earlier section. To add a boundary, choose the **Boundary** tab in the **Corridor Properties <corridor name>** dialog box and then right-click on the surface name in the **Name** column; a shortcut menu will be displayed, as shown in Figure 8-19.

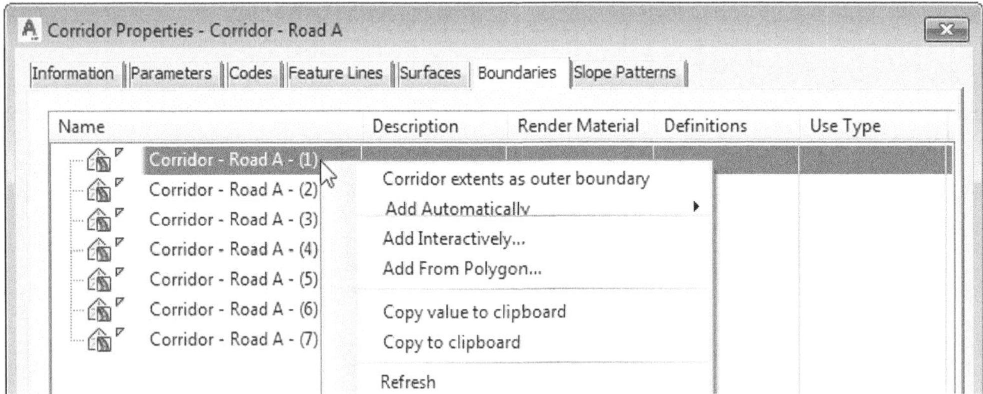

Figure 8-19 *The shortcut menu displaying various options*

Now, choose the required option from this shortcut menu to add the boundary to the corridor surface. Figure 8-20 shows the corridor surface created after adding the surface boundary. The options for adding boundaries are discussed next.

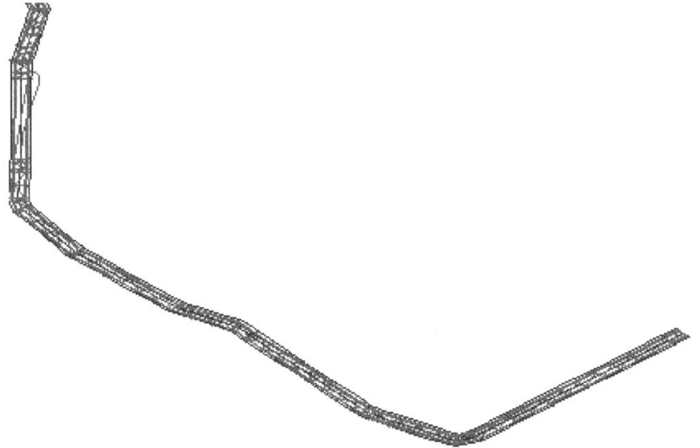

Figure 8-20 *Corridor surface created after adding the surface boundary*

Add Automatically

This option is used to add a surface boundary using feature line codes. When you choose the **Add Automatically** option from the shortcut menu; a cascading menu will be displayed. Choose the required feature line codes from the cascading menu displayed, as shown in Figure 8-21. The chosen feature line codes will be automatically added as the boundary of the corridor surface. This option is available only in case of a single baseline and a single assembly corridor.

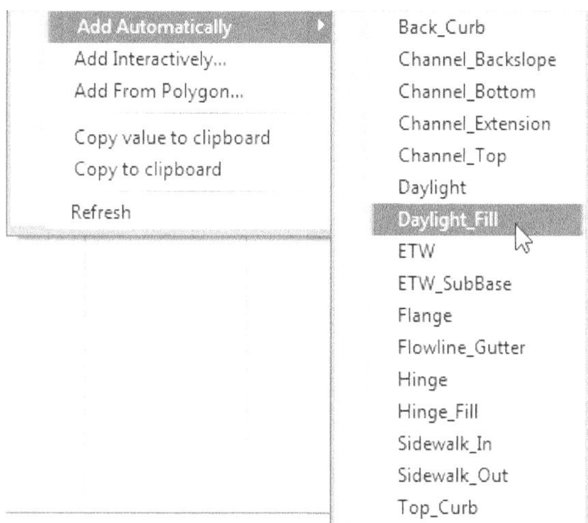

Figure 8-21 *Choosing a feature line code to be added as a boundary*

Add Interactively

This option is used to add a boundary to a multi-based corridor surface. Using this option, you can choose the codes from the feature line that you want to add to the surface. When you choose the **Add Interactively** option from the shortcut menu; the **Corridor Properties** dialog box will be closed and you will be prompted to select a first point on a corridor feature line. Pick a point on the required feature line; you will notice that a red colored boundary line is displayed at the point you have picked. Now, follow the prompt displayed and pick more points to define the boundary. To close the boundary, enter **C** at the command prompt and press ENTER; the **Corridor Properties** dialog box will be displayed again. Also, the boundary will be added in the **Name** column of this dialog box.

Add From Polygon

This option is used to define the boundary for the corridor surface using an existing polygon. When you choose the **Add From Polygon** option from the shortcut menu; the **Corridor Properties** dialog box will be closed and you will be prompted to select the polygon. Select the required polygon from the drawing; the **Corridor Properties <corridor name>** dialog box will be displayed again and a boundary will be added in the surface head of the **Name** column.

After creating the boundary for the corridor surface, you need to specify the type of boundary in the **Use Type** column in the **Boundary** tab of the **Corridor Properties <corridor name>** dialog box. By default, the value in the **Use Type** column is set to **Outside Boundary**. As a result, a boundary will be created outside the selected corridor surface. If you select the **Hide Boundary** option from the drop-down list, void areas in the corridor surface will be created. If you select the **Render Only** option from the drop-down list, you can create a boundary to assign different render materials to different parts of the corridor region. After creating the boundary, choose the **OK** button in the **Corridor Properties** dialog box. The corridor surface will be triangulated as per the options specified in the **Use Type** column.

Editing the Corridor Boundary

To edit the boundary added to the corridor surface, you need to select the corridor from the drawing and then right-click to display a shortcut menu. Choose **Corridor Properties** from the shortcut menu; the **Corridor Properties <corridor Name>** dialog box will be displayed. Choose the **Boundaries** tab from this dialog box and expand the required corridor surface node in the **Name** column.

To modify the name of the boundary, click on the existing name and then enter the desired name for the boundary in the edit box displayed. Similarly, click in the **Description**, **Render Material**, and **User Type** columns and modify the corresponding values. To view and modify the boundary definitions except for the one that is created from a polygon, click in the **Definitions** column; the **Corridor Boundary Definition** dialog box will be displayed, as shown in Figure 8-22.

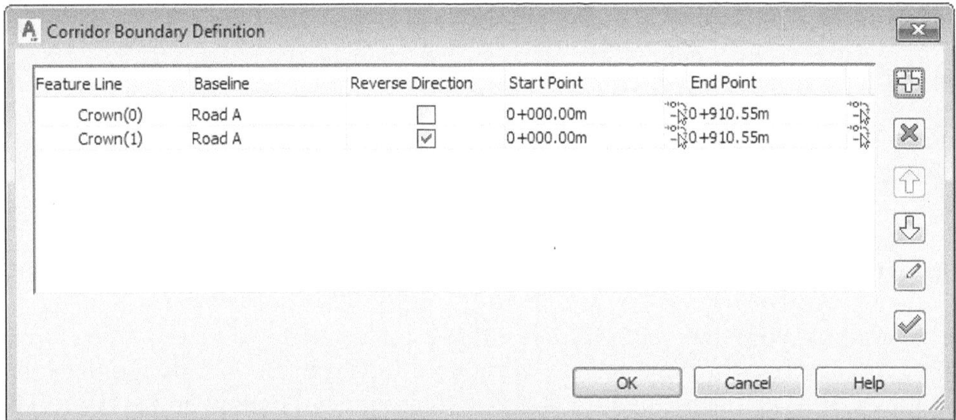

Figure 8-22 *The* ***Corridor Boundary Definition*** *dialog box*

Note

You can change the render material of the boundary from the ***Render Material*** *column of the* ***Boundary*** *tab provided the* ***Render Only*** *option is selected from the* ***User Type*** *column for the selected boundary.*

You can use this dialog box to edit the start and end points of the boundary. To modify the start point of the boundary, click on the start point value in the **Start Point** column and enter a new value. Alternatively, choose the button on the right of the start point value; the **Corridor Boundary Definition** dialog box will be closed and you will be prompted to specify the station on screen. Specify the start point station graphically in the drawing; the **Corridor Boundary Definition** dialog box will be displayed again. Similarly, modify the values of the end point of the boundary in the **End Point** column. To reverse the direction of the boundary, select the check box in the **Reverse Direction** column. To add a new feature line in the **Corridor Boundary Definition** dialog box, choose the + button then select the feature line from the corridor surface in your drawing. On doing so, a new feature line will be added to the boundary definition. You can also delete a feature line from the boundary definition. To do so, select the required feature line name from the **Corridor Boundary Definition** dialog box and then choose the X button; the selected feature line will be deleted from the boundary definition. To preview the boundary in the drawing, choose the button with the pencil symbol from the **Corridor Boundary Definition** dialog box; the dialog box will disappear and the boundary will be highlighted in green. Notice that now if you perform the zooming operations, the highlighted boundary will disappear. Next, after previewing the boundary in your drawing, you can verify whether or not the boundary polygon is well formed. To do so, choose the button; a message will be displayed at the bottom of the **Corridor Boundary Definition** dialog box, indicating whether or not the boundary definition is well formed.

Once you have modified the boundary definition, choose the **Apply** button to view the changes. Next, choose the **OK** button to close the dialog box. The surface boundary will be edited.

CALCULATING EARTHWORK VOLUMES

Ribbon: Analyze > Volumes and Materials > Volumes Dashboard
Command: VOLUMESDASHBOARD

AutoCAD Civil 3D allows you to compare the corridor surface with the existing ground surface as well as perform the calculation for the total earthwork. In Civil 3D, the calculation of the earthwork volume is performed by comparing two TIN surfaces. To perform the earthwork volume calculation process, choose the **Volumes Dashboard** tool from the **Volumes and Materials** panel of the **Analyze** tab; the **PANORAMA** window will be displayed with the **Volumes Dashboard** tab. Choose the **Create new volume surface** button; the **Create Surface** dialog box will be displayed. In this dialog box, click in the **Value** field of the **Base Surface** column; a browse button will be displayed. Choose the browse button; the **Select Base Surface** dialog box is displayed. In this dialog box, select the required surface as the base surface. Similarly, select a comparison surface in the **Value** field corresponding to the **Comparison Surface** column. Specify other required options such as the surface style, cut and fill factors, and choose the **OK** button; the **Create Surface** dialog box will be closed and new record will be added to the **Volumes Dashboard** tab, refer to Figure 8-23.

The various options in this tab are discussed in detail in the **Volumes Dashboard** section of Chapter 4.

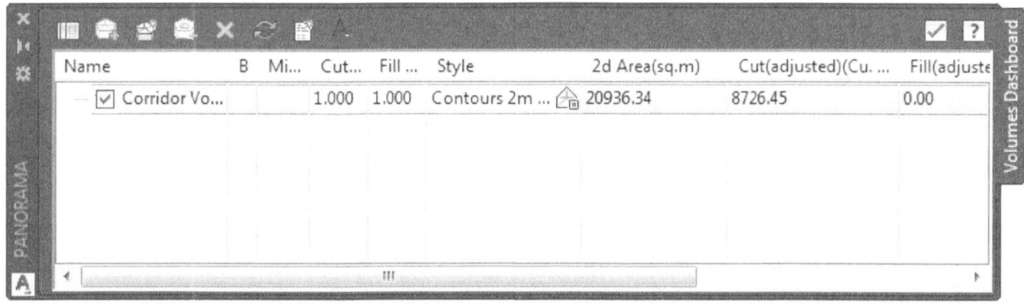

Figure 8-23 *The* ***PANORAMA*** *window displaying the* ***Volumes Dashboard*** *tab*

CREATING CIVIL 3D OBJECTS USING CORRIDOR

Civil 3D provides you with some tools that can be used to create objects from a corridor. These tools are discussed next.

Create Polyline From Corridor

Ribbon: Home > Create Design > Create Polyline From Corridor
Command: CREATEPOLYLINEFROMCORRIDOR

The **Create Polyline From Corridor** tool is used to create a polyline from the selected corridor feature line. To do so, choose the **Create Polyline From Corridor** tool from the **Create Design** panel; you will be prompted to select a corridor feature line. Select the required feature line from the corridor in the drawing; the polyline is created.

Note, due to the proximity of feature lines in the drawing, more than one feature line might be selected while selecting the feature line. In this case, the **Select a Feature Line** dialog box will be displayed. You can select the required feature line from this list of feature lines displayed in the dialog box and choose the **OK** button; the corridor feature line will be converted to a 3D polyline. Press ESC to end the command.

Create Feature Line from Corridor

Ribbon: Home > Create Design > Feature Line drop-down > Create Feature Line from Corridor
Command: FEATURELINESFROMCORRIDOR

You can create a grading feature line from the corridor and use it for feature line or projection grading. To do so, choose the **Create Feature Line from Corridor** tool from the **Create Design** panel; you will be prompted to select the corridor feature line. Select the corridor feature line in the drawing; the **Select a Feature Line** dialog box will be displayed. Select the required feature line from this dialog box and choose the **OK** button; the **Create Feature Line from Corridor** dialog box will be displayed. In this dialog box, specify the site, name, layer, and also choose the smoothing options for the grading feature line to be created. In this dialog box, the **Create dynamic link to the corridor** check box is selected by default. As a result, a dynamic link is created and maintained between the grading feature line and the corridor. Choose the **OK** button from this dialog box; the selected feature line will be converted into a grading line. Press ESC to end the command.

Create Alignment from Corridor

Ribbon: Home > Create Design > Alignment drop-down > Create Alignment from Corridor
Command: CREATEALIGNFROMCORRIDOR

An alignment can also be created from an existing corridor. This alignment is created along the horizontal path of the corridor feature line and is used to create profile views, special labeling, target alignments, and so on. To create an alignment from the corridor, choose the **Create Alignment from Corridor** tool from the **Create Design** panel; you will be prompted to select a corridor feature line. Select the corridor; the **Select a Feature Line** dialog box will be displayed. Select the required feature line from the dialog box and choose the **OK** button; the **Create Alignment from Objects** dialog box will be displayed. Enter the required information in the dialog box and choose the **OK** button. On doing so, the **Create Profile - Draw New** dialog box will be displayed. In this dialog box, specify the profile name in the **Name** edit box and choose the **OK** button; the **Create Profile - Draw New** dialog box will be closed. Press ESC to end the command. The required alignment will be created and listed in the **Alignments** node of the **Prospector** tab in the **TOOLSPACE** palette.

Create Profile from Corridor

Ribbon: Home > Create Design > Profile drop-down > Create Profile from Corridor
Command: CREATEPROFILEFROMCORRIDOR

To create a profile from the corridor, choose the **Create Profile from Corridor** tool from the **Create Design** panel; you will be prompted to select a corridor feature line. On doing so, the **Select a Feature Line** dialog box will be displayed. Select the required feature line from the dialog box and choose the **OK** button; the **Create Profile - Draw New** dialog box will be displayed. In this dialog box, set various parameters for the profile you want to create and then choose the **OK** button. Now, press ESC to end the command. Zoom in to view the profile view. The profile will be added to the **Profiles** sub node of the **Alignments** node in the **Prospector** tab.

Create COGO Points from Corridor

Ribbon: Home> Create Ground Data > Points drop-down > Create COGO Points from Corridor
Command: CREATEPOINTSFROMCORRIDOR

You can create the Civil 3D points using the corridor codes. To do so, choose the **Create COGO Points from Corridor** tool from the **Create Ground Data** panel; the **Create COGO Points** dialog box will be displayed, refer to Figure 8-24. Select the **For entire corridor range** radio button in this dialog box to create COGO points along the entire length of the corridor. You can also create the COGO points at a specified range along the corridor by selecting the **For user specified range** radio button in the **Create COGO Points** dialog box. Note that when you choose this radio button, the **Baseline start** and **Baseline end** edit boxes will be activated. Specify the start and the end station in the **Baseline start** and **Baseline end** edit boxes. The corridor codes that fall along the specified range of the baseline will be converted to COGO points.

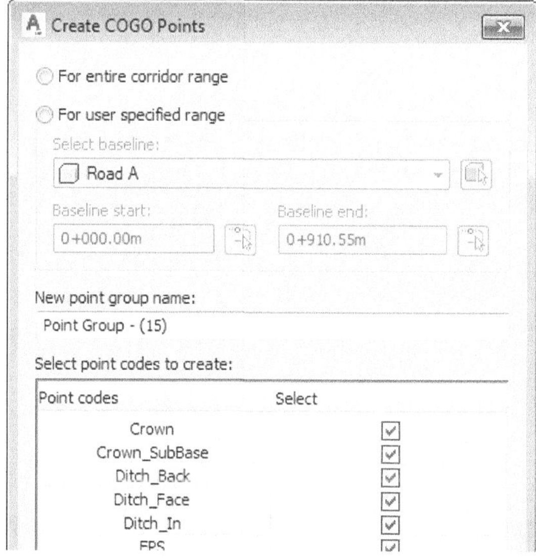

***Figure 8-24** Partial view of the **Create COGO Points** dialog box*

Now, in the **New point group name** edit box of the **Create COGO Points** dialog box, specify the name of the point group to which all COGO points will be added. Next, you need to select the point codes that will help in creating the points. To do so, you need to select the point codes from the **Select point codes to create** area. Select the check boxes in the **Select** column to select the corresponding point codes located in the **Point codes** column. Now, choose the **OK** button in the **Create COGO Points** dialog box; the dialog box will be closed and the COGO points will be generated for the specified corridor region using the selected point codes. The created points are added in the point group that you have specified and can be viewed under the **Point Groups** node of the **Prospector** tab in the **TOOLSPACE** palette.

Creating Surfaces from Corridor

Ribbon:	Home> Create Ground Data > Surfaces drop-down > Create Surface from Corridor
Command:	CORRIDOREXTRACTSURFACES

You can create a static surface object that is not linked to the corridor model using this tool. To create a corridor surface, choose the **Create Surface from Corridor** tool from the **Create Ground Data** panel; the **Create Corridor Surfaces** dialog box will be displayed. In this dialog box, a list of all the existing corridor surfaces is displayed. By default, all the check box under the **Select** column in this list are selected. Clear the check box for the surface which you do not intend to export. Next, click on the default value in the **Surface Style** column to select a surface style; the **Pick Corridor Surface Style** dialog box will be displayed. Select the required surface style from the drop-down list in this dialog box and choose the **OK** button; the selected surface style will be assigned to the corridor surface. Now, choose the **OK** button in the **Create Corridor Surfaces** dialog box; the dialog box will be closed and static surfaces are created for the surfaces corresponding to the selected check box. The names for these created surfaces are added to the **Surfaces** node of the **Prospector** tab.

SELECTING AND EDITING CORRIDOR STATION

Ribbon:	Corridor(contextual tab)> Modify Corridor Sections > Section Editor
Command:	VIEWEDITCORRIDORSECTION

After you have created the corridor, you can view and edit the cross-section of the corridor at each station. To edit a section, choose the **Corridor** tool from the **Design** panel of the **Modify** tab; the **Corridor** tab will be displayed. Next, choose the **Section Editor** tool from the **Modify Corridor Sections** panel; the **Section Editor** contextual tab will be displayed, as shown in Figure 8-25. You can use various tools from the **Section Editor** tab to view and edit the corridor sections. The buttons in this tab are discussed next.

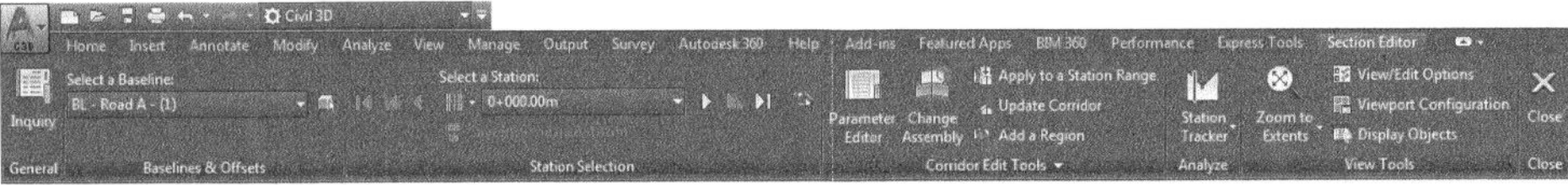

*Figure 8-25 The **Section Editor** tab*

Selecting the Baselines and Offsets of a Corridor

You can specify the baseline for a corridor or controlling offset for which you want to view or edit the sections. To do so, select the desired baseline name from the **Select a Baseline** drop-down list in the **Baselines & Offsets** panel of the **Section Editor** tab. Alternatively, you can select the alignment from the drawing by choosing the button on the right of the drop-down list and then picking the point from the drawing.

Selecting a Station

You can use the various buttons available in the **Station Selection** panel to display the stations of the corridor sections. These buttons are discussed next.

Start station

Choose the **Go to First Station** button to display the cross-section of the corridor baseline at the first station.

Previous station

Choose the **Go to Previous Station** button to view the cross-section of the corridor baseline at the previous station.

Next station

Choose the **Go to Next Station** button to view the cross-section of the corridor at the station after the current station. You can also select the next or the previous stations from the **Select a station** drop-down list.

End station

Choose the **Go to Last Station** button to display the cross-section view of the corridor at the last station.

Go to Previous Region

Choose this button to display the previous region of the corridor in the cross-section view, refer to Figure 8-26. The last station of the region will be displayed in the **Select a Station** drop-down list.

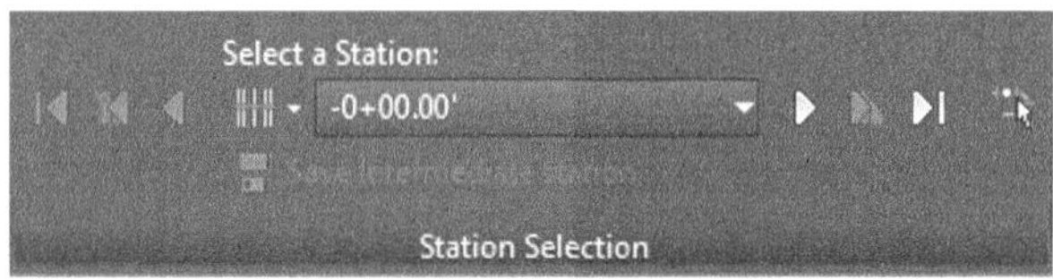

***Figure 8-26** The **Station Selection** panel*

Go to Next Region

Choose this button to display the first station on the next region of the corridor in the cross-section view. The first station of the next region of the corridor will be displayed in the **Select a Station** drop-down list.

Station Type Drop-down List

This drop-down allows you to display the stations which will be visible in the **Select a Station** drop-down list. If you select the **All Baseline Station** option; the **Select a Station** drop-down list will display all the stations of the baseline. If you select the **Region Station** option; the **Select a Station** drop-down list will display the list of all the stations of the selected region of the corridor.

Similarly, you can select the **Overridden Stations** and the **Non-region Stations** options to display the corresponding stations in the **Select a Station** drop-down list.

Save Intermediate Station

On choosing this button, you will be able to save the intermediate station which you have added in the corridor. Also, after saving the intermediate station, it will be displayed in the **Select a Station** drop-down list.

Editing a Corridor Section

There are various tools which can be used to edit the corridor section. These tools are available in the **Corridor Edit Tools** panel of the **Section Editor** contextual tab. Some of the tools used for editing a corridor in this panel and the **View Tools** panel are discussed next.

Parameter Editor

Ribbon: Section Editor (Contextual Tab) > Corridor Edit Tools > Parameter Editor

This button allows you to modify the parameters of the subassemblies which have been defined for the corridor. Choose this button from the **Corridor Edit Tools** panel to display the **CORRIDOR PARAMETERS** window, refer to Figure 8-27. In this window, the **Design Value** column displays the values that have been set for the subassembly parameter.

You cannot directly edit the parameter value in the **Design Value** column. To override the value in **Design Value** column, enter the new value in the corresponding cell in the **Value** column. This will override the value in the **Design Value** column. The **Design Value** column will now display the updated value with the (i) symbol representing the value in the cell has been overridden and the corresponding cell in the **Override** column displays **True** with the check box selected.

The **Comment** column in the table of the **CORRIDOR PARAMETERS** window is provided to add any additional information. In this column, you can add a comment for further reference.

Note

*The default value in the **Override** column of the **CORRIDOR PARAMETER** window is **False** with a cleared check box, refer to Figure 8-27.*

*To display the **Section Editor** tab in the ribbon, select the required corridor in the drawing and right-click; a shortcut menu will be displayed. Choose the **Modify Corridor Sections** option from the shortcut menu; a cascading menu will be displayed. Select the **Corridor Section Editor** from the cascading menu; the **Section Editor** tab will be displayed in the ribbon.*

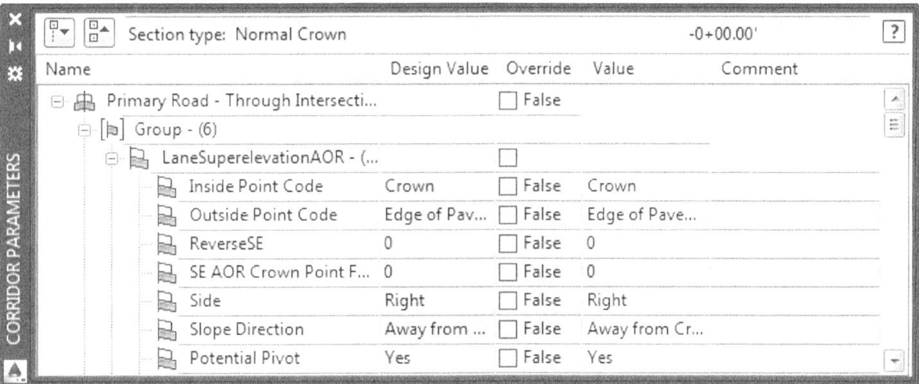

Figure 8-27 The ***CORRIDOR PARAMETERS*** *window*

Change Assembly

Ribbon: Section Editor (Contextual Tab) > Corridor Edit Tools > Change Assembly

This tool is used to replace the assembly used in the given corridor region, with another assembly. To do so, choose the **Change Assembly** tool from the **Corridor Edit Tools** panel; the **Change Assembly** dialog box will be displayed, as shown in Figure 8-28. In this dialog box, select the required assembly from the **Replace current assembly** list box. Alternatively, you can choose the **Select from drawing** button to select the assembly from the drawing area. Next, choose the **OK** button to close the dialog box and wait for the process to complete. Once the process is completed, you will notice that the cross-section editor shows the replaced assembly.

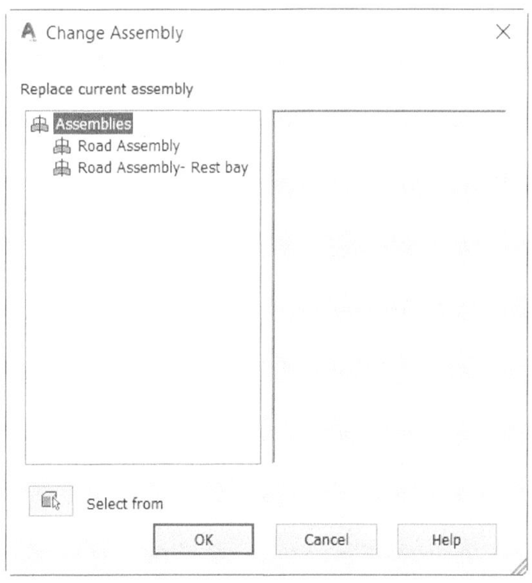

Figure 8-28 The ***Change Assembly*** *dialog box*

Apply to a Station Range

Ribbon: Section Editor (Contextual Tab) > Corridor Edit Tools > Apply to a Station Range

Apply to a Station Range This tool is used to apply the overrides made in the subassembly using the **Panorama Editor** or by grip editing. To do so, invoke the **Apply to a Station Range** dialog box tool from the **Corridor Edit Tools** panel; the **Apply to a Range of Stations** dialog box will be displayed. In this dialog box, specify the start and end stations in the **Start station** and **End station** edit boxes, respectively. By default, the first and last stations are selected in the **Start station** and **End station** edit boxes, respectively. Choose the **OK** button to close the dialog box and wait till the process is completed. You can view the corridor with the applied changes in the drawing.

Add Point

Ribbon: Section Editor (Contextual Tab) > Corridor Edit Tools > Add Point
Command: VECSADDPOINT

Add Point This tool is used to add a point at the midpoint of any link. Choose the **Add Point** tool from the **Corridor Edit Tools** panel; you will be prompted to specify a link to add a point. Select the link from the section view displayed. Next, you will be prompted to specify the point code; specify the point code in the command line and then press ENTER. The point will be added at the middle of the selected link.

There are various other tools such as **Add Link**, **Add Subassembly**, **Delete Point**, **Delete Link**, and **Delete Subassembly** available for editing the corridor section in the **Corridor Edit Tools** panel. You can use these tools to perform various editing operations.

View/Edit Options

Ribbon: Section Editor (Contextual Tab) > View Tools > View/Edit Options
Command: VECSOPTIONS

View/Edit Options You can use this tool to specify various properties for the grid, grid text, and default style. To do so, choose the **View/Edit Options** tool from the **View Tools** panel; the **View/Edit Corridor Section Options** dialog box will be displayed, refer to the Figure 8-29. The properties in this dialog box are discussed next.

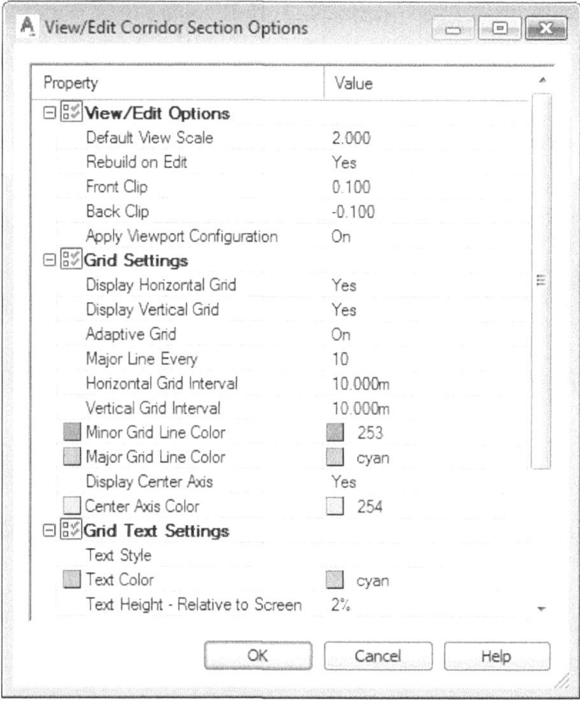

***Figure 8-29** The **View/Edit Corridor Section Options** dialog box*

Use the **Default View Scale** property in the **View/Edit Options** node to specify the scale factor to be used when viewing the corridor sections. To edit this value, click in the **Value** field of the **Default View Scale** property of the **View/Edit Options** node to enter the required value in the edit box and press ENTER.

Use the **Rebuild on Edit** tool to rebuild the corridor model automatically when you edit a subassembly using the tools in the **Section Editor** tab. Click in the **Value** cell of the **Rebuild on Edit** property; a drop-down list will be displayed. Choose the **Yes** option from the drop-down list. This will automatically update the corridor model when you edit a subassembly that is specified in the corridor model.

You can specify the extent of visibility of 3D objects in a corridor section, measured forward or backward from the sampled section. To do so, click in the **Value** field of the **Front Clip** or **Back Clip** property, change the value of the clipping range in the respective edit boxes, and press ENTER.

You can also set the display of the station tracker in multiple viewports. To ensure that the station tracker is displayed in the viewport, click in the **Value** field of the **Apply Viewport Configuration** property to display the drop-down list.

Specify the style for the code using the **Code Set Style** parameter for the corridor section view. To edit a new value, click in the **Value** field of the **Code Set Style** property; the **Browse** button will be displayed. Now, choose this button; the **Code Set Style** dialog box will be displayed. Select the required option from the drop-down list and choose the **OK** button to apply the selected code set style.

In the **View/Edit Corridor Section Options** dialog box, you can also set various settings of the grid and grid text. Set the parameters in this dialog box and then choose the **OK** button to accept the settings.

CHECKING THE CORRIDOR VISIBILITY

Civil 3D provides various tools to check the visibility of the corridor model. These tools enable you to visually inspect your model along a specified path for the given section or entire length of the corridor. You can specify the path for checking the visibility by using Civil 3D objects such as the alignment, profile, feature line or 3D polyline.

The **Drive** tool and the **Check Sight Distance** tool, which are used to check corridor visibility are discussed next.

Drive

Ribbon:	Corridor (Contextual Tab) > Analyze > Drive
Command:	DRIVE

The **Drive** tool is simulation tool and is used to simulate driving along the corridor. To invoke the **Drive** tool, choose the corridor from the drawing; the **Corridor: <corridor name>** contextual tab is displayed. Choose the **Drive** tool from the **Analyze** panel of this tab; you will be prompted to select a corridor feature line. Select the required feature line object from the drawing. Civil 3D will process your request and display the simulated corridor in the drawing area. Figure 8-30 shows the simulated corridor.

Note

*In case more than one feature line is selected, the **Select a Feature Line** dialog box will be displayed with a list of the selected feature lines. Select the required feature line object from the displayed list and then choose the **OK** button in the dialog box*

Figure 8-30 *Partial view of a corridor simulation*

Along with the corridor simulation, a **Drive** tab is also added to the ribbon, refer to Figure 8-31. The various tools and panels in the **Drive** tab are discussed next.

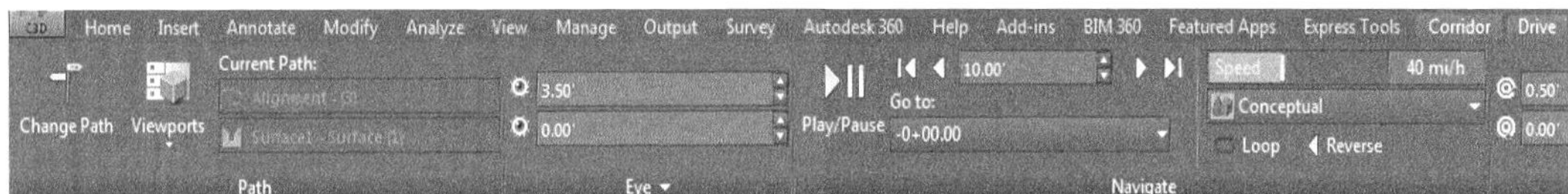

Figure 8-31 *Partial view of the* ***Drive*** *tab*

Tip
*You can also access the **Drive** tool by choosing the **Drive** button in the **Design** panel of the **Analyze** tab.*

Path Panel

The **Path** panel is used to display the basic information of the selected path along which the corridor is simulated. This information is displayed in the two text boxes under the **Current Path** head panel. The corridor name and the selected feature line (path) are displayed in the **Drive: First Level Path** and **Drive: Second Level Path** text boxes, respectively. To change the simulation path, choose the **Change Path** button; you will be prompted to specify simulation path from the drawing. Select the corridor feature line, 3D polyline, alignment, or profile; the simulation will set to the selected path.

Eye Panel

The options in the **Eye** panel are used to set the location of the observer's eye with respect to the selected simulation path. You can set the height of the observer's eye using the **Eye Height** text box. Use the spinner in this text box to increase or decrease the value for observer's eye height. Increasing the value in the **Eye Height** text box will elevate the observer's eye height and decreasing the value will lower the height. Similarly set the value for the observer's offset in the **Eye Offset** text box. The **Eye Offset** specifies the observer's position to the left (offset) or right (offset) of the selected path.

Navigate Panel

This panel contains the tools such as the **Play/Pause**, **Start Station**, **End Station**, **Previous Station**, **Next Station,** and **Go to** drop-down list. These tools are used to navigate to the required station along the corridor. This panel also contains the **Loop** and **Reverse** tools. Use the **Loop** tool to play the simulation continuously. You can use the **Reverse** tool to change the direction of simulation along the corridor. You can also change the speed of motion for simulation by using the **Speed** slider. The drop-down below the **Speed** slider defines the visual style used while playing the simulation. Select the appropriate style for your simulation. Note that the **Conceptual**, **Realistic** and **Shaded** visual styles are resource intensive styles and may take a while to render the simulation.

Target Panel

Use the options in the target panel to specify the parameters for the target. You can specify the relative target height in the **Target Height** edit box and the target offset in the **Target Offset** edit box, respectively. Use the spinner corresponding to these text boxes to increase or decrease the parameter value. You can also specify the distance between the target and observer (Target Distance) in the **Target Distance** edit box.

Sight Distance

Ribbon:	Corridor (Contextual Tab) > Analyze > Sight Distance
Command:	SIGHTDISTANCECHECK

This tool is used to analyze the sight distance along the corridor. To use this tool, you need to invoke the **Sight Distance Check** wizard. To do so, select the corridor from the drawing; the **Corridor: <corridor name>** contextual tab is displayed in the ribbon. In this tab, choose the **Sight Distance** tool from the **Analyze** panel; the **General** page of the **Sight Distance Check** wizard will be displayed, refer to the Figure 8-32. Alternatively, you can invoke the **Sight Distance Check** wizard by choosing the **Check Sight Distance** tool from the **Analyze > Design >Visibility check** drop-down.

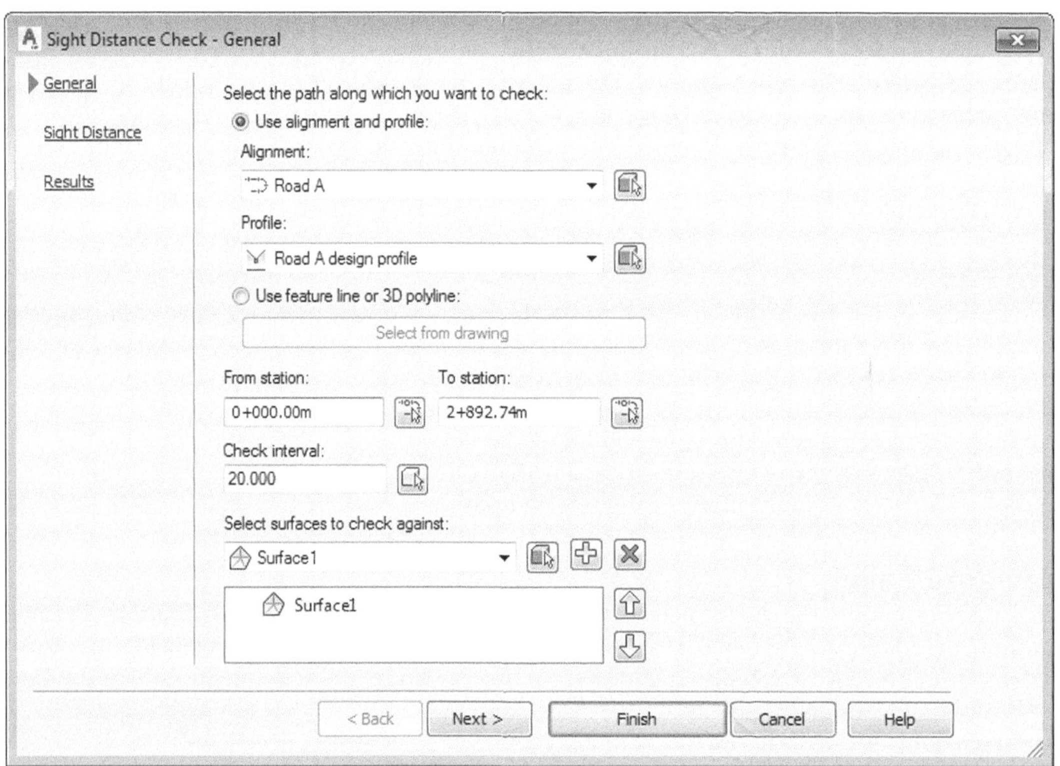

*Figure 8-32 The **General** page of the **Sight Distance Check** wizard*

In the **General** page, you can specify the path along which you want to check the corridor visibility. You can check the visibility along a specified profile and alignment or you can use a feature line or a polyline to define the path for checking the visibility.

To check visibility along an existing alignment and profile, select the **Use alignment and profile** radio button. Next, select the required alignment and profile from the respective drop-down lists. Alternatively, you can select the alignment and profile from the drawing by choosing the **Select from the drawing** button. The **From station** and **To station** edit boxes will display the start and end station of the selected entity. If you wish to check visibility along an existing feature line or a 3D polyline, select the **Use feature line or 3D polyline** radio button; the **Select from drawing** button will be activated and the drop-down under the **Use alignment and profile** radio button will be deactivated. Choose the **Select from the drawing** button; you will be prompted to select the required object from the drawing. Select the object from the drawing; the **From point** and **To point** text boxes will be activated. These text boxes will now display the start and end point coordinate of the selected object. Specify the interval for checking the visibility in the **Check interval** text box. Next, select the surface against which the visibility check are to be performed from the **Select surfaces to check against** drop-down list and add it to the surface list displayed below this drop-down by choosing the **Add** button. If multiple surfaces exist at a given location, then the visibility check is performed against the surface with the highest priority. You can change the priority of surface by moving them in the surface list using the up and down arrow buttons displayed on the right of the list.

On specifying the required options and parameters in the **General** page, choose the **Next** button; the **Sight Distance** page of the wizard will be displayed. In this page of the wizard, specify the visibility distance to be checked in the **Minimum site distance** text box. Also specify the values for the driver's eye height and eye offset in the **Eye height** and **Eye Offset** text boxes, respectively. Similarly, specify the target height and offset in **Target height** text box and **Target offset** text box, respectively. Alternatively, use the corresponding **Pick from the drawing** button to specify the value in the drawing. Choose the **Next** button; the **Result** page of the wizard will be displayed.

You can use the options in the **Results** page for displaying the result of the analysis. In this page, the list of visibility analysis components is displayed in table. To display the component in the result of the visibility check, select the check box corresponding to the component. You can also specify the layer in which the components are drawn in the drawing. To do so, click in the **Layer** cell; the **Layer Selection** dialog box will be displayed. Select the required layer and choose the **OK** button. The **Layer Selection** dialog box will be closed and the selected layer name will be displayed in the **Layer** column for the component. Next, choose the hatch pattern for the obstructed area. To do so, choose the corresponding button; the **Hatch properties** dialog box will be displayed. Select the required hatch pattern in this dialog box and choose the **OK** button. The **Hatch properties** dialog box will be closed and the selected hatch pattern will be displayed in the **Results** page of the wizard. Select the **Create sight analysis report** check box to generate analysis report. To specify the file type for the generated report, choose the file type from the options given in the **Choose a file type** drop-down list. Finally, specify the location to save the report in the **Save to** text box. Choose the **Finish** button to perform the analysis as per the options specified.

EXTRACTING CORRIDOR SOLIDS AND BODIES

In AutoCAD Civil 3D, several types of AutoCAD entities such as Bodies, Solids, and Solids (Swept Solids) can be extracted from the corridor model shapes and links. After extraction, these entities can then be used for visualization. They can also be used for calculating mass properties such as volume. These entities can be imported and used by other solid modeling applications that are unable to interact directly with AutoCAD Civil 3D corridor models.

To extract the corridor solids and bodies, choose the **Extract Corridor Solids** tool from the **Corridor Tools** panel of **Corridor** (Contextual Tab); you will be prompted to select the corridor regions to export as solids. Select the corridor region in the drawing or you can select the **Station range**, **within Polygon**, or **All regions** option in the command prompt. After specifying the required option, the **Extract Corridor Solids** wizard will be displayed, as shown in Figure 8-33. The various options available in the pages of this wizard are used to extract corridor solids and bodies from a corridor model. The pages of this wizard are discussed next.

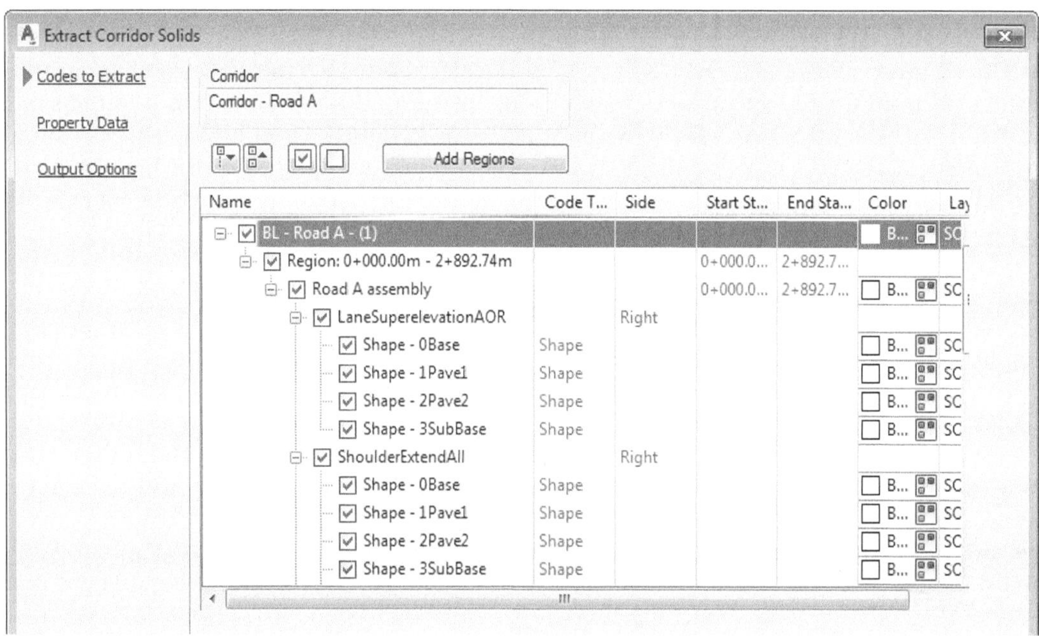

*Figure 8-33 Partial view of the **Extract Corridor Solids** wizard*

Codes to Extract Page

The options in this page are used to specify the corridor elements that are to be extracted. The text box in the **Corridor** area displays the name of the selected corridor. In the **Codes to Extract** page, a list box will be displayed showing the list of available types of codes (shape or link) that are available in the selected corridor region. The list consists of the corridor baseline as the parent node followed by corridor regions as the sub-nodes. Under the corridor regions sub-node, the subassemblies will be displayed. Choose the **Expand Tree** button to expand all the nodes in the list box. Similarly, choose the **Collapse Tree** button to collapse the nodes in the list box. To select the check box for all the shapes and links at once, choose the **Turn on all the shapes and links** button. Similarly, to clear the check box for all the shapes and links at once, select the **Turn off all the shapes and links** button. To add another regions to the current selection set, choose the **Add Regions** button; AutoCAD Civil 3D will prompt you to select the regions from the drawing. After adding the desired corridor regions, select the desired codes in the **Name** column of the list box and choose the **Next** button. On choosing the **Next** button, the **Property Data** page of the **Extract Corridor Solids** wizard will be displayed.

Property Data Page

The options in this page are used to specify the properties associated with the exported solids. The specified properties will be visible in the **Extended Data** tab of the **Properties** palette for the extracted solids. AutoCAD Civil 3D has three property set definitions that will be applied to the corridor and 3D solids.

To specify the model information, select the **Corridor Model Information** node; the property sheet on the right will be loaded with the properties for model information. Select the desired check box in the **Visible** column to include the property for model information. Similarly, to include the shape information for corridor and 3D solids, select the desired check box in the **Visible** column of the **Corridor Shape Information** node.

To add a custom property data, select the **Corridor Property Data - User Defined** node and right-click in the property sheet on the right; a shortcut menu will be displayed. Choose **Add** from the shortcut menu; a new entry will be created and displayed in the property sheet. You can edit the parameters for this user defined property simply by double-clicking. After specifying the desired property set definitions for the corridor and 3D solids, choose **Next**; the **Output Options** page will be displayed.

Output Options Page

This page is used to specify the output options for the exported AutoCAD solids and bodies, as shown in figure 8-34. From the **Output object type** drop-down list, you can select the type of entity to be extracted from a corridor model. The options in this drop-down are **AutoCAD 3D Bodies (based on corridor sampling)**, **AutoCAD 3D Solids (based on corridor sampling)**, and **AutoCAD 3D Solids (swept solids)**. In the **Output destination options** area of this page, if you choose the **Insert into current drawing** radio button, the extracted solids or bodies will get placed in the current drawing and will cover the whole originating corridor. If you choose the **Add to an existing drawing** radio button, the extracted solid bodies will be added to an existing drawing specified by you. If you choose the **Add to a new drawing** radio button, the extracted solids or bodies will be added to a new drawing specified by you. To specify the location for the new drawing, enter a name in the edit box below the **Add to a new drawing** radio button. You can also click on the browse button located next to the blank field and select the desired drawing in which you want to add the extracted solids or bodies.

Note that, when you choose to insert the extracted solids and bodies into the current drawing, you can select the **Dynamic link to corridor** check box. On selecting this check box, the extracted solids and bodies will be dynamically linked to the corridor. Whenever the corridor will be rebuilt, the solids or bodies will be updated.

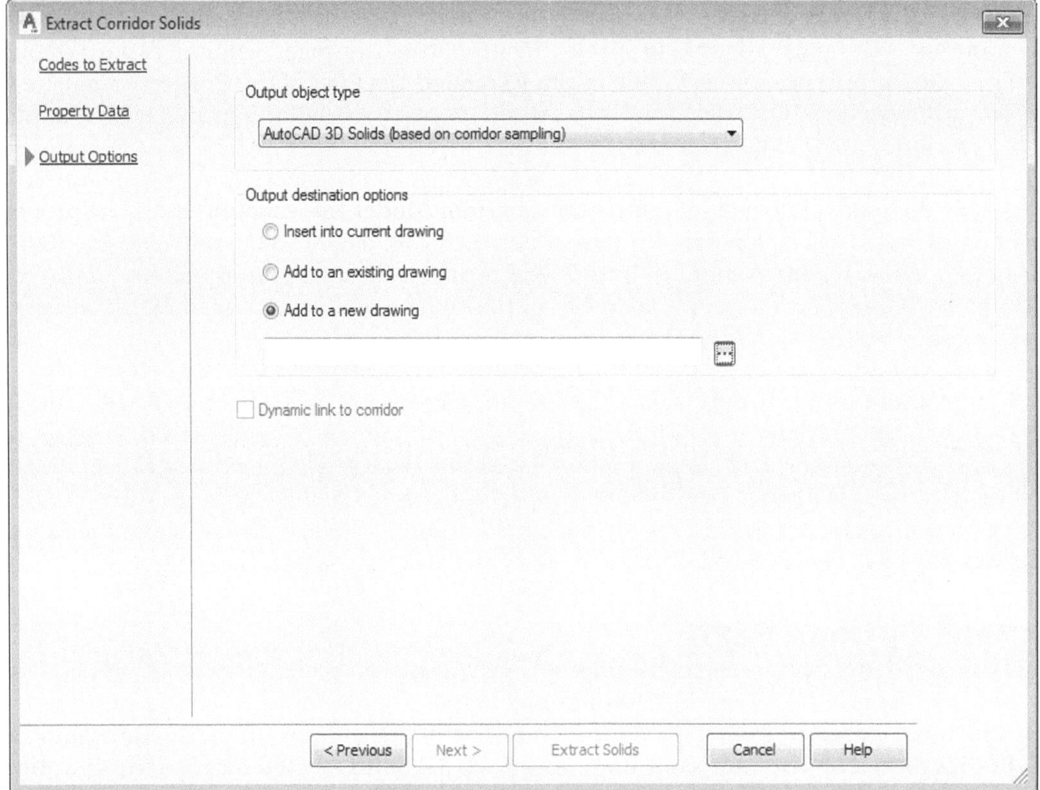

*Figure 8-34 The **Output Options** page of the **Extract Corridor Solids** wizard*

RESTORING CORRIDOR BOWTIES

In AutoCAD Civil 3D, if a corridor is created with fixed width and the corridor tangents intersect at corner, the inner and outer corners of corridors are cleared automatically. It does not happen so with non-fixed subassemblies such as daylighting subassemblies. In non-fixed width subassemblies, you needed to edit and rebuild those corridors. However, in Civil 3D 2018, a new tool **Clear Corridor Bowties** has been introduced which can be used to clear such corners.

To clear corridor bowties, invoke the **Clear Corridor Bowties** tool from the **Corridor Tools** panel of **Corridor** contextual tab; you will be prompted to select the subentity. Select the alignment leading to the bowtie area; you will be prompted to select the subentity. Select the alignment leading out of it; a rubber band jig will appear and you will be prompted to select the insertion point to solve the corridor bowties (daylights). Select that point and press ENTER; the corridor bowties (daylights) will tie to the solution point and eliminate the corners. Repeat the same procedure to clear other corridor bowties and then press ESC to terminate the command.

Figures 8-35 and 8-36 show the corner bowties before and after using the **Clear Corridor Bowties** tool, respectively and the line in red colour shows the baseline.

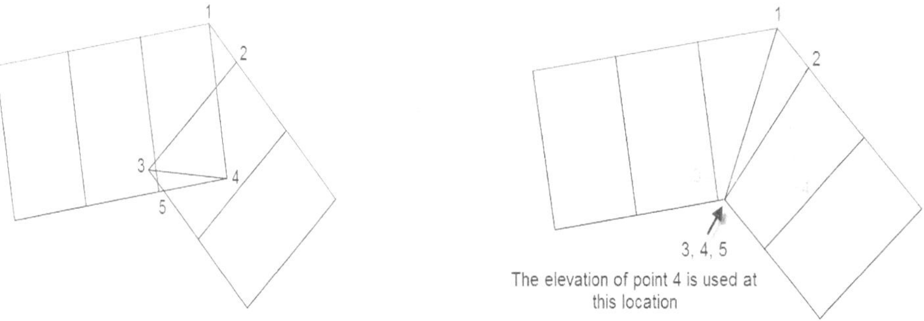

Figure 8-35 *Corners prior to clearing the bowtie* ***Figure 8-36*** *Corners after clearing the bowtie*

To restore corridor bowties, invoke the **Restore Corridor Bowties** tool from the **Corridor Tools** panel of the **Corridor** contextual tab; you will be prompted to select the bowtie you want to restore. Select the bowtie and press ENTER; the bowtie will be restored.

INTRODUCTION TO PARCELS

In Civil 3D, parcels are objects which acts as a topology in a site. The entire project site will always be covered accurately with this topology. A site boundary is the outermost polygon containing interior land blocks and the smaller division of these blocks are referred as parcel objects. A site acts as a bucket for the parcel objects. Sites and parcels are closely related and they maintain active relationships with their boundaries and alignments. A site boundary can be divided into smaller parcels by inserting alignments within its boundary. For example, when you create an alignment in a site, the site will be divided into two parcels with the alignment acting as the dividing line. Also, if the alignment is deleted, the parcels combine and return to the original conditions.

In AutoCAD Civil 3D, parcels comprises series of points, lines, and curves and are always represented by closed areas with a label at the center or the centroid. A Civil 3D drawing may contain multiple sites and sites may contain multiple parcels. Therefore, you usually start with a site boundary and then divide the site into smaller parcels.

Key Points for Designing a Parcel

In Civil 3D, you should always keep in mind some keypoints before creating the parcels at the required site. These keypoints are discussed next:

1. In a site, the parcels create the topology for that site and therefore, they are dynamically related to each other. This also means that any changes made to a parcel results related changes to the other adjacent parcels in the site. However, the parcels in one site are not related to parcels in a different site.

2. Parcels within a site cannot overlap each other and if two parcels overlap then a third parcel is created from the overlapping area. However, if the parcel overlap is required without the creation of a new parcel then you should place them in separate sites, as objects in different sites do not relate with each other.

3. On moving a parcel from one site to another, the relationship of the parcel with the other parcels in the original site will be lost.

4. If an alignment is created in a site which closes itself by making a loop, a parcel will automatically be generated by the enclosed area.

CREATING PARCELS

You can create parcels by using the existing objects in your drawing such as lines, curves, polylines or by using the **Parcel Layout Tools** toolbar. You can also create right of way parcel using the **Create Right of Way** tool.

Once a parcel is created, it is added to the **Parcel** sub-node under the **Sites** node in the **Prospector** tab of the **TOOLSPACE** palette. Various methods to create parcels are discussed next.

Creating Parcels using Polylines

Ribbon:	Home > Create Design > Parcel drop-down > Create Parcel from Objects
Command:	CREATEPARCELFROMOBJECTS

The simplest and most common method of creating a parcel is by using the AutoCAD drawing objects. Using this method, you can automatically convert the existing line work into parcels or parcel segments. Before using this tool, you require lines, arcs, or polylines to be present in your drawing and also all the objects should be closed polygons.

To convert the drawing objects into parcel objects, choose the **Create Parcel from Objects** tool from the **Create Design** panel of the **Home** tab; you will be prompted to select a line, an arc, or a polyline object. In the drawing, select the object you have drawn. Also, you can enter **X** in the command line to select the polyline from the Xref drawing. On selecting the required object from the drawing or from the Xref drawing, press ENTER; the **Create Parcels - From Objects** dialog box will be displayed, as shown in Figure 8-37. This dialog box is used to specify the information about the parcel. The options in this dialog box are discussed next.

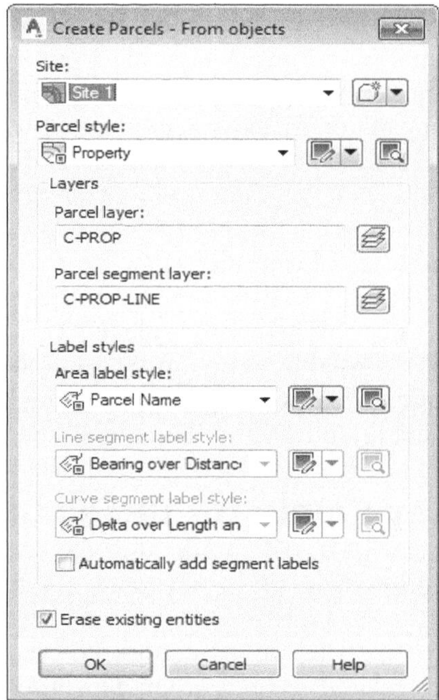

Figure 8-37 The ***Create Parcels - From objects*** *dialog box*

Site

You can specify the site for the parcel by selecting the required site from the **Site** drop-down.

Alternatively, you can select the site directly from the drawing or create a new one. To do so, choose the down arrow on the right of the **Site** drop-down list. On choosing the down arrow, the flyout menu will be displayed. Choose the **Pick from Drawing** option to select the site from the drawing or choose the **Create a New** option from the flyout to create a new one.

Parcel style

You can select a parcel style from the **Parcel style** drop-down list. To create a new style or edit the existing style, click on the down arrow next to the **Parcel style** drop-down list; a flyout menu will be displayed. Choose the required option from the flyout to create or edit the parcel style.

Layers Area

The **Parcel layer** text box in the **Layers** area displays the default layer (**C-PROP**) on which the parcel will be created. To select a new layer, choose the button on the right of the **Parcel layer** text box; the **Object Layer** dialog box will be displayed. You can use this dialog box to select a new layer for the parcel.

Similarly, the **Parcel segment layer** text box displays the default layer (**C-PROP-LINE**) on which the parcel segment will be created.

Label styles Area

The **Label styles** area in the **Create Parcels - From objects** dialog box displays the default label styles for the parcel and the parcel segments. In the **Area label style** drop-down list, you can select the area label style for the new parcel. From the **Line segment label style** and **Curve segment label style** drop-down lists, you can select the label style to line segment and curve segment for the new parcel segments, respectively. Note that the **Line segment label style** and **Curve segment label style** drop-down lists will only be activated, when you select the **Automatically add segment labels** check box.

Select the **Erase existing entities** checkbox to delete the entities such as polylines that are used to create the parcel. Clear the check box to retain the entity.

Creating Parcels Using the Parcels Layout Tools

Ribbon: Home > Create Design > Parcel drop-down > Parcel Creation Tools
Command: CREATEPARCELBYLAYOUT

AutoCAD Civil 3D allows you to create a parcel based on some complex designs by using the parcel layout tools. These tools can be accessed from the **Parcel Layout Tools** toolbar. These tools enable you to create new integrated designs for parcels.

Creating a parcel using the parcel layout tools is a two-step process. The first step includes the selecting of required parcel layout tool which you will use to draft the parcel from the **Parcel Layout Tools** toolbar. The second step involves naming the parcel, specifying the site, parcel layer, and parcel style.

To create a parcel using the parcel layout tools, choose **Parcel Creation Tools** from the **Create Design** panel; the **Parcel Layout Tools** toolbar will be displayed, as shown in Figure 8-38, and you will be prompted to select the required tool from the toolbar.

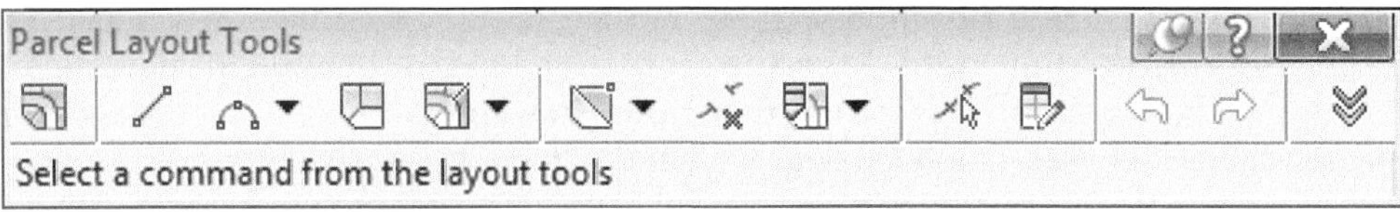

*Figure 8-38 The **Parcel Layout Tools** toolbar*

To create and edit the parcel, these tools help you to be more creative and can convert the AutoCAD lines, arcs or curves into parcel objects. When you select the required tool from the toolbar; the **Create Parcels - Layout** dialog box will be displayed, refer to Figure 8-39.

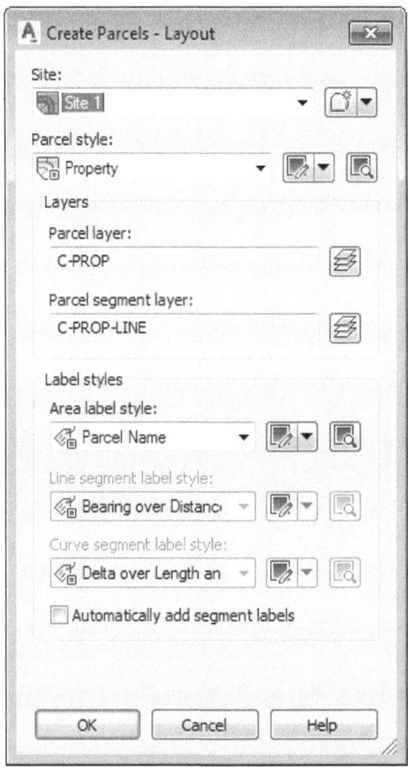

*Figure 8-39 The **Create Parcels - Layout** dialog box*

The options in this dialog box are same as discussed earlier for the **Create Parcels - From Objects** dialog box.

PARCELS LAYOUT TOOLS TOOLBAR

The tools in the **Parcel Layout Tools** toolbar are used to design a parcel object. These tools are discussed next. Figure 8-40 shows the **Parcel Layout Tools** toolbar.

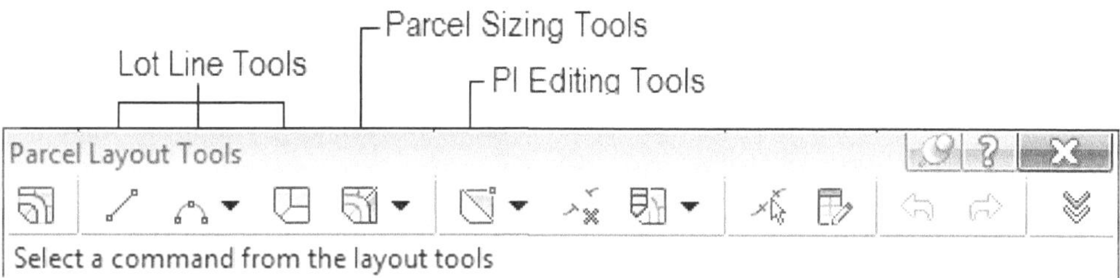

*Figure 8-40 The **Parcel Layout Tools** toolbar*

Lot Line Tools

The lot lines represents the parcels in 2-D plane. To create lot lines, available tools are discussed next.

Add Fixed Line - Two Points

This tool is used to create plot lines. It is same as creating a line segment. To create a line segment, choose the **Add Fixed Line - Two Points** tool from the **Parcels Layout Tools** toolbar; the **Create Parcels - Layout** dialog box will be displayed. Choose the **OK** button from the **Create Parcels - Layout** dialog box and then specify the start and end points in the drawing.

Add Fixed Curve - Three Points

This tool is used to add fixed curve to a parcel geometry by specifying three points in the drawing. This tool is similar to the AutoCAD three point arc command. To draw a fixed curve, choose the **Add Fixed Curve - Three Points** tool from the **Parcels Layout Tools** toolbar; the **Create Parcels - Layout** dialog box will be displayed. Specify the required settings in this dialog box and choose the **OK** button; the dialog box will be closed and you will be prompted to specify the start point and then follow the prompt displayed in the command line to add a fixed curve.

Add Fixed Curve - Two points and radius

This tool is used to add a fixed curve by specifying the two points and the radius for the curve. To access this tool, choose the down arrow on the right side of the **Fixed Curve (Three Points)** tool and select the **Add Fixed Curve - Two points and radius** tool from the drop-down menu.

Draw Tangent - Tangent with No Curves

This tool is used to create a parcel geometry which consists of tangents without curves. The parcel object is created by selecting and joining the consecutive points end-to-end in a sequential series which results in the creation of lot lines in a connected series. To invoke this tool, choose the **Draw Tangent - Tangent with No Curves** tool from the **Parcels Layout Tools** toolbar; the **Create Parcels - Layout** dialog box will be displayed. Specify the required settings in this dialog box and choose the **OK** button; the dialog box will be closed and you will be prompted to specify the start, intermediate, and the end point. Click in the drawing area to specify the points and press ENTER to end the command.

Parcel Sizing Tools

The parcel sizing tools accurately guides the position of the lot lines according to the user-defined parameters. These tools are used to create and edit attached lot lines. You can access these tools from the **Slide Line - Create** drop-down in the **Parcels Layout Tools** toolbar.

When you choose the desired parcel sizing tool from the drop-down, the **Create Parcels - Layout** dialog box will be displayed and also a property sheet is displayed at the bottom of the toolbar, refer to Figure 8-41. You can specify or change the parameters for new size of the parcel. The parameters of the property sheet are discussed later in the chapter.

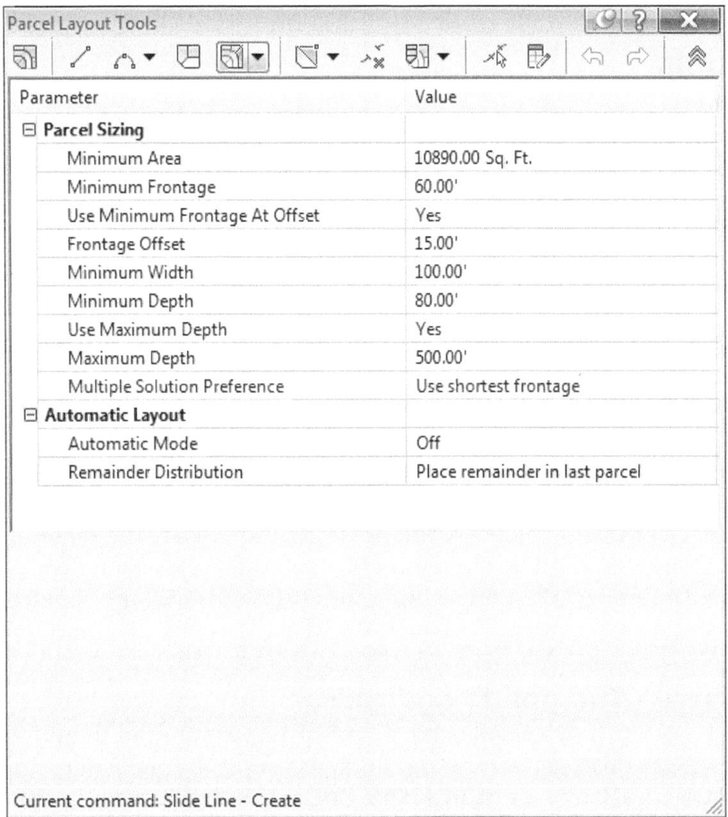

Figure 8-41 *The property sheet displayed at the bottom of the* ***Parcel Layout Tools*** *toolbar*

Slide Line - Create

This tool is used to create one or more lot lines by defining the start and end points along the frontage. Optionally for the lot lines, you can also specify the angle relative to the frontage or you can specify the absolute direction for the lot line. To invoke this tool, choose the **Slide Line - Create** tool from the **Slide Line - Create** drop-down list in the **Parcel Layout Tools** toolbar; the **Create Parcels - Layout** dialog box will be displayed and also a property sheet will be displayed at the bottom of the toolbar, refer to Figure 8-41. Specify the required settings in the dialog box and property sheet; you will be prompted to select the parcel which is to be divided by the lot lines. After that follow the prompts in the command line.

Slide Line - Edit

This tool is used to shift the position of the lot lines. You can also change the lot line's frontage angle and the absolute direction.

Swing Line - Create

Using this tool, you can define the lot lines to subdivide a parcel into two or more parcels. The lot line will be defined by specifying the start and end points along the frontage and then by specifying the location for the swing point on the opposite side of the selected frontage. The position of the swing point determines the size of the parcels. Therefore, to adjust the size of the parcels, change the location of the swing point. To invoke this tool, choose the **Swing Line - Create** tool from the **Slide Line - Create** drop-down list in the **Parcel Layout Tools** toolbar; the **Create Parcels - Layout** dialog box will be displayed and also a property sheet is displayed at the bottom of the toolbar, refer to Figure 8-42. Specify the required settings in the dialog box and property sheet; you will be prompted to select the parcel which is to be divided by the lot lines. After that follow the prompts in the command line.

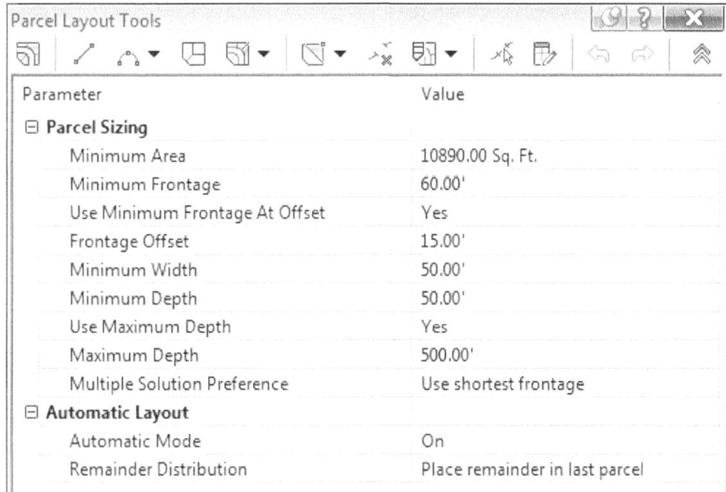

***Figure 8-42** The property sheet displayed under the **Parcel Layout Tools** toolbar*

PI Editing Tools

The **PI** (Point of Intersection) tools are used to add, delete, or break apart the PI of the parcel lot lines. The **PI** tools are discussed next.

Insert PI

This tool is used to create a point of intersection by inserting a vertex on the parcel segment. To insert PI, choose the **Insert PI** button from the **Parcel Layout Tools** toolbar; you will be prompted to select a lot line. On selecting the lot line, you are prompted to pick a point to insert the PI. Click at the location where you want to add the PI. Figure 8-43 shows a PI added to a fixed line.

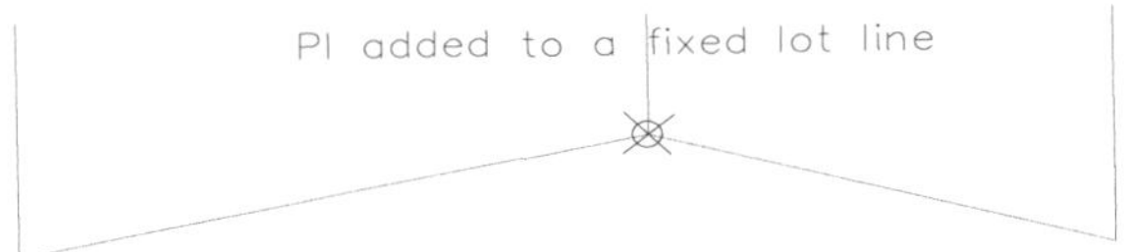

Figure 8-43 PI added to a fixed lot line

Delete PI

This tool is used to delete a point of intersection and create a single lot line between the vertices on either side of the selected lot line. If you remove a PI between two lot lines, the result would be a combination of two lot lines. To delete a PI, choose the **Delete PI** button from the **Parcel Layout Tools** toolbar; you will be prompted to select the lot line. On selecting the lot line, you will be prompted to pick a point near PI that you want to delete. Click in the drawing area near a PI; the PI will be removed. Press ENTER to end the command.

Break Apart PI

This tool is used to separate the point of intersection where the endpoints of two lot lines meet, thus resulting in two separate lot lines. To seperate the point of intersection, choose the **Break Apart PI** button from the **Parcel Layout Tools** toolbar; you will be prompted to select a lot line. On selecting the lot line, you will be prompted to pick a point near a PI that you want to split. Click in the drawing near PI, specify the distance by which you want to split it by specifying the points in the drawing or by entering the distance in the command line; the lot line will split into two different parts. Figure 8-44 shows the two split parts of the fixed lot line using the **Break Apart PI** tool.

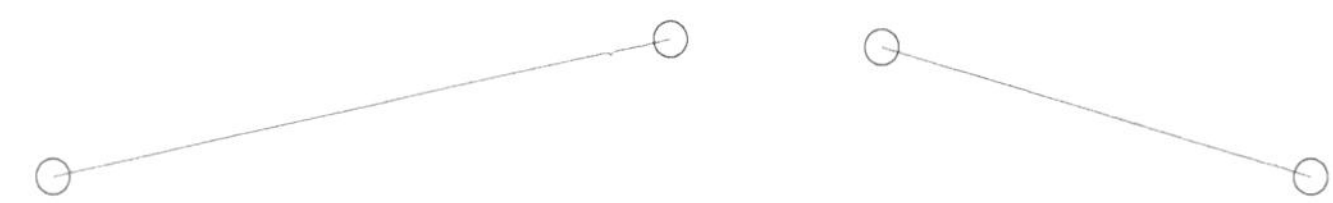

Figure 8-44 Fixed lot line after breaking apart from the PI

Other Tools

Apart from the lot line tools, parcel sizing tools and PI editing tools, there are some other tools in the **Parcel Layout Tools** toolbar. These tools are discussed next.

Delete Sub-entity

This tool is used to delete a parcel entity. To delete a parcel entity, choose the **Delete Sub-entity** tool; you will be prompted to select the subentity to be removed. Select the subentity; the selected subentity will be removed from the drawing.

Parcel Union

This tool is used to join two adjacent parcels. To do so, choose the **Parcel Union** tool from the **Parcel Layout Tools** toolbar; you will be prompted to select the destination parcel. The destination parcel selected by you determines the identity and properties of the joined parcel. On selecting the destination parcel; you are prompted to select the parcels to be joined. Select the required parcels and press ENTER. The parcel union will be created. Press ESC to exit the command.

Dissolve Parcel Union

This tool is used to restore the separate identity of the joined parcels. To do so, choose the **Dissolve Parcel Union** tool from the **Parcel Layout Tools** toolbar; you are prompted to select the parcel. When you select the parcel; the parcel will be separated into individual entities.

Pick Sub-entity

The **Pick Sub-entity** tool is used to pick a parcel entity as well as to view and modify its parameters in the **Parcel Layout Parameters** window. To display the **Parcel Layout Parameters** window, choose the **Sub-entity Editor** tool from the **Parcel Layout Tools** toolbar; the window will be displayed. Next, choose the **Pick Sub-entity** tool from the **Parcel Layout Tools** toolbar; you will be prompted to select the sub-entity. Select the sub-entity from the drawing; the parameters and their values corresponding to that sub-entity will be displayed in the respective columns of the **Parcel Layout Parameters** window. You can view the parameters of the selected entity and also modify the values that are editable.

Sub-entity Editor

This tool is used to open the **Parcel Layout Parameters** window, wherein you can view and edit the parameters of the selected sub-entity or a parcel.

PARCEL SIZING PARAMETERS

The **Parcel Sizing** parameters determines the dimensions of the parcels that are to be created using the tools in the **Parcel Layout Tools** toolbar. To create the parcels according to these parameters, first you need to define the parameters in the property sheet, refer to Figure 8-45. Some of the different parameters listed in the property sheet are explained next.

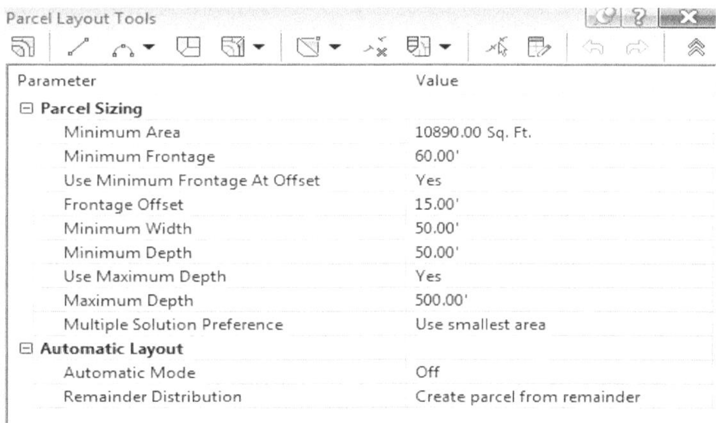

Parameter	Value
⊟ Parcel Sizing	
Minimum Area	10890.00 Sq. Ft.
Minimum Frontage	60.00'
Use Minimum Frontage At Offset	Yes
Frontage Offset	15.00'
Minimum Width	50.00'
Minimum Depth	50.00'
Use Maximum Depth	Yes
Maximum Depth	500.00'
Multiple Solution Preference	Use smallest area
⊟ Automatic Layout	
Automatic Mode	Off
Remainder Distribution	Create parcel from remainder

***Figure 8-45** The property sheet displaying various **Parcel Sizing** parameters*

Minimum Area

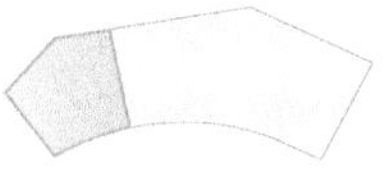

This option determines the minimum area for the new parcels. It should always be greater than zero and is commonly used by the designers to meet the minimum area requirements in the designing zone.

Minimum Frontage

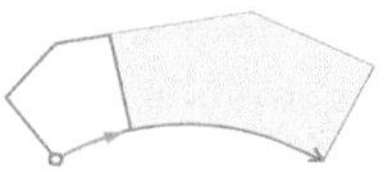

This sizing parameter sets the minimum width of a parcel which is coincident with the ROW or with a road ROW.

Use Minimum Frontage at Offset

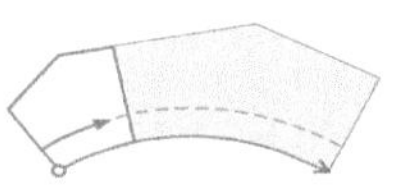

This parameter specifies whether to consider any offset while defining the frontage for the lot. To do so, choose the **Yes** option in the **Value** field of this parameter. This option helps in creating large number of smaller lots, mostly while creating the lots along a curved path.

Frontage Offset

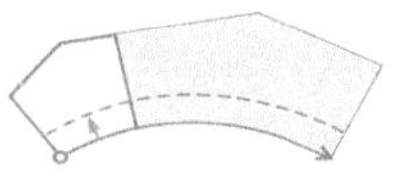

Using this parameter, you can set the default value for the frontage offset. While creating the parcels this offset value will be considered only if the **Yes** option is selected in the value field of **Use Minimum Frontage At Offset** drop-down list.

Minimum Width

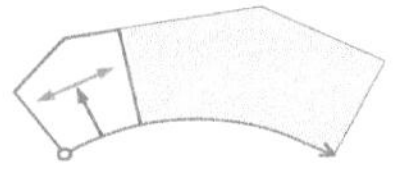

This parameter is used to specify the minimum width for the parcel to be created.

Minimum Depth

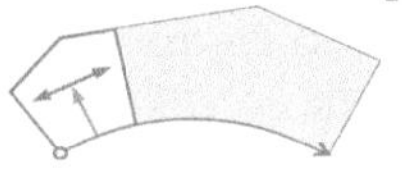

This parameter is used to specify the minimum depth allowed for the parcel. The minimum depth is measured perpendicularly from the mid-point of the frontage.

Use Maximum Depth

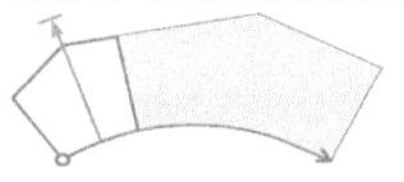

This parameter specifies whether to consider the maximum depth criteria while creating the parcel or not. Click in the value field of this parameter and select **Yes** to use the maximum depth criterion for creating parcel.

Maximum Depth

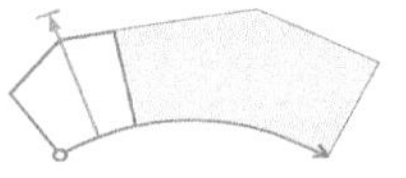

This parameter is used to specify the maximum depth allowed for the parcel, measured perpendicularly from the mid-point of the frontage.

Multiple Solution Preference

Sometimes, there are multiple valid solutions available while creating new parcels. In such cases, when multiple solutions occur, you can choose the solution to be displayed by using the options in the **Multiple Solutions Preference** drop-down list. The two options available in the drop-down list are discussed next.

Use Shortest Frontage

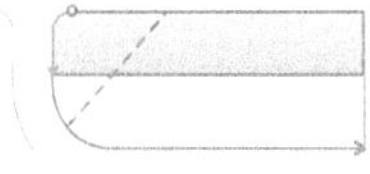

The **Use Shortest Frontage** option is selected from the **Multiple Solution Preference** drop-down list, the parcels will be created using the shortest frontage criteria and the parcels with the shortest frontage will be displayed.

Use Smallest Area

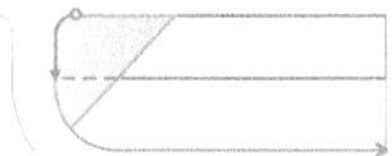

If the **Use Smallest Area** option is selected from the **Multiple Solution Preference** drop-down list, the parcels will be created using the smallest area criteria and the parcels with the smallest area will be displayed.

In addition to the parcel sizing parameters, parcel layout parameters are also available in the property sheet. The parcel layout parameters play their role only during the creation of multiple parcels. The parcel layout parameters are clubbed under the **Automatic Layout** node in the property sheet. The parameters under this node are discussed next.

Automatic Mode

Using this parameter, you can specify the mode for the creation of parcels. Using the options in the **Automatic Mode** drop-down list, you can specify whether to create multiple parcels automatically or create them one by one using command prompts.

Automatic Mode - On

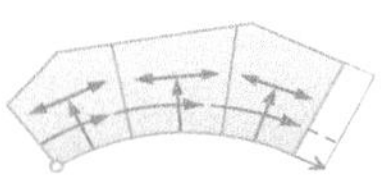

If the **Automatic Mode** is turned on then the multiple parcels will be created automatically within the selected area as per the specified sizing parameters. To enable the automatic mode, click in the value field of the **Automatic Mode** parameter and choose the **On** option from the drop-down list.

Automatic Mode - Off

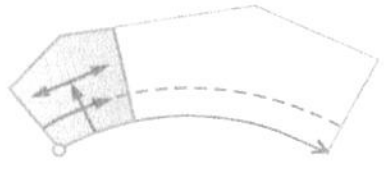

If the **Automatic Mode** is turned off then the parcels will be created one by one by specifying the information in the command prompt for each individual parcel. To disable the automatic mode, click in the value field of the **Automatic Mode** parameter and choose the **Off** option from the drop-down list.

Remainder Distribution

This parameter helps to specify the remaining area, which got left after the completion of all the parcels created according to the specified size requirements. The options available for the **Remainder Distribution** option are discussed next.

Create parcel from remainder

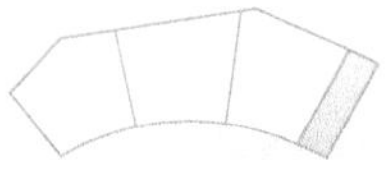

Choose the **Create parcel from remainder** option from the **Remainder Distribution** drop-down list to create a new parcel from the remainder area.

Place remainder in last parcel

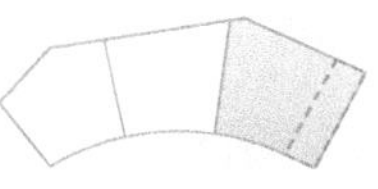

Choose the **Place remainder in last parcel** option from the **Remainder Distribution** drop-down list to add the remainder area to the last parcel.

Redistribute remainder

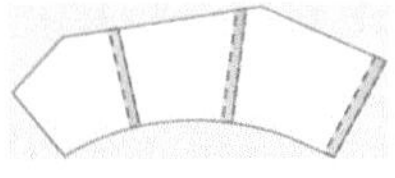

Choose the **Redistribute remainder** option from the **Remainder Distribution** drop-down to equally distribute the remainder area to every parcel.

RIGHT OF WAY (ROW) PARCEL

The ROW parcel is a parcel that usually represents the piece of land, which could be constructed as a road, sidewalk, or other utility purposes. It is generally used for the community and maintained by the local government or municipality. In Civil 3D, the ROW parcel is created as a constant width parcel along each side of the alignment.

Creating Right of Way Parcels

Ribbon: Home > Create Design > Parcel drop-down > Create Right of Way
Command: CREATEPARCELROW

To create the **Right of Way** parcel, you need to create the alignment representing a road or a sidewalk linked to the site. After creating the alignment, choose the **Create Right of Way** tool from the **Parcel** drop-down under the **Create Design** panel of the **Home** tab; you will be prompted to select a parcel. Select the parcel and press ENTER; the **Create Right Of Way** dialog box will be displayed showing various parameters to offset the parcel boundaries from both sides of the alignment, as shown in Figure 8-46.

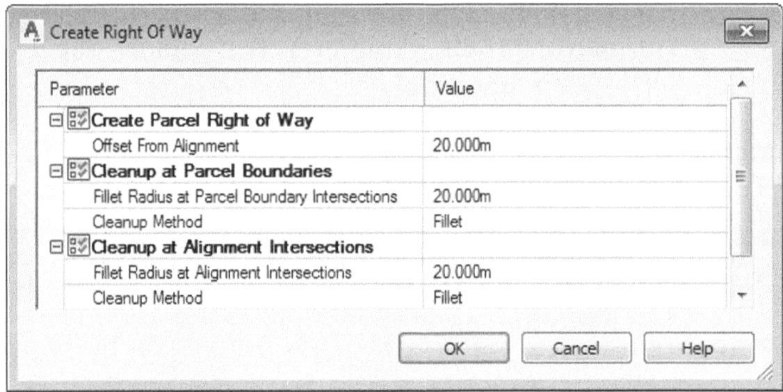

*Figure 8-46 The **Create Right Of Way** dialog box*

Create Parcel Right of Way

Specify the offset distance of each side of the right-of-way from alignment in the value field of **Offset From Alignment**.

Cleanup at Parcel Boundaries

Specify the fillet radius or the chamfer distance at parcel boundary intersections. If you select the **None** option for the **Cleanup Method** option, no cleanup will be used at parcel boundary intersections. If you select the **Fillet** option for **Cleanup Method**, a fillet will be used at parcel boundary intersections which connects the parcel boundaries with an arc tangent to the boundaries having a radius specified in the value field of **Fillet Radius at Parcel Boundary Intersections**. Similarly, by using the **Chamfer** option, a chamfer will be used at parcel boundary intersections that connect parcel boundaries with an angled line at a chamfer distance specified in the value field of **Fillet Radius at Parcel Boundary Intersections**.

Cleanup at Alignment Intersections

Specify the fillet radius or chamfer distance at alignment intersections. If you select the **None** option under the drop-down of **Cleanup Method**, no cleanup will be used at alignment intersections. By using the **Fillet** option for **Cleanup Method**, a fillet will be used at alignment intersections connecting the alignment boundaries with an arc tangent to the boundaries having a radius specified in the value field of **Fillet Radius at Alignment Intersections**. Similarly by using **Chamfer** option, a chamfer will be used at alignment intersections which connects the alignment boundaries with an angled line at a chamfer distance specified in the value field of **Fillet Radius at Alignment Intersections**.

PARCEL PROPERTIES

You can view and edit the properties of a single parcel or a group of parcels. In both the cases, you can change the parcel style, area label style, parcel number, and address. An additional property is included in site parcel properties which specifies the display order of parcels within the site, including the site parcel itself. To edit parcel properties, select and right-click on a parcel area label in the drawing; a shortcut menu will be displayed. Choose the **Parcel Properties** option; the **Parcel Properties - <Parcel Name>** dialog box with **Information** tab as default will be displayed as shown in Figure 8-47. The options in this dialog box are discussed next.

***Figure 8-47** Partial view of the **Parcel Properties - Property : 1** dialog box*

Information Tab

The **Information** tab is chosen by default. You can use this tab to view or modify the general information of the parcel such as name, description, and object style.

Name
You can specify a name for the parcel in the **Name** edit box. By default, the **Name** edit box is disabled. You can enable it by clearing the **Use name template in parcel style** check box.

Description
You can enter the description about the parcel in the **Description** edit box.

Object Style
You can select the parcel style from the **Object Style** drop-down list. To create a new style or to edit the existing style, click on the down arrow next to the **Object Style** drop-down list; a flyout will be displayed. Choose the required option from the flyout.

Use name template in parcel style
You can specify whether the parcel name is based on the parcel style name template or has to be set manually. If this check box is selected, the parcel name is (re)set based on the parcel style name template. Clear the check box if you want to manually enter a parcel name in the name field.

Show tooltips
You can specify whether to display the tooltip for the object in the drawing (not over toolbar icons).

Composition Tab
This tab is used to change a parcel area label style or to view the parcel area or perimeter.

Area selection label style
You can select an existing label style from the **Area selection label style** drop-down list or create a new one. To create a new style or edit the existing style, click on the down arrow next to the **Area selection label style** drop-down list; a flyout will be displayed. Choose the required option from the flyout to create or edit the area selection label style.

Area
It displays the area of the parcel.

Perimeter
It displays the perimeter of the parcel.

Analysis Tab
This tab is used to view the analysis result, change the analysis type, segement process order, or point of beginning.

Inverse analysis
It provides a report of distances, direction, curve data, and start and end co-ordinates for each parcel segment starting at specified point of beginning.

Mapcheck analysis

It provides the same information as the Inverse analysis, except that all start and end co-ordinates for each parcel segment are computed in relation to the co-ordinates of point of beginning and the previous segment. Mapcheck reports inspect the plotted drawing for omission of segment labels to avoid errors introduced into legal documents.

Enable mapcheck across chord

On selecting this check box, Mapcheck traverse is computed for curve segments using their chord lengths. Otherwise, it is computed using their curve length.

Point of beginning

You can specify the initial node for parcel boundary by choosing the **point of beginning selector** button. When you choose the button, the **Parcel Properties** dialog box will close and you will be prompted to pick a new starting point. Pick the approriate starting point; **The Parcel Properties** dialog box reapears with updated point of beginning co-ordinates.

Process segment order counterclockwise

Select this check box to specify that segments will be processed in counter-clockwise order.

User Defined Properties Tab

This tab is used to review or change user-defined parcel properties.

Parcel Number

In this field you can specify the number assigned to the parcel.

Parcel Address

In this field you can specify the address of the parcel.

Parcel Tax ID

In this field you can specify the Tax ID number assigned to the parcel.

TUTORIALS

Tutorial 1 Creating a Corridor

In this tutorial, you will create a corridor. Next, edit the corridor to create multiple regions and assign a new assembly (for the new region) to create a rest bay, as shown in Figure 8-48.

(Expected time: 30 min)

The following steps are required to complete this tutorial:

a. Download and open the file.
b. Create a corridor.
c. View the corridor.
d. Create regions.
e. Save the file.

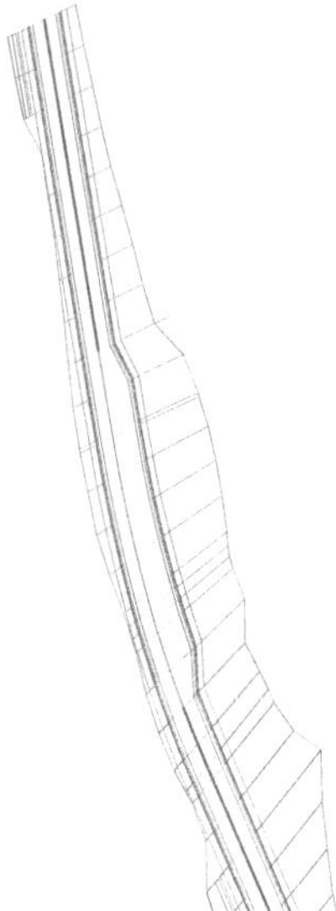

Figure 8-48 Partial view of the Corridor showing the added rest bay

Downloading and Opening the File

1. Download *c08_c3d_2018_tut.zip* file from *http://www.cadcim.com*. Next, save and extract the file at *C:\c3d_2018*.

2. Choose **Open** from the **Application Menu**; the **Select File** dialog box is displayed.

3. In the dialog box, browse to the location *C:\c3d_2018\c08_c3d_2018_tut.*

4. Select the file *c08_c3d_2018_tut01.dwg* and then choose the **Open** button to open the file. Ignore the error message if displayed.

Creating a Corridor

In this section of the tutorial, you will create a corridor model using proposed road alignment, proposed profile, assembly, and existing ground surface.

1. Choose the **Corridor** tool from the **Create Design** panel of the **Home** tab; the **Create Corridor** dialog box is displayed.

2. Enter **Road Corridor** in the **Name** edit box.

3. Ensure that the **Proposed Road** option is selected in the **Alignment** drop-down list. Next, select the **Road Profile** option from the **Profile** drop-down list.

4. Select the **Road Assembly** and **Existing Ground** options from the **Assembly** and **Target Surface** drop-down lists, respectively.

5. Next, clear the **Set baseline and region parameters** check box and then choose the **OK** button; the **Create Corridor** dialog box is closed and Civil 3D starts executing the corridor creation process.

On the completion of the process, the **Road Corridor** is added to the **Corridors** node of the **Prospector** tab in the **TOOLSPACE**. Ignore the messages in the **PANORAMA** window if displayed and close the window.

Viewing the Corridor

1. Select and right-click on **Road Corridor** from the **Corridors** node in the **TOOLSPACE**; a shortcut menu is displayed.

2. Choose the **Select** option from the shortcut menu; the corridor is selected in the drawing window.

3. With the corridor selected, right-click in the drawing area; a shortcut menu is displayed.

4. Choose the **Isolate Objects** option from the shortcut menu; a cascading menu is displayed. Choose the **Isolate Selected Objects** option from the cascading menu, as shown in Figure 8-49; objects other than the selected corridor get hidden.

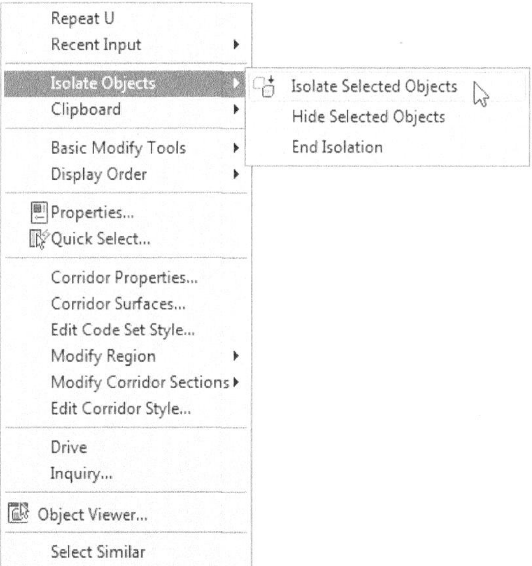

Figure 8-49 *Choosing the* ***Isolate Selected Objects*** *option*

5. Enter **ZE** in the command bar; the drawing will zoom to the corridor in the drawing area, refer to Figure 8-50.

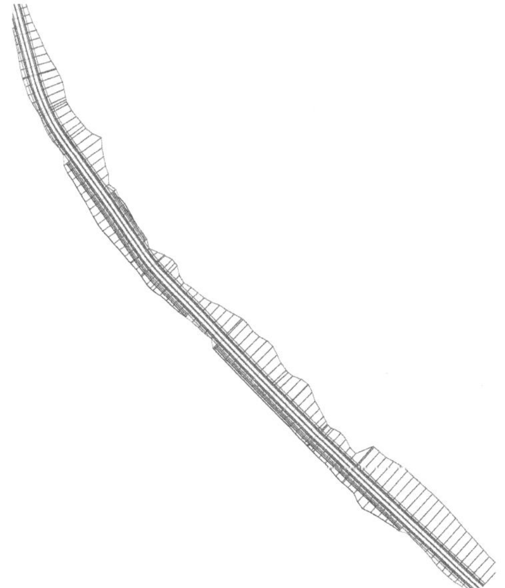

Figure 8-50 *Full view of the isolated* ***Road Corridor*** *object*

Tip

You can also view the corridor model in the ***Object Viewer*** *window. To do so, select the corridor model in the drawing and right-click; a shortcut menu will be displayed. Choose the* ***Object Viewer*** *option from the shortcut menu; the corridor model is displayed in the new* ***Object Viewer*** *window, as shown in Figure 8-51.*

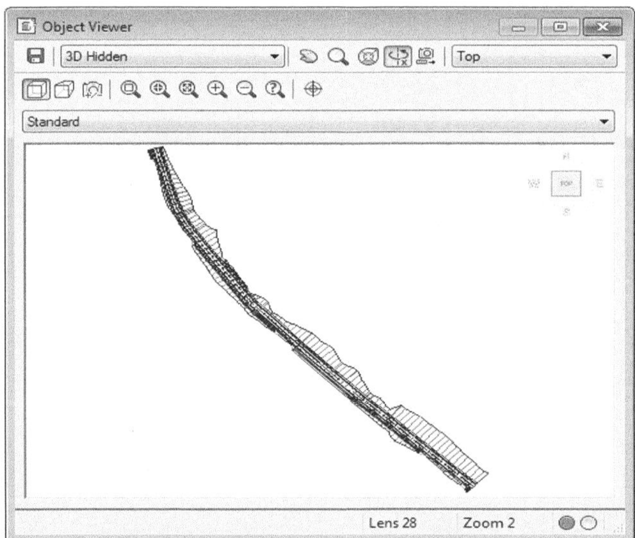

Figure 8-51 *The corridor model displayed in the* ***Object Viewer*** *window*

6. Right-click in the drawing; a shortcut menu is displayed. Choose **Isolate Object** from the shortcut menu; a cascading menu is displayed. Choose **End Object Isolation** from the cascading menu; the hidden objects are displayed again in the drawing area.

Creating Regions

1. Expand the **Corridors** node in the **Prospector** tab of the **TOOLSPACE**. Right-click on the **Road Corridor**; a shortcut menu is displayed. Choose **Properties** from the shortcut menu; the **Corridor Properties - Road Corridor** dialog box is displayed.

2. Choose the **Parameters** tab in this dialog box. Expand the **BL - Proposed Road - (1)** node in the **Name** column, if not already expanded. Right-click on **RG - Road Assembly - (1)** under the baseline **BL - Proposed Road - (1)** node; a shortcut menu is displayed.

3. Choose the **Split Region** option from the shortcut menu, as shown in Figure 8-52; the **Corridor Properties - Road Corridor** dialog box is closed and you are prompted to select a station along the alignment.

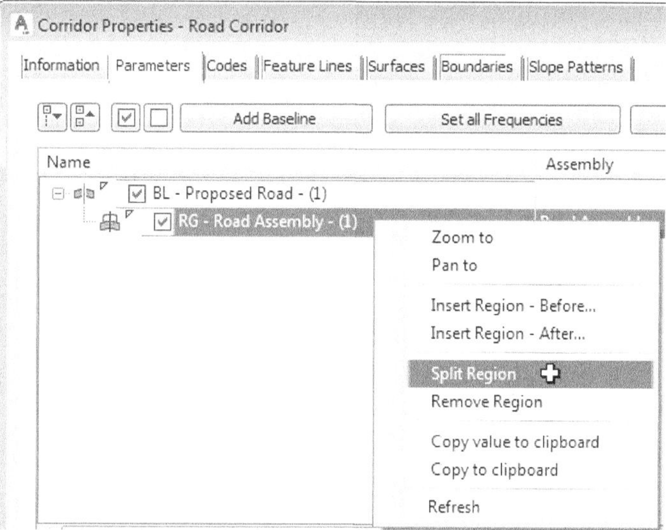

Figure 8-52 *Choosing the **Split Region** option from the shortcut menu*

4. Select a point along the alignment at station 2+00.00; a region is created at the selected station and you are prompted to specify another station.

5. Choose a point along the alignment at station **4+00.00**, as shown in Figure 8-53; a region is created at the selected station and you are prompted to specify another station.

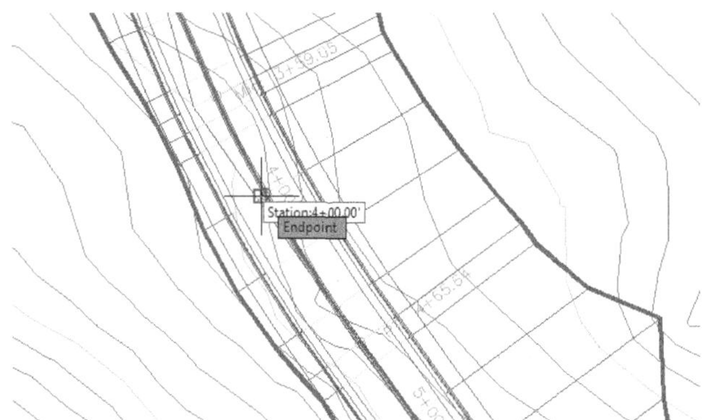

Figure 8-53 *Specifying a point along the alignment at station* ***4+00.00***

6. Press ENTER to exit region creation; the **Corridor Properties - Road Corridor** dialog box is displayed again, refer to Figure 8-54.

Tip

In case the corridor regions are not created at exact station values mentioned in the steps then edit the ***Start Station*** *and* ***End Station*** *values manually for the regions in the* ***Corridor Properties*** *dialog box.*

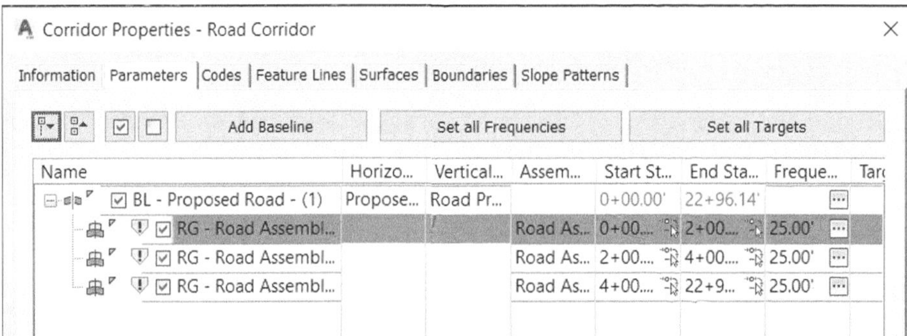

Figure 8-54 *Partial view of the* ***Corridor Properties - Road Corridor*** *dialog box with created regions*

7. Click on the **Name** cell of the newly created region **RG - Road Assembly - (1) (1)**; an edit box is displayed. Rename the region as **RG - Road Assembly - Rest Bay** in this edit box.

8. Next, click in the cell of the **Assembly** column corresponding to the **RG - Road Assembly - Rest Bay**; the **Edit Corridor Region** dialog box is displayed.

9. In the **Edit Corridor Region** dialog box, select the **Road Assembly- Rest bay** option from the **Assembly** drop-down list. Next, choose the **OK** button; the **Edit Corridor Region** dialog box is closed. The **Road Assembly-Rest bay** name is displayed in the **Assembly** column for the **RG - Road Assembly - Rest Bay** region in the **Corridor Properties - Road Corridor** dialog box. Ignore the message in the **PANORAMA** window if displayed.

10. Next, choose the **OK** button; the **Corridor Properties - Rebuild** message box is displayed, as shown in Figure 8-55.

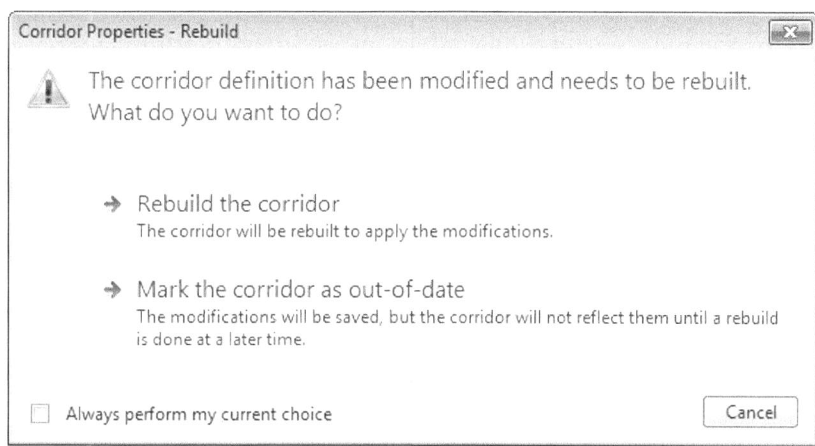

Figure 8-55 *The* ***Corridor Properties - Rebuild*** *message box*

11. Choose the **Rebuild the corridor** option from the message box; the message box is closed and the corridor model is rebuilt.

After completing the rebuild process, follow the steps explained in the **Viewing the Corridor** section of this tutorial to view the corridor model.

12. Zoom to the corridor along station 2+00.00 to 4+00.00. Notice the rest bay is added to the corridor, refer to Figure 8-56.

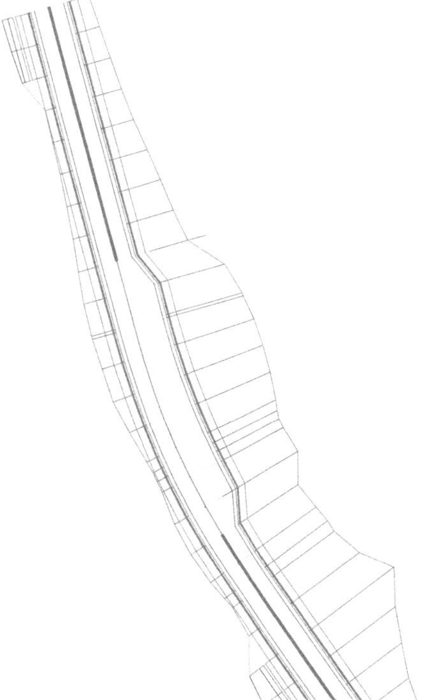

Figure 8-56 *Partial view of the Corridor showing the added rest bay*

Saving the File

1. Choose **Save As** from the **Application Menu**; the **Save Drawing As** dialog box is displayed.

2. In this dialog box, browse to the following location:

   C:\c3d_2018\c08_c3d_2018_tut

3. In the **File name** edit box, enter **c08_tut01a**.

4. Choose the **Save** button; the file is saved with the name *c08_tut01a.dwg* at the specified location.

Tutorial 2 Creating Corridor - Surface and Boundary

In this tutorial, you will use the corridor model (created in tutorial 1) to create a surface and a surface boundary. You will also create polylines from the corridor feature lines.

(Expected time: 45 min)

The following steps are required to complete this tutorial:

a. Download and open the file.
b. Create a corridor surface.
c. Create a boundary for the corridor surface.
d. Create polylines from corridor.
e. Create alignment from the corridor
f. Create profile from the corridor.
g. Save the file.

Downloading and Opening the File

1. Download *c08_c3d_2018_tut.zip* file, if not downloaded earlier, from *www.cadcim.com*. Next, save and extract the file at *C:\c3d_2018* location.

2. Choose **Open** from the **Application Menu**; the **Select File** dialog box is displayed.

3. In the dialog box, browse to the location *C:\c3d_2018\c08_c3d_2018_tut.*

4. Select the file *c08_c3d_2018_tut02.dwg* and then choose the **Open** button to open the file. Ignore the error message if displayed.

Creating the Corridor Surface

In this section of the tutorial, you will create a new corridor surface using the **Top** code for the **Links** in the corridor model.

1. Expand the **Corridors** node in the **Prospector** tab of the **TOOLSPACE**. Right-click on the **Road Corridor**; a shortcut menu is displayed. Choose **Properties** from the shortcut menu; the **Corridor Properties - Road Corridor** dialog box is displayed.

2. Choose the **Create a corridor surface** button in the **Surfaces** tab; the **Road Corridor Surface - (1)** surface is added to the **Corridor Properties - Road Corridor** dialog box.

3. Rename the surface name as **Proposed Road Corridor Surface** in the **Name** column.

4. Ensure that the **Links** and **Top** options are selected in the **Data type** and **Specify code** drop-down lists, respectively. Choose the **Add surface item** button displayed on the right of the **Specify code** drop-down; surface item **Top** is added to the **Proposed Road Corridor Surface** node.

5. Select the check box in the **Add as Breakline** column, refer to Figure 8-57.

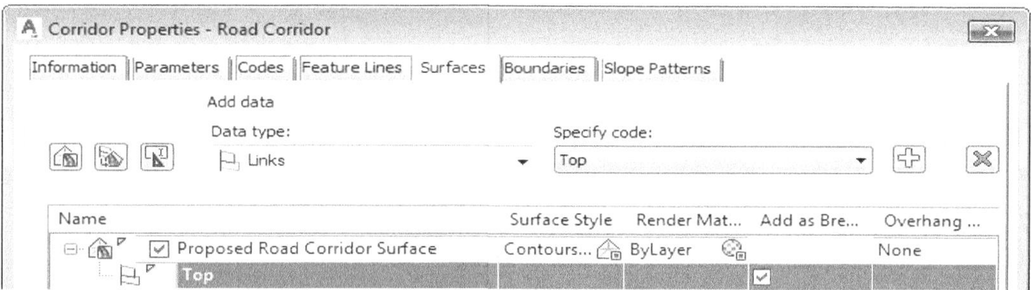

***Figure 8-57** Partial view of the **Corridor Properties - Road Corridor** dialog box with check box selected in the **Add as Breakline** column*

6. Click on the style name in the **Surface Style** column corresponding to **Proposed Road Corridor Surface**; the **Pick Corridor Surface Style** dialog box is displayed.

7. Select the **Road Corridor Surface** option from the **Pick Corridor Surface Style** drop-down list, refer to Figure 8-58.

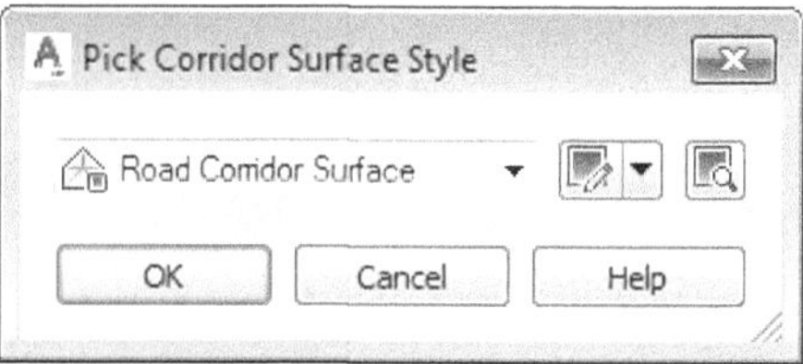

***Figure 8-58** **Road Corridor Surface** selected in the **Pick Corridor Surface Style** drop-down*

8. Choose the **OK** button; the **Pick Corridor Surface Style** dialog box is closed and the selected style is assigned to the corridor surface.

9. Next, choose the **OK** button in the **Corridor Properties - Road Corridor** dialog box; the **Corridor Properties - Rebuild** message box is displayed.

10. Choose the **Rebuild the corridor** option in the message box; the message box is closed and the surface is created, refer to Figure 8-59. Ignore the **PANORAMA** window.

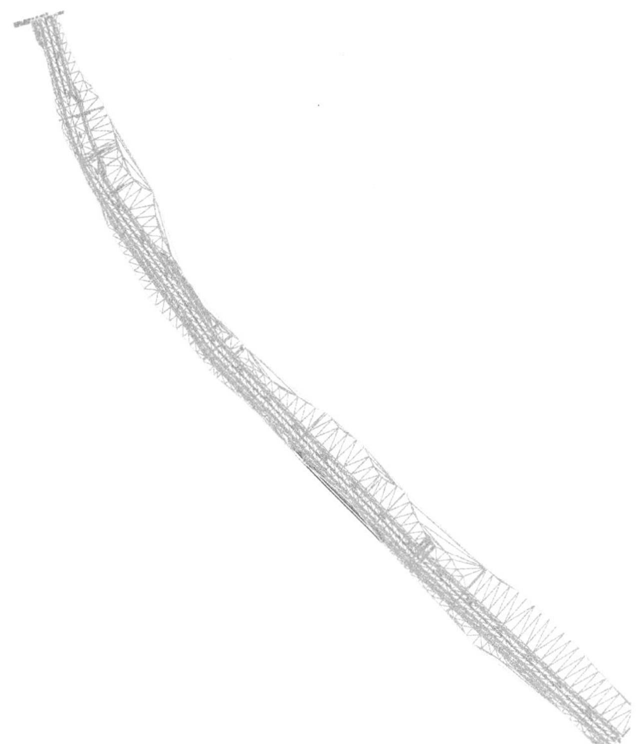

Figure 8-59 A view of the Proposed Road Corridor Surface

Adding the Surface Boundary

1. In the **Prospector** tab of the **TOOLSPACE** palette, expand the **Corridors** node and select the **Road Corridor** subnode. Right-click on the **Road Corridor** subnode; a shortcut menu is displayed.

2. Select the **Properties** option from the shortcut menu; the **Corridor Properties - Road Corridor** dialog box is displayed.

3. Choose the **Boundaries** tab in this dialog box. Note that the corridor surface name **Proposed Road Corridor Surface** is displayed in the **Name** column.

4. Select the surface name and right-click; a shortcut menu is displayed.

5. Choose **Add Automatically** from the menu; a cascading menu is displayed.

6. Choose the **Daylight** option from the cascading menu, refer to Figure 8-60; **Corridor Boundary (1)** is added to the **Corridor Properties - Road Corridor** dialog box.

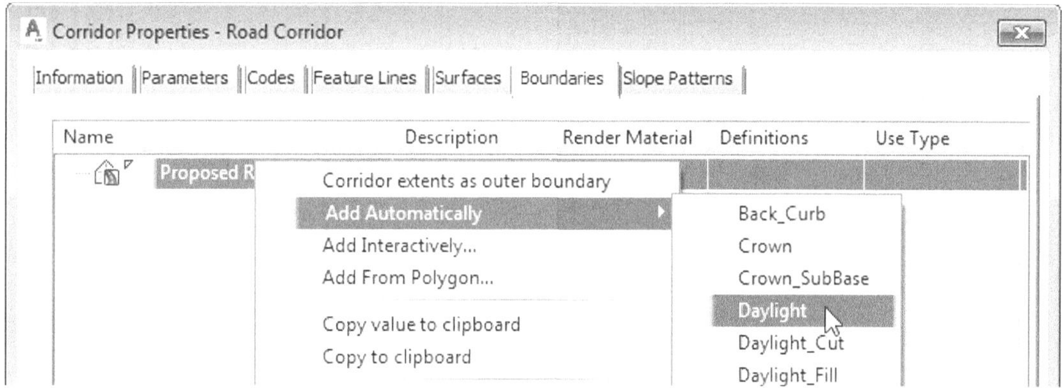

Figure 8-60 *Choosing the* ***Daylight*** *option from the shortcut menu*

7. Next, choose the **OK** button in the **Corridor Properties - Road Corridor** dialog box; the **Corridor Properties - Rebuild** message box is displayed.

8. Choose the **Rebuild the Corridor** option in this message box; the message box is closed and surface is created with the specified boundary. Figures 8-61 and 8-62 show the surface triangulation for the corridor surface creation without and with surface boundary, respectively.

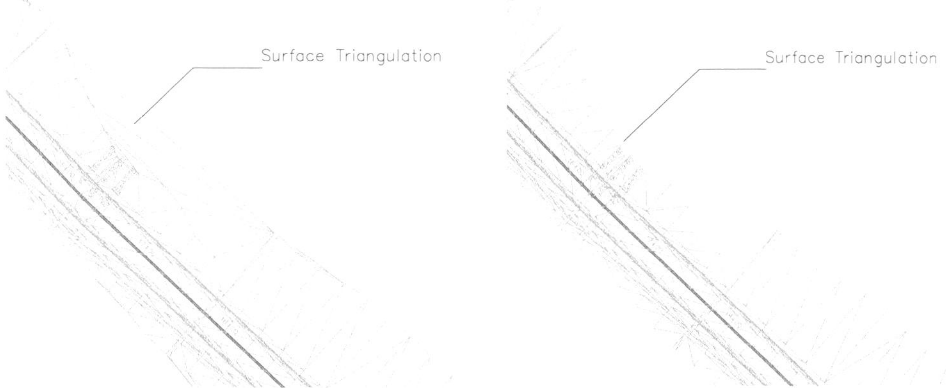

Figure 8-61 *Corridor surface triangulation without surface boundary*

Figure 8-62 *Corridor surface triangulation with surface boundary*

Creating Polylines from Corridor

In this section, you will create polylines from the feature lines of the corridor model. As you need to select feature lines in this section, it is recommended that you change the display order of the corridor model and bring it on the top to select feature lines easily.

1. Select the corridor model from the drawing and right-click on it; a shortcut menu is displayed.

2. Choose the **Display Order** option from the shortcut menu; a cascading menu is displayed.

3. Choose the **Bring to Front** option from the cascading menu, as shown in Figure 8-63; the corridor model is displayed on the top of other objects in the drawing.

4. Select the corridor from the drawing; the **Corridor: Road Corridor** tab is displayed in the ribbon.

5. Choose the **Polyline from Corridor** tool from the **Launch Pad** panel of the **Corridor: Road Corridor** tab, refer Figure 8-64; the **Select a Feature Line** dialog box is displayed.

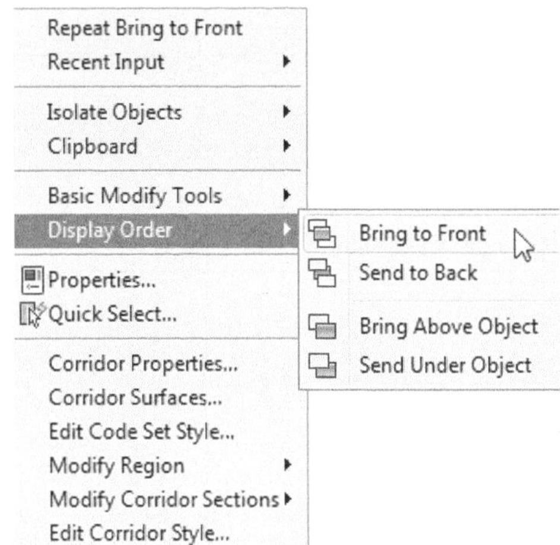

Figure 8-63 *Choosing the* ***Bring to Front*** *option*

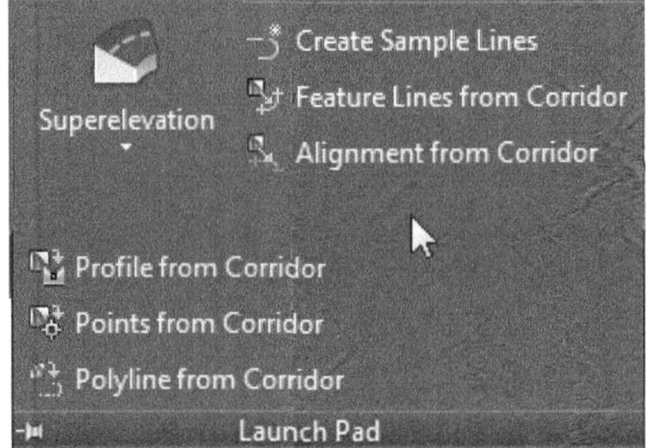

Figure 8-64 *The* ***Launch Pad*** *panel of the* ***Corridor: Road Corridor*** *tab*

7. In the **Select a Feature Line** dialog box, choose the **Cancel** button. You are prompted to select a corridor feature line from the drawing.

8. Select the outer most feature line on the right of the corridor, refer to Figure 8-65; the **Select a Feature Line** dialog box is displayed, as shown in Figure 8-66.

9. Select the **Daylight** feature line from the list and choose the **OK** button; the polyline is created and is added to the drawing. Also, you are prompted to select another corridor feature.

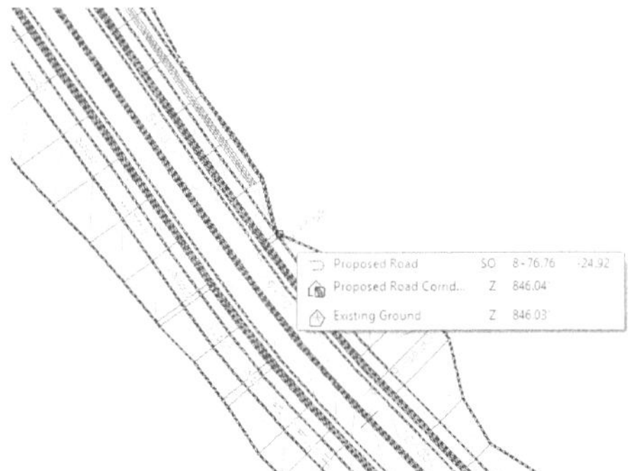

Figure 8-65 Selecting the feature line from the corridor

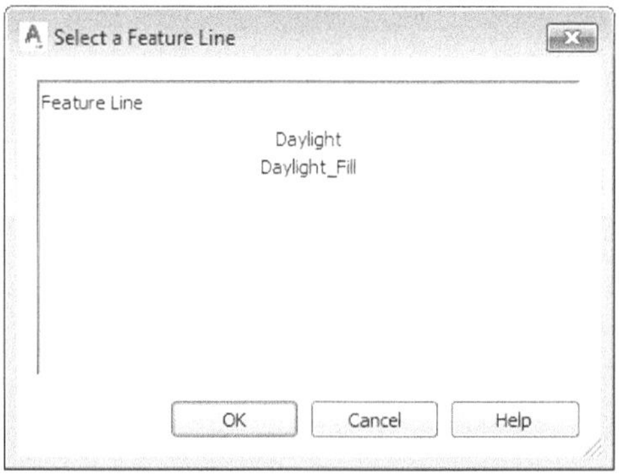

Select a Feature Line

Feature Line

Daylight

Daylight_Fill

OK Cancel Help

*Figure 8-66 The **Select a Feature Line** dialog box*

10. Select the outermost feature line on the left of the corridor; the **Select a Feature line** dialog box is displayed.

11. Select the **Daylight** feature line from the list and choose the **OK** button; another polyline is created and is added to the drawing, as shown in Figure 8-67. Now, you will be prompted again to select a corridor feature line.

12. Press ESC to end the command.

Creating Alignment from the Corridor

1. Choose the **Create Alignment from Corridor** tool from **Home > Create Design > Alignment** drop-down; you are prompted to select a corridor feature line.

2. Zoom in station **1+00** of the corridor and select the **Sidewalk_Out** feature line (second line from the right), refer to Figure 8-67; the **Select a Feature Line** dialog box is displayed.

3. Select the **Sidewalk_Out** feature line from the dialog box and then choose the **OK** button; the **Create Alignment from Objects** dialog box is displayed, as shown in Figure 8-68.

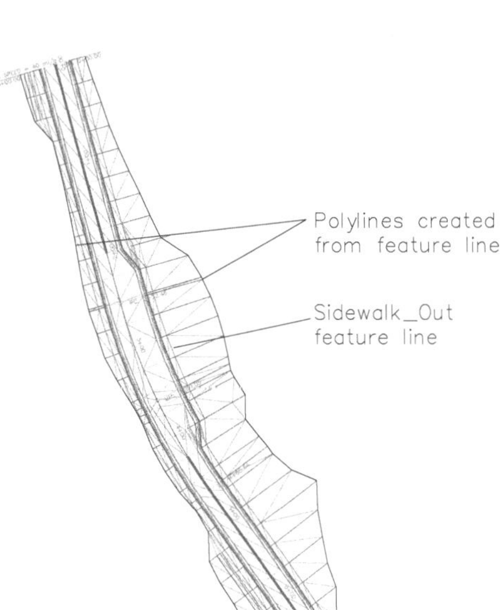

Figure 8-67 *Partial view of corridor with polylines created from feature lines*

Figure 8-68 *The **Create Alignment from Objects** dialog box*

4. In this dialog box, enter **Alignment - Side Walk** in the **Name** edit box.

5. Choose the **OK** button; the **Create Alignment from Objects** dialog box is closed and the **Create Profile - Draw New** dialog box is displayed.

6. Choose the **Cancel** button from the **Create Profile - Draw New** dialog box; the dialog box is closed without creating the profile. Press ESC to terminate the command. The alignment is added to the drawing, refer to Figure 8-69.

Notice that the created alignment has been added to the **Offset Alignments** sub node under the alignment node of the **Prospector** tab.

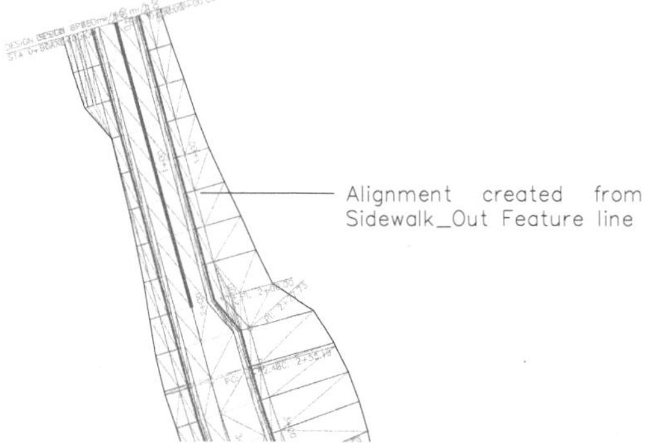

Figure 8-69 *Partial view of the alignment created from feature line*

Creating Profile from Corridor

1. Choose the **Create Profile from Corridor** tool from **Home > Create Design > Profile** drop-down; you are prompted to select a corridor feature line.

2. Zoom in station **1+00.00** and select the first **magenta** colored feature line from left, refer to Figure 8-70; the **Select a Feature Line** dialog box is displayed.

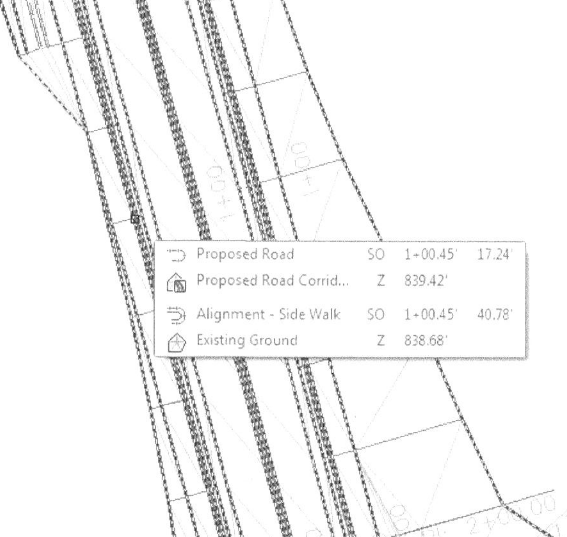

Figure 8-70 *Selecting the feature line from the corridor*

3. Select the **Sidewalk_In** feature line from the dialog box and then choose the **OK** button; the **Select a Feature Line** dialog box is closed and the **Create Profile - Draw New** dialog box is displayed.

4. Enter **Sidewalk-In Profile** in the **Name** edit box of the dialog box.

5. Choose the **OK** button; the dialog box is closed and the **Sidewalk-In Profile** is added to the profile view in the drawing, refer to Figure 8-71.

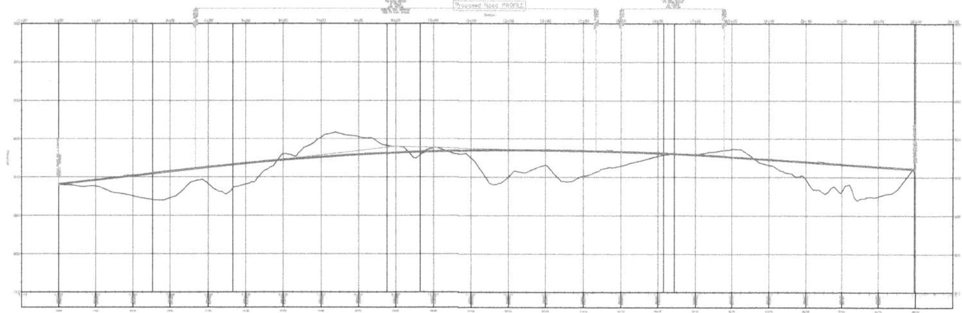

Figure 8-71 *The profile view with the profile created from corridor feature line*

6. Press ESC to end the command.

Saving the File

1. Choose **Save As** from the **Application Menu**; the **Save Drawing As** dialog box is displayed.

2. In this dialog box, browse to the following location:

   C:\c3d_2018\c08_c3d_2018_tut

3. In the **File name** edit box, enter **c08_tut02a**.

4. Choose the **Save** button; the file is saved with the name *c08_tut02a.dwg* at the specified location.

Tutorial 3 Checking Corridor Visibility

In this tutorial, you will check the line of site along the corridor. Also, create a drive simulation along the road corridor. You will also extract the corridor solid from the corridor.

(Expected time: 45 min)

The following steps are required to complete this tutorial:

a. Download and open the file.
b. Analyze the corridor visibility using the **Site Distance** tool.
c. Create drive simulation.
d. Extract AutoCAD 3D solid using the **Extract corridor solids** tool.
e. View the extracted corridor solid.
f. Save the file.

Downloading and Opening the File

1. Download *c08_c3d_2018_tut.zip* file, if not downloaded earlier, from www.cadcim.com. Next, save and extract the file at *C:\c3d_2018* location.

2. Choose **Open** from the **Application Menu**; the **Select File** dialog box is displayed.

3. In the dialog box, browse to the location *C:\c3d_2018\c08_c3d_2018_tut* where you have saved the file.

4. Select the file *c08_c3d_2018_tut03.dwg* and then choose the **Open** button to open the file. Ignore the error message if displayed.

Corridor Visibility Analysis

1. Select the corridor in the drawing; the **Corridor: Road Corridor** tab is displayed in the ribbon.

2. Choose the **Sight Distance** tool from the **Analyze** panel of the **Corridor: Road Corridor** tab; the **General** page of the **Sight Distance Check** wizard is displayed, as shown in Figure 8-72.

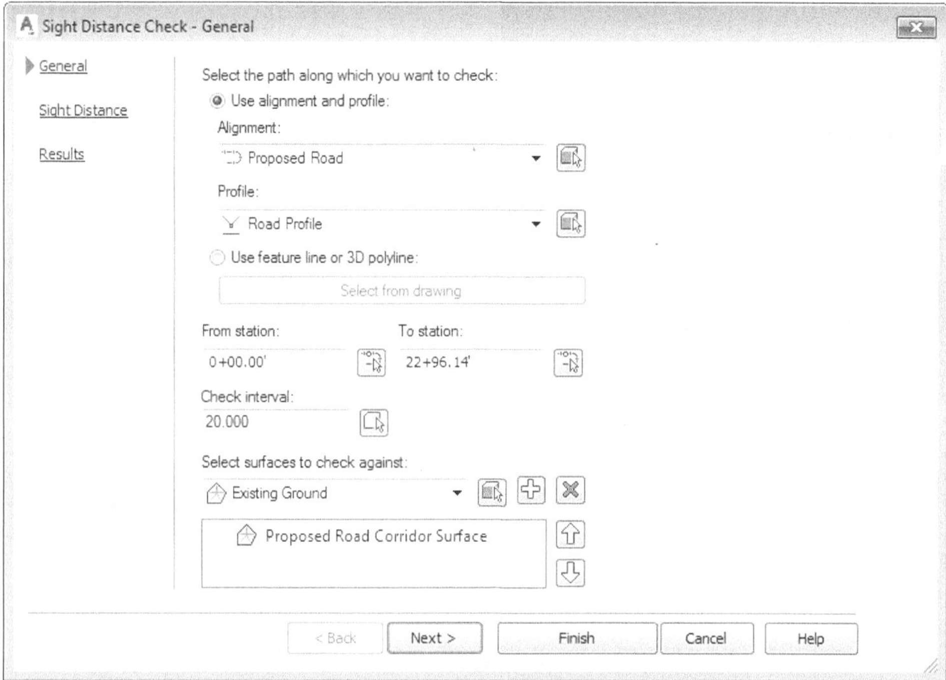

***Figure 8-72** The **General** page of the **Sight Distance Check** wizard*

3. Ensure the **Use alignment and profile** radio button is selected. Next, select the **Proposed Road** and **Road Profile** options from the **Alignment** and **Profile** drop-down lists, respectively.

4. Enter **25** in the **Check interval** edit box.

5. Select the **Proposed Road Corridor Surface** option from the **Select surfaces to check against** drop-down list.

6. Choose the **Next** button; the **Sight Distance** page of the wizard is displayed.

7. Set the minimum site distance to **350** and eye offset as **6.00** in the **Minimum sight distance** and **Eye Offset** edit boxes, respectively.

8. Choose the **Next** button; the **Results** page of the wizard is displayed.

9. In the **Select items you want to draw in the model:** area, clear all the check boxes except the **Visibility sight lines** and the **Eye path** components.

Note

*If the **Browse** button corresponding to **Save to** edit box is disabled, to enable it you need to select the **Create sight analysis report** check box.*

10. Choose the **Browse** button corresponding to the **Save to** edit box; the **Save As** dialog box is displayed.

11. In this dialog box, browse to the following location:

    C:\c3d_2018\c08_c3d_2018_tut

12. In the **File name** edit box, enter **c08_c3d_2018_tut03.txt**.

13. Choose the **Save** button; the **Save As** dialog box is closed.

14. Choose the **Finish** button in the **Results** page of the **Sight Distance Check** wizard; the wizard is closed and Civil 3D performs the analysis for the specified parameters.

On completion of the process, a graphical representation of visibility analysis is added to the corridor, refer to Figure 8-73. Note that the corridor is now displaying the components for the sight distance check. The visibility report for the defined path is also created and saved in the file location specified in the wizard. Figure 8-74 shows the Sight Analysis Report for the visibility check.

Creating the Drive Simulation

1. Select the corridor model in the drawing; the **Corridor: Road Corridor** tab is displayed in the ribbon.

2. Select the **Drive** tool from the **Analyze** panel of the **Corridor: Road Corridor** tab; you are prompted to select the corridor feature line.

3. Zoom in to station **1+00.00** and select the feature line for the outer edge of right lane, as shown in Figure 8-75; the **Select a Feature Line** dialog box is displayed.

4. In the dialog box, select the **ETW** feature line and then choose the **OK** button; the dialog box is closed and the **Drive** tab is displayed in the ribbon.

Note

Drive simulation is a system intensive process and may take some time depending on your computer's processing capability.

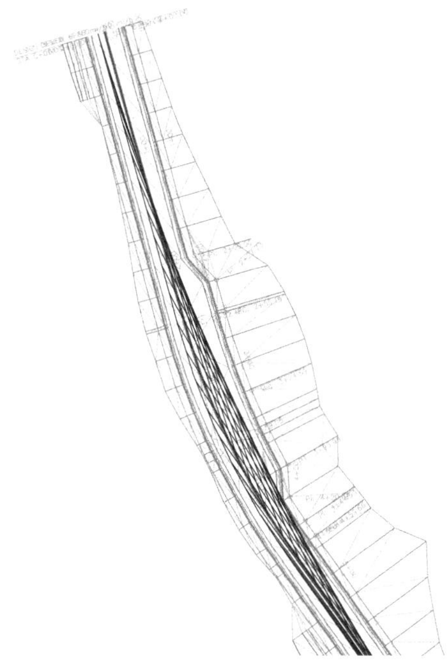

Figure 8-73 *Partial view of the corridor with graphical representation of the sight distance check*

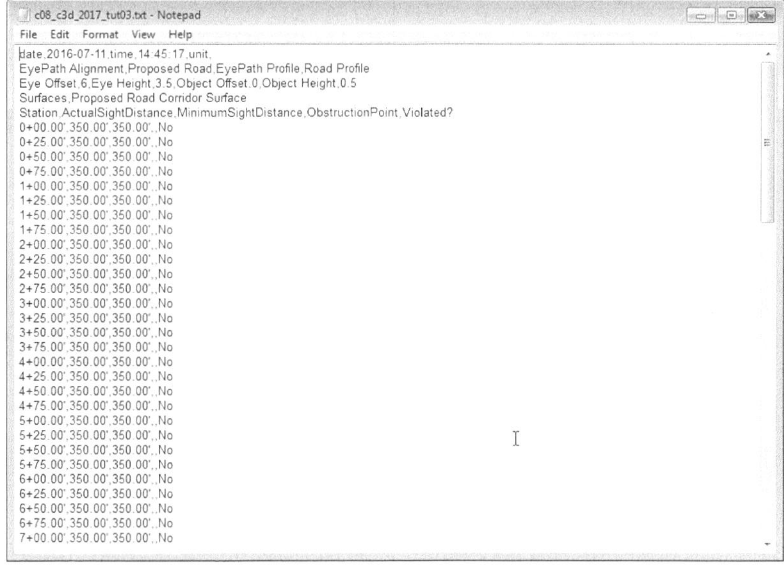

date,2016-07-11,time,14:45:17,unit,
EyePath Alignment,Proposed Road,EyePath Profile,Road Profile
Eye Offset,6,Eye Height,3.5,Object Offset,0,Object Height,0.5
Surfaces,Proposed Road Corridor Surface
Station,ActualSightDistance,MinimumSightDistance,ObstructionPoint,Violated?
0+00.00',350.00',350.00',,No
0+25.00',350.00',350.00',,No
0+50.00',350.00',350.00',,No
0+75.00',350.00',350.00',,No
1+00.00',350.00',350.00',,No
1+25.00',350.00',350.00',,No
1+50.00',350.00',350.00',,No
1+75.00',350.00',350.00',,No
2+00.00',350.00',350.00',,No
2+25.00',350.00',350.00',,No
2+50.00',350.00',350.00',,No
2+75.00',350.00',350.00',,No
3+00.00',350.00',350.00',,No
3+25.00',350.00',350.00',,No
3+50.00',350.00',350.00',,No
3+75.00',350.00',350.00',,No
4+00.00',350.00',350.00',,No
4+25.00',350.00',350.00',,No
4+50.00',350.00',350.00',,No
4+75.00',350.00',350.00',,No
5+00.00',350.00',350.00',,No
5+25.00',350.00',350.00',,No
5+50.00',350.00',350.00',,No
5+75.00',350.00',350.00',,No
6+00.00',350.00',350.00',,No
6+25.00',350.00',350.00',,No
6+50.00',350.00',350.00',,No
6+75.00',350.00',350.00',,No
7+00.00',350.00',350.00',,No

Figure 8-74 *The partial view of the Sight Analysis Report*

Figure 8-75 *Selecting the feature line at station **1+00.00***

On completing the processing, Civil 3D creates a conceptual view of the corridor and displays it in the drawing window, refer to Figure 8-76.

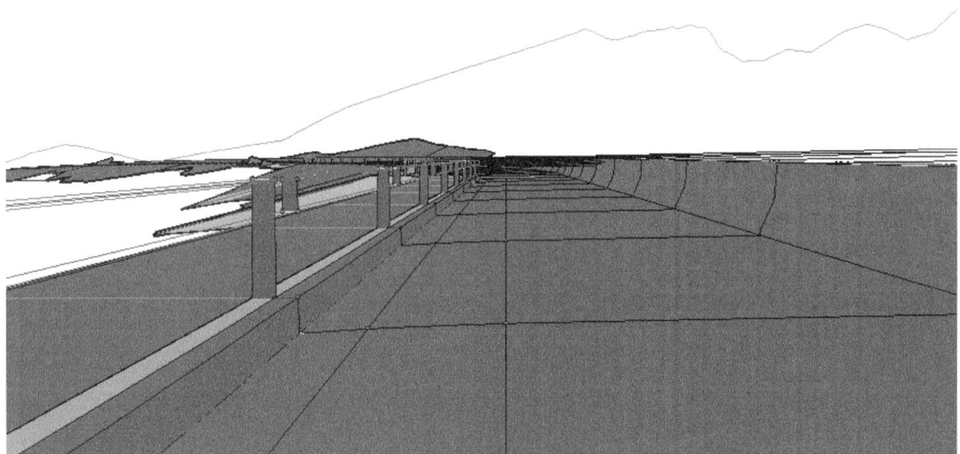

Figure 8-76 *The conceptual view of corridor simulation using the **Drive** tool*

5. Set the observers offset value with respect to the selected feature line to **6** in the **Eye Offset** edit box of the **Eye** panel.

6. Choose the **Loop** button in the **Navigate** panel to play the simulation continuously.

7. Set the height of the target as **2.5** and its offset as **5** in the **Target Height** and **Target Offset** edit boxes of the **Target** panel, respectively.

8. Expand the **Target** panel and set the target distance to **350** in the **Target Distance** edit box. Next, choose the **Show target** button. Note that the target is displayed in green color in the simulation.

9. Choose the **Play/Pause** button in the **Navigate** panel to play the simulation.

10. Choose the **Play/Pause** button; the simulation is paused. Next, choose the **Reverse** button and choose the **Play/pause** button again; the simulation starts in reverse direction.

11. After the simulation is finished, choose the **Close** button from the **Close** panel of the **Drive** tab; the **Drive** tab will be closed.

Extracting Corridor Solids

In this section of the tutorial you will extract solids from the corridor model.

1. Select the corridor from the drawing; the **Corridor: Road Corridor** tab is displayed. In this tab, choose the **Extract Corridor Solids** option from the **Corridor Tools** panel. You are prompted to select corridor regions to export as solids.

2. Select **All Regions** from the command prompt; the **Extract Corridor Solids** wizard is displayed, as shown in Figure 8-77.

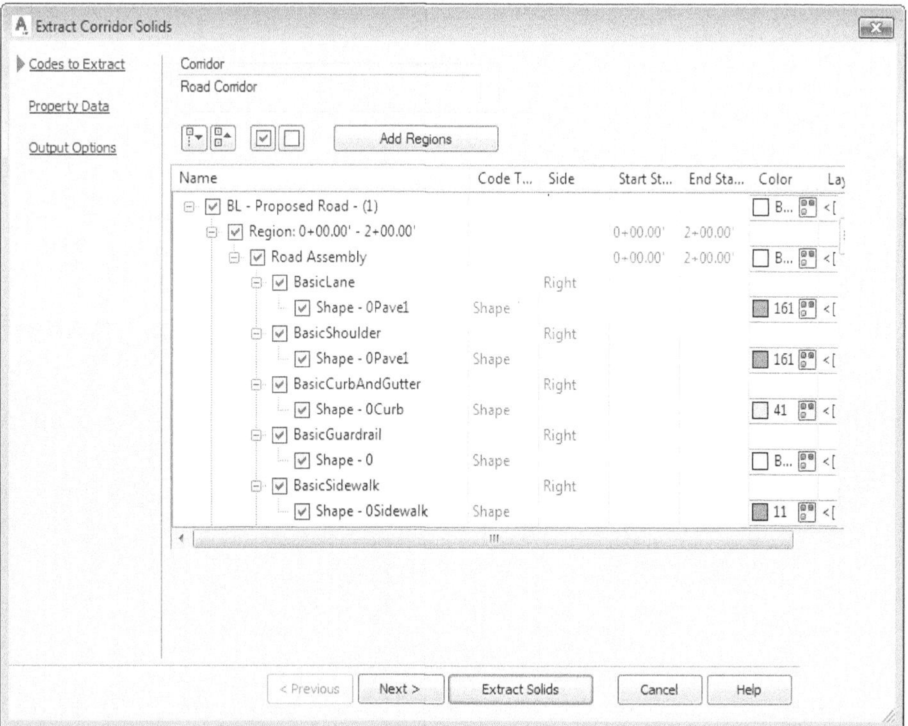

Figure 8-77 *The **Extract Corridor Solids** wizard with the **Codes to Extract** page displaying the added baseline region with different field properties*

3. Choose the **Turn on all the shapes and links** button and click the **Next button** twice; the **Output Options** page of the **Extract Corridor Solids** wizard is displayed.

4. In this page, select the **AutoCAD 3D Solids (based on corridor sampling)** option from the **Output object type** drop-down list, if it is not selected by default.

6. Select the **Add to a new drawing** radio button in the **Output destination options** area of this page and then choose the browse button located on the right side of the edit box; the **Select the output file** dialog box is displayed.

7. In this dialog box, browse to the location *C:\c3d_2018\c08_c3d_2018_tut*. Enter **Extracted corridor model** in the **File name** edit box and then choose the **Save** button; the **Select the output file** dialog box is closed and the specified path is displayed in the edit box of the **Output Options** page.

8. Choose the **Extract Solids** button; the **Extract Corridor Solids** wizard is closed.

Viewing the Extracted Corridor Solid

1. Choose **Open** from the **Application Menu**; the **Select File** dialog box is displayed.

2. In this dialog box, browse to the location *C:\c3d_2018\c08_c3d_2018_tut* where you have saved the file.

3. Select *Extracted corridor model.dwg* file and then choose the **Open** button to open the file.

4. Enter **ZE** in the command line and then press ENTER; the extracted corridor solid will be displayed.

5. Choose the **Orbit** tool from the **Navigate 2D** panel of the **View** tab and orient the model to view it in a 3D view. Figure 8-78 shows the extracted corridor solid in a 3D view.

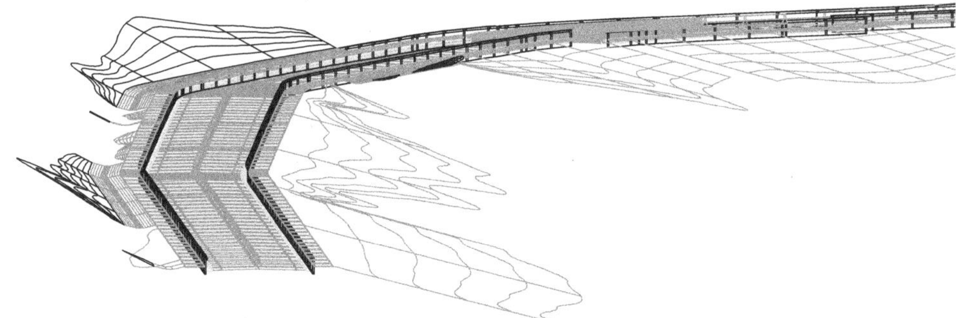

Figure 8-78 *Extracted corridor solid*

Saving the File

1. Choose **Save As** from the **Application Menu**; the **Save Drawing As** dialog box is displayed.

2. In this dialog box, browse to the location C:\c3d_2018\c08_c3d_2018_tut.

3. In the **File name** edit box, enter **c08_tut03a**.

4. Choose the **Save** button; the file is saved with the name *c08_tut03a.dwg* at the specified location.

Tutorial 4 Creating Parcels

In this tutorial, you will create parcels from objects and right-of-way parcels. You will also use parcel segments using parcel creation tools. **(Expected time: 30 min)**

The following steps are required to complete this tutorial:

a. Download and open the file.
b. Create a parcel from object.
c. Create a Right of Way parcel.
d. Create parcel segments.
e. Save the file.

Downloading and Opening the File

1. Download *c08_c3d_2018_tut.zip* file if not downloaded earlier from *http://www.cadcim.com*. Next, save and extract the file at *C:\c3d_2018\c08_c3d_2018_tut*.

2. Choose **Open** from the **Application Menu**; the **Select File** dialog box is displayed.

3. In the dialog box, browse to the location *C:\c3d_2018\c08_c3d_2018_tut*.

4. Select the file *c08_c3d_2018_tut04.dwg* and then choose the **Open** button to open the file. Ignore the error message if displayed.

Creating a Parcel from Object

In this section of the tutorial, you will create a new parcel using the objects already present in the drawing.

1. Invoke the **Create Parcel from Objects** tool from the **Parcel** drop-down in the **Create Design** panel of the **Home** tab. You will be prompted to select lines, arcs or polylines to convert into parcels or Xrefs.

2. Select the rectangular object from the drawing area and press ENTER. The **Create Parcels - From objects** dialog box is displayed.

3. Select the **Name Square Foot & Acres** option from the **Area label style** drop-down list.

4. Choose the **OK** button to close the dialog box.

5. Notice that the rectangle object in the drawing area is now converted into a parcel with a label inside the rectangle describing the parcel name and area (foot & acres), as shown in Figure 8-79.

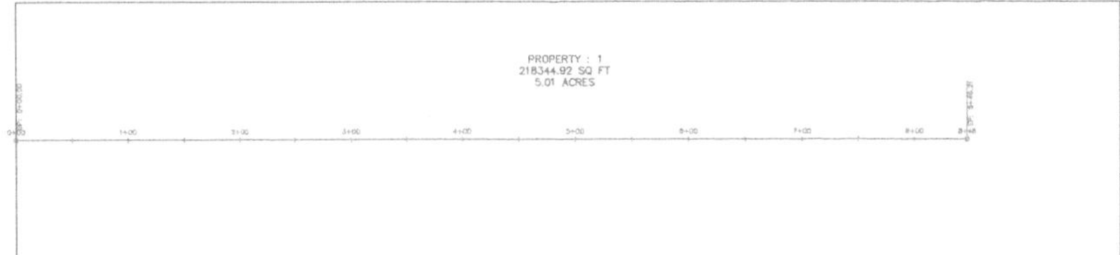

Figure 8-79 Parcel created from rectangular object

Creating a Right of Way Parcel

In this section of the tutorial, you will create a new parcel representing a piece of land for road using the **Create Right of Way** parcel tool.

1. Choose the **Create Right of Way** tool from the **Parcel** drop-down in the **Create Design** panel of the **Home** tab. You will be prompted to select parcels.

2. Select the previously created parcel label in the drawing area and press ENTER; the **Create Right of Way** dialog box is displayed.

3. Accept the default values and choose the **OK** button; a new parcel representing piece of land for road will be created along the alignment in the drawing area with fillet being used at parcel boundary intersections, as shown in Figure 8-80.

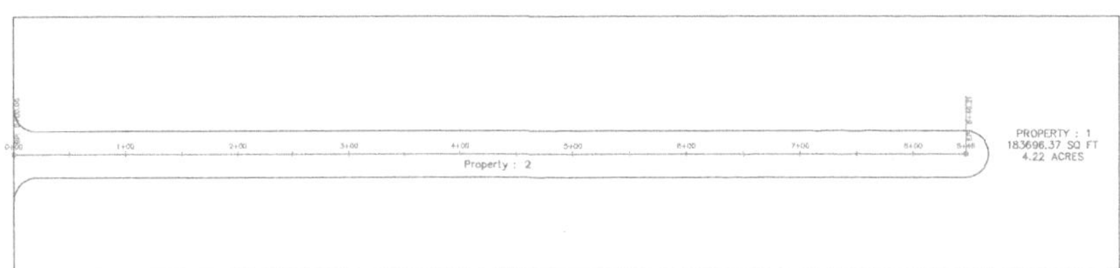

Figure 8-80 Parcel representing piece of land for road along alignment

Creating Parcel Segments

In this section of the tutorial, you will create parcel segments representing final individual plots using the parcel creation tools.

1. Invoke the **Parcel Creation Tools** from the **Parcel** drop-down in the **Create Design** panel of the **Home** tab; the **Parcel Layout Tools** dialog box is displayed.

2. Set **5000** in the value field corresponding to **Minimum Area** in the property sheet of the **Parcel Layout Tools** toolbar.

3. Select **No** option from the drop-down list corresponding to **Use Minimum Frontage At Offset**.

4. Select the **Slide Line - Create** tool from the **Parcel Layout Tools** toolbar; the **Create Parcels - Layout** dialog box is displayed. 

5. Select the **Name Square Foot & Acres** option from the **Area label style** drop-down list in the **Create Parcels - Layout** dialog box.

6. Choose the **OK** button; the **Create Parcels - Layout** dialog box is closed and you will be prompted to select the parcel to be subdivided.

7. Select the **Property : 1** label of the parcel created earlier; you will be prompted to select start point on frontage.

8. Click on the endpoint of one fillet and then on the other endpoint of another fillet, refer to Figure 8-81.

9. A frontage line for parcel segments will be created in yellow color as shown in Figure 8-82.

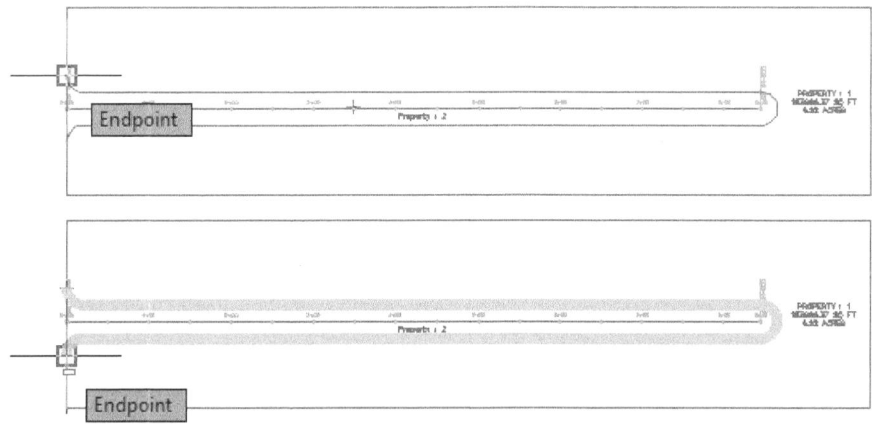

Figure 8-81 *Frontage line to be created from endpoint of one fillet to another*

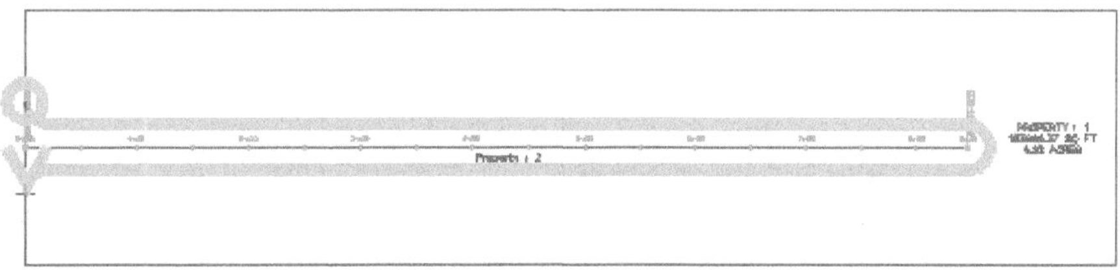

Figure 8-82 *Frontage line created in yellow color*

10. Press ENTER after creating the frontage line; temporary parcel segments will be created as a suggestion, as shown in Figure 8-83 with area not less than 5000 square feet as specified earlier as the parameters.

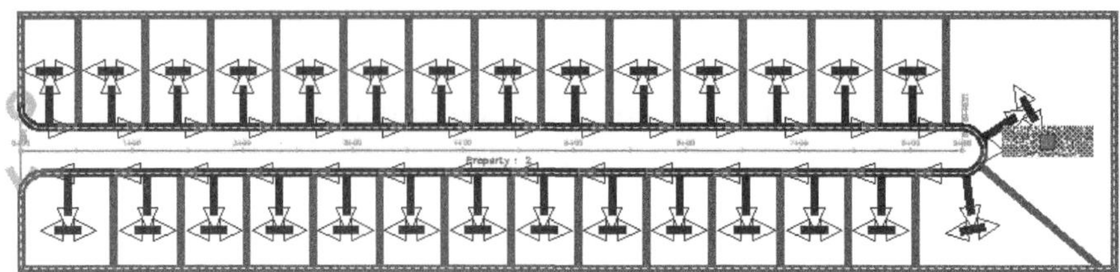

Figure 8-83 *Temporary parcel segments created within* ***Property : 1*** *parcel*

11. Also, you will be prompted to accept the result. Select the **Yes** option from the command line and press ENTER; parcel segments will be created, as shown in Figure 8-84.

12. Press ESC to terminate the command and close the **Parcel Layout Tool** toolbar.

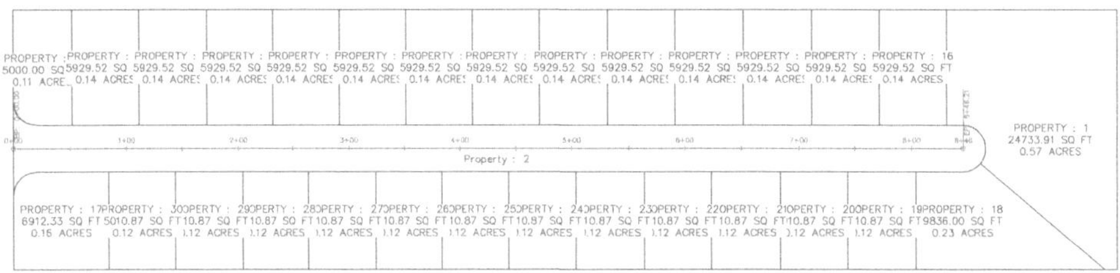

Figure 8-84 *Parcel segments created as new parcels representing new properties*

Saving the File

1. Choose **Save As** from the **Application Menu**; the **Save Drawing As** dialog box is displayed.

2. In this dialog box, browse to the following location:

   C:\c3d_2018\c08_c3d_2018_tut

3. In the **File name** edit box, enter **c08_tut04a**.

4. Choose the **Save** button; the file is saved with the name *c08_tut04a.dwg* at the specified location.

Self-Evaluation Test

Answer the following questions and then compare them to those given at the end of this chapter:

1. Which of the following tools is used to compare the corridor surface with the existing ground surface and calculate the total earthwork required?

   a) **Volumes Dashboard** b) **Create Surface from Corridor**
   c) **Create Surface from Grading** d) None of the these

2. Which of the following drop-down lists in the **Create Corridor** dialog box is used to select a set of building blocks (components) of a roadway?

   a) **Alignment** b) **Profile**
   c) **Assembly** d) **Target Surface**

3. Which of the following tabs of the **Corridor Properties** dialog box is used to display the slope between the feature lines?

   a) **Slope Pattern** b) **Feature Lines**
   c) **Surface** d) **Codes**

4. Which of the following options is used to divide a given region into two or more sections?

   a) **Split Region** b) **Insert Region - Before**
   c) **Remove Region** d) **Insert Region - After**

5. Which of the following tool is used to simulate the driving along a given corridor?

   a) **Sight Distance** b) **Point to Point**
   c) **Zone of Visual Influence** d) **Drive**

6. Which of the following tools is used to create a parcel along a specified offset distance from alignment?

   a) **Side Line - Create** b) **Right of Way Parcel**
   c) **Create Parcel From Objects** d) All of these

7. A corridor is a combination of alignment, profile and _________, which provides horizontal, vertical, and the cross-sectional geometry.

8. The _________ are the longitudinal lines that connect the identical point codes in a corridor.

9. The __________ button in the **Baseline and Region Parameters** dialog box is used to add a new alignment to the corridor.

10. On choosing the **Set All Targets** button in the **Baseline and Region Parameters** dialog box, the _________ dialog box is displayed.

11. The __________ tab in the **Corridor Properties** dialog box contains options to create a corridor surface.

12. Adding __________ to the corridor surface helps remove the extra triangulation.

13. The _________ tool helps you to create an alignment from a corridor.

14. You can choose the ________ option from the **TOOLSPACE** to extract the corridor solids.

15. A corridor model cannot have more than one baseline. (T/F)

16. You can add breaklines while creating a corridor surface. (T/F)

17. Civil 3D allows you to compare the corridor surface with the existing ground surface and calculate the quantity of the total earthwork calculations. (T/F)

Review Questions

Answer the following questions:

1. The alignment used in creating a corridor is referred as __________.

2. You can create __________ surface using the **Surfaces** tab in the **Corridor Properties** dialog box.

3. The __________ option in the shortcut menu in the **Boundaries** tab allows you to add a surface boundary automatically using the feature line codes.

4. The options in the __________ tab of the **Corridor Properties** dialog box are used to specify the boundary definition.

5. There are __________ methods to add a boundary to a surface.

6. The options in the __________ tab of the **Corridor Properties** dialog box are used to specify the corridor baseline, regions, and other parameters.

7. A corridor is a three-dimensional model of a design encompassing the horizontal geometry and the cross-sectional geometry. (T/F)

8. You can create a corridor surface while you are creating the corridor. (T/F)

9. The **Frequency to Apply Assemblies** dialog box is used to specify the settings for the frequency at which assemblies are placed in a corridor. (T/F)

10. You cannot assign a surface style to a corridor surface created by using the **Corridor Properties** dialog box. (T/F)

EXERCISES

1. Log on to *www.cadcim.com* and browse to *Textbooks > Civil/GIS > Civil 3D > Exploring AutoCAD Civil 3D 2018*. Next, select *c08_c3d_2018_exer.zip* file from the **Exercise Files** drop-down list. Choose the corresponding **Download** button to download the data file.

2. Now, save and extract the downloaded folder to the following location:

   C:\c3d_2018

Note

While opening the exercise files, the ***PANORAMA*** *window may appear with an error message. Close this window to proceed further.*

Exercise 1

Create a corridor, as shown in Figure 8-85, using the *c08_c3d_2018_ex01.dwg* file. Create corridor for Region 2 and hide Region 1 of the corridor. Use the following parameters:

(Expected time: 30 min)

Corridor name: **Canal 2**
Surface Style for Region 2: **Canal Surface**
Assembly: **Canal 2**
End Station for Region 1: **135+00.00'**
Start Station for Region 2: **195+00.00'**

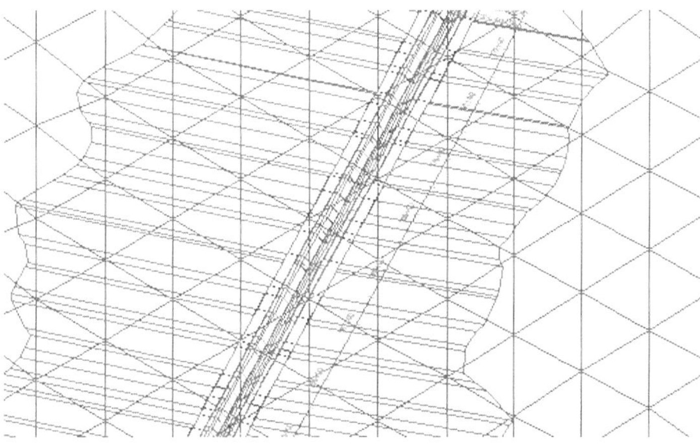

Figure 8-85 *The corridor model*

Exercise 2

Open the *c08_c3d_2018_ex02.dwg* file and create a corridor surface and add a boundary to it, as shown in Figure 8-86. Use the following parameters:

(Expected time: 30 min)

Surface name: **Pipe Datum**
Data Type: **Links**
Specify Code: **Datum**
Surface Style: **Pipe Trench**
Boundary: **Add Automatically > Trench_ Daylight**

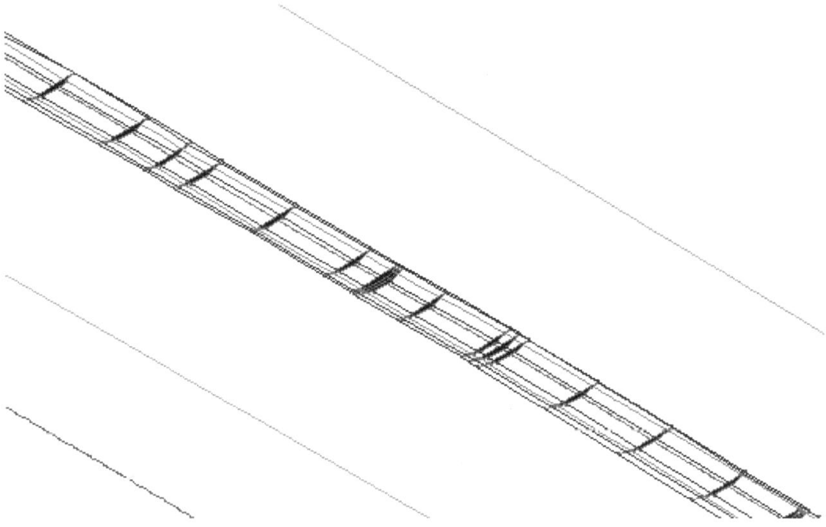

Figure 8-86 *The corridor surface with the boundary*

Answers to Self-Evaluation Test

1. a, **2.** c, **3.** a, **4.** a, **5.** d, **6.** b, **7.** assembly, **8.** feature lines, **9. Add Baseline**, **10. Target mapping**, **11. Surfaces**, **12.** surface boundary, **13. Create Alignment from Corridor**, **14. Extract corridor solids**, **15.** F, **16.** T, **17.** T

Chapter 9

Sample Lines, Sections, and Quantity Takeoffs

Learning Objectives

After completing this chapter, you will be able to:

- *Understand sections*
- *Know about sample lines*
- *Create sample lines using different methods*
- *Edit sample lines*
- *Create section views*
- *Understand section view data bands*
- *Add section labels*
- *Understand quantity takeoffs*
- *Compute materials*
- *Generate takeoff reports*

OVERVIEW

In AutoCAD Civil 3D, a cross section provides a graphical view of the terrain or surface elevations along a linear cut feature at a certain angle across a horizontal alignment. To create a cross section, you need at least two Civil 3D objects such as an alignment and a surface. Thus, a cross section consists of elevation data along any linear feature. The major components of a section are vertices or points at which one grade line ends and another grade line starts. The other component of the section is the line segment that represents the surface grade between two vertices or grade break points.

In Civil 3D, you can create sections from surfaces, corridors, corridor surfaces, and pipe networks along a linear object.

A section is created along the sample line and is displayed using a section view. These section views are the graphical representation of the elevation data or an assembly (in case of corridor sections) at a given station. Figure 9-1 shows a typical cross section view of a road corridor.

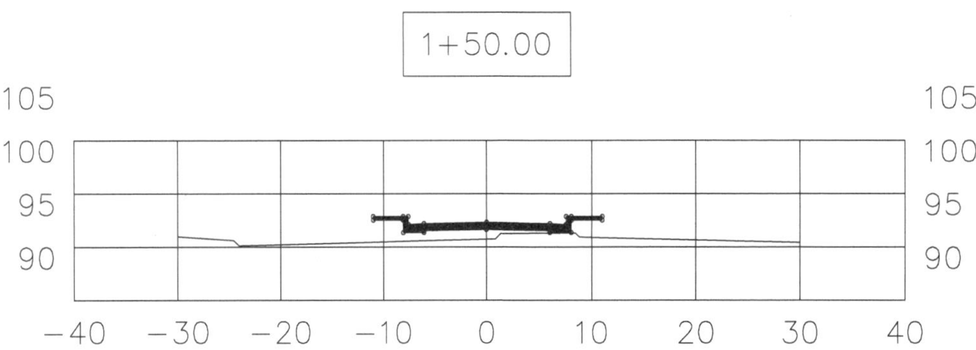

Figure 9-1 *A typical section view of a road corridor*

SAMPLE LINES

A sample line is a linear object that is used for creating a cross section across an alignment or a corridor. A sample line represents the direction along which the section is cut. A sample line consists of a linear feature and sample line label. A group of sample lines is called sample line group. You can create multiple groups of sample lines for a single alignment. The sample line group controls the display of sample lines, sections, and section views. The sample line group is available in the parent alignment node in the **Prospector** tab of the **TOOLSPACE** palette.

Sample lines are created using the **Sample Lines** tool. Before you start creating sample lines, you need to have an alignment. It is better to create a corridor and corridor surfaces before creating sample lines because corridor can provide you more information such as materials used and surfaces with cut and fill areas.

Creating Sample Lines

Ribbon: Home > Profile & Section Views > Sample Lines
Command: CREATESAMPLELINES

To create sample lines, choose the **Sample Lines** tool from the **Profile & Section Views** panel; you will be prompted to select an alignment from the drawing. Alternatively, press ENTER to select alignment from the list; the **Select Alignment** dialog box will be displayed. Select the required alignment from this dialog box and then choose the **OK** button; the dialog box will be closed and the **Sample Line Tools** toolbar will be displayed, as shown in Figure 9-2. In case you are creating a sample line for the first time for a given alignment, the **Create Sample Line Group** dialog box will also be displayed along with the **Simple Line Tools** toolbar. Options in this dialog box are discussed later in this chapter.

*Figure 9-2 The **Sample Line Tools** toolbar*

In the **Create Sample Line Group** dialog box specify the required parameters and choose the **OK** button; the dialog box will be closed and you will be prompted to specify a station. You can specify stations by using different options available in the **Sample Line Tools** toolbar. The tools in the **Sample Line Tools** toolbar are used to create and edit sample lines along the alignment. The options in the toolbar are discussed next.

Click to edit name template Tool

This tool is used to edit the default name of the sample line. Choose the **Click to edit name template** button; the **Name Template** dialog box will be displayed. In this dialog box, specify the name of the sample line to be created in the **Name** edit box and then choose the **OK** button; the dialog box will be closed and the name of the sample line group that you have specified will be displayed in the text box.

Alignment picker Button

This button is used to select an alignment for creating a sample line. Choose this button from the **Sample Line Tools** toolbar; you will be prompted to select an alignment. Select the alignment from the drawing or press ENTER to display the **Select Alignment** dialog box. Select the required alignment from the list of alignment(s) displayed in this dialog box and then choose the **OK** button; the dialog box will be closed and the alignment will be selected for creating the sample line.

Current sample line group Drop-down

You can select the required sample line group from this drop-down. You can also create a new sample line group or edit an existing sample line group. To do so, choose the down-arrow on the right of the **Current sample line group** drop-down; a flyout is displayed, as shown in Figure 9-3. The tools in the flyout are discussed next.

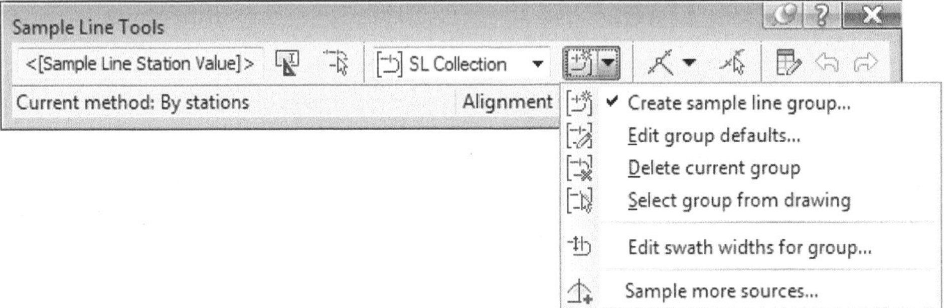

Figure 9-3 Flyout showing different tools

Create sample line group Tool

Choose this tool from the **Sample lines Tools** toolbar; the **Create Sample Line Group** dialog box is displayed, as shown in Figure 9-4. Use this dialog box to create a new sample line group and then choose the **OK** button; the name of the sample line group will be added in the **Sample line group** drop-down list. The options in this dialog box are discussed next.

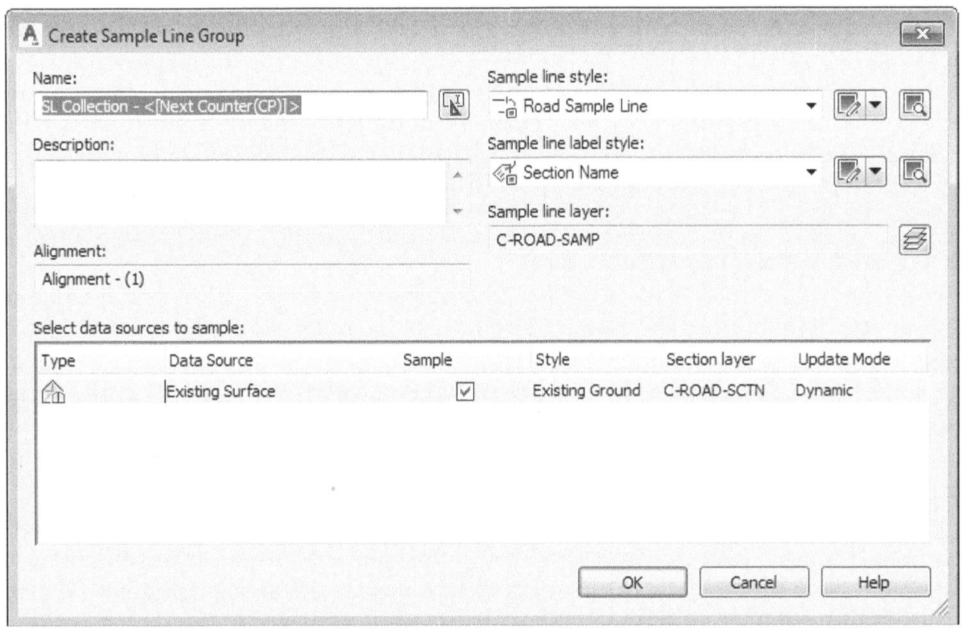

*Figure 9-4 The **Create Sample Line Group** dialog box*

In the **Create Sample Line Group** dialog box, enter the name of the sample line group in the **Name** edit box. Optionally, enter description of the sample line in the **Description** text box. Now, select a line style and label style from the **Sample line style** and **Sample line label style** drop-down lists, respectively. The **Sample line layer** option in this dialog box is used to specify the layer on which the sample line will be created. To create a new layer for the sample line, choose the button on the right of the **Sample line layer** option; the **Object Layer** dialog box will be displayed. You can use the **Object Layer** dialog box to create a new layer and then choose the **OK** button to close the dialog box. The layer created will be displayed in the **Sample line layer** text box. The **Alignment** text box is used to display the name of the parent alignment to which the sample line group belongs. In the **Create Sample Line Group** dialog box, the **Select data sources to sample** list box displays the type of existing data source and the section style. The columns of this list box are discussed next.

Type: The **Type** column displays the symbol of the corresponding data sources.

Data Source: The **Data Source** column displays the name of the data source from where elevations will be sampled. You can use a surface, corridor, corridor surface, or a pipe network as a data source.

Sample: The **Sample** column displays a check box. By default, the check box is selected. As a result, the **Data Source** field corresponding to the selected check box will be used to sample elevations. Clear the check box, if you do not want a given **Data Source** to be used to sample elevation.

Style: The **Style** column displays the default style of the section. To change the style, click in the cell of this column; the **Pick Section Style** dialog box will be displayed. Select the required style from this dialog box and then choose the **OK** button to close the dialog box.

Section Layer: The **Section layer** column in this list box displays the default layer on which the section will be created. To modify the layer, click in this column cell; the **Object Layer** dialog box will be displayed. Select the required layer from the dialog box and choose the **OK** button.

Update Mode: The **Update Mode** column displays the status of the updated mode of the section. To specify the status of the update mode, click in the cell of the **Update Mode** column; a drop-down list will be displayed. Select an option from this list to set the updating mode. Selecting the **Dynamic** option from the drop-down list enables the sections to update dynamically to reflect the changes made in the sample lines. Selecting the **Static** option from the drop-down list will not affect the sections even if you modify the sample lines geometry or position.

Edit group defaults Tool

If you choose this tool, the **Edit Sample Line Group** dialog box will be displayed, as shown in Figure 9-5. Specify the options in this dialog box to edit details of the selected sample line group and then choose the **OK** button; the selected sample line group will be modified and added to the **Current sample line group** tool. Now, you can select this group from the **Current sample line group** drop-down list in the **Sample Line Tools** toolbar.

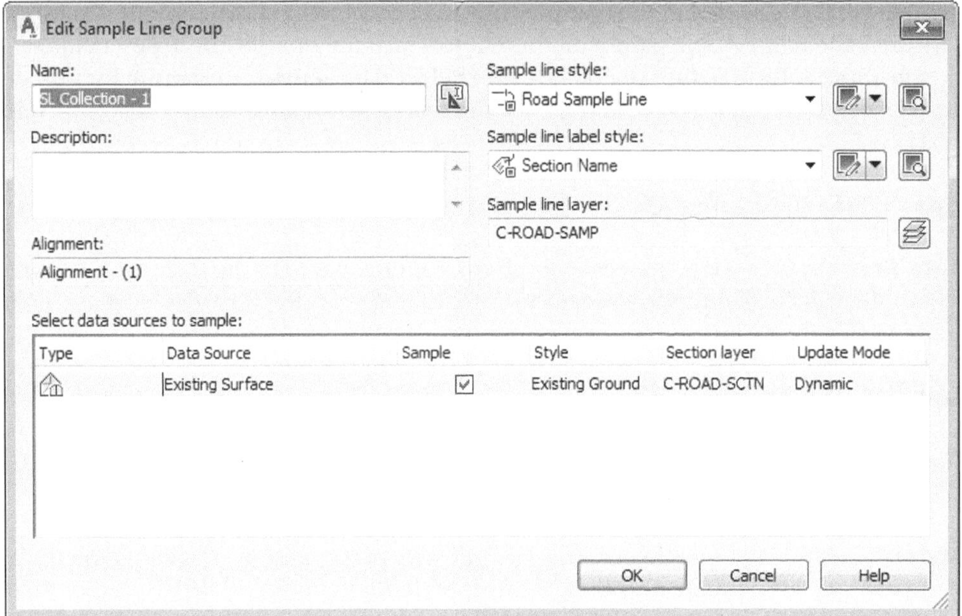

Figure 9-5 The ***Edit Sample Line Group*** *dialog box*

Delete current group Tool

Select the sample line group that you need to delete from the **Sample line group** drop-down list and then choose the **Delete current group** tool to delete it.

Select group from drawing Tool

Choose this tool to select a sample line group from the drawing. On choosing this tool, you will be prompted to select the alignment sample line. Select the sample line in the drawing; the group name of the selected sample line will be displayed in the **Current sample line group** drop-down list.

Edit swath widths for group Tool

On choosing this tool, the **Edit Sample Line Widths** dialog box will be displayed. Specify the left and right swath width values in the **Left swath width** and **Right swath width** edit boxes, respectively, and then choose the **OK** button. The swath width is the width of sample line to the left or right of the alignment. On choosing the **OK** button, the length of all the sample lines in the selected group is extended or trimmed to match the specified widths.

Sample more sources Tool

On choosing the **Sample more sources** tool from the flyout, the **Section Sources** dialog box will be displayed, as shown in Figure 9-6.

In this dialog box, select the sources to be sampled from the **Available sources** list box and then choose the **Add** button to add the selected source to the **Sampled sources** list box. After specifying all sampled sources, choose the **OK** button; the dialog box will be closed and the selected sample sources will be added to the current sample line group.

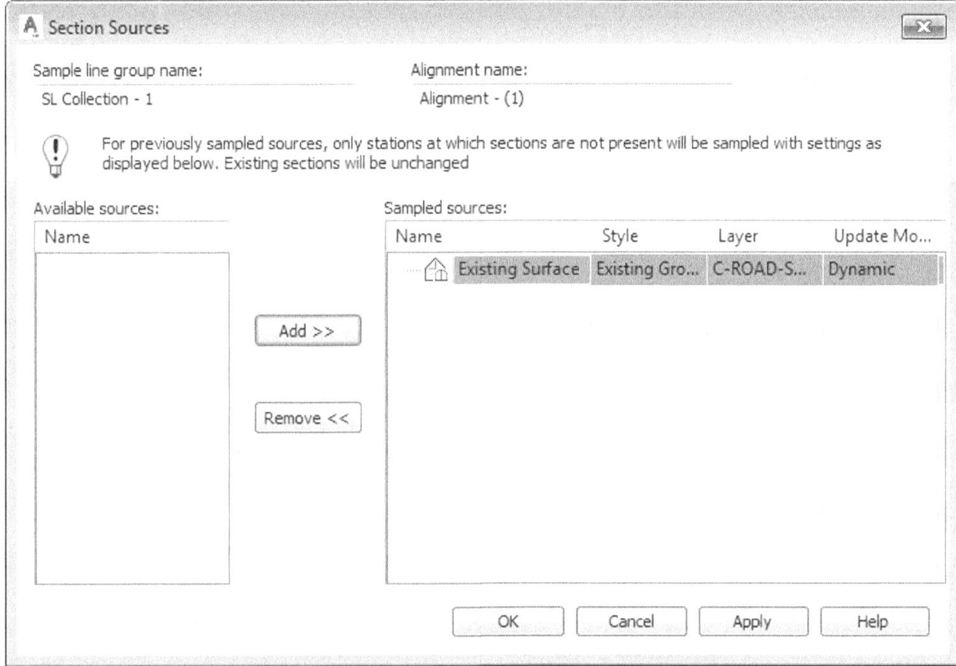

*Figure 9-6 The **Section Sources** dialog box*

Sample line creation methods

This drop-down is next to the **Create sample line group** drop-down. Choose the down arrow on the right of this button; a flyout with different tools for creating sample lines will be displayed, as shown in Figure 9-7. The tools displayed in the flyout are discussed next.

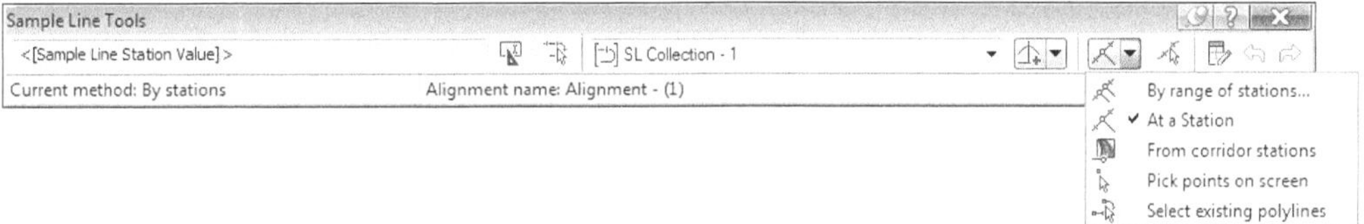

Figure 9-7 Flyout displaying the sample lines creation tools

By range of stations Tool

This tool is used to create sample lines along a given alignment for a specified range of station on that alignment. On choosing this tool, the **Create Sample Lines - By Station Range** dialog box will be displayed. This dialog box is used to set the criteria for creating the sample lines.

To specify a range of station for creating sample lines along the alignment, set the values of the **From alignment start** and **To alignment end** properties to **False** in the **Station Range** head in the **Create Sample Lines - By Station Range** dialog box. On doing so, the **Value** cells of the **Start Station** and **End Station** property will be activated. Click in the **Value** cell corresponding to the **Start Station** and **End Station** property, respectively, and enter the required station value in the column. Alternatively, choose the button displayed on the right of the value in the **Value** field of the selected property to select the station from the drawing.

Note

*If you set the values of the **Start station** and **End station** properties to **True**, the sample line will be created for the entire length of the alignment.*

In the **Left Swath Width** collection, you can set the value of the **Snap to an alignment** property to **True**. This will enable the sample lines to snap the swath widths to the alignment offsets. On doing so, the **Alignment** property value will be activated. Click in the **Value** field of the **Alignment** property; a button will be displayed on the right in the **Value** column. Choose the button; the **Sample line left swath offset alignment** dialog box will be displayed. Select an option from the drop-down list in the dialog box and choose the **OK** button; the dialog box will be closed and the sample line will snap the swath width to the selected offset on the left of the alignment.

By default, the value of the **Snap to an alignment** property is set to **False** to enable the sample line to snap the swath width to the specified swath distance. The **Width** property of the **Left Swath Width** collection specifies the width of the left swath. You can specify the swath width in the value field of the **Width** property. Similarly, you can specify the value of the right swath for the sample line in the **Right Swath Width** collection. You can also set the values of **Sampling Increments** and **Additional Sample Controls** collections in this dialog box. Once you have specified the settings, choose the **OK** button; the dialog box will be closed.

Note

*The method of creating sample lines as well as the alignment with which sample lines are associated are displayed at the bottom of the **Sample Line Tools** toolbar.*

At a station Tool

This tool is used to create a sample line by specifying an individual station. On choosing this tool, you will be prompted to specify the station. Select the required station from the drawing; you will be prompted to specify the left swath width. Enter the width in the command line or specify it by picking points from the drawing. Similarly, specify the right swath width when prompted to do so.

From corridor stations Tool

This tool is used to create sample lines by specifying corridor stations. On choosing this tool, the **Create Sample Lines - From Corridor Stations** dialog box will be displayed. In this dialog box, specify the settings for sample lines, as explained in the **By range of stations** method.

Note

*The **From corridor stations** tool will be active only if a corridor has been created for the alignment.*

Pick points on screen Tool

This tool is used to create a sample line by picking points from the screen. On choosing this tool, you will be prompted to specify the start point. Select the start point from the drawing; you will be prompted to specify the end point. Specify the end point and press ENTER; a sample line will be created between the two points. Press ESC to exit the command.

Select existing polylines Tool

This tool is used to create a sample line from the existing polylines. On choosing this tool, you will be prompted to select polylines from the drawing. Select the required polylines and press ENTER; the polylines will be converted into sample lines. Press ENTER again to end the command.

Select/Edit Sample Line Button

This button is used to select and then edit the sample line parameters. Choose the **Select/Edit Sample Line** button from the **Sample Line Tools** toolbar; the **Edit Sample Line** dialog box will be displayed. Note that this dialog box is empty. Now, select the required sample line from the drawing; the dialog box will be populated with the parameters and values related to the selected sample line, as shown in Figure 9-8. You can edit only those parameters which are displayed in black while the parameters displayed in grey cannot be edited.

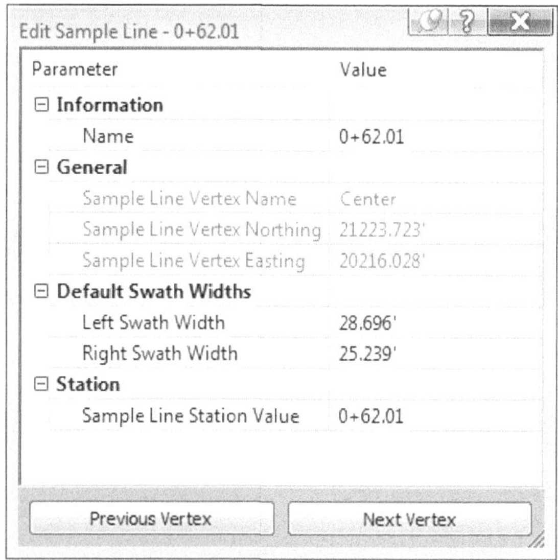

Figure 9-8 The ***Edit Sample Line*** *dialog box with the parameters and values related to the selected sample line*

Sample Line Entity View Button

This button is used to toggle the display of the **Edit Sample Line** dialog box. Choose the **Sample Line Entity View** button from the **Sample Line Tools** toolbar; the **Edit Sample Line** dialog box will be displayed. Next, choose the **Select/Edit Sample Line** button. Select the required sample line from the drawing; the dialog box will be populated with sample line parameters. Now, choose the **Sample Line Entity View** button again; the dialog box will disappear. Thus, you can toggle the display of the **Edit Sample Line** dialog box.

To create a sample line, specify the sample line parameters and choose the sample line creation method in the **Sample Line Tools** toolbar. Depending on the method selected for sample line creation, specify the location/ region for sample line creation. On creating the sample lines, press ENTER; the toolbar will be closed. Next, you need to create section views to display the section of the surface along the sample line.

Note

Sample lines are added in the ***Sample Line Groups*** *sub-node under the parent alignment head in the* ***Alignments*** *node of the* ***Prospector*** *tab. Sections are added in the* ***Sections*** *sub-node of the parent sample line node.*

Sample Line Properties

To view and edit the properties of a sample line, select the required sample line from the drawing and right-click; a shortcut menu will be displayed. Choose the **Sample Line Properties** option from the shortcut menu; again select the required sample line from the drawing; the **Sample Line Properties** dialog box will be displayed, as shown in Figure 9-9.

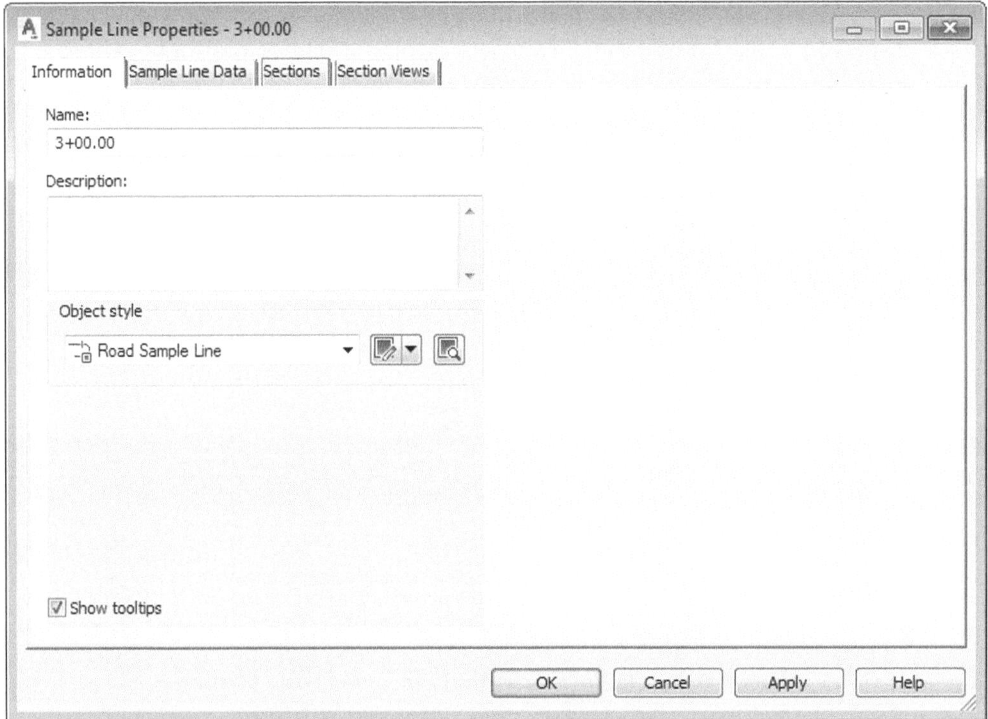

Figure 9-9 The ***Sample Line Properties - 3+00.00*** *dialog box*

Alternatively, to invoke the **Sample Line Properties** dialog box, expand the **Sample Line Groups** sub-node with which the required sample line is associated. Right-click on the required sample line; a shortcut menu is displayed. Choose the **Properties** option from the shortcut menu; the **Sample Line Properties** dialog box will be displayed. The tabs in this dialog box are discussed next.

Information Tab

The **Information** tab is used to edit the name of a sample line in the **Name** edit box. You can select an option from the **Object style** drop-down list to specify the style for the sample line.

Sample Line Data Tab

The **Sample Line Data** tab is used to view the sample line properties. In this tab, the **Lock to the station** check box is selected by default. As a result, the relative position of the sample line with respect to the station on the alignment is maintained. If the geometry of an alignment is updated with the **Lock to the station** check box selected then the position of the sample with respect to the alignment station is maintained.

Clearing the check box will allow the sample line to remains in its location. The sample line maintains its geometry and recomputes the station where it intersects the alignment.

Sections Tab

The **Sections** tab displays the properties of sample lines that are used to create section views. You can modify the update mode, layer, and style of sample line in this tab. The **Offsets** column in this tab specifies the left and right offset values of the section view that is created along the sample line. The **Elevations** column specifies the minimum and maximum elevations of the sections created using the sample line.

Section Views Tab

The **Section Views** tab is used to view and edit the properties of the section views associated with sample line. Using this tab, you can modify the layer and style of the section view created from sample line.

Sample Line Group Properties

To view the sample line group properties, expand the **Alignments** node from the **Prospector** tab of the **TOOLSPACE** palette. Next, expand the required alignment node with which the sample line group is associated. Now, expand the **Sample Line Groups** sub-node under the alignment node; the existing sample line groups will be listed in this node. Right-click on the required sample line group; a shortcut menu will be displayed. Choose the **Properties** option from the shortcut menu; the **Sample Line Group Properties** dialog box will be displayed. The tabs in this dialog box are discussed next.

Information Tab

This tab is used to view the name of the sample line group. You can modify the name of the sample line group by entering a new name in the **Name** edit box. Optionally, you can enter a description for the sample line group in the **Description** text box.

Sample Lines Tab

This tab is used to view and edit the properties of sample lines included in the sample line group. You can modify the values for the layer, style, left offset, and right offset of the sample line in the respective columns. After editing the required value, choose the **Edit Group Labels** button; the **Sample Line Labels - <sample line group name>** dialog box will be displayed. You can use this dialog box to modify the sample line labels style for the group. After specifying the parameters, close the dialog box.

Sections Tab

This tab is used to view and edit the properties of the section included in the sample line group. The **Name** column in the **Sections list** list box of this tab displays the name of the sections associated with the selected sample line group. In this area, you can use various options to modify the style of the section, update mode, and layer of sections from respective columns. Next, choose the **Sample more sources** button; the **Section Sources** dialog box will be displayed. You can use this dialog box to sample the sections of the selected sample line group. Then, close the dialog box.

Section Views Tab

This tab is used to view and edit the properties of section views associated with the selected sample line group. The **Section View** column in the **Section views list** list box displays the name of section views. In this tab, you can modify the group label style, section view style, band set style, and section display settings. The **Section Display** column displays the section display settings. To modify these settings, choose the browse button in the **Section Display** column; the **Section Display Controls - Section View Group - <group name>** dialog box will be displayed. You can use this dialog box to modify the display options of the section views of the sample line group. After specifying the parameters, close the dialog box.

To display the profile grade point in the section view, choose the button in the **Profile Grade** column; the **Profile Grade Points - Section View Group - <group name>** dialog box will be displayed. You can use this dialog box to select the required alignment whose profile grade is to be displayed in the section view. After specifying the parameters, close the dialog box.

Material List Tab

This tab is used to view and edit the material list of the sample line group. You can also add and delete materials using this tab. To add a new material to the list, choose the button on the right of the **Add new material** button; the **Name Template** dialog box will be displayed. Specify the name of the material in this dialog box and choose the **OK** button. Next, choose the **Add new material** button; the material will be added in the **Material Name** column.

In the **Define material** area of this tab, you can specify the data type as surface or corridor from the **Data type** drop-down list. The data type option specifies the type of data which is compared and processed when defining the material.

Now, choose the button displayed in the right of the **Select surface** drop-down list; the selected surface or the corridor shape will be added in the **Material Name** column under the added material.

The **Condition** column in the **Material List** tab specifies the criteria for material calculation. There are five different types of conditions: **Above**, **Below**, **Base**, **Compare**, and **Include**. The **Above** condition specifies that the material above the selected surface will be included while defining the material. The **Below** condition specifies that the area below the selected surface will be included while defining the material. The **Base** condition specifies that the selected surface is the surface to be compared against the **Compare** surface. This condition is used when the quantity type in the **Quantity Type** column is set to **Earthworks**. The **Include** condition specifies that the corridor shape is included in the structure type definition.

The **Quantity Type** column specifies the type of quantity to be calculated. To specify the quantity type, click in the cell of the **Quantity Type** column and select the required type from the drop-down list. There are five options in the drop-down list namely, **Cut**, **Fill**, **Cut and Refill**, **Earthworks**, and **Structures**. The **Cut** option is used to calculate the quantity of material to be removed. The **Fill** option is used to calculate the quantity of the material to be added. The **Cut and Refill** option is used to specify the area to be cut and refilled with the fill material. The **Earthworks** option is used to calculate the total cut and fill area by comparing two surfaces (EG and FG surfaces). The **Structures** option is used to calculate the volume of the corridor shapes such as volume of the sidewalk in a corridor.

The **Cut Factor** and **Fill Factor** columns display the total expansion and contraction factors of the cut and fill materials (soil). Generally, the volume of the material expands after its removal and gets compacted while filling. The expansion and contraction of the material depends upon the soil types and soil conditions. The cut and fill factors indicate the requirements of additional material volume. The **Refill Factor** column specifies the factor to determine the quantity of the cut material that can be reused as fill material.

The **Shape Style** column in the **Material List** tab displays the default style to display the material in a section view. To modify the style, click in the **Shape Style** column of the corresponding material in the material list; the **Pick Material Section Style** dialog box will be displayed. Select the required option from the dialog box and choose the **OK** button.

The **Curve Tolerance** column in the **Material List** tab specifies the value of the curve correction tolerance of curves. To edit this value, select the check box in this column and enter the value in the column.

The **Gap** column is used to define or apply gap in the material. A gap indicates a non continuity in a material along its length. To define a gap, click in the **Gap** column corresponding to a material list (the material list is indicated with an icon in the **Material Name** column); the **Define Gaps** dialog box is displayed. To apply gap during material calculation, click in the **Gap** column corresponding to a material level (indicated by an icon in the **Material Name** column) in this dialog box; the **Apply Gaps** dialog box is displayed. Use this dialog box to apply gaps and to define **Run Ins** and **Run Outs**.

Once you have specified parameters for all the tabs discussed earlier, choose the **OK** button and close the dialog box.

Editing Sample Lines

Ribbon: Sample Line > Modify > Edit Sample Line
Command: EDITSAMPLELINE

To edit sample lines parameters, select the sample line from the drawing; the **Sample Line - <station number>** tab will be displayed. In this tab, choose the **Edit Sample Line** tool from the **Modify** panel; the **Edit Sample Line** dialog box will be displayed along with the **Sample Line Tools** toolbar. Also, you will be prompted to select a sample line in the command line. Select the required sample line; the **Edit Sample Line** dialog box will be populated with the selected sample line parameters. You can edit the required parameters either by using this dialog box or by using the **Sample Line Tools** toolbar, as explained earlier in this chapter.

To edit the sample line style, select the **Edit Sample Line Style** tool from the **Sample Line Properties** drop-down from the **Modify** panel of the **Sample Line** tab; the **Sample Line Style - <Sample Line Style Name>** dialog box is displayed. You can use this dialog box to edit the sample line style. Alternatively, you can invoke this dialog box from the **Settings** tab of the **TOOLSPACE** palette. To do so, in the **Settings** tab, expand **Sample Line > Sample Line Styles** sub-node. Next, select the required sample line and right-click on it; a shortcut menu will be displayed. Choose the **Edit** option from the shortcut menu, as shown in Figure 9-10; the **Sample Line Style** dialog box will be displayed.

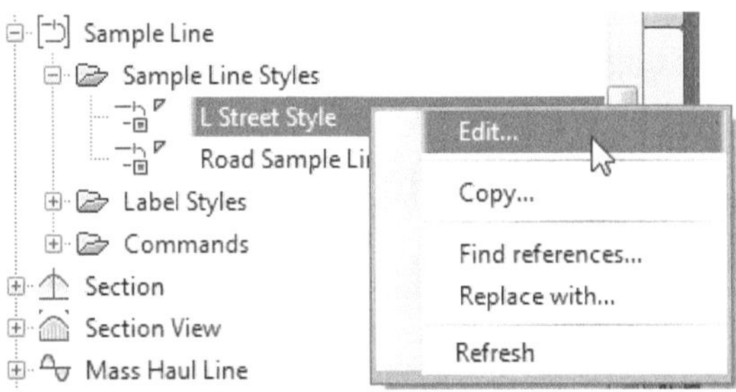

Figure 9-10 *Choosing the **Edit** option from the shortcut menu*

CREATING SECTION VIEWS

After defining a sample line group and creating the sample lines, you will create section views. In AutoCAD Civil 3D, you can create two types of section views, single section view and multiple section view. Section views are added to the collection of parent sample line in the **Prospector** tab. The processes to create different section views are discussed next.

Creating a Single Section View

Ribbon:	Home > Profile & Section Views > Section Views drop-down > Create Section View
Command:	CREATESECTIONVIEW

To create a single section view at a particular station, choose the **Create Section View** tool from the **Profile & Section Views** tab; the **General** page of the **Create Section View** wizard will be displayed, as shown in Figure 9-11.

The **Create Section View** wizard is composed of various pages such as the **General**, **Offset Range**, **Elevation Range**, **Section Display Options**, **Data Bands**, and **Section View Tables**. Each page hosts a number of tools and options for setting the criteria and the parameters to display in the section view. The pages in this wizard are discussed next.

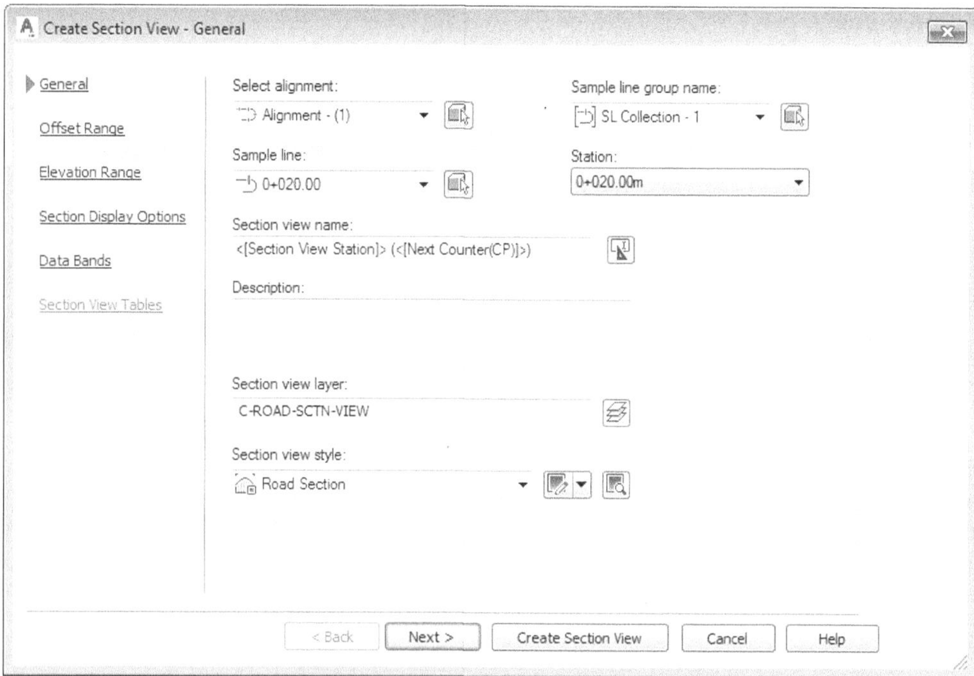

*Figure 9-11 The **General** page of the **Create Section View** wizard*

General Page

The **General** page in the **Create Section View** wizard displays the general parameters to be set for the section view. This page is displayed by default when you invoke the wizard. This page is used to specify the basic information such as parent alignment, sample line group name, sample line, station, style, and layer about the section view to be generated. The options in this page are discussed next.

Select alignment

The **Select alignment** drop-down list is used to specify the name of the parent horizontal alignment for which the section view is to be created. Select the name of the parent alignment from the drop-down list. Alternatively, you can use the **Select from the drawing** button corresponding to the drop-down list to select an alignment from the drawing area.

Sample line group name

This drop-down list is used to specify the name of the sample line group of the sample line. On selecting an alignment in the **Select alignment** drop-down list, the **Sample line group name** drop-down list is populated with the names of the sample group associated with that alignment. Select the name of the sample line group from the drop-down list. Alternatively, choose the alignment sample line from the drawing by choosing the **Select from the drawing** button available next to this drop-down list.

Sample line

This drop-down list is used to specify the sample line from which the section view will be created. On specifying a sample group, the **Sample line** drop-down list is populated with the names of all the sample lines in the selected sample line group. To specify the sample line, select the name of the sample line group from this drop-down list. Alternatively, choose the sample line from the drawing by choosing the **Select from the drawing** button available next to this drop-down list.

Station

This drop-down list is used to specify the station value of the sample line from which the section view will be created. You can view the list of available station values from the **Station** drop-down list. Note that if you change the station value, there will be a change in the sample line value in the **Sample line** drop-down list and vice-versa.

Section view name

The **Section view name** edit box is used to specify the default name of the section view. Choose the **Click to edit name template** button on the right of this edit box; the **Name Template** dialog box will be displayed. Enter a name for the section view in the **Name** edit box of this dialog box and then choose the **OK** button. Optionally, enter a description of the section view in the **Description** text box.

Section view layer

This text box displays the name of the layer on which the section view will be created. To edit this layer, choose the button on the right of this text box; the **Object Layer** dialog box will be displayed. In this dialog box, specify the layer using various options and then choose the **OK** button; the dialog box will be closed and the layer will be specified for the section view.

Section view style

This drop-down list displays the default section view styles. To specify a style of the section view, select an option from the **Section view style** drop-down list. In case you want to edit the default style or create a new layer, choose the down arrow on the right of this area; a flyout will be displayed. Choose the option to edit the default style or create a new style.

After specifying the required options on the **General** page, choose the **Next** button; the **Offset Range** page of the wizard will be displayed.

Offset Range Page

This page enables you to set the offset range such as the left and right swath of the section view. The option on this page is discussed next.

Offset range Area

The **Offset range** area of the **Offset Range** page is used to specify the range of offset by using two radio buttons: **Automatic** and **User specified**. The **Automatic** radio button is selected by default. As a result, the offset range is set automatically. The minimum and maximum lengths of swaths are displayed in the **Left** and **Right** text boxes next to the selected radio button. You can also specify the offset range manually. To do so, select the **User specified** radio button and enter the length of the left and right ranges in the respective edit boxes available next to this radio button.

After specifying the offset range on this page, choose the **Next** button; the **Elevation Range** page of the wizard will be displayed.

Elevation Range Page

This page enables you to set the maximum and minimum elevation ranges of the section view. The option on this page is discussed next.

Elevation range Area

The **Elevation range** area is used to specify the maximum and minimum range of elevation by using two radio buttons: **Automatic** and **User specified**. The **Automatic** radio button is selected by default. As a result, the maximum and minimum elevation ranges are set automatically. The minimum and maximum elevations are displayed in the **Minimum** and **Maximum** text boxes next to the radio button selected. You can also specify the elevation range manually. To do so, select the **User specified** radio button and enter the maximum and minimum elevations in the respective edit boxes, available next to the radio button.

After specifying the options in this page, choose the **Next** button; the **Section Display Options** page will be displayed.

Section Display Options Page

On this page, you can set the section display option. The **Name** column in this area displays the name of the current sections. Clear the check box available in the **Draw** column, if you do not want to draw a section view of a particular section listed in the **Name** column. Select the required radio button in the **Clip Grid** column to specify the extents of the section view grid. The extents of the section view grid will be adjusted according to the section for which you have selected the radio button in the **Clip Grid** column. The **Label set** column displays the label style set for the section view. To change the existing label style or to hide labels, click in the cell of this column; the **Select Label Set** dialog box will be displayed. Select the required option from the drop-down list in the dialog box or select the **_No Labels** option to hide labels, and then choose the **OK** button. The **Style** column displays the default section style. Click on the default style in the column; the **Pick Section style** dialog box will be displayed. Select the required option from the drop-down list in the dialog box and then choose the **OK** button; the dialog box will be closed.

Choose the **Next** button in the wizard; the **Data Bands** page will be displayed.

Data Bands Page

This page is used to specify the properties of data bands associated with the section view. Various options in this page are discussed next.

Select band set

This area is used to specify the set of band styles used in the section view. You can select a specific band style from the drop-down list in this area. You can also use this area to create a new band style, edit the existing band style, or copy the existing band style. To perform any of these operations, choose the down-arrow next to the drop-down list and then choose the required option from the flyout.

List of bands

This area is used to specify the location and band properties of the section view. The **Location** drop-down list in this area is used to specify the position of band with respect to the section view. Select the required option from the drop-down list to set the position of the band. Next, use the **Set band properties** area to specify the band type, style, and surfaces sampled by the sample line that supplies data for the band, including any corridor surface.

Section View Tables Page

This page is used to set the volume table properties of the section view. Choose the **Section View Tables** option from the wizard to display various options in this page.

Note

The ***Section View Tables*** *page will not be available in the* ***Create Section View*** *wizard if the material list is not available for the drawing.*

Once you have specified the settings for the section view, choose the **Create Section View** button from the **Create Section View** wizard; the wizard will be closed and you will be prompted to specify the origin of the section view. Click at the required location on the screen; the section view will be created and added to the drawing, as shown in Figure 9-12.

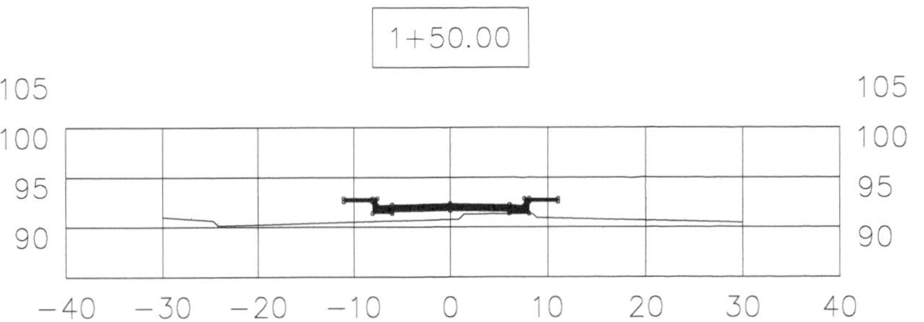

Figure 9-12 *A section view created at station 1+50.00*

The section view displays the title of the section view at top, section line, and elevations along the Y-axis on the left and right sides of the section view, respectively. The station values are displayed along the X-axis. The section view also displays swath widths and offsets labeled in the section view, depending upon the settings of the selected section label style.

Creating Multiple Section Views

Ribbon:	Home > Profile & Section Views > Section Views drop-down > Create Multiple Views
Command:	CREATEMULTIPLESECTIONVIEW

To create multiple section views, choose the **Create Multiple Views** tool from the **Profile & Section Views** panel; the **General** page of the **Create Multiple Section Views** wizard will be displayed, as shown in Figure 9-13. This wizard is used to create multiple section views from the existing sections. The pages in this wizard are the same as those discussed in the **Create Section View** wizard except for the **Section Placement** page which is discussed next.

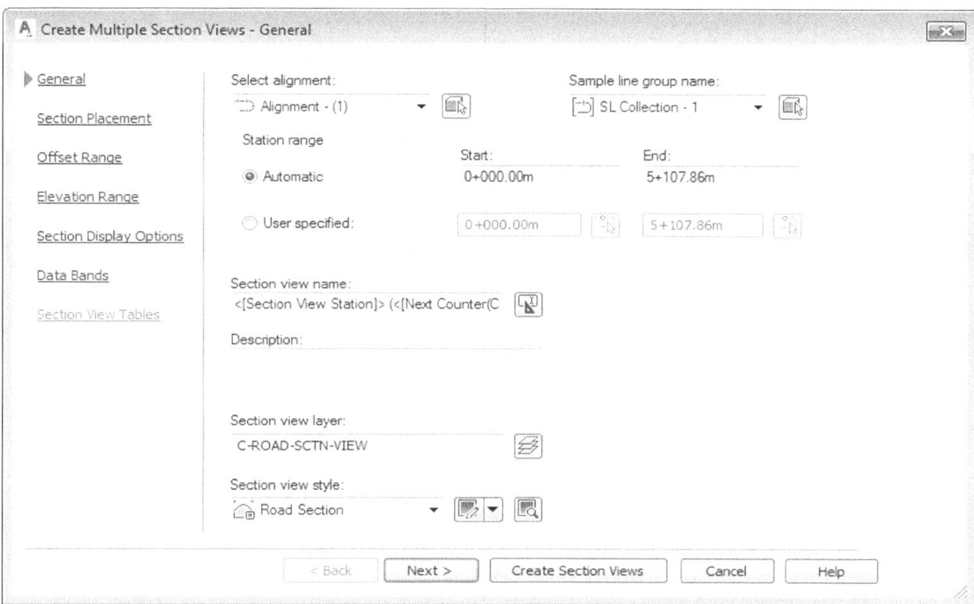

*Figure 9-13 The **General** page of the **Create Multiple Section Views** wizard*

To display the **Section Placement** page, choose the **Next** button in the **General** page of the **Create Multiple Section Views** wizard.

Section Placement Page

This page is used to specify the placement of the section or sections in the drawing area. The different areas in this page are discussed next.

Placement Options

This area consists of the **Production** and **Draft** radio buttons. To use a layout from a template file for placing the section views, select the **Production** radio button. On selecting this radio button, the **Template for cross section sheet** edit box becomes active. To specify the template in the edit box, choose the browse button on its right; the **Select Layout as Sheet Template** dialog box will be displayed. In this dialog box, specify the drawing template file name and the layout and then choose the **OK** button to close this dialog box. If you want to place the section views in a grid format, select the **Draft** radio button.

You can also arrange multiple section views in rows and columns, and plot them on a sheet. To specify a group plot style to multiple section views, you can select an option from the **Group Plot Style** drop-down list in the **Placement Options** area of this page. You can also create a new group plot style for multiple section views. To do so, choose the down arrow on the right of the **Group Plot Style** drop-down list; a flyout will be displayed. Choose the **Create New** option from the flyout, as shown in Figure 9-14. On doing so, the **Group Plot Style - New Group Plot Style** dialog box will be displayed, as shown in Figure 9-15. In the **Information** tab of this dialog box, enter a style name in the **Name** edit box. Next, choose the **Array** tab. The options in this tab are used to specify the settings for the layout of section views on a sheet.

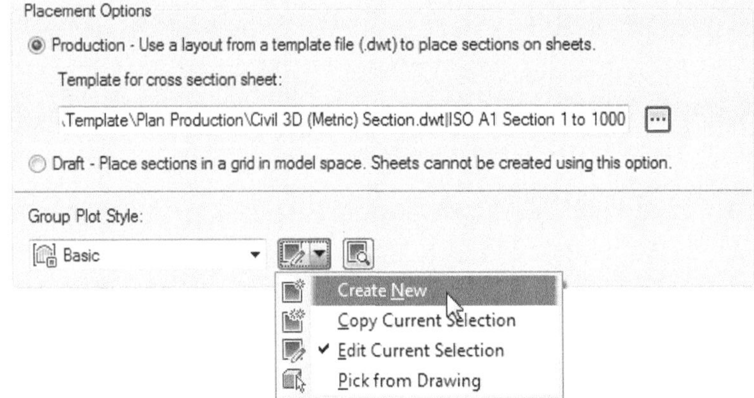

***Figure 9-14** Choosing the **Create New** option from the flyout*

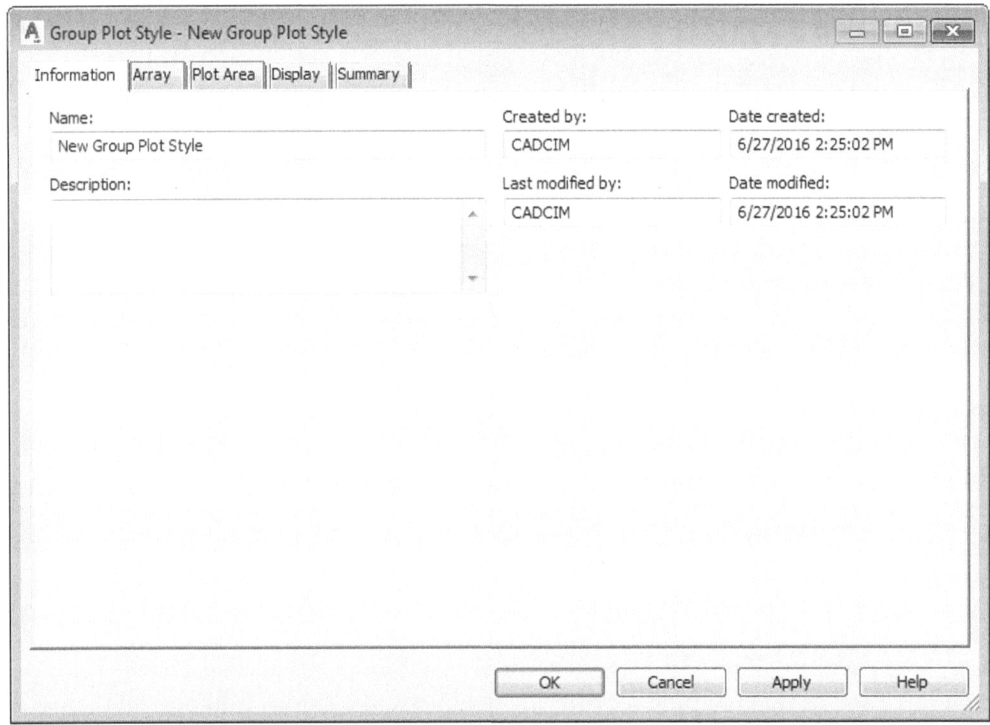

***Figure 9-15** The **Group Plot Style - New Group Plot Style** dialog box*

Tip

*You can also invoke the **Group Plot Style - New Group Plot Style** dialog box from the **Settings** tab of the **TOOLSPACE**. To do so, expand the **Section View** node in the **Settings** tab and right-click on the **Group Plot Style** sub-node; a shortcut menu will be displayed. Choose the **New** option from the shortcut menu to display the dialog box.*

In the **Plot rules** area of the **Array** tab, the **By rows** radio button is selected by default. As a result, section views are plotted in rows. You can select the **By columns** radio button to plot views in columns. Next, select an option from the **Start corner** drop-down list to specify the start corner of the plot section views.

From the **Align section views about** drop-down list, select an option to align the section view. The options in the **Cell sizes** drop-down list are used to specify the size or area of section views. In the **Space between adjacent section views** area, specify the spacing between two adjacent section views in a column and a row in the respective edit boxes.

Next, choose the **Plot Area** tab from the dialog box. This tab is used to select the method of plotting section views. In the **Plot area grid details** area, specify the horizontal major and horizontal minor grid values in the respective edit boxes. Similarly, specify the vertical major and vertical minor grid values in the respective edit boxes. Next, specify the gap value in the **Gap** edit box of the **Gap between successive pages** area. Choose the **OK** button to return to the **Section Placement** page of the **Create Multiple Section Views** wizard. Set the required options in the remaining pages of the wizard and choose the **Create section Views** button; the wizard will be closed and you will be prompted to select the section view origin in the drawing. Choose the point by clicking in the drawing; the multiple section view will be added to your drawing. The multiple section view object will be added in the **Section View Groups** sub-node of the **Prospector** tab in the **TOOLSPACE** palette. To view the section view name, choose the **Prospector** tab and expand **Alignments > Sample Line Groups** sub-node to display the existing sample line groups. Now, expand the required sample line group to view the sample lines of that group. Next, expand the required sample line node. Each sample line node consists of the **Sections** and **Section View Groups** sub-nodes, as shown in Figure 9-16. The sections sampled from the parent sample line are listed in the **Sections** sub-node and the section views created are added and displayed under their parent section view group in the **Section View Groups** sub-node.

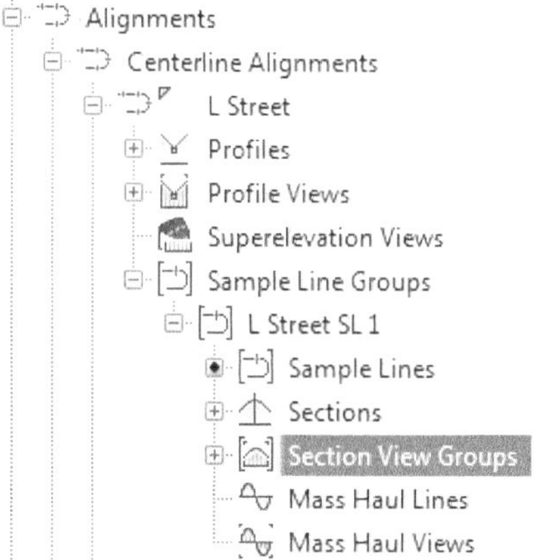

Figure 9-16 *The expanded* ***Sample Line Groups*** *sub-node*

Section View Band Set

A section view band set is a set of data bands that displays annotation of the section view and other related objects such as station offset, elevations, and so on. You can place the section view band set above or below the section view. The band set consists of two types of bands, **Section**

Data and **Section Segment**. The **Section Data** band is used to annotate major offsets from the centerline, section 1 and section 2 elevations, distance from centerline, and section segment grade points. The **Section Segment** data is used to annotate the length of section segments.

Creating a Band Style

Band types have their own band styles that are created and managed in the respective **Section data** and **Section Segment** sub-nodes in the **Settings** tab. You can create your own styles and use them in section views. To do so, expand **Section View > Band Style > Section Data** in the **Settings** tab. Next, right-click on the **Section Data** node and choose the **New** option from the shortcut menu; the **Section Data Band Style - New Section Data Band Style** dialog box will be displayed. In this dialog box, enter a style name in the **Name** edit box of the **Information** tab.

Next, choose the **Band Details** tab. The options in this tab are used to specify the settings for band layout, title text, style, composing label, and so on. Figure 9-17 shows the **Band Details** tab of the **Section Data Band Style - New Section Data Band Style** dialog box. Choose the **Compose label** button from the **Title text** area; the **Label Style Composer - Band Title** dialog box will be displayed. Use this dialog box to specify the title text name, content, text height, color, and so on. After specifying all parameters, choose the **OK** in the dialog box; the dialog box will be closed.

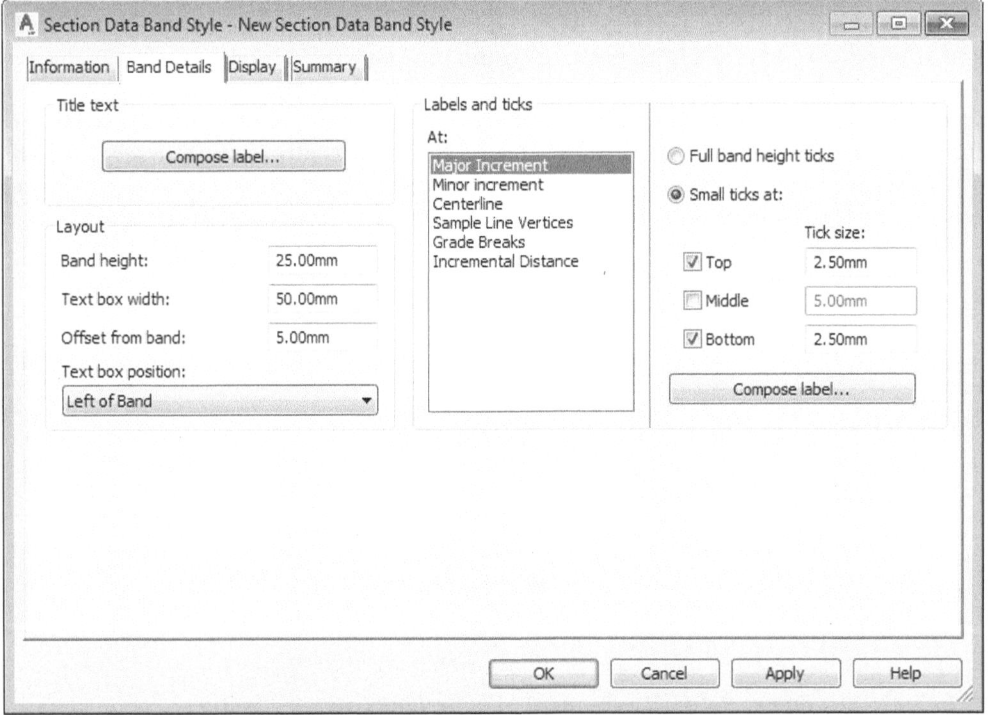

Figure 9-17 The options displayed in the ***Band Details*** *tab*

In the **Layout** area of the **Band Details** tab, enter the height of the band in the **Band height** edit box, enter the width of the band in the **Text box width** edit box, and enter the distance of the text box from the band in the **Offset from band** edit box. Select an option from the **Text box position** drop-down list to add the text box to the left or right of the section band.

In the **Labels and ticks** area, select the points where you want to add labels. For example, selecting the **Major Increment** option will enable you to add labels only at major intervals along the band. Also, the ticks will be placed at major intervals only. Similarly, you can add labels and ticks at minor increments, centerline, sample line vertices, grade breaks, and incremental distance by selecting the corresponding option from the **Labels and ticks** area. On the right side of this area, select the **Full band height ticks** radio button to specify the ticks to be drawn at full band height.

When you select the **Centerline** option from the **Labels and ticks** area, the **Full band height ticks** radio button will be selected by default. For any other option selected in the **Labels and ticks** area, the **Small ticks at** radio button as well as the **Top** and **Bottom** check boxes will be selected by default. The **Tick size** edit box will display the value of the tick size at the top, middle, and bottom of the band. You can edit these values in the respective edit boxes. You can also choose ticks to be placed by selecting the corresponding check boxes.

Choose the **Compose label** button displayed below the **Tick size** edit boxes; the **Label Style Composer** dialog box will be displayed, based on the option selected from the **Labels and ticks** area. You can use this dialog box to compose the labels to be added at the selected point such as Major Increment, Centerline, and so on. Then, choose the **OK** button to close the **Label Style Composer** dialog box. Next, set the required options in the **Display** tab of the **Section Data Band Style - New Section Data Band Style** dialog box. Next, choose the **OK** button from the dialog box; the dialog box will be closed and the new band style will be added to the **Section Data** node in the **Settings** tab.

Similarly, you can create a new band style for the **Section Segment** band style. After you have created band styles for both the **Section Data** and **Section Segment** band styles, you can add them to a band set and create a new band set style to add to section views.

Creating a Band Set Style

To create a band set style, expand **Section View > Band Styles > Band Sets** in the **Settings** tab. Next, right-click on the **Band Sets** node and choose the **New** option from the shortcut menu; the **Section View Band Set - New Section View Band Set** dialog box will be displayed. In this dialog box, specify the name of the style in the **Name** edit box of the **Information** tab.

Then, choose the **Bands** tab, refer to Figure 9-18. This tab is used to specify the data bands to be added to the set along with band styles and positions. Select the band to be added from the **Band type** drop-down list. Next, select an option from the **Select band style** drop-down list. In the **Location** drop-down list, select an option to add the band set at top or bottom of the section view. Next, choose the **Add** button; the band will be added in the **List of bands** area. Similarly, add another data band and choose the **OK** button; the dialog box will be closed and the data band set style will be added to the **Band Sets** sub-node in the **Settings** tab.

Applying the Band Set

You can apply a band set before or after creating section views. To add a data band after the section views are created or to edit a data band set style, select the section view in the drawing and right-click; a shortcut menu will be displayed. Choose the **Section View Properties** option from the shortcut menu; the **Section View Properties - <station number>** dialog box will be displayed.

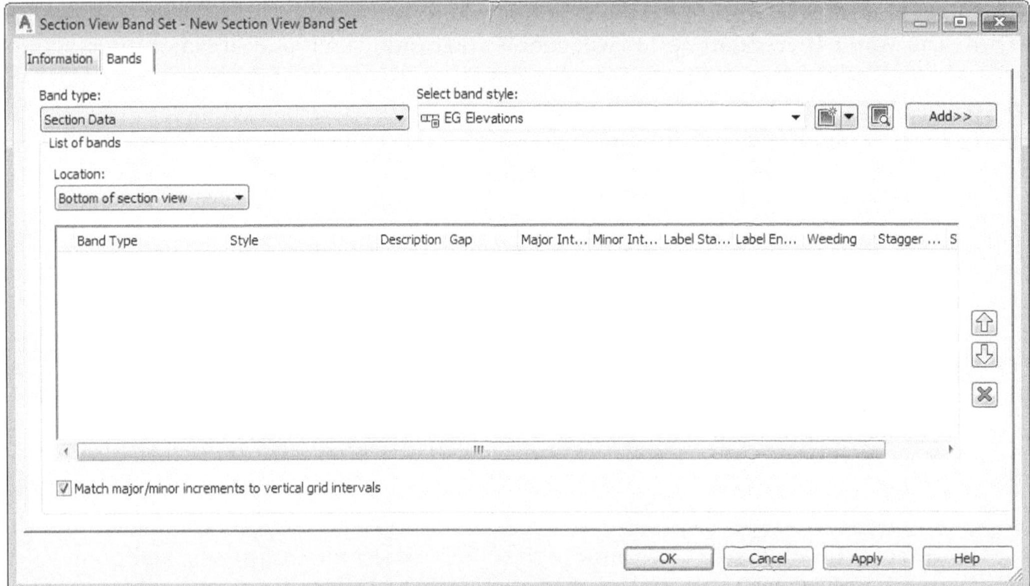

***Figure 9-18** The **Bands** tab of the **Section View Band Set - New Section View Band Set** dialog box*

Choose the **Bands** tab from the dialog box. Next, select the band type, and band type style, and then choose the **Add** button to add them in the **List of bands** area. You can also choose the **Import band set** button from the **Section View Properties - <section view name>** dialog box to import an existing band set to be added into the current section view. On doing so, the **Band Set** dialog box will be displayed. Select the required option from the drop-down list in the dialog box and choose the **OK** button; the bands in the band set will be added in the **List of bands** area. Next, choose the **OK** button from the **Section View Properties - <section view name>** dialog box; the dialog box will be closed and the band set will be added to the section view at the specified location.

To apply band set to multiple section views, select any of the section views from the drawing and right-click; a shortcut menu will be displayed. Choose the **Section View Group Properties** option from the shortcut menu; the **Section View Group Properties - <section view group name>** dialog box will be displayed. Choose the **Section Views** tab from this dialog box and then choose the button in the **Change Band Set** column; the **Section View Group Bands - <section view group name>** dialog box will be displayed, as shown in Figure 9-19. Select an option from the **Select band style** drop-down list in this dialog box. This dialog box is used to select source surface for data band annotation. The **Location** drop-down list in the **List of bands** area in this dialog box specifies the location of the data band annotation in the section view. Select the required option from the drop-down list to specify the location. The **Band Type** column in the **List of bands** area displays the type of data band specified in the band set property. The **Style** column in this area specifies the style specified in the band set properties.

Now, click in the cell of the **Surface 1** column for the required band type and select the required option from the drop-down list. **Surface 1** is the surface sampled by sample lines to provide data for data bands. This surface can also include any type of corridor surface.

Similarly, click in the cell of the **Surface 2** column and select the required surface from the drop-down list for the required band type. **Surface 2** is the additional surface sampled by sample lines to provide data for the **Section Data** band only. This surface can also include any type of corridor surface. After specifying source surfaces and location for data bands, choose the **OK** button; the dialog box will be closed and the **Section View Group Properties - <section view group name>** dialog box will be displayed. Choose the **OK** button from the dialog box; the dialog box will be closed and the data bands will be added to multiple section views.

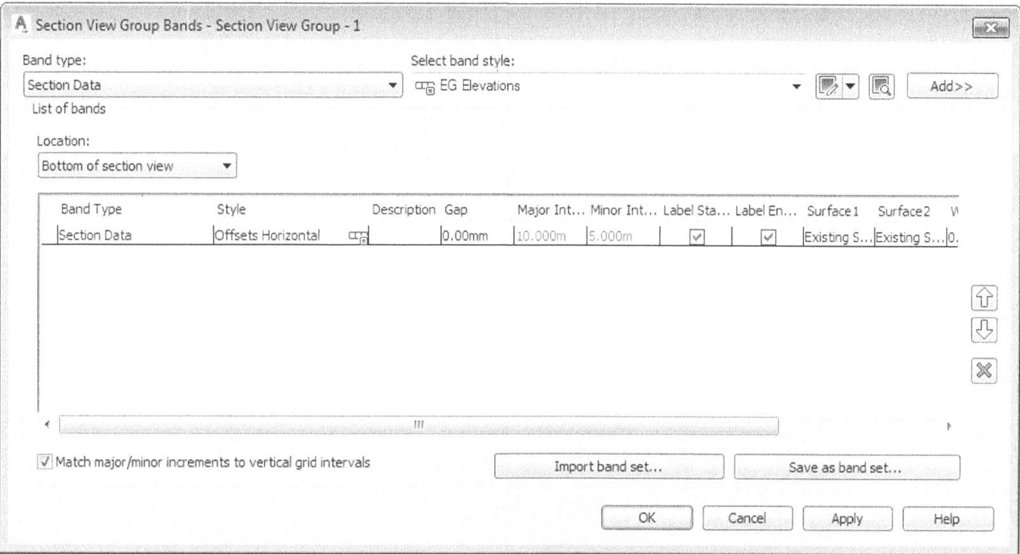

*Figure 9-19 The **Section View Group Bands** dialog box*

Adding Section View Labels

Ribbon: Annotate > Labels & Tables > Add Labels drop-down > Section View > Add Section View Labels
Command: ADDSECTIONVIEWLABELS

To add grade or offset labels to a section view, choose the **Section View** option from the **Labels & Tables** panel; a flyout will be displayed. Choose the **Add Section View Labels** tool from the flyout, as shown in Figure 9-20; the **Add Labels** dialog box will be displayed. Make sure the **Section View** option is selected from the **Feature** drop-down list. Next, select the required option such as **Grade**, **Offset Elevation**, or **Projection** from the **Label type** drop-down list to specify the label type. Also, select the label style for the selected label type from the corresponding label style drop-down list. Next, choose the **Add** button; you will be prompted to pick the label location. Select the required location. Next, press ESC to end the command. Now, choose the **Close** button from the **Add Labels** dialog box to close it.

Note

*The options in the **Label type** drop-down list vary depending upon the type of option selected from the **Feature** drop-down list.*

Tip

*To add the **Grade** labels or the **Offset Elevation** labels using default label styles, choose the **Section View** tool from the **Labels and Tables** panel; a flyout will be displayed. From the flyout, choose the **Grade or Offset Elevation** option and follow the prompts in the command line.*

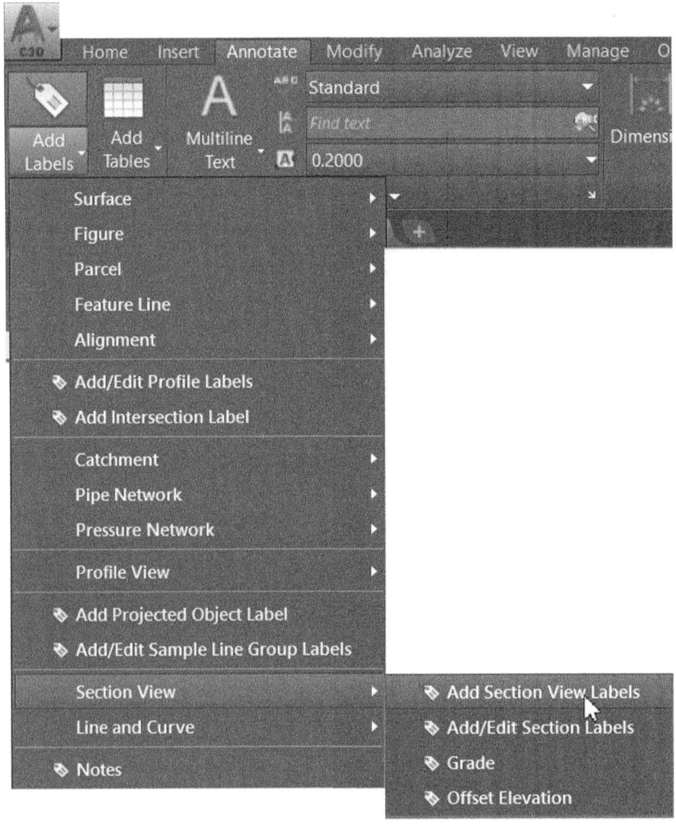

***Figure 9-20** Choosing the **Add Section View Labels** tool*

The **Grade**, **Projection** and **Offset Elevation** label styles are listed in the **Label Styles** sub-node of the **Section View** node in the **Settings** tab. To create a new label style, choose the **Settings** tab and expand **Section View > Label Styles**. Next, select the required **Offset Elevation**, **Projection** or **Grade** sub-node and right-click on it; a shortcut menu will be displayed. Choose the **New** option from the shortcut menu; the **Label Style Composer - New Section View Offset Elevation Label Style**, **Label Style Composer - New Section View Projection Label Style** or **Label Style Composer - New Section View Depth Grade Label Style** dialog box will be displayed depending upon the sub-node you have selected. You can use these dialog boxes to create a new label style.

Section View Properties

To view and edit the section view properties, choose the required section view in the drawing and right-click; a shortcut menu is displayed. Choose the **Section View Properties** option from the shortcut menu; the **Section View Properties - <section view name>** dialog box will be displayed. You can use this dialog box to view and edit the properties of the section view, section view style, bands, and profile grade lines associated with the selected section view.

Editing Sections

To edit section of a section view, choose the required section from the drawing; the **Section** tab will be displayed in the Ribbon. In the **Section** tab, choose the **Edit Section Geometry** tool from the **Modify Section** panel; the **Section Editor** dialog box will be displayed, as shown in Figure 9-21. You can edit the values of the section parameters in this dialog box.

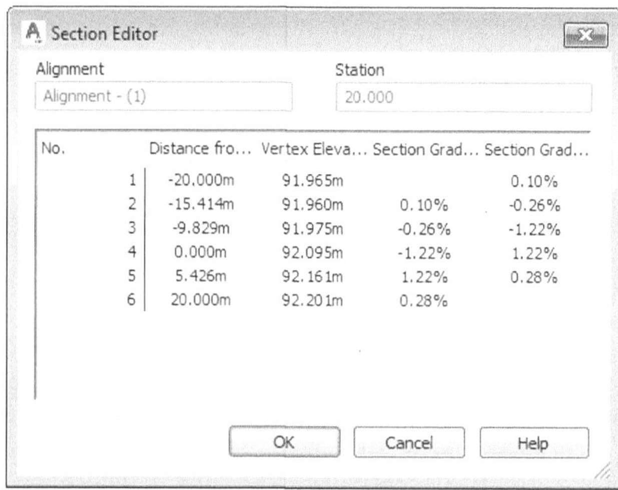

*Figure 9-21 The **Section Editor** dialog box*

Note

*The **Edit Section Geometry** option is used to edit the static sections whose update mode is set to **Static**. If you edit dynamic sections using this option, the **Section Editor** dialog box will not allow you to modify the values in the columns.*

Move Sections Views to a Different Section View Group

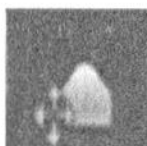

You can now move section views between different section view groups and update the sheet layout. The section views that you want to move and the destination section view group must share the same sample line group. To move section views to a different section view group, choose the required section from the drawing; the **Section** tab will be displayed in the Ribbon. In the **Section** tab, choose the **Move to Section View Group** tool from the **Modify View** panel; the **Select a Section View Group** dialog box will be displayed, as shown in Figure 9-22. You can select the required destination section view group from the drop-down list.

The moved section view object will be added in the **Section View Groups** sub-node of the **Prospector** tab in the **TOOLSPACE** palette. To view the move section view group name, choose the **Prospector** tab and expand **Alignments > Sample Line Groups** sub-node to display the existing sample line groups. Now, expand the required sample line group to view the section view group. Next, expand the required section view group.

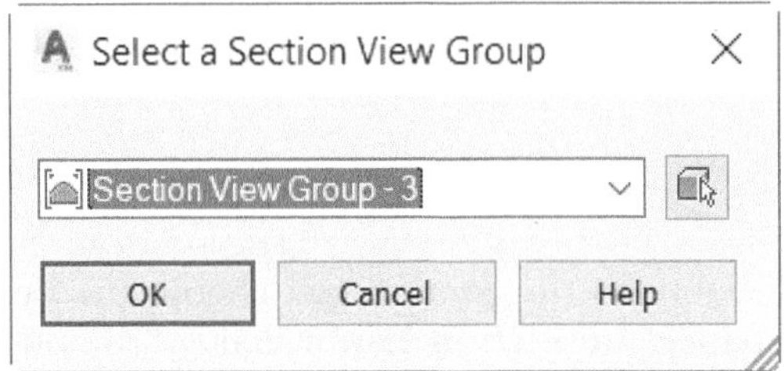

Figure 9-22 ***Select a Section View Group*** *dialog box*

QUANTITY TAKEOFFS

Civil 3D provides you with two types of quantity takeoffs namely, earthworks and material volumes. You can generate the formatted reports of earthwork and material volumes. The Earthwork takeoff represents the amount of total material to be added to or removed from the existing site. This is done by comparing the existing surface with the datum of the assembly. The datum of the assembly is the bed over which different layers of materials (rubble, concrete, and so on) to build the road are laid. The main purpose of the earthwork calculation is to modify the design such that a balance is maintained between the total cut and fill material.

The material volume takeoffs represent the material needed on the site. The subassembly of the corridor assembly provides information about the materials used. The quantity of the material takeoff is determined by the subassembly shapes (Structures) such as **Pave1**, **Curb**, **Sidewalk**, and so on.

To compute the quantity takeoffs for earthworks, you need to create a material list and define the conditions for quantity takeoffs, as mentioned earlier in this chapter. To define the criteria or conditions for quantity takeoffs, choose the **Settings** tab in the **TOOLSPACE** palette and expand the **Quantity Takeoff** node. Select the **Quantity Takeoff Criteria** sub-node and right-click on it; a shortcut menu will be displayed. Choose the **New** option from the shortcut menu; the **Quantity Takeoffs Criteria - New Quantity Takeoff Criteria** dialog box will be displayed. This dialog box is used to create material list and set the criteria for quantity takeoffs. In the next section, you will learn about creating the material list and defining the criteria for quantity takeoffs.

Defining the Quantity Takeoff Criteria

To define the quantity takeoff criteria, choose the **Information** tab from the **Quantity Takeoff Criteria - New Quantity Takeoff Criteria** dialog box and then enter the name for quantity takeoff criteria in the **Name** edit box. Now, choose the **Material List** tab. The options in this tab are used to create the material list and set the criteria for quantity takeoffs.

To create the material list, choose the button next to the **Add new material** button; the **Name Template** dialog box will be displayed. Enter the required material name in the **Name** edit box and choose the **OK** button; the dialog box will be closed. Now, choose the **Add new material** button; the material will be added in the **Material Name** column. Next, click in the **Quantity Type** column and select **Earthworks** option from the drop-down list. Now, you need to add data to the material list. To do so, select the required options from the **Data type** drop-down list and the **Select surface** drop-down list in the **Define material** area. Then, choose the button next to the **Select surface** drop-down list; the data will be added to the material list of the **Material Name** column. Similarly, select another surface from the **Select surface** drop-down list and add it to the list. In the **Condition** column, set the value of one of the surfaces to **Base** and another to **Compare**, refer to Figure 9-23.

Note

Civil 3D calculates quantity takeoffs by comparing two surfaces. You must specify and add two surfaces to the material list to calculate quantity takeoffs. Similarly, select and add two corridor shapes from the ***Select corridor shape*** *drop-down list, when the* ***Corridor Shape*** *option is selected from the* ***Data type*** *drop-down list.*

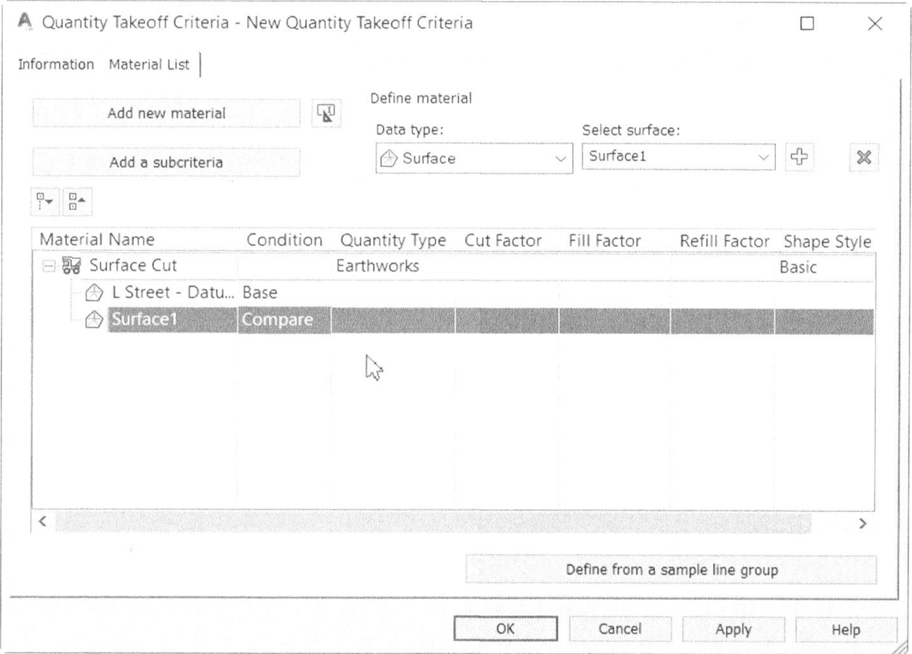

Figure 9-23 The options displayed in the ***Material List*** *tab of the* ***Quantity Takeoff Criteria - New Quantity Takeoff Criteria*** *dialog box*

Optionally, modify the cut, fill, and refill factors in their respective columns. Next, modify the material section style in the **Shape Style** column, if required. Similarly, you can add more material lists with different criteria and add data to them.

You can also create the material list using the **Sample Line Group Properties** dialog box and then use the created list to define the criteria of quantity takeoff. To do so, choose the **Define from a sample line group** button from the **Quantity Takeoff Criteria - New Quantity Takeoff Criteria** dialog box; the **Define Material Criteria** dialog box will be displayed. Select the required sample line group from the **Select sample line group** drop-down list in the dialog box and choose the **OK** button.

After you have created the material list and the criteria of the quantity takeoff in the **Quantity Takeoff Criteria - New Quantity Takeoff Criteria** dialog box, choose the **OK** button; the dialog box will be closed and the new quantity takeoff criteria will be added in the **Quantity Takeoff Criteria** sub-node in the **Settings** tab.

Computing Materials

Ribbon: Analyze > Volumes and Materials > Compute Materials
Command: COMPUTEMATERIALS

To compute materials, choose the **Compute Materials** tool from the **Volumes and Materials** panel; the **Select a Sample Line Group** dialog box will be displayed. Select the required alignment and the sample line group from the **Select alignment** and **Select sample line group** drop-down lists, respectively. Choose the **OK** button; the **Compute Materials - <sample line group name>** dialog box will be displayed, as shown in Figure 9-24.

Select the required quantity takeoff criteria from the **Quantity takeoff criteria** drop-down list. Enter the curve correction tolerance value in the edit box on the right of the **Curve correction tolerance** check box. Choose the **Map objects with same name** button to map surfaces and corridor shapes with the same name as they have in the drawing. Next, choose the **OK** button; the dialog box will be closed and the materials and quantities will be computed. To view the quantities of cut and fill volumes, you need to generate volume reports. Civil 3D creates volume reports in the printable format or in the form of tables that can be added in the drawing. The method of generating reports is discussed next.

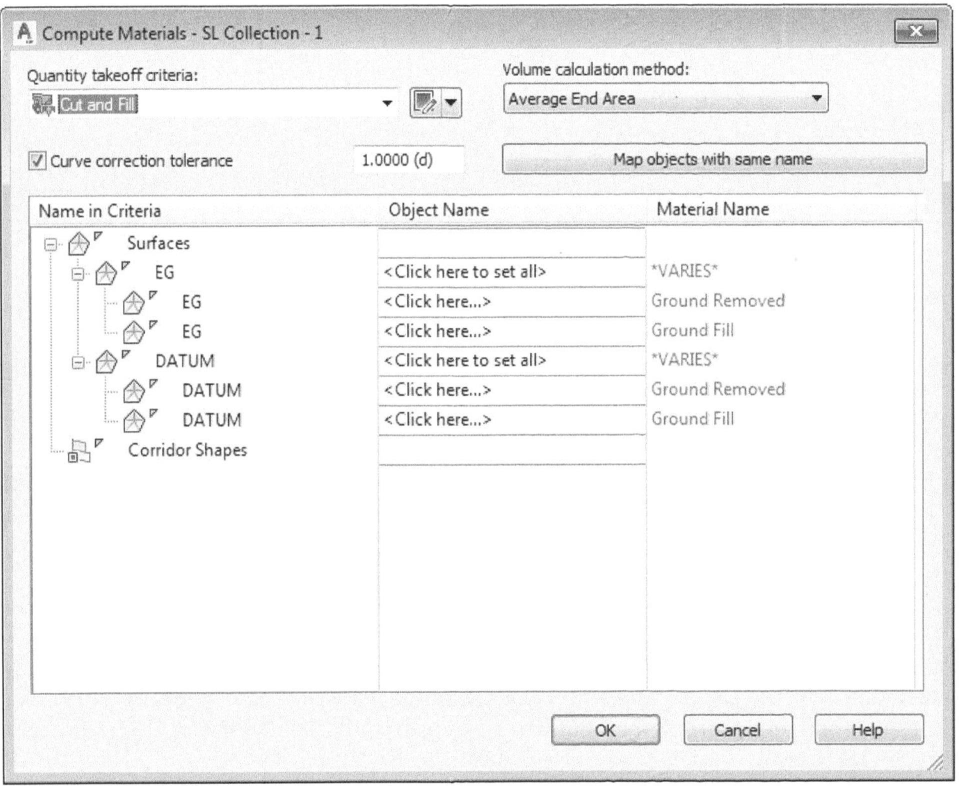

Figure 9-24 *The* ***Compute Materials - <sample line group name>*** *dialog box*

Generating Volume Reports

Ribbon: Analyze > Volumes and Materials > Volume Report
Command: GENERATEQUANTITIESREPORT

To view the total volume of cut and fill quantity reports, choose the **Volume Report** tool from the **Volumes and Materials** panel; the **Report Quantities** dialog box will be displayed, as shown in Figure 9-25.

The **Select alignment** drop-down list in this dialog box displays the existing alignment. Select the required alignment from the drop-down list. Similarly, select an option from the **Select sample line group** drop-down list.

Next, select the material list for which you want to compute materials from the **Select material list** drop-down list. The **Select a style sheet** text box is used to display the path and name of the style to be used to generate volume report. To select the style sheet, choose the button on the right of the **Select a style sheet** area; the **Select Style Sheet** dialog box will be displayed. In this dialog box, there are three types of style sheets. These sheets are discussed next.

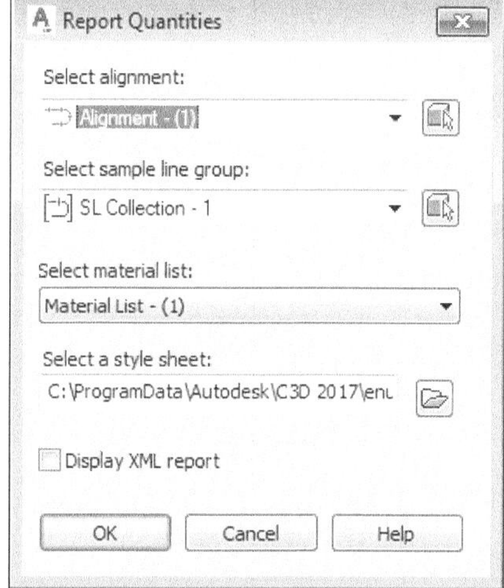

*Figure 9-25 The **Report Quantities** dialog box*

earthwork.xsl
This style sheet generates the reports of station-by-station values in a tabular format for cut and fill volumes, incremental volumes, and cumulative net volume.

Mass Haul - Multiple Materials.xsl
This type of style sheet is used if you have defined multiple material types to be removed. You can generate material-by-material reports at each station as well as aggregate volume reports for mass-hauls and then create mass-hauls curves.

Select Material.xsl
This style sheet is used to generate station-by-station value reports for the selected materials. You can use this sheet to generate reports of all the selected materials defined in the criteria and cumulative volumes that are reported at each station.

You can select any of these style sheets according to your requirement. Then, choose the **Open** button to return to the **Report Quantities** dialog box. In this dialog box, select the **Display XML report** check box to generate the XML report of the computed volumes or materials. Now, choose the **OK** button; the **Report Quantities** dialog box will be closed and the **Internet Explorer** message box will be displayed. Choose **Yes** from the message box; the volume report will be generated, as shown in Figure 9-26. Figure 9-27 shows the material report generated after selecting the **Select Material.xsl** style sheet.

Volume Report

Project: C:\Users\TIET\appdata\local\temp\c09_c3d_2018_tut03_1_25073_5629.sv$
Alignment: L Street
Sample Line Group: L Street SL 1
Start Sta: 0+50.000
End Sta: 19+00.000

Station	Cut Area (Sq.ft.)	Cut Volume (Cu.yd.)	Reusable Volume (Cu.yd.)	Fill Area (Sq.ft.)	Fill Volume (Cu.yd.)	Cum. Cut Vol. (Cu.yd.)	Cum. Reusable Vol. (Cu.yd.)	Cum. Fill Vol. (Cu.yd.)	Cum. Net Vol. (Cu.yd.)
0+50.000	0.46	0.00	0.00	108.67	0.00	0.00	0.00	0.00	0.00
1+00.000	0.00	0.42	0.42	146.25	236.04	0.42	0.42	236.04	-235.61
1+50.000	0.00	0.00	0.00	153.11	277.19	0.42	0.42	513.23	-512.81
2+00.000	0.00	0.00	0.00	136.97	252.02	0.42	0.42	765.25	-764.82

Figure 9-26 *Volume report showing the total cut and fill volumes*

Material Report

Project: C:\Users\TIET\appdata\local\temp\c09_c3d_2018_tut03_1_25073_5629.sv$
Alignment: L Street
Sample Line Group: L Street SL 1
Start Sta: 0+50.000
End Sta: 19+00.000

	Area Type	Area	Inc.Vol.	Cum.Vol.
		Sq.ft.	Cu.yd.	Cu.yd.
Station: 0+50.000				
	Surface Cut	0.46	0.00	0.00
	Surface Fill	108.67	0.00	0.00
	Concrete In Ditch	3.30	0.00	0.00
	Concrete In Sidewalk	4.00	0.00	0.00

Figure 9-27 *Material report*

You can also create the material volume table. To do so, choose the **Material Volume Table** tool from the **Volume and Materials** panel in the **Analyze** tab; the **Create Material Volume Table** dialog box will be displayed. Use this dialog box to create the material volume table. Table styles are created and managed in the **Table Styles** sub-node of the **Section View** node of the **Settings** tab.

Adding Tables

Ribbon: Analyze > Volumes and Materials > Total Volume Table
Command: ADDTOTALVOLUMETABLE

You can also view the cut and fill volumes in tabular form by adding the volume table or the material volume in the drawing. To do so, choose the **Total Volume Table** tool from the **Volumes and Materials** panel; the **Create Total Volume Table** dialog box will be displayed, as shown in Figure 9-28.

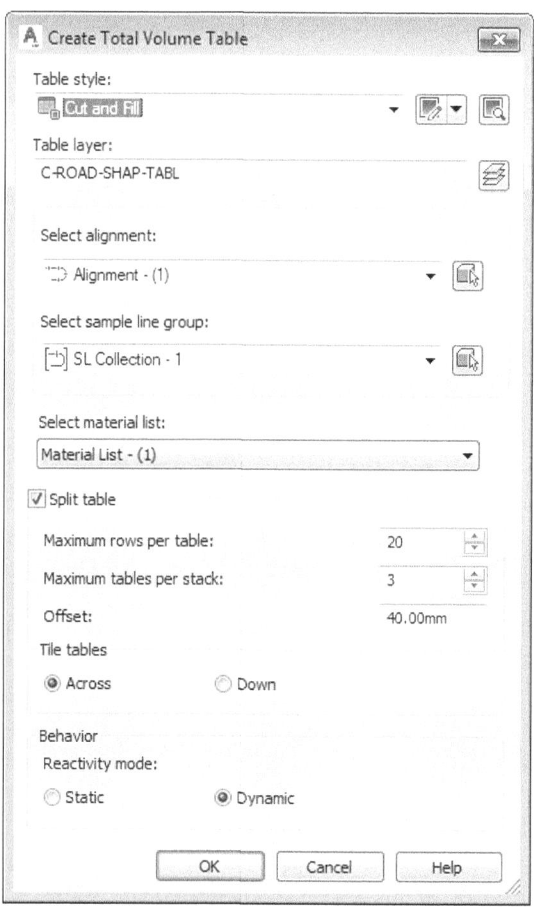

Figure 9-28 *The **Create Total Volume Table** dialog box*

This dialog box is used to create tables by using the volume data from the material list. To do so, select the required table style from the **Table style** drop-down list. The **Table layer** text box is used to display the default layer on which the table will be created. Select the required alignment from the **Select alignment** drop-down list. Next, select the required sample line group from the **Select sample line group** drop-down list. In the **Split table** area, ensure that the **Split table** check box is selected so that the table is split to adjust with the screen. You can specify the maximum number of rows in a table using the **Maximum rows per table** spinner in the **Split table** area. Specify the behavior of the table by selecting the **Static** or **Dynamic** radio button in the **Behavior** area. Once you have specified the settings for the volume table, choose the **OK** button; the dialog box will be closed and you will be prompted to specify the upper left corner of the table. Click at the required location on the screen; **Total Volume Table** will be created, as shown in Figure 9-29.

Total Volume Table						
Station	Fill Area	Cut Area	Fill Volume	Cut Volume	Cumulative Fill Vol	Cumulative Cut Vol
0+50.00	108.67	0.46	0.00	0.00	0.00	0.00
1+00.00	146.25	0.00	236.04	0.42	236.04	0.42
1+50.00	153.11	0.00	277.19	0.00	513.23	0.42
2+00.00	136.97	0.00	252.02	0.00	765.25	0.42
2+50.00	130.05	0.00	238.39	0.00	1003.64	0.42
3+00.00	102.42	0.04	207.32	0.04	1210.96	0.46
3+50.00	98.48	1.47	173.71	1.73	1384.68	2.19
4+00.00	92.40	0.97	176.75	2.26	1561.42	4.46
4+50.00	69.11	2.39	149.55	3.11	1710.97	7.57
5+00.00	79.32	1.41	137.43	3.51	1848.40	11.08
5+50.00	105.03	0.17	170.69	1.47	2019.09	12.55
6+00.00	62.96	1.31	155.55	1.38	2174.64	13.92
6+50.00	64.01	0.96	115.63	2.45	2290.27	16.38
7+00.00	35.05	17.04	88.35	19.69	2378.63	36.07
7+50.00	21.03	21.65	48.10	41.73	2426.72	77.81
8+00.00	11.11	38.55	24.66	70.13	2451.38	147.94
8+50.00	18.61	34.94	27.51	68.05	2478.89	215.99
9+00.00	17.17	40.26	33.13	69.64	2512.02	285.63
9+50.00	9.05	59.28	24.28	92.17	2536.31	377.79
10+00.00	5.77	80.10	13.72	129.05	2550.03	506.85

Figure 9-29 Total Volume Table *displaying the cut and fill volumes*

TUTORIALS

Tutorial 1 Section View

In this tutorial, you will create a sample line group by using the **From Corridor Stations** method and then create a section view at the selected station, as shown in Figure 9-30.

(Expected time: 1 hr)

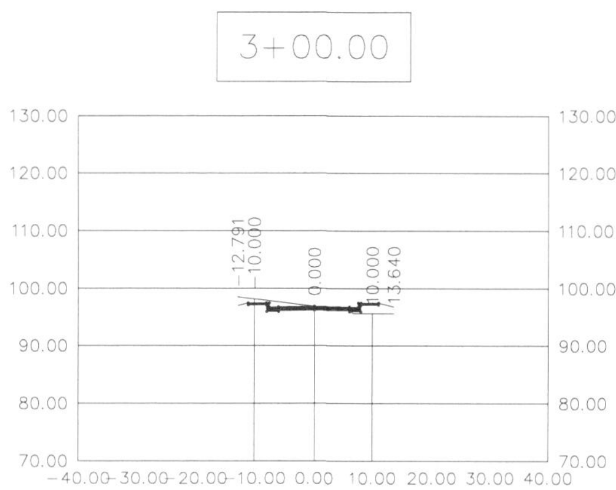

Figure 9-30 *The created section view at the selected station*

The following steps are required to complete this tutorial:

a. Download and open the file.
b. Create the sample line group.
c. Create the cross section at the selected station.
d. Edit the section label style.
e. Save the file.

Downloading and Opening the File

1. Download and extract the *c09_c3d_2018_tut.zip* file from *http://www.cadcim.com,* as explained in Chapter 2.

2. Choose **Open > Drawing** from the **Application Menu**; the **Select File** dialog box is displayed.

3. In the dialog box, browse to the location *C:\c3d_2018\c09_c3d_2018_tut.*

4. Select the file *c09_c3d_2018_tut01.dwg* and then choose the **Open** button to open the file.

Ignore any error messages if displayed in the **PANORAMA** window while opening the drawing file.

Creating a Sample Line Group

1. Choose the **Sample Lines** tool from the **Profile & Section Views** panel of the **Home** tab; you are prompted to select an alignment.

2. Press ENTER; the **Select Alignment** dialog box is displayed.

3. Select **Stephen Road** from the **Select Alignment** dialog box and then choose the **OK** button; the **Sample Line Tools** toolbar with the **Create Sample Line Group** dialog box is displayed.

4. In this dialog box, choose the **Click to edit name template** button on the right of the **Name** edit box; the **Name Template** dialog box is displayed. 

5. In the **Name Template** dialog box, enter **Stephen Collection** in the **Name** edit box and choose the **OK** button; the **Name Template** dialog box is closed.

6. Select **Stephen Style** option from the **Sample line style** drop-down list in the **Create Sample Line Group** dialog box.

7. Next, select **SR Label Style** from the **Sample line label style** drop-down list and then choose the **OK** button; the **Create Sample Line Group** dialog box is closed.

8. Make sure that the **Stephen Collection** option is selected in the **Current sample line group** drop-down list of the **Sample Line Tools** toolbar and then choose the down-arrow next to the **Sample line creation methods** button; a drop-down list is displayed.

9. Choose the **From corridor stations** tool from the drop-down list, as shown in Figure 9-31; the **Create Sample Lines - From Corridor Stations** dialog box is displayed.

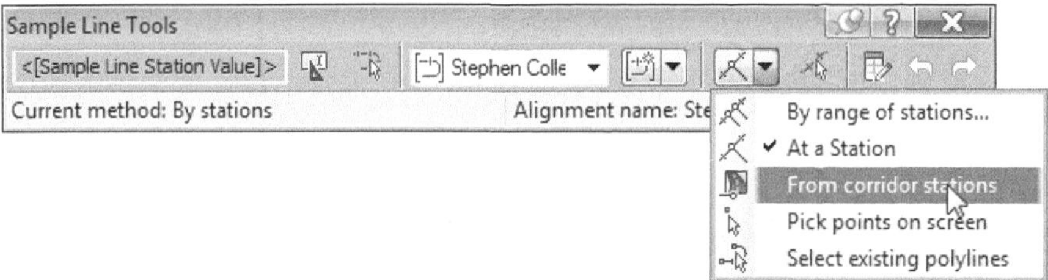

*Figure 9-31 Choosing the **From corridor stations** tool from the flyout*

10. In the **Station Range** category of this dialog box, set the value of the **To alignment end** property to **False**.

11. For the **End Station** property, enter **5+19.91'** in the **Value** column and then press ENTER.

12. In the **Left Swath Width** category, click in the value field of the **Width** property; a button is displayed on the right of the **Value** column. 

13. Choose the button; the **Create Sample Line - From Corridor Stations** dialog box is closed and you are prompted to specify the distance.

14. Zoom in the first station at the start of the corridor and click at the top center of the alignment, as shown in Figure 9-32; you are prompted to specify second point.

15. Drag the cursor to the left, as shown in Figure 9-33, and then click on the screen to specify the left swath width. On doing so, the **Create Sample Lines - From Corridor Stations** dialog box is displayed again and the swath width is displayed in the **Value** column.

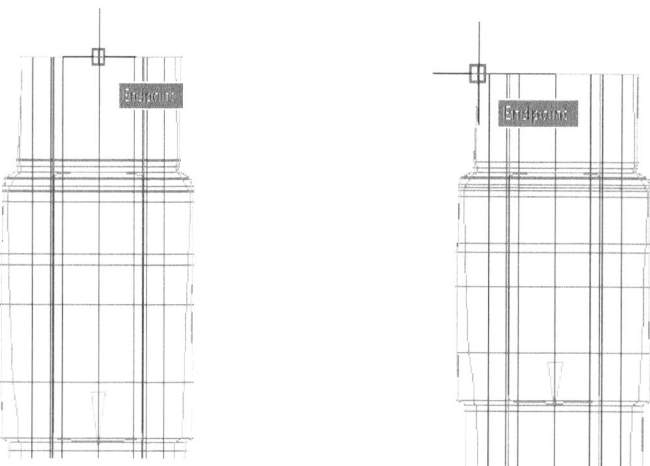

Figure 9-32 Clicking at the top center of the alignment

Figure 9-33 Dragging the cursor on the left to specify the swath width

16. Now, set the value of the swath width in the **Right Swath Width** edit box to **13.640**.

17. Choose the **OK** button; the **Create Sample Lines - From Corridor Stations** dialog box is closed.

18. Next, press ESC to exit the command.

19. Close the **PANORAMA** window, if it is displayed; sample lines are created from corridor stations, as shown in Figure 9-34.

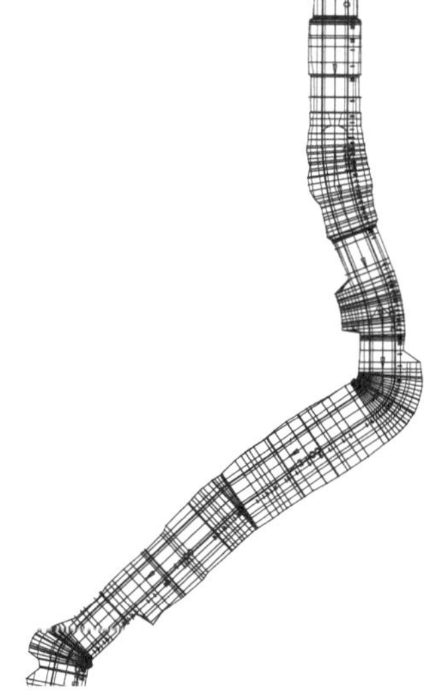

Figure 9-34 Sample lines created from corridor stations

Creating the Section View

1. Choose the **Create Section View** tool from **Home > Profile & Section Views > Section Views** drop-down; the **General** page of the **Create Section View** wizard is displayed.

2. Choose the **Click to edit name template** button, next to the **Section view name** edit box on this page; the **Name Template** dialog box is displayed.

3. In the **Name Template** dialog box, enter **Stephen Section** in the **Name** edit box and then choose the **OK** button; the dialog box is closed.

4. Next, choose the down-arrow next to the **Section view style** drop-down list; a flyout is displayed.

5. Choose the **Create New** option from the flyout; the **Section View Style - New Section View Style** dialog box is displayed.

6. Choose the **OK** button to accept the default settings in this dialog box.

7. Next, from the **Section view style** drop-down list on the **General** page, select **New Section View Style**, if it is not selected by default.

8. Select the **3+00.0** option from the **Sample line** drop-down list.

9. Next, choose the **Section Display Options** option from the left panel of this wizard; the **Section Display Options** page is displayed.

10. In the **Select sections to draw** list box of the **Section Display Options** page, clear the check box in the **Draw** column for the **corridor 1 Top surface** row to exclude drawing of the top surface of the corridor in the section view.

11. Now, choose the **Create Section View** button; the **Create Section View** wizard is closed and you are prompted to specify the origin of the section view.

12. Click anywhere in the drawing; the section view is created, as shown in Figure 9-35. Press ESC to exit the command.

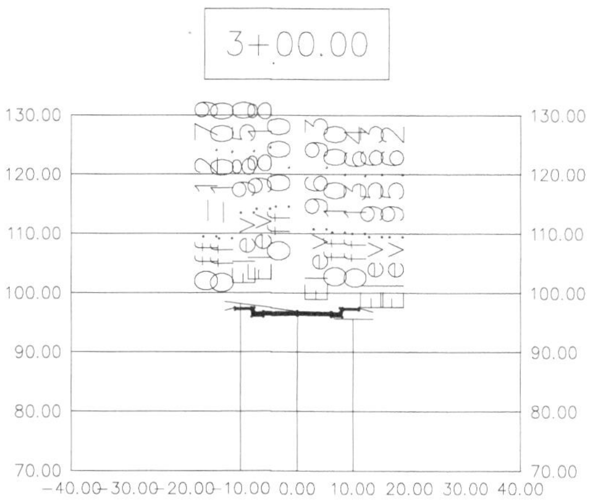

Figure 9-35 The section view created at alignment station **3+00.00**

Editing the Section Label Style

1. Select the section view from the drawing and right-click; a shortcut menu is displayed.
2. Choose **Section View Properties** option from the shortcut menu; the **Section View Properties - Stephen Section** dialog box is displayed,
3. Choose the **Sections** tab from this dialog box, refer to Figure 9-36.
4. Click on **<Edit>** in the **Labels** column corresponding to **Stephen Collection - 3+00.00 - Surface1** (first row); the **Section Labels - Stephen Collection - 3+00.00 - Surface 1(1093)** dialog box is displayed. Make sure that the **Major Offset** and **Basic** options are selected in the **Type** and **Section Major Offset Label Style** drop-down lists, respectively, of the dialog box.
5. Click on the icon displayed in the **Style** column; the **Pick Label Style** dialog box is displayed. 

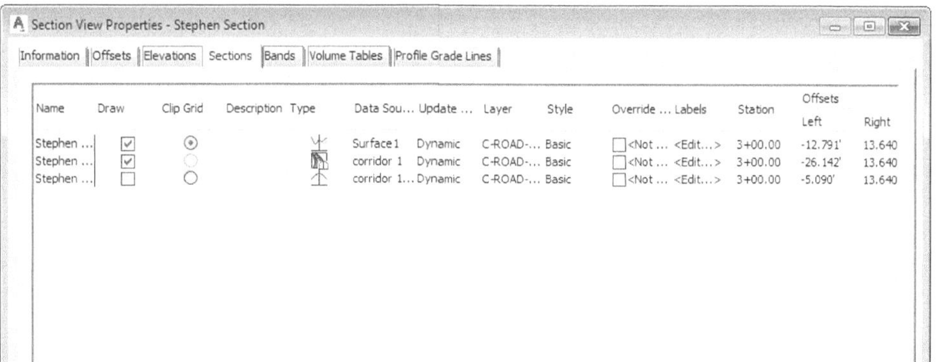

Figure 9-36 Partial view of the options displayed in the ***Sections*** *tab of the* ***Section View Properties - Stephen Section*** *dialog box*

6. Select **Stephen Major** from the drop-down list in the dialog box, as shown in Figure 9-37.

Figure 9-37 *Selecting the* ***Stephen Major*** *option from the drop-down list*

7. Choose the **OK** button; the **Pick Label Style** dialog box is closed.

8. Choose **OK** in the **Section Labels - Stephen Collection - 3+00.00 - Surface1(1093)** dialog box; the dialog box is closed and the **Section View Properties - Stephen Section** dialog box is displayed.

9. Now, choose the **OK** button in the **Section View Properties - Stephen Section** dialog box; the dialog box is closed and the section view is displayed, as shown in Figure 9-38. Similarly, you can create a section view at any station by selecting the required sample line.

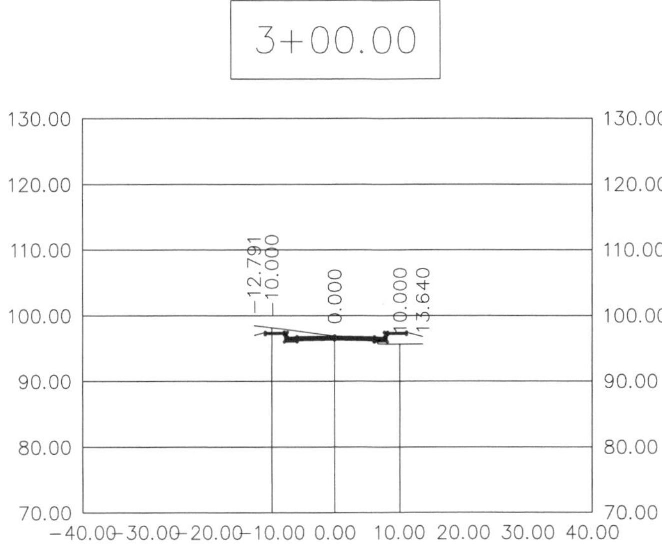

Figure 9-38 *The* ***Stephen Section*** *view created at station* ***3+00.00***

Saving the File

1. Choose **Save As** from the **Application Menu**; the **Save Drawing As** dialog box is displayed.

2. In this dialog box, browse to the following location:

C:\c3d_2018\c09_c3d_2018_tut

3. In the file name edit box, enter **c09_tut01a.**

4. Choose the **Save** button; the file is saved with the name *c09_tut01a.dwg* at the specified location.

Tutorial 2 Multiple Section View

In this tutorial, you will create a Band style and Multiple section views, as shown in Figure 9-39. Also, you will create a plot style to plot views on the sheet. **(Expected time: 1 hr)**

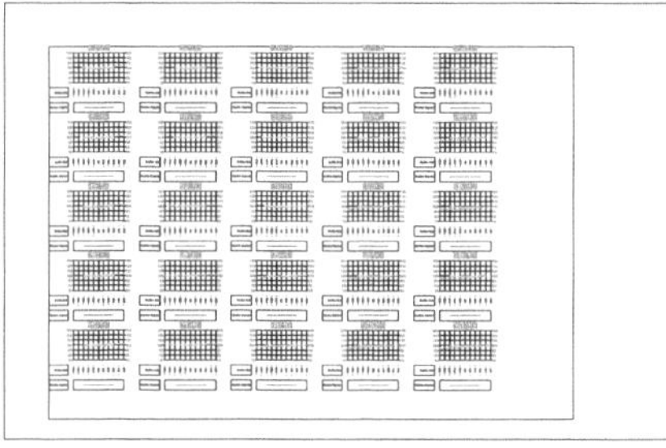

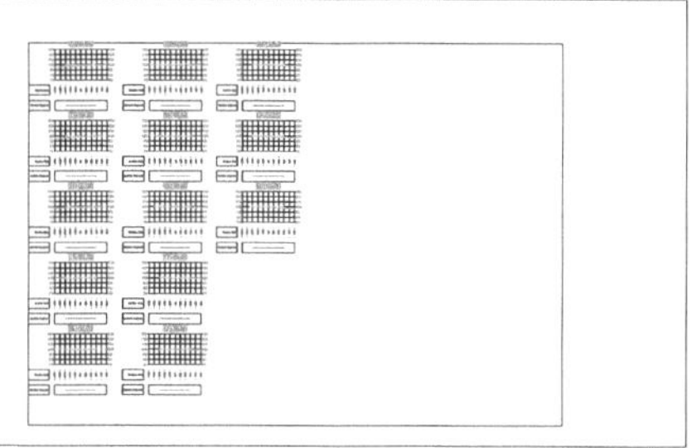

Figure 9-39 *The Band style and Multiple section views*

The following steps are required to complete this tutorial:

a. Download and open the file.
b. Create a section data band style.
c. Create a band set style.
d. Create multiple section views.
e. Create the plot style.
f. Assign the plot style.
g. Save the file.

Opening the File

1. Download the *c09_c3d_2018_tut.zip* file from *http://www.cadcim.com* as explained in Chapter 2.

2. Choose **Open > Drawing** from the **Application Menu**; the **Select File** dialog box is displayed.

3. In the dialog box, browse to the location *C:\c3d_2018\c09_c3d_2018_tut.*

4. Select the file *c09_c3d_2018_tut02.dwg* and then choose the **Open** button to open the file.

This file consists of two alignments, a corridor, two sample line groups, and profile view sections.

Creating the Section Data Band Style

1. Choose the **Settings** tab in the **TOOLSPACE** palette and then expand **Section View > Band Styles > Section Data** in this tab.

2. Right-click on the **Section Data** node; a shortcut menu is displayed.

3. Choose the **New** option from the shortcut menu; the **Section Data Band Style - New Section Data Band Style** dialog box is displayed.

4. In this dialog box, enter **L Street Band Data** in the **Name** edit box of the **Information** tab of this dialog box.

5. Next, choose the **Band Details** tab in this dialog box.

6. Choose the **Compose label** button from the **Title text** area of the **Band Details** tab; the **Label Style Composer - Band Title** dialog box is displayed.

7. Set the following values for the properties in the **Label Style Composer - Band Title** dialog box:

   Name: **Surface1 Elevation** Text Height: **0.0700"** Color: **red**

   Choose the **OK** button; the dialog box is closed.

8. In the **Layout** area of the **Band Details** tab, set the following values:

   Band height: **0.5000"** Text box width: **1.0000"** Offset from band: **0.2500"**

9. In the **Text box position** drop-down list of the **Layout** area, select the **Left of Band** option, if it is not selected by default.

10. Select the **Major Increment** option from the **At** list box in the **Labels and ticks** area, if it is not selected by default.

11. Next, ensure that the **Top** and **Bottom** check boxes are selected and then set the tick sizes for both the top and bottom ticks to **0.0400"**, as shown in Figure 9-40.

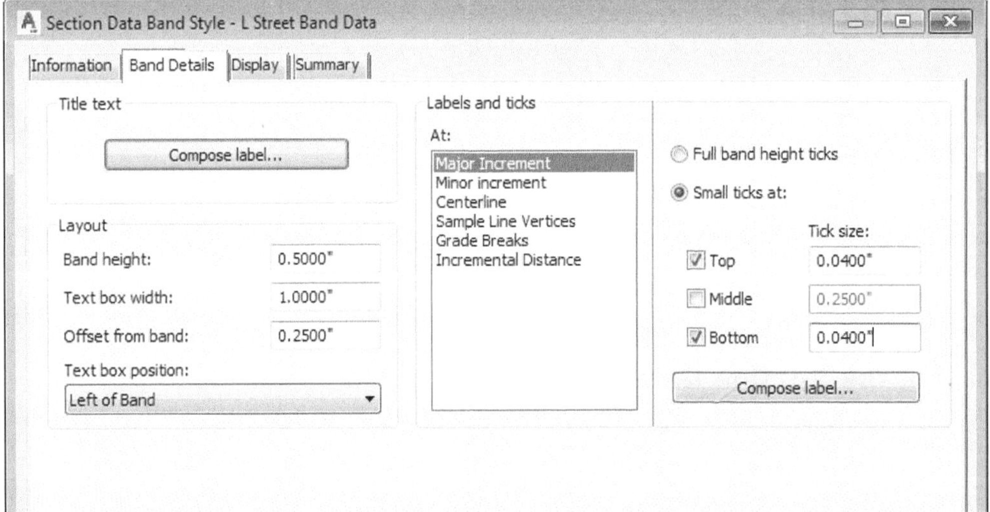

Figure 9-40 *Partial view of the Setting the options in the* ***Band Details*** *tab*

12. Now, choose the **Compose label** button from the **Label and ticks** area; the **Label Style Composer - Major Increment** dialog box is displayed.

13. Click in the **Value** field of the **Contents** property; a browse button is displayed on its right.

14. Choose this button; the **Text Component Editor - Contents** dialog box is displayed.

15. Select and delete the text in the **Editor** window on the right of the dialog box.

16. Next, select **Section1 Elevation** from the **Properties** drop-down list, as shown in Figure 9-41.

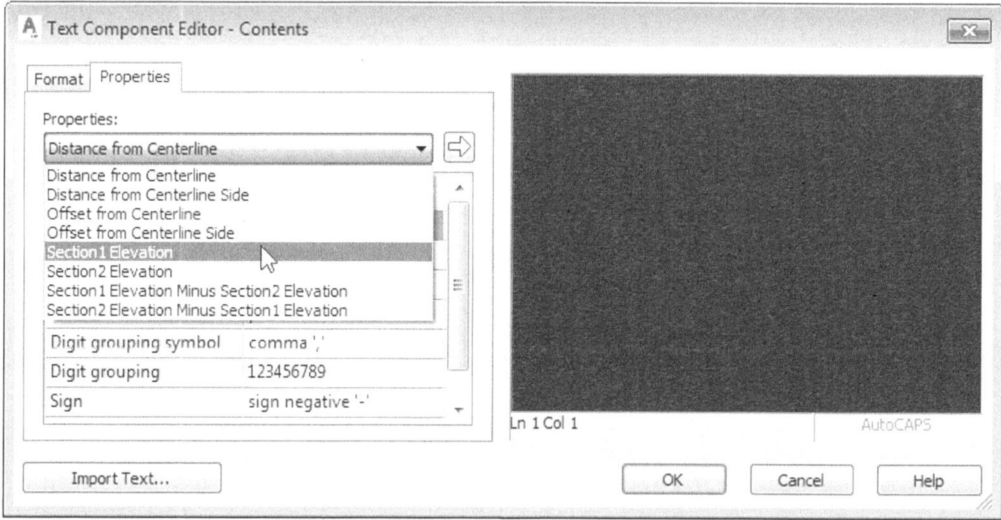

Figure 9-41 *Selecting the* ***Section1 Elevation*** *option from the* ***Properties*** *drop-down list*

17. Choose the arrow button adjacent to the **Properties** drop-down list and then choose the **OK** button to close the **Text Component Editor - Contents** dialog box.

18. In the **Property** column of the **Label Style Composer - Major Increment** dialog box, set the **Text Height** to **0.0500"**, if it is not set by default.

19. Set the **Color** to **red** and then choose the **OK** button from the **Label Style Composer - Major Increment** dialog box to close it; the dialog box is closed.

20. Choose the **OK** button from the **Section Data Band Style - L Street Band Data** dialog box; the dialog box is closed and the **L Street Band Data** style is added to the **Section Data** node in the **Settings** tab.

Creating a Band Set Style

1. Expand **Section View > Band Styles > Band Sets** in the **Settings** tab of the **TOOLSPACE** palette.

2. Right-click on the **Band Sets** sub-node; a shortcut menu is displayed and then choose the **New** option; the **Section View Band Set - New Section View Band Set** dialog box is displayed.

3. Enter **L Street Band Set** in the **Name** edit box of the **Information** tab.

4. Next, choose the **Bands** tab. In this tab, select the **Section Data** option from the **Band type** drop-down list in this dialog box, if it is not selected by default.

5. Next, select the **L Street Band Data** option from the **Select band style** drop-down list.

6. Make sure that the **Bottom of section view** option is selected in the **Location** drop-down list.

7. Choose the **Add** button; the **Section Data** band is added in the **List of bands** area.

8. Now, select the **Section Segment** and **Segment Length** options from the **Band type** and **Select band style** drop-down lists, respectively.

9. Choose the **Add** button; the **Section Segment** band is added to the **Lists of bands** area, refer to Figure 9-42.

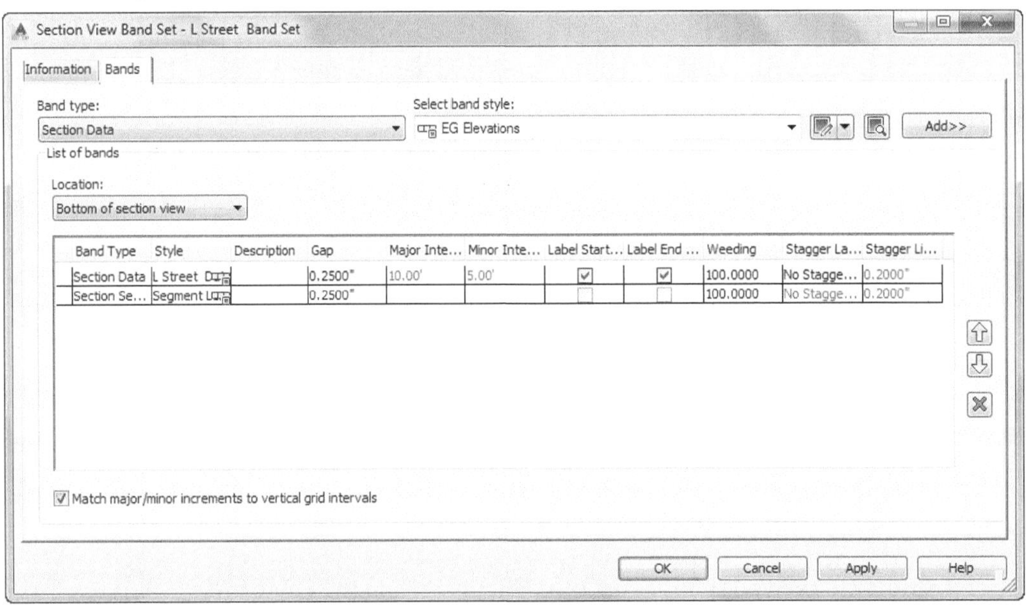

*Figure 9-42 The band type added to the **List of bands** area of the **Bands** tab*

10. Next, choose the **OK** button; the **Section View Band Set - L Street Band Set** dialog box is closed and the **L Street Band Set** style is added to the **Band Sets** node in the **Settings** tab.

Creating Multiple Section Views

1. Choose the **Create Multiple Views** tool from **Home > Profile & Section Views > Section Views** drop-down; the **General** page of the **Create Multiple Section Views** wizard is displayed.

2. In this page, choose the button corresponding to the **Section view name** text box; the **Name Template** dialog box is displayed.

3. Enter **L Street Views** in the **Name** edit box of the dialog box and choose the **OK** button; the **Name Template** dialog box is closed.

4. Now, make sure that the **L Street** alignment and the **L Street SL 1** sample line group are selected from the **Select alignment** and **Sample line group name** drop-down lists, respectively.

5. Accept the default value for the **Section view style**. Next, choose the **Data Bands** option displayed on the left side of the page; the **Data Bands** page of the **Create Multiple Section Views** wizard is displayed.

6. In this page, select the **L Street Band Set** option from the **Select band set** drop-down list, as shown in Figure 9-43.

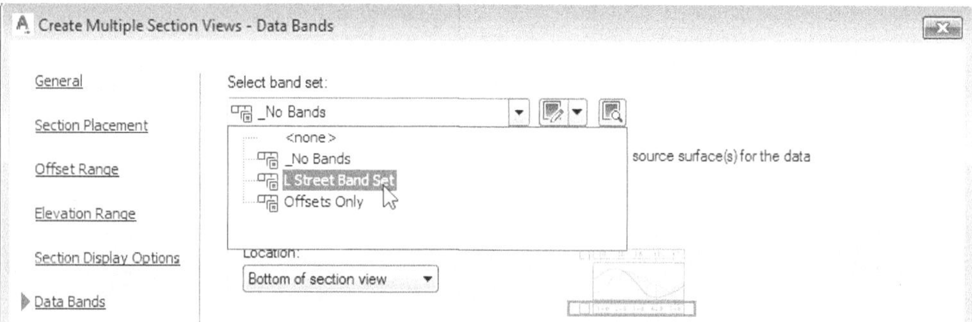

***Figure 9-43** Selecting the **L Street Band Set** style in the **Data Bands** page*

7. Now, choose the **Create Section Views** button; the **Create Multiple Section Views** wizard is closed and you are prompted to identify the **Section view origin**.

8. Click anywhere in the drawing area; multiple section views are created. Next, close the **PANORAMA** window, if it is displayed.

9. Zoom in the section view and the data bands added below each section view, refer to Figure 9-44.

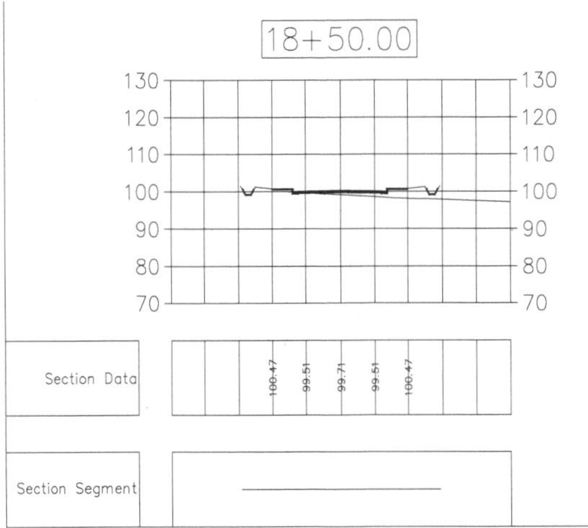

Figure 9-44 Section view and data bands created at station 18+50.00

Creating the Plot Style

1. Choose the **Settings** tab from the **TOOLSPACE** palette and expand **Section View > Group Plot Styles** in the **Settings** tab; the existing plot style is displayed in the **Group Plot Styles** sub-node.

2. Select the **Group Plot Styles** node and right-click on it; a shortcut menu is displayed.

3. Choose the **New** option from the shortcut menu, as shown in Figure 9-45; the **Group Plot Style - New Group Plot Style** dialog box is displayed.

4. Enter **L Street Plot** in the **Name** edit box of the **Information** tab.

5. Now, choose the **Array** tab and select the **By columns** radio button from the **Plot rules** area.

6. Select the **Upper Left** option from the **Start corner** drop-down list and the **Left** option from the **Align section views about** drop-down list.

7. In the **Space between adjacent section views** area, enter **0.5000"** in the **Column** and **Row** edit boxes.

8. Now, choose the **OK** button; the **Group Plot Style - L Street Plot** dialog box is closed and the **L Street Plot** style is added to the **Group Plot Styles** sub-node in the **Settings** tab.

Assigning the Plot Style

1. Select any of the multiple section views from the drawing and right-click; a shortcut menu is displayed.

2. Choose the **Section View Group Properties** option from the shortcut menu, as shown in Figure 9-46; the **Section View Group Properties - Section View Group - 3** dialog box is displayed.

Figure 9-45 Choosing the ***New*** *option from the shortcut menu*

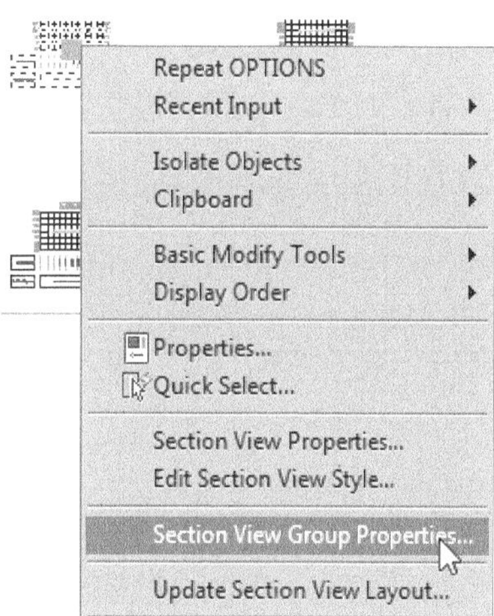

Figure 9-46 Choosing the ***Section View Group Properties*** *option*

3. Choose the **Section Views** tab and click on the **Plot By Page** value in the **Group Plot Style** column; the **Pick Section view group plot style** dialog box is displayed.

4. Select the **L Street Plot** option from the drop-down list in this dialog box.

5. Next, choose the **OK** button; the **Pick Section view group plot style** dialog box is closed.

6. Choose the **OK** button from the **Section View Group Properties - Section View Group - 3** dialog box; the dialog box is closed and multiple section views are displayed, as shown in Figure 9-47.

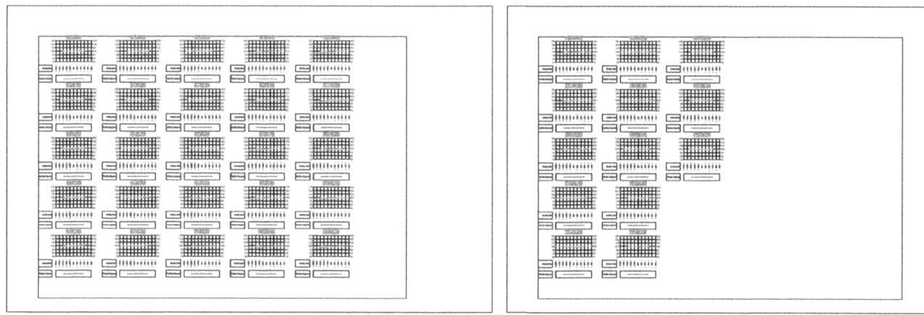

Figure 9-47 Multiple section views displayed after applying the L Street Plot style

Saving the File

1. Choose **Save As** from the **Application Menu**; the **Save Drawing As** dialog box is displayed.

2. In this dialog box, browse to the following location:

   C:\c3d_2018\c09_c3d_2018_tut

3. In the file name edit box, enter **c09_tut02a**.

4. Choose the **Save** button; the file is saved with the name *c09_tut02a.dwg* at the specified location.

Tutorial 3 Quantity Takeoffs

In this tutorial, you will create a material list and then set the criteria for the cut and fill volumes, and material takeoffs. Also, you will generate a volume and material report and add the volume table in the drawing, as shown in Figure 9-48. **(Expected time: 30 min)**

Total Volume Table						
Station	Fill Area	Cut Area	Fill Volume	Cut Volume	Cumulative Fill Vol	Cumulative Cut Vol
0+50.00	108.67	0.46	0.00	0.00	0.00	0.00
1+00.00	146.25	0.00	236.04	0.42	236.04	0.42
1+50.00	153.11	0.00	277.19	0.00	513.23	0.42
2+00.00	136.97	0.00	252.02	0.00	765.25	0.42
2+50.00	130.05	0.00	238.39	0.00	1003.64	0.42
3+00.00	102.42	0.04	207.32	0.04	1210.96	0.46
3+50.00	98.48	1.47	173.71	1.73	1384.68	2.19
4+00.00	92.40	0.97	176.75	2.26	1561.42	4.46
4+50.00	69.11	2.39	149.55	3.11	1710.97	7.57
5+00.00	79.32	1.41	137.43	3.51	1848.40	11.08
5+50.00	105.03	0.17	170.69	1.47	2019.09	12.55
6+00.00	62.96	1.31	155.55	1.38	2174.64	13.92
6+50.00	64.01	0.96	115.63	2.45	2290.27	16.38
7+00.00	35.05	17.04	88.35	19.69	2378.63	36.07
7+50.00	21.03	21.65	48.10	41.73	2426.72	77.81
8+00.00	11.11	38.55	24.66	70.13	2451.38	147.94
8+50.00	18.61	34.94	27.51	68.05	2478.89	215.99
9+00.00	17.17	40.26	33.13	69.64	2512.02	285.63
9+50.00	9.05	59.28	24.28	92.17	2536.31	377.79
10+00.00	5.77	80.10	13.72	129.05	2550.03	506.85

Figure 9-48** The **Total Volume Table

The following steps are required to complete this tutorial:

a. Download and open the file.
b. Set the criteria for quantity takeoff
c. Create a material list for the calculation of materials.
d. Compute the materials.
e. Generate a volume report.
f. Generate a material report.
g. Add the material table in the drawing.
h. Save the file.

Downloading and Opening the File

1. Download the *c09_c3d_2018_tut.zip* file from *http://www.cadcim.com*, if you have not downloaded it as explained in Chapter 2.

2. Choose **Open > Drawing** from the **Application Menu**; the **Select File** dialog box is displayed.

3. In the dialog box, browse to the location *C:\c3d_2018\c09_c3d_2018_tut*.

4. Select the file *c09_c3d_2018_tut03.dwg* and then choose the **Open** button to open the file.

The drawing file consists of a corridor, a profile view, and an assembly. It also consists of an existing surface, corridor surfaces, a profile view, multiple section views, and a pipe trench assembly.

Ignore any error messages if displayed in the **PANORAMA** window while opening the drawing file.

Setting the Criteria for the Quantity Takeoff

1. Choose the **Settings** tab in the **TOOLSPACE** palette and then expand **Quantity Takeoff > Quantity Takeoff Criteria** in this tab.

2. Right-click on the **Quantity Takeoff Criteria** node; a shortcut menu is displayed.

3. Choose the **New** option from the shortcut menu; the **Quantity Takeoff Criteria - New Quantity Takeoff Criteria** dialog box is displayed.

4. Enter **Cut and Fill Criteria** in the **Name** edit box of the **Information** tab.

5. Now, choose the **Material List** tab.

6. In the **Material List** tab, choose the **Material Name Template** button placed next to the **Add new material** button; the **Name Template** dialog box is displayed.

7. Enter **Surface Cut** in the **Name** edit box of the **Name Template** dialog box and choose the **OK** button; the **Name Template** dialog box is closed.

8. Now, choose the **Add new material** button in the **Material List** tab; **Surface Cut** is added in the **Material Name** column. Next, make sure that quantity type is set to **Cut** in the **Quantity Type** column.

9. In the **Define material** area of the **Material List** tab, ensure that the **Surface** option is selected in the **Data type** drop-down list. Also, select the **Surface1** option from the **Select surface** drop-down list, as shown in Figure 9-49.

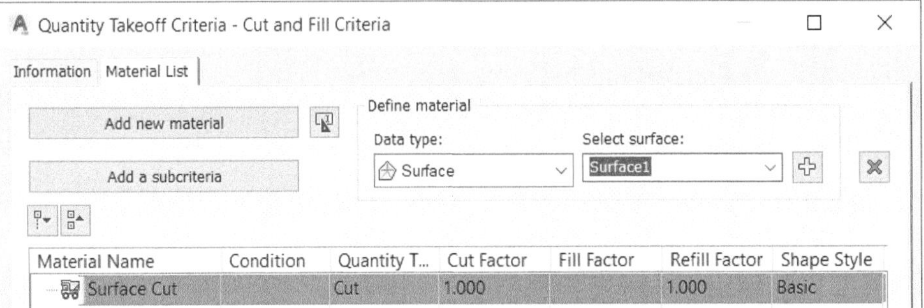

*Figure 9-49 Selecting the **Surface1** option from the **Select surface** drop-down list*

10. Now, choose the button next to the **Select surface** drop-down list; the selected surface is added to the **Material Name** column. 

11. Next, select the **L Street-Datum** option from the **Select surface** drop-down list and add the surface to the **Material Name** column.

12. For **Surface1**, ensure that the condition is set to **Above** in the **Condition** column for calculating the volume of the surface to be removed.

13. For the **L Street-Datum** surface, click on the default value in the **Condition** column and select **Below** from the drop-down list displayed.

14. Now, repeat the procedure followed in steps 6 through 13 and add a new material, **Surface Fill** in the **Material Name** column with quantity type set to **Fill** in the **Quantity Type** column.

15. Set the parameters for the different surfaces in the **Condition** column of the **Quantity Takeoff Criteria - Cut and Fill Criteria** dialog box, as shown in Figure 9-50.

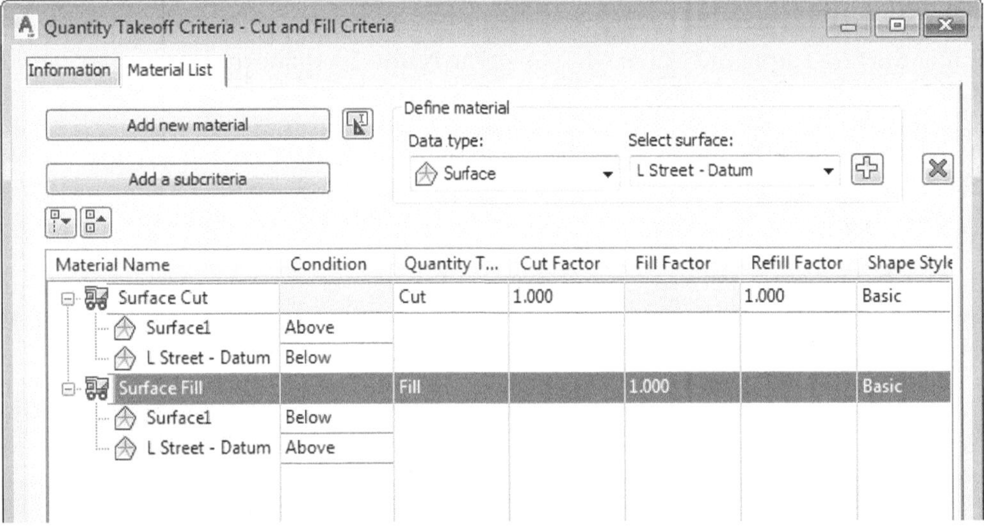

*Figure 9-50 Partial view of the **Quantity Takeoff Criteria - Cut and Fill Criteria** dialog box*

Creating Material Quantity Take Off Criteria

1. In the **Quantity Takeoff Criteria - Cut and Fill Criteria** dialog box, choose the **Material Name Template** button; the **Name Template** dialog box is displayed.

2. Enter **Concrete In Ditch** in the **Name** edit box and choose the **OK** button; the **Name Template** dialog box is closed.

3. In the **Quantity Takeoff Criteria - Cut and Fill Criteria** dialog box, choose the **Add new material** button; the material name is added to the list.

4. Click on the **Cut** option in the **Quantity Type** column and then select the **Structures** option from the drop-down list displayed.

5. Select the **Corridor Shape** option from the **Data type** drop-down list.

6. Next, select the **Ditch** option from the **Select corridor shape** drop-down list.

7. Choose the **Add** button from the **Define material** area in the **Material List** tab; the selected data type and the corridor shape are added under the **Concrete In Ditch** material.

8. Repeat the procedure followed in steps 1 through 5 to add another items to the material list and name them as **Concrete In Sidewalk**, **Concrete In Curb**, and **Asphalt**.

9. Select the **Sidewalk**, **Curb**, and **Pavel** options from the **Select corridor shape** drop-down list, refer to Figure 9-51, and add it to the **Concrete In Sidewalk**, **Concrete In Curb**, and **Asphalt** materials, respectively, as explained earlier.

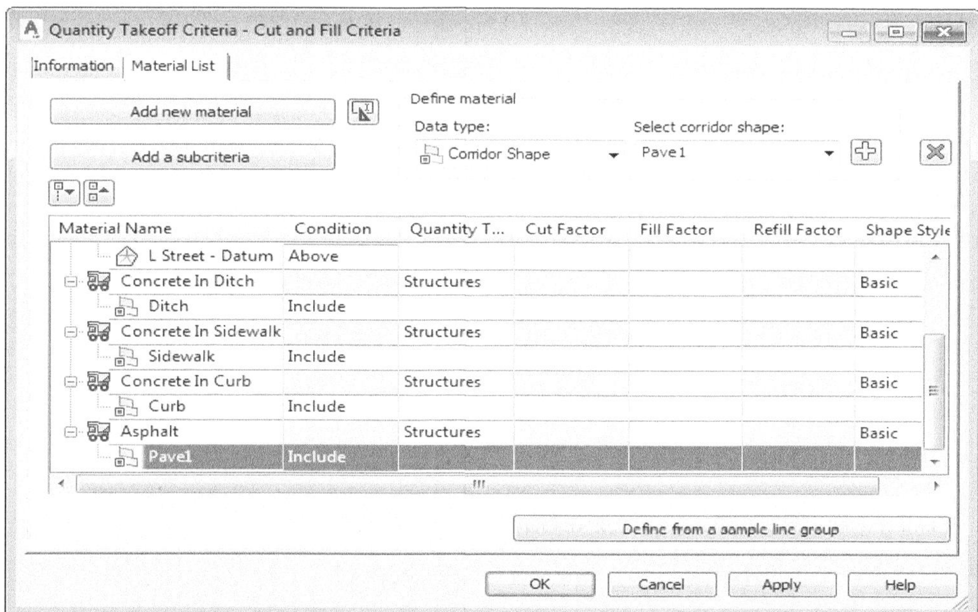

*Figure 9-51 The **Sidewalk**, **Curb**, and **Pavel** options selected in the **Quantity Takeoff Criteria - Cut and Fill Criteria** dialog box*

10. Now, choose the **OK** button in the **Quantity Takeoff Criteria - Cut and Fill Criteria** dialog box; the dialog box is closed and the takeoff criteria is added to the **Quantity Takeoff Criteria** node.

Computing Materials

1. Choose **Compute Materials** tool from the **Volumes and Materials** panel of the **Analyze** tab; the **Select a Sample Line Group** dialog box is displayed.

2. Make sure that the **L Street** alignment and the **L Street SL 1** option are selected from the **Select alignment** and **Select sample line group** drop-down lists, respectively, of the dialog box.

3. Next, choose the **OK** button; the **Compute Materials - L Street SL 1** dialog box is displayed.

4. Select the **Cut and Fill Criteria** option from the **Quantity takeoff criteria** drop-down list.

5. Now, choose the **Map objects with same name** button in the **Compute Materials - L Street SL 1** dialog box; the surface and corridor shapes are mapped automatically with the same name, as shown in Figure 9-52.

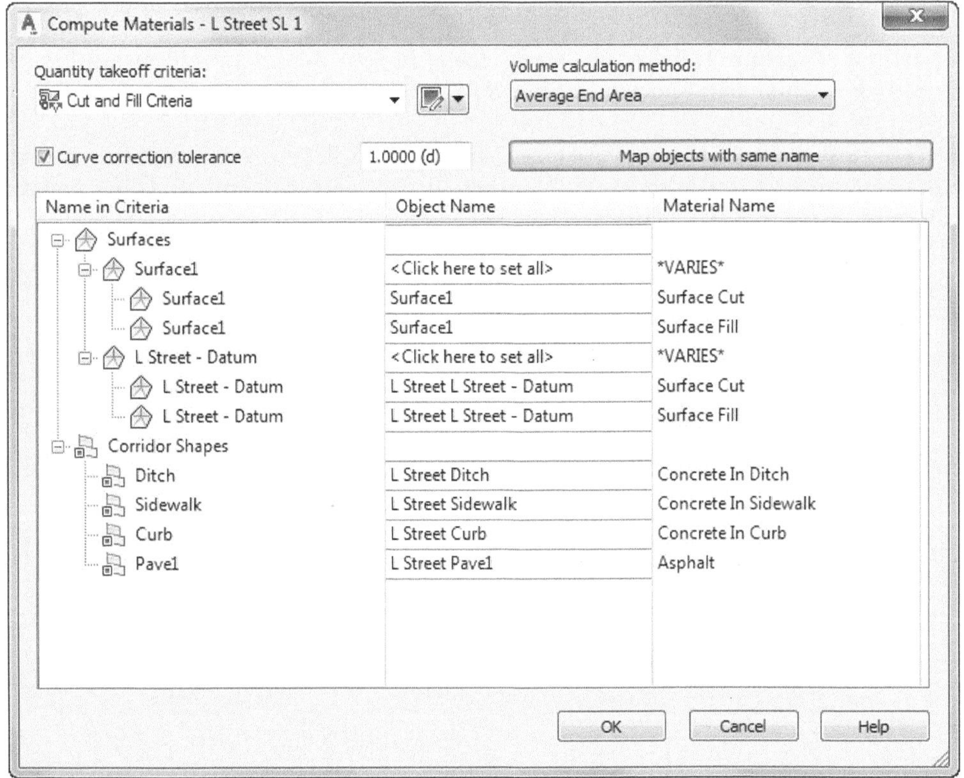

Figure 9-52 The ***Compute Materials - L Street SL 1*** *dialog box displaying takeoff criteria*

6. Choose the **OK** button in the **Compute Materials - L Street SL 1** dialog box; the dialog box is closed and the materials are computed.

7. Close the **PANORAMA** window, if any displayed.

Generating the Volume Report

1. Choose the **Volume Report** tool from the **Volumes and Materials** panel of the **Analyze** tab; the **Report Quantities** dialog box is displayed. 

2. Ensure that the **L Street**, **L Street SL 1**, and **Material List - (1)** options are selected from the **Select alignment**, **Select sample line group**, and **Select material list** drop-down lists, respectively.

3. Next, choose the button adjacent to the **Select a style sheet** edit box; the **Select Style Sheet** dialog box is displayed. 

4. Select the *earthwork.xsl* sheet style from this dialog box and choose the **Open** button; the **Select Style Sheet** dialog box is closed.

5. Now, choose the **OK** button from the **Report Quantities** dialog box; the dialog box is closed and the **Internet Explorer** message box is displayed, as shown in Figure 9-53.

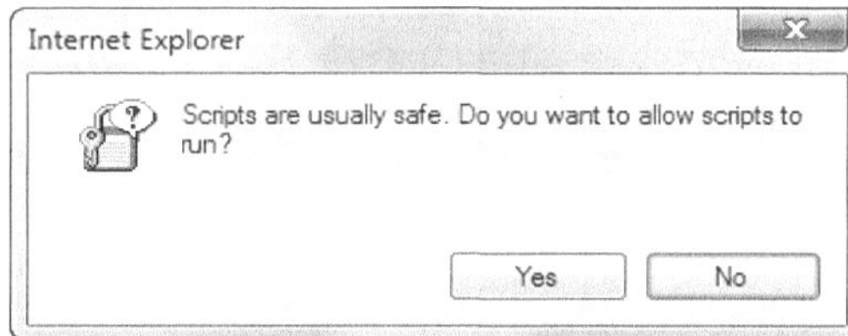

Figure 9-53 *The* ***Internet Explorer*** *message box*

6. Choose the **Yes** button; the message box is closed and the volume report is generated, as shown in Figure 9-54.

Volume Report

Project: C:\Users\TIET\appdata\local\temp\c09_c3d_2018_tut03_1_25073_5629.sv$
Alignment: L Street
Sample Line Group: L Street SL 1
Start Sta: 0+50.000
End Sta: 19+00.000

Station	Cut Area (Sq.ft.)	Cut Volume (Cu.yd.)	Reusable Volume (Cu.yd.)	Fill Area (Sq.ft.)	Fill Volume (Cu.yd.)	Cum. Cut Vol. (Cu.yd.)	Cum. Reusable Vol. (Cu.yd.)	Cum. Fill Vol. (Cu.yd.)	Cum. Net Vol. (Cu.yd.)
0+50.000	0.46	0.00	0.00	108.67	0.00	0.00	0.00	0.00	0.00
1+00.000	0.00	0.42	0.42	146.25	236.04	0.42	0.42	236.04	-235.61

Figure 9-54 *Partial view of the generated volume report*

Generating the Material Report

1. Repeat the procedure followed in steps 1 through 3 mentioned in the previous section.

2. Select the *Select Material.xsl* sheet style from the **Select Style Sheet** dialog box and choose the **Open** button.

3. Now, choose the **OK** button from the **Report Quantities** dialog box; the dialog box is closed and the **Internet Explorer** message box is displayed.

4. Choose the **Yes** button from the message box; the message box is closed and the material report is generated, as shown in Figure 9-55.

Material Report

Project: C:\Users\TIET\appdata\local\temp\c09_c3d_2018_tut03_1_25073_5629.sv$
Alignment: L Street
Sample Line Group: L Street SL 1
Start Sta: 0+50.000
End Sta: 19+00.000

	Area Type	Area	Inc.Vol.	Cum.Vol.
		Sq.ft.	Cu.yd.	Cu.yd.
Station: 0+50.000				
	Surface Cut	0.46	0.00	0.00
	Surface Fill	108.67	0.00	0.00
	Concrete In Ditch	3.30	0.00	0.00
	Concrete In Sidewalk	4.00	0.00	0.00
	Concrete In Curb	3.98	0.00	0.00
	Asphalt	16.08	0.00	0.00
Station: 1+00.000				
	Surface Cut	0.00	0.42	0.42

Figure 9-55 *Partial view of the generated material report*

Adding Tables

1. Choose the **Total Volume Table** tool from the **Volumes and Materials** panel of the **Analyze** tab; the **Create Total Volume Table** dialog box is displayed.

2. Choose the **OK** button in this dialog box; you are prompted to specify the upper left corner.

3. Click at the location in the drawing; the **Total Volume Table** is created, as shown in Figure 9-56.

Saving the File

1. Choose **Save As** from the **Application Menu**; the **Save Drawing As** dialog box is displayed.

2. In this dialog box, browse to the following location:

   C:\c3d_2018\c09_c3d_2018_tut

Total Volume Table						
Station	Fill Area	Cut Area	Fill Volume	Cut Volume	Cumulative Fill Vol	Cumulative Cut Vol
0+50.00	108.67	0.46	0.00	0.00	0.00	0.00
1+00.00	146.25	0.00	236.04	0.42	236.04	0.42
1+50.00	153.11	0.00	277.19	0.00	513.23	0.42
2+00.00	136.97	0.00	252.02	0.00	765.25	0.42
2+50.00	130.05	0.00	238.39	0.00	1003.64	0.42
3+00.00	102.42	0.04	207.32	0.04	1210.96	0.46
3+50.00	98.48	1.47	173.71	1.73	1384.68	2.19
4+00.00	92.40	0.97	176.75	2.26	1561.42	4.46
4+50.00	69.11	2.39	149.55	3.11	1710.97	7.57
5+00.00	79.32	1.41	137.43	3.51	1848.40	11.08
5+50.00	105.03	0.17	170.69	1.47	2019.09	12.55
6+00.00	62.96	1.31	155.55	1.38	2174.64	13.92
6+50.00	64.01	0.96	115.63	2.45	2290.27	16.38
7+00.00	35.05	17.04	88.35	19.69	2378.63	36.07
7+50.00	21.03	21.65	48.10	41.73	2426.72	77.81
8+00.00	11.11	38.55	24.66	70.13	2451.38	147.94
8+50.00	18.61	34.94	27.51	68.05	2478.89	215.99
9+00.00	17.17	40.26	33.13	69.64	2512.02	285.63
9+50.00	9.05	59.28	24.28	92.17	2536.31	377.79
10+00.00	5.77	80.10	13.72	129.05	2550.03	506.85

*Figure 9-56 The **Total Volume Table***

3. In the file name edit box, enter **c09_tut03a**.

4. Choose the **Save** button; the file is saved with the name *c09_tut03a.dwg* at the specified location.

Self-Evaluation Test

Answer the following questions and then compare them to those given at the end of this chapter:

1. Which of the following tools is used to create sample lines along a given length of an alignment?

   a) **By range of stations** b) **At a station**
   c) **From corridor stations** d) **Pick points on screen**

2. Which of the following tabs in the **Sample Line Group Properties** dialog box is used to view and edit the material lists for a sample line group and also add and delete materials from the list?

   a) **Section Views** b) **Material List**
   c) **Sections** d) **Sample Lines**

3. Which of the following tools is used to display the view of an existing ground and corridor across a given alignment along a given line?

   a) **Create Multiple Views** b) **Create Profile View**
   c) **Create Section View** d) **Create Multiple Profile Views**

4. Which of the following tools is used to change the properties of the sample line group in the **Sample Line Tools** toolbar?

   a) **Create sample line group** b) **Edit group defaults**
   c) **Delete current group** d) **Select group from drawing**

5. To create a cross section in an AutoCAD Civil 3D drawing, you need at least an alignment and a __________.

6. A __________ is a Civil 3D object used to cut sections across an alignment or any linear feature.

7. The __________tool is used to create sample lines by specifying the station range.

8. The __________ dialog box is used to add labels to section views.

9. The __________ dialog box is used to create a new group plot style.

10. The **Edit Sections** option is used to edit the sections whose update mode is set to __________.

11. A sample line consists of a linear feature and a sample line label. (T/F)

12. To create sample lines, choose the **Sample Lines** tool from the **Profile & Section Views** panel of the **Home** tab. (T/F)

13. Sample lines are created using the **Sample Layout Tools** toolbar. (T/F)

14. You can create multiple section views using the **Create Section View** wizard. (T/F)

Review Questions

Answer the following questions:

1. The __________ dialog box is used to select sources or elements to be sampled by sample lines.

2. The _________ tab is used to edit properties of sections that are included in the selected sample line group.

3. The __________ dialog box is used to select and then edit the sample line parameters.

4. The ________ is a set of data bands that display the band style of the section view.

5. The Earthwork takeoff represents the amount of total material to be added or removed from the existing site. (T/F)

6. Civil 3D allows you to calculate only Earthwork Takeoffs. (T/F)

7. To compute quantity takeoffs for earthworks and material volumes, you need to define the quantity takeoffs criteria. (T/F)

8. Volume report displays material volumes. (T/F)

9. Section views are the graphical representation of elevation data or an assembly (in case of corridor sections) placed at a particular station. (T/F)

10. You can create multiple groups of sample lines for single alignment. (T/F)

EXERCISE

1. Log on to *www.cadcim.com* and browse to *Textbooks > Civil/GIS > Civil 3D > Exploring AutoCAD Civil 3D 2018*. Next, select *c09_c3d_2018_exer.zip* file from the **Exercise Files** drop-down list. Choose the corresponding **Download** button to download the data file.

2. Now, save and extract the downloaded folder to the following location:

   C:\c3d_2018

Note

*While opening the exercise files, the **PANORAMA** window may appear with an error message. Close this window to proceed further.*

Exercise 1

Open the *c09_c3d_2018_ex01.dwg* file and create a group plot style and multiple section views, as shown in Figure 9-57. **(Expected time: 30 min)**

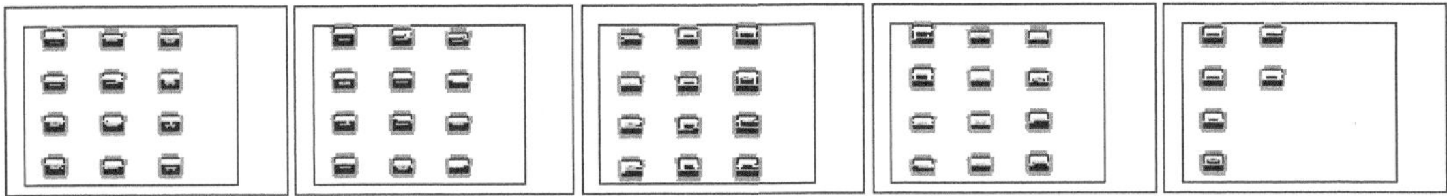

Figure 9-57 *Multiple section views*

Use the following settings for the group plot style:

- Maximum in a row: **7**
- Space between adjacent sections in a row and column: **2.0000"**
- Save the drawing as *c09_ex_01a.dwg*
- Accept the default values for all other options

Answers to Self-Evaluation Test

1. a, **2.** b, **3.** c, **4.** b, **5.** Surface, **6.** Sample line, **7. By range of stations**, **8. Add Labels**, **9. Group Plot Style**, **10. Static**, **11.** T, **12.** T, **13.** T, **14.** F

Chapter 10

Feature Lines and Grading

Learning Objectives

After completing this chapter, you will be able to:

- *Create feature lines*
- *Edit feature lines*
- *Work with feature line properties and styles*
- *Understand grading objects and grading groups*
- *Understand grading criteria sets*
- *Create grading and grading styles*
- *Edit grading*
- *Apply grading styles and properties*

OVERVIEW

A feature line is a Civil 3D object that is used to represent important features in a drawing such as ridge line and pavement edges. Feature lines are essentially 3D polylines with some additional properties and data that a polyline does not possess. In the grading process, the feature lines are used to create a closed or open geometric figure (Footprint) to which the grading criteria can be applied.

Grading is a process of modeling finished ground. In this process, you add surfaces to the site at different elevations and slopes to achieve the required level of surface. This process is carried out throughout the design process. For example, at the initial stage of site development, rough grading is done by the planner to verify the proposed site plans. After verifying the site plan, the rough grading data is used to estimate the required design road grades by creating the grading objects and groups, baseline geometry, and surfaces. Finally, the grading of finished ground is done to ensure that the maximum and minimum slope criteria are fulfilled.

Grading objects and feature lines are two main prerequisites for completing a grading process. While the grading groups are created using the grading layout tools, the features lines are created using feature lines tool. Before you proceed further with the grading process, you need to understand the concept of feature line object as well as different tools associated with it.

FEATURE LINES

Feature lines can be created by using various feature line tools. You can use these tools to create feature lines or convert existing polylines, lines, arcs, and 3D polylines into feature lines. You can also create feature lines using corridor, alignments, and stepped offset. The feature line tools can be accessed from the **Feature Line** drop-down in the **Create Design** panel of the **Home** tab. Figure 10-1 shows various tools in the **Feature Line** drop-down.

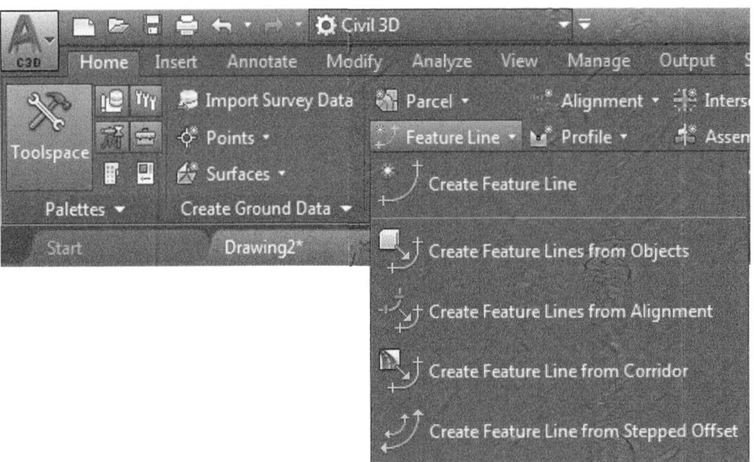

Figure 10-1 *Various tools in the* ***Feature Line*** *drop-down*

Creating Feature Lines by Using the Create Feature Line Tool

Ribbon: Home > Create Design > Feature Line drop-down > Create Feature Line
Command: DRAWFEATURELINE

The **Create Feature Line** tool is used to create straight or curved segments as feature lines. To do so, choose the **Create Feature Line** tool from the **Create Design** panel; the **Create Feature Lines** dialog box will be displayed, as shown in Figure 10-2.

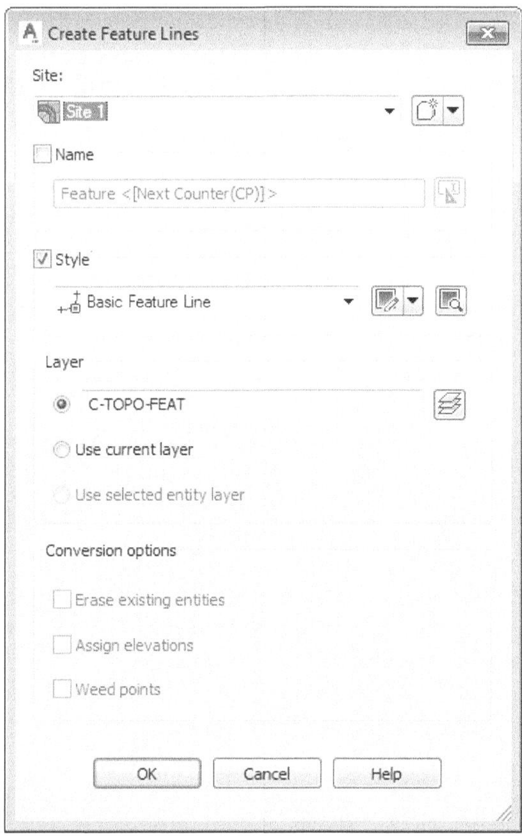

***Figure 10-2** The **Create Feature Lines** dialog box*

You can specify the settings for creating the feature lines in this dialog box. Select the site at which you need to create the feature lines from the **Site** drop-down list. Alternatively, choose the down arrow on the right of the drop-down list; a flyout will be displayed. Choose the **Pick from Drawing** option from the flyout to select the site graphically from the drawing. Next, select the **Name** check box and choose the **Click to edit name template** button on its right; the **Name Template** dialog box will be displayed. In this dialog box, enter the name of the feature line in the **Name** edit box and choose the **OK** button; the **Name Template** dialog box will be closed. If you do not want to name all feature lines to be created, clear the **Name** check box and select it only when you want to name them.

The **Style** area is used to specify the style settings for the feature line. To assign a style to the feature line, select the **Style** check box; the options in the **Style** area will be activated. By default, the **Basic Feature Line** option is selected in the drop-down list below the **Style** check box. You can select the required style for the feature line from the options displayed in this drop-down list. Clear the **Style** check box, if you do not want to assign any style to the feature line.

The **Layer** area is used to display the default layer on which the feature line will be created. The default layer selected is **C-TOPO-FEAT**. To modify the layer, choose the button on the right of the **Layer** area; the **Object Layer** dialog box will be displayed. You can use this dialog box to select a new layer on which the feature line will be created. In the **Layer** area of the **Create Feature Lines** dialog box, you can select the **Use current layer** radio button to create the feature line on the current layer used in the drawing. The **Use selected entity layer** radio button will be activated only when you are creating the feature line from the objects. You can select this radio button to create the feature line on the same layer as that of the object from which it is created.

There are three check boxes available in the **Conversion options** area. These check boxes are used to define the conversion options for a feature line created from an object. The check boxes will be enabled only if you invoke the **Create Feature Lines** dialog box by choosing the **Create Feature Lines from Objects** tool. The **Erase existing entities** option is used to specify whether the object from which the feature line is created is to be retained or deleted. You can select the **Assign elevations** check box to assign the elevation to the converted feature line. You can select the **Weed points** check box to weed the points in the resulting feature line.

After specifying various parameters in the **Create Feature Lines** dialog box, choose the **OK** button; the dialog box will be closed and you will be prompted to specify the start point in the command line. Click at the required location in the drawing to specify the point. On doing so, you will be prompted to specify the elevation for the point. Enter the point elevation in the command line and press ENTER. Alternatively, to assign the point elevation obtained from the surface, enter **S** in the command line. Note that a numeric value is displayed in the command line which is the elevation of the surface at the specified point. To accept this value, press ENTER; the elevation value will be assigned to the feature line. By entering the elevation value in the command line, you can create a straight feature line or a curved feature line. The procedure to create straight and curve feature line is described next.

Note

If your drawing contains more than one surface then on entering **S** *in the command line, the* ***Select Surface*** *dialog box will be displayed. You can select the required surface that you want to take as reference from this dialog box.*

Creating a Straight Feature Line

On entering the elevation value in the command line, you will be prompted to specify the next point or the arc. Click in the drawing to specify the next point; you will be prompted to specify the grade or Slope/Elevation/Difference/Surface/Transition. While specifying points for the feature line, you can change parameters for creating feature lines by using the following shortcuts:

a. Enter **G** in the command line to add a grade between the first and the second point of the feature line.

b. Enter **SL** in the command line to specify the slope parameter and press ENTER. Enter the required slope value and press ENTER again.

c. Enter **E** in the command line to specify the elevation parameter and press ENTER. Specify the required elevation value and press ENTER again.

d. Enter **D** in the command line for the elevation difference and press ENTER. Enter the required elevation difference between the first and second points and then press ENTER.

e. Enter **SU** in the command line to specify surface elevation and press ENTER. Select the surface to obtain elevation from the drawing. After you have specified the points, press ENTER to end the command.

Creating a Curved Feature Line

To create a curved feature line, enter **A** in the command line when you are prompted to specify the next point or arc and then press ENTER. On doing so, you will be prompted to specify the arc second point or direction. Click in the drawing to specify the second point of the arc. Once you have specified the arc points, you will be prompted to specify the elevation for the points. Specify the elevation value of the arc points by choosing any of the options discussed earlier and press ENTER to end the command; the curved feature line will be created.

Editing Feature Lines

Civil 3D provides you with different tools to help edit the elevation/grade and the geometry of a feature line. The feature lines can also be edited by using the grip editing method. Some of the methods used to edit the feature line elevations are discussed next.

Editing Elevations by Using the Elevation Editor

Ribbon: Modify > Edit Elevations > Elevation Editor
Command: GRADINGELEVEDITOR

You can change the elevations of the feature lines by using the options in the **Grading Elevation Editor** tab of the **PANORAMA** window. To invoke the **PANORAMA** window with the **Grading Elevation Editor** tab chosen, choose the **Elevation Editor** tool from the **Edit Elevations** panel of the **Modify** tab; you will be prompted to select the object. Select the required feature line from the drawing; the **PANORAMA** window with the **Grading Elevation Editor** tab chosen will be displayed, refer to Figure 10-3.

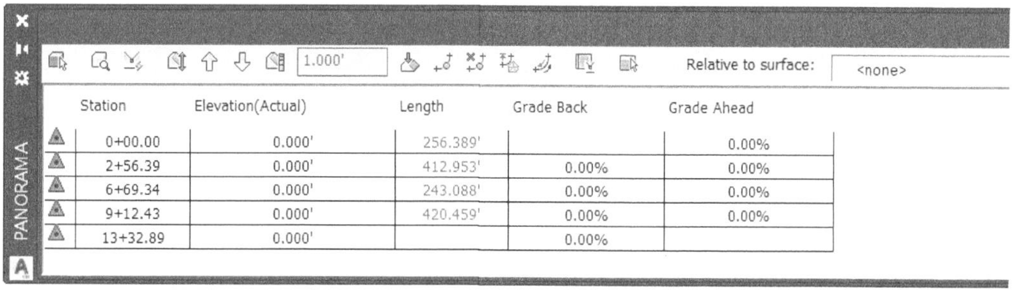

Station	Elevation(Actual)	Length	Grade Back	Grade Ahead
0+00.00	0.000'	256.389'		0.00%
2+56.39	0.000'	412.953'	0.00%	0.00%
6+69.34	0.000'	243.088'	0.00%	0.00%
9+12.43	0.000'	420.459'	0.00%	0.00%
13+32.89	0.000'		0.00%	

Figure 10-3 *The* ***PANORAMA*** *window with the* ***Grading Elevation Editor*** *tab*

In the **PANORAMA** window, the vertices of the feature lines are displayed in the **Station** column and the symbols on the left of these points indicate their type, refer to Figure 10-3. The green colored triangular symbols represent the major horizontal geometry points such as the vertices of the feature lines. The green colored triangular symbol with a + sign represents a common point between the two feature lines. The white colored triangular symbol with a + sign indicates the intersection point of two feature lines. The **Elevation** column displays the elevation of all the feature line points. To edit the elevation of points, double-click in the **Elevation** column and edit the elevation value.

Note

You cannot edit the elevation value of the intersection point of two feature lines in the ***Elevation*** *column in the* ***Grading Elevation Editor*** *tab of the* ***PANORAMA*** *window.*

The **Length** column displays the length of the selected feature line segments. The **Grade Ahead** column specifies the grade of the selected segment in the forward direction. To change the grade of the selected station, double-click in the **Grade Ahead** column and then edit the values. On doing so, the elevation value of the second point of the feature line will be modified in the **Elevation** column. The **Grade Back** column specifies the grade of the selected feature line segment from its end to start. On modifying the grade back value, the start elevation of the selected segment will get changed. The options in the **PANORAMA** window are discussed next.

Select a feature line, parcel line, or survey figure

Choose this button to select the required feature line, parcel line, or survey figure to be edited in the drawing. On choosing this button, you will be prompted to select the object. Select the required feature line from the drawing; the vertices of feature line points and their respective elevations will be displayed in the **PANORAMA** window.

Zoom To

The **Zoom To** button is used to zoom to the required feature line point. Select the required point from the **PANORAMA** window and then choose the **Zoom To** button to zoom to that point.

Quick Profile

The **Quick Profile** button is used to create a quick profile of the selected feature line. Select the required feature line and choose this button; the **Create Quick Profiles** dialog box will be displayed. Enter the required information in the dialog box and choose the **OK** button; the dialog box will be closed and you will be prompted to specify the origin of the profile. Click in the drawing area to create the profile view of the feature line.

Raise/Lower

The **Raise/Lower** button is used to increase or decrease the elevation of the feature line in a row. To increase or decrease the elevation of the feature line, select the required row from the **PANORAMA** window and choose this button; the elevation of the selected point will be highlighted in the edit box at top. Next, change the elevation value in the edit box and press ENTER. To edit the elevations of multiple rows, press and hold the SHIFT key and select the required rows from the **PANORAMA** window.

Set Increment

The **Set Increment** button is used to set the increment value for raising or lowering the elevation values of the points or the selected points. When you choose this button, the edit box on its right will be enabled. Enter the required increment value in the edit box and press ENTER.

Raise Incrementally

The **Raise Incrementally** button is used to raise the elevation of the selected feature line points as per the increment value set in the **Set Increment** edit box. On choosing this button, the elevation value in each row changes automatically according to the increment value. To change the elevation in a particular row, select the required row and choose the **Raise Incrementally** button to raise the elevation.

Lower Incrementally

The **Lower Incrementally** button is used to lower the elevation of the points on the selected feature line as per the value set in the **Set Increment** edit box. On choosing this button, the values in the Elevation column changes automatically according to the value specified in the edit box.

Flatten Grade or Elevations

Choose the **Flatten Grade or Elevations** button to flatten the elevation or the grade of the selected rows in the **PANORAMA** window equivalent to the elevation of the row that you have selected last. You need to select at least two rows to flatten the grade or elevations. When you choose this button, the **Flatten** dialog box will be displayed. Select the **Constant Elevation** radio button in this dialog box to flatten the elevation in the row or select the **Constant Grade** button to flatten the grade values. Choose the **OK** button; the **Flatten** dialog box will be closed. Also, the elevation or grade values specified in the last row selected will be assigned to all other selected rows, depending upon the radio button selected in the **Flatten** dialog box.

Insert Elevation Point

Choose the **Insert Elevation Point** button to insert an intermediate elevation point between the start point and the end point of the selected feature line. On choosing this button, you will be prompted to specify the location of the elevation point. Click at the required location in the drawing; the **Insert PVI** dialog box will be displayed. Specify the station and the elevation of the point in the **Station** and **Elevation** edit boxes, respectively and choose the **OK** button; the dialog box will be closed and a new elevation point will be added in the **PANORAMA** window.

Delete Elevation Point

Choose this button to delete an intermediate elevation point between the first and last station of the feature line. Select the point from the **PANORAMA** window and choose the **Delete Elevation Point** button; the selected point will be deleted.

Elevations from Surface

You can choose the **Elevations from Surface** button to obtain the elevation values from the surface. Select the required point or row from the **PANORAMA** window and choose this button; the **Set Elevations from Surface** dialog box will be displayed. Select the required surface to obtain elevation from the select from list drop-down list. Next, choose the **OK** button; the **Set Elevations from Surface** dialog box will be closed and the elevation of the selected point or row will be modified. If only one surface is available in the drawing, the **Select surface** dialog box will not be displayed and the elevation values of all points will be modified according to the elevation of the existing surface.

Note

If the selected feature line or the feature line point does not lie on the selected surface, Civil 3D will display a warning message.

Reverse the Direction

Choose this button to change the direction of feature lines. On doing so, the order of points will also be reversed and the labeling and stationing of the feature line will be affected.

Show Grade Breaks Only

Choose the **Show Grade Breaks Only** button to display only the start point and the end point of a feature line and any grade breaks in between these two points.

Unselect all rows

Choose the **Unselect all rows** button to deselect the selected rows in the **PANORAMA** window.

After you have edited the required feature lines, close the **PANORAMA** window. The feature lines created will be added to the **Sites** collection of the **Prospector** tab of the **TOOLSPACE** palette.To view the feature lines, expand the **Sites** collection and then expand the required site node. You will notice that a black colored symbol is displayed on the right of the **Feature Lines** option. This symbol indicates that feature lines have been added in the drawing. Select the **Feature Lines** option from the **Site** collection in the **Prospector** tab to view feature lines and their information in the **Prospector** list view of the **TOOLSPACE** palette, refer to Figure 10-4.

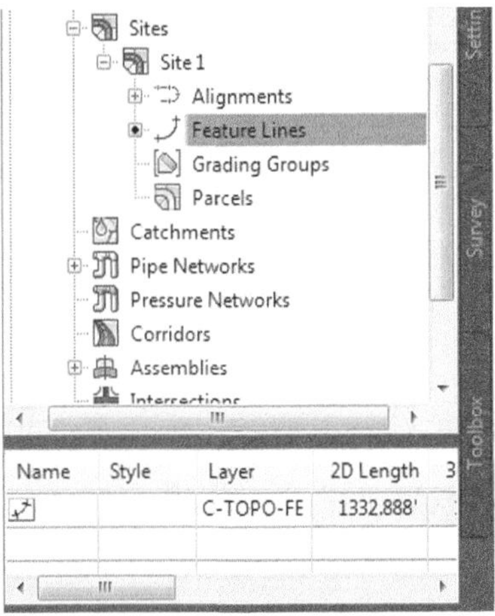

***Figure 10-4** The feature lines displayed in the **Prospector** list view*

Using the Quick Elevation Edit Tool

Ribbon: Modify > Edit Elevations > Quick Elevation Edit
Command: QUICKEDITFEATUREELEVS

The **Quick Elevation Edit** tool is used to quickly edit the elevation or the grade of the selected feature line points. To edit elevations, choose the **Quick Elevation Edit** tool from the **Edit Elevations** panel of the **Modify** tab; you will be prompted to specify the point in the drawing.

Tip

*You can also access the **Quick Elevation Edit** tool from the **Edit Elevations** panel of the **Feature Line** tab (contextual tab).*

Note

*You can show or hide the **Edit Geometry** and **Edit Elevations** panels in the **Feature Line** tab by choosing the **Edit Geometry** and **Edit Elevations** tools, respectively from the **Modify** panel of this tab.*

If you want to edit the elevation of the feature line in the current site, hover the cursor over the required feature line or 2D figure; the cursor will snap to the nearest point of the feature line and you will notice green colored triangles, circles, and arrows displayed on it. The green triangles will be displayed when the cursor hovers over the vertex of the feature line or at an intersection point. The circles will be displayed to highlight elevation points and the arrows will be displayed to highlight feature line segments. Also, the grey colored glyphs will be displayed at the points whose elevation and grade cannot be edited. The elevation and grade values of feature lines points will be displayed at the tooltips, as you move or hover your cursor over the feature line or the required figure. Next, to edit the elevation or the grade of the feature line vertices or other points, click near the point to be edited; the elevation or the grade value will be displayed in the command line. Enter a new elevation or grade value in the command line and press ENTER; the elevation or the grade of the point will be edited. Move and hover the cursor again in the same location; the edited elevation or the grade value will be displayed in the tooltip.

You can select a site in different ways. When you are prompted to specify a point or site/reference, enter **S** (Site) in the command line and then press ENTER; you will be prompted to select an object in site or press ENTER to select from the list. Press ENTER; the **Site** dialog box will be displayed. Next, select the site from the **Site** dialog box and then choose the **OK** button to close this dialog box.

To quickly edit the feature line elevation by using reference, enter **R** in the command line when you are prompted to specify point or site/reference and press ENTER; you will be prompted to specify the reference point either by specifying it at the command prompt or by picking it from the drawing. As you enter the value in the command line, the cursor will snap to the existing feature line points and you will be prompted to specify a point. Click in the drawing to select the required point; a yellow colored line will be drawn between the reference point and the selected point to be edited and you will be prompted to specify grade or slope/elevation/difference. Use the required keywords and edit the slope, grade, elevation, or difference in the elevation values. Similarly, you can choose various tools from the **Edit Elevations** panel to edit the elevations and grades of the feature lines.

The edit options of the feature lines can also be accessed from the **Prospector** Item View. To do so, select the required feature line in the **Name** column of the **Prospector** Item View and right-click; a shortcut menu will be displayed. Choose the required options from the shortcut menu and edit the selected feature line.

Editing the Feature Line Geometry

As a feature line is more complex than a line or a polyline feature, Civil 3D provides you with a number of tools to edit the feature line geometry. These tools can be accessed from the **Edit Geometry** panel of the **Modify** tab. This panel consists of tools such as **Break**, **Trim**, **Fillet**, **Smooth**, **Join**, and **Edit Curve**. The **Fillet** and **Smooth** tools in this panel are discussed next.

Filleting Feature Lines

Ribbon:	Modify > Edit Geometry > Fillet
Command:	FILLETFEATURE

You can fillet feature lines using the **Fillet** tool. To use this tool, choose the **Fillet** tool from the **Edit Geometry** panel; you will be prompted to select the object. Select the required feature lines or a 2D element. On doing so, you will be prompted to specify corner. Enter **R** in the command line to specify all joint radius. Press ENTER; you will be prompted to specify the radius. Specify the radius in the command line and press ENTER again; you will be prompted to specify corner. Click at the required corner of the feature line or enter **A** in the command line to create fillet at all corners of the feature line. Press ENTER; corners will be filleted as per the specified option. Figures 10-5 and 10-6 show a feature line before and after using the **Fillet** tool, respectively.

*Figure 10-5 Feature lines before using the **Fillet** tool*

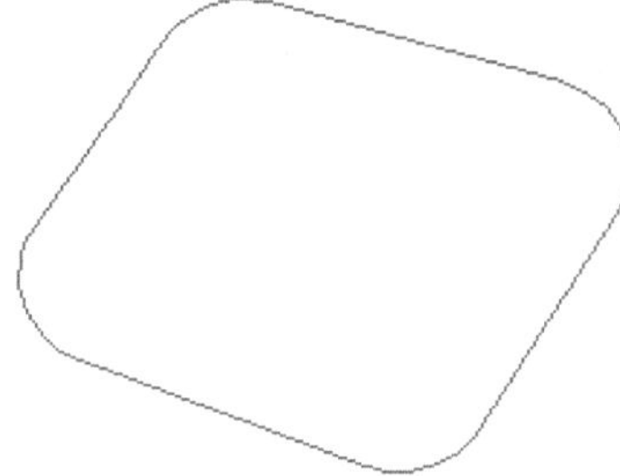

*Figure 10-6 Feature lines after using the **Fillet** tool*

Smoothening the Feature Lines

Ribbon:	Modify > Edit Geometry > Smooth
Command:	SMOOTHFEATURE

AutoCAD Civil 3D allows you to smoothen the vertices or edges of feature lines or 2D figures by adding arcs and curves to it. To smoothen the edges of a feature line, choose the **Smooth** tool from the **Edit Geometry** panel; you will prompted to select the feature lines to be smoothened. Select the required feature line or 2D figure from the drawing and press ENTER; the selected feature line will be smoothened by adding arcs and curves. You can also straighten the existing curved feature lines. To do so, enter **S** in the command line and press ENTER. Next, select the required feature lines from the drawing and press ENTER again to straighten the smooth feature lines. Figures 10-7 and 10-8 show the feature lines before and after using the **Smooth** tool. You can use other tools from the **Edit Geometry** panel and edit the feature line geometry.

Figure 10-7 *Feature line before using the **Smooth** tool*

Figure 10-8 *Feature line after using the **Smooth** tool*

Creating Dynamic Feature Lines

New

In Civil 3d 2018, Feature line elevations can be obtained from a surface and can also be relative to a surface, so if a surface is updated, the feature line will also be updated. The update behavior of relative feature lines is different depending on whether the feature line was set to be relative to a surface when it was created or it was created at fixed or non-dynamic elevations and then set to be relative.

You can specify that a feature line is relative to a surface while creating or editing it. To do so, choose the **Elevation Editor** tool from the **Edit Elevations** panel of the **Modify** tab; you will be prompted to select the object. Select the required feature line from the drawing; the **PANORAMA** window with the **Grading Elevation Editor** tab chosen will be displayed.

In the **PANORAMA** window, choose the **Elevation from Surface** button to obtain **Set Elevation from Surface** dialog box. Using this command, you can edit the feature lines so that it obtain its elevations from a surface and also relative to that surface. In this dialog box, select the reference surface from the **Select From list** drop-down list. Then, select the **Insert Intermediate Grade Break Points** and **Relative Elevations to Surface** check boxes; the edit box next to **Relative Elevations to Surface** option will become active. Specify the value of relative elevation in the edit box and then choose the **OK** button; **Set Elevation from Surface** dialog box will be closed.

Notice the changes in relative elevation of the feature lines in the **Grading Elevation Editor** tab, as shown in Figure 10-9.

Station	Elevation(Relative)	Elevation(Actual)	Length	Grade Back	Grade Ahead	Elevation Derived From
0+00.00	10.000'	112.288'	19.870'		1.22%	Relative to Surface
0+19.87	10.000'	112.531'	38.198'	-1.22%	0.72%	Relative to Surface
0+58.07	10.000'	112.805'	10.793'	-0.72%	0.58%	Relative to Surface
0+68.86	10.000'	112.867'	31.006'	-0.58%	0.43%	Relative to Surface
0+99.87	10.000'	113.000'	2.751'	-0.43%	0.61%	Relative to Surface
1+02.62	10.000'	113.017'	1.306'	-0.61%	1.79%	Relative to Surface
1+03.92	10.000'	113.040'	41.533'	-1.79%	1.19%	Relative to Surface
1+45.46	10.000'	113.533'	34.543'	-1.19%	0.63%	Relative to Surface
1+80.00	10.000'	113.753'	12.158'	-0.63%	0.04%	Relative to Surface

Figure 10-9 Partial view of the changes in relative elevation of the feature line in ***Grading Elevation Editor***

Setting the Properties and Style of the Feature Line

To view and edit the feature line properties and style, select the required feature line and right-click in the drawing; a shortcut menu will be displayed. Choose **Feature Line Properties** from the shortcut menu; the **Feature Line Properties: Site 1** dialog box will be displayed, as shown in Figure 10-10.

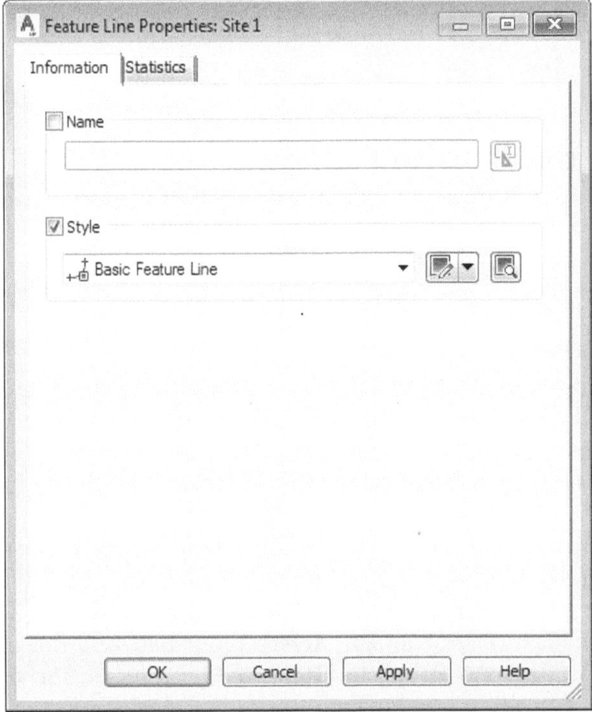

Figure 10-10 The ***Feature Line Properties: Site 1*** *dialog box*

In this dialog box, the **Information** tab displays the **Name** and **Style** areas where you can specify the name and style of the feature line, respectively. To specify the name of the feature line, if it is not specified already, select the check box next to the **Name** area; the **Name** area will become active. Choose the **Click to edit name template** button in the **Name** area; the **Name Template** dialog box will be displayed. In this dialog box, specify the name in the **Name** edit box and then choose the **OK** button; the **Name Template** dialog box will be closed. The **Style** area in the **Information** tab of the **Feature Line Properties: Site 1** dialog box is used to display the current feature line style. Select the **Style** check box to make this area active. Now, you can select the required option from the drop-down list in the **Style** area to specify the style of the feature line. You will learn how to create a new feature line later in this chapter.

The **Statistics** tab of the **Feature Line Properties: Site 1** dialog box displays the information about the feature properties and their values in the **Property** and **Value** columns. It also displays information about the breakline data. After specifying all the properties, choose the **OK** button to close the dialog box and save the settings.

Creating a New Feature Line Style

To create a new feature line style, choose the **Settings** tab in the **TOOLSPACE** palette and expand **General > Multipurpose Styles > Feature Line Styles**. Right-click on the **Feature Line Styles** node and choose the **New** option from the shortcut menu displayed; the **Feature Line Style - New Feature Line Style** dialog box will be displayed.

In the **Information** tab of the dialog box, specify a style name in the **Name** edit box. Optionally, you can enter the description of the feature line style in the **Description** edit box. In the **Profile** tab of the **Feature Line Style - New Feature Line Style** dialog box, select an option from the **Beginning Vertex Marker Style** drop-down list to specify the marker style for the beginning vertex. Similarly, select the options from the **Internal Vertex Marker Style** and **Ending Vertex, Marker Style** drop-down lists to specify the marker style for the internal and ending vertices respectively. In the **Object Display** area of the **Section** tab, select an option from the **Crossing Marker Style** drop-down list to specify the marker style for the crossing. In the **Display** tab, select the view direction from the **View Direction** drop-down list. Set the visibility, color, linetype, and other display properties of the feature line in the **Component display** area of the **Display** tab and choose the **OK** button; the **Feature Line Style - New Feature Line Style** dialog box will be closed. And, the defined feature line style is added to the **Feature Line Styles** sub-node in the **General** node of the **Settings** tab. You can view the existing style by expanding the **Feature Line Styles** sub-node. You can also view the styles in the Item View by selecting the **Feature Line Styles** sub-node from the **General** node of the **Settings** tab.

Tip

*You can also invoke the **Feature Line Style** dialog box from the **Information** tab of the **Feature Line Properties: <site name>** dialog box. To do so, click on the down arrow next to the **Style** edit box in the **Style** area and then choose the **Create New** option from the flyout displayed.*

Adding Labels to Feature Lines

Ribbon: Annotate > Labels & Tables > Add Labels drop-down > Feature Line > Add Feature Line Labels
Command: ADDFEATURELINELABELS

To add labels to feature lines, choose the **Add Feature Line Labels** tool from the **Labels & Tables** panel; the **Add Labels** dialog box will be displayed. Select the **Line and Curve** option from the **Feature** drop-down list to label lines and curved segments in the feature line. Next, select the **Single Segment** option from the **Label type** drop-down list to label the single segment of the feature line. You can select the **Multiple Segment** option from the **Label type** drop-down list to label all segments of the feature line. Then, select the required option from the **Line label style** and **Curve label style** drop-down list. Choose the **Add** button from the **Add Labels** dialog box; you will be prompted to select a point on the entity. Select the required feature line segment in the drawing; the segment will be labeled.

To create a new feature line label style for the line and curved segment, choose the **Settings** tab in the **TOOLSPACE** palette and then expand **General > Label Styles > Line**. Select the **Line** option and right-click on it; a shortcut menu will be displayed. Choose the **New** option from the shortcut menu; the **Label Style Composer - New General Line Label Style** dialog box will be displayed. Use this dialog box to specify the settings for the new label style to label the feature lines. Similarly, select and right-click on the **Curve** option and choose the **New** option from the shortcut menu displayed; the **Label Style Composer - New General Curve Label Style** dialog box will be displayed. Use this dialog box to create a new label style to label the curved segments of the feature line.

GRADING OBJECTS

After you have created the feature lines, the next step is to create grading objects from them. The feature line acts as a baseline for these grading objects. Besides using the feature line as a baseline for grading, it can also be added as a breakline in a surface.

The object on which the grading applied is called a grading object. A grading object consists of footprint, daylight line, projection line, and center marker, refer to Figure 10-11. To create a grading object, you need to set the grading criteria which is explained next.

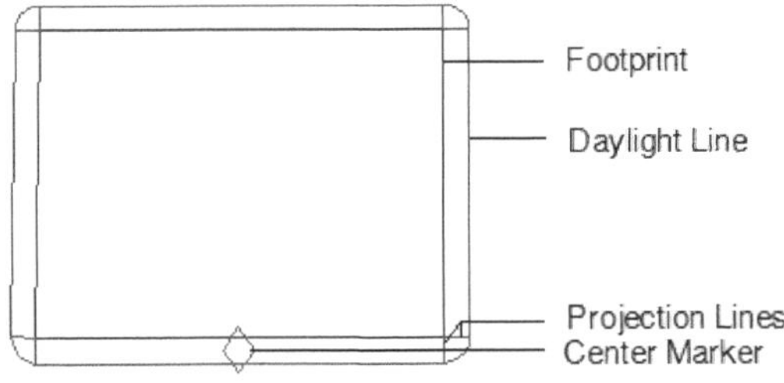

Figure 10-11 *Different parts of a grading object*

A footprint is basically a feature line or a closed 2D figure created using the feature line. A daylight line is a line that is created by grading a target at some distance, slope, or an elevation. The projection lines are the lines that connect the footprint and the daylight lines. A center marker is a diamond-shaped marker that represents the centroid of the grading object. The area bounded by grading lines is called the face of the grading.

In Civil 3D, every grading object consists of a baseline (feature line) and a criteria set. A criteria set is a collection of criteria on the basis of which grading is carried out. The grading criteria are the settings which specify the grading method. The criteria contains parameters that define how grading is created from an object. The criteria set define the geometry of a grading object. Civil 3D allows you to create multiple grading objects with different criteria and use them as criteria sets according to the site design. Every grading object has a criteria set assigned to it. The various components of grading objects are discussed next.

Creating Criteria Sets

To create a criteria set, choose the **Settings** tab in the **TOOLSPACE** palette. Next, expand **Grading > Grading Criteria Sets** to view the default criteria set. Right-click on the **Grading Criteria Sets** sub-node and choose the **New** option from the shortcut menu; the **Grading Criteria Set Properties - Grading Criteria Set (1)** dialog box will be displayed. Enter a name of the criteria set in the **Name** edit box. Optionally, you can enter a description in the **Description** text box. Next, choose the **OK** button; the dialog box will be closed and the criteria set will be added to the **Grading Criteria Sets** node. After you have created the criteria set, you need to create and add different criteria to this criteria set. To add the criteria, select the criteria set created and right-click on it; a shortcut menu will be displayed. Choose the **New** option from the shortcut menu displayed; the **Grading Criteria - New Grading Criteria** dialog box will be displayed, as shown in Figure 10-12.

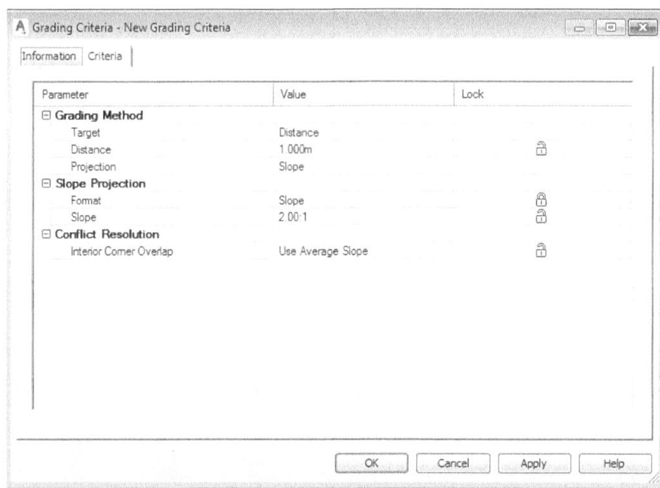

*Figure 10-12 Parameters in the **Criteria** tab of the **Grading Criteria - New Grading Criteria** dialog box*

This dialog box consists of two tabs: **Information** and **Criteria**. In the **Information** tab, enter the name of the criteria in the **Name** edit box. Optionally, you can enter a description of the criteria in the **Description** text box. Next, choose the **Criteria** tab which is used to define the grading criteria. Grading parameters are displayed under three categories: **Grading Method**,

Slope Projection, and **Conflict Resolution**, refer to Figure 10-11. The parameters in the **Grading Method** and **Slope Projection** categories vary according to the **Target** and **Projection** options selected. The parameters under these options are discussed next.

Target

This parameter is available in the **Grading Method** category and is used to specify the target selected for grading. The boundary of the grading object depends upon on the target value selected. For example, if the **Surface** option is selected as the target value, the projection lines of the grading object will extend till they match the surface according to the criteria. There are four options available to specify the target value namely **Surface**, **Elevation**, **Relative Elevation**, and **Distance**. To specify a target value, click in the **Value** field of the **Target** parameter; a drop-down list will be displayed. Select the required option from the drop-down list. The options in this drop-down list are discussed next.

Surface

The **Surface** option is selected for extending the grading projection line to match to the selected target surface.

Elevation

The **Elevation** option is selected when you want the grading projection lines to project upward or downward from the footprint to a given elevation. The elevation can be specified in the **Value** field of the **Elevation** parameter that is displayed after selecting the target.

Relative Elevation

The **Relative Elevation** option can be specified when you want the projection lines to extend up or down from the footprint to the required height or depth. When this option is selected, the **Relative Elevation** parameter is displayed. Enter the required relative elevation in the **Value** field of the **Relative Elevation** parameter.

Distance

The **Distance** option can be selected when you want the projection lines to project outward at the specified horizontal distance. Specify the distance in the **Value** field of the **Distance** parameter that is displayed after selecting the target.

Projection

The projection parameter defines the projection method that is used to access the target. The projection options vary according to the type of target selected. To select a projection, click in the **Value** field of this parameter and select the projection from the drop-down list displayed. Various types of projections are discussed next.

Slope

The **Slope** option is selected to create grading by projecting a specific slope value to the target at a specified slope value. This option is used with the **Relative Elevation** and **Distance** targets. Specify the slope value in the **Value** field of the **Slope** parameter. You can also specify the slope value in percentage by setting the value of the **Format** parameter to **Grade**.

Relative Elevation

This projection is applicable when the target value is set to **Distance**. The **Relative Elevation** option is selected to project the grading lines to an elevation relative to the elevation of the footprint of the grading object.

Cut/Fill Slope

This projection is applicable when the target value is set to **Surface** or **Elevation**. The **Cut/Fill Slope** option is used to create a grading by projecting the slope to a target surface or elevation located up or below the footprint. These two targets can be both above and below the footprint. On selecting the **Cut/Fill Slope** option, the **Search Order** parameter becomes available. This parameter specifies the type of slope (Cut or Fill) to be used first to create a grading. This option is used where both the cut and fill slopes can exist such as steep slopes. If the value of the **Search Order** parameter is set to **Cut first**, the grading object will grade up from the footprint and vice versa.

Cut Slope

This type of projection is applicable when the target value is set to **Surface** or **Elevation**. The **Cut Slope** option is used to allow the grading object to use only the cut slope and grade up to the target. Specify the required cut slope value in the **Value** field of the **Slope** parameter. On selecting this option, grading object will not be created if the target is below the footprint.

Fill Slope

This type of projection is also applicable when the target value is set to **Surface** or **Elevation**. The **Fill Slope** projection is used to allow the grading object to use only the fill slope value to grade down to the target. Specify the required fill slope value in the **Value** field of the **Slope** parameter. Grading will not be created if the target is above the footprint.

Distance

This type of projection is also applicable when the target value is set to **Relative Elevation**. The **Distance** projection is used to allow the grading object to project the target at a fixed horizontal distance from the footprint. Specify the horizontal distance in the **Value** field of the **Distance** parameter.

Format

The **Format** parameter is available in the **Slope Projection** category. This parameter determines how the slope will be represented. Click in the **Value** field of the **Format** parameter and select the **Slope** or **Grade** option from the drop-down list. On selecting the **Slope** option, you can specify the slope in the run : rise format. On selecting the **Grade** option, you can specify the grade value as a percent decimal.

Interior Corner Overlap

This parameter is under the **Conflict Resolution** node of the **Criteria** tab and is used to determine how the projections of the interior corners of the daylight will be cleaned up when the corners of the footprint are at different elevations. Click in the **Value** field of this parameter and select the required option from the drop-down list. You can select the **Use Average Slope** option from the drop-down list to average the slopes of projection lines to reach the same daylight point. The **Hold Slope As Minimum** option can be selected to hold the specified grade or slope as minimum and increase the slope projected from the footprint on one side. The **Hold Slope As Maximum** option is selected from the drop-down list to hold the slope or grade as maximum and flatten the slope projected from the footprint on the other side.

You can lock the values of some parameters by clicking on the lock symbol in the **Lock** column. On doing so, you will not be prompted to enter the values of the locked parameters while creating the grading object. After you have defined the grading criteria, choose the **OK** button from the **Grading Criteria - New Grading Criteria** dialog box; the dialog box will be closed and the grading criteria will be added in the **Grading Criteria Sets** sub-node. Similarly, you can create multiple criteria sets with different criteria.

Creating a Grading Group

You have learned to create feature lines, grading objects, and grading criteria sets. Now, you will learn to create grading groups. Grading groups are created to organize grading into different groups for creating surfaces and earthwork computations.

To create a grading group, choose the **Prospector** tab. Expand the **Sites** node and then expand the required site to which the grading group is to be added. Choose the **Grading Groups** node under the site name and right-click on it; a shortcut menu will be displayed. Choose **New** from the shortcut menu; the **Create Grading Group** dialog box will be displayed, as shown in Figure 10-13.

*Figure 10-13 The **Create Grading Group** dialog box*

In this dialog box, choose the **Click to edit name template** button next to the **Name** edit box; the **Name Template** dialog box will be displayed. Enter a grading group name in the **Name** edit box and choose the **OK** button; the **Name Template** dialog box will be closed. In the **Create Grading Group** dialog box, enter a description in the **Description** text box. Then, select the **Automatic surface creation** check box to create a surface from the grading group automatically. The **Use the Group Name** check box is selected by default and is used to create the surface with the same name as the group name. Note that this check box will get activated after the **Automatic surface creation** check box is selected. Clear the check box if you do not want the surface to be created with the group name. Next, select an option from the **Surface style** drop-down list in the **Automatic surface creation** area. Select the **Volume base surface** check box. On doing so, the drop-down list in the **Volume base surface** area will be activated. Select a base surface from the drop-down list in the **Volume base surface** area. The selected base surface and the grading group surface will be used to calculate the volumes. Now, choose the **OK** button; the **Create Grading Group** dialog box will be closed and the **Create Surface** dialog box will be displayed (if the **Automatic surface creation** check box is selected). Select the required option from the **Type** drop-down list and choose the **OK** button; the **Create Surface** dialog box will be closed and the surface will be added in the **Surfaces** node of the **Prospector** tab. Also, the grading group will be added to the **Grading Groups** sub-node of the **Site** node.

Tip

*You can also invoke the **Create Grading Group** dialog box by choosing the **Create Grading Group** tool from **Home > Create Design > Grading** drop-down.*

You have learned about feature lines, grading objects, criteria, and groups. Now, you will learn how to create a grading. The method of creating a grading is discussed next.

Using the Grading Creation Tools Toolbar

Ribbon: Home > Create Design > Grading drop-down > Grading Creation Tools
Command: GRADINGTOOLS

The **Grading Creation Tools** toolbar is used to create a new grading, edit the existing grading, and apply the grading criteria and styles. To invoke this toolbar, choose the **Grading Creation Tools** from the **Create Design** panel in the **Home** tab. The **Grading Creation Tools** toolbar contain various tools for grading, as shown in Figure 10-14. These tools are discussed next.

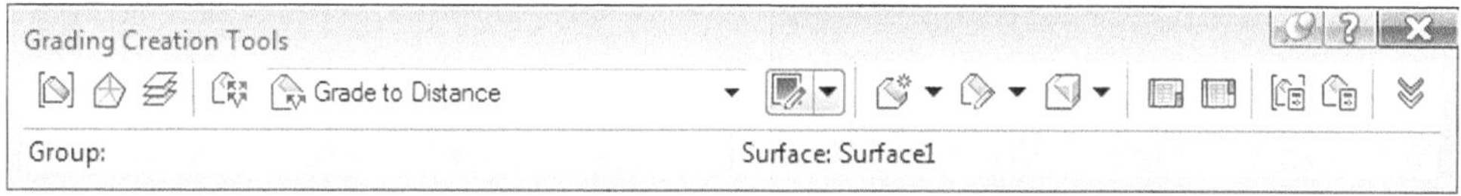

*Figure 10-14 The **Grading Creation Tools** toolbar*

Set the Grading Group Tool

The **Set the Grading Group** tool from the **Grading Creation Tools** toolbar is used to select or create a grading group. On invoking this tool, the **Create Grading Group** dialog box will be displayed. Note that if one or more grading groups exist in the drawing then on choosing the **Set the Grading Group** tool, the **Select Grading Group** dialog box will be displayed, as shown in Figure 10-15.

Select the required site with which the group is associated from the **Site name** drop-down list. Next, select an option from the **Group name** drop-down list. After you have selected the required site and group name, choose the **OK** button; the dialog box will be closed and the group name will be displayed at the bottom of the toolbar.

Note

*To create a new group from the **Select Grading Group** dialog box, choose the **Create a Grading Group** button in the **Select Grading Group** dialog box; the **Create a Grading Group** dialog box will be displayed. You can use this dialog box to create a new grading group.*

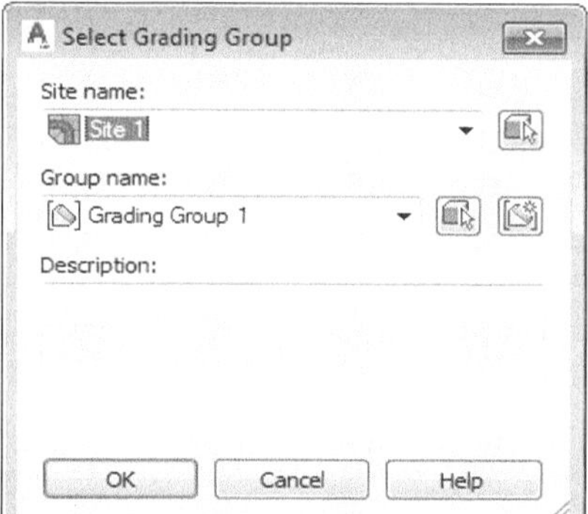

*Figure 10-15 The **Select Grading Group** dialog box*

Set the Target surface Tool

This tool is used to specify the surface to be used as a target. On choosing this tool, the **Select surface** dialog box will be displayed. Select the required surface from the drop-down list in the dialog box and choose the **OK** button; the dialog box will be closed and the selected surface will be set as the target surface.

Set the Grading layer Tool

This tool is used to specify a layer for the grading. On choosing this tool, the **Set Grading Layers** dialog box will be displayed. You can use this dialog box to select a layer for the grading.

Select a Criteria Set Tool

This tool is used to select the required criteria set for grading. On choosing this tool, the **Select a Criteria Set** dialog box will be displayed. Select the required criteria set from the drop-down list in the dialog box and choose the **OK** button. Next, select the required criteria from the criteria set using the **Select a Grading Criteria** drop-down list available next to this tool.

To edit the selected criteria or to add a new criteria to the criteria set, choose the down arrow on the right of this tool; a flyout will be displayed, refer to Figure 10-16. Choose the required option from the flyout to edit or create a new criteria. The **Edit Current Selection** option is chosen by default in the flyout.

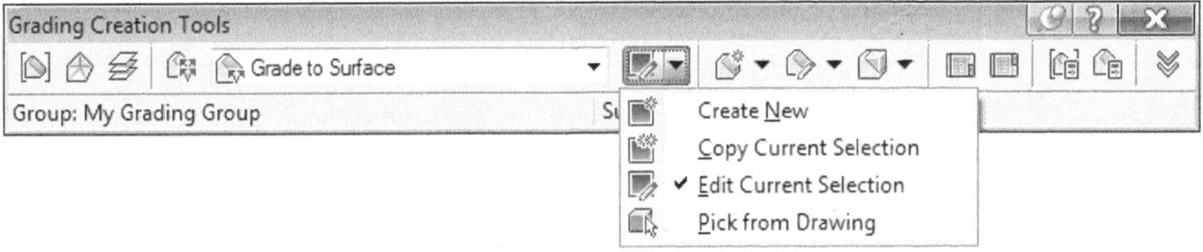

Figure 10-16 *Various options displayed in the flyout*

Create Grading Tool

After you have selected the required grading group, criteria set, and criteria, choose the **Create Grading** tool to create a grading. On doing so, you will be prompted to select the feature. Select the required feature line or a figure from the drawing; you will be prompted to select the grading side. Click in the drawing to specify the grading side; you will be prompted to specify whether the grading is to be applied to the entire length. Press ENTER to accept the default **<Yes>** option. Next, you will be prompted to specify the distance; enter a value in the command line and press ENTER. On doing so, you will be prompted to specify the slope; enter the slope value in the command line; the grading will be created. Next, press ENTER to end the command.

Note

The prompts displayed in the command line vary according to the criteria and settings specified in the ***Grading Criteria*** *dialog box.*

Edit Grading Tool

This tool is used to edit the grading parameters. On choosing this tool, the **Select a point in the grading or [Site]:** prompt will be displayed in the command line. Select the required grading from the drawing; you will be prompted to specify the distance. Enter the required distance in the command line and follow the prompts to edit the grading. Note that the prompts displayed in the command line vary according to the criteria selected for grading. When you choose the down arrow on the right of this tool, a flyout will be displayed. The **Edit Grading** option is chosen by default in the flyout. The other options in the flyout are discussed next.

Delete Grading Tool

Choose the **Delete Grading** tool from the **Grading Creation Tools** toolbar, as shown in Figure 10-17 and select the grading to be deleted from the drawing; the grading (daylight line) will be deleted.

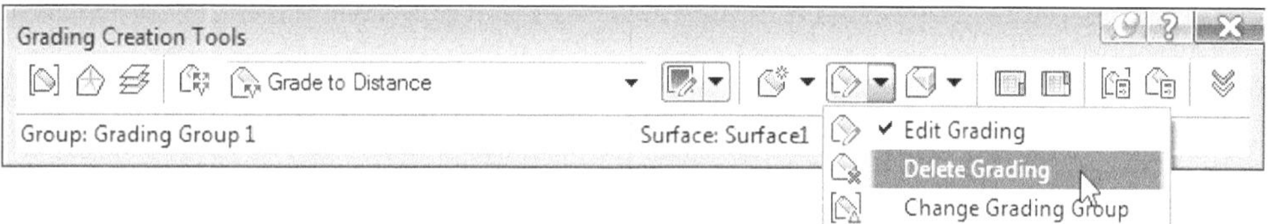

*Figure 10-17 Choosing the **Delete Grading** tool*

Change Grading Group Tool

This tool is used to change the existing group of the grading. Invoke this tool and select the grading for which you want to change the grading group. On doing so, the **Select Grading Group** dialog box will be displayed. Select the required group from the dialog box and then choose the **OK** button; the dialog box will be closed and the grading group of the selected grading will be changed.

Note

*The **Change Grading Group** tool can be used only when there are two or more grading groups available in the drawing.*

Grading Volume Tools Tool

This tool is used to adjust the cut and fill volumes for a grading group. To work with this tool, you need to have a surface in the drawing which is created from a grading group. Therefore, this tool can only be invoked when the **Automatic surface creation** check box is selected in the **Create Grading Group** dialog box. The **Grading Volume** tools are discussed in detail later in this chapter.

Grading Editor Tool

This tool is used to edit the grading criteria. Invoke this tool and select the required grading; the **Grading Editor PANORAMA** window will be displayed. You can use this window to edit the grading criteria.

Elevation Editor Tool

This tool is used to edit the elevation of feature lines. Invoke this tool and select the required object from the drawing; the **Grading Elevation Editor Panorama** window will be displayed. You can use this window to edit the elevation of the feature line points.

Grading Group Properties Tool

This tool is used to view the properties of the selected grading group. On invoking this tool, the **Grading Group Properties** dialog box will be displayed, as shown in Figure 10-18.

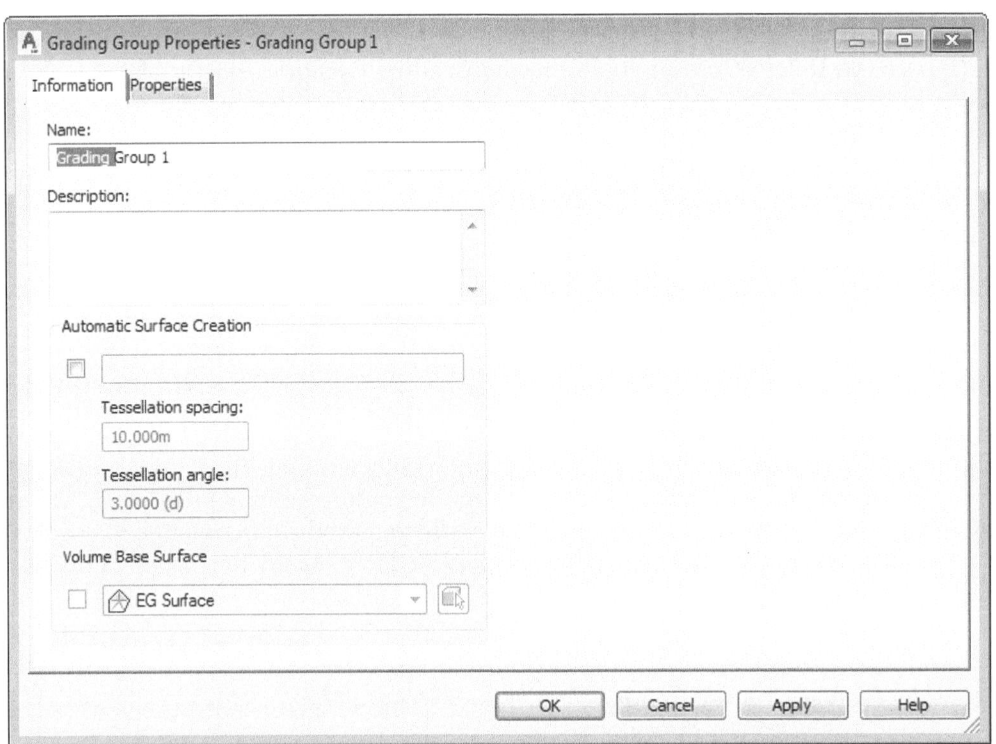

Figure 10-18 The ***Grading Group Properties*** *dialog box*

Tip

Alternatively, to display the ***Grading Group Properties*** *dialog box, select the required grading from the drawing and right-click to display a shortcut menu. Choose the* ***Grading Group Properties - Group 1*** *option from the shortcut menu; the dialog box will be displayed.*

The **Information** tab in this dialog box displays general information about the grading group. Edit the name of the group in the **Name** edit box, if required. Optionally, enter a description of the grading group in the **Description** text box. The options in the **Automatic Surface Creation** area and the **Volume Base Surface** area are already set in the **Create Grading Group** dialog box. You can change the settings in this area, if required.

The **Properties** tab of this dialog box is used to review the grading group properties. This tab displays the count for which specific grading criteria and styles have been used by the grading group. Once you have edited or reviewed the grading group properties, choose the **Apply** button to apply the changes in the **Grading Group Properties** dialog box and then choose the **OK** to close the dialog box.

Grading Properties Tool

Choose this tool to display the **Grading Properties** dialog box. The options in this dialog box are used to view the properties of the individual grading group. Invoke the **Grading Properties** tool and select the required point in the grading; the **Grading Properties** dialog box will be displayed, as shown in Figure 10-19.

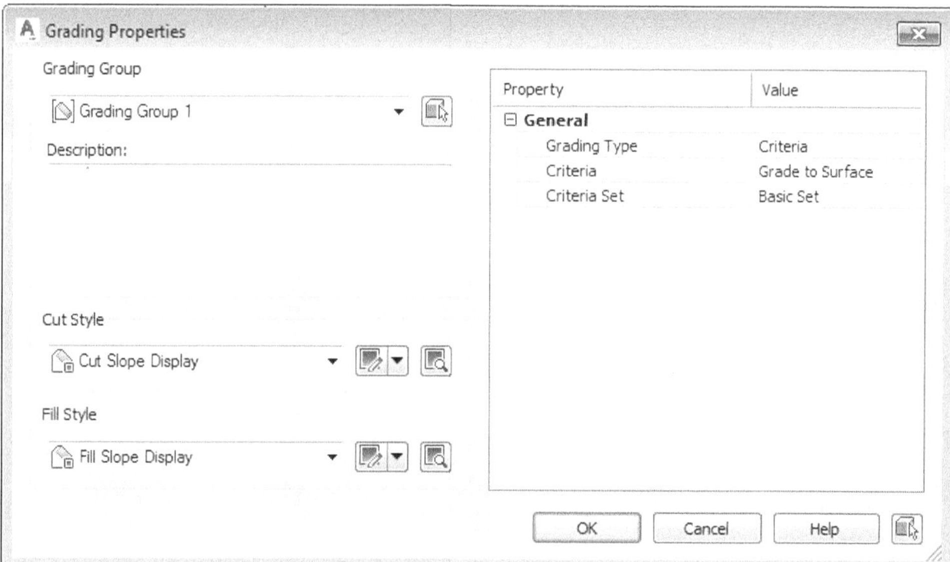

*Figure 10-19 The **Grading Properties** dialog box*

Tip

*You can also display the **Grading Properties** dialog box by using the shortcut menu. To do so, select the required grading from the drawing and right-click; a shortcut menu will be displayed. Choose **Grading Properties** from the shortcut menu.*

You can edit the grading group and grading style in this dialog box. After you have edited the group name and the grading style, choose the **OK** button to close the dialog box.

Expand the Toolbar

This tool is used to expand the **Grading Creation Tools** toolbar, as shown in Figure 10-20. This toolbar is used to display the existing criteria values and styles. To hide the expanded toolbar, choose this tool again. Close the toolbar after the grading has been created. Figure 10-21 shows the grading in the **Conceptual** and **3D Wireframe** visual styles.

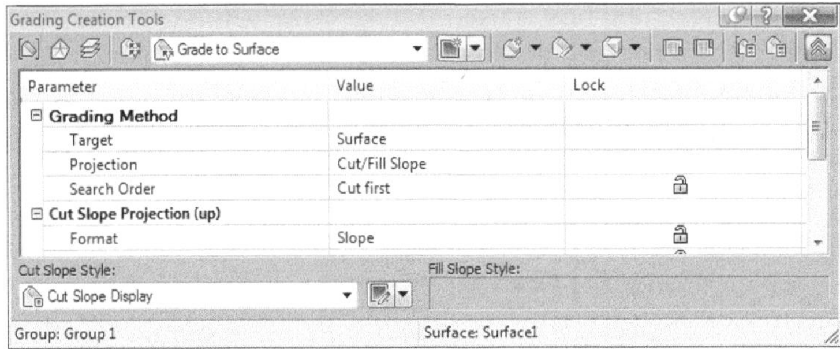

*Figure 10-20 The expanded **Grading Creation Tools** toolbar*

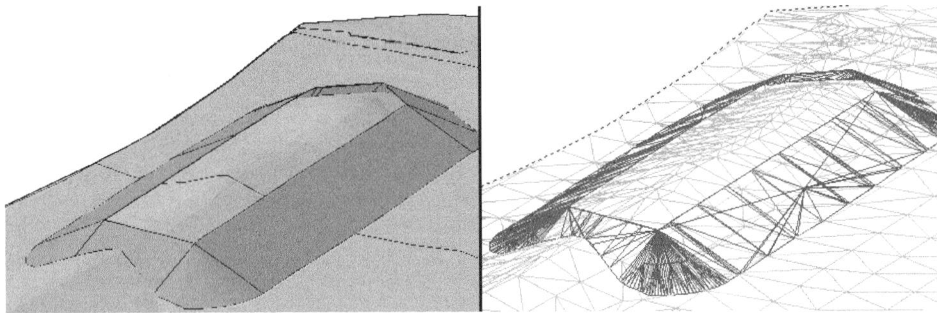

*Figure 10-21 The **Conceptual** and **3D wireframe** views of the grading created on the surface*

Editing Gradings Using the Grading Editor Tool

Ribbon: Grading > Modify > Grading Editor
Command: GRADINGEDITOR

You can edit a grading by using the **Grading Editor** tab in the **PANORAMA** window. To display the **Grading Editor** tab in the **PANORAMA** window, select grading from the drawing; the **Grading** tab will be displayed in the ribbon. Next, choose the **Grading Editor** tool from the **Modify** panel of this tab; the **Grading Editor** tab in the **PANORAMA** window will be displayed, as shown in Figure 10-22.

You can edit the grading parameters in this window. To do so, click in the **Value** field and then specify a new value in it. Note that you can edit only the values in black color. After you have edited the required parameters, close the **PANORAMA** window.

You can also edit a grading by using grips. The grip edit is used to edit the footprint geometry and the location of different vertices and elevation points. To edit a grading by using grips, zoom to the feature line or the footprint of the grading and select it; grips will be displayed at every vertex of the feature line, and also at every elevation point.

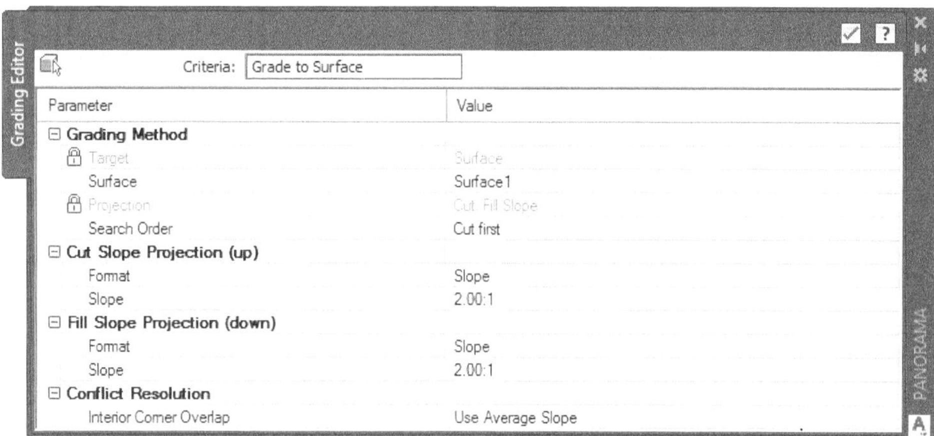

Figure 10-22 *The **Grading Editor** tab in the **PANORAMA** window*

Select the required grip and drag it to change the location of the selected grip. Figure 10-23 shows the grips displayed on selecting the footprint and Figure 10-24 shows the footprint geometry after dragging the grip of the footprint.

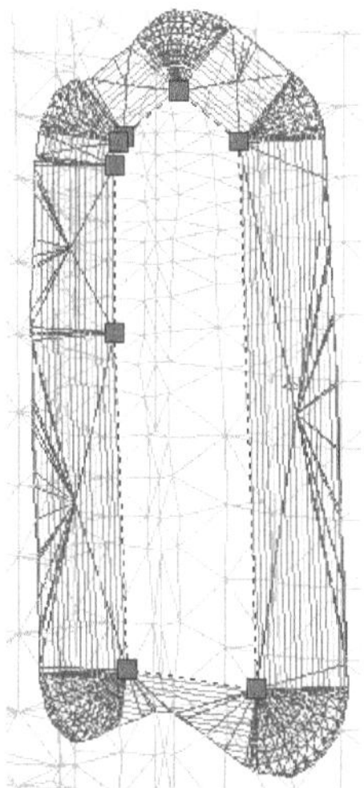

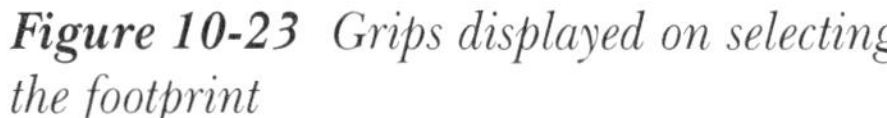

Figure 10-23 *Grips displayed on selecting the footprint*

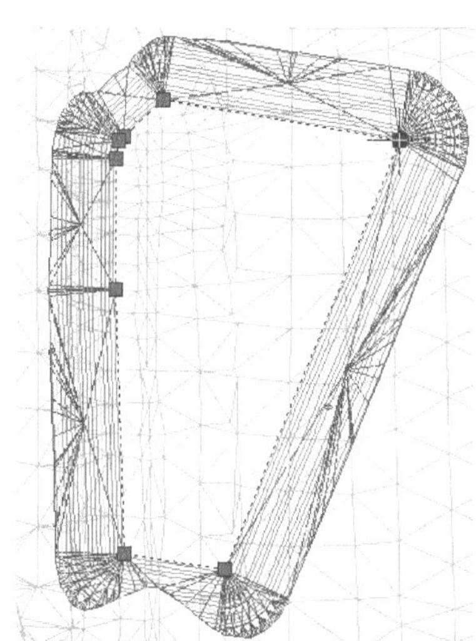

Figure 10-24 *Footprint geometry after dragging the grip of the footprint*

The most common method of editing the grading is by using the command line prompts. To quickly edit the cut or slope format and slope values, choose the **Edit Grading** tool from the **Modify** tab; you will be prompted to select a point in the grading or site. Click on a point in the grading and press ENTER; you will be prompted to specify the cut format in terms of grade or slope. Enter **G** for grade or **S** for slope in the command line and press ENTER. Next, follow the prompts and enter the required values in the command line; the format will be edited.

To edit the elevation, grade, or slope of the footprint vertices and elevation points, invoke the **Elevation Editor** tool from the **Grading Creation Tools** toolbar, as explained earlier in this chapter. On doing so, you will be prompted to select the object. Select the required footprint (feature line) from the drawing; the **Grading Elevation Editor** tab in the **PANORAMA** window will be displayed, as shown in Figure 10-25.

Station	Elevation(Actual)	Length	Grade Back	Grade Ahead
377+21.14	337.788'	25.488'	7.63%	-13.94%
377+46.62	334.236'	25.490'	13.94%	-13.87%
377+72.11	330.700'	8.354'	13.87%	-13.84%
377+80.47	329.543'	10.212'	13.84%	-13.83%
377+90.68	328.131'	12.642'	13.83%	-9.74%
378+03.32	326.901'	8.067'	9.74%	-8.63%
378+11.39	326.205'	31.303'	8.63%	-8.60%
378+42.69	323.513'	11.047'	8.60%	-8.99%
378+53.74	322.520'	7.896'	8.99%	-8.98%
378+61.64	321.810'	30.526'	8.98%	-8.97%
378+92.16	319.071'	12.663'	8.97%	-10.86%
379+04.83	317.696'	20.468'	10.86%	-9.86%
379+25.29	315.678'	10.178'	9.86%	-9.49%
379+35.47	314.712'	7.938'	9.49%	-9.49%
379+43.41	313.959'	29.752'	9.49%	-9.49%
379+73.16	311.135'	33.438'	9.49%	-10.11%

*Figure 10-25 The **Grading Elevation Editor** tab of the **PANORAMA** window*

In the first column of the **Grading Elevation Editor** tab in the **PANORAMA** window, intermediate points and vertices are displayed as symbols. To edit the elevation of the vertex or point, double-click in the **Elevation** column for the required vertex or point and then specify the elevation. You can double-click in the **Grade Ahead** and **Grade Back** columns and specify the grades as required. After you have edited the elevation and grade values, close this window.

Creating the Grading Infill

Ribbon: Grading > Modify > Creating Grading Infill
Command: CREATEGRADINGINFILL

Grading infill refers to filling of open areas or voids in a grading. The grading infill does not have any criteria. To create a grading infill, select the grading from the drawing; the **Grading** tab will be displayed. Next, choose the **Create Grading Infill** tool from the **Modify** panel; you will be prompted to select the area to infill. Move the cursor to the grading area; the area to be infilled will be highlighted. Click in the required area; the grading infill will be created. Alternatively, invoke the **Create Infill** tool from the **Grading Creation Tools** toolbar to create the grading infill. Figure 10-26 shows the grading without infill and Figure 10-27 shows the grading after creating the grading infill in the empty areas.

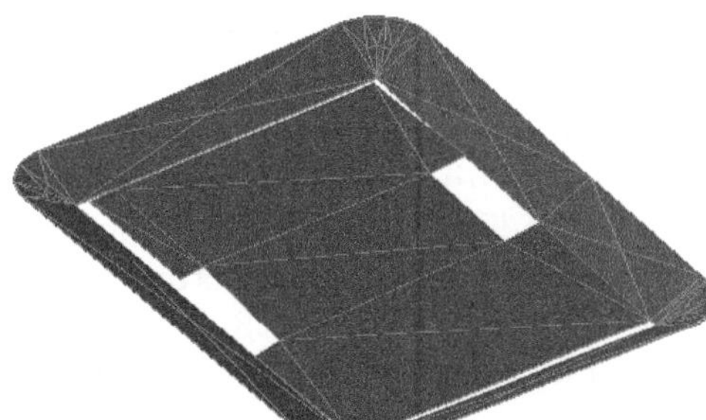

Figure 10-26 Grading without infill

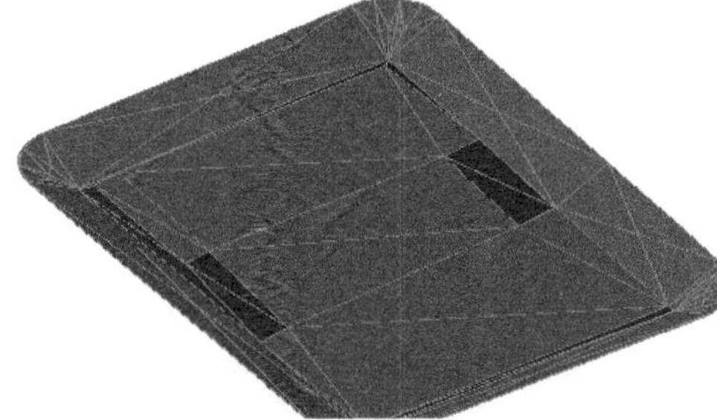

Figure 10-27 Grading after creating the grading infill

Grading Transition

Civil 3D allows you to add a transition to fill the empty area between gradings. The transition grading is the area that merges with grading on its both sides. You can also add a new grading with a transitional value to the existing grading. To add a transition, invoke the **Create Transition** tool from the **Grading Creation Tool** toolbar, as shown in Figure 10-28; you will be prompted to select a feature line.

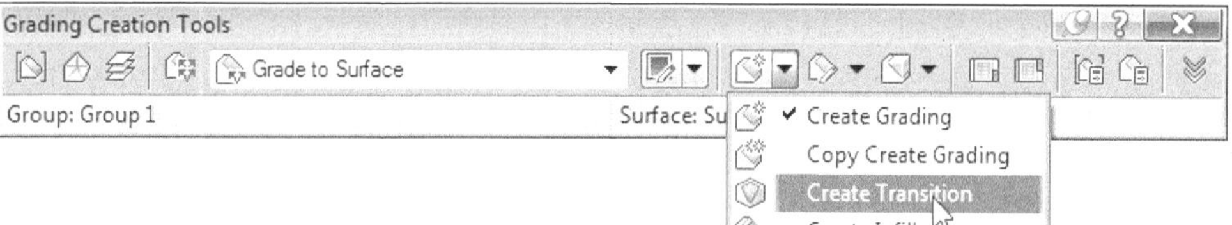

Figure 10-28 Choosing the ***Create Transition*** *tool from the* ***Grading Creation Tool*** *toolbar*

Select the feature line of the required grading from the drawing. Next, specify the grading side and then specify the starting point, station, and distance. Similarly, specify the endpoint, follow the prompts displayed, and add a transitional grading as required. Figure 10-29 shows a grading transition added between two different gradings.

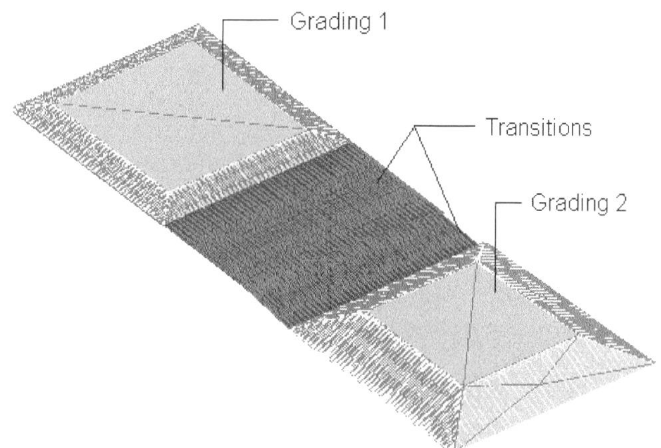

Figure 10-29 The transitional gradings added between Grading 1 and Grading 2

Grading Utilities

In AutoCAD Civil 3D, you can use grading utilities to adjust the total cut and fill volumes in a grading design, and to create a detached surface from the grading groups. Before calculating the cut and fill volumes, you need to select the check box in the **Automatic Surface Creation** area of the **Grading Group Properties** dialog box and create a surface. The method of computing the cut and fill volumes and creating a detached surface from the grading groups is discussed next.

Viewing and Adjusting Surface Volumes

Ribbon: Analyze > Volumes and Materials > Grading Volume Tools
Command: GRADINGVOLUMETOOLS

You can use the **Grading Volume Tools** tool to view and adjust the elevation of a grading design and then optimize the requirement for cut and fill. Before using this tool, you need to ensure that the **Automatic surface creation** check box is selected in the **Create Grading Group** dialog box. If the check box is not selected, select the required grading for which you want to calculate volumes and right-click; a shortcut menu will be displayed. Choose the **Grading Group Properties** option from the shortcut menu; the **Grading Group Properties - <group name>** dialog box will be displayed. Select the check box in the **Automatic surface creation** area of this dialog box. Also, select the check box in the **Volume Base Surface** area, if you want the surface to be the base surface for volume computations. Next, choose the **OK** button to close the dialog box.

To calculate the grading volume, choose the **Grading Volume Tools** tool from the **Volumes and Materials** panel; the **Grading Volume Tools** dialog box will be displayed, as shown in Figure 10-30. The options in the toolbar are discussed next.

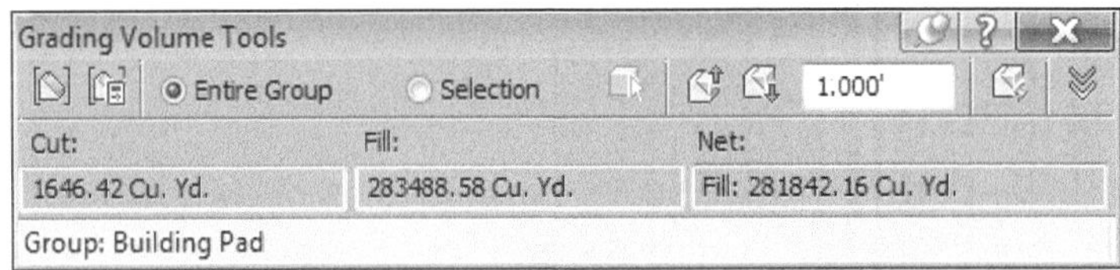

Figure 10-30 The ***Grading Volume Tools*** *dialog box*

In the **Grading Volume Tools** dialog box, the **Set the Grading Group** button allows you to select the grading group. On choosing this button, the **Select Grading Group** dialog box will be displayed. In this dialog box, specify the group name and the site name and then choose the **OK** button to close the dialog box.

To specify the properties of the grading group, choose the **Grading Group Properties** button; the **Grading Group Properties - <group name>** dialog box will be displayed. Specify the required properties in this dialog box and then choose the **OK** button to return to the toolbar. To adjust the elevation of the entire grading group, select the **Entire Group** radio button. If you need to adjust the elevation of a section of the grading group, select the **Selection** radio button. To raise the elevation of the grading group or section of the grading group, choose the **Raise the Grading Group** button. Similarly, to lower the elevation of the grading group or section of the grading group, choose the **Lower the Grading Group** button and enter a value in the text box next to the button. To automatically balance the volume of the grading group, choose the **Automatically raise/lower to balance volumes** button; the **Auto-Balance Volumes** dialog box will be displayed. Enter a value in the **Required Volume** text box and choose the **OK** button to close the dialog box; the adjusted volume will be displayed in the **History** table. To view the **History** table, expand the **Grading Volume Tools** toolbar by choosing the button on its topright corner of the toolbar. Close the dialog box after the grading volume calculation is done.

Creating a Detached Surface

Ribbon: Home > Create Ground Data > Surfaces drop-down> Create Surface from Grading
Command: CREATEDETACHEDGRADINGSURF

You can create a detached (static) surface from the grading group. The detached surface is the one in which the changes do not reflect if the grading object is changed. To create a detached surface from the grading group, choose the **Create Surface from Grading** tool from the **Surfaces** drop-down in the **Create Ground Data** panel; the **Select Grading Group** dialog box will be displayed. Select the required grading group from this dialog box and choose the **OK** button; the dialog box will be closed and the **Create Surface** dialog box will be displayed.

Specify the surface name in the **Value** field of the **Name** property. Select a surface style from the **Value** field of the **Style** property and choose the **OK** button; the dialog box will be closed and the surface will be created and added to the **Surfaces** node.

Note

*You can also create a dynamic surface from the grading group. The dynamic surface changes according to the changes made in the grading group or grading object. To create a dynamic surface from the grading group, select the **Automatic surface creation** check box in the **Create Grading Group** dialog box.*

Grading Style

To create a grading style, choose the **Settings** tab from the **TOOLSPACE** palette and then expand **Grading > Grading Styles** to view the default style. Now, right-click on **Grading Styles** sub-node; a shortcut menu will be displayed. Choose the **New** option from this menu; the **Grading Style - New Grading Style** dialog box will be displayed.

In the **Information** tab of the dialog box, enter a name of the style in the **Name** edit box. Choose the **Center Marker** tab to specify the size of the marker. In this tab, select the required option from the **Size** drop-down list in the **Options** area to calculate the marker size. The **Percentage of Screen** option is the default option selected from the drop-down list. This option allows the size of the marker to be calculated as the fixed percentage of the drawing window. Specify the percentage in the edit box on the right. The **Plotted Size** option is selected from the **Size** drop-down list to specify the size of the marker based on the current drawing unit. On selecting the **Fixed Size** option from the **Size** drop-down list, you can specify the marker size based on the current drawing units. Now, choose the **Slope Patterns** tab from the dialog box, refer to Figure 10-31. This tab is used to select a pattern to represent the grading slopes. Select the **Slope pattern** check box in the **Options** area.

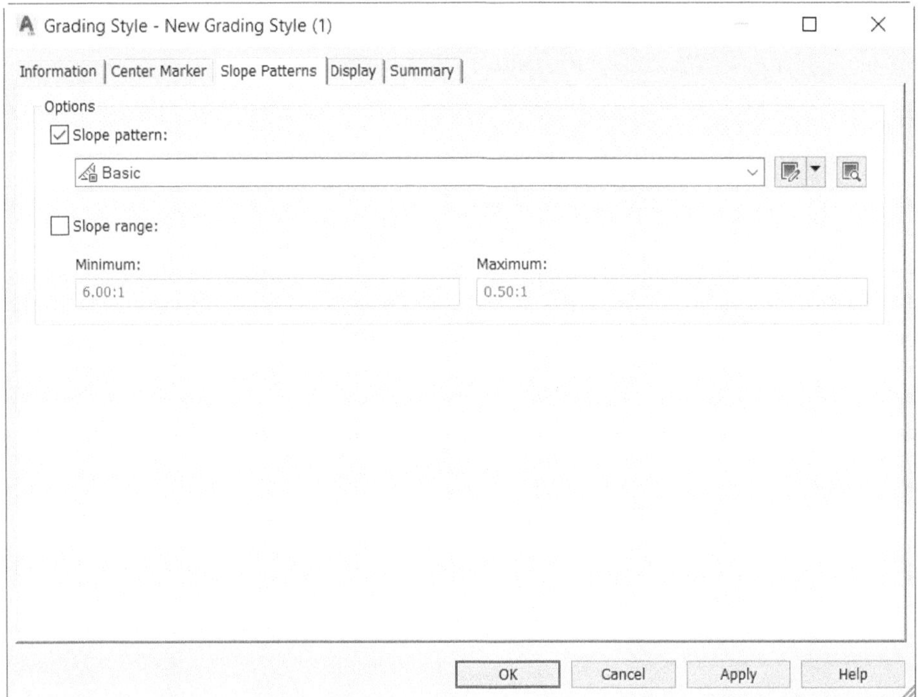

Figure 10-31 The ***Slope Patterns*** *tab of the* ***Grading Style - New Grading Style*** *dialog box*

Then, select an option from the drop-down list below the **Slope pattern** check box. To create a new slope pattern, choose the down arrow on the right side of the drop-down list; a flyout will be displayed. Choose the **Create New** option from the flyout; the **Slope Pattern Style - New Slope Pattern Style** dialog box will be displayed. You can use this dialog box to create a new slope pattern style. To apply the slope pattern with the current grading style to a specified range of slope values, select the **Slope range** check box that will be activated after you have selected the **Slope pattern** check box; the **Minimum** and **Maximum** edit boxes will be enabled. Specify the minimum and maximum slope range for the slope pattern in the respective edit boxes.

Choose the **Display** tab to set the appearance and display of different components of grading. Select the view direction from the **View Direction** drop-down list and specify the display settings for the selected view direction. Next, choose the **OK** button after specifying all parameters; the dialog box will be closed and the style that you have created will be added in the **Grading Styles** sub-node of the **Grading** node in the **Settings** tab.

To apply the grading style to a grading, select the grading marker in the drawing and right-click on it to display a shortcut menu. Choose **Grading Properties** option from the shortcut menu; the **Grading Properties** dialog box will be displayed. In this dialog box, select the options from the drop-down list in the **Style** area. After you have selected the style, choose the **OK** button to close the dialog box.

TUTORIALS

Tutorial 1 Creating Feature Lines

In this tutorial, you will first create a feature line style and then feature lines from the existing polylines. Additionally, you will edit feature lines and create grading from them, as shown in Figure 10-32. **(Expected time: 30 min)**

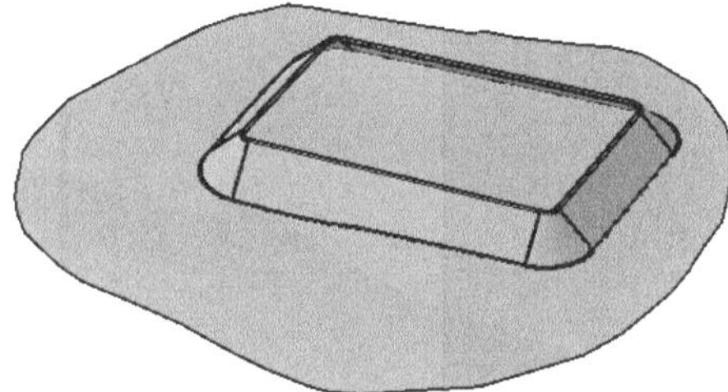

Figure 10-32 *Grading created from the feature lines*

The following steps are required to complete this tutorial:

a. Download and open the file.
b. Create a new feature line style.
c. Convert polylines into feature lines.
d. Edit the feature lines geometry.
e. Edit the feature lines elevations.
f. Create grading.
g. Save the file.

Downloading and Opening the File

1. Download the *c10_c3d_2018_tut.zip* file from *http://www.cadcim.com* as explained in Chapter 2.

2. Choose **Open** from the **Application Menu**; the **Select File** dialog box is displayed.

3. In the dialog box, browse to the location *C:\c3d_2018\c10_c3d_2018_tut.*

4. Select the *c10_c3d_2018_tut01.dwg* file and then choose the **Open** button to open the file.

Creating a Feature Line Style

1. Choose the **Settings** tab from the **TOOLSPACE** palette and expand **General > Multipurpose Styles > Feature Line Styles** to view the existing feature line styles.

2. Right-click on **Feature Line Styles**; a shortcut menu is displayed. Choose the **New** option from this menu; the **Feature Line Style - New Feature Line Style** dialog box is displayed. Accept the default name of the style displayed in the **Name** edit box of the **Information** tab.

3. Next, choose the **Profile** tab. In the **Object Display** area of this tab, select the **Basic X** option from the **Beginning Vertex Marker Style** drop-down list, as shown in Figure 10-33.

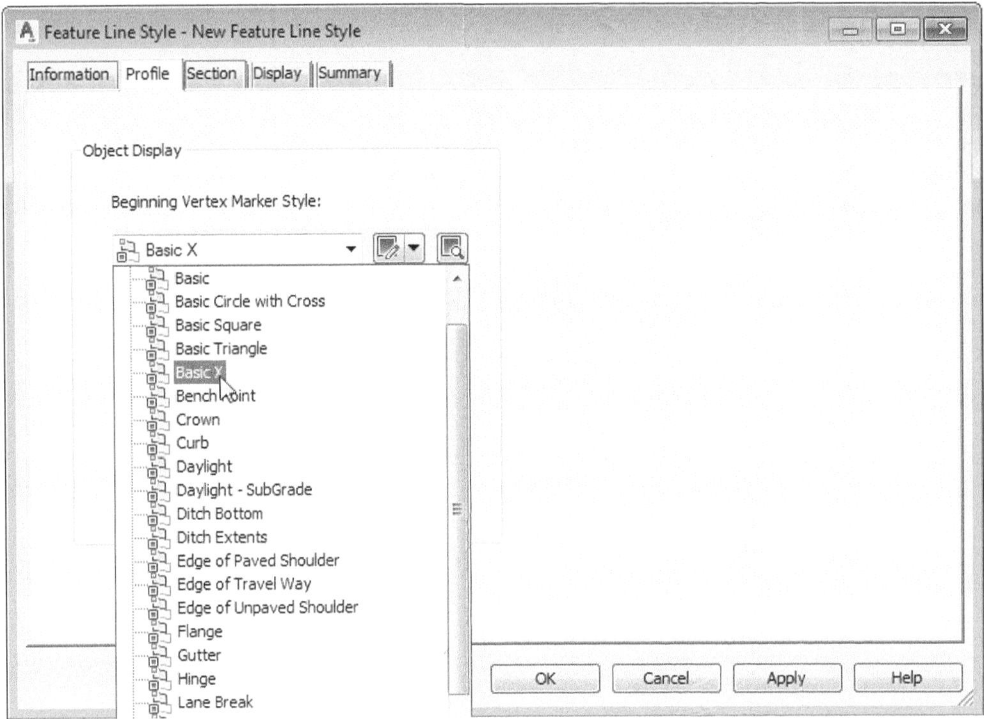

Figure 10-33 Selecting the ***Basic X*** *option from the* ***Beginning Vertex Marker Style*** *drop-down list*

4. Select the **Basic X** option from both the **Internal Vertex Marker Style** and **Ending Vertex Marker Style** drop-down lists.

5. Next, choose the **Section** tab and then select the **Basic X** option from the **Crossing Marker Style** drop-down list.

6. Next, choose the **Display** tab. Ensure that the **Plan** option is selected in the **View Direction** drop-down list.

7. Set the color of the **Feature Line** layer to red and Lineweight to **0.40** mm in the **Component display** list box.

8. Choose the **OK** button; the **Feature Line Style - New Feature Line Style** dialog box is closed and the **New Feature Line Style** style is added to the **Feature Line Styles** node. You will use this line style to display the feature lines.

After creating a feature line style, you need to create feature lines from the polyline objects.

Converting Polylines into Feature Lines

1. Choose the **Create Feature Lines from Objects** tool from **Home > Create Design > Feature Line** drop-down; you are prompted to select objects from the drawing to convert polyline into a feature line.

2. Select the polyline from the drawing, refer to Figure 10-34 and then press ENTER; the **Create Feature Lines** dialog box is displayed.

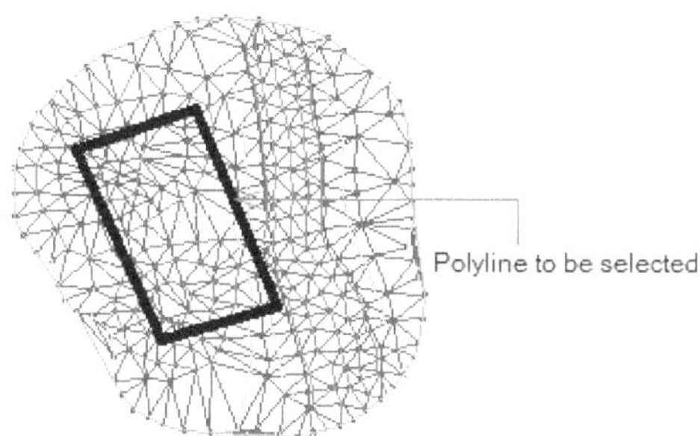

Figure 10-34 *Polyline to be selected from the drawing*

3. Select the **Name** check box in the dialog box; the **Click to edit name template** button  is enabled.

4. Choose the **Click to edit name template** button; the **Name Template** dialog box is displayed.

5. Enter **Building Pad** in the **Name** edit box and choose the **OK** button; the **Name Template** dialog box is closed.

6. Next, in the **Create Feature Lines** dialog box, select the **Style** check box; the drop-down list below the check box is activated.

7. Select the **New Feature Line Style** option from the drop-down list.

8. Choose the **OK** button; the **Create Feature Lines** dialog box is closed and the polylines are converted into feature lines.

Editing the Feature Line Geometry

1. Choose the **Fillet** tool from the **Edit Geometry** panel of the **Modify** tab; you are prompted to select the object. 

Note

You can toggle the display of the ***Edit Geometry*** *panel in the* ***Feature Line*** *tab by choosing the* ***Edit Geometry*** *tool in the* ***Modify*** *panel.*

2. Select the building pad feature lines from the drawing; you are prompted to specify a corner or All/Join/Radius.

3. Enter **R** in the command line and press ENTER; you are prompted to specify radius. Enter **15** in the command line and then press ENTER; you are again prompted to specify corner or All/Join/Radius.

4. Enter **A** for all the corners and press ENTER; all the corners of the building pad get filleted, as shown in Figure 10-35. Press ESC to end the command.

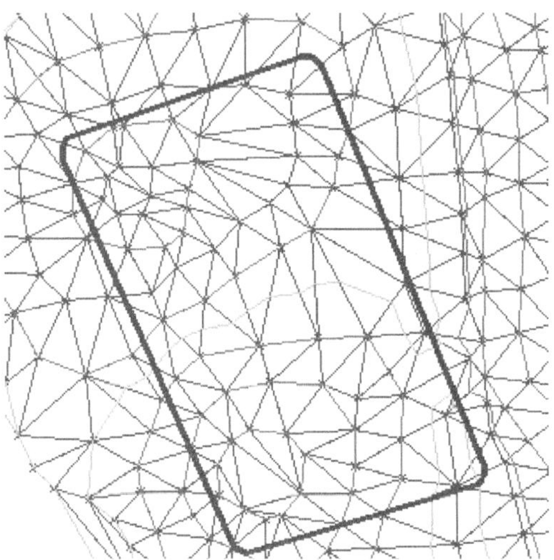

Figure 10-35 Feature lines of the building pad after using the ***Fillet*** *tool*

Editing the Feature Line Elevation

1. Choose the **Elevation Editor** tool from the **Edit Elevations** panel of the **Modify** tab; you are prompted to select an object from the drawing. Select the **Building Pad** feature line; the **Grading Elevation Editor** tab in the **PANORAMA** window is displayed, as shown in Figure 10-36.

2. Choose the **Set Increment** button in the **Grading Elevation Editor** tab of the **PANORAMA** window; the edit box on the right of the button is enabled. 

Station	Elevation(Actual)	Length	Grade Back	Grade Ahead
0+00.00	0.000'	235.959'		0.00%
2+35.96	0.000'	16.788'	0.00%	0.00%
2+52.75	0.000'	393.156'	0.00%	0.00%
6+45.90	0.000'	14.268'	0.00%	0.00%
6+60.17	0.000'	223.269'	0.00%	0.00%
8+83.44	0.000'	16.807'	0.00%	0.00%
9+00.25	0.000'	400.007'	0.00%	0.00%
13+00.25	0.000'	14.969'	0.00%	0.00%
13+15.22	0.000'		0.00%	

Figure 10-36 The ***Grading Elevation Editor*** *tab of the* ***PANORAMA*** *window*

3. Enter **150.000** in the edit box and then choose the **Raise Incrementally** button from the **Grading Elevation Editor** tab; the elevation of the vertices of all the feature lines is raised by the value specified in the edit box. 

4. Now, choose the green tick mark button; the **PANORAMA** window is closed. 

Creating a Grading

1. Choose the **Grading Creation Tools** tool from **Home > Create Design > Grading** drop-down; the **Grading Creation Tools** toolbar is displayed.

2. Choose the **Set the Grading Group** button from the toolbar; the **Create Grading Group** dialog box is displayed. 

3. Specify **Group 1** as the group name in the **Name** edit box of the dialog box.

4. Choose the **OK** button; the **Create Grading Group** dialog box is closed and the group name is displayed at the bottom of the **Grading Creation Tools** toolbar.

5. In the **Select a Grading Criteria** drop-down list of the **Grading Creation Tools** toolbar, select the **Grade to Surface** option, as shown in Figure 10-37.

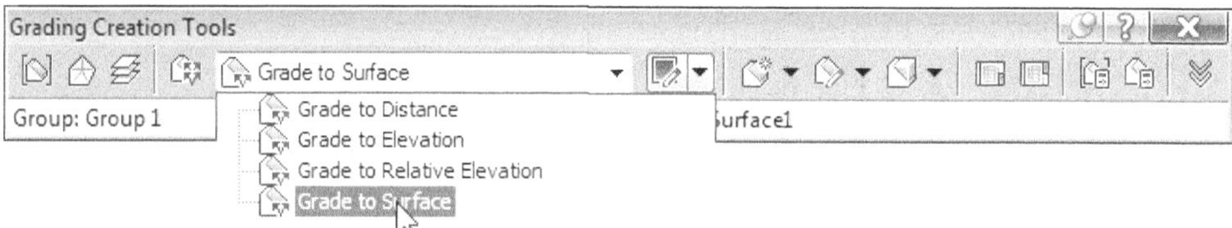

*Figure 10-37 Selecting the **Grade to Surface** option from the **Select a Grading Criteria** drop-down list*

6. Now, choose the **Create Grading** button; you are prompted to select a feature. 

7. Select the feature lines from the drawing; you are prompted to select the grading side. Click in the area outside the closed feature line to specify the grading side; you are prompted whether to apply grading to the entire length or not.

8. Press ENTER to accept the default **Yes** option; you are prompted to specify the cut format.

9. Again, press ENTER; you are prompted to specify the cut slope.

10. Enter **1:1** as cut slope value in the command line and then press ENTER; you are prompted to specify fill format.

11. Again, press ENTER; you are prompted to specify the fill slope. Enter **1:1** as the fill slope value in the command line and then press ENTER; you are prompted to select a feature.

12. Press ESC to exit the command and close the **Grading Creation Tools** toolbar.

13. Choose the **Conceptual** option from **View > Visual Styles > Visual Styles** drop-down.

14. Next, choose the **NE Isometric** option from the **Views** panel in the **View** tab to view grading.

15. Use the **ViewCube** tool to view the grading from different angles. Figure 10-38 shows the Conceptual view of the Building Pad grading with NE Isometric orientation.

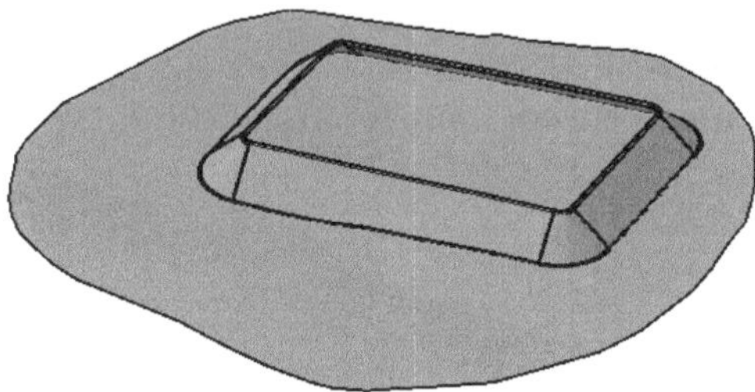

***Figure 10-38** The grading in the Conceptual view with the NE Isometric orientation*

Saving the File

1. Choose **Save As** from the **Application Menu**; the **Save Drawing As** dialog box is displayed.

2. In this dialog box, browse to the following location:

   C:\c3d_2018\c10_c3d_2018_tut

3. Save the file as *c10_tut01a*.

Tutorial 2 Creating Pond Grading

In this tutorial, you will create a pond basin by drawing the feature lines. Also, you will create criteria set for the pond and then grade the pond, as shown in Figure 10-39.

(Expected time: 30 min)

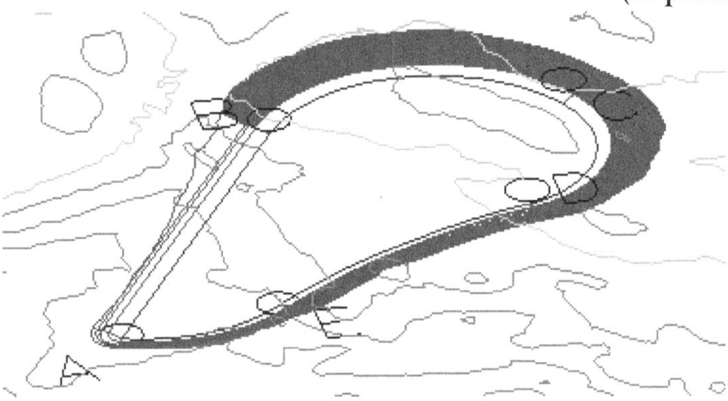

***Figure 10-39** Pond after creating the grading*

The following steps are required to complete this tutorial:

a. Download and open the file.
b. Draw feature lines to create the pond outline.
c. Create a grading criteria set for the pond grading.
d. Grade the pond.
e. Save the drawing file.

Downloading and Opening the File

1. Download the *c10_c3d_2018_zip* file from *http://www.cadcim.com* as explained in Chapter 2, if you have not downloaded it earlier.

2. Choose **Open** from the **Application Menu**; the **Select File** dialog box is displayed.

3. In the dialog box, browse to the location *C:\c3d_2018\c10_c3d_2018.*

4. Next, select the *c10_c3d_2018_tut02.dwg* file and then choose the **Open** button to open the file. Ignore any error messages, if displayed. The file consists of a surface and few circular marks. You will first create the pond boundary feature lines by connecting the centers of these circles. You can use the **OSNAP** command to snap to the centers of the circles.

Drawing the Feature Lines

1. Choose the **Create Feature Line** tool from **Home > Create Design > Feature Line** drop-down; the **Create Feature Lines** dialog box is displayed.

2. Enter **Pond Boundary** in the **Name** edit box of the dialog box and choose the **OK** button; the dialog box is closed and you are prompted to specify the start point of the feature line.

3. Zoom in to view the circles in the drawing and then press the F3 button. The **Object Snap** feature is activated.

4. Snap to the center of the circle **A** and then click to specify the start point of the feature line, as shown in Figure 10-40.

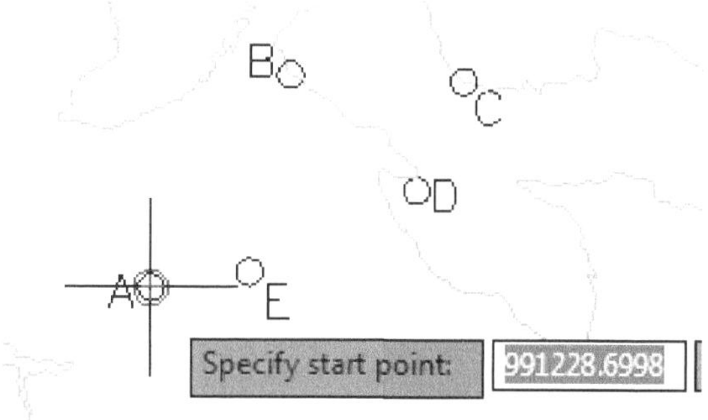

Figure 10-40 *Selecting the center of the circle to specify the start point of the feature line*

5. On specifying the start point of the feature line, you are prompted to specify the elevation. Enter **300** in the command line and press ENTER; you are prompted to specify the next point.

6. Click at the center of the circle **B**, as shown in Figure 10-41.

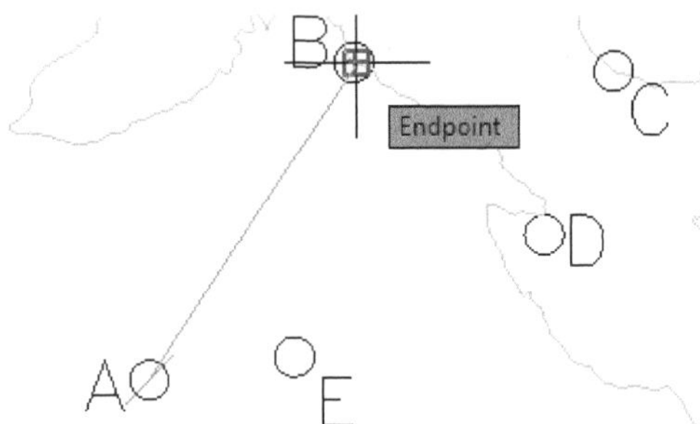

Figure 10-41 Specifying the second point

7. Specify the elevation as **300** in the command line and again press ENTER; you are prompted to specify the next point or the arc length.

8. Next, enter **A** in the command line and press ENTER; you are prompted to specify the arc endpoint.

9. Click at the center of the circle **C** to create a curved feature line.

10. Next, enter **300** as elevation in the command line and then press ENTER.

11. Again, click at the center of the circle **D** to create another curved feature line segment, as shown in Figure 10-42; you are prompted to enter the elevation.

12. Enter **300** as the elevation value in the command line and then press ENTER.

13. Similarly, click at the center of the circle **E** and enter **300** as the elevation in the command line. Next, press ENTER.

14. Now, enter **C** in the command line and press ENTER to end the command. You have drawn the pond boundary by using the feature lines. Figure 10-43 shows the pond boundary created.

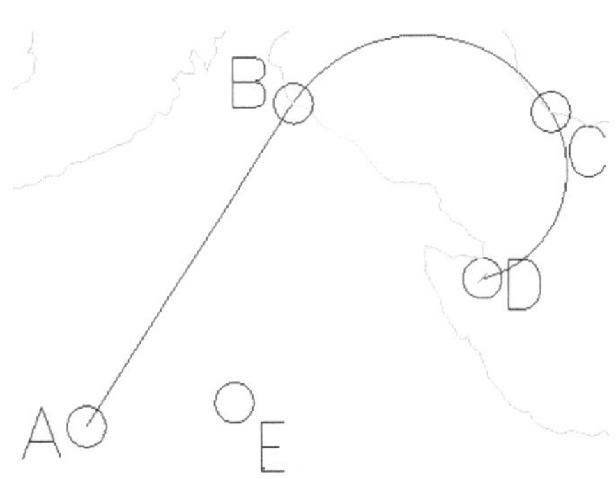

Figure 10-42 Drawing the curved feature line segment

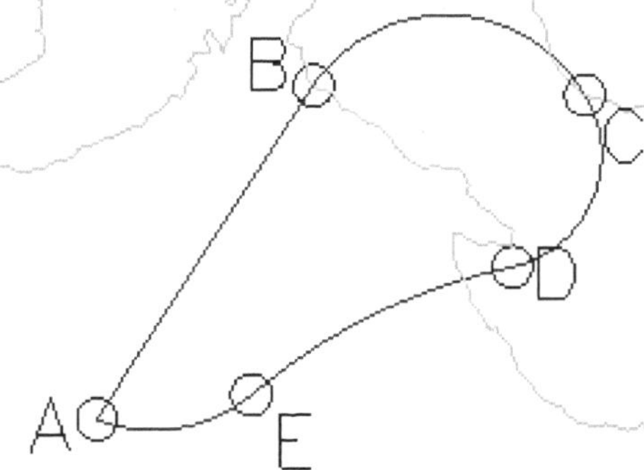

Figure 10-43 Pond boundary

Creating the Grading Criteria Set

1. Choose the **Settings** tab from the **TOOLSPACE** palette and expand **Grading > Grading Criteria Sets**.

2. Now, right-click on the **Grading Criteria Sets** sub-node and choose the **New** option from the shortcut menu displayed; the **Grading Criteria Sets Properties - Grading Criteria Set (1)** dialog box is displayed.

3. Enter **Pond Grading** in the **Name** edit box and choose the **OK** button; the dialog box is closed and **Pond Grading** is added to the **Grading Criteria Sets** sub-node.

4. Right-click on **Pond Grading** and choose the **New** option from the shortcut menu displayed; the **Grading Criteria - New Grading Criteria** dialog box is displayed.

5. In this dialog box, enter **Elevation - 3:1** in the **Name** edit box of the **Information** tab and then choose the **Criteria** tab.

6. In the **Grading Method** area of this tab, set the value of the **Target** property to **Elevation** and then set all the other parameters, as specified below:

   Grading Method Head
   Elevation: 360.000'

   Cut Slope Projection (up) Head
   Slope 3.00:1

   Fill Slope Projection (down) Head
   Slope 3.00:1

7. Click on the lock symbol in the **Lock** column and lock the values for the **Elevation** property in the **Grading Method** area. Also, lock the values for the **Slope** property in the **Cut Slope Projection (up)** and **Fill Slope Projection (down)** areas, refer to Figure 10-44.

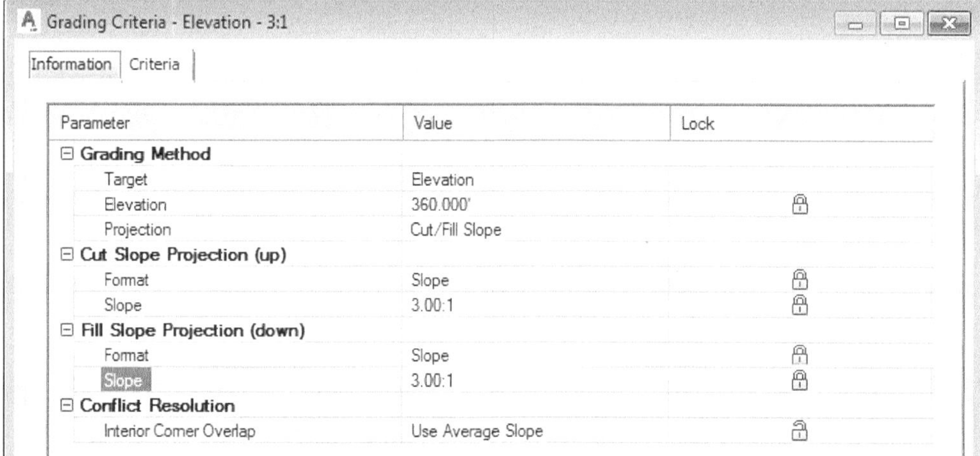

Figure 10-44 *Partial view of the parameters specified in the* ***Criteria*** *tab*

8. Choose the **OK** button to close the **Grading Criteria - Elevation-3:1** dialog box. In this way, one elevation-based criteria is created. Next, expand the **Pond Grading** node and then right-click on it; a shortcut menu is displayed. Choose the **Refresh** option from this menu.

9. Next, expand the **Pond Grading** sub-node in the **Grading Criteria Sets** node of the **Settings** tab and right-click on the **Elevation - 3:1** sub-node. Choose the **Copy** option from the shortcut menu displayed; the **Grading Criteria - Elevation - 3:1[Copy]** dialog box is displayed.

10. Enter **Elevation - 4:1** in the **Name** edit box and choose the **Criteria** tab in the dialog box.

11. Set the value of the **Elevation** property to **360.000',** if it is not set by default. Similarly, set the value for the **Slope** property in the **Cut Slope Projection(up)** node to **4.00:1** and the value for the **Slope** property under the **Fill Slope Projection(down)** node to **4.00:1**. Ensure that all values are locked. Choose the **OK** button to close the dialog box. In this way, the second elevation-based criteria is created.

12. Right-click on the **Elevation - 4:1** sub-node in the **Settings** tab of the **TOOLSPACE** and choose the **Copy** option from the shortcut menu displayed; the **Grading Criteria - Elevation - 4:1 [Copy]** dialog box is displayed.

13. In this dialog box, enter **Berm** in the **Name** edit box of the **Information** tab and then choose the **Criteria** tab.

14. Specify the following values in the **Criteria** tab of the **Grading Criteria-Berm** dialog box, as shown in Figure 10-45 and enter the following parameters specified below

Slope Projection Head
Format : **Grade**
Grade : **3.00%**

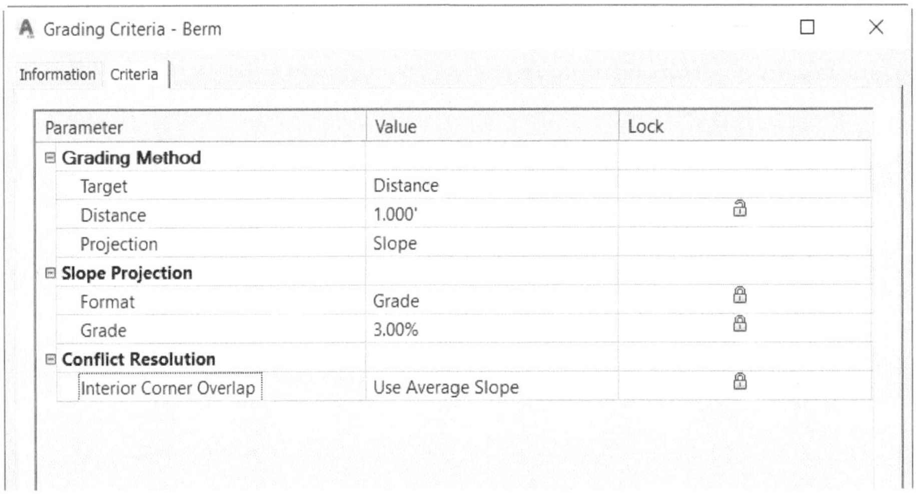

Grading Criteria - Berm

Information Criteria

Parameter	Value	Lock
⊟ **Grading Method**		
Target	Distance	
Distance	1.000'	
Projection	Slope	
⊟ **Slope Projection**		
Format	Grade	
Grade	3.00%	
⊟ **Conflict Resolution**		
Interior Corner Overlap	Use Average Slope	

Figure 10-45 *Partial view of the parameters to be specified for the* ***Berm*** *grading criteria*

15. Next, choose the **OK** button; the dialog box is closed.

16. Using the procedure given in steps 12 and 13, create a grading criteria set with the name **Surface**.

17. In the **Criteria** tab, set the value of the **Target** property to **Surface**, and the value for the **Slope** under the **Cut Slope Projection (up)** and **Fill Slope Projection (down)** nodes to **3:1**. Next, choose the **OK** button; the dialog box is closed.

Grading the Pond

1. Choose the **Grading Creation Tools** tool from **Home > Create Design > Grading** drop-down; the **Grading Creation Tools** toolbar is displayed.

2. Choose the **Set the Grading Group** button from the toolbar; the **Select Grading Group** dialog box is displayed.

3. In this dialog box, select the **Pond Grade** option from the **Group name** drop-down list and choose the **OK** button; the **Select Grading Group** dialog box is closed.

4. Next, choose the **Select a Criteria Set** button from the **Grading Creation Tools** toolbar; the **Select a Criteria Set** dialog box is displayed.

5. Select the **Pond Grading** option from the drop-down list in the dialog box and choose the **OK** button; the **Select a Criteria Set** dialog box is closed.

6. Now, select the **Elevation - 3:1** option from the **Select a Grading Criteria** drop-down list, as shown in Figure 10-46. Next, choose the **Create Grading** button; you are prompted to select a feature.

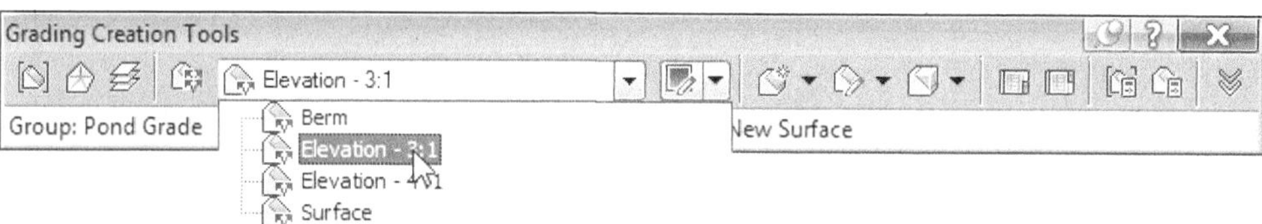

Figure 10-46 *Selecting the* ***Elevation-3:1*** *option from the* ***Select a Grading Criteria*** *drop-down list*

7. Select the pond boundary that you have drawn; you are prompted to specify the grading side.

8. Click on the outer side of the pond boundary to specify the grading side; you are prompted to specify whether you want to apply grading to the entire length. Press ENTER to select the **Yes** option. Civil 3D starts the grading process. Wait until the process is completed. Figure 10-47 shows the grading created using the **Elevation - 3:1** criteria.

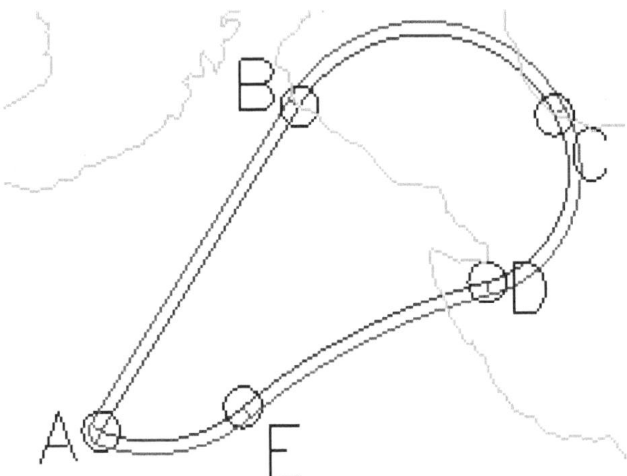

Figure 10-47 *The first grading created using the* ***Elevation-3:1*** *criteria*

9. Now, select the **Berm** option from the **Select a Grading Criteria** drop-down list in the **Grading Creation Tools** toolbar and select the outer edge of the grading that you have created.

10. Press ENTER to grade the entire length of the pond; you are prompted to specify the distance.

11. Enter **100** in the command line and then press ENTER; you are prompted to specify the grade. Press ENTER to accept the default value for grading. Wait till the pond grading is created and displayed in the drawing, as shown in Figure 10-48.

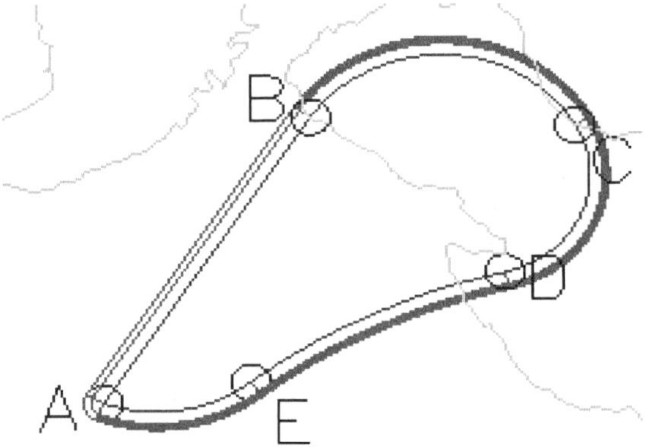

Figure 10-48 *Berm created using the* ***Berm*** *criteria set*

12. Now, select **Elevation - 4:1** from the **Select a Grading Criteria** drop-down list in the **Grading Creation Tools** toolbar and select the outer edge of the berm created.

13. Press ENTER to apply the grading to the entire length of the pond. In this way, the third grading is completed.

14. Again, select the **Berm** option from the **Select a Grading Criteria** drop-down list; you are prompted to select a feature.

15. Select the outer edge of the grading; you are prompted to specify whether you want to apply grading to the entire length. Press ENTER to apply grading to the entire length of the pond; you are prompted to enter the grade distance.

16. Enter **50** in the command line and press ENTER; you are prompted to specify grade. Accept the default value and press ENTER; you are prompted to select a feature.

17. Now, select the **Surface** option from the **Select a Grading Criteria** drop-down list. Next, choose the **Create Grading** tool from the toolbar; you are prompted to select the feature.

18. Select the outer edge of pond grading; you are prompted to specify if the grading is to be applied to the entire length. Press ENTER to apply the grading to the entire length. Wait till the daylight calculations are completed and the final grading of the pond is created. The final view of the pond is displayed in the drawing, as shown in Figure 10-49.

19. Close the toolbar and press ESC to exit.

Note

The final grading of the pond might take some more time to complete as compared to the earlier pond gradings. You can check the status of the progress of the creation of grading in the progress bar at the lower right corner of the screen.

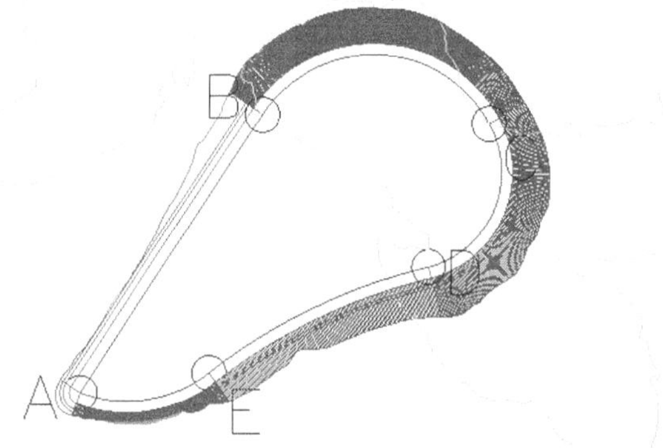

Figure 10-49 *The pond after creating final grading*

Viewing the Pond in 3D

1. Choose **3D Wireframe** option from the **Visual Styles** panel of the **View** tab.

2. Use **ViewCube** to spin and view the pond grading from different directions, as shown in Figure 10-50. You can remove the circles from thc drawing.

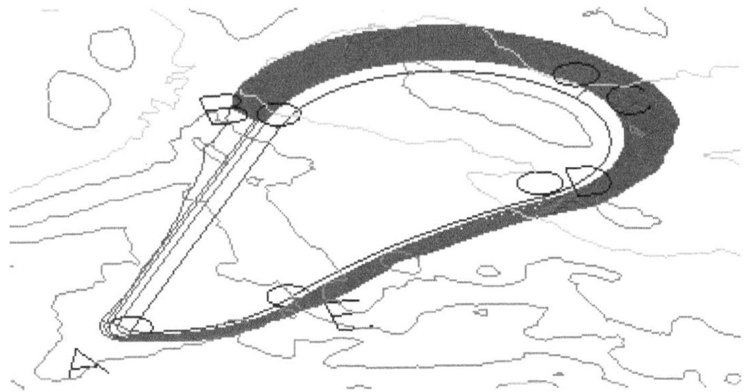

Figure 10-50 The 3D view of the pond after the completion of the grading

Saving the File

1. Choose **Save As** from the **Application Menu**; the **Save Drawing As** dialog box is displayed.

2. In this dialog box, browse to the following location:

   C:\c3d_2018\c10_c3d_2018

3. Save the file as *c10_tut02a*.

Self-Evaluation Test

Answer the following questions and then compare them to those given at the end of this chapter:

1. Which of the following features of Civil 3D defines the relationship between the Civil 3D object and terrain?

   a) Grading criteria   b) Feature line
   c) Surface   d) Alignment

2. Which of the following tools in the **Grading Volume Tools** dialog box calculates grading values for the cut and fill volumes so as to achieve the specified target value for net volume?

   a) **Raise the Grading Group**
   b) **Lower the Grading Group**
   c) **Automatically Raise/lower to Balance Volumes**
   d) None of the above

3. Which of the following is created using the **Create Detached Surface** tool?

   a) Static surface b) Cut/Fill volume surface
   c) Composite surface d) Dynamic surface

4. Which of the following features is created using the **Create Feature Line** tool?

   a) New feature line segments
   b) Feature line from AutoCAD object
   c) Feature line from an alignment
   d) All of the above

5. Which of the following options is used to reduce the number of vertices on a feature line while creating a feature line from an AutoCAD object or an alignment?

   a) **Erase existing entities** b) **Weed points**
   c) **Smooth** d) **Fit Curve**

6. Grading is a process of modeling __________ ground.

7. The two prerequisites for the grading process are __________ and feature line.

8. The __________ is defined as an open or closed geometric figure that represents the object to be graded.

9. The elevation of the feature line can be changed by using the options in the __________ tab of the **PANORAMA** window.

10. The __________ refers to a fill applied to the open areas or voids for creating grading.

11. The __________ tool in the **Grading** (contextual) tab is used to edit the grading criteria.

12. The feature line is a Civil 3D object that is used to represent important features in the drawing such as the ridge line, pavement edges, and so on. (T/F)

13. In Civil 3D, feature line is another name of 3D polyline. (T/F)

14. You can use the **Create Feature Line** tool to convert existing polylines, lines, arcs, and 3D polylines into feature lines. (T/F)

15. The target parameter is used to specify the target or the criteria selected to create a grading. (T/F)

Review Questions

Answer the following questions:

1. The __________ projection is used to allow the projection of a grading object to the target at a fixed horizontal distance from the footprint.

2. The __________ button is used to raise the elevation of the selected feature line points as per the increment value set in the edit box in the **Grading Elevation Editor** tab of the **PANORAMA** window.

3. Civil 3D allows you to add a transition to fill the areas between the grading by using the _________ tool.

4. The __________ button is used to create a quick profile for the selected feature line.

5. The **Grading Volume Tools** tool is used to adjust the cut and fill volumes for a grading group. (T/F)

6. The **Insert Elevation Point** button is used to insert an intermediate elevation point only at the end point of the selected feature line. (T/F)

7. The grading infill cannot be used without creating any criteria. (T/F)

8. The surface created from a grading group is a static surface and reflects the changes made in the grading object. (T/F)

9. You can use the **Grading Volume Tools** tool only when there is a surface in the drawing which is created from a grading group. (T/F)

10. The center marker is a diamond shaped marker that represents the centroid of the grading object. (T/F)

EXERCISE

1. Log on to *www.cadcim.com* and browse to *Textbooks > Civil/GIS > Civil 3D > Exploring AutoCAD Civil 3D 2018*. Next, select *c10_c3d_2018_exer.zip* file from the **Exercise Files** drop-down list. Choose the corresponding **Download** button to download the data file.

2. Now, save and extract the downloaded folder to the following location:

   C:\c3d_2018

Note

*While opening the exercise files, the **PANORAMA** window may appear with an error message. Close this window to proceed further.*

Exercise 1

Open the *c10_c3d_2018_ex01.dwg* file and use the baseline in the drawing file. Next, create the grading object using the criteria in the order given below. **(Expected time: 30 min)**

1.	Lane Distance:	**Applied to the main outer circle** **Distance-21**
2.	Lane Elevation:	**Applied to Lane 1** **Elevation-95** **Fill Slope-1:1**
3.	Lane Relative Elevation:	**Applied to Lane 2** **Relative Elevation-7**
4.	Lane Surface:	**Applied to Lane 3** **Surface** **Fill Slope-2:1** **Cut Slope-2:1**

Apart from the values given, accept all the default values of the properties when you are prompted to do so. Save the file as *c10_ex01a*. The final grading for this exercise is shown in Figure 10-51.

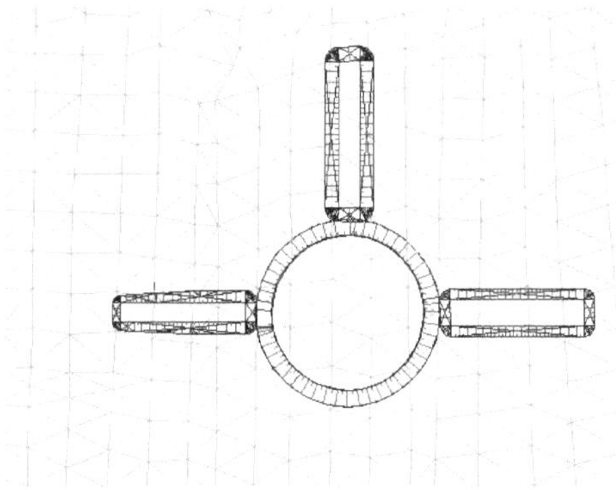

Figure 10-51 *The lanes and the main circle after grading*

Answers to Self-Evaluation Test

1. a, **2.** c, **3.** a, **4.** a, **5.** b, **6.** finished, **7.** Grading group, **8.** footprint, **9. Grading Elevation Editor Panorama**, **10.** grading infill, **11. Edit Grading**, **12.** T, **13.** F, **14.** F, **15.** T

Chapter 11

Pipe Networks

Learning Objectives

After completing this chapter, you will be able to:

- *Understand the pipe network object and its parts*
- *Understand the part builder and the part catalog*
- *Create the network parts list*
- *Create part styles*
- *Understand part rules*
- *Create the pipe network using the network layout tools*
- *Create the pipe network from objects*
- *Draw network parts in a profile view*
- *Edit pipe networks*
- *Add labels to the pipe network*
- *Run the interference check*

OVERVIEW

Pipe networks are an integral part of a design site. A well-designed pipe network, be it a sewage system, storm drainage system, or a water supply system, is an essential aspect of a designed land site. For example, a storm drainage system avoids flooding in an area which occurs due to excessive surface runoff. Runoff is part of the rainwater, snow melt, or irrigation water that occurs when there is more water than land can absorb, it flows over the ground and returns back to the streams or rivers. The calculation of runoff is an important factor in the site design as the runoff causes erosion of soil, leading to a change in the landscape. Also, excessive runoff may lead to the flooding of an area. The engineers should be aware of the retention capacity of the site and the amount of runoff that the site will detain after being developed. If the excess of runoff is not checked, it may lead to floods and other disturbances.

Hydraulic systems, storm sewers, sanitary sewers, detention ponds and culverts are some of the features that are designed to deal with the flow of water and help diverting the excess runoff to avoid flood. AutoCAD Civil 3D has the ability to analyze and design such hydraulic systems and help the engineers enhance and improve their designs. In AutoCAD Civil 3D, the pipe network objects allow you to draft 2D and 3D models of the hydraulic systems along with the visual effects and useful data. AutoCAD Civil 3D enables you to perform various water management and analysis tasks using three application extensions that are installed on your computer with the installation of Civil 3D. These application extensions are briefly discussed next:

Hydraflow Express Extension: This application allows you to perform hydraulic or hydrology studies on culverts, inlets, weirs, and channels. You can model and design culverts with different shapes using this application extension.

Hydraflow Hydrographs Extension: This extended application of AutoCAD Civil 3D allows you to design and model the detention ponds and watersheds.

Hydraflow Storm Sewers Extension: This application of Civil 3D allows you to import the pipe networks from AutoCAD Civil 3D and modify the pipe designs, perform designs calculations, modify slopes, and then export the modified pipe network back to Civil 3D.

These extensions can be accessed and opened by choosing the **Launch Storm Sewers / Launch Hydrographs / Launch Express** tool from the **Design** panel of the **Analyze** tab. In this chapter, you will learn about pipe networks and other related topics. First, you must get familiar with different terms related to the pipe network object that are discussed next.

PIPE NETWORK

The pipe network object is a collection of different pipes and structures, such as manholes and catch basins that form a pipe system. The pipe network also specifies and maintains the relationship between different parts of the network and other Civil 3D objects, such as surfaces, alignments, and labels. The pipe networks are added in plan views and can consist of both pipes and structures or pipes and structures individually.

AutoCAD Civil 3D provides you with various inbuilt styles to display the pipes and structures with visual effects and data. You can use these styles to display the pipes and structures in plan, profile, or section views as required.

The pipe network objects are listed in the **Networks** sub-node of the **Pipe Networks** node in the **Prospector** tab of the **TOOLSPACE** palette. The information about the pipe network is displayed in the **Prospector Item View** of the **Prospector** tab. Figures 11-1 and 11-2 show a 2D view and a conceptual 3D view of a pipe network, respectively. The pipe network consists of various components and parameters such as pipes, structure and null structure. These components and parameters are discussed next.

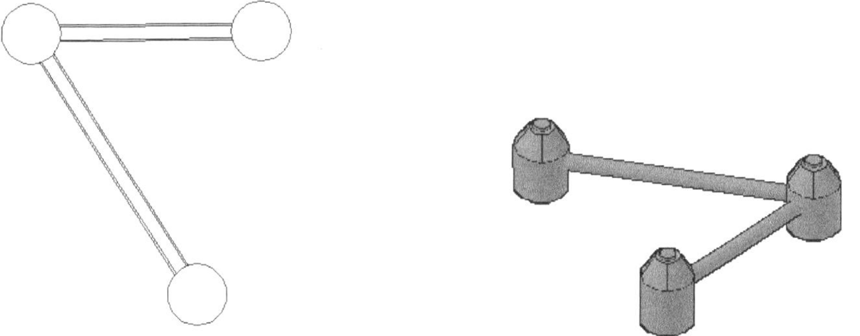

Figure 11-1 *The 2D view of a pipe network* ***Figure 11-2*** *The 3D view of a pipe network*

Pipes

A pipe object can be defined as a tube or a conduit that carries fluid under the gravitational force or pressure applied externally (pumped fluids). Pipes are available in various sizes and shapes such as rectangular, elliptical, oval, or circular. A pipe can be made from different materials such as steel, concrete, PVC, or iron. To create a pipe network in Civil 3D, you can use the default pipes provided in the Civil 3D library or create your own pipes as required. Civil 3D allows you to create and use different pipe styles to control the appearance of pipes in a plan, section, or profile view. The pipe styles are created and managed in the **Settings** tab of the **TOOLSPACE** palette.

Creating a Pipe Style

To create a pipe style, choose the **Settings** tab and expand the **Pipe** node. Next, right-click on **Pipe Styles** and choose **New** from the shortcut menu displayed; the **Pipe Style - New Pipe Style** dialog box will be displayed. The tabs in this dialog box are discussed next.

Information Tab

This tab is used to specify a pipe style name. You can specify this name in the **Name** edit box of the **Information** tab.

Plan Tab

This tab is used to specify the settings for the pipe display and the dimensions in the plan view, as shown in Figure 11-3. From the **Pipe wall sizes** area of this tab, select the **Use part dimensions** radio button to draw the inner and outer pipe wall dimensions according to the actual dimensions of the pipe part. The **User defined** radio button can be selected to draw the inner and outer pipe wall dimensions, as required. Select an option from the **Size options** drop-down list. Next, specify the inner and outer pipe wall diameters in the **Inner diameter** and **Outer diameter** edit boxes, respectively.

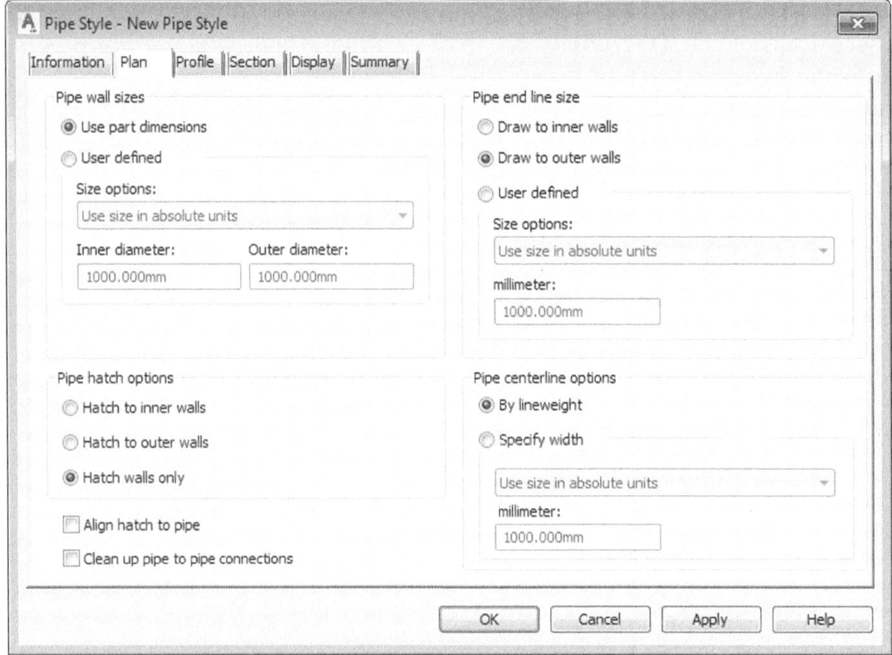

***Figure 11-3** The **Pipe Style - New Pipe Style** dialog box with the **Plan** tab chosen*

The **Pipe end line size** area of the tab provides the options to draw and specify the dimension of the pipe ends. Select the **Draw to inner walls** radio button to draw the pipe end lines equal to the size of the inner walls of the pipe. Similarly, select the **Draw to outer walls** radio button to draw the pipe end lines to the size of the outer walls of the pipe. The **User defined** radio button is selected to specify the pipe ends size as required. Select an option of the pipe end from the **Size options** drop-down list and specify the size of the pipe in the **inch** edit box. In case you have selected the **Use size as percentage of screen** option from the **Size options** drop-down list, then you can specify the size in the **Percent** edit box.

The **Pipe hatch options** area provides you with the options to apply a hatch pattern to the pipe. Select the **Hatch to inner walls** radio button to apply a hatch pattern only to the inner walls of the pipe but not in the area between the outer and inner pipe walls. The **Hatch to outer walls** radio button can be selected to apply a hatch pattern to the entire area of the pipe including the pipe wall. Select the **Hatch walls only** radio button to apply the hatch pattern only to the pipe walls. Figure 11-4 shows a hatch pattern applied to different areas of pipe walls.

From the **Pipe centerline options** area, select the **By lineweight** radio button to draw the pipe centerline based on the existing lineweight of the pipe. The width of the pipe will depend on the lineweight of the pipe. To create a pipe centerline with the required dimensions, select the **Specify width** radio button and specify the width of the pipe centerline using any option available in the drop-down list in this area. Select the **Draw to inner/ Draw to outer walls** option to specify the width of the pipe centerline based on the inner or outer walls of the pipes. If you select the **Use drawing scale** option from the drop-down list, the edit box in this area will be enabled. You can specify a value in the edit box according to the drawing units. For example, if the drawing unit is Metric, the value will be specified in meters. This value will be multiplied with the current drawing scale to determine the width of the pipe centerline. Similarly, on selecting the **Use size as percentage of screen** option, the pipe centerline width will be specified based on the percentage value specified in the **Percent** edit box.

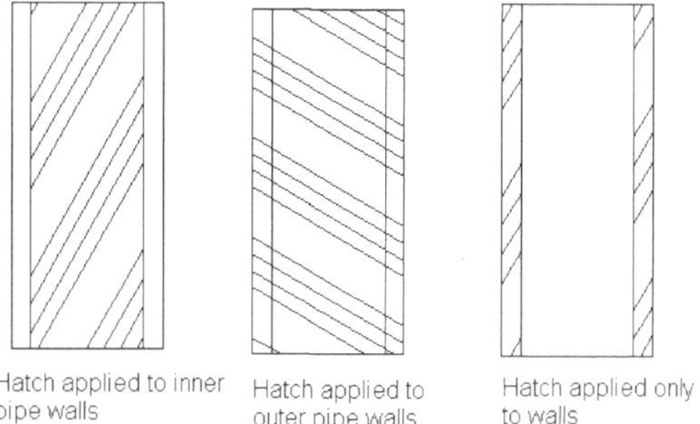

Figure 11-4 *Hatch patterns applied to different areas of the pipe walls*

Select the **Align hatch to pipe** check box to align the hatch pattern with the pipe, if the pipe is inclined at different angles. Select the **Clean up pipe to pipe connection** and check box to enable the clean up of the pipes in the plan view. The pipe cleanup is a process of cleaning up or removing the display of the junctions where the multiple adjoining pipes are connected to the other pipes using the null structures. The pipe to pipe connections are visible in the plan or profile views.

Profile Tab

The options in this tab are the same as that explained in the **Plan** tab except for the **Crossing pipe hatch options** area. The **Crossing pipe hatch options** area is used to specify pipe crossing with a hatch pattern. Use various parameters in this tab to specify the settings for the appearance of the pipe in a profile view.

Section Tab

This tab is used to specify the display of the hatch patterns in the section view of the pipe. Select the required radio button from the **Display as hatched pipe** area of this tab to apply a hatch pattern to the pipes in a section view.

Display Tab

In this tab, you can specify the visibility, color, and other properties of the pipe components in a plan view, model view, profile view, and the section views of the pipe. Also, you can specify the hatch pattern and angle for the hatch lines of the pattern in the **Component hatch display** area of this tab.

Summary Tab

In the **Summary** tab, you can review the information of the pipe style as well as edit the values, if required.

After setting the required parameters, choose the **OK** button; the **Pipe Style - New Pipe Style** dialog box will be closed and the pipe style will be added in the **Pipe Styles** sub-node of the **Pipe** node in the **Settings** tab.

Structures

A structure represents the manholes, catch basins, headwalls, and other parts of a pipe network. The structures are more complex than pipes. AutoCAD Civil 3D provides some in-built structures with specified dimensions and shapes. There are four types of structures available in Civil 3D: **Inlets-Outlets**, **Junction Structures with Frames**, **Junction Structures without Frames**, and **Null** structures. You can modify these structures as required and then use them in the network. Like pipes, structures too have different styles that control their display in the drawing.

Creating a Structure Style

To create a new structure style, choose the **Settings** tab and expand the **Structure** node. Next, right-click on **Structure Styles** and choose **New** from the shortcut menu; the **Structure Style - New Structure Style** dialog box will be displayed. Various tabs in this dialog box are discussed next.

Information Tab

Enter a name for the structure style in the **Name** edit box. You can also enter a short description about the structure style in the **Description** edit box, if required.

Model Tab

The options in this tab are used to define the appearance of the 3D object used to represent the structure in the model view. Use the **Structure** area of this tab to specify the method to be used while defining and drawing the structure. You can select the **Use catalog defined 3D part** radio button from this area to use the 3D object defined in the part catalog for displaying the structure in 3D view. You will learn about the part catalog later in this chapter. Select the **Use simple 3D part** radio button to enable the **3D part type** drop-down list. You can select the 3D figure of the required shape from this drop-down list. You can view the selected 3D figure in the **Preview** area of this tab, refer to Figure 11-5.

Plan Tab

The options in this tab are used to define the appearance of the structure in 2D plan view. In the **Structure** area of this tab, select the **Use outer part boundary** radio button to display the structure in a 2D plan view, as an outline of the 3D object specified in the **Model** tab. To use an AutoCAD block as the 2D view of the structure, select the **User defined part** radio button and choose the button on the right of the **Block name** drop-down list. On doing so, the **Select Drawing File** dialog box will be displayed. Select a file containing the AutoCAD block and choose the **Open** button to assign a block to the structure. The block will be added to the drawing and its name will be displayed in the **Block name** drop-down list. After specifying the shape of the structure, select an option from the **Size options** drop-down list to specify its size.

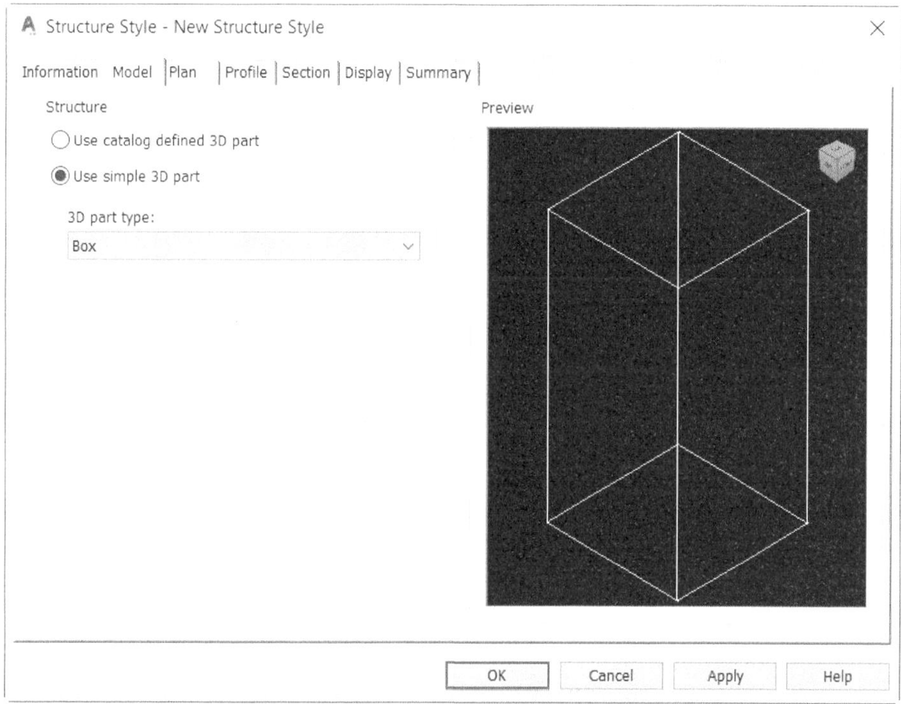

***Figure 11-5** The **Structure Style - New Structure Style** dialog box with the selected 3D figure in the **Preview** area of the **Model** tab*

Profile Tab

Use this tab to specify the display of the 3D object representing the structure in the profile view. The **Display as solid** radio button is selected by default and it enables the use of 3D object in the parts catalog to display the structure in a 3D view. You cannot see the preview of this option. Select the **Display as boundary** radio button to use the actual outer boundary of the structure defined in the parts catalog to display the structure in the profile view. Select the **Display as block** radio button to use an AutoCAD block to represent the structure in a profile view. Select an insertion point for the AutoCAD block from the **Block insertion location** drop-down list. You can add the block at the rim or at the sump of the structure.

Choose the button on the right of the **Block name** drop-down list; the **Select Drawing File** dialog box will be displayed. Select the required file and choose the **Open** button to exit the dialog box; a block will be assigned to the structure. Now, select an option from the **Size options** drop-down list to define the size of the structure.

Section Tab

Use this tab to specify the display of the 3D object representing the structure in a section view. The options in this tab are the same as those discussed in the **Profile** tab.

Display Tab

Use this tab to specify the visibility, color, lineweight, and other properties of the structure object in the plan, model, profile, and the section views. Also, specify the hatch patterns for the structure of all the views in the **Component hatch display** area of this tab.

Summary Tab

Use the **Summary** tab to review all the values specified for the structure style in different tabs and edit the values, if required.

After you have specified the settings for creating the new structure style in the dialog box, choose the **OK** button; the new structure style will be displayed in the **Structure Styles** sub node of the **Structure** node.

Null Structures

The null structure is a special type of structure created at the junction of two pipes. This type of structure is automatically added in the pipe network when a pipe is connected with the other pipe without using any other type of structure. The main use of the null structure is to connect the pipes, as shown in Figure 11-6. You can hide the null structures in a drawing view by creating and assigning different styles to them.

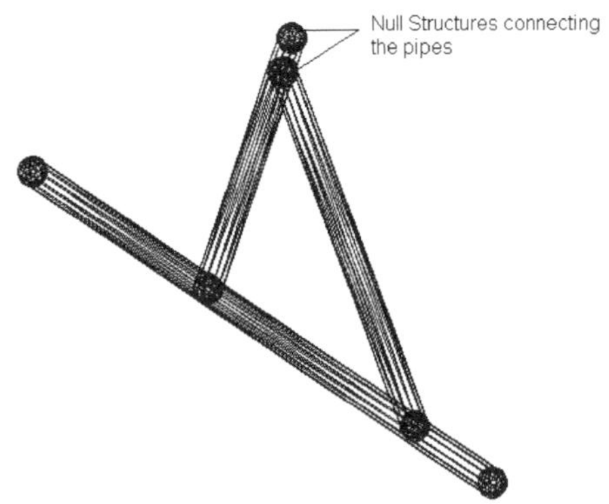

Figure 11-6 *The null structures connecting the pipes*

Note

*The names of the pipes, structures, and the null structure objects cannot be added to the **Prospector** tab of the **TOOLSPACE** palette, but the information related to them can be viewed in the list view. To do so, select a pipe network in the **Prospector** tab; the information about this network will be displayed in the list view, as shown in Figure 11-7.*

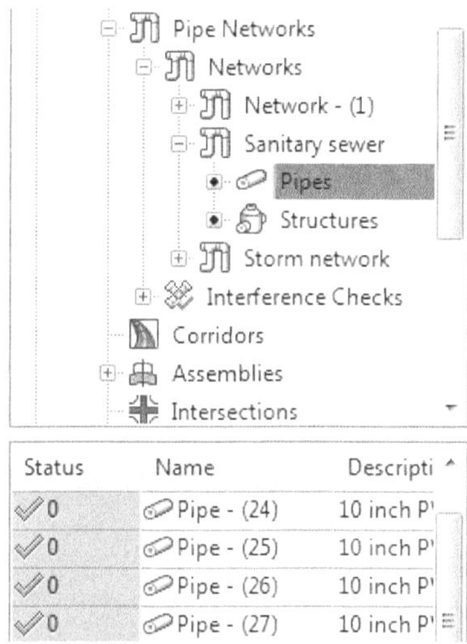

***Figure 11-7** The **Prospector** list view displaying information about **Sanitary sewer** pipe network*

Part Catalog

AutoCAD Civil 3D provides you with the part catalog consisting of various in-built parts (pipes and structures) of different sizes, shapes, materials, and behavior used in a pipe network. After deciding the parts that you want to use to create a design, you can find those parts in the part catalog. The part catalog is automatically saved at the location *C:\ProgramData\Autodesk\C3D 2018\enu\Pipes Catalog* while installing AutoCAD Civil 3D 2018.

A Civil 3D part catalog has two basic domains to select **Pipes** and **Structures**. Both the **Pipes** and the **Structures** domains consist of Metric and Imperial pipe catalogs in the corresponding folders. These folders together form the content of the part catalog. To display and use this catalog, browse to *C:\ProgramData\Autodesk\C3D 2018\enu\Pipes Catalog\US Imperial Pipes*. Each sub-folder in this folder can be expanded to view the type of pipes. Select the required pipe from the left pane of the catalog to view the image, specifications, and available sizes of the selected pipe type.

Similarly, open the *US Imperial Structures.html* file from the **US Imperial Structures** folder. The default structure catalog consists of four different categories representing four types of structures.

Setting the Part Catalog

Ribbon: Home > Create Design > Set Pipe Network Catalog
Command: SETNETWORKCATALOG

To set a part catalog, choose the **Set Pipe Network Catalog** tool from the **Create Design** panel; the **Pipe Network Catalog Settings** dialog box will be displayed, as shown in Figure 11-8. Select the required pipe and structure catalog from the respective **Pipe catalog** and **Structure catalog** drop-down lists and choose the **OK** button to exit the dialog box.

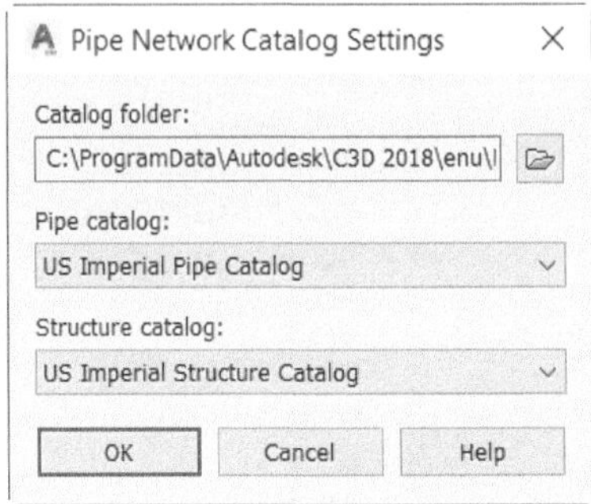

*Figure 11-8 The **Pipe Network Catalog Settings** dialog box*

Parts List

A parts list is a subset of components which are derived from a master catalog of components of a pipe network. A parts list is a collection of required parts (pipes and structures) of a pipe network. The parts list enables you to store the selected pipes, structures, styles, render materials, rule sets, and so on separately in a parts list so that you do not need to navigate and look for the required parts in the part catalog. Thus, the parts list saves time and helps you to use the required parts to create the pipe network in an organized way. You can create different parts list for different projects based on the project requirement. Civil 3D has some default parts list that are stored in the Civil 3D template. However, you can also create your own multiple parts list and then use them in the project.

The parts lists are added in the **Part Lists** sub-node of the **Pipe Network** node in the **Settings** tab of the **TOOLSPACE** palette. Before creating a parts list, you need to specify the part catalog from which the parts list would be derived. Specify the catalog using the **Set Pipe Network Catalog** tool as described earlier. The method of creating a new parts list is discussed next.

Creating a Network Parts List

Ribbon:	Home > Create Design > Create Network Parts List
Command:	CREATENETWORKPARTSLIST

To create a network parts list, choose the **Create Network Parts List** tool from the **Create Design** panel; the **Network Parts List - New Parts List** dialog box will be displayed. The options in this dialog box are discussed next.

Information Tab

Use this tab to specify the name for the part list. Enter a name for the part list in the **Name** edit box. You can also enter a short description about the part in the **Description** edit box.

Pipes Tab

This tab is used to add pipe parts to the parts list. To add the required pipe parts, right-click on **New Parts List** in the **Name** column and choose the **Add part family** option from the shortcut menu displayed, refer to Figure 11-9; the **Part Catalog** dialog box will be displayed. Select the check boxes on the left of the required pipe names to add them to the part list, as shown in Figure 11-10. Next, choose the **OK** button to close the **Part Catalog** dialog box and return to the **Network Parts List - New Parts List** dialog box. Expand the **New Parts**

List node in the **Name** column of the **Pipes** tab to view the added pipe parts.

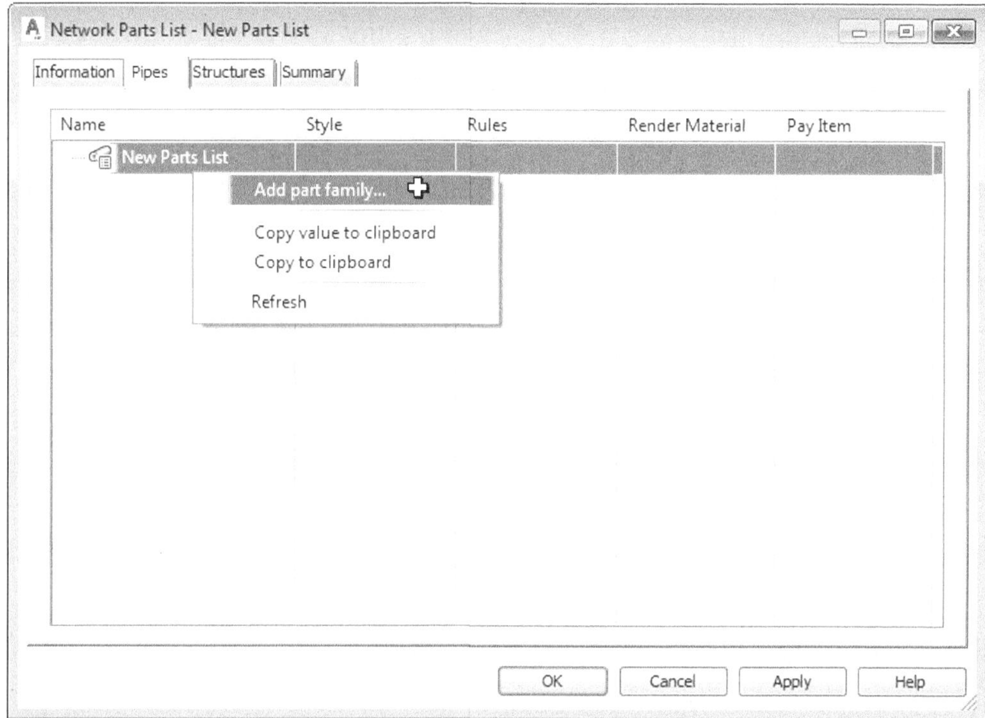

Figure 11-9 Choosing the ***Add part family*** *option from the shortcut menu to add pipe parts*

Structures Tab

This tab is used to add the structure part families to the corresponding list. The null structure is added to the parts list in the **Structures** tab by default. To add a new structure to the parts list, right-click on **New Parts List** in the **Name** column and choose the **Add part family** option from the shortcut menu displayed. On doing so, the **Part Catalog** dialog box will be displayed. Select the check boxes on the left of the required pipe names, refer to Figure 11-11. Next, choose the **OK** button; the selected structures will be added in the **Name** column of the **Structures** tab.

Summary Tab

Use the **Summary** tab to review all the values specified for the structure style in different tabs and edit the values if required.

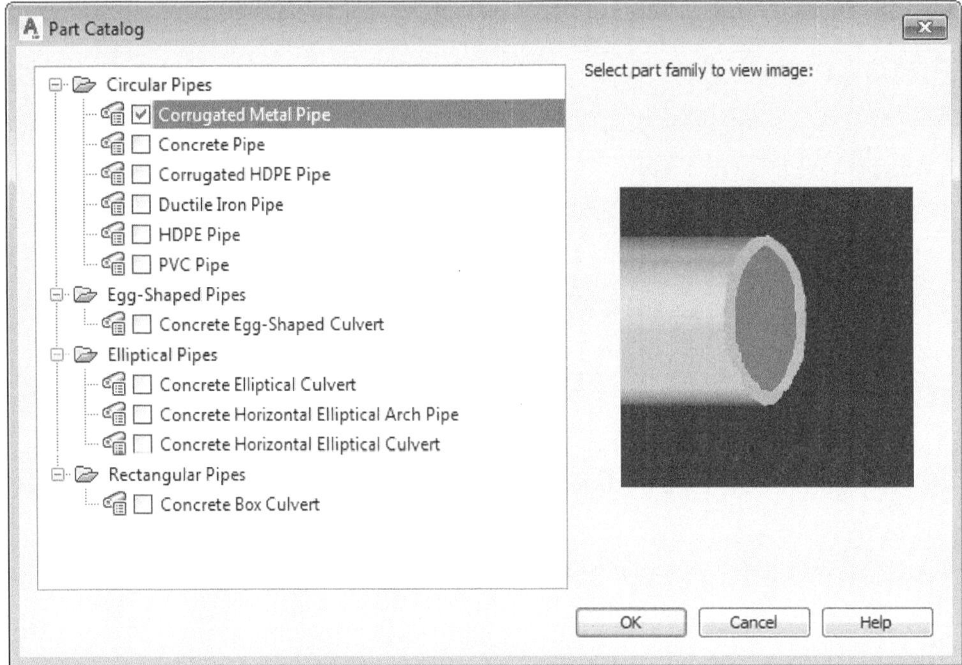

***Figure 11-10** The **Corrugated Metal Pipe** check box selected in the **Part Catalog** dialog box*

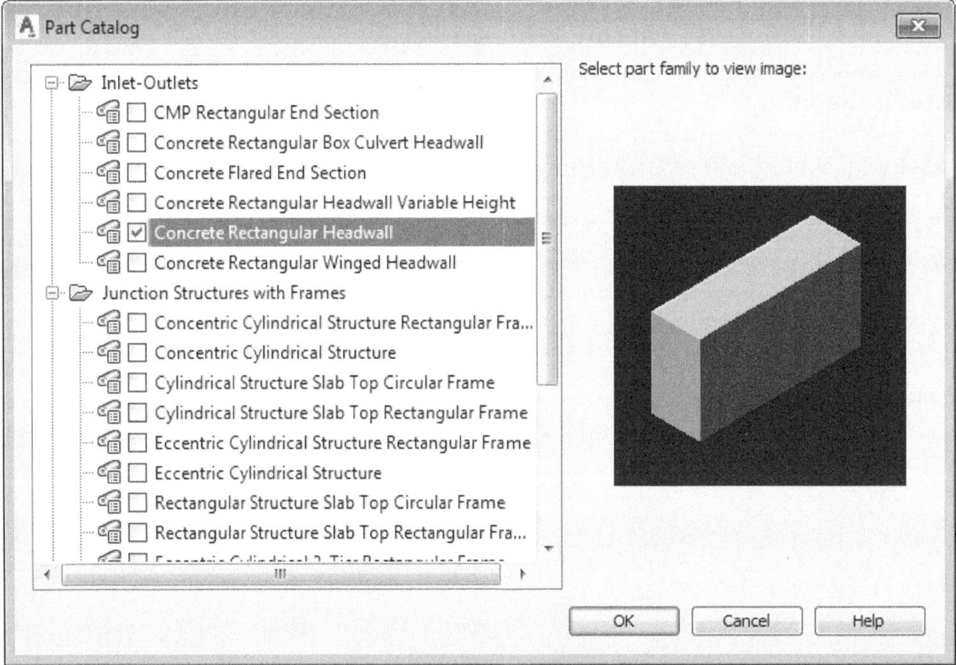

***Figure 11-11** The required structures selected in the **Part Catalog** dialog box to add to the parts list*

Adding Part Sizes

In the parts list, you can select, add, or edit various sizes and parameters of the pipe and structure parts of the pipe network. To add a pipe part size, right-click on the required pipe part name in the **Name** column and choose the **Add part size** option from the shortcut menu; the **Part Size Creator** dialog box will be displayed, as shown in Figure 11-12.

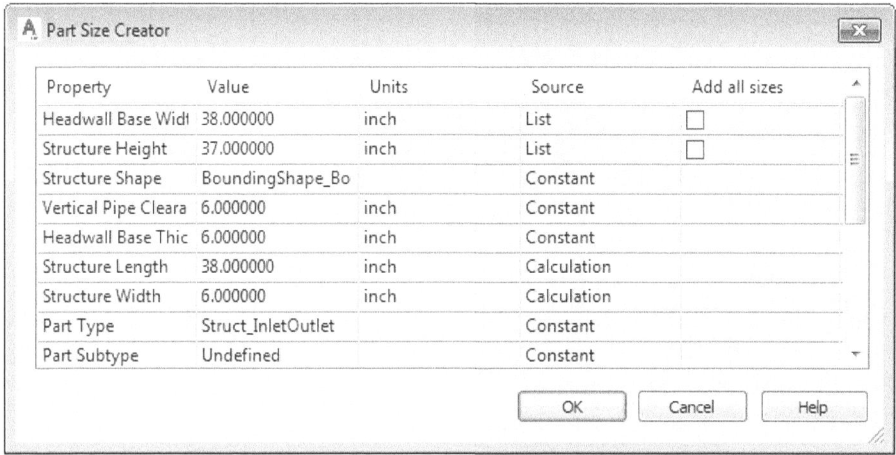

***Figure 11-12** The **Part Size Creator** dialog box*

Specify the size of the required properties in the **Value** column. For example, to set the head wall base width, you can click in the **Value** field of the **Headwall Base Width** property and enter the required diameter value from the drop-down list displayed. Similarly, you can click on the **Value** fields of the other properties. After specifying the properties, choose the **OK** button; the dialog box will be closed and the selected part of the specified size will be added in the **Name** column under the respective pipe part sub-node in the **Structures** tab.

Part Builder

AutoCAD Civil 3D allows you to create and modify pipe network parts available in the part catalog of Civil 3D using the **Part Builder** tool. You can also build the customized network parts using the Part Builder. Remember that the Part Builder should be used by the experienced Civil 3D users who are well acquainted with the parametric modeling and pipe network parts. The method of creating pipe network parts using the Part Builder is discussed next.

Note

Before you start using the Civil 3D Part Builder, save a copy of the part catalog to retain the default parts. As mentioned earlier, the catalogs can be accessed from C:\ProgramData\Autodesk\C3D 2018\enu\Pipes Catalog\US Imperial Structures. This will help you to avoid deleting or changing the default parts in the catalogs.

Using the Part Builder

Ribbon: Home > Create Design > Part Builder

Before using the **Part Builder** tool, set the required pipe network catalog and choose the **Part Builder** tool from the **Create Design** panel; the **Getting Started - Catalog Screen** dialog box will be displayed, as shown in Figure 11-13. The options in this dialog box are discussed next.

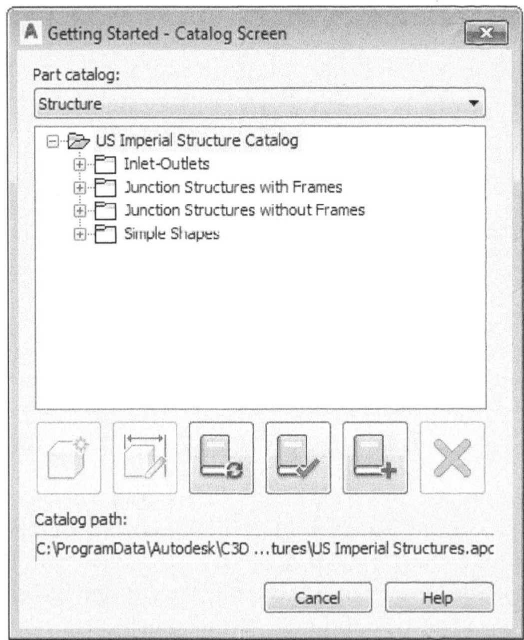

*Figure 11-13 The **Getting Started - Catalog Screen** dialog box*

Part catalog

The **Part catalog** drop-down list allows you to select the required part catalog (Pipe/Structure) to be used in your drawing. The **Structure** option is selected by default in this drop-down list. As a result, the catalog of the selected option will be listed below it. The catalog displayed in the list box will be either in the US Metric or Imperial unit system. When you expand the displayed catalog in the list, the type or chapters will be displayed under it. Select the required type from the list and then use the other options in the **Getting Started - Catalog Screen** dialog box for adding a new part or modifying an existing part in the selected catalog.

Note

*The parts in the selected catalog will be drawn in Metric or in Imperial units depending upon the type of catalog (Metric/Imperial) selected in the **Pipe Network Catalog Settings** dialog box. This dialog box can be invoked by choosing the **Set Pipe Network Catalog** tool from the **Create Design** panel of the **Home** tab.*

New Parametric Part

The Civil 3D parts in the parts catalog are parametric in nature. This means that they are dynamically linked to some specified parameters and can be updated if the parameters are changed.

To create a new parametric part, select any node listed in the area below the **Part Catalog** drop-down list and then choose the **New Parametric Part** button; the **New Part** dialog box will be displayed. Enter the required part name and description in the dialog box and choose the **OK** button; the dialog box will be closed and the part builder parametric modeling environment will be invoked, as shown in Figure 11-14. Note that the **Part family validation successful** or **Part family validation failed** message will be displayed depending on the validation status of the part created.

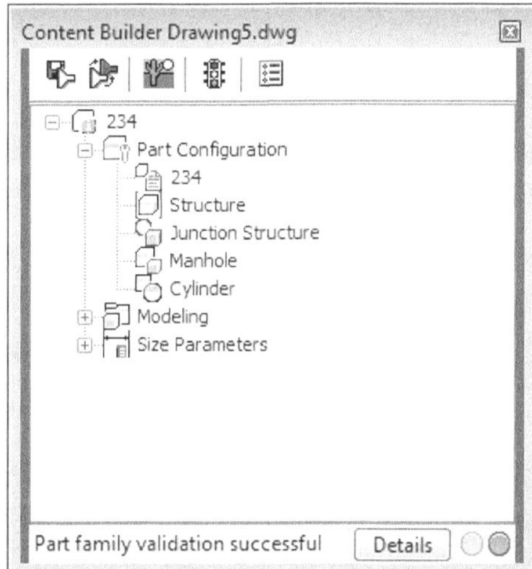

***Figure 11-14** The part builder parametric modeling environment*

Modify Part Sizes

This button is used to modify an existing part. To do so, expand the required node in the dialog box and select the part that you want to edit; the **Modify Part Sizes** button will be activated. Now, choose this button to open the **Part Builder** interface and edit the part size and parameters.

Catalog Regen

You can use this button to regenerate or refresh the part catalog after editing the part or making changes in the part catalog.

Catalog Test

Choose the **Catalog Test** button to validate and test the catalog after making changes or editing any part of the catalog.

New Chapter

This button is used to add a new chapter in the part catalog. To do so, select a catalog name from the top in the area of the **Getting Started - Catalog Screen** dialog box and then choose the **New Chapter** button; the **New Chapter** dialog box will be displayed. Enter the required name for the chapter in the **Name** edit box of the dialog box and choose the **OK** button; the dialog box will be closed and the chapter will be added.

Delete

This button is used to delete any part from the catalog. To do so, select the required part from the chapter folder and choose the **Delete** button to delete it.

Part Rules

The part rules are a set of rules that govern the elevation, location, and the way the pipes are connected to the structures. These rules also help you to keep a check and warn you if certain criteria are violated after creating or editing the pipe network parts. Civil 3D has some built in set of rules that are automatically applied to each part of the pipe network. You can also create your own set of rules and use them to design the pipe network.

The part rules are divided into two parts: Pipe Rules and Structure Rules. The combination of these rules is called a rule set. The rules can be applied to the pipe network parts as a rule set. The pipe rules and structure rules are discussed next.

Pipe Rules

The pipe rules govern the elevation, length, slope, and other properties of the pipe object in the pipe network. There are five rules in Civil 3D, namely cover and slope, cover only, length check, pipe to pipe match, and set pipe end location. These rules and their associated parameters are discussed next.

Cover and Slope Rule

This rule governs the slope and cover of the pipe. It ensures that the pipe slopes in the required direction and the minimum cover is maintained. This rule also helps you check if the pipe is placed closed to the ground. The parameters associated with the cover and slope rule are discussed next.

Maximum Cover: This parameter specifies the maximum extent of soil over the length of the pipe. The maximum cover should not exceed the value specified for this parameter. This parameter provides a validation check to the rule by warning you whenever there would be a violation.

Maximum Slope: This parameter specifies the maximum slope in percentage that pipe should maintain. The default value specified for this parameter is **8%**.

Minimum Cover: This parameter specifies the minimum thickness of soil cover over the pipe along its length. The pipes are designed initially in such a way that they maintain the minimum cover.

Minimum Slope: This parameter specifies the minimum slope value that a pipe should maintain.

Cover Only Rule

This rule is applicable for the pressure based pipe system where the slope of the pipe is not the primary criterion for the design. This rule ensures that the minimum and maximum cover values are maintained along the length of the pipe. The parameters associated with this rule are the **Minimum Cover** and the **Maximum Cover** and have already been discussed.

Note that the default values of these two parameters are different from the parameter values of the **Cover and Slope** rule.

Length Check Rule

This rule helps you to check if the pipe length exceeds the value specified for the maximum pipe length or is less than minimum pipe length value. The rule does not change the values of the pipe length but will warn you if the maximum and minimum pipe length criteria are not met. This rule is useful for designing long continuous pipes. The parameters associated with this rule are as follows:

Minimum Length. This parameter allows you to set the minimum value for the pipe length. The pipe length should not be less than this minimum value. If the length of the pipe is shorter than the specified length, a warning icon will be displayed with the object name in the List View.

Maximum Length. This parameter allows you to set the maximum length of the pipe. If the pipes are drawn exceeding the value specified for this parameters, a warning icon will be displayed with the object name in the List View.

Pipe to Pipe Match Rule

This rule is applicable to the pipes created without structures or when connecting one pipe to another using the null structures. This rule can also be useful in a condition where you need to place a pipe, to break an existing pipe, or connect the pipe end of an existing pipe with another pipe end. The rule can be used to specify the match points for the continuous pipes. In case of gravity systems, the pipes may need to match at the pipe crown and in case of pressure systems, they may need to match at their centerlines. The **Pipe to Pipe Match** rule also allows you to specify a pipe drop value across a pipe to pipe connection if required. The parameters governing this rule are as follows:

Match Location: This parameter specifies if the match location for the pipes is the pipe invert, crown, or the pipe centerline.

Drop Value: This parameter allows you to specify an additional drop at the pipe to pipe connections.

Set Pipe End Location

This rule allows you to specify the end and start location of the pipe. Using this rule, you can specify if the pipe starts/ends are at the **Structure Center**, **Structure Inner Wall**, or **Structure Outer Wall**. You can also use this rule to specify the required offset for the start and end locations.

Creating a Pipe Rule Set

The pipe set rules are available in the **Pipe Rule Set** sub-node of the **Pipe** node in the **Settings** tab. To create a new pipe rule set, choose the **Settings** tab and expand **Pipe > Pipe Rule Set**. Now, right-click on **Pipe Rule Set** and choose the **New** option from the shortcut menu; the **Pipe Rule Set - New Pipe Rules** dialog box will be displayed. The tabs in this dialog box are discussed next.

Information Tab

This tab is used to specify a pipe rule set name. You can specify this name in the **Name** edit box of the **Information** tab.

Rules Tab

This tab is used to add new pipe rules or edit the existing rules. To add new rules, choose the **Add Rule** button in this tab; the **Add Rule** dialog box will be displayed. This dialog box is used to add the required pipe rules to the **Rules** tab. Select the category to which the rules will be applied from the **Category** drop-down list. The **Storm Sewer** option is selected by default in the **Category** drop-down list. From the **Rule name** drop-down list, select the required rule to be added to the rule set, refer to Figure 11-15. The four different types of pipe rules available in the drop-down list have already been discussed.

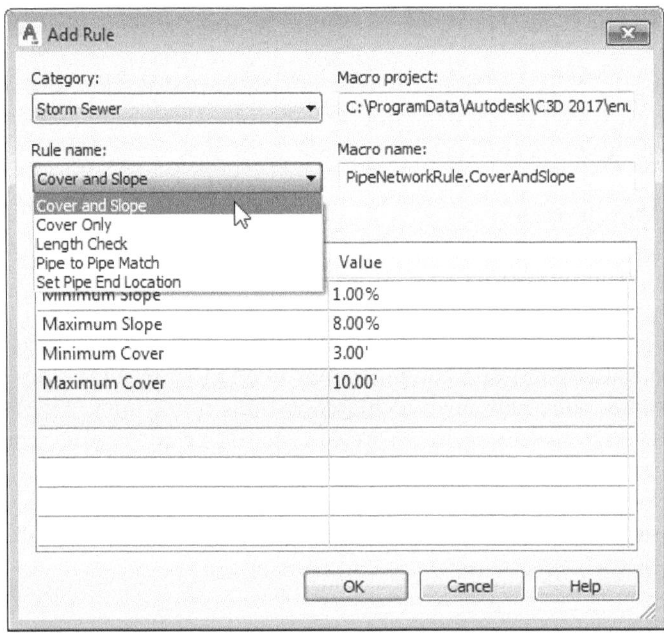

*Figure 11-15 Selecting the **Cover and Slope** option from the **Rule name** drop-down list*

Note that on selecting the required rule from the **Rule name** drop-down list, its associated parameters and default values will be displayed in the **Rule parameters** table. After selecting the required rules, choose the **OK** button to close the **Add Rule** dialog box; the selected rule and its parameters will be added in the **Rules** tab of the **Pipe Rule Set - New Pipe Rules** dialog box. Edit the values of the parameters in the **Value** column as per the project requirement and choose the **OK** button again; the **Pipe Rule Set - New Pipe Rules** dialog box will be closed and the pipe rule set will be added in the **Pipe Rule Set** node of the **Pipe** collection in the **Settings** tab.

Note

*Remember that you cannot edit the values of the rule parameters in the **Add Rule** dialog box. To edit the values of rule parameters, expand the desired rule node by clicking on the + sign in the **Rules** tab of the **Pipe Rule Set - New Pipe Rules** dialog box and then edit the value for the required parameter.*

Structure Rules

The structure rules govern the location, size, and depth of the structures at the time of their creation. These rules also warn you if any pipe connected to the structure violates the rules or is not connected properly to the structures. Like the pipe objects, structure names are also displayed with a warning icon in the Item View if the structure rules are violated. The three different structure rules and their associated parameters are discussed next.

Maximum Pipe Size Check

This rule checks that the pipe diameter or width of the pipe entering the structure does not exceed the specified value. In other words, it ensures that the pipe entering the structure is of suitable dimensions and can fit easily in the structure. The parameter associated with this rule is discussed next.

Maximum Pipe Diameter or width: This parameter allows you to specify the maximum value of the pipe diameter for the circular pipes and width for the rectangular pipes.

Pipe Drop Across Structure

This rule ensures that all the pipes connected to a structure enter or exit the structure according to the specified drop value. This rule is applicable only to gravity-based systems. First of all, it ensures that if a new pipe is connected to the structure in an existing pipe network and that the pipe exiting the structure is not higher than the lowest exiting pipe entering the structure. Secondly, it also checks that the new pipe entering the structure is not lower than the highest pipe exiting the structure. Third, a specified drop distance is always maintained between the lowest pipe entering the structure and the highest pipe exiting the system.

The drop value is based on the pipe centerlines, inverts, or pipe crowns. The rule applies a check to validate whether the drop exceeds a specified distance or the maximum drop value is violated. The associated parameters governing this rule are as follows:

Drop Reference Location: This parameter allows you to specify the drop location by referencing the pipe invert, crown, or pipe centerline elevation. **Invert** is the default value specified to this parameter.

Drop Value: This value specifies the drop value between the lowest pipe entering the structure and the highest pipe exiting the structure.

Maximum Drop Value: This parameter allows you to set the maximum drop value between the lowest incoming pipe and the highest outgoing pipe.

Set Sump Depth

This rule specifies the vertical distance from the invert of the lowest pipe attached to the structure to the inside bottom of the structure. This vertical distance is called the sump depth. The **Sump Depth** parameter associated with this rule allows you to specify the required sump depth. This parameter validates and generates a rule violation for the part, if the specified value is exceeded.

Creating a Structure Rule Set

The structure rule sets are available in the **Structure Rule Set** sub-node of the **Structure** node of the **Settings** tab. To create a new structure rule set, choose the **Settings** tab and expand the **Structure > Structure Rule Set**. Now, right-click on **Structure Rule Set** and then choose the **New** option from the shortcut menu; the **Structure Rule Set - New Structure Rules** dialog box will be displayed. The options in this dialog box are the same as those discussed in the **Pipe Rule Set - New Pipe Rules** dialog box. Select the required structure rule from the **Rule name** drop-down list of the **Add Rules** dialog box displayed on choosing the **Add Rule** button from the **Rules** tab. Next, choose the **OK** button; the dialog box will be closed and the selected rule and its parameters will be added in the **Rules** tab. Edit the parameter values, if required and choose the **OK** button to close the **Structure Rule Set - New Structure Rules** dialog box. The rule set will be added in the **Structure Rule Set** sub-node of the **Structure** node in the **Settings** tab.

CREATING A PIPE NETWORK

AutoCAD Civil 3D provides a set of tools to design pipe network for transporting fluid using earth's gravitational force. The objects in the network can be created by using the pipe network layout tools or by using the objects such as polyline, line, and feature line. The methods of creating the pipe network are discussed next.

Using the Network Layout Tools

Ribbon:	Home > Create Design > Pipe Network drop-down > Pipe Network Creation Tools
Command:	CREATENETWORK

To create a pipe network using the pipe network layout tools, choose the **Pipe Network Creation Tools** tool from the **Create Design** panel; the **Create Pipe Network** dialog box will be displayed, as shown in Figure 11-16. This dialog box is used to specify the information about the pipe network to be created. The options in the dialog box are discussed next.

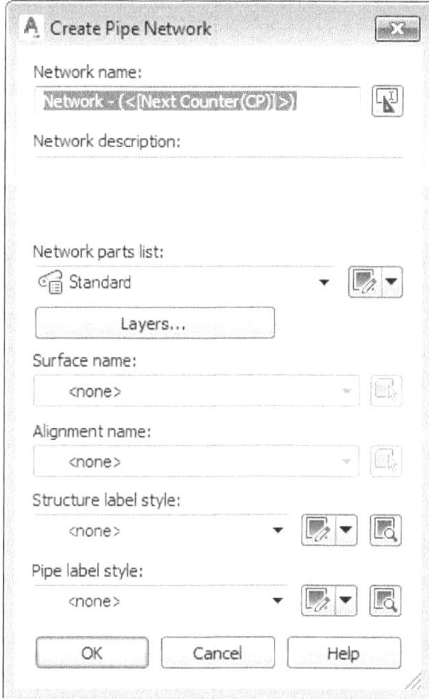

Figure 11-16 *The* ***Create Pipe Network*** *dialog box*

Network name

This edit box displays the default name of the pipe network. To specify a desired name, choose the **Click to edit the name template** button located next to this edit box; the **Name Template** dialog box will be displayed. Enter the required name in the **Name** edit box of the dialog box and choose the **OK** button to exit.

Network description

In this text box, the description about the pipe network is specified.

Network parts list

You can select the required option from the **Network parts list** drop-down list. You can choose the **Layers** button below the **Network parts list** drop-down list to display the **Pipe Network Layers** dialog box. In this dialog box, you can create and specify the layers on which the pipe network will be created in the plan, section, and profile views.

Surface name

You can select the required option from the **Surface name** drop-down list. You can then associate the selected surface with the pipe network. Alternatively, choose the **Select from the drawing** button on the right of the drop-down list to select the alignment from the drawing. This drop-down list is available only if the drawing consists of a surface. This option can be used for creating pipe parts in a profile view where you need a surface and an alignment to create the profile view.

Alignment name

Select the alignment associated with the pipe network from the **Alignment name** drop-down list. Alternatively, choose the **Select from the drawing** button on the right of the drop-down list to select the alignment from the drawing. The drop-down list is available only if the drawing consists of an alignment.

Structure label style

This option allows you to specify a label style for labeling the structures of the pipe network. Select the required option from the **Structure label style** drop-down list.

Pipe label style

This drop-down list allows you to specify a label style to label the pipe objects in the pipe network. To specify the required pipe label style, select the required option from the **Pipe label style** drop-down list.

After specifying the information about the pipe network, choose the **OK** button; the **Create Pipe Network** dialog box will be closed and the **Network Layout Tools - <network name>** toolbar will be displayed, refer to Figure 11-17. Note that the specified name of the pipe network in the dialog box will be added in the **Networks** sub-node of the **Pipe Networks** node of the **Prospector** tab. Now, choose the **Parts List** tool from the **Network Layout Tools - <network name>** toolbar; the **Select Parts List** dialog box is displayed. Select the required part list in this dialog box and then choose the **OK** button to exit the dialog box. You can invoke this tool if you have created your own part list or else, accept the default parts list. Next, select the required option to be added in the network from the **Structure List** drop-down list. Similarly, select the required option from the **Pipe List** drop-down list. Now, invoke the **Pipes and Structures** tool. On doing so, you will be prompted to specify the insertion point of the structure. Click in the drawing to specify the insertion point; you will be prompted to specify the insertion point of the next structure. Specify the insertion point; a pipe connecting the two structures will be displayed in the network.

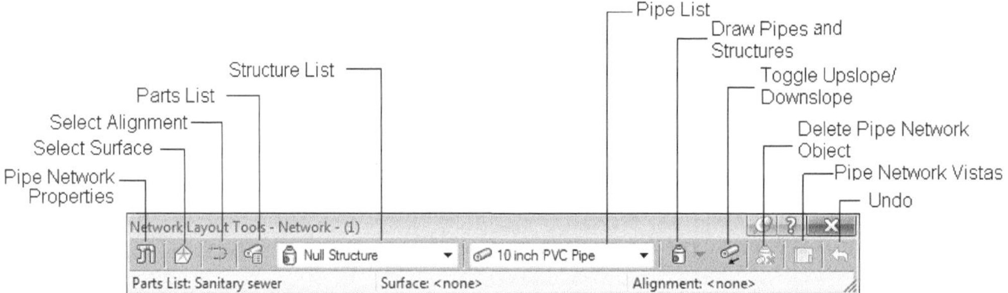

*Figure 11-17 The **Network Layout Tools - Network - (1)** toolbar*

The pipe network can be created by using three different tools namely **Pipes and Structures**, **Pipes only**, and **Structures only**. These tools are discussed next.

Pipes and Structures Tool

This tool allows you to create a pipe network with both the pipes and structures parts. To create a pipe network, choose the **Pipes and Structures** tool from the **Network Layout Tools** toolbar and create a pipe network with a series of structures connected to the pipes. Figure 11-18 shows a pipe network with both pipes and structure parts.

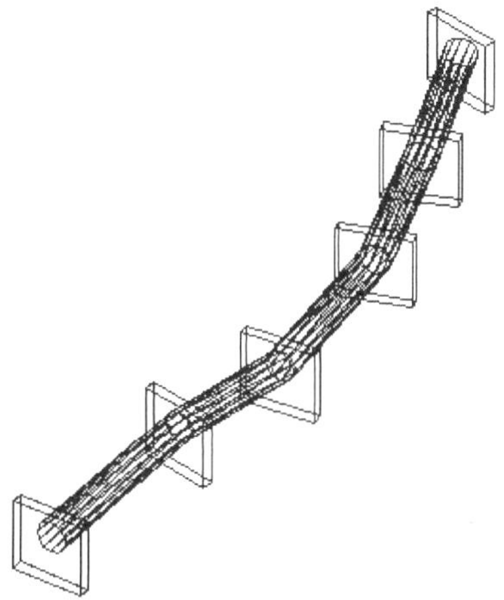

Figure 11-18 *A pipe network with both pipes and structure parts*

Pipes Only Tool

The **Pipes Only** tool allows you to create a network by only drawing the pipes. In this case, the network will have only the null structures joining the pipes. To create a pipe network by using only pipes, choose the down-arrow on the right of the **Pipes and Structures** tool to display a flyout. Next, and choose the **Pipes Only** tool from the flyout displayed. Next, click in the drawing to specify the first pipe point. Follow the prompts and click in the drawing again to specify other pipe points. Figure 11-19 shows a part of the network with only the pipes connected with the null structures.

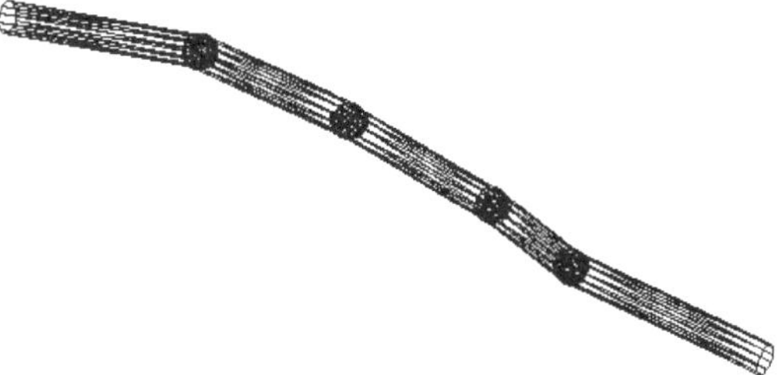

Figure 11-19 *A part of the network with only the pipes connected with the null structures*

Structures Only Tool

This tool allows you to draw only the structures in an existing pipe network. To use this mode, choose the down-arrow next to the **Pipes and Structures** tool from the **Network Layout Tools - <network name>** toolbar and then choose the **Structures Only** tool from the flyout displayed. Next, click in the drawing at the required location to specify the structure insertion points for the structures. Figure 11-20 shows the structures added to the existing pipe.

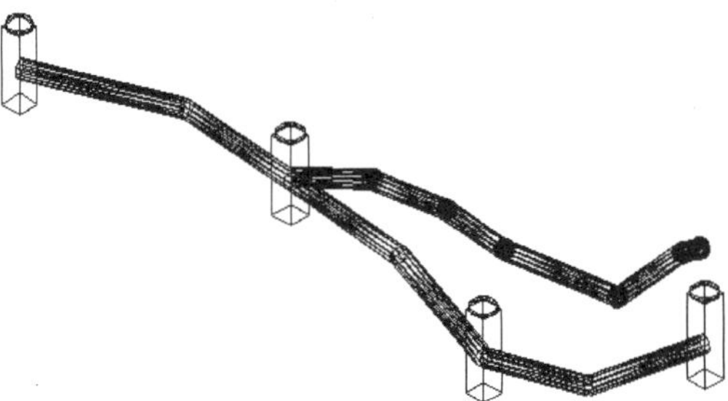

Figure 11-20 *The structures added to the pipe*

After you have created the pipe network using any of the three tools, you can check if any of the part rule is violated. To do so, choose the **Pipe Network Vistas** button from the toolbar; the **PANORAMA** window with the **Pipes** and **Structures** tabs will be displayed. To check the status of the pipe rule, choose the **Pipes** tab in the **PANORAMA** window. In case the rules have been violated, the violation icon will be displayed in the **Status** column for the pipes which have violated the rules, as shown in Figure 11-21.

Similarly, choose the **Structures** tab in the **PANORAMA** window and check the status of the structures in the **Status** column. You can also use the **PANORAMA** window to edit the pipe and structure parameters such as name, description, render material, and style.

Alternatively, you can also check the status of the pipes in the **Prospector** list view. To do so, expand **Pipe Networks > Networks** in the **Prospector** tab and then expand the required network. Next, select **Pipes** or **Structures** from the expanded node to view the respective information in the list view. You can use the **Network Layout Tools - <network name>** to draw the pipe network according to the design and the project requirement. This method provides you the flexibility of selecting the network parts, part styles, and the mode of creating the pipe network.

Status	Name	Descripti...	Style	Rule Set	Override ...	Render ...	Shape	Inner Dia...	Inner
2	Pipe - (1	24 x 24 inch	Double Line	Basic	No	ByLayer	Rectangular		24.000
1	Pipe - (2	24 x 24 inch	Double Line	Basic	No	ByLayer	Rectangular		24.000
2	Pipe - (3	24 x 24 inch	Double Line	Basic	No	ByLayer	Rectangular		24.000
1	Pipe - (4	24 x 24 inch	Double Line	Basic	No	ByLayer	Rectangular		24.000
2	Pipe - (5	24 x 24 inch	Double Line	Basic	No	ByLayer	Rectangular		24.000
2	Pipe - (6	24 x 24 inch	Double Line	Basic	No	ByLayer	Rectangular		24.000
1	Pipe - (7	24 x 24 inch	Double Line	Basic	No	ByLayer	Rectangular		24.000
1	Pipe - (8	24 x 24 inch	Double Line	Basic	No	ByLayer	Rectangular		24.000
2	Pipe - (9	24 x 24 inch	Double Line	Basic	No	ByLayer	Rectangular		24.000

Figure 11-21 *The violation icon displayed in the* ***Status*** *column for the pipes violating the pipe rules*

Creating Pipe Networks from Objects

Ribbon: Home > Create Design > Pipe Network drop-down > Create Pipe Network from Object
Command: CREATENETWORKFROMOBJECT

You can create a pipe network from the existing AutoCAD entities such as line, polylines, splines, arcs, and feature lines. AutoCAD Civil 3D converts these entities to a pipe network and then inserts structures at the end points or vertices of these drawing entities. To create a pipe network from an object, choose the **Create Pipe Network from Object** tool from the **Create Design** panel; you will be prompted to select an object or an Xref in the command line. Select the existing entity in the drawing; you will notice an arrow displayed on the selected entity showing the direction of flow. Press ENTER to accept the default direction or enter **R** in the command line and then press ENTER; the direction of flow will be reversed. Again, press ENTER to display the **Create Pipe Network from Object** dialog box, as shown in Figure 11-22.

The options in the dialog box are the same as those explained in the **Create Pipe Network** dialog box. You can select the **Erase existing entity** check box to remove the entity from which the network is created. Select the **Use vertex elevations** check box to use the elevations of vertices along the selected entity to set the elevations of the pipes created in the network. On selecting this check box, the options in the **Vertex Elevation Reference** area will become active. You can select an option from this area to specify the location on the pipe where the vertex elevation is located. Note that when you select an option from this area, the rules set for the pipe network will no longer be applicable.

After you have specified the required information in the **Create Pipe Network from Object** dialog box, choose the **OK** button; the dialog box will be closed and a pipe network will be created with the structures inserted at the vertices of the selected entity.

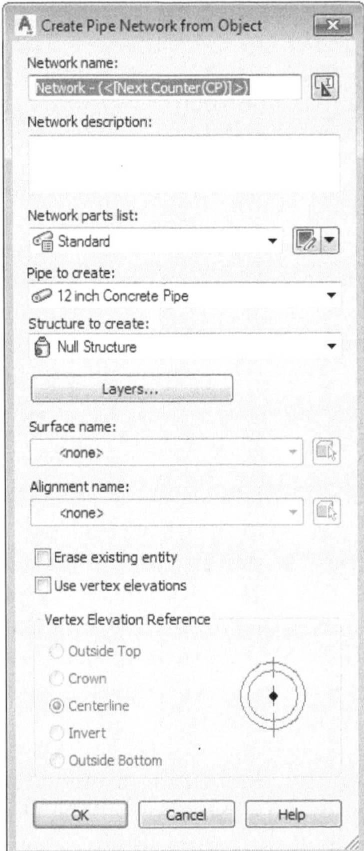

*Figure 11-22 The **Create Pipe Network from Object** dialog box*

DRAWING PIPE NETWORK PARTS IN A PROFILE VIEW

You can view the parts of an existing pipe network in a profile view to evaluate the vertical positions of the network parts based on your design. This will help you to visualize and compare the pipe network elevation with those of the road design. You can view the entire pipe network or the required pipe network parts in a profile or a section view.

To draw the network parts in a profile view, you need to have a pipe network, a profile view, and an alignment providing the station data in your drawing. To draw, select the profile view; the **Profile View: <profile view name>** tab will be displayed. Next, choose the **Draw Parts in Profile View** tool from the **Launch Pad** panel of the **Profile View :<profile view name>** tab; you will be prompted to select the pipe network or a part of pipe network that you want to display in the profile view. Select the required network part in the drawing and press ENTER; you are now prompted to select the profile view in which you want to display the network parts. Select the required profile view in which you want to display the network parts; the selected network parts will be displayed in the profile view, as shown in Figure 11-23.

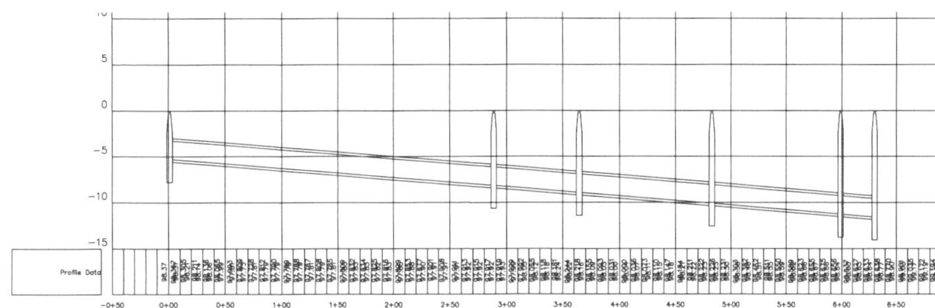

Figure 11-23 *The network parts displayed in the profile view*

To display the required parts in the profile view, select the profile view in the drawing and right-click to display the shortcut menu. Choose the **Profile View Properties** option from the shortcut menu; the **Profile View Properties - <profile view name>** dialog box will be displayed. Choose the **Pipe Networks** tab from the dialog box; all the parts of the pipe network will be displayed. By default, all the check boxes in the **Draw** column of this tab are selected indicating that all the parts of the pipe network will be drawn in the profile view, refer to Figure 11-24. Clear the check boxes in the **Draw** column for the parts that you do not want to draw in the profile view. Select the check boxes in the **Draw** column for the parts that you want to draw and clear the remaining ones. In this way, you can remove the unwanted parts from the profile view without deleting them.

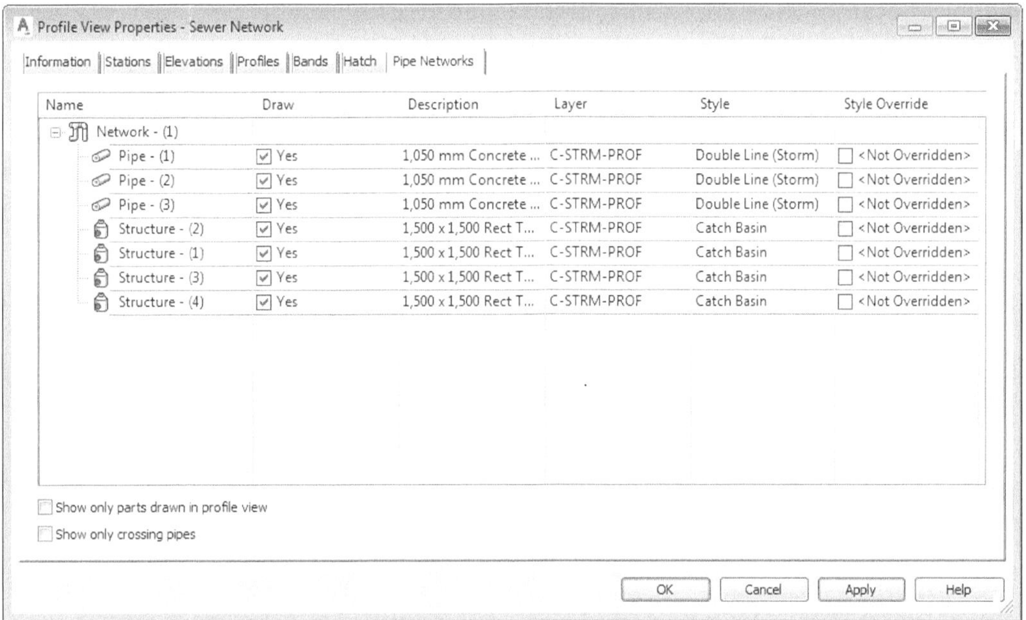

Figure 11-24 *The pipes displayed in the **Pipe Networks** tab of the **Profile View Properties - Sewer Network** dialog box*

To override the existing parts style, select the corresponding check box for pipe or structure in the **Style Override** column; the **Pick Pipe Style** or **Pick Structure Style** dialog box will be displayed, depending upon the part for which you want to change the style. Select the required option from the drop-down list in this dialog box and choose the **OK** button; the existing part style will be overridden by the selected style. Next, choose the **OK** button; the **Profile View Properties - <profile view name>** dialog box will be closed and the selected network parts will be drawn in the profile view with the selected style.

It is important to remember that the pipe networks drawn in the profile view may not be sketched according to the actual length of the network. This is due to the fact that the profile views are created and cut according to the alignments. Sometimes the pipe centerline does not correspond to the alignment or may not cross the alignment, thus resulting in the inappropriate representation of the pipe length and the pipe slope in the profile view. Also note that the network structures will not be displayed in the profile view if the location at which the structure is inserted lies outside the profile view. Therefore, you must ensure that the structure's insertion point is within the profile view limits to enable its display in the profile view.

Editing a Pipe Network in a Profile View

You can edit the vertical position or elevation of the network parts in the profile view, though other properties, such as pipe length and width cannot be changed. Note that you cannot modify the X and Y coordinates of the pipe network parts in a profile view, but the vertical position of the parts can be modified using the grips. To do so, select the required pipe part in the profile view; the grip controls will be displayed. You will notice a square grip at the centre and triangular grips at the end of the selected pipe, as shown in Figure 11-25. Use the square grip to adjust the elevation or vertical position of the pipe without affecting the current slope. The triangular grips are used to change the elevation of one end of the pipe, while maintaining the elevation of the other end.

On selecting a structure from the profile view, two triangular grips will be displayed at the top and bottom of the selected structure, as shown in Figure 11-26. Use these grips to adjust the location of the structure vertically. The top grip is the rim (insertion) grip that helps you adjust the rim depth and the bottom grip is the sump depth that helps you adjust the sump depth.

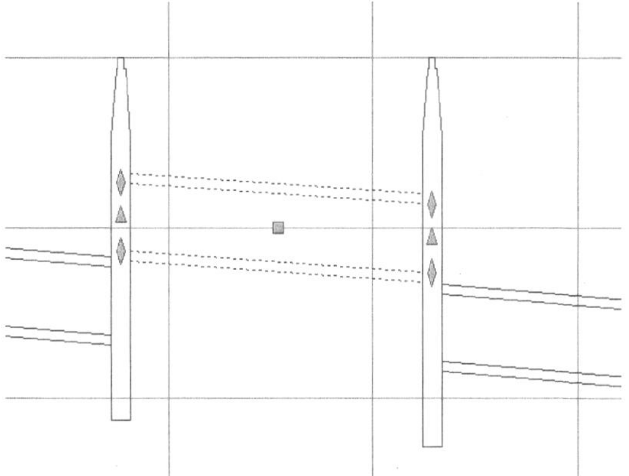

***Figure 11-25** The square and the triangular grips displayed at the center and ends of the selected pipe*

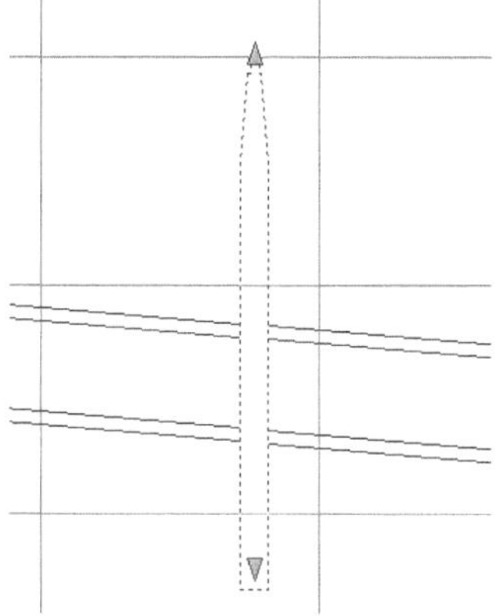

***Figure 11-26** The triangular grips displayed on selecting the structure*

The properties to be changed by the group editing depend upon how the structure properties are defined. The junction structures have an in-built resize behavior controlled by the structure properties. For example, if the sump behavior of a structure is controlled by the sump depth, then using the sump grip will modify the sump depth. Similarly, if the sump behavior of the structure is controlled by elevation, then adjusting the sump grip will modify the sump elevation in the profile view. If the **Automatic Surface Adjustment** property of the structure is set to **True** in the **Part Properties** tab of the **Structure Properties - <structure name>** dialog box, then the grip editing the rim grip point will modify the surface adjustment value and the rim will change according to the changes made in the surface. But, if the value of the **Automatic Surface Adjustment** property is set to **False** then the grip editing the rim will modify the insertion point of the rim and it will be locked even if you modify the reference surface. You can use the sump depth grip (at the bottom) to move the sump up to the lowest connected pipe but you cannot move it up beyond that point. You can also use this grip to move the sump down. In this case, the sump will move to the new location without affecting the connected pipes or the rim. On the other hand, you can use the rim grip (at the top) and move the structure's rim to a new location without affecting the pipes and the elevation. But you will not be allowed to move the grip down beyond the pipe clearance area. Note that the built in resize behavior is applicable only to the junction structures and not to the null structures or the inlet/outlet structures.

The resize behavior properties can be accessed in the **Part Properties** tab of the **Structure Properties** dialog box of the selected structure. To display this dialog box, select the required structure in the profile view and right-click on it. Choose **Structure Properties** option from the shortcut menu displayed.

NETWORK PROPERTIES

To access and edit the pipe network properties such as network name, labels, layers, profile and section view settings, select any part of the network in the drawing and right-click; a shortcut menu will be displayed. Choose the **Network Properties** option from the shortcut menu displayed; the **Pipe Network Properties - <network name>** dialog box will be displayed, refer to Figure 11-27. The **Information** tab of this dialog box displays the name of the selected pipe network. Modify the name in the **Name** edit box, if required.

Choose the **Layout Settings** tab to view and edit the parameters used for the pipe network in the plan view. The **Labels** area displays the label styles used to label the pipes and structures in the plan view, refer to Figure 11-27. Select the required options from the **Structure plan label style** and **Pipe plan label style** drop-down lists. Select an option from the **Network parts list** drop-down list to define the part list used for the selected pipe network. You can select the required part list from the drop-down list or create a new part list. To create a new part list, choose the down arrow from the button on the right of this drop-down list; a flyout will be displayed. Select the **Create New** option from the flyout to create a new part list. The **Default object reference** area displays the name of the surface and alignment objects to which the pipe network is referenced. If the network is not referenced to any surface or alignment, the **none** option will be selected by default in the **Surface name** and **Alignment name** drop-down lists in this area.

The **Default network layers** area displays the layers in which the pipes and structures will be drawn in the plan view. Choose the **Select Layers** buttons on the right in this area to display the **Object Layer** dialog box. You can use this dialog box to change the default layer. The **Name**

templates area displays the default names of the templates used for creating the pipes and structures in the network. Choose the button on the right of the **Pipes** or **Structures** edit box to display the **Name Template** dialog box. Enter a name for the pipe or structure in the **Name** edit box in this dialog box and choose the **OK** button to exit.

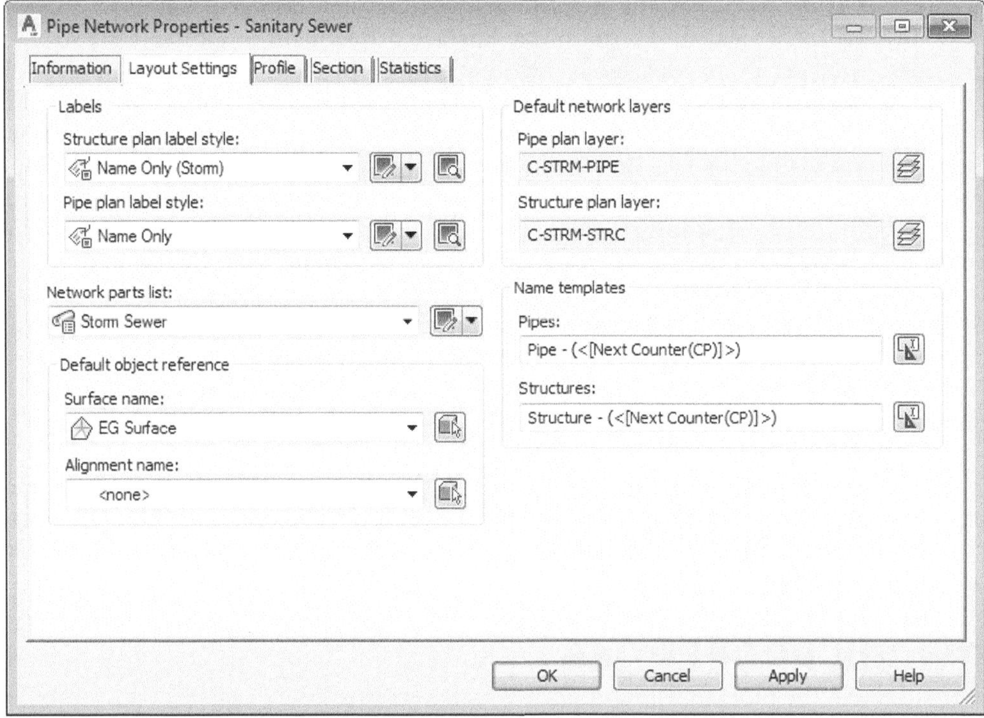

*Figure 11-27 The **Pipe Network Properties** dialog box*

The **Profile** tab displays the label styles used to label the pipes and structures in the network in the profile view. If no styles are used, the **none** option will be selected by default in the **Structure profile label style** and the **Pipe profile label style** drop-down lists in the **Labels** area. You can select the required option from these drop-down lists to specify the label style. The **Default profile layers** area displays name of the default layers on which the pipes and structures will be drawn in the profile view. Choose the button on the right of the **Pipe profile layer** text box; the **Object Layer** dialog box will be displayed. You can modify the default layers by using the options in the dialog box.

The **Section** tab displays the name of the default layer to display the network objects in a section view. You can modify the default layer by choosing the **Select Layers** button next to the **Pipe network section layer** text box in the **Default section layers** area.

The **Statistics** tab of the **Pipe Network Properties - <network name>** dialog box displays the network statistics for the selected network. Expand the **General**, **Pipes**, and **Structures** categories in this tab to view their statistics. After you have viewed or edited the network properties, choose the **OK** button to exit the **Pipe Network Properties - <network name>** dialog box.

Structure Properties

To view and edit the properties of a structure in a network, select the required structure from the drawing and right-click; a shortcut menu will be displayed. Choose **Structure Properties** from the shortcut menu; the **Structure Properties - <structure name>** dialog box will be displayed, refer to Figure 11-28. The tabs in this dialog box are discussed next.

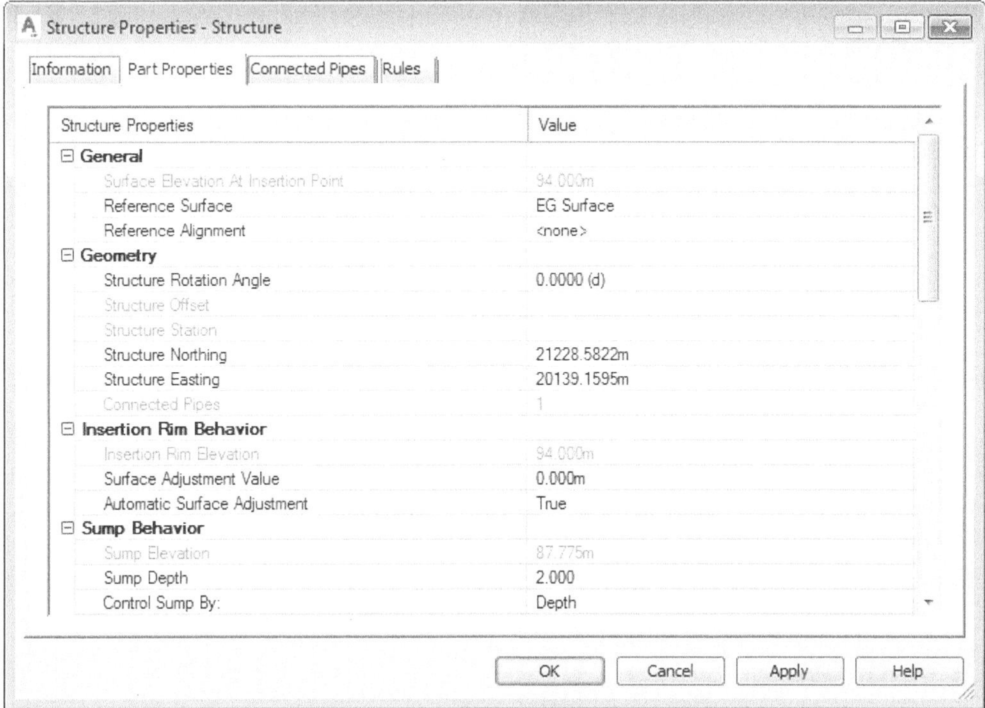

*Figure 11-28 The **Structure Properties** dialog box*

Information Tab

This tab displays the general information about the selected structure, such as its name, style, and description. You can edit the name of the structure using the **Name** edit box and select the required style for the structure in this tab. The options in the **Style** and **Render Material** drop-down lists under the **Object styles** area are used to select a style and to assign a new render material to the structure, respectively.

Part Properties Tab

This tab displays various properties associated with the selected structure along with their current values, refer to Figure 11-28. These properties define different attributes of the pipe structure including size, shape, behavior of elevation adjustment, and so on.

The structure properties are divided into six categories: **General**, **Geometry**, **Insertion Rim Behavior**, **Hydraulic Properties**, **Sump Behavior**, and **Part Data**. The properties in the **General** category specify the general properties of the structure such as the name of the surface and alignment associated with it. Some of the properties in this tab are structure specific. For example, the rim and sump behavior properties are used for the junction structures only.

The properties in the **Geometry** category determine the geometrical behavior of the structure such as its rotation, northing, and easting. The properties in the **Insertion Rim Behavior** category are confined to the junction structures and specify the elevation and adjustment behavior of the rim of the structure. The properties in the **Sump Behavior** category specify the structure elevation, depth, and sump behavior. The properties in the **Hydraulic Properties** category specify the hydraulic grade line and energy grade line. The properties in the **Part Data** category specifies the part information such as the part name, part size and part shape. You can edit the properties displayed in black. But the properties displayed in grey are read only and cannot be edited. This is because the properties specifying the basic properties of the part cannot be edited.

Connected Pipes Tab

This tab displays information about the pipes connected to the selected structure. You can also edit different pipe properties that are connected to the structure. For example, you can edit the pipe diameter, invert elevation, and slope using this tab. Using the options in this tab, you can quickly edit the properties of the pipe and set the pipe-in and pipe-out elevations in case of multiple pipes entering and exiting the structure.

Rules Tab

This tab is used to view the existing rule set and rule values. You can modify the rule set and the associated values and also check the violation status of the rules in this tab. To modify the rules set, select the required rule set from the **Rule set** drop-down list. You can also edit an existing rule set. To do so, choose the down arrow button on the right of the **Rule set** drop-down list; a flyout will be displayed. Choose the **Edit current selection** option from the flyout; the **Structure Rule Set <rule set name>** dialog box will be displayed. You can modify the values of the rules, and add or delete rules using this dialog box.

Pipe Properties

To view and edit the pipe properties, select the required pipe part from the drawing and right-click; a shortcut menu will be displayed. Next, choose the **Pipe Properties** option from the shortcut menu; the **Pipe Properties - <pipe name>** dialog box will be displayed. The options in this dialog box are discussed next.

Information Tab

This tab displays the pipe name, description, and pipe style.

Part Properties Tab

This tab displays the properties associated with the pipe in five different categories: **General**, **Geometry**, **Resize Behavior**, **Hydraulic Properties**, and **Part Data**. The **General** category properties specify the general characteristics of the pipe such as the pipe flow direction, surface, and the alignment associated with the pipe. If the pipe is not referenced to any surface or an alignment, the **none** value will be displayed in the **Value** fields of the **Reference Surface** and **Reference Alignment** properties. The **Geometry** category also specifies the geometrical behavior of a pipe such as its bearing, the name of the structures connected at the start and end of the selected pipe, and so on. The **Resize Behavior** category specifies the behavior of the pipe, if it is resized. The properties in the **Hydraulic Properties** category specify the hydraulic grade line up, energy grade line down, and flow rate. The properties in the **Part Data** category specify various part properties such as part name, shape and size. You cannot modify the properties displayed in gray but the properties and values displayed in black color can be modified.

Rules Tab

This tab is used to view and change the pipe rule set or the associated values. You can also check the status of the pipe parts in the **Status** column to find out whether the rules are violated or not.

EDITING A PIPE NETWORK IN PLAN LAYOUT

Civil 3D provides you with different methods for editing the pipe networks in a plan layout. You can use the **Network Layout Tools** toolbar, **TOOLSPACE** Item View, and the grip editing methods to edit the pipe network as required. These editing methods are discussed next.

Using the Pipe Network Layout Tools Toolbar

Ribbon: Pipe Networks: <Network Name> > Modify > Edit Pipe Network
Command: EDITNETWORK

To edit the pipe network by using the **Pipe Network Layout tools** toolbar, choose the **Edit Pipe Network** tool from the **Modify** panel of the **Pipe Networks: <Network Name>** tab; the **Network Layout Tools - <network name>** toolbar will be displayed. You can choose various tools from this toolbar to add, change, or delete the network parts. You can also modify the associated surface, alignment, and the part list using this toolbar. Some of the tools in this toolbar are discussed next.

Pipe Network properties

On invoking this tool, the **Pipe Network Properties <network name>** dialog box will be displayed. You can check or edit the properties of the pipe networks in this dialog box.

Select Surface

On invoking this tool, the **Select Surface** dialog box will be displayed. You can use this dialog box to change the surface referenced used by the pipe network. This tool can be used only if a surface has been referenced to a pipe network.

Select Alignment

Choose this tool to modify an alignment referenced by the pipe network. On invoking this tool, the **Select Alignment** dialog box will be displayed. Use this dialog box to change the alignment referenced by the pipe network.

Parts List

Invoke the **Parts List** tool to display the **Select Parts List** dialog box, as shown in Figure 11-29. This dialog box can be used to modify the existing parts list, create a new parts list, or to modify the existing parts list. To change the existing part list, select various options from the drop-down list. You can also choose the down arrow button on the right of this drop-down list and then choose the required option from the flyout displayed.

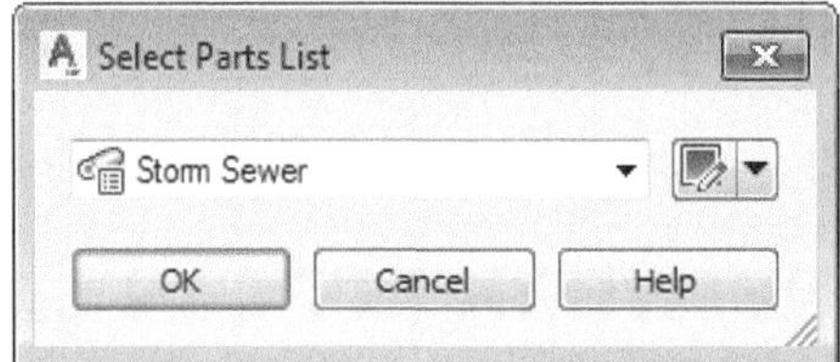

*Figure 11-29 The **Select Parts List** dialog box*

Toggle Upslope/Downslope

This tool is used to toggle between the uphill and downhill direction of the pipe network. By default, the downhill slope is selected which is indicated by the arrow pointing downward in this icon. You can invoke this tool to set the upward slope of the network, which will be indicated by the arrow pointing upward in the icon. This tool is used to ensure that the pipe rules are correctly followed.

Pipe Network Vistas

Invoke this tool to display the **PANORAMA** window. The **Pipes** tab allows you to edit the pipe data such as its name, description, style, rule set, rotation, and other properties. It also displays the status of a rule and indicates whether the rule is violated or not. The check mark in the **Status** column indicates that the pipe is drawn according to the rule set, refer to Figure 11-30.

Status	Name	Descripti...	Style	Rule Set	Override ...	Render ...	Type	Inner Dia...	Inner
✓0	Structure - ı	Eccentric St	Sanitary Sev	Basic	No	ByLayer	Junction Stı	48.000"	
✓0	Structure - ı	Eccentric St	Sanitary Sev	Basic	No	ByLayer	Junction Stı	48.000"	
✓0	Structure - ı	Eccentric St	Sanitary Sev	Basic	No	ByLayer	Junction Stı	48.000"	
✓0	Structure - ı	Eccentric St	Sanitary Sev	Basic	No	ByLayer	Junction Stı	48.000"	
✓0	Structure - ı	Eccentric St	Sanitary Sev	Basic	No	ByLayer	Junction Stı	48.000"	
✓0	Structure - ı	Eccentric St	Sanitary Sev	Basic	No	ByLayer	Junction Stı	48.000"	
✓0	Structure - ı	Eccentric St	Sanitary Sev	Basic	No	ByLayer	Junction Stı	48.000"	
✓0	Structure - ı	Eccentric St	Sanitary Sev	Basic	No	ByLayer	Junction Stı	48.000"	
✓0	Structure - ı	Eccentric St	Sanitary Sev	Basic	No	ByLayer	Junction Stı	48.000"	

*Figure 11-30 The **PANORAMA** window showing the status of the rule*

Editing Pipes and Structures Using the TOOLSPACE Item View

You can also edit the pipes and structures in a network using the **TOOLSPACE** Item View. To do so, choose the **Prospector** tab in the **TOOLSPACE** palette and expand **Pipe Networks > Networks** sub-node. Next, expand the required network and select **Pipes** or **Structures** of the network. On doing so, the pipe data or the structure data will be displayed in the **Item View** depending upon the selection. Now, click in various column cells and edit the required values.

Grip Editing of the Pipe Network

AutoCAD Civil 3D gives you the flexibility of using the grips to edit the pipe networks. Each time you select a pipe or a structure, the control grips will be displayed. You can use these grips to move or resize the pipe and the structure objects. Select the required pipe in the plan view; grips will be displayed at the center and the ends of the pipe, as shown in Figure 11-31.

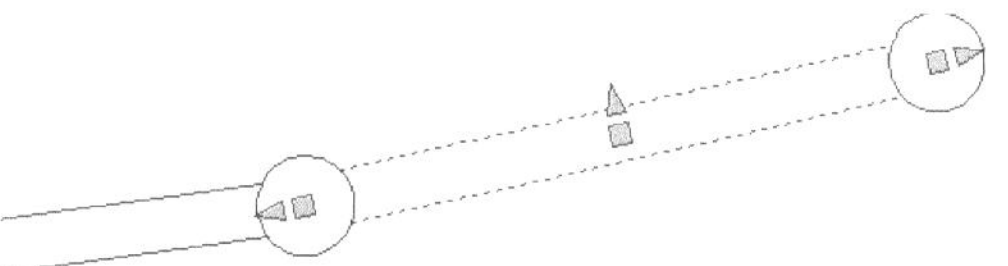

Figure 11-31 *Grips displayed on selecting the pipe object*

Figure 11-32 through 11-35 shows the use of the grip while editing the pipe object. The square grip helps you to change the location of the pipe object, whereas the triangular grip helps you to change the size of the pipe. The triangular grip at the center helps you to change the width or the pipe diameter and the triangular grips at the two ends of the pipe help you to lengthen or shorten the pipes.

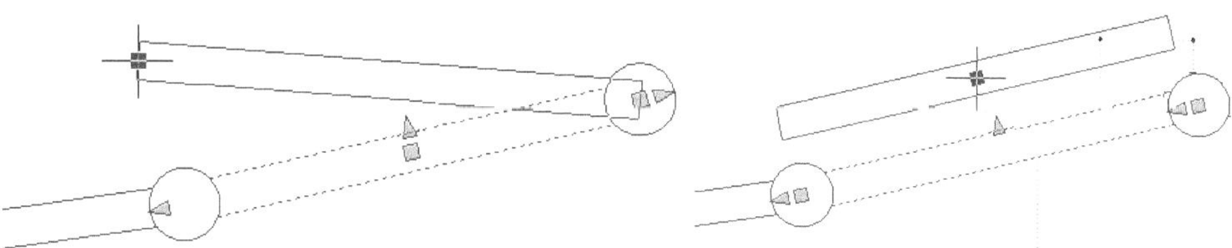

Figure 11-32 *Using the square grip to move the pipe end*

Figure 11-33 *Using the square grip at the center to move the entire pipe object*

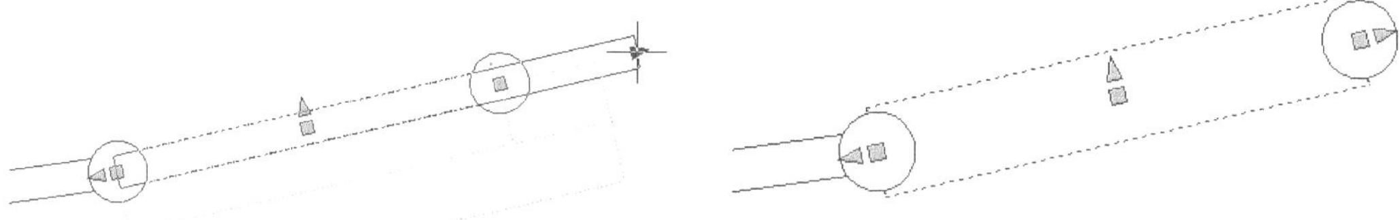

Figure 11-34 *Using the triangular grip at the end to lengthen the pipe*

Figure 11-35 *Using the triangular grip at the center to change the pipe diameter*

Click on the required grips and drag them to view the desired result. The square grip at the center of the pipes helps you to move the entire pipe to a new location. The square grips at the two ends of the pipe helps you to move the selected end to a new location, keeping the other pipe end fixed at the same location.

While using the grips to edit the pipe object, you must remember that the structures connected to the selected pipe will not move or change with the pipe or pipe ends. They will remain at their original positions. You can use the square grip at the end to insert the pipe end into another structure. On doing so, an orange colored glyph will be displayed next to the grip.

While grip editing the pipes, the connected structures are not affected. But in case of structures, the grip editing affects the pipes connected to it. For example, if you change the location of the structure using the grip, the pipe connected to the structure will automatically be relocated along with the structure. However, the elevations of the pipe ends will be retained. In case of a structure, only a square grip will be displayed in the plan and 3D views.

ADDING PIPE NETWORK LABELS

Ribbon: Annotate > Labels & Tables > Add Labels drop-down > Pipe Network > Add Pipe Networks Labels
Command: ADDNETWORKLABELS

You can label the pipe network or some parts of the network using the in-built label styles. The label styles can be created and managed in the **Settings** tab of the **TOOLSPACE** palette. You can access the pipe and structure labels styles in the **Pipe** and **Structure** nodes respectively. The labels can be added while creating the network or they can be added after the pipe network is created. To add the label while creating the network, select the required label style in the **Create Pipe Network** dialog box.

To add the pipe network labels after the pipe network is created, choose the **Pipe Network** tool from the **Add Labels** drop-down in the **Labels & Tables** panel of the **Annotate** tab; a flyout will be displayed with different tools to label the pipe network. Choose the **Add Pipe Network Labels** tool from the flyout displayed, as shown in Figure 11-36. On doing so, the **Add Labels** dialog box will be displayed.

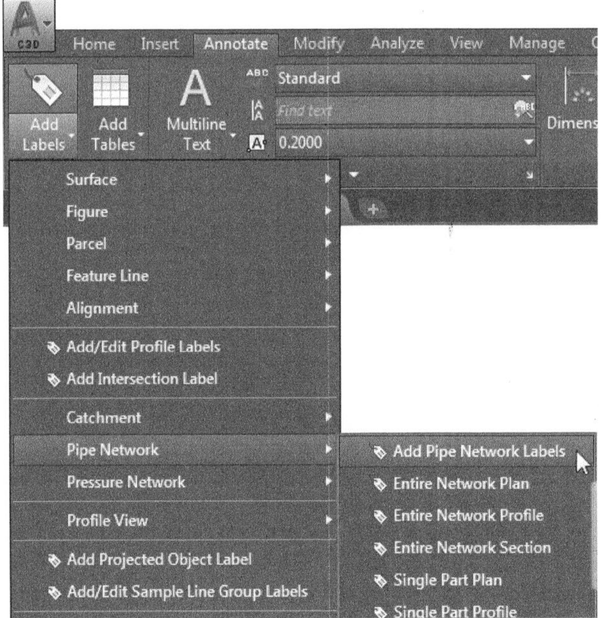

*Figure 11-36 Choosing the **Add Pipe Network Labels** tool from the flyout*

Ensure that the **Pipe Network** option is selected in the **Feature** drop-down list. Next, in this dialog box, select the **Entire Network Plan** option from the **Label type** drop-down list to label the entire network in the plan view. Now, to assign a label style for a pipe, select an option from the **Pipe label style** drop-down list. Alternatively, choose the down arrow on the right of this drop-down list to display a flyout and then choose the **Create New** option from this flyout to create a new label style or choose the **Edit Current Selection** option to edit the current style. Similarly, to label a structure, select an option from the **Structure label style** drop-down list. Now, choose the **Add** button; you will be prompted to select a part contained in the network that is to be labeled. Select any pipe or structure object in the pipe network. On doing so, all the pipe and structure objects in the pipe network will be labeled.

In the **Add Labels** dialog box, specify the label type for the network from the **Label type** drop-down list. To label only a part of the network in the plan, profile, or section view, select the **Single Part Plan/Profile/Section** option from the **Label type** drop-down list. Select the required label style for the pipe and structure from the **Pipe label style** and **Structure label style** drop-down lists, respectively. After selecting the required label styles, choose the **Add** button to add the labels. After you have added the labels, choose the **Close** button from the **Add Labels** dialog box to exit.

Tip

You can also choose the direct option to label the required network part. To do so, choose the ***Pipe Network*** *option from* ***Annotate > Labels & Tables > Add Labels****; a flyout will be displayed. Choose the required option from this flyout, refer to Figure 11-36.*

Note

If you choose a direct labeling option from the flyout, refer to Figure 11-36, you will not have the flexibility of selecting the label styles from the ***Add Labels*** *dialog box. Therefore, it is recommended that you use the default label styles to label the network.*

ADDING TABLES

You can view the network pipe and structure data in a tabular form and add the tables to the drawing. These tables help you to view the consolidated information about the structure and pipe objects that are used to draw the pipe network.

Adding a Structure Table

Ribbon: Annotate > Labels & Tables > Add Tables drop-down > Pipe Network > Add Structure
Command: ADDNETWORKSTRUCTTABLE

To add the table for structures, choose the **Pipe Network** option from the **Add Tables** drop-down; a flyout will be displayed. Choose the **Add Structure** option from the flyout displayed; the **Structure Table Creation** dialog box will be displayed, as shown in Figure 11-37. In this dialog box, select the required option from the **Table style** drop-down list. You can also create a new style for structure table. To do so, choose the down arrow on the right of the **Table style** drop-down list; a flyout will be displayed. Choose **Create New** option from the flyout; the **Table Style - New Structure Table Style** dialog box will be displayed. Specify the required options in this dialog box and choose the **OK** button to close the dialog box.

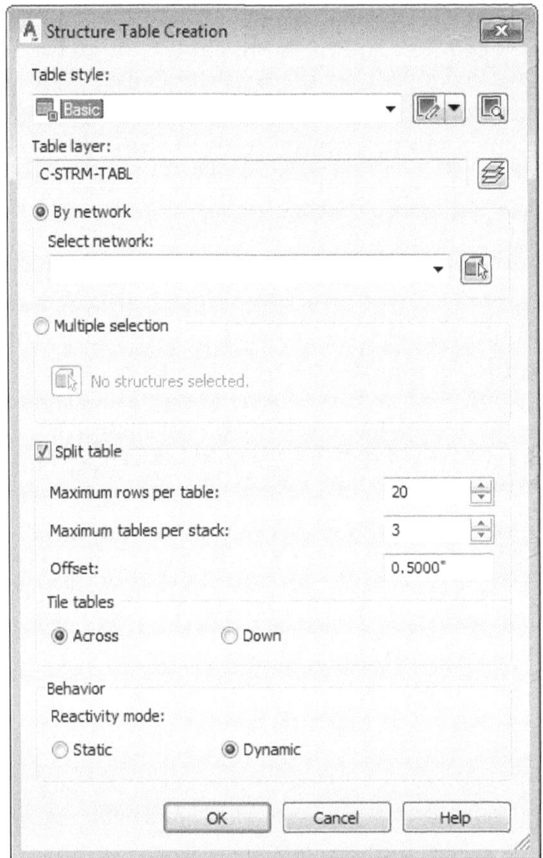

*Figure 11-37 The **Structure Table Creation** dialog box*

The **Table layer** text box displays the default layer on which the label will be created. Choose the button on the right of this text box to change the layer. Next, you will add the structure data of all the structure objects in the network. To do so, select the required option from the **Select network** drop-down list in the **By network** area. The **Select network** drop-down list remains active as the **By network** radio button is selected by default. Alternatively, choose the **Select from the drawing** button on the right to select the required network from the drawing.

To add information about multiple network structures to the structure table, select the **Multiple Selection** radio button in this dialog box. On selecting this radio button, the **Pick On-Screen** button gets activated. Choose this button to select the required structures from the plan view; the information about the selected structure will be added to the structure table.

The options in the **Split table** area of the **Structure Table Creation** dialog box allow you to format the table. Use the spinners in this area to specify the maximum rows per table and the maximum tables per stack. In the **Behavior** area, the **Dynamic** radio button is selected by default. As a result the table is updated automatically if any of the structure is changed in the network. After setting the parameters in this dialog box, choose the **OK** button; the dialog box will be closed and you will be prompted to specify the upper left corner of the table. Click in the drawing at the required location to add the structure table. The information displayed in the table depends upon the table style. You can create your own table style and configure the settings to display the required information in the table, refer to Figure 11-38.

Structure Table	
Structure Name	Structure Details
Structure – (15)	RIM = 0.000 SUMP = –7.292 Pipe – (10) INV OUT = –5.292
Structure – (16)	RIM = 0.000 SUMP = –10.163 Pipe – (10) INV IN = –8.163 Pipe – (11) INV OUT = –8.163
Structure – (17)	RIM = 0.000 SUMP = –10.924 Pipe – (11) INV IN = –8.924
Structure – (18)	RIM = 0.000 SUMP = –12.095 Pipe – (13) INV OUT = –10.095
Structure – (19)	RIM = 0.000 SUMP = –13.262 Pipe – (13) INV IN = –11.262
Structure – (20)	RIM = –4.955 SUMP = –13.580

*Figure 11-38 The **Structure table** displaying the structure details*

Adding a Pipe Table

Ribbon: Annotate > Labels & Tables > Add Tables drop-down > Pipe Network > Add Pipe
Command: ADDNETWORKPIPETABLE

To add the tables for the pipe, choose the **Pipe Network** option from the **Add Tables** drop-down; a flyout will be displayed with different options. Choose the **Add Pipe** option from the flyout displayed; the **Pipe Table Creation** dialog box will be displayed. The options in this table are same as discussed for the **Structure Table Creation** dialog box. After you have specified the settings and selected the required network or the pipe objects, choose the **OK** button; the **Pipe Table Creation** dialog box will be closed and you will be prompted to specify the upper left corner of the table. Click in the drawing to specify the table corner; the pipe table will be added to the drawing displaying the pipe details, as shown in Figure 11-39. Like the Structure table, you can configure the settings for the pipe table in the table style and display the required information about the pipe object in the table.

Pipe Table			
Pipe Name	Size	Length	Slope
Pipe – (10)	24.000	287.117	1.00%
Pipe – (11)	24.000	76.153	1.00%
Pipe – (12)	24.000	117.107	1.00%
Pipe – (13)	24.000	116.654	1.00%
Pipe – (14)	54.000	31.906	1.00%

Figure 11-39 The Pipe table displaying the pipe details

INTERFERENCE CHECK

AutoCAD Civil 3D provides you with a utility called **Interference Check** that helps you to identify and highlight the network parts that intersect, collide, or physically overlap each other. This is one of the most important utilities for checking the validity of a pipe network. It helps you to ensure that the parts of the network are not too close to each other. Interference check can be run for two different pipe networks or between the selected parts of the same network.

After running the interference check, Civil 3D highlights the parts or areas where the interference is found. You can have a better view of the results of the interference check by rotating the model in a 3D view or by drawing the pipe networks in a profile or section view. AutoCAD Civil 3D has some in-built styles to highlight and display the interferences in the network. But you can create your own style to display the interference check results. The procedure to create a style for the interference check is discussed next.

Creating the Style for the Interference Check

Choose the **Settings** tab of the **TOOLSPACE** palette and expand **Pipe Networks > Interference Styles** sub-node. Now, right-click on the **Interference Style** option and choose the **New** option from the shortcut menu; the **Interference Style - New Interference Style** dialog box will be displayed.

In the **Information** tab of this dialog box, enter a name for the style and then choose the **View Options** tab. The options in this tab are used to specify the appearance of the interference, refer to Figure 11-40. From the **Symbol Options** area of this tab, select a marker style to identify the interference visually through a symbol in the plan view.

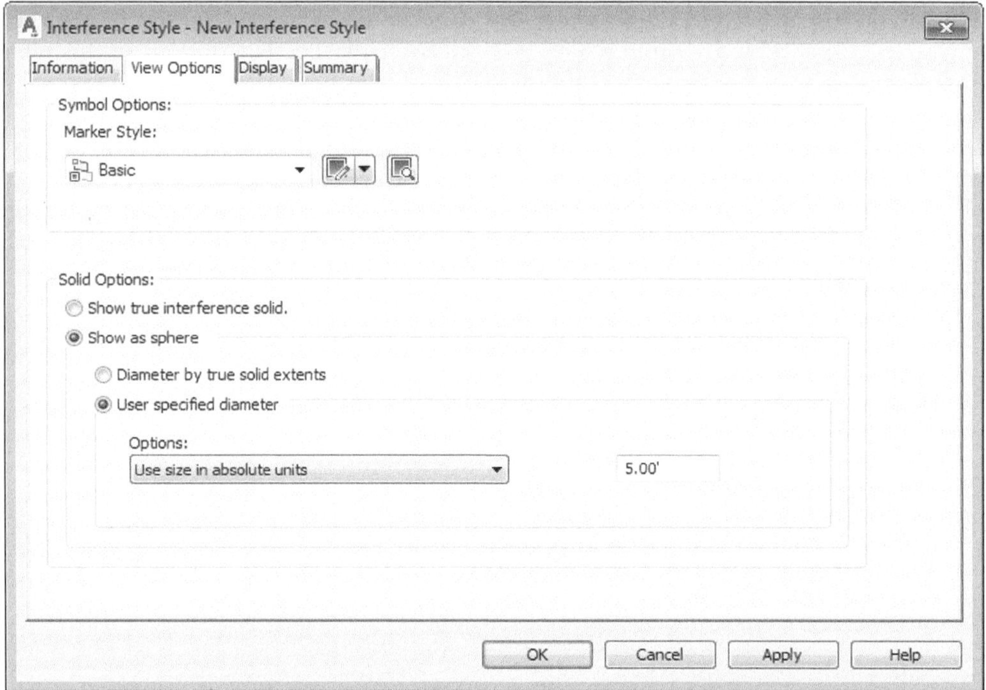

*Figure 11-40 The **Interference Style - New Interference Style** dialog box*

From the **Solid Options** area of this tab, you can select the required option to identify the interference by a solid in a model view. For example, you can select the **Show true interference solid** radio button to display the interference as a solid based on the true overlap shape of the network parts colliding with each other. Similarly, you can select the **Show as sphere** radio button to display the interference as a sphere that will be added in the drawing at the interference location. You can specify the diameter of the sphere by selecting the **User specified diameter** radio button. Note that when you select this radio button, you need to specify the options in the **Options** drop-down list and the edit box displayed below the radio button. Selecting the **Diameter by true solid extents** radio button will add the sphere at the centroid of the interference solid and its size will be equal to the extent of the collision.

The **Display** tab is used to specify the visibility of the symbol or the solid representing the interference, color, lineweight, and other properties in different views. Select the required model, plan, or a section view from the **View Direction** drop-down list and then specify the other properties for the display of the interference symbol or solid. After you have specified the settings for the interference style, choose the **OK** button to exit the dialog box; the style will be added in the **Interference Style** sub-node.

Running the Interference Check

You can run the interference check to identify and highlight the parts of a network that intersect or are within a specified distance from each other. To do so, right-click on the **Interference Checks** sub-node of the **Pipe Network** node in the **Prospectors** tab; a shortcut menu will be displayed. Choose the **Create Interference Check** option from the shortcut menu; you will be prompted to select a part from the first network. Select the required network part of the network from the drawing; you will be prompted to select another part from the same network or from a different network. Select the required part in the drawing; the **Create Interference Check** dialog box will be displayed, as shown in Figure 11-41. In this dialog box, specify a name for the interference check in the **Name** edit box. You can also enter a description in the **Description** text box if required. Now, select an option from the **Network 1** the drop-down list. Alternatively, choose the **Select from the drawing** button on the right and select the first network from the drawing. Similarly, select the required option from the **Network 2** drop-down list. Next, select the required option from the **Interference style** drop-down list and from the **Render material** drop-down list.

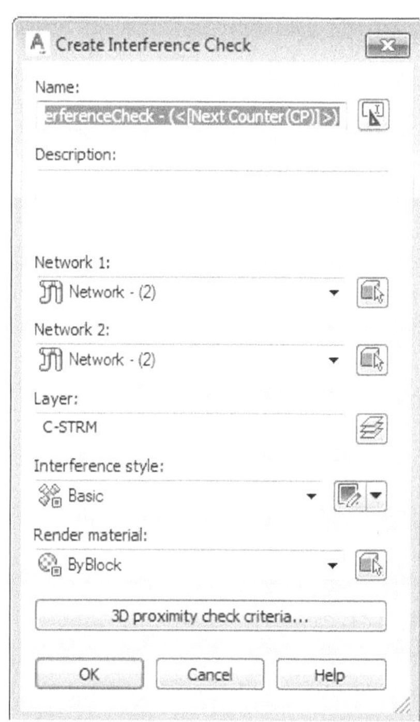

Figure 11-41 The ***Create Interference Check*** *dialog box*

Next, you can also choose the **3D proximity check criteria** button in the **Create Interference Check** dialog box to check if the parts in the selected pipe network(s) are distant by the specified distance from each other. On doing so, the **Criteria** dialog box will be displayed, as shown in Figure 11-42.

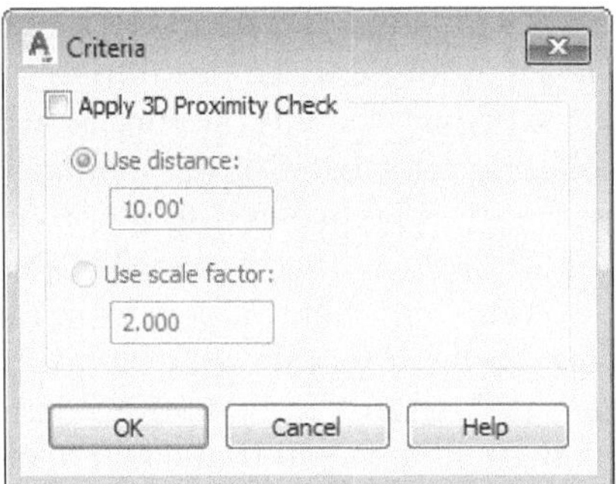

*Figure 11-42 The **Criteria** dialog box*

You can use the options in this dialog box to specify the parameters for checking the proximity of parts in the network. To enable the proximity check, ensure that the **Apply 3D Proximity Check** check box in this dialog box is selected.

Select the **Use distance** radio button if you want to check the proximity by specifying the proximity distance. On doing so, the edit box below this radio button will be activated. Next, specify the proximity distance value in the edit box below this radio button. On running the interference check with this radio button selected, Civil 3D will search and identify the pipe network parts that are at less distance than the specified one. These parts will be highlighted as the interference.

Alternatively, you can also select the **Use scale factor** radio button and specify the required scale factor in the edit box. On running the interference check, Civil 3D will search, identify, and mark all the pipe network parts at a distance from each other as per the scale factor specified. After specifying the desired settings in the **Criteria** dialog box, choose the **OK** button; the **Criteria** dialog box will be closed.

Next, choose the **OK** button in the **Create Interference Check** dialog box; the dialog box will be closed and Civil 3D will start searching for the parts that collide, or are too close to each other and display a message box. This message box indicates that a check has been run and also displays the number of the interferences found. Choose the **OK** button from the message box; the message box will be closed and the interferences will be displayed according to the interference style.

Note that even if you do not enable the 3D proximity check criteria, you can still run the interference check. However, the interference will be marked only at the location where the parts physically collide with each other. In this case, the distance criteria will not be considered. Figures 11-43 and 11-44 show the interference using the **Show true interference solid** and **Show as sphere** options, respectively.

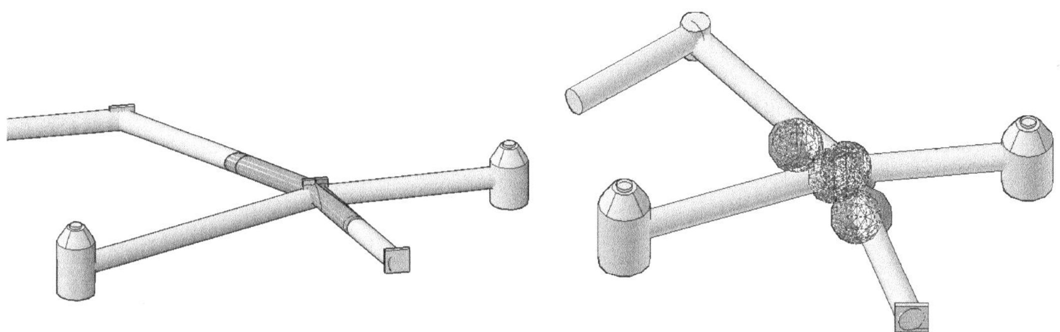

Figure 11-43 *The interference displayed by true interference solid*

Figure 11-44 *The interference displayed by spheres*

The interference checks that you perform are listed in the **Prospector** tab of the **TOOLSPACE** palette. To view these checks, expand **Pipe Networks > Interference Checks** in the **Prospector** tab; various checks will be displayed. To view the details of an interference check, select the name of the required interference check; the details will be displayed in the Item View. If you make any changes in the pipe network or in the interference style, the out-of-date symbol will be displayed in the **Prospector** tab. To rectify this, select the required interference check name and right-click. Next, choose the **Rerun Interference check** option from the shortcut menu displayed.

SWAPPING PARTS

AutoCAD Civil 3D allows you to replace the existing network parts with new parts. To replace the existing network parts with new parts, select a pipe or the structure parts in the drawing and right-click; a shortcut menu will be displayed. Choose the **Swap Part** option from the shortcut menu; the **Swap Part Size** dialog box will be displayed, as shown in Figure 11-45. Select the required part from this dialog box and choose the **OK** button to exit the dialog box. The selected part will be swapped with the part selected from the **Swap Part Size** dialog box.

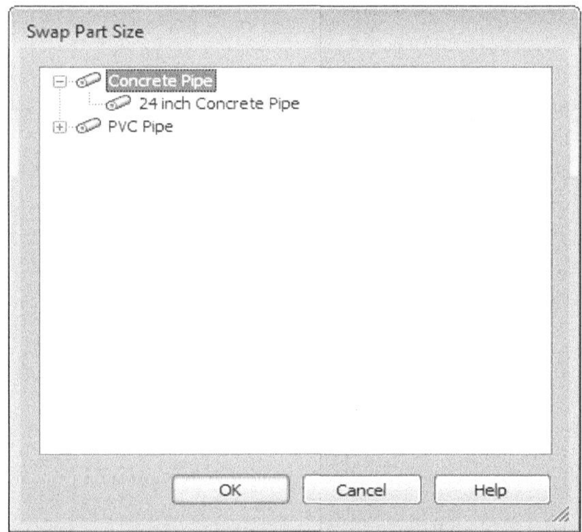

Figure 11-45 *The **Swap Part Size** dialog box*

The **Swap Part Size** dialog box displays only the available parts. Note that the parts can be swapped only if they are of the same type. For example, you can swap a junction structure only with a junction structure and a pipe with a pipe. The null structure is an exception because it can be swapped with a junction structure. Remember that even after swapping, the elevation of the parts is retained.

TUTORIALS

Tutorial 1 Sanitary Sewer Network

In this tutorial, you will create a sanitary sewer network, as shown in Figure 11-46, using the **Network Layout Tools** toolbar. You will also create a parts list and part label styles.

(Expected time: 30 min)

The following steps are required to complete this tutorial:

a. Download and open the file.
b. Create the parts list.
c. Create the structure label style.
d. Add another component to the label.
e. Create the sanitary sewer network using the **Network Layout Tools** toolbar.
f. Reference the label text.
g. Save the file.

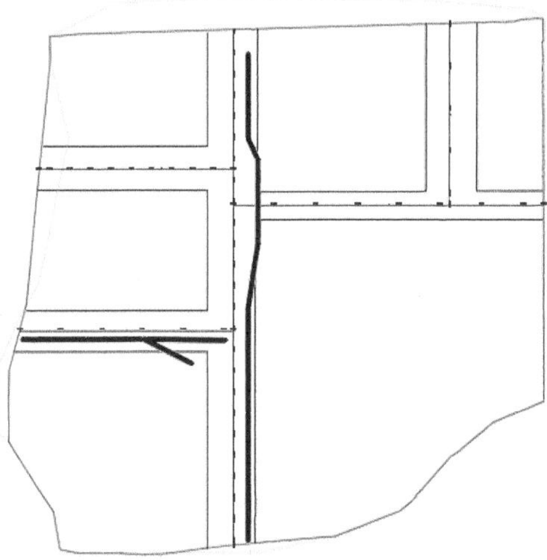

Figure 11-46 *The sanitary sewer network created along the alignments*

Downloading and Opening the File

1. Download *c11_c3d_2018_tut.zip* file from *http://www.cadcim.com*. Next, save and extract the file at *C:\c3d_2018* location.

2. Choose **Open** from the **Application Menu**; the **Select File** dialog box is displayed.

3. In the dialog box, browse to the location *C:\c3d_2018\c11_c3d_2018_tut*.

4. Select the file *c11_c3d_2018_tut01.dwg* and then choose the **Open** button to open the file. Ignore any warnings, if displayed. Now, expand the **Surfaces** node in the **Prospector** tab of the **TOOLSPACE** palette; the **EG** and **FG** surfaces will be displayed. In the opened drawing, the **EG** (existing ground) surface is indicated by a yellow border in the drawing and the **FG** (finished ground) surface is indicated by a red border. The drawing consists of five alignments.

Creating the Parts List

1. Choose the **Create Network Parts List** tool from the **Create Design** panel of the **Home** tab; the **Network Parts List - New Parts List** dialog box is displayed. Choose the **Information** tab.

2. Enter **Sanitary Sewer** in the **Name** edit box of the **Information** tab and then choose the **Pipes** tab.

3. Right-click on **New Parts List** in the **Name** column and choose **Add part family** from the shortcut menu displayed; the **Part Catalog** dialog box is displayed, as shown in Figure 11-47.

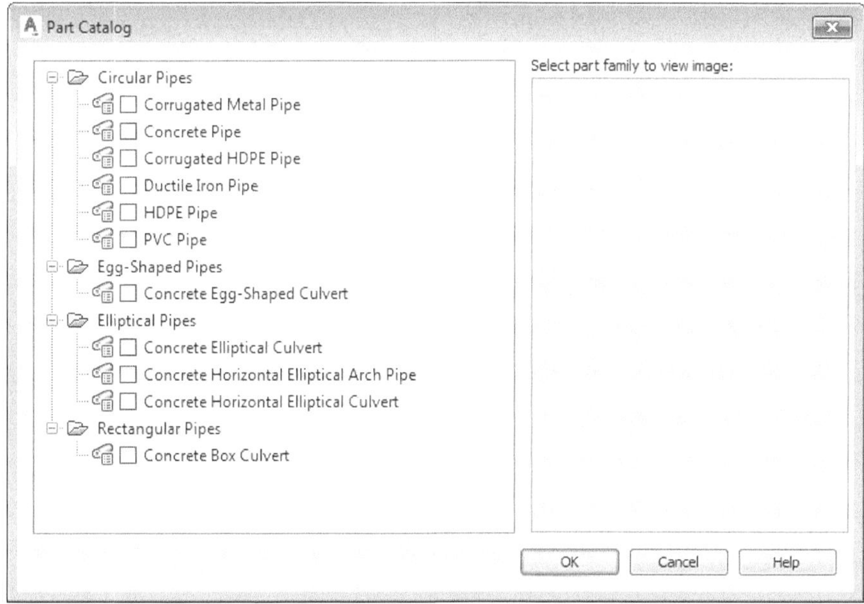

***Figure 11-47** The **Part Catalog** dialog box*

4. Select the **PVC Pipe** check box and then choose the **OK** button; the dialog box is closed and the selected part family is added to the parts list in the **Name** column.

5. Expand the **Sanitary Sewer** sub-node in the **Name** column and right-click on **PVC Pipe**; a shortcut menu is displayed.

6. Choose **Add part size** from the shortcut menu; the **Part Size Creator** dialog box is displayed.

7. Double-click in the **Value** field of the **Inner Pipe Diameter** property and select **6.000000** from the drop-down list, as shown in Figure 11-48. Next, choose the **OK** button; the selected part size is added to the **PVC Pipe** node created in the **Name** column.

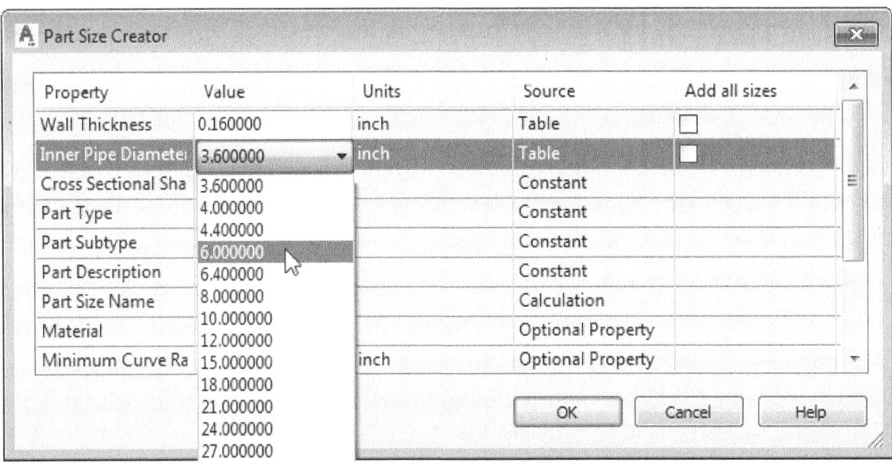

*Figure 11-48 Selecting the **6.000000** value from the **Inner Pipe Diameter** drop-down list*

8. Repeat the procedure followed in steps 6 and 7, and select **10.000000** and **12.000000** as the inner pipe diameters to add two more part sizes. As a result, three pipes of different sizes are added to the **PVC Pipe** node, as shown in Figure 11-49.

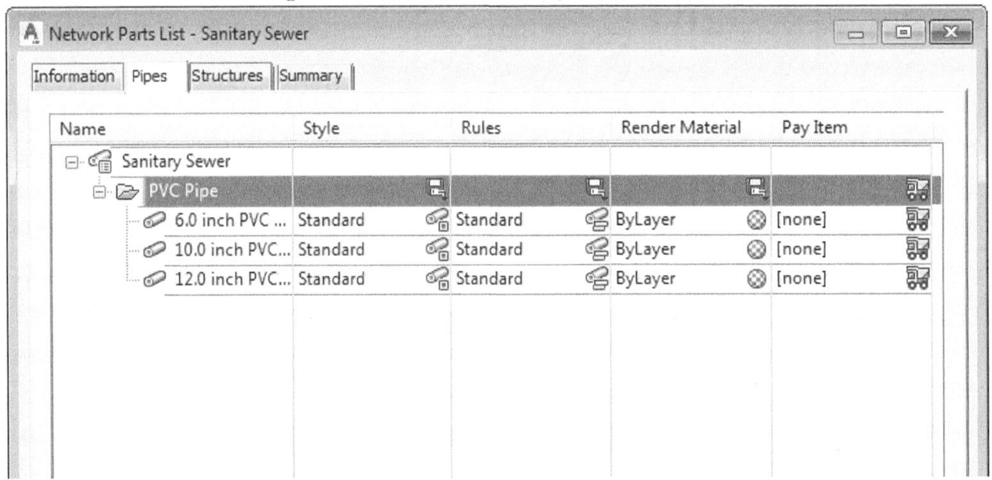

*Figure 11-49 Partial view of three pipes of different sizes added to the **PVC Pipe** node*

9. Now, choose the **Structures** tab in the **Network Parts List - Sanitary Sewer** dialog box and right-click in the dialog box; a shortcut menu is displayed. Choose **Refresh** from the shortcut menu; the item list now displays **Sanitary Sewer** under the **Name** column. Right-click on **Sanitary Sewer** in the **Name** column; a shortcut menu is displayed.

10. Choose the **Add part family** option from the shortcut menu; the **Part Catalog** dialog box is displayed.

11. Select the **Concentric Cylindrical Structure** check box from the **Junction Structures with Frames** category and choose the **OK** button to exit the **Part Catalog** dialog box; the structure part family is added to the part family.

12. Expand the **Sanitary Sewer** and then right-click on **Concentric Cylindrical Structure** in the **Name** column; a shortcut menu is displayed. Choose the **Add part size** option from the shortcut menu; the **Part Size Creator** dialog box is displayed.

13. In this dialog box, ensure that the value of the **Inner Structure Diameter** property is set to **48.000000**. Next, choose the **OK** button to exit. The structure with the specified diameter is added to the part list.

14. Repeat the procedure followed in steps 12 and 13 to add two other structures with the inner structure diameter values as **60.000000** and **72.000000** to the parts list. The structure family and the part sizes are added to the part list, as shown in Figure 11-50.

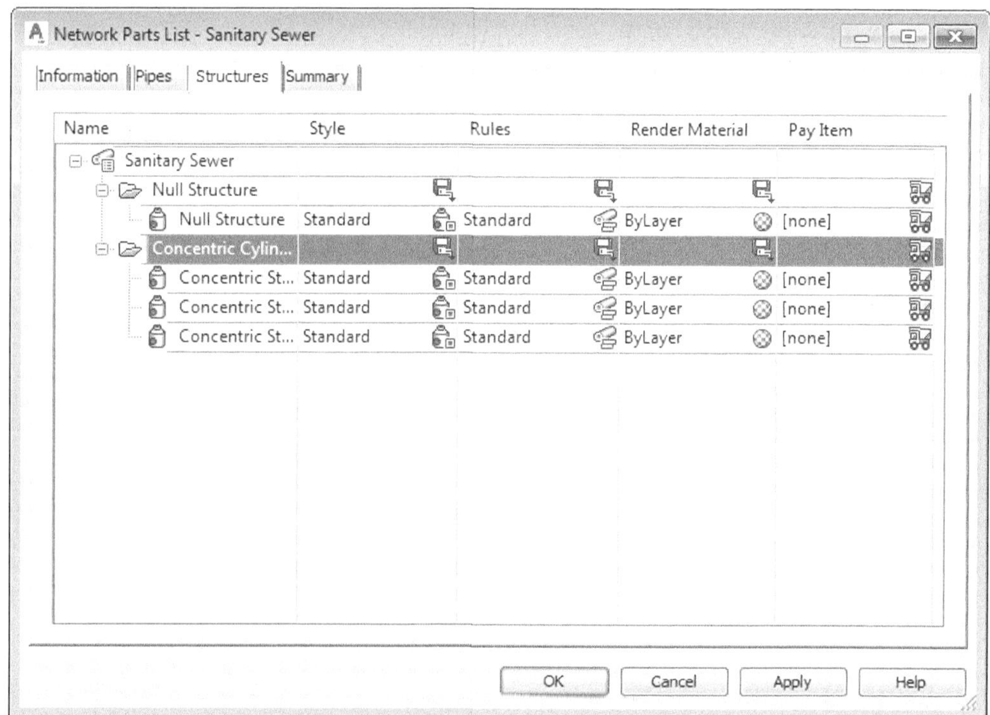

Figure 11-50 *The* ***Concentric Cylindrical Structure*** *family and the part sizes added to the* ***Sanitary Sewer*** *part list*

15. Choose the **OK** button from the **Network Parts List - Sanitary Sewer** dialog box to close it. Now, you have created the parts list consisting of the required parts. This part list is added to the **Parts Lists** sub-node of the **Pipe Network** in the **Settings** tab and will be used to create the sanitary sewer network.

Creating the Structure Label Style

1. Choose the **Settings** tab from the **TOOLSPACE** palette and expand **Structure > Label Styles** sub-node.

2. Right-click on the **Label Styles** sub-node and choose the **New** option from the shortcut menu displayed; the **Label Style Composer - New Structure Label Style** dialog box is displayed. The **Information** tab is chosen by default in this dialog box.

3. Enter **Structure Style** in the **Name** edit box and then choose the **Layout** tab.

Note that **Structure Text** is the default selected component in the **Component name** drop-down list of this tab.

4. Click in the **Value** field of the **Contents** property and choose the browse button; the **Text Component Editor - Contents** dialog box is displayed.

5. Select the text in the **Editor** window and delete it.

6. Now, select the **Name** option from the **Properties** drop-down list and choose the button located on the right of this drop-down list; the text **<[Name(CP)]>** is added in the **Text Editor** window. Next, click in the **Editor** window and bring the cursor to the next line.

7. Now, select the **Insertion Rim Elevation** option from the **Properties** drop-down list and set the **Precision** modifier to **0.01**.

8. Again, choose the button located on the right of the **Properties** drop-down list to add the property to the **Text Editor** window, as shown in Figure 11-51.

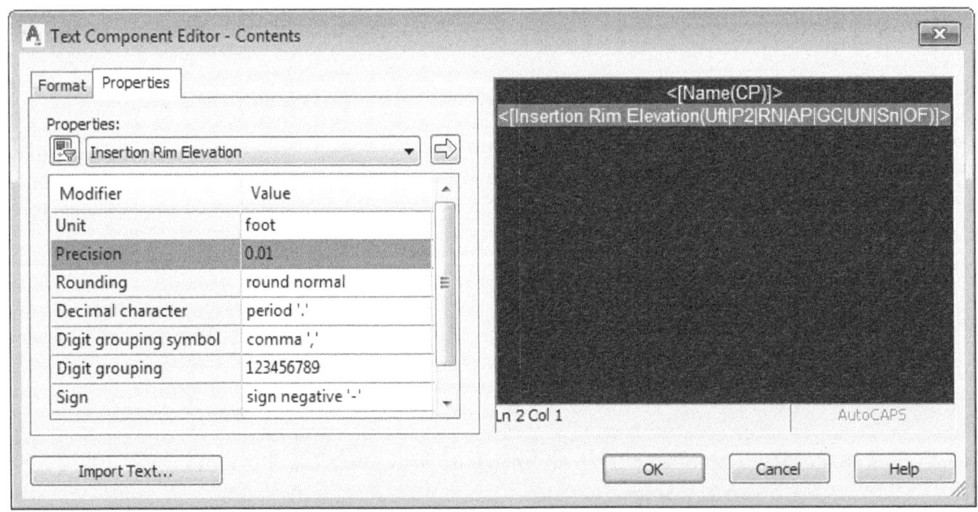

Figure 11-51 *The **Precision** property added to the **Text Editor** window*

9. In the **Editor** window, type **RIM** before the **<Insertion Rim Elevation>** text and align it below the **Name** property.

10. Choose the **OK** button; the **Text Component Editor - Contents** dialog box is closed.

11. In the **Label Style Composer - Structure Style** dialog box, click on the **Create Text component** button; a flyout is displayed. Choose the **Reference Text** option from the flyout, as shown in Figure 11-52; the **Select Type** dialog box is displayed.

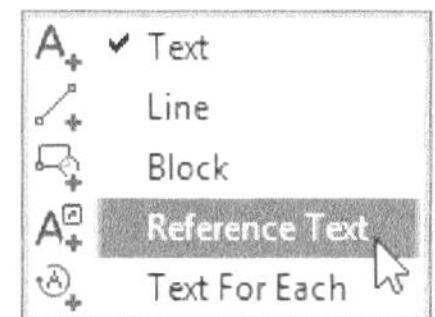

***Figure 11-52** Choosing the **Reference Text** option from the **Create Text Component** flyout*

12. Select the **Surface** option from the dialog box and choose the **OK** button; the dialog box is closed.

13. Click in the **Value** field of the **Name** property and enter **FG**.

14. Set the required parameters as given below:

    Anchor Component: **Structure Text** Anchor Point: **Bottom Center**

15. Click in the **Value** field of the **Contents** property and choose the browse button; the **Text Component Editor - Contents** dialog box is displayed.

16. Delete the text in the **Editor** window and select the **Surface Elevation** option from the **Properties** drop-down list.

17. Set the **Precision** to **0.01** and choose the arrow button located on the right of the **Properties** drop-down list to add text to the **Editor** window.

18. Enter **FG** before the text in the **Editor** window, as shown in Figure 11-53.

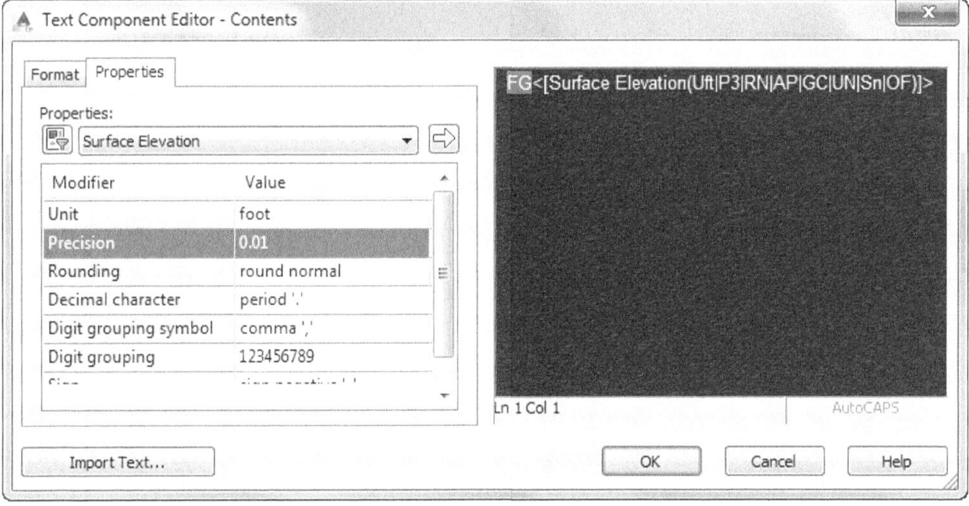

***Figure 11-53** The text entered in the **Editor** window*

19. Choose the **OK** button to exit the **Text Component Editor - Contents** dialog box and return to the **Label Style Composer - Structure Style** dialog box.

20. Enter **0.300"** in the **Value** field of the **Text Height** property. You will notice that in the preview area, **???** symbol is displayed in the label as you have not yet selected the surface to be referenced.

Adding Another Component to the Label

1. Choose the down arrow on the right of the **Create Reference Text Component** button in the **Layout** tab of the **Label Style Composer - Structure Style** dialog box and choose the **Text For Each** option from the flyout displayed; the **Select Type** dialog box is displayed.

2. Select the **Structure all pipes** option from the list box displayed in the dialog box if it is not selected by default and then choose the **OK** button; the **Select Type** dialog box is closed.

3. In the **Label Style Composer - Structure Style** dialog box, click in the **Value** field of the **Contents** property and then choose the browse button; the **Text Component Editor - Contents** dialog box is displayed.

4. Delete the text in the **Editor** window and select the **Connected Pipe Invert Elevation** option from the **Properties** drop-down list.

5. Set the precision to **0.01** and then add the property to the **Editor window** by using the arrow button located on the right of the **Properties** drop-down list.

6. Add **Invert** before the label text in the **Editor** window and choose the **OK** button to close the **Text Component Editor - Contents** dialog box.

7. In the **Label Style Composer - Structure Style** dialog box, set the parameters as given below:

   Anchor Component: **FG**
   Attachment: **Top center**
   Anchor Point: **Bottom Center**
   Text Height: **0.300"**

Note
The defined text will be used to display the pipe inverts elevation at the structure.

8. Choose the **OK** button to close the **Label Style Composer - Structure Style** dialog box.

Creating the Sanitary Sewer Pipe Network

1. Choose the **Pipe Network Creation Tools** tool from **Home > Create Design > Pipe Network** drop-down; the **Create Pipe Network** dialog box is displayed.

2. Specify the following values in this dialog box:

   Network name: **Sanitary Sewer Network**
   Network description: **Along the Main Street**

Network parts list:	**Sanitary Sewer**
Surface name:	**FG**
Alignment name:	**Main Street**
Structure label style:	**sewer style**

3. Choose the **OK** button to close the dialog box; the **Network Layout Tools - Sanitary Sewer Network** toolbar is displayed.

4. Select the **Concentric Structure 48 dia 18 frame 24 cone 5 wall 6 floor** option from the **Structure List** drop-down list and then select **10 inch PVC Pipe** from the **Pipe List** drop-down list.

5. Now, invoke the **Pipes and Structures** tool from the drop-down next to the **Pipe List** in the **Network Layout Tools** toolbar; you are prompted to specify the insertion point for the structure.

6. Enter **'SO** in the command line and press ENTER to activate the transparent command for the station offset.

7. Next, select the **Main Street** alignment; you are prompted to specify a station along the alignment.

8. Enter **50** in the command line and press ENTER; you are prompted to specify the offset distance from the station.

9. Enter **-36** in the command line and press ENTER.

10. Follow the prompts in the command line and add a structure at station **200** and **250** each at an offset distance of **-36**, refer to Figure 11-54. You will notice that the structures are placed at the specified stations of the alignment and a pipe connecting the two structures is drawn automatically.

11. Again, enter **350** in the command line and press ENTER to add a structure at station **3+50.00**. Next, enter **-60** as the offset distance and then press ENTER; the structure is placed outside the white boundary line, as shown in Figure 11-55.

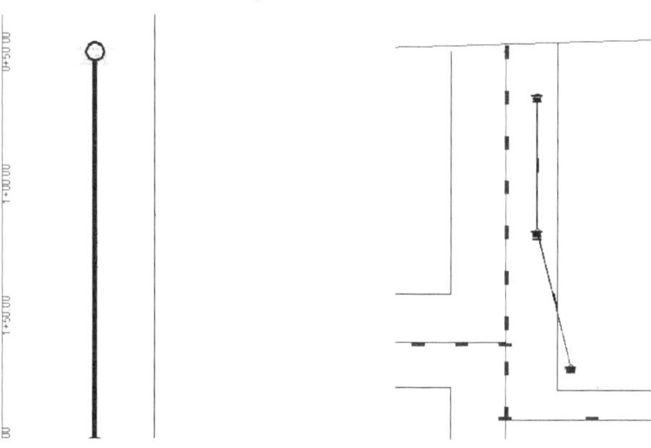

Figure 11-54 *A pipe connecting the structures added at stations*

Figure 11-55 *Structures and pipe parts placed outside the boundary*

12. Repeat the procedure given in steps 8 and 9, and add a structure at station **500** at an offset distance of **-60**, at station **650** at an offset distance of **-36**, and at stations **9+00.00**, **10+50.00**, and **12+00.00** each at an offset distance of **-36**.

13. Press ENTER twice to exit the command; the sanitary sewer network along the **Main Street** alignment is created and displayed, as shown in Figure 11-56.

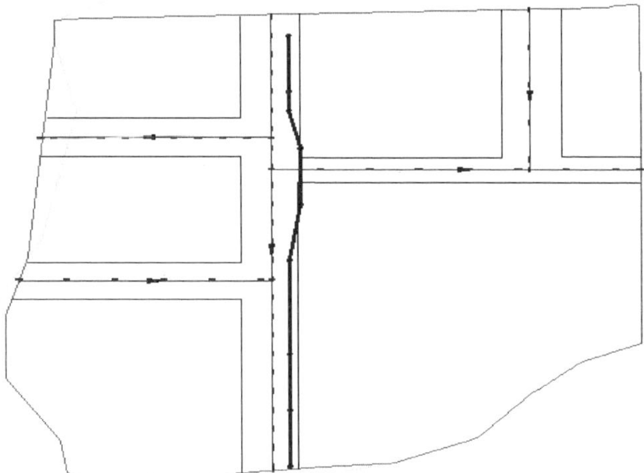

Figure 11-56 *The sanitary sewer network created along the* ***Main Street*** *alignment*

14. Now, select the **Concentric Structure 60 dia 18 frame 24 cone 5 wall 6 floor** option from the **Structure List**. Next, select the **6 inch PVC Pipe** option from the **Pipe List** drop-down list in the **Network Layout Tools** toolbar.

Note

If the ***Network Layout Tools*** *toolbar is not displayed, select any part of the network from the drawing and right-click. Choose* ***Edit Network*** *from the shortcut menu displayed to enable the toolbar.*

15. Invoke the **Draw Pipes and Structures** tool from the **Network Layout Tools** toolbar and click near the first station of the **MG Road** alignment (second alignment on the left) to add a structure, as shown in Figure 11-57.

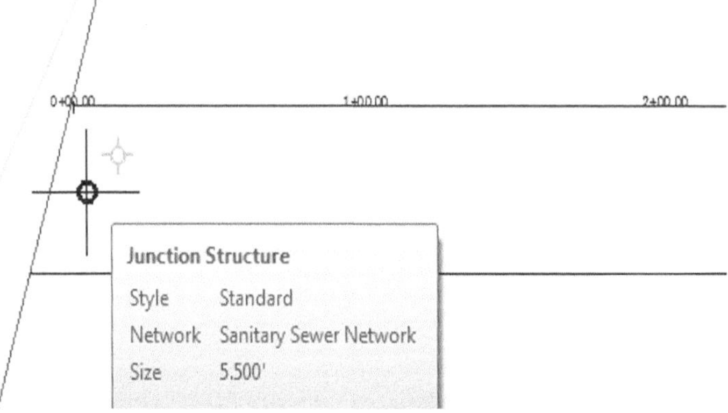

Figure 11-57 *Adding a structure near the first station of the* ***MG Road*** *alignment*

16. Next, click again between the stations **1+00.00** and **2+00.00** to place another structure.

17. Now, select the **10 inch PVC Pipe** option from the **Pipe List** drop-down list and click in the drawing area to add structures near stations **3+00.00** and **5+00.00**.

18. Press ENTER to exit the command.

19. Select **Concentric Structure 60 dia 18 frame 24 cone 5 wall 6 floor** from the **Structure List** drop-down list and **12 inch PVC Pipe** from the **Pipe List** drop-down list in the **Network Layout Tools** toolbar.

20. Choose the **Pipes and Structures** tool from the drop-down next to the **Pipe List** in the **Network Layout Tools** toolbar and then choose **Structures Only** from the flyout displayed, as shown in Figure 11-58.

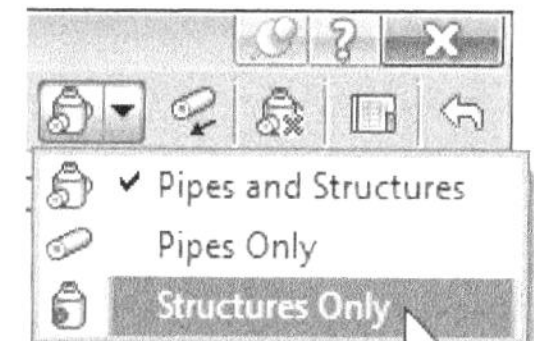

*Figure 11-58 Choosing the **Structures Only** option from the flyout*

21. Now, add a structure outside the alignment right-of-way, as shown in Figure 11-59.

22. Choose **Pipes Only** from the flyout.

23. Move the cursor near the structure added in step 20, and click when the orange colored circular glyph is displayed, as shown in Figure 11-60. This glyph indicates the insertion or the connection point to connect the pipe.

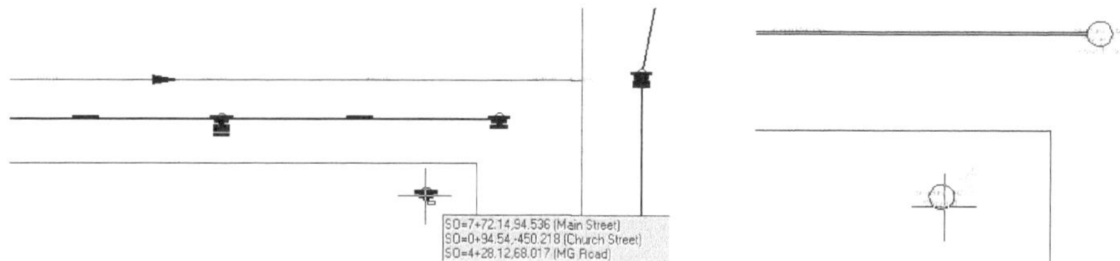

Figure 11-59 Adding the structure outside the right-of-way

Figure 11-60 The orange colored glyph displayed at the insertion point

24. Now, move the cursor to the structure added near station **3+00.00**; the orange glyph is displayed. Next, click in the drawing; the pipe connecting the two structures is created, as shown in Figure 11-61.

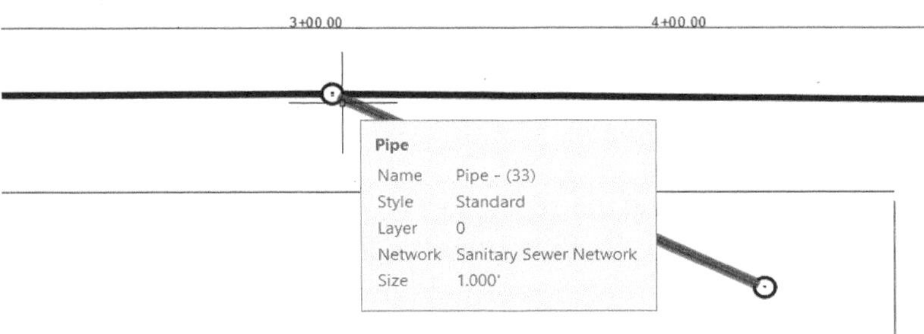

Figure 11-61 *The pipe created between two structures*

25. Press ENTER to terminate the command.

Referencing the Label Text

1. Zoom in the center of the structure of any of the structure labels and you will notice that the **???** symbol is displayed in the structure label as mentioned earlier. To get rid of this symbol, you need to reference the required surface to the label text.

2. Select any of the structure labels from the drawing and right-click; a shortcut menu is displayed.

3. Choose **Label Properties** from the shortcut menu to display the **PROPERTIES** window.

4. Click on the default value **none** of the **sewer style::FG::surface** property under the **Reference Text Objects** head; a drop-down list is displayed.

5. Select **FG** from the drop-down list, as shown in Figure 11-62. Close the **PROPERTIES** window.

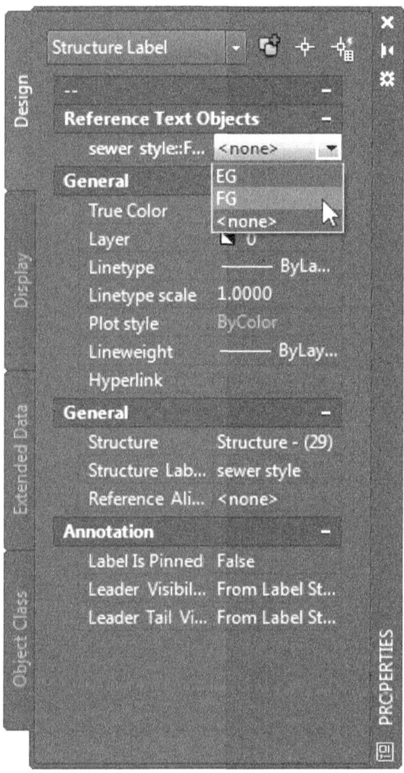

***Figure 11-62** Selecting the **FG** option from the drop-down list of the **sewer style** property*

6. Zoom in the selected structures again; you will notice that the **???** symbol is replaced with the elevation of the **FG** surface, refer to Figures 11-63 and 11-64.

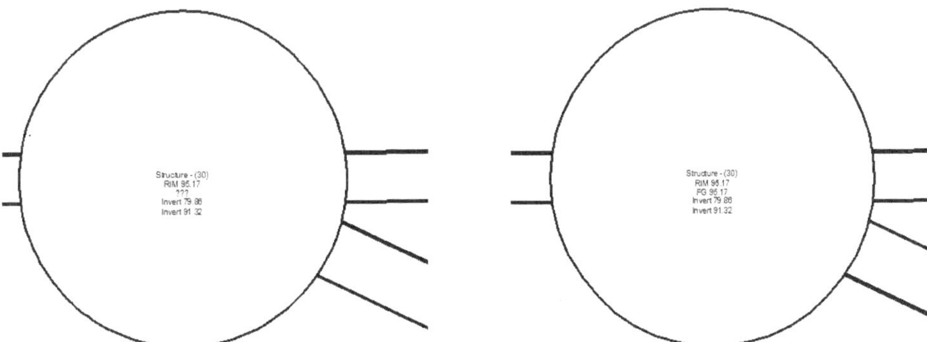

***Figure 11-63** The structure label without the referenced object*

***Figure 11-64** The structure label after referencing the surface object with the label*

7. Zoom in to any other structure; you will notice the **???** symbol. To reference the value in all the structures in one go, right-click on any structure label; a shortcut menu is displayed.

Choose the **Select Similar** option from the shortcut menu displayed; all the labels for the structures will be selected. Now, right-click and select the **FG** surface as the reference object for the label text, as explained in steps 3 to 5.

8. Zoom in to check the structure labels and view the elevation of the **FG** surface.

Saving the File

1. Choose **Save As** from the **Application Menu**; the **Save Drawing As** dialog box is displayed.

2. In this dialog box, browse to the following location:

   C:\c3d_2018\c11_c3d_2018_tut

3. Save the file as *c11_tut01a*.

Tutorial 2 Storm Network

In this tutorial, you will create a storm network from the polyline object, as shown in Figure 11-65. Also, you will run the interference check for the existing sanitary sewer network and storm network, add labels, and draw storm network parts in the profile view.

(Expected time: 30 min)

The following steps are required to complete this tutorial:

a. Download and open the file.
b. Create the storm network from the polyline object in the drawing.
c. Run the interference check.
d. Add labels to the network.
e. Draw storm network parts in the profile view.
f. Save the file.

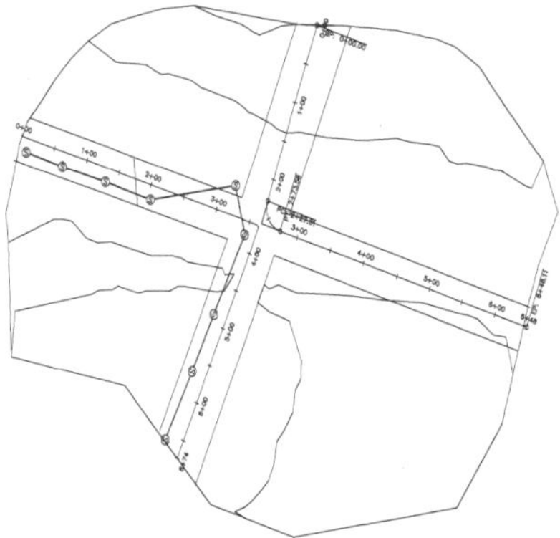

Figure 11-65 *The storm network created from the polyline object*

Downloading and Opening the File

1. Download *c11_c3d_2018_tut.zip* file if not downloaded earlier from *http://www.cadcim.com*. Next, save and extract the file at *C:\c3d_2018* location.

2. Choose **Open** from the **Application Menu**; the **Select File** dialog box is displayed.

3. In the dialog box, browse to the location *C:\c3d_2018\c11_c3d_2018_tut*.

4. Select the file *c11_c3d_2018_tut02.dwg* and then choose the **Open** button to open the file. The drawing file consists of alignments, a sanitary sewer network, profile view, and a blue colored polyline object that you will use to create the storm network.

Creating the Storm Network

1. Choose the **Create Pipe Network from Object** tool from **Home > Create Design > Pipe Network** drop-down; you are prompted to select an object.

2. Zoom in the sanitary network on the left side of the drawing and select the blue colored polyline object before station **2+00**; you are prompted to specify the flow direction.

3. Press ENTER to accept the default direction; the **Create Pipe Network from Object** dialog box is displayed.

4. Enter the following values in the dialog box:

   Network Name: **Storm network**
   Network Parts List: **Storm network** (default)
   Pipe to create: **21 inch PVC** (default)
   Structure to create: **Slab Top Cylindrical Structure 18 dia 18 dia Frm 4 FrHt 4 Slab 3 Wall 4 Floor**

5. Choose the **OK** button; the **Create Pipe Network from Object** dialog box is closed and the storm network is created from the polyline object.

6. Select the created pipe in the network and then right-click in the drawing; a shortcut menu is displayed.

7. Choose **Pipe Properties** from the shortcut menu; the **Pipe Properties - Pipe - <number>** dialog box is displayed. In this dialog box, choose the **Information** tab if not chosen by default.

8. Select the **Double Line (Storm)** option from the **Style** drop-down list in the **Object styles** area.

9. Choose the **OK** button; the dialog box is closed. Notice the pipe in the drawing. The pipe style has changed and it is displayed in blue color, as shown in Figure 11-66.

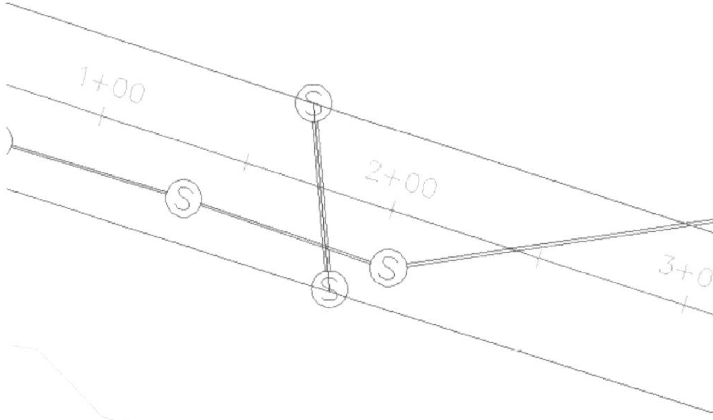

Figure 11-66 The storm network displayed with the selected pipe style

10. Select the first storm network structure created previously and right-click; a shortcut menu is displayed. Now, choose the **Structure Properties** option from the shortcut menu; the **Structure Properties - Structure - <number>** dialog box is displayed.

11. In the **Information** tab, select the **Storm Sewer Manhole** option from the **Style** drop-down list in the **Object styles** area and choose the **OK** button; the dialog box is closed and the style is assigned to the first storm network structure.

12. Assign the style for the second storm network structure as explained in steps 10 and 11. The structures are displayed with a different style, refer to Figure 11-67.

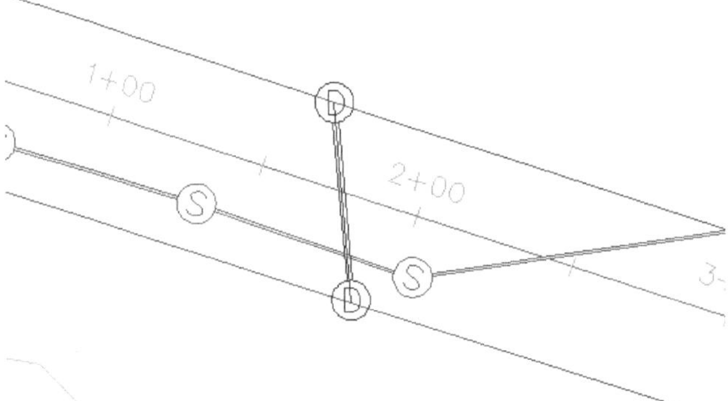

Figure 11-67 The storm network structures after changing part styles

Running the Interference Check

1. Select and right-click on the **Interference Checks** subnode in the **Pipe Network** node of the **Prospector** tab; a shortcut menu is displayed. Choose the **Create Interference Check** option from the shortcut menu; you are prompted to select an object from the first network.

2. Select the pipe part of the storm network; you are prompted to select a part from the same or another network.

3. Next, select the pipe part of the sanitary network where the storm network crosses the sanitary network; the **Create Interference Check** dialog box is displayed.

4. Enter **Storm sewer interference** in the **Name** edit box and ensure that **Storm network** and **Sanitary sewer** options are selected in the **Network 1** and **Network 2** drop-down lists, respectively.

5. Keeping the default interference style, choose the **3D proximity check criteria** button; the **Criteria** dialog box is displayed.

6. Select the **Apply 3D Proximity Check** check box if not selected by default and ensure that the **Use distance** radio button is selected.

7. Retain the default value 10.0' for distance in the edit box below the **Use distance** radio button. Next, choose the **OK** button to close the dialog box and return to the **Create Interference Check** dialog box.

8. Choose the **OK** button; the **Create Interference Check** dialog box is closed and the **AutoCAD Civil 3D 2018** message box is displayed showing the number of interferences found, refer to Figure 11-68.

9. Choose the **OK** from the message box; the interference marker is displayed in the plan view, as shown in Figure 11-69.

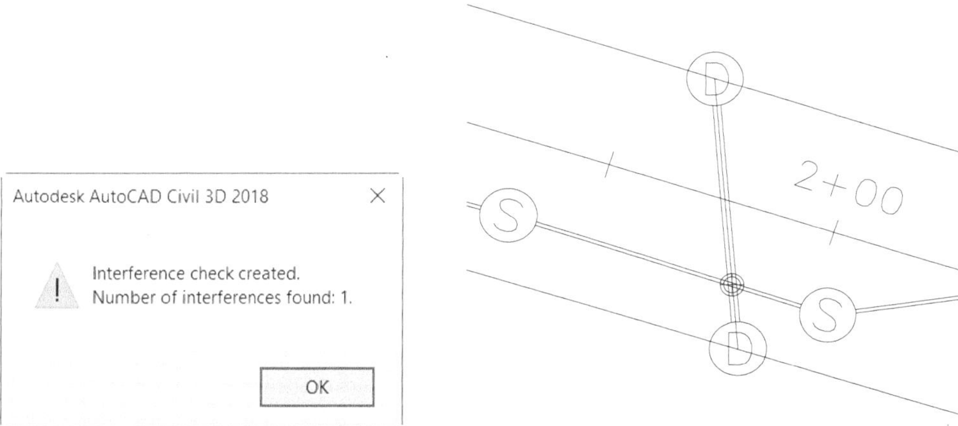

Figure 11-68 *The **AutoCAD Civil 3D 2018** message box*

Figure 11-69 *The interference marker displayed in the plan view*

10. Choose the **SW Isometric** option from the list box in the **Views** panel of the **View** tab; 3D view of the storm network and the sanitary sewer interference is displayed, refer to Figure 11-70.

Note

The interference is represented by using a sphere marker that is determined on the basis of the default interference style settings. This marker indicates that the network parts in this area are not within the tolerance distance specified in the ***3D proximity criteria*** *dialog box. This marker is not displayed in case of physical collisions between the network parts.*

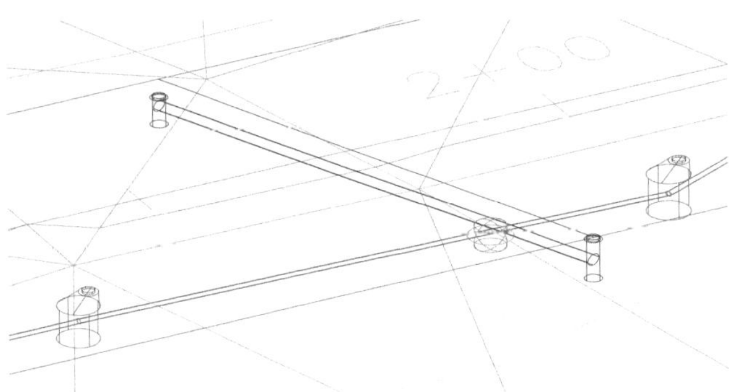

Figure 11-70 *The 3D view of the interference marker displayed*

11. Choose the **Top** option from the list box in the **Views** panel of the **View** tab to return to the plan view.

Adding Network Labels

1. Choose the **Pipe Network** tool from **Annotate > Labels & Tables > Add Labels** drop-down; a flyout is displayed. From this flyout, choose the **Add Pipe Network Labels** option; the **Add Labels** dialog box is displayed.

2. Ensure that **Entire Network Plan** is selected in the **Label type** drop-down list.

3. In the **Add Labels** dialog box, select **Length Material and Slope** and **Data with Connected Pipes (Sanitary)** from the **Pipe label style** and **Structure label style** drop-down lists, respectively, if these options are not selected by default.

4. Now, choose the **Add** button and select any part of the **Sanitary sewer** network; the pipe and the structure parts of the sanitary sewer network are labeled. Next, choose the **Close** button to close the **Add Labels** dialog box. The pipe label shows the pipe diameter and the pipe slope. The structure labels show the structure name, sump elevation, and invert elevations of the incoming and outgoing pipes that are connected to the structure, refer to Figure 11-71.

Note

In the structure labels, the values of the station and offset are not displayed and the RIM elevation shows ***0*** *value. This is because the structure labels are not yet referenced to the surface and the alignment.*

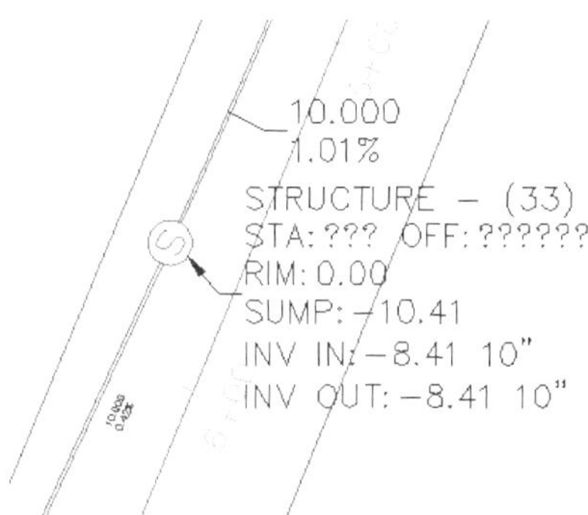

Figure 11-71 *The structure and the pipe labels added to the* ***Sanitary sewer*** *network*

5. Select any structure from the network and right-click to display a shortcut menu.

6. Choose **Structure Properties** from the shortcut menu displayed; the **Structure Properties - Structure - <number>** dialog box is displayed.

7. Choose the **Part Properties** tab and click in the **Value** field of the **Reference Surface** property; a browse button is displayed. Choose this button; the **Reference Surface** dialog box is displayed. Select the **Finished Surface** option from the drop-down list. Choose the **OK** button to close the **Reference Surface** dialog box.

8. Click in the **Value** field of the **Reference Alignment** property; a browse button is displayed. Choose the browse button; the **Reference Alignment** dialog box is displayed. Select the **Xaviers Street** option from the drop-down list. Next, choose the **OK** button; the **Reference Alignment** dialog box is closed.

9. Now, choose the **OK** button; the **Structure Properties - Structure - <number>** dialog box; the dialog box is closed.

10. Zoom in to view the structure labels and note that the labels show the station value, station offset value, and also the RIM elevation, refer to Figure 11-72.

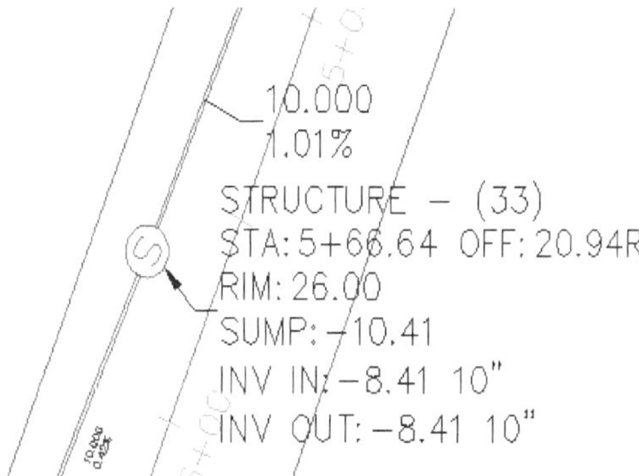

Figure 11-72 *The structure and the pipe labels after referencing the label texts to a surface and alignment*

11. Repeat the procedure followed in steps 5 through 9. For all the structures of the **Sanitary sewer** network, specify the reference surface, reference alignment to label the station (STA), station offset (OFF), and RIM components of the structure label.

12. Repeat steps 1 to 3. Next select the **Data with Connected Pipes (Storm)** from the **Structure label style** drop-down list.

13. Repeat steps 5 to 9 to specify the reference surface and alignment for the **Storm network** structure parts.

Drawing Parts in the Profile View

1. Select the **Finished Surface** profile represented by red color from the drawing; the **Profile: Finished Surface - Surface <Number>** tab is displayed. Choose the **Draw Parts in View** tool from the **Launch Pad** panel of this tab; you are prompted to select the required networks or select parts of the network to add to the profile view.

2. Select any network part of the **Sanitary sewer** and press ENTER; you are prompted to select the profile view.

3. Select the **Sewer Network** profile view from the drawing; the sewer network parts are displayed in the profile view.

4. Choose the **Pipe Network** option from **Annotate > Labels & Tables > Add Labels** drop-down; a flyout is displayed. In this flyout, choose the **Add Pipe Network Labels** option; the **Add Labels** dialog box is displayed.

5. In the dialog box, select the **Entire Network Profile** option from the **Label type** drop-down list.

6. Now, choose the **Add** button and select the magenta colored structure of the **Sanitary sewer** in the profile view; the labels are added to the structures in the profile view and the **Add Labels** dialog box is closed. Figure 11-73 shows the labels added.

7. Choose the **Close** button to close the **Add Labels** dialog box.

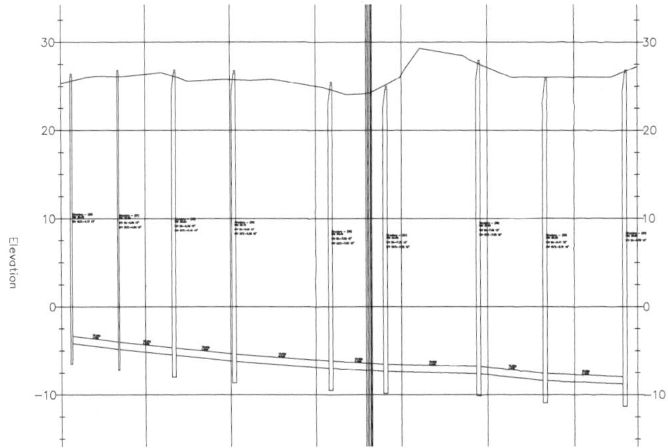

Figure 11-73 *The storm network parts drawn in a profile view with labels added to the network*

Saving the File

1. Choose **Save As** from the **Application Menu**; the **Save Drawing As** dialog box is displayed.

2. In this dialog box, browse to the following location:

   C:\c3d_2018\c11_c3d_2018_tut

3. Save the file as *c11_tut02a*.

Self-Evaluation Test

Answer the following questions and then compare them to those given at the end of this chapter:

1. Which of the following rules ensures that the minimum cover is met along the length of the pipe?

   a) **Cover Only** b) **Length check**
   c) **Pipe to Pipe Match** d) **Set Pipe End Location** Rule

2. Which of the following tools is used to create a pipe network from an AutoCAD line object?

   a) **Pipe Network Creation Tools**
   b) **Create Pipe Network from Object**
   c) **Create Pressure Network from GIS Industry Model**
   d) None of the above

3. Which of the following structures is regarded as a special type of structure and is created automatically at the junction of two pipes?

   a) **Null Structure** b) **Inlets-Outlets**
   c) **Junction Structures with Frames** d) **Junction Structures without Frames**

4. Which of the following options allows you to choose a **Label Type** for labeling a pipe network?

   a) **Add Pipe Network Label** b) **Single Part Plan**
   c) **Entire Network Plan** d) **Single Part Profile**

5. Which of the following tools is used to view the vertical alignment of a pipe network?

   a) **Alignment Creation Tools** b) **Pipe Network Creations Tool**
   c) **Draw Parts in Profile** d) **Create Pipe Network from Object**

6. A __________ is a collection of different pipes and structures.

7. A __________ can be defined as a tube or a conduit that carries water under pressure.

8. The __________ is a collection of selected parts (pipes and structures) of a pipe network.

9. The __________ is a set of rules that governs the elevation and location of the structures as well as the way the pipes will be connected to the structures.

10. The __________ tab in the **Pipe Network Properties** dialog box displays the label styles used to label pipes and structures of the network in the profile view.

11. The null structure is a special type of structure created at the junction of two pipes. (T/F)

12. You can use the **3D Proximity Check** criterion while running the interference check. (T/F)

13. The **Part catalog** dialog box consists of various in-built parts (pipes and structures) used in a pipe network. (T/F)

14. The parts list enables you to store the selected pipes, structures, styles, render materials, and rule sets separately in a list. (T/F)

Review Questions

Answer the following questions:

1. Which of the following AutoCAD Civil 3D software extensions allows you to design and model detention ponds?

   (a) **Hydraflow Express Extension** (b) **Hydraflow Storm Sewer Extension**
   (c) **Hydraflow Hydrographs Extension** (d) None of these

2. Which of the following rules determines the elevation and location of a pipe?

   (a) **Part Rules** (b) **Structure Rules**
   (c) **Pipe Rules** (d) None of these

3. You can view the components of an existing pipe network in a __________ to evaluate their vertical positions based on your design.

4. The __________ helps you to identify and highlight the network parts that intersect and collide physically with each other.

5. The __________ allows you to create and modify pipe network parts available in the **Part Catalog** of Civil 3D.

6. You cannot create pipe network from existing AutoCAD entities such as line, polylines, splines, arcs, and feature lines. (T/F)

7. Runoff is the excess water flowing on the earth's surface due to rain, meltwater, or other sources. (T/F)

8. The tools in the **Network Layout Tools** toolbar can be used to edit the pipe network. (T/F)

9. The **Pipe to Pipe Match** rule is applicable for the pipes created without structures or in case one pipe is connected to another using null structures. (T/F)

10. AutoCAD Civil 3D has four different categories of in-built pipes. (T/F)

EXERCISES

1. Log on to *www.cadcim.com* and browse to *Textbooks > Civil/GIS > Civil 3D > Exploring AutoCAD Civil 3D 2018*. Next, select *c11_c3d_2018_exer.zip* file from the **Exercise Files** drop-down list. Choose the corresponding **Download** button to download the data file.

2. Now, save and extract the downloaded folder to the following location:

   C:\c3d_2018

Note

*While opening the exercise files, the **PANORAMA** window may appear with an error message. Close this window to proceed further.*

Exercise 1

Use the *c11_c3d_2018_tut02.dwg* file and create a water pipeline parts list and water pipeline network, as shown in Figure 11-74, using the **Network Layout Tools** toolbar. Also, run the interference check. **(Expected time: 30 min)**

Use the following parameters:

Parts List name:	**Water Pipeline**
Pipe Parts:	**Concrete Pipe**
Part Size:	**36.000000 inch inner pipe diameter**
Structure Part:	**No**
Network Name:	**Water Pipe Network** (**Create Pipe Network dialog box)**
Network parts List:	**Water Pipeline**
Surface name:	**Finished Surface**
Alignment name:	**Rosewood street**
Toggle Upslope/DownSlope:	**UpSlope** (**Network Layout Tools** toolbar)
Network Tool:	**Draw Pipes Only tool**
Starting station of the pipe network:	**6+48**
Station Offset:	**18**

Click after an interval of 100 at every station till the station 3+00. For example, the stations can be at 6+00, 5+00, 4+00, and 3+00 and then at 2+50, 2+00, 100, and 0+00 all at an offset distance of 18, refer to Figure 11-74. Also, run the interference check between the sanitary sewer and the water pipeline network using the 3D Proximity check criteria. Use the distance of 18 inch as the tolerance.

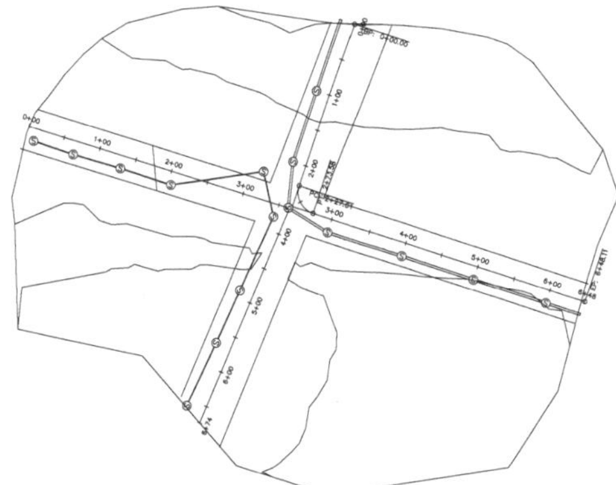

Figure 11-74 *The water pipeline network created along the* ***Rosewood street*** *alignment*

Exercise 2

Open the *c11_c3d_2018_ex02.dwg* file and create a pipe network from the feature line in the drawing. Also, add labels to the pipe network, refer to Figure 11-75.

(Expected time: 30 min)

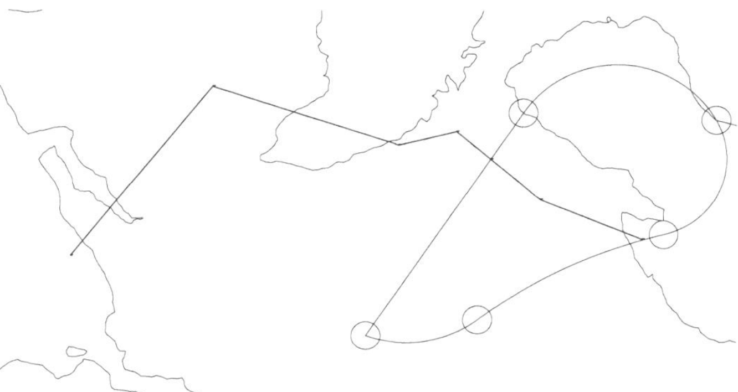

Figure 11-75 *The drainage network*

Answers to Self-Evaluation Test

1. a, **2.** b, **3.** a, **4.** a, **5.** c, **6.** pipe network, **7.** pipe object, **8.** parts list, **9.** part rules, **10. Profile**, **11.** T, 12. T, **13.** T, **14.** T

Chapter 12

Pressure Networks

Learning Objectives

After completing this chapter, you will be able to:

- *Define pressure network components*
- *Create the pressure network in a plan layout*
- *Draw and refine the pressure network in a profile view*
- *Create a pressure network from objects*
- *Edit and access pressure network properties*
- *Add labels and tables to pressure network objects*
- *Validate a pressure network*

PRESSURE NETWORK

Pressure network is a network consisting of pressure pipes, fittings, and appurtenances in which pressure energy is used to deliver a liquid or a gaseous substance from the storage source to the destination. In AutoCAD Civil 3D, a set of tools are used to design pressure networks. To design a pressure network, you need to define a list of network components called parts list. After defining the parts list, you will create the pressure network in horizontal plane and refine the network design in the vertical plane. The procedure to define network components (parts list) is discussed next.

Defining Network Components

To design a pressure network, you first need to create a parts list. A parts list contains a list of components that will be used in the network and is derived from the part catalog. A part catalog enlists the components of the pressure network. To create a parts list, first you need to set a network catalog and then create parts list.

Setting a Pressure Network Catalog

Ribbon:	Home > Create Design > Set Pressure Network Catalog
Command:	SETPRESSURENETWORKCATALOG

A catalog serves as the source for the components that are used to create the parts list. To set the catalog, choose the **Set Pressure Network Catalog** tool from the **Create Design** panel of the **Home** tab; the **Set Pressure Network Catalog** dialog box will be displayed, as shown in Figure 12-1. In this dialog box, choose the button located on the right of the **Catalog folder** text box; the **Catalog Folder** dialog box will be displayed. Browse and select the required catalog folder on your system and then choose the **Open** button. On doing so, the **Catalog Folder** dialog box will be closed and the path of the selected folder will be displayed in the **Catalog folder** text box of the **Set Pressure Network Catalog** dialog box. Select the catalog from the **Catalog database file** drop-down list and then choose the **OK** button. In AutoCAD Civil 3D, 150 fittings, 13 pipes, 50 valves, and 1 hydrant are available as pressure network catalogs across three catalog categories. The HDPE catalog includes 24 fittings, 2 pipes, and 14 valves. The PVC catalog includes 78 fittings, 6 pipes, 18 valves, and 1 hydrant. The steel catalog includes 48 fittings, 5 pipes, and 18 valves.

Creating a Pressure Network Parts List

To create a parts list, expand the **Pressure Network** node in the **Settings** tab of the **TOOLSPACE** palette. Next, select and right-click on the **Parts Lists** node; a shortcut menu will be displayed. Choose the **New** option from the shortcut menu, as shown in Figure 12-2; the **Pressure Network Parts List - <Parts List Name>** dialog box will be displayed. A brief description of the tabs in this dialog box is given next.

Information

The options in this tab are used to specify the general information for the parts list. You can assign the parts list name in the **Name** edit box. Optionally, you can write a description about the parts list in the **Description** edit box.

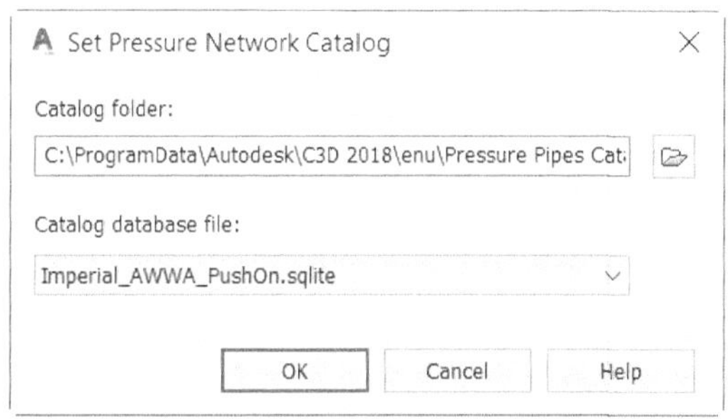

Figure 12-1 The ***Set Pressure Network Catalog*** *dialog box*

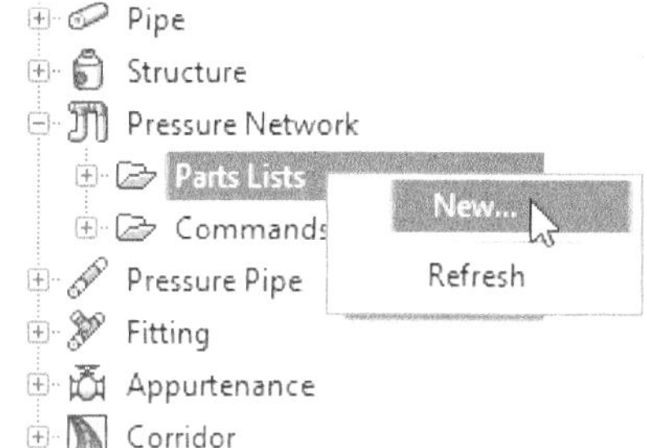

Figure 12-2 Choosing the ***New*** *option*

Pressure Pipes

In this tab, you can add different types of pipes to the parts list based on the material and size of the pipe. To specify the material for the pipe, select and right-click on the **New Parts List** displayed in the **Name** column of list box; a shortcut menu will be displayed. Choose the **Add material** option from the shortcut menu, as shown in Figure 12-3; the **Pressure Network Catalog** dialog box is displayed. In this dialog box, select the check box corresponding to the required pipe material and then choose the **OK** button; the **Pressure Network Catalog** dialog box will be closed and the pipe material will be added to the parts list. Also, you will notice that the **New Part List** is renamed to the part list name entered in the **Name** edit box of the **Information** tab.

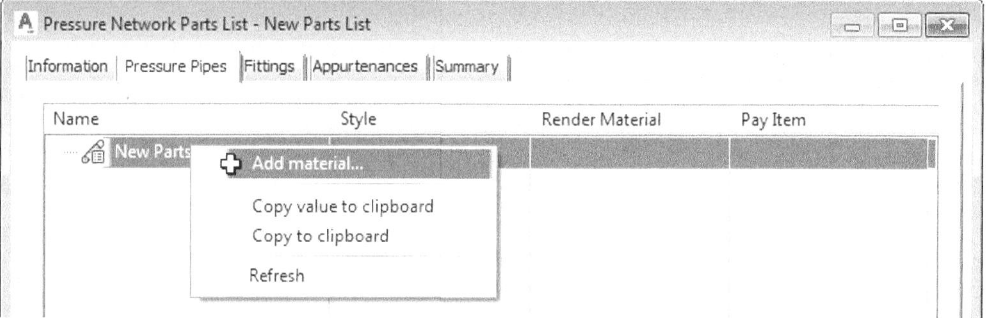

Figure 12-3 Choosing the ***Add material*** *option from the shortcut menu*

Expand the part list name node in the **Name** column; the added material name will be displayed in the node. To add different pipe sizes to the parts list, right-click on the material name; a shortcut menu will be displayed. Choose the **Add size** option from the shortcut menu, as shown in Figure 12-4; the **Add Pressure Pipe Sizes** dialog box will be displayed. In this dialog box, you cannot edit the values for the properties that are displayed in the gray cell. To edit the value of a property, double-click in the **Value** cell corresponding to the required property. Depending upon the property selected, an edit box or a drop-down list will be displayed in the selected cell. Specify the required value in the cell and then choose the **OK** button in the dialog box. On doing so, the selected pipe size will be added in the pipe material node in the **Pressure Pipes** tab of the **Pressure Network Parts List** dialog box. Expand the pipe material node to view the added pipe size, refer to Figure 12-5.

Tip

To add pipes of all sizes available in the catalog, choose the ***Add all sizes*** *check box in the* ***Add Pressure Pipe Sizes*** *dialog box.*

To edit or delete a pipe after it has been added to the material node, select and right-click; a shortcut menu is displayed. Choose an appropriate option from the shortcut menu to proceed.

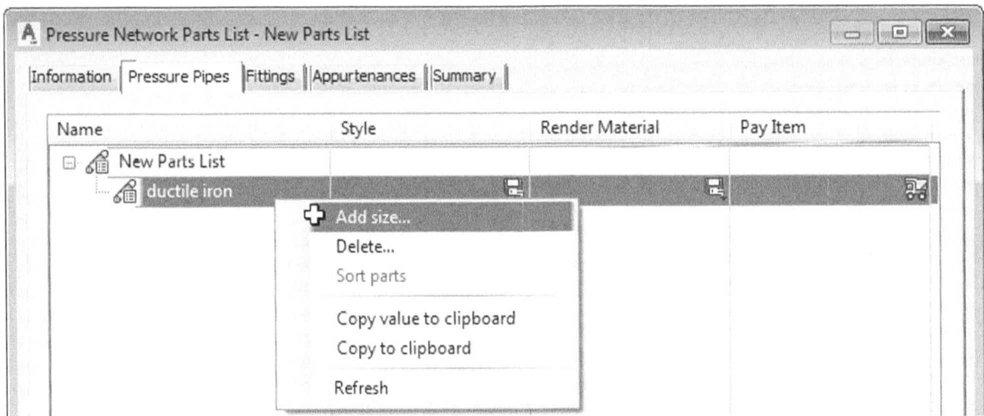

Figure 12-4 *Choosing the* ***Add size*** *option from the shortcut menu*

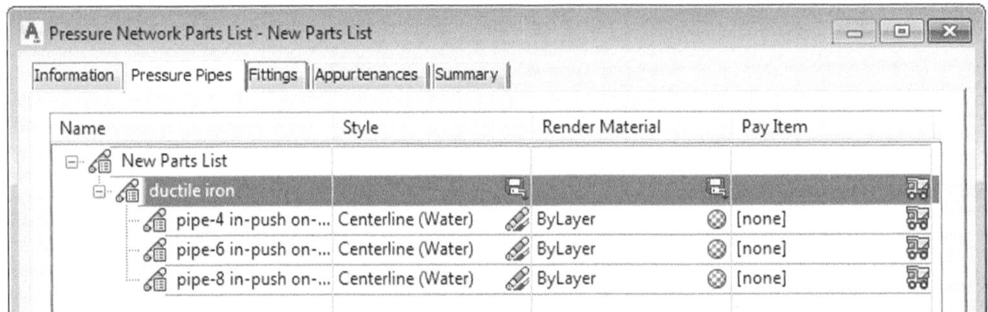

Figure 12-5 *Partial view of the* ***Pressure Network Parts List - New Parts List*** *dialog box showing pipes of various sizes added to the list*

In the **Style** column, you can assign a style to the pipes. To assign a style to a pipe, choose the button displayed in the **Style** column corresponding to the required pipe or part; the **Pressure pipe styles** dialog box will be displayed. Select the required style from the **Select a style** drop-down list and then choose the **OK** button in the dialog box; the selected style will be assigned to the pipe. You can also create a new pipe style or edit an existing one. To do so, click on the down arrow displayed on the right of the **Select a style** drop-down list; a menu is displayed. Choose the required option from the menu to proceed.

To assign a render material to a pipe, choose the button displayed in the **Render Material** column corresponding to the required pipe; the **Select Render Material** dialog box will be displayed. Select the required render material from the options displayed in the **Select from list** drop-down list. Alternatively, you can select the render material from the drawing. To do so, choose the button displayed on the right of the drop-down list; you are prompted to select an object. Select an object in the drawing and choose the **OK** button in the **Select Render Material** dialog box to assign the render material to the selected pipe.

In this version of AutoCAD Civil 3D, you can also assign pay items to the pressure pipes. To assign a pay item to a pressure pipe, choose the button displayed in the **Pay Item** column corresponding to the required pipe or item; the **Pay Item List** dialog box will be displayed. A pre loaded pay item list is displayed in the list box of this dialog box. Select the required pay item from this pay item list for the selected pipe and choose the **OK** button; the **Pay Item List** dialog box is closed and the required pay item is assigned to the selected pressure pipe.

Note that if the pay item list is not pre loaded and you choose the button in the **Pay Item** column to assign the pay item then the Civil 3D will show the **Pay item list not loaded** message box informing that no pay item list is loaded in the project. To load a pay item list, select the **Load master pay item list** option from the message box; the **Open Pay Item File** dialog box is displayed. In this dialog box, specify the pay item list you need to load in the project and then follow the procedure explained above.

To assign a style to all the pipes in the list, choose the button displayed in the **Style** cell corresponding to the material name, the **Pressure pipe styles** dialog box is displayed. Set the required style using this dialog box, as explained earlier. Similarly, to assign the render material to all the pipes, choose the button displayed in the **Render Material** cell corresponding to the material name; the **Select Render Material** dialog box is displayed. Assign the required render material using the options in this dialog box.

Fittings

In this tab, you can add various fittings to your parts list. To add a fitting, first you need to select the type of fitting that you want to add to the parts list. Next, you will specify the various sizes for the fitting. To specify the type of fitting, right-click on the **New Part List** in the **Name** column; a shortcut menu will be displayed. Choose **Add type** from the shortcut menu; the **Pressure Network Catalog** dialog box is displayed. In this dialog box, select the check boxes corresponding to the required fitting type, refer to Figure 12-6. Choose the **OK** button; the **Pressure Network Catalog** dialog box is closed and the selected fittings are added to the parts list. Also, you will notice that the **New Part List** is renamed to the part list name entered in the **Name** edit box of the **Information** tab.

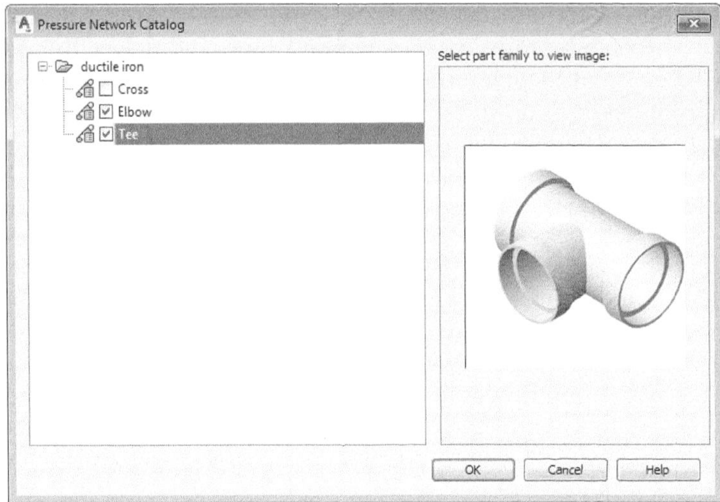

Figure 12-6 *The* ***Pressure Network Catalog*** *dialog box showing the type of fittings selected*

To see the added fittings in the list box, expand the parts list name node. The added fittings are displayed, as shown in Figure 12-7.

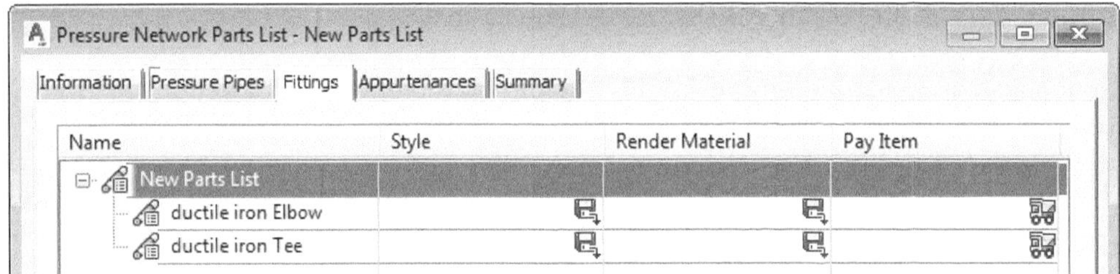

Figure 12-7 *Partial view of the* ***Pressure Network Parts List - New Parts List*** *dialog box showing the list of fittings added to the parts list*

Next, to add different sizes of fittings, right-click on the fittings name in the parts list node; a shortcut menu is displayed. Choose the **Add size** option from the menu; the **Add Fitting Sizes** dialog box is displayed. In this dialog box, you cannot edit the value for the fitting properties that are displayed in gray colored cell. Choose the **OK** button to add the fittings size to the parts list, refer to Figure 12-8.

You can add style and render material to all or individual fittings. In addition, you can specify pay items for them. To do so, choose the corresponding buttons in the **Style**, **Render Material**, or **Pay Item** column and follow the procedure explained earlier.

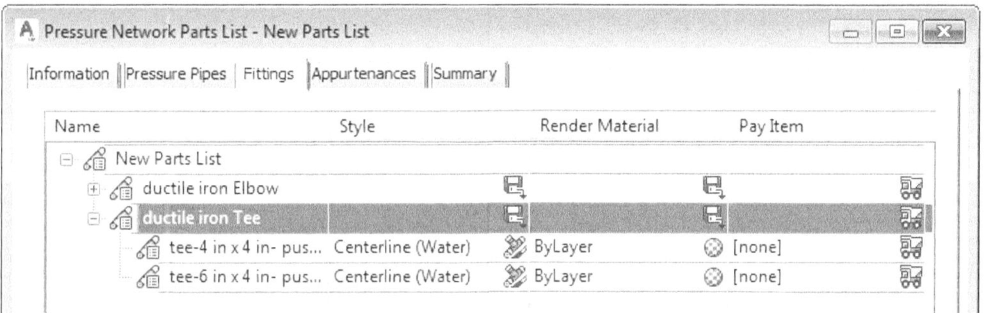

Figure 12-8 Partial view of the ***Pressure Network Parts List - New Parts List*** *dialog box showing fittings of various sizes*

Appurtenances

In this tab, you can add various appurtenances to the parts list. The method of adding appurtenances to a parts list is similar to that of adding fittings. First, you will specify the type of appurtenance. To do so, right-click on the **New Parts List** in the **Name** column; a shortcut menu will be displayed. Choose the **Add type** option from the shortcut menu; the **Pressure Network Catalog** dialog box is displayed. Select the check box corresponding to the required type and then choose the **OK** button. The **Pressure Network Catalog** dialog box will be closed and the selected appurtenance will be added to the parts list. Also, you will notice that the **New Part List** is renamed to the part list name entered in the **Name** edit box of the **Information** tab. Next to specify the appurtenance size, expand the parts list node in the **Name** column. Right-click on the appurtenance name; a shortcut menu is displayed. Choose the **Add size** option in this menu; the **Add Appurtenance Sizes** dialog box is displayed. In this dialog box, you cannot edit the value for the fitting properties that are displayed in gray colored cell. Edit the value for the required property of the appurtenance and choose the **OK** button; the appurtenances are added to the parts list. Next, you can specify the style and the render material for the appurtenances. Figure 12-9 shows appurtenances added to the parts list.

Next, on creating the parts list, choose the **OK** button in the **Pressure Network Parts List** dialog box; the dialog box is closed.

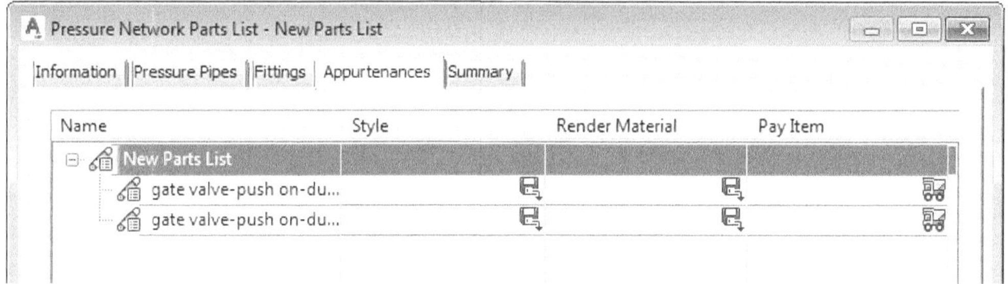

Figure 12-9 Partial view of the ***Pressure Network Parts List - New Parts List*** *dialog box showing the appurtenances of various sizes added to the parts list*

Creating a Pressure Network

Ribbon:	Home > Create Design > Pipe Network drop-down > Pressure Network Creation Tools
Command:	CREATEPRESSURENETWORK

Civil 3D provides a set of tools to design a pressure network. You will design a pressure network in a horizontal layout and then refine the networks elevation information in profile view.

To create a pressure network, choose the **Pressure Network Creation Tools** tool from the **Home > Create Design > Pipe Network** drop-down; the **Create Pressure Pipe Network** dialog box is displayed, as shown in Figure 12-10. In this dialog box, the **Network name** text box displays the name of the pressure network. To specify a name, choose the **Click to edit the name template** button located next to the text box; the **Name Template** dialog box will be displayed. Enter the desired name in the **Name** edit box of this dialog box and choose the **OK** button to exit. Optionally, you can include the information about the network in the **Network description** text box.

To assign the label style to the pipes, fittings and appurtenances, choose the required label style option from the drop-down list corresponding to that component. For example, to assign a label style to the pressure pipe, select an option from the **Pressure Pipe Label Style** drop-down list. You can also create a new label style or edit an existing style. To do so, click on the down arrow corresponding to the label style drop-down list; an options list is displayed. Select the required option from the displayed list to proceed.

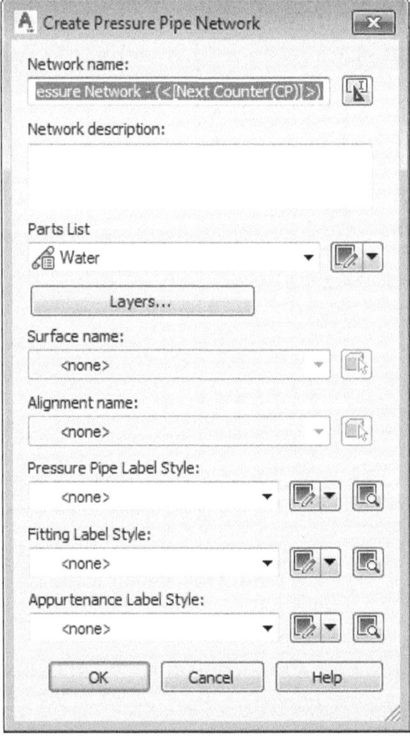

Figure 12-10 The ***Create Pressure Pipe Network*** *dialog box*

To specify the parts list, surface, and alignment associated with the network, choose the required option from the **Parts List**, **Surface name**, and **Alignment name** drop-down list, respectively. You can also set or change the associated surface, alignment and parts list using the options in the **Pressure Network Plan Layout** tab. These options are discussed in detail further in this chapter.

To assign a layer to a pressure network component in the plan and profile layout, choose the **Layers** button in the **Create Pressure Pipe Network** dialog box; the **Pressure Network Layers** dialog box will be displayed, refer to Figure 12-11. This dialog box contains various text boxes. These text boxes display the layer assigned to each component of the network. You can change the layer for any network component. To change a layer for any given component, choose the button corresponding to that component in the **Pressure Network Layers** dialog box; the **Object Layer** dialog box is displayed. In this dialog box, choose the button displayed on the right of the **Base layer name** text box; the **Layer Selection** dialog box is displayed. Choose the required layer for the selected network component in this dialog box and then choose the **OK** button in the **Layer Selection** dialog box to close it. Next, close the **Object Layer** dialog box by choosing the **OK** button. In the **Pressure Network Layers** dialog box, the name of the selected layer for the component is displayed in the text box corresponding to that component. Choose the **OK** button to close the dialog box.

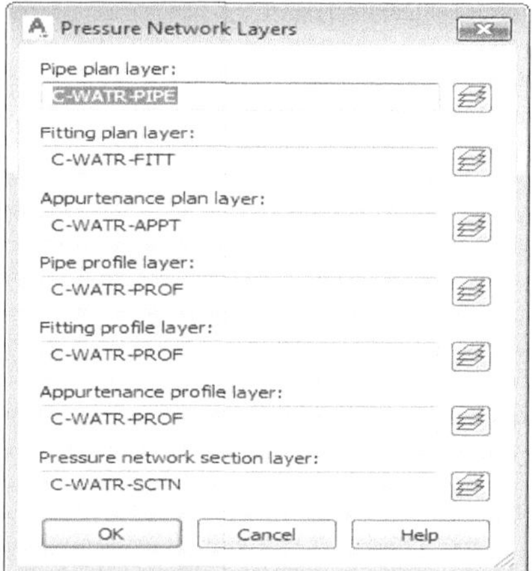

Figure 12-11 *The **Pressure Network Layers** dialog box*

After specifying the options in the **Create Pressure Pipe Network** dialog box, choose the **OK** button; the dialog box is closed and the created network is added to the **Pressure Networks** node in the **Prospector** tab of **TOOLSPACE**. Also, the **Pressure Network Plan Layout** tab is displayed in the ribbon, refer to Figure 12-12. Also, you are prompted to specify a point in the drawing to begin designing the pressure network in the horizontal (plan) layout.

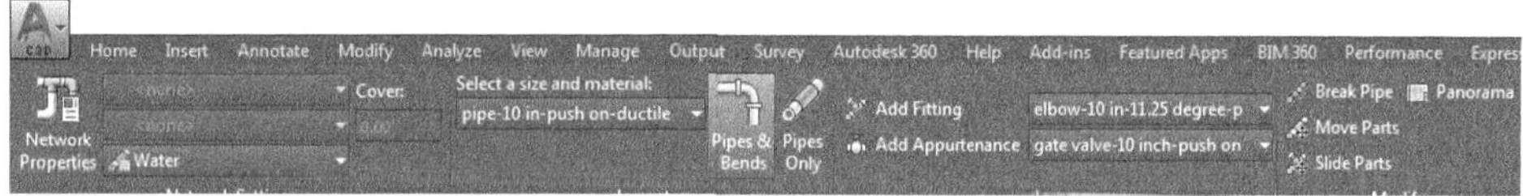

Figure 12-12 *The partial view of the **Pressure Network Plan Layout** tab*

The method to design the pressure network in a plan layout (horizontal) is discussed next.

Designing a Pressure Network in Plan Layout

In the **Pressure Network Plan Layout < Network Name>** tab, you can use various options and tools to design the pressure network in horizontal layout. To create a pipe network, first, you need to choose the pipe size and its material from the **Layout** panel. Next, you need to choose a tool to add the pipes in the network. You can also add the fittings and appurtenances to the network using the tools in the **Insert** panel.

The tools and options in the **Pressure Network Plan Layout < Network Name>** tab are arranged in different panels which are discussed next.

Network Settings Panel

The tools and options in this panel are used to set the parameters for the pressure network. Choose the **Network Properties** button from this panel; the **Pressure Pipe Network Properties - <Network Name>** dialog box will be displayed. The options in this dialog box are used to set or change the network parameters of surface, alignment, parts list, label style, and network layers for the plan and profile layouts of the network.

In the **Network Settings** panel, you can also change the associated surface, alignment, and the parts list for the network by choosing the corresponding options from the **Reference Surface**, **Reference Alignment** and **Pressure Network Parts List** drop-down lists displayed in the panel. The **Cover** edit box in the panel is used to specify the depth at which the component of the network will lie below the reference surface.

Note

If you enter a negative value in the ***Cover*** *edit box, the pressure network will be created above the reference surface.*

Layout Panel

In the **Layout** panel, you can specify the size and material of the pipe for creating the pressure network. To do so, choose the required options from the **Select a size and material** drop-down list. From this panel, you can also select a method of inserting pipes in the layout. You can choose the **Pipes Only** tool to create a pipe network without any bends. Choosing this option for creating pipe network will limit the angle of change in direction between two pipes. For more flexibility while changing the direction between two pipe segments, use the **Pipes & Bends** tools. This tool inserts a bend between two pipe segments. This tool permits a wide angle of deflection between two pipes when compared to **Pipes Only** tool.

Insert Panel

The tool and options in the **Insert** panel are used to insert fittings and appurtenances into the network. To add fittings in a network, first you need to specify the size of the network component to be inserted. To do so, choose the required size from the **Fittings** drop-down list. Next, choose the **Add Fittings** tool; you are prompted to specify the location of the component in the network. Click on the required location in the drawing to add the fitting component to the network.

Similarly, you can add the appurtenances in the network using the **Appurtenance** drop-down list and the **Add Appurtenance** tool.

Modify Panel

The **Modify** panel consists of the **Break Pipe**, **Move Parts**, **Slide Parts,** and **Panorama** tools. These tools are used to modify the pressure network. Use the **Break Pipe** tool to split an existing pipe into two pipe segments. The split segments remain connected as the part of the original pipe. To break a pipe, choose the **Break Pipe** tool; you are prompted to specify the location at which the pipe is to be broken. Click on the required location on the pipe to break it. The **Move Parts** tool is used to move or reposition the parts of an existing pressure pipe network to a new location in the drawing. To move the parts of a pressure pipe network, choose the **Move Parts** tool; you will be prompted to select the parts. After selecting the part, you will be prompted to specify the base point. Specify the base point for the selected network part; you will be prompted to specify the destination point. Click at the required point in the drawing; the selected parts are moved to the specified location in the drawing. Similarly, the **Slide Parts** tool is used to slide connected parts along another pressure pipe. Choose the **Panorama** tool in the panel to invoke the **PANORAMA** window. You can use the **PANORAMA** window to view and edit pressure network properties. Figure 12-13 shows the **PANORAMA** window for a pressure network.

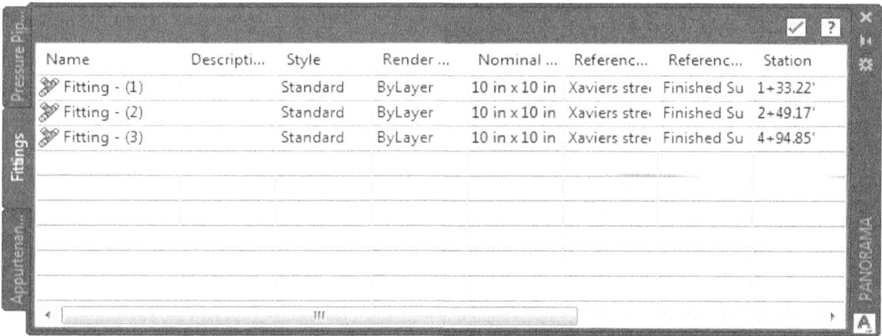

Figure 12-13 The PANORAMA window displaying a typical pressure pipe network

The **PANORAMA** window has three tabs, namely **Pressure Pipes**, **Fittings,** and **Appurtenances**. These tabs contain detailed information about the corresponding network component such as the name, description, reference surface and alignment, diameter of the component, elevation, and coordinates for the point insertion (start point and end point in case of pipe). You can use the panorama window to edit the network component. Note that you cannot edit the values displayed in gray colored cells.

Compass Panel

The tools and options in this panel are used to set the parameters for the compass that is displayed at the end of a pipe segment while creating a pressure network using the **Pipes & Bend** and **Pipes Only** tools. The tick mark on the compass indicates the allowable deflection between two pipes. You can change the color of the compass by choosing the color option from the **Compass Color** drop-down list. You can also change the diameter of the compass in the **Compass Size** edit box. Civil 3D allows you to toggle the display of the compass in the drawing by choosing the **Compass Visibility** button. Figures 12-14 and 12-15 show the compass for the pipes created using the **Pipes Only** and **Pipes & Bends** tools, respectively. Note the permissible limit of direction change indicated by the ticks in the compass for the pipes created using different methods.

After creating the pressure network in a plan layout, you might require refining the vertical design of the pressure network.

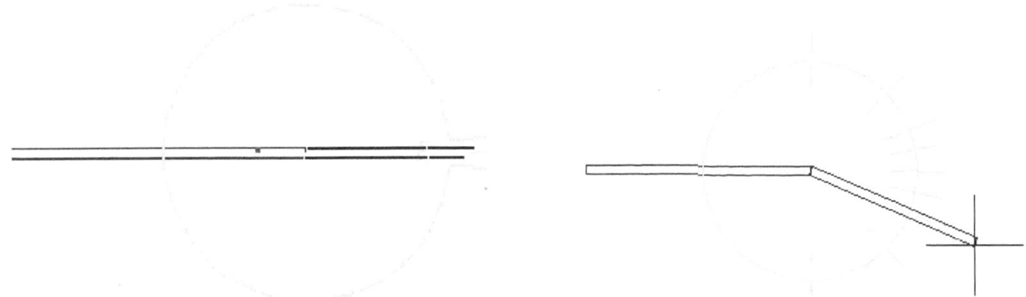

***Figure 12-14** Compass for the pipes created using the **Pipes Only** tool*

***Figure 12-15** Compass for the pipes created using the **Pipes & Bends** tool*

Designing a Pressure Network in Profile Layout

You can create a profile view of a pressure pipe network by using the pipe alignment. To create an alignment, choose any component of the pressure network; the **Pressure Network: <Network Name>** contextual tab will be displayed, refer to Figure 12-16. The tools in this tab can be used to design the network in the profile view.

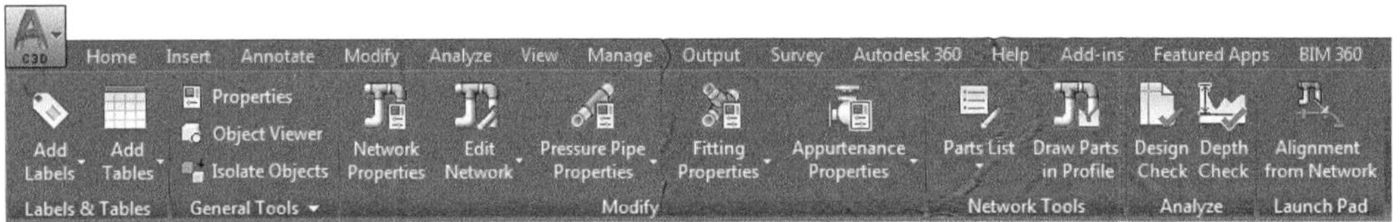

***Figure 12-16** The various options in the **Pressure Networks: <Network Name>** tab*

You will first create an alignment and profile view for the pressure network and then you shall refine the pressure network in the profile layout.

Creating Pressure Network Alignment and Profile View

To create a pressure pipe network alignment, choose the **Alignment from Network** tool from the **Launch Pad** tab of the **Pressure Networks: <Network Name>** tab; you will be prompted to select the pressure network components. Choose one or more network components and press ENTER; the **Create Alignment - From Pressure Network** dialog box is displayed, refer to Figure 12-17.

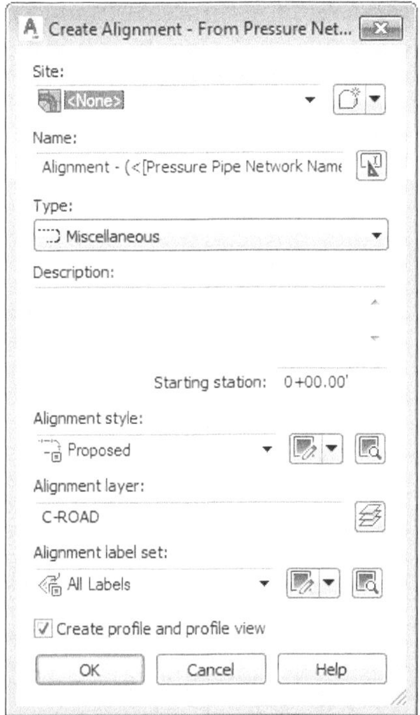

*Figure 12-17 The **Create Alignment - From Pressure Network** dialog box*

Tip

*You can also invoke the **Create Alignment - From Pressure Network** dialog box by choosing the **Create Alignment from Pressure Network** tool from the **Home > Create Design > Alignment** drop-down. On choosing this tool, you will be prompted to select the network components. Choose the components from the drawing and press ENTER; the **Create Alignment - From Pressure** dialog box will be displayed.*

In the **Create Alignment - From Pressure Network** dialog box, assign the alignment name in the **Name** edit box. Optionally, write the alignment description in the **Description** edit box. Select any style, layer, and the label set for the alignment from the options in the **Alignment style**, **Alignment layer**, and **Alignment label set** drop-down lists, respectively. Select the **Create profile and profile view** check box and choose the **OK** button; the **Create Profile from Surface** dialog box is displayed. In this dialog box, make sure that the alignment for the pressure pipe network is selected in the **Alignment** drop-down list. Select the required surface from the **Select surfaces** list. Next, choose the **Add** button; a record is added in the **Profile Lists** area. Next, choose the **Draw in profile view** button; the **Create Profile View** wizard is displayed.

For setting the options in the pages (except the **Pipe/Pressure Network** page) of **Create Profile View** wizard, refer to the section Creating a Surface Profile in Chapter 6, of this textbook. Next, set the options in the **Pipe/Pressure Network** page.

In the **Pipe/Pressure Network** page of the **Create Profile View** wizard, refer to Figure 12-18, the **Select stacked view to specify options for** list box lists all the stacked views and allows you to select the required profile view for which you want to specify the display options. The number of profile views listed in this list box depends upon the number specified in the **Stacked Profile** page of the wizard.

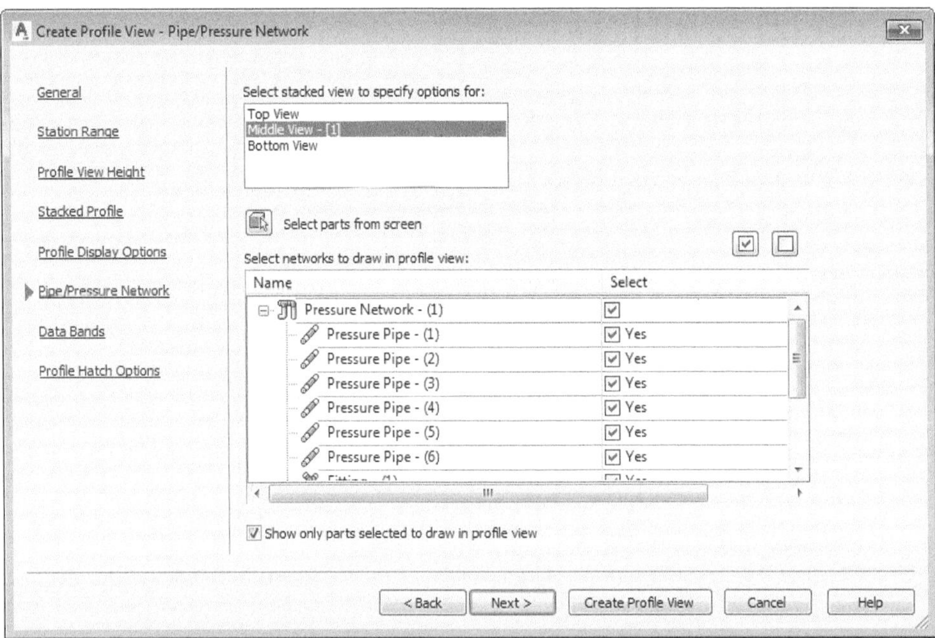

***Figure 12-18** The **Pipe/Pressure Network** page of the **Create Profile View** wizard*

Note

*The **Select stacked view to specify options for** list box will be available only if the **Show offset profiles by vertically stacking profile views** check box is selected in the **General** page of the wizard.*

In the **Select pipe networks to draw in profile view** list, select the check box corresponding to the pipe name to include it in the profile view. Alternatively, you can select the pipes from the drawing by choosing the **Select parts from screen** button. On choosing the button, you will be prompted to select the pipe in the drawing. Select the required pipes from the drawing and press ENTER.

After setting the required options in the **Create Profile View** wizard, choose the **Create Profile View** button; you will be prompted to specify the location of the origin of the profile view. Pick an appropriate location in the drawing; the profile view will be created for the selected pipe alignment, refer to Figure 12-19.

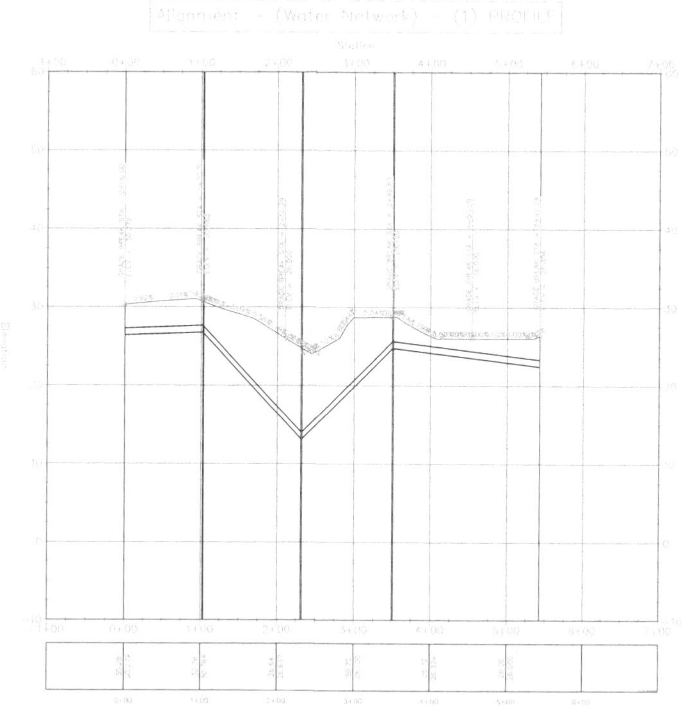

Figure 12-19 The profile view of the pressure pipe network

Editing Pressure Network in Profile Layout

Profile Layout Tools

To edit the pressure network in profile layout, choose the **Profile Layout Tools** from the **Edit Network** drop-down in the **Modify** panel of the **Pressure Network: <Network Name>** contextual tab; the **Pressure Network Profile Layout: <Network Name>** contextual tab is displayed, refer to Figure 12-20.

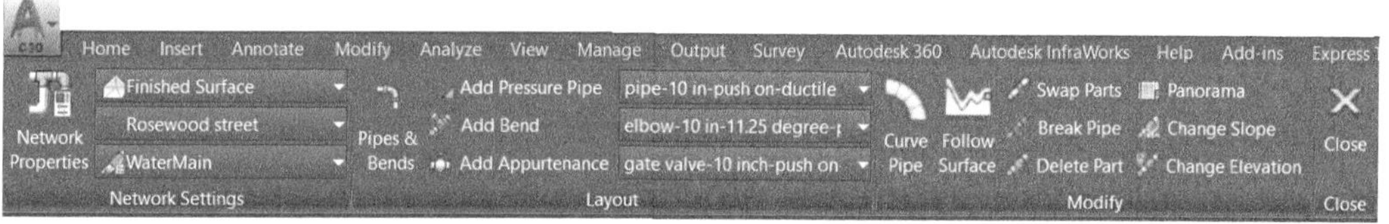

*Figure 12-20 The **Pressure Network Profile Layout: Water Network** tab*

You can use the options in the **Network Settings** panel of this tab to specify the surface, alignment, and parts list in the pressure network. The options in this panel are similar to the options in the **Network Settings** panel of the **Pressure Network Plan Layout: <Network Name>** tab described earlier.

You can use the options and tools in the **Layout** panel of the **Pressure Network Profile Layout** tab to add pipes, bends, and appurtenances in the network. In a profile view, you can insert an appurtenance to an open connection (end) of the pipe. To insert an appurtenance, choose the required appurtenance size from the **Appurtenances** drop-down list of the **Layout** panel. Next, choose the **Add Appurtenance** tool; you are prompted to specify the location.

Click on the open connection of the pipe to add the appurtenance. Similarly, to add a bend to a pipe, choose the bend size from the **Bends** drop-down list in the **Layout** panel. Next, choose the **Add Bend** tool; you are prompted to specify the location for the bend to be inserted. Choose an open connection of the pipe; you are prompted to specify the bend direction; specify the direction as clockwise or anti-clockwise; the bend is added to the pipe.

Note

1. In a profile view, you can add bends and appurtenances only to open connections on pressure pipes.

2. You cannot insert a bend along a running pipe or to any open connection on other fittings or appurtenances.

You can use the tools in the **Modify** panel of the **Pressure Network Profile Layout** tab to modify the pressure network in a profile view.

To edit the geometry of a pipe segment in a profile view, you will first create a gap in the existing pipe network. To do so, choose the **Break Pipe** tool from the **Modify** panel and click at the required point on the pipe; a break in the pipe will be created. Next, choose the **Delete Part** tool in the **Modify** panel and choose a pipe segment; the selected pipe segment will be deleted and a gap is created in the pipe.

After creating a gap in the pipe, you will add pipe segment(s) in the network so as to bypass a vertical obstacle or achieve the required depth for the pipe. To do so, select the **Add Pressure Pipe** tool from the **Layout** panel; you are prompted to select the part at start of the range. Choose the open end of the pipe segment on the either side of the gap created earlier; you are prompted to select the part at the end of the range. Click in the drawing to add a segment; the **Pressure Network - Use plan Layout Tools** message box will displayed informing that profile layout tools may not establish the network path currently and Civil 3D recommends the use of plan layout tools. Therefore, choose **YES** to continue adding pipe segments so as to achieve the required pipe geometry in the profile view. Finally, choose the other open end of the gap to complete the required modification in the geometry of the pipe.

You can also bridge the pipe gap using the **Pipes & Bends** tool. While bridging the gaps in a same direction, the pipes are added linearly and when the direction changes, bends are added to the pipes. Note that you can only use the bends that are defined in the parts list.

Note

While adding a pipe to a profile view using the ***Pipes & Bends*** *tool, you must start adding parts from an existing pipe; else you will be prompted to add a pipe.*

You can also use the **Curve Pipe** tool from the **Modify** panel to bypass an obstruction in a profile view. On choosing the tool, you will be prompted to select the pipe in the profile view. Select a pipe segment; you will be prompted to specify the radius. Specify the radius; you will be prompted to define the type of curve. Specify **C** or **S** for crest and sag, respectively and press ENTER; the curve will be inserted at the selected segment.

You can choose the **Follow Surface** tool in the **Modify** panel to modify the pipe segment in a network so that its geometry in profile follows the surface terrain. On choosing this tool, you will be prompted to choose the start part in the network. Select the required part(s) and press ENTER; you will be prompted to specify the depth. Specify the required depth for the pipe and press ENTER; the selected part of the network will be split into multiple segments and rearranged at the specified depth to follow the terrain above.

Note

*While using the **Follow Surface** tool, specifying a negative depth value will create a pipe above the ground surface.*

Creating Pressure Networks from Objects

Ribbon: Home > Create Design > Pipe Network drop-down > Create Pressure Network from Object

Command: CREATEPRESSURENETWORKFROMOBJ

In AutoCAD Civil 3D, existing Civil 3D objects such as lines, polylines, arcs, and feature lines can be converted into a network of connected pressure pipes and bends. AutoCAD Civil 3D converts these entities to a pressure pipe network and then inserts structures at the end points or vertices of these entities. To create a pressure pipe network from an object, choose the **Create Pressure Network from Object** tool from the **Create Design** panel; you will be prompted to select an object or an Xref. Select the existing entity in the drawing; arrows will be displayed on the selected entity showing the direction of flow. Press ENTER to accept the default direction or enter **R** in the command line and then press ENTER; the direction of flow will be reversed. Again, press ENTER; the **Create Pressure Pipe Network from Object** dialog box will be displayed, as shown in Figure 12-21.

In this dialog box, to specify the parts list, surface, and alignment associated with the network, choose the required option from the **Network parts list**, **Surface name**, and **Alignment name** drop-down lists, respectively. You can select the desired pressure pipe size and material from the **Size and material** drop-down list. In the **Elevation Reference** area of this dialog box, you can use various options to specify the elevation for the pressure pipes. You can enter the desired elevation in the **Depth of cover** edit box. The elevation value entered in this edit box is measured between the reference surface and the top outside surface of the pipe. Select the **Use vertex elevations** radio button, if you need to set the elevations of the pressure pipes created in the network such that they follow the elevation of the vertices along the selected entity. On selecting this radio button, the options below it will be activated. Now, you can select any of these options to specify the location on the pressure pipe where the vertex elevation is located.

You can remove the entity using which the network is created by selecting the **Erase existing entity** check box.

After specifying the required parameters in the **Create Pressure Pipe Network from Object** dialog box, choose the **OK** button; the dialog box will be closed and a pressure pipe network will be created from the selected entity.

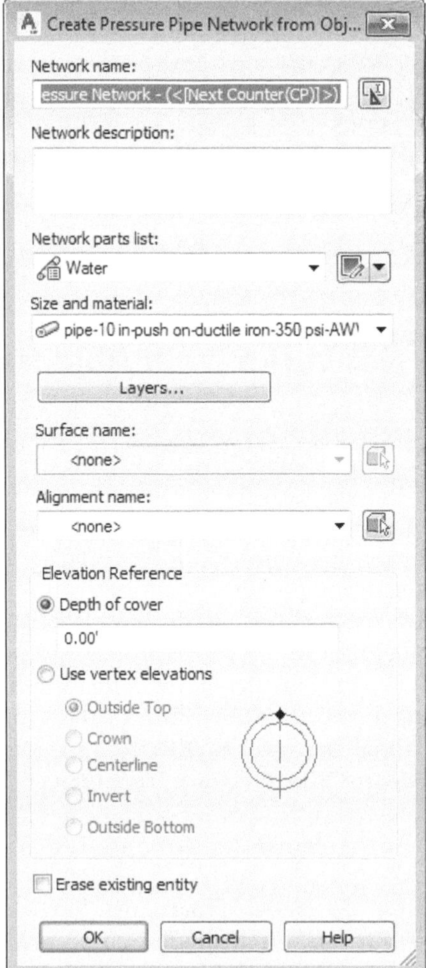

*Figure 12-21 The **Create Pressure Pipe Network from Object** dialog box*

PRESSURE NETWORK PROPERTIES

To access and edit the pressure pipe network properties such as network name, labels, layers, profile, and section view settings, select any part of the network in the drawing and right-click; a shortcut menu will be displayed. Choose the **Pressure Network Properties** option from the shortcut menu displayed; the **Pressure Pipe Network Properties - <network name>** dialog box will be displayed, refer to Figure 12-22. The **Information** tab of this dialog box displays the name of the selected pipe network. Modify the name in the **Name** edit box, if required.

Choose the **Layout Settings** tab to view and edit the parameters used for the pipe network in the plan view. The **Labels** area displays the label styles used to label the pressure pipes, fittings, and appurtenances in the plan view, refer to Figure 12-22. You can select the required options from the **Pressure pipe plan label style**, **Fitting plan label style**, and **Appurtenance plan label style** drop-down lists. Next, select an option from the **Pressure Parts List** drop-down list to define the part list used for the selected pressure pipe network. You can select the required part list from the drop-down list or create a new part list. To create a new part list, choose the down arrow on the button on the right of this drop-down list; a flyout will be displayed. Choose the **Create New** option from the flyout to create a new part list. The **Default object reference** area displays the name of the surface and alignment objects to which the pipe network is referenced. If the network is not referenced to any surface or alignment, the **none** option will be selected by default in the **Surface name** and **Alignment name** drop-down lists in this area. If you change the referenced surface or alignment from this area, it will not affect any existing pressure network objects. It will affect only those which were created after the change was made.

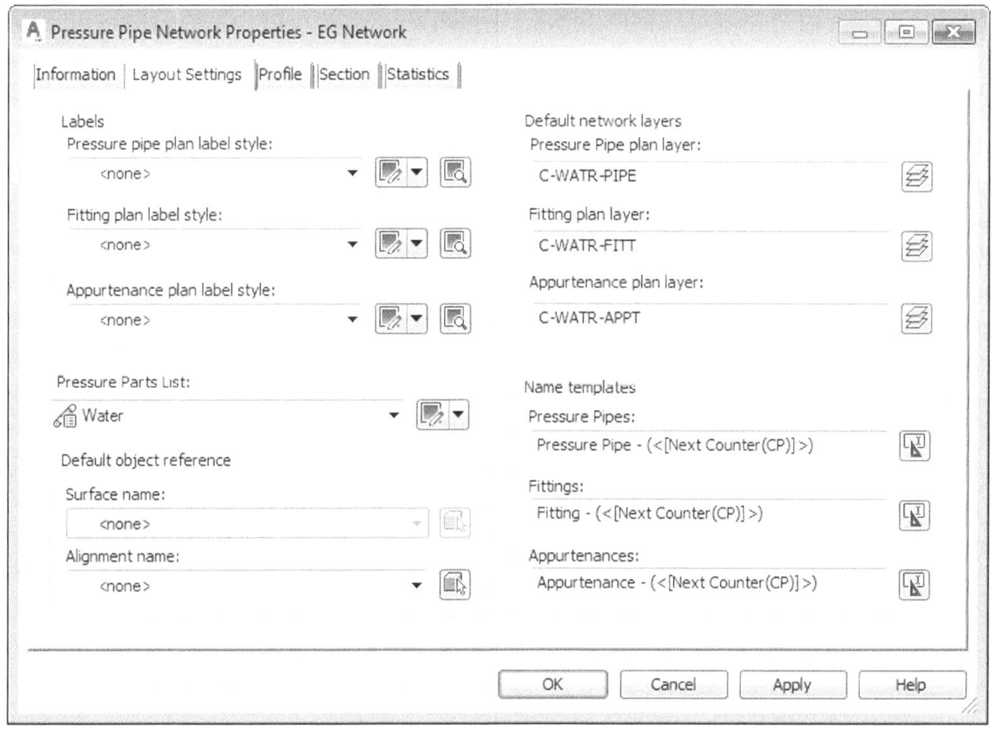

***Figure 12-22** The **Pressure Pipe Network Properties - EG network** dialog box*

The **Default network layers** area displays the layers in which the pressure pipes, fittings, and appurtenances are drawn in the plan view. Choose the **Select Layers** buttons on the right in this area to display the **Object Layer** dialog box. You can use this dialog box to change the default layer. The **Name templates** area displays the default names of the templates used for creating pressure pipes, fittings, and appurtenances in the network. Choose the button on the right of the **Pressure Pipes**, **Fittings**, or **Appurtenances** edit boxes to display the **Name Template** dialog box. Enter a name for the selected item in the **Name** edit box in this dialog box and choose the **OK** button to exit.

The **Profile** tab displays the label styles which are used to label the pressure network objects when displayed in the profile view. If no styles are used, the **none** option will be selected by default in the **Pressure pipe profile label style**, **Fitting profile label style**, and **Appurtenance profile label style** drop-down lists in the **Labels** area. You can select the required option from these drop-down lists to specify the label style. The **Default profile layers** area displays name of the default layers on which the pressure network objects are drawn in the profile view. You can also modify the default layers. To do so, choose the button on the right of the required pressure network object text box; the **Object Layer** dialog box will be displayed. You can modify the default layers by using the options in this dialog box.

The **Section** tab displays the name of the default layer for the pressure network objects in a section view. You can modify the default layer by choosing the **Select Layers** button next to the **Pressure network section layer** text box in the **Default section layers** area.

The **Statistics** tab of the **Pressure Pipe Network Properties - <network name>** dialog box displays the network statistics for the current pressure network. Expand the **General** category in this tab to view the statistics of the network objects. After you have viewed or edited the network properties, choose the **OK** button to exit the **Pressure Pipe Network Properties - <network name>** dialog box.

Pressure Pipe Properties

To view and edit the pressure pipe properties, select the required pressure pipe part from the drawing and right-click; a shortcut menu will be displayed. Next, choose the **Pressure Pipe Properties** option from this menu; the **Pressure Pipe Properties - <pipe name>** dialog box will be displayed, as shown in Figure 12-23. The options in this dialog box are discussed next.

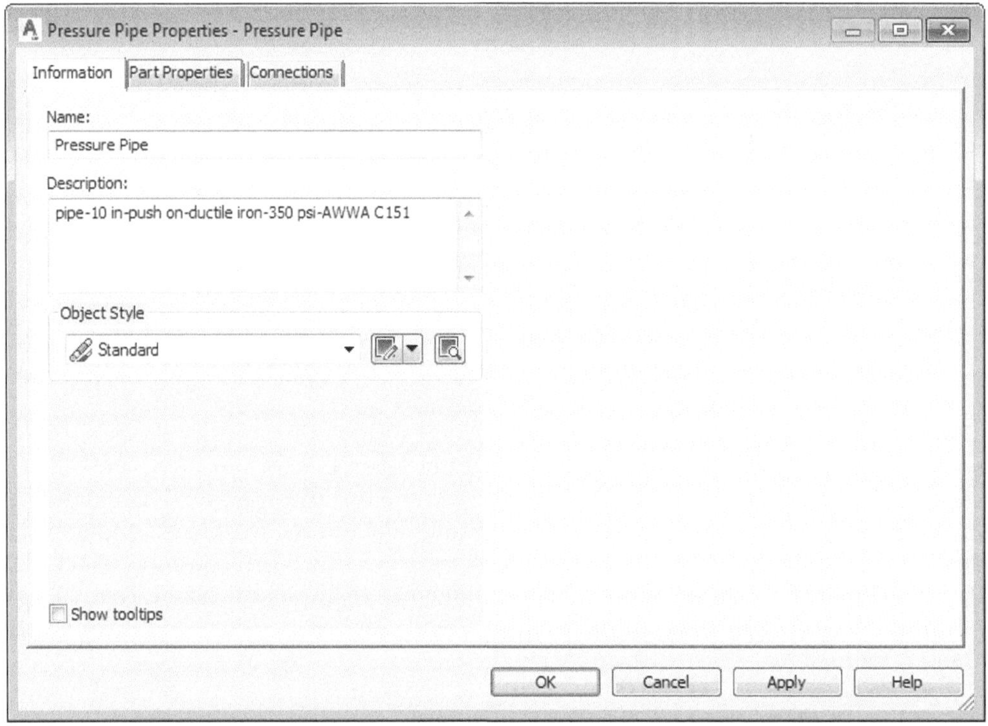

***Figure 12-23** The **Pressure Pipe Properties - <pipe name>** dialog box*

Information Tab
This tab displays the pressure pipe name, description, and style.

Part Properties Tab
This tab displays the properties associated with the pipe in three different categories: **General**, **Geometry**, and **Part Data**. The **General** category properties specify the general characteristics of the pressure pipe such as the surface and the alignment associated with the pipe. If the pipe is not referenced to a surface or an alignment the **none** value will be displayed in the **Value** fields of the **Reference Surface** and **Reference Alignment** properties. The **Geometry** category also specifies the geometrical behavior of a pipe, such as its bearing, the name of the parts connected at the start and end of the selected pipe, start and end station of the pipe, start and end offset of the pipe, slope of the pipe, and so on. The properties in the **Part Data** category specify various part properties such as part family name, size, cut length, and so on. If the value field of a property listed in the **Part Data** category is blank then it means that the part does not have a value defined for that property in the **Part Catalog**. You cannot modify the properties displayed in gray but the properties and values that are displayed in black color can be modified.

Connections Tab
This tab displays the parts that are connected to the currently selected pressure pipe. The **Name** column displays the name of each part that is connected to the pipe. The **Allowable Deflection** and **Actual Deflection** columns display the allowed deflection as specified in the **Part Catalog** and the actual deflection that is applied to the part, respectively. The **Nominal Diameter** column displays the nominal diameter of the pipe at the connection port.

Fittings and Appurtenances Properties
To view and edit the fittings or appurtenances properties, select the required fitting or appurtenance and right click; a shortcut menu will be displayed. Depending upon the part selected, choose the **Fitting Properties** or the **Appurtenance Properties** from this menu; the **Fitting Properties - <fitting name>** or **Appurtenance Properties - <appurtenance name>** dialog box will be displayed. The options in these dialog boxes are same as in the **Pressure Pipe Properties - <pipe name>** dialog box which have already been explained in the **Pressure Pipe Properties** section of this chapter.

EDITING PRESSURE NETWORK
Civil 3D provides you with different methods for editing the pressure networks in both the plan and profile views. You can use the **Pressure Network Plan Layout: <Network Name>** tab or the **Pressure Network Profile Layout: <Network Name>** tab for editing the network in the plan and profile views, respectively. You can also use the **TOOLSPACE** item view and the grip editing methods to edit the pressure network in both the plan and profile views as required. These editing methods are discussed next.

Using the Pressure Network Plan Layout or Profile Layout Tab

Ribbon: Pressure Networks: <Network Name> > Modify > Edit Network
Command: EDITPRESSURENETWORK

To edit pressure network in plan view, select it; the **Pressure Networks: <Network Name>** contextual tab is displayed. Select the **Plan Layout Tools** option from the **Edit Network** drop-down list in the **Modify** panel of this tab; the **Pressure Network Plan Layout - <Network Name>** tab will be displayed. You can choose various tools from this tab to add, change, or delete the network parts. You can also modify the associated surface and the alignment. All the options and commands in this tab have been explained in detail in the **Creating Pressure Networks** > **Designing a Pressure Network in Plan Layout** section of this chapter.

Editing the pressure network in profile view using the tab has already been explained earlier in this chapter.

Editing Pressure Network Objects Using the TOOLSPACE Item View

You can also edit the pressure network objects such as pressure pipes, fittings, and appurtenances using the **TOOLSPACE** item view. To do so, choose the **Prospector** tab in the **TOOLSPACE** palette and expand **Pressure Networks > Networks** sub-node. Next, expand the required network and select any of the pressure network objects. On doing so, the data for the selected object will be displayed in the **Item View** list area. Now, click in the desired column cells to edit the required values.

Grip Editing of the Pressure Pipe Network

Enhanced

AutoCAD Civil 3D gives you the flexibility of using grips to edit the pressure networks. Each time you select a pressure network object, the control grips will be displayed. You can use these grips to move or resize the objects. For example, select the required pressure pipe from the plan view; square grips will be displayed at the center of the pipe, as shown in Figure 12-24.

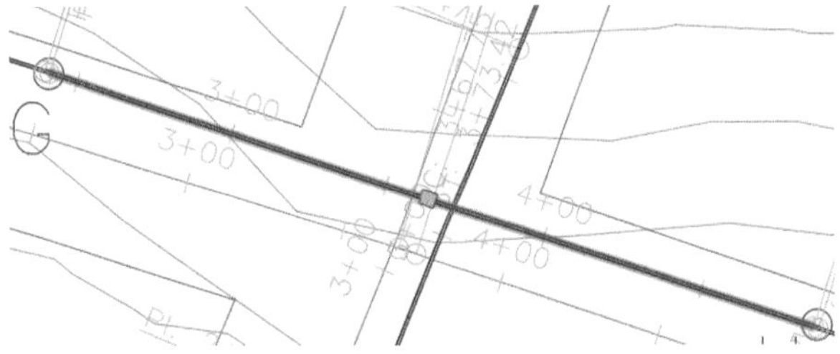

Figure 12-24 *Grips displayed on selecting the pipe object before changing the location*

The square grip helps you to change the location of the pipe object. After changing the location, select the particular pressure pipe; grips will be displayed at the center and the ends of the pipe, as shown in Figure 12-25.

Figures 12-26 through 12-28 show the use of the grips while editing the pressure pipe object.

The plus sign grip at the end helps you to add the pressure network objects such as fittings and appurtenances to the pipe end and the triangular grips at the two ends of the pipe help you to lengthen or shorten the pipes.

Figure 12-25 *Grips displayed on selecting the pipe object after changing the location*

Figure 12-26 *Using the triangular grip at the end to lengthen the pipe*

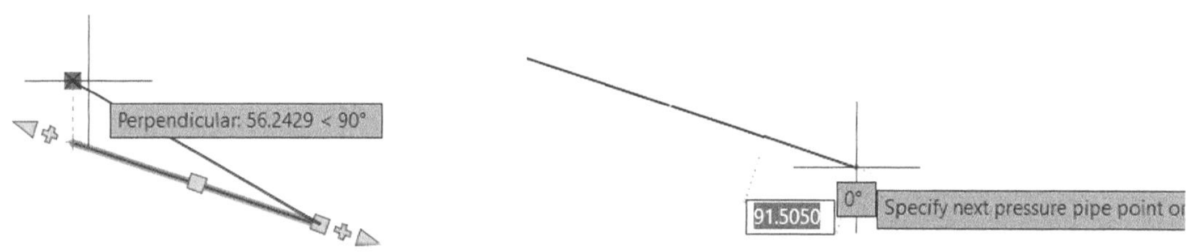

Figure 12-27 *Using the square grip to move the pipe end*

Figure 12-28 *Using the plus sign grip at the end to add another pressure pipe object*

Click on the required grips and drag them to view the desired result. The square grip at the center of the pipe help you to move the entire pipe to a new location. The square grips at the two ends of the pipe helps you to move the selected end to a new location, keeping the other pipe end fixed at the same location.

While using the grips to edit the pressure pipe object, you must remember that the fittings or appurtenance connected to the selected pipe will not move or change with the pipe or pipe ends. They will remain at their original positions.

ADDING PRESSURE NETWORK LABELS

Ribbon: Annotate > Labels & Tables > Add Labels drop-down > Pressure Network > Add Pressure Networks Labels
Command: ADDPRESSURENETWORKLABELS

You can label the pressure network or some parts of the network using the in-built label styles. The label styles can be created and managed in the **Settings** tab of the **TOOLSPACE** palette. You can access the pressure pipes, fittings, and appurtenance labels styles in the **Pressure Pipe**, **Fitting**, and **Appurtenance** nodes, respectively. The labels can be added while creating the network or can also be added after the pressure network is created. To add the labels while creating the network, select the required label style from the **Create Pressure Pipe Network** dialog box.

To add the pressure network labels, after the pressure network is created, choose **Pressure Network > Add Pressure Network Labels** from the **Add Labels** drop-down, as shown in Figure 12-29. On doing so, the **Add Labels** dialog box will be displayed, as shown in Figure 12-30.

*Figure 12-29 Choosing the **Add Pipe Network Labels** tool from the flyout*

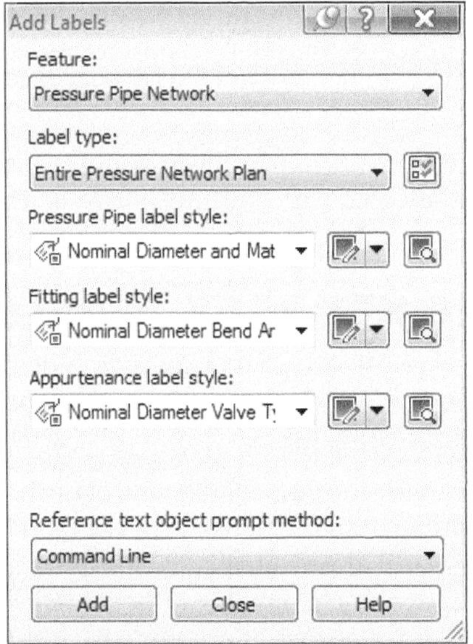

*Figure 12-30 The **Add Labels** dialog box*

Ensure that the **Pressure Pipe Network** option is selected in the **Feature** drop-down list. Next, in the **Add Labels** dialog box, select the **Entire Pressure Network Plan** option from the **Label type** drop-down list to label the entire network in the plan view. Now, to assign a label style for a pressure pipe, select an option from the **Pressure Pipe label style** drop-down list. You can also create a new label style. To do so, choose the down arrow on the right of this drop-down list to display a flyout and then choose the **Create New** option from this flyout to create a new label style. Also, you can edit the current style by choosing the **Edit Current Selection** option from the flyout. Similarly, to specify a label style for fittings and appurtenances, select an option from the **Fitting label style** and **Appurtenance label style** drop-down lists. Now, choose the **Add** button; you will be prompted to select a part contained in the network that is to be labeled. Select any object in the pressure network. On doing so, all the pressure network objects in the pressure network will get labeled.

In the **Add Labels** dialog box, specify the label type for the network from the **Label type** drop-down list. To label a single part of the pressure network in the plan or profile view, select the **Single Pressure Part Plan** or **Single Pressure Part Profile** option from the **Label type** drop-down list. Select the required label styles for the selected pressure network objects from the required label style drop-down lists, respectively. Select the required label styles and then choose the **Add** button to add the labels. After you have added the labels, choose the **Close** button from the **Add Labels** dialog box; the dialog box will be close.

Note

If you choose a direct labeling option from the flyout, refer to Figure 12-29, you will not have the flexibility of selecting the label styles from the ***Add Labels*** *dialog box. Therefore, it is recommended that you use the default label styles to label the network.*

ADDING PRESSURE NETWORK TABLES

To view the pressure network objects data in a tabular form, you can add the tables in the drawing. These tables help you to view the consolidated information about the objects that are used to draw the pressure network.

Adding a Pressure Pipe Table

Ribbon: Annotate > Labels & Tables > Add Tables drop-down > Pressure Network > Add Pressure Pipe
Command: ADDPRESSUREPIPETABLE

To add the table for structures, choose **Pressure Network > Add Pressure Pipe** from the **Add Tables** drop-down; the **Pressure Pipe Table Creation** dialog box will be displayed, as shown in Figure 12-31. In this dialog box, select the required option from the **Table style** drop-down list. You can also create a new style for the pressure pipe table. To do so, choose the down arrow button on the right of the **Table style** drop-down list; a flyout will be displayed. Choose **Create New** option from the flyout; the **Table Style - New Pressure Pipe Table Style** dialog box will be displayed. Specify the required options in this dialog box and choose the **OK** button; the dialog box is closed.

The **Table layer** text box in the **Pressure Pipe Table Creation** dialog box displays the default layer on which the table will be created. Choose the button on the right of this text box to change the layer. Next, you will add the pressure pipe data of all the pressure pipes in the network. To do so, select the required option from the **Select network** drop-down list in the **By network** area. The **Select network** drop-down list remains active as the **By network** radio button is selected by default. Alternatively, choose the **Select from the drawing** button on the right of this drop-down list to select the required network from the drawing.

To add information about multiple pressure network pipes to the structure table, select the **Multiple Selection** radio button in this dialog box. On selecting this radio button, the **Pick On-Screen** button gets activated. Choose this button to select the required pressure pipes from the plan view; the information about the selected pressure pipes will be added to the pressure pipe table.

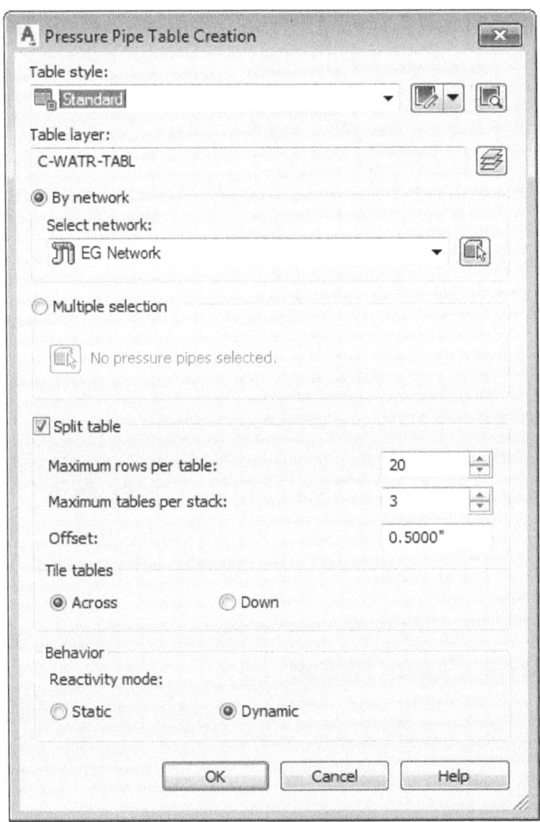

*Figure 12-31 The **Pressure Pipe Table Creation** dialog box*

The options in the **Split table** area of the **Pressure Pipe Table Creation** dialog box allow you to format the table. Use the spinners in this area to specify maximum rows per table and maximum tables per stack. In the **Behavior** area, the **Dynamic** radio button is selected by default to enable the table to update automatically if any of the pressure is changed in the network. After setting the parameters in this dialog box, choose the **OK** button; the dialog box will be closed and you are prompted to specify the upper left corner of the table. Click in the drawing at the required location to add the **Pressure Pipe Table**. The information displayed in the table depends upon the table style. You can create your own table style and configure the settings to display the required information in the table, refer to Figure 12-32.

Pressure Pipe Table			
PRESSURE PIPE NAME	SIZE	LENGTH	MATERIAL
Pressure Pipe – (1)	10 in x 10 in	724.86	Ductile Iron
Pressure Pipe – (2)	10 in x 10 in	372.51	Ductile Iron
Pressure Pipe – (3)	10 in x 10 in	331.54	Ductile Iron
Pressure Pipe – (4)	10 in x 10 in	336.38	Ductile Iron
Pressure Pipe – (5)	10 in x 10 in	245.42	Ductile Iron

Figure 12-32 *The* ***Pressure Pipe Table*** *displaying the pressure pipe details*

Adding a Fitting Table

Ribbon: Annotate > Labels & Tables > Add Tables drop-down > Pressure Network > Add Fitting
Command: ADDFIITINGTABLE

To add a table for the fittings, choose **Pressure Network** > **Add Fitting** from the **Add Tables** drop-down; the **Fitting Table Creation** dialog box will be displayed. The options in this dialog box are same as discussed for the **Pressure Pipe Table Creation** dialog box. After you have specified the settings and selected the required network or the fitting objects, choose the **OK** button; the **Fitting Table Creation** dialog box will be closed and you are prompted to specify the upper left corner of the table. Click in the drawing to specify the table corner; the **Fitting Table** will be added to the drawing displaying the fitting details, as shown in Figure 12-33. Like the **Pressure Pipe Table**, you can configure the settings for the **Fitting Table** in the table style and display the required information about the fitting object in the table.

Fitting Table		
Fitting Name	Horizontal Angle	Vertical Angle
Fitting – (1)	11.2393	0.4907
Fitting – (3)	14.7551	17.0427
Fitting – (4)	9.7227	5.7080

Figure 12-33 *The* ***Fitting Table*** *displaying the fitting details*

Adding an Appurtenance Table

Ribbon: Annotate > Labels & Tables > Add Tables drop-down > Pressure Network > Add Appurtenance
Command: ADDAPPURTTABLE

To add a table for appurtenances, choose the **Pressure Network** > **Add Appurtenance** from the **Add Tables** drop-down; the **Appurtenance Table Creation** dialog box will be displayed. The options in this dialog box are same as discussed for the **Pressure Pipe Table Creation** dialog box and by using these options, you can create a table for the appurtenances.

VALIDATING A PRESSURE NETWORK

In AutoCAD Civil 3D, you can validate the designed pressure network created by you by running a design check and a depth check on the network. Performing these checks helps in verifying the pressure network for various design parameters such as deflection, diameter, open connections, radius of curvature, and so on. You can also check whether the designed pressure network is within the allowed minimum and maximum depth.

After running the design and the depth checks, Civil 3D highlights the area where the pressure network violates the specified settings and parameters by placing the warning symbols into the drawing. When you hover the cursor over a warning symbol, a tooltip will be displayed which describes the violation.

Note

Both the design check and the depth check are run separately on a pressure network because the design check can only be run on multiple branches of the pressure network, whereas the depth check can be run on one branch at a time.

Performing Design Check

As mentioned above, by running the design check on a pressure network, you can check the network for parameters such as deflection, diameter, open connections, and radius of curvature. To run the design check, select the required pressure network graphically; the **Pressure Network Plan Layout:<network name>** contextual tab will be displayed. Next, choose **Design Check** from the **Analyze** panel of this tab; the **Run Design Check** dialog box will be displayed, as shown in Figure 12-34. In this dialog box, from the **Select parameter to check** area, select check boxes corresponding to the parameters for which you need to validate the pressure network and then choose the **OK** button; the **Run Design Check** dialog box will be closed and the warning symbols will be displayed automatically at the location where pressure network violates the specified parameters.

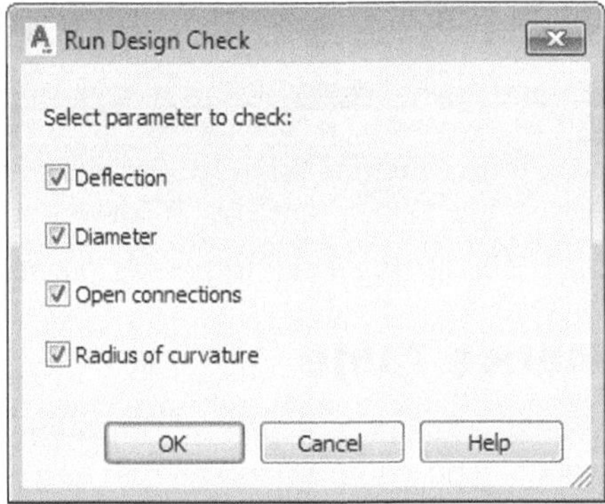

Figure 12-34 The ***Run Design Check*** *dialog box*

Performing Depth Check

In a pressure pipe network, pipe elevations are determined according to the specified depth, below a terrain from the ground level. Therefore, running a depth check ensures that the specified minimum cover value is satisfied along the full length of the pressure pipe and also validates that both the minimum and the maximum cover values are not violated at any length of the pressure pipe network. To run the depth check, select the required pressure network pipe; the **Pressure Network Plan Layout:<Network Name>** contextual tab will be displayed. Next, choose **Depth Check** from the **Analyze** panel of this tab; you will be prompted to select a path along the pressure network in the plan or profile view. Select the required pressure pipe and press ENTER; the **Run Depth Check** dialog box will be displayed. In this dialog box, under the **Select parameter to check** area, specify the minimum and maximum cover of depth in the **Minimum depth of cover** and **Maximum depth of cover** edit boxes, respectively. Note that, you can enter the values in these edit boxes only after selecting their respective check box, refer to Figure 12-35. Next, choose the **OK** button; the **Run Depth Check** dialog box will be closed. Now, if the selected pressure pipe violates the value of any of the specified parameters then a warning symbol will be displayed in the drawing. Hover the cursor over the warning symbol; a tooltip showing the violation information is displayed.

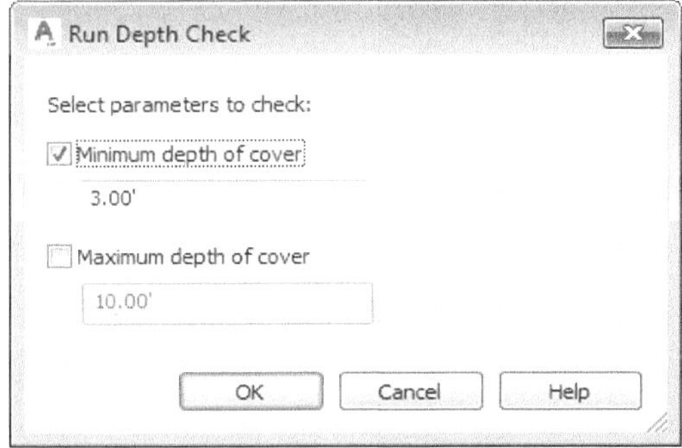

*Figure 12-35 The **Run Depth Check** dialog box*

TUTORIALS

Tutorial 1 — Pressure Network - I

In this tutorial, you will create a parts list for the pressure network. Using the parts list, you will design the pressure network in plan layout. Also, you need to refine the network in the profile layout, refer to Figure 12-36. **(Expected time: 60 min)**

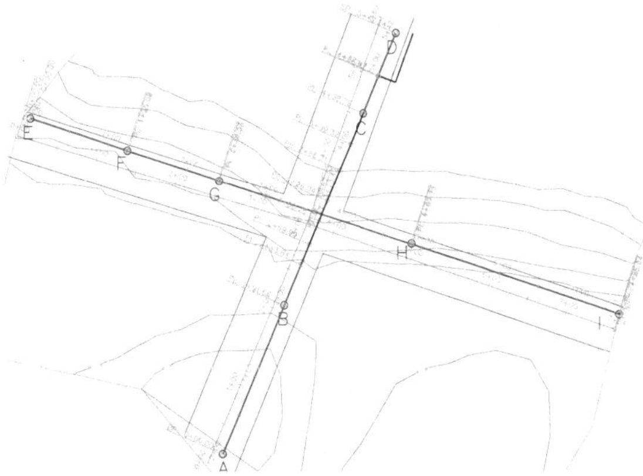

Figure 12-36 The pressure network in plan layout

The following steps are required to complete this tutorial:

a. Download and open the file.
b. Set the pressure network catalog.
c. Create the parts list.
d. Create pressure network in a plan layout.
e. Refine pressure network design in a profile layout.
f. Save the file.

Downloading and Opening the File

1. Download *c12_c3d_2018_tut.zip* file if not downloaded earlier from *www.cadcim.com*. Next, save and extract the file at *C:\c3d_2018* location.

2. Choose **Open > Drawing** from the **Application Menu**; the **Select File** dialog box is displayed.

3. In the dialog box, browse to the location *C:\c3d_2018\c12_c3d_2018_tut.*

4. Select the file *c12_c3d_2018_tut01.dwg* and then choose the **Open** button to open the file.

The drawing contains a ground surface and a set of two road alignments in North-South and East-West orientations. The drawing also has a pressure network along the Xaviers street (East-West orientation). An alignment and a profile view of this pressure pipe network is also included in the drawing.

Setting the Pressure Network Catalog

1. Choose the **Set Pressure Network Catalog** tool from the **Create Design** panel of the **Home** tab; the **Set Pressure Network Catalog** dialog box is displayed.

   In this dialog box, the **Catalog folder** text box displays the following path:
   C:\ProgramData\Autodesk\C3D 2018\enu\Pressure Pipes Catalog\Imperial

2. Select the **Imperial_AWWA_PushOn.sqlite** option, if not selected by default, from the **Catalog database file** drop-down list.

Tip

*1. To set the location of the catalog folder, choose the **Open** button displayed on the right of the **Catalog Folder** text box; the **Catalog Folder** dialog box is displayed. Browse to the folder location and choose the **Open** button in the dialog box.*

2. By default, the Imperial catalog folder is located in the AutoCAD installation folder as given below:~ \Autodesk\C3D 2018\enu\Pressure Pipes Catalog\Imperial

3. Choose the **OK** button; the dialog box closes and the pressure network is set to the selected catalog file.

Creating the Parts List

1. Expand the **Pressure Network** node in the **Settings** tab of **TOOLSPACE** and right-click on **Parts Lists** in the **Pressure Network** node; a shortcut menu is displayed.

2. Choose the **New** option from the shortcut menu; the **Pressure Network Parts List - New Part List** dialog box is displayed.

3. In the **Information** tab of this dialog box, enter **WaterMain** in the **Name** edit box. Next, choose the **Pressure Pipes** tab.

4. Right-click on **New Parts List** in the **Name** column; a shortcut menu is displayed. Choose **Add material** from the shortcut menu; the **Pressure Network Catalog** dialog box is displayed, as shown in Figure 12-37.

Figure 12-37 *Partial view of the* ***Pressure Network Catalog*** *dialog box*

5. Select the **ductile iron** check box and then choose the **OK** button; the dialog box is closed. Also, **WaterMain** is displayed in the **Name** column of the **Pressure Pipes** tab of the **Pressure Network Parts List - WaterMain** dialog box.

6. In this dialog box, expand the **WaterMain** sub-node in the item list and right-click on **ductile iron**; a shortcut menu is displayed.

7. Choose **Add size** from the shortcut menu; the **Add Pressure Pipe Sizes** dialog box is displayed.

8. Ensure that the **Value** field corresponding to the **Nominal Diameter** is set to **10.000000**, refer to Figure 12-38. Choose the **OK** button; the **Add Pressure Pipe Sizes** dialog box is closed and the selected part size is added to the **ductile iron** node of the list in the **Pressure Pipes** tab of the **Pressure Network Parts List - WaterMain** dialog box, refer to Figure 12-39.

Add Pressure Pipe Sizes

Property	Value	Unit	Add all sizes
Nominal Diameter	10.000000	in	☐
Inner Diameter	10.000000	in	
Outer Diameter	11.100000	in	
Wall Thickness	0.550000	in	
Cut Length	18.000000	ft	
Allowable Deflection	5.000000	deg	
Minimum Flex Radius	0.000000	ft	

OK Cancel Help

Figure 12-38 *The* ***Add Pressure Pipe Sizes*** *dialog box*

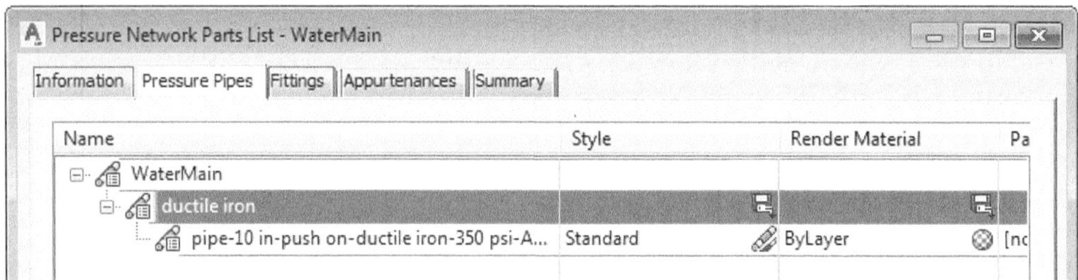

*Figure 12-39 Partial view of the **Pressure Network Part List - WaterMain** dialog box showing the pipe of selected size added to the list*

9. Next, choose the **Fittings** tab, and right-click on **New Parts List** in the **Name** column; a shortcut menu is displayed.

10. Choose the **Add type** option from the menu; the **Pressure Network Catalog** dialog box is displayed.

11. In this dialog box, select the check boxes corresponding to **Elbow** and **Tee** and choose the **OK** button; the dialog box is closed and in the **Fittings** tab of the **Pressure Network Parts List** dialog box, the name **New Parts List** is replaced with the name **WaterMain**. Also, the selected fittings are added to the **WaterMain** node.

12. Expand the **WaterMain** node, as shown in Figure 12-40 and right-click on the **ductile iron Elbow**; a shortcut menu is displayed.

13. Choose the **Add size** option from the menu; the **Add Fitting Sizes** dialog box is displayed.

14. In this dialog box, double-click in the **Value** column corresponding to the **Bend Angle**; a drop-down list is displayed. Select the **11.250000** option from the drop-down list.

15. Next, double-click in the **Value** column corresponding to the **Nominal Diameter**; a drop-down list is displayed. Select **10.000000x10.000000** from the drop-down list.

16. Next, choose the **OK** button; the dialog box is closed and the selected bend angle is added to the **ductile iron Elbow** sub-node.

17. Repeat the procedure given in steps 12 to 16 to add different sizes of elbow to the list using the data given in the table below, refer to Figure 12-40.

Nominal Diameter	Bend Angle
10.000000x10.000000	22.5
10.000000x10.000000	45
10.000000x10.000000	90

18. Right-click on the **ductile iron Tee** node; a shortcut menu is displayed.

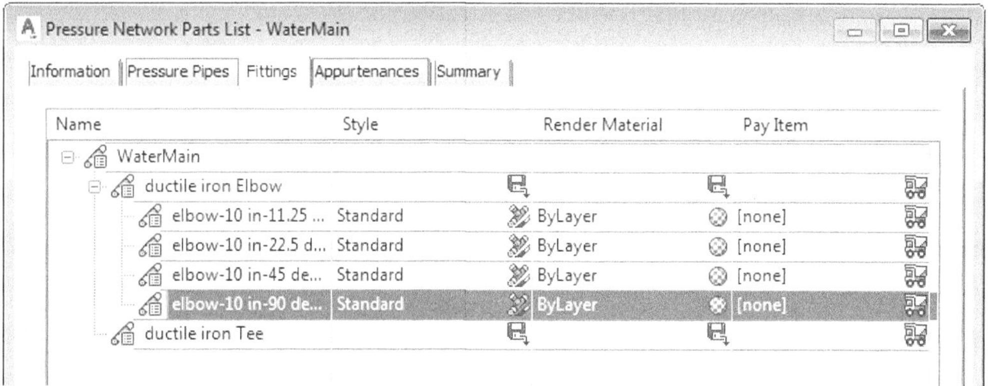

Figure 12-40 *Partial view of the* ***Pressure Network Parts List*** *dialog box showing the elbow fittings of various sizes added to the parts list*

19. Choose the **Add size** option from the menu; the **Add Fitting Sizes** dialog box is displayed.

20. In the dialog box, double-click on the **Value** cell corresponding to the **Nominal Diameter**; a drop-down list is displayed. Select **10.000000** from the drop-down list. Similarly, set the value of **Allowable Deflection** as **5.000000** if not set by default.

21. Next, choose the **OK** button; the dialog box is closed and the selected Tee is added to the **ductile Iron Tee** sub-node.

22. Choose the **Appurtenances** tab from the **Pressure Network Parts Lis**t dialog box. Right-click on the **New Parts List** in the **Name** column; a shortcut menu is displayed.

23. Choose the **Add type** option from the menu; the **Pressure Network Catalog** dialog box is displayed.

24. Select the check box corresponding to **gate value-push on-ductile iron-200 psi** and choose the **OK** button; the dialog box is closed and in the **Appurtenances** tab of the **Pressure Network Parts List** dialog box, the name **New Parts List** is replaced with the name **WaterMain**. Also, the selected appurtenance is added to the **WaterMain** node.

25. Expand the **WaterMain** node. Right-click on the **gate value-push on-ductile iron-200 psi** node; a shortcut menu is displayed.

26. Choose the **Add size** option from the menu; the **Add Appurtenance Sizes** dialog box is displayed.

27. In the dialog box, double-click on the **Value** cell corresponding to the **Nominal Diameter**; a drop-down list is displayed. Select **10.000000x10.000000** from the drop-down list and then choose the **OK** button; the **Add Appurtenance Sizes** dialog box is closed.

28. Choose the **OK** button in the **Pressure Network Parts List** dialog box; the dialog box is closed and the created parts list **WaterMain** is added to the **Parts Lists** node of the **Settings** tab, refer to Figure 12-41.

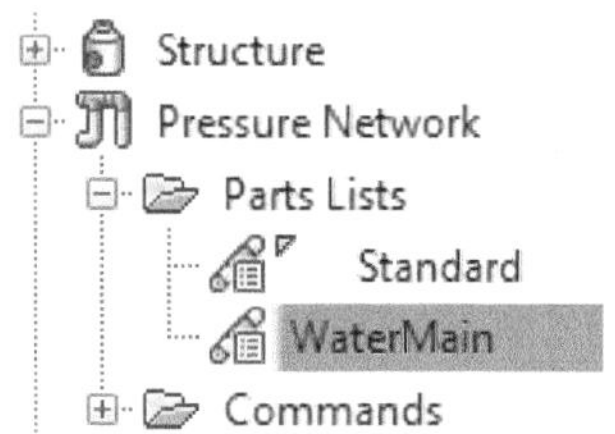

*Figure 12-41 The **WaterMain** part list in the **Parts Lists** node*

Creating Pressure Network in Plan Layout

1. Choose **Pressure Network Creation Tools** from **Home > Create Design > Pipe Network** drop-down; the **Create Pressure Pipe Network** dialog box is displayed.

2. In this dialog box, enter **RosewoodStreetWaterMain** in the **Network name** edit box.

3. Select the **WaterMain** option from the **Parts List** drop-down list.

4. Select the **Finished surface** and **Rosewood street** options from the **Surface name** and **Alignment name** drop-down lists, respectively.

5. Choose the **OK** button in the **Create Pressure Pipe Network** dialog box; the dialog box is closed and the **RosewoodStreetWaterMain** pressure network is created and added to the **Pressure Networks** node in the **Prospector** tab. Also, the **Pressure Network Plan Layout: RosewoodStreetWaterMain** conceptual tab is displayed in the Ribbon.

6. Choose the **Pipes Only** tool from the **Layout** panel of this tab; you are prompted to specify the first point of the pressure network.

7. Zoom to the circle marked **A** along the **Rosewood street** alignment and click at the center of the circle; you are prompted to specify the next point of the pressure network pipe.

8. Click at the center of the circle **B**; the pipe segment is created between circles **A** and **B**. Notice that a yellow colored compass is displayed at the circle **B** and you are prompted to specify the next point.

Note that the deflection of next pipe segment is restricted within the tick marks displayed on the compass. This angle of deflection is specified while creating the parts list using the **Allowable Deflection** property.

9. Click at the center of the circle **C** to create a pipe segment between circles **B** and **C**. Similarly, create a pipe segment between the circles **C** and **D**.

10. Press ESC to terminate the command. Now, you have created a pipe segment along the **Rosewood street** alignment, refer to Figure 12-42.

Next, you will add pipe fittings, appurtenances, and pipe segments to your network.

11. Zoom in to pipe segment between circles **C** and **D**.

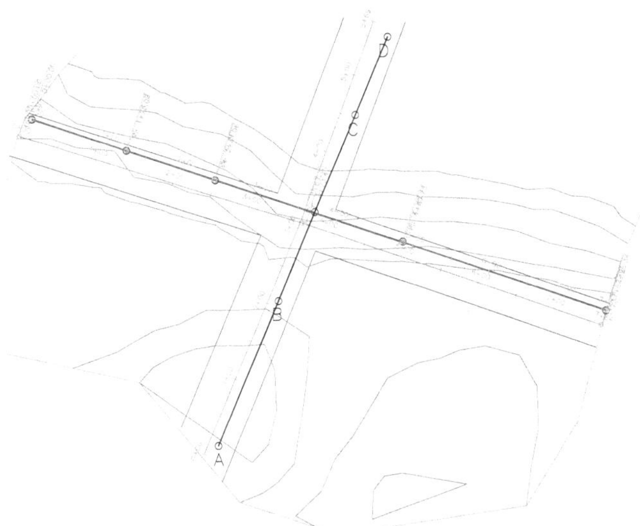

*Figure 12-42 The pressure pipe network along the **Rosewood street** alignment*

12. Choose the **tee-10 in x 10 in- push on- ductile iron 350 psi-AWWA C111/C153** option from the **Fittings** drop-down list in the **Insert** panel of the **Pressure Network Plan Layout: RosewoodStreetWaterMain** tab.

13. Choose the **Add Fitting** tool from the **Insert** panel; you are prompted to specify the placement point for the fitting. Ensure that the object snap is turned off.

14. Click on the pipe at a suitable location between circles **C** and **D**, refer to Figure 12-43; the tee is added to the pipe network at the specified location.

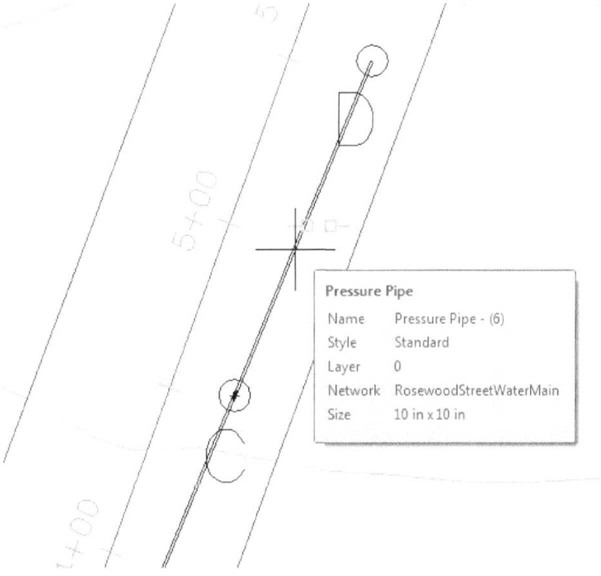

Figure 12-43 Adding the fitting in the pipe segment

15. Turn on the object snap option. Choose the **Pipes & Bends** tool from the **Layout** panel of the **Pressure Network Plan Layout : RosewoodStreetWaterMain** tab; you are prompted to specify the first pressure pipe point.

16. Specify the open end of the tee as the start point for the pipe, refer to Figure 12-44; you are prompted to specify the next point.

17. Specify the second point on the right of the **Rosewood street** alignment beyond the red line; refer to Figure 12-45; a yellow colored compass is displayed at the specified location and you are prompted to specify the next point.

Note that while using the **Pipes & Bends** tool, the compass shows more number of ticks as compared to the ticks on the compass while using the **Pipes Only** tool. The ticks displayed on the compass show the deflection of pipe that can be achieved by using the bends that are specified in the parts list.

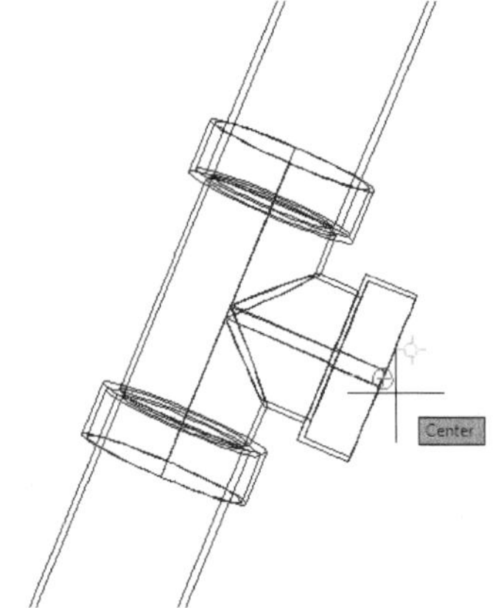

Figure 12-44 *Specifying the first point at the open end of tee*

18. Specify the next point such that it is parallel to pipe segments **C** and **D** and press the ESC key to exit the command. The pipe network is created, as shown in Figure 12-46.

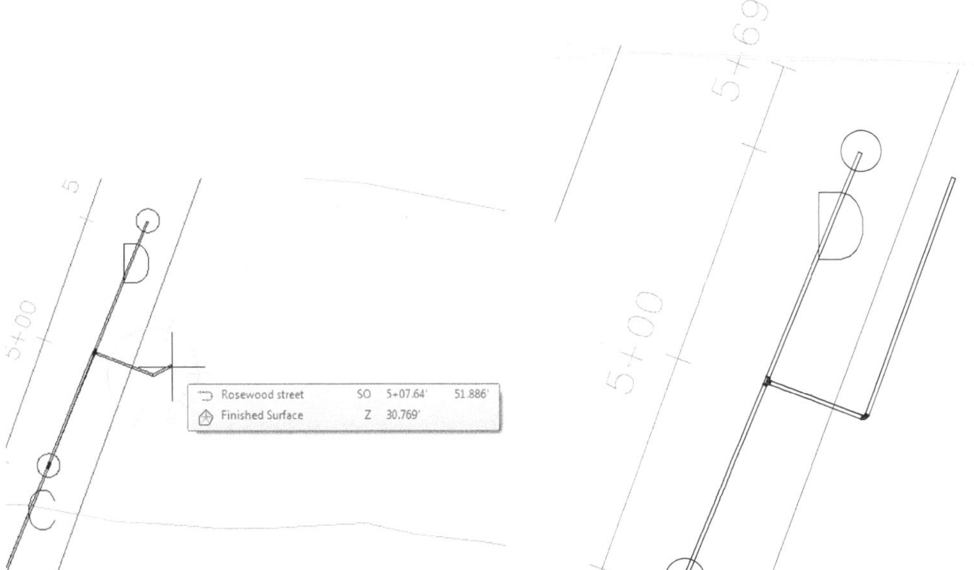

Figure 12-45 *Specifying the second point of the pressure pipe network*

Figure 12-46 *The pressure pipe network*

19. Ensure that the **gate valve-10 inch-push on- ductile iron- 200 psi-AWWA C111/C500** is selected in the **Appurtenances** drop-down list in the **Insert** panel of the **Pressure Network Plan Layout: RosewoodStreetWaterMain** tab. Next, choose the **Add Appurtenance** tool; you are prompted to specify the location of the appurtenance.

20. Click at a suitable location along the newly added pipe segment; the appurtenance is added, as shown in Figure 12-47. Press ESC to exit the command.

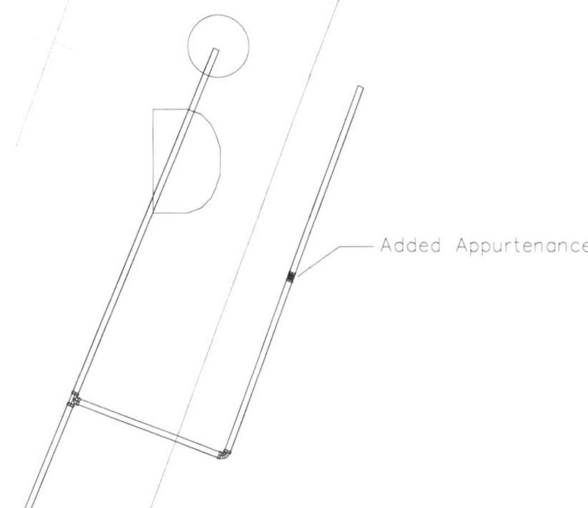

Figure 12-47 The pressure pipe network with the inserted appurtenance

Refining the Network Design in the Profile Layout

In this section, you will refine the two pipe networks in your drawing. You will begin with creating the profile view for the **RosewoodStreetWaterMain** pipe network.

1. Select any segment of the **RosewoodStreetWaterMain** pipe network; the **Pressure Networks: RosewoodStreetWaterMain** contexual tab is displayed in the Ribbon.

2. Choose the **Alignment from Network** tool from the **Launch Pad** panel of the tab; you are prompted to select the first pressure network part. Click on the pipe segment near circle **A**; you are prompted to select the next pressure network part.

3. Click on the pipe segment near circle **D**; the entire pipe along the **Rosewood street** alignment is selected.

4. Press ENTER; the **Create Alignment - From Pressure Network** dialog box is displayed.

5. Enter **RosewoodStreetWaterMain** in the **Name** edit box. Make sure the **Create profile and profile view** check box is selected.

6. Retain the other default settings and choose the **OK** button; the **Create Alignment - From Pressure Network** dialog box is closed and the **Create Profile from Surface** dialog box is displayed.

7. In this dialog box, select the **RosewoodStreetWaterMain** in the **Alignment** drop-down list, if it is not selected by default, and then select **Finished Surface** from the **Select surfaces** list.

8. Choose the **Add** button; a record is added to the **Profile list** area.

9. Choose the **Draw in profile view** button; the **Create Profile from Surface** dialog box is closed and the **General** page of the **Create Profile View** wizard is displayed.

10. In this page, make sure **RosewoodStreetWaterMain** is selected in the **Select alignment** drop-down list. Retain the default settings in the page and choose the link **Profile View Height** page in the left pane of the wizard; the **Profile View Height** page of the wizard is displayed.

11. Select the **User specified** radio button in the **Profile view height** area of the page; the text boxes corresponding to this radio button are activated.

12. In these text boxes, enter **10** and **50** as the minimum and maximum profile view height values, respectively.

13. Accept the default settings for all the options in the other pages of the wizard and choose the **Create Profile View** button in the wizard; you are prompted to select the origin for the profile view.

14. Specify a suitable point as the origin of the profile view; the profile view of the pressure pipe network is created in the drawing, as shown in Figure 12-48.

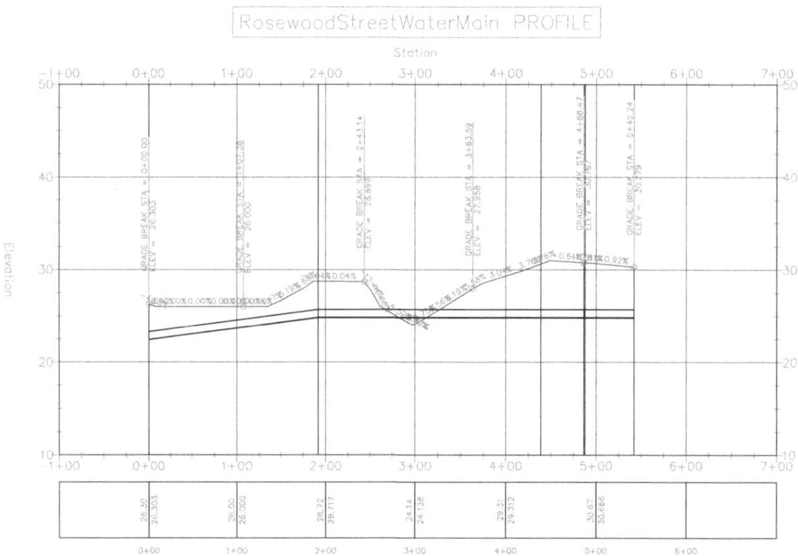

***Figure 12-48** The profile layout of the **RosewoodStreetWaterMain profile** pressure network*

The profile view of the **RosewoodStreetWaterMain** pressure network shows the pipe segment above the existing surface at station 3+00.00 along the pipe alignment. Now, edit this network and ensure that the entire pipe network is below the existing ground surface. To do so, you will begin with breaking the pipe segment. Next, you will delete the section that is above the ground surface and then redesign the network below the ground surface.

15. Type BREAKPRESSUREPIPE in the command window and press ENTER; you are prompted to pick a point on the pipe to break.

16. Zoom in to pipe segment between circle **B** and circle **C** and click on pipe segment near circle **B**, as shown in Figure 12-49.

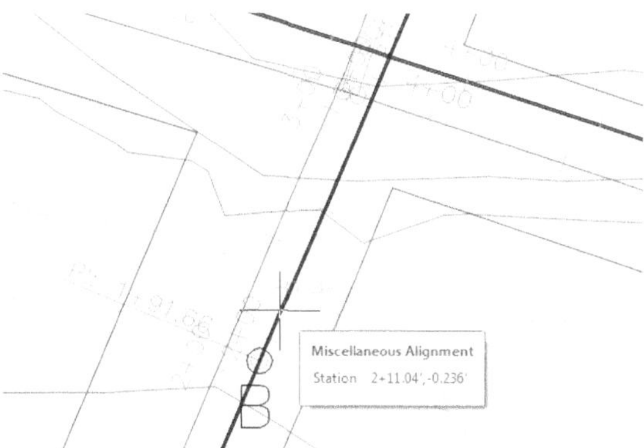

Figure 12-49 *Specifying first breakpoint on the selected pressure pipe*

17. Press ENTER to activate the BREAKPRESSUREPIPE command and click on the pipe segment near circle C, as shown in Figure 12-50.

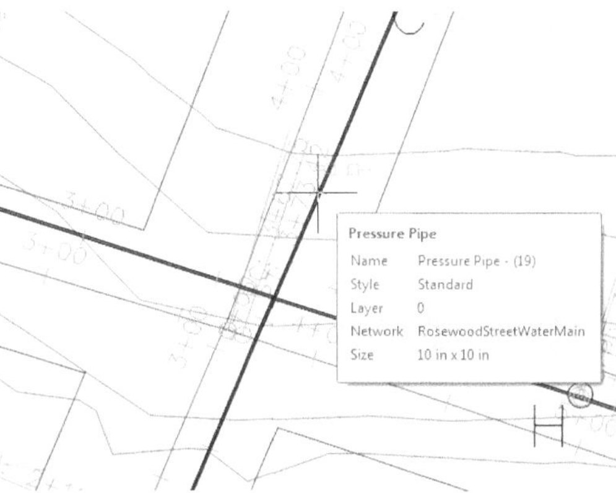

Figure 12-50 *Specifying second breakpoint on the selected pressure pipe*

Note that the pipe segment between circle **B** and circle **C** is divided into three segments in the **RosewoodStreetWaterMain** profile view.

18. Select the pipe segment between circle **J** and circle **K**, as shown in Figure 12-51; the **PressureNetworks: RosewoodStreetWaterMain** contexual tab is displayed in the Ribbon.

19. Choose **Profile Layout Tools** from **Pressure Networks: RosewoodStreetWaterMain > Modify > Edit Network** drop-down; the **Pressure Network Profile Layout: RosewoodStreetWaterMain** contexual tab is displayed.

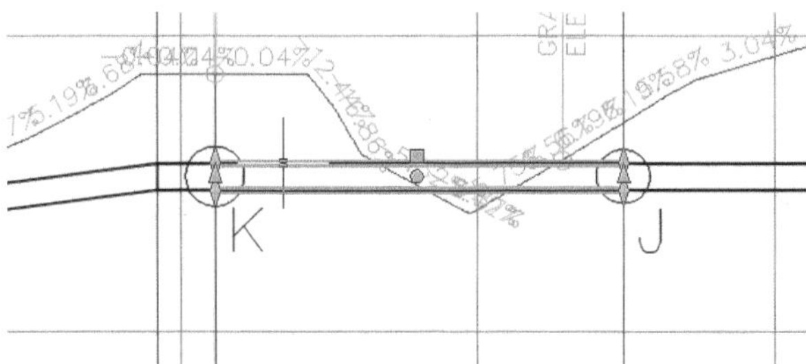

Figure 12-51 Selecting the pressure pipe segment above the ground surface

20. Choose the **Delete Part** tool from the **Modify** panel of the **Pressure Network Profile Layout: RosewoodStreetWaterMain** tab; you are prompted to select the section to be deleted.

21. Click on the section between circles **J** and **K**; the selected pipe segment is deleted.

Now, you will create a new pipe section between circles **J** and **K** below the existing ground surface.

22. Choose the **Add Pressure Pipe** tool from the **Layout** panel of the **Pressure Network Profile Layout: RosewoodStreetWaterMain** tab; you are prompted to select the network part at the start.

23. Choose the pipe segment at circle **K**; you are prompted to choose the network part at the end.

24. Select the pipe segment at **J**; you are prompted to specify the first pressure pipe point.

25. Zoom in and click at the pipe end at circle **K**; you are prompted to specify the next pipe point.

26. Specify the next pipe point, as shown in Figure 12-52; a pipe segment is created between the specified points and you are prompted to specify the next point.

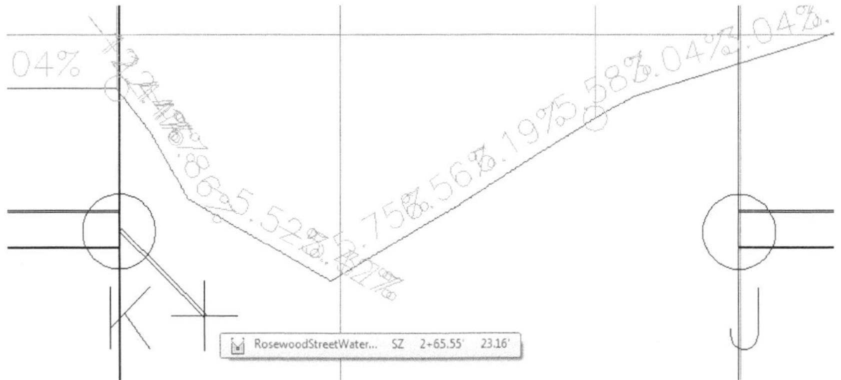

Figure 12-52 Specifying the second pressure pipe network point

27. Continue specifying the points to create the pipe network, as shown in Figure 12-53. Finally, specify the last point at the open end of the pipe at circle **J** to close the gap and then press ESC.

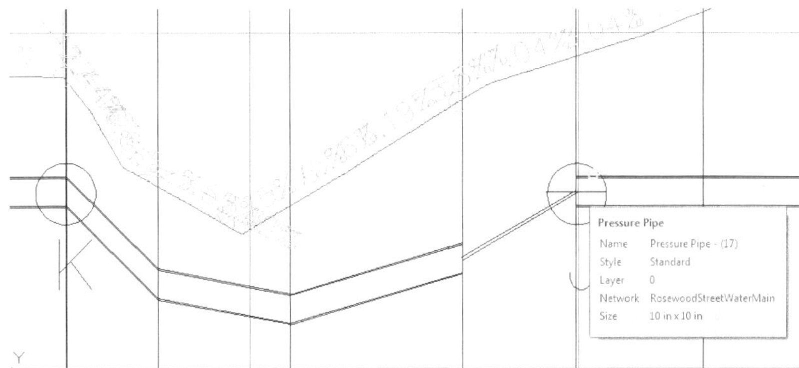

Figure 12-53 *Specifying the last pressure pipe network point*

You have now bridged the gap in the pipe network and the new segment is now below the surface. Notice that though the pipe segment is below the ground, its depth from the surface is not uniform. Next, you will create a pipe segment that will follow the ground terrain.

28. Zoom in to the profile layout of **XaviersStreetWaterMain** in the drawing.

Notice that the pipe network is below the ground surface but the pipe segments do not follow the terrain, refer to Figure 12-54.

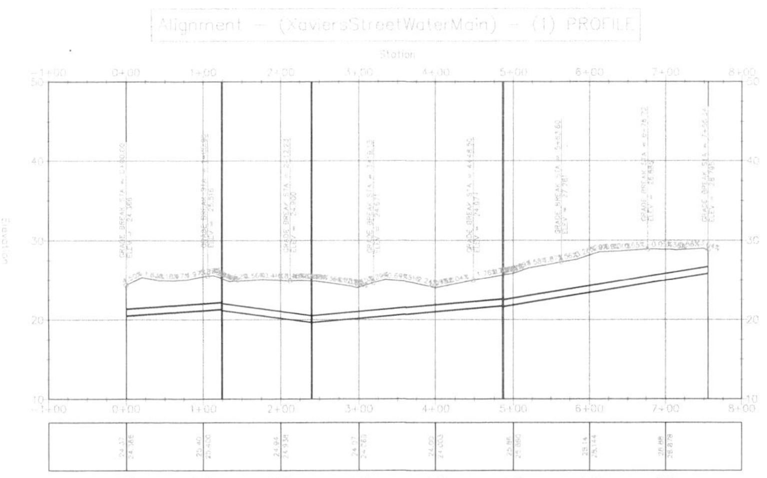

Figure 12-54 *The profile layout of the* ***XaviersStreetWaterMain*** *pipe network*

29. Choose any component of the **XaviersStreetWaterMain** pipe network in its profile layout; the **Pressure Networks: XaviersStreetWaterMain** tab is displayed in the Ribbon.

30. In this tab, choose **Profile Layout Tools** from the **Edit Network** drop-down of the **Modify** panel; the **Pressure Network Profile Layout: XaviersStreetWaterMain** tab is displayed in the Ribbon.

31. Press ENTER and choose the **Follow Surface** tool from the **Modify** panel of this tab; you are prompted to select the network part.

32. Click on the first pipe segment from the left (along alignment station); you are prompted to select the next part.

33. Choose the last segment; all the pipes are selected and you are prompted to select the next part.

34. Press ENTER to finish the selection process; you are prompted to specify the depth of the pipe below the surface.

35. Enter **3** as the depth value at the command bar and press ENTER; the pipe is redesigned and follows the surface terrain closely, as shown in Figure 12-55.

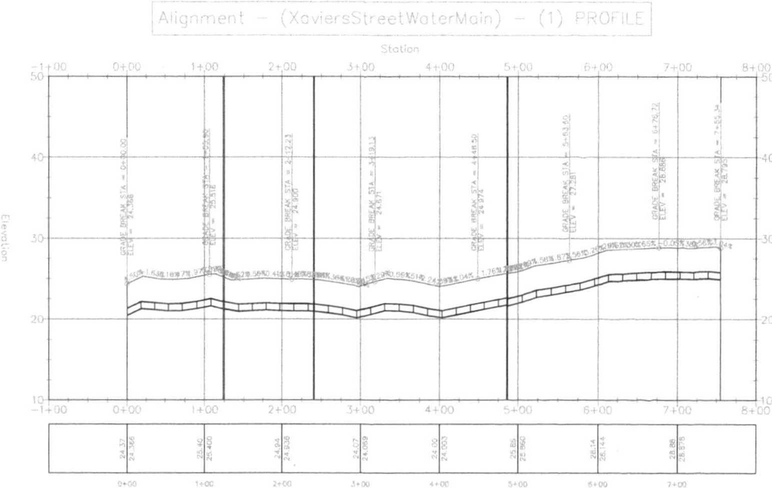

Figure 12-55 The profile layout of the ***XaviersStreetWaterMain*** *pipe network displaying the result of the* ***Follow Surface*** *tool*

36. Zoom in to the right end of the pipe and choose the **Add Appurtenance** tool from the **Layout** panel of the **Pressure Network Profile Layout: XaviersStreetWaterMain** tab; you are prompted to specify the location of the appurtenance.

37. Click at the open end of the pipe on the right; the appurtenance is added at the end of the pipe segment, as shown in Figure 12-56.

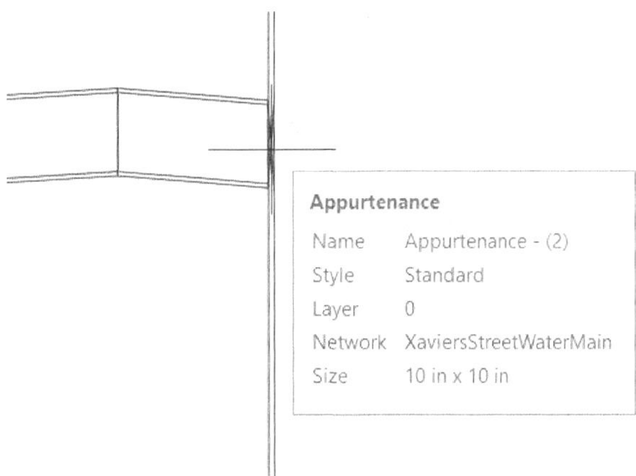

Figure 12-56 *Appurtenance is added at the end of the pipe segment*

Notice that the appurtenance is also added at the right end of the xaviers street pipe in the plan view.

Saving the File

1. Choose **Save As** from the **Application Menu**; the **Save Drawing As** dialog box is displayed.

2. In this dialog box, browse to the following location:

   C:\c3d_2018

3. Save the file as *c12_tut01a*.

Tutorial 2 — Pressure Network - II

In this tutorial, you will create a pressure network from a polyline object, as shown in Figure 12-57 and run the design and the depth checks on the created pressure network. Also, you will add labels to the created pressure network. **(Expected time: 30 min)**

Figure 12-57 *The Pressure network created from the polyline object*

The following steps are required to complete this tutorial:

a. Download and open the file.
b. Create the pressure network from the polyline object in the drawing.
c. Run the design and depth checks.
d. Add labels to the network.
e. Save the file.

Downloading and Opening the File

1. Download *c12_c3d_2018_tut.zip* file if not downloaded earlier from *www.cadcim.com*. Next save and extract the file at *C:\c3d_2018*.

2. Choose **Open > Drawing** from the **Application Menu**; the **Select File** dialog box is displayed.

3. In this dialog box, browse to location *C:\c3d_2018\c12_c3d_2018_tut* where you have saved the file.

4. Select the file *c12_c3d_2018_tut02.dwg* and then choose the **Open** button to open it. This drawing file consists of a surface, a profile view, and an alignment which you will use to create the pressure network.

Creating the Pressure Network

1. Choose the **Create Pressure Network from Object** tool from **Home > Create Design >Pipe Network** drop-down; you are prompted to select an object.

2. Zoom in to the drawing and select the polyline object from the drawing displayed below the alignment; you are prompted to select the flow direction.

3. Press ENTER to accept the default direction; the **Create Pressure Pipe Network from Object** dialog box is displayed.

4. Enter the following details in the dialog box:

   Network name: **Water Main**
   Network parts list: **Water**
   Size and material: **pipe-12 in- push on- ductile iron- 350 psi- AWWA C151**
   Surface name: **EG surface**
   Alignment name: **EG Road**
   Depth of cover: **3.00'**

5. Also, select the **Erase existing entity** check box and choose the **OK** button; the **Create Pressure Pipe Network from Object** dialog box is closed and the pressure network is created from the selected entity.

6. Select any pressure pipe entity from the network and right-click; a shortcut menu is displayed.

7. Choose the **Edit Pressure Pipe Style** option from the shortcut menu; the **Pressure Pipe Style- Standard** dialog box is displayed. In this dialog box, choose the **Display** tab.

8. In the **Component display** area of this tab, select the **Color** cell corresponding to the **Outside Pipe Walls** parameter; the **Select Color** dialog box is displayed. Choose the red color from this dialog box and choose the **OK** button; the **Select Color** dialog box is closed; the red color is assigned to the **Outside Pipe Walls** parameter.

9. Similarly, assign red color to the **Inside Pipe Walls** and **Pipe End Line** parameters.

10. Next, choose the **OK** button in the **Pressure Pipe Style- Standard** dialog box; the dialog box is closed.

Notice that the color of the pressure pipe in the drawing has changed and it is displayed in red color.

Running the Design and the Depth Checks

1. Select all the pressure pipes of network; the **Pressure Networks: Water Main** contextual tab is displayed.

2. Choose the **Design Check** option from the **Analyze** panel of this tab; the **Run Design Check** dialog box is displayed.

3. In this dialog box, ensure that the **Diameter**, **Open connections**, and **Radius of curvature** check boxes in the **Select parameter to check** area are selected and then choose the **OK** button; the **Run Design Check** dialog box is closed and a message is displayed in the command line that design check is complete.

   Two violations are detected and marked as yellow colored warning symbols in the drawing.

4. Hover the cursor over the warning symbol; a tooltip describing the violation is displayed, as shown in Figure 12-58.

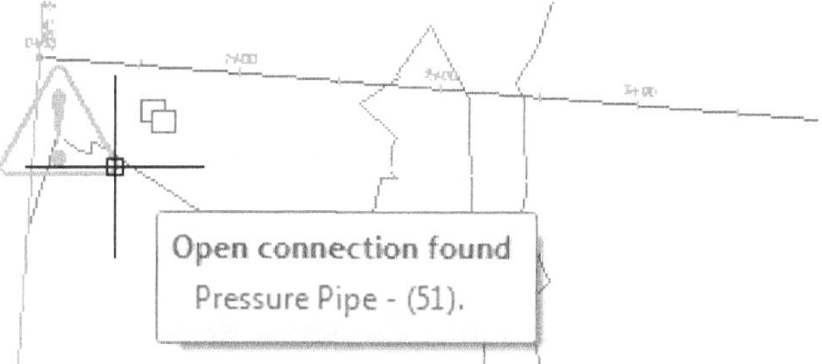

Figure 12-58 *Yellow colored warning symbol with the tooltip showing the violation*

5. Now, select the **Depth Check** option from the **Analyze** panel of the **Pressure Networks: WaterMain** contextual tab; you are prompted to select a path along the pressure network in the plan or profile view.

6. Next, select the left most pipe segment in the network; you are prompted to select the next point on the path.

7. Select the right most pipe segment; all the pipes in the pressure network are selected.

8. Next, press ENTER; the **Run Depth Check** dialog box is displayed.

9. In this dialog box, in the **Select parameters to check** area, select the check box corresponding to **Minimum depth of cover** if it is not selected by default and then enter the value **2.00'** in the edit box.

10. Choose the **OK** button; the **Run Depth Check** dialog box is closed and a message is displayed in the command line that two warnings symbols marking the violations are displayed in the drawing, as shown in Figure 12-59.

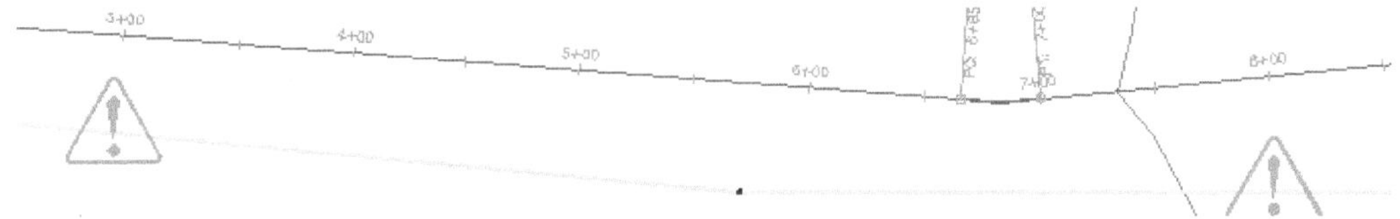

Figure 12-59 Warning symbols showing the violation for depth

Adding Pressure Network Labels

1. Choose the **Pressure Network** option from **Annotate > Labels & Tables > Add Labels** drop-down; a flyout is displayed. From this flyout, choose the **Add Pressure Network Labels** option; the **Add labels** dialog box is displayed.

2. Ensure that the **Entire Pressure Network Plan** option is selected in the **Label type** drop-down list.

3. Next, select the **Standard** option from the **Pressure Pipe label style** and **Fitting label style** drop-down lists.

4. Now, choose the **Add** button; you are prompted to select a part in the pressure network. Select any part of the **Water Main** pressure network; the pressure pipes and the fittings of the pressure network are labeled. Next, choose the **Close** button to close the **Add Labels** dialog box.

The added label shows the pressure pipe and fitting name or number and the name of the layer on which the pressure network is created, refer to Figure 12-60.

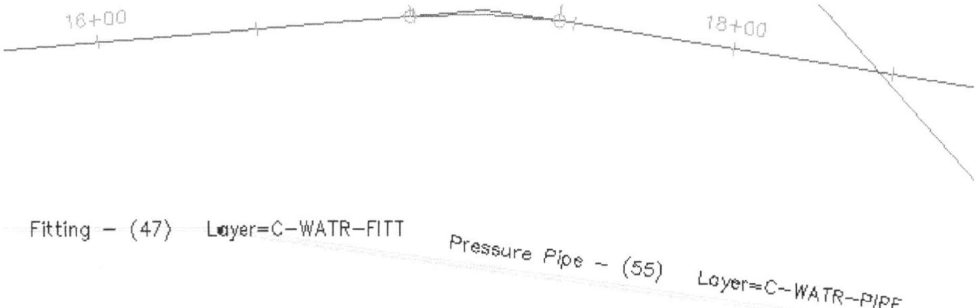

Figure 12-60 The pressure pipe and fitting labels added to the ***Water Main*** *pressure network*

Saving the File

1. Choose **Save As** from the **Application Menu**; the **Save Drawing As** dialog box is displayed.

2. In this dialog box, browse to the following location:

   C:\c3d_2018\c12_c3d_2018.tut

3. Save the file as *c12_tut02a*.

Self-Evaluation Test

Answer the following questions and then compare them to those given at the end of this chapter:

1. Which of the following options ensures that the minimum cover is met along the length of the pressure pipe?

   a) **Depth Check** b) **Length check**
   c) **Design Check** d) **Set Pipe End Location**

2. Which of the following tools is used to create a pressure network from an AutoCAD line object?

   a) **Pressure Network Creation Tools**
   b) **Create Pressure Network from Object**
   c) **Create Pressure Network from GIS Industry Model**
   d) None of the above

3. Which of the following options can validate a pressure network for parameters such as deflection, diameter, open connection, and radius of curvature?

   a) **Design Check** b) **Depth Check**
   c) **Pipe to Pipe Match** d) **Length Check**

4. Which of the following options allows you to choose a **Label Type** for labeling a pressure network?

   a) **Add Pressure Network Label** b) **Single Part Plan**
   c) **Entire Network Plan** d) **Single Part Profile**

5. Which of the following tools is used to view the vertical alignment of a pressure network?

   a) **Alignment Creation Tools** b) **Pressure Network Creations Tools**
   c) **Draw Parts in Profile** d) **Create Pressure Network from Object**

6. The ________ is a collection of pressure pipes, fittings and appurtenances.

7. To create a pressure network, you first need to create a ________ .

8. To create a pressure network, choose ______________ from **Home > Create Design > Pipe Network** drop-down.

9. The tick mark on the ________ indicates the allowable deflection between two pipes.

10. In the **Pressure Network Plan Layout < Network Name>** tab, you can use various options and tools to design the pressure network in the ___________ layout.

11. While designing a pressure network in a profile view, you can add fittings and appurtenances only to the open connections on pressure pipes. (T/F)

12. If there is any violation of parameters on running the depth or the design check, warning symbols are displayed on the pressure network. (T/F)

13. You can run design checks and depth checks simultaneously on a pressure network. (T/F)

14. The **Part catalog** dialog box consists of various in-built parts (pipes, fittings and appurtenances) used in a pressure network. (T/F)

15. The parts list enables you to store the selected pressure pipes, fittings and appurtenaces separately in a list. (T/F)

Review Questions

Answer the following questions:

1. Which of the following parameters, determine the pressure pipe elevation in a pressure network?

    a) Deflection
    b) Radius of curvature
    c) Depth
    d) None of the above

2. Which of the following tabs in the **Pressure Pipe Properties-<pipe name>** dialog box displays the properties associated with the pipe?

    a) **Properties** b) **Summary**
    c) **Connection** d) None of these

3. The __________ helps in highlighting the network parts which violate the specified parameters.

4. The __________ allows you to create and modify pressure network parts available in the **Part Catalog** of Civil 3D.

5. You can view the parts of an existing pressure network in a __________ to evaluate the vertical positions of the network parts based on your design.

6. A catalog serves as the source for the components that are used to create the parts list. (T/F)

7. The tools in the **Pressure Network Plan Layout: <Network Name>** tab can be used to edit the pipe network. (T/F)

8. You can also edit the pressure network objects such as pressure pipes, fittings, and appurtenances using the **TOOLSPACE** Item View. (T/F)

EXERCISE

1. Log on to *www.cadcim.com* and browse to *Textbooks > Civil/GIS > Civil 3D > Exploring AutoCAD Civil 3D 2018*. Next, select *c08_c3d_2018_exer.zip* file from the **Exercise Files** drop-down list. Choose the corresponding **Download** button to download the data file.

2. Now, save and extract the downloaded folder to the following location:

   C:\c3d_2018

Note

*While opening the exercise file, the **PANORAMA** window may appear with an error message. close this window to proceed further.*

Exercise 1

Open the *c12_c3d_2018_ex01.dwg* file and create a pressure network from the feature line in the drawing, refer to Figure 12-61. Also, add labels to the pressure network.

(Expected time: 30min)

Figure 12-61 *The feature line from which the pressure network will be created*

Network name:	**Water Main**
Network parts list:	**Water**
Size and material:	**pipe-12 in- push on- ductile iron- 350 psi- AWWA C151**
Surface name:	**Ground surface**
Depth of cover:	**3.00'**

Answers to Self-Evaluation Test

1. a, **2.** a, **3.** a, **4.** a, **5.** c, **6.** pressure network, **7.** parts list, **8. Pressure Network Creation Tools**, **9.** compass, **10.** horizontal, **11.** T, **12.** T, **13.** F, **14.** T, **15.** T

Chapter 13

Working with Plan Production Tools and Data Shortcuts

Learning Objectives

After completing this chapter, you will be able to:

- *Understand the plan production tools*
- *Create view frames*
- *Create sheets and sheet sections*
- *Create data shortcuts*
- *Create data references*
- *Promote and synchronize references*

PLAN PRODUCTION TOOLS

AutoCAD Civil 3D provides you with comprehensive tools that help you create construction documents and sheet sets containing the layout of plan and profile views. These tools are known as plan production tools. Sheet sets display the alignment sections and the profile views.

There are various tools in Civil 3D that you can use to create a view frame, a view frame group, and a match line. These features along with the in-built Civil 3D templates and viewports help you to generate the required sheets sets in an organized and easy way.

In AutoCAD Civil 3D 2018, new drawing templates, namely *Civil 3D (Imperial) Plan over Plan.dwt* , *Civil 3D (Metric) Plan over Plan.dwt*, *Civil 3D (Imperial) Profile over Profile.dwt*, and *Civil 3D (Metric) Profile over Profile.dwt*, have been added to create plan/plan and profile/profile sheets. In addition, new plan production tools are introduced that enable you to create construction documents more quickly by allowing you to create plan(s) only, profile(s) only sheets

Creating View Frames

Ribbon: Output > Plan Production > Create View Frames
Command: CREATEVIEWFRAMES

Before explaining the process of creating a view frame, the objects view frame and match lines that are created by using the tools in the **Plan Production** panel are discussed first.

View Frame

View frames are rectangular frames that are placed along the alignment, aligned to north direction, or rotated at a specific angle. These frames divide the alignment into different regions, as shown in Figure 13-1. These regions are displayed separately in different sheets. The prerequisites of drawing a view frame are alignment, profiles, and drawing templates.

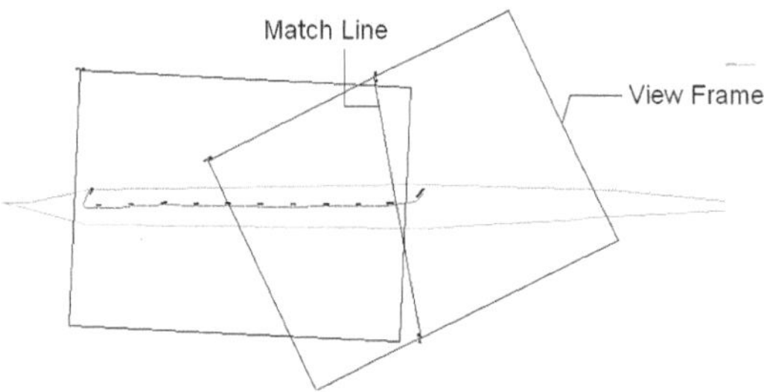

Figure 13-1 *The view frames dividing the alignment into different regions*

Tip

*In **plan(s) only** sheets, the sheets created will contain plan views only (no profile views). Similarly, in **profile(s) only**, the sheets created will contain profile views only.*

The first important requirement for creating a view frame is an alignment. View frames are primarily designed to create the alignment plan and profile views on a sheet. If you want to create a sheet with both the plan and profile views, you should create the required profile views. The next requirement for creating a view frame is a drawing template. The drawing templates are the in-built AutoCAD based sheet templates with predefined viewports in which the alignment section or regions created by the view frames will be displayed.

View frames have their own styles and label styles. Each view frame has a default label attached to one of its corners. AutoCAD Civil 3D has some default view frame styles and label styles. However, you can create your own view frame style and view frame label styles. View frame styles are created and managed in the **Settings** tab of the **TOOLSPACE** palette. To access the default view frame styles and view frame label styles, expand **View Frame > View Frame Styles** in the **Settings** tab; the default view frame style will be displayed in the **View Frame Styles** sub-node of the **View Frame** node. To create a new style, right-click on the **View Frame Styles** sub-node and choose the **New** option from the shortcut menu displayed; the **View Frame Style - New View Frame Style** dialog box will be displayed. You can use this dialog box to create a new frame style as required.

Similarly, expand **View Frame > Label Styles > View Frame** in the **Settings** tab to view the default label style of the view frame. To create a new label style, right-click on the **View Frame** sub-node and choose the **New** option from the shortcut menu displayed; the **Label Style Composer - New View Frame Label Style** dialog box will be displayed. You can use this dialog box to create a new label style for view frames.

Label styles are used to define the display settings for label in the view frame such as the name, group name, and view frame number. They are also used to display the alignment station from which the view frame starts or ends.

View Frame Groups

A collection of view frames is called view frame group. View frame groups are automatically created when you create view frames in a drawing. These groups are listed in the **View Frame Groups** node in the **Prospector** tab of the **TOOLSPACE** palette.

Match Lines

A match line is a line that indicates the location where one frame matches or intersects with the other in a view frame group, refer to Figure 13-1. Match lines are only displayed in paper space and plans. They are designed to visually indicate locations (start and end stations) along an alignment. These lines are created automatically and have labels attached to them by default. They have their own object styles and label styles like the view frames have.

The styles and the label styles of match lines are created and listed in the **Match Line** node in the **Settings** tab of the **TOOLSPACE** palette. You can create your own match line labels to display the name and number of the match line, view frame group, and match line station. Now, you will learn the procedure of creating a view frame.

The first step for generating sheets is to create the view frames along an alignment. To create view frames, choose the **Create View Frames** tool from the **Plan Production** panel of the **Output** tab; the **Create View Frames - Alignment** wizard will be displayed, refer to Figure 13-2. There are different pages in this wizard. By default, the **Alignment** page is displayed in the **Create View Frames** wizard. Different pages and options in the wizard are discussed next.

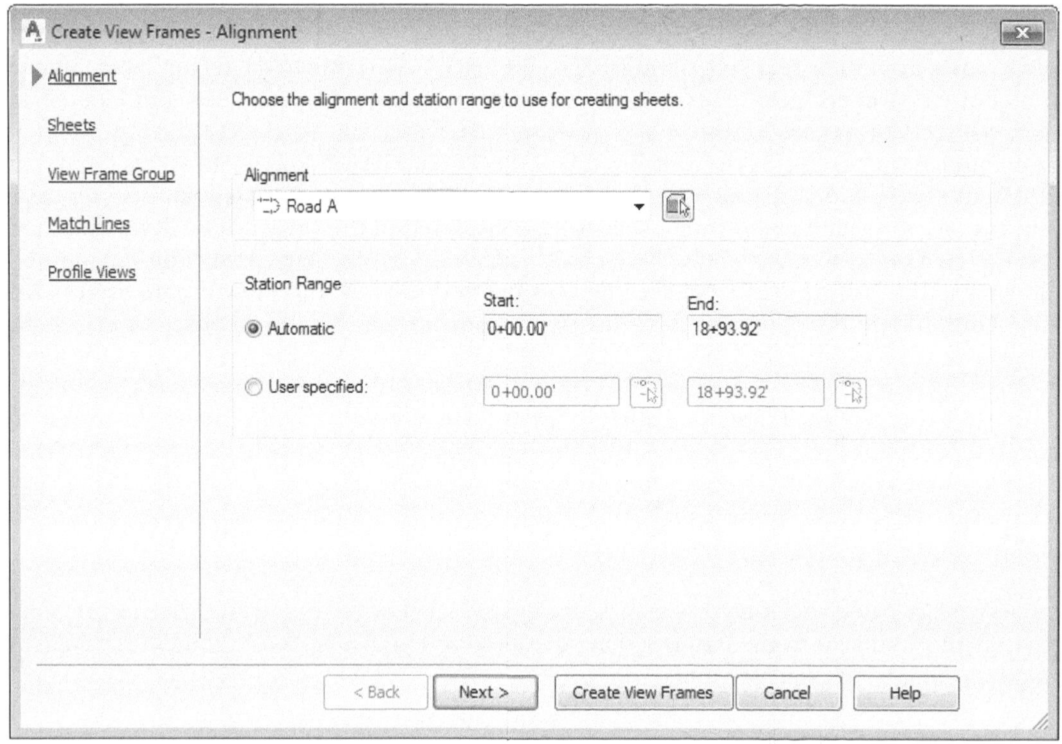

*Figure 13-2 The **Alignment** page of the **Create View Frames** wizard*

Alignment Page

This page is used to specify the required alignment and the station range to create view frames. Select the desired alignment from the drop-down list available in the **Alignment** area. Alternatively, choose the **Select from the drawing** button to select the alignment from the drawing.

In the **Station Range** area, specify the station range by selecting the **Automatic** or **User specified** radio button. By default, the **Automatic** radio button is selected and therefore, the view frames are automatically created along the complete station range. On the other hand, selecting the **User specified** radio button will allow to you to specify the required station range over which the frames will be created. You can specify the range either by entering the start and end station values in the respective edit boxes or by choosing the buttons to select the stations directly from the drawing, refer to Figure 13-2. After specifying the settings in the alignment page, choose the **Next** button to display the **Sheets** page.

Sheets Page

This page is used to select the type of sheets to be created, the required template for the selected sheets, and set the placement of the view frames in the drawing.

In the **Sheet Settings** area, select a radio button to specify the sheet type. To draw both the plan and profile views of the drawing, select the **Plan and Profile** radio button; the two viewports will be created in the sheet, one for the plan view and the other for the profile view. The preview of the sheet will be displayed on the right in this page. Select the **Plan(s) only** radio button if you want to draw only the plan view in the sheet. In this case, there will be two viewports to display the plan/plan sheet. To draw only the profile/profile view in the sheet, select the **Profile only(s)** radio button.

Next, choose the browse button on the right of the **Template for Plan and Profile sheet** edit box; the **Select Layout as Sheet Template** dialog box will be displayed. Note that the name of the edit box depends upon the radio button selected. You can use this dialog box to select the template (*.dwt*) file that will be used to create a view frame group. In the **Select Layout as Sheet Template** dialog box, you can use various options to define the folder path, drawing template (*.dwt*) file, and a layout name that will be used for creating new sheets.

To define a folder path and the template file in the **Select Layout as Sheet Template** dialog box, choose the browse button next to the **Drawing template file name** edit box; the **Select Layout as Sheet template** dialog box will be displayed. In this dialog box, browse to the location *C:\Users\<user name>\AppData\Local\Autodesk\C3D 2018\enu\Template\Plan Production*. Next, select the required template file and then choose the **Open** button; the dialog box will be closed and the path and name of the selected sheet will be displayed in the **Drawing template file name** edit box.

Now, you can specify the name of the layout in the drawing template file that will be used for the new sheet(s). To do so, select a layout from the list displayed in the **Select a layout to create new sheets** area of the **Select Layout as Sheet Template** dialog box. Then, choose the **OK** button to exit this dialog box. After selecting the sheet and template, you need to set the options to orient and place view frames in the **View Frame Placement** area. If you select the **Along alignment** radio button from this area, the view frames will be oriented along the alignment. If you select the **Rotate to north** radio button, the view frames will be oriented toward the north direction of the drawing. You can select the **Set the first view frame before the start of the alignment by** check box to set the first view frame at a distance before the start of the alignment. This is done to display all the necessary data near the start of the view frame. You can specify the offset distance in the edit box that will be activated when you select this check box. Now, choose the **Next** button to display the **View Frame Group** page.

View Frame Group Page

This page is used to specify the group name, description, label style, and other information of the view frame group. In the **View Frame Group** area, enter a name of the view frame group in the **Name** edit box or choose the **Edit View frame Group name** button on the right of this area to display the **Name Template** dialog box. You can use this dialog box to specify the name of the view frame group then close the dialog box. Optionally, enter the description about the view frame group in the **Description** text box in the **View Frame Group** page.

The **Layer** text box in the **View Frame** area displays the default layer on which the frame will be drawn. Choose the button on the right of the **Layer** text box; the **Object Layer** dialog box will be displayed. You can use this dialog box to select a different layer. In the **Name** edit box in the **View Frame** area, you can specify a name for the view frame that will be drawn in the drawing. Next, select an option from the drop-down list in the **Style** text box. You can also create your own view frame style or edit the existing view frame style. To do so, choose the down arrow on the right of the drop-down list in the **Style** text box; a flyoutwill be displayed. Choose the option from the flyout to create a new style or edit the default style. Next, select an option from the **Label style** drop-down list. The **Label location** drop-down list on this page displays the different locations to place the view frame. Select an option from this drop-down list to place the view frame. For example, on selecting the **Top right** option from the drop-down list, the view frame labels will be placed at the top right corner of each view frame. After selecting the parameters, choose the **Next** button; the **Match Lines** page will be displayed.

Match Lines Page

Match lines are only displayed in model space and plan views. This page of the wizard displays various options that determine how the match lines will appear in these views. Select the **Insert match lines** check box in this page to insert match lines on the view frames. If you select the **Plan and Profile** sheet or **Profile only** for the sheet settings in the **Sheets** page then the **Insert match lines** check box will be automatically selected and then you will not be able to clear this check box.

Using the options available in the **Positioning** area, you can specify the location of the match lines and also adjust their position, if required. In this area, select the **Snap station value down to the nearest** check box; the edit box below this check box will be activated, as shown in Figure 13-3. Enter the required value in the edit box; the location of the match lines will be adjusted and rounded off according to the value specified in the edit box. In the **Positioning** area, you can also select the **Allow additional distance for repositioning (Increases view overlap)** check box to specify the maximum distance by which you can move the match lines from their original position and the distance to which the views on the adjacent sheets will overlap.

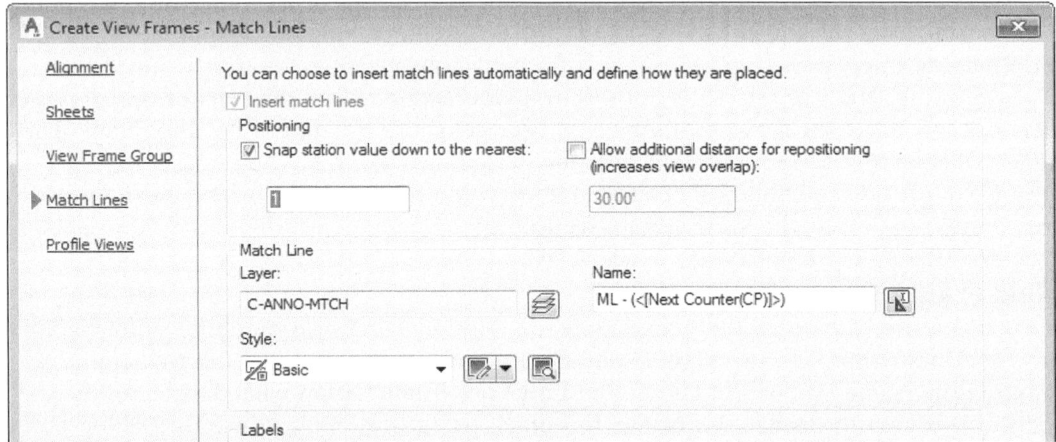

*Figure 13-3 The edit box below the **Snap station value down to the nearest** check box activated in the **Positioning** area*

The options in the **Match Line** area are used to specify the name, layer, and style of match lines. In this area, choose the button on the right of the **Layer** text box to display the **Object layer** dialog box. In this dialog box, select the layer on which the view frames will be created. Next, choose the **Edit View Frame Match line name** button on the right of the **Name** edit box; the **Name Template** dialog box will be displayed. Enter a name of the match line in this dialog box and choose the **OK** button to close it. Note that if you do not specify a name for the match line, Civil 3D will name the match lines automatically and number them accordingly. Select the required option from the **Style** drop-down list.

The **Labels** area on the **Match Lines** page provides you with the options to specify the style and location of the match line. Each match line has two labels, one on the right side and the other on the left side. In the **Left label style** or **Right label style** drop-down list, select the option to specify the label on the left or right side of the match line. You can also create a new style for the left or right labels, or edit the existing style. To do so, choose the down-arrow either on the right of the **Left label style** or **Right label style** drop-down list; a flyout will be displayed. Choose the required options from the flyout.

Next, you can specify the location for the label that will be placed on the left or right side of a match line. To do so, select an option from the **Left label location** or **Right label location** drop-down list in the **Labels** area. Now, choose the **Next** button from this page; the **Profile Views** page will be displayed.

Profile Views Page

This page is used to specify the profile view style and the band set style displayed in the profile views that are created on the sheets. In the **Profile View Style** area, select an option from the **Select profile view style** drop-down list. You can also create a new profile view style by choosing the **Create New** option from the flyout that will be displayed on choosing the down-arrow button on the right of the **Select profile view style** drop-down list.

Next, in the **Band Set** area, select an option from the **Select band set style** drop-down list. You can create a new band set style by choosing the **Create New** option from the flyout displayed on choosing the down arrow on the right of the **Select band set style** drop-down list.

After you have specified the required options in the **Create View Frames** wizard pages, choose the **Create View Frames** button; the wizard will be closed and the rectangular view frames will be created along the selected alignment. Note that the match lines will be labeled at both the ends and will be added under the **View Frame Groups** node in the **Prospector** tab, refer to Figure 13-4.

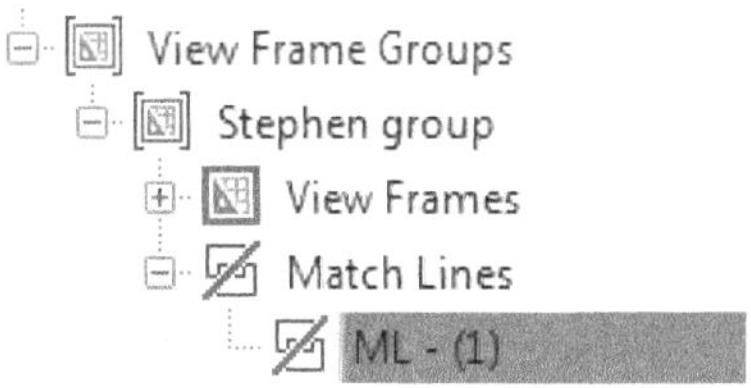

Figure 13-4 *The* ***ML - (1)*** *match line added to the* ***Stephen group*** *view group sub-node*

The next step after creating the view frame group and match lines is to create sheets. The method of creating sheets is discussed next.

Creating Sheets

Ribbon: Output > Plan Production > Create Sheets
Command: CREATESHEETS

To create a sheet, choose the **Create Sheets** tool from the **Plan Production** panel; the **Create Sheets** wizard with the **View Frame Group and Layouts** page selected by default will be displayed, as shown in Figure 13-5. The different pages and their options in the **Create Sheets** wizard are discussed next.

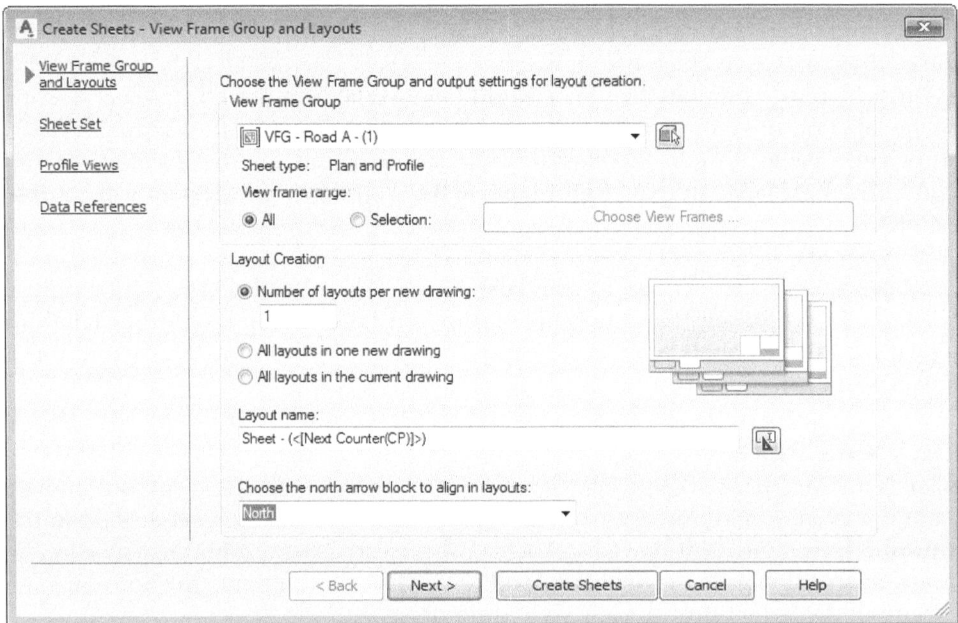

*Figure 13-5 The **View Frame Group and Layouts** page of the **Create Sheets** wizard*

View Frame Group and Layouts Page

This page is used to select the required view frame group and specify layout settings for the sheet. In the **View Frame Group** area, select an option from the drop-down list to create the sheet. Alternatively, choose the **Select from the drawing** button on the right of this drop-down list and select the required view frame directly from the drawing. The **All** radio button is selected by default in this area. As a result, the sheet is created for each view frame in the view frame group selected. To select one or more view frames, select the **Selection** radio button; the **Choose View Frames** button will be activated. Choose this button; the **Select View Frames** dialog box will be displayed. Select the required view frames from this dialog box and choose the **OK** button to close it.

Note

*Use the CTRL key to select more than one viewframe in the **Select View Frames** dialog box.*

The options in the **Layout Creation** area of this page are used to specify the settings for creating the layouts. In this area, the **Number of layouts per new drawing** radio button is selected by default and **1** is specified as the default value in the edit box below the radio button. As a result, one new sheet is created in each new drawing. This option is useful if different people are working on different sheets. You can change the value in the edit box according to the number of layouts required in each new drawing. For example, if you enter **2**, you can create two new layouts (sheets) for each new drawing. The total number of sheets to be created depends upon the length of the alignment selected and the size of the viewport in the template referenced.

Note

*You can create from 1 to 255 layouts in a new drawing by specifying the required value in the edit box below the **Number of layouts per drawing** radio button.*

Select the **All layouts in one new drawing** radio button to create all the layouts (sheets) in new drawing. This option is useful only if you want to create 10 or less than 10 sheets. The number of sheets created in the drawing depends upon the length of the alignment and the size of the viewports. If you want to create less than 10 sheets, select the **All layouts in the current drawing** radio button.

Next, enter a suitable name for the layouts in the **Layout name** edit box or choose the **Edit layout name** button; the **Name Template** dialog box will be displayed. Enter the required name in the **Name** edit box of this dialog box and then choose the **OK** button to exit. The **Choose the north arrow block to align in layouts** drop-down list displays names of all the blocks existing in the template selected. Select the required block from this drop-down list to align it to the north of the sheet. After specifying the required values and parameters in the **View Frame Group and Layouts** page, choose the **Next** button from the **Create Sheets** wizard; the **Sheet Set** page will be displayed. The options in the **Sheet Set** page are discussed next.

Sheet Set Page

This page is used to specify the name and location of the sheet set, sheet set file, and sheet file. The options in the **Sheet Set** area are used to create a new sheet set or select the existing set to add the sheets to the drawing. Select the **New sheet set** radio button and enter a suitable name for the sheet set in the **New sheet set** edit box below it.

Note

*By default, the name in the edit box below the **New sheet set** radio button will be the same as selected in the drop-down list in the **View Frame Group** area of the **View Frame Group and Layouts** page in the **Create Sheets** wizard.*

To add sheets to an existing sheet set, select the **Add to existing sheet set** radio button and choose the browse button on the right; the **Browse the Sheet set file** dialog box will be displayed. Browse to the required location, select the existing sheet set and choose the **Open** button; the dialog box will be closed. The **Sheet files storage location** edit box in the **Sheets** area of the **Sheet Set** page is used to specify the location of the sheet set. You can use this edit box to select a location for the new sheet set. To select a location for the new sheet set, choose the browse button on the right of this edit box; the **Browse for Sheet Set Folder** dialog box will be displayed. In the dialog box, select the folder in which the new sheet set will be placed and then choose the **Open** button to close this dialog box. On doing so, the location of the new sheet set will be updated and will be displayed in the **Sheet files storage location** edit box.

Note

1. If you select the ***Add to existing sheet set*** *radio button, the location of the existing sheet set will be displayed in the* ***Sheets files storage location*** *edit box, provided there is an existing sheet set in the drawing.*

2. If you select the ***Add to existing sheet set*** *radio button then all other options in the* ***Sheet Set*** *page will become inactive.*

The options in the **Sheets** area are used to specify the name of the sheet file and the location to save the sheet file. The **Sheet files storage location** edit box displays the path and location where the current sheet files will be saved. Alternatively, you can choose the browse button on the right of this edit box and select the location to save the files in the **Browse for Folder** dialog box displayed. Next, enter the name in the **Sheet file name** edit box and then choose the **Next** button in the wizard; the **Profile Views** page will be displayed. The options on this page are discussed next.

Profile Views Page

The options in this page are used to edit some of the profile view options. You can also view the profile view and data band styles selected during the view frame creation using the options in this page. The **Profile view settings** area on this page displays the name of the profile view style as well as the name of the data band style to be used to create sheets. The options in the **Other profile view options** area are used to edit some profile view settings. Select the **Get other settings from an existing profile view** radio button to use the profile view settings from another profile view in the current drawing. On selecting this radio button, the drop-down list below this radio button will become active. Select the required option from the drop-down list. Alternatively, choose the **Select from the drawing** button on the right of the drop-down list to select the required profile view directly from the drawing.

Select the **Choose settings** radio button in the **Other profile view options** area of this page; the **Profile View Wizard** button will be activated. Next, choose this button; the **Create Multiple Profile Views - Profile View Height** wizard will be displayed. You can use this wizard to create multiple profile views and add them to the model space in the file containing the sheets.

The options in the **Align views** area are used to align the data of the plan and profile views. Note that these options will not be available if you are creating only the plan or profile views. Select the required option from this area to align the data. The preview of the alignment of the data of the plan and profile views will be displayed on the right in the **Align Views** area, refer to Figure 13-6. After selecting the parameters in this page, choose the **Next** button to display the **Data References** page.

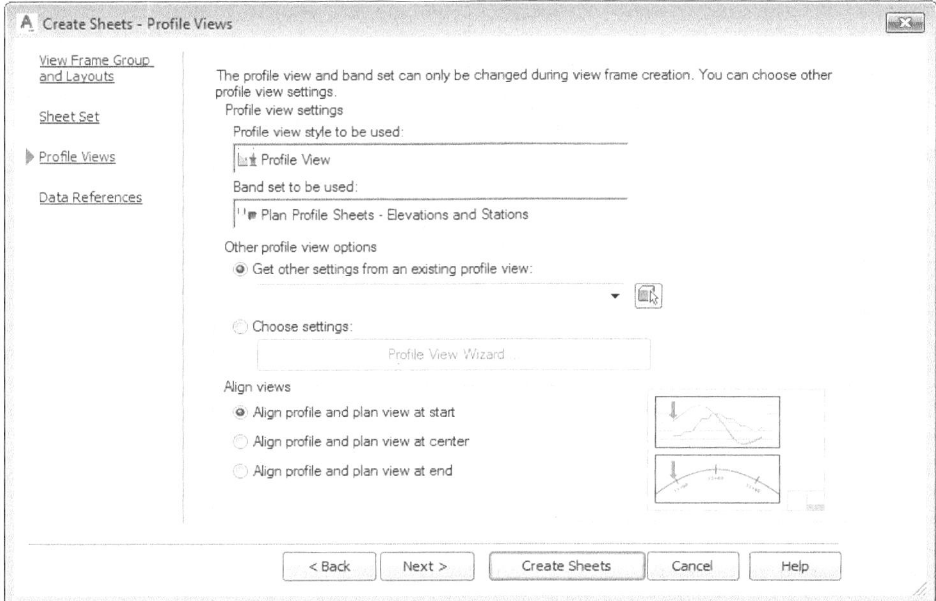

*Figure 13-6 The **Profiles Views** page of the **Create Sheets** wizard*

Data References Page

This page is used to select the data that you want to reference in the sheet. In the list box of this page, the check boxes corresponding to the objects required for creating the sheets are selected by default and cannot be cleared. However, you can select additional set of data by selecting the corresponding check box, refer to Figure 13-7.

You can also choose the **Pick from drawing** button and then select the required objects from the drawing. After selecting the objects, choose the **Create Sheets** button from the **Create Sheets** wizard; the **AutoCAD Civil 3D 2018** message box will be displayed. This message box will inform you that the drawing will be saved in order to complete the current process of creating the sheets. Next, choose the **OK** button from the message box to proceed; the wizard will be closed and you will be prompted to specify the origin of the profile view, if you have selected the option to create sheets with profile views. Now, click at the required location in the drawing to specify the origin of the profile view; the **Create Sheet Progress Dialog** dialog box will be displayed. Once the process of creating the sheet is completed, the **PANORAMA** window will be displayed with the **Events** tab chosen and the **Sheet Set Manager** palette displayed. The **Events** tab of the **PANORAMA** window displays the information about location and number of the sheet sets created. The **Sheet Set Manager** palette displays the new sheets created in a sheet set. To view a particular sheet, double-click on the name of the sheet in the **Sheet Set Manager** palette.

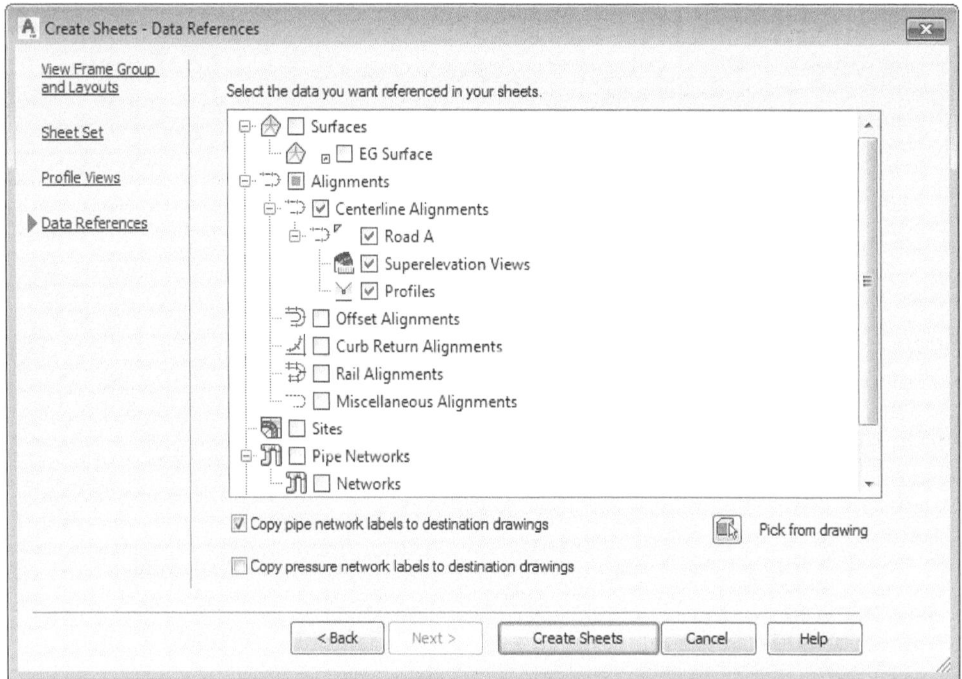

Figure 13-7 The ***Data References*** *page of the* ***Create Sheets*** *wizard*

Note

If you have selected the ***All layouts in the current drawing*** *radio button in the* ***Layout Creation*** *area of the* ***View Frame Group and Layouts*** *page, the profile views will be displayed in the current drawing when you specify the origin.*

DATA SHARING

Any Civil Engineering project requires a team of engineers to work simultaneously for effective implementation and management of the project. This would require effective data management and data sharing tools. AutoCAD Civil 3D provides you with such effective tools. These tools help the team members to access the project data simultaneously and work independently on the project. These tools are discussed next in detail.

Data Shortcut

The data shortcut is a method that allows you to create external references for different Civil 3D objects. These references can be inserted into one or more drawings and can be worked upon by multiple users simultaneously. The references or data shortcuts are XML files representing a shortcut to Civil 3D objects and contain information about the objects for identifying them in the source drawings. Using the data shortcut, you can divide a project or model into separate drawings. These drawings are called source drawings and contain the objects that you can share. Prior to AutoCAD Civil 3D 2017, data shortcuts can only be created for alignments, surfaces, profiles, view frame groups, and pipe networks. Now, you can create data shortcuts for corridors also. When a data shortcut is created for corridors, the data shortcuts for alignments and profiles related to the corridors are automatically created. Additionally, you can save the geometry of the referenced surface into the current drawing. The objects in the source drawings can be used in other drawings provided you create a data reference for it.

Note

*The data shortcuts are created and managed in the **Master View** of the **TOOLSPACE** palette.*

Working with Data Shortcuts

Before creating data shortcuts, you need to set a working folder. The working folder is the parent folder which contains all project folders for data shortcuts. This folder is stored at a location that is accessible to all users. The default location of the working folder for the data shortcut projects is *C:\Civil 3D Projects*. The same working folder is used for Vault Projects as well.

Setting a Working Folder

Ribbon: Manage > Data Shortcuts > Set Working Folder
Command: SETWORKINGFOLDER

To set a working folder, choose the **Set Working Folder** tool from the **Data Shortcuts** panel of the **Manage** tab; the **Browse For Folder** dialog box will be displayed, as shown in Figure 13-8. Select the required working folder from the **Set Working Folder** list box and then choose the **OK** button; the working folder will be set.

***Figure 13-8** The **Browse For Folder** dialog box*

Creating a New Data Shortcut Folder

To create a new data shortcut folder, right-click on the **Data Shortcuts** node in the **Prospector** tab of the **TOOLSPACE** palette and choose the **New Data Shortcuts Project Folder** option from the shortcut menu displayed; the **New Data Shortcut Folder** dialog box will be displayed, as shown in Figure 13-9.

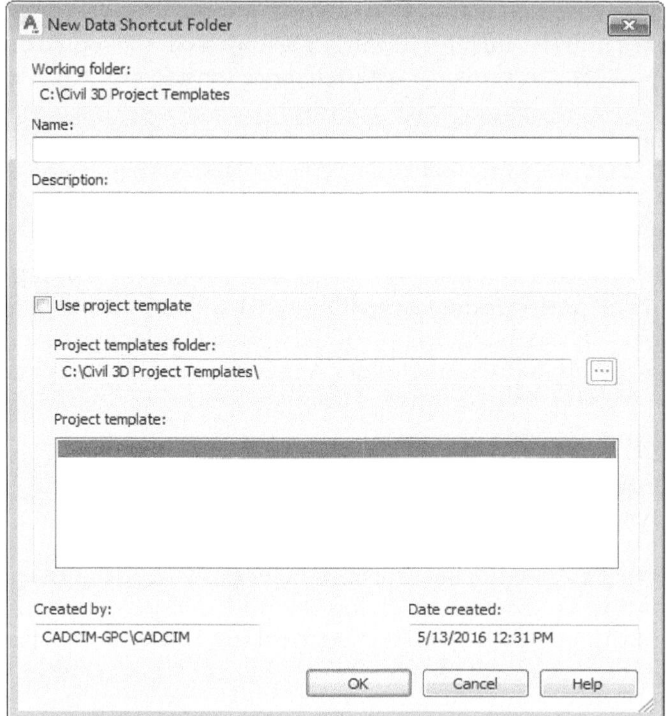

Figure 13-9 *The* ***New Data Shortcut Folder*** *dialog box*

In this dialog box, the **Working folder** text box displays the name of the parent working folder where all the project folders containing the data shortcuts will be saved. Enter the name of the data shortcut folder in the **Name** edit box. Optionally, enter a short description in the **Description** text box. Next, select the **Use project template** check box to use the default template that contains a set of subfolders. The **Project templates folder** edit box displays the path and name of the default project template folder. You can select some other project template folder. To do so, choose the browse button on the right of this edit box; the **Browse For Folder** dialog box will be displayed. Select the required folder and choose the **OK** button to exit this dialog box. The **Project template** text box in the **New Data Shortcut Folder** dialog box displays the name of the default project template, **_Sample Projects**. Note that you can also create your own project template. Now, choose the **OK** button; the **New Data Shortcut Folder** dialog box will be closed and the data shortcut folder will be created. To browse to the working folder and the data shortcut folders, use the explorer of the operating system. After creating the new data shortcut folder, you can create data shortcuts of the required Civil 3D objects in the drawing.

Note

While browsing a folder in the data shortcut folder, separate subfolders are created for source drawing and other data.

Tip

You can also invoke the ***Browse For Folder*** *dialog box by right-clicking on the* ***Data Shortcuts*** *node in the* ***Prospector*** *tab and then choosing the* ***Set Working Folder*** *option from the shortcut menu displayed.*

Creating Data Shortcuts

Ribbon: Manage > Data Shortcuts > Create Data Shortcuts
Command: CREATEDATASHORTCUTS

To create a data shortcut, choose the **Create Data Shortcuts** tool from the **Data Shortcuts** panel; the **Create Data Shortcuts** dialog box will be displayed, as shown in Figure 13-10. Select the check boxes corresponding to the objects whose shortcuts you want to create in the **Object** column of this dialog box. For example, to create a data shortcut for alignment, select the check box next to the **Alignments** node; all existing alignments in the current drawing will be selected automatically. You can clear the check box if you do not want to create data shortcut for a particular alignment. Similarly, select the required objects from the dialog box and choose the **OK** button; the dialog box will be closed and data shortcuts will be created and added in the **Data Shortcuts** node in the **Prospector** tab of the **TOOLSPACE** palette. In AutoCAD Civil 3D, you can create sub folders within the **Data Shortcuts** node in the **Prospector** tab. To do so, right-click on the data shortcut node for surfaces, alignments, etc. and choose the **Create Folder** option; the **Create Folder** dialog box will be displayed. In the **Create Folder** dialog box, enter the sub folder name in the **New Folder Name** edit box and choose **OK**; the sub folder with the specified name will be created, as shown in Figure 13-11.

You can also view the data shortcuts that have been created. For example, to view the shortcut created for an alignment object, expand **Data Shortcuts > Alignments** in the **Prospector** tab, refer to Figure 13-11. The names of the objects for which the data shortcuts have been created will be displayed in their respective nodes.

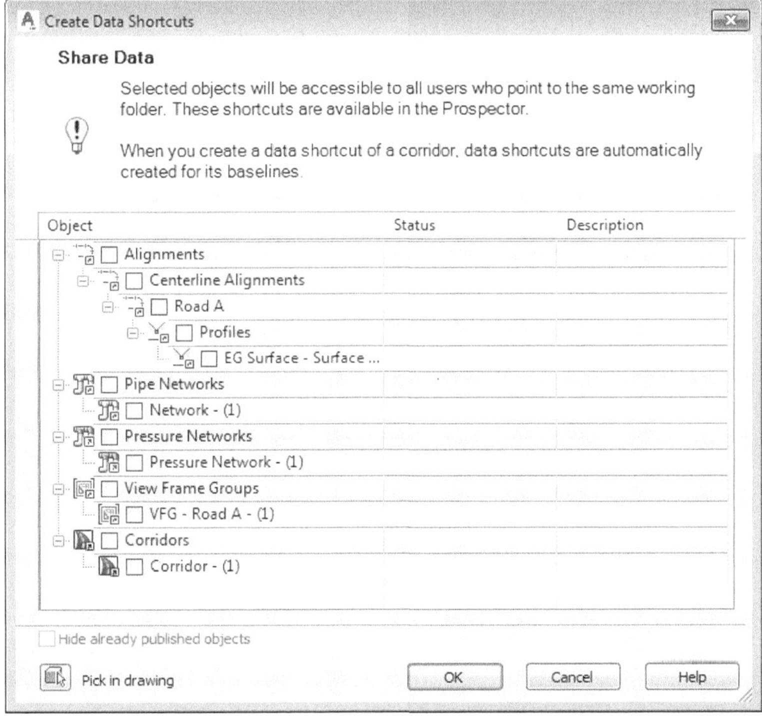

***Figure 13-10** The **Create Data Shortcuts** dialog box*

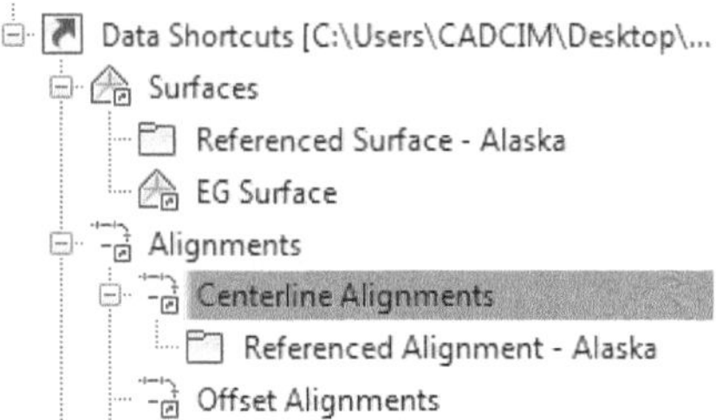

Figure 13-11 *Data shortcuts and sub folders created within the* ***Data Shortcuts*** *node in the* ***Prospector*** *tab*

Data Reference

A data reference is a link to use data shortcut objects in a new drawing. The referenced objects provide you with the flexibility to apply a temporary object style, annotation, and perform various analyses with them. The properties of these referenced objects can also be viewed in the drawing.

Data reference is a two step process, first is to create a data shortcut and second is to create a data reference. The procedure of creating a data reference is explained next.

Creating Data Reference

Data references help you to import references of objects created in data shortcuts into other drawings. Data references are lightweight copies of original objects and need very little space. When you import the referenced data shortcuts into an active drawing, you can edit objects to some extent without actually affecting the source drawings. The referenced data shortcut objects can only be imported into the active drawings. These objects are also called consumer drawings. Note that you can import only one such copy into an active drawing. To reference a data shortcut for a surface into a new drawing, expand **Data Shortcuts > Surfaces** in the **Prospector** tab. Next, right-click on the data shortcut created for the surface and choose **Create Reference** from the shortcut menu displayed, as shown in Figure 13-12.

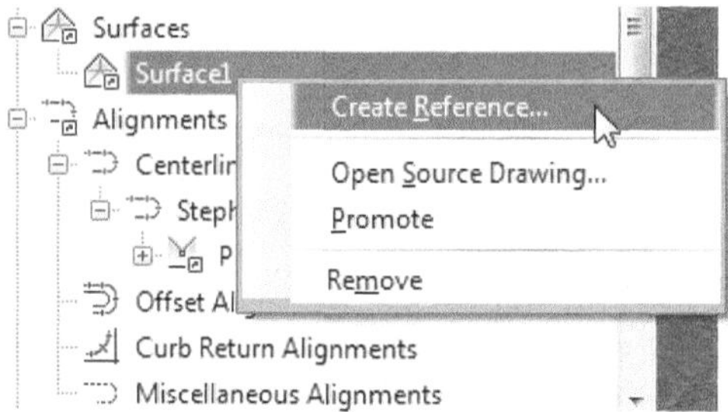

Figure 13-12 *Choosing the* ***Create Reference*** *option*

On doing so, the **Create Surface Reference** dialog box will be displayed, as shown in Figure 13-13. Enter a new name of the surface, if required. Select an option from the **Value** field of the **Style** property and then choose the **OK** button; the **Create Surface Reference** dialog box will be closed and the surface will be displayed in the drawing according to the surface style selected. Thus, you have created a data shortcut, data reference, and imported the surface object in a new drawing or a consumer drawing.

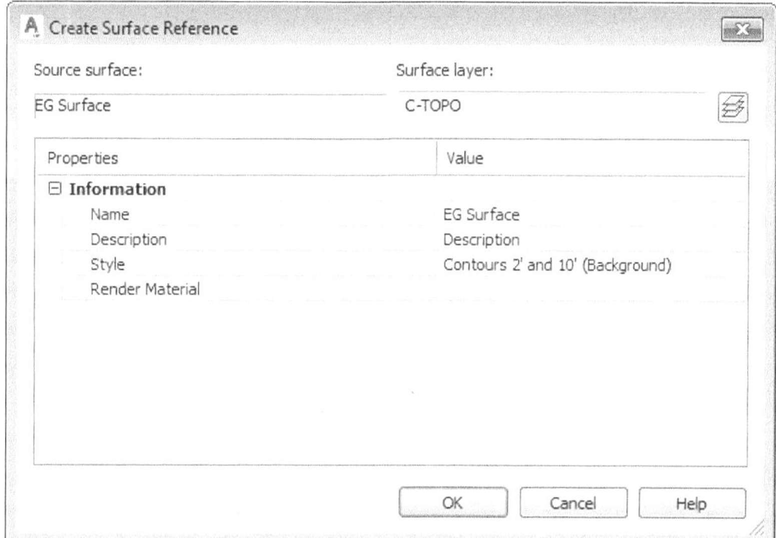

***Figure 13-13** The **Create Surface Reference** dialog box*

Similarly, you can import alignments, pipe networks, view frame groups, and profiles in the consumer drawing and work on them without affecting the source drawings. After creating the data references, choose **File > Save As** from the **Application Menu**; the **Save Drawing As** dialog box will be displayed. Navigate to the location *C:\Civil 3D Project Templates_Sample Project\Production Drawings* and save the drawing. All data shortcut project drawings can be saved in the **Production Drawings** subfolder of the data shortcut folder.

Promoting References

Ribbon: Manage > Data Shortcuts > Promote All Data References
Command: PROMOTEALLREFERENCES

When a reference is promoted, the copy of the object referenced in the current drawing becomes an independent and editable object. Also, the promoted object is not affected by any updation in the original object in the source drawing.

To promote all the references in a drawing, choose the **Promote All Data References** tool from the **Data Shortcuts** panel; the **Promote All Data References** message box will be displayed. This message box informs that you have chosen to replace all the data references in the current file with the objects that they reference. Next, you can choose the **Promote all referenced objects into the current file** button to promote all referenced objects in the drawing.

To promote only one or two referenced objects to the current file, expand the **Data Shortcuts** folder and then the required object folder. For example, if you want to promote a surface object, expand the **Surfaces** folder and right-click on the reference surface and choose **Promote** from the shortcut menu displayed, as shown in Figure 13-14; the **Create Surface Reference** dialog box will be displayed. Enter the required information in this dialog box and choose the **OK** button; the individual surface will be promoted.

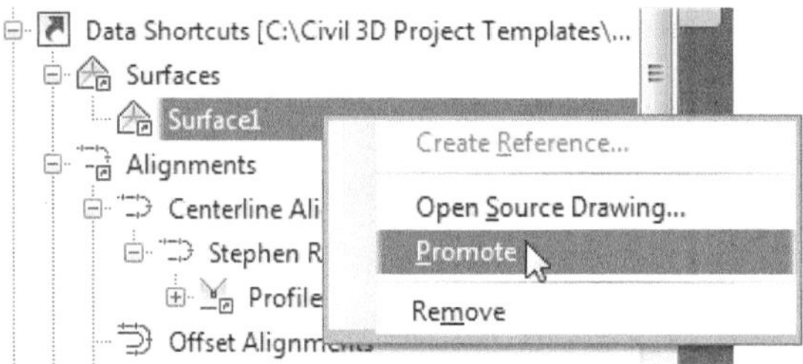

*Figure 13-14 Choosing the **Promote** option to promote the surface reference*

Similarly, you can promote individual reference objects such as alignments, profiles, pipe networks, and so on.

Synchronizing Data References

Ribbon: Manage > Data Shortcuts > Synchronize References
Command: SYNCHRONIZEREFERENCES

When the source drawing is updated or modified, you need to synchronize or update the referenced object. To do so, choose the **Synchronize References** tool from the **Data Shortcuts** panel; the reference object will be updated according to the changes made in the original surface in the source drawing. Alternatively, to synchronize or update the referenced object, expand the object node such as the **Surfaces** node in the **Prospector** tab of the **TOOLSPACE** palette. Next, right-click on the out-of-date reference surface indicated by the out-of-date symbol and then choose the **Synchronize** option from the shortcut menu displayed. Similarly, you can synchronize and update all other reference objects. Civil 3D will display a message whenever a source object is changed or updated.

TUTORIALS

Tutorial 1 View Frames and Sheets

In this tutorial, you will create view frames and sheets using plan production tools, refer to Figure 13-15. **(Expected time: 30 min)**

The following steps are required to complete this tutorial:

a. Download and open the file.
b. Create view frames.
c. Create sheets.
d. Save the file.

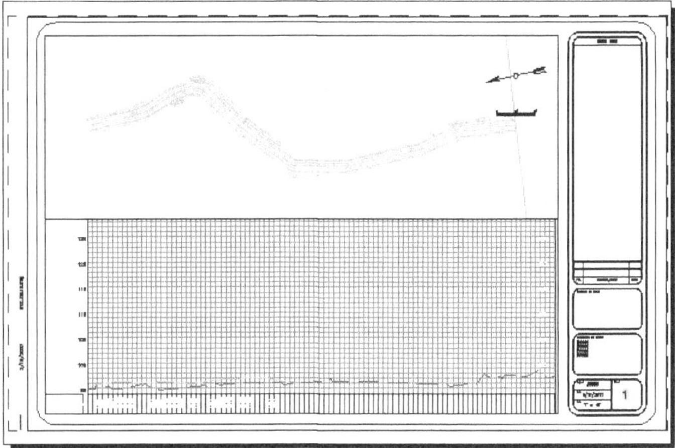

Figure 13-15 The sheet with plan and profile views

Downloading and Opening the File

1. Download the *c13_c3d_2018_tut.zip* file from *http://www.cadcim.com* and save the downloaded file as explained in Chapter 2.

2. Choose **Open > Drawing** from the **Application Menu**; the **Select File** dialog box is displayed.

3. In this dialog box, browse to the location *C:\c3d_2018\c13_c3d_2018_tut* and select the file *c13_c3d_2018_tut01.dwg*.

4. Choose the **Open** button to open the file. Ignore the error message if displayed in the **PANORAMA** window.

Creating View Frames

1. Choose the **Create View Frames** tool from the **Plan Production** panel of the **Output** tab; the **Create View Frames** wizard with the **Alignment** page is displayed.

2. In the **Alignment** page of this wizard, select the **Stephen Road** option from the drop-down list in the **Alignment** area if it is not selected by default.

3. Select the **Automatic** radio button in the **Station Range** area of the **Alignment** page of the wizard.

4. Choose the **Next** button; the **Sheets** page of the **Create View Frames** wizard is displayed.

5. In the **Sheet Settings** area of the **Sheets** page, select the **Plan and Profile** radio button. Next, choose the browse button displayed on the right of the **Template for Plan and Profile sheet** edit box; the **Select Layout as Sheet Template** dialog box is displayed, as shown in Figure 13-16.

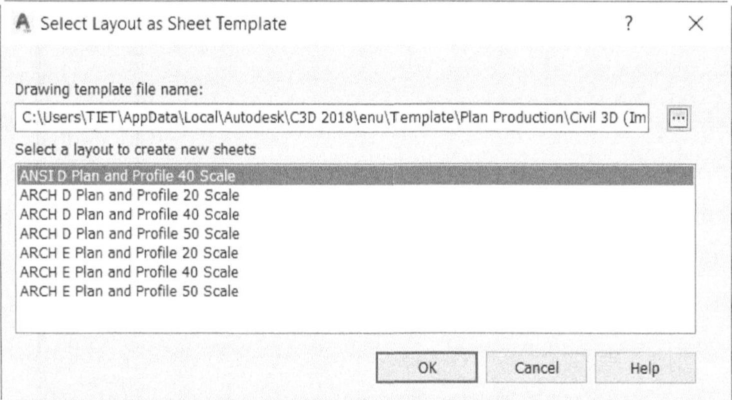

Figure 13-16 *The* ***Select Layout as Sheet Template*** *dialog box*

6. In this dialog box, choose the browse button on the right of the **Drawing template file name** edit box; the **Select Layout as Sheet Template** dialog box is displayed.

7. In this dialog box, browse to the location *C:\Users\<username>\AppData\Local\Autodesk\C3D 2018\enu\Template\Plan Production* and then select the *Civil 3D (Imperial) Plan and Profile.dwt* template file if it is not selected by default.

8. Choose the **Open** button to return to the **Select Layout as Sheet Template** dialog box. In this dialog box, ensure that the **ANSI D Plan and Profile 40 Scale** option is selected in the **Select a layout to create new sheets** list box. Next, choose the **OK** button; the dialog box is closed.

9. In the **View Frame Placement** area of the **Sheets** page, make sure that the **Along alignment** radio button is selected. Choose the **Next** button; the **View Frame Group** page of the **Create View Frames** wizard is displayed.

10. In this page, enter **Stephen group** in the **Name** edit box of the **View Frame Group** area.

11. Accept all the default values in the **View Frame** area and choose the **Next** button; the **Match Lines** page of the wizard is displayed.

12. Accept the default values in this page and then choose the **Next** button; the **Profile Views** page of the **Create View Frames** wizard is displayed.

13. Retain the default settings in this page and choose the **Create View Frames** button from the wizard; the view frames are created, as shown in Figure 13-17.

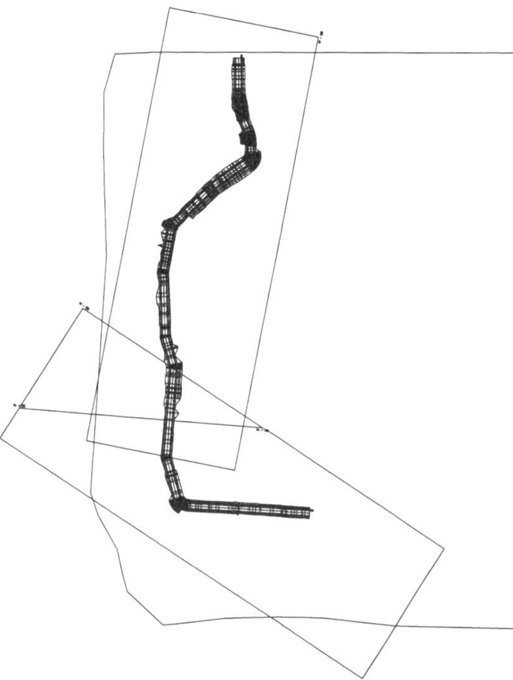

Figure 13-17 *The* ***Stephen group*** *view frames*

Creating Sheets

1. Choose the **Create Sheets** tool from the **Plan Production** panel of the **Output** tab; the **View Frame Group and Layouts** page of the **Create Sheets** wizard is displayed.

2. In the **Layout Creation** area of this page, enter **Stephen sheet** in the **Layout name** edit box.

3. In the **Choose the north arrow block to align in layouts** drop-down list, select the **North** option.

4. Retain all other default settings in the **View Frame Group and Layouts** page and choose the **Next** button; the **Sheet Set** page of the **Create Sheets** wizard is displayed.

5. In the **Sheet Set** area, ensure that the **New sheet set** radio button is selected. Next, choose the Browse button on the right of the **Sheet set storage location** edit box; the **Browse for Sheet Set Folder** dialog box is displayed.

6. Browse to the location *C:\Users\<user name>\Documents\Autodesk* in this dialog box and select the folder *My Civil 3D Tutorial Data*.

Note

If the My Civil 3D Tutorial Data folder is not available at C:\Users\<user name>\Documents\Autodesk, create a new folder and rename it as My Civil 3D Tutorial Data.

7. Choose the **Open** button; the **Browse for Sheet Set Folder** dialog box is closed and the **Sheet Set** page of the **Create Sheets** wizard is displayed.

8. In the **Sheets** area of the **Sheet Set** page of the wizard, choose the Browse button next to the **Sheet files storage location** edit box; the **Browse for Folder** dialog box is displayed.

9. Navigate to the location *C:\Users\<user name>\Documents\Autodesk\My Civil 3D Tutorial Data* and choose the **Open** button to return to the **Sheet Set** page.

10. Enter **Stephen sheet file** in the **Sheet file name** edit box and choose the **Next** button; the **Profile Views** page is displayed.

11. Retain the default settings in the **Profile Views** page and choose the **Next** button to display the **Data References** page.

12. Ensure that the **Alignments** check box is selected. Select the **Surfaces** check box to draw the surface in the sheet.

13. Choose the **Create Sheets** button in the wizard; the **AutoCAD Civil 3D 2018** message box is displayed, as shown in Figure 13-18.

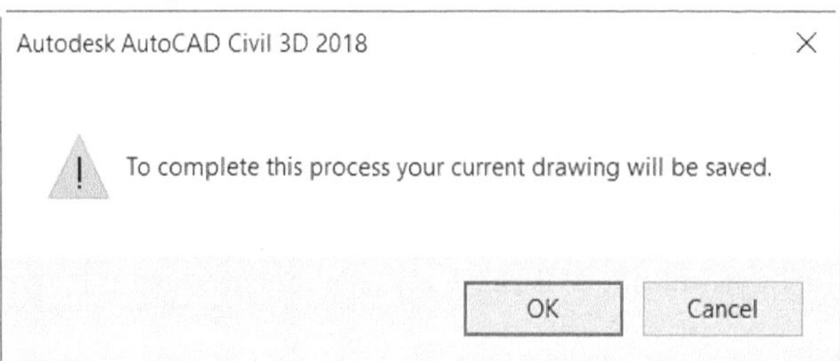

***Figure 13-18** The **AutoCAD Civil 3D 2018** message box*

14. Choose the **OK** button; the message box is closed and you are prompted to specify the origin for the profile view.

15. Click in the drawing area; the **Create Sheets Progress Dialog** window is displayed showing the progress of the sheets creation. After the sheet creation process is completed, the **SHEET SET MANAGER** palette and the **PANORAMA** window are displayed. Close the **PANORAMA** window.

16. Right-click on the first sheet **1-Stephen sheet** in the **SHEET SET MANAGER** palette and then choose the **Open** option from the shortcut menu displayed, as shown in Figure 13-19. On doing so, the sheet is displayed in a new drawing, as shown in Figure 13-20. In addition, the **PANORAMA** window is displayed. Ignore the message and close the **PANORAMA** window.

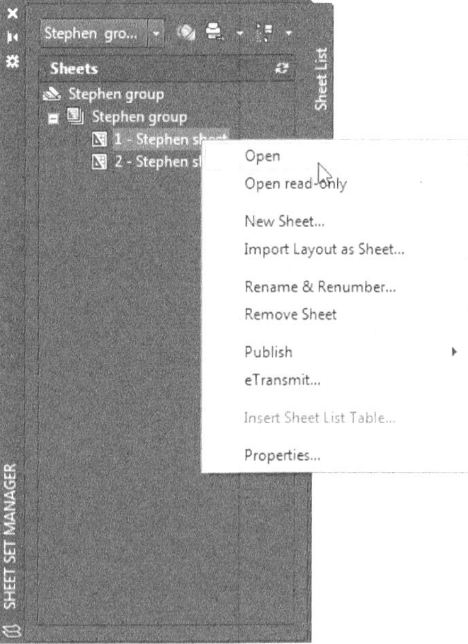

*Figure 13-19 Choosing the **Open** option from the shortcut menu*

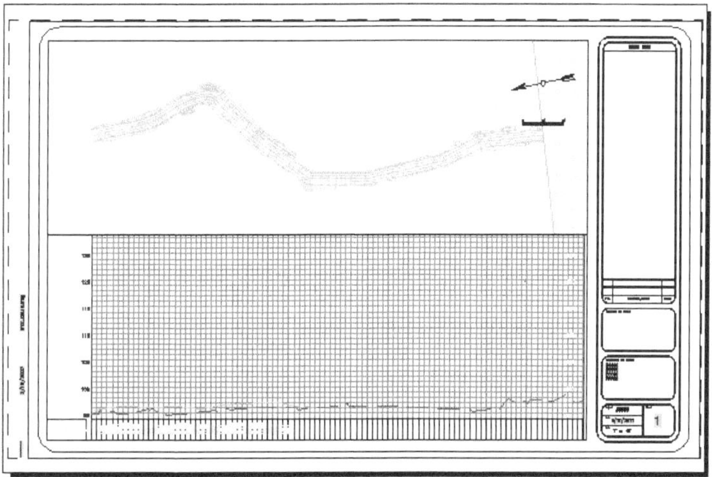

Figure 13-20 The sheet displayed in a new drawing

Saving the File

1. Choose **Save As** from the **Application Menu**; the **Save Drawing As** dialog box is displayed.

2. In this dialog box, browse to the following location:

   C:\c3d_2018\c13_c3d_2018_tut

3. In the **File name** edit box, enter **c13_tut01a**.

4. Choose the **Save** button; the file is saved with the name *c13_tut01a.dwg* at the specified location.

5. Choose the **Close** button from the **Application Menu**; the file is closed.

Tutorial 2 Data Shortcuts

In this tutorial, you will create data shortcuts for different objects.

(Expected time: 30 min)

The following steps are required to complete this tutorial.

a. Download and open the file.
b. Set up the Working Folder.
c. Create data shortcut folder.
d. Create data shortcuts.
e. Create data references.
f. Save the file.

Downloading and Opening the File

1. Choose **Open > Drawing** from the **Application Menu**; the **Select File** dialog box is displayed.

2. In this dialog box, browse to the location *C:\c3d_2018\c13_c3d_2018_tut* and select the file *c13_c3d_2018_tut02.dwg*.

3. Choose the **Open** button to open the file.

Setting Up the Working Folder

1. Select **Master View**, if it is not selected by default, from the drop-down list displayed at the left of the **Prospector** tab in the **TOOLSPACE** palette, refer to Figure 13-21.

2. In the **Prospector** tab of the **TOOLSPACE** palette, right-click on the **Data Shortcuts** node and choose the **Set Working Folder** option from the shortcut menu; the **Browse For Folder** dialog box is displayed.

3. Browse to *C:\Users\<user name>\Documents\Autodesk\My Civil 3D Tutorial Data* and choose the **OK** button; the **Browse For Folder** dialog box is closed. Note that My Civil 3D Tutorial Data is the working or parent folder in which all the project and data shortcut folders will be saved.

Note

If the My Civil 3D Tutorial Data folder is not available, create a new folder and rename it as My Civil 3D Tutorial Data.

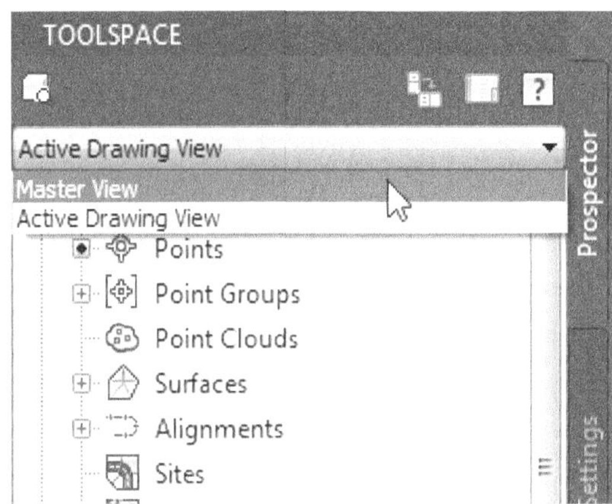

*Figure 13-21 Selecting the **Master View** option*

Creating a New Data Shortcut Folder

1. Right-click on the **Data Shortcuts** node and choose the **New Data Shortcuts Project Folder** option from the shortcut menu; the **New Data Shortcut Folder** dialog box is displayed.

2. Enter **New Data Shortcut Folder** in the **Name** edit box.

3. Select the **Use project template** check box and then choose the browse button on the right of **Project templates folder**; the **Browse For Folder** dialog box is displayed.

4. Browse to the location *C:\Civil 3D Project Templates* and select the *Civil 3D Project Templates* folder. If the folder is not available at the location, create a new folder and name it as **Civil 3D Project Templates**.

5. Choose the **OK** button to close the **Browse For Folder** dialog box and return to the **New Data Shortcut Folder** dialog box.

6. Choose the **OK** button in the **New Data Shortcut Folder** dialog box to exit it.

Associating Project to Current Drawing

1. Right-click on the **Data Shortcuts** node and choose **Associate Project to Current Drawing** from the shortcut menu displayed; the **Associate Project to Current Drawing** dialog box is displayed.

2. Ensure that the **New Data Shortcut Folder** option is selected in the **Select Project** drop-down and choose **OK**.

Creating Data Shortcuts

1. Save the current drawing file. Next, in the **Prospector** tab of the **TOOLSPACE** palette, right-click on the **Data Shortcuts** node and choose **Create Data Shortcuts** from the shortcut menu displayed; the **Create Data Shortcuts** dialog box is displayed, as shown in Figure 13-22.

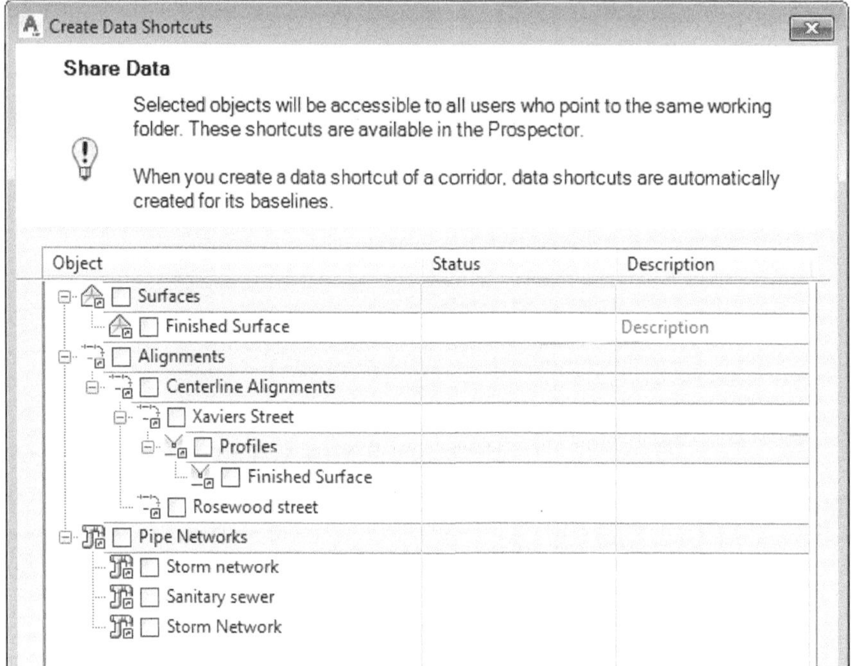

Figure 13-22 *Partial view of the* ***Create Data Shortcuts*** *dialog box*

Note

The ***AutoCAD Civil 3D*** *message box is displayed if the current drawing file is not saved.*

2. Select the **Surfaces**, **Alignments**, and **Pipe Networks** check boxes in the **Create Data Shortcuts** dialog box. Ensure that the **Rosewood street** and **Storm Network** check boxes are cleared.

   The data shortcuts for **Rosewood street** and **Storm Network** will not be created.

3. Choose the **OK** button; the **Create Data Shortcuts** dialog box is closed and the data shortcuts for surface, alignment, and the pipe network objects are created.

4. Expand the **Data Shortcuts** node in the **Prospector** tab, and then expand the **Surfaces**, **Alignments**, and **Pipe Networks** sub-nodes to view the data shortcuts created from the objects, refer to Figure 13-23.

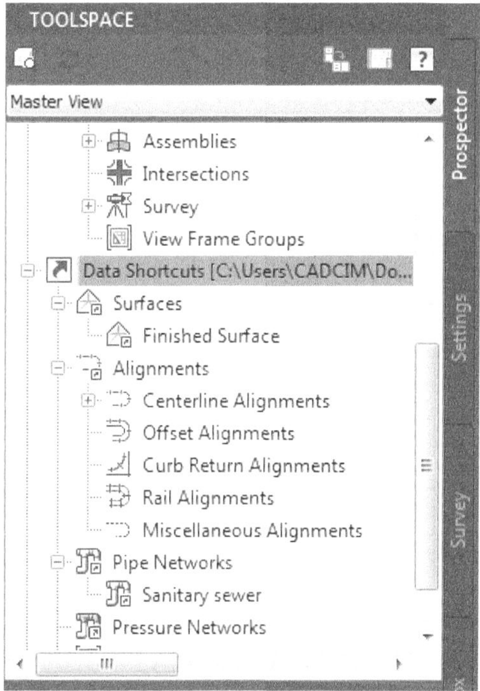

Figure 13-23 The ***Data Shortcuts*** *node expanded*

5. Open the Windows Explorer and browse to the location *Documents\Autodesk\My Civil 3D Tutorial Data\New Data Shortcut Folder_Shortcuts*.

6. Click on the **Surfaces**, **Alignments**, and **PipeNetworks** folders and notice that an XML file for the objects is created in these subfolders.

7. Close the Windows Explorer.

Referencing Data Shortcuts

1. Choose **New > Drawing** from the **Application Menu**; the **Select template** dialog box is displayed.

2. Select the *_AutoCAD Civil 3D (Imperial) NCS.dwt* file and choose the **Open** button to open a new drawing.

3. Choose **Save As > Drawing** from the **Application Menu**; the **Save Drawing As** dialog box is displayed.

4. Browse to *New Data Shortcut Folder* created earlier and then enter **Tutorial 2** in the **File name** edit box.

5. Choose the **Save** button; the **Save Drawing As** dialog box is closed and the file is saved with the specified name.

6. Expand **Data Shortcuts > Surfaces** in the **Prospector** tab of the **TOOLSPACE** palette if not expanded.

7. Right-click on **Finished Surface** and choose the **Create Reference** option from the shortcut menu displayed, as shown in Figure 13-24; the **Create Surface Reference** dialog box is displayed, as shown in Figure 13-25.

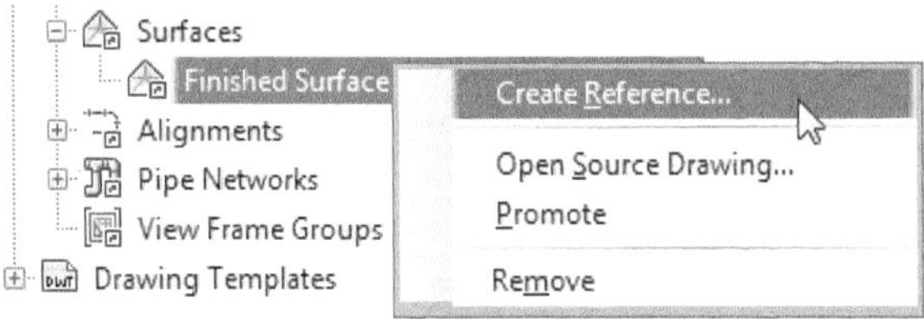

Figure 13-24 *Choosing the* ***Create Reference*** *option*

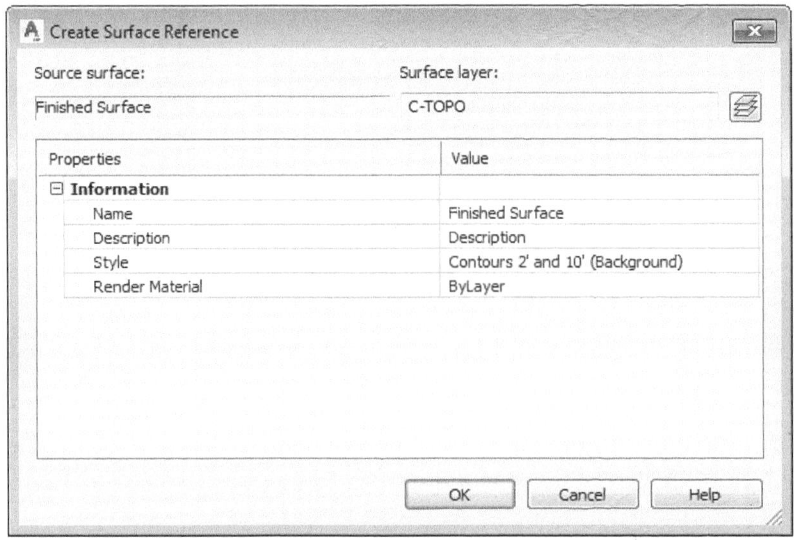

Figure 13-25 *The* ***Create Surface Reference*** *dialog box*

8. In the **Value** column of the **Name** property, enter **Surface reference** as the name of the surface.

9. Retain the other default settings and choose the **OK** button; the **Create Surface Reference** dialog box is closed. Also, **Finished Surface** will be referenced and displayed in the drawing of Tutorial 2, as shown in Figure 13-26. If the surface is not displayed, enter **ZE** in the command line to zoom and view the surface. The surface is referenced in a new drawing and added to the **Surfaces** node of the **Prospector** tab.

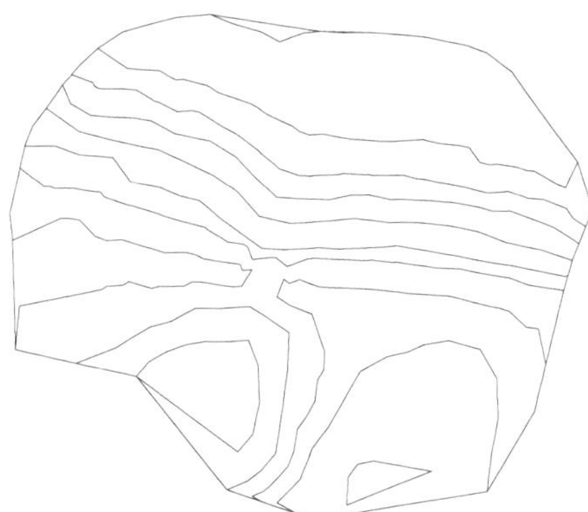

Figure 13-26 *The referenced* ***Finished Surface*** *in the drawing of Tutorial 2*

Referencing the Alignment

1. Right-click on **Xaviers Street** from **Data Shortcuts > Alignments > Centerline Alignments** in the **Prospector** tab; a shortcut menu is displayed.

2. Choose the **Create Reference** option from the shortcut menu; the **Create Alignment Reference** dialog box is displayed.

3. Enter **Xaviers Street Reference** in the **Name** edit box of this dialog box.

4. Retain the default settings for other parameters and choose the **OK** button to exit the dialog box; the **Xaviers Street** alignment is displayed in the drawing, as shown in Figure 13-27.

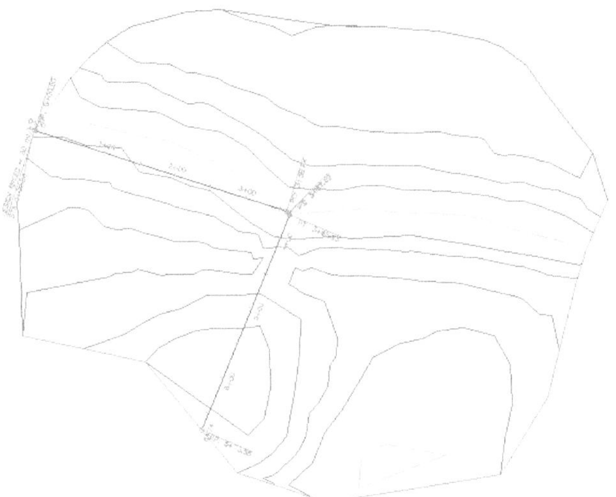

Figure 13-27 *The surface with the* ***Xaviers Street*** *alignment*

Referencing the Pipe Network

1. Right-click on the **Sanitary sewer** option from the **Data Shortcuts > Pipe Networks** in the **Prospector** tab; a shortcut menu is displayed.

2. Choose the **Create Reference** option from the shortcut menu; the **Create Pipe Network Reference** dialog box is displayed.

3. Enter **Sanitary Sewer Reference** in the **Network name** edit box.

4. Select the **none** option from the **Structure label style** drop-down list if it is not selected by default and then choose the **OK** button to exit the dialog box. On doing so, the sewer reference network is displayed in the drawing, as shown in Figure 13-28. Ignore the warning message displayed in the **PANORAMA** window.

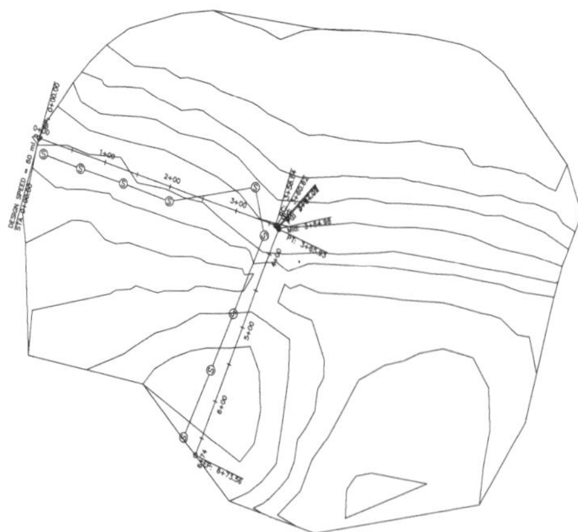

Figure 13-28 *The surface with the sewer reference network*

Saving the File

1. Choose **Save As > Drawing** from the **Application Menu**; the **Save Drawing As** dialog box is displayed.

2. In this dialog box, browse to the following location:

   C:\c3d_2018\c13_c3d_2018_tut

3. In the **File name** edit box, enter **c13_tut02a**.

4. Choose the **Save** button; the file is saved with the name *c13_tut02a.dwg* at the specified location.

Self-Evaluation Test

Answer the following questions and then compare them to those given at the end of the chapter:

1. The __________ tool is used to create the sheets that display the alignment sections and the profile views.

2. The ______________ divide the alignment into different sections for visual presentation using sheets.

3. The _________ are used to maintain continuity between the frames of different sheets in a sheet set.

4. When a reference is __________, the copy of the object referenced in the current drawing becomes an independent and editable object.

5. A data shortcut can be defined as an ___________ for different Civil 3D objects that can be inserted into one or more drawings.

6. To create data shortcuts, choose the __________ tool from the **Data Shortcuts** panel of the **Manage** tab.

7. The data shortcuts are created and managed in the __________ tab of the **TOOLSPACE** palette.

8. The data shortcuts are __________ files that provide reference copies of AutoCAD objects that can be inserted in drawings.

9. A collection of view frames is called as the __________.

10. The **Sheets** page of the **Create View Frames** wizard provides __________, __________, and __________ options to generate a sheet.

11. The last step in generating sheets is to create the view frames along an alignment. (T/F)

12. To create a view frame, choose the **Create View Frames** tool in the **Plan Production** panel of the **Output** tab. (T/F)

13. A data shortcut is a link that can be used to access the data objects in a new drawing. (T/F)

14. You can assign different label styles to the left and right labels of Match Lines. (T/F)

15. You cannot create view frames for a user specified station range. (T/F)

Review Questions

Answer the following questions:

1. Which of the following is a plan production tool?

   a) **Create View Frames** b) **Sheets**
   c) **Data Reference** d) None of these

2. A __________ is a straight line that indicates locations where one frame matches or intersects with the other in a view frame group.

3. The first important requirement for creating a view frame is an _________.

4. The_________ tool is used to synchronize or update reference objects.

5. A sheet is a collection of view frames. (T/F)

6. To set a working folder, choose the **Set Working Folder** tool from the **Data Shortcuts** panel of the **Manage** tab. (T/F)

7. You can create a data shortcut by using the **Create Data Shortcuts** option. (T/F)

8. The **Promote All Data References** tool is used to promote all references in a drawing. (T/F)

9. If you create a reference to an object, you cannot modify the geometry of the object. However, you can access its properties and data, apply styles and annotation to it, and perform some types of analyses on the object. (T/F)

EXERCISE

1. Log on to *www.cadcim.com* and browse to *Textbooks > Civil/GIS > Civil 3D > Exploring AutoCAD Civil 3D 2018*. Next, select *c13_c3d_2018_exer.zip* file from the **Exercise Files** drop-down list. Choose the corresponding **Download** button to download the data file.

2. Now, save and extract the downloaded folder to the following location:

   C:\c3d_2018

Note

*While opening the exercise file, the **PANORAMA** window may appear with an error message. Close this window to proceed further*

Exercise 1

Open the *c13_c3d_2018_ex01.dwg* drawing file and create the view frames shown in Figure 13-29. Also, create the sheets using the view frames. **(Expected time: 30 min)**

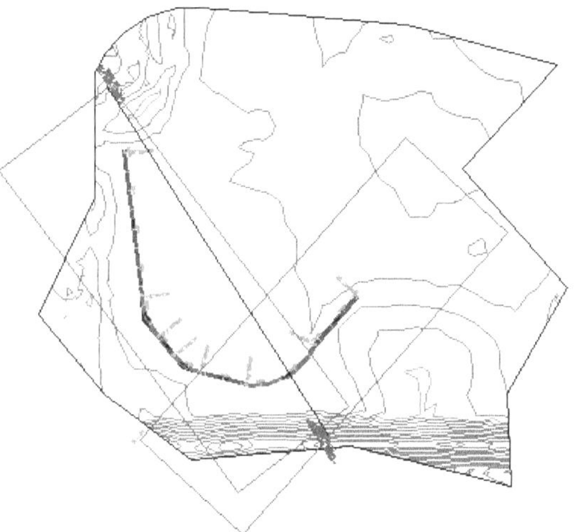

Figure 13-29 *Surface with view frames*

Answers to Self-Evaluation Test

1. Create Sheets, **2. View Frames**, **3.** match lines, **4.** promoted, **5.** external reference, **6. Create Data Shortcuts**, **7. Prospector**, **8. XML**, **9. View Frame Groups**, **10. Plan(s) only**, **Profile(s) only**, **Plan and Profile**, **11.** F, **12.** T, **13.** T, **14.** T, **15.** F

Index

A

B

C

D

E

F

G

Q

R

S

T

U

V

W

Other Titles of Interest- BPB/TICKOO SERIES

Publication by BPB/TICKOO SERIES

The following is the list of some of the publications by BPB/TICKOO series

AutoCAD Textbooks

- AutoCAD 2018: A Problem-Solving Approach, Basic and Intermediate, 24th Edition
- AutoCAD 2018: A Problem-Solving Approach, 3D and Advanced, 24th Edition

Autodesk Inventor Textbooks

- Autodesk Inventor 2018 for Designers, 18th Edition
- Autodesk Inventor 2017 for Designers, 17th Edition

AutoCAD MEP Textbooks

- AutoCAD MEP 2018 for Designers, 4th Edition

AutoCAD Plant 3D Textbooks

- AutoCAD Plant 3D 2018 for Designers, 4th Edition

NX Textbooks

- NX 12.0 for Designers, 11th Edition
- NX 11.0 for Designers, 10th Edition

NX Mold Textbooks

- Mold Design Using NX 11.0: A Tutorial Approach

SolidEdge Textbooks

- Solid Edge ST 10 for Designers, 15th Edition

SolidWorks Textbooks

- SOLIDWORKS 2018 for Designers, 16th Edition
- SOLIDWORKS 2017 for Designers, 15th Edition

SolidWorks Simulation Textbooks

- SOLIDWORKS Simulation 2018: A Tutorial Approach
- SOLIDWORKS Simulation 2016: A Tutorial Approach

Creo Parametric

- Creo Parametric 4.0 for Designers, 4th Edition
- PTC Creo Parametric 3.0 for Designers, 3rd Edition

CATIA Textbook
- CATIA V5-6R2017 for Designers, 15th Edition
- CATIA V5-6R2016 for Designers, 14th Edition

AutoCAD Electrical Textbooks
- AutoCAD Electrical 2018 for Electrical Control Designers, 9th Edition
- AutoCAD Electrical 2017 for Electrical Control Designers, 8th Edition

Autodesk Revit Architecture Textbooks
- Exploring Autodesk Revit 2018 for Architecture, 14th Edition
- Exploring Autodesk Revit 2017 for Architecture, 13th Edition

Autodesk Revit Structure Textbooks
- Exploring Autodesk Revit Structure 2018, 8^{h} Edition
- Exploring Autodesk Revit Structure 2017, 7th Edition

Bentley STAAD.Pro Textbooks
- Exploring Bentley STAAD.Pro (CONNECT Edition), 3rd Edition
- Exploring Bentley STAAD.Pro V8i (SELECT series 6)

AutoCAD Map 3D Textbooks
- Exploring AutoCAD Map 3D 2018, 8th Edition
- Exploring AutoCAD Map 3D 2017, 7th Edition

Autodesk Navisworks Textbooks
- Exploring Autodesk Navisworks 2017, 4th Edition

Oracle Primavera Textbooks
- Exploring Oracle Primavera P6 R8.4
- Exploring Oracle Primavera P6 v7.0

3ds Max Textbooks
- Autodesk 3ds Max 2018: A Comprehensive Guide, 18th Edition
- Autodesk 3ds Max 2017: A Comprehensive Guide, 17th Edition

Autodesk Maya Textbooks
- Autodesk Maya 2018: A Comprehensive Guide, 10th Edition
- Autodesk Maya 2017: A Comprehensive Guide, 9th Edition

CINEMA 4D Textbooks
- MAXON CINEMA 4D Studio R19: A Tutorial Approach, 6th Edition
- MAXON CINEMA 4D Studio R18: A Tutorial Approach, 5th Edition

ZBrush Textbooks

- Pixologic ZBrush 4R8: A Comprehensive Guide, 4th Edition
- Pixologic ZBrush 4R7: A Comprehensive Guide, 3rd Edition

Computer Programming Textbooks

- Introducing PHP/MySQL